Honda CBR1000RR Fireblade

Service and Repair Manual

by Matthew Coombs

Models covered
CBR1000RR-4. 998cc. 2004
CBR1000RR-5. 998cc. 2005
CBR1000RR-6. 998cc. 2006
CBR1000RR-7. 998cc. 2007

(4604-304)

ABCDE
FGHIJ
KLMNO
PQRST

A book in the Haynes Service and Repair Manual Series

ISBN: 978 1 84425 604 4

Library of Congress Control Number 2006935381

Printed in the USA

Haynes Publishing
Sparkford, Yeovil, Somerset BA22 7JJ, England

Haynes North America, Inc
861 Lawrence Drive, Newbury Park, California 91320, USA

Haynes Publishing Nordiska AB
Box 1504, 751 45 Uppsala, Sweden

Contents

LIVING WITH YOUR HONDA CBR1000RR FIREBLADE

Introduction

Pre-ride checks

MAINTENANCE

Routine maintenance and servicing

Contents

REPAIRS AND OVERHAUL

The Birth of a Dream

by Julian Ryder

There is no better example of the Japanese post-war industrial miracle than Honda. Like other companies which have become household names, it started with one man's vision. In this case the man was the 40-year old Soichiro Honda who had sold his piston-ring manufacturing business to Toyota in 1945 and was happily spending the proceeds on prolonged parties for his friends. However, the difficulties of getting around in the chaos of post-war Japan irked Honda, so when he came across a job lot of generator engines he realised that here was a way of getting people mobile again at low cost.

A 12 by 18-foot shack in Hamamatsu became his first bike factory, fitting the generator motors into pushbikes. Before long he'd used up all 500 generator motors and started manufacturing his own engine, known as the 'chimney', either because of the elongated cylinder head or the smoky exhaust or perhaps both. The chimney made all of half a horsepower from its 50 cc engine but it was a major success and became the Honda A-type.

Less than two years after he'd set up in Hamamatsu, Soichiro Honda founded the Honda Motor Company in September 1948. By then, the A-type had been developed into the 90 cc B-type engine, which Mr Honda decided deserved its own chassis not a bicycle frame. Honda was about to become Japan's first post-war manufacturer of complete motorcycles. In August 1949 the first prototype was ready. With an output of three horsepower, the 98 cc D-type was still a simple two-stroke but it had a two-speed transmission and most importantly a pressed steel frame with telescopic forks and hard tail rear end. The frame was almost triangular in profile with the top rail going in a straight line from the massively braced steering head to the rear axle. Legend has it that after the D-type's first tests the entire workforce went for a drink to celebrate and try and think of a name for the bike. One man broke one of those silences you get when people are thinking, exclaiming 'This is like a dream!' 'That's it!' shouted Honda, and so the Honda Dream was christened.

Honda C70 and C90 OHV-engined models

> 'This is like a dream!' 'That's it' shouted Honda

Mr Honda was a brilliant, intuitive engineer and designer but he did not bother himself with the marketing side of his business. With hindsight, it is possible to see that employing Takeo Fujisawa who would both sort out the home market and plan the eventual expansion into overseas markets was a masterstroke. He arrived in October 1949 and in 1950 was made Sales Director. Another vital new name was Kiyoshi Kawashima, who along with Honda himself, designed the company's first four-stroke after Kawashima had told them that the four-stroke opposition to Honda's two-strokes sounded nicer and therefore sold better. The result of that statement was the overhead-valve 148 cc E-type which first ran in July 1951 just two months after the first drawings were made. Kawashima was made a director of the Honda Company at 34 years old.

The E-type was a massive success, over 32,000 were made in 1953 alone, a feat of mass-production that was astounding by the standards of the day given the relative complexity of the machine. But Honda's lifelong pursuit of technical innovation sometimes distracted him from commercial reality. Fujisawa pointed out that they were in danger of ignoring their core business, the motorised bicycles that still formed Japan's main means of transport. In May 1952 the F-type Cub appeared, another two-stroke despite the top men's reservations. You could buy a complete machine or just the motor to attach to your own bicycle. The result was certainly distinctive, a white fuel tank with a circular profile went just below and behind the saddle on the left of the bike, and the motor with its horizontal cylinder and bright red cover just below the rear axle on the same side of the bike. This was the machine that turned Honda into the biggest bike maker in Japan with 70% of the market for bolt-on bicycle motors, the F-type was also the first Honda to be exported. Next came the machine that would turn Honda into the biggest motorcycle manufacturer in the world.

The C100 Super Cub was a typically audacious piece of Honda engineering and marketing. For the first time, but not the last, Honda invented a completely new type of motorcycle, although the term 'scooterette' was coined to describe the new bike which had many of the characteristics of a scooter but the large wheels, and therefore stability, of a motorcycle. The first one was sold in August 1958, fifteen years later over nine-million of them were on the roads of the world. If ever a machine can be said to have brought mobility to the masses it is the Super Cub. If you add in the electric starter that was added for the C102 model of 1961, the design of the Super Cub has remained substantially unchanged ever since, testament to how right Honda got it first time. The Super Cub made Honda the world's biggest manufacturer after just two years of production.

The CB250N Super Dream became a favorite with UK learner riders of the late seventies and early eighties

Honda's export drive started in earnest in 1957 when Britain and Holland got their first bikes, America got just two bikes the next year. By 1962 Honda had half the American market with 65,000 sales. But Soichiro Honda had already travelled abroad to Europe and the USA, making a special

The GL1000 introduced in 1975, was the first in Honda's line of GoldWings

Carl Fogarty in action at the Suzuka 8 Hour on the RC45

An early CB750 Four

point of going to the Isle of Man TT, then the most important race in the GP calendar. He realised that no matter how advanced his products were, only racing success would convince overseas markets for whom 'Made in Japan' still meant cheap and nasty. It took five years from Soichiro Honda's first visit to the Island before his bikes were ready for the TT. In 1959 the factory entered five riders in the 125 class. They did not have a massive impact on the event being benevolently regarded as a curiosity, but sixth, seventh and eighth were good enough for the team prize. The bikes were off the pace but they were well engineered and very reliable.

The TT was the only time the West saw the Hondas in '59, but they came back for more the following year with the first of a generation of bikes which shaped the future of motorcycling – the double-overhead-cam four-cylinder 250. It was fast and reliable – it revved to 14,000 rpm – but didn't handle anywhere near as well as the opposition. However, Honda had now signed up non-Japanese riders to lead their challenge. The first win didn't come until 1962 (Aussie Tom Phillis in the Spanish 125 GP) and was followed up with a world-shaking performance at the TT. Twenty-one year old Mike Hailwood won both 125 and 250 cc TTs and Hondas filled the top five positions in both races. Soichiro Honda's master plan was starting to come to fruition, Hailwood and Honda won the 1961 250 cc World Championship. Next year Honda won three titles. The other Japanese factories fought back and inspired Honda to produce some of the most fascinating racers ever seen: the awesome six-cylinder 250, the five-cylinder 125, and the 500 four with which the immortal Hailwood battled Agostini and the MV Agusta.

When Honda pulled out of racing in '67 they had won sixteen rider's titles, eighteen manufacturer's titles, and 137 GPs, including 18 TTs, and introduced the concept of the modern works team to motorcycle racing. Sales success followed racing victory as Soichiro Honda had predicted, but only because the products advanced as rapidly as the racing machinery. The Hondas that came to Britain in the early '60s were incredibly sophisticated. They had overhead cams where the British bikes had pushrods, they had electric starters when the Brits relied on the kickstart, they had 12V electrics when even the biggest British bike used a 6V system. There seemed no end to the technical wizardry. It wasn't that the technology itself was so amazing but just like that first E-type, it was the fact that Honda could mass-produce it more reliably than the lower-tech competition that was so astonishing.

When in 1968 the first four-cylinder CB750 road bike arrived the world of motorcycling changed for ever, they even had to invent a new word for it, 'Superbike'. Honda raced again with the CB750 at Daytona and won the

World Endurance title with a prototype DOHC version that became the CB900 roadster. There was the six-cylinder CBX, the CX500T – the world's first turbocharged production bike, they invented the full-dress tourer with the GoldWing, and came back to GPs with the revolutionary oval-pistoned NR500 four-stroke, a much-misunderstood bike that was more a rolling experimental laboratory than a racer. Just to show their versatility Honda also came up with the weird CX500 shaft-drive V-twin, a rugged workhorse that powered a new industry, the courier companies that oiled the wheels of commerce in London and other big cities.

It was true, though, that Mr Honda was not keen on two-strokes – early motocross engines had to be explained away to him as lawnmower motors! However, in 1982 Honda raced the NS500, an agile three-cylinder lightweight against the big four-cylinder opposition in 500 GPs. The bike won in its first year and in '83 took the world title for Freddie Spencer. In four-stroke racing the V4 layout took over from the straight four, dominating TT, F1 and Endurance championships with the RVF750, the nearest thing ever built to a Formula 1 car on wheels. And when Superbike arrived Honda were ready with the RC30. On the roads the VFR V4 became an instant classic while the CBR600 invented another new class of bike on its way to becoming a best-seller. The V4 road bikes had problems to start with but the VFR750 sold world-wide over its lifetime while the VFR400 became a massive commercial success and cult bike in Japan. The original RC30 won the first two World Superbike Championships is 1988 and '89, but Honda had to wait until 1997 to win it again with the RC45, the last of the V4 roadsters. In Grands Prix, the NSR500 V4 two-stroke superseded the NS triple and became the benchmark racing machine of the '90s. Mick Doohan secured his place in history by winning five World Championships in consecutive years on it.

In yet another example of Honda inventing a new class of motorcycle, they came up with the astounding CBR900RR FireBlade, a bike with the punch of a 1000 cc motor in a package the size and weight of a 750. It became a cult bike as well as a best seller, and with judicious redesigns continues to give much more recent designs a run for their money.

When it became apparent that the high-tech V4 motor of the RC45 was too expensive to produce, Honda looked to a V-twin engine to power its flagship for the first time. Typically, the VTR1000 FireStorm was a much more rideable machine than its opposition and once accepted by the market formed the basis of the next generation of Superbike racer, the VTR-SP-1.

One of Mr Honda's mottos was that technology would solve the customers' problems, and no company has embraced cutting-edge technology more firmly than Honda. In fact Honda often developed new technology, especially in the fields of materials science and metallurgy. The embodiment of that was the NR750, a bike that was misunderstood nearly as much as the original NR500 racer. This limited-edition technological tour-de-force embodied many of Soichiro Honda's ideals. It used the latest techniques and materials in every component, from the oval piston, 32-valve V4 motor to the titanium coating on the windscreen, it was – as Mr Honda would have wanted – the best it could possibly be. A fitting memorial to the man who has shaped the motorcycle industry and motorcyles as we know them today.

The CX500 – Honda's first V-Twin and a favorite choice of dispatch riders

Still Crazy After All These Years

You could never accuse any Honda with a 'double-R' suffix to its name of being anything other than a very focussed motorcycle. However, there have been times during the Fireblade's history when it has not been seen as the ultimate super-sports motorcycle. There were various reasons for this surprising state of affairs, such as the 'Blade's oddball capacity that did not fit into a racing capacity class, Honda's deliberate

The VFR400R was a cult bike in Japan and a popular grey import in the UK

The CBR1000RR-5 in Repsol Honda trim

The revised CBR1000RR-6 model

attempt to keep the bike usable on the road, and the opposition in the shape of the Yamaha R1 and Suzuki GSX-R moving the goal posts. Mind you, there wouldn't have been a game, let alone goal posts, without the original 'Blade.

The 1992 FireBlade (note the capital 'B') was one of those rare bikes that totally redefined not just its class but a whole sector of the market. It was just under 900cc and packed the punch of a litre-bike in a package the size and weight of a 600. It was the concept of Honda R&D chief engineer Tadeo Baba, one of the few Japanese industry figures to achieve fame outside their own company, The 'Blade was his creation and his child (his word) from inception up to and including the 2003 model. The Fireblades (note that the name now lacks that capital 'B' in the middle) in this manual were designed by a team led by HRC engineer Heijiro Yoshimura. There is a great deal of significance in those sets of initials: R&D means what it says on the tin, research and development; HRC is Honda's independent racing company, which means it's about the race track. And this generation of Fireblades is made for the track like no other, chiefly because of the change in World Championship regulations that opened up Superbike racing to 1000cc fours. For the first time there was a reason to push the 'blade's capacity to the full litre and take advantage of MotoGP technology.

The change in Grand Prix regulations in 2002 opened up the class to four-strokes and Honda stunned the opposition with the RCV211, a V5 of deceptively simple elegance and brutal efficiency. It was by far the most successful bike of the 990cc formula that lasted from the inception of MotoGP in 2002 through to the change to 800cc for the 2007 season. Now that the Fireblade was going to be the homologation machine for top-level Superbike racing, it benefited from original research done on the RCV. It even got to look like the GP bike. Most of those lessons bore fruit in the chassis department rather than the engine although the motor did get two-stage fuel injection and was considerably shortened by stacking the gearbox shafts. It got a race-mechanic friendly cassette gearbox as well.

The frame is deceptively simple thanks to advanced die-casting techniques and along with the swinging arm bears a striking resemblance to the MotoGP machine. The effect is, of course, strengthened by the outline of the fairing and the exhaust exiting under the seat: Just like Nicky and Dani's.

But the bits lifted almost directly off the RCV are to be found in the suspension department. At the back, the rear suspension is Unit Pro-Link. This variation on Honda's long established rising-rate linkage is said to isolate the frame from stresses transmitted from the swinging arm and suspension. The whole shock absorber and linkage are mounted on the swinging arm with the only attachment to the main chassis being one end of the linkage rods. At the front, the 'blade also got Honda's electro-hydraulic steering damper (HESD). Originally developed as a crash-proof racing item, basically, it's a vane connected to the top fork yoke by a linking rod and moving in an oil-filled chamber under the influence of the forks turning. An internal valve allows the 'damping' seen by the vane to vary according to riding conditions. The engine management module controls the valve.

The new Fireblade was considered ready for a full-on factory assault on Superbike racing. HRC sent Ryuichi Kyonari to the UK to develop the bike for the Suzuka 8 Hours in the British Superbike Championship while keeping the World Superbike Championship at arm's length owing to political problems with the control-tyre rule. A 'blade duly won the 8 Hour in the hands of Ukawa and Izutsu although Kiyo had to wait until 2006 for his BSB title. In the World Superbike Championship Chris Vermeulen gave the new 'blade three wins in its first season despite his Ten Kate team having minimal factory support. Just like those mould-breaking early 'Blades, it was clear that the new Fireblade designed for the track was going to change the status quo irrevocably.

Acknowledgements

Our thanks are due to Bransons of Yeovil who supplied the machines featured in the illustrations throughout this manual. We would also like to thank NGK Spark Plugs (UK) Ltd for supplying the colour spark plug condition photographs, the Avon Rubber Company for supplying information on tyre fitting and Draper Tools Ltd for some of the workshop tools shown.

Thanks are also due to Julian Ryder who wrote the introduction 'The Birth of a Dream' and to Honda (UK) Ltd. who supplied model photographs.

About this Manual

The aim of this manual is to help you get the best value from your motorcycle. It can do so in several ways. It can help you decide what work must be done, even if you choose to have it done by a dealer; it provides information and procedures for routine maintenance and servicing; and it offers diagnostic and repair procedures to follow when trouble occurs.

We hope you use the manual to tackle the work yourself. For many simpler jobs, doing it yourself may be quicker than arranging an appointment to get the motorcycle into a dealer and making the trips to leave it and pick it up. More importantly, a lot of money can be saved by avoiding the expense the shop must pass on to you to cover its labour and overhead costs. An added benefit is the sense of satisfaction and accomplishment that you feel after doing the job yourself.

References to the left or right side of the motorcycle assume you are sitting on the seat, facing forward.

We take great pride in the accuracy of information given in this manual, but motorcycle manufacturers make alterations and design changes during the production run of a particular motorcycle of which they do not inform us. No liability can be accepted by the authors or publishers for loss, damage or injury caused by any errors in, or omissions from, the information given.

Illegal copying

Frame and engine numbers

The frame serial number is stamped into the right-hand side of the steering head. The engine number is stamped into the crankcase at the back of the engine. Both of these numbers should be recorded and kept in a safe place so they can be given to law enforcement officials in the event of a theft. There is also a colour code label on the top of the rear mudguard, visible after removing the passenger seat, and a VIN plate on the left-hand frame spar. The throttle bodies also have an ID number stamped into them.

The frame serial number, engine serial number, and colour code should also be kept in a handy place (such as with your driver's licence) so they are always available when purchasing or ordering parts for your machine.

The procedures in this manual identify model years by their code letters and number, e.g. RR-4 (2004). The model code is printed on the colour code label.

Model code	Production year
CBR1000RR-4	2004
CBR1000RR-5	2005
CBR1000RR-6	2006
CBR1000RR-7	2007

The VIN plate (arrowed) is riveted to the left-hand frame spar

The colour code label is on the top of the rear mudguard under the passenger seat

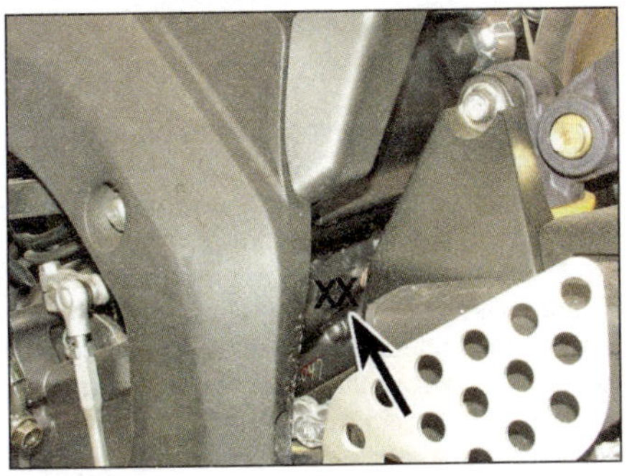

The engine number (arrowed) is stamped into the crankcase at the back of the engine

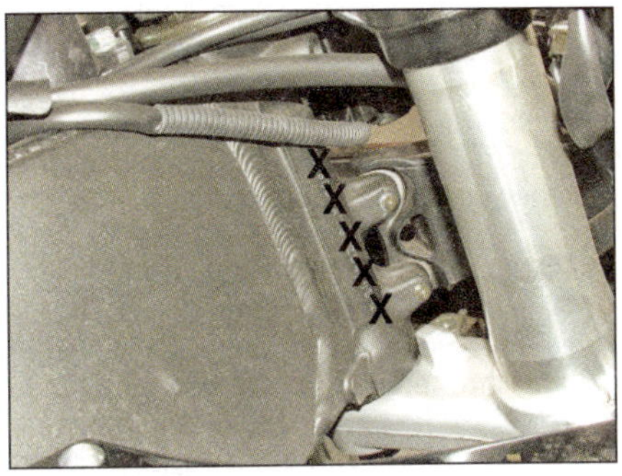

The frame number is stamped into the right-hand side of the steering head

Buying spare parts

Once you have found all the identification numbers, record them for reference when buying parts. Since the manufacturers change specifications, parts and vendors (companies that manufacture various components on the machine), providing the ID numbers is the only way to be reasonably sure that you are buying the correct parts.

Whenever possible, take the worn part to the dealer so direct comparison with the new component can be made. Along the trail from the manufacturer to the parts shelf, there are numerous places that the part can end up with the wrong number or be listed incorrectly.

The two places to purchase new parts for your motorcycle – the franchised or main dealer and the parts/accessories store – differ in the type of parts they carry. While dealers can obtain every single genuine part for your motorcycle, the accessory store is usually limited to normal high wear items such as chains and sprockets, brake pads, spark plugs and lubes.

Used parts can be obtained from breakers yards for roughly half the price of new ones, but you can't always be sure of what you're getting. Once again, take your worn part to the breaker for direct comparison, or when ordering by mail order make sure that you can return it if you are not happy.

Whether buying new, used or rebuilt parts, the best course is to deal directly with someone who specialises in your particular make.

Professional mechanics are trained in safe working procedures. However enthusiastic you may be about getting on with the job at hand, take the time to ensure that your safety is not put at risk. A moment's lack of attention can result in an accident, as can failure to observe simple precautions.

There will always be new ways of having accidents, and the following is not a comprehensive list of all dangers; it is intended rather to make you aware of the risks and to encourage a safe approach to all work you carry out on your bike.

Asbestos

- Certain friction, insulating, sealing and other products - such as brake pads, clutch linings, gaskets, etc. - contain asbestos. Extreme care must be taken to avoid inhalation of dust from such products since it is hazardous to health. If in doubt, assume that they do contain asbestos.

Fire

- Remember at all times that petrol is highly flammable. Never smoke or have any kind of naked flame around, when working on the vehicle. But the risk does not end there - a spark caused by an electrical short-circuit, by two metal surfaces contacting each other, by careless use of tools, or even by static electricity built up in your body under certain conditions, can ignite petrol vapour, which in a confined space is highly explosive. Never use petrol as a cleaning solvent. Use an approved safety solvent.
- Always disconnect the battery earth terminal before working on any part of the fuel or electrical system, and never risk spilling fuel on to a hot engine or exhaust.
- It is recommended that a fire extinguisher of a type suitable for fuel and electrical fires is kept handy in the garage or workplace at all times. Never try to extinguish a fuel or electrical fire with water.

Fumes

- Certain fumes are highly toxic and can quickly cause unconsciousness and even death if inhaled to any extent. Petrol vapour comes into this category, as do the vapours from certain solvents such as trichloro-ethylene. Any draining or pouring of such volatile fluids should be done in a well ventilated area.
- When using cleaning fluids and solvents, read the instructions carefully. Never use materials from unmarked containers - they may give off poisonous vapours.
- Never run the engine of a motor vehicle in an enclosed space such as a garage. Exhaust fumes contain carbon monoxide which is extremely poisonous; if you need to run the engine, always do so in the open air or at least have the rear of the vehicle outside the workplace.

The battery

- Never cause a spark, or allow a naked light near the vehicle's battery. It will normally be giving off a certain amount of hydrogen gas, which is highly explosive.
- Always disconnect the battery ground (earth) terminal before working on the fuel or electrical systems (except where noted).
- If possible, loosen the filler plugs or cover when charging the battery from an external source. Do not charge at an excessive rate or the battery may burst.
- Take care when topping up, cleaning or carrying the battery. The acid electrolyte, evenwhen diluted, is very corrosive and should not be allowed to contact the eyes or skin. Always wear rubber gloves and goggles or a face shield. If you ever need to prepare electrolyte yourself, always add the acid slowly to the water; never add the water to the acid.

Electricity

- When using an electric power tool, inspection light etc., always ensure that the appliance is correctly connected to its plug and that, where necessary, it is properly grounded (earthed). Do not use such appliances in damp conditions and, again, beware of creating a spark or applying excessive heat in the vicinity of fuel or fuel vapour. Also ensure that the appliances meet national safety standards.
- A severe electric shock can result from touching certain parts of the electrical system, such as the spark plug wires (HT leads), when the engine is running or being cranked, particularly if components are damp or the insulation is defective. Where an electronic ignition system is used, the secondary (HT) voltage is much higher and could prove fatal.

Remember...

✗ **Don't** start the engine without first ascertaining that the transmission is in neutral.

✗ **Don't** suddenly remove the pressure cap from a hot cooling system - cover it with a cloth and release the pressure gradually first, or you may get scalded by escaping coolant.

✗ **Don't** attempt to drain oil until you are sure it has cooled sufficiently to avoid scalding you.

✗ **Don't** grasp any part of the engine or exhaust system without first ascertaining that it is cool enough not to burn you.

✗ **Don't** allow brake fluid or antifreeze to contact the machine's paintwork or plastic components.

✗ **Don't** siphon toxic liquids such as fuel, hydraulic fluid or antifreeze by mouth, or allow them to remain on your skin.

✗ **Don't** inhale dust - it may be injurious to health (see Asbestos heading).

✗ **Don't** allow any spilled oil or grease to remain on the floor - wipe it up right away, before someone slips on it.

✗ **Don't** use ill-fitting spanners or other tools which may slip and cause injury.

✗ **Don't** lift a heavy component which may be beyond your capability - get assistance.

✗ **Don't** rush to finish a job or take unverified short cuts.

✗ **Don't** allow children or animals in or around an unattended vehicle.

✗ **Don't** inflate a tyre above the recommended pressure. Apart from overstressing the carcass, in extreme cases the tyre may blow off forcibly.

✓ **Do** ensure that the machine is supported securely at all times. This is especially important when the machine is blocked up to aid wheel or fork removal.

✓ **Do** take care when attempting to loosen a stubborn nut or bolt. It is generally better to pull on a spanner, rather than push, so that if you slip, you fall away from the machine rather than onto it.

✓ **Do** wear eye protection when using power tools such as drill, sander, bench grinder etc.

✓ **Do** use a barrier cream on your hands prior to undertaking dirty jobs - it will protect your skin from infection as well as making the dirt easier to remove afterwards; but make sure your hands aren't left slippery. Note that long-term contact with used engine oil can be a health hazard.

✓ **Do** keep loose clothing (cuffs, ties etc. and long hair) well out of the way of moving mechanical parts.

✓ **Do** remove rings, wristwatch etc., before working on the vehicle - especially the electrical system.

✓ **Do** keep your work area tidy - it is only too easy to fall over articles left lying around.

✓ **Do** exercise caution when compressing springs for removal or installation. Ensure that the tension is applied and released in a controlled manner, using suitable tools which preclude the possibility of the spring escaping violently.

✓ **Do** ensure that any lifting tackle used has a safe working load rating adequate for the job.

✓ **Do** get someone to check periodically that all is well, when working alone on the vehicle.

✓ **Do** carry out work in a logical sequence and check that everything is correctly assembled and tightened afterwards.

✓ **Do** remember that your vehicle's safety affects that of yourself and others. If in doubt on any point, get professional advice.

- If in spite of following these precautions, you are unfortunate enough to injure yourself, seek medical attention as soon as possible.

Note: *The Pre-ride checks outlined in the owner's manual covers those items which should be inspected before riding the motorcycle.*

Engine oil level

Before you start:

✔ Start the engine and let it idle for 3 to 5 minutes.

Caution: Do not run the engine in an enclosed space such as a garage or workshop.

✔ Stop the engine and hold the motorcycle upright. Allow it to stand undisturbed for 2 to 3 minutes to allow the oil level to stabilise. Make sure the motorcycle is on level ground.

Bike care:

● If you have to add oil frequently, check whether you have any oil leaks from the engine joints, oil seals and gaskets. If not, the engine could be burning oil, in which case there will be white smoke coming out of the exhaust (see *Fault Finding*).

The correct oil:

● Modern, high-revving engines place great demands on their oil. It is very important that the correct oil for your bike is used.

● Always top up with a good quality oil of the specified type and viscosity and do not overfill the engine.

Caution: Do not use chemical additives or oils labelled "ENERGY CONSERVING". Such additives or oils could cause clutch slip.

Oil type	API grade SG or higher conforming to JASO MA.
Oil viscosity	SAE 10W40*

**If you are using the motorcycle constantly in extreme conditions of heat or cold, other more suitable viscosity ranges may be used – refer to the viscosity table to select the oil best suited to your conditions.*

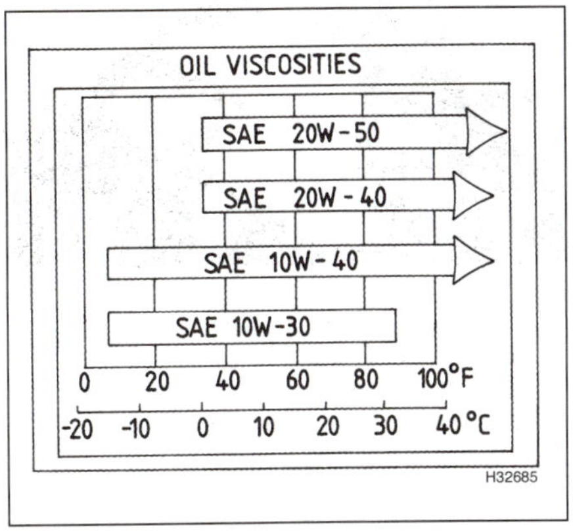

Oil viscosity table: select the oil best suited to your conditions

1 The oil level inspection window is located on the right-hand side of the engine and is visible via the aperture (arrowed) in the lower fairing panel. If necessary wipe the window so that it is clean.

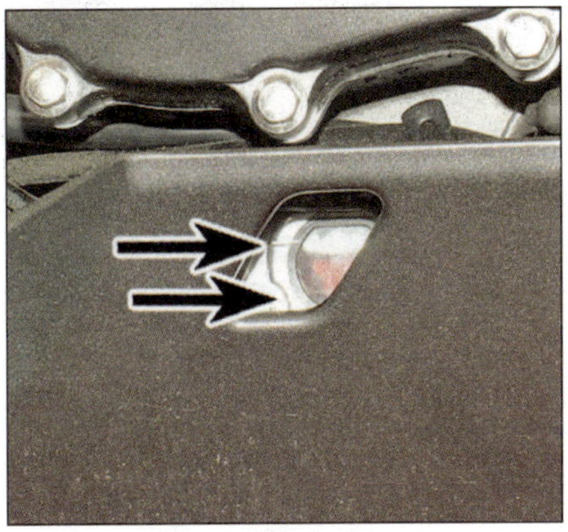

2 With the motorcycle vertical, the oil level should lie between the upper and lower level lines (arrowed).

3 If the level is on or below the lower line, unscrew the oil filler cap from the clutch cover.

4 Top up the engine with the recommended grade and type of oil to bring the level almost up to the upper line on the inspection window. Do not overfill. On completion, make sure the filler cap is secure in the cover.

Coolant level

Warning: DO NOT remove the radiator pressure cap to add coolant. Topping up is done via the coolant reservoir tank filler. DO NOT leave open containers of coolant about, as it is poisonous.

Before you start:

✔ Make sure you have a supply of coolant available (a mixture of 50% distilled water and 50% corrosion inhibited ethylene glycol anti-freeze is needed).

✔ Always check the coolant level when the engine is at normal working temperature. Take the motorcycle on a short run to allow it to reach normal temperature.

Caution: Do not run the engine in an enclosed space such as a garage or workshop.

✔ Stop the engine and hold the motorcycle upright, ensuring it is on level ground.

Bike care:

● Use only the specified coolant mixture. It is important that anti-freeze is used in the system all year round, and not just in the winter. Do not top the system up using only water, as the system will become too diluted.

● Do not overfill the reservoir tank. If the coolant is significantly above the UPPER level line at any time, the surplus should be siphoned or drained off to prevent the possibility of it being expelled out of the overflow hose.

● If the coolant level falls steadily, check the system for leaks (see Chapter 1). If no leaks are found and the level continues to fall, it is recommended that the machine is taken to a Honda dealer for a pressure test.

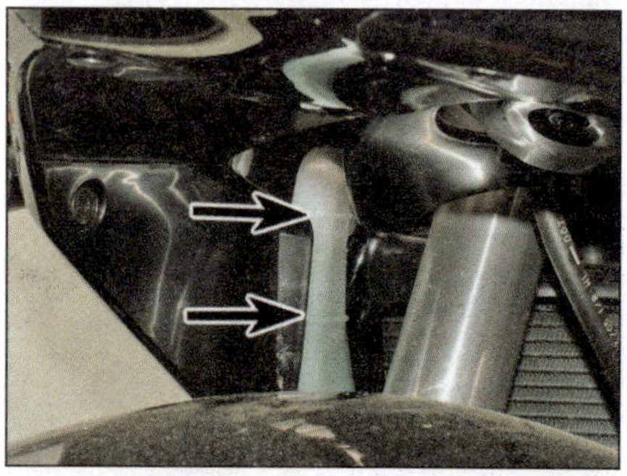

1 The coolant reservoir is located at the front of the radiator on the right-hand side and is visible by looking under the fairing. If necessary wipe the reservoir so that it is clean. With the motorcycle held upright, the coolant level should lie between the upper and lower level lines (arrowed) marked on the reservoir.

2 If the coolant level is on or below the LOWER line, remove the right-hand fairing side panel (see Chapter 7). Remove the reservoir filler cap.

3 Top the reservoir up with the recommended coolant mixture to the UPPER level line, using a suitable funnel if required. Fit the cap securely. Install the fairing side panel (see Chapter 7).

Brake fluid levels

Warning: Hydraulic fluid can harm your eyes and damage painted surfaces, so use extreme caution when handling and pouring it and cover surrounding surfaces with rag. Do not use fluid that has been standing open for some time, as it is hygroscopic (absorbs moisture from the air) which can cause a dangerous loss of braking effectiveness.

Before you start:

✔ The front brake fluid reservoir is on the right-hand handlebar. The rear brake fluid reservoir is located under the seat cowling on the right-hand side.

✔ Make sure you have a supply of DOT 4 hydraulic fluid.

✔ Wrap a rag around the reservoir being worked on to ensure that any spillage does not come into contact with painted surfaces.

✔ When checking the fluid in the front reservoir, place the motorcycle on its sidestand and turn the handlebars to full right lock.

✔ When checking the fluid in the rear reservoir support the motorcycle upright.

Bike care:

● The fluid in the front and rear brake master cylinder reservoirs will drop as the brake pads wear down. If the fluid level is low check the brake pads for wear (see Chapter 1), and replace them with new ones if necessary (see Chapter 6). Do not top the reservoir(s) up until the new pads have been fitted, and then check to see if topping up is still necessary - when the caliper pistons are pushed back to accommodate the extra thickness of the new pads some fluid will be displaced back into the reservoir.

● If either fluid reservoir requires repeated topping up there is a leak somewhere in the system, which must be investigated immediately.

● Check for signs of fluid leakage from the hydraulic hoses and/or brake system components – if found, rectify immediately (see Chapter 6).

● Check the operation of both brakes before taking the machine on the road; if there is evidence of air in the system (spongy feel to lever or pedal), it must be bled (see Chapter 6).

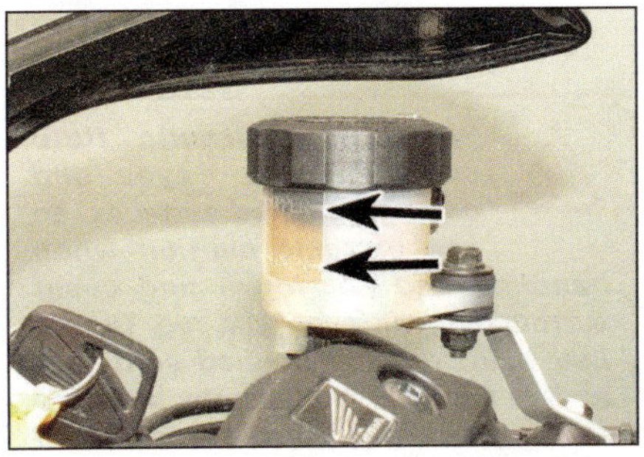

1 The front brake fluid level is visible through the window in the reservoir body – it must be between the UPPER and LOWER level lines (arrowed).

2 On RR-4 and RR-5 models, if the level is on or below the LOWER line, undo the reservoir cap screws. Remove the cap, diaphragm plate and diaphragm - the float can remain in the reservoir.

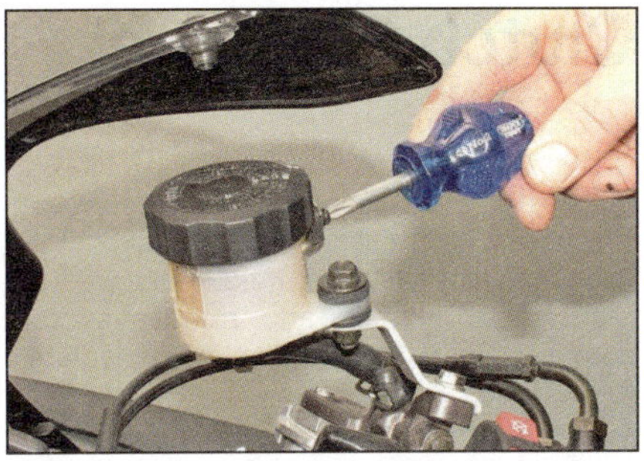

3 On RR-6 and RR-7 models, if the level is on or below the LOWER line, undo the cap clamp screw. Remove the cap, diaphragm plate and diaphragm.

4 Top up with new clean DOT 4 hydraulic fluid, until the level is up to the UPPER line on the reservoir. Do not overfill and take care to avoid spills (see **Warning** opposite).

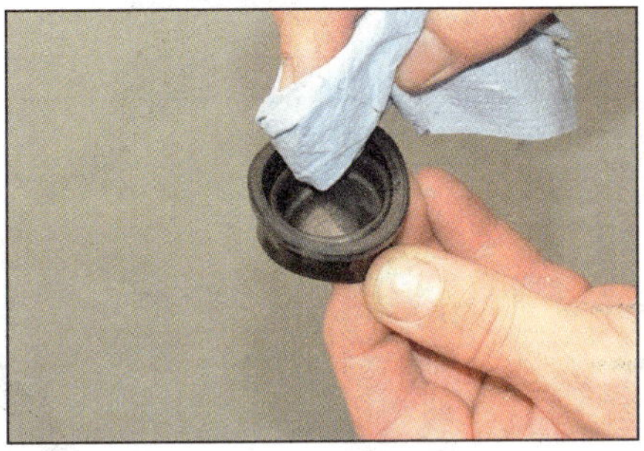

5 Wipe any moisture off the diaphragm with a tissue.

6 Ensure that the diaphragm is correctly seated before installing the plate and cap. Secure the reservoir cover with its screws (RR-4 and RR-5) or clamp (RR-6 and RR-7).

Front brake - steps 1-6

Rear brake - steps 7-11

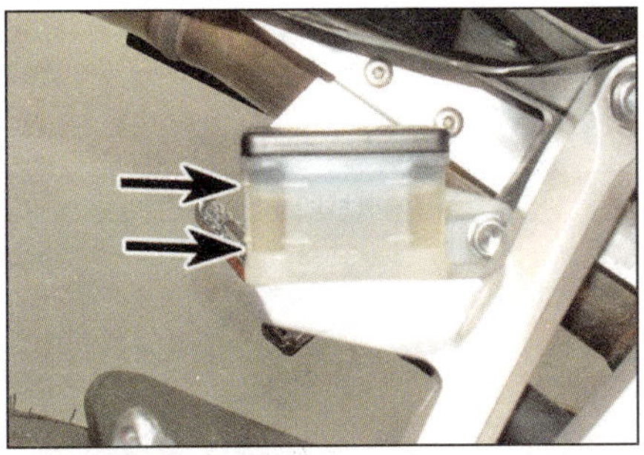

7 The rear brake fluid level is visible through the reservoir body – it must be between the UPPER and LOWER level lines (arrowed).

8 If the level is on or below the LOWER line, remove the seat cowling (see Chapter 7). Undo the two reservoir cover screws, and remove the diaphragm plate and diaphragm.

9 Top up with new clean DOT 4 hydraulic fluid, until the level is up to the UPPER line. Do not overfill and take care to avoid spills (see **Warning** opposite).

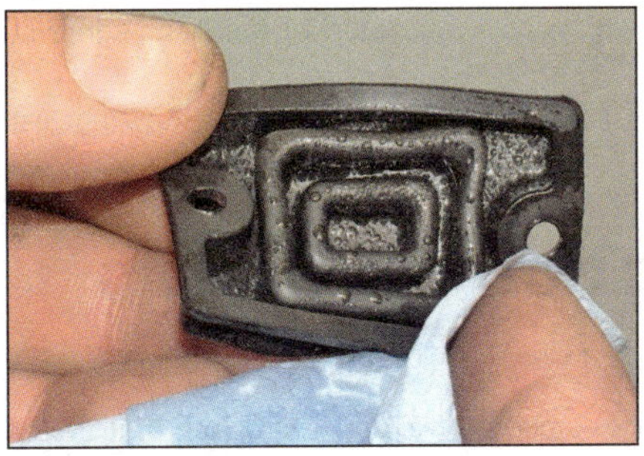

10 Wipe any moisture off the diaphragm with a tissue.

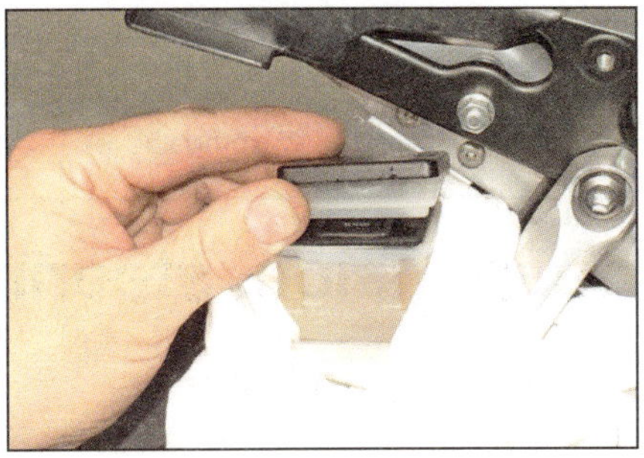

11 Ensure that the diaphragm is correctly seated before installing the plate and cover. Secure the cover with its screws. Install the seat cowling.

Clutch fluid level

Bike care:

- If the fluid reservoir requires repeated topping-up there is a leak somewhere in the system, which must be investigated immediately.
- Check for signs of fluid leakage from the hydraulic hose and release system components – if found, rectify immediately (see Chapter 2).
- Check the operation of the clutch before taking the machine on the road; if there is evidence of air in the system (spongy feel to the lever, difficulty selecting gears and clutch drag), it must be bled (see Chapter 2).

Before you start:

✔ The clutch fluid reservoir is on the left-hand handlebar.

✔ Make sure you have a supply of DOT 4 hydraulic fluid.

✔ Wrap a rag around the reservoir to ensure that any spillage does not come into contact with painted surfaces.

✔ When checking the fluid, place the motorcycle on its sidestand and turn the handlebars to full left lock.

Warning: Hydraulic fluid can harm your eyes and damage painted surfaces, so use extreme caution when handling and pouring it and cover surrounding surfaces with rag. Do not use fluid from an opened container as it is hygroscopic (absorbs moisture from the air) which can cause a loss of clutch effectiveness.

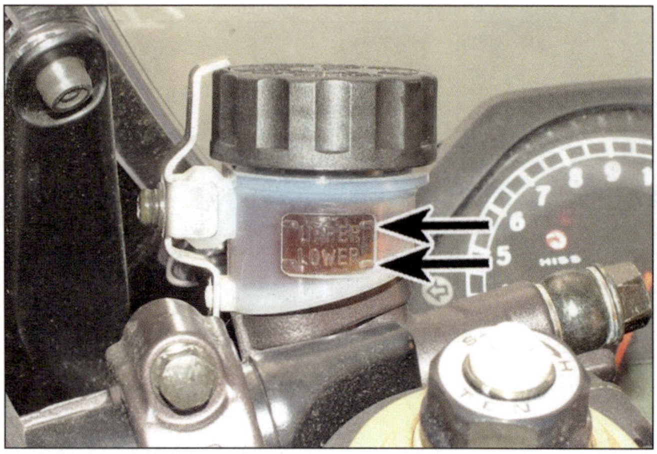

1 The clutch fluid level is visible through the window in the reservoir body – it must be between the UPPER and LOWER level lines (arrowed).

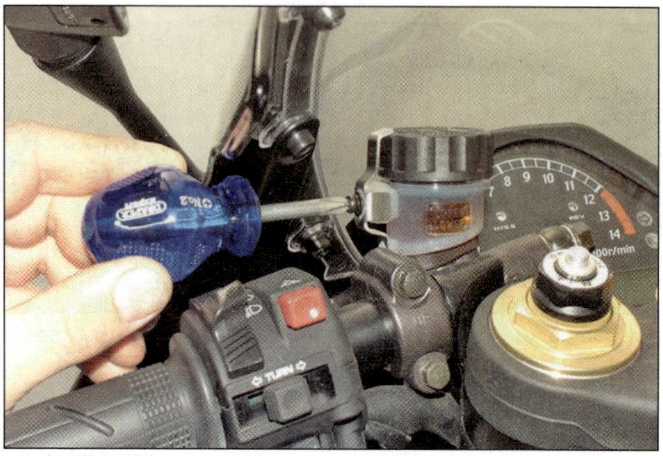

2 If the level is on or below the LOWER line, undo the cap clamp screw. Remove the cap, diaphragm plate and diaphragm.

3 Top up with new DOT 4 hydraulic fluid, until the level is up to the UPPER line on the reservoir. Do not overfill and take care to avoid spills (see **Warning** above).

4 Wipe any moisture off the diaphragm with a tissue.

5 Ensure that the diaphragm is correctly seated before installing the plate and cap. Secure the reservoir cover with its clamp.

Suspension, steering and drive chain

Suspension and Steering:

- Check that the front and rear suspension operates smoothly without binding (see Chapter 1).
- Check that the suspension is adjusted as required (see Chapter 5).
- Check that the steering moves smoothly from lock-to-lock.

Drive chain:

- Check that the chain isn't too loose or too tight, and adjust it if necessary (see Chapter 1).
- If the chain looks dry, lubricate it (see Chapter 1).

Tyres

The correct pressures:

● The tyres must be checked when **cold**, not immediately after riding. Note that tyre pressure is affected by ambient temperature and atmospheric pressure and so can change daily.

● Incorrect tyre pressures will cause abnormal tread wear and unsafe handling. Low tyre pressures may cause the tyre to slip on the rim or come off.

● Use an accurate pressure gauge. Many forecourt gauges are wildly inaccurate. If you buy your own, spend as much as you can justify on a quality gauge.

● Proper air pressure will increase tyre life and provide maximum stability and ride comfort.

Front	Rear
36 psi (2.50 Bar)	42 psi (2.90 Bar)

Tyre care:

● Check the tyres carefully for cuts, tears, embedded nails or other sharp objects and excessive wear. Operation of the motorcycle with excessively worn tyres is extremely hazardous, as traction and handling are directly affected.

● Pick out any stones or nails which may have become embedded in the tyre tread. If left, they will eventually penetrate through the casing and cause a puncture.

● Ensure the dust cap is in place. If air escapes when the cap is removed the valve could be lose in its core - a simple tool that is cheaply available and sometimes incorporated in the cap is needed to tighten the valve. Check the condition of the valve.

● If tyre damage is apparent, or unexplained loss of pressure is experienced, seek the advice of a tyre fitting specialist without delay.

Tyre tread depth:

● At the time of writing UK law requires that tread depth must be at least 1 mm over 3/4 of the tread breadth all the way around the tyre, with no bald patches. Many riders, however, consider 2 mm tread depth minimum to be a safer limit. Honda recommend a minimum of 1.5 mm on the front and 2 mm on the rear, but note that German law requires a minimum of 1.6 mm for each tyre.

● Many tyres now incorporate wear indicators in the tread. Identify the location marking on the tyre sidewall to locate the indicator bar and replace the tyre if the tread has worn down to the bar.

1 Remove the dust cap from the valve. Do not forget to fit the cap after checking the pressure.

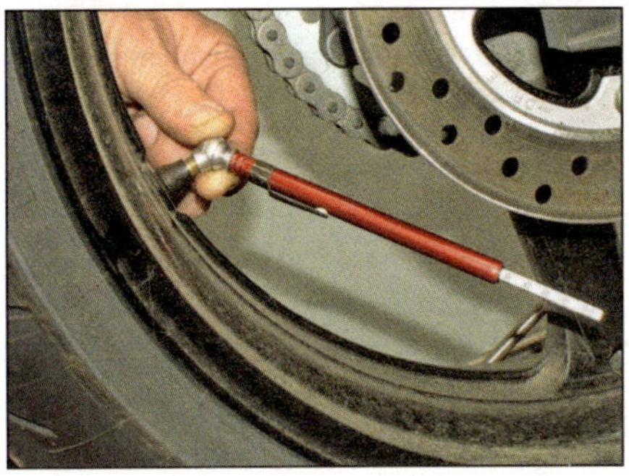

2 Check the tyre pressures when cold.

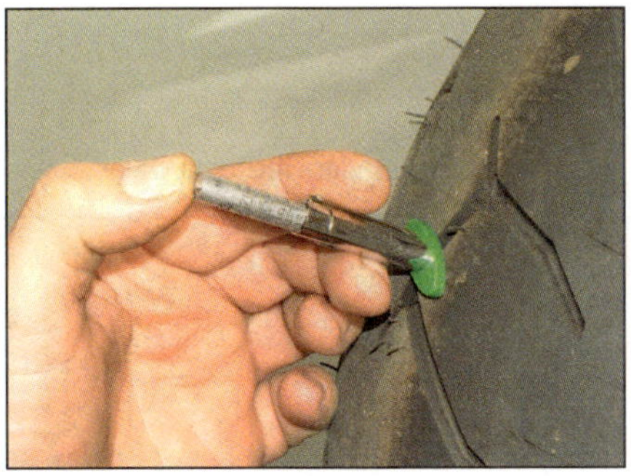

3 Measure tread depth at the centre of the tyre using a depth gauge.

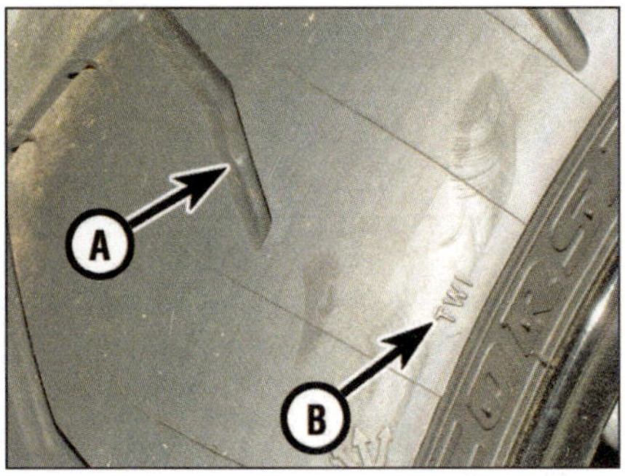

4 Tyre tread wear indicator (A) and its location marking (B) on the edge or sidewall (according to manufacturer).

Legal and safety

Lighting and signalling:

● Take a minute to check that the headlight, tail light, brake light, licence plate light, instrument lights and turn signals all work correctly.

● Check that the horn sounds when the button is pressed.

● A working speedometer, graduated in mph, is a statutory requirement in the UK.

Safety:

● Check that the throttle grip rotates smoothly when opened and snaps shut when released, in all steering positions. Also check for the correct amount of freeplay (see Chapter 1).

● Check that the brake lever and pedal, clutch lever and gearchange lever operate smoothly. Lubricate them at the specified intervals or when necessary (see Chapter 1).

● Check that the engine shuts off when the kill switch is operated. Check the starter interlock circuit (see Chapter 1).

● Check that sidestand return springs hold the stand up securely when retracted.

Fuel:

● This may seem obvious, but check that you have enough fuel to complete your journey. If you smell petrol (gasoline) or notice signs of fuel leakage, rectify the cause immediately.

● Ensure you use the correct grade fuel – see Chapter 4 Specifications.

2004 CBR1000RR-4

The design concept for the new Fireblade was weight saving and mass centralisation to improve handling. The new CBR1000RR retained the in-line four cylinder liquid-cooled engine configuration of the previous CBR954RR model, but in a more compact form. The main differences were in the transmission area with an hydraulically actuated clutch and cassette-type gearbox.

The PGM-FI fuel injection system fitted to previous Fireblade models was replaced by PGM-DSFI (programmed dual-stage fuel injection), which incorporates two injectors per cylinder. The primary injectors are mounted in the throttle bodies below the throttle valve and operate all the time the engine is running. The secondary injectors are mounted in the top of the air filter housing and spray fuel into the air entering the throttle bodies above the throttle valves. These secondary injectors operate when the throttle is opened wide at engine speeds over 5500 rpm. An electronic engine management system controls both the injection system and the ignition system.

The fuel system incorporates a variable intake and exhaust system, with the flow of air through the air box controlled using a two-position valve, and the flow of gases through the exhaust system controlled by Honda's EGCV or exhaust gas control valve.

The engine sits in a twin-beam aluminium frame which uses the engine as a stressed member. Front suspension is by fully adjustable upside-down oil-damped 43 mm forks with cartridge dampers. Rear suspension is Honda's new unit Pro-link with a fully adjustable single shock absorber via a three-way rising rate linkage, and mimicks the floating design used for the RC211V Moto GP bike by incorporating the upper shock absorber mount in the swingarm as opposed to It being bolted to the frame.

A radical new feature is Honda's electronically controlled hydraulic rotary steering damper (HESD), which enables high-speed stability without the loss of low speed balance and control; it ensures progressive damping in accordance with information received on vehicle speed and acceleration by the system's control unit, which is integrated with the engine management system's control module (ECM).

The front brake system has two radial-mounted twin-opposed piston calipers acting on 310 mm floating discs. The rear brake system has a single piston sliding caliper acting on a conventional 220 mm disc.

Colour schemes were white/red/blue, black/silver and red/black.

CBR1000RR-5 2005 model

There were no significant changes from the RR-4 (2004) model.

Colour schemes were red/blue/silver, black, blue/black/silver, and Repsol Honda replica colours.

CBR1000RR-6 2006 model

Development work on the cylinder head involved refined intake port design and larger exhaust ports, which combined with the use of dual valve springs on the intake valves enabled a higher maximum engine speed, and a smaller combustion chamber, thereby increasing the compression ratio. The crankshaft was strengthened without adding weight, while the camshafts were reduced in weight.

Full EURO 3 exhaust emissions compliance was achieved using a pollution control system and catalyser.

Dimensional frame and swingarm changes improved handling, and a redesigned radiator and exhaust reduced weight further. Changes to the braking system involved larger diameter 320 mm front brake discs and a modified rear caliper. The bodywork was restyled and the coolant reservoir and air filter housing were modified.

Colour schemes were black/grey, red/black and silver/black.

CBR1000RR-7 2007 model

There are no significant changes from the RR-6 (2006) model.

Colour schemes were red/blue/white, black, red/black, and Repsol Honda replica colours.

Engine

Type	Four-stroke in-line four
Capacity	998 cc
Bore	75.0 mm
Stroke	56.5 mm
Compression ratio	
RR-4 and RR-5 models	11.9 to 1
RR-6 and RR-7 models	12.2 to1
Cooling system	Liquid cooled
Clutch	Wet multi-plate
Transmission	Six-speed constant mesh
Final drive	Chain and sprockets
Camshafts	DOHC, chain-driven
Fuel system	PGM-DSFI fuel injection
Exhaust system	Four-into-one with under seat silencer
Ignition system	Computer-controlled digital transistorised with electronic advance

Chassis

Frame type	Twin spar aluminium box-section
Rake and Trail	
RR-4 and RR-5 models	23.45°, 102 mm
RR-6 and RR-7 models	23.25°, 100 mm
Fuel tank	
Capacity (including reserve)	18.0 litres
Reserve volume	approx. 3.5 litres
Front suspension	
Type	43 mm oil-damped cartridge-type upside down telescopic forks
Travel	110 mm
Adjustment	Spring pre-load, rebound and compression damping
Rear suspension	
Type	Single floating shock absorber, rising rate linkage, box-section aluminium swingarm
Travel (at axle)	
RR-4 and RR-5 models	135 mm
RR-6 and RR-7 models	133 mm
Adjustment	Spring pre-load, rebound and compression damping
Wheels	17 inch 3-spoke alloys
Tyres	
Front	120/70-ZR17 (58W) Radial
Rear	190/50-ZR17 (73W) Radial
Front brake	
RR-4 and RR-5 models	Twin 310 mm floating discs with four piston calipers
RR-6 and RR-7 models	Twin 320 mm floating discs with four piston calipers
Rear brake	Single 220 mm disc with single piston sliding caliper

Dimensions and weights

Overall length	
RR-4 and RR-5 models	2025 mm
RR-6 and RR-7 models	2030 mm
Overall width	720 mm
Overall height	1120 mm
Wheelbase	
RR-4 and RR-5 models	1410 mm
RR-6 and RR-7 models	1400 mm
Seat height	820 mm
Ground clearance	130 mm
Weight (dry)	
RR-4 and RR-5 models	179 kg
RR-6 and RR-7 models	174 kg
Weight (wet)	
RR-4 and RR-5 models	210 kg
RR-6 and RR-7 models	205 kg
Maximum weight capacity	
UK and European models	180 kg
US models	166 kg
Canada models	170 kg

Chapter 1
Routine maintenance and servicing

Contents

Degrees of difficulty

Easy, suitable for novice with little experience	**Fairly easy,** suitable for beginner with some experience	**Fairly difficult,** suitable for competent DIY mechanic	**Difficult,** suitable for experienced DIY mechanic	**Very difficult,** suitable for expert DIY or professional

Engine

Cylinder numbering	1 to 4 from left to right
Spark plug type	
NGK	IMR9C-9HES
Denso	VUH27ES
Spark plug electrode gap	0.8 to 0.9 mm
Engine idle speed	1200 ± 100 rpm
Valve clearances (COLD engine)	
Intake valves	0.13 to 0.19 mm
Exhaust valves	0.27 to 0.33 mm

Cycle parts

Drive chain slack	25 to 35 mm
Throttle cable freeplay	2 to 4 mm
Tyre pressures (cold)	see *Pre-ride checks*
Steering head bearing pre-load (see text)	
RR-4 and RR-5 models	12 to 19 N
RR-6 and RR-7 models	13 to 19 N

Lubricants and fluids

Engine oil	see Pre-ride checks
Engine oil capacity	
Oil change	3.0 litres
Oil and filter change	3.1 litres
Following engine overhaul – dry engine, new filter	3.8 litres
Coolant type	50% distilled water, 50% corrosion inhibited ethylene glycol anti-freeze
Coolant capacity	
Radiator and engine	
RR-4 and RR-5 models	3.5 litres
RR-6 and RR-7 models	3.3 litres
Reservoir	0.4 litres
Brake and clutch fluid	DOT 4
Drive chain	SAE 80 or 90 gear oil or chain lubricant suitable for O-ring chains
Steering head bearings	Urea based multi-purpose grease with EP2 rating
Swingarm pivot bearings	Multi-purpose grease with EP2 rating
Suspension linkage bearings	Multi-purpose grease with EP2 rating
Gearchange linkage rod ball joints	Multi-purpose grease with EP2 rating
Bearing seal lips	Multi-purpose grease
Gearchange lever/rear brake pedal/footrest pivots	Multi-purpose grease
Clutch lever pivot	Silicone grease
Sidestand pivot	Multi-purpose grease
Throttle twistgrip	Multi-purpose grease
Front brake lever pivot and piston tip	Silicone grease
Clutch lever pivot and piston tip	Silicone grease
Rear brake caliper slider pin boots	Silicone grease
Throttle cables	Cable lubricant
Exhaust gas control valve cables	Molybdenum oil (50% molybdenum disulphide grease, 50% engine oil)

Torque settings

Cooling system drain bolt	12 Nm
Engine oil drain plug	29 Nm
Engine oil filter	26 Nm
Fork clamp bolts (top yoke)	23 Nm
Handlebar clamp bolts	26 Nm
Handlebar end weight screw	10 Nm
Rear axle nut	113 Nm
Spark plugs	16 Nm
Steering head bearing adjuster nut	
RR-4 and RR-5 models	20 Nm
RR-6 and RR-7 models	27 Nm
Steering stem nut	103 Nm
Timing inspection cap	18 Nm

Note: *The Pre-ride checks outlined in the owner's manual cover those items which should be inspected before every ride. Also perform the pre-ride inspection at every maintenance interval (in addition to the procedures listed). The intervals listed below are the intervals recommended by the manufacturer for the models covered in this manual.*

Pre-ride

- ☐ See 'Pre-ride checks' at the beginning of this manual

After the initial 600 miles (1000 km)

Note: *This check is usually performed by a Honda dealer after the first 600 miles (1000 km) from new. Thereafter, maintenance is carried out according to the following intervals of the schedule.*

Every 500 miles (800 km)

- ☐ Check, adjust, clean and lubricate the drive chain (Section 1)

Every 4000 miles (6000 km) or 6 months

- ☐ Check and adjust the engine idle speed (Section 2)
- ☐ Check the brake pads for wear (Section 3)
- ☐ Check the clutch (Section 4)

Every 8000 miles (12,000 km) or 12 months

Carry out all the items under the 4000 mile (6000 km) check, plus the following:

- ☐ Check the fuel system and hoses (Section 5)
- ☐ Check and adjust the throttle cables (Section 6)
- ☐ Change the engine oil and fit a new filter (Section 7)
- ☐ Check the cooling system (Section 8)
- ☐ Check the pulse secondary air injection (PAIR) system (Section 9)
- ☐ Check the brake system and brake light switch operation (Section 3)
- ☐ Check the sidestand and starter interlock circuit (Section 10)
- ☐ Check the front and rear suspension (Section 11)
- ☐ Check and adjust the steering head bearings (Section 12)
- ☐ Check the condition of the wheels, wheel bearings and tyres (Section 13)
- ☐ Lubricate the clutch, gearchange and brake levers, brake pedal, sidestand pivot, and the throttle and exhaust valve cables (Section 14)
- ☐ Check the tightness of all nuts, bolts and fasteners (Section 15)

Every 12,000 miles (18,000 km) or 18 months

Carry out all the items under the 4000 mile (6000 km) check, plus the following:

- ☐ Fit new air filter elements (Section 16)
- ☐ Check the EVAP (evaporative emission control) system (California models only) (Section 17)

Every 12,000 miles (18,000 km) or two years

Carry out all the items under the 4000 mile (6000 km) check, plus the following:

- ☐ Change the brake fluid and clutch fluid (Sections 3 and 4)

Every 16,000 miles (24,000 km) or two years

Carry out all the items under the 8000 mile (12,000 km) check, plus the following:

- ☐ Check and adjust the valve clearances (Section 18)
- ☐ Check the spark plugs (Section 19)
- ☐ Check the exhaust gas control valve (Section 20)

Every 24,000 miles (36,000 km) or two years

Carry out all the items under the 12,000 mile (18,000 km) and 8000 mile (12,000 km) checks, plus the following:

- ☐ Change the coolant (Section 8)

Every 32,000 miles (48,000 km)

Carry out all the items under the 16,000 mile (24,000 km) check, plus the following:

- ☐ Fit new spark plugs (Section 19)

Non-scheduled maintenance

- ☐ Check the battery (Section 21)
- ☐ Fit new brake and clutch master cylinder and caliper/release cylinder seals (Sections 3 and 4)
- ☐ Fit new brake and clutch hoses (Sections 3 and 4)
- ☐ Clean the fuel strainer (Section 5)
- ☐ Fit new fuel system hoses (Section 5)
- ☐ Change the front fork oil (Section 11)
- ☐ Re-grease the swingarm and suspension linkage bearings (Section 11)
- ☐ Re-grease the steering head bearings (Section 12)

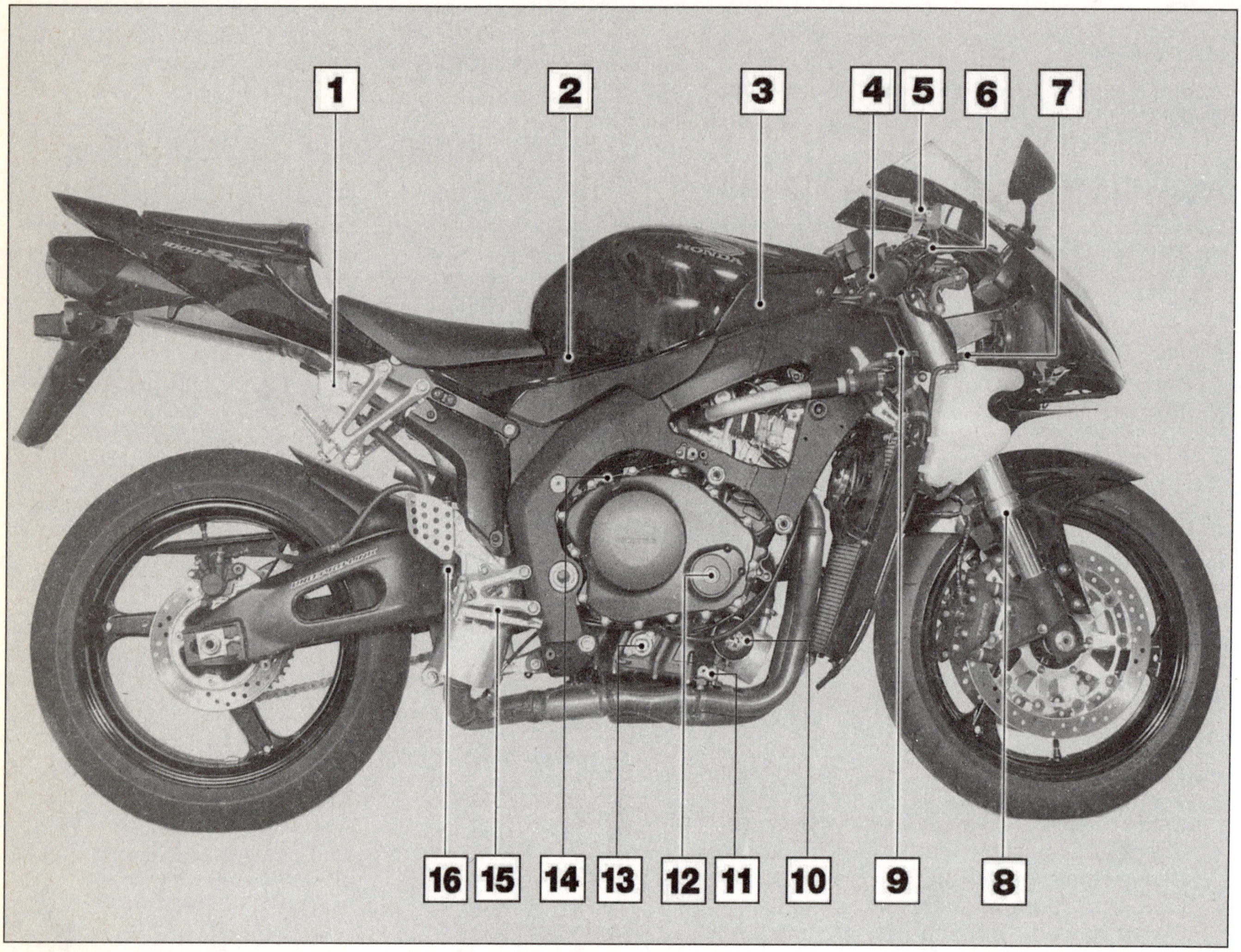

Component locations on right side

1 Rear brake fluid reservoir
2 Fuel strainer/filter
3 Air filter
4 Steering head bearing adjuster
5 Front brake fluid reservoir
6 Throttle cable upper adjuster
7 Coolant reservoir tank filler cap
8 Front fork seals
9 Coolant pressure cap
10 Engine oil filter
11 Engine oil drain plug
12 Timing inspection cap
13 Engine oil inspection window
14 Engine oil filler cap
15 Rear brake light switch
16 Rear brake pedal height adjuster

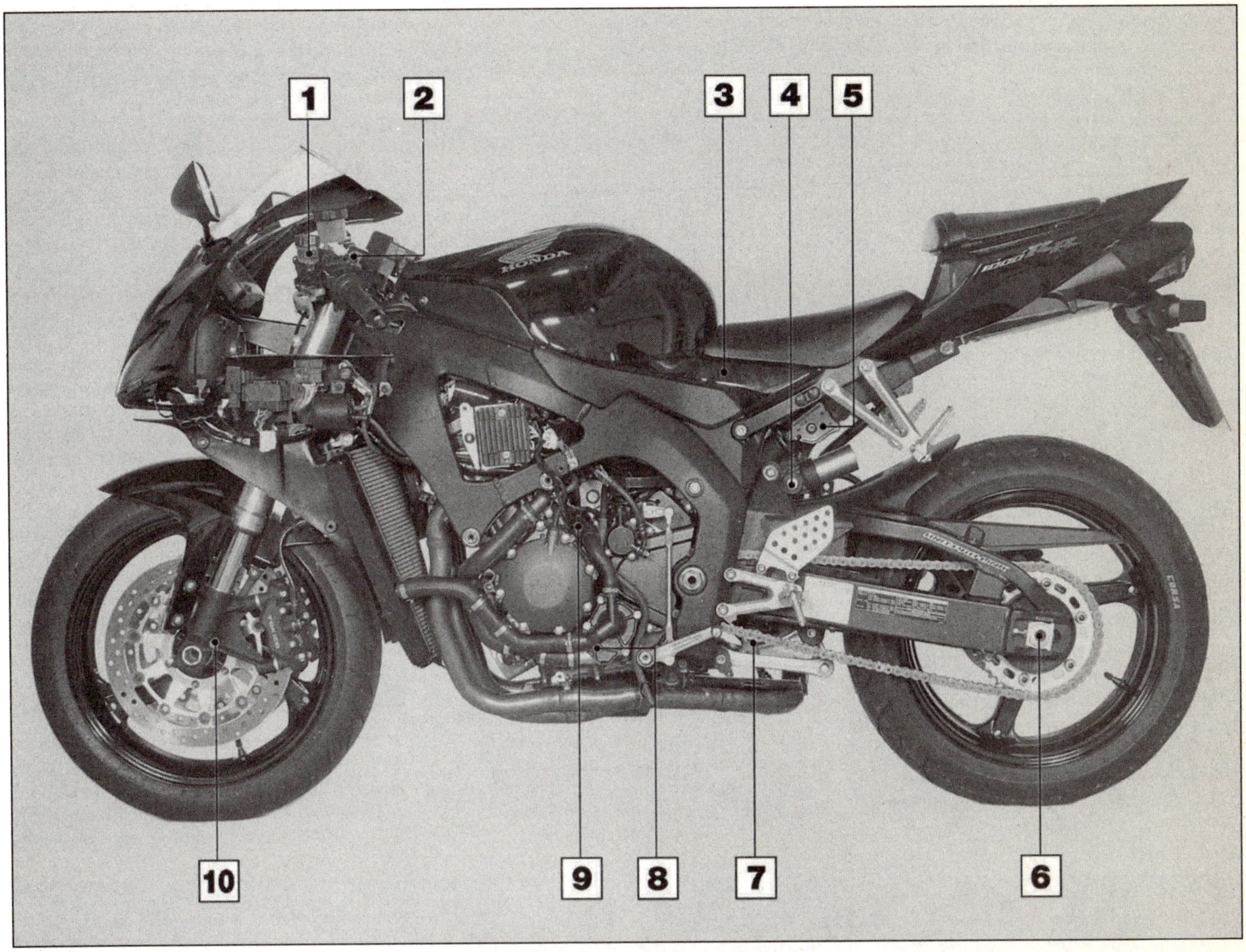

Component locations on left side

1 Clutch fluid reservoir
2 Fork pre-load and rebound damping adjuster
3 Battery
4 Rear shock compression damping adjuster
5 Exhaust gas control valve (EGCV)
6 Drive chain adjuster
7 Rear shock rebound damping adjuster
8 Coolant drain plug
9 Idle speed adjuster knob
10 Fork compression damping adjuster

Introduction

1 This Chapter is designed to help the home mechanic maintain his/her motorcycle for safety, economy, long life and peak performance.

2 Deciding where to start or plug into the routine maintenance schedule depends on several factors. If your motorcycle has been maintained according to the warranty standards and has just come out of warranty, start routine maintenance as it coincides with the next mileage or calendar interval. If you have owned the machine for some time but have never performed any maintenance on it, start at the nearest interval and include some additional procedures to ensure that nothing important is overlooked. If you have just had a major engine overhaul, then start the maintenance routine from the beginning. If you have a used machine and have no knowledge of its history or maintenance record, combine all the checks into one large service initially and then settle into the specified maintenance schedule.

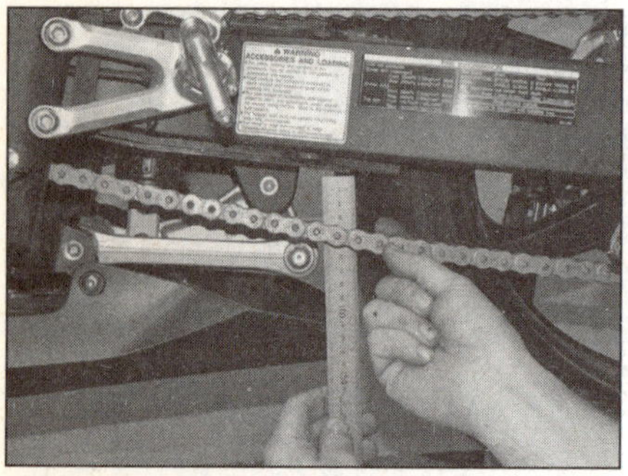

1.3 Push up on the chain and measure the slack

3 Before beginning any maintenance or repair, clean the machine thoroughly, especially around the oil filter, valve cover, body panels, drive chain, suspension, wheels, etc. Cleaning will help ensure that dirt does not contaminate the engine and will allow you to detect wear and damage that could otherwise easily go unnoticed. If you use a pressure washer make sure you do not direct the jet at wheel bearing and suspension seals and at the steering head, or at any electrical/ignition components and connectors.

4 Certain maintenance information is sometimes printed on labels attached to the motorcycle. If the information on the labels differs from that included here, use the information on the label.

1 Drive chain and sprockets

Check chain slack

1 A neglected drive chain won't last long and will quickly damage the sprockets. Routine chain adjustment and lubrication isn't difficult and will ensure maximum chain and sprocket life.

2 To check the chain, place the bike on its sidestand and shift the transmission into neutral. Make sure the ignition switch is OFF.

3 Push up on the bottom run of the chain and measure the slack midway between the two sprockets, then compare your measurement to that listed in this Chapter's Specifications **(see illustration)**. As the chain stretches with wear, adjustment will periodically be necessary (see below). Since the chain will rarely wear evenly, roll the bike forward so that another section of chain can be checked (having an assistant to do this makes the task a lot easier); do this several times to check the entire length of chain, and mark the tightest spot.

Caution: Riding the bike with excess slack in the chain could lead to damage.

4 In some cases where lubrication has been neglected, corrosion and dirt may cause the links to bind and kink, which effectively shortens the chain's length and makes it tight **(see illustration)**. Thoroughly clean and work free any such links, then highlight them with a marker pen or paint. Take the bike for a ride.

5 After the bike has been ridden, repeat the measurement for slack in the highlighted area. If the chain has kinked again and is still tight, replace it with a new one (see Chapter 6). A rusty, kinked or worn chain will damage the sprockets and can damage transmission bearings. If in any doubt as to the condition of a chain, it is far better to install a new one than risk damage to other components and possibly yourself.

6 Check the entire length of the chain for damaged rollers, loose links and pins, and missing O-rings and replace it with a new one if necessary. **Note:** *Never install a new chain on old sprockets, and never use the old chain if you install new sprockets – replace the chain and sprockets as a set.*

Adjust chain slack

7 Move the bike so that the chain is positioned with the tightest point at the centre of its bottom run, then put it on the sidestand.

8 Slacken the rear axle nut **(see illustration)**.

9 Slacken the locknut on the adjuster bolt on

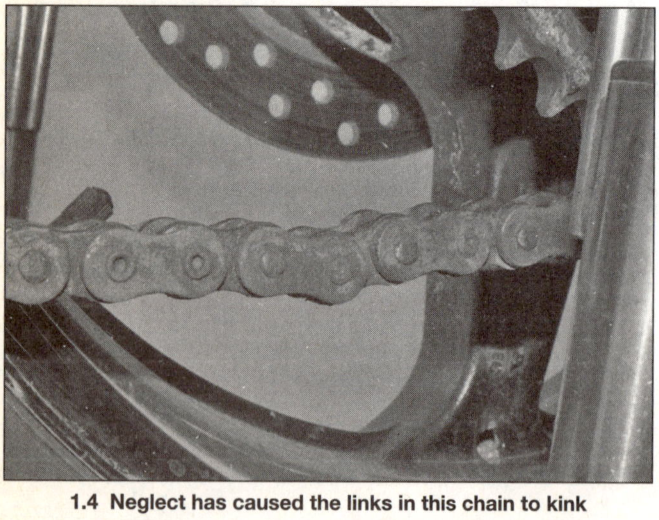

1.4 Neglect has caused the links in this chain to kink

1.8 Slacken the axle nut (arrowed)

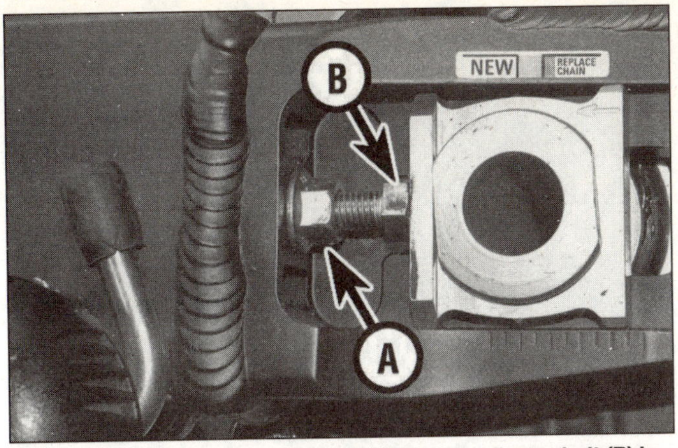

1.9a Slacken each locknut (A) and turn each adjuster bolt (B) by an equal amount . . .

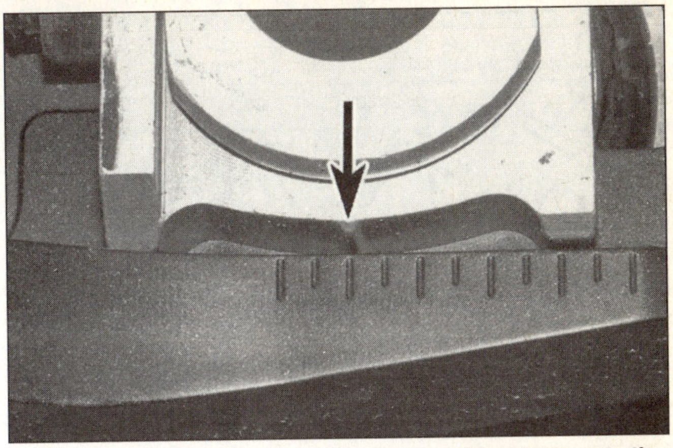

1.9b . . . then check the alignment marks as described – note the index point (arrowed) on the marker

each side of the swingarm **(see illustration)**. Turn each adjuster bolt evenly until the amount of freeplay specified at the beginning of the Chapter is obtained at the centre of the bottom run of the chain – if the chain was slack turn the bolts anti-clockwise; if the chain was tight turn them clockwise, then move the wheel forwards in the swingarm to take up the gap between the adjustment marker blocks and the bolt heads. Following adjustment, check that the bottom index point on each adjustment marker is in the same position in relation to the marks on the swingarm **(see illustration)**. It is important the alignment is the same on each side otherwise the rear wheel will be out of alignment with the front. Always make sure that the front edge of each marker is butted against the end of the adjuster bolt. If there is a difference in the positions, adjust one of them so that its position is exactly the same as the other. Check the chain freeplay again and readjust if necessary.

10 Also check the alignment of the wear decal on the left-hand side with the top index point on the marker **(see illustration)**. When the index line or point meets the red REPLACE CHAIN zone, the drive chain has stretched excessively and must be replaced with a new one (see Chapter 6).

11 When adjustment is complete, tighten the adjuster bolt locknuts **(see illustration 1.9a)**. Tighten the axle nut to the torque setting specified at the beginning of the Chapter **(see illustration)**. Recheck the adjustment as above, then place the machine on an auxiliary stand and spin the wheel to make sure it runs freely.

Clean and lubricate the chain

12 If required, wash the chain using a dedicated aerosol cleaner, or in paraffin (kerosene) or a suitable non-flammable or high flash-point solvent that will not damage the O-rings, using a soft brush to work any dirt out if necessary. Wipe the cleaner off the chain and allow it to dry. If the chain is excessively dirty remove it from the machine and allow it to soak in the paraffin or solvent (see Chapter 6).

Caution: Don't use petrol (gasoline), an unsuitable solvent or other cleaning fluids which might damage the internal sealing properties of the chain. Don't use high-pressure water to clean the chain. The entire process shouldn't take longer than ten minutes, otherwise the O-rings could be damaged.

13 The best time to lubricate the chain is after the motorcycle has been ridden. When the chain is warm, the lubricant will penetrate the joints between the side plates better than when cold. **Note:** *Honda specifies SAE 80 to SAE 90 gear oil or an aerosol chain lube that it is suitable for O-ring or X-ring (sealed) chains; do not use any other chain lubricants – the solvents could damage the chain's sealing rings.* Apply the lubricant to the area where the sideplates overlap – not the middle of the rollers **(see illustration)**.

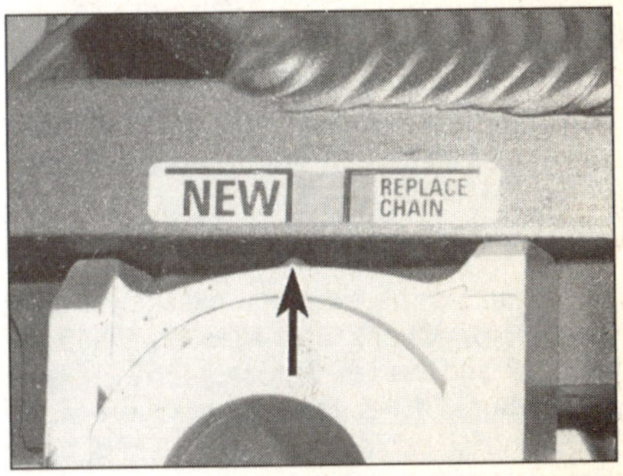

1.10 Here the index point (arrowed) is in the green zone, so the chain is in good order

1.11 Tighten the axle nut to the specified torque

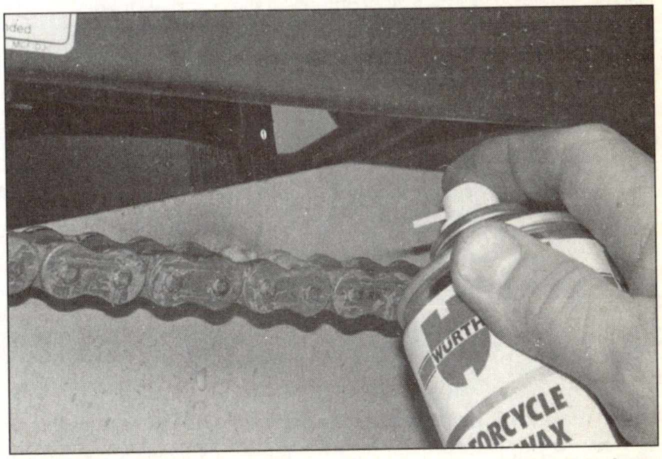

1.13 Apply the lubricant to the overlapping sections of the sideplates

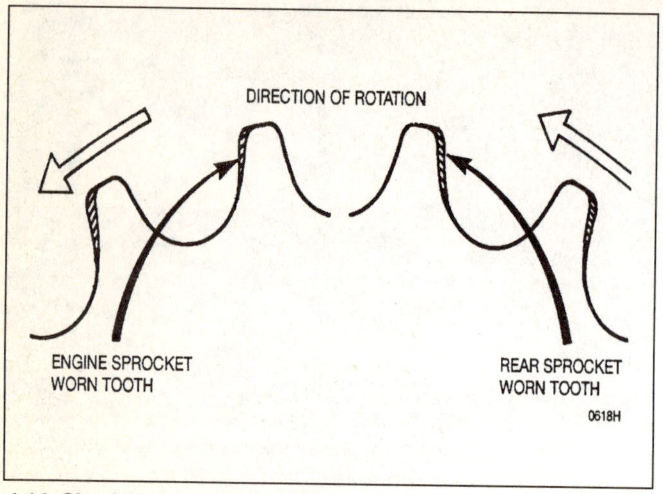

1.14 Check the sprockets in the areas indicated to see if they are worn excessively

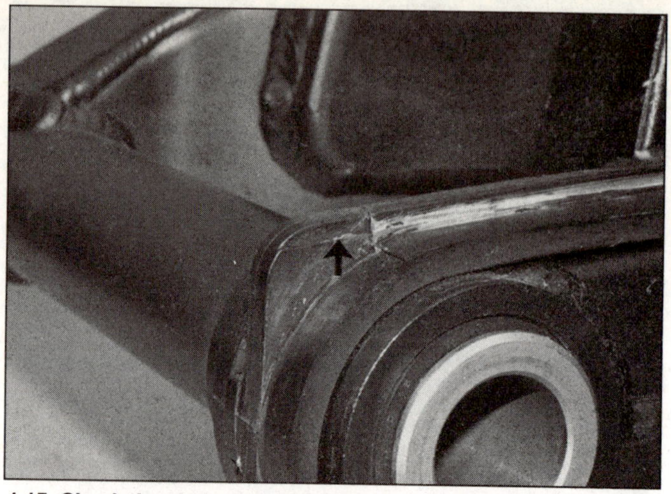

1.15 Check the chain slider for wear and damage – note the wear limit arrows

HAYNES HiNT ***Apply the lubricant to the top of the lower chain run, so centrifugal force will work the oil into the chain when the bike is moving. After applying the lubricant, let it soak in a few minutes before wiping off any excess.***

Warning: Take care not to get any lubricant on the tyre or brake system components. If any of the lubricant inadvertently contacts them, clean it off thoroughly using a suitable solvent or dedicated brake cleaner before riding the machine.

Check sprocket wear

14 Remove the front sprocket cover (see Chapter 6). Check the teeth on the front sprocket and the rear sprocket for wear **(see illustration)**. If the sprocket teeth are worn excessively, replace the chain and both sprockets with a new set.

15 With the sprocket cover removed check the amount of wear on the chain slider on the front of the swingarm **(see illustration)** – if the rubbing surfaces of the slider have worn to the markers remove the swingarm and replace the slider with a new one (see Chapter 5).

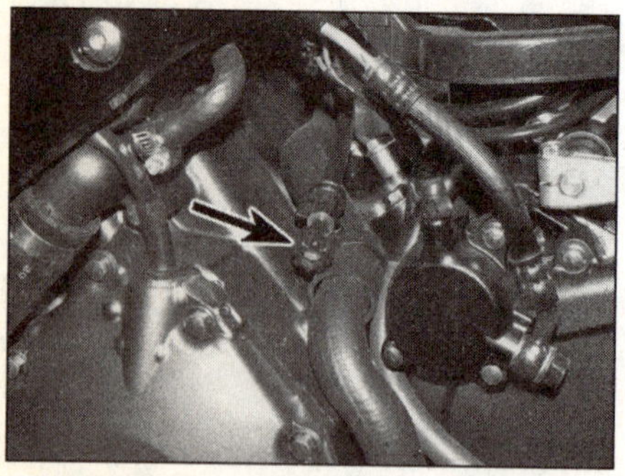

2.2 Idle speed adjuster (arrowed)

2 Idle speed

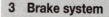

1 The engine should be at normal operating temperature when its idle speed is checked. Take the machine for a 10 to 15 minute ride, then place it on its sidestand with the engine running and the transmission in neutral. Check the idle speed shown on the tachometer with the figure specified at the beginning of this Chapter.

2 If adjustment is required, locate the knurled idle speed adjuster knob on the left-hand side of the machine between the frame and the fairing side panel **(see illustration)**. Turn the knob until the engine idles at the speed specified – turn it clockwise to increase idle speed and anti-clockwise to decrease it.

3 Snap the throttle open and shut a few times, then recheck the idle speed and if necessary readjust it.

4 If a smooth, steady idle can't be achieved check the starter valves (see Chapter 4).

5 The idle speed should be checked and adjusted after checking the valve clearances, and when it is obviously too high or too low. Before adjusting the idle speed, make sure the valve clearances were checked at the previous prescribed interval, and the spark plugs are in good condition and the air filter is clean. Also, turn the handlebars from side-to-side and check the idle speed does not change as you do. If it does, the throttle cables may not be adjusted or routed correctly, or may be worn out. This is a dangerous condition that can cause loss of control of the bike. Be sure to correct this problem before proceeding.

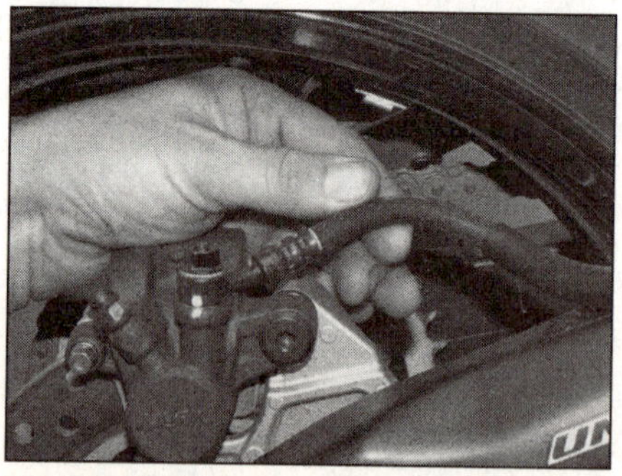

3.3 Check all hoses and unions, for cracks and leaks

3 Brake system

Brake system check

1 A routine general check of the brake system will ensure that any problems are discovered and remedied before the rider's safety is jeopardised.

2 Check the brake lever and pedal for loose fixings, improper or rough action, excessive play, bends, and other damage. Replace any damaged parts with new ones (see Chapter 5). Clean and lubricate the lever and pedal pivots if their action is stiff or rough (see Section 14).

3 Make sure all brake component fasteners are tight. Check the brake pads for wear (see below) and make sure the fluid level in the reservoirs is correct (see *Pre-ride checks*). Look for leaks at the hose connections and check for cracks in the hoses and unions **(see illustration)**. If the lever or pedal is spongy, bleed the brakes (see Chapter 6).

4 Make sure the brake light operates when the front brake lever is pulled in. The front brake light switch, mounted on the underside of the master cylinder, is not adjustable. If it fails to operate properly, check it (see Chapter 8).

5 Make sure the brake light is activated just before the rear brake takes effect. The rear brake light switch is mounted below the rider's right-hand footrest bracket. If adjustment is necessary, hold the switch and turn the

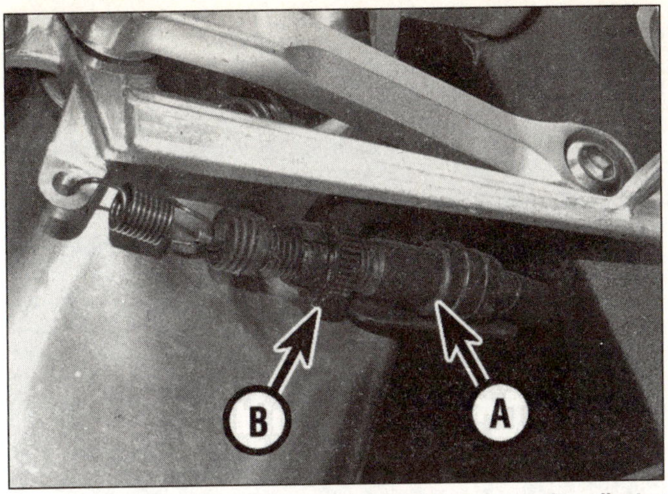

3.5 Hold the rear brake light switch body (A) and turn the adjuster ring (B) as required

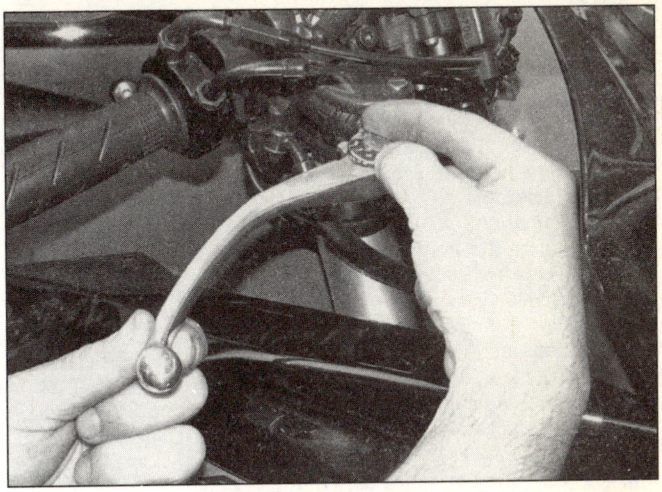

3.6 Front brake lever span adjuster

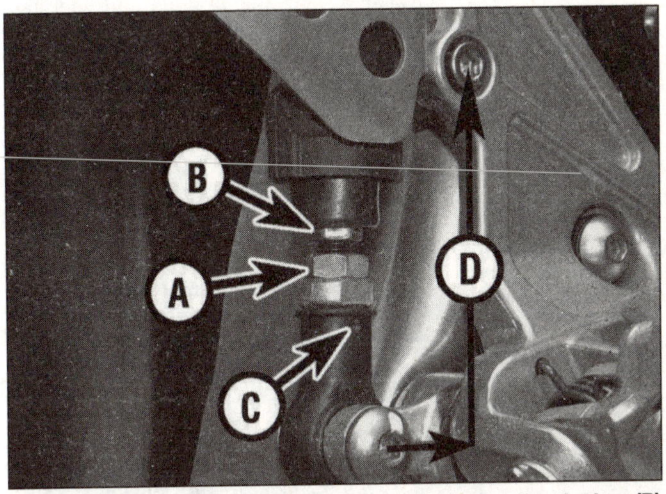

3.7 Slacken the locknut (A) and turn the pushrod using the hex (B) to adjust pedal height. Check that some of the pushrod is visible in the hole (C). The specified setting is with D at 75 mm

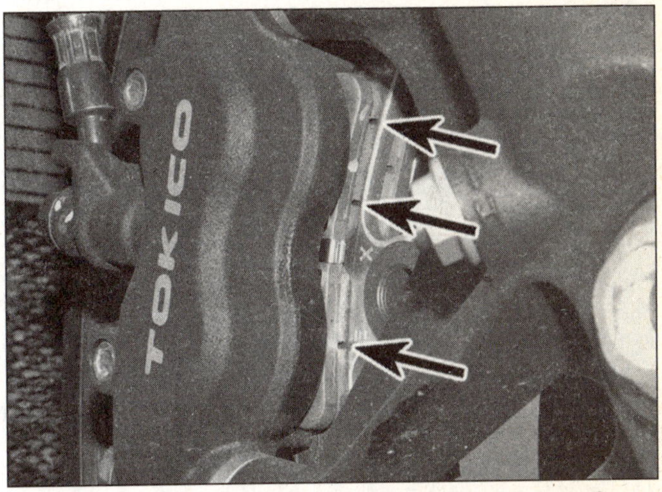

3.8a Front brake pad wear indicator cut-outs (arrowed)

adjuster ring on the switch body until the brake light is activated when required – do not turn the switch itself **(see illustration)**. If the brake light comes on too late or not at all, turn the ring clockwise (when looked at from the front) so the switch is drawn out of the bracket. If the brake light comes on too soon or is permanently on, turn the ring anti-clockwise so the switch is drawn into the bracket. If the switch doesn't operate the brake light, check it (see Chapter 8).

6 The front brake lever has a span adjuster which alters the distance of the lever from the handlebar **(see illustration)**. Each setting is identified by a number on the adjuster which aligns with the arrow on the lever. Turn the adjuster ring until the setting which best suits the rider is obtained. Do not set the adjuster between the defined settings.

7 The height of the rear brake pedal can be adjusted to suit the rider's preference. Slacken the rose joint locknut on the master cylinder pushrod, then turn the pushrod using a spanner on the hex at the top of the rod until the pedal is at the desired height **(see illustration)**. Always make sure the pushrod blocks the hole in the top of the clevis (check using a small screwdriver) – if not, the rod-to-clevis joint will be insecure. Note that Honda specify that the distance D between the bottom mounting bolt for the master cylinder and the rose joint bolt should be 75 mm. On completion tighten the locknut. Adjust the rear brake light switch after adjusting the pedal height (see Step 5).

Brake pad wear check

8 Each brake pad has wear indicators in the form of cut-outs in the friction material. The wear indicators should be plainly visible by looking at the edges of the friction material from the best vantage point – on the front brake look at the bottom edge of the pad from below the caliper, and on the rear brake look at the rear edge of the pad from behind the caliper, but note that an accumulation of road dirt and brake dust could make them difficult to see **(see illustrations)**.

3.8b Rear brake pad wear indicator cut-out (arrowed)

9 If the indicators aren't visible, then the amount of friction material remaining should be, and it will be obvious when the pads need replacing. Honda do not specify a minimum thickness for the friction material, but anything less than 1 mm should be considered excessively worn. **Note:** *Some after-market pads may use different indicators to those on the original equipment.* Also check for uneven wear in the front brake pads, which is indicative of a sticking or seized piston. If found, the calipers must be overhauled (see Chapter 6).
10 If the pads are worn to or beyond the wear indicator (i.e. the bottom of the cut-out on the front pads or the beginning of the cut-out on the rear pads) or there is little friction material remaining, they must be replaced with new ones, though it is advisable to fit new pads before they become this worn.
11 If the pads are dirty or if you are in doubt as to the amount of friction material remaining, remove them for inspection (see Chapter 6). If the pads are excessively worn, also check the brake discs (see Chapter 6).
12 Refer to Chapter 6 for details of pad removal and installation.

Brake fluid change

13 The brake fluid should be changed at the prescribed interval or whenever a master cylinder or caliper overhaul is carried out. Refer to Chapter 6, Section 11 for details. Ensure that all the old fluid is be pumped from the hydraulic system and that the level in the fluid reservoir is checked and the brakes tested before riding the motorcycle.

Brake hoses

14 The hoses will deteriorate with age and should be replaced with new ones regardless of their apparent condition (see Chapter 6).
15 Always replace the banjo union sealing washers with new ones when fitting new hoses. Refill the system with new brake fluid and bleed the system as described in Chapter 6.

Brake caliper and master cylinder seals

16 Brake system seals will deteriorate over a period of time and lose their effectiveness, leading to sticky operation of the brake master cylinders or the pistons in the brake calipers, or fluid loss. Although seal replacement is not subject to a specific time or mileage interval, it is advised after a high mileage has been covered and particularly if fluid leakage or a sticking caliper action is apparent.
17 Replace all the seals in each caliper as a set – a rebuild kit for each caliper is available; master cylinder seals are supplied as a kit along with a new piston and spring (see Chapter 6).

4 Clutch

Clutch check

1 All models are fitted with an hydraulic clutch. Make sure the fluid level in the reservoir is correct (see *Pre-ride checks*).
2 Check the clutch lever for loose fixings, improper or rough action, excessive play, bends, and other damage. Replace any damaged parts with new ones (see Chapter 5). Clean and lubricate the lever pivot if its action is stiff or rough (see Section 14).
3 Check the operation of the clutch. If there is evidence of air in the system (spongy feel to the lever, difficulty in engaging gear, drag when in gear), bleed the clutch (see Chapter 2). If the lever feels stiff or sticky, overhaul the release mechanism (see Chapter 2).
4 Look for leaks at the hose and pipe connections and check for cracks in the hoses, pipe and unions – a hose runs from the master cylinder and joins to a section of pipe that runs along the inside of the frame on the left-hand side and down to the release cylinder where it joins to a final short section of hose.
5 The clutch lever has a span adjuster which alters the distance of the lever from the handlebar **(see illustration)**. Each setting is identified by a number on the adjuster which aligns with the arrow on the lever. Turn the adjuster ring until the setting which best suits the rider is obtained. Do not set the adjuster between the defined settings.

Clutch fluid change

6 The clutch fluid should be changed at the prescribed interval or whenever a master cylinder or release cylinder overhaul is carried out. Refer to Chapter 2 for details. Ensure that all the old fluid is be pumped from the system and that the level in the fluid reservoir is checked and the clutch tested before riding the motorcycle.

Clutch hoses

7 The hoses will deteriorate with age and the hose/pipe (which comes as one complete piece) should be replaced with a new one regardless of its apparent condition (see Chapter 2).
8 Always replace the banjo union sealing washers with new ones when fitting new hose. Refill the system with new fluid and bleed the system as described in Chapter 2.

4.5 Clutch lever span adjuster

Clutch master and release cylinder seals

9 Clutch release mechanism seals will deteriorate over a period of time and lose their effectiveness, leading to sticky operation of the master cylinder or the piston in the release cylinder, or fluid loss. Although seal replacement is not subject to a specific time or mileage interval, it is advised after a high mileage has been covered and particularly if fluid leakage or poor clutch action is apparent.
10 A rebuild kit for the master cylinder is available; and new O-rings and seals are available for the release cylinder along with a new piston and spring if necessary (see Chapter 2).

5 Fuel system

Warning: Petrol (gasoline) is extremely flammable, so take extra precautions when you work on any part of the fuel system. Don't smoke or allow open flames or bare light bulbs near the work area, and don't work in a garage where a natural gas-type appliance is present. If you spill any fuel on your skin, rinse it off immediately with soap and water. When you perform any kind of work on the fuel system, wear safety glasses and have a fire extinguisher suitable for a Class B type fire (flammable liquids) on hand.

Check fuel hoses, EVAP hoses and system components

1 Raise the fuel tank (see Chapter 4) and check the tank, the fuel hoses, the vacuum hoses, the tank drain and breather hoses, and on California models the EVAP system hoses (see Section 17), for signs of leaks, deterioration or damage **(see illustrations)**. In particular check that there are no leaks from the fuel hoses or hose unions. Replace any hose that is cracked or deteriorated with a new one (see Chapter 4).
2 If the joint between the fuel pump mounting plate and the tank is leaking, ensure the mounting bolts are tightened to the specified torque setting (see Chapter 4) **(see illustration 5.1a)**; if the leak persists, remove the pump and fit a new gasket (see Chapter 4).
3 Inspect the joints between the fuel rails,

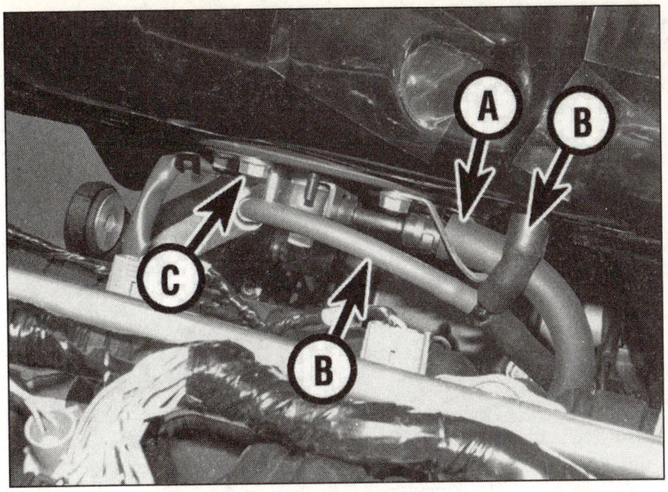

5.1a Check the fuel supply hose (A), the tank drain and breather hoses (B) and pump mounting plate (C) . . .

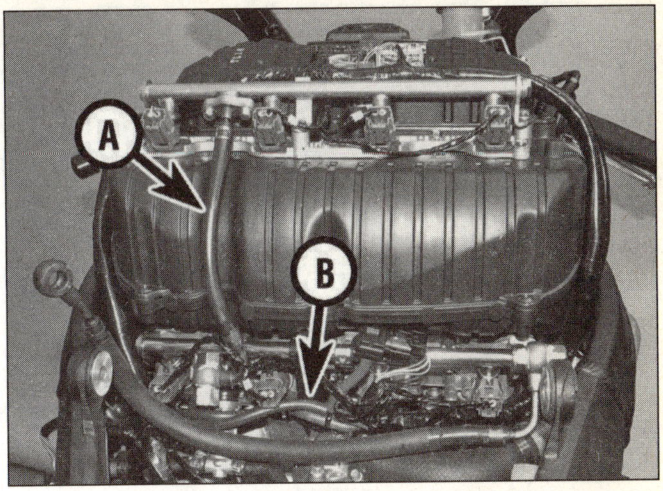

5.1b . . . the fuel hose (A) linking the fuel rails, the vacuum hoses (B) . . .

the injectors and the throttle bodies **(see illustration)**. If there are any leaks, remove the fuel rail(s) and fit new seals and O-rings to the injectors (see Chapter 4).

Fuel strainer and filter

4 Cleaning of the fuel strainer is advised after a particularly high mileage has been covered, although no interval is specified. It is also necessary if fuel starvation is suspected. Remove the pump from the fuel tank to access the strainer (see Chapter 4). The strainer is in the form of a wad of mesh in the bottom of the pump – it is difficult to clean, but as it is not available separately it is preferable to clean it than to replace the whole pump.
5 The filter is integral with the fuel pump, and is not available as a separate component. If after checking all other possibilities a blocked filter is the cause of fuel starvation a new pump assembly must be installed (see Chapter 4).

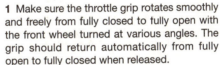

6 Throttle cables

1 Make sure the throttle grip rotates smoothly and freely from fully closed to fully open with the front wheel turned at various angles. The grip should return automatically from fully open to fully closed when released.
2 If the throttle sticks, this is probably due to a cable fault. Remove the cables (see Chapter 4) and lubricate them (see Section 14). Check that the inner cables slide freely and easily in the outer cables. If not, replace the cables with new ones.
3 With the cables removed, make sure the throttle twistgrip rotates freely on the handlebar – dirt combined with a lack of lubrication can cause the action to be stiff. If necessary, unscrew the handlebar end-weight and slide the twistgrip off the handlebar **(see illustration)**. Clean any old grease from the bar and the inside of the tube. Smear some new grease of the specified type onto the bar, then refit the twistgrip. When fitting the end-weight, align the boss with the cut-out on the inner weight inside the handlebar. Clean the threads of the end-weight retaining screw, then apply a suitable non-permanent thread locking compound and tighten it to the torque setting specified at the beginning of the Chapter. Install the cables, making sure they are correctly routed (see Chapter 4). If this fails to improve the operation of the throttle, the cables must be replaced with new ones. Note that in very rare cases the fault could lie in the throttle bodies. Remove the air filter housing (see Chapter 4) and check the action of the throttle pulley.
4 With the throttle operating smoothly, check for a small amount of freeplay in the

5.3 . . . and the injector joints (arrowed) as described

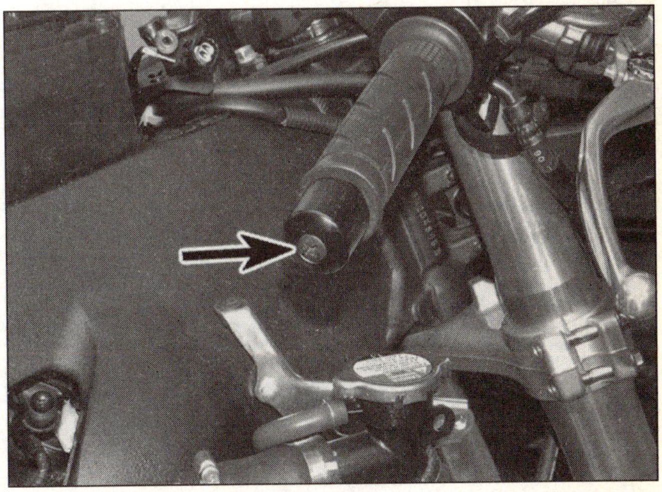
6.3 Undo the screw (arrowed) to free the end-weight and twistgrip

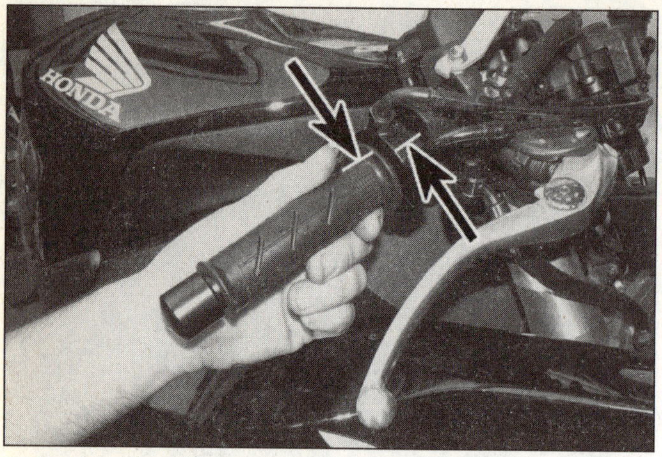

6.4 Throttle cable freeplay is measured in terms of twistgrip rotation

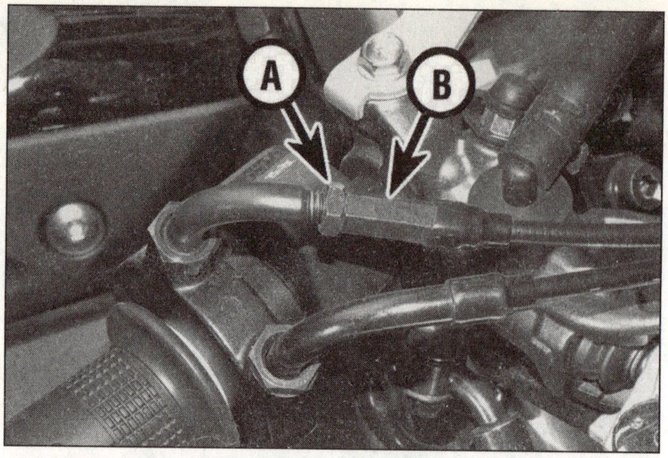

6.5 Slacken the adjuster locknut (A) and turn the adjuster (B) as required – throttle end

cables, measured in terms of the amount of twistgrip rotation before the throttle opens, and compare the amount to that listed in this Chapter's Specifications **(see illustration)**. If it's incorrect, adjust the cables to correct it as follows.

5 Initially adjust freeplay using the adjuster in the throttle opening cable where it leaves the throttle pulley housing on the handlebar. Loosen the locknut and turn the adjuster in or out as required until the specified amount of freeplay is obtained (see this Chapter's Specifications), then retighten the locknut **(see illustration)**.

6 If the adjuster has reached its limit of adjustment, reset it to its start point by turning it fully in, so that freeplay is at a maximum, then remove the air filter housing (see Chapter 4), and adjust the cable at the throttle body end.

7 The adjuster is on the lower cable in the bracket. Slacken the adjuster locknut, then screw the adjuster in or out as required, making sure the lower nut remains captive in the bracket, thereby threading itself along the adjuster as you turn it, until the specified amount of freeplay is obtained, then tighten the locknut **(see illustration)**. Subsequent adjustments can be made at the throttle end when required. If the cable cannot be adjusted as specified, replace it with a new one (see Chapter 4). Check that the throttle twistgrip operates smoothly and snaps shut quickly when released.

Warning: Turn the handlebars all the way through their travel with the engine idling. Idle speed should not change. If it does, the cables may be routed incorrectly. Correct this condition before riding the bike.

7 Engine oil and filter

Special tool: *A filter removing tool is necessary for this job* ***(see illustration 7.6a)****.*

Warning: Be careful when draining the oil, as the exhaust pipes, the engine, and the oil itself can cause severe burns.

1 Consistent routine oil and filter changes are the single most important maintenance procedure you can perform. The oil not only lubricates the internal parts of the engine, transmission and clutch, but it also acts as a coolant, a cleaner, a sealant, and a protector. Because of these demands, the oil takes a terrific amount of abuse and should be replaced often with new oil of the recommended grade and type. The oil filter should be changed with every oil change.

HAYNES HiNT ***Saving a little money on the difference in cost between a good oil and a cheap oil won't pay off if the engine is damaged***

2 Before changing the oil, warm up the engine so the oil will drain easily. Make sure the bike is on level ground. Remove the lower fairing (see Chapter 7). The oil drain plug is at the front of the sump on the bottom of the engine, and the filter is at the front on the right-hand side.

3 Position a clean drain tray below the engine. Unscrew the oil filler cap from the clutch cover to vent the crankcase and to act as a reminder that there is no oil in the engine **(see illustration)**.

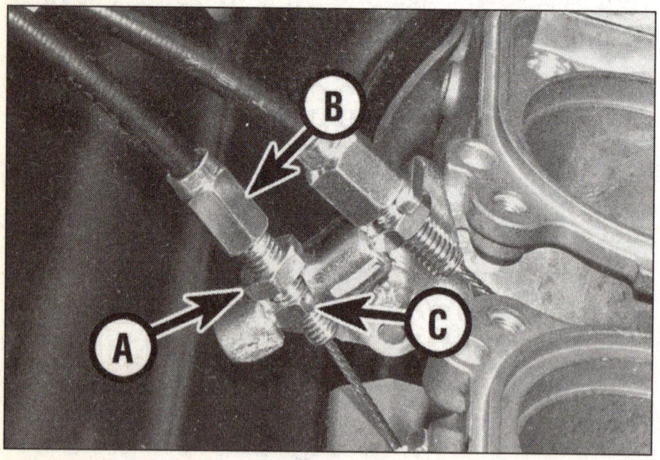

6.7 Throttle cable adjuster locknut (A), adjuster (B) and lower nut (C)

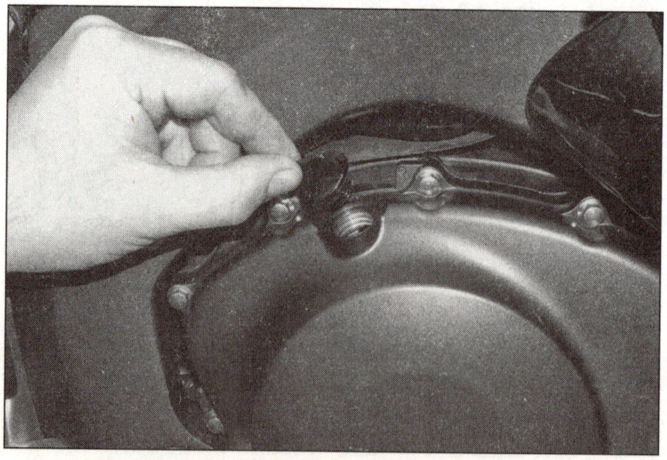

7.3 Unscrew the oil filler cap to act as a vent . . .

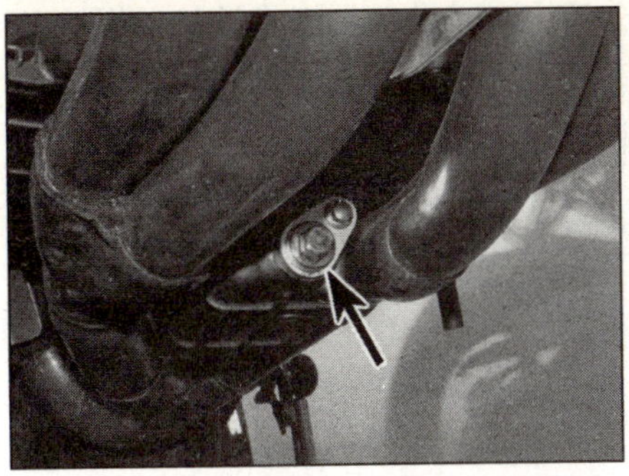

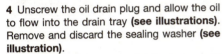

7.4a . . . then unscrew the oil drain plug (arrowed) . . .

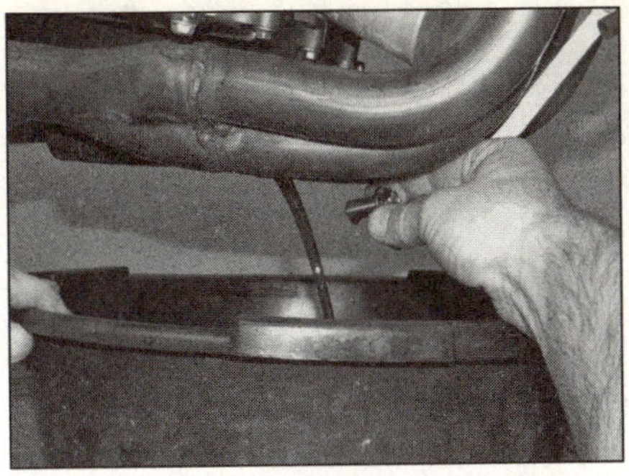

7.4b . . . and allow the oil to completely drain

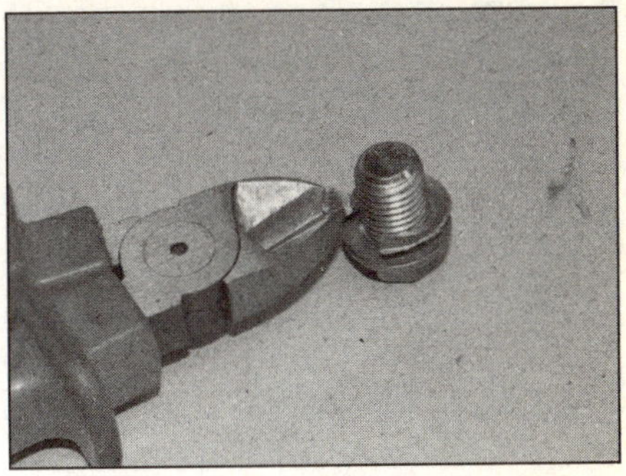

7.4c Depending on the type the sealing washer may need to be cut off

4 Unscrew the oil drain plug and allow the oil to flow into the drain tray **(see illustrations)**. Remove and discard the sealing washer **(see illustration)**.

5 When the oil has completely drained, fit a new sealing washer onto the plug and fit the plug into the sump, and tighten it to the torque setting specified at the beginning of the Chapter **(see illustration)**. Do not overtighten it as the threads in the sump are easily damaged.

6 Now place the drain tray below the oil filter. Unscrew the filter using a filter socket (one can be obtained with the new filter from Honda dealers under part No. 07AAA-PLCA100 in the USA or 07HAA-PJ70101 in other markets, or otherwise there are commercially available equivalents available), filter pliers, or a filter removing strap or a chain-wrench, and tip any residual oil into the drain tray **(see illustrations)**. The filter socket is preferable because it provides a means of tightening the new filter to the correct torque.

7 Smear clean engine oil onto the rubber seal on the new filter and thread the filter onto the engine **(see illustrations)**. Tighten it to the specified torque setting using the filter socket if available, or tighten the filter as tight as possible by hand, or by the number of turns specified on the filter itself or its packaging. **Note:** *Do not use a strap or chain-type filter removing tool to tighten the filter as you will damage it.*

8 Refill the engine to the proper level using the recommended type and amount of oil (see Specifications). With the motorcycle vertical, the oil level should lie between the maximum and minimum level lines on the inspection window (see *Pre-ride checks*). Check the condition of the O-ring on the filler cap and replace it with a new one if it is damaged or worn. Install the filler cap **(see illustration 7.3)**.

9 Start the engine and let it run for two or three minutes (make sure that the oil pressure light extinguishes after a few seconds). Shut it off, wait a few minutes, then check the oil level again. If necessary, add more oil to bring the level close to the maximum line, but do not go above it. Check around the drain plug and the oil filter for leaks.

10 If leaks are evident, and the plug and filter are correctly tightened using a new washer and a lubricated seal, there is another cause which must be investigated before riding the bike.

11 Install the lower fairing (see Chapter 7).

12 The old oil drained from the engine cannot be re-used and should be disposed of properly. Check with your local refuse disposal

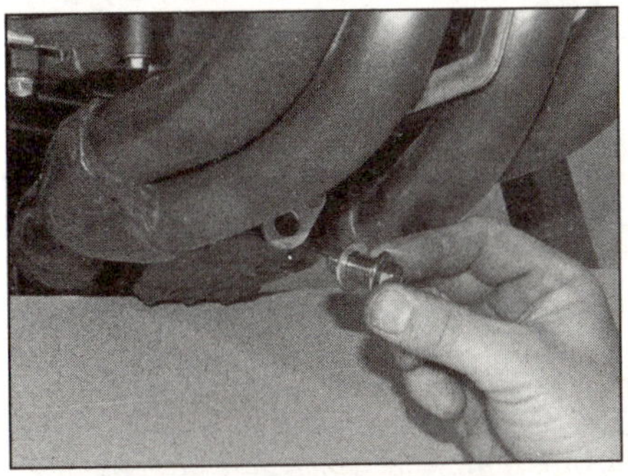

7.5 Install the drain plug using a new sealing washer

7.6a Unscrew the filter using a filter removing socket . . .

7.6b . . . or a filter removing strap . . .

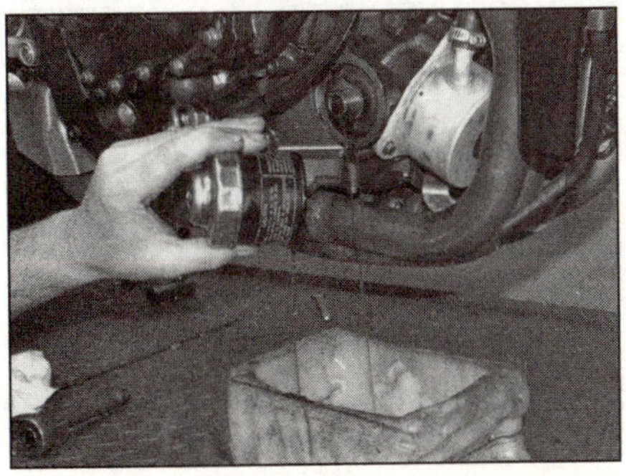

7.6c . . . and allow the oil to drain

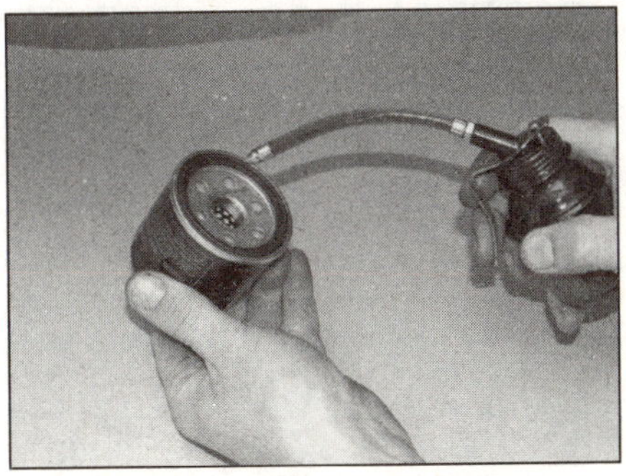

7.7a Smear clean oil onto the seal . . .

7.7b . . . then install the filter and tighten it as described

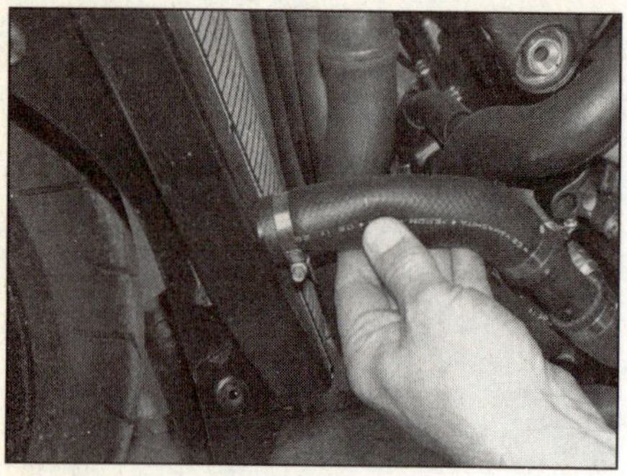

8.2 Check all the coolant hoses as described

8.3a Check all hose connections, the inlet union (A), the pump (B) . . .

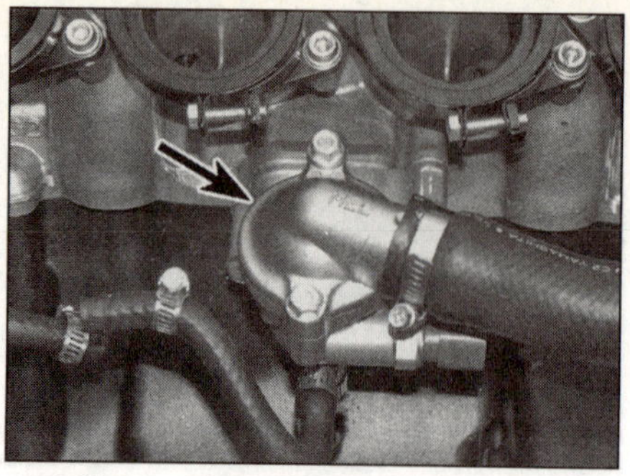

8.3b . . . and the thermostat housing (arrowed)

company, disposal facility or environmental agency to see whether they will accept the used oil for recycling. Don't pour used oil into drains or onto the ground.

> **HAYNES HiNT** ***Check the old oil carefully – if it is very metallic coloured, then the engine is experiencing wear from break-in (new engine) or from insufficient lubrication. If there are flakes or chips of metal in the oil, then something is drastically wrong internally and the engine will have to be disassembled for inspection and repair. If there are pieces of fibre-like material in the oil, the clutch is experiencing excessive wear and should be checked.***

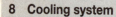

8 Cooling system

Check

> ***Warning: The engine must be cool before beginning this procedure.***

1 Check the coolant level in the reservoir (see *Pre-ride checks*).

2 Remove the lower fairing and the fairing side panels (see Chapter 7). Check the entire cooling system for evidence of leaks. Examine each rubber coolant hose along its entire length. Look for cracks, abrasions and other damage. Squeeze each hose at various points to see whether they are dried out or hard **(see illustration)**. They should feel firm, yet pliable, and return to their original shape when released. If necessary, replace them with new ones (see Chapter 3).

3 Check for evidence of leaks at each cooling system hose connection, at the inlet union on the left-hand end of the cylinder block, at the outlet union and thermostat housing on the back of the cylinder head, and around the pump on the left-hand side of the engine **(see illustrations)**. Tighten the hose clips carefully to prevent future leaks. If the pump is leaking around the cover, check that the bolts are tight. If they are, remove the cover and replace the O-ring with a new one (see Chapter 3). If oil is leaking around the crankcase, remove the pump and replace the body O-ring with a new one (see Chapter 3).

4 To prevent leakage of coolant from the cooling system to the lubrication system and vice versa, two seals are fitted on the pump shaft. On the bottom of the pump housing there is a drain hole **(see illustration)**. If either seal fails, the drain allows the coolant or oil to escape and prevents them mixing. The seal on the water pump side is of the mechanical type which bears on the rear face of the impeller. The second seal, which is mounted behind the mechanical seal is of the normal feathered lip type. If on inspection the drain shows signs of leakage, remove the pump and replace it with a new one – it comes as an assembly, and the seals are not available separately (see Chapter 3).

5 Check the radiator in front of the engine for leaks and other damage **(see illustration)**. Leaks in the radiator leave tell-tale scale deposits or coolant stains on the outside of the core below the leak. If leaks are noted, remove the radiator (see Chapter 3) and have it repaired or replace it with a new one – do not use a liquid leak stopping compound to try to repair leaks.

6 Check the radiator fins for mud, dirt and insects, which may impede the flow of air through it **(see illustration 8.5)**. If the fins are dirty, remove the radiator (see Chapter 3) and clean it using water or low pressure compressed air directed through the fins from the inner side of the radiator. If the fins are bent or distorted, straighten them carefully with a screwdriver. If the air flow is restricted by bent or damaged fins over more than 20% of the radiator's surface area, replace the radiator with a new one.

> ***Warning: Do not remove the pressure cap when the engine is hot. It is good practice to cover the cap with a heavy cloth and turn the cap slowly anti-clockwise. If you hear a hissing sound (indicating that there is still pressure in the system), wait until it stops, then continue turning the cap until it can be removed.***

7 Remove the pressure cap from the radiator filler neck by turning it anti-clockwise until it reaches the stop. Now press down on the cap and continue turning it until it can be removed **(see illustration)**.

8 Check the condition of the coolant in the system. If it is rust-coloured or if accumulations of scale are visible, drain, flush and refill the

8.4 Check the pump drain hole (arrowed) for signs of leakage

8.5 Check the radiator and fins (arrowed) as described

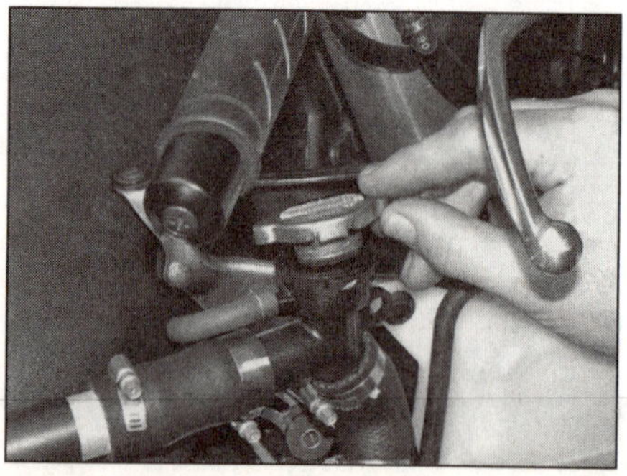

8.7 Remove the pressure cap as describe

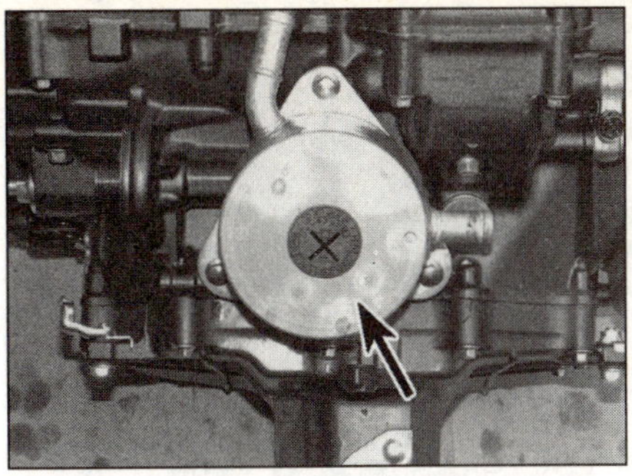

8.12 Check the oil cooler (arrowed) for leaks and damage

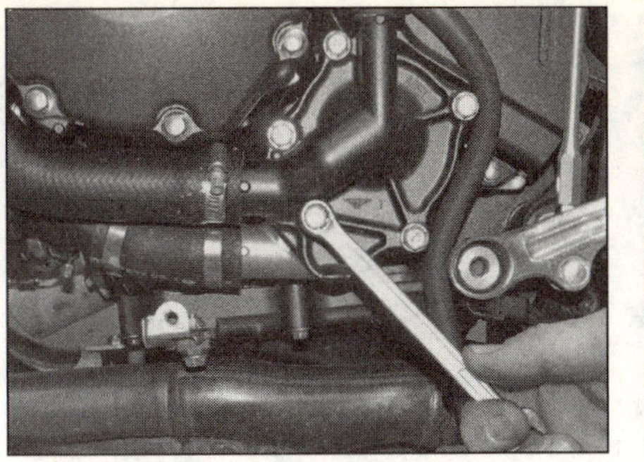

8.15a Unscrew the drain bolt . . .

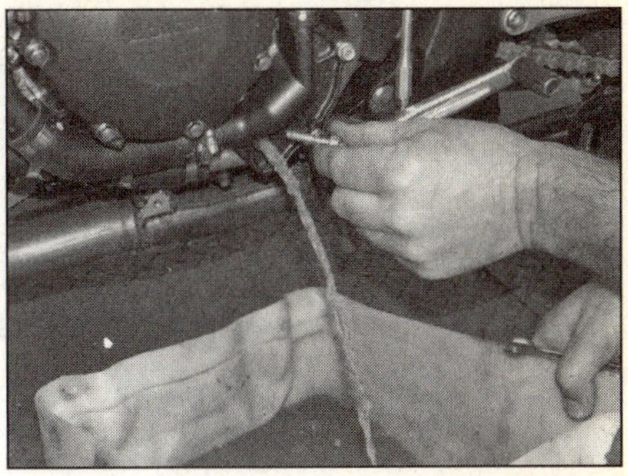

8.15b . . . and allow the coolant to drain

system with new coolant (see below). Check the antifreeze content of the coolant with an antifreeze hydrometer. If the system has not been topped-up with the correct coolant mixture (see *Pre-ride checks*) the coolant will be too weak to offer adequate protection. If the hydrometer indicates a weak mixture, drain, flush and refill the system (see below).

9 Check the cap seal for cracks and other damage. If in doubt about the pressure cap's condition, have it tested by a Honda dealer or fit a new one.

10 Fit the cap by turning it clockwise until it reaches the first stop then push down on it and continue turning until it can turn no further. Start the engine and let it reach normal operating temperature, then check for leaks again. As the coolant temperature increases, the electric fan (mounted on the back of the radiator) should come on automatically and the temperature should begin to drop. If it does not, refer to Chapter 3 and check the fan and fan circuit carefully.

11 If the coolant level is consistently low, and no evidence of leaks can be found, have the entire system pressure checked by a Honda dealer.

12 Check the oil cooler on the front of the engine (next to the oil filter) for any signs of oil leakage between it and the engine **(see illustration)**. If there is leakage check the cooler bolts are tight. If the leakage persists you will have to fit a new O-ring between the cooler and the engine (see Chapter 2). Check that the coolant hoses are secure on the unions, and that there is no evidence of coolant leakage from the body of the cooler. If there is, the cooler is damaged and must be replaced with a new one.

Change the coolant

⚠ ***Warning: Allow the engine to cool completely before performing this maintenance operation. Also, don't allow anti-freeze to come into contact with your skin or the painted surfaces of the motorcycle. Rinse off spills immediately with plenty of water. Anti-freeze is highly toxic if ingested. Never leave anti-freeze lying around in an open container or in puddles on the floor; children and pets are attracted by its sweet smell and may drink it. Check with local authorities (councils) about disposing of anti-freeze. Many communities have collection centres which will see that anti-freeze is disposed of safely. Anti-freeze is also combustible, so don't store it near open flames.***

Draining

13 Support the motorcycle upright on a level surface using an auxiliary stand. Remove the lower fairing and the right-hand fairing side panel (see Chapter 7).

14 Remove the pressure cap from the top of the radiator by covering it with a heavy cloth and turning it anti-clockwise until it reaches a stop **(see illustration 8.7)**. If you hear a hissing sound (indicating there is still pressure in the system), wait until it stops. Now press down on the cap and continue turning the cap until it can be removed. Also remove the coolant reservoir cap.

15 Position a suitable container beneath the water pump on the left-hand side of the engine. Unscrew the cooling system drain bolt and allow the coolant to completely drain – note that the bolt is long and coolant will start to dribble out around the bolt before it is fully unscrewed **(see illustrations)**. Retain the old sealing washer for use during flushing.

16 Now place the container on the right-hand side of the engine below the reservoir. Disconnect the radiator overflow hose from the bottom of the reservoir and allow the reservoir to drain into the container **(see illustration)**.

Flushing

17 Flush the system with clean tap water by inserting a hose in the radiator filler neck. Allow the water to run through the system until it is clear and flows out cleanly. If the radiator is extremely corroded, remove it (see Chapter 3) and have it cleaned by a specialist. Also flush the reservoir, then fit the radiator overflow hose back onto the radiator filler neck.

18 Clean the drain hole in the water pump then install the drain bolt using the old sealing washer **(see illustration 8.24)**.

19 Fill the cooling system with clean water mixed with a flushing compound **(see illustration 8.25)**. Make sure the flushing compound is compatible with aluminium components, and follow the manufacturer's instructions carefully. Fit the radiator cap.

20 Start the engine and allow it to reach normal operating temperature. Let it run for about ten minutes.

21 Stop the engine. Let it cool for a while, then cover the pressure cap with a heavy rag and turn it anti-clockwise to the first stop, releasing any pressure that may be present in the system. Once the hissing stops, push down on the cap and remove it completely.

22 Drain the system once again.

23 Fill the system with clean water and repeat Steps 20 to 22.

Refilling

24 Install the drain bolt using a new sealing washer and tighten it to the torque setting specified at the beginning of the Chapter **(see illustration)**.

25 Fill the system to the base of the radiator filler neck with the proper coolant mixture (see this Chapter's Specifications) **(see**

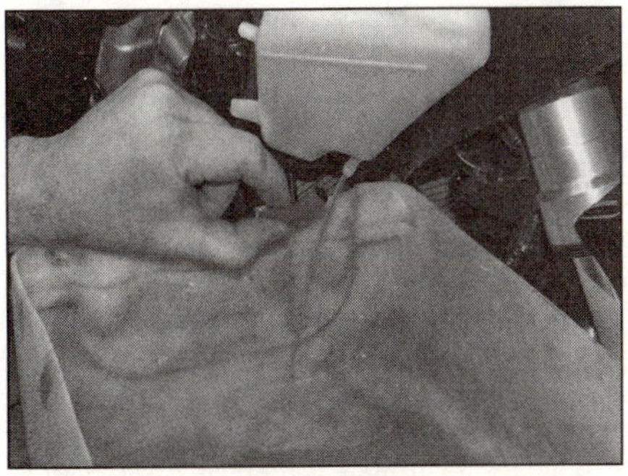

8.16 Detach the hose and allow the reservoir to drain

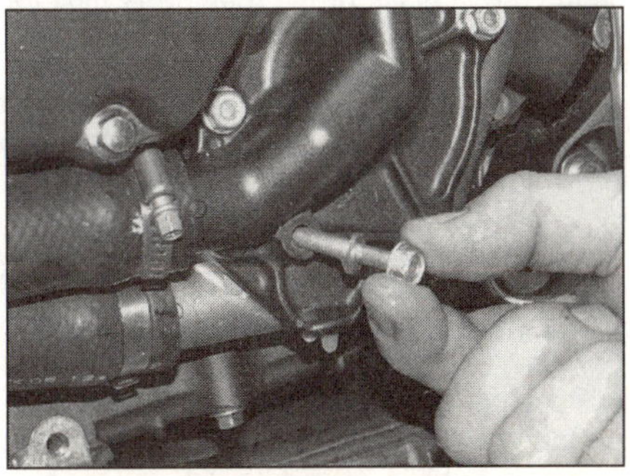

8.24 Use new sealing washers on the drain bolts

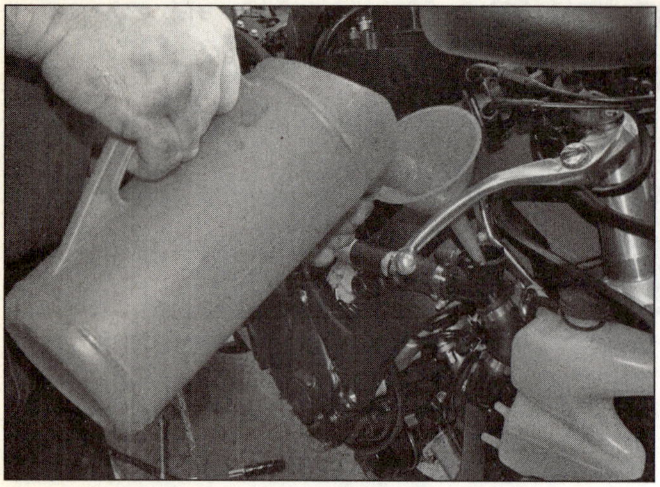

8.25 Fill the system and bleed it as described

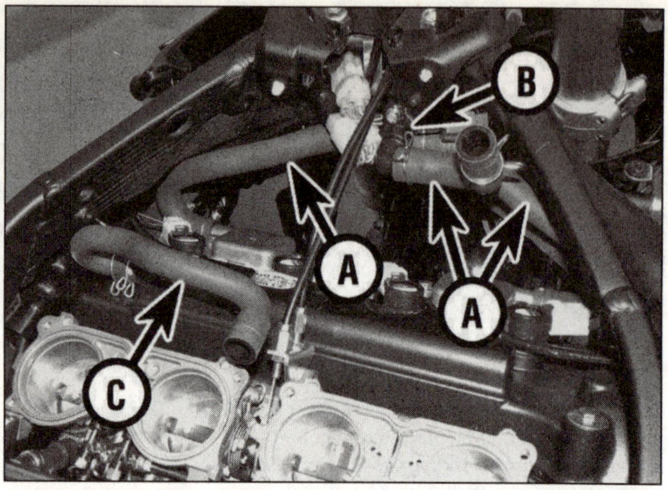

9.3 Check the PAIR system hoses (A) as described. PAIR control valve (B). Crankcase breather hose (C)

illustration). **Note:** *Pour the coolant in slowly to minimise the amount of air entering the system, and when full carefully waggle the bike from side to side to dislodge any trapped air.* Fill the reservoir to the UPPER level line (see *Pre-ride checks)*.

26 Start the engine and allow it to idle for 2 to 3 minutes. Flick the throttle twistgrip part open 3 or 4 times, so that the engine speed rises to approximately 4000 to 5000 rpm, then stop the engine. Any air trapped in the system should bleed back to the radiator filler neck.

27 If necessary, top up the coolant level to the base of the radiator filler neck, then install the pressure cap. Also top up the coolant reservoir to the UPPER level line.

28 Start the engine and allow it to reach normal operating temperature, then shut it off. Let the engine cool then remove the pressure cap as described in Step 14. Check that the coolant level is still up to the base of the upper radiator filler neck. If it's low, add the specified mixture until it reaches the base of the filler neck. Refit the cap.

29 Check the coolant level in the reservoir and top up if necessary.

30 Check the system for leaks. Install the fairing panels (see Chapter 7).

31 Do not dispose of the old coolant by pouring it down the drain. Instead pour it into a heavy plastic container, cap it tightly and take it into an authorised disposal site or service station – see ***Warning*** at the beginning of this Section.

10.1 Check the springs (arrowed) as described

Hose renewal

32 The hoses will deteriorate with age and should be replaced with new ones regardless of their apparent condition (see Chapter 3).

9 PAIR (Pulse secondary air supply) system

1 To reduce the amount of unburned hydrocarbons released in the exhaust gases, a pulse secondary air supply (PAIR) system is fitted. The system consists of the control valve (mounted under the front of the air filter housing), the reed valves (fitted in the valve cover) and the hoses linking them. The control valve is actuated electronically by the ECM.

2 Under certain operating conditions, a signal from the ECM opens up the PAIR control valve which then allows filtered air to be drawn through the reed valves and cylinder head passages and into the exhaust ports. The air mixes with the exhaust gases, causing any unburned particles of the fuel in the mixture to be burnt in the exhaust port/pipes. This process changes a considerable amount of hydrocarbons and carbon monoxide into relatively harmless carbon dioxide and water. The reed valves in the valve cover are fitted to prevent the flow of exhaust gases back up the cylinder head passages and into the air filter housing.

3 The system is not adjustable and requires little maintenance. Remove the air filter housing and air intake duct to access and inspect the components (see Chapter 4). Check that the hoses are not kinked or pinched, are in good condition and are securely connected at each end **(see illustration)**. While you are there also check the crankcase breather hose. Replace any hoses that are cracked, split or generally deteriorated with new ones.

4 Refer to Chapter 4 for further information on the system and for checks if it is believed to be faulty.

10 Sidestand and starter interlock circuit

1 Check the stand springs for damage and distortion **(see illustration)**. The springs must be capable of retracting the stand fully and holding it retracted when the motorcycle is in use. If a spring is sagged or broken it must be replaced with a new one.

2 Lubricate the stand pivot regularly (see Section 14).

3 Check the stand and its mount for bends and cracks. Stands can often be repaired by welding.

4 Check the operation of the starter interlock circuit as follows:

- Make sure the transmission is in neutral, then retract the stand and start the engine. Pull in the clutch lever and select a gear. Extend the sidestand. The engine should stop as the sidestand is extended.
- Make sure the engine is in neutral and the sidestand is down, then start the engine. Pull the clutch lever in and select a gear. The engine should cut out.
- Check that when the sidestand is down the engine can only be started if the transmission is in neutral, and when the sidestand is up and the transmission is in gear the engine can only be started if the clutch lever is pulled in.

5 If the circuit does not operate as described, check the sidestand switch, neutral switch, diode and clutch switch, and the circuit between them (see Chapter 8).

11.2 Compress the forks to check their action. Check the slider (A) for pitting and signs of oil leakage

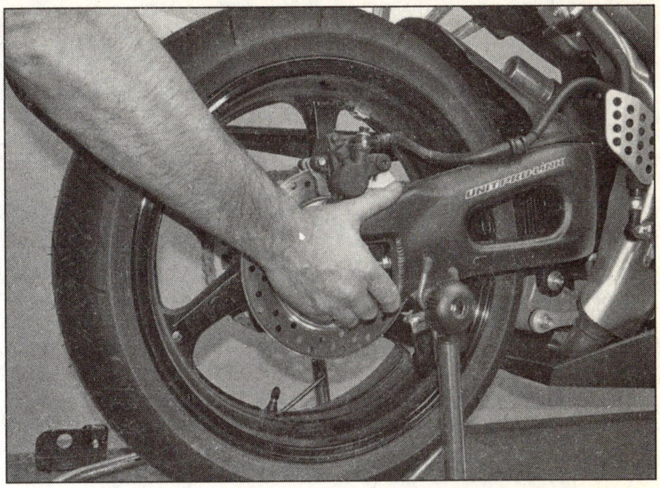

11.9 Checking for play in the swingarm bearings

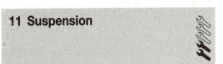

11 Suspension

1 The suspension components must be maintained in top operating condition to ensure rider safety. Loose, worn or damaged suspension parts decrease the motorcycle's stability and control.

Front suspension check

2 While standing alongside the motorcycle, apply the front brake and push on the handlebars to compress the forks several times. See if they move up-and-down smoothly without binding **(see illustration)**. If binding is felt, the forks should be disassembled and inspected (see Chapter 5).

3 Inspect the fork sliders for scratches, corrosion and pitting which will cause seal failure **(see illustration 11.2)** – if the damage is excessive, new tubes should be installed (see Chapter 5).

4 Inspect the area below the dust seal for signs of oil leakage, then carefully lever the seal down using a flat-bladed screwdriver and inspect the area around the fork oil seal **(see illustration 11.2)**. If leakage is evident, the seals must be replaced with new ones (see Chapter 5). If there is evidence of corrosion between the oil seal retaining ring and its groove in the fork tube, spray the area with a penetrative lubricant, otherwise the ring will be difficult to remove if needed. Press the dust seal back into the bottom of the fork tube on completion.

5 The forks are adjustable for spring pre-load, rebound damping and compression damping and it is essential that both fork legs are adjusted equally. Refer to Chapter 5 and check the settings on each fork if in doubt.

6 Check the tightness of all suspension nuts and bolts to be sure none have worked loose, referring to the torque settings specified at the beginning of Chapter 5.

Rear suspension check

7 Inspect the rear shock absorber for fluid leakage and tightness of its mountings. If leakage is found, the shock must be replaced with a new one (see Chapter 5).

8 With the aid of an assistant to support the bike, compress the rear suspension several times. It should move up-and-down freely without binding. If any binding is felt, the worn or faulty component must be identified and checked (see Chapter 5). The problem could be due to either the shock absorber, the suspension linkage components or the swingarm components.

9 Support the motorcycle on an auxiliary stand so that the rear wheel is off the ground. Grab the swingarm and rock it from side-to-side – there should be no discernible movement at the rear **(see illustration)**. If there's a little movement or a slight clicking can be heard, inspect the tightness of all the swingarm and rear suspension mounting bolts and nuts, referring to the torque settings specified at the beginning of Chapter 5, and re-check for movement.

10 Next, grasp the top of the rear wheel and pull it upwards – there should be no discernible freeplay before the shock absorber begins to compress **(see illustration)**. Any freeplay felt in either check indicates worn bearings in the suspension linkage or swingarm, or worn shock absorber mountings. The worn components must be identified and replaced with new ones (see Chapter 5).

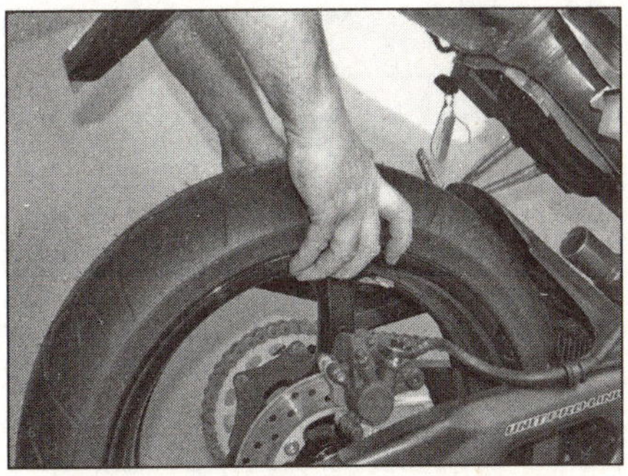

11.10 Checking for play in the rear shock mountings and suspension linkage bearings

11 To make an accurate assessment of the swingarm bearings, remove the rear wheel (see Chapter 6) and the bolt securing the suspension linkage rods to the linkage arm (see Chapter 5). Grasp the rear of the swingarm with one hand and place your other hand at the junction of the swingarm and the frame. Try to move the rear of the swingarm from side-to-side. Any wear (play) in the bearings should be felt as movement between the swingarm and the frame at the front. If there is any play, the swingarm will be felt to move forward and backward at the front (not from side-to-side). Next, move the swingarm up and down through its full travel. It should move freely, without any binding or rough spots. If there is any play in the swingarm or if it does not move freely, remove the bearings for inspection (see Chapter 5).

Front fork oil change

12 Although there is no set interval for changing the fork oil, note that the oil will degrade over a period of time and lose its damping qualities. Refer to Chapter 5, Sections 6 and 7 for details of front fork removal, oil draining and refilling. The forks do not need to be completely disassembled to change the oil.

Rear suspension bearing lubrication

13 Although there is no set interval for regreasing the suspension linkage bearings, over a considerable mileage (or through incorrect use of jet washers) the seals may fail allowing the ingress of dirt and water and the grease in the bearings will be washed out or will harden.

14 The suspension linkage and the swingarm should be disassembled periodically and the bearings cleaned and re-greased as necessary (see Chapter 5, Sections 13 and 16).

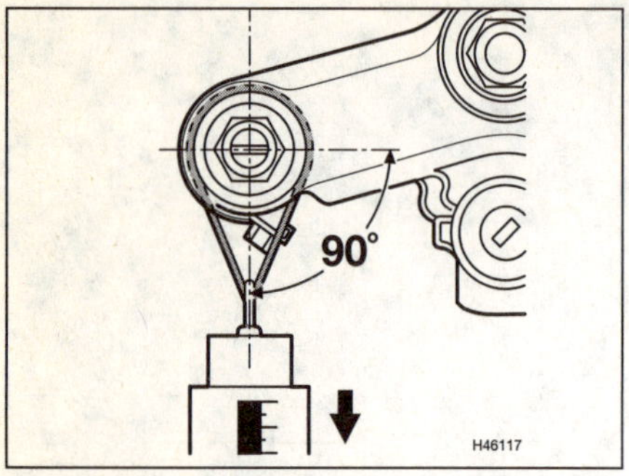

12.4 Steering head bearing pre-load check

12.5 Checking for play in the steering head bearings

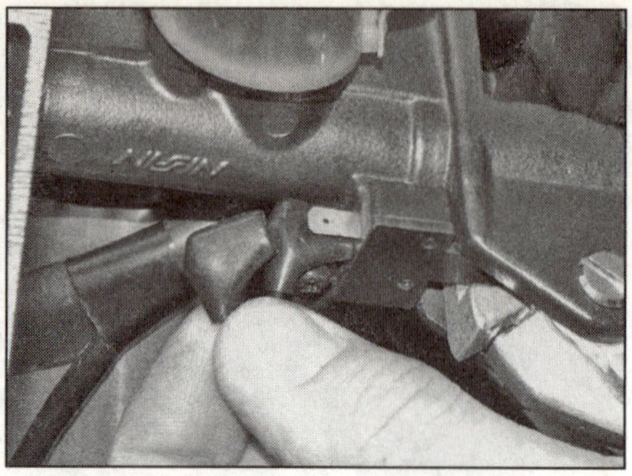

12.7a Disconnect the wiring connectors . . .

12 Steering head bearings

Freeplay check and adjustment

1 Steering head bearings can become dented, rough or loose during normal use of the machine. In extreme cases, worn or loose steering head bearings can cause steering wobble – a condition that is potentially dangerous.

Check

2 Remove the lower fairing (see Chapter 7). Raise the front wheel off the ground using an auxiliary stand. Always make sure that the bike is properly supported and secure.

3 Point the front wheel straight-ahead and slowly move the handlebars from lock to lock. Any dents or roughness in the bearing races will be felt – if the bearings are too tight the bars will not move smoothly and freely. Again point the wheel straight-ahead, and tap the front of the wheel to one side. The wheel should 'fall' under its own weight to the limit of its lock, indicating that the bearings are not too tight (take into account the restriction that cables and wiring may have, and for best accuracy refer to Chapter 5 and remove the steering damper). Check for similar movement to the other side.

4 If available, and with the steering damper removed (see Chapter 5), attach one end of a spring balance (graduated zero to 30 N) to the fork tube between the top and bottom yokes. With the steering straight-ahead, pull on the balance and check the reading at which the handlebars start to turn **(see illustration)**. If the reading is below the minimum value specified in the pre-load range given in the Specifications at the beginning of the Chapter, the steering head is too loose, if the reading is above the maximum value specified the steering head is too tight. If the steering doesn't perform as described, and it's not due to the resistance of cables or hoses, then the bearings should be adjusted as described below.

5 Next, grasp the bottom of the forks and gently pull and push them forward and backward **(see illustration)**. Any looseness or freeplay in the steering head bearings will be felt as front-to-rear movement of the forks. If play is felt, adjust the bearings as described below.

> **HAYNES HiNT** ***Make sure you are not mistaking any movement between the bike and stand, or between the stand and the ground, for freeplay in the bearings. Do not pull and push the forks too hard – a gentle movement is all that is needed. Freeplay between the fork slider and the fork tube due to worn bushes can also be misinterpreted as steering head bearing play – do not confuse the two.***

12.7b . . . then unscrew the bolts (arrowed) and displace the master cylinder

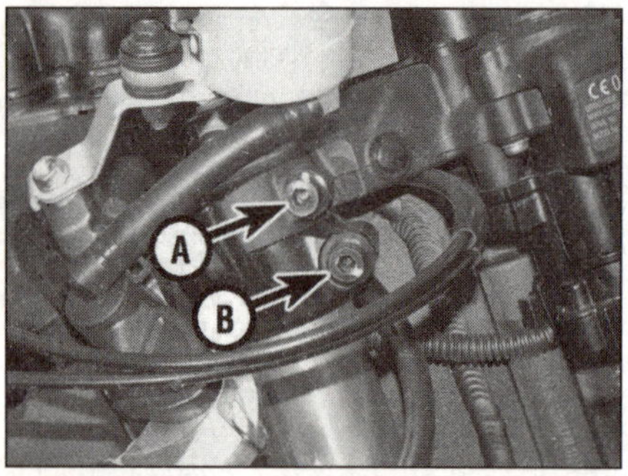

12.8a Slacken the fork clamp bolt (A) and handlebar clamp bolt (B) on each side

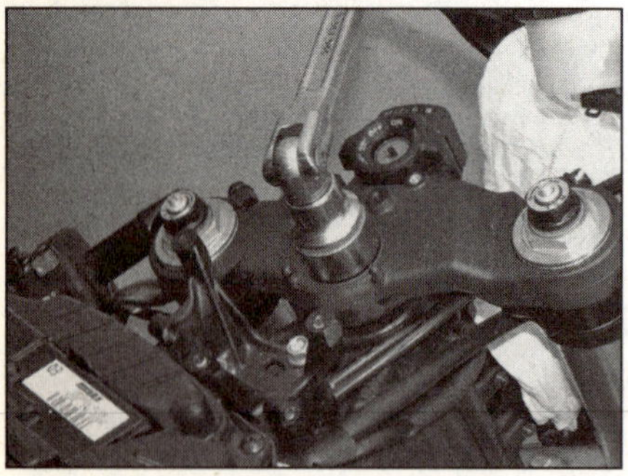

12.8b Unscrew the steering stem nut . . .

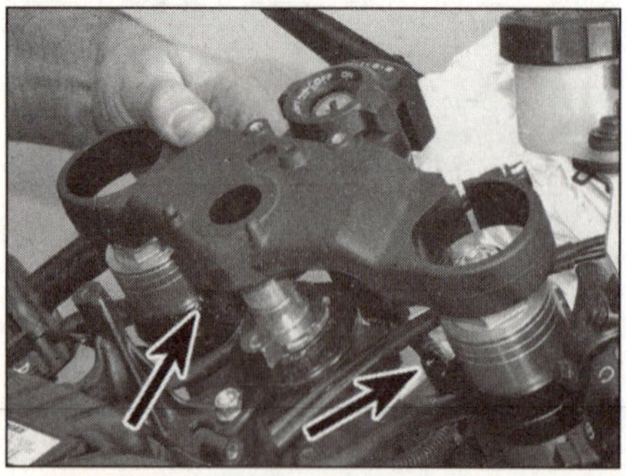

12.9 . . . and gently ease the yoke up off the forks, noting how the handlebar clamp lugs (arrowed) locate in the holes

Adjustment

Special tool: *A suitably sized C-spanner is useful for this procedure* ***(see illustration 12.11)****.*

6 As a precaution, remove the fuel tank cover (see Chapter 4) and the fairing (see Chapter 7). Though not actually necessary, this will prevent the possibility of damage should a tool slip. Remove the steering damper (see Chapter 5).

7 On RR-4 and RR-5 models displace the clutch master cylinder from the handlebar (see Chapter 2) – there is no need to detach the hydraulic hose **(see illustration)**. Keep the master cylinder reservoir upright to prevent possible fluid leakage.

8 Slacken the fork clamp bolts in the top yoke and the handlebar clamp bolts **(see illustration)**. Unscrew the steering stem nut and on RR-6 and RR-7 models remove the washer **(see illustrations)**.

9 Gently ease the top yoke up off the fork tubes and position it clear of the head bearings, using a rag to protect other components **(see illustration)**.

12.10a Bend down the tabs securing the locknut . . .

12.10b . . . then unscrew the locknut . . .

10 Bend the lockwasher tabs out of the notches in the locknut **(see illustration)**. Unscrew the locknut using either your fingers (it shouldn't be tight), a C-spanner or a suitable drift located in one of the notches **(see illustration)**. Remove the lockwasher **(see illustration)** and inspect its tabs for cracks or signs of fatigue – replace it with a new one if necessary; otherwise the old one can be re-used, but note that Honda recommend using a new one as a matter of course.

11 Slacken the adjuster nut slightly until pressure is just released, then tighten it until all freeplay is removed, yet the steering is able to move freely **(see illustration)**. The object is to set the adjuster nut so that the bearings are under a very light loading, just enough to remove any freeplay, but not so much that the steering is prevented from moving freely from side-to-side. If the Honda service tool (part No. 07916-3710101 or 3710100 according to country) or a suitable peg spanner (which can be made by cutting castellations into an old socket) is available, tighten the adjuster nut to the torque setting specified at the beginning of the Chapter, then turn the steering from lock-to-lock five times, then slacken it and tighten it again to the specified torque setting. However do not rely on the torque setting method alone and assume the loading to be correct – check the physical feel as described as well. If you have the spring balance (see Step 4), set the adjuster nut so that the steering starts to move at around the mid-point of the pre-load range given in the Specifications at the beginning of the Chapter.

Caution: Take great care not to apply excessive pressure because this will cause premature failure of the bearings.

12 If the bearings cannot be correctly adjusted, disassemble the steering head and check the bearings and races (see Chapter 5).

13 With the bearings correctly adjusted, fit the lockwasher, using a new one if the tabs are weakened or cracked, onto the adjuster nut and fit the two short tabs into the slots in the adjuster nut **(see illustration 12.10c)**.

14 Hold the adjuster nut to prevent it from moving, then fit the locknut and tighten it finger-tight **(see illustration 12.10b)**. Tighten the locknut further (but no more than 90°) until its notches align with the remaining lockwasher tabs, making sure the adjuster nut does not turn as well (though that is unlikely). Secure the locknut in position by bending up the long lock washer tabs into its notches **(see illustration)**.

12.10c . . . and remove the lockwasher

12.11 Adjust the bearings as described using either a C-spanner or a drift

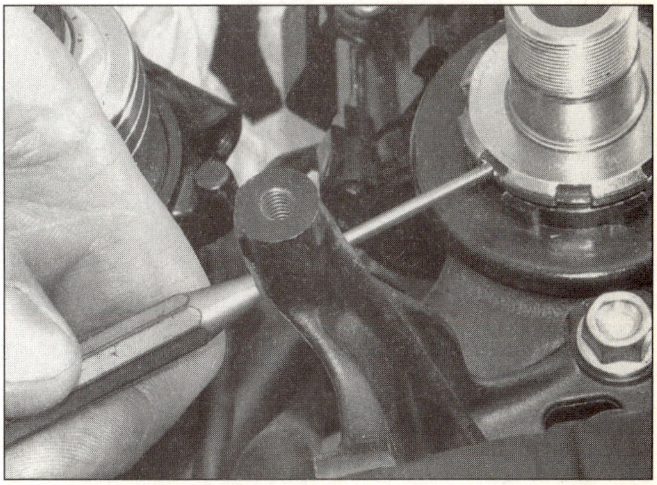

12.14 Bend the tabs up into the notches in the locknut

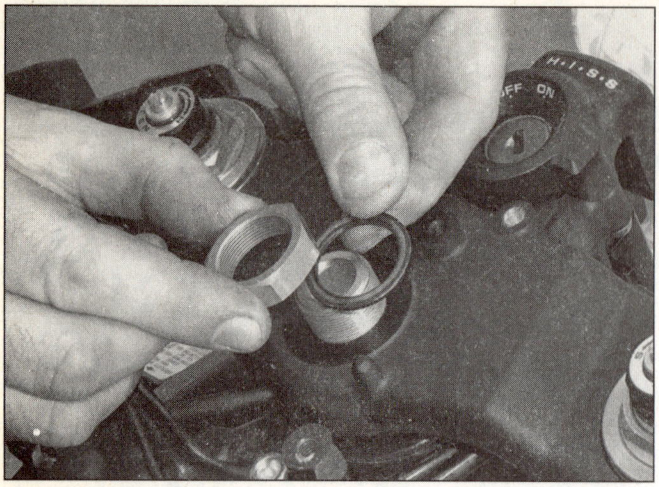

12.15a Fit the steering stem nut, on RR-6 and RR-7 models with its washer . . .

12.15b . . . and tighten the nut to the specified torque

15 Fit the top yoke onto the steering stem, locating the lug on the top of each handlebar clamp into its hole in the underside of the yoke **(see illustration 12.9)**. Install the steering stem nut, with its washer on RR-6 and RR-7 models, and tighten it to the torque setting specified at the beginning of the Chapter **(see illustrations)**.

16 Tighten the fork clamp bolts to the specified torque **(see illustration 12.8a)**. Make sure the handlebars are correctly aligned and push each handlebar up against the top yoke then tighten the handlebar clamp bolts to the specified torque.

17 Check the bearing adjustment as described above and re-adjust if necessary.

18 Install the steering damper (see Chapter 5), the clutch master cylinder (see Chapter 2), the fuel tank cover (see Chapter 4) and the fairing (see Chapter 7).

Lubrication

19 Over a considerable time the grease in the bearings will be dispersed or will harden allowing the ingress of dirt and water.

20 The steering head should be disassembled periodically and the bearings cleaned and re-greased (see Chapter 5, Section 10).

13 Wheels and tyres

Wheels

1 Cast wheels are virtually maintenance free, but they should be kept clean and checked periodically for cracks and other damage. Also check the wheel runout and alignment (see Chapter 6). Never attempt to repair damaged cast wheels; they must be renewed if damaged. Check that the wheel balance weights are fixed firmly to the wheel rim. If you suspect that a weight has fallen off, have the wheel rebalanced by a motorcycle tyre specialist.

Tyres

2 Check the tyre condition and tread depth thoroughly – see *Pre-ride checks*. Check the valve rubber for signs of damage or deterioration and have it replaced with a new one if necessary by a tyre fitting specialist. Also, make sure the valve stem cap is in place and tight **(see illustration)**.

Wheel bearings

3 Wheel bearings will wear over a considerable mileage and should be checked periodically to avoid handling problems.

4 Support the motorcycle upright using an auxiliary stand so that the wheel being examined is off the ground. Check for any play in the bearings by pushing and pulling the wheel against the hub **(see illustration)**. Also rotate the wheel and check that it turns smoothly and without any grating noises.

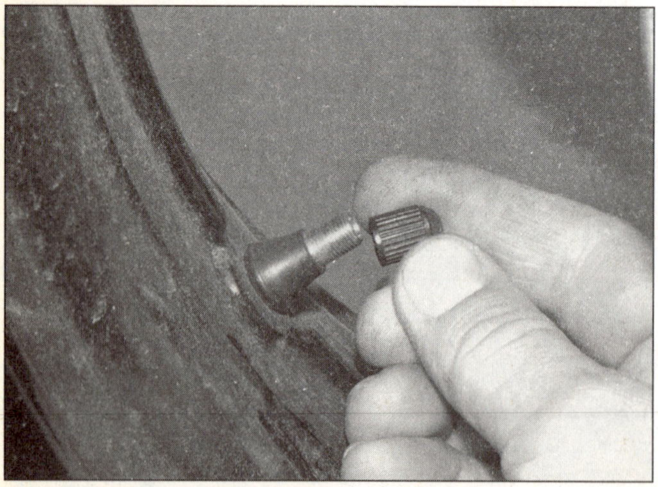

13.2 Check each valve as described and make sure a cap is fitted

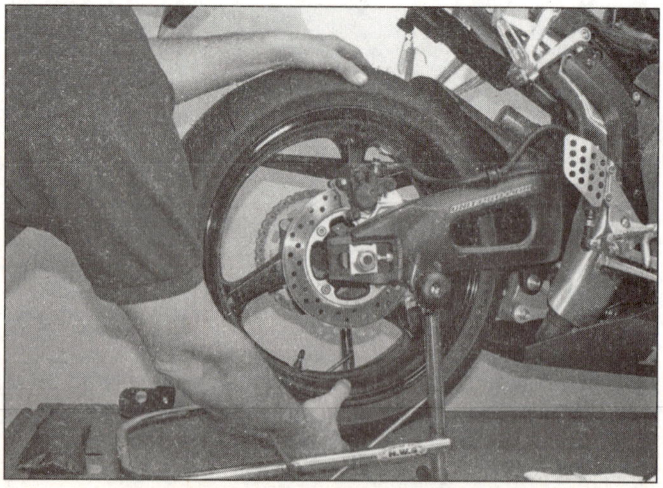

13.4 Checking for play in the wheel bearings

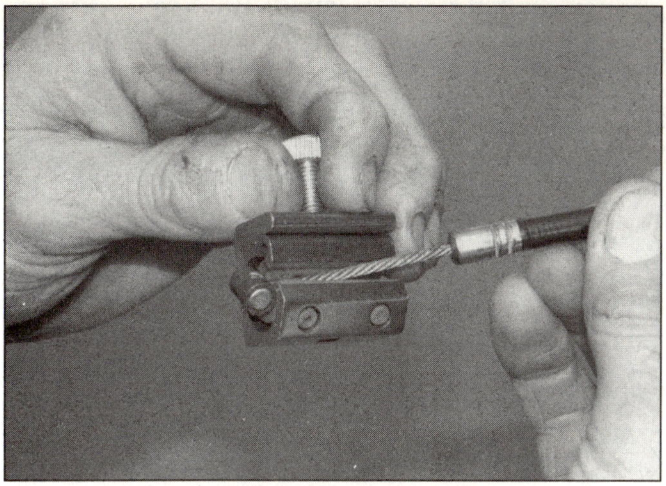

14.3a Fit the cable into the adapter . . .

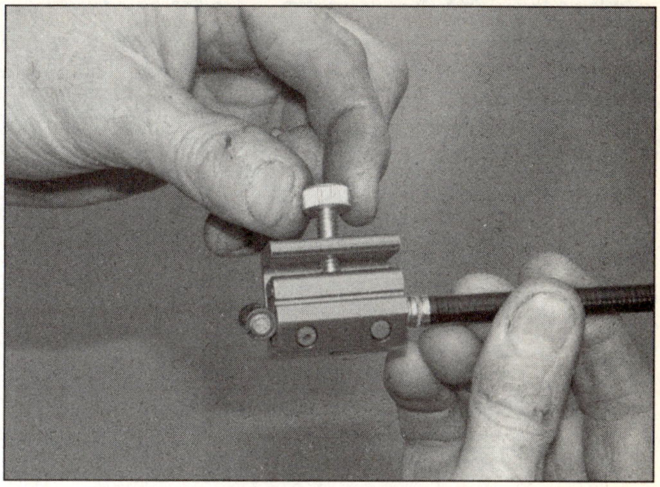

14.3b . . . and tighten the screw to seal it in . . .

5 If any play is detected in the hub, or if the wheel does not rotate smoothly (and this is not due to brake or transmission drag), the wheel should be removed and the bearings inspected for wear or damage (see Chapter 6).

14 Stand, lever pivot and cable lubrication

Pivot points

1 Since the controls, cables and various other components of a motorcycle are exposed to the elements, they should be checked and lubricated periodically to ensure safe and trouble-free operation.

2 The footrest pivots, clutch and brake lever pivots, brake pedal and gearchange lever pivots and linkage and sidestand pivot should be lubricated frequently. In order for the lubricant to be applied where it will do the most good, the component should be disassembled (see Chapter 5). The lubricant recommended by Honda for each application is listed at the beginning of the Chapter. If aerosol chain or cable lubricant is being used, it can be applied to the pivot joint gaps and will usually work its way into the areas where friction occurs, so less disassembly of the component is needed (however it is always better to do so and clean off all corrosion, dirt and old lubricant first). If motor oil or light grease is being used, apply it sparingly as it may attract dirt (which could cause the controls to bind or wear at an accelerated rate). **Note:** *A good lubricant for the control lever pivots is a dry-film lubricant (available from many sources by different names).*

Cables

Special tool: *A cable lubricating adapter is necessary for this procedure **(see illustration 14.3c)**.*

3 To lubricate the cables, disconnect the relevant cable at its upper end, then lubricate it with a pressure adapter and aerosol lubricant **(see illustrations)**. See Chapter 4 for both throttle and exhaust gas control valve (EGCV) cable removal procedures.

15 Nuts and bolts

1 Since vibration of the machine tends to loosen fasteners, all nuts, bolts, screws, etc. should be periodically checked for proper tightness.

2 Pay particular attention to the following, referring to the relevant Chapter:

- Spark plugs
- Engine oil drain plug
- Lever and pedal bolts
- Footrest and sidestand bolts
- Engine mounting bolts
- Shock absorber and suspension linkage bolts; swingarm pivot bolt, nut and locknut
- Handlebar clamp bolts
- Front fork clamp bolts (top and bottom yoke) and fork top bolts
- Steering stem nut
- Front wheel axle bolt and axle clamp bolts
- Rear wheel axle nut
- Front sprocket bolt and rear sprocket nuts
- Brake caliper and master cylinder mounting bolts, front brake caliper body bolts
- Brake hose banjo bolts and caliper bleed valves
- Brake disc bolts
- Exhaust system bolts/nuts

3 If a torque wrench is available, use it along with the torque settings given at the beginning of this and other Chapters.

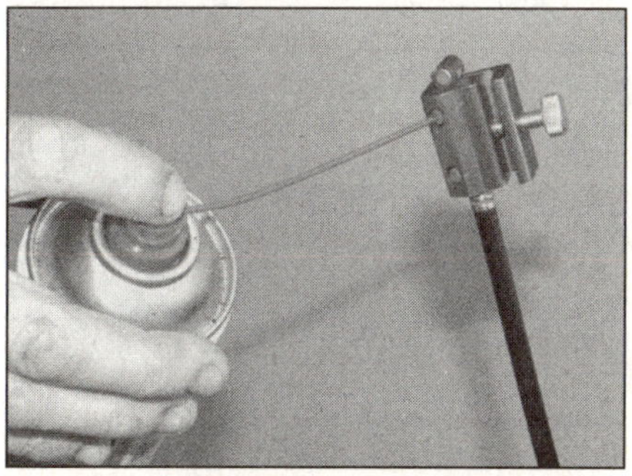

14.3c . . . then apply the lubricant using the nozzle provided inserted in the hole in the adapter

16 Air filters

Caution: If the machine is continually ridden in wet or dusty conditions, the filter should be replaced more frequently.

1 Remove the fuel tank cover (see Chapter 4). On RR-6 and RR-7 models undo the screws securing the ECM holder and remove it, then lift the ECM back so it rests on the secondary fuel rail **(see illustration)**.

2 Disconnect the intake air temperature (IAT)

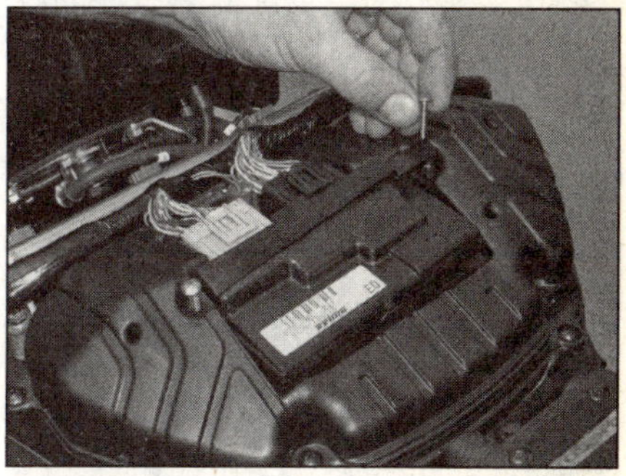

16.1 Undo the screws, remove the holder and lift the ECM off the air filter cover

16.2a Disconnect the IAT sensor wiring connector

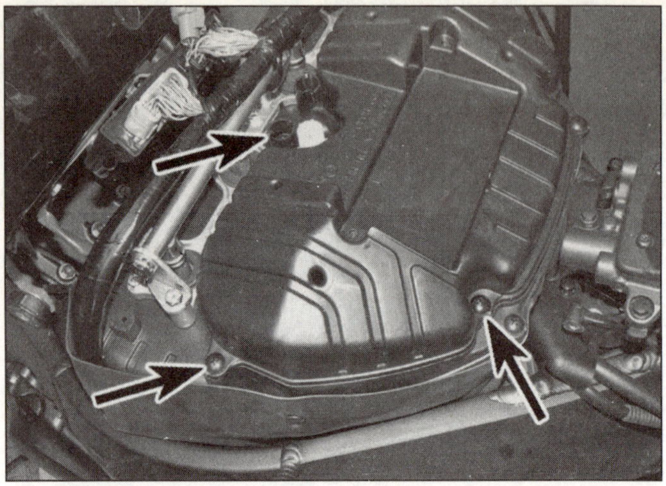

16.2b Undo the screws (arrowed) on each side . . .

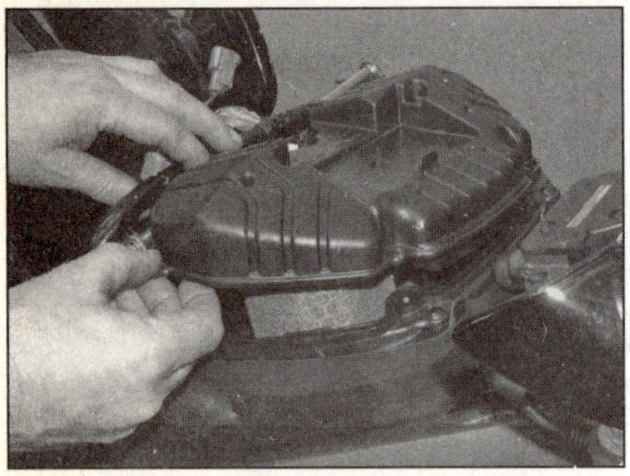

16.2c . . . and remove the cover

sensor wiring connector **(see illustration)**. Undo the screws securing the air filter housing cover and lift it off the housing **(see illustrations)**.

3 Remove the filter elements from the housing, noting how they locate, and discard them **(see illustration)**.

4 Fit the new filter elements into the housing, aligning the sections on the base with the cut-outs, and making sure they seat properly **(see illustration 16.3)**.

5 Install the filter housing cover **(see illustration 16.2c)**. Connect the IAT (intake air temperature) sensor wiring connector **(see illustration 16.2a)**. On RR-6 and RR-7 models locate the ECM on the cover and fit the holder **(see illustration 16.1)**. Install the fuel tank cover (see Chapter 4).

6 To clean the filter between renewal intervals, tap it on a hard surface to dislodge any dirt and use compressed air to clear the element, directing the air in the opposite way to normal flow, i.e. from the outside **(see illustration)**. Do not use any solvents or cleaning agents on the element.

17 EVAP (Evaporative emission control) system (California models)

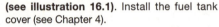

1 Raise the fuel tank (see Chapter 4). Visually inspect all the system hoses between the fuel tank, the purge control solenoid valve, and the canister for kinks and splits and any other damage or deterioration. Make sure that the hoses are securely connected with a clamp on each end. Replace any hoses that are damaged or deteriorated.

2 Check the EVAP canister and the valve for cracks or other damage.

3 See Chapter 4 for further information and tests on the system. Note that there is an emission control system hose routing diagram on a label stuck to the side of the fuel tank, and an information label under the passenger seat.

18 Valve clearances

Special tool: *A set of feeler gauges is necessary for this job* ***(see illustration 18.7)****.*

1 The engine must be completely cool for this maintenance procedure, so let the bike stand overnight before beginning.

2 Remove the spark plugs (see Section 19). Remove the valve cover (see Chapter 2).

3 Make a chart or sketch of all valve positions so that a note of each clearance can be made against the relevant valve. The cylinders are numbered 1 to 4 from left to right. The intake valves are at the back of the cylinder head and the exhaust valves are at the front.

4 Unscrew the timing inspection cap from the clutch cover **(see illustration)**. Check the condition of its O-ring and obtain a new one if necessary.

5 To check the valve clearances the engine must be turned so that the valve being checked is closed. The engine can be turned using a suitable spanner or a socket on the timing rotor bolt and turning it in a clockwise direction only **(see illustration 18.6a)**.

6 Turn the engine clockwise until the line

16.3 Remove the filter elements, noting how they locate

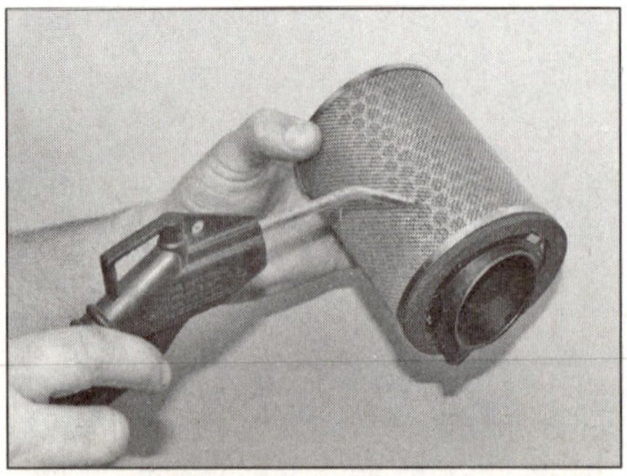

16.6 Direct the air in the opposite direction of normal flow

18.4 Remove the timing inspection cap

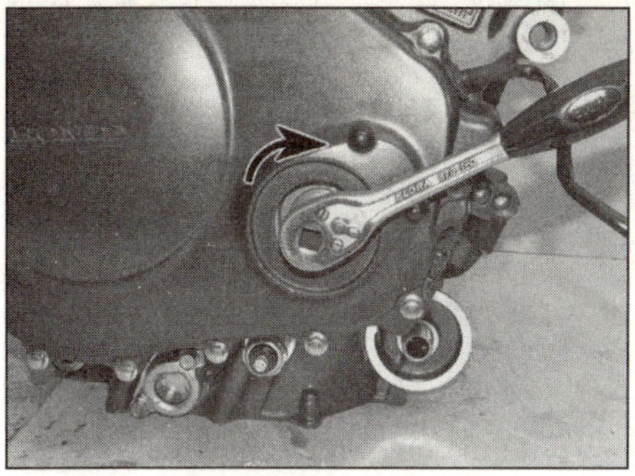

18.6a Turn the engine clockwise using the bolt . . .

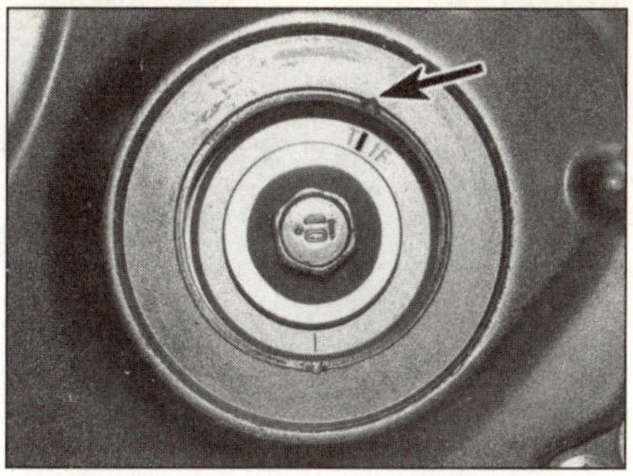

18.6b . . . until the line next to the T mark aligns with the notch (arrowed) . . .

18.6c . . . and the camshaft sprocket marks are as shown

next to the T mark on the timing rotor aligns with the static timing mark, which is a notch in the inspection hole rim, and the IN and EX marks on the intake and exhaust camshaft sprockets respectively are facing away from each other and are flush with the cylinder head top surface **(see illustrations)**. If the sprocket marks are facing towards each other, rotate the engine clockwise one full turn (360°) until the line next to the T mark again aligns with the static timing mark. The sprocket marks will now be facing away.

7 With the engine in this position, check the clearances on the Nos. 1 and 3 cylinder intake valves, remembering there are two valves per cylinder. Insert a feeler gauge of the same thickness as the correct valve clearance (see Specifications) between the camshaft lobe and the follower of each valve and check that it is a firm sliding fit – you should feel a slight drag when the you pull the gauge out **(see illustration)**. If not, use the feeler gauges to obtain the exact clearance. Record the measured clearance on the chart.

8 Now rotate the engine 180° clockwise until the line next to the T mark on the timing rotor is diametrically opposite the static timing mark – the scribed line on the rotor will now be in the 12 o'clock position **(see illustration)**. With the engine in this position, check the clearances on the Nos. 2 and 4 cylinder exhaust valves using the method described in Step 7.

9 Now rotate the engine 180° clockwise until the line next to the T mark aligns with the static timing mark again **(see illustration 18.6b)**. With the engine in this position, check the clearances on the Nos. 2 and 4 cylinder intake valves using the method described in Step 7.

10 Now rotate the engine 180° clockwise until the line next to the T mark on the timing rotor is once again diametrically opposite the static timing mark and the scribed line is at the 12 o'clock position **(see illustration 18.8)**. With the engine in this position, check the clearances on the Nos. 1 and 3 cylinder exhaust valves using the method described in Step 7.

11 When all clearances have been measured and charted, identify whether the clearance on any valve falls outside the specified range. If any do, the shim must be replaced with one of a thickness which will restore the correct clearance.

12 Shim replacement requires removal of the camshafts (see Chapter 2). Place rags over the spark plug holes and the cam chain tunnel to prevent a shim from dropping into the engine on removal. Work on one valve at a time to prevent the possibility of mixing up the followers, which must be returned to their original location. If you want to remove more than one shim and follower at a time, store them in a marked container or bag, denoting which cylinder and which valve the shim and follower are from, so that they do not get mixed up.

13 With the camshaft removed, remove the cam follower of the valve in question using a magnet or the suction created by a valve lapping tool, but long nosed pliers can be used with care **(see illustration)**. Retrieve the shim either from the inside of the follower or pick it out of the top of the valve spring retainer using

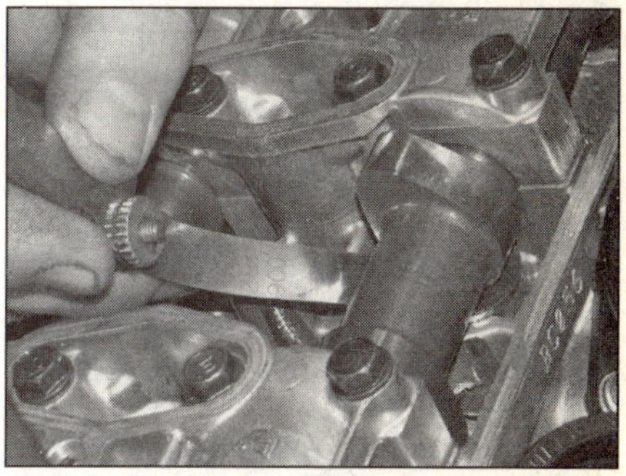

18.7 Insert the feeler gauge between the base of the cam lobe and the top of the follower as shown

either a magnet, a screwdriver with a dab of grease on it (the shim will stick to the grease), or a very small screwdriver and a pair of pliers **(see illustrations)**. Do not allow the shim to fall into the engine.

18.8 Turn the engine 180° so the marks are aligned as shown

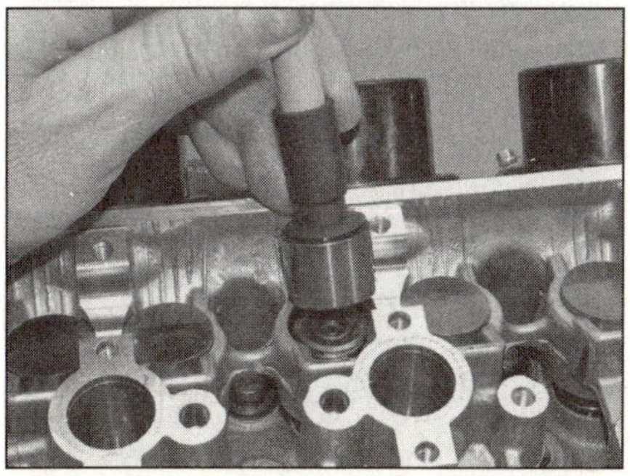

18.13a Carefully lift out the follower using grips, a lapping tool or a magnet . . .

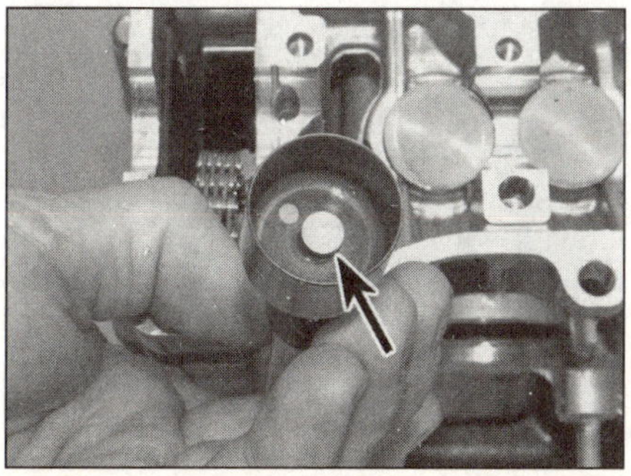

18.13b . . . and retrieve the shim (arrowed) from inside it . . .

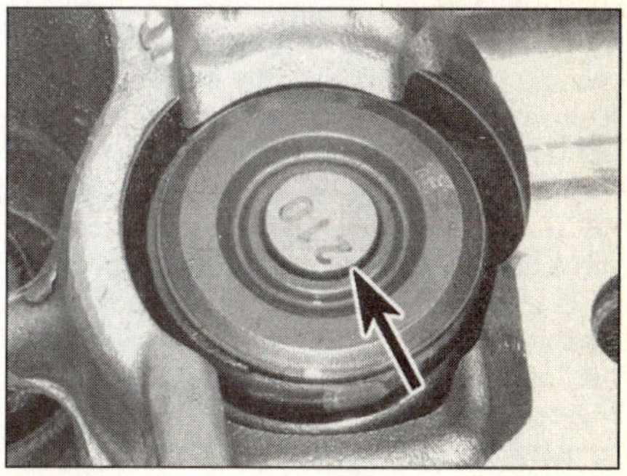

18.13c . . . or from the top of the valve

18.14a The shim size is marked on one face . . .

18.14b . . . but check the thickness of the shim using a micrometer

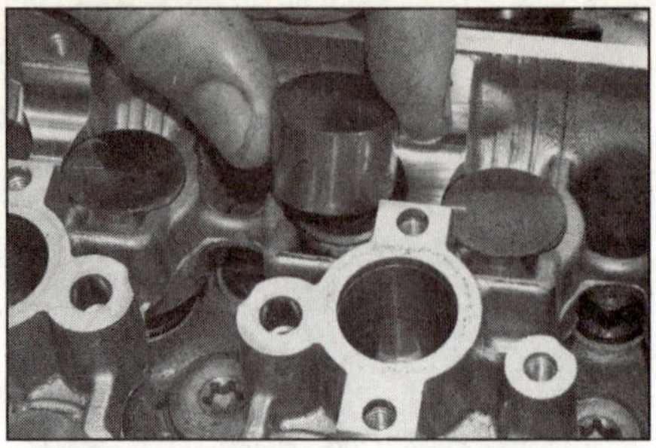

18.17 Fit the follower onto the valve

14 A size mark should be stamped on one face of the shim – a shim marked 175 is 1.75 mm thick **(see illustration)**. If the mark is not visible measure the shim thickness using a micrometer **(see illustration)**. It is recommended that the shim is measured anyway to check whether it has worn.

15 Calculate the required replacement shim by using the formula a = (b – c) + d, where a is the required replacement shim size, b is the measured valve clearance, c is the specified valve clearance, and d is the existing shim thickness. For example:

The measured clearance of an intake valve is 0.22 mm, so b = 0.22

The specified clearance range for an intake valve is 0.13 to 0.19 mm, the mid-point being 0.16 mm, so c = 0.16

The thickness of the existing shim is 2.00 mm, so d = 2.0

Therefore, the required replacement shim a = 0.22 – 0.16 + 2.0 (a = 2.06 mm). The nearest available size to this 2.05 mm (Step 16).

Note: *If the required replacement shim is greater than 2.900 mm (the largest available), the valve is probably not seating correctly due to a build-up of carbon deposits and should be checked and cleaned or resurfaced as required (see Chapter 2).*

16 Shims are available in 0.025 mm increments from 1.200 mm to 2.900 mm. Obtain the replacement shim, then lubricate it with molybdenum disulphide oil (a 50/50 mixture of molybdenum disulphide grease and engine oil) and fit it into the recess in the top of the valve spring retainer with the size mark facing up **(see illustration 18.13c)**.

17 Check that the shim is correctly seated, then lubricate the follower with molybdenum disulphide oil and fit it onto the valve, making sure it fits squarely in its bore **(see illustration)**. Repeat the process for any other valves until the clearances are correct, then install the camshafts (see Chapter 2).

18 Rotate the crankshaft clockwise several turns to seat the new shim(s), then check the clearances again. Install the valve cover (see Chapter 2).

19 Install all disturbed components in a reverse of the removal sequence. Install the timing inspection cap using a new O-ring if required, and smear the O-ring and the cap threads with grease **(see illustration 18.4)**. Tighten the cap to the torque setting specified at the beginning of the Chapter.

20 On completion, check and adjust the idle speed (see Section 2).

19 Spark plugs

Check

Special tool: *A wire gauge is necessary for measuring the spark plug gap* ***(see illustration 19.7b)****.*

Note 1: *The spark plug caps are integral with the ignition coils. To avoid damaging the wiring, always disconnect the wiring connectors before removing the coils. Do not attempt to lever the coils off the plugs or pull them off with pliers. Do not drop the coils.*

Note 2: *All models are equipped with plugs that have an iridium coated centre electrode. The plugs must be treated differently to conventional plugs, so be sure to follow the procedure as described – do not treat them in the same way as conventional plugs or replace them with conventional plugs.*

1 Make sure your spark plug socket is the correct size (16 mm hex) before attempting to remove the plugs – a suitable one is supplied in the motorcycle's tool kit which is stored under the passenger seat.

2 Remove the air filter housing and the air intake duct (see Chapter 4).

3 Clean the area around each coil to prevent any dirt falling into the spark plug channels.

4 Check that the cylinder location is marked on each coil wiring sleeve, then disconnect the coil wiring connectors **(see illustration)**. Pull the coil off each spark plug **(see illustration)**.

5 Using either the plug removing tool supplied in the bike's toolkit or a deep 16 mm spark plug socket, unscrew and remove the plugs from the cylinder head **(see illustrations)**. Lay

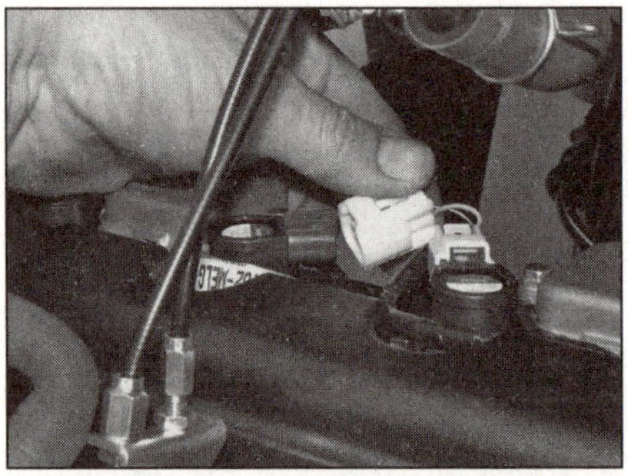

19.4a Disconnect the coil wiring connector . . .

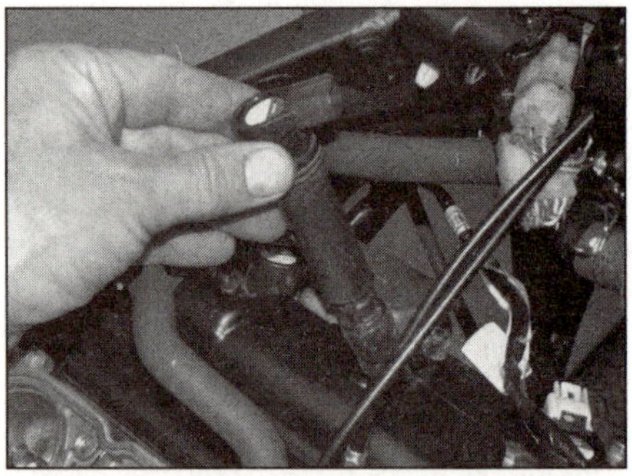

19.4b . . . then pull the coil up off the plug

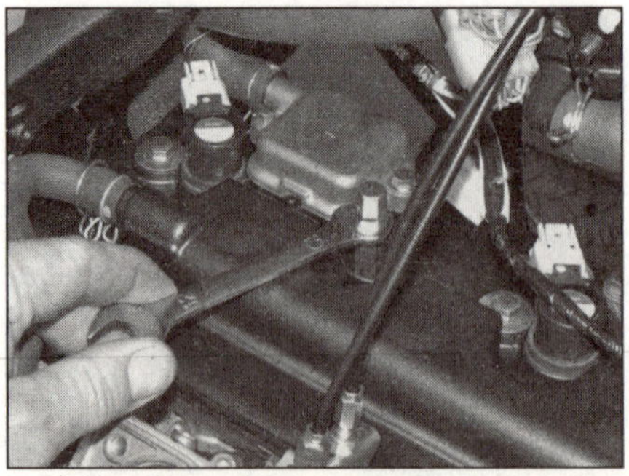

19.5a Unscrew the plug . . .

19.5b . . . and lift it out with the tool – the rubber insert should grip around the plug top

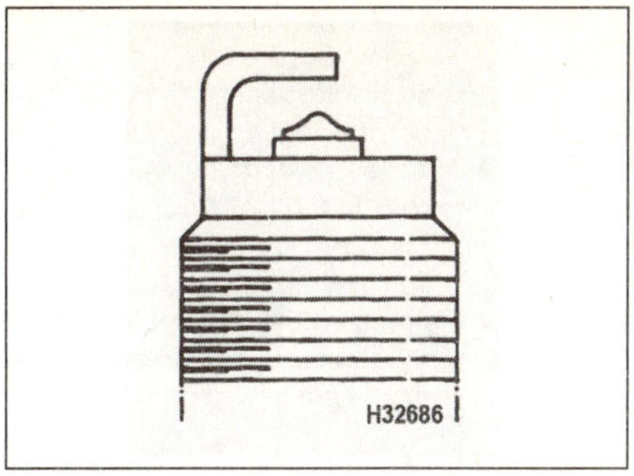

19.7a If the centre electrode has rounded off the plug is worn

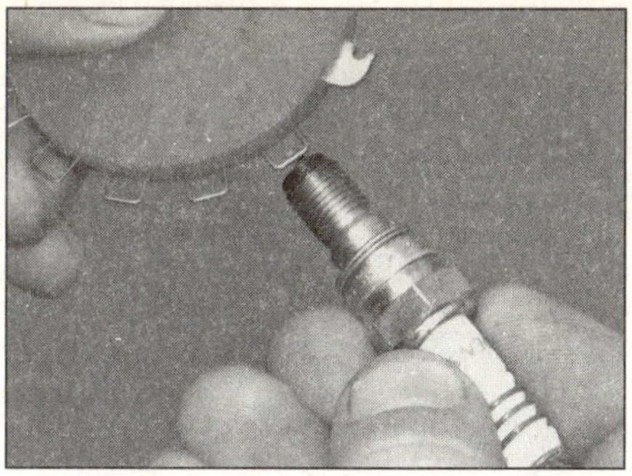

19.7b Using a wire type gauge to measure the spark plug electrode gap

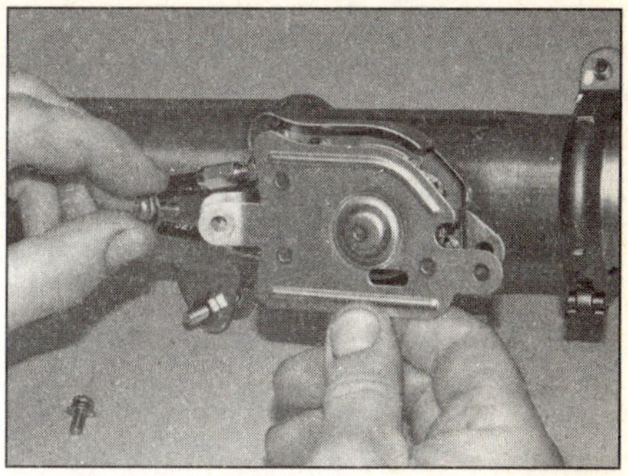

20.2 Undo the screws and remove the cover – RR-6 model shown, exhaust removed

each plug out in relation to its cylinder; if any plug shows up a problem it will then be easy to identify the troublesome cylinder.

6 Check the condition of the electrodes, referring to the spark plug reading chart at the end of this manual if signs of contamination are evident. Note that contaminated iridium plugs should not be cleaned – discard them and install new ones.

7 Examine the pointed iridium-tipped centre electrode; if the tip has rounded off, the plug is worn **(see illustration)**. Measure the gap between the electrodes with a wire type gauge only **(see illustration)** – do not use blade type feeler gauges because the iridium tip might be damaged. The gap should be as given in the Specifications at the beginning of this chapter; if the electrodes have worn and the gap is wider than it should be, or for some reason the gap is narrower than it should be (if the plug has been dropped for instance) a new plug must be installed. Do not bend the outer electrode to adjust the gap.

8 Check the threads, the washer and the ceramic insulator body for cracks and other damage.

9 Note that Honda advise that the specified iridium plugs only must be fitted – do not substitute with conventional plugs.

10 Fit the plug into the end of the tool, then use the tool to insert the plug **(see illustration 19.5b)**. Since the cylinder head is made of aluminium, which is soft and easily damaged, thread the plugs as far as possible into the head turning the tool by hand. Once the plugs are finger-tight, the job can be finished with a spanner on the tool supplied or a socket drive **(see illustration 19.5a)**. If a torque wrench can be applied, tighten the spark plugs to the torque setting specified at the beginning of the Chapter. Otherwise, if new plugs are being used tighten them by 1/2 a turn after the washer has seated, and if the old plugs are being reused tighten them by 1/8 to 1/4 turn after they have seated. Do not over-tighten them.

HAYNES HiNT ***As the plugs are quite recessed, slip a short length of hose over the end of the plug to use as a tool to thread it into place. The hose will grip the plug well enough to turn it, but will start to slip if the plug begins to cross-thread in the hole – this will prevent damaged threads.***

11 Install the coils, making sure they locate correctly onto the plugs **(see illustration 19.4b)**. Reconnect the coil wiring connectors, making sure they are securely connected to the correct cylinder – each wiring sleeve should be marked with its cylinder number **(see illustration 19.4a)**. Install the air filter housing and the air intake duct (see Chapter 4).

HAYNES HiNT ***Stripped plug threads in the cylinder head can be repaired with a thread insert – see 'Tools and Workshop Tips' in the Reference section.***

Renewal

12 At the prescribed interval, whatever the condition of the existing spark plugs, remove the plugs as described above and install new ones.

20 Exhaust gas control valve (EGCV)

1 Remove the left-hand fairing side panel (see Chapter 7).

2 Unscrew the two exhaust control valve cover bolts and remove the cover **(see illustration)**.

3 Locate the engine management system data link connector (DLC), which is a red blanked single-sided 4-pin connector that may be wrapped in insulating tape **(see illustrations)**.

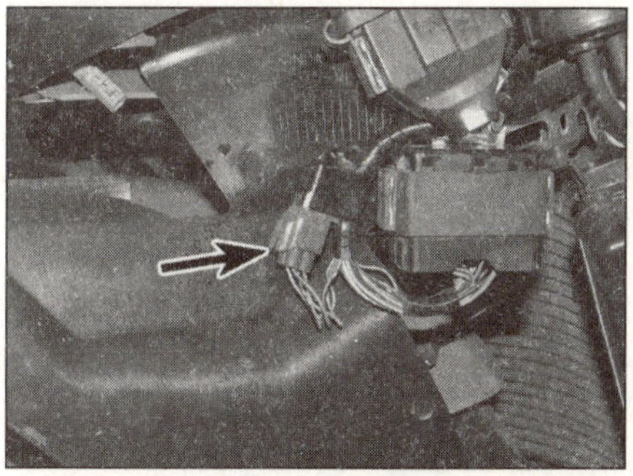

20.3a Data link connector (arrowed) – RR-4 and RR-5 models

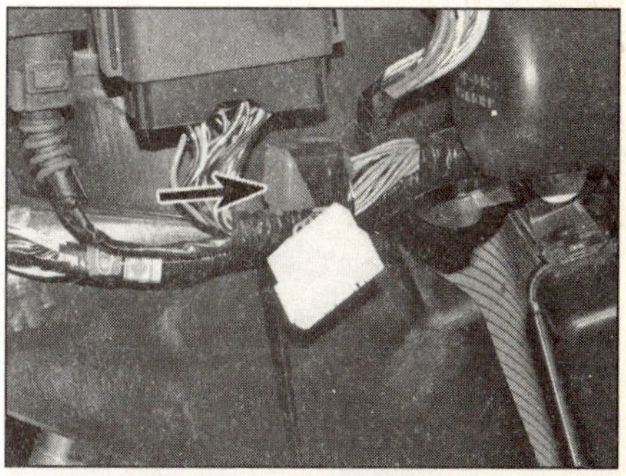

20.3b Data link connector (arrowed) – RR-6 and RR-7 models

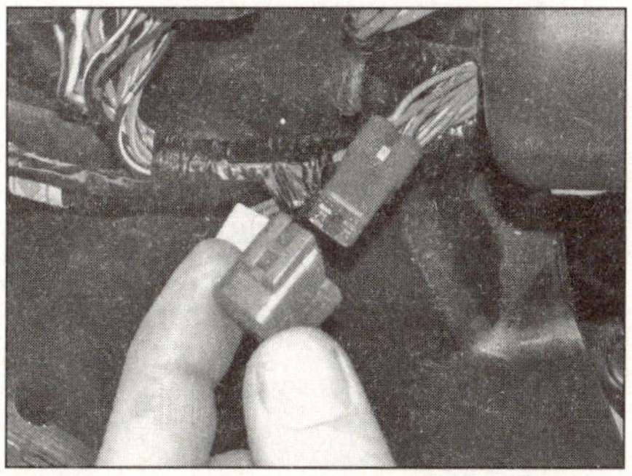

20.3c Removing the blanking cap on RR-6 and RR-7 models

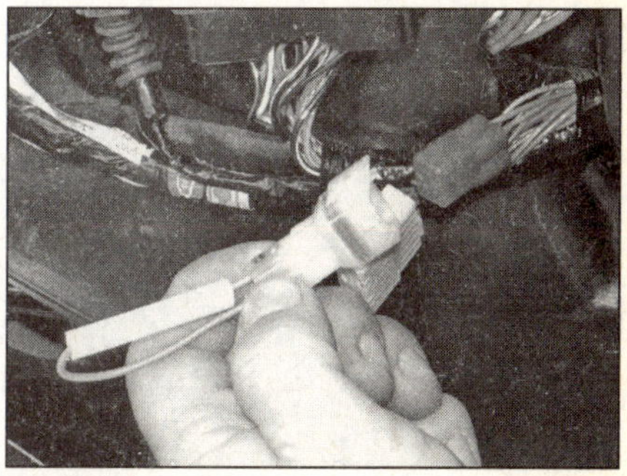

20.3d Honda's SCS connector being fitted to the DLC connector

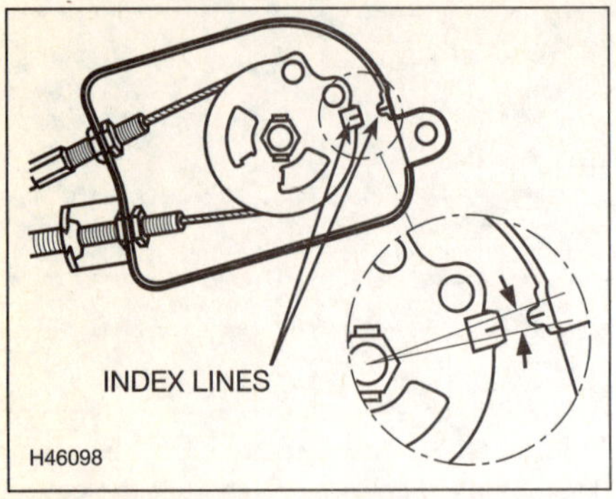

20.4a Control valve pulley index line alignment – RR-4 and RR-5 models

On RR-4 and RR-5 models disconnect the wired side of the connector from the taped blank side. On RR-6 and RR-7 models remove the tape if necessary, and the blanking cap. Turn the ignition ON. Either fit the Honda SCS service connector (Part No. 070PZ-ZY30100, available from your dealer), or bridge the green and brown wire terminals of the connector with a piece of electrical wire – do not confuse the brown wire with the adjacent brown/yellow wire, on which the yellow stripe is thin and depending on the light may be difficult to distinguish **(see illustrations)**.

4 Check the position of the index line on the control valve pulley – it should align with the index line on the valve housing **(see illustrations)**. If the index lines are out

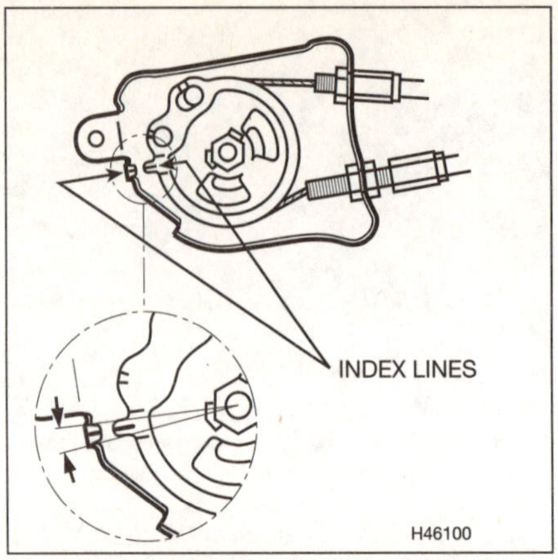

20.4b Control valve pulley index line alignment – RR-6 and RR-7 models

of alignment adjust the cable(s) as follows according to model.

5 On RR-4 and RR-5 models fully slacken the locknuts on the spring-loaded lower cable **(see illustration)**. Now slacken the nuts holding the adjuster on the upper cable and turn them as required to alter the position of the adjuster until the index lines align, then tighten the nuts **(see illustration)**. Now tighten the locknuts on the lower cable. Remove and reconnect the SCS connector or jumper wire and recheck the alignment of the index lines, readjusting if necessary.

6 On RR-6 and RR-7 models slacken the nuts holding the adjuster on the lower cable and turn them as required to alter the position of the adjuster until the index lines align, then tighten the nuts **(see illustration)**. Remove and reconnect the SCS connector or jumper wire and recheck the alignment of the index lines, readjusting if necessary.

7 Smear some grease over the cable ends in the pulley. Apply some copper grease to the exhaust valve cover bolt threads and fit the cover.

21 Battery

1 All models covered in this manual are fitted with a sealed MF (maintenance free) battery. **Note:** *Do not attempt to remove the battery caps to check the electrolyte level or battery specific gravity.* Removal will damage the caps, resulting in electrolyte leakage and battery damage. All that should be done is to check that the terminals are clean and tight and that the casing is not damaged or leaking. See Chapter 8 for further details.

2 If the machine is not in regular use, disconnect the battery and give it a refresher charge every month to six weeks (see Chapter 8).

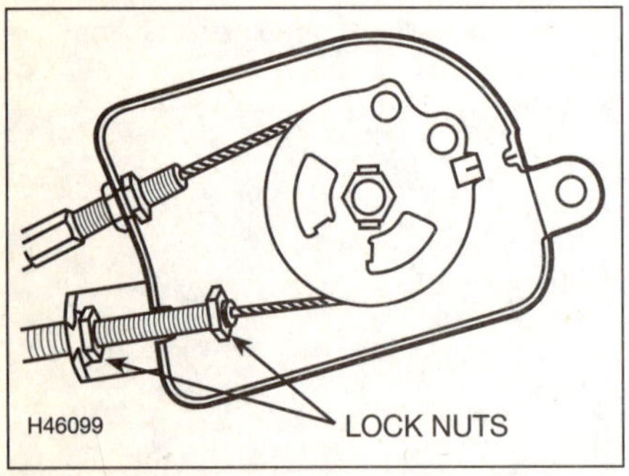

20.5a Slacken the locknuts on the lower cable . . .

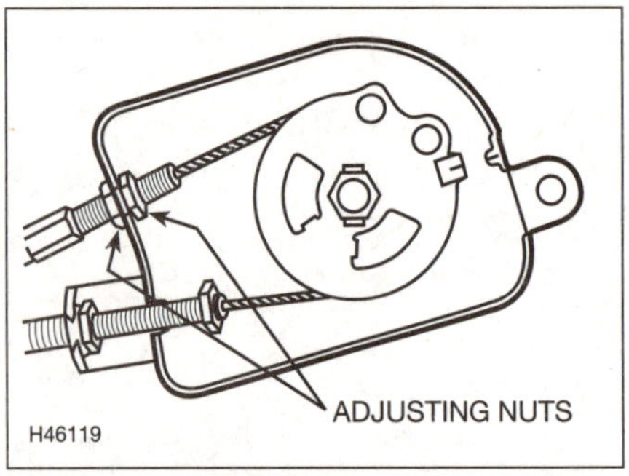

20.5b . . . then adjust the upper cable using the nuts – RR-4 and RR-5 models

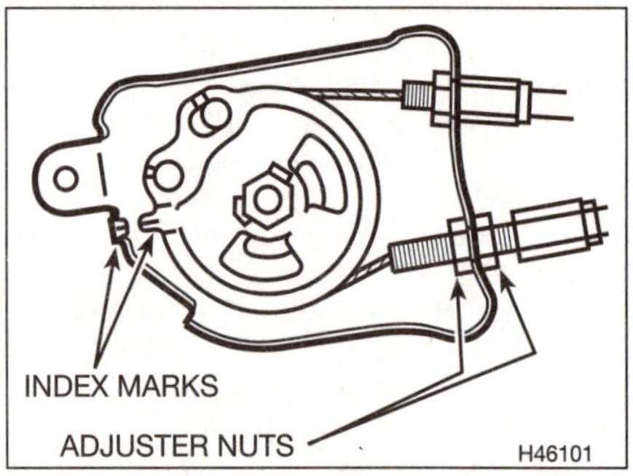

20.6 Cable adjusting nuts – RR-6 and RR-7 models

Chapter 2
Engine, clutch and transmission

Contents

Degrees of difficulty

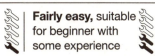

Easy, suitable for novice with little experience	**Fairly easy,** suitable for beginner with some experience	**Fairly difficult,** suitable for competent DIY mechanic	**Difficult,** suitable for experienced DIY mechanic	**Very difficult,** suitable for expert DIY or professional

Specifications

General

Type	Four-stroke in-line four
Capacity	998.4 cc
Cylinder numbering	1 to 4 from left to right
Firing order	1-2-4-3
Bore	75.0 mm
Stroke	56.5 mm
Compression ratio	
RR-4 and RR-5 models	11.9 to 1
RR-6 and RR-7 models	12.2 to 1
Cooling system	Liquid cooled
Lubrication	Wet sump, trochoid pump
Clutch	Wet multi-plate
Transmission	Six-speed constant mesh, cassette loading
Final drive	Chain

Camshafts and followers

Intake lobe height	
RR-4 and RR-5 models	
Standard	37.02 to 37.10 mm
Service limit (min)	37.00 mm
RR-6 and RR-7 models	
Standard	37.22 to 37.30 mm
Service limit (min)	37.20 mm
Exhaust lobe height	
Standard	36.66 to 36.74 mm
Service limit (min)	36.64 mm
Oil clearance	
Standard	0.020 to 0.062 mm
Service limit (max)	0.10 mm
Runout (max)	0.05 mm
Camshaft follower diameter	
Standard	25.978 to 25.993 mm
Service limit (min)	25.97 mm
Camshaft follower bore diameter	
Standard	26.010 to 26.026 mm
Service limit (min)	26.04 mm

Cylinder head

Warpage (max)	0.10 mm

Valves, guides and springs

Valve clearances	see Chapter 1
Stem diameter	
Intake valve	
Standard	3.975 to 3.990 mm
Service limit (min)	3.965 mm
Exhaust valve	
Standard	3.965 to 3.980 mm
Service limit (min)	3.955 mm
Guide bore diameter – intake and exhaust valves	
Standard	4.000 to 4.012 mm
Service limit (max)	4.040 mm
Stem-to-guide clearance	
Intake valve	
Standard	0.010 to 0.037 mm
Service limit	0.075 mm
Exhaust valve	
Standard	0.020 to 0.047 mm
Service limit	0.085 mm
Seat width – intake and exhaust valves	
Standard	0.90 to 1.10 mm
Service limit (max)	1.50 mm
Valve guide height above cylinder head	
Intake valve	16.1 to 16.4 mm
Exhaust valve	15.5 to 15.8 mm
Valve spring free length	
RR-4 and RR-5 models	
Intake	
Standard	39.5 mm
Service limit (min)	38.7 mm
Exhaust	
Standard	39.5 mm
Service limit (min)	38.7 mm
RR-6 and RR-7 models	
Intake – inner spring	
Standard	36.56 mm
Service limit (min)	35.83 mm
Intake – outer spring	
Standard	40.65 mm
Service limit (min)	39.8 mm
Exhaust	
Standard	40.04 mm
Service limit (min)	39.24 mm

Starter clutch

Starter driven gear hub OD	
Standard	45.657 to 45.673 mm
Service limit (min)	45.642 mm
Starter idle gear ID	
Standard	10.013 to 10.035 mm
Service limit (max)	10.05 mm
Starter idle gear shaft OD	
Standard	9.991 to 10.000 mm
Service limit (min)	9.98 mm

Clutch

Friction plates	8
Plain plates	7
Friction plate thickness	
Type A (innermost and outermost plates)	
Standard	3.72 to 3.88 mm
Service limit (min)	3.4 mm
Type B	
Standard	3.22 to 3.38 mm
Service limit (min)	2.9 mm
Plain plate warpage (max)	0.3 mm
Spring free length	
Standard	56.8 mm
Service limit (min)	55.7 mm
Clutch guide OD	
Type A, no marking	
Standard	35.004 to 35.012 mm
Service limit (min)	34.994 mm
Type B, with marking	
Standard	34.996 to 35.004 mm
Service limit (min)	34.986 mm
Clutch guide ID (both types)	
Standard	27.993 to 28.003 mm
Service limit (max)	28.012 mm
Primary driven gear ID	
Type A	
Standard	41.008 to 41.016 mm
Service limit (min)	41.026 mm
Type B	
Standard	41.000 to 41.008 mm
Service limit (min)	41.018 mm
Input shaft OD at clutch guide	
Standard	27.980 to 27.990 mm
Service limit (max)	27.960 mm

Clutch release mechanism

Clutch fluid	DOT 4
Master cylinder bore ID	
Standard	12.700 to 12.743 mm
Service limit (max)	12.755 mm
Piston OD	
Standard	12.657 to 12.684 mm
Service limit (max)	12.645 mm

Oil pump

Oil pressure (at oil pressure switch, with engine warm) . . . 71 psi (4.9 Bar) @ 6000 rpm, oil @ 80°C

	Standard	**Service limit (max)**
Inner rotor tip-to-outer rotor clearance	0.15 mm	0.20 mm
Outer rotor-to-body clearance	0.15 to 0.21 mm	0.35 mm
Rotor end-float	0.04 to 0.09 mm	0.17 mm
Oil pump drive sprocket ID	35.025 to 35.145 mm	35.155 mm
Oil pump drive sprocket guide ID	28.000 to 28.021 mm	28.030 mm
Oil pump drive sprocket guide OD	34.975 to 34.991 mm	34.965 mm
Input shaft OD at sprocket guide	27.980 to 27.990 mm	27.960 mm

Selector drum and forks

Selector fork end thickness	
Standard	5.93 to 6.00 mm
Service limit (min)	5.90 mm
Selector fork bore ID	
Standard	12.000 to 12.018 mm
Service limit (max)	12.03 mm
Selector fork shaft OD	
Standard	11.957 to 11.968 mm
Service limit (min)	11.95 mm
Cylinder bores	
Bore	
Standard	75.000 to 75.015 mm
Service limit (max)	75.100 mm
Warpage (max)	0.10 mm
Ovality (out-of-round) (max)	0.10 mm
Taper (max)	0.10 mm
Cylinder compression	
RR-4 and RR-5 models	159 psi (11.0 Bar) @ 350 rpm
RR-6 and RR-7 models	178 psi (12.2 Bar) @ 350 rpm

Connecting rods

Small-end internal diameter	
Standard	17.030 to 17.042 mm
Service limit (max)	17.048 mm
Small-end-to-piston pin clearance	
Standard	0.030 to 0.046 mm
Service limit	0.070 mm
Big-end side clearance	
Standard	0.05 to 0.20 mm
Service limit (max)	0.25 mm
Big-end oil clearance	
Standard	0.030 to 0.052 mm
Service limit (max)	0.06 mm

Pistons

Piston diameter (measured 4 mm up from skirt, at 90° to piston pin axis)	
Standard	74.960 to 74.980 mm
Service limit (min)	74.895 mm
Piston-to-bore clearance	
Standard	0.020 to 0.055 mm
Service limit (min)	0.10 mm*
Piston pin diameter	
Standard	16.994 to 17.000 mm
Service limit (min)	16.980 mm
Piston pin bore diameter in piston	
Standard	17.002 to 17.008 mm
Service limit (max)	17.030 mm
Piston pin-to-piston pin bore clearance	
Standard	0.002 to 0.014 mm
Service limit	0.04 mm

**If the piston-to-bore clearance exceeds the service limit, the cylinders can be rebored – Honda supply +0.25 oversize pistons and rings. Following rebore, the piston-to-bore clearance must be as standard for normal pistons*

Piston rings

	Standard	Service limit (max)
Ring end gap (installed)		
Top ring	0.22 to 0.32 mm	0.52 mm
Second ring	0.48 to 0.63 mm	0.82 mm
Oil ring side-rail	0.20 to 0.70 mm	1.0 mm
Ring-to-groove clearance		
Top ring	0.050 to 0.085 mm	0.125 mm
Second ring		
RR-4 and RR-5 models	0.015 to 0.050 mm	0.075 mm
RR-6 and RR-7 models	0.015 to 0.045 mm	0.070 mm

Crankshaft and bearings

Main bearing oil clearance	
Standard	0.019 to 0.037 mm
Service limit (max)	0.05 mm
Runout (max)	0.05 mm

Transmission

Gear ratios (no. of teeth)	
Primary reduction	1.604 to 1 (77/48T)
Final reduction	
European models	
RR-4 and RR-5 models	2.500 to 1 (40/16T)
RR-6 and RR-7 models	2.625 to 1 (42/16T)
US and Canada models	
RR-4 and RR-5 models	2.562 to 1 (41/16T)
RR-6 and RR-7 models	2.625 to 1 (42/16T)
1st gear	2.538 to 1 (33/13T)
2nd gear	1.941 to 1 (33/17T)
3rd gear	1.578 to 1 (30/19T)
4th gear	1.380 to 1 (29/21T)
5th gear	1.250 to 1 (25/20T)
6th gear	1.160 to 1 (29/25T)
Input shaft 5th and 6th gears ID	
Standard	31.000 to 31.025 mm
Service limit (max)	31.04 mm
Input shaft 5th and 6th gears bush OD	
Standard	30.955 to 30.980 mm
Service limit (min)	30.935 mm
Input shaft 5th and 6th gears gear-to-bush clearance	
Standard	0.020 to 0.070 mm
Service limit (max)	0.10 mm
Input shaft 5th gear bush ID	
Standard	27.985 to 28.006 mm
Service limit (max)	28.016 mm
Input shaft OD at 5th gear bush point	
Standard	27.967 to 27.980 mm
Service limit (min)	27.957 mm
Input shaft-to-bush clearance at 5th gear bush point	
Standard	0.005 to 0.039 mm
Service limit (max)	0.06 mm
Output shaft 1st gear ID	
Standard	28.000 to 28.021 mm
Service limit (max)	28.04 mm
Output shaft 2nd, 3rd and 4th gears ID	
Standard	33.000 to 33.025 mm
Service limit (max)	33.04 mm
Output shaft 2nd gear bush OD	
Standard	32.955 to 32.980 mm
Service limit (min)	32.935 mm
Output shaft 3rd and 4th gears bush OD	
Standard	32.950 to 32.975 mm
Service limit (min)	32.93 mm
Output shaft 2nd gear gear-to-bush clearance	
Standard	0.020 to 0.070 mm
Service limit (max)	0.10 mm
Output shaft 3rd and 4th gears gear-to-bush clearance	
Standard	0.025 to 0.075 mm
Service limit (max)	0.11 mm
Output shaft 2nd gear bush ID	
Standard	29.985 to 30.006 mm
Service limit (max)	30.021 mm
Output shaft OD at 2nd gear bush point	
Standard	29.967 to 29.980 mm
Service limit (min)	29.96 mm
Output shaft-to-bushing clearance at 2nd gear bush point	
Standard	0.005 to 0.039 mm
Service limit (max)	0.06 mm

Torque settings

Cam chain front guide blade pivot bolt	12 Nm
Cam chain tensioner blade pivot bolt	10 Nm
Cam chain tensioner bolts	10 Nm
Camshaft holder bolts	12 Nm
Camshaft sprocket bolts	20 Nm
Camshaft position (CMP) sensor rotor bolts	12 Nm
Clutch hose banjo bolt	34 Nm
Clutch master cylinder clamp bolts	12 Nm
Clutch nut	127 Nm
Clutch spring bolts	12 Nm
Connecting rod bolts	
Torque setting – new bolts	20 Nm
Torque setting – oil clearance check (old bolts)	14 Nm
Angle setting	+ 90°
Crankcase breather separator bolts	12 Nm
Crankcase bolts	
Crankshaft journal 9 mm bolts	
Torque setting	20 Nm
Angle setting	+ 150°
Lower crankcase 8 mm bolt	24 Nm
Lower crankcase 7 mm bolts	18 Nm
Upper crankcase 8 mm bolts	24 Nm
Upper crankcase 7 mm bolts	18 Nm
Cylinder head 9 mm bolts	51 Nm
Engine mountings	
Upper and lower rear mounting bolt nuts	64 Nm
Upper and lower rear mounting adjuster bolts	15 Nm
Upper and lower rear mounting adjuster bolt locknuts (see text)	
Actual	54 Nm
Indicated (with special tool)	49 Nm
Front and middle mounting bolts	64 Nm
Oil pressure switch	12 Nm
Oil pump cover bolts	8 Nm
Oil pump driven sprocket bolt	15 Nm
Selector drum bearing retainer bolts	12 Nm
Selector drum cam bolt	12 Nm
Starter clutch bolt	93 Nm
Stopper arm bolt	12 Nm
Timing inspection cap	18 Nm
Transmission cassette plate bolts	29 Nm
Transmission shaft bearing retainer bolts	12 Nm
Valve cover bolts	10 Nm

1 General information

The engine unit is a liquid-cooled in-line four cylinder. The sixteen valves are operated by double overhead camshafts which are chain driven off the right-hand end of the crankshaft. The crankcase divides horizontally.

The crankcase incorporates a wet sump, pressure-fed lubrication system which uses a dual rotor trochoidal oil pump that is chain-driven off the back of the clutch. The system has an oil strainer in the pick-up, a pressure relief valve in the feed from the pump to the filter, an oil filter, an oil cooler, and an oil pressure switch in the main gallery.

The alternator is on the left-hand end of the crankshaft. The water pump is on the left-hand side of the engine, and its drive shaft is keyed to the oil pump drive shaft. The ignition timing triggers are on the outside of the starter clutch body which is on the right-hand end of the crankshaft. The crankshaft position sensor is mounted in the clutch cover.

Power from the crankshaft is routed to the transmission via the clutch. The clutch is of the wet, multi-plate type and is gear-driven off the crankshaft. The clutch is hydraulically operated. The transmission is a six-speed constant-mesh unit of the cassette type which allows removal and installation with the engine in the frame. Final drive to the rear wheel is by chain and sprockets.

2 Component access

Operations possible with the engine in the frame

The components and assemblies listed below can be removed without having to remove the engine from the frame. If however, a number of areas require attention at the same time, removal of the engine is recommended.

Valve cover
Cam chain tensioner and blades
Camshafts and cam chain
Cylinder head
Clutch
Gearchange mechanism
Alternator
Oil filter and oil cooler
Oil sump, oil pump, oil strainer and oil pressure relief valve
Starter motor
Starter clutch/timing rotor
Water pump
Selector drum and forks
Transmission shafts

Operations requiring engine removal

It is necessary to remove the engine from the frame to gain access to the following components.

Crankshaft and bearings
Connecting rods and bearings
Pistons, piston rings and cylinder bores

3 Engine wear assessment

Cylinder compression check

Special tool: *A compression gauge is required to perform this test.*

1 Poor engine performance may be caused by leaking valves, incorrect valve clearances, a leaking head gasket, or worn pistons, piston rings or cylinder walls. A cylinder compression check will highlight these conditions and can also indicate the presence of excessive carbon deposits in the cylinder head.

2 The only tools required are a compression gauge (with a threaded adapter to fit the spark plug holes in the cylinder head) and a 16 mm spark plug socket. Depending on the outcome of the initial test, a squirt-type oil can may also be needed.

3 Make sure the valve clearances are correctly set (see Chapter 1) and that the cylinder head bolts are tightened to the correct torque setting (see Section 11).

4 Refer to *Fault Finding Equipment* in the Reference section for details of the compression test, and to the Specifications at the beginning of this Chapter for cylinder compression figures.

Engine oil pressure check

Special tool: *An oil pressure gauge is required to perform this test.*

5 The oil pressure warning light should come on when the ignition (main) switch is turned ON and extinguish a few seconds after the engine is started. If the oil pressure light comes on whilst the engine is running, low oil pressure is indicated – stop the engine immediately and carry out an oil level check (see *Pre-ride checks*).

6 An oil pressure check must be carried out if the warning light comes on when the engine is running yet the oil level is good. It can also provide useful information about the condition of the engine's lubrication system.

7 To check the oil pressure, a suitable gauge and adapter (which screws into the main oil gallery in place of the oil pressure switch) will be needed. Honda can provide a gauge and adapter (part Nos. 07506-3000001 and 07406-0030000) for this purpose, or one can be obtained from a tool supplier. You will also need some rags to catch and mop up any residual oil that is lost between removing the oil pressure switch and installing the gauge – place the bike on its sidestand so that the oil gathers at the other end of the gallery to reduce spillage.

8 Remove the lower fairing (see Chapter 7). Check the oil level (see *Pre-ride checks*). Warm the engine up to normal operating temperature then stop it.

9 Pull the rubber boot off the oil pressure switch, then undo the screw and detach the wiring connector **(see illustrations)**. Counter-hold the switch base hex using an open-ended spanner and unscrew the switch. Screw the gauge adapter in its place. Connect the oil pressure gauge to the adapter.

3.9a Pull the rubber boot off the switch . . .

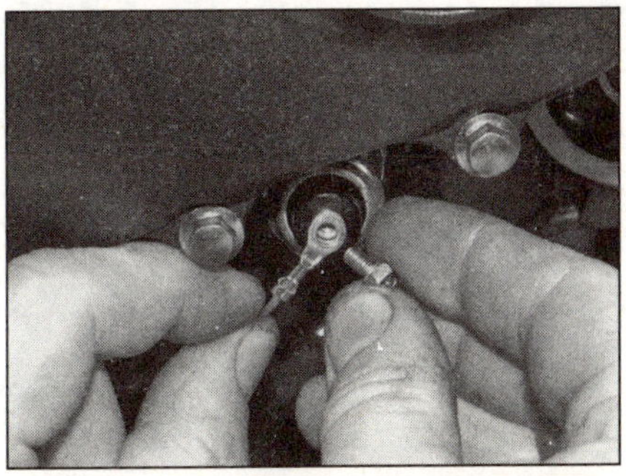

3.9b . . . then undo the screw and detach the wiring connector

10 Start the engine and briefly increase the engine speed to 6000 rpm whilst watching the gauge reading. The oil pressure should be similar to that given in the Specifications.

11 If the pressure is significantly lower than the standard, either the pressure relief valve is stuck open, the oil pump or its drive mechanism is faulty, the oil strainer or filter is blocked, or there is other engine damage. Also make sure the correct grade oil is being used. Begin diagnosis by checking the oil filter, strainer and relief valve, then the oil pump (see Sections 21 and 22). If those items check out okay, chances are the bearing oil clearances are excessive and the engine needs to be overhauled.

12 If the pressure is too high, either an oil passage is clogged, the relief valve is stuck closed or the wrong grade of oil is being used.

13 Stop the engine and unscrew the gauge and adapter from the crankcase.

Warning: Be careful when removing the pressure gauge adapter as the exhaust pipes, the engine and the oil itself can cause severe burns.

14 Apply a suitable sealant to the upper portion of the pressure switch threads (3 to 4 mm away from the tip), then thread the switch into the engine. Counter-hold the base and tighten the switch to the torque setting specified at the beginning of the Chapter. Check the oil level (see *Pre-ride checks*). Connect the wiring and secure it with the screw, then fit the boot over the switch **(see illustrations 3.9b and a)**.

15 Install the lower fairing (see Chapter 7).

4 Engine removal and installation

Caution: The engine is very heavy. Engine removal and installation should be carried out with the aid of at least one assistant; personal injury or damage could occur if the engine falls or is dropped.

Note 1: *A peg spanner is required to slacken and tighten the adjuster bolt locknuts on the upper and lower rear engine mounting bolts. If the Honda service tool (Part no 07VMA-MBB0100 or MBB0101) is not available, a suitable one will have to obtained commercially or fabricated from a piece of steel tubing, or an old socket* ***(see illustrations 4.23b and c).***

Removal

1 Support the bike upright using an auxiliary stand that will not interfere with engine removal, making sure it is on level ground,

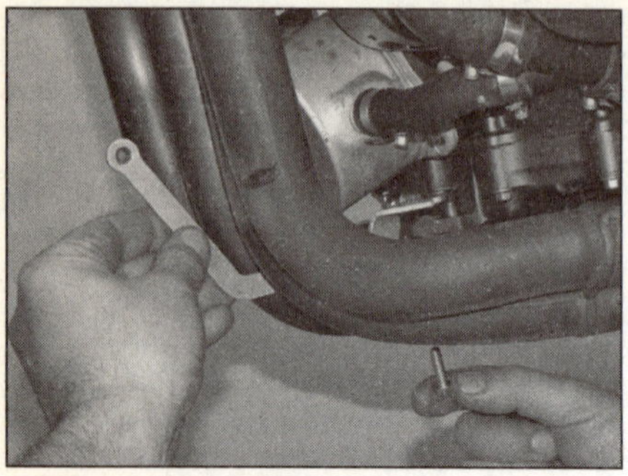

4.7 Unscrew the bolt and remove the bracket

4.10a Speed sensor wiring connector (arrowed) – RR-4 and RR-5 models

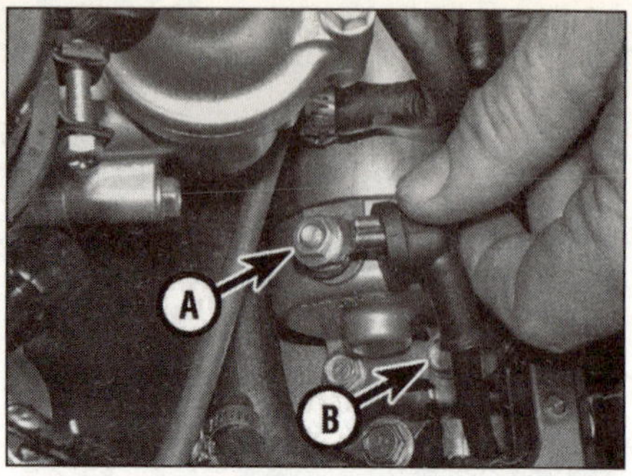

4.10b Unscrew the nut (A) and the bolt (B) and detach the leads

and block the front wheel or tie the front brake on. Work can be made easier by raising the machine to a suitable working height on an hydraulic ramp or a suitable platform. Make sure the motorcycle is secure and will not topple over (also see *Tools and Workshop Tips* in the Reference section).

2 Remove the lower fairing and fairing side panels, and to avoid the possibility of damage the fairing (see Chapter 7).

3 If the engine is dirty, particularly around its mountings, wash it thoroughly. This will make work much easier and rule out the possibility of caked on lumps of dirt falling into some vital component.

4 Drain the engine oil and coolant (see Chapter 1). If required remove the oil filter (see Chapter 1).

5 Disconnect the negative (–) lead from the battery (see Chapter 8).

6 Remove the fuel tank along with the drain and breather hoses, noting their routing (see Chapter 4). Remove the air filter housing and the throttle bodies (see Chapter 4). Plug the engine intake manifolds with clean rag.

7 Remove the radiator along with its hoses, noting their routing (see Chapter 3). Also remove the coolant reservoir along with its hoses, again noting their routing (see Chapter 3). Detach and remove any coolant hoses not already removed as required depending on what work is to be carried out, noting their positions and routing. Remove the radiator bottom mounting bracket **(see illustration)**.

8 Remove the exhaust downpipe assembly, leaving the silencer in place (see Chapter 4).

9 Remove the air intake duct (see Chapter 4). Remove the ignition coils (see Chapter 4).

10 On RR-4 and RR-5 models disconnect the speed sensor (natural 3-pin) wiring connector **(see illustration)**. If required, remove the starter motor (see Chapter 8). If you want to leave the starter motor in situ, pull back the rubber cover on its terminal, then unscrew the nut and disconnect the lead **(see illustration)**. Also unscrew the mounting bolt securing the earth lead and detach the lead.

11 On RR-6 and RR-7 models disconnect the speed sensor (black 3-pin) wiring connector **(see illustration)**. Release the starter motor and earth cables from the wiring harness guide, then detach the guide from its clip and from the frame **(see illustrations)**. Remove the starter motor (see Chapter 8).

12 Disconnect the wiring connector from the ECT sensor **(see illustration)**. Disconnect the black 2-pin engine sub-harness (neutral and oil pressure switch) wiring connector **(see illustration)**.

13 Disconnect the crankshaft position (CKP)

4.11a Disconnect the wiring connector . . .

4.11b . . . then release the wires (arrowed) . . .

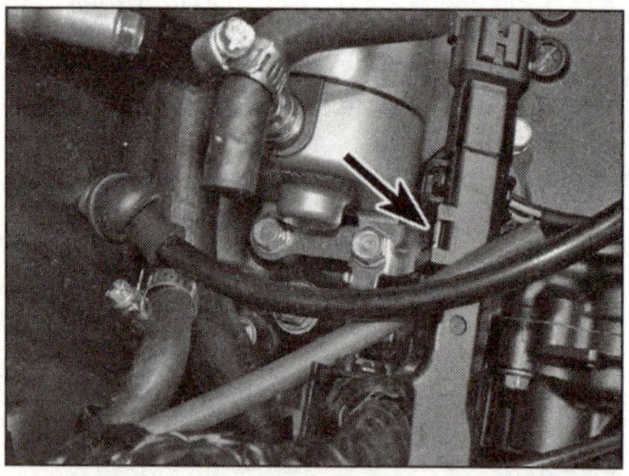

4.11c . . . and detach the guide from its clip (arrowed) . . .

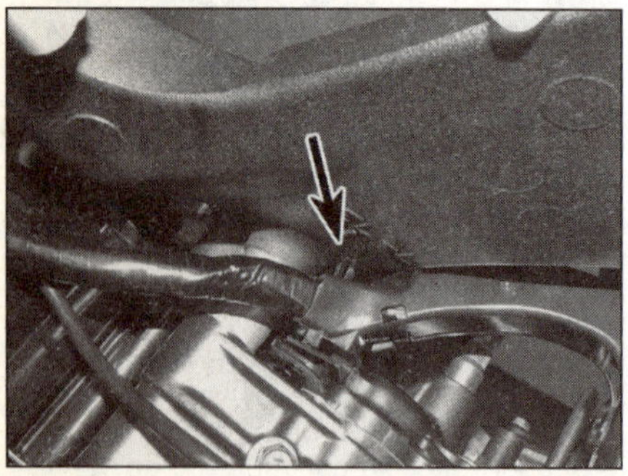

4.11d . . . and pull its peg from the hole in the frame (arrowed)

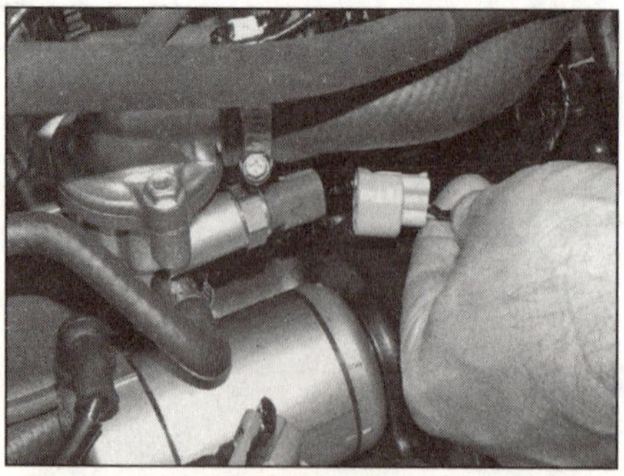

4.12a Disconnect the ECT sensor wiring connector . . .

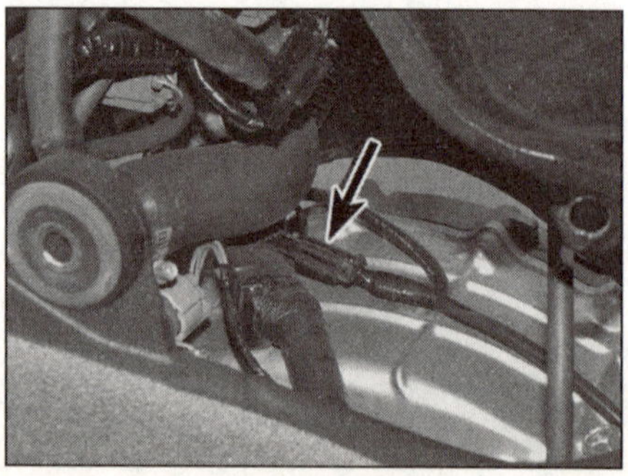

4.12b . . . and the engine sub-harness connector (arrowed)

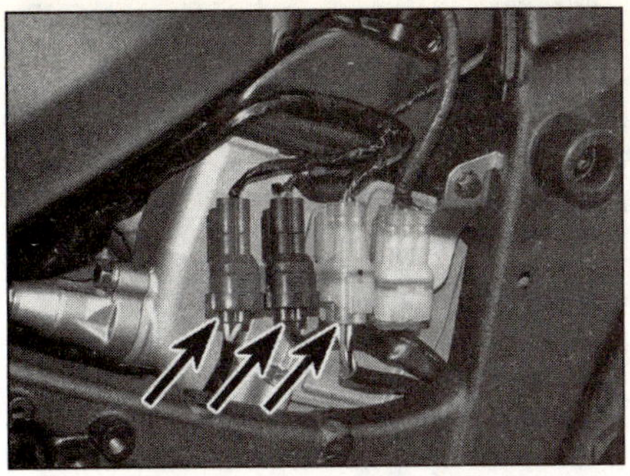

4.13a Disconnect the wiring connectors (arrowed) – RR-6 and RR-7 model with oxygen sensor shown

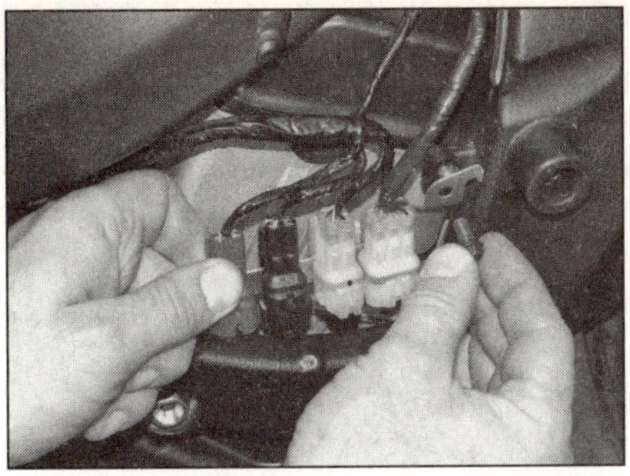

4.13b Unscrew the bolt and detach the plate . . .

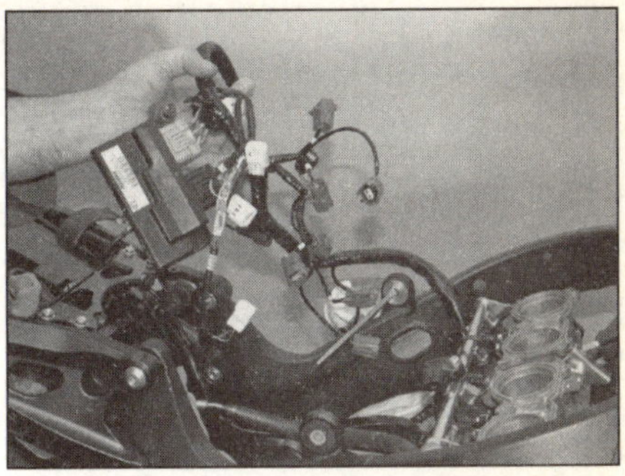

4.13c . . . and fold the wiring back off the engine

sensor (red 2-pin) wiring connector, the rear brake light switch (black 2-pin) wiring connector, and where fitted the oxygen sensor (natural 4-pin) wiring connector **(see illustration)** – the front connector for the ignition coil sub-harness can stay connected. Unscrew the bolt securing the connector mounting plate, then draw the ignition coil sub-harness off the valve cover and fold the whole lot (including the ECM on RR-6 and RR-7 models) back and out of the way **(see illustrations)**. Release the brake light switch and, where fitted, the oxygen sensor wiring from its guides on or under the clutch cover (according to model), then draw the connectors down noting their routing between the frame and the engine and position them clear **(see illustrations)**.

14 On RR-4 and RR-5 models release the tie securing the wiring connector boots on the left-hand side and disconnect the sidestand switch (green 2-pin) wiring connector, and the alternator (natural 3-pin) wiring connector **(see illustration)**. Feed the wiring back to its source, noting its routing and freeing it from any guides. On RR-6 and RR-7 models release the tie securing the wiring connector boots on the left-hand side and disconnect the alternator (natural 3-pin) wiring connector **(see illustration)**. Trace the wiring from the sidestand switch and disconnect it at the black 2-pin wiring connector **(see illustration)**. Feed the wiring back to its source, noting its routing and freeing it from any guides.

15 Disconnect the camshaft position (CMP) sensor (black or natural 2-pin) wiring connector **(see illustration)**.

16 Detach the PAIR system hoses **(see illustration)** and the crankcase breather hose from the valve cover, and remove the breather hose.

4.13d Brake light switch wiring guides (arrowed) – RR-4 and RR-5 model without oxygen sensor

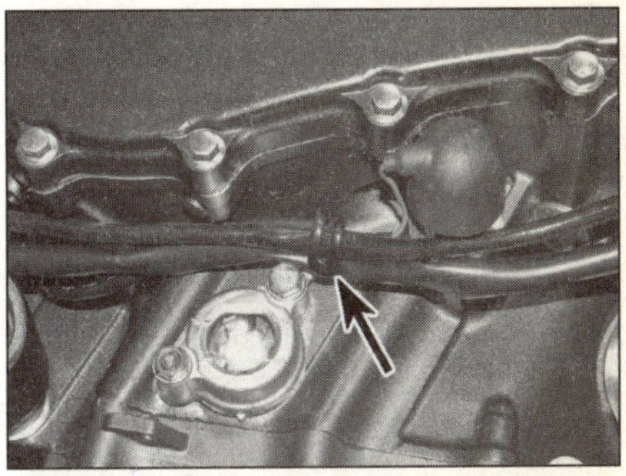

4.13e Brake light switch and oxygen sensor wiring guide (arrowed) – RR-6 and RR-7 model

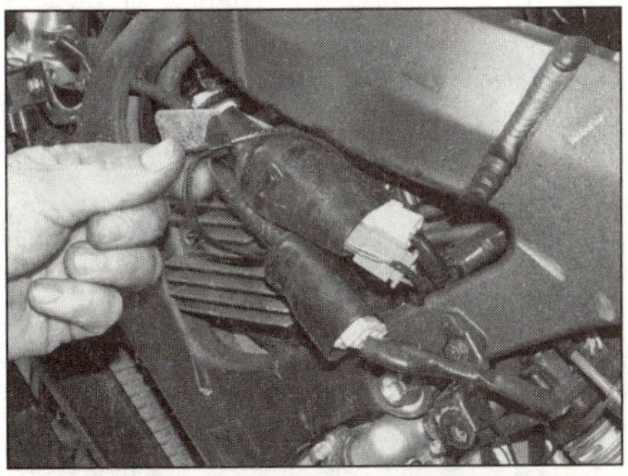

4.14a On RR-4 and RR-5 models draw the connectors out of the boots and disconnect them

4.14b On RR-6 and RR-7 models disconnect the alternator wiring connector . . .

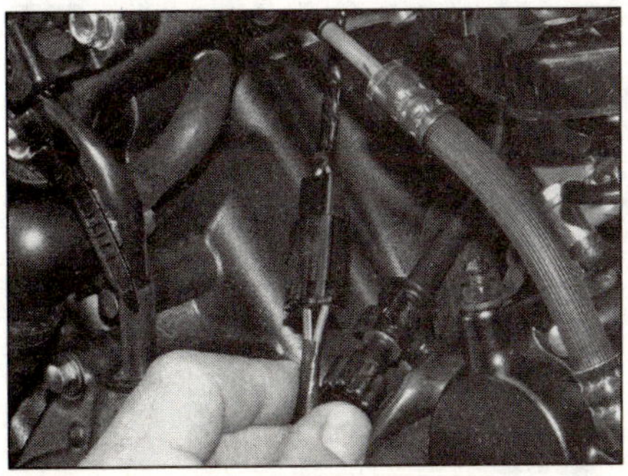

4.14c . . . and the sidestand switch wiring connector

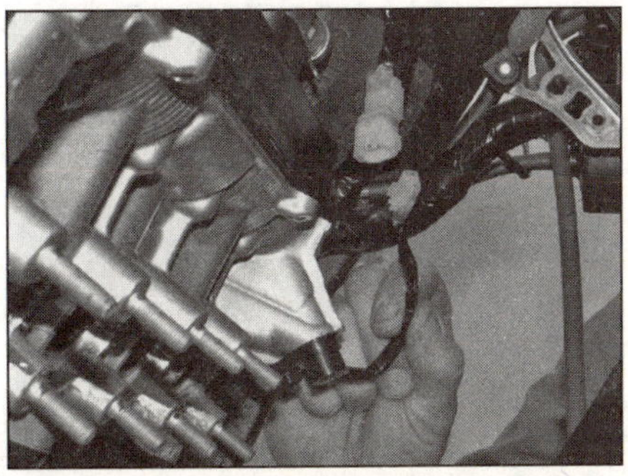

4.15 Disconnect the CMP sensor wiring connector – RR-6 and RR-7 model shown

4.16 Detach the hoses (arrowed) from the valve cover

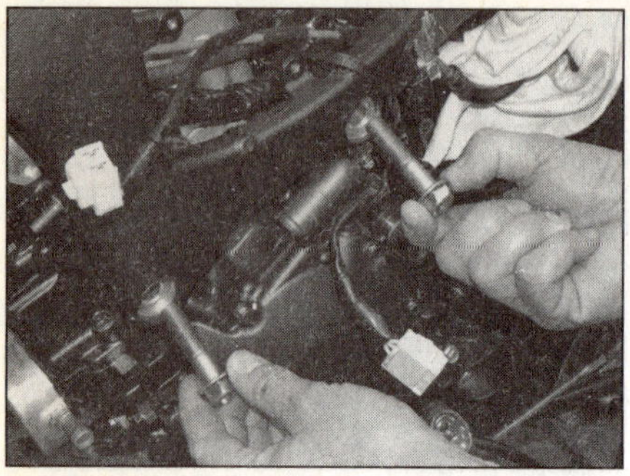

4.20 Unscrew and remove the front and middle left-hand bolts

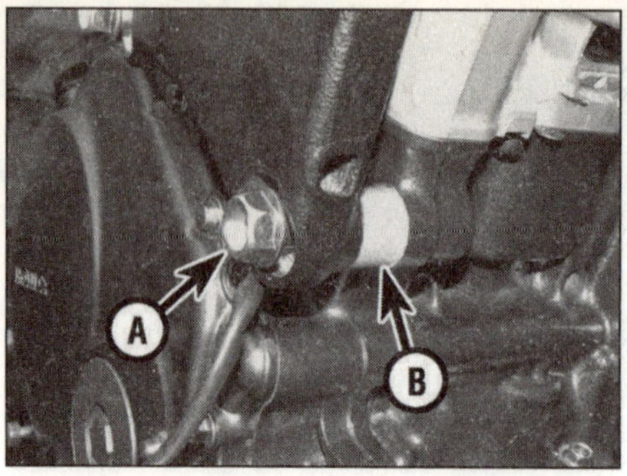

4.21a Unscrew the front right-hand bolt (A) and remove the spacer (B) . . .

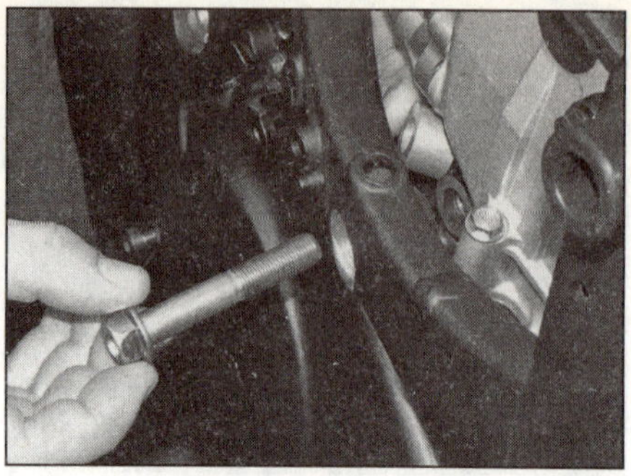

4.21b . . . then remove the middle right-hand bolt and its spacer

17 Remove the front sprocket (see Chapter 6). Slip the drive chain off the end of the output shaft and let it rest against the front of the swingarm.

18 If required, remove the thermostat housing (see Chapter 3).

4.22 Unscrew the nut from each rear mounting bolt

19 At this point, position an hydraulic or mechanical jack under the engine with a block of wood between the jack head and sump. Make sure the jack is centrally positioned so the engine will not topple in any direction when the last mounting bolt is removed. Raise the jack to take the weight of the engine, but make sure it is not lifting the bike and taking the weight of that as well. The idea is to support the engine so that there is no pressure on any of the mounting bolts once they have been slackened, so they can be easily withdrawn. Note that it may be necessary to alter the position of the jack as some of the bolts are removed to relieve the stress transferred to the other bolts.

20 Unscrew the front and middle mounting bolts on the left-hand side **(see illustrations)**.

21 Unscrew the front and middle mounting bolts on the right-hand side and remove their spacers from between the engine and frame **(see illustrations)**. Note that the front bolts are shorter than the middle ones on each side.

22 Unscrew the nut on the left-hand end of each rear mounting bolt, counter-holding the bolt head if necessary **(see illustration)**.

23 Slacken the adjuster bolt locknut on the right-hand end of each bolt using a suitable peg spanner (see Note above) **(see illustrations)**. The locknut can remain loose on the adjuster bolt, or remove it if required.

24 Unscrew the upper and lower rear mounting bolts, thereby turning the adjuster bolts with which they engage, until the flange on the inner end of each adjuster bolt just contacts the frame **(see illustration)**.

25 Check that the engine is properly supported by the jack. Withdraw the upper rear mounting bolt from the right-hand side and remove the spacers **(see illustration)**.

26 Withdraw the lower rear mounting bolt from the right-hand side **(see illustration)**.

4.23a Slacken the locknut (arrowed) on each adjuster . . .

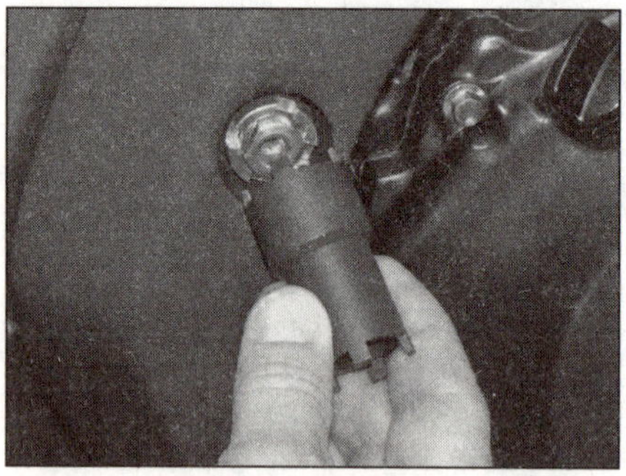

4.23b . . . using a suitable peg spanner . . .

4.23c . . . or one made from an old socket

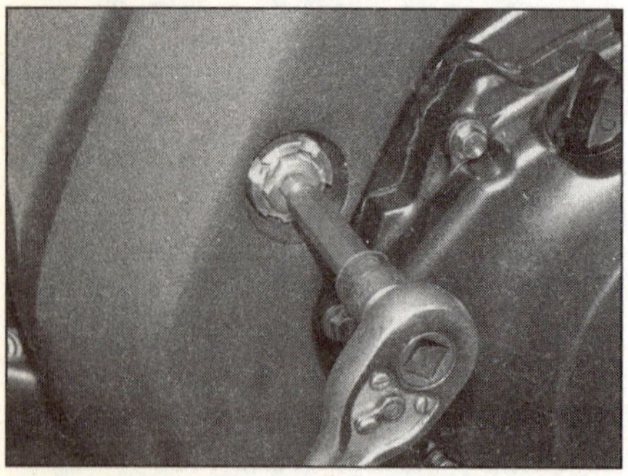

4.24 Unscrew each adjuster bolt using an Allen key in the mounting bolt head

4.25 Withdraw the upper bolt and remove the spacers . . .

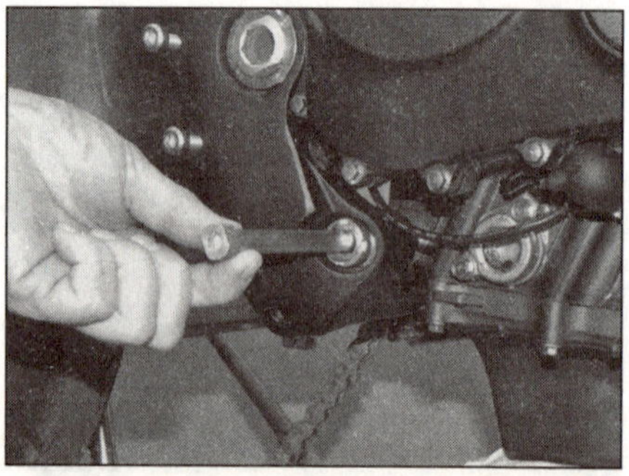

4.26 . . . then withdraw the lower bolt

4.28 Remove the adjuster bolts if required

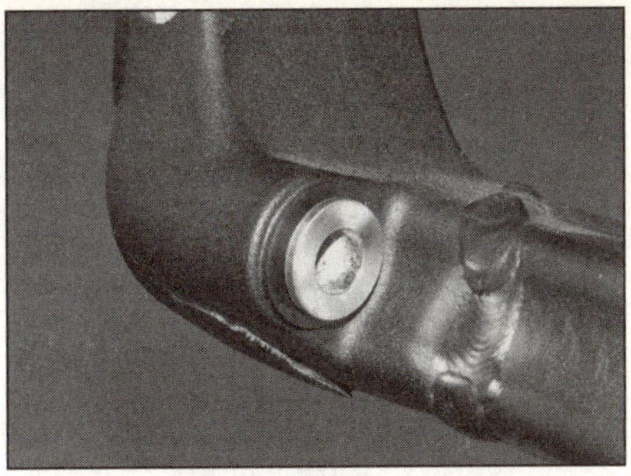

4.29 Thread the adjuster bolts all the way in

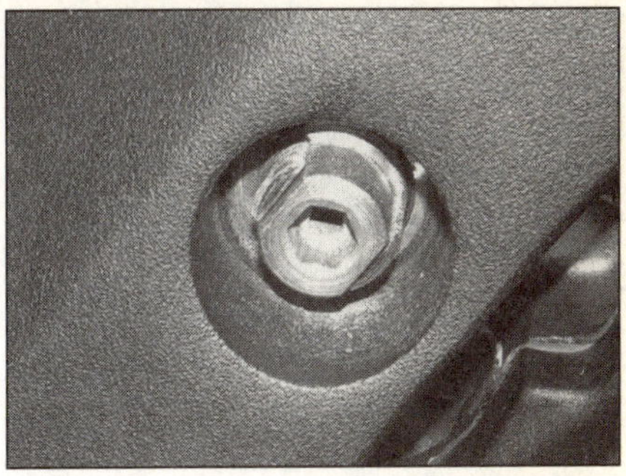

4.31 Engage the bolt head flats in the adjuster bolt flats

27 The engine can now be removed from the frame (see ***Caution*** above). Check that all wiring, cables and hoses are free and clear, then carefully lower the jack a bit and manoeuvre the engine forward until it clears the swingarm. Fully lower the jack, then with the aid of an assistant remove the jack from under the engine and remove the engine.

28 If required thread the adjuster bolts out of the frame **(see illustration)** – remove the locknut from its outer end first if not already done.

Installation

Note 2: *To prevent corrosion which could lead to bolts being seized, smear copper grease onto the bolt shafts, not the threads, to prevent the possibility of them seizing in the collars or the engine or frame.*

29 If removed thread the adjuster bolts into the upper and lower rear mountings on the right-hand side from the inside until the flanges contact the frame **(see illustration)**.

30 Manoeuvre the engine into position under the frame and lift it onto the jack. Raise the engine to align all the mounting bolt holes, making sure that all cables and wiring are correctly routed and do not get trapped. Note that it may be necessary to adjust the jack as some of the bolts are installed and tightened to realign the other bolt holes.

31 Install the upper and lower rear mounting bolts from the right-hand side, fitting the spacers between the engine and frame on each side with the upper bolt **(see illustrations 4.26 and 4.25)**. Fit the head of each bolt into its adjuster bolt so they lock together **(see illustration)**.

32 Fit the front and middle bolts on each side, with the spacers between the engine and frame on the right-hand side, and fitting the shorter bolts at the front, and tighten them finger-tight **(see illustrations 4.21b and a and 4.20)**.

33 Turn the adjuster bolts on the upper and lower rear engine mounts by turning the mounting bolts using a hex key until they just contact the engine **(see illustration 4.24)**.

34 Tighten the adjuster bolt on the lower rear mount to the torque setting specified at the beginning of the Chapter **(see illustration)**. After tightening it make sure the flats on the bolt head are central in the adjuster bolt – any pressure on either side makes the locknut difficult to fit (if it was removed). If removed, thread the locknut onto the adjuster bolt **(see illustration 4.35b)**. Tighten the locknut to the specified torque setting using the Honda special tool or a peg spanner (see Note 1 above) **(see illustration)**. If you do not have the Honda special tool, which is offset and allows the adjuster bolt to be counter-held while tightening the locknut, it is advisable to make a reference mark between the adjuster bolt and the frame to make sure that it does not turn as the locknut is being tightened. If you have the special tool, tighten the locknut to the 'indicated' specified torque setting, which allows for the extra leverage provided by the offset. If you are using a standard or fabricated peg spanner tighten the locknut to the 'actual' specified torque setting.

35 Repeat Step 34 for the upper rear mount **(see illustrations)**.

36 Fit the nut onto the left-hand end of the lower rear bolt, then counter-hold the bolt head and tighten the nut to the torque setting specified at the beginning of the Chapter **(see**

4.34a Tighten the adjuster bolt to the specified torque . . .

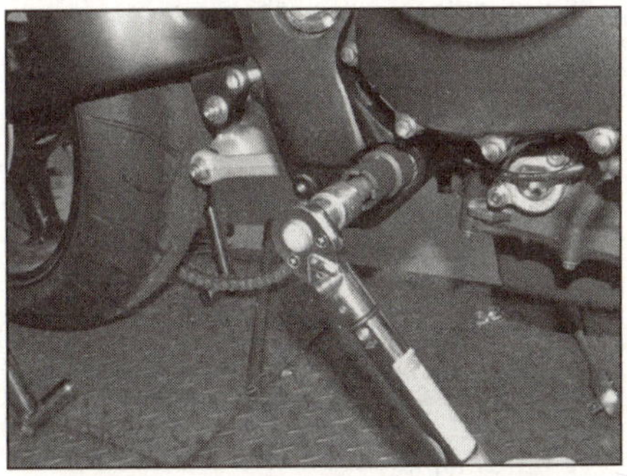

4.34b . . . then tighten the locknut

4.35a Tighten the adjuster bolt to the specified torque . . .

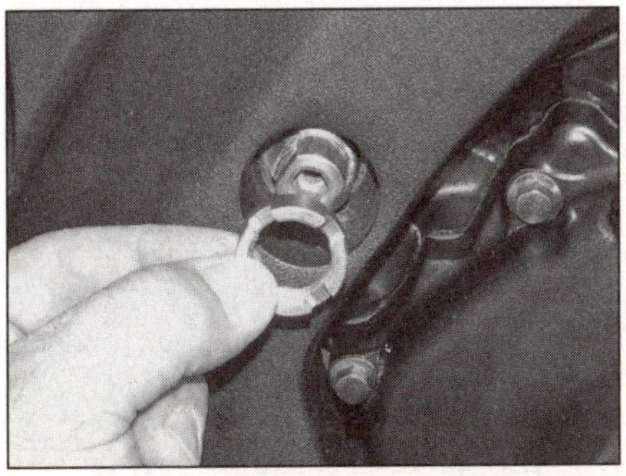

4.35b . . . then fit the locknut if removed . . .

4.35c . . . and tighten it to the specified torque

illustration 4.22). Repeat for the upper rear bolt.

37 Tighten the front and middle bolts on the left-hand side to the specified torque **(see illustration 4.20)**.

38 Tighten the front and middle bolts on the right-hand side to the specified torque.

39 The remainder of the installation procedure is the reverse of removal, referring to the relevant Chapters where directed, and noting the following points:

- Use new gaskets on the exhaust pipe connections.
- Make sure all wires, cables and hoses are correctly routed and connected, and secured by any clips or ties.
- Refill the engine with oil and coolant (see Chapter 1).
- Adjust the throttle cable freeplay.
- Adjust the drive chain (see Chapter 1).
- Start the engine and check that there are no oil or coolant leaks. Adjust the idle speed (see Chapter 1).

5 Engine overhaul information

1 Before beginning the engine overhaul, read through the related procedures to familiarise yourself with the scope and requirements of the job. Overhauling an engine is not all that difficult, but it is time-consuming. Check on the availability of parts and make sure that any necessary special tools are obtained in advance.

2 Most work can be done with a typical workshop hand tools, although a number of precision measuring tools are required for inspecting parts to determine if they are worn.

3 To ensure maximum life and minimum trouble from a rebuilt engine, everything must be assembled with care in a spotlessly clean environment.

Disassembly

4 Before disassembling the engine, thoroughly clean and degrease its external surfaces. This will prevent contamination of the engine internals, and will also make the job a lot easier and cleaner. A high flash-point solvent, such as paraffin (kerosene) can be used, or better still, a proprietary engine degreaser such as Gunk. Use old paintbrushes and toothbrushes to work the solvent into the various recesses of the casings. Take care to exclude solvent or water from the electrical components and intake and exhaust ports.

Warning: The use of petrol (gasoline) as a cleaning agent should be avoided because of the risk of fire.

5 When clean and dry, position the engine on the workbench, leaving suitable clear area for working. Gather a selection of small containers, plastic bags and some labels so that parts can be grouped together in an easily identifiable manner. Also get some paper and a pen so that notes can be taken. You will also need a supply of clean rag, which should be as absorbent as possible.

6 Before commencing work, read through the appropriate section so that some idea of the necessary procedure can be gained. When removing components note that great force is seldom required, unless specified (checking the specified torque setting of the particular bolt being removed will indicate how tight it is, and therefore how much force should be needed). In many cases, a component's reluctance to be removed is indicative of an incorrect approach or removal method – if in any doubt, re-check with the text.

7 When disassembling the engine, keep 'mated' parts together (including gears, pistons, connecting rods, valves, etc, that have been in contact with each other during engine operation). These 'mated' parts must be reused or replaced as an assembly.

8 A complete engine disassembly should be done in the following general order with reference to the appropriate Sections.

Remove the valve cover
Remove the camshafts
Remove the cylinder head
Remove the starter motor (see Chapter 8)
Remove the starter clutch
Remove the cam chain and blades
Remove the clutch
Remove the gearchange mechanism
Remove the transmission shafts/selector drum and forks
Remove the alternator (see Chapter 8)
Remove the oil sump
Remove the oil pump
Separate the crankcase halves
Remove the crankshaft
Remove the connecting rods and pistons

Reassembly

9 Reassembly is accomplished by reversing the general disassembly sequence.

6 Oil cooler

Note: *The oil cooler can be removed with the engine in the frame. If the engine has been removed, ignore the steps which do not apply.*

Removal

1 The cooler is located on the front of the engine next to the oil filter. Remove the lower fairing and the fairing side panels (see Chapter 7).

2 Drain the engine oil and coolant (see Chapter 1).

3 Remove the exhaust downpipe assembly, leaving the silencer in place (see Chapter 4).

4 Slacken the clamp securing each hose to the cooler and detach the hoses.

5 Unscrew the three bolts and remove the cooler **(see illustrations)**. Discard the O-ring as a new one must be used.

6 Check the cooler body for cracks and dents and any evidence of coolant leakage and replace it with a new one if necessary. Also check the hoses for splits, cracks, hardening and deterioration and fit new ones if required.

Installation

7 Installation is the reverse of removal, noting the following:

- Ensure the mating surfaces of the crankcase and the cooler are clean and dry.
- Use a new O-ring on the cooler body and smear it with clean engine oil. Make sure it seats in its groove **(see illustration)**.
- Make sure the coolant hoses are pressed fully onto their unions and are secured by the clamps.
- Fill the engine with the specified amount and type of oil (see Chapter 1).
- Refill the cooling system (see Chapter 1).

6.5a Unscrew the bolts (arrowed) . . .

6.5b . . . and remove the cooler

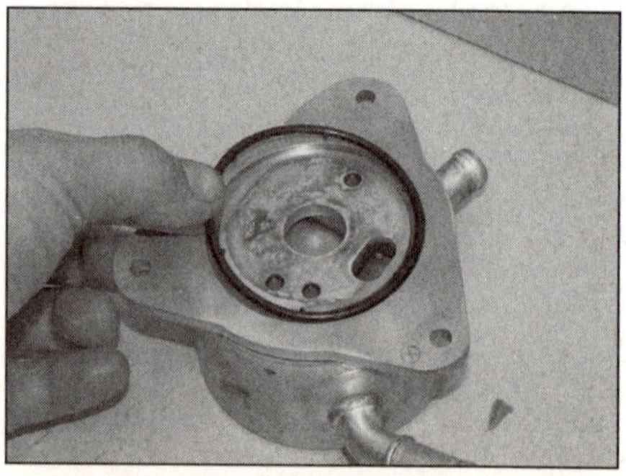

6.7 Fit a new O-ring into the groove

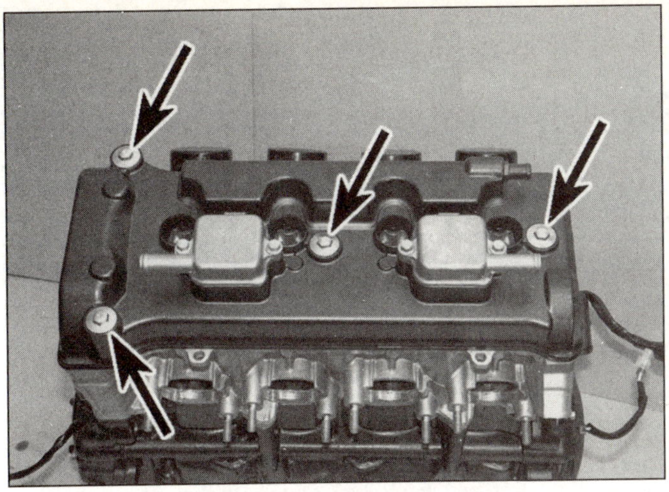

7.4a Unscrew the bolts (arrowed) . . .

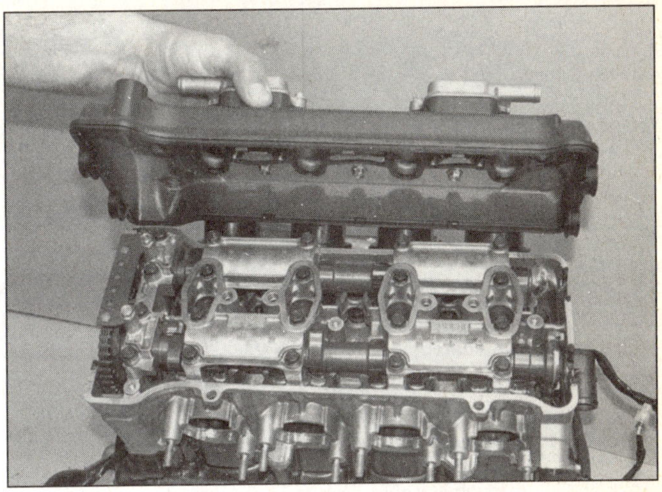

7.4b . . . and remove the cover

7 Valve cover

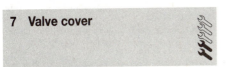

Note: *The valve cover can be removed with the engine in the frame. If the engine has been removed, ignore the steps which do not apply.*

Removal

1 Remove the air filter housing, the air intake duct and the throttle bodies (see Chapter 4).

2 Detach the PAIR system hoses and the crankcase breather hose from the valve cover, and remove the breather hose **(see illustration 4.16)**.

3 Remove the ignition coils (see Chapter 4). Secure the wiring out of the way.

4 Unscrew the four valve cover bolts and lift the cover off the cylinder head – if the engine is in the frame take care when removing it as it is quite a tight fit and both the cover and the frame are easily scratched (use some tape on the ends of the cover or on the frame if required) **(see illustrations)**. If the cover is stuck, do not try to lever it off with a screwdriver. Tap it gently around the sides with a rubber hammer or block of wood to dislodge it. Note the rubber washers for the bolts and remove them if they are loose **(see illustration 7.13)**.

5 The rubber gasket is normally glued into the groove in the cover, and is best left there if it is reusable. If the gasket is in any way damaged, deformed or deteriorated, remove it **(see illustration 7.12a)**.

6 Note the four dowels that link the PAIR system air passages between the valve cover and cylinder head and remove them for safekeeping if they are loose (which is unlikely), taking care not to drop them if they are not in the valve cover **(see illustration)**.

7 If required, unscrew the crankcase breather separator bolts and remove the separator **(see illustration 7.6)**. Discard the gasket. Clean out the breather chamber.

8 If required, remove the PAIR system reed valves (see Chapter 4).

Installation

9 If removed, fit the breather separator onto the valve cover using a new gasket. Apply a suitable non-permanent thread locking compound to the bolts and tighten them to the torque setting specified at the beginning of the Chapter **(see illustration 7.6)**.

10 If removed, install the PAIR system reed valves (see Chapter 4).

11 If removed, fit the PAIR system dowels into the valve cover **(see illustration 7.6)**.

12 Examine the valve cover gasket for signs of damage or deterioration and fit a new one if necessary. If a new one is used, clean all traces of the old glue from the groove in the cover and clean it and the cylinder head mating surface with solvent. Fit the new gasket into the groove, using a suitable glue, sealant or grease to hold it in place **(see illustration)**. Also apply a suitable sealant to the cut-outs in the cylinder head **(see illustration)**.

13 Position the valve cover on the cylinder head, making sure the gasket stays in place **(see illustration 7.4b)**. If removed, fit the rubber washers into the cover, using new ones if required, and making sure they are installed with the UP mark facing up **(see illustration)**.

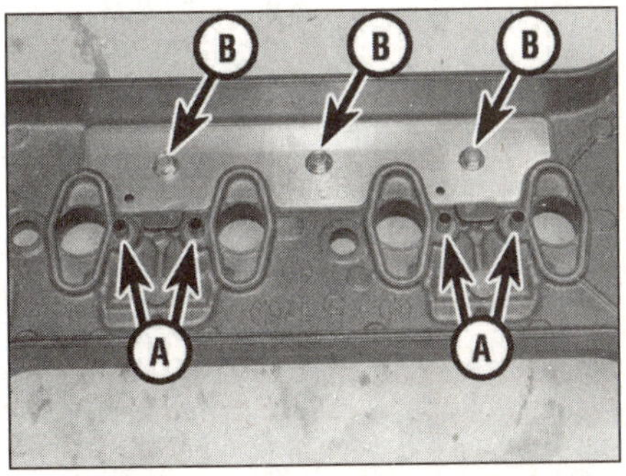

7.6 PAIR system air passage dowels (A), breather separator bolts (B)

7.12a Make sure the gasket locates in the groove and stays there

7.12b Apply sealant to the cutouts (arrowed) in the cylinder head

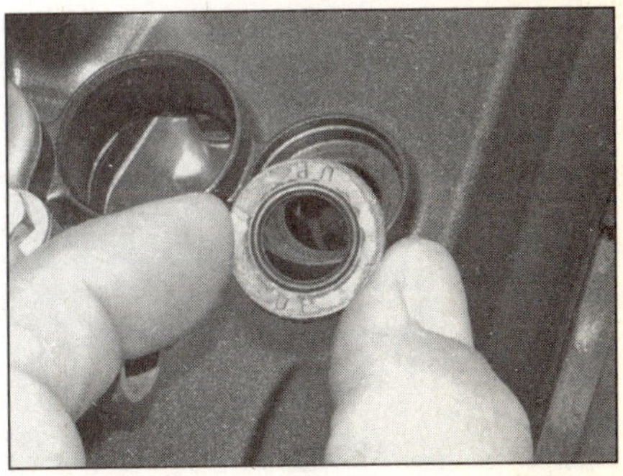

7.13 Make sure the UP marks on the washers face up

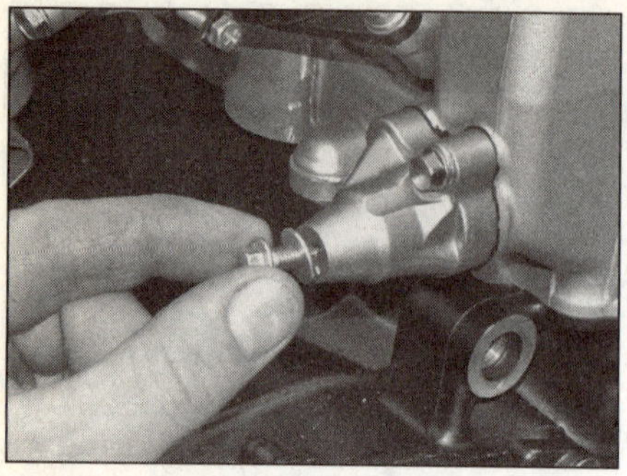

8.2 Unscrew the cap bolt and remove the washer

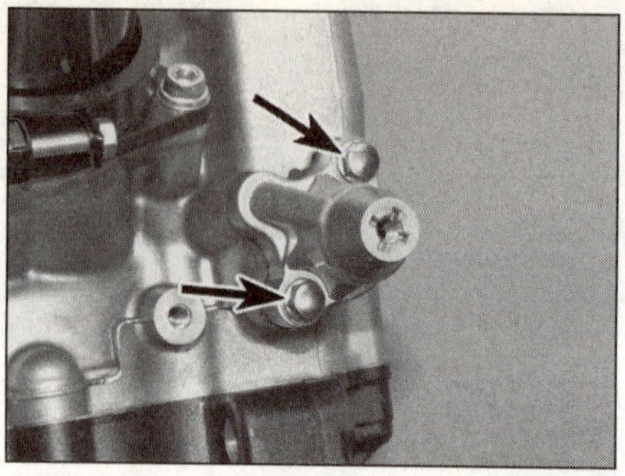

8.4a Slacken the mounting bolts (arrowed) slightly . . .

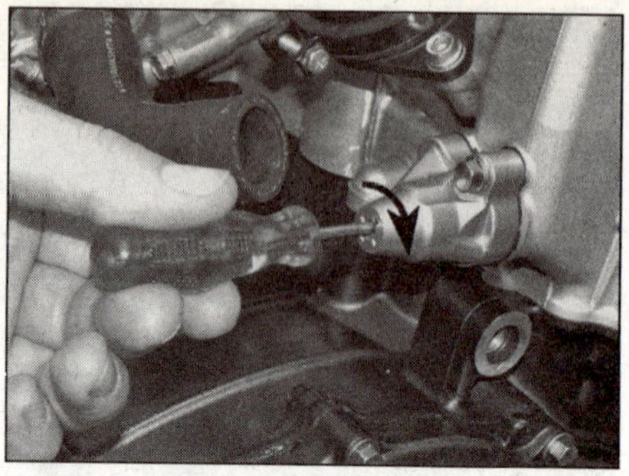

8.4b . . . then insert the screwdriver and retract the plunger

Install the cover bolts and tighten them to the specified torque setting **(see illustration 7.4a)**.
14 Install the remaining components in the reverse order of removal.

8 Cam chain tensioner

Note: *The cam chain tensioner can be removed with the engine in the frame. If the engine has been removed, ignore the steps which do not apply.*

Removal

1 Remove the fairing right-hand side panel (see Chapter 7).
2 Unscrew the tensioner cap bolt and remove the sealing washer **(see illustration)**.
3 If the Honda tensioner holding tool (part no. 07ZMG-MCAA400) is available, fit it onto the end of the tensioner and turn it clockwise until the plunger is fully retracted and held. Unscrew the tensioner mounting bolts, then withdraw the tensioner from the engine **(see illustration 8.4a)**.
4 If a holding tool is not available, first slacken the tensioner mounting bolts slightly **(see illustration)**. Insert a small flat-bladed screwdriver in the end of the tensioner so that it engages the slotted plunger **(see illustration)**. Turn the screwdriver clockwise until the plunger is fully retracted and hold it in this position while unscrewing the tensioner mounting bolts. Remove the bolts, then withdraw the tensioner from the engine and release the screwdriver **(see illustration 8.8a)** – the plunger will spring back out once the screwdriver is removed, but can be easily reset on installation.
5 Discard the gasket and sealing washer as new ones must be used on installation. Do not attempt to dismantle the tensioner.

Installation

6 Check that the plunger moves smoothly when wound into the tensioner and springs back out freely when released **(see illustration 8.8a)**. Ensure the tensioner and cylinder block surfaces are clean and dry.
7 If the Honda holding tool is being used and has been removed, fit it onto the end of the tensioner and turn it clockwise until the plunger is fully retracted and held. Fit a new gasket onto the tensioner body, then install the tensioner with its mounting bolts and tighten them to the torque setting specified at the beginning of the Chapter **(see illustration 8.8b)**. Remove the tool, then install the tensioner cap bolt with a new sealing washer and tighten it **(see illustration 8.2)**.
8 If the tool is not available, insert a small flat-bladed screwdriver in the end of the tensioner so that it engages the slotted plunger **(see illustration)**. Turn the screwdriver clockwise until the plunger is fully retracted and hold it in this position whilst the tensioner is installed. Fit a new gasket onto the tensioner body, then install the tensioner with its mounting bolts and tighten them to the torque setting specified at the beginning of the Chapter **(see illustration)**. Release and remove the screwdriver, then install the tensioner cap bolt with a new sealing washer and tighten it **(see illustration 8.2)**.
9 Install the fairing side panel (see Chapter 7).

9 Camshafts and followers

Note: *The camshafts can be removed with the engine in the frame. Place clean rags over the spark plug holes and the cam chain tunnel to prevent any component from dropping into the engine.*

Removal

1 Remove the spark plugs (see Chapter 1). Remove the valve cover (see Section 7). To prevent the possibility of damage remove the camshaft position (CMP) sensor (see Chapter 4).
2 Unscrew the timing inspection cap from the clutch cover **(see illustration)**. Check the condition of its O-ring and obtain a new one if necessary.
3 The engine must be turned so that the No. 1 piston is at TDC (top dead centre) on its compression stroke. Turn the engine using a suitable spanner or socket on the timing rotor bolt and turning it in a clockwise direction only

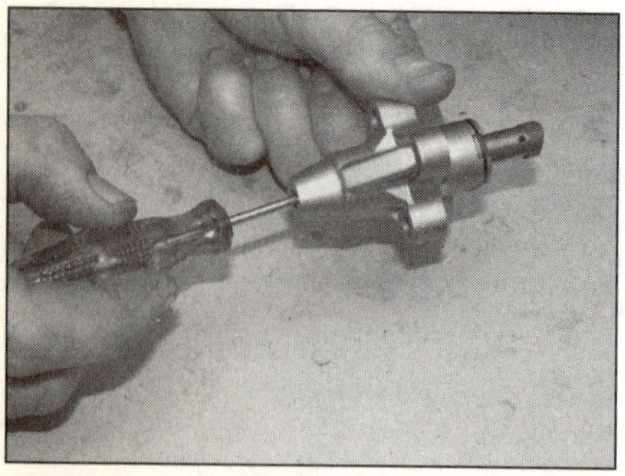

8.8a Insert the screwdriver and retract the plunger . . .

8.8b . . . then fit a new gasket and install the tensioner

9.2 Remove the timing inspection cap

9.3a Turn the engine clockwise using the bolt . . .

9.3b . . . until the line next to the T mark aligns with the notch (arrowed) . . .

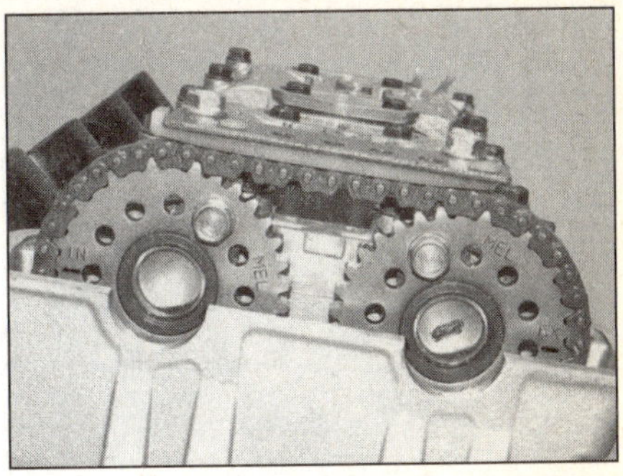

9.3c . . . and the camshaft sprocket marks are as shown

9.4 Unscrew the bolts and remove the guide

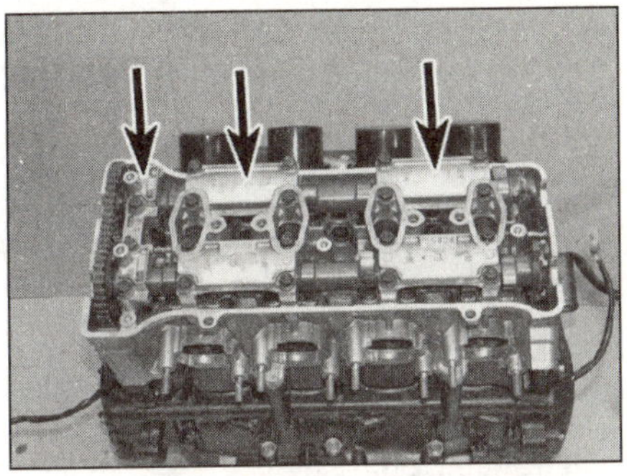

9.5a Camshaft holders (arrowed)

9.5b Note the ID letter and the bolt numbers on each holder

until the line next to the T mark on the timing rotor aligns with the static timing mark, which is a notch in the inspection hole rim, and the IN and EX marks on the intake and exhaust camshaft sprockets respectively are facing away from each other and are flush with the cylinder head top surface **(see illustrations)**. If the marks are facing towards each other, rotate the engine clockwise one full turn (360°) until the line next to the T mark again aligns with the static timing mark. The sprocket marks will now be facing away.

4 Either remove the cam chain tensioner (see Section 8), or if you prefer, using the tensioner holding tool as described in Section 8, Step 3, retract and lock the tensioner plunger. Unscrew the bolts securing the cam chain top guide and remove it **(see illustration)**.

5 There are three camshaft holders, each bridging both camshafts **(see illustration)**. Of the two larger holders, the one on the right-hand side is marked R and the one on the left-hand side L, and these letters are at the front **(see illustration)**. Note the numbers marked on the holders, adjacent to each bolt. These numbers denote the tightening sequence for the holder bolts.

6 Unscrew the camshaft holder bolts, slackening them evenly and a very little at a time in a reverse of the tightening sequence marked on the holders. Remove the bolts, noting which fits where as some are different, and lift off the holders, noting how they fit **(see illustration)**. Note the sealing washers fitted with the eight bolts around the spark plug bores **(see illustration 9.30d)**. Remove the sealing rings from their grooves around the spark plug holes on the underside of the holders, noting how they also locate around the PAIR system air passage dowels **(see illustration)**. Discard them as new ones must be used. Do not remove the dowels unless they are loose and liable to drop out.

Caution: Make sure the holders lift up squarely and evenly and do not stick on a dowel or distort from some of the bolts being slackened more than the others as they or a camshaft could easily break.

7 The camshafts are marked for identification – on RR-4 and RR-5 models the intake camshaft is marked IN and the exhaust camshaft is marked EX **(see illustration)**. On RR-6 and RR-7 models the intake camshaft is marked DI and the exhaust camshaft is

9.6a Unscrew the bolts as described and remove the holders

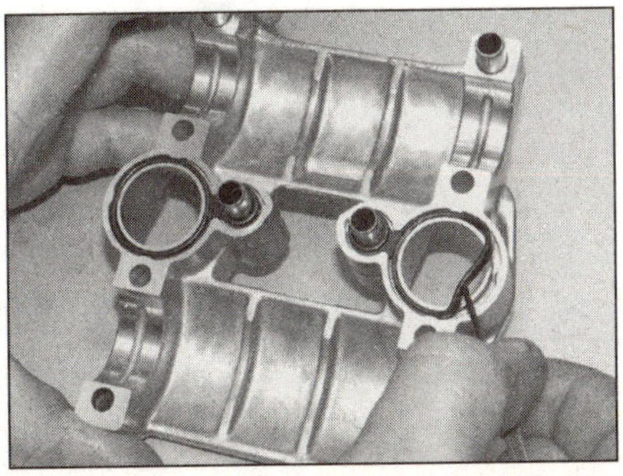

9.6b Remove the sealing rings and discard them

9.7a Camshaft identity marks – RR-4 and RR-5 models

9.7b Camshaft identity marks – RR-6 and RR-7 models

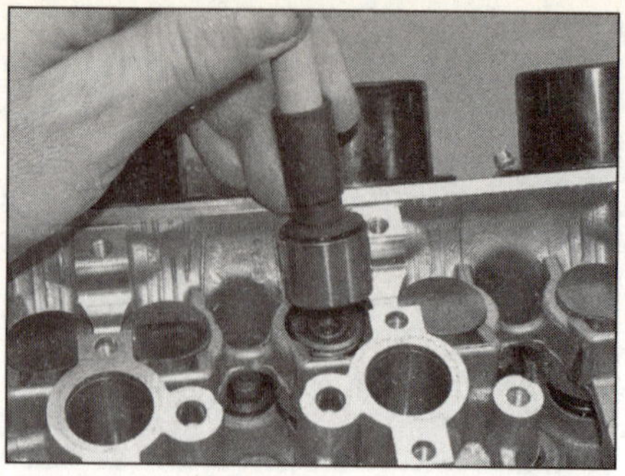

9.9a Carefully lift out the follower using a lapping tool, grips or a magnet . . .

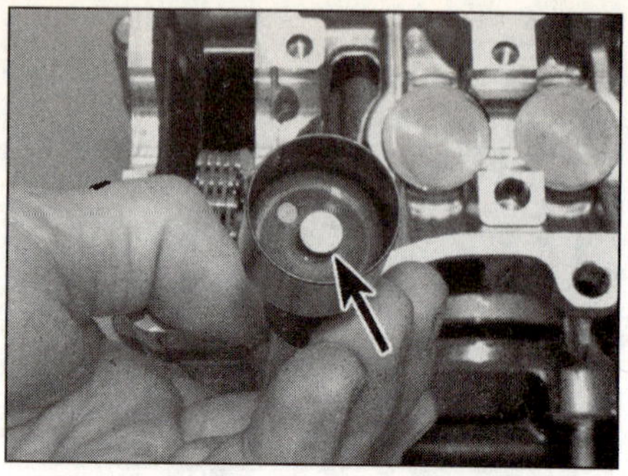

9.9b . . . and retrieve the shim (arrowed) from inside it . . .

marked DE **(see illustration)**. If the marks aren't clear make your own as the camshafts must be installed in their original location.

8 Remove the intake camshaft first, then the exhaust. Carefully lift each camshaft in turn off the head and disengage the sprocket from the chain **(see illustrations 9.29a and 9.28a)**. Wire the chain to another component or secure it using a rod of some sort to prevent it from dropping. While the camshafts are out do not rotate the crankshaft. Place rags over the spark plug holes and the cam chain tunnel to prevent anything from dropping into the engine on removal.

9 If the followers and shims are being removed from the cylinder head, obtain a container which is divided into sixteen compartments, and label each compartment with the location of a valve, i.e. intake or exhaust camshaft, left or right valve. If a container is not available, use labelled plastic bags (egg cartons also do very well!). Remove the cam follower of the valve in question using a magnet or the suction created by a valve lapping tool, but long nosed pliers can be used with care **(see illustration)**. Retrieve the shim either from the inside of the follower or pick it out of the top of the valve spring retainer using either a magnet, a screwdriver with a dab of grease on it (the shim will stick to the grease), or a very small screwdriver and a pair of pliers **(see illustrations)**. Do not allow the shim to fall into the engine.

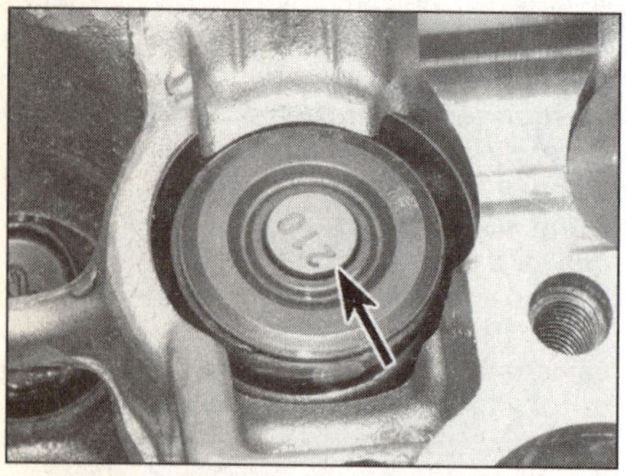

9.9c . . . or from the top of the valve

10 If required unscrew the sprocket bolts and take the sprockets off the camshafts **(see illustration)**. Both sprockets are identical and are therefore interchangeable, but mark them according to their camshaft so they can be installed in their original position. Also make alignment marks between the sprocket and the camshaft so that the sprocket can be installed the correct way round to avoid confusion when setting up the timing.

11 Note the alignment and fitting of the camshaft position (CMP) sensor rotor on the left-hand end of the exhaust camshaft and remove it if required – it is secured by two bolts **(see illustration)**.

Inspection

12 Inspect the bearing surfaces of the camshaft holders and cylinder head and the corresponding journals on the camshafts. Look for score marks, deep scratches and evidence of spalling (a pitted appearance). Check the oil passages for clogging.

13 Check the camshaft lobes for heat discoloration (blue appearance), score marks, chipped areas, flat spots and spalling. Measure the height of each lobe with a micrometer **(see illustration)** and compare the results to the minimum height listed in this Chapter's Specifications. If damage is noted or wear is excessive, the camshaft must be replaced with a new one.

14 Check the amount of camshaft runout by supporting each end on V-blocks, and measuring any runout using a dial gauge. If the runout exceeds the specified limit the camshaft must be replaced with a new one.

> **HAYNES HiNT** ***Refer to Tools and Workshop Tips in the Reference section for details of how to read a micrometer and dial gauge.***

15 Next, check the camshaft journal oil clearances. In order to negate the probability of the camshafts rotating (due to the fact that some of the lobes will be depressing their valves) as the holder bolts are tightened down, which will disturb the Plastigauge and lead to a false measurement, the valves should be removed from the cylinder head. To do this the head must be removed from the engine (see Sections 11 and 12). Clean the camshafts and the bearing surfaces in the cylinder head and camshaft holder with a clean lint-free cloth, then lay each camshaft in its correct location in the cylinder head (see Step 6).

16 Cut some strips of Plastigauge and lay one piece on each journal, parallel with the camshaft centreline. Make sure the camshaft holder dowels are installed **(see illustration 9.30a)**. If

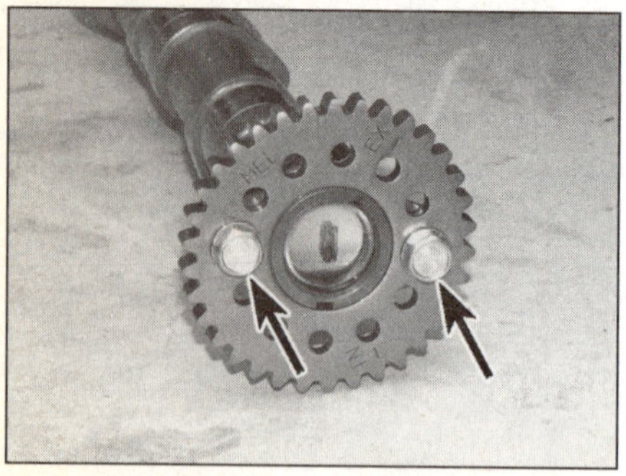

9.10 Camshaft sprocket bolts (arrowed)

9.11 CMP sensor bolts (arrowed)

9.13 Measure the height of the camshaft lobes with a micrometer

the valves are installed, install the holders and tighten the bolts as described in Step 30. If the valves have been removed, install the holders as described in Step 30, noting that you can do each holder separately rather than all three at the same time, and tighten the bolts evenly and a little at a time in a criss-cross sequence to the specified torque setting, making sure the holders are pulled down squarely onto the dowels. While doing this, don't let the camshafts rotate, or the Plastigauge will be disturbed and you will have to start again.

17 Now unscrew the camshaft holder bolts as described in Step 6 (valves installed) or evenly and a little at a time in a criss-cross sequence (valves removed), and lift off the holder.

18 To determine the oil clearance, compare the crushed Plastigauge (at its widest point) on each journal to the scale printed on the Plastigauge container. Compare the results to this Chapter's Specifications. If the oil clearance is greater than specified, replace the camshaft with a new one and recheck the clearance. If the clearance is still too great, also replace the cylinder head and holder with new ones.

> **HAYNES HiNT** ***Before replacing the camshafts, cylinder head or holders because of damage, check with motorcycle cylinder head specialists to see whether worn components can be renewed. Due to the cost of new components it is recommended that all options be explored.***

19 Except in cases of oil starvation, the cam chain should wear very little. If the chain has stretched excessively, which makes it difficult to maintain proper tension, or if it is stiff or the links are binding or kinking, replace it with a new one. Refer to Section 10 for replacement.

20 Check the sprockets for wear, cracks and other damage, and replace them with new ones if necessary (see Steps 10 and 24). If the sprockets are worn, the cam chain is also worn, and so probably is the sprocket on the crankshaft. If severe wear is apparent, the entire engine should be disassembled for inspection.

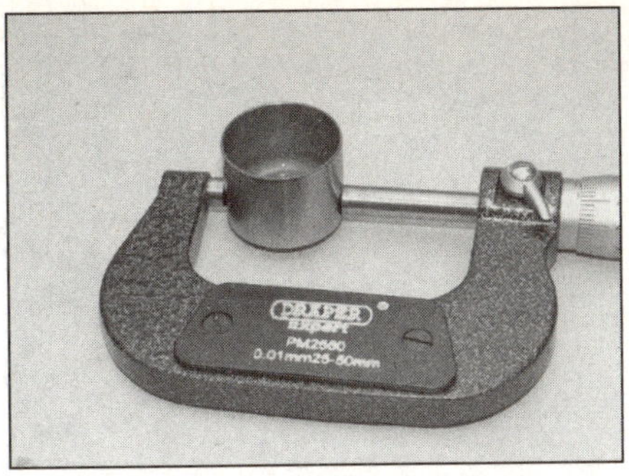

9.22a Measure the external diameter of each follower . . .

9.22b . . . and the internal diameter of each bore

21 Inspect the cam chain guides and tensioner blade (see Section 10).

22 Inspect the outer surface of each cam follower for evidence of scoring or other damage. If a follower is in poor condition, it is probable that the bore in the cylinder head in which it works is also damaged. Check for clearance between each follower and its bore. Measure the outer diameter of each follower and the inner diameter of its bore and compare the results to the Specifications **(see illustrations)**. If any follower is worn beyond its service limit replace it with a new one. If any bore is worn beyond its limit, is seriously out-of-round or tapered, replace the cylinder head with a new one.

Installation

23 If removed, fit the CMP sensor rotor onto the left-hand end of the exhaust camshaft – align it so that when the No. 1 cylinder (left-hand) lobes are facing up, the OUT mark on the rotor is at the bottom and faces out **(see illustration 9.11)**. Apply a suitable non-permanent thread locking compound to the bolts and tighten them to the specified torque setting. If necessary, tighten the bolts after the camshafts are installed so the shaft can be counter-held easily.

24 If separated, fit the sprockets onto the camshafts. Make sure they are installed the correct way round and in their original location as identified by the marks made on removal (Step 10) **(see illustration and 9.10)**. Apply a suitable non-permanent thread locking compound to the sprocket bolts and tighten them to the torque setting specified at the beginning of the Chapter.

25 If removed, lubricate each shim and its follower with molybdenum disulphide oil (a 50/50 mixture of molybdenum disulphide grease and engine oil). Fit each shim into its recess in the top of the valve spring retainer with the size mark facing up, making sure it is correctly seated **(see illustration 9.9c)**. **Note:** *It is most important that the shims and followers are returned to their original valves otherwise the valve clearances will be inaccurate.* Install each follower, making sure it fits squarely in its bore **(see illustration)**.

26 Make sure the bearing surfaces on the camshafts and in the cylinder head are clean, then apply molybdenum disulphide oil (a 50/50 mixture of molybdenum disulphide grease and

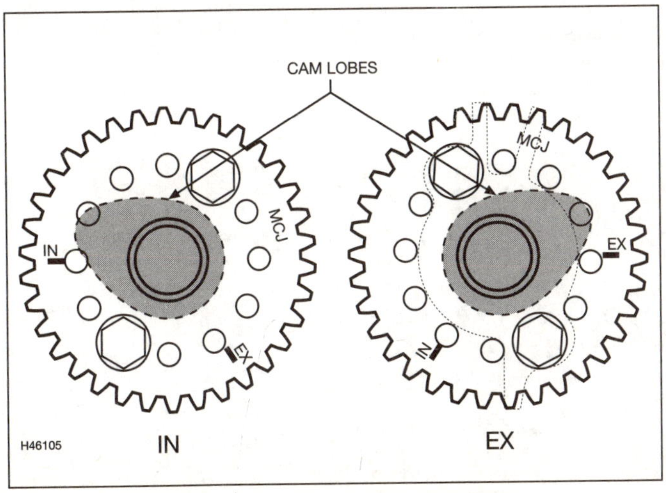

9.24 Camshaft sprocket alignment
Cylinder No. 1 cam lobe positions shown

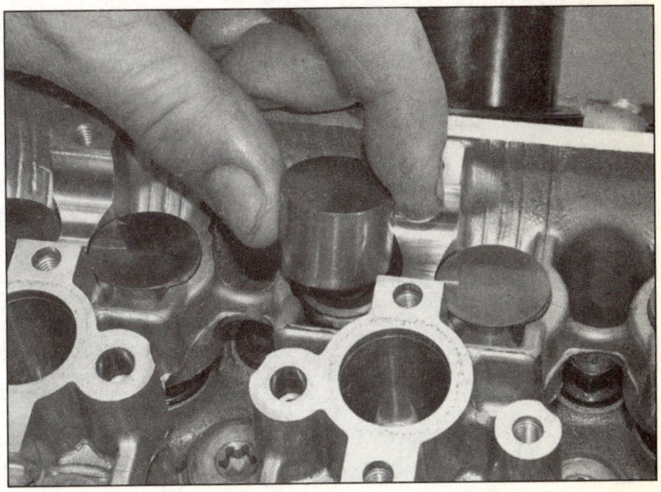

9.25 Fit each shim into its recess, then fit the follower onto the valve

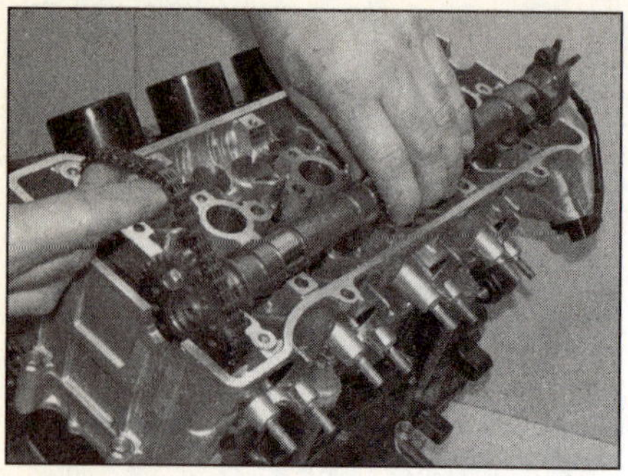

9.28a Install the exhaust camshaft as described . . .

9.28b . . . so the EX mark is positioned as shown

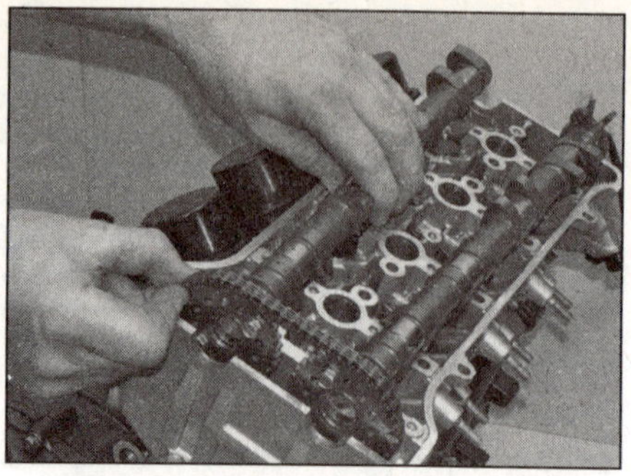

9.29a Install the intake camshaft as described . . .

engine oil) to each of them. Also apply it to the camshaft journals and lobes. Make sure that none gets on the mating surfaces between the holder and the head, or in the bolt holes.

27 Check that the line next to the T mark on the timing rotor aligns with the notch in the inspection hole rim **(see illustration 9.3b)**.

28 Lay the exhaust camshaft (marked EX or DE) onto the head with the EX mark on the sprocket facing forward and level with the cylinder head top mating surface, and the No. 1 cylinder lobes facing forward **(see illustrations and 9.24)**. Fit the cam chain around the sprocket as you install the camshaft, pulling up on the chain to remove all slack in the front run between the crankshaft and the camshaft.

29 Lay the intake camshaft (marked IN or DI) onto the head with the IN mark on the sprocket facing back and level with the cylinder head top mating surface, and the No. 1 cylinder lobes facing diagonally back and up **(see illustrations and 9.24)**. Fit the cam chain around the sprocket as you install the camshaft, pulling on it to remove all slack from between the two camshaft sprockets. Any slack in the chain must lie in the rear run of the chain between the intake camshaft and the crankshaft so that it is later taken up by the tensioner.

30 Make sure the bearing surfaces in the camshaft holders are clean. Make sure the camshaft holder bolt dowels and PAIR system air passage dowels are installed **(see illustration)**. Fit new sealing rings into the grooves around the spark plug holes on the underside of the main holders, making sure they also locate around the PAIR system air passage dowels. Apply molybdenum disulphide oil (a 50/50 mixture of molybdenum disulphide grease and engine oil) to the bearing surfaces. Lay the holders in the head making sure they are correctly positioned (see Step 6) **(see illustrations)**. Apply clean engine oil to the threads and under the heads of all the camshaft holder bolts. Install the bolts, not forgetting new sealing washers with the eight bolts around the spark plug bores, and fitting the six longer bolts into the front and rearmost right-hand holes, and tighten them finger-tight **(see illustrations)**. First gradually and evenly tighten the centre bolts Nos. 5-6-7-8 in that order until the dowels in the holder enter their bores in the head. Now tighten all the bolts evenly and a little at a time in the correct sequence (i.e. 1 to 20), again making sure the holder is being pulled down squarely.

9.29b . . . so the IN mark is as shown

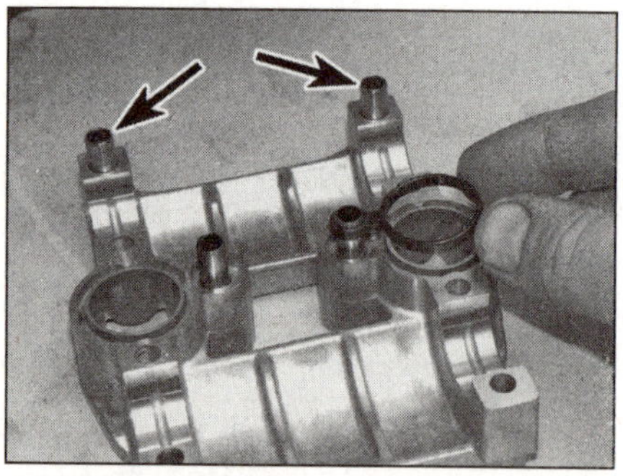

9.30a Camshaft holder dowels (arrowed). Fit new sealing rings over the air passage dowels and into the grooves around the plug holes

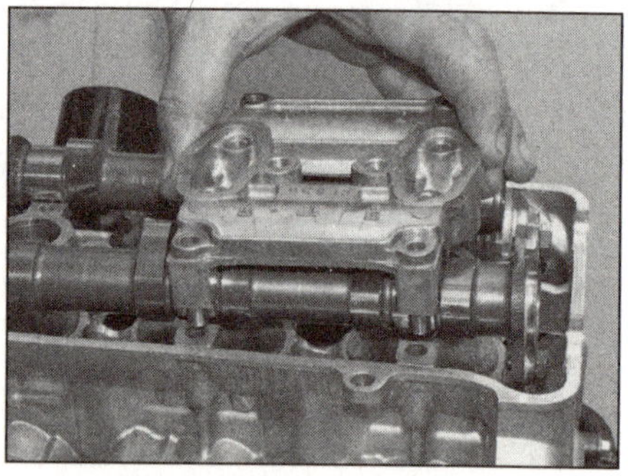

9.30b Install the holders . . .

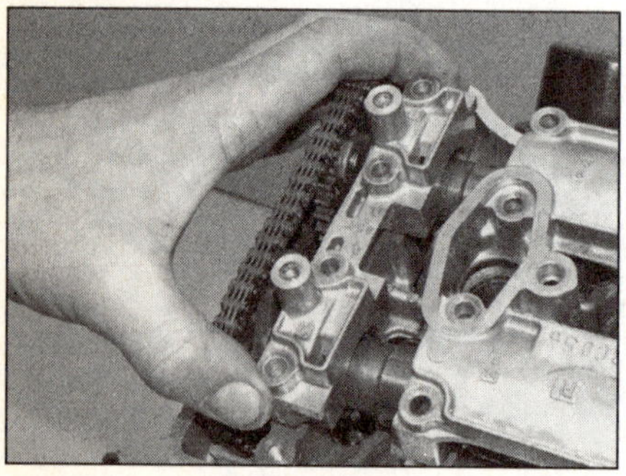

9.30c . . . making sure they are correctly positioned

9.30d Do not forget the sealing washers with the spark plug bore bolts . . .

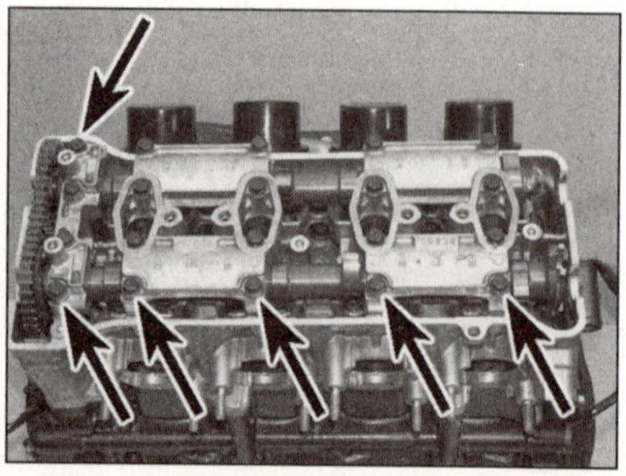

9.30e . . . and fit the longer bolts as shown (arrowed)

Caution: Whilst tightening the bolts, make sure the holders are being pulled evenly and squarely down and are not binding on the dowels or tilting to one side – if they do, adjust the relevant bolts until the holders are again square to the head. A holder or camshaft is likely to break if they are not tightened down evenly and squarely.

31 If the tensioner tool was used to retract and hold the tensioner plunger, remove it to release the plunger. If the tensioner was removed, use a piece of wooden dowel to press on the back of the cam chain tensioner blade via the tensioner bore in the cylinder block to ensure that any slack in the cam chain is taken up and transferred to the rear run of the chain (where it will later be taken up by the tensioner). At this point check that all the timing marks are still in exact alignment as described in Step 3 **(see illustrations 9.3b and c and 9.28b and 9.29b)**. Note that it is easy to be slightly out (one tooth on the sprocket) without the marks appearing drastically out of alignment. If the marks are out, verify which sprocket is misaligned, then either reinstall the tensioner locking tool and retract the plunger, or remove the wooden dowel. Unscrew the sprocket's bolts and slide it off the camshaft, then disengage it from the chain. Move the camshaft round as required, then fit the sprocket back into the chain and onto the camshaft, and check the marks again. With everything correctly aligned, apply a suitable non-permanent thread locking compound to the sprocket bolts and tighten them to the torque setting specified at the beginning of the Chapter.

Caution: If the marks are not aligned exactly as described, the valve timing will be incorrect and the valves may strike the pistons, causing extensive damage to the engine.

32 Install the cam chain top guide and tighten its bolts **(see illustration 9.4)**. Either install the cam chain tensioner (see Section 8), or remove the tensioner holding tool, according to the method you used earlier.

33 Turn the engine clockwise through two full turns and check again that all the timing marks still align (see Step 3) **(see illustrations 9.3b and c and 9.28b and 9.29b)**. Check the valve clearances and adjust them if necessary (see Chapter 1).

34 Install the timing inspection cap using a new O-ring if required, and smear the O-ring and the cap threads with grease **(see illustration 9.2)**. Tighten the cap to the torque setting specified at the beginning of the Chapter.

35 Install the valve cover (see Section 8). Install the CMP sensor (see Chapter 4). Install the spark plugs (see Chapter 1).

10 Cam chain, tensioner blades and front guide

Note: *The cam chain and its blades can be removed with the engine in the frame. If the engine has been removed, ignore the steps which do not apply.*

Removal

1 Remove the camshafts – this procedure involves removing the top guide blade (see Section 9).

2 Remove the starter clutch (see Section 13).

3 Unscrew the tensioner blade pivot bolt and draw the blade out of the engine, noting the washer that fits behind it **(see illustrations)**.

4 Draw the cam chain off the crankshaft sprocket and out of the engine **(see illustration)**. Slide the sprocket off the end of the crankshaft, noting the offset wide splines that mean it can only be installed in one position.

5 Unscrew the front guide blade pivot bolt and draw the blade out of the engine **(see illustrations)**. Note the washer with the bolt and the collar that fits from the inside **(see illustration)**.

Inspection

Cam chain and sprockets

6 Check the chain for binding, kinks and any obvious damage and replace it with a new one if necessary. Check the camshaft and crankshaft sprocket teeth for wear and replace the cam chain, camshaft sprockets and crankshaft with a new set if necessary.

Tensioner and guide blades

7 Check the sliding surface and edges of the blades for excessive wear, deep grooves,

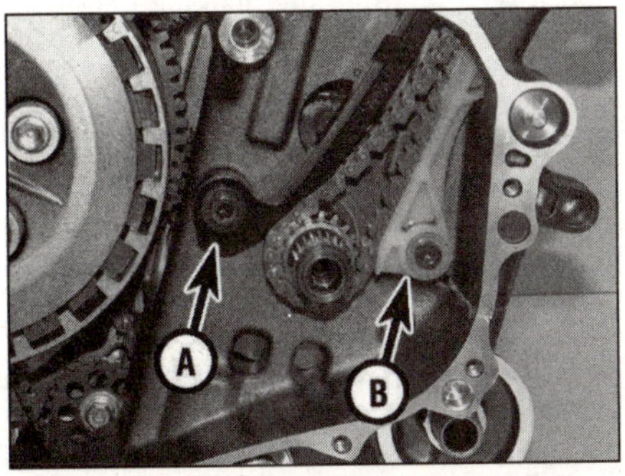

10.3a Tensioner blade (A), front guide blade (B)

10.3b Unscrew the pivot bolt, noting the washer behind the blade

10.4 Remove the cam chain and slide the sprocket off the shaft

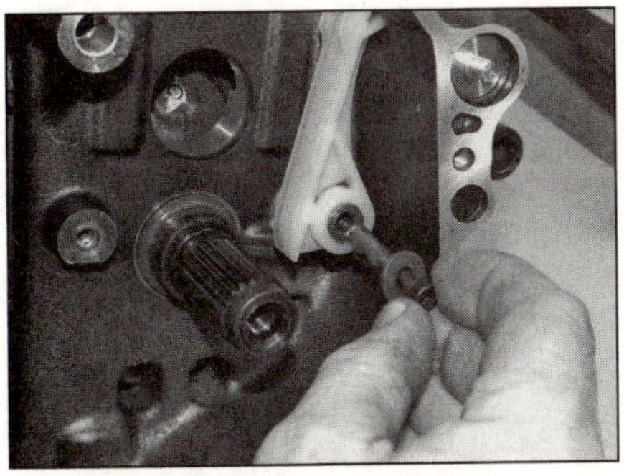
10.5a Unscrew the pivot bolt . . .

10.5b . . . and draw the blade out of the engine

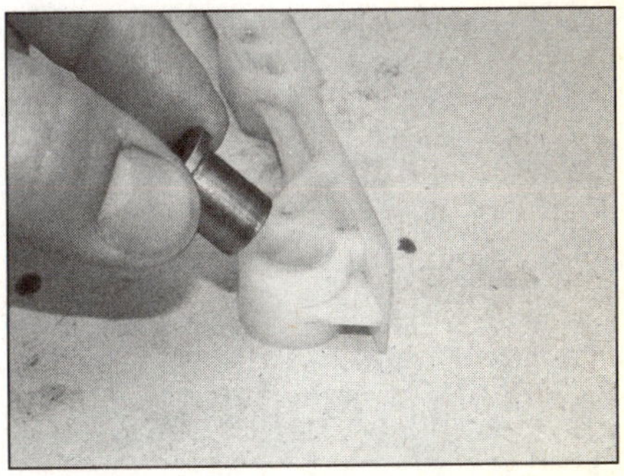
10.5c Note the collar in the pivot

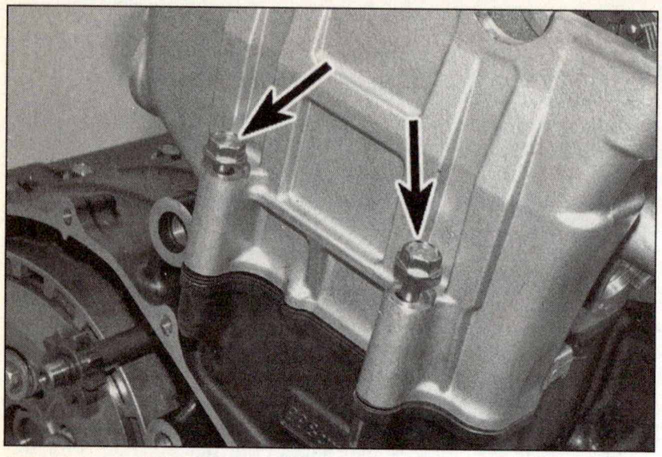

11.4a Cylinder head 6 mm bolts (arrowed)

11.4b Cylinder head 9 mm bolts (arrowed)

cracking and other obvious damage, and replace them with new ones if necessary.

Installation

8 Installation of the sprocket, chain and blades is the reverse of removal. Do not omit the washer that fits behind the tensioner blade **(see illustration 10.3a)**, or the collar in the guide blade **(see illustration 10.5c)**. Apply a suitable non-permanent thread locking compound to the blade pivot bolts and tighten them to the torque settings specified at the beginning of the Chapter.

11 Cylinder head

Note: *The cylinder head can be removed with the engine in the frame, though the procedure is easier with the engine removed, in which case ignore the Steps which do not apply.*

Removal

1 Remove the valve cover (see Section 7).
2 Remove the camshafts, followers and shims (see Section 9). If not already done, remove the cam chain tensioner (see Section 8). If the engine is in the frame remove the tensioner blade and guide blade (see Section 10).
3 Either remove the thermostat housing, or detach the coolant hoses from it (see Chapter 3).
4 The cylinder head is secured by two 6 mm bolts and ten 9 mm bolts with fitted washers (i.e. they can't be separated from the bolts) **(see illustrations)**. First unscrew and remove the 6 mm bolts. Now unscrew and remove the 9 mm bolts, slackening them evenly and a little at a time in a criss-cross pattern working from the outside to the middle until they are all loose.
5 Hold the cam chain up and pull the cylinder head up off the block, removing it from the front if the engine is in the frame, and pass the cam chain down through the tunnel **(see illustration)**. Do not let the chain fall into the crankcase – secure it with a piece of wire or metal bar to prevent it from doing so. If the head is stuck, tap around the joint faces with a soft-faced mallet. Do not attempt to free the head by inserting a screwdriver between the head and block mating surfaces – you'll damage them.
6 Remove the cylinder head gasket and discard it as a new one must be used. If they are loose, remove the dowels from the crankcase or the underside of the cylinder head **(see illustration 11.10)**.
7 Check the cylinder head gasket and the mating surfaces on the cylinder head and crankcase for signs of leakage, which could indicate warpage. Refer to Section 12 and check the cylinder head gasket surface for warpage.
8 Clean all traces of old gasket material from the cylinder head and crankcase. If a scraper is used, take care not to scratch or gouge the soft aluminium. Be careful not to let any of the gasket material fall into the crankcase, the cylinder bore or the oil and coolant passages.

Installation

9 Lubricate the cylinder bores with engine oil. If removed, fit the dowels into the crankcase **(see illustration 11.10)**.
10 Ensure both cylinder head and crankcase mating surfaces are clean. Lay the new head gasket over the cam chain and blades and onto the crankcase, locating it over the dowels and making sure all the holes are correctly aligned **(see illustration)**. Never reuse the old gasket.
11 Carefully fit the cylinder head onto the block, making sure it locates correctly onto the dowels **(see illustration 11.5)**. Feed the cam chain up through the tunnel as you install the head, then secure it in place with a piece of wire to prevent it from falling back down.
12 Apply some molybdenum disulphide oil (a 50/50 mixture of molybdenum disulphide grease and engine oil) to the threads and the underside of the heads of all the bolts. Note that if new bolts are being installed, first remove any anti-rust coating by cleaning them with solvent. Install the bolts and tighten them all finger-tight **(see illustration)**. Tighten the

11.5 Carefully lift the head up off the block

11.10 Install the dowels (arrowed) then lay the new gasket on the block

11.12 Lubricate and install the bolts and tighten them as described to specified torque setting

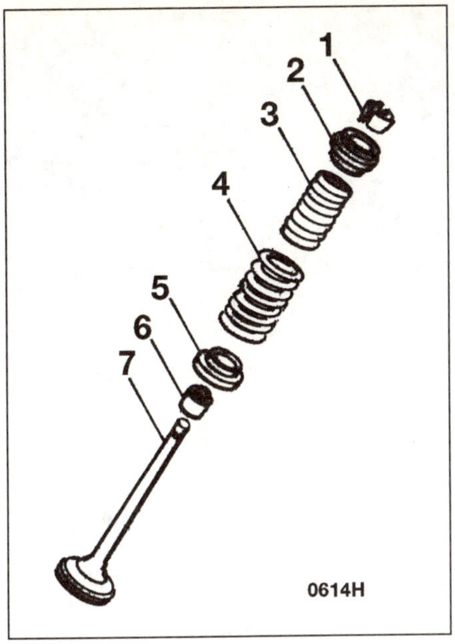

12.5 Valve components

1 *Collets*
2 *Spring retainer*
3 *Inner valve spring (intake valve on RR-6 and RR-7 models)*
4 *Valve spring*
5 *Spring seat*
6 *Valve stem oil seal*
7 *Valve*

9 mm bolts evenly and a little at a time in a criss-cross pattern working from the middle to the outside to the torque setting specified at the beginning of the Chapter. Now tighten the 6 mm bolts **(see illustration 11.4a)**.

13 Install the remaining components in a reverse of their removal sequence, referring to the relevant Sections or Chapters (see Steps 1 to 3).

12 Cylinder head and valve overhaul

1 Because of the complex nature of this job and the special tools and equipment required, most owners leave servicing of the valves, valve seats and valve guides to a professional. However, you can make an initial assessment of whether the valves are seating correctly, and therefore sealing, by pouring a small amount of solvent into each of the valve ports. If the solvent leaks past any valve into the combustion chamber area the valve is not seating correctly and sealing.

2 With the correct tools (a valve spring compressor is essential – make sure it is suitable for motorcycle work), you can also remove the valves and associated components from the cylinder head, clean them and check them for wear to assess the extent of the work needed, and, unless seat cutting or guide

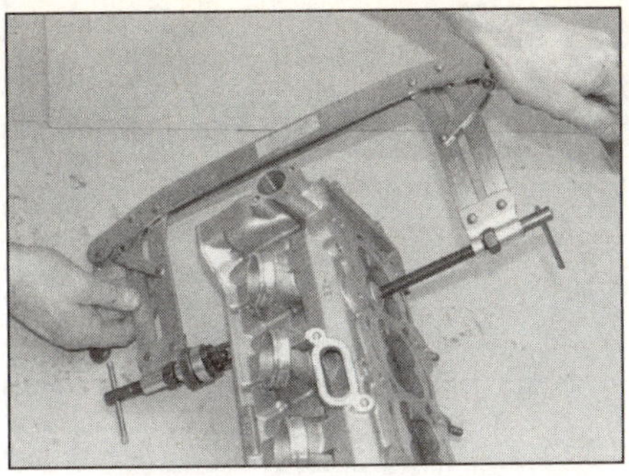

12.6a Compressing the valve spring(s) using a valve spring compressor

replacement is required, grind in the valves and reassemble them in the head.

3 A dealer service department or specialist can replace the guides and re-cut the valve seats.

4 After the valve service has been performed, be sure to clean it very thoroughly before installation on the engine to remove any metal particles or abrasive grit that may still be present from the valve service operations. Use compressed air, if available, to blow out all the holes and passages.

Disassembly

5 Before proceeding, arrange to label and store the valves along with their related components in such a way that they can be returned to their original locations without getting mixed up **(see illustration)**. Either use the same container as the cam followers and shims are stored in (see Section 9), or obtain a separate container and label each compartment accordingly. Alternatively, labelled plastic bags will do just as well. RR-4 and RR-5 models have one spring per valve, while RR-6 and RR-7 models have two springs per intake valve and one per exhaust valve.

6 Compress the valve spring on the first valve with a spring compressor, making sure it is

HAYNES HiNT

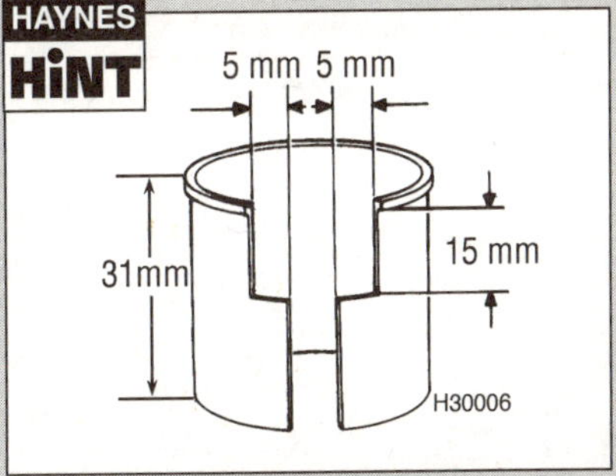

Protect the follower bore in the cylinder head from scratches by the valve spring compressor using either the Honda tool (Part No. 07HMG-MR70002) or by fabricating a shield from a 35 mm film canister. Cut the canister to the dimensions shown.

12.6b Make sure the compressor locates correctly both on the top of the spring retainer . . .

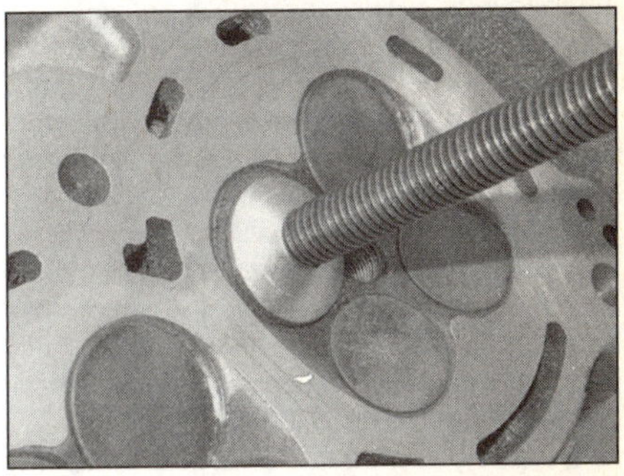

12.6c . . . and on the bottom of the valve

correctly located onto each end of the valve assembly **(see illustration)**. On the top of the valve the adaptor needs to be about the same size as the spring retainer – if it is too big it will contact the follower bore and mark it, and if it is too small it will be difficult to remove and install the collets **(see illustration)**. On the underside of the head make sure the plate on the compressor only contacts the valve and not the soft aluminium of the head **(see illustration)** – if the plate is too big for the valve, use a spacer between them. Do not compress the springs any more than is absolutely necessary.

Caution: Take great care not to mark the cam follower bore with the spring compressor.

7 Remove the collets, using a magnet or a screwdriver with a dab of grease on it **(see illustration)**. Carefully release the valve spring compressor and remove the spring retainer,

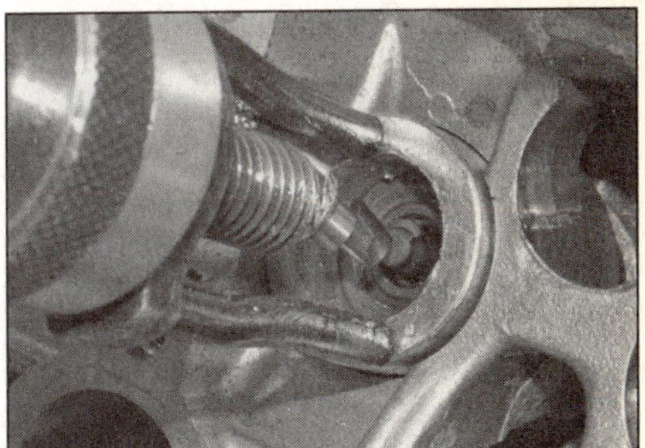

12.7a Remove the collets . . .

12.7b ... the spring retainer ...

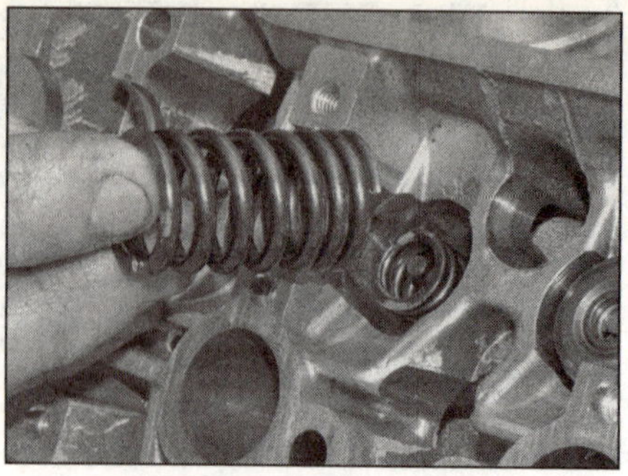

12.7c ... the spring(s) ...

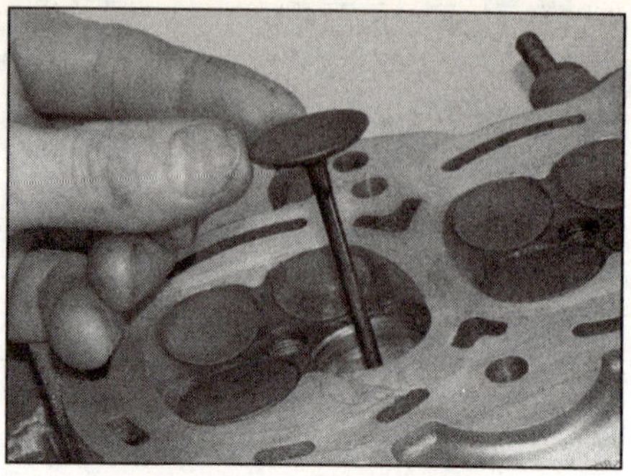

12.7d ... and the valve

noting which way up it fits, the spring(s) and the valve **(see illustrations)**. If the valve binds in the guide and won't pull through, push it back into the head and deburr the area around the collet groove with a very fine file or whetstone **(see illustration)**.

8 Pull the valve stem seal off the top of the valve guide with pliers and discard it (the old seals should never be reused), then remove the spring seat noting which way up, it fits – using a magnet is the easiest way to remove the seat from the head **(see illustrations)**.

9 Repeat the procedure for the remaining valves. Remember to keep the parts for each valve together so they can be reinstalled in the same location.

10 Clean the cylinder head with solvent and dry it thoroughly. Compressed air will speed the drying process and ensure that all holes and recessed areas are clean. **Note:** *Do not use a wire brush mounted in a drill motor to clean the combustion chambers as the head material is soft and may be scratched or eroded away by the wire brush.*

11 Clean all of the valve springs, collets, retainers and spring seats with solvent and dry them thoroughly. Do the parts from one valve at a time so that no mixing of parts between valves occurs.

12 Scrape off any deposits that may have formed on the valve, then use a motorised wire brush to remove deposits from the valve heads and stems. Again, make sure the valves do not get mixed up.

Inspection

13 Inspect the head very carefully for cracks and other damage. If cracks are found, a new head is required. Check the camshaft bearing surfaces for wear and evidence of seizure. Check the camshafts and holders for wear as well (see Section 9).

14 Using a precision straight-edge and a feeler gauge set to the warpage limit listed in the specifications at the beginning of the Chapter, check the head gasket mating surface for warpage. Refer to Tools and Workshop Tips in the Reference section for details of how to use the straight-edge. If the head is warped beyond the limit specified at the beginning of this Chapter, consult a Honda dealer or take it to a specialist repair shop for an opinion, though be prepared to buy a new one.

15 Examine the valve seats in the combustion chamber. If they are pitted, cracked or burned, the head will require work beyond the scope of the home mechanic. Measure the valve seat width and compare it to this Chapter's Specifications **(see illustration)**. If it exceeds the service limit, or if it varies around its circumference, overhaul is required.

16 Working on one valve and guide at a time, measure the valve stem diameter **(see illustration)**. Clean the valve's guide using a guide reamer to remove any carbon build-up – insert the reamer from the underside of the head and turn it clockwise only. Now measure the inside diameter of the guide (at both ends and in the centre of the guide) with a small bore gauge, then measure the gauge

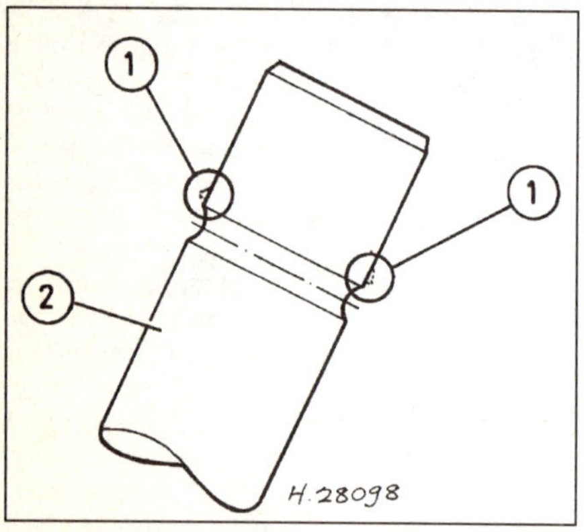

12.7e If the valve stem (2) won't pull through the guide, deburr the area above the collet groove (1)

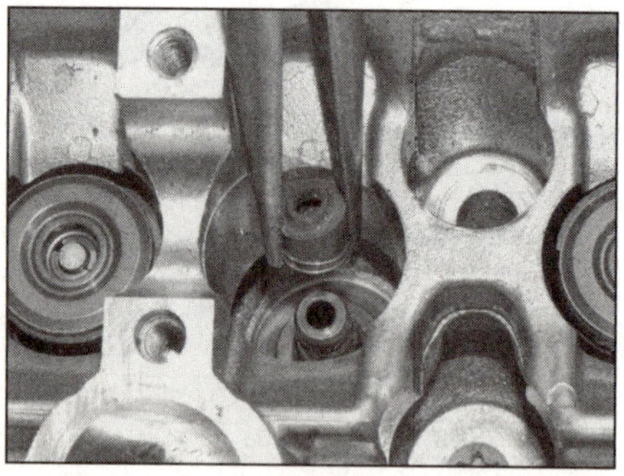

12.8a Pull the seal off the valve stem ...

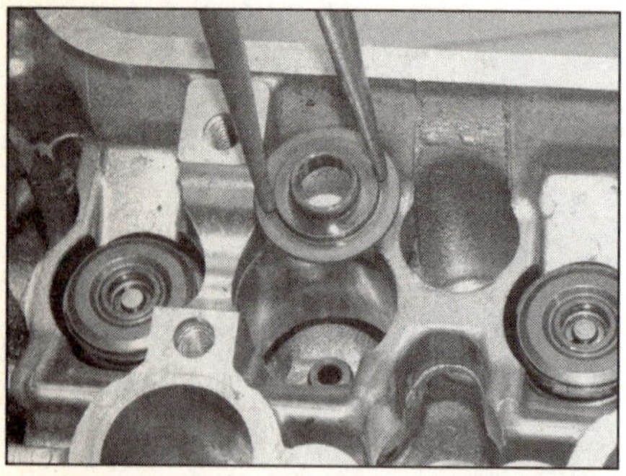

12.8b ... then remove the spring seat

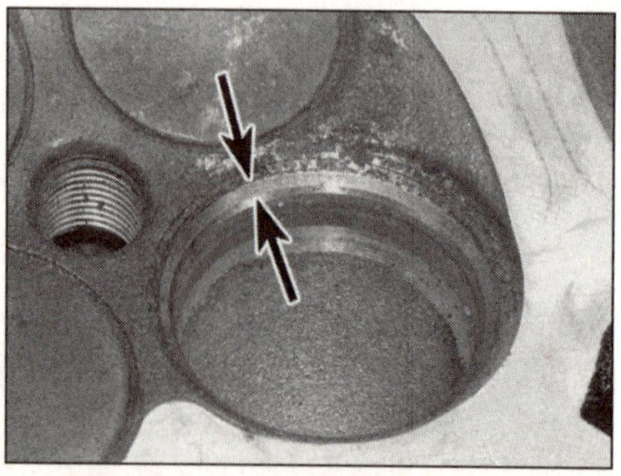

12.15 Measure the valve seat width

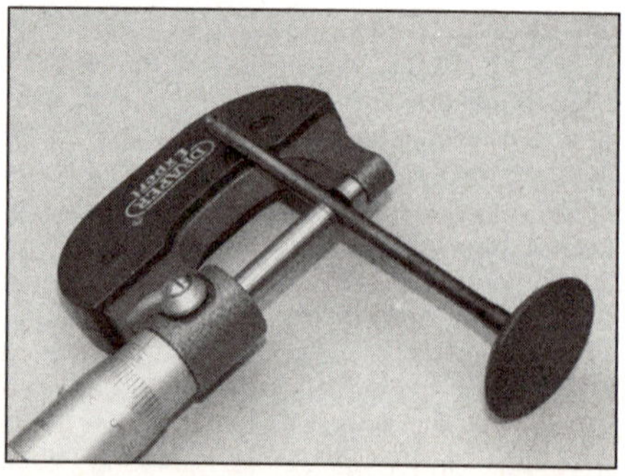

12.16a Measure the valve stem diameter with a micrometer

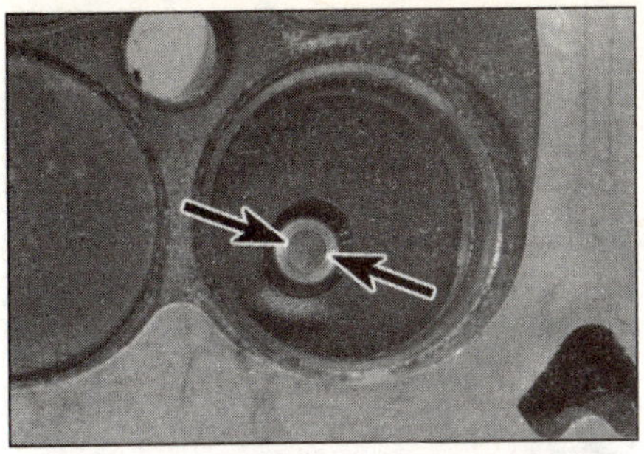

12.16b Measure the valve guide with a small bore gauge, then measure the bore gauge with a micrometer

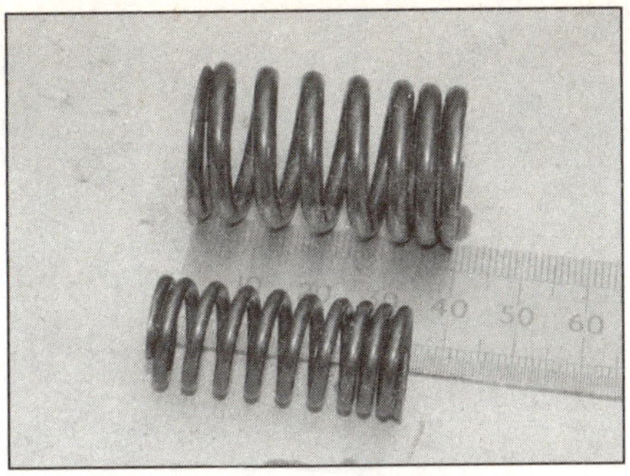

12.19 Measure the free length of the valve springs and check them for bend

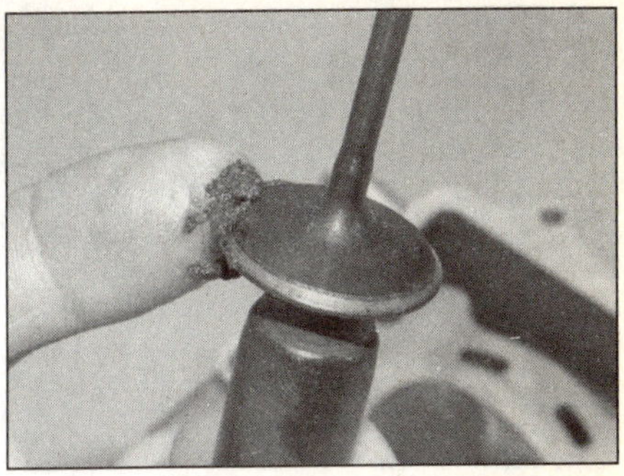

12.23 Apply dabs of paste round the valve face

with a micrometer **(see illustration)**. Measure the guide at the ends and at the centre to determine if it is worn in a bell-mouth pattern (more wear at the ends). Subtract the stem diameter from the valve guide diameter to obtain the valve stem-to-guide clearance. If the stem-to-guide clearance is greater than listed in this Chapter's Specifications, replace whichever component is beyond its specification limits with a new one. If the valve guide is within specifications, but is worn unevenly, it should be replaced with a new one. Repeat for the other valves.

17 Carefully inspect each valve face, stem and collet groove area for cracks, pits and burned spots.

18 Rotate the valve and check for any obvious indication that it is bent, in which case it must be replaced with a new one. Check the end of the stem for pitting and excessive wear. The presence of any of the above conditions indicates the need for valve servicing.

19 Check the end of each valve spring for wear and pitting. Measure the spring free lengths and compare them to the specifications **(see illustration)**. If any spring is shorter than specified it has sagged and must be replaced with a new one. Also place the spring upright on a flat surface and check it for bend by placing a ruler against it, or alternatively lay it against a set square. If the bend in any spring is excessive, it must be replaced with a new one.

20 Check the spring seats, retainers and collets for obvious wear and cracks. Any questionable parts should not be reused, as extensive damage will occur in the event of failure during engine operation.

21 If the inspection indicates that no overhaul work is required, the valve components can be reinstalled in the head.

Reassembly

22 Unless a valve service has been performed, before installing the valves in the head they should be ground in (lapped) to ensure a positive seal between the valves and seats. This procedure requires coarse and fine valve grinding compound and a valve grinding tool (either hand-held or drill driven – note that some drill-driven tools specify using only a fine grinding compound). If a grinding tool is not available, a piece of rubber or plastic hose can be slipped over the valve stem (after the valve has been installed in the guide) and used to turn the valve.

23 Apply a small amount of coarse grinding compound to the valve face **(see illustration)**. Smear some molybdenum disulphide oil (a 50/50 mixture of molybdenum disulphide grease and engine oil) to the valve stem, then slip the valve into the guide **(see illustration 12.29)**. **Note:** *Make sure each valve is installed in its correct guide and be careful not to get any grinding compound on the valve stem.*

24 Attach the grinding tool to the valve and rotate the tool between the palms of your hands. Use a back-and-forth motion (as though rubbing your hands together) rather than a circular motion (i.e. so that the valve rotates alternately clockwise and anti-clockwise rather than in one direction only) **(see illustration)**. If a motorised tool is being used, take note of the correct drive speed for it – if your drill runs too fast and is not variable, use a hand tool instead. Lift the valve off the seat and turn it at regular intervals to distribute the grinding compound properly. Continue the grinding procedure until the valve face and seat contact area is of uniform width, and unbroken around the entire circumference.

25 Carefully remove the valve and wipe off all traces of grinding compound, making sure none gets in the guide. Use solvent to clean the valve and wipe the seat area thoroughly with a solvent soaked cloth.

26 Repeat the procedure with fine valve grinding compound, then use solvent to clean the valve and flush the guide, and wipe the seat area thoroughly with a solvent soaked cloth. Repeat the entire procedure for the remaining valves. On completion thoroughly clean the entire head again, then blow through all passages with compressed air. Make sure all traces of the grinding compound have been removed before assembling the head.

27 Working on one valve at a time, lay the spring seat in place in the cylinder head with its shouldered side facing up **(see illustration)**. As it is easy to cock the seat on the top of the valve guide, and then tricky to get it to sit properly, install it using a rod as a guide for it to slide down.

28 Fit a new valve stem seal onto the guide, using finger pressure, a stem seal fitting tool or an appropriate size deep socket, to push the seal squarely onto the end of the valve guide until it is felt to clip into place **(see illustration)**.

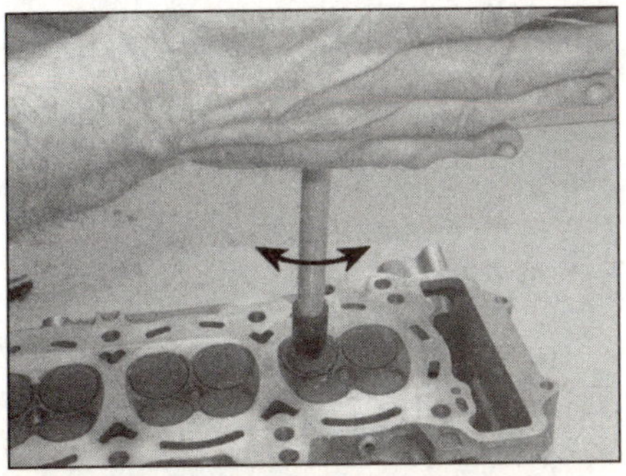

12.24 Rotate the valve grinding tool back and forth between the palms of your hands

12.27 Fit the spring seat using a rod to guide it if necessary

12.28 Fit a new valve stem seal and press it squarely into place

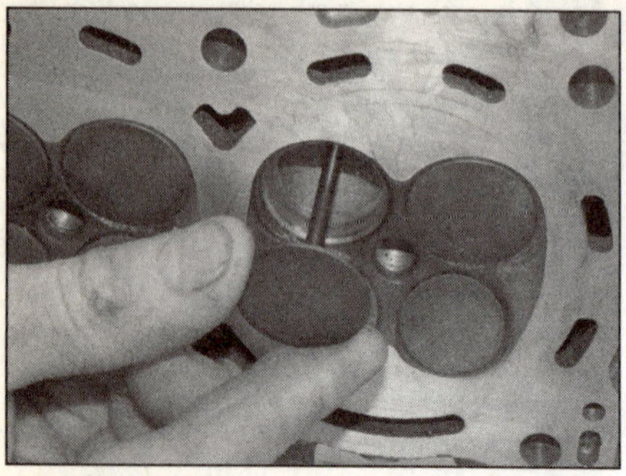

12.29 Lubricate the stem and slide the valve into its correct location

12.30a Fit the inner valve spring . . .

12.30b . . . and the outer valve spring . . .

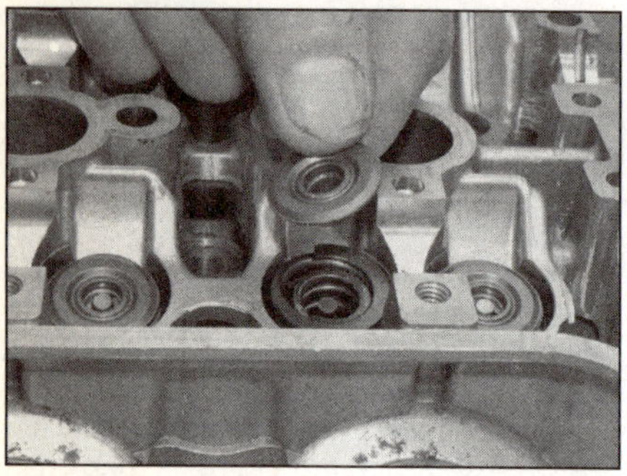

12.30c . . . then fit the spring retainer

12.31 Locate each collet in its groove in the top of the valve stem

12.33 Seat the collets as described

Make sure the seal does not get cocked sideways as it could be damaged – using a rod as a guide as for the seat helps.

29 Coat the valve stem with molybdenum disulphide oil (a 50/50 mixture of molybdenum disulphide grease and engine oil), then install it into its guide, rotating it slowly to avoid damaging the seal **(see illustration)**. Check that the valve moves up-and-down freely in the guide.

30 Next, install the spring(s), with the closer-wound coils facing down into the cylinder head **(see illustrations)**. Fit the spring retainer, with its shouldered side facing down so that it fits into the top of the spring(s) **(see illustration)**.

31 Apply a small amount of grease to the collets to help hold them in place. Compress the valve spring(s) with a spring compressor, making sure it is correctly located onto each end of the valve assembly (see Step 6) **(see illustrations 12.6a, 12.6b and 12.6c)**. Do not compress the spring(s) any more than is necessary to slip the collets into place. Locate each collet in turn into the groove in the valve stem using a screwdriver with a dab of grease on it **(see illustration)**. Carefully release the compressor, making sure the collets seat and lock in the retaining groove.

32 Repeat the procedure for the remaining valves. Remember to keep the parts for each valve together and separate from the other valves so they can be reinstalled in the same location.

33 Support the cylinder head on blocks so the valves can't contact the work surface, then tap the end of each valve stem lightly to seat the collets in their grooves **(see illustration)**.

34 After the cylinder head and camshafts have been installed, check the valve clearances and adjust as required (see Chapter 1).

13 Starter clutch and gears

Note: *The starter clutch can be removed with the engine in the frame. If the engine has been removed, ignore the steps which do not apply.*

Check

1 The operation of the starter clutch can be checked while it is in situ. Remove the starter motor (see Chapter 8). Check that the reduction gear is able to rotate freely clockwise as you look at it via the starter motor aperture, but locks when rotated anti-clockwise. If not, the starter clutch is faulty and should be removed for inspection.

13.2 Remove the idle gear and shaft

Removal

2 Remove the clutch cover (see Section 14, Steps 1 to 3). Withdraw the idle gear shaft and remove the gear **(see illustration)**.

3 To prevent the crankshaft from turning while unscrewing the starter clutch bolt, either engage 6th gear and have an assistant hold the rear brake on hard with the rear tyre in firm contact with the ground, or alternatively wedge a thick piece of rag material between the primary drive and driven gears at the top as shown **(see illustration)**.

13.3 Wedge some rag between the gears (arrowed) to jam them while unscrewing the bolt

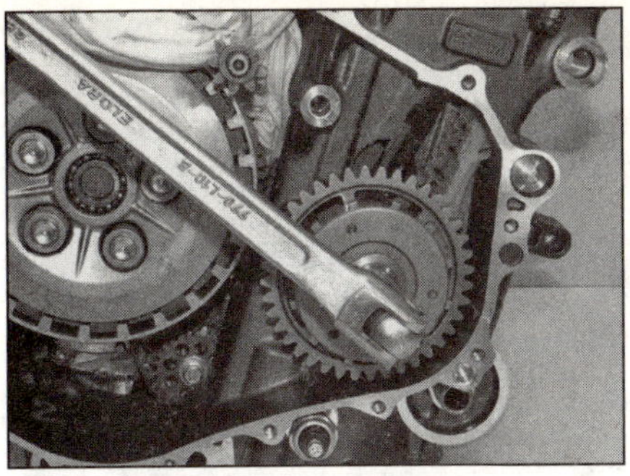

13.4a Unscrew the bolt . . .

13.4b . . . then slide the starter clutch off . . .

13.4c . . . and remove the thrust washer

13.5 Remove the reduction gear

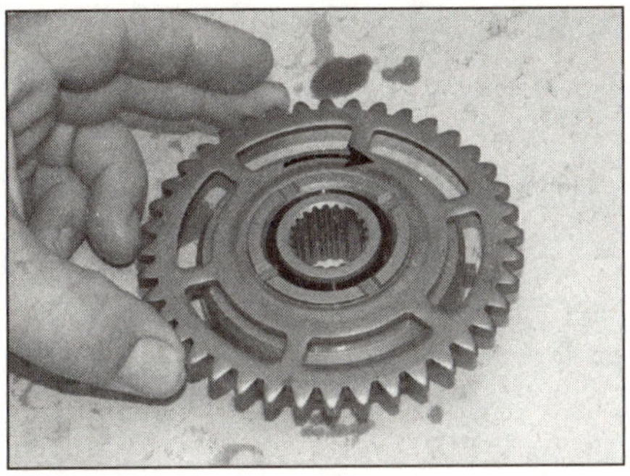

13.6 Check the operation of the clutch as described

13.7 Withdraw the driven gear and remove the bearing

4 Unscrew the bolt and remove the washer **(see illustration)**. Slide the starter clutch off the shaft, noting the offset wide splines that mean it can only be installed in one position **(see illustration)**. Remove the inner thrust washer **(see illustration)**.

5 If you need to remove the reduction gear first remove the clutch (see Section 14). Remove the reduction gear **(see illustration)**.

Inspection

6 With the starter clutch face down on a workbench, check that the starter driven gear rotates freely clockwise and locks against the rotor anti-clockwise **(see illustration)**. If it doesn't, the starter clutch should be dismantled for further investigation.

7 Withdraw the starter driven gear from the starter clutch **(see illustration)**. If the gear appears stuck, rotate it clockwise as you withdraw it to free it from the starter clutch. Remove the needle bearing.

8 Check the condition of the sprags inside the clutch body – if they are damaged, marked or flattened at any point, the sprag assembly must be replaced with a new one **(see illustration)**. To remove the sprag assembly release the circlip that holds it in its housing and note which way round it fits. Install the new assembly in a reverse sequence, with the white paint mark facing out of the housing. Secure the sprag assembly with the circlip. Apply clean engine oil to the sprags.

9 Check the external surface on the driven gear hub **(see illustration 13.7)**. Measure the outside diameter of the hub and check that it has not worn beyond the service limit specified. Check the needle roller bearing and the bearing surfaces on the starter driven gear hub and the starter clutch housing boss. If the bearing surfaces show signs of excessive wear or the bearing itself is worn or damaged, they should be replaced with new ones.

10 Check the teeth of the reduction and idle gears and the corresponding teeth of the starter driven gear and starter motor drive shaft. Replace the gears and/or starter motor if worn or chipped teeth are discovered on related gears. Also check the idle gear shaft for damage, and check that the gear is not a loose fit on it. Measure the external diameter of the shaft and the diameter of its bore in the idle gear replace them with new ones if worn beyond the service limits specified at the beginning of the Chapter. Check the reduction gear shaft ends and the bores they run in for wear.

Installation

11 Lubricate the outside of the starter driven gear hub with clean engine oil, then fit the gear into the clutch, rotating it clockwise as you do so to spread the sprags and allow the hub to enter **(see illustration 13.6)**. Lubricate the needle roller bearing with clean engine oil and fit it over the starter clutch boss **(see illustration)**.

12 If removed, lubricate the reduction gear shaft ends with clean engine oil then locate the inner end of the shaft in its bore in the crankcase, engaging it with the starter motor shaft teeth if installed **(see illustration 13.5)**. Install the clutch (see Section 14).

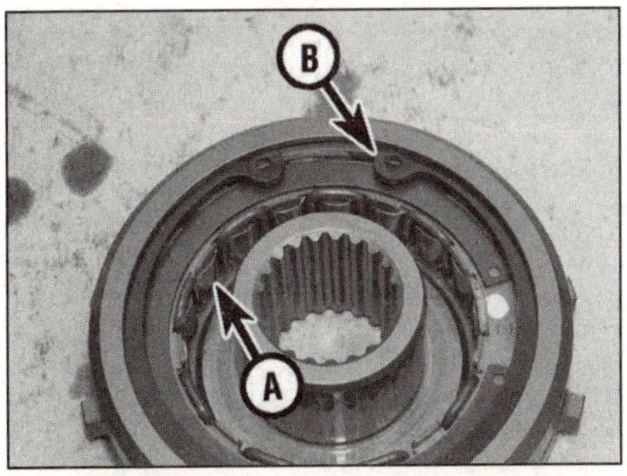

13.8 Check the sprags (A). The sprag assembly is held by the circlip (B)

13.11 Fit the bearing between the hub and the boss

13.14a Fit the lubricated bolt with its washer

13.14b Wedge the rag between the gears at the bottom (arrowed) . . .

13.14c . . . to prevent rotation while tightening the bolt

13 Slide the inner thrust washer onto the crankshaft and against the cam chain sprocket **(see illustration 13.4c)**. Align the wide splines on the starter clutch with those on the crankshaft and slide the starter clutch on with the driven gear on the inside **(see illustration 13.4b)**.

14 Apply clean oil to the threads and under the head of the starter clutch bolt. Install the bolt with its washer and tighten it to the torque setting specified at the beginning of the Chapter, noting that if rag was used to prevent crankshaft rotation it must now be wedged between the primary drive and driven gears at the bottom as shown **(see illustrations)**.

15 Lubricate the idle gear shaft with clean engine oil and fit it into the gear. Locate the idle gear, shouldered side inwards **(see illustration 13.2)**, between the reduction gear and the driven gear and slide the shaft into its bore in the crankcase **(see illustration)**.

16 Install the clutch cover (see Section 14, Steps 30 to 32).

14 Clutch

Note 1: *The clutch can be removed with the engine in the frame. If the engine has been removed, ignore the steps which don't apply.* **Note 2:** *The clutch nut must be discarded and a new one used on installation – it is best to obtain the new nut in advance.*

13.15 Engage the idle gear with the reduction gear and driven gear

Removal

1 Remove the lower fairing and the fairing right-hand side panel (see Chapter 7). Drain the engine oil (see Chapter 1).

2 Trace the crankshaft position (CKP) sensor wiring from the top of the clutch cover and disconnect it at the red 2-pin wiring connector **(see illustration)**. Feed the connector down to the cover, noting its routing.

14.2 Disconnect the CKP sensor red 2-pin wiring connector (arrowed)

3 Working evenly in a criss-cross pattern, unscrew the clutch cover bolts **(see illustration)** – on RR-4 and RR-5 models noting the three wiring guides fitted with the bolts **(see illustration 4.13d)**. Remove the cover. Note that there is a thrust washer and a wave washer on the end of the idle gear shaft which may come away with the cover and could therefore drop from it – if they stay on the end of the shaft remove them for safekeeping **(see illustration)**. Be prepared to catch any residual oil. Remove the two dowels from either the cover or the crankcase if they are loose.

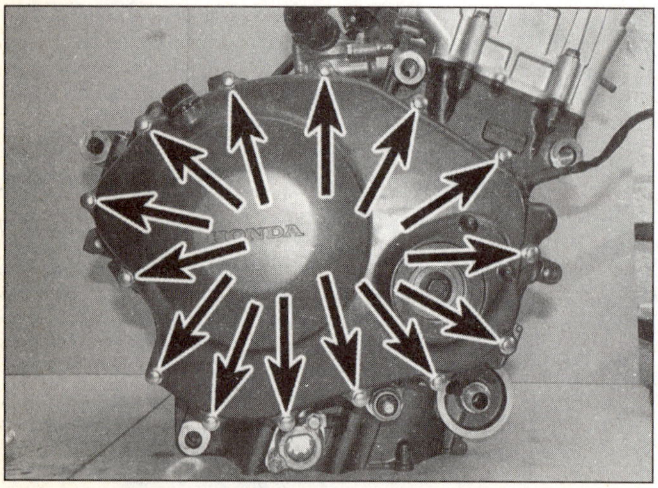

14.3a Unscrew the bolts (arrowed) and remove the cover

14.3b Remove the thrust washer and the wave washer (arrowed) from the shaft

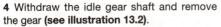

14.5a Unscrew the bolts (arrowed) and remove the springs . . .

14.5b . . . then remove the pressure plate

14.5c Withdraw the pushrod if required

4 Withdraw the idle gear shaft and remove the gear **(see illustration 13.2)**.

5 Working in a criss-cross pattern, gradually slacken the clutch spring bolts until pressure is released **(see illustration)**. To prevent the assembly from turning, cover it with a rag and hold it securely – the bolts are not very tight. If available, have an assistant to hold the clutch while you unscrew the bolts. Remove the bolts and springs, then remove the pressure plate **(see illustration)**. Remove the lifter from either the back of the pressure plate or the end of the shaft **(see illustration 14.28a)**. If required withdraw the pushrod from the shaft **(see illustration)**.

6 Remove the clutch friction and plain plates, hooking them out when necessary, noting how they fit and keeping them in order **(see illustrations 14.27c, b and a)**. Note how the tabs on the outer friction plate locate in the shallow slots in the housing, while the rest sit in the deep slots. The outer and inner friction plates are different to the rest – they have a larger internal diameter and are identified as plate Type A. The inner plain plate differs to the rest in that it has a different surface coating. Remove the anti-judder spring and spring seat, noting which way round they fit **(see illustrations 14.26b and a)**.

7 The clutch nut rim is staked against the input shaft. Unstake the nut using a hammer and punch – take care not to damage the threads on the end of the shaft **(see illustration)**. To remove the clutch nut, the input shaft must be locked. This can be done in several ways. If the engine is in the frame, engage 6th gear and have an assistant hold the rear brake on hard with the rear tyre in firm contact with the ground. Alternatively, the Honda service tool (Pt. No. 07724-0050002), or a similar commercially available can be used to stop the clutch centre from turning whilst the nut is slackened **(see illustration)**. Unscrew the nut and remove the lock washer and the thrust washer **(see illustrations 14.25b and a)**. Discard the nut as a new one must be used on installation.

8 Remove the clutch centre and the thrust washer from the shaft **(see illustrations 14.24b and a)**.

9 Ease out the clutch guide and needle bearing from between the clutch housing and the input shaft – this can be done using a magnet and by sliding the housing on the shaft to help push them along **(see illustration)**. Remove the clutch housing. Note how the holes in the back of the housing engage with the pins on the oil pump drive sprocket.

14.7a Unstake the nut . . .

10 If required, draw the oil pump drive sprocket guide out to create slack in the chain, then remove the sprocket and chain **(see illustration)**.

Inspection

11 After an extended period of service the clutch friction plates will wear and promote clutch slip. Measure the thickness of each friction plate using a Vernier caliper **(see illustration)**. If any plate has worn to or beyond the service limits given in the Specifications at the beginning of the Chapter, or if any of the plates smell burnt or are glazed, the friction plates must be replaced with a new set.

12 The plain plates should not show any signs of excess heating (bluing). Check for

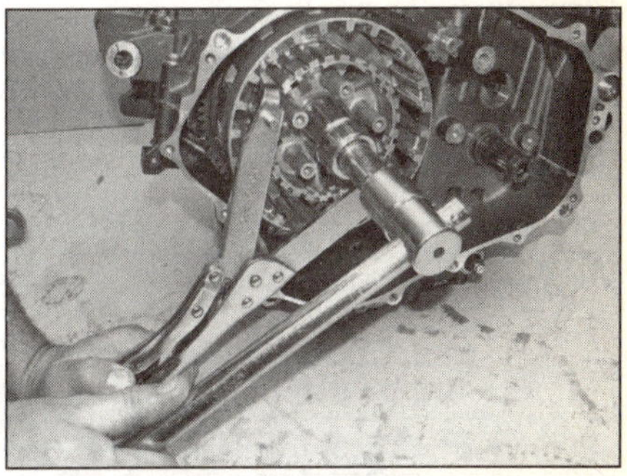

14.7b . . . then unscrew it as described and remove the washers

14.9 Ease the bearing and guide out from the middle of the housing then remove the housing

14.10 Ease the guide out from the middle of the sprocket then remove the sprocket and chain

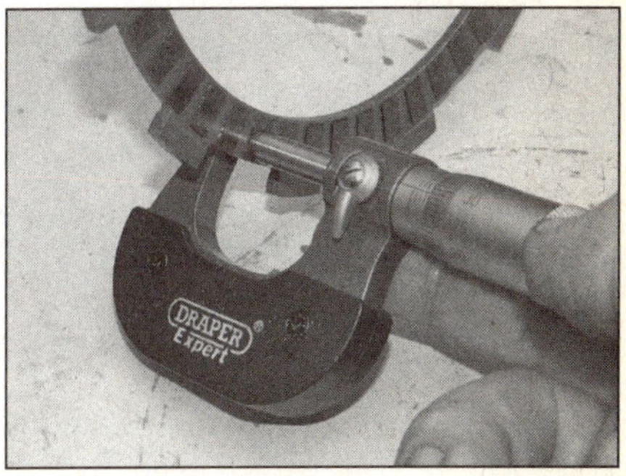

14.11 Measuring clutch friction plate thickness

14.12 Check the plain plates for warpage

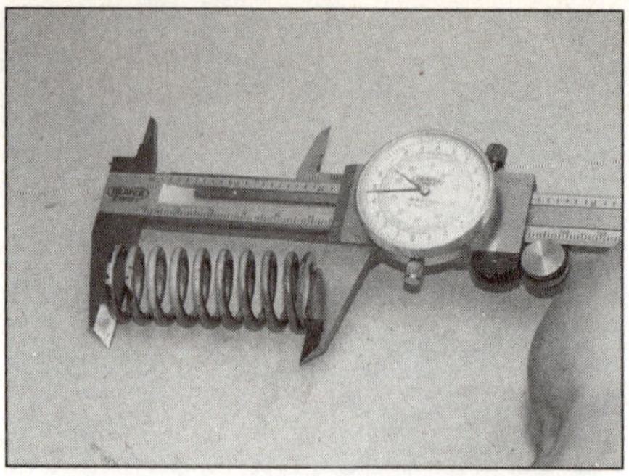
14.13 Measure the free length of the clutch springs and check them for bend

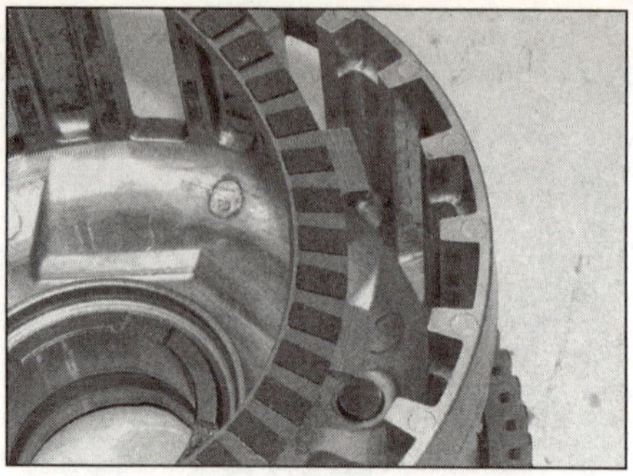
14.14a Check the friction plate tabs and housing slots . . .

warpage using a flat surface and feeler gauges **(see illustration)**. If any plate exceeds the maximum permissible amount of warpage, or shows signs of bluing, all plain plates must be replaced with a new set.

13 Measure the free length of each clutch spring using a Vernier caliper **(see illustration)**. Place each spring upright on a flat surface and check it for bend by placing a ruler against it, or alternatively lay it against a set square. If any spring is below the minimum free length specified or if the bend in any spring is excessive, replace all the springs as a set. Also check the anti-judder spring and spring seat for damage or distortion and replace them with new ones if necessary.

14 Inspect the friction plates and the clutch housing for burrs and indentations on the edges of the protruding tabs on the plates and/or the slots in the housing **(see illustration)**. Similarly check for wear between the inner teeth of the plain plates and the slots in the clutch centre **(see illustration)**. Wear of this nature will cause clutch drag and slow disengagement during gear changes as the plates will snag when the pressure plate is lifted. With care a small amount of wear can be corrected by dressing with a fine file, but if this is excessive the worn components should be replaced with new ones.

15 Inspect the needle roller bearing and the bearing surfaces on the clutch guide and in the clutch housing **(see illustrations)**. If there are any signs of wear, pitting or other damage the affected parts must be replaced with new ones. A new bearing must be selected according to marks on the primary driven gear and clutch guide. On RR-4 and RR-5 models the primary driven gear will be marked A or B, and the guide will either be marked or not on its outer (grooved) rim. On RR-6 and RR-7 models the primary driven gear will be marked with a white or black dot, and the guide will either be marked or not on its outer (grooved) rim. Refer to the table below for your model to select the correct bearing.

RR-4 and RR-5 models	**Guide with mark**	**Guide without mark**
Primary driven gear marked A	Bearing B	Bearing A
Primary driven gear marked B	Bearing C	Bearing B

RR-6 and RR-7 models	**Guide with mark**	**Guide without mark**
Primary driven gear marked white	Bearing B	Bearing A
Primary driven gear marked black	Bearing C	Bearing B

16 Using a Vernier caliper, measure the internal and external diameter of the clutch guide, the internal diameter of the clutch housing and the external diameter of the input shaft where the guide sits **(see illustrations 14.15a and b)**. Make sure you refer to the correct specifications for the guide on your model – on models with a marked guide the marking is on the outer (grooved) rim. Compare the measurements to the specifications at the beginning of the Chapter and replace any part that is worn beyond its service limit with a new one. Similarly measure the internal and external diameter of the oil pump drive sprocket guide, the internal diameter of the sprocket and the external diameter of the input shaft where the guide sits.

17 Check the pressure plate and its bearing for signs of wear or damage and roughness **(see illustration 14.28a)**. Check that the bearing outer race is a good fit in the centre, and that the inner race rotates freely without any rough spots.

18 Check the pushrod is not bent by rolling it on a flat surface. Check the lifter for signs of wear or damage. Replace any parts necessary with new ones. The hydraulic release mechanism is covered in Section 15.

19 Check the teeth of the primary driven gear on the back of the clutch housing and

14.14b . . . and the plain plate teeth and centre slots as described

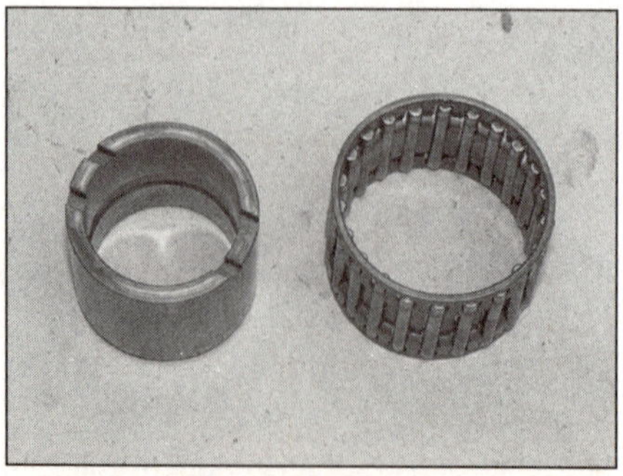
14.15a Check the bearing and the bearing surfaces on the guide . . .

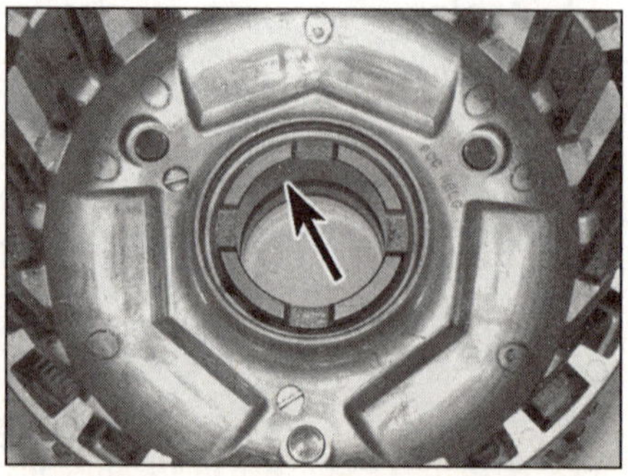
14.15b . . . in the housing (arrowed)

14.19 Primary drive gear (arrowed)

14.22a Slide the drive sprocket onto the guide . . .

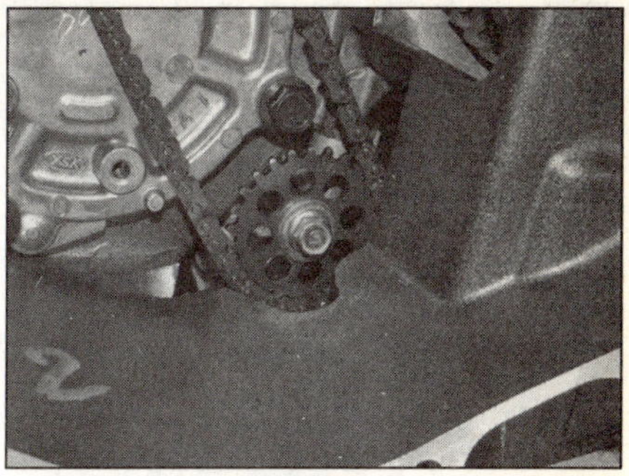

14.22b . . . and fit the chain over the driven sprocket

the corresponding teeth of the primary drive gear on the crankshaft **(see illustration)**. Replace the clutch housing and/or crankshaft with a new one if worn or chipped teeth are discovered.

Installation

20 Remove all traces of old sealant from the crankcase and clutch cover surfaces. Note that if removed the starter reduction gear must be installed now as it cannot be fitted once the clutch is in place – see Section 13, Step 12.

21 Smear the inside and outside of the oil pump drive sprocket guide and the inside of the sprocket with molybdenum disulphide oil (a 50/50 mixture of molybdenum disulphide grease and engine oil). Slip the chain around the sprocket.

22 Slide the sprocket onto the shaft, making sure the pins face out, and engage the lower end of the chain with the driven sprocket **(see illustrations)**. Slide the guide onto the input shaft with the grooved end outwards and into the drive sprocket **(see illustration 14.10)**.

23 Smear the inside and outside of the clutch guide, the inside of the clutch housing and the needle bearing with molybdenum disulphide oil (a 50/50 mixture of molybdenum disulphide grease and engine oil). Position the clutch housing on the shaft and hold it in position as the clutch guide and needle bearing are slipped onto the shaft and into the centre of the housing **(see illustrations)**. Make sure that the primary drive and driven gear teeth engage and the pins on the oil pump drive sprocket locate in the holes in the rear of the housing – turn the driven sprocket with your finger while pressing on the housing until the pins are felt to locate and the housing moves in a bit further, then double-check by making sure the sprocket can't turn independently of the housing.

14.23a Position the housing over the shaft, engaging the gears and locating it on the sprocket pins . . .

14.23b . . . then slide the guide and bearing in

24 Slide the thrust washer onto the shaft **(see illustration)**. Slide the clutch centre onto the shaft splines **(see illustration)**.

25 Fit the thrust washer and the spring washer with its OUT mark facing out **(see**

14.24a Fit the thrust washer . . .

14.24b . . . and the clutch centre

14.25a Fit the thrust washer and the spring washer, with the OUT mark facing out

14.25b Fit a new clutch nut . . .

14.25c . . . and tighten it to the specified torque

14.25d Stake the nut against the detent in the shaft end

14.26a Fit the anti-judder spring seat . . .

14.26b . . . and spring . . .

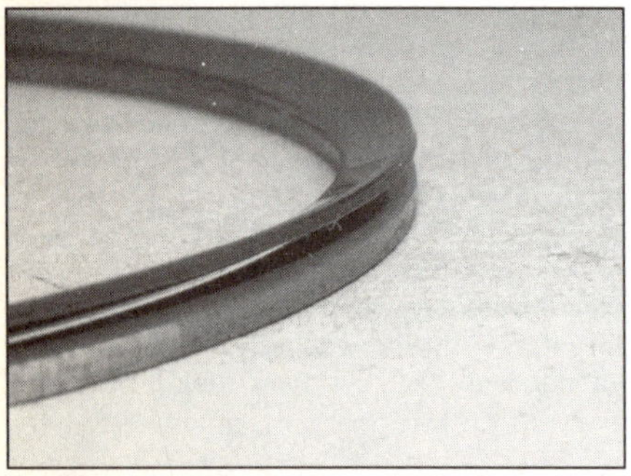

14.26c . . . so the spring's outer edge is raised off the seat

14.27a Identify the friction plate with the larger internal diameter and fit that first, locating it over the anti-judder assembly . . .

14.27b . . . then fit a plain plate

14.27c Locate the tabs on the outer friction plate into the shallow slots in the housing

illustration). Smear the ***new*** clutch nut threads and seating face with oil, then thread it onto the input shaft and, using the method employed on removal to lock the shaft (see Step 7), tighten the nut to the torque setting specified at the beginning of the Chapter **(see illustrations)**. Stake the rim of the nut into the indent on the end of the shaft **(see illustration)**.

26 Fit the anti-judder spring seat into the clutch centre, then fit the spring so that its outer edge is raised off the seat and facing outwards **(see illustrations)**.

27 Coat each clutch plate with engine oil prior to installation, then build up the plates as follows. Fit a friction plate with the larger internal diameter (Type A) over the spring and spring seat **(see illustration)**, then fit the plain plate with the different surface coating, then alternate standard friction plates (Type B) and plain plates until all except the other friction plate with the larger internal diameter (Type A) are installed, then fit that with its tabs fitting into the shallow slots in the housing **(see illustrations)**.

28 Lubricate the bearing in the pressure plate, the lifter and the pushrod with oil. Fit the lifter into the bearing **(see illustration)**. Slide the pushrod into the shaft if removed **(see illustration 14.5c)**. Fit the pressure plate onto the clutch, engaging the protrusions on its inner rim in the slots in the clutch centre **(see illustration)**. Install the springs and the

14.28a Fit the lifter into the bearing

14.28b Fit the pressure plate, making sure it locates in the slots . . .

14.28c . . . then install the springs and bolts and tighten them as described

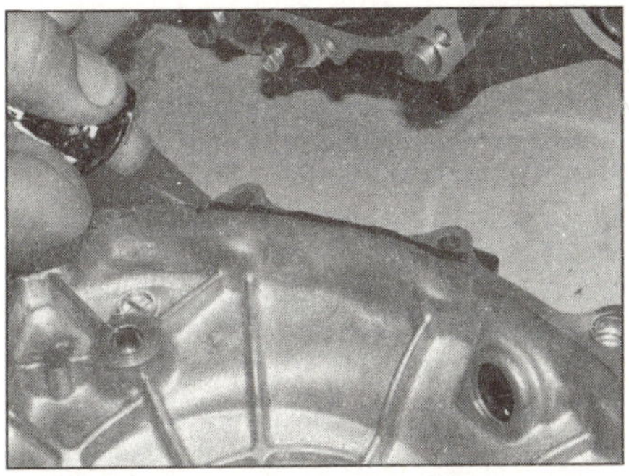
14.31a Apply the sealant as described

14.31b Make sure the dowels (arrowed) are fitted . . .

14.31c . . . and install the cover

bolts and tighten them evenly in a criss-cross sequence to the specified torque setting **(see illustration)**. Counter-hold the clutch housing to prevent it turning when tightening the spring bolts.

29 Lubricate the idle gear shaft with clean engine oil and fit it into the gear. Locate the idle gear, shouldered side inwards **(see illustration 13.2)**, between the reduction gear and the driven gear and slide the shaft into its bore in the crankcase **(see illustration 13.15)**.

30 Fit the wave washer and the thrust washer onto the end of the starter idle gear shaft **(see illustration 14.3b)**. Lubricate the reduction and idle gear shaft outer ends with oil.

31 Apply a smear of a suitable sealant (such as Three Bond 1207B or equivalent RTV sealant – ask your dealer) 10 to 15 mm each side of the crankcase joints on the mating surface with the clutch cover. Also apply the sealant to the entire mating surface on the clutch cover **(see illustration)**. Fit the two dowels into the crankcase if removed **(see illustration)**. Install the cover **(see illustration)**. Install all the bolts finger-tight, not forgetting the three wiring clamps on RR-4 and RR-5 models **(see illustration 4.13d)**, then tighten them evenly and a little at a time in a criss-cross pattern **(see illustration 14.3a)**.

32 Reconnect the crankshaft position sensor wiring connector, making sure the wiring is correctly routed **(see illustration 14.2)**. Fill the engine with the correct quantity and type of oil (see Chapter 1). Install the fairing panels (See Chapter 7).

15 Clutch release mechanism

Master cylinder

Note: *If the master cylinder is being overhauled (usually due to sticking or poor action, or fluid leaks) read through the entire procedure first and make sure that you have obtained all the new parts required, including some new DOT 4 brake/clutch fluid – a rebuild kit is available that includes the pushrod, boot, circlip, piston assembly (incorporating seal and cup) and spring, but note that the reservoir O-rings must be obtained separately.*

Removal

Warning: If the master cylinder is in need of an overhaul all old fluid should be flushed from the system (see Step 44). Overhaul must be done in a spotlessly clean work area to avoid contamination and possible failure of the hydraulic system components. Do not, under any circumstances, use petroleum-based solvents to clean the parts – use DOT 4 fluid or denatured alcohol. To prevent damage from spilled fluid, always cover paintwork when working on the system.

1 Disconnect the wiring connectors from the clutch switch **(see illustration)**.

2 If the master cylinder is just being displaced, follow this Step only: unscrew the master cylinder clamp bolts and remove the back of the clamp, noting how it fits, then position the master cylinder assembly clear of the handlebar **(see illustration)**. Ensure no strain is placed on the hydraulic hose. Keep the reservoir upright to prevent air entering the system.

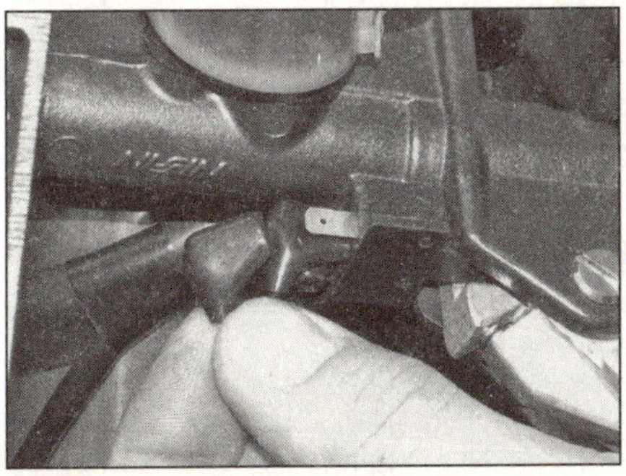
15.1 Pull the connectors off the switch terminals

15.2 Master cylinder clamp bolts (arrowed)

15.4 Free the clamp and slacken the cap

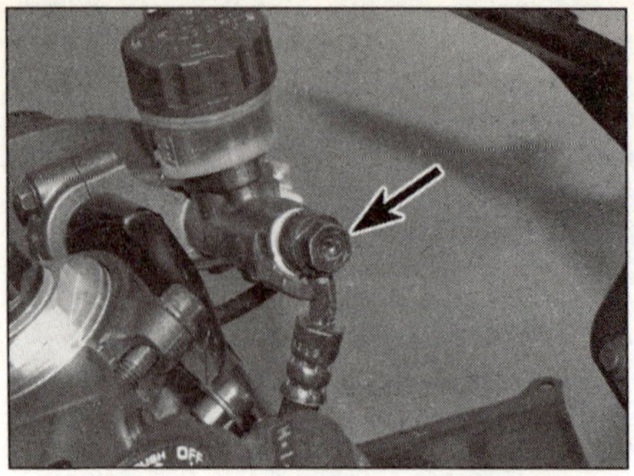

15.5 Clutch hose banjo bolt (arrowed)

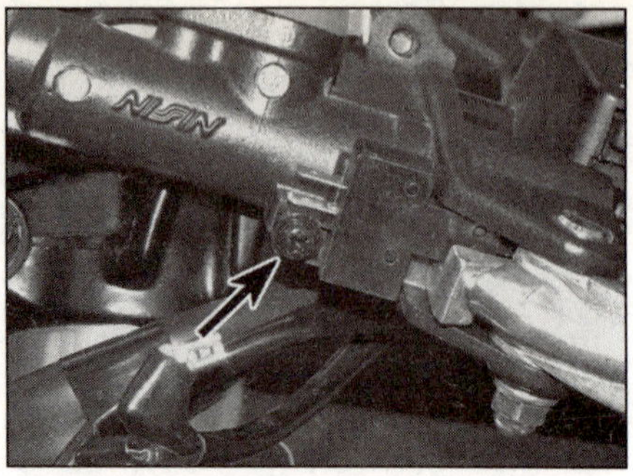

15.8 Clutch switch screw (arrowed)

3 Remove the clutch lever (see Chapter 5).

4 Undo the reservoir cap clamp screw then slacken the reservoir cap **(see illustration)**.

5 Unscrew the clutch hose banjo bolt and detach the banjo union, noting its alignment with the master cylinder **(see illustration)**. Use plastic foodwrap to seal the banjo union and secure the hose in an upright position to minimise fluid loss. Discard the sealing washers as new ones must be fitted on reassembly.

6 Unscrew the master cylinder clamp bolts and remove the back of the clamp, noting how it fits, then lift the master cylinder and reservoir away from the handlebar **(see illustration 15.2)**.

7 Remove the reservoir cap, diaphragm plate and diaphragm. Drain the brake fluid from the master cylinder and reservoir into a suitable container. Wipe any remaining fluid out of the reservoir with a clean rag.

8 If required, undo the screw securing the clutch switch and remove the switch **(see illustration)**.

Overhaul

9 If required undo the screw inside the reservoir and remove the reservoir and its O-rings **(see illustration)**. Discard the O-rings as new ones must be used.

10 Carefully remove the pushrod and rubber boot from the master cylinder. Depress the piston and use circlip pliers to remove the circlip, then slide out the piston assembly and the spring, noting how they fit. If they are difficult to remove, apply low pressure compressed air to the fluid outlet. Lay the parts out in the proper order to prevent confusion during reassembly.

11 Clean all parts with clean brake/clutch fluid. If compressed air is available, blow it through the fluid galleries to ensure they are clear (make sure the air is filtered and unlubricated).

Caution: Do not, under any circumstances, use a petroleum-based solvent to clean brake parts.

12 Check the master cylinder bore for corrosion, scratches, nicks and score marks. If the necessary measuring equipment is available, compare the dimensions of the piston and bore to those given in the Specifications at the beginning of this Chapter. If damage or wear is evident, the master cylinder must be replaced with a new one. If the master cylinder is in poor condition, then the release cylinder should be checked as well.

13 The pushrod, dust boot, circlip, piston components and spring are all included in the master cylinder rebuild kit. Use all of the new parts, regardless of the apparent condition of the old ones. Lubricate the master cylinder bore with new brake fluid.

14 Smear the cup and seal with new brake fluid. Fit them into their grooves in the piston so their flared ends will fit into the master cylinder first.

15 Fit the spring wide end first into the master cylinder.

16 Lubricate the piston with clean brake fluid and slide it into the master cylinder and up against the spring. Make sure the lips on the cup and seal do not turn inside out. Push the piston in to compress the spring and install the new circlip. Smear the pushrod and rubber boot with silicone grease. Fit the pushrod into the rubber boot so the lips locate in the groove and press the boot into place in the end of the cylinder.

17 If removed fit new reservoir O-rings smeared with fluid onto the master cylinder then locate the reservoir. Apply a thread locking compound to the screw and tighten it lightly. Inspect the reservoir diaphragm and fit a new one if it is damaged or deteriorated.

Installation

18 If removed, fit the clutch switch onto the master cylinder **(see illustration 15.8)**.

19 Attach the master cylinder to the handlebar, aligning the clamp joint with the punch mark on the top of the handlebar, then fit the back of the clamp with its UP mark facing up **(see**

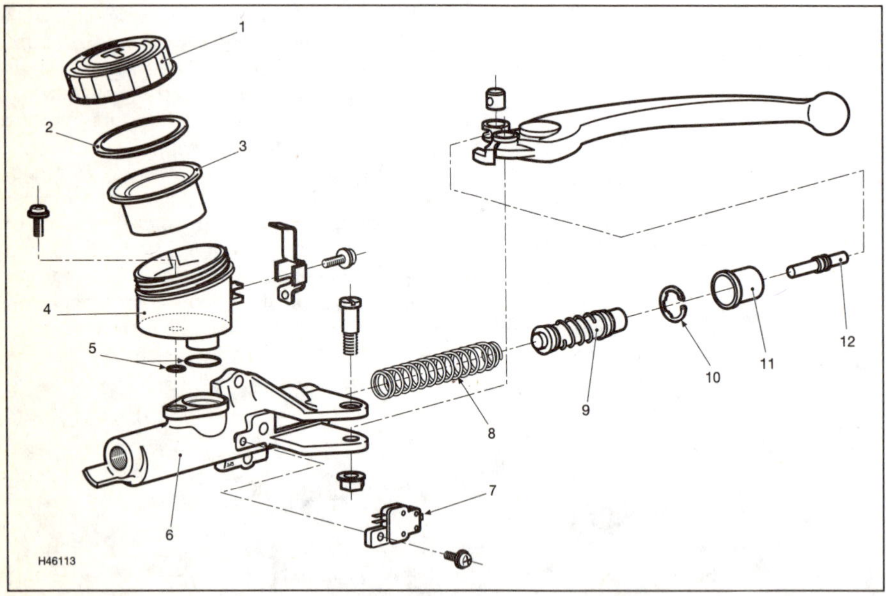

15.9 Clutch master cylinder assembly

1 Reservoir cap
2 Diaphragm plate
3 Diaphragm
4 Reservoir
5 O-rings
6 Master cylinder
7 Brake light switch
8 Spring
9 Piston (incorporating seal and cup)
10 Circlip
11 Rubber boot
12 Pushrod

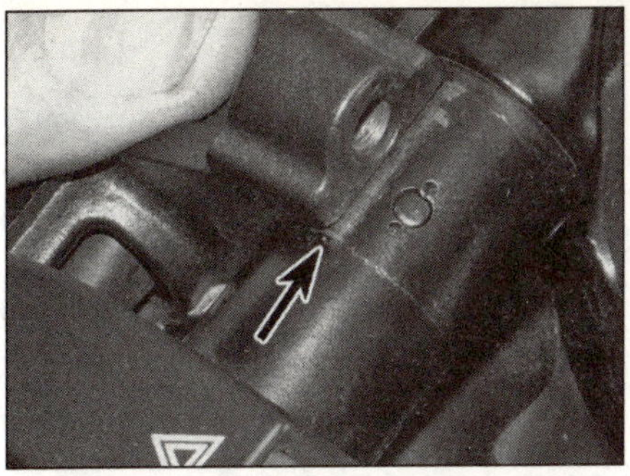

15.19a Align the mating surface with the punch mark (arrowed) . . .

15.19b . . . and fit the clamp with the UP mark the correct way

15.26 Clutch hose banjo bolt (arrowed)

15.27a Release cylinder bolts (arrowed)

15.27b Withdraw the pushrod if required

15.27c Secure the piston with a cable tie if the cylinder is not being overhauled

illustrations). Tighten the upper bolt to the torque setting specified at the beginning of this Chapter, followed by the lower bolt.

20 Connect the clutch hose to the master cylinder, using new sealing washers on each side of the banjo fitting. Align the hose as noted on removal **(see illustration 15.5)**. Tighten the banjo bolt to the torque setting specified at the beginning of this Chapter.

21 Install the clutch lever (see Chapter 5).

22 Connect the clutch switch wiring **(see illustration 5.1)**.

23 Fill the fluid reservoir with new DOT 4 fluid (see *Pre-ride checks*). Refer to Step 44 and bleed the air from the system.

24 Check the operation of the clutch before riding the motorcycle.

Release cylinder

Caution: Disassembly, overhaul and reassembly of the slave cylinder must be done in a spotlessly clean work area to avoid contamination and possible failure of the hydraulic system components.

Removal

25 To prevent the possibility of damage from spilled fluid, cover the lower fairing and left-hand fairing side panel in rag, or remove them (see Chapter 7).

26 If required unscrew the clutch hose banjo bolt and detach the banjo union, noting its alignment with the release cylinder **(see illustration)**. Seal the banjo union using plastic foodwrap and secure the hose in an upright position to minimise fluid loss. Discard the sealing washers as new ones must be fitted on reassembly.

27 Unscrew the release cylinder bolts and remove the cylinder from the sprocket cover **(see illustration)**. Remove the dowels if they are loose. Remove the gasket and discard it as a new one must be used. If required withdraw the pushrod **(see illustration)**. Fit a cable tie around the release cylinder as shown to prevent the piston creeping out if required **(see illustration)**.

Overhaul

28 Clean the exterior of the cylinder with denatured alcohol or brake system cleaner.

29 Withdraw the piston from cylinder **(see illustration)**. If the piston cannot be withdrawn by hand, it can be pushed out by applying compressed air to the clutch hose union hole. Only low pressure should be required, such as is generated by a foot pump. Wrap the release cylinder in a wad of rag to prevent the piston being forcibly expelled.

30 Remove the spring, noting how it fits.

31 Carefully remove the fluid seals and pushrod seal from the piston, noting which way round the pushrod seal fits. Discard the fluid seals as new ones must be used. Replace the pushrod seal with a new one if necessary.

32 Clean the piston and cylinder with clean brake fluid or denatured alcohol. If compressed air is available, use it to dry the

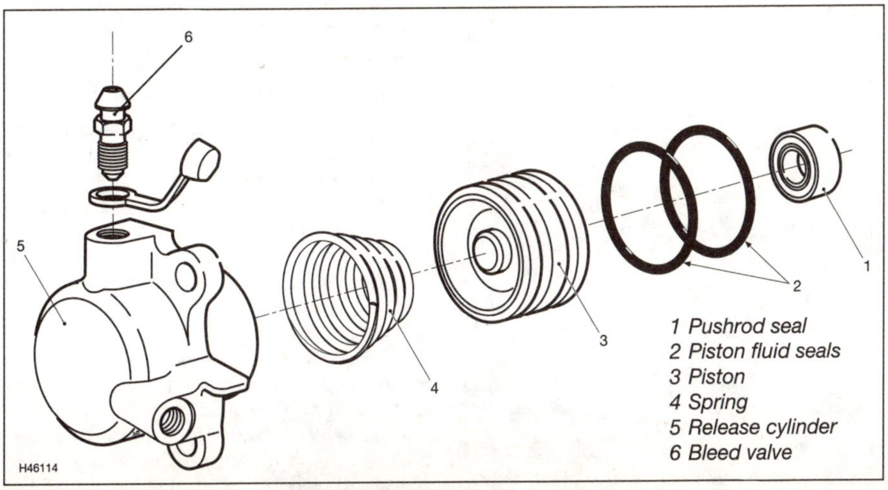

15.29 Release cylinder assembly

15.39 Fit a new gasket onto the dowels (arrowed)

15.40a Smear some silicone grease onto the pushrod and its seal lips (arrowed) . . .

15.40b . . . then fit the release cylinder

parts thoroughly (make sure it's filtered and unlubricated).

Caution: Do not, under any circumstances, use a petroleum-based solvent to clean master cylinder parts.

33 Inspect the cylinder bore and piston for signs of corrosion, nicks and burrs and loss of plating. If surface defects are present, the cylinder assembly must be replaced with a new one. If it is in bad shape the master cylinder should also be checked. No specifications are given to check piston and bore wear.

34 Lubricate the new piston fluid seals with silicone grease, and smear some on the piston between the seal grooves. Fit the seals into the grooves.

35 Fit the new pushrod seal to the piston and smear it with grease.

36 Fit the narrow end of the spring over the boss on the inner end of the piston.

37 Lubricate the cylinder with clean fluid and fit the spring and piston into the bore. Make sure the spring remains correctly positioned and take great care to ensure the fluid seals are not dislodged or damaged as they enter the bore. Using your thumbs, push the piston all the way in, making sure it enters the bore squarely.

Installation

38 Remove all traces of gasket from the cylinder and cover sealing surfaces.

39 Ensure the locating dowels are fitted and fit a new gasket onto the sprocket cover **(see illustrations)**. If removed make sure the pushrod is straight and clean and smear it with oil, then slide it into place **(see illustration 15.27b)**.

40 Apply a smear of silicone grease to the pushrod end and the seal lips **(see illustration)**. Fit the release cylinder, aligning it with the pushrod and locating dowels **(see illustration)**. Install the bolts and tighten them.

41 Position a new sealing washer on each side of the clutch hose end fitting then connect the hose to the cylinder. Ensure it is correctly positioned against its stop then tighten the banjo bolt to the specified torque **(see illustration 15.26)**.

42 Fill the master cylinder to the correct level with new DOT4 hydraulic fluid (see *Pre-ride checks*) and bleed the hydraulic system (see Step 44).

43 Check for leaks and thoroughly test the operation of the clutch before installing the fairing panels.

Clutch release mechanism bleeding

44 Bleeding the clutch is simply the process of removing air from the clutch fluid reservoir, the hose and the release cylinder. Bleeding is necessary whenever an hydraulic connection is loosened, after a component or hose is replaced with a new one, or when the release cylinder is overhauled. Leaks in the system may also allow air to enter, but leaking clutch fluid will reveal their presence and warn you of the need for repair.

45 To bleed the clutch, you will need some new DOT 4 brake/clutch fluid, a length of clear vinyl or plastic hose, a small container partially filled with clutch fluid, some rags, a spanner to fit the release cylinder bleed valve.

46 Cover the lower fairing panel with rag to prevent damage in the event that clutch fluid is spilled.

47 Refer to *Pre-ride checks* and remove the reservoir cap, diaphragm plate and diaphragm and slowly pump the clutch lever a few times, until no air bubbles can be seen floating up from the holes in the bottom of the reservoir. This bleeds the air from the master cylinder end of the line. Temporarily refit the reservoir cap.

48 Pull the dust cap off the bleed valve **(see illustration)**. Attach one end of the clear vinyl or plastic hose to the bleed valve and submerge the other end in the clean clutch fluid in the container. **Note:** *To avoid damaging the bleed valve during the procedure, loosen it and then tighten it temporarily with a ring spanner before attaching the hose. With the hose attached, the valve can then be opened and closed either with an open-ended spanner, or by leaving the ring spanner located on the valve and fitting the hose above it.*

15.48 Clutch release cylinder bleed valve (arrowed)

49 Check the fluid level in the reservoir. Do not allow the fluid level to drop below the lower mark during the procedure.

50 Carefully pump the clutch lever three or four times and hold it in while opening the bleed valve. When the valve is opened, clutch fluid will flow out of the release cylinder into the clear tubing, and the lever will move toward the handlebar. If there is air in the system there will be air bubbles in the clutch fluid coming out of the release cylinder.

51 Tighten the bleed valve, then release the clutch lever gradually. Top-up the reservoir and repeat the process until no air bubbles are visible in the clutch fluid leaving the release cylinder and the lever action no longer feels spongy. On completion, disconnect the bleeding equipment and install the dust cap over the bleed valve.

52 Check the fluid level in the reservoir, then install the diaphragm, diaphragm plate and cap (see *Pre-ride checks*). Wipe up any spilled clutch fluid. Check the entire system for fluid leaks.

Changing the clutch fluid

53 Changing the clutch fluid is a similar process to bleeding the clutch and requires the same materials plus a suitable tool for siphoning the fluid out of the reservoir such as a syringe, though if one isn't available it is no problem to displace the resevoir and tip the fluid out. Also ensure that the container is large enough to take all the old fluid when it is flushed out of the system.

54 Follow Steps 46 and 48, then remove the reservoir cap, diaphragm plate and diaphragm and siphon the old fluid out of the reservoir. Fill the reservoir with new clutch fluid, then carefully pump the clutch lever three or four times and hold it in while opening the release cylinder bleed valve. When the valve is opened, clutch fluid will flow out of the release cylinder into the clear tubing.

55 Tighten the bleed valve, then release the clutch lever gradually. Keep the reservoir topped-up with new fluid to above the LOWER level at all times or air may enter the system and greatly increase the length of the task. Repeat the process until new fluid can be seen emerging from the release cylinder bleed valve.

> **HAYNES HiNT** ***Old clutch fluid is invariably darker in colour than new fluid, making it easy to see when all old fluid has been expelled from the system.***

56 Disconnect the hose, then make sure the bleed valve is tightened to the specified torque setting and install the dust cap.

57 Top-up the reservoir, then install the diaphragm, diaphragm plate and cap (see *Pre-ride checks*). Wipe up any spilled clutch fluid. Check the entire system for fluid leaks.

16 Gearchange mechanism

Note: *The gearchange mechanism can be removed with the engine in the frame. If the engine has been removed, ignore the steps which don't apply.*

Removal

1 Make sure the transmission is in neutral. Remove the clutch release cylinder as described in the previous section and the gearchange linkage and front sprocket cover (see Chapter 6). Fully slacken the drive chain to access the gearchange mechanism cover bottom bolt (see Chapter 1). If necessary remove the front sprocket (see Chapter 6).

2 Unscrew the gearchange mechanism cover bolts and remove the cover **(see illustration)**. Remove the dowels if they are loose. Discard the gasket as a new one must be used.

3 Note how the gearchange shaft centralising spring ends fit on each side of the locating pin in the casing, and how the pawls on the selector arm locate onto the pins on the end

16.2 Unscrew the bolts (arrowed) and remove the cover

of the selector drum cam. Note the washer on the gearchange shaft and remove it if required – there is also one on the inner end of the shaft.

4 Grasp the end of the shaft and withdraw the shaft/arm assembly **(see illustration)**. Retrieve the inner washer from the crankcase if it didn't come with the shaft.

5 To access and remove the gearchange mechanism stopper arm, which is on the right-hand end of the selector drum, remove the clutch (see Section 14) – there is no need to remove the oil pump drive sprocket and chain. Block the holes into the sump with clean rag to prevent anything falling in. Note how the stopper arm spring ends locate and how the roller on the arm locates in the neutral detent on the selector drum cam, then unscrew the stopper arm bolt and remove the arm, the

16.4 Withdraw the shaft/arm assembly, noting how it fits

washer and the spring, noting how they fit **(see illustration)**.

Inspection

6 Check the selector arm for cracks, distortion and wear of its pawls, and check for any corresponding wear on the pins on the selector drum end **(see illustrations)**. Inspect the shaft centralising spring for fatigue, wear or damage **(see illustration)**. To replace the shaft spring, slide the inner washer off the shaft, then remove the circlip and slide the spring off the shaft, noting how its ends locate. Fit the new spring, locating the ends on each side of the tab, and secure it with the circlip, making sure it locates in its groove. Slide the washer against the circlip. Also check that the centralising spring locating pin in the crankcase is securely tightened **(see illustration)**. If it is loose, remove it and apply

16.5 Note how the spring ends locate, and how the roller sits in the neutral detent, then unscrew the bolt (arrowed) and remove the arm

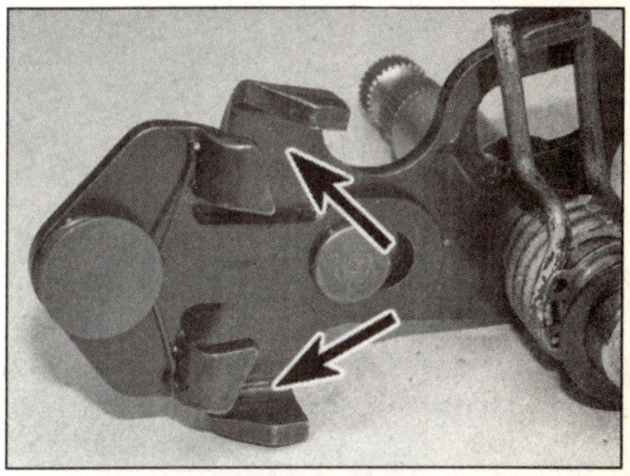

16.6a Check the selector arm pawls (arrowed) . . .

16.6b . . . and the pins on the end of the drum

16.6c Centralising spring (A), inner washer (B), circlip (C)

16.6d Make sure the locating pin (arrowed) is tight

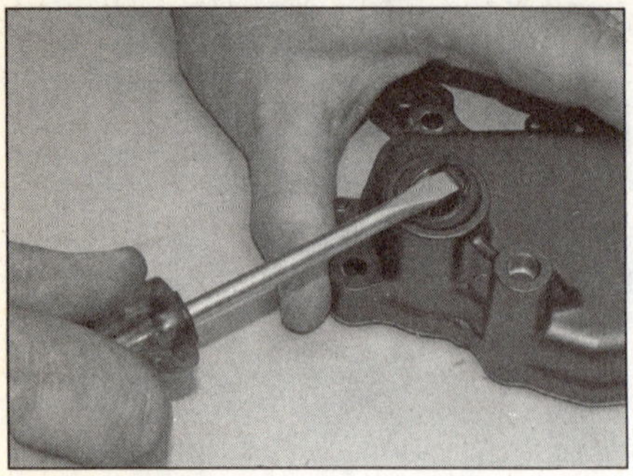

16.8a Lever out the seal

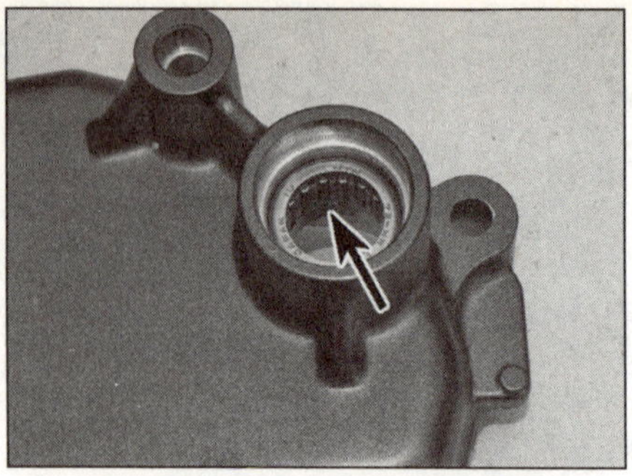

16.8b Check the bearing (arrowed)

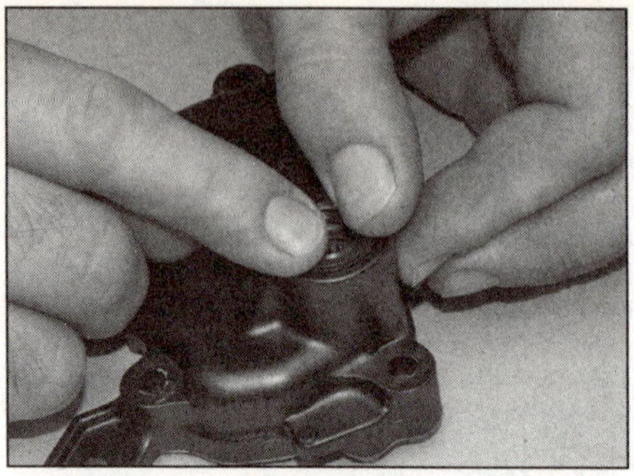

16.8c Press the new seal into its housing

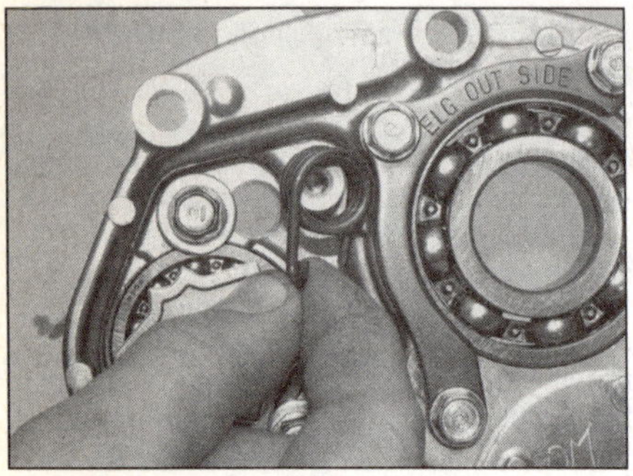

16.9a Fit the spring onto its post

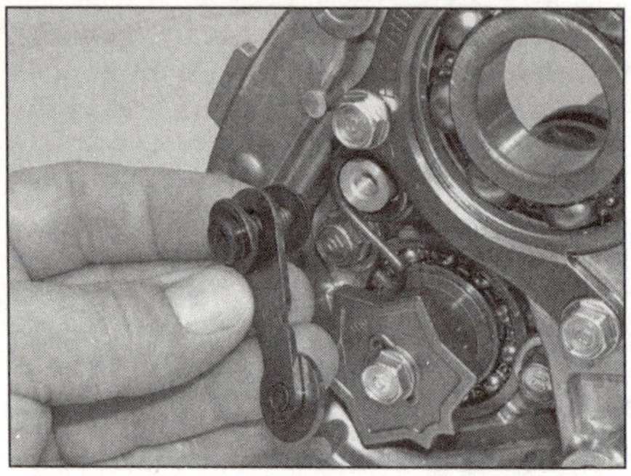

16.9b Fit the bolt through the arm and fit the washer onto the bolt – note that the arm is installed with the roller on the inside

a non-permanent thread locking compound to its threads, then tighten it.

7 Check the stopper arm roller and the detents in the selector drum cam for any wear or damage, and make sure the roller turns freely. Inspect the stopper arm return spring for fatigue, wear or damage **(see illustration 16.5)**. If required, remove the selector drum cam by counter-holding it and unscrewing the bolt in its centre – take care how you hold it as its rim must not be marked **(see illustration 20.5)**. Note the locating pins in the end of the drum and remove them for safekeeping if required **(see illustration 20.14a)**. Remove the collar if required **(see illustration 20.6a)**. On installation fit the collar with its shouldered end innermost. Fit the cam locating pins into their holes then locate the cam on the end of the drum with the OUT mark facing out – it can only fit one way **(see illustrations 20.14a and b)**. Apply a suitable non-permanent thread locking compound to the cam bolt and tighten it to the torque setting specified at the beginning of the Chapter, counter-holding the drum as before **(see illustration 20.14c)**.

8 Check the gearchange shaft for straightness and damage to the splines. If the shaft is bent you can attempt to straighten it, but if the splines are damaged the shaft must be replaced with a new one. Also check the condition of the shaft oil seal in the cover. If it is damaged, deteriorated or shows signs of leakage it must be replaced with a new one – lever out the old seal with a seal hook or screwdriver **(see illustration)**. With the seal removed, check the condition of the needle bearing, and replace that with a new one as well if necessary **(see illustration)**. Fit the new bearing and press or drive the new seal squarely into place using your fingers, a seal driver or suitable socket **(see illustration)**.

Installation

9 If removed, locate the stopper arm return spring onto its post, then fit the bolt through the stopper arm and fit the washer **(see illustrations)**. Apply a suitable non-permanent thread locking compound to the bolt. Install the arm, locating the roller onto the neutral detent on the selector drum and making sure the spring ends are positioned correctly. Tighten the bolt to the torque setting specified at the beginning of the Chapter. Check that the arm and spring ends are correctly positioned **(see illustration 16.5)**. Install the clutch (see Section 14).

10 Check that the shaft centralising spring is properly positioned and slide the washers onto each end of the shaft if removed **(see illustration)**. Slide the shaft into place **(see illustration 16.4)**, locating the selector arm pawls onto the pins on the selector drum and the centralising spring ends onto each side of the locating pin in the crankcase **(see illustration)**.

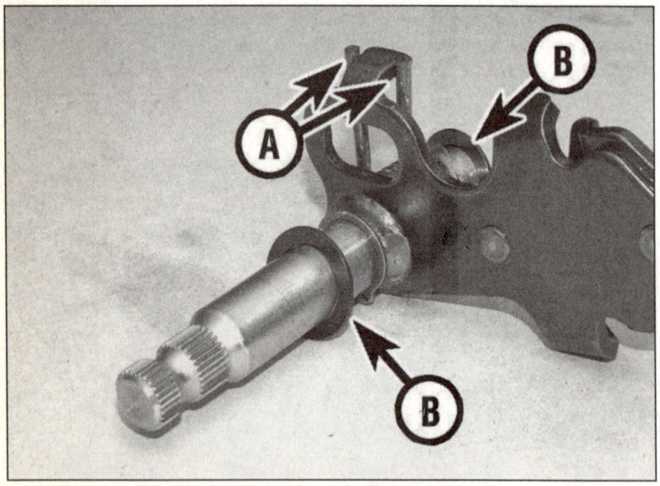

16.10a Make sure the spring ends (A) and washers (B) are correctly fitted

16.10b Make sure everything is correctly positioned

11 Remove the rag that was blocking the sump. Apply some grease to the lips of the gearchange shaft oil seal in the cover, and wrap a single layer of insulating tape around the splines on the shaft to protect the seal. Fit the dowels and a new gasket onto the cover **(see illustration)**. Apply a smear of a suitable sealant (such as Three Bond 1207B or equivalent RTV sealant – ask your dealer) 10 to 15 mm each side of the crankcase joints on the mating surface with the cover, then fit the cover over the shaft **(see illustrations)**. Apply a thread locking compound to the bottom cover bolt **(see illustration)**. Install and tighten the bolts. Remove the insulating tape from around the gearchange shaft splines.

12 Install the front sprocket and/or cover as required, followed by the gearchange linkage (see Chapter 6), and adjust the drive chain (see Chapter 1). Install the clutch release cylinder.

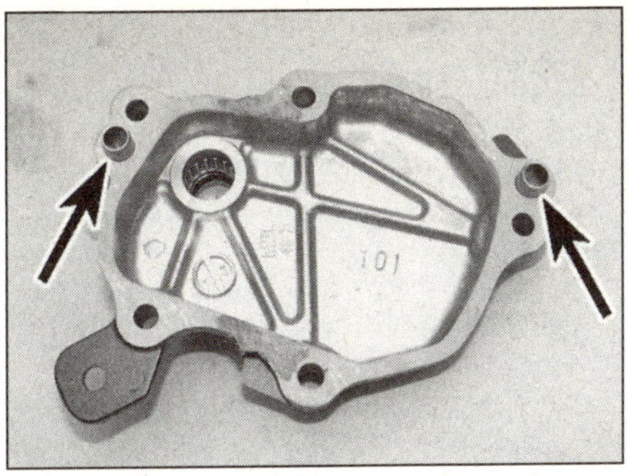

16.11a Fit a new gasket onto the dowels (arrowed) . . .

16.11b . . . and apply some sealant to the crankcase joints . . .

16.11c . . . then install the cover

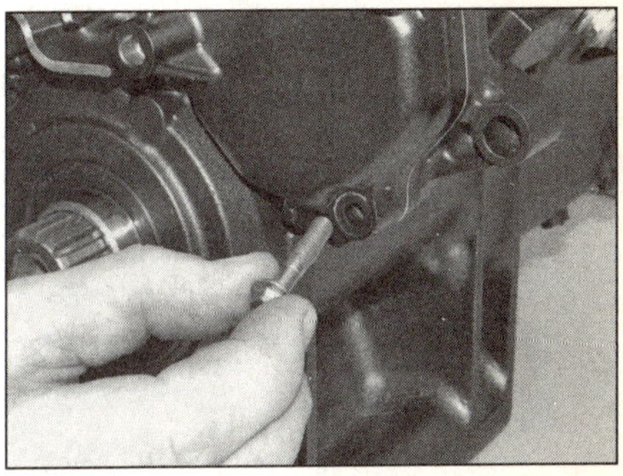

16.11d Apply a thread lock to the bottom bolt

17 Transmission cassette removal and installation

Note: *The transmission cassette can be removed with the engine in the frame.*

Removal

1 Remove the clutch and the oil pump drive sprocket and chain (see Section 14). Remove the front sprocket (see Chapter 6) and the gearchange mechanism (see Section 16).

2 Stuff some rag into the opening to the sump. Unscrew the cassette plate bolts **(see illustration)**. Grasp the transmission input shaft and pull the cassette out of the crankcase, pushing or tapping the end of the output shaft with a soft-faced hammer to help ease it out if necessary **(see illustration)**. Note that there is an oil jet in the crankcase which may come away with the cover and drop free (hence the rag) – if not retrieve the jet from its bore **(see illustration)**. Remove the three dowels from either the cassette plate or the crankcase if they are loose **(see illustration 17.6)**.

3 Support the plate on blocks of wood with the transmission shafts pointing up. If required remove the selector forks, the transmission shafts and the selector drum (see Sections 18 and 20). The transmission shaft and selector drum bearings are covered in those Sections. Note that the transmission output shaft oil seal should be replaced with a new one if the cassette is removed, and the bearing must be removed first as the seal is shouldered on its inner side – see Section 18.

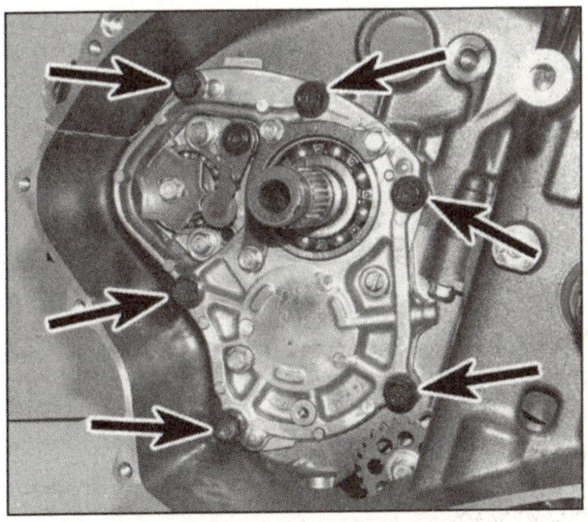

17.2a Unscrew the bolts (arrowed) . . .

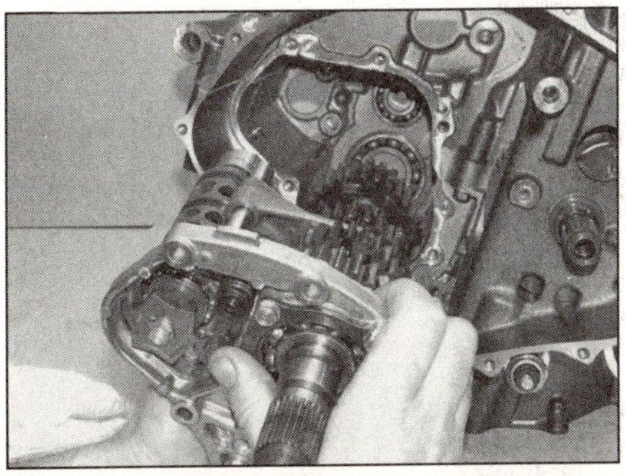

17.2b . . . and draw the cassette out of the crankcase

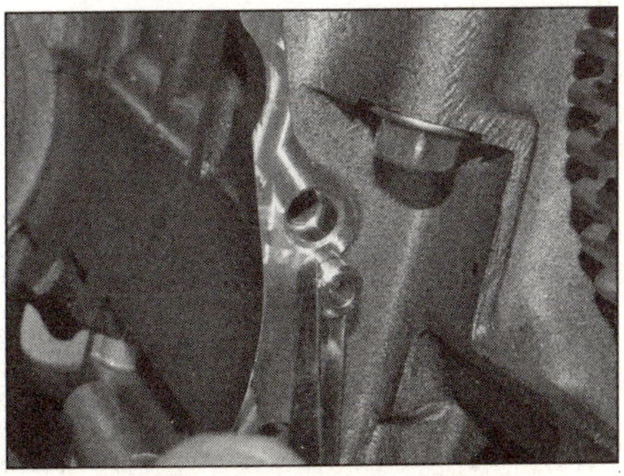

17.2c Remove the oil jet

Installation

4 Support the plate on blocks of wood with the transmission shafts pointing up. Make sure both transmission shafts are correctly seated and their related pinions and the selector forks are all correctly engaged.

5 Position the gears in the neutral position and check the shafts are free to rotate easily and independently (i.e. the input shaft can turn whilst the output shaft is held stationary).

6 Clean the oil jet in solvent and blow it through with compressed air if available, then fit it into its bore in the crankcase with its smaller diameter end facing in **(see illustration 17.2c)**. Fit the three dowels into the cassette plate if removed **(see illustration)**.

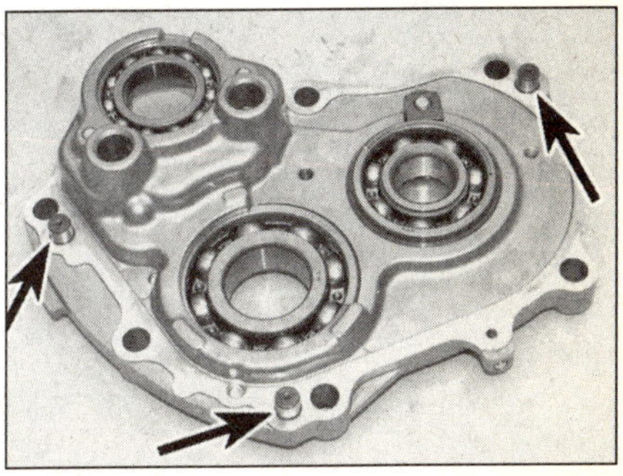

17.6 Make sure the dowels (arrowed) are fitted

17.8 Make sure the shaft ends and dowels all locate correctly

7 Lubricate the transmission shafts, gears, selector drum tracks, selector forks and shafts with oil. Smear some grease on the new output shaft oil seal lips.

8 Fit the transmission assembly into the crankcase, making sure the inner ends of the shafts and drum locate correctly in their bores or bearings **(see illustration 17.2b)**. Push the cassette plate fully against the crankcase making sure it locates onto the dowels **(see illustration)**.

9 Fit the bolts and tighten them evenly and a little at a time in a criss-cross pattern to the torque setting specified at the beginning of the Chapter **(see illustration 17.2a)**.

10 Install the oil pump drive sprocket and chain and the clutch (see Section 14). Install the gearchange mechanism (see Section 16) and the front sprocket (see Chapter 6).

18 Transmission shaft and bearing removal and installation

Shaft removal

1 Remove the transmission cassette (see Section 17).

2 Support the plate on blocks of wood with the transmission shafts pointing up.

3 Remove the selector forks and shafts (Section 20, Step 3).

4 Grasp both transmission shafts together, in particular holding the 1st gear pinion on the plate end of the output shaft as it can drop off, and lift them out of the plate, noting that there is a thrust washer on the end of the output shaft will is also likely to drop off **(see illustration)**.

5 If necessary, the transmission shafts can be disassembled and inspected for wear or damage (see Section 19).

Bearing removal and installation

6 After removing the shafts, refer to Tools and Workshop Tips (Section 5) in the Reference Section and check the transmission shaft bearings in the crankcase and plate. Replace the bearings with new ones if necessary.

7 To remove the input shaft bearing in the plate unscrew the three bolts and remove the retainer **(see illustration)**. The output shaft bearing is held on the inside of the plate by a retainer secured by a bolt from the outside **(see illustration)**. The output shaft bearing in the crankcase is held by a retainer secured by a bolt on the inside **(see illustration)**. The

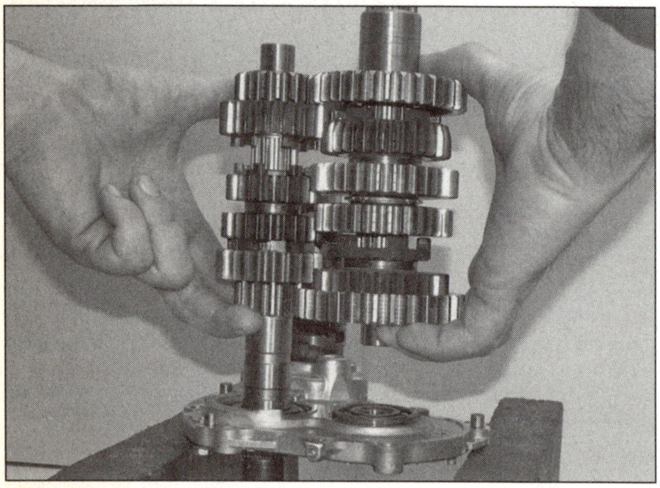

18.4 Grasp both shafts, and holding the bottom gear and thrust washer on the end of the output shaft, and lift them out of the plate

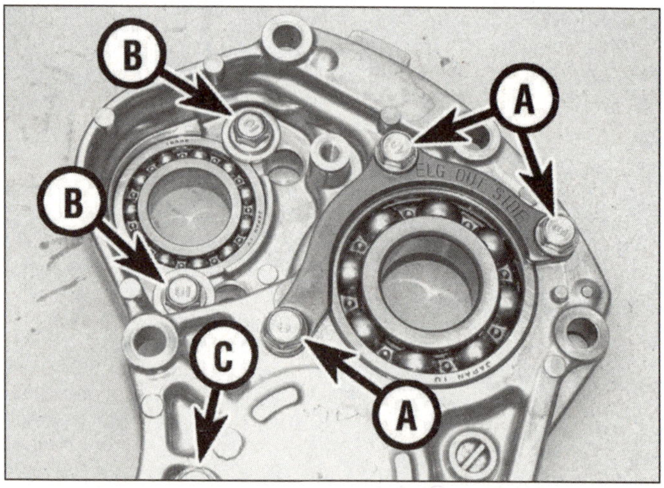

18.7a Input shaft bearing retainer bolts (A), output shaft bearing retainer bolt (C), selector drum bearing retainer bolts (B) . . .

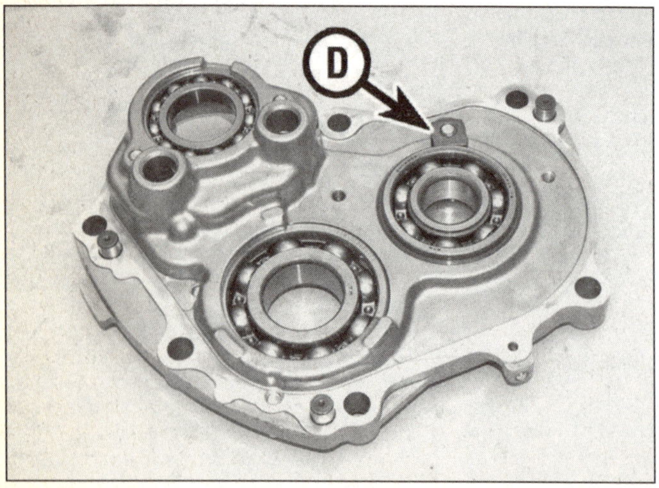

18.7b . . . output shaft bearing retainer (D)

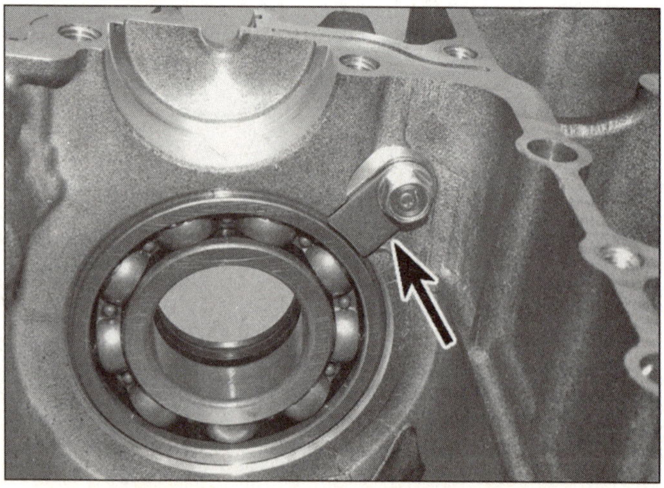

18.7c Output shaft crankcase bearing retainer (arrowed)

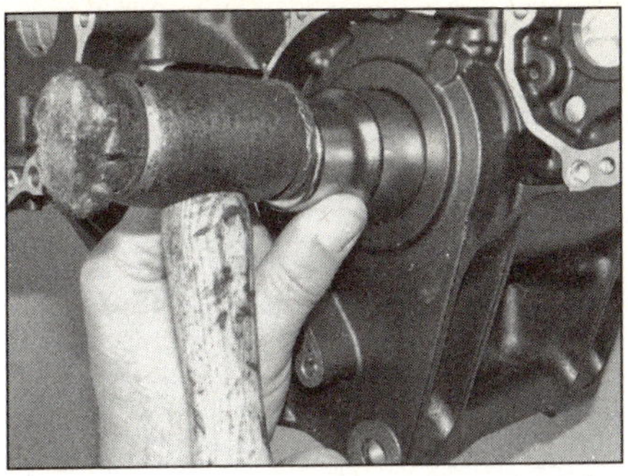

18.8a Drive the seal and bearing out at the same time

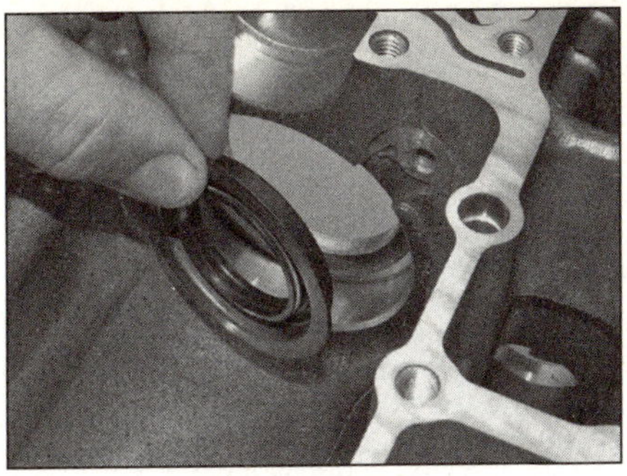

18.8b Make sure the seals . . .

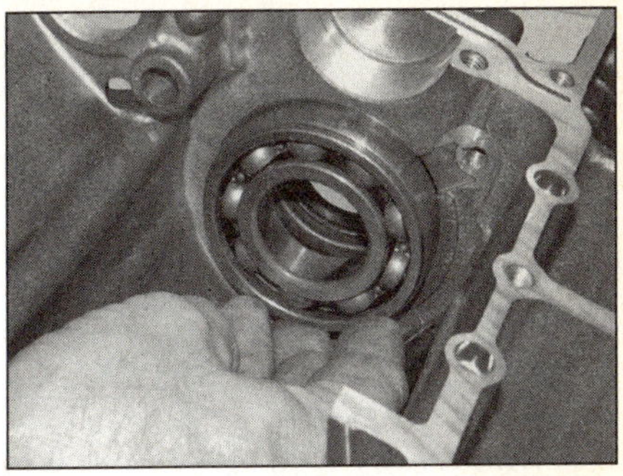

18.8c . . . are fitted the correct way round

input shaft bearing in the crankcase can only be removed after the crankcase has been split into halves as it has a locating pin which prevents it being driven out **(see illustration 23.11c)**.

8 Remove the bearings using a puller, or by driving them out with a socket, using heat to free them if necessary – note that you can drive the output shaft bearing and oil seal out at the same time using a socket on the seal **(see illustration)**. Alternatively the output shaft oil seal can be driven out from the crankcase after removing the bearing. Fit the new seal from the inside and make sure its shoulder seats correctly in the housing **(see illustrations)**. Fit the output shaft crankcase bearing with its lipped rim on the inside so that its retainer seats on the lip **(see illustration)**. Fit the output shaft cassette plate bearing with its lipped rim on the inside of the plate so that its retainer seats on the lip.

9 Apply thread lock to the retainer bolts and tighten them to the torque setting specified at the beginning of the Chapter, and fit the input shaft retainer with the marked side facing out, and the output shaft retainers with the shaped end fitting onto the lipped bearing outer race.

Shaft installation

10 Position both transmission shafts together so their related pinions engage.

11 Make sure the thrust washer is on the right-hand end of the output shaft **(see illustration 19.36c)**. Grasp the shafts as shown, using your finger to keep the thrust washer and 1st gear pinion in place, and locate them in the cassette plate, making sure they seat correctly **(see illustration)**.

18.8d The application of heat to the bearing housing makes them easier to remove and install

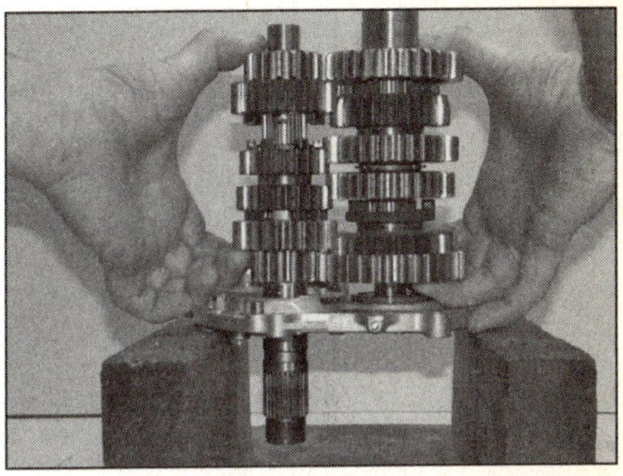

18.11 Slide the shafts into the cassette making sure the washer stays on the end of the output shaft

12 Make sure both transmission shafts are correctly seated and their related pinions are correctly engaged.

13 Install the selector forks and shafts (see Section 20, Steps 17 and 18).

14 Install the transmission cassette (see Section 17).

19 Transmission shaft overhaul

1 Remove the transmission shafts from the plate (see Section 18). Always disassemble the transmission shafts separately to avoid mixing up the components.

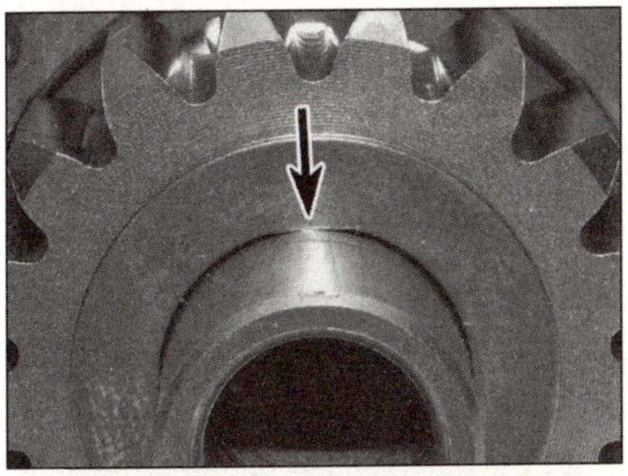

19.2a The washer has an out-of-round section (arrowed) on its inner rim that locates in the groove

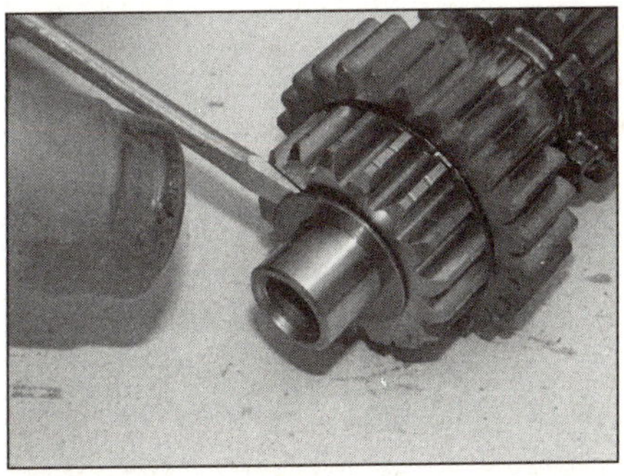

19.2b Carefully lever the washer out of the groove, using some heat if necessary

HAYNES HiNT ***When disassembling the transmission shafts, place the parts on a long rod or thread a wire through them to keep them in order and facing the proper direction.***

Input shaft

Disassembly

2 The thrust washer on the left-hand end of the shaft has a slightly out-of round section on its inner rim that locates in a groove in the shaft **(see illustration)** – this prevents the washer and 2nd gear pinion sliding off the end of the shaft when removing and installing the transmission cassette. To remove the washer slip one or two flat-bladed screwdrivers behind it at the out-of-round section and lever it out of the groove and towards the end of the shaft **(see illustration)**. Use a heat gun on the washer to expand it if required – we found it helped. If the washer becomes distorted to the extent it cannot be reused discard it and obtain a new one.

3 Slide the 2nd gear pinion off the shaft, noting which way round it fits **(see illustration 19.19)**.

4 Slide the tabbed lockwasher off the shaft, then turn the slotted splined washer to offset the splines and slide it off the shaft, noting how they fit together **(see illustrations 19.18c, b and a)**. Slide the 6th gear pinion and its splined bush off the shaft, followed by

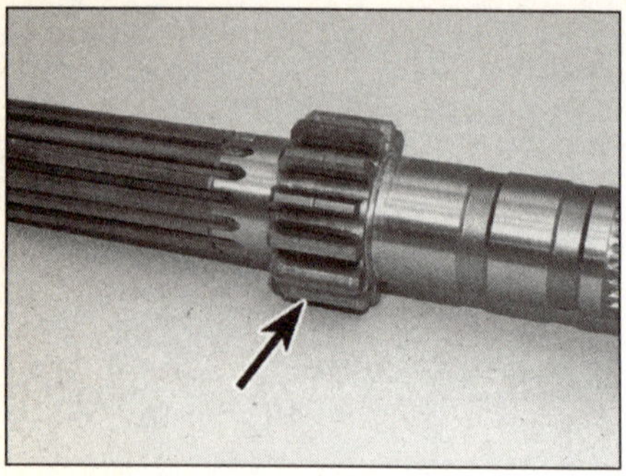

19.6 1st gear pinion (arrowed) is part of the shaft

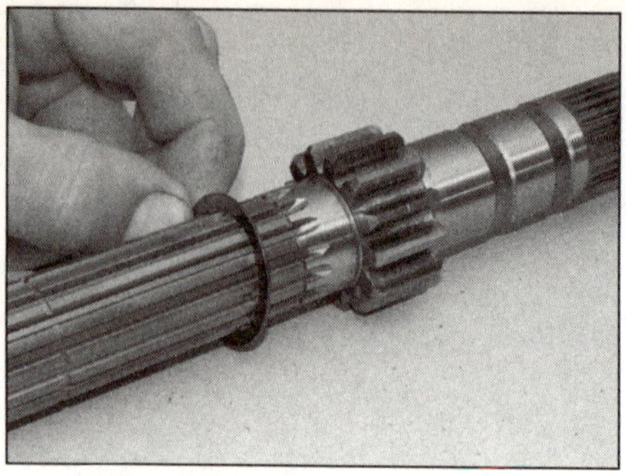

19.15a Slide the thrust washer . . .

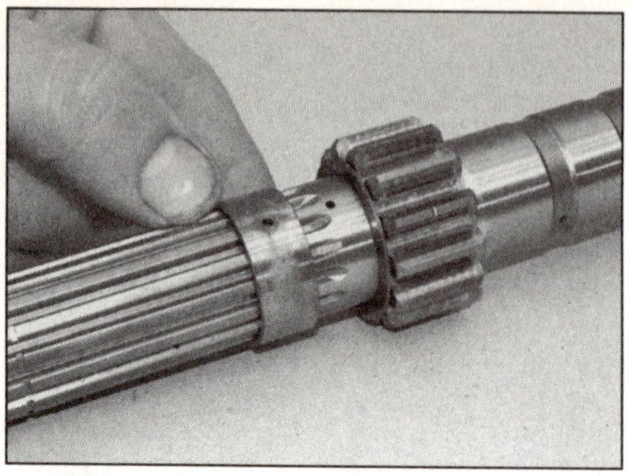

19.15b . . . the 5th gear pinion bush . . .

the splined washer **(see illustrations 19.17c, b and a)**.

5 Remove the circlip securing the combined 3rd/4th gear pinion, then slide the pinion off the shaft **(see illustrations 19.16b and a)**.

6 Remove the circlip securing the 5th gear pinion, then slide the splined washer, the pinion and its bush, and the thrust washer off the shaft **(see illustrations 19.15e, d, c, b and a)**. The 1st gear pinion is integral with the shaft **(see illustration)**.

Inspection

7 Wash all of the components in clean solvent and dry them off.

8 Check the gear teeth for cracking, chipping, pitting and other obvious wear or damage. Any pinion that is damaged as such must be replaced with a new one.

9 Inspect the dogs and the dog holes in the gears for cracks, chips, and excessive wear especially in the form of rounded edges. Make sure mating gears engage properly. Replace the paired gears as a set if necessary.

10 Check for signs of scoring or bluing on the pinions, bushes and shaft. This could be caused by overheating due to inadequate lubrication. Check that all the oil holes and passages are clear. Replace any damaged pinions or bushes.

11 Check that each pinion moves freely on the shaft or its bush but without undue freeplay. Check that each bush moves freely on the shaft but without undue freeplay. If the necessary equipment is available the individual components for which dimensions are given in the Specifications at the beginning of this Chapter can be measured to assess the extent of wear.

12 The shaft is unlikely to sustain damage unless the engine has seized, placing an unusually high loading on the transmission, or the machine has covered a very high mileage. Check the surface of the shaft, especially where a pinion turns on it, and replace the shaft if it has scored or picked up, or if there are any cracks. Damage of any kind can only be cured by replacement.

13 Check the washers and circlips and replace any that are bent or appear weakened or worn. Use new ones if in any doubt. Note that it is good practice to renew all circlips when overhauling gearshafts.

Reassembly

14 During reassembly, apply molybdenum disulphide oil (a 50/50 mixture of molybdenum disulphide grease and clean engine oil) to the mating surfaces of the shaft, pinions and bushes. Install the stamped circlips and washers so that their chamfered side faces away from the thrust side. When installing the circlips, do not expand their ends any further than is necessary, and locate the ends so the gap between them aligns with a spline groove as shown.

15 Slide the thrust washer onto the left-hand end of the shaft, followed by the 5th gear pinion bush **(see illustrations)**. Fit the 5th gear pinion onto the bush with its dogs facing away from the integral 1st gear **(see illustration)**. Slide the splined washer onto the shaft, then fit the circlip, making sure that it locates correctly in the groove in the shaft **(see illustrations)**.

16 Slide the combined 3rd/4th gear pinion onto the shaft with the larger 4th gear pinion facing the 5th gear pinion **(see illustration)**. Fit

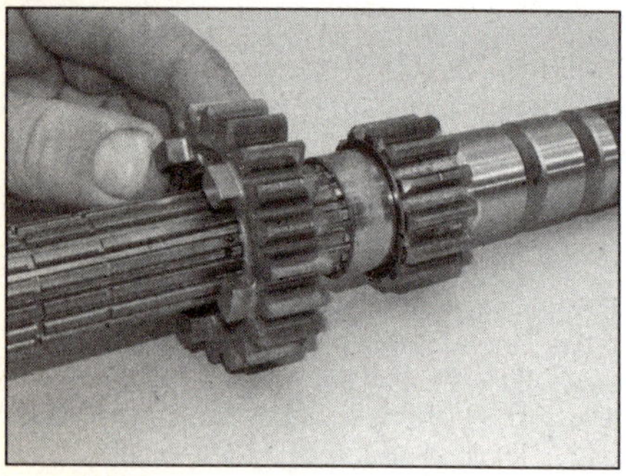

19.15c . . . the 5th gear pinion . . .

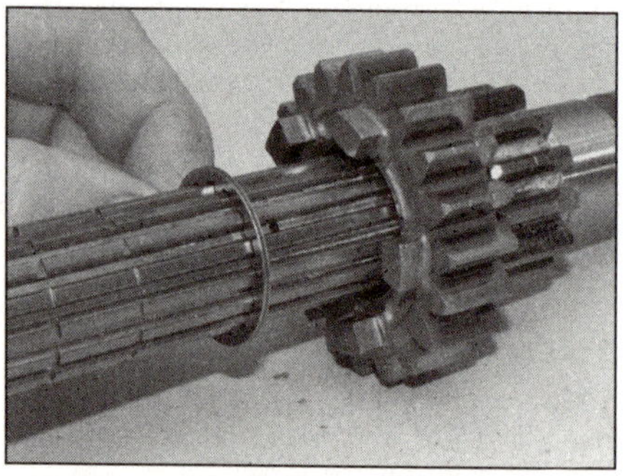

19.15d . . . and the splined washer onto the shaft . . .

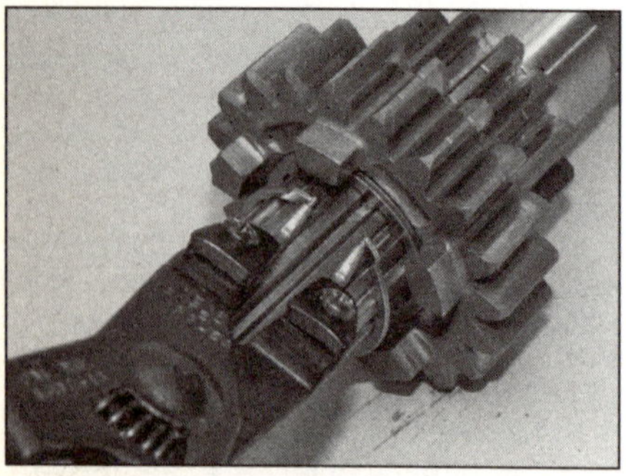

19.15e . . . and secure them with the circlip . . .

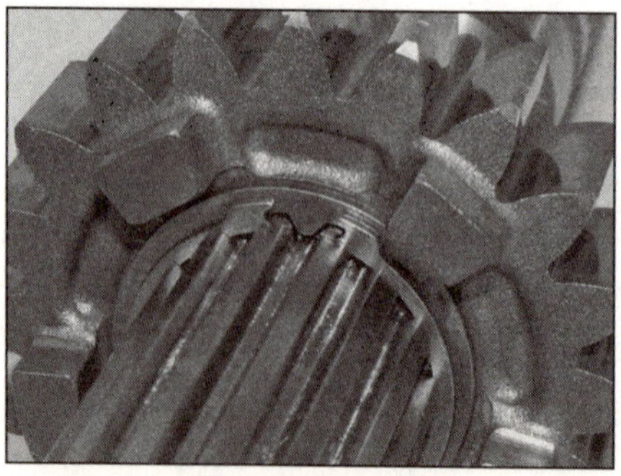

19.15f . . . making sure it locates properly in its groove

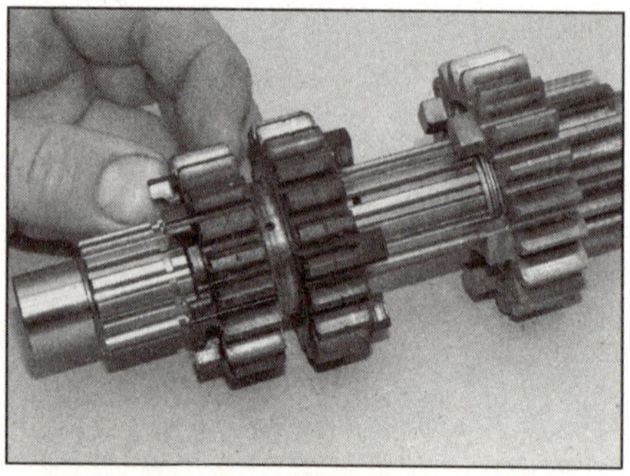

19.16a Slide the combined 3rd/4th gear pinion onto the shaft . . .

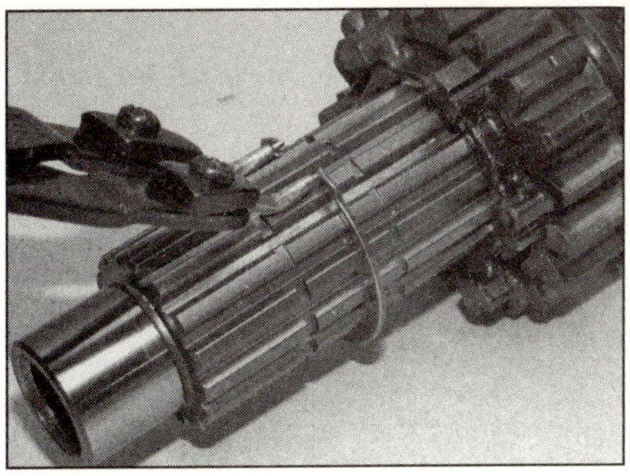

19.16b . . . and secure it with the circlip . . .

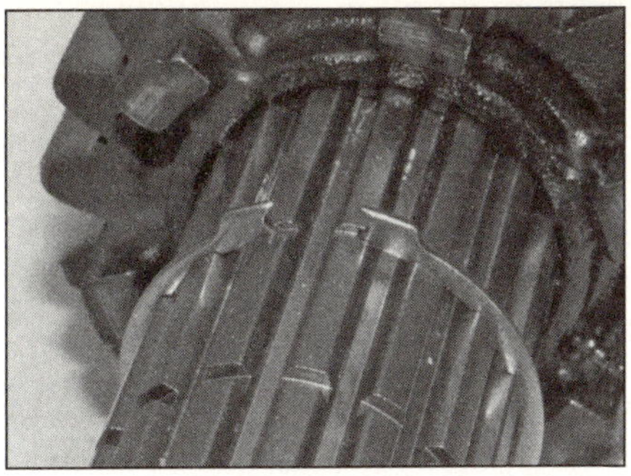

19.16c . . . making sure it locates properly in its groove

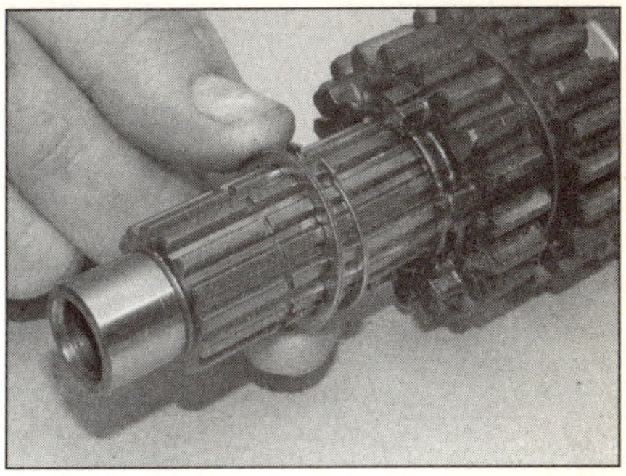

19.17a Slide the splined washer . . .

the circlip, making sure it is locates correctly in its groove in the shaft **(see illustrations)**.

17 Slide the splined washer onto the shaft, followed by the 6th gear pinion splined bush, aligning the oil hole in the bush with the hole in the shaft. Slide the 6th gear pinion onto the bush, making sure its dogs face the 3rd/4th gear pinion **(see illustrations)**.

18 Slide the slotted splined washer onto the shaft and locate it in its groove, then turn it in the groove so that the splines on the washer align with the splines on the shaft and secure the washer in the groove **(see illustrations)**. Slide the tabbed lockwasher onto the shaft and locate the tabs in the slots in the outer rim of the splined washer **(see illustration)**.

19 Slide the 2nd gear pinion onto the end of the shaft with the chamfered side of the teeth facing the 6th gear pinion **(see illustration)**.

20 Fit the special thrust washer onto the end of the shaft and drive it down to the groove using a suitable socket until the out-of-round section on its inner rim locates in the groove **(see illustrations and 19.2a)**.

19.17b . . . the 6th gear pinion splined bush . . .

19.17c . . . and the 6th gear pinion onto the shaft

19.18a Slide on the slotted splined washer . . .

19.18b . . . and locate it as shown . . .

19.18c . . . then slide on the tabbed lockwasher and locate its tabs in the slots

19.19 Slide the 2nd gear pinion onto the shaft

19.20a Fit the washer onto the shaft . . .

19.20b . . . and drive it down so its rim locates in the groove

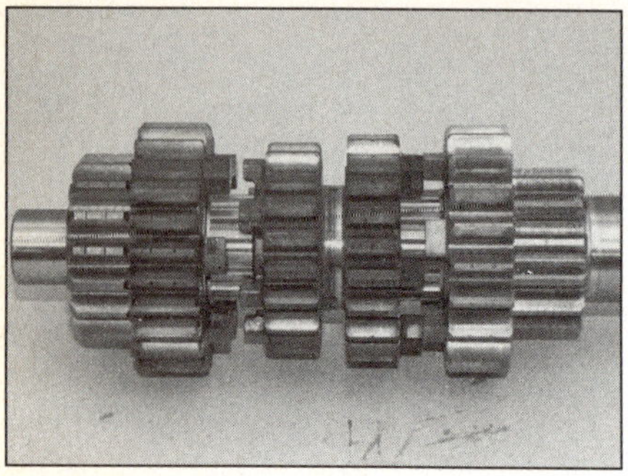
19.21 The complete input shaft should be as shown

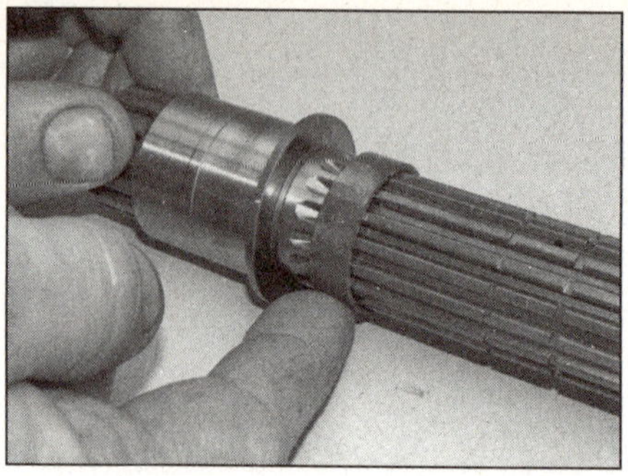
19.30a Slide the 2nd gear pinion bush . . .

19.30b . . . the 2nd gear pinion . . .

21 Check that all components have been correctly installed **(see illustration)**.

Output shaft

Disassembly

22 Slide the thrust washer off the shaft, followed by the 1st gear pinion and its needle roller bearing, the thrust washer and the 5th gear pinion **(see illustrations 19.36c, b and a, and 19.35b and a)**.

23 Remove the circlip securing the 4th gear pinion, then slide the splined washer, the pinion and its splined bush off the shaft **(see illustrations 19.34d, c, b and a)**.

24 Slide the tabbed lockwasher off the shaft, then turn the slotted splined washer to offset the splines and slide it off the shaft, noting how they fit together **(see illustrations 19.33c, b and a)**.

25 Slide the 3rd gear pinion and its splined bush, followed by the splined washer, off the shaft **(see illustrations 19.32c, b and a)**.

26 Remove the circlip securing the 6th gear pinion, then slide the pinion off the shaft **(see illustrations 19.31b and a)**.

27 Remove the circlip securing the 2nd gear pinion, then slide the splined washer, the pinion and its bush off the shaft **(see illustrations 19.30d, c, b and a)**.

Inspection

28 Refer to Steps 7 to 13 above.

Reassembly

29 During reassembly, apply molybdenum disulphide oil (a 50/50 mixture of molybdenum disulphide grease and clean engine oil) to the mating surfaces of the shaft, pinions and bushes. Install the stamped circlips and washers so that their chamfered side faces away from the thrust side. When installing the circlips, do not expand their ends any further than is necessary, and locate the ends so the gap between then aligns with a spline groove as shown.

30 Slide the 2nd gear pinion bush onto the shaft, then slide the 2nd gear pinion onto the bush with its dog holes facing away from the collar, followed by the splined washer **(see illustrations)**. Fit the circlip, making sure it is locates correctly in its groove in the shaft **(see illustrations)**.

31 Slide the 6th gear pinion onto shaft with its selector fork groove facing away from the 2nd gear pinion, then fit the circlip, making sure it is locates correctly in its groove in the shaft **(see illustrations)**.

19.30c . . . and the splined washer onto the shaft . . .

19.30d . . . and secure them with the circlip . . .

19.30e . . . making sure it locates in the groove

19.31a Slide the 6th gear pinion onto the shaft . . .

19.31b . . . and secure it with the circlip . . .

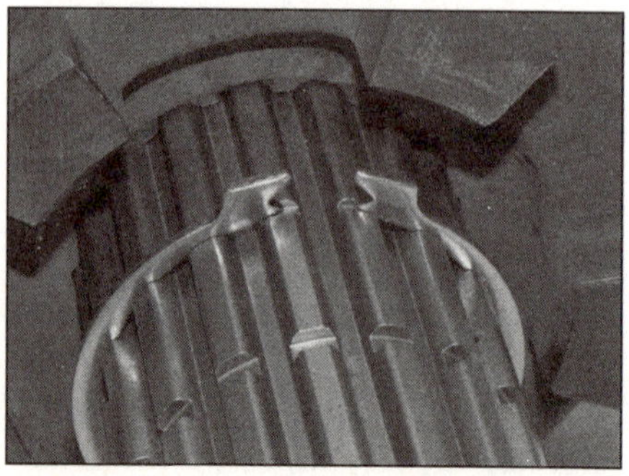
19.31c . . . making sure it locates in the groove

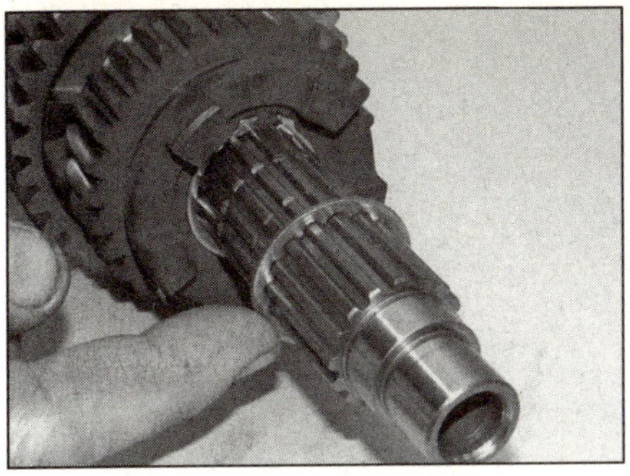

19.32a Slide the splined washer . . .

19.32b . . . the 3rd gear pinion splined bush . . .

19.32c . . . and the 3rd gear pinion onto the shaft

32 Slide the splined washer and the 3rd gear pinion splined bush onto the shaft, making sure the oil hole in the bush aligns with the hole in the shaft, then slide the 3rd gear pinion onto its bush with its dog holes facing the 6th gear pinion **(see illustrations)**.

33 Slide the slotted splined washer onto the shaft and locate it in its groove, then turn it in the groove so that the splines on the washer align with the splines on the shaft and secure the washer in the groove **(see illustrations)**. Slide the tabbed lockwasher onto the shaft and locate the tabs in the slots in the outer rim of the splined washer **(see illustration)**.

34 Slide the 4th gear pinion splined bush onto the shaft, making sure the oil hole in the bush aligns with the hole in the shaft **(see illustration)**. Slide the 4th gear pinion onto its bush with its dog holes face away from the 3rd gear pinion **(see illustration)**. Slide the splined washer on, then fit the circlip, making sure it is locates correctly in its groove in the shaft **(see illustrations)**.

19.33a Slide the slotted splined washer onto the shaft . . .

19.33b . . . and locate it as shown

19.33c Slide the lockwasher onto the shaft and engage it with the slotted washer

19.34a Slide the 4th gear pinion splined bush . . .

19.34b . . . the 4th gear pinion . . .

19.34c . . . and the splined washer onto the shaft . . .

19.34d . . . and secure them with the circlip . . .

19.34e . . . making sure it locates in the groove

19.35a Slide the 5th gear pinion . . .

19.35b . . . and the thrust washer onto the shaft

19.36a Slide the needle bearing . . .

35 Slide the 5th gear pinion onto the shaft with its selector fork groove facing the 4th gear pinion, followed by the thrust washer **(see illustrations)**.

36 Slide the 1st gear pinion needle roller bearing onto the shaft, then slide the 1st gear pinion onto the bearing with its dog holes facing the 5th gear pinion **(see illustrations)**. Fit the thrust washer **(see illustration)**.

37 Check that all components have been correctly installed **(see illustration)**.

19.36b . . . the 1st gear pinion . . .

19.36c . . . and the thrust washer onto the shaft

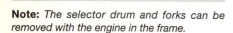

20 Selector drum and forks

Note: *The selector drum and forks can be removed with the engine in the frame.*

Removal

1 Remove the transmission cassette (see Section 17).

2 If not already done support the plate on blocks of wood with the transmission shafts pointing up.

3 Before removing the selector forks, note that the forks for the output shaft are marked RL, and the fork for the input shaft is marked C. If no letters are visible, mark them yourself using a felt pen. Withdraw the shaft supporting the input shaft fork and remove the fork, noting how it locates **(see illustrations 20.18b and a)**. Withdraw the shaft supporting the output shaft forks and remove the forks, noting how they locate **(see illustrations 20.17e, d, c, b and a)**. Once removed, slide the forks back onto the shafts to keep them mated **(see illustration)**.

4 If required (though they can stay in place) refer to Section 18, Step 4 and remove the transmission shafts.

5 If not already done, refer to Section 16, Step 5 and remove the stopper arm. Counter-hold the selector drum using a rod passed through its middle and unscrew the selector

19.37 The assembled output shaft should be as shown

20.3 Keep the forks and shafts mated and the forks the correct way up. Note the identification markings on the forks

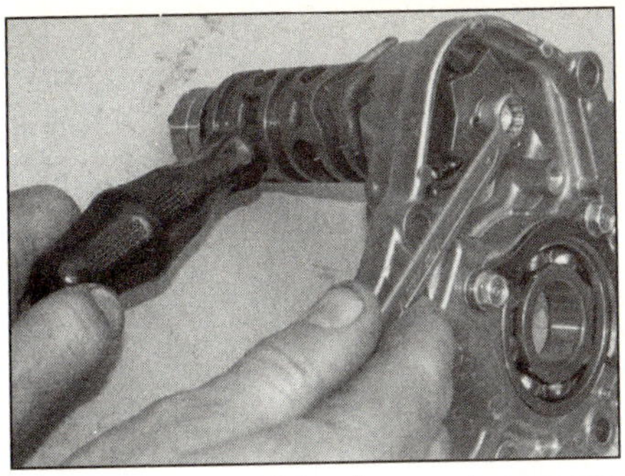

20.5 Counter-hold the drum and unscrew the cam bolt

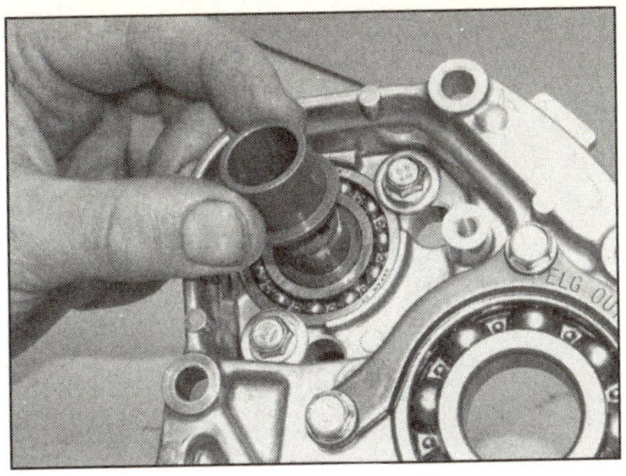

20.6a Remove the collar . . .

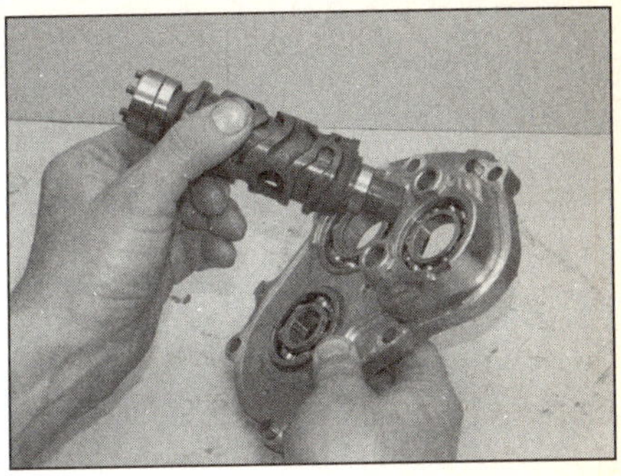

20.6b . . . and then the drum

cam bolt **(see illustration)**. Note the locating pins in the end of the drum and remove them for safekeeping **(see illustration 20.14a)**.

6 Remove the collar, then withdraw the selector drum from the plate **(see illustrations)**.

Inspection

7 Inspect the selector forks for any signs of wear or damage, especially around the fork ends where they engage with the groove in the pinion. Check that each fork fits correctly in its pinion groove. Check closely to see if the forks are bent. If the forks are in any way damaged they must be replaced with new ones.

8 Measure the thickness of the fork ends and compare the readings to the specifications **(see illustration)**. Replace the forks with new ones if they are worn beyond their specifications.

9 Check that the forks fit correctly on their shaft **(see illustration)**. They should move freely with a light fit but no appreciable freeplay. Measure the internal diameter of the fork bores and the corresponding diameter of the fork shaft **(see illustration)**. Replace the forks and/or shafts with new ones if they are worn beyond their specifications. Check that the shaft holes in the plate and crankcase are neither worn nor damaged.

10 Check each selector fork shaft is straight by rolling it along a flat surface. A bent shaft will cause difficulty in selecting gears and make the gearchange action heavy. Replace the shaft with a new one if it is bent.

11 Inspect the selector drum grooves and selector fork guide pins for signs of wear or damage **(see illustration)**. If either component shows signs of wear or damage the fork(s) and drum must be replaced with new ones.

12 Check that the bearing on the selector drum rotates freely and has no sign of freeplay between it and the casing **(see illustration)**. To fit a new bearing, remove the selector drum pin boss by unscrewing the bolt in its centre – pass a rod through the drum to counter-hold it **(see illustration)**. Note the locating pin in the end of the drum and remove it for safekeeping if required. Remove the old bearing and fit a new one (see *Tools and Workshop Tips* in the Reference Section if necessary). Install the pin boss, seating it on the locating pin. Apply a suitable non-permanent thread locking compound to the bolt and tighten it, counter-holding the drum as before.

13 Also check the bearing in the cassette

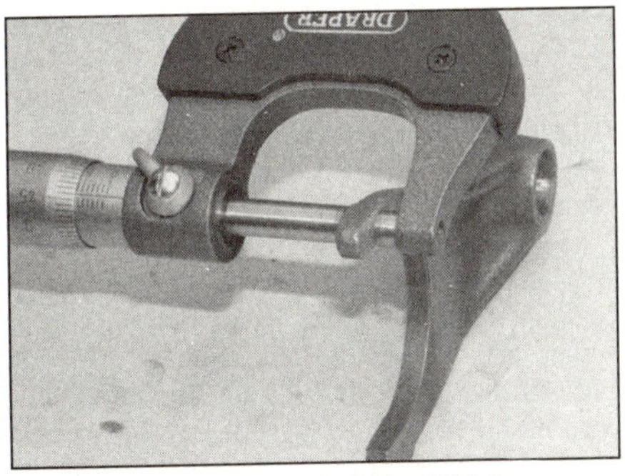

20.8 Measure the fork end thickness

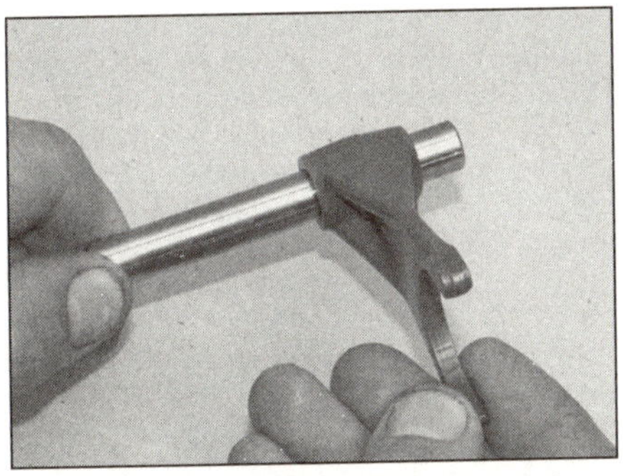

20.9a Check the fit of each fork on the shaft . . .

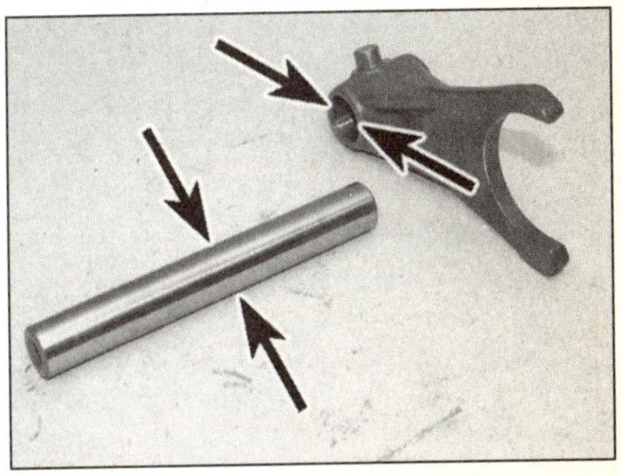

20.9b . . . then measure the fork bore ID and the fork shaft OD

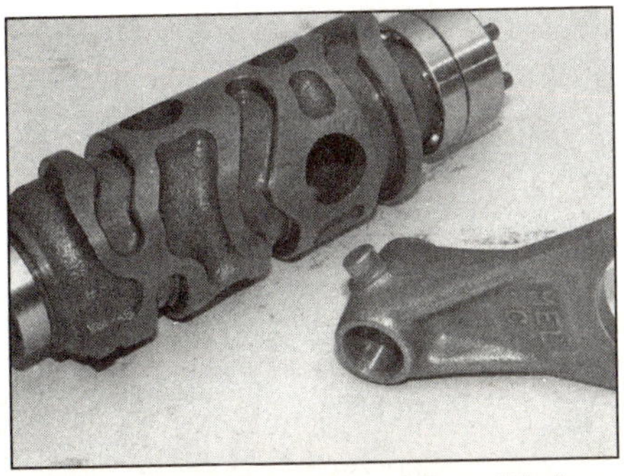

20.11 Check the guide pins and their grooves in the drum

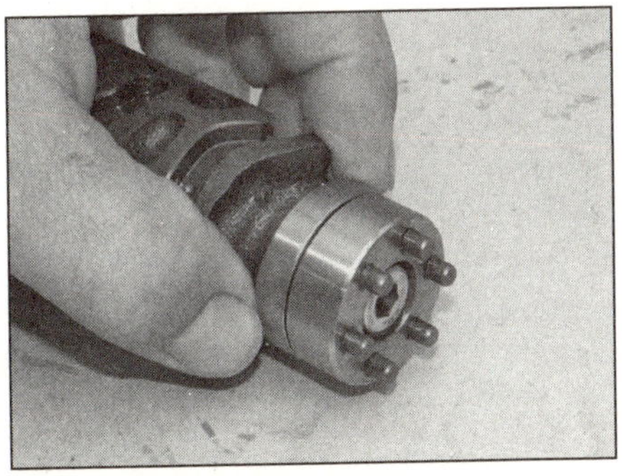

20.12a Check the bearing

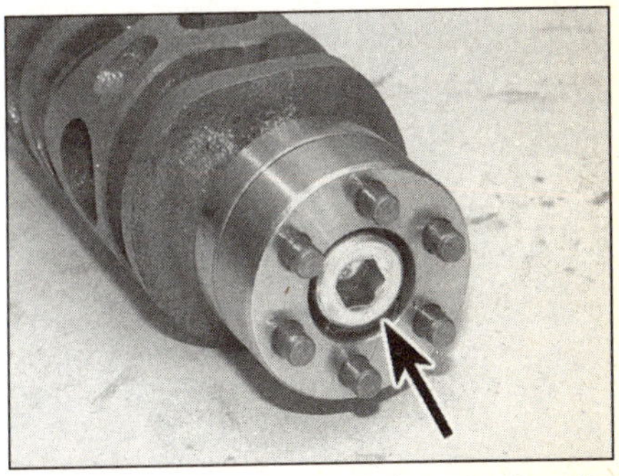

20.12b Unscrew the bolt (arrowed) and remove the pin boss to release the bearing

20.14a Fit the locating pins . . .

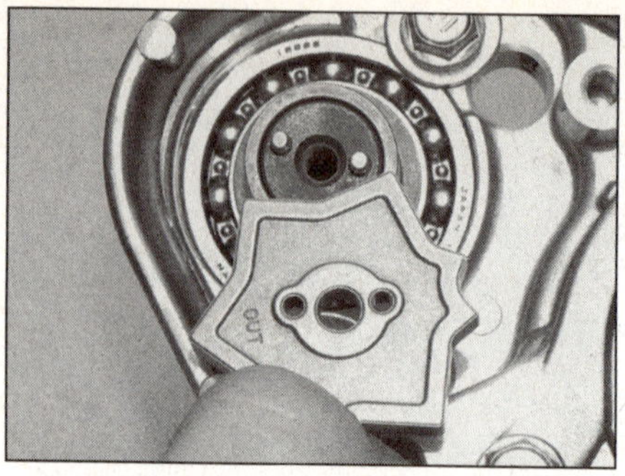

20.14b . . . then locate the cam, with the OUT mark facing out, onto the pins

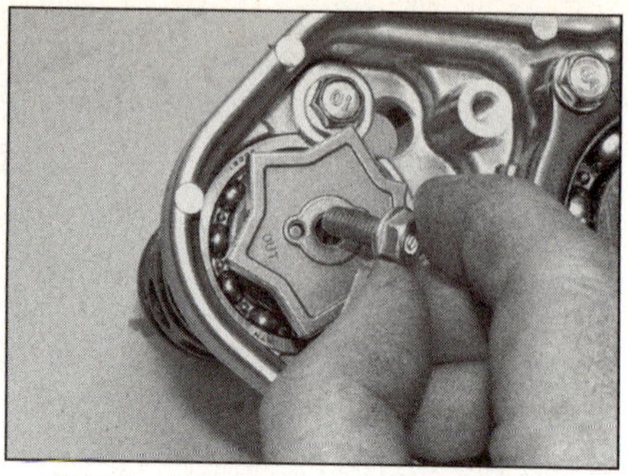

20.14c Apply thread lock to the bolt

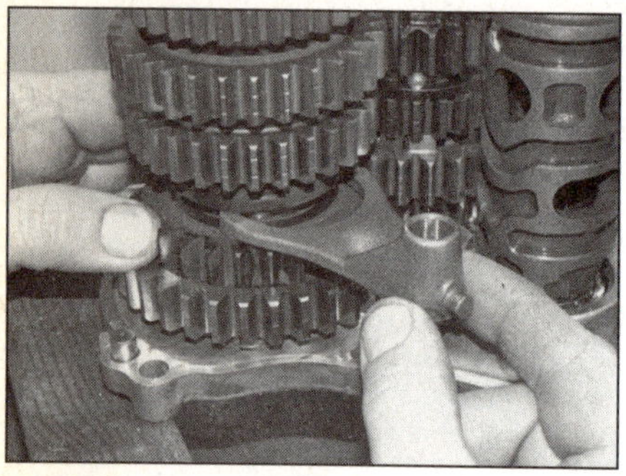

20.17a Locate the 5th gear fork in its pinion . . .

20.17b . . . and pivot it so the guide pin locates in its groove

20.17c Locate the 6th gear fork in its pinion . . .

plate **(see illustration 18.7a)**. To remove the bearing unscrew the two retainer bolts. If the bearing is tight remove it using a puller, or by driving it out with a socket, using heat to free it if necessary. On installation apply thread lock to the retainer bolts and tighten them to the torque setting specified at the beginning of the chapter.

Installation

14 Slide the selector drum into its bearing in the plate and fit the collar with its shouldered end innermost **(see illustrations 20.6b and a)**. Fit the cam locating pins into their holes then locate the cam on the end of the drum with the OUT mark facing out – it can only fit one way **(see illustrations)**. Apply a suitable non-permanent thread locking compound to the cam bolt and tighten it to the torque setting specified at the beginning of the Chapter, counter-holding the drum as before **(see illustration and 20.5)**. Turn the selector drum so the neutral detent in the cam is correctly positioned for the stopper arm.

15 Refer to Section 16, Step 9 and install the stopper arm.

16 If removed install the transmission shafts (see Section 18, Step 11).

17 Lubricate the selector fork ends and bores and the shafts with clean engine oil as you fit them. Fit the fork for the 5th gear pinion on the output shaft into its groove with the RL mark facing the cassette plate, then locate the fork's guide pin in its groove in the selector drum, lifting the gear slightly to align it if required **(see illustrations)**. Fit the fork for the 6th gear pinion on the output shaft into its groove with the RL mark facing away from the cassette plate, then locate the fork's guide pin in its groove in the selector drum **(see illustrations)**. Slide the shaft through each fork and into its bore in the plate **(see illustration)**.

18 Now fit the fork for the 3rd/4th gear pinion on the input shaft into its groove with the C mark facing away from the cassette plate **(see illustration)**. Locate the fork's guide pin in its groove in the selector drum, lifting the gear slightly to align them if required, then slide the

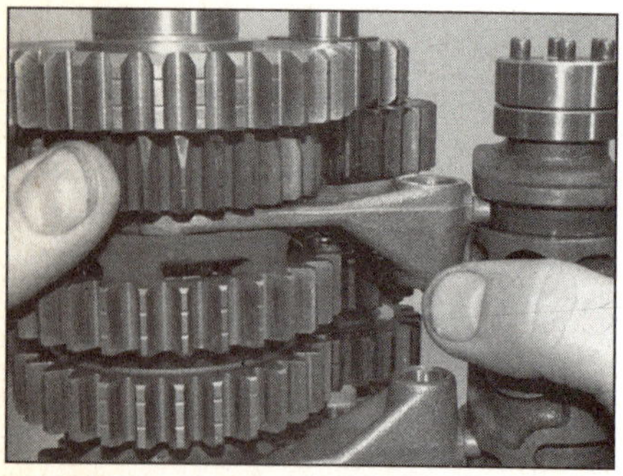

20.17d . . . and pivot it so the guide pin locates in its groove

20.17e Slide the shaft through the forks and into its bore in the plate

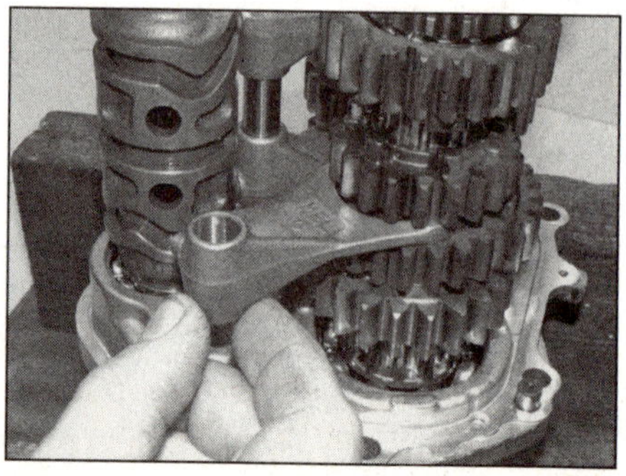

20.18a Locate the 3rd/4th gear fork in its pinion . . .

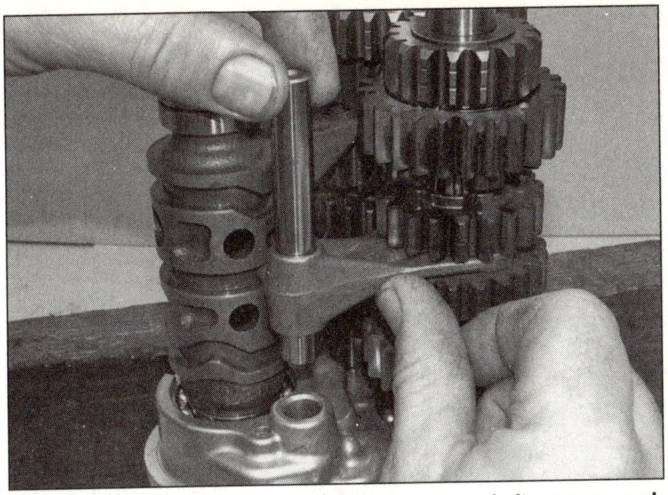

20.18b . . . then pivot it so the guide pin locates in its groove and slide the shaft through

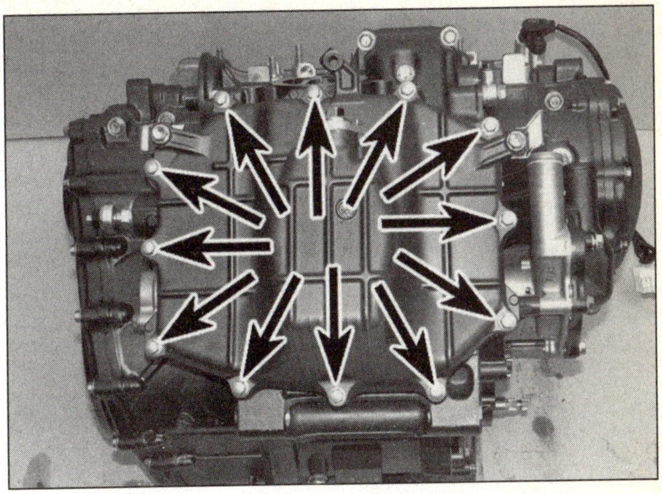

21.3 Unscrew the bolts (arrowed) and remove the sump

shaft through the fork and into its bore in the plate **(see illustration)**.

19 Install the transmission cassette (see Section 17).

21 Oil sump, oil strainer and pressure relief valve

Note: *The oil sump, strainer and pressure relief valve can be removed with the engine in the frame. If the engine has been removed, ignore the steps which don't apply.*

Removal

1 Remove the lower fairing and the fairing side panels (see Chapter 7). Drain the engine oil (see Chapter 1).

2 While the oil is draining, remove the exhaust downpipe assembly, leaving the silencer in place (see Chapter 4).

3 Unscrew the sump bolts, slackening them evenly in a criss-cross sequence to prevent distortion, and remove the sump **(see illustration)**.

4 Pull the strainer out of the oil pump, noting how it locates **(see illustration)**. Remove the rubber seal and discard it as a new one must be used **(see illustration)**.

5 Pull the pressure relief valve out of its socket – it also is a push-fit **(see illustration)**. Discard the O-ring as a new one must be used.

Inspection

6 Remove all traces of sealant from the sump and crankcase mating surfaces, and clean the inside of the sump with solvent. Blow the sump dry with compressed air if available. If you need to remove the oil drain plug threaded base, refit the drain plug lightly then unscrew the base bolt. Remove the base and discard the O-ring, and thread the drain plug out of the base. When fitting the base use a new O-ring and make sure it locates in the groove, and apply a suitable non-permanent thread locking compound to the base bolt. Fit the drain plug into the base then tighten the base bolt to the torque setting specified at the beginning of the Chapter. Remove the drain plug again if required – you will need to fit a new sealing washer before refilling with oil (see Chapter 1).

7 Clean the oil strainer in solvent and remove any debris caught in the mesh. If the strainer gauze is damaged, replace the strainer with a new one.

8 Push the relief valve plunger into the valve body and check that it moves smoothly and freely against spring pressure **(see illustration)**. If not, remove the circlip, noting that it is under spring pressure, then remove the washer, spring and plunger. Clean all components in solvent, then check the plunger and the valve body for evidence of scoring, wear and any other damage. If any is found, replace the relief valve with a new one – individual components are not available. Otherwise, coat the plunger with oil and fit it closed end first back into the valve and recheck the movement. If it is good, install the spring and washer and secure them with the circlip.

21.4a Remove the strainer, noting how the tab locates in the groove . . .

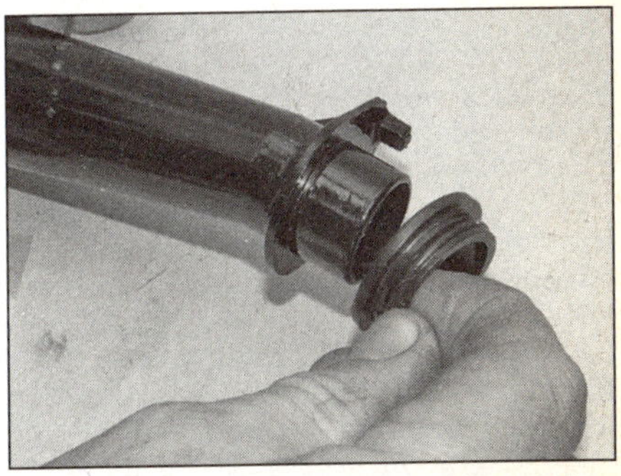

21.4b . . . and remove the rubber seal

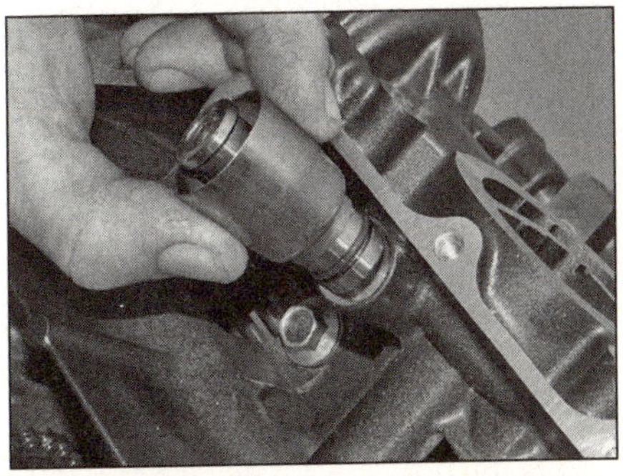

21.5 Pull the relief valve out of its socket

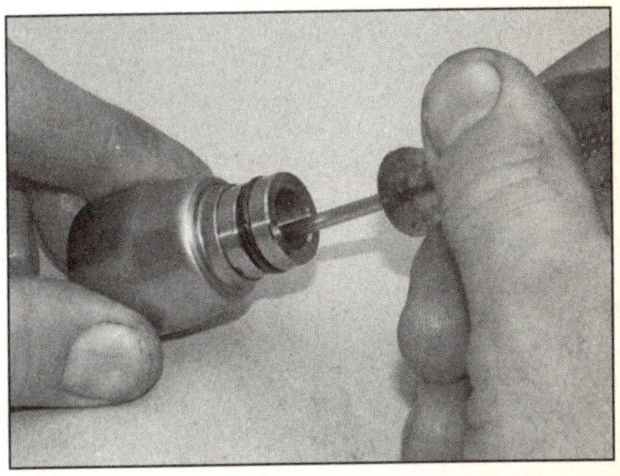

21.8 Push the plunger into the body and check that it moves smoothly

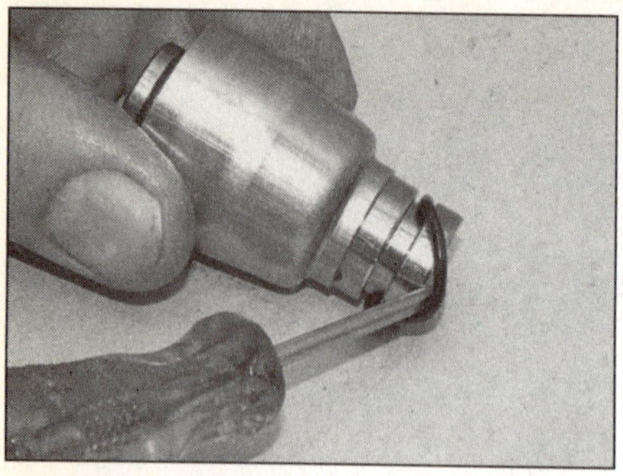

21.9 Fit a new O-ring onto the relief valve body

21.10a Lubricate the rubber seal and fit it into the crankcase

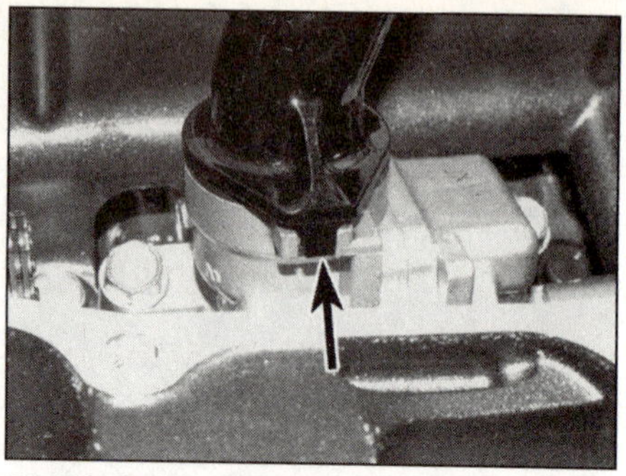

21.10b Locate the tab in the slot (arrowed)

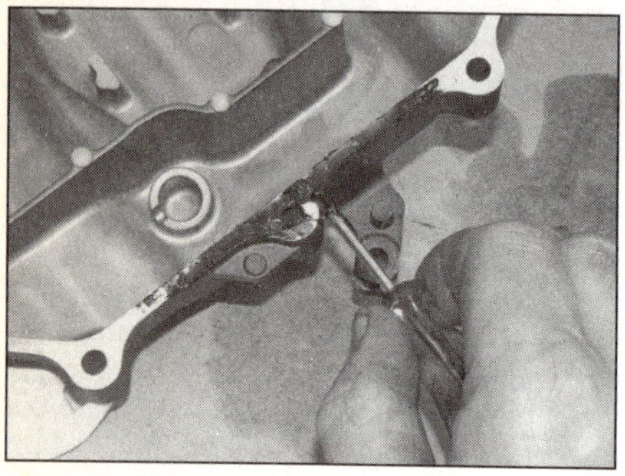

21.11a Apply the sealant . . .

21.11b . . . then install the sump

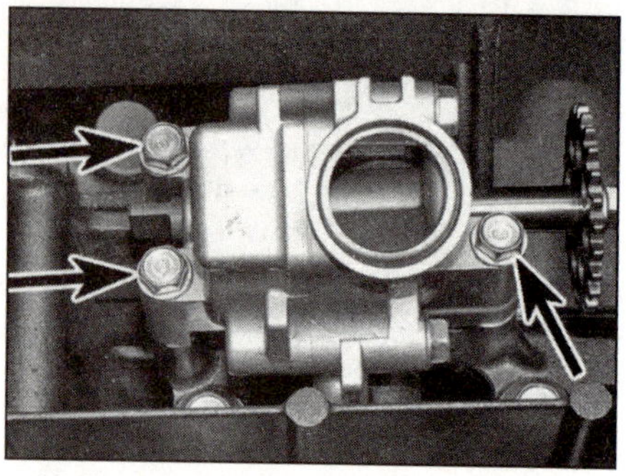

22.3a Unscrew the bolts (arrowed) and remove the pump

Installation

9 Fit a new O-ring onto the relief valve and smear it with clean oil, then push the valve into its socket **(see illustration and 21.5)**.

10 Fit a new rubber seal smeared with clean oil into the strainer socket in the pump **(see illustration)**. Do not fit it onto the strainer as it will distort when the strainer is fitted. Fit the strainer, locating the tab in the cut-out **(see illustration)**.

11 Clean the mating surfaces of the sump and crankcase with solvent. Apply a suitable sealant (such as Three Bond 1207B or equivalent RTV sealant – ask your dealer) to the sump mating surface **(see illustration)**. Position the sump onto the crankcase and install the bolts finger-tight **(see illustration)**. Tighten the bolts evenly and a little at a time in a criss-cross pattern **(see illustration 21.3)**.

12 Install the exhaust system (see Chapter 4), but do not yet fit the fairing panels.

13 Fill the engine with the correct type and quantity of oil as described in Chapter 1. Start the engine and check that there are no leaks around the sump.

14 Install the fairing side panels and the lower fairing (see Chapter 7).

22 Oil pump

Note: *The oil pump can be removed with the engine in the frame. If the engine has been removed, ignore the steps which don't apply.*

Removal

1 Remove the clutch and the oil pump drive sprocket and chain (see Section 14).

2 Remove the sump and the oil strainer (see Section 21).

3 Unscrew the three bolts securing the pump to the crankcase, then remove the pump, noting how it fits **(see illustration)**. Remove the dowels from either the crankcase or the pump if they are loose **(see illustration)**. Remove the oil passage collar and O-ring and discard the O-ring – a new one must be used.

Inspection

4 If required lock the oil pump driven sprocket to prevent it from turning and unscrew the bolt **(see illustration 22.5a)**. Remove the driven sprocket.

5 Unscrew the bolts securing the cover to the pump body, then remove the cover **(see illustrations)**.

6 Remove the drive pin and thrust washer

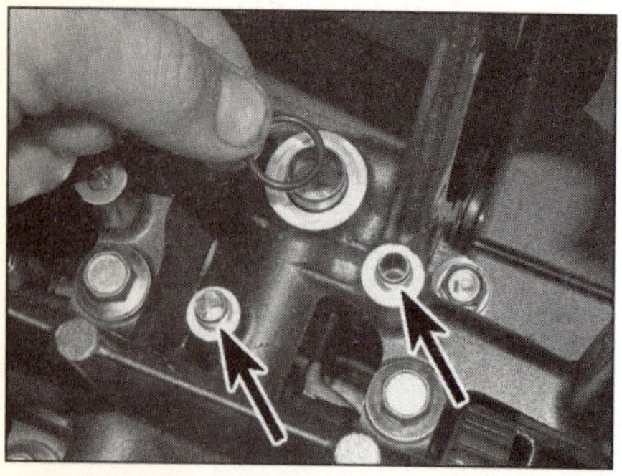

22.3b Remove the O-ring and collar, and the dowels (arrowed) if loose

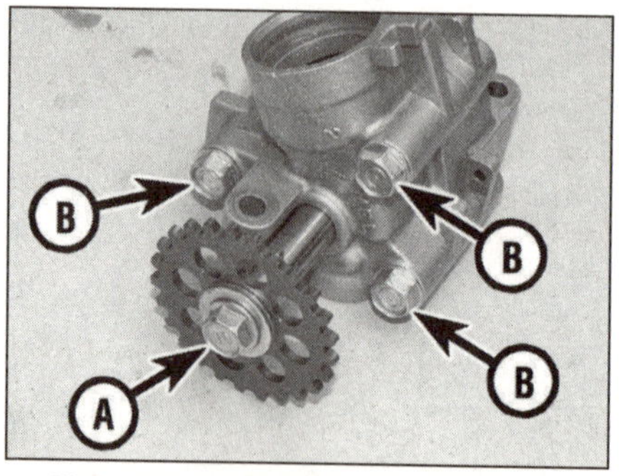

22.5a Driven sprocket bolt (A) and oil pump cover bolts (B)

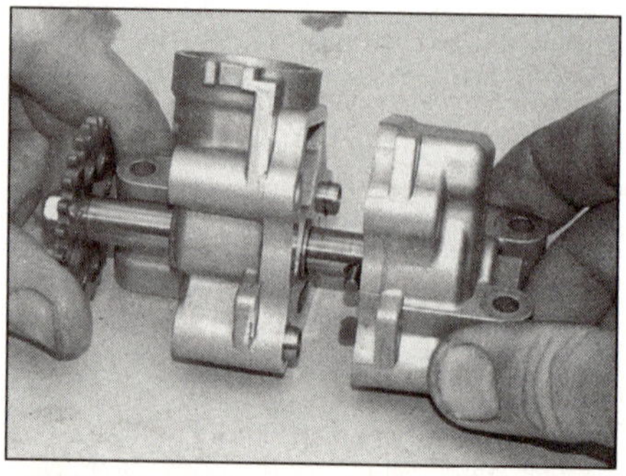

22.5b Draw the pump body off the shaft

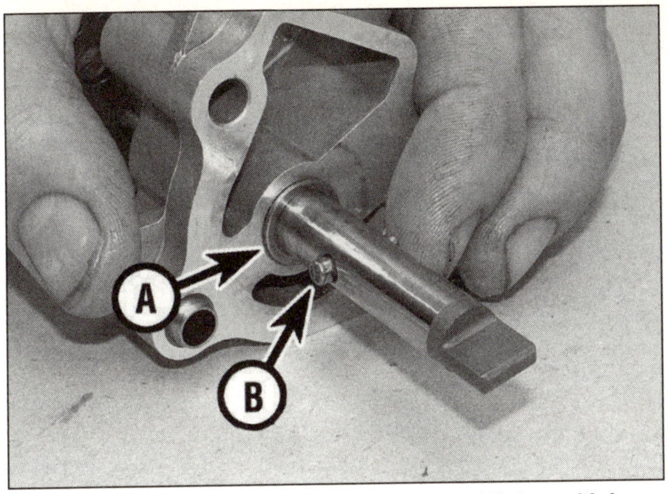

22.6 Remove the drive pin (B) and the washer (A) then withdraw the shaft

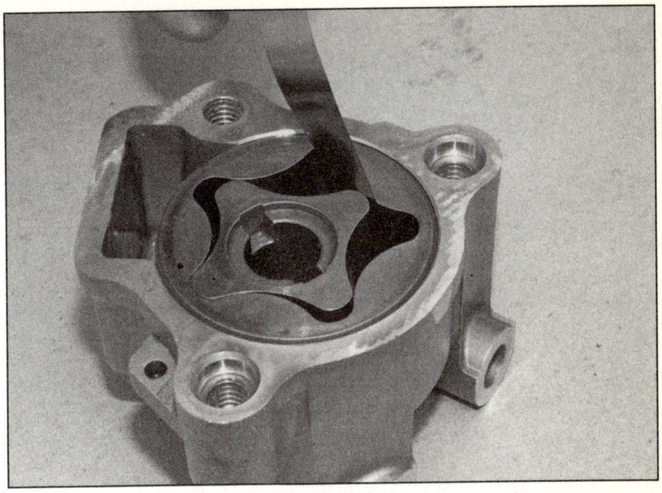
22.9 Measure the inner rotor tip-to-outer rotor clearance as shown (shaft shown removed for clarity)

then withdraw the shaft from the cover **(see illustration)**. Remove the inner and outer rotors from the body, noting which way round they fit.

7 Clean all the components in solvent.

8 Inspect the pump body, shaft and rotors for scoring and wear. If any damage, scoring or uneven or excessive wear is evident, replace the pump with a new one (individual components are not available).

9 Fit the inner and outer rotors into the pump body, then slide the shaft through the inner rotor. Align the rotors as shown and measure the clearance between the inner rotor tip and the outer rotor with a feeler gauge and compare it to the service limit listed in the specifications at the beginning of the Chapter **(see illustration)**. If the clearance measured is greater than the maximum listed, replace the pump with a new one.

10 Measure the clearance between the outer rotor and the pump body with a feeler gauge and compare it to the maximum clearance listed in the specifications at the beginning of the Chapter **(see illustration)**. If the clearance measured is greater than the maximum listed, replace the pump with a new one.

11 Lay a straight-edge across the rotors and the pump body and, using a feeler gauge, measure the rotor end-float (the gap between the rotors and the straight-edge) **(see illustration)**. If the clearance measured is greater than the maximum listed, replace the pump with a new one.

12 Check the pump drive chain and drive and driven sprockets for wear or damage, and replace them with a new set if necessary.

13 If the pump is good, make sure all the components are clean, then lubricate them with new engine oil.

14 Fit the outer rotor into the pump body. Fit the inner rotor into the outer rotor with the cut-outs in the inner rotor facing out.

15 Fit the dowels into the cover if removed. Slide the drive shaft through the cover, making sure the end with the driven sprocket bolt hole is on the outer side so the tabbed end fits through the pump body. Slide the thrust washer onto the shaft then fit the drive pin into its hole in the shaft **(see illustration 22.6)**. Turn

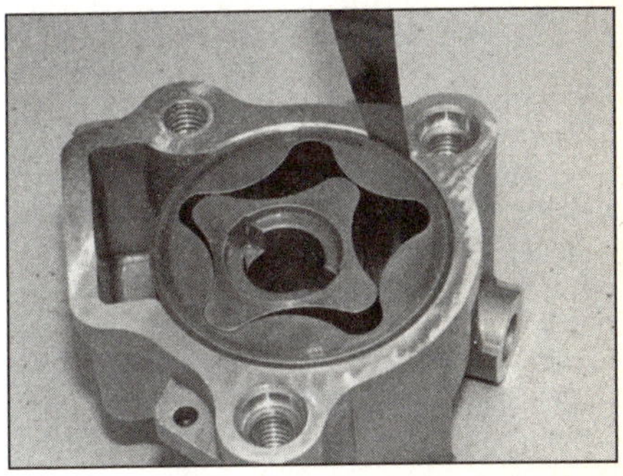
22.10 Measure the outer rotor-to-body clearance as shown

the shaft to align the drive pin ends with the cut-outs in the inner rotor **(see illustration)**. Fit the cover onto the pump, locating the drive pin ends into the cut-outs **(see illustration 22.5b)**. Fit the bolts and tighten them to the torque setting specified at the beginning of the Chapter **(see illustration 22.5a)**.

16 Rotate the pump shaft by hand and check it turns the rotors smoothly and freely.

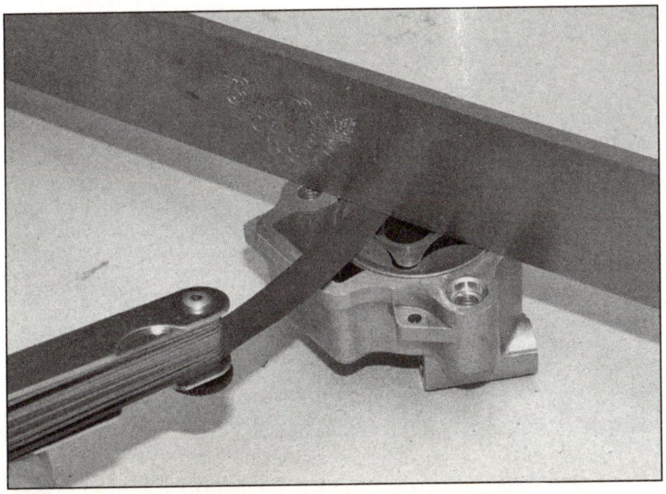
22.11 Measure rotor end-float as shown

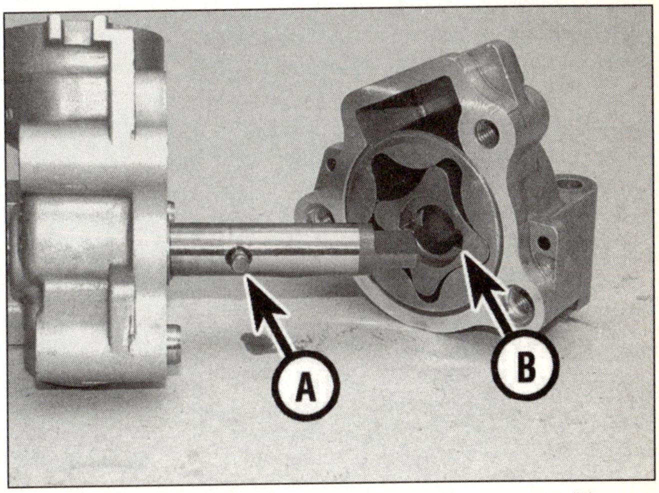

22.15 Align the drive pin ends (A) with the cut-outs (B)

22.19a Fit the sump onto its dowels and collar

22.19b Make sure the shafts engage correctly

22.20 Prime the pump with oil before fitting the sump

17 If removed, locate the driven sprocket on the shaft with the OUT mark facing out, then apply a suitable non-permanent thread locking compound to the sprocket bolt and tighten it to the torque setting specified at the beginning of the chapter, counter-holding the sprocket as before **(see illustration 22.5a)**.

Installation

18 Fit the pump locating dowels if removed **(see illustration 22.3b)**. Fit the oil passage collar then fit a new O-ring smeared with clean oil around the collar.

19 Install the pump, rotating the drive shaft to align the tab on its end with the slot in the water pump shaft **(see illustrations)**. Make sure it locates correctly on the dowels and collar, then fit the mounting bolts and tighten them, noting that the longer bolt fits into the hole near the sprocket.

20 Install the oil pump drive sprocket and chain and the clutch (see Section 14). Pour some clean engine oil into the pump via the strainer socket and rotate the shaft to prime it **(see illustration)**. Install the oil strainer and the sump (see Section 21).

23 Crankcase separation and reassembly

Note 1: *To separate the crankcase halves, the engine must be removed from the frame.*

Note 2: *The 9 mm main journal crankcase bolts are of the stretch type, which can only be used in a running engine once, though they can be used when performing the oil clearance check detailed in Section 26. The new bolts come pre-coated with an oil additive which must not be cleaned off.*

Special tool: *A degree disc is required for tightening the crankshaft journal bolts **(see illustration 23.22c)**.*

Separation

1 To access the pistons, connecting rods, crankshaft, balancer shaft and the main and big-end bearings, the crankcase must be split into its two halves.

2 Before the crankcases can be separated the following components must be removed:

Valve cover (Section 7)
Camshafts (Section 9) – see Note 3
Cylinder head (Section 11) – see Note 3
Alternator (Chapter 8)
Starter clutch (Section 13)
Cam chain and blades (Section 10) – see Note 3
Gearchange mechanism (Section 16)
Clutch, oil pump drive chain and sprocket (Section 14)
Transmission cassette (Section 17)
Water pump (Chapter 3)
Oil cooler (Section 6)
Starter motor (Chapter 8)
Oil sump, strainer and pressure relief valve (Section 21)
Oil pump (Section 22)
Speed sensor (Chapter 8)

Note 3: *If the crankcases are being separated to inspect the crankshaft without removing it, the camshafts and cylinder head can remain in situ. To remove the crankshaft without removing the connecting rods and pistons, the camshafts must be removed but the head can stay in place. However, if removal of the connecting rod assemblies is intended, full disassembly of the top-end is necessary. If required the cam chain can remain loose on the crankshaft after the camshafts have been removed, and can be taken off after the crankshaft has been removed.*

3 Pull the rubber boot off the oil pressure switch, then undo the terminal screw and detach the wiring **(see illustration)**. Pull the wiring connector off the neutral switch **(see illustration)**.

4 Unscrew the oil level inspection window bolts and remove the window **(see illustration)**. Discard the O-ring as a new one must be used. On RR-6 and RR-7 models note the wiring clamp secured by the upper bolt.

5 Unscrew the six 7 mm upper crankcase bolts evenly, a little at a time and in a criss-cross sequence until they are finger-tight, then remove them, noting the one at the front fitted with a sealing washer **(see**

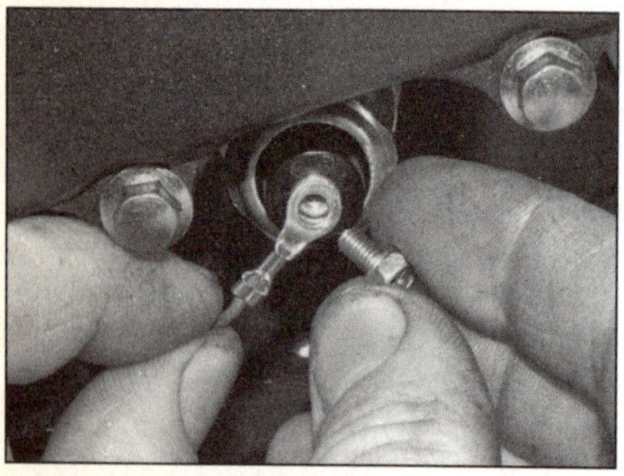

23.3a Disconnect the wiring from the oil pressure switch . . .

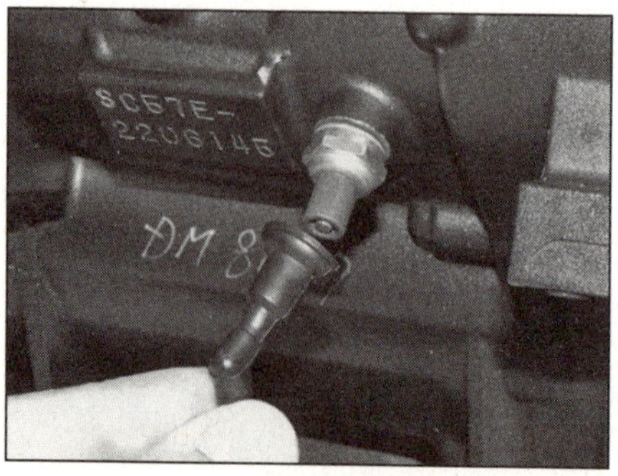

23.3b . . . and the neutral switch

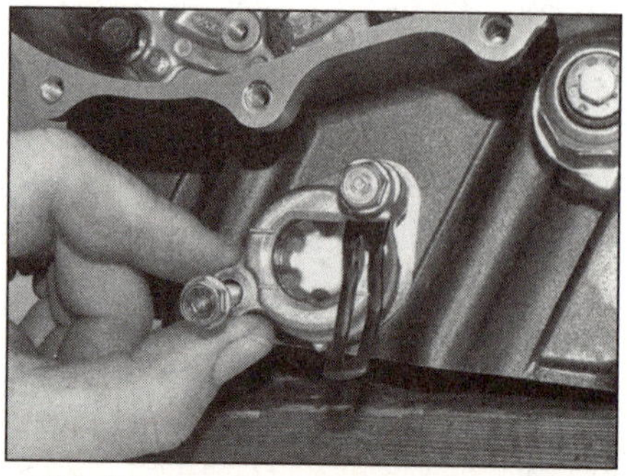

23.4 Unscrew the bolts and remove the window, on RR-6 and RR-7 models noting the wiring clamp

23.5a Upper crankcase 7 mm bolts (A) . . .

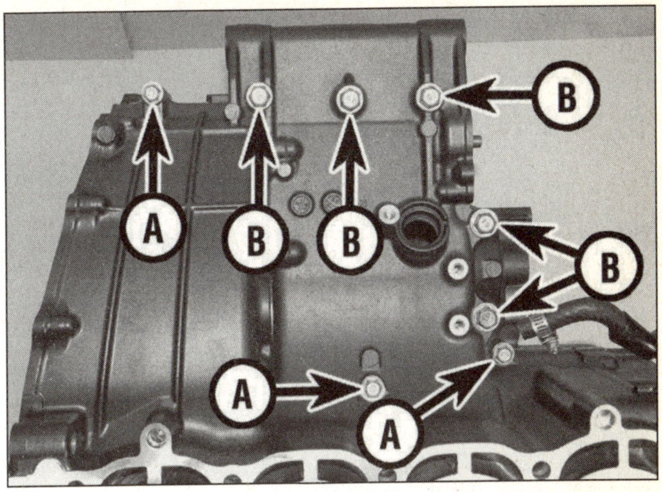

23.5b . . . and 8 mm bolts (B)

23.8a Lower crankcase 7 mm bolts (arrowed) . . .

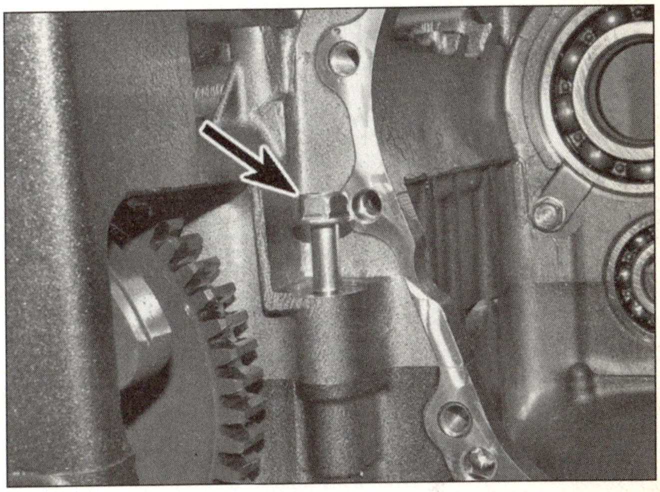

23.8b . . . and 8 mm bolt (arrowed)

illustrations). **Note:** *As each bolt is removed, store it in its relative position in a cardboard template of the crankcase halves. This will ensure all bolts and washers are installed in the correct location on reassembly.* Note that any sealing washers should be replaced with new ones on reassembly, though it is wise to keep the old ones with the bolts for the time being as a guide to refitting.

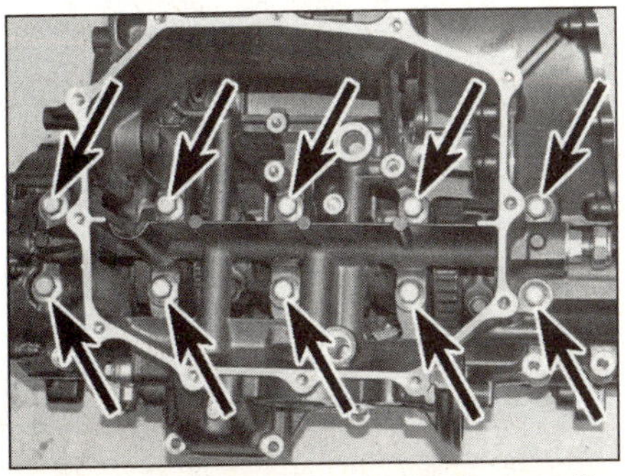

23.9 Crankshaft journal bolts (arrowed)

6 Unscrew the five 8 mm upper crankcase bolts evenly, a little at a time and in a criss-cross sequence until they are finger-tight, then remove them.

7 Turn the engine upside down.

8 Unscrew the six 7 mm and one 8 mm lower crankcase bolts evenly, a little at a time and in a criss-cross sequence until they are finger-tight, then remove them **(see illustrations)**.

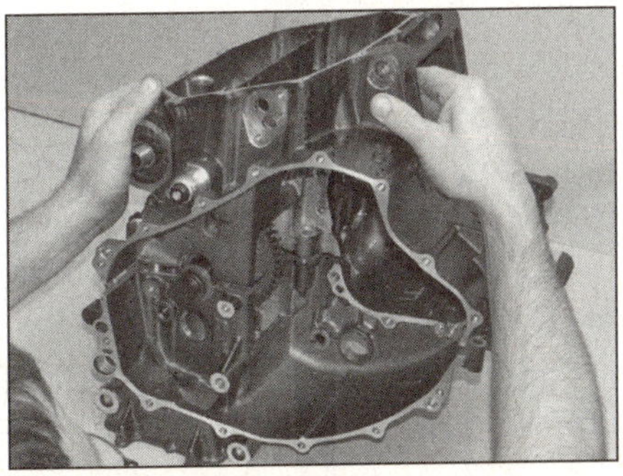

23.10 Carefully separate the crankcase halves

Note: *As each bolt is removed, store it in its relative position in a cardboard template of the crankcase halves. This will ensure all bolts are installed in the correct location on reassembly.*

9 Now unscrew the ten 9 mm crankshaft journal bolts evenly, a little at a time and in a **reverse** of the tightening sequence **(see illustration 23.22b)**, i.e. starting from the outside and working to the centre, until they are finger-tight, then remove them **(see illustration)**.

10 Carefully lift the lower crankcase half off the upper half, using a soft-faced hammer to tap around the joint to initially separate the halves if necessary **(see illustration)**. **Note:** *If the halves do not separate easily, make sure all fasteners have been removed. Do not try and separate the halves by levering against the crankcase mating surfaces as they are easily scored and may leak oil in the future if damaged.* The lower crankcase half will come away with the balancer shaft, leaving the crankshaft in the upper crankcase half.

11 Remove the three locating dowels from the crankcase if they are loose (they could

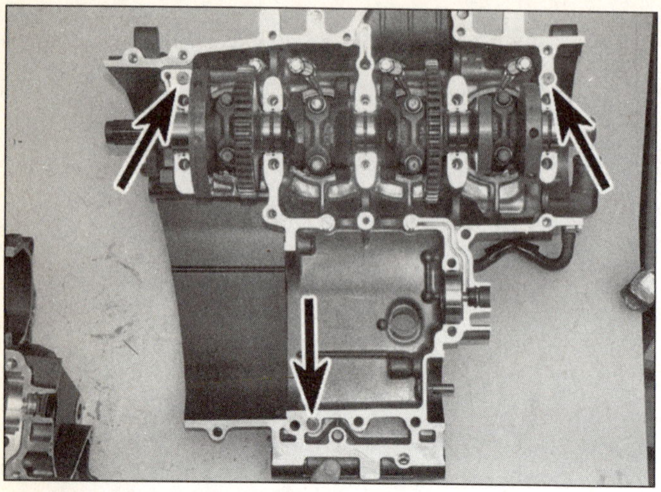

23.11a Remove the dowels (arrowed) if they are loose . . .

23.11b . . . and the oil orifices (arrowed)

23.11c Remove the bearing noting how the pin locates in the hole (arrowed) . . .

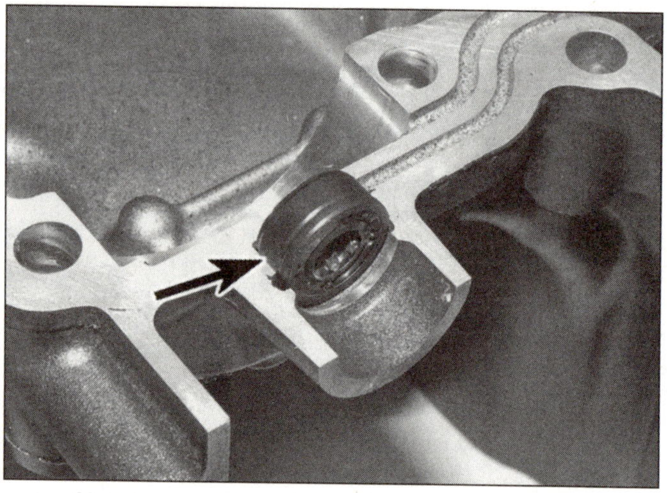

23.11d . . . and the clutch pushrod oil seal (arrowed)

be in either crankcase half), and the two oil orifices, noting how they fit **(see illustrations)**. Remove the transmission input shaft bearing, noting how the pin locates in the hole **(see illustration)**. Remove the clutch pushrod oil seal and discard it – a new one must be used **(see illustration)**. Check the condition of the input shaft bearing and replace it with a new one if necessary.

12 Refer to Sections 24 to 30 for the removal, inspection and installation of the components housed within the crankcases.

Reassembly

13 Remove all traces of sealant from the crankcase mating surfaces.

14 Make sure the crankshaft, connecting rods and pistons and the balancer shaft and their bearings are in place in the upper and lower crankcase halves. Fit a new clutch pushrod oil seal, locating its lip in the groove as shown **(see illustration 23.11d)**. Fit the transmission input shaft bearing, locating its pin in the hole **(see illustration 23.11c)**.

15 Generously lubricate the crankshaft and balancer shaft, particularly around the bearings, with clean engine oil, then use a rag soaked in high flash-point solvent to wipe over the mating surfaces of both crankcase halves to remove all traces of oil.

16 If removed, install the three locating dowels and the two oil orifices in the upper crankcase half **(see illustrations 23.11a and b)**. Make sure the orifices are installed the correct way up and so their flat sides locate correctly in the bores **(see illustration)**.

17 To enable easy engagement of the balancer shaft driven gear with its drive gear on the crankshaft the backlash adjustment must be set to a maximum (more information on backlash and its importance is given in Section 30). If not already done (if the balancer shaft was removed from the crankcase – see Section 30), first make an alignment mark on the balancer shaft holder with the punch mark on the end of the balancer shaft – this will give a good indication as to the starting point for resetting the backlash adjustment after the crankcases have been assembled **(see**

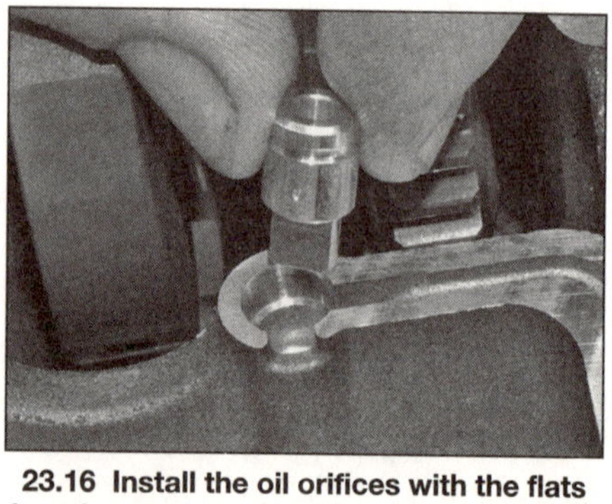

23.16 Install the oil orifices with the flats locating against the corresponding flats in their bores

23.17 **Make an alignment mark, then slacken the pinch bolt (arrowed) and turn the shaft so the punch mark is at the bottom**

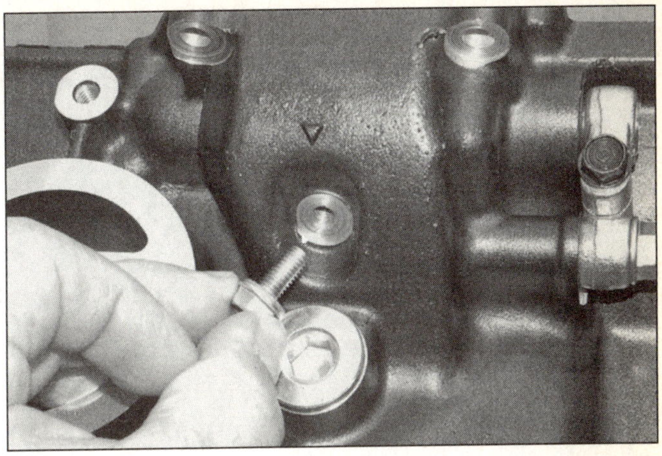

23.18a **Unscrew the bolt . . .**

illustration). Slacken the balancer shaft holder pinch bolt, then turn the shaft until the punch mark on its end is facing down (the shaft provides an eccentric adjustment which alters the backlash).

18 Now both the balancer shaft and the crankshaft must be correctly positioned. Unscrew and remove the bolt below the balancer **(see illustration)**. Discard its sealing washer. Obtain either the Honda special tool (part No. 90004-MM5-000, which is an M6 x 18 mm bolt with a coned end) or an equivalent (make sure the thread pitch is identical to the bolt removed and ground at the end so it is coned instead of flat) **(see illustration)**. Identify the hole in the balancer shaft into which the bolt end must locate, then turn the shaft until the hole aligns with the bolt hole in the crankcase, then thread the special bolt into the crankcase until its shaped end locates in the hole in the balancer, thereby locking it to prevent it turning **(see illustration)**. Set the crankshaft so that the No. 1 (left-hand) piston is at top dead centre in its bore, then turn it slightly as required until the centre of the 5th spline anti-clockwise from the wide spline on the right-hand (starter clutch) end aligns with the lower triangular mark on the crankcase as shown **(see illustration)**. Make sure the No. 1 piston is correctly set at TDC because there are two wide splines on the crankshaft, and if the wrong one is aligned the engine will be out of balance.

19 Apply a small amount of suitable sealant (Three-Bond 1207B or equivalent RTV sealant – ask your dealer) to the outer mating surface of the lower crankcase half as shown **(see illustration)**.

Caution: Apply the sealant only to the shaded areas. Do not apply an excessive amount as it will ooze out when the case halves are assembled and may obstruct oil passages. Do not apply the sealant close to any of the bearing shells or surfaces, or oil passages.

23.18b **. . . then find or buy a suitable replacement as described . . .**

23.18c **. . . to locate in the hole (arrowed) in the shaft**

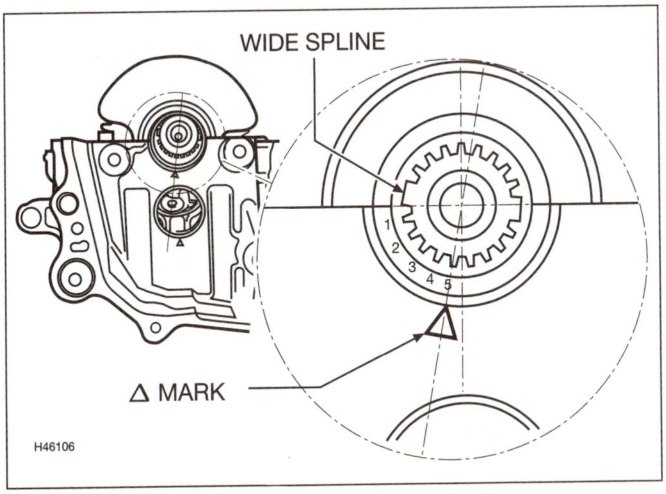

23.18d **Make sure the crankshaft is correctly aligned as shown**

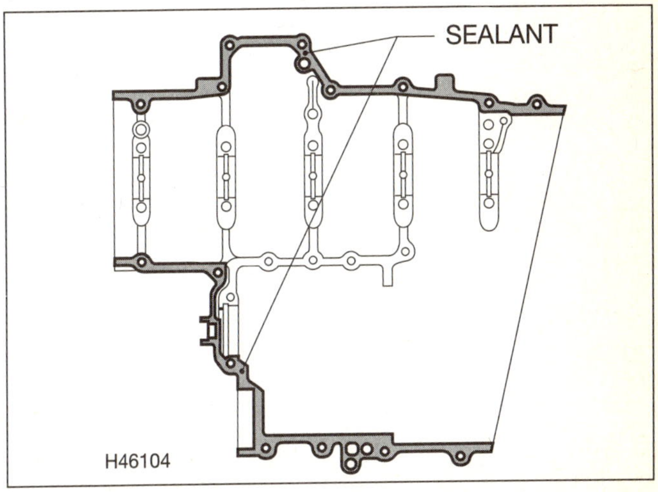

23.19 **Apply the sealant to the shaded area shown**

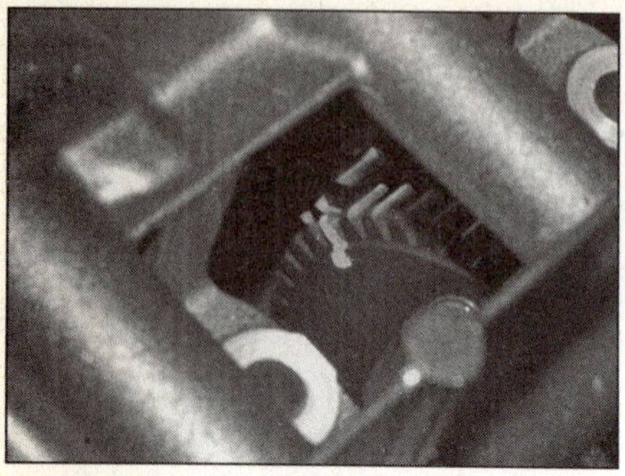

23.20 Make sure the painted teeth mesh together

23.22a Use new bolts for the crankshaft journals and fit the longer ones at the alternator end

23.22b Tighten the bolts as described in the sequence shown to the specified torque . . .

20 Check again that all components are in position, and that the bearing shells are still correctly located in the lower crankcase half. Carefully fit the lower crankcase half down onto the upper crankcase half, making sure the dowels and oil orifices locate correctly **(see illustration 23.10)**. As the balancer shaft and crankshaft gears engage, the paint marks on their teeth should match as shown – note that the crankshaft may turn slightly as the teeth mate **(see illustration)**. Check that the lower crankcase half is correctly seated.

21 To double check alignment, or if the paint marks are not visible, temporarily fit the starter clutch and timing rotor assembly onto the end of the crankshaft aligning the wide splines (see Section 13), and check that the line next to the 'T' mark on the timing rotor aligns with the higher triangle mark on the crankcase. If the marks do not align, or if you are not sure, remove the lower crankcase and start again, noting that you may have to clean and re-seal the mating surfaces. Remove the special bolt locking the balancer shaft and replace it with the original bolt, but using a new sealing washer **(see illustration 23.18a)**. Tighten the bolt.

Caution: The crankcase halves should fit together without being forced. If the casings are not correctly seated, remove the lower crankcase half and investigate the problem. Do not attempt to pull them together using the crankcase bolts as the casing will crack and be ruined.

22 Install the ten NEW 9 mm crankshaft journal bolts, fitting the four longer bolts into the outer ends **(see illustration and 23.9)**. Secure all bolts finger-tight at first, then tighten them evenly and a little at a time in the numerical sequence shown to the torque setting specified at the beginning of the Chapter **(see illustration)**. Now, using a degree disc, tighten each bolt in turn by a further 150°, again following the numerical sequence **(see illustration)**.

23 Clean the threads of the six 7 mm and one 8 mm lower crankcase bolts and insert them in their original locations **(see illustrations 23.8a and b)**. Secure all bolts finger-tight at first, then tighten the 8 mm bolt to the specified torque. Now tighten the 7 mm bolts evenly and a little at a time in a criss-cross sequence starting in the middle and working outwards to the specified torque setting.

24 Turn the engine over. Clean the threads of the six 7 mm bolts and the five 8 mm bolts and insert them in their original locations **(see illustrations 23.5a and b)** – do not forget to fit a new sealing washer with the 7 mm bolt at the front **(see illustration)**. Secure the bolts finger-tight at first, then tighten the 8 mm bolts evenly and a little at a time in a criss-cross sequence starting in the middle and working outwards to the specified torque setting, followed by the 7 mm bolts.

25 With all crankcase fasteners tightened, check that the crankshaft and balancer shaft rotate smoothly and easily, but at this stage do not worry about any noise from the gear teeth. Refer to Section 30 and adjust the backlash following the static adjustment procedure.

26 Fit a new O-ring smeared with oil into the groove on the inside of the oil level inspection window **(see illustration)**. Fit the window, not forgetting the wiring clamp on RR-6 and RR-7 models, and tighten the bolts **(see illustration 23.4)**. Reconnect the engine sub-loom wiring to the neutral switch and oil pressure switch **(see illustrations 23.3b and a)**. Install all other removed assemblies in a reverse of the sequence given in Step 2.

24 Crankcases and cylinder bores

Crankcases

1 After the crankcases have been separated, remove the crankshaft and its bearing shells, connecting rods and pistons, balancer shaft, speed sensor, neutral switch and oil pressure switch, referring to the relevant Sections of this Chapter, and to Chapter 8 for the speed sensor and oil pressure and neutral switches. If there are any other components or assemblies that have not been removed as part of your stripdown procedure, for example the starter motor or the coolant inlet union, remove these as well, referring to the relevant Chapter.

2 Unscrew the bolt securing each piston oil jet and remove the jets with their holders **(see**

23.22c . . . and then through the specified angle using a degree disc

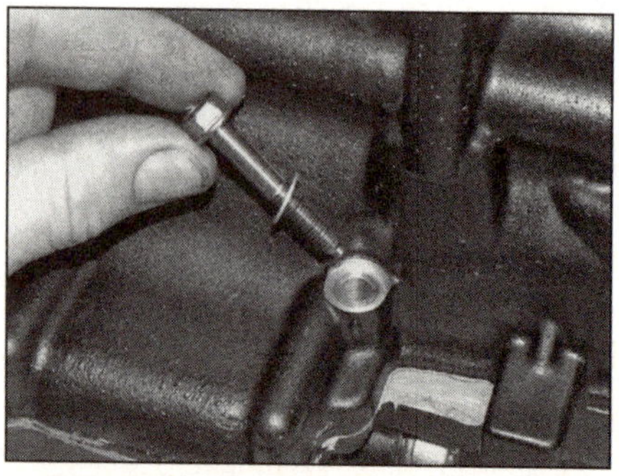

23.24 Use a new sealing washer on this bolt

23.26 Fit a new O-ring onto the oil level window

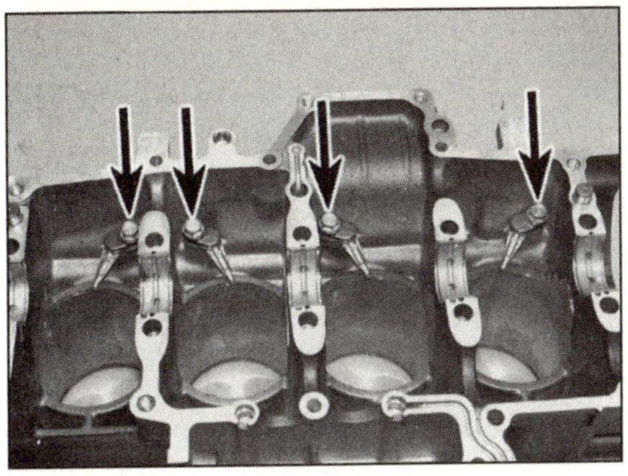

24.2a Piston oil jet bolts (arrowed)

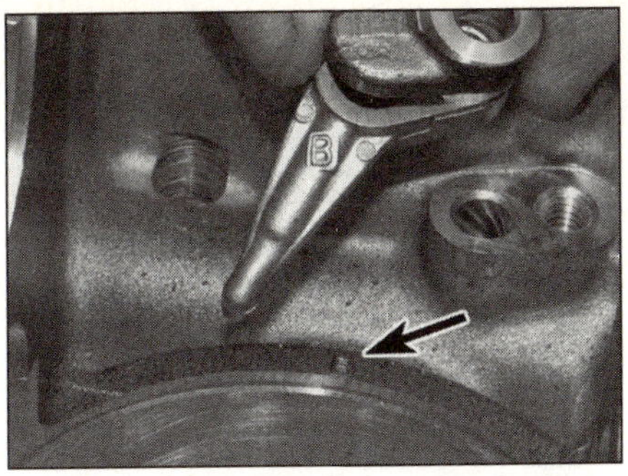

24.2b Note the letter on each jet which matches the letter on the cylinder rim (arrowed)

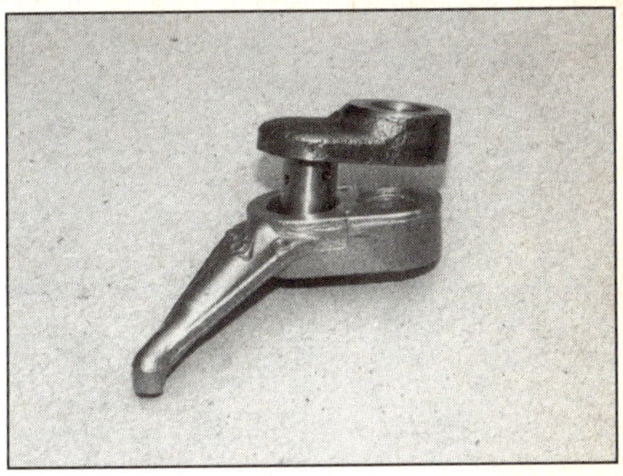

24.8a Fit the holders into the jets

illustration) – note that each jet is marked with the letter A or B that corresponds to the letter marked on the bottom rim of its cylinder **(see illustration)**. Separate the jets from the holders **(see illustration 24.8a)**.

3 Clean the crankcases thoroughly with new solvent and dry them with compressed air. Blow out all oil passages with compressed air. Clean the inside of the oil level inspection window. Clean and blow through the piston oil jets and holders.

4 Remove all traces of old gasket sealant from the mating surfaces. Clean up minor damage to the surfaces with a fine sharpening stone or grindstone.

Caution: Be very careful not to nick or gouge the crankcase mating surfaces or oil leaks may result. Check both crankcase halves very carefully for cracks and other damage.

5 Small cracks or holes in aluminium castings can be repaired with an epoxy resin adhesive as a temporary measure. Permanent repairs can be done by argon-arc welding (only a specialist in this process should carry out this work), or alternatively small repairs can be made using one of the low temperature welding kits. If any damage is found that can't be repaired, replace the crankcase halves as a set.

6 Damaged threads can be economically reclaimed using a diamond section wire insert, for example of the Heli-Coil type (though there are other makes), which are easily fitted after drilling and re-tapping the affected thread.

7 Sheared studs or screws can usually be removed with extractors, which consist of a tapered, left-hand thread screw of very hard steel. These are inserted into a pre-drilled hole in the stud, and usually succeed in dislodging the most stubborn stud or screw. If a stud has sheared above its bore line, it can be removed using a conventional stud extractor which avoids the need for drilling.

HAYNES HiNT ***Refer to Tools and Workshop Tips for details of installing a thread insert and using screw extractors.***

8 Fit the holders into the piston oil jets **(see illustration)**. Fit the jets, making sure the ones marked A are fitted into the Nos. 2 and 3 cylinders and the ones marked B are fitted into the Nos. 1 and 4 cylinders, corresponding to the marks on the cylinder rim **(see illustration 24.2b)**. Apply a suitable non-permanent thread locking compound to the jet bolts and tighten them **(see illustration)**.

9 Install all components and assemblies, referring to the relevant Sections of this and the other Chapters, before reassembling the crankcase halves. Fit a new O-ring smeared with oil into the groove in the oil level inspection window then fit it onto the crankcase and tighten its bolts.

Cylinder bores

Note: *Do not attempt to separate the cylinder liners from the cylinder block. The liners are made of an aluminium/ceramic powdered metal composite and so great care must be taken not to scratch or gouge them.*

10 Check the cylinder walls carefully for scratches and score marks.

11 Using a precision straight-edge and a feeler gauge set to the warpage limit listed in the specifications at the beginning of the Chapter, check the block gasket mating surface for warpage. Refer to Tools and Workshop Tips in the Reference section for details of how to use the straight-edge. If warpage is excessive the crankcases must be replaced with new ones.

12 Using telescoping gauges and a micrometer (see Tools and Workshop Tips), check the dimensions of each cylinder to assess the amount of wear, taper and ovality. Measure near the top (but below the level of the top piston ring at TDC), centre and bottom (but above the level of the oil ring at BDC) of the bore, both parallel to and across the crankshaft axis **(see illustrations)**. Compare the results to the specifications at the beginning of the Chapter. If the cylinders are worn, oval or tapered beyond the service limit they can be re-bored – an oversize (+ 0.25) set of pistons and rings and available. Note that the engineer carrying out the re-bore must be aware of the piston-to-bore clearance for the oversize pistons and rings (see Specifications).

13 If the precision measuring tools are not available, take the upper crankcase to a Honda dealer or specialist motorcycle repair shop for assessment and advice.

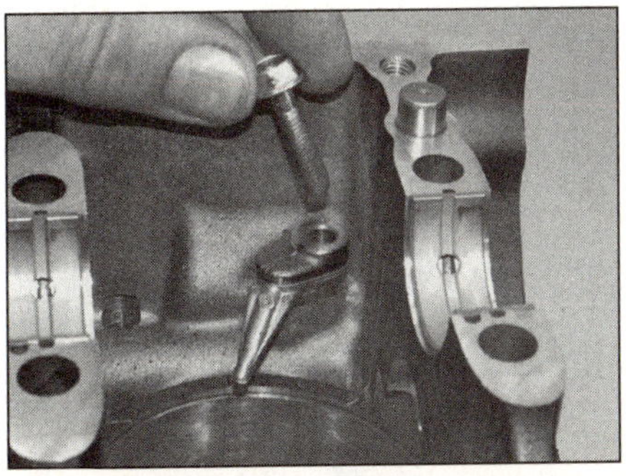

24.8b Apply a thread lock to the bolts

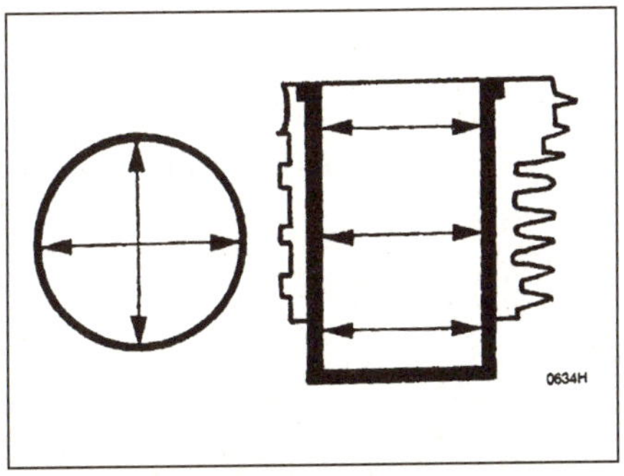

24.12a Measure the cylinder bore in the directions shown . . .

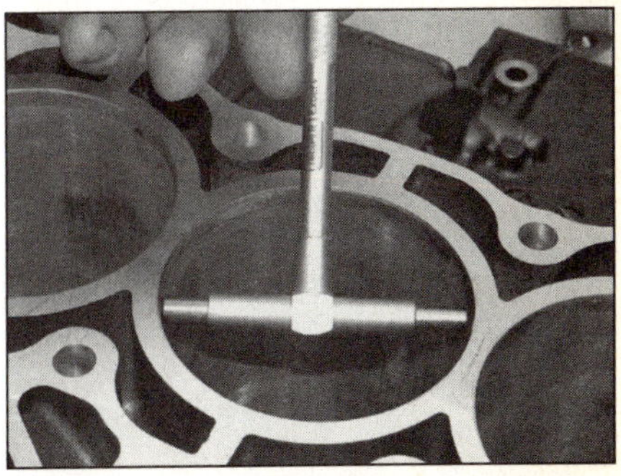

24.12b . . . using a telescoping gauge, then measure the gauge with a micrometer

25 Connecting rod and main bearing information

1 Even though new main and connecting rod bearings are generally fitted during engine overhaul, the old bearings should be retained for close examination as they often reveal valuable information about the condition of the engine.

2 Bearing failure occurs mainly because of lack of lubrication, the presence of dirt or other foreign particles, overloading the engine and/or corrosion. Regardless of the cause of bearing failure, it must be corrected before the engine is reassembled to prevent it from happening again.

3 When examining the bearings, lay them out on a clean surface in the same general position as their location on the crankshaft journals. This will enable you to match any noted bearing problems with the corresponding crankshaft journal.

4 Dirt and other foreign particles get into the engine in a variety of ways. They may be left in the engine during assembly or they may pass through filters or breathers, then get into the oil and from there into the bearings. Metal chips from machining operations and normal engine wear are often present. Abrasives are sometimes left in engine components after reconditioning operations, especially when parts are not thoroughly cleaned using the proper cleaning methods. Whatever the source, foreign objects often end up imbedded in the soft bearing material and are easily recognised. Large particles will not imbed in the bearing and will score or gouge the bearing and journal. The best prevention for this cause of bearing failure is to clean all parts thoroughly and keep everything spotlessly clean during engine reassembly. Regular oil and filter changes are also recommended.

5 Lack of lubrication or lubrication breakdown has a number of interrelated causes. Excessive heat (which thins the oil), overloading (which squeezes the oil from the bearing face) and oil leakage or throw off (from excessive bearing clearances, worn oil pump or high engine speeds) all contribute to lubrication breakdown. Blocked oil passages will starve a bearing of lubrication and destroy it. When lack of lubrication is the cause of bearing failure, the bearing material is wiped or extruded from the steel backing of the bearing. Temperatures may increase to the point where the steel backing and the journal turn blue from overheating.

HAYNES HiNT ***Refer to Tools and Workshop Tips for bearing fault finding.***

6 Riding habits can have a definite effect on bearing life. Full throttle low, speed operation, or labouring the engine, puts very high loads on bearings, which tend to squeeze out the oil film. These loads cause the bearings to flex, which produces fine cracks in the bearing face (fatigue failure). Eventually the bearing material will loosen in pieces and tear away from the steel backing. Short trip riding leads to corrosion of bearings, as insufficient engine heat is produced to drive off the condensed water and corrosive gases produced. These products collect in the engine oil, forming acid and sludge. As the oil is carried to the engine bearings, the acid attacks and corrodes the bearing material.

7 Incorrect bearing installation during engine assembly will lead to bearing failure as well. Tight fitting bearings which leave insufficient bearing oil clearances result in oil starvation. Dirt or foreign particles trapped behind a bearing insert result in high spots on the bearing which lead to failure.

8 To avoid bearing problems, clean all parts thoroughly before reassembly, double check all bearing clearance measurements and lubricate the new bearings with clean engine oil during installation.

26 Crankshaft and main bearings

Note 1: *To remove the crankshaft the engine must be removed from the frame and the crankcase halves separated.*

Note 2: *The crankshaft journal bolts can only be used in a running engine once, though they can be used when performing the oil clearance check.*

Special tool: *A degree disc is required for tightening the crankshaft journal bolts if performing an oil clearance check* ***(see illustration 23.22c)****.*

Removal

1 Remove the engine from the frame (see Section 4) and separate the crankcase halves (see Section 23).

2 Refer to Section 27 and detach the connecting rods from the crankpins. Push the rods and pistons up to the tops of the bores so that the bottom ends are clear of the crankshaft, taking care to keep the rods clear of the cylinder liners – it is best to protect the liners with some rag **(see illustration 27.4c)**. **Note:** *If no work is to be carried out on the piston/connecting rod assemblies there is no need to remove them from the bores. If you do need to remove them, continue to refer to Section 27.*

3 Lift the crankshaft out of the upper crankcase half, bringing the cam chain with it if it hasn't been removed, and taking care not to dislodge the main bearing shells **(see illustration)**. Wrap some rag around each connecting rod to protect the cylinder walls.

4 If necessary remove the main bearing shells from the crankcase halves using a small screwdriver inserted in the notch to lift them out, but make sure you keep them in order **(see illustration)**. If they are being reused they must be returned to their original location.

Inspection

5 Clean the crankshaft with solvent, squirting it under pressure through all the oil passages. If available, blow the crank dry with compressed air, and also blow through the oil passages. Check the primary drive gear and the balancer drive gear for wear or damage. If any of the gear teeth are excessively worn, chipped or broken, the crankshaft must be replaced with a new one. If wear or damage is found, also inspect the primary driven gear on the back of the clutch housing (see Section 14), and the balancer shaft driven gear (see Section 30).

6 Refer to Section 25 and examine the main bearing shells. If they are scored, badly scuffed or appear to have been seized, new bearings must be installed. Always replace the main bearings as a set selected as described in Steps 21 and 22. If they are badly damaged, check the corresponding crankshaft journals. Evidence of extreme heat, such as discoloration, indicates that lubrication failure has occurred. Be sure to thoroughly check the oil pump and pressure relief valve as well as all oil holes and passages before reassembling the engine.

7 Give the crankshaft journals a close visual examination, paying particular attention where damaged bearings have been discovered. If the journals are scored or pitted in any way a new crankshaft will be required. Note that undersizes are not available, precluding the option of regrinding the crankshaft.

26.3 Lift the crankshaft out of the crankcase

26.4 Remove the shells from their housings

26.13 Place a strip of Plastigauge on each bearing journal

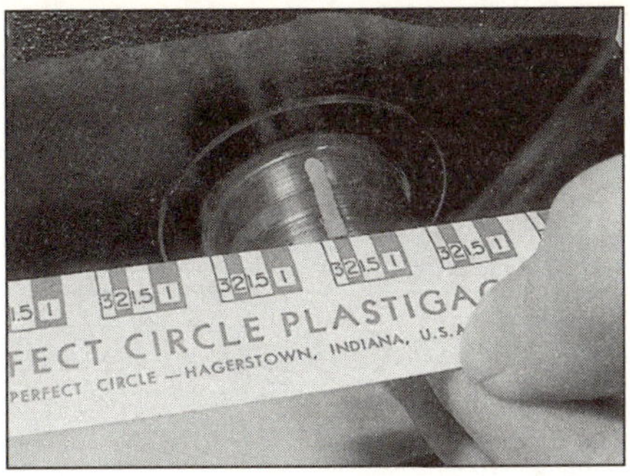

26.16 Measure the crushed Plastigauge using the scale on the pack

26.19 Measure the diameter of the main journal as shown

8 Place the crankshaft on V-blocks and check the runout at the main bearing journals using a dial gauge. Compare the reading to the maximum specified at the beginning of the Chapter. If the runout exceeds the limit, the crankshaft must be replaced with a new one.

Oil clearance check

9 Whether new bearing shells are being fitted or the original ones are being reused, the main bearing oil clearance should be checked before the engine is reassembled. Main bearing oil clearance is measured with a product known as Plastigauge.

10 Remove the shells if not already done **(see illustration 26.4)**. Clean the backs of the shells and the bearing housings in both crankcase halves.

11 Press the bearing shells into their cut-outs, ensuring that the tab on each shell engages in the notch in the crankcase **(see illustration 26.24)**. Make sure the bearings are fitted in the correct locations and take care not to touch any shell's bearing surface with your fingers.

12 Ensure the shells and crankshaft are clean and dry. Lay the crankshaft in position in the upper crankcase **(see illustration 26.3)**. Install the three crankcase dowels if removed **(see illustration 23.11a)**.

13 Cut five lengths of the appropriate size Plastigauge (they should be slightly shorter than the width of the crankshaft journals). Place a strand of Plastigauge on each (cleaned) journal, avoiding the oil hole **(see illustration)**. During the procedure make sure the crankshaft is not rotated at all as this will disturb the Plastigauge and give false readings, in which case you must start again.

14 Carefully fit the lower crankcase half onto the upper half **(see illustration 23.10)**. Check that the lower half is correctly seated. Install the ten 9 mm crankshaft journal bolts, fitting the four longer bolts into the outer ends **(see illustrations 23.9 and 23.22a)**. Secure all bolts finger-tight at first, then tighten them evenly and a little at a time in the numerical sequence shown to the torque setting specified at the beginning of the Chapter **(see illustration 23.22b)**. Now, using a degree disc, tighten each bolt in turn by a further 150°, again following the numerical sequence **(see illustration 23.22c)**.

15 Slacken each bolt evenly and a little at a time in a reverse of the tightening sequence, i.e. starting from the outside and working to the centre, until they are all finger-tight, then remove the bolts. Carefully lift off the lower crankcase half, making sure the Plastigauge is not disturbed.

16 Compare the width of the crushed Plastigauge on each crankshaft journal to the scale printed on the Plastigauge envelope to obtain the main bearing oil clearance **(see illustration)**. Compare the reading to the specifications at the beginning of the Chapter.

17 On completion carefully scrape away all traces of the Plastigauge material from the crankshaft journal and bearing shells; use a fingernail or other object which is unlikely to score them.

18 If the clearance is within the range listed in this Chapter's Specifications and the bearings are in perfect condition, they can be reused.

19 If the clearance on any journal is beyond the service limit, measure the journal to see if it has worn **(see illustration)**. If it has refer to Steps 21 and 22 and use the specifications given in the bearing selection table to determine whether different shells that correspond with the actual journal diameter (as opposed to its given size code) can be used. If the journal is the correct diameter for its given size code, replace the bearing shells with new ones according to the size codes. Check the oil clearance once again. Always replace all of the shells at the same time.

20 If the crankshaft has worn beyond the narrowest diameter given it must be replaced with a new one, and new shells selected according to that crankshaft.

Main bearing shell selection

21 Replacement bearing shells for the main bearings are supplied on a selected fit basis. Code letters and numbers stamped on the crankshaft and crankcase, or the actual measured size of the crankshaft journal, are used to identify the correct replacement bearings. The crankshaft main bearing journal size numbers are stamped on the outside of the left-hand crankshaft web and will be either a 1, 2 or 3 **(see illustration)**. The first number, after the L, is for the left-hand journal, and the numbers correspond consecutively for each journal. The corresponding main bearing housing size letters are stamped into the left-hand side of the upper crankcase half and will be either an A, B or C **(see illustration)**. The left-hand letter corresponds to the left-

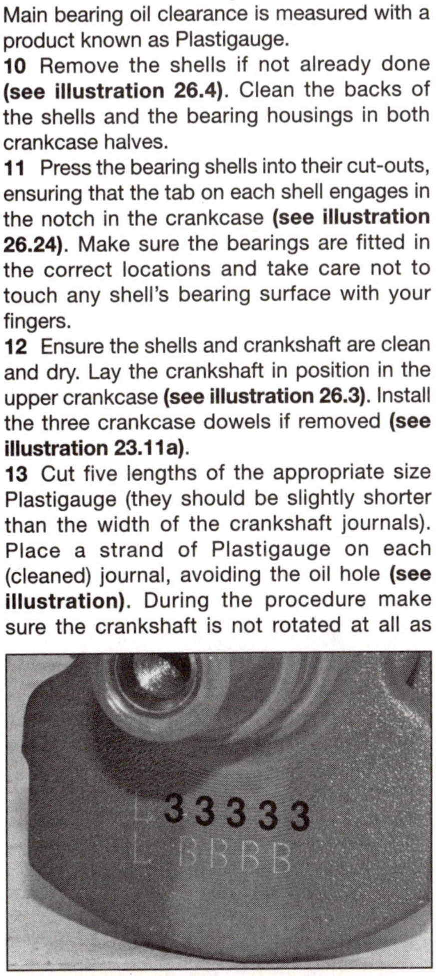

26.21a Main bearing journal size numbers

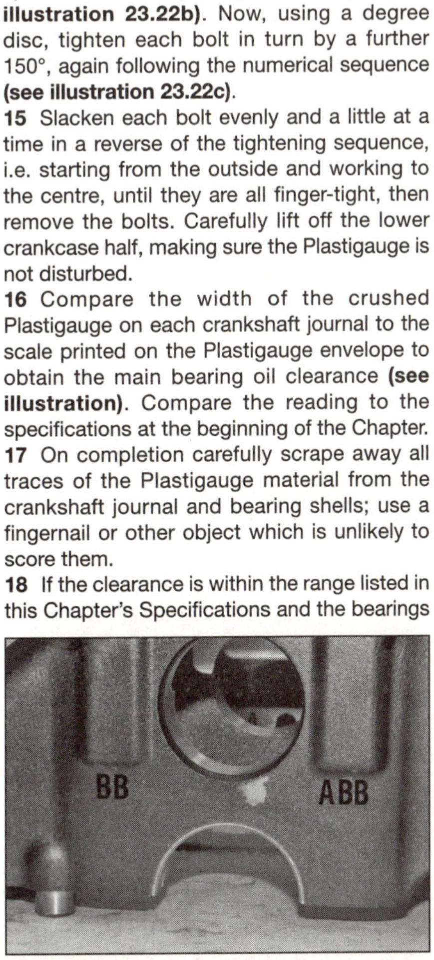

26.21b Main bearing housing size letters

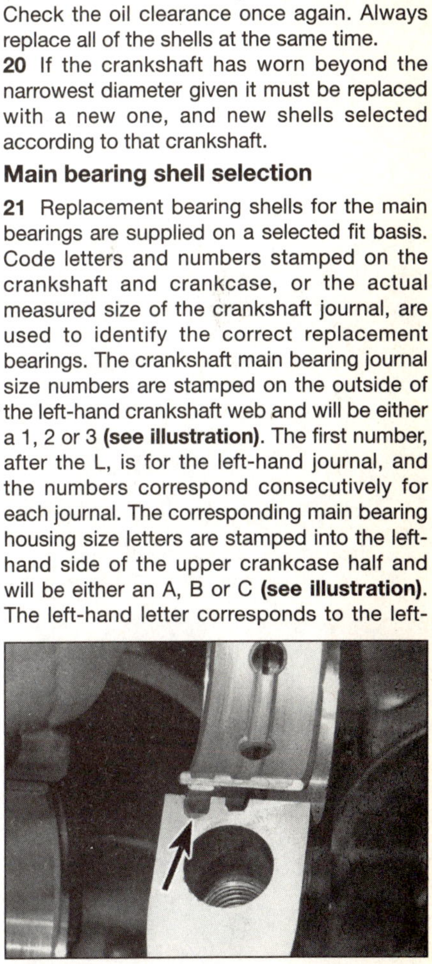

26.24 Fit the shells, locating the tabs in the notches (arrowed)

	Main bearing housing code		
Main bearing journal code	**A**	**B**	**C**
1 (34.000 to 34.006 mm)	Red	Pink	Yellow
2 (33.994 to 34.000 mm)	Pink	Yellow	Green
3 (33.988 to 33.994 mm)	Yellow	Green	Brown

hand journal, and the letters correspond consecutively from left to right.

22 A range of bearing shells is available. To select the correct bearing for a particular journal, use the table above and cross-refer the main bearing journal size number or measured size with the main bearing housing size letter to determine the colour code of the bearing required. For example, if the journal code is 3, and the housing code is A, then the bearing required is yellow. The colour is marked on the side of the shell **(see illustration 27.22)**.

Installation

23 Clean the backs of the bearing shells and the bearing cut-outs in both crankcase halves. If new shells are being fitted, ensure that all traces of the protective grease are cleaned off using paraffin (kerosene). Wipe the shells and crankcase halves dry with a lint-free cloth. Make sure all the oil passages and holes are clear, and blow them through with compressed air if it is available.

24 Press the bearing shells into their locations. Make sure the tab on each shell engages in the notch in the casing **(see illustration)**. Make sure the bearings are fitted in the correct locations and take care not to touch any shell's bearing surface with your fingers. Lubricate each shell with molybdenum disulphide oil (a 50/50 mixture of molybdenum disulphide grease and clean engine oil).

25 Lower the crankshaft into position in the upper crankcase, making sure all bearings remain in place **(see illustration 26.3)**.

26 Refer to Section 27 and fit the connecting rods and caps onto the crankshaft.

27 Reassemble the crankcase halves (see Section 23).

27 Connecting rods and bearings

Note 1: *To remove the connecting rods the engine must be removed from the frame and the crankcases separated.*

Note 2: *The connecting rod bolts can only be used in a running engine once, though they can be used when performing the oil clearance check.*

Special tools: *A piston ring compressor is necessary for the installation procedure* ***(see illustration 27.25b)****. A degree disc is also required for tightening the bolts to the correct torque* ***(see illustration 27.28b)****.*

Removal

1 Remove the engine from the frame (see Section 4) and separate the crankcase halves (see Section 23).

2 Before detaching the rods from the crankshaft, measure the side clearance (the gap between the connecting rod big-end and the crankshaft web) with a feeler gauge **(see illustration)**. If the clearance is greater than the service limit listed in this Chapter's Specifications, replace the rods with new ones. If the clearance is still excessive, replace the crankshaft with a new one.

3 Using paint or a felt marker pen, mark the relevant cylinder identity on each connecting rod and cap **(see illustration 27.2)**. Mark across the cap-to-connecting rod join that faces the front of the engine to ensure that everything is fitted the correct way around and onto the correct rod on reassembly. Note that the number already across the rod and cap indicates rod size grade **(see illustration 27.21b)**.

4 Unscrew the connecting rod cap bolts **(see illustration)**. Separate the caps from the crankpin, noting the locating pins **(see illustration)**. Push the rods and pistons up to the tops of the bores so that the bottom ends are clear of the crankshaft, taking care to keep the rods clear of the cylinder liners – it is best to protect the liners with some rag **(see illustration)**. Remove the crankshaft (see Section 26). Wrap some rag around each connecting rod to protect the cylinder walls.

5 Turn the crankcase on its side. Push each piston/connecting rod assembly up its bore and remove it from the top making sure the connecting rod does not mark the cylinder walls **(see illustration)**. The piston crown is marked with a dot that faces the intake side of the cylinder, and the bearing shell notch in the big-end of the connecting rod faces the same way, to the back of the engine (intake side).

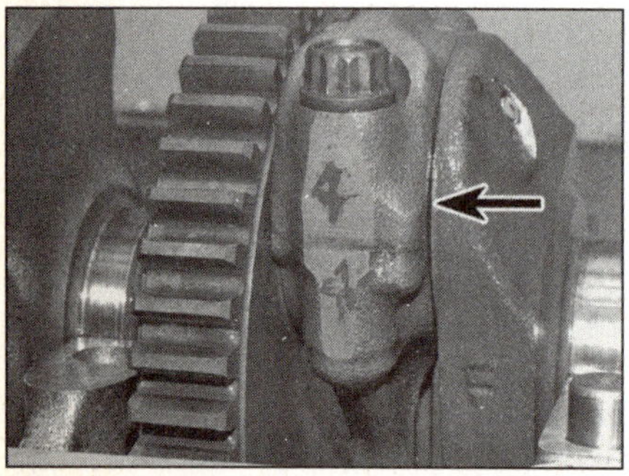

27.2 Measure the gap (arrowed) between the big-end and the web using a feeler gauge

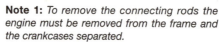

27.4a Unscrew the bolts (arrowed) . . .

27.4b . . . and remove the connecting rod caps

27.4c Push the rods off the crankpins and up the bores

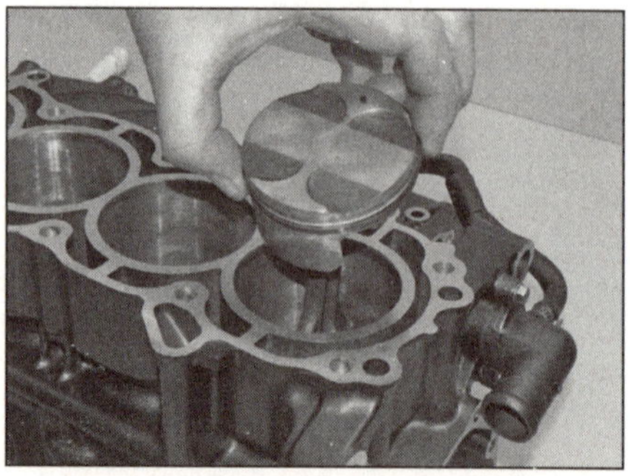

27.5 Carefully lift the piston and rod assembly out of the bore. Note the alignment mark on the intake side

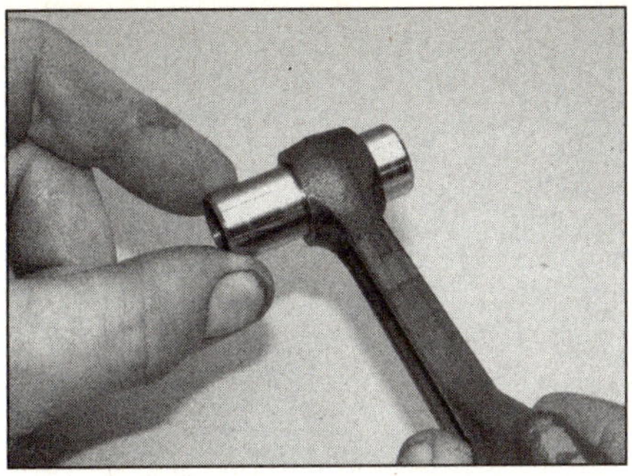
27.9a Check for freeplay between the rod and pin

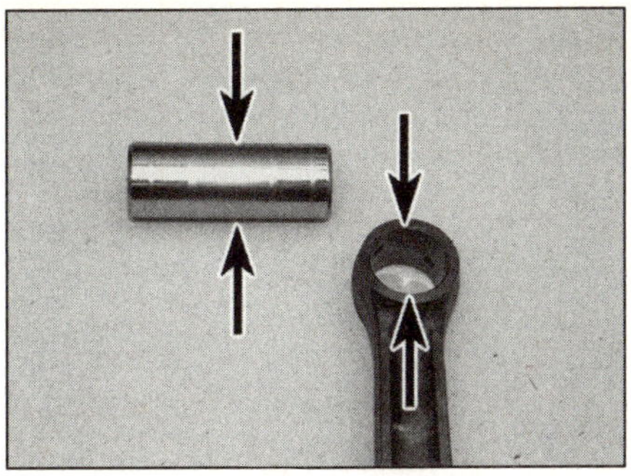
27.9b Measure the external diameter of the pin and the internal diameter of the rod small-end

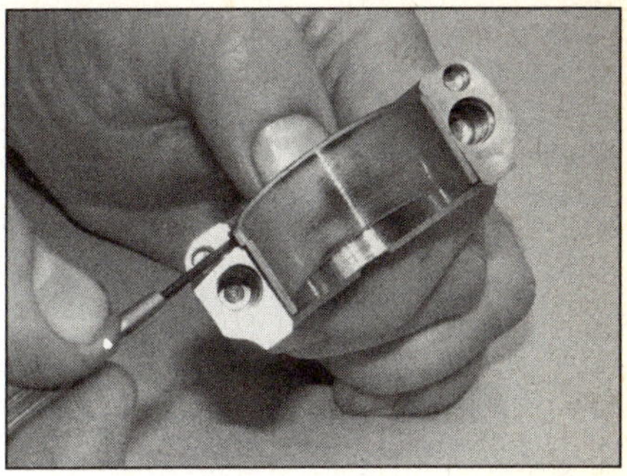
27.10 Remove the shells as shown

HAYNES HiNT *To ease removal of the pistons, carefully remove any ridge of carbon built up on the top of each cylinder bore using a scraper, knife blade or scouring pad. If there is a pronounced wear ridge, remove it using a ridge reamer.*

Caution: Do not try to remove the piston/connecting rod from the bottom of the cylinder bore. The piston will not pass the crankcase main bearing webs. If the piston is pulled right to the bottom of the bore the oil control ring will expand and lock the piston in position. If this happens it is likely the ring will break.

6 Keep the rod, cap, bolts (if they are to be used for an oil clearance check), and the bearing shells (if they are to be reused) together in their correct positions to ensure correct installation – fit the caps back onto the rods and finger-tighten the bolts to make sure.

7 Remove the pistons from the connecting rods if required (see Section 28), but note that if you are doing a big-end oil clearance check they are best left in place as they will prevent the rod rotating on the crankpin and disturbing the Plastigauge.

Inspection

8 Check the connecting rods for cracks and other obvious damage.

9 Apply clean engine oil to the piston pin, insert it into the connecting rod small-end and check for any freeplay between the two **(see illustration)**. Measure the pin external diameter at its centre, and the small-end bore diameter, then calculate the difference to obtain the small-end-to-piston pin clearance **(see illustration)**. Compare the result to the specifications at the beginning of the Chapter. If the clearance is greater than specified, replace the components that are worn beyond their specified limits with new ones.

10 Refer to Section 25 and examine the connecting rod bearing shells. If they are scored, badly scuffed, corroded, or appear to have seized, new shells must be installed. Remove the shells from the rods and caps using a small screwdriver inserted in the notch to lift them out **(see illustration)**. Always replace the shells in the connecting rods as a set. If they are badly damaged, check the corresponding crankpin. Evidence of extreme heat, such as discoloration, indicates that lubrication failure has occurred. Be sure to thoroughly check the oil pump and pressure relief valve as well as all oil holes and passages before reassembling the engine.

11 Have the rods checked for twist and bend by a Honda dealer if you are in doubt about their straightness.

Oil clearance check

12 Whether new bearing shells are being fitted or the original ones are being reused, the connecting rod bearing oil clearance should be checked prior to reassembly. Check the clearance on two rods at a time, doing Nos. 1 and 4 together and Nos. 2 and 3 together, turning the crankshaft as required so their crankpins are positioned to give best access.

13 Remove the shells from the rods and caps **(see illustration 27.10)**. Clean the backs of the bearing shells and the bearing housings in both the connecting rod and cap.

14 Press the bearing shells into their housings, making sure the tab on each shell engages the notch in the connecting rod/cap **(see illustration 27.24)**. Make sure the bearings are fitted in the correct location and take care not to touch any shell's bearing surface with your fingers. Refer to Step 25 and fit the rods and pistons into their bores. Turn the crankcase over and lay the crankshaft in the upper crankcase half (make sure the main bearing shells are installed), and position it so the crankpins being checked are central and uppermost. Pull the connecting rods onto the crankpins, making sure they are the correct way round so previously made markings align (Step 3) **(see illustration 27.4c)**.

15 Cut a length of the appropriate size Plastigauge (it should be slightly shorter than the width of the crankpin). Place a strand of Plastigauge on each crankpin journal being checked, making sure it is not over the oil hole. Fit the caps onto the rods **(see illustrations 27.4b)**. Make sure each cap is fitted the correct way around so the previously made markings align **(see illustration 27.2)**. Apply some clean oil to the threads and under the heads of the connecting rod bolts **(see illustration 27.28a)**. Install the bolts and tighten them evenly and a little at a time to the oil clearance (old bolt) torque setting specified at the beginning of the Chapter all the time ensuring that the crankshaft does not rotate. Now, using a degree disc, tighten each bolt in turn by a further 90° **(see illustration 27.28b)**. It is highly advisable to have an assistant to hold the crankshaft down in the crankcase while tightening the bolts as it could jump out.

16 Slacken the bolts and remove the connecting rod caps. Compare the width of the crushed Plastigauge on the crankpin to the scale printed on the Plastigauge envelope to obtain the connecting rod bearing oil clearance. Compare the reading to the specifications at the beginning of the Chapter.

17 On completion carefully scrape away all traces of the Plastigauge material from the crankpin and bearing shells using a fingernail or other object which is unlikely to score the shells. Repeat the procedure for the other two rods.

18 If the clearance is within the range listed in this Chapter's Specifications and the bearings are in perfect condition, they can be reused.

19 If the clearance is beyond the service limit, measure the crankpin to see if it has worn, and if it has refer to Steps 21 and 22 and use the specifications given in the bearing selection table to determine whether different shells that correspond with the actual crankpin diameter (as opposed to its given size code) can be used. If the crankpin is the correct diameter for its given size code, replace the bearing shells with new ones according to the size codes. Check the oil clearance once again. Always replace all of the shells at the same time.

20 If the crankshaft has worn beyond the narrowest diameter given it must be replaced with a new one, and new shells selected according to that crankshaft.

Bearing shell selection

21 Replacement bearing shells for the big-end bearings are supplied on a selected fit basis. Code letters and numbers stamped

27.21a Crankpin journal size letters

27.21b Connecting rod size number

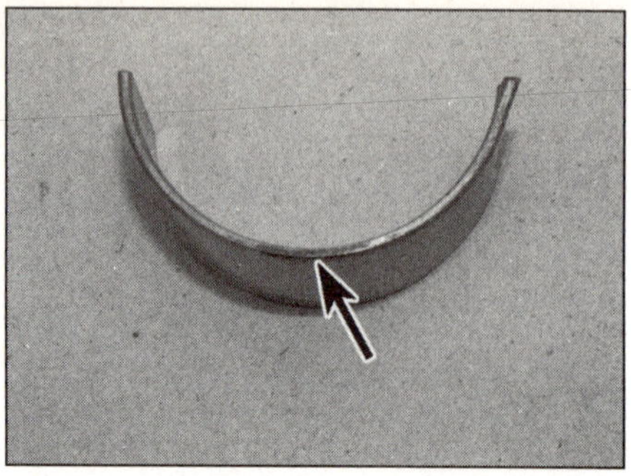
27.22 The colour is on the side of the shell

on the crankshaft and connecting rod, or the actual measured size of the crankpin journal, are used to identify the correct replacement bearings. The crankpin journal size letters are stamped on the outside of the left-hand crankshaft web, and will be either an A, B or C **(see illustration)**. The first letter after the L is for the No. 1 cylinder connecting rod (left-hand journal), and the letters correspond consecutively for each cylinder. The connecting rod size code number is marked across the flat face of the connecting rod and cap and will be either a 1, 2 or 3 **(see illustration)**.

22 A range of bearing shells is available. To select the correct bearing shell colour code for a particular big-end, use the table below and cross-refer the crankpin journal size letter or measured size with the connecting rod size number. For example, if the crankpin size is B, and the connecting rod size is 1, then the bearing required is green. The colour is marked on the side of the shell **(see illustration)**.

	Connecting rod code		
Crankpin journal code	**1**	**2**	**3**
A (36.497 to 36.503 mm)	Yellow	Green	Brown
B (36.491 to 36.497 mm)	Green	Brown	Black
C (36.485 to 36.491 mm)	Brown	Black	Blue

Installation

23 Fit the pistons onto the connecting rods (see Section 28).

24 Clean the backs of the bearing shells and the bearing housings in both cap and rod. If new shells are being fitted, ensure that all traces of any protective grease are cleaned off using paraffin (kerosene). Wipe the shells, cap and rod dry with a clean lint free cloth. Install the bearing shells in the connecting rods and caps, making sure the tab on each shell engages the notch in the connecting rod/cap **(see illustration)**. Lubricate the shells with molybdenum disulphide oil (a 50/50 mixture of molybdenum disulphide grease and clean engine oil).

25 Position the crankcase the correct way up. Lubricate the pistons, rings and cylinder bores with clean engine oil. Wrap some rag round the bottom of each connecting rod. Fit a piston ring compressor around the first piston being installed and tighten it to compress the rings – a compressor is required because there is very little lead-in for the rings to be easily fed in by hand **(see illustration)**. Locate the piston/connecting assembly on the top of the bore with the dot on the piston crown on the intake side **(see illustration 27.5)** and tap the top of the piston using a wooden or plastic tool (such as the handle end of a hammer) until the piston is completely in the bore **(see illustration)**. If resistance is felt a ring may be catching on the rim – do not try

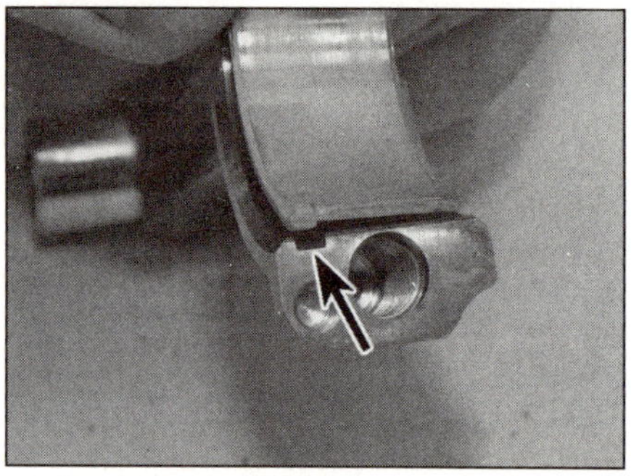
27.24 Fit the shells, locating the tabs in the notches (arrowed)

27.25a Fit the compressor over the piston and rings and compress the rings by tightening the bands on the compressor using an Allen key

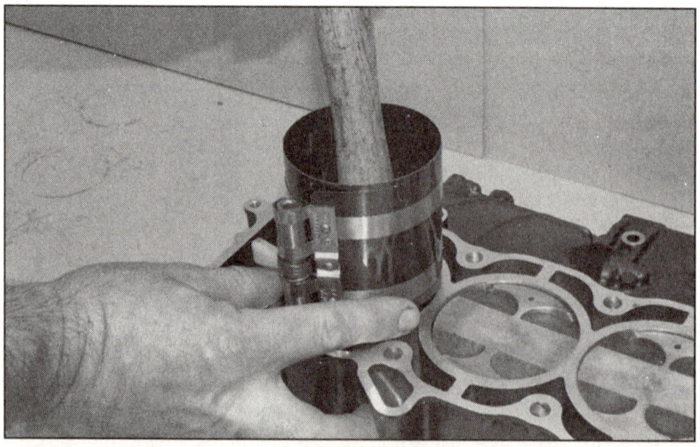
27.25b Fit the rod into the bore and rest the compressor on the crankcase then tap the top of the piston with a soft-faced tool so that it enters

27.28a Install the lubricated bolts and tighten them as described first to the specified torque . . .

27.28b . . . and then through the specified angle

to force it in as rings are easily broken. Tighten the compressor a bit more to squash the ring. Install the other pistons/rods in the same way.

26 Carefully turn the crankcase upside down. Install the crankshaft (see Section 26), and position it so two of the crankpins (i.e. either for Nos. 1 and 4 cylinders, or for Nos. 2 and 3) are central and uppermost.

27 Lubricate the crankpins with molybdenum disulphide oil (a 50/50 mixture of molybdenum disulphide grease and clean engine oil). Remove the rag and carefully pull the corresponding connecting rods onto the crankpins, taking care not to mark the cylinders **(see illustration 27.4c)**. Fit the caps onto the rods, locating the pins in the holes **(see illustration 27.4b)**. Make sure the previously made markings align, and that the rods are facing the right way (see Step 3).

28 Apply some clean oil to the threads and under the heads of the NEW connecting rod bolts, then fit them and tighten them finger-tight **(see illustration)**. First tighten them evenly and a little at a time to the new bolt torque setting specified at the beginning of the Chapter. Now, using a degree disc, tighten each bolt in turn by a further 90° **(see illustration)**. It is highly advisable to have an assistant to hold the crankshaft down in the crankcase while tightening the bolts as it could jump out.

29 Check that the crankshaft is free to rotate easily, then position it with the remaining crankpins easily accessible and install the other connecting rods in the same way. Check to make sure that all components have been returned to their original locations using the marks made on disassembly.

30 Check that the rods rotate smoothly and freely on the crankpins. If there are any signs of roughness or tightness, remove the rods and recheck the bearing clearance. Sometimes tapping the bottom of the connecting rod cap will relieve tightness, but if in doubt, recheck the clearances.

31 Reassemble the crankcase halves (see Section 23).

28 Pistons

Note: *To remove the pistons the engine must be removed from the frame and the crankcase halves separated.*

Removal

1 Remove the connecting rods (see Section 27).

2 Before removing the piston from the connecting rod, use a sharp scriber or felt marker pen to write the cylinder identity on the crown of each piston (or on the inside of the skirt if the piston is dirty and going to be cleaned). Each piston crown should already be marked with a dot (though it may be invisible until the piston is cleaned) and this dot faces the intake side of the cylinder, the same way as the bearing shell notch in the big-end of the connecting rod **(see illustration)**.

3 Carefully prise out the circlip on one side of the piston using needle-nose pliers or a small flat-bladed screwdriver inserted into the notch **(see illustration)**. Push the piston pin out from the other side to free the piston from the connecting rod **(see illustration)**. Remove the other circlip and discard them as new ones must be used. When the piston has been removed, slide its pin back into its bore so that related parts do not get mixed up.

> **HAYNES HiNT** ***If a piston pin is a tight fit in the piston bosses, use a heat gun to heat the piston – this will expand the alloy piston sufficiently to release its grip on the pin. If the piston pin is particularly stubborn, extract it using a drawbolt tool, but be careful to protect the piston's working surfaces.***

4 Using your thumbs or a piston ring removal and installation tool, carefully remove the rings from the pistons **(see illustrations 29.10, 29.9a and b, 29.7c, b and a)**. Do not nick or gouge the pistons in the process. Carefully note which way up each ring fits and in which groove as they must be installed in their original positions if being reused. The upper surface of the top ring should be marked with the letter R at one end, and the second (middle) ring marked RN **(see illustration 29.9a)**. The top and middle rings can also be identified by the fact that the top ring is narrower in width than the second (middle) ring, and their cross-section profiles are different.

5 Scrape all traces of carbon from the tops of the pistons. A hand-held wire brush or a piece of fine emery cloth can be used once most of the deposits have been scraped away. Do not, under any circumstances, use a wire brush mounted in a drill motor to remove deposits from the pistons; the piston material is soft and will be eroded away by the wire brush.

6 Use a piston ring groove cleaning tool to remove any carbon deposits from the ring grooves. If a tool is not available, a piece broken off an old ring will do the job. Be very

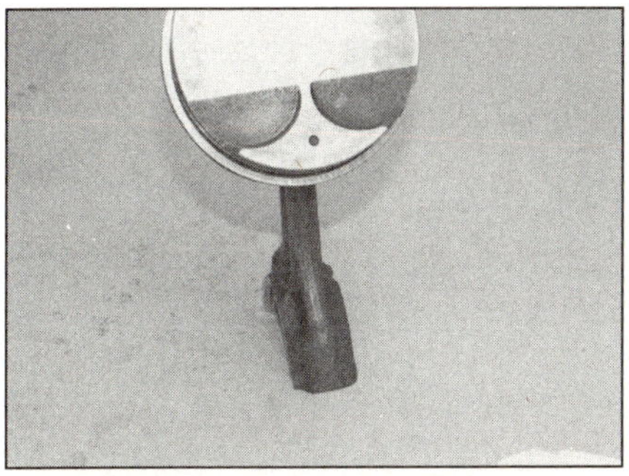

28.2 Note the dot on the piston which faces the intake side, as does the bearing notch in the big-end

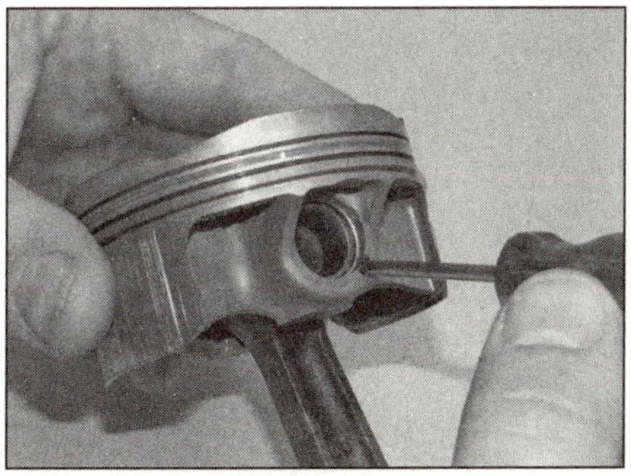

28.3a Prise out the circlip using a suitable tool in the notch . . .

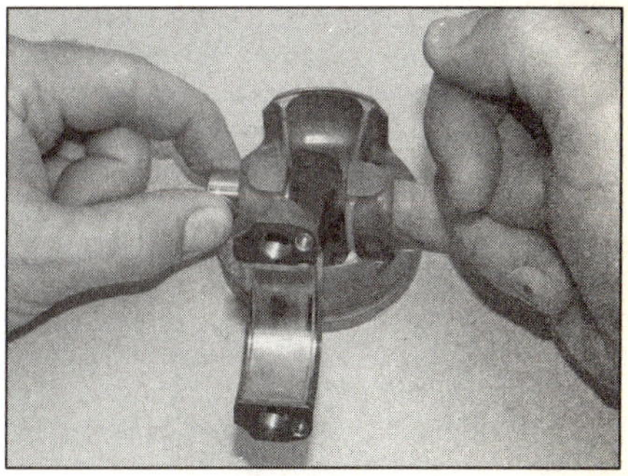

28.3b . . . then push out the pin and separate the piston from the rod

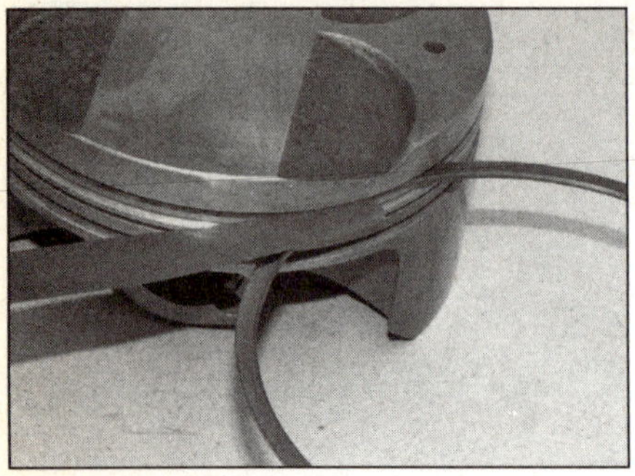

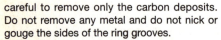

28.10 Measure the piston ring-to-groove clearance with a feeler gauge

28.11 Measure the piston diameter with a micrometer at the specified distance from the bottom of the skirt

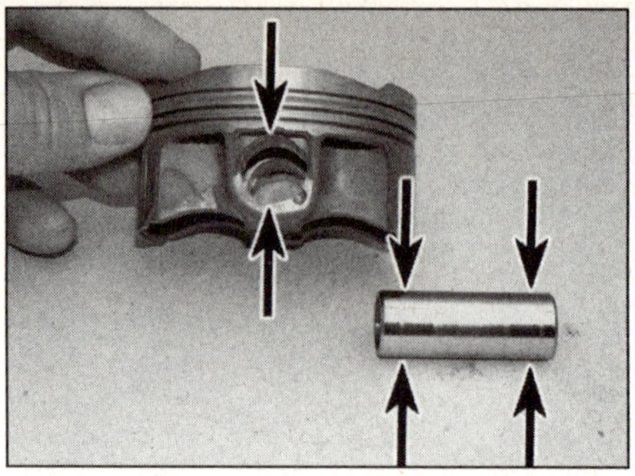

28.12 Measure the external diameter of the pin near each end and the internal diameter of the bore in the piston

careful to remove only the carbon deposits. Do not remove any metal and do not nick or gouge the sides of the ring grooves.

7 Once the deposits have been removed, clean the pistons with solvent and dry them thoroughly. If the identification mark previously made on the piston is cleaned off, be sure to re-mark it with the correct identity. Make sure the oil return holes below the oil ring groove are clear.

Inspection

8 Carefully inspect each piston for cracks around the skirt, at the pin bosses and at the ring lands. Normal piston wear appears as even, vertical wear on the thrust surfaces of the piston. If the skirt is scored or scuffed, the engine may have been suffering from overheating and/or abnormal combustion, which causes excessively high operating temperatures. Also check that the circlip grooves are not damaged.

9 A hole in the top of the piston, in one extreme, or burned areas around the edge of the piston crown, indicate that pre-ignition or knocking under load have occurred. If you find evidence of any problems the cause must be corrected or the damage will occur again (see Fault Finding in the *Reference* section).

10 Measure the piston ring-to-groove clearance by laying each piston ring in its groove and slipping a feeler gauge in beside it **(see illustration)**. Make sure you have the correct ring for the groove (see Step 4). Check the clearance at three or four locations around the groove. If the clearance is greater than specified, replace both the piston and rings as a set. If new rings are being used, measure the clearance using the new rings. If the clearance is greater than that specified, the piston is worn and must be replaced with a new one.

11 Check the piston-to-bore clearance by measuring the bore (see Section 24), then measure the piston 4 mm up from the bottom of the skirt and at 90° to the piston pin axis **(see illustration)**. Make sure each piston is matched to its correct cylinder. Refer to the Specifications at the beginning of the Chapter and subtract the piston diameter from the bore diameter to obtain the clearance. If it is greater than the specified figure, the piston must be replaced with a new one (assuming the bore itself is within limits).

12 Apply clean engine oil to the piston pin, insert it into the piston and check for any freeplay between the two. Measure the pin external diameter near each end, and the pin bores in the piston **(see illustration)**. Calculate the difference to obtain the piston pin-to-piston pin bore clearance. Compare the result to the specifications at the beginning of the Chapter. If the clearance is greater than specified, replace the components that are worn beyond their specified limits. If not already done, repeat the measurements between the pin and the connecting rod small-end (see Section 27).

Installation

13 Inspect and install the piston rings (see Section 29).

14 Lubricate the piston pin, the piston pin bore and the connecting rod small-end bore with molybdenum disulphide oil (a 50/50 mixture of molybdenum disulphide grease and clean engine oil).

15 When fitting the pistons onto the connecting rods make sure the dot on the piston crown faces the intake side of the cylinder, the same way as the bearing shell notch in the big-end of the connecting rod **(see illustration 28.2)**.

16 Fit a ***new*** circlip into one side of the piston (do not reuse old circlips). Line up the piston on its correct connecting rod, and insert the piston pin from the other side **(see illustration)**. Secure the pin with the other ***new*** circlip **(see illustration)**. When fitting the circlips, compress them only just enough to fit them in the piston, and make sure they are properly seated in their grooves with the open end away from the removal notch.

17 Install the connecting rods (see Section 27) and reassemble the crankcase halves (see Section 23).

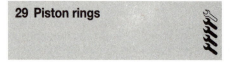

29 Piston rings

Inspection

1 It is good practice to replace the piston rings with new ones when an engine is being overhauled. Before installing the new rings, check their end gaps with the rings installed in the bore, as follows.

2 Lay out each piston with its ring set and keep them together so the rings will be matched with the same piston and bore during the end gap measurement procedure and engine assembly. If the old rings are being reused, make sure they are matched with their correct piston and cylinder.

3 To measure the installed ring end gap, insert the top ring into the top of the bore and square it up with the bore walls by pushing it

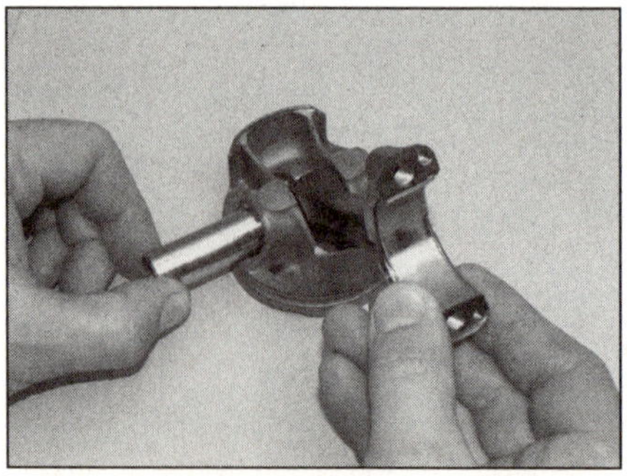

28.16a Slide the pin through the piston and rod . . .

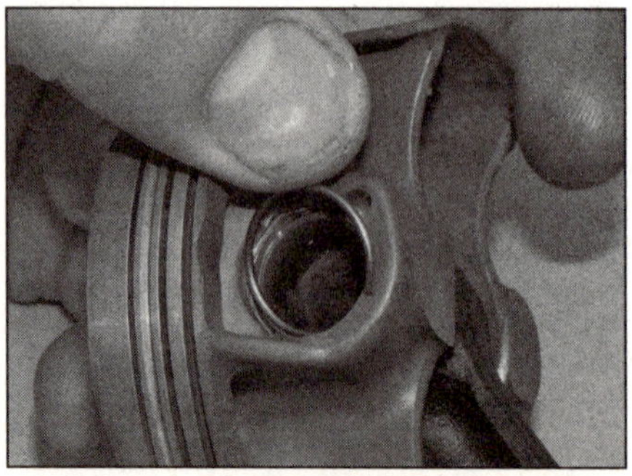

28.16b . . . and secure it with the new circlips

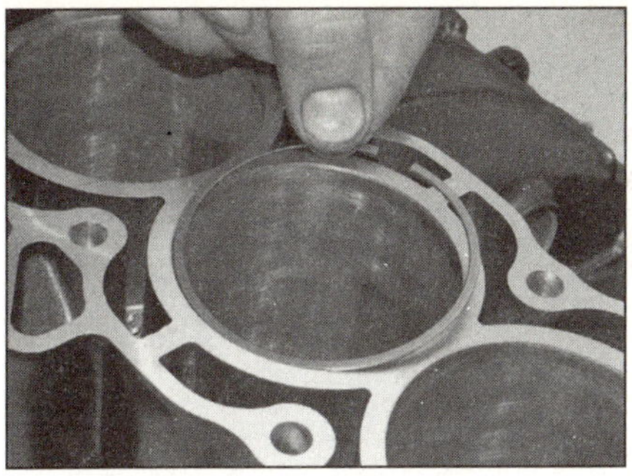

29.3a Fit the ring in its bore . . .

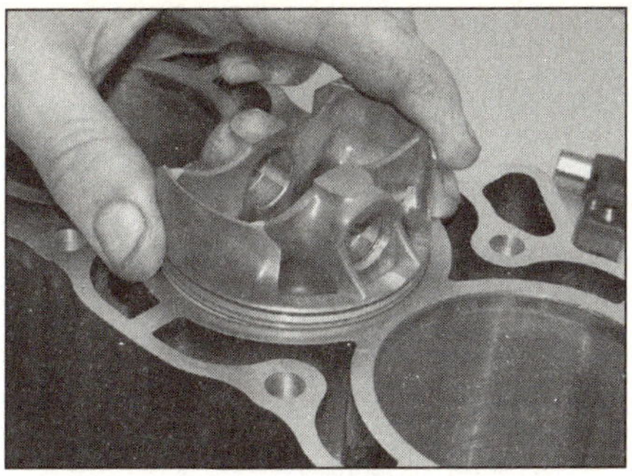

29.3b . . . and square it up using the piston . . .

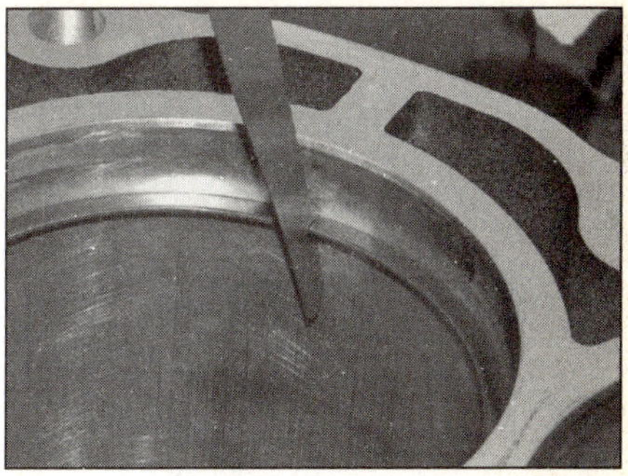

29.3c . . . then measure the end gap using a feeler gauge

in with the top of the piston **(see illustrations)**. The ring should be about 20 mm below the top edge of the bore. Slip a feeler gauge between the ends of the ring and compare the measurement to the specifications at the beginning of the Chapter **(see illustration)**.

4 If the gap is larger or smaller than specified, double check to make sure that you have the correct rings before proceeding; excess end gap is not critical unless it exceeds the service limit.

5 If the service limit is exceeded with new rings, check the bore for wear (see Section 24). If the gap is too small, the ring ends may come in contact with each other during engine operation, which can cause serious damage.

6 Repeat the procedure for the middle ring and the oil control ring side-rails, but not the expander ring. Remember to keep the rings, pistons and bores matched up.

Installation

7 Install the oil control ring (lowest on the piston) first. It is composed of three separate components, namely the expander and the upper and lower side-rails. Slip the expander into the groove, making sure the ends don't overlap, then fit the lower side-rail **(see illustrations)**. Do not use a piston ring installation tool on the side-rails as they may be damaged. Instead, place one end of the side-rail into the groove between the expander and the ring land. Hold it firmly in place and slide a finger around the piston while pushing the rail into the groove. Next, fit the upper side-rail in the same manner **(see illustration)**. Check that the ends of the expander have not overlapped.

8 After the three oil ring components have been installed, check to make sure that both the upper and lower side-rails can be turned smoothly in the ring groove.

9 Install the second (middle) ring next – it should be marked with the letters RN at one end, and it can also be identified by its cross-section profile **(see illustration)**. Make sure that the ring is installed with the identification letter facing up. Fit the ring into the middle groove in the piston **(see illustration)**. Do not expand the ring any more than is necessary to slide it into place. To avoid breaking the ring, use a piston ring installation tool.

10 Finally, install the top ring, marked with the letter R, in the same manner into the top groove in the piston **(see illustration)**. Make sure the identification letter near the end gap is facing up.

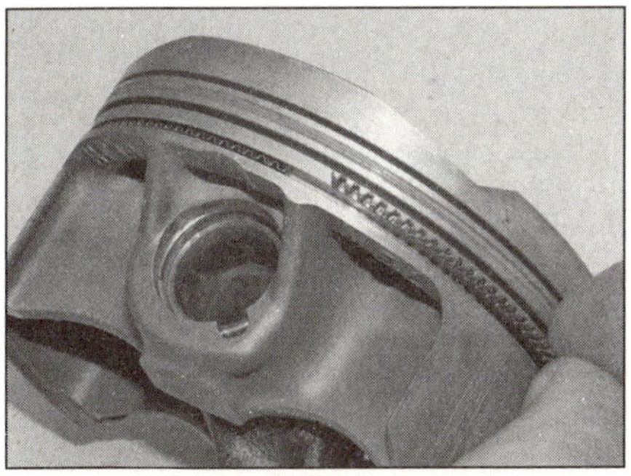

29.7a Fit the oil ring expander in its groove . . .

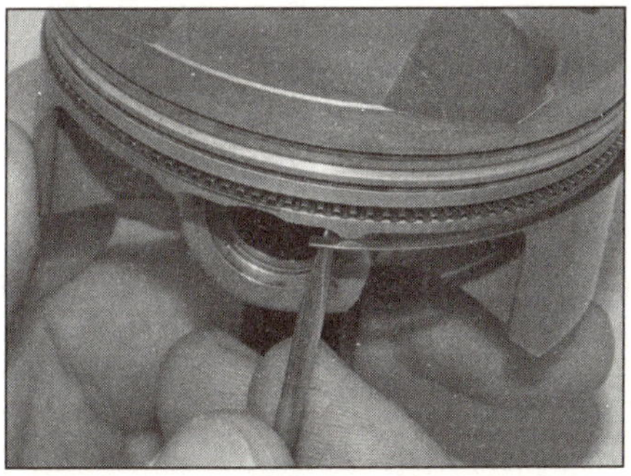

29.7b . . . then fit the lower side rail . . .

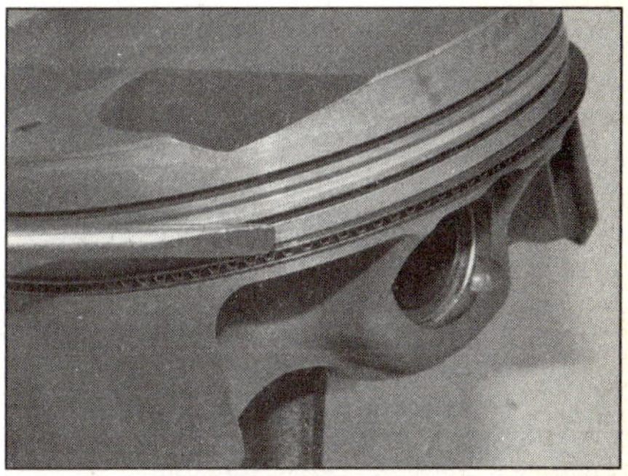

29.7c . . . and the upper side rail on each side of it

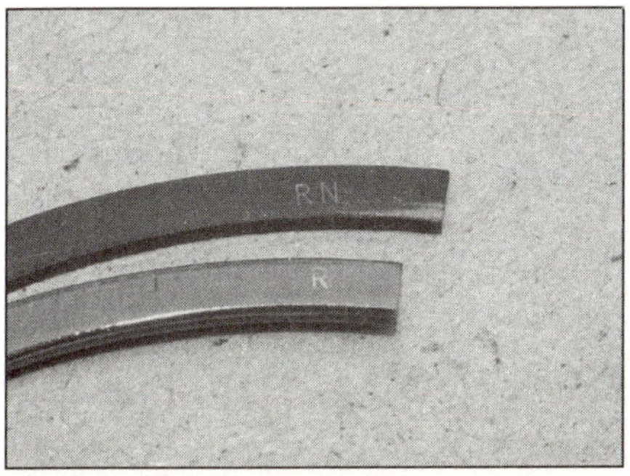

29.9a Note the marking on each ring and make sure it faces up

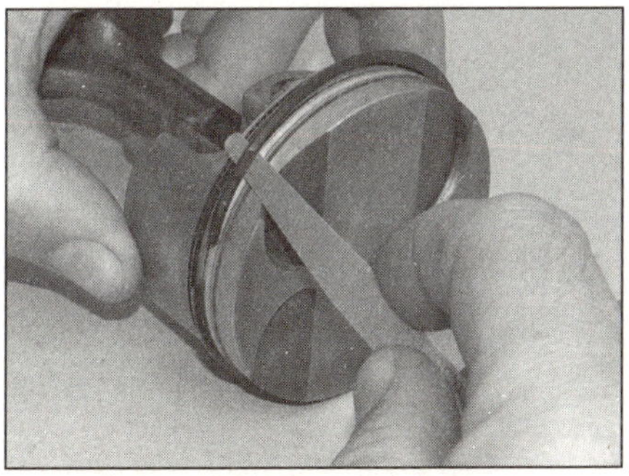

29.9b Install the middle ring . . .

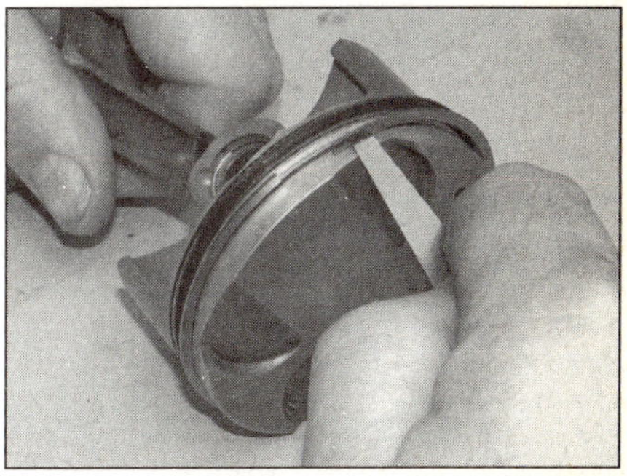

29.10 . . . and the top ring as described

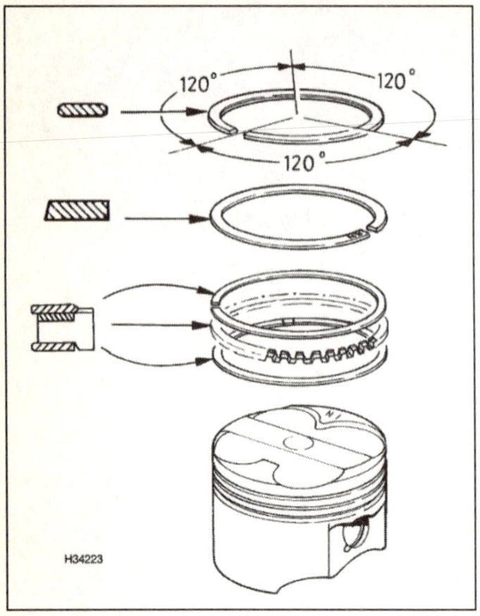

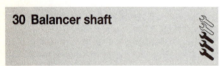

29.11 Piston ring installation details – stagger the ring end gaps as shown

11 Once the rings are correctly installed, check they move freely without snagging and stagger their end gaps as shown **(see illustration)**.

30 Balancer shaft

Note: *To remove the balancer shaft the engine must be removed from the frame and the crankcase halves separated.*

Removal

1 Separate the crankcase halves (see Section 23) – the balancer shaft is in the lower half.

2 Make an alignment mark on the balancer shaft holder with the punch mark on the end of the balancer shaft – this will give a good indication as to the starting point for resetting the backlash adjustment when the crankcases are reassembled **(see illustration)**. Slacken the balancer shaft holder pinch bolt, then unscrew the holder mounting bolt and slide the holder off the shaft **(see illustration)**.

3 Support the balancer gear/weight assembly, then withdraw the shaft and remove the gear/

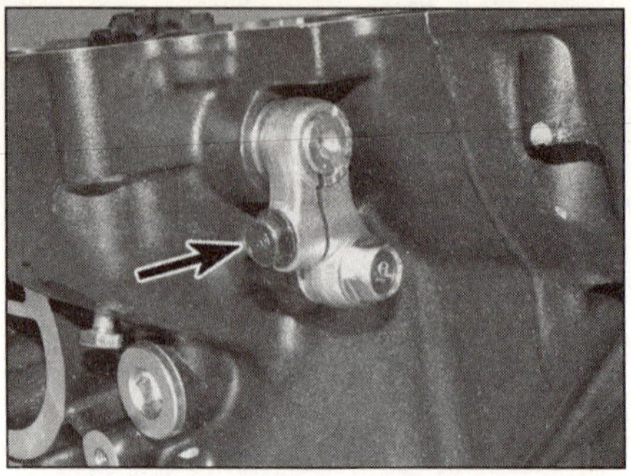

30.2a Make an alignment mark between the shaft and the holder, then slacken the pinch bolt (arrowed) . . .

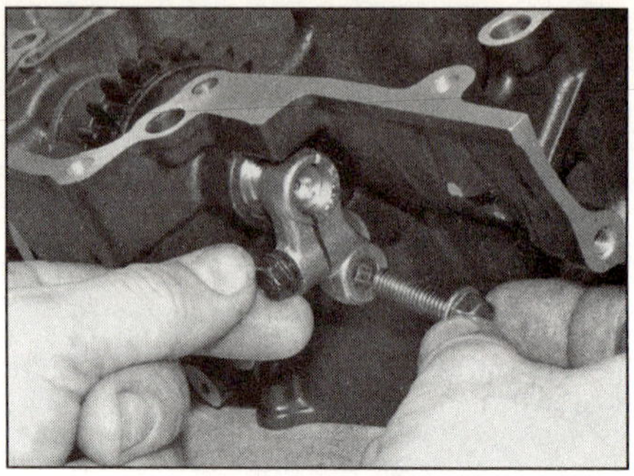

30.2b . . . unscrew the mounting bolt and slide the holder off

weight **(see illustration)**. Discard the shaft O-ring as a new one must be used.

Inspection

4 Inspect the teeth on the gear for signs of wear or damage, and replace it with a new one if necessary. If damage is found, check the teeth on the drive gear on the crankshaft. The gear/weight can be disassembled if required – all components are available individually.

5 Remove the washer from each end of the gear/weight, noting which fits where **(see illustrations 30.9d and e)**. Slide the shaft back into the gear/weight and check that it runs freely and smoothly in the bearings. If there is any evidence of wear on the shaft, or it is a sloppy fit in the bearings, and the bearings are good, replace the shaft with a new one. If the bearings do not run smoothly and freely, or if there is any wear or damage evident, replace them with new ones. Note that all components are matched by size and should be replaced either as a set, or by matching them using the coded markings (see Steps 7 and 8). Withdraw the shaft and the bearings **(see illustration 30.9c)**. Clean them with solvent.

6 Separate the weight from the gear **(see illustration 30.9b)**. Check the condition of the rubber dampers in the gear for damage, deformation and deterioration, and replace them with new ones if necessary **(see illustration 30.9a)**.

Bearing selection

7 Replacement bearings for the balancer are supplied on a selected fit basis according to the internal diameter (ID) of the end it runs in. Code letters stamped on the weight web are used to identify the correct replacement bearings, which are colour-coded. The balancer gear/weight size code letters (the right-hand one for the gear end and the left-hand one for the weight end) will be either an A, B or C **(see illustration)**.

8 Measure the internal diameter of each end of the balancer and check it according to its letter against the specifications given in the table below to check the weight bearing surface has not worn. If it has worn beyond its specification replace the balancer with a new one and select new bearings according to the numbers on the new one. If the balancer has not worn, select new bearings according to the letters. For example, if the gear end size is B, then the bearing required for the gear end of the shaft is white. The colour is marked on the bearing.

Balancer gear/ weight ID codes	Bearing colour
A (26.996 to 27.000 mm)	Blue
B (26.991 to 26.996 mm)	White
C (26.987 to 26.991 mm)	Green

Installation

9 Smear the dampers with grease, then fit them onto the gear **(see illustration)**. Fit the

30.3 Withdraw the shaft and lift the balancer out

30.7 Balancer gear and weight size code letters

30.9a Fit the dampers onto the gear . . .

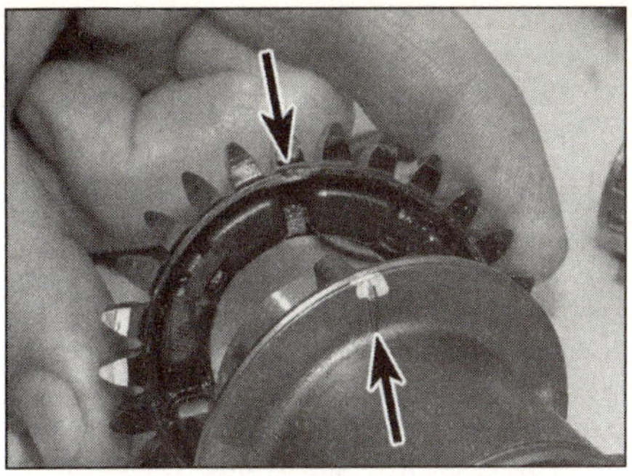

30.9b . . . then fit the gear onto the balancer, aligning the marks

30.9c Fit the bearings into the bore . . .

30.9d . . . then fit the shouldered washer . . .

gear onto the balancer, aligning the mark on the inner rim with the line on the balancer, and making sure the dampers locate correctly **(see illustration)**. Lubricate the bearings with clean oil and slide them into the balancer, making sure they are correctly located according to the codes (see Steps 7 and 8) **(see illustration)**. Fit the shouldered washer onto the gear end and the dished washer onto the weight end **(see illustrations)**.

10 Fit a new O-ring onto the balancer shaft and smear it with clean oil **(see illustration)**. Position the balancer gear/weight assembly in the crankcase with the weight facing the left-hand end, then slide the shaft in with the O-ring on the outer end **(see illustration 30.3)**.

11 Turn the shaft using a screwdriver until the punch mark faces down **(see illustration)**. Fit the holder onto the end of the shaft and tighten its mounting bolt **(see illustration 30.2b)**. Temporarily tighten the shaft pinch bolt.

12 Reassemble the crankcase halves (see Section 23).

13 Carry out the static backlash adjustment procedure (see below).

14 Turn the engine clockwise through 360° (one full turn) and check that the crankshaft and balancer marks still align (see Section 23). Finish rebuilding the engine and install it (see Section 4).

30.9e . . . and the dished washer

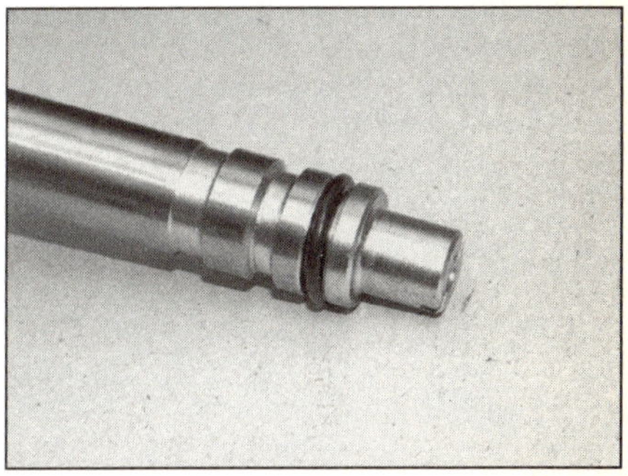

30.10 Fit a new O-ring into the outer groove

15 Carry out the dynamic backlash adjustment procedure (see below).

Backlash adjustment

Note: *A backlash adjustment is provided so that the gears mesh at their optimum point for quiet running with minimal wear. If the amount of backlash is too great, the shafts will clatter. If the gears are running tight, they will whine, and wear very quickly. At the optimum point the gears will run very quietly – it is easy to tell the difference with the engine running. Adjustment is possible due to the offset which allows eccentric movement of the balancer gear in relation to its drive gear when the shaft is turned. The static adjustment procedure allows the backlash to be set up in roughly the optimum position, but the dynamic procedure should always be carried out as well to fine tune the setting.*

Static adjustment

Note: *This procedure must be carried out when the engine is cold.*

16 Slacken the balancer shaft holder pinch bolt **(see illustration 30.2a)**.

17 Turn the shaft slightly anti-clockwise using a screwdriver in the slotted end, then turn it clockwise until resistance is felt – at this point backlash between the gears has been eliminated **(see illustration)**. Now turn the shaft anti-clockwise so the slot moves one graduation as marked on the holder, then temporarily tighten the pinch bolt.

30.11 Turn the shaft so the punch mark is at the bottom

30.17 Turn the shaft using a screwdriver

18 Now carry out the dynamic adjustment procedure (see below).

Dynamic adjustment

Note: *This procedure must be carried out when the engine is warm.*

19 Remove the lower fairing (see Chapter 7). Start the engine and allow it to warm up, then let it idle.
20 Slacken the balancer shaft holder pinch bolt **(see illustration 30.2a)**.
21 Turn the shaft slightly one way then the other to find the point at which the gears run at their quietest. Too far one way and the gears will whine (no backlash), too far the other and they will clatter (excessive backlash). Rev the engine and check that there is no unwanted noise at varying speeds.
22 On completion, tighten the pinch bolt. Install the lower fairing (see Chapter 7).

31 Running-in procedure

1 Make sure the engine oil and coolant levels are correct (see *Pre-ride checks*). Make sure there is fuel in the tank.
2 Turn the engine kill switch to the ON position and shift the gearbox into neutral. Turn the ignition ON.
3 Start the engine and allow it to run at a moderately fast idle until it reaches operating temperature.

Warning: If the oil pressure warning light doesn't go off, or it comes on while the engine is running, stop the engine immediately.

4 If a lubrication failure is suspected, stop the engine immediately and try to find the cause. If an engine is run without oil, even for a short period of time, severe damage will occur.
5 Check carefully for oil and coolant leaks and make sure the transmission and controls, especially the brakes, function properly before road testing the machine.
6 Treat the machine gently for the first few miles to make sure oil has circulated throughout the engine and any new parts installed have started to seat.
7 Even greater care is necessary if new pistons/rings or a new crankcase/bores have been fitted, and the bike will have to be run in as when new. This means greater use of the transmission and a restraining hand on the throttle until at least 300 miles (500 km) have been covered. There's no point in keeping to any set speed limit – the main idea is to keep from labouring the engine and to gradually increase performance up to the 300 miles (500 km) mark. Experience is the best guide, since it's easy to tell when an engine is running freely.
8 Upon completion of the road test, and after the engine has cooled down completely, recheck the valve clearances (see Chapter 1) and check the engine oil and coolant levels (see *Pre-ride checks*).

Chapter 3
Cooling system

Contents

Degrees of difficulty

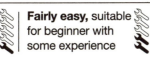

Easy, suitable for novice with little experience	**Fairly easy,** suitable for beginner with some experience	**Fairly difficult,** suitable for competent DIY mechanic	**Difficult,** suitable for experienced DIY mechanic	**Very difficult,** suitable for expert DIY or professional

Specifications

Coolant

Mixture type and capacity	see Chapter 1

ECT sensor

Resistance @ 80°C	2.1 to 2.6 K-ohms
Resistance @ 120°C	650 to 730 ohms

Thermostat

Opening temperature	80 to 84°C
Fully open	95°C
Valve lift	8 mm (min)

Radiator

Cap valve opening pressure	16 to 20 psi (1.1 to 1.4 Bar)

Torque settings

Cooling fan blade nut	3 Nm
Cooling fan motor nuts	5 Nm
Cooling fan mounting bracket bolts	9 Nm
ECT sensor	23 Nm
Thermostat cover bolts	12 Nm
Water pump bolts	12 Nm

1 General information

The cooling system uses a water/anti-freeze coolant to carry away excess heat from the engine and maintain as constant a temperature as possible. The cylinders are surrounded by a water jacket from which the heated coolant is circulated by thermo-syphonic action in conjunction with a water pump, which is driven by the oil pump. The hot coolant passes upwards to the thermostat and through to the radiator. The coolant then flows across the core of the radiator, then to the water pump and back to the engine (via the oil cooler) where the cycle is repeated.

A thermostat is fitted in the system to prevent the coolant flowing through the radiator when the engine is cold, therefore accelerating the speed at which the engine reaches normal operating temperature. A dual circuit sensor (containing the temperature gauge sensor and the ECT (engine coolant temperature) sensor) mounted in the thermostat housing transmits information to the digital temperature display on the instrument panel, and to the ECM (electronic control module). A cooling fan fitted to the back of the radiator aids cooling in extreme conditions by drawing extra air through. The fan motor is controlled by a relay which receives a signal from the ECM which in turn receives information from the ECT sensor.

The complete cooling system is partially sealed and pressurised, the pressure being controlled by a valve contained in the spring-loaded radiator cap. By pressurising the coolant the boiling point is raised, preventing premature boiling in adverse conditions. The overflow pipe from the system is connected to a reservoir into which excess coolant is expelled under pressure. The discharged coolant automatically returns to the radiator by the vacuum created when the engine cools.

Warning: Do not remove the pressure cap from the radiator when the engine is hot. Scalding hot coolant and steam may be blown out under pressure, which could cause serious injury. When the engine has cooled, place a thick rag, like a towel, over the pressure cap; slowly rotate the cap anti-clockwise to the first stop. This procedure allows any residual pressure to escape. When the steam has stopped escaping, press down on the cap while turning it anti-clockwise and remove it.

Caution: Do not allow anti-freeze to come in contact with your skin or painted surfaces of the motorcycle. Rinse off any spills immediately with plenty of water. Anti-freeze is highly toxic if ingested. Never leave anti-freeze lying around in an open container or in puddles on the floor; children and pets are attracted by its sweet smell and may drink it. Check with the local authorities about disposing of used anti-freeze. Many communities will have collection centres which will see that anti-freeze is disposed of safely.

Caution: At all times use the specified type of anti-freeze, and always mix it with distilled water in the correct proportion. The anti-freeze contains corrosion inhibitors which are essential to avoid damage to the cooling system. A lack of these inhibitors could lead to a build-up of corrosion which would block the coolant passages, resulting in overheating and severe engine damage. Distilled water must be used as opposed to tap water to avoid a build-up of scale which would also block the passages.

2 Cooling fan and relay

Cooling fan

Check

1 If the engine is overheating and the cooling fan isn't coming on, first check the cooling fan fuse (see Chapter 8). If the fuse is good, check the relay as described below.

2 To test the cooling fan motor, remove the right-hand fairing side panel (see Chapter 7). Disconnect the fan wiring connector **(see illustration)**. Using a 12 volt battery and two jumper wires with suitable connectors, connect the battery positive (+) lead to the black/blue wire terminal on the fan side of the wiring connector, and the battery negative (–) lead to the black wire terminal on the connector. Once connected the fan should operate. If it does not, and the connector and wiring between it and the motor is good, then the fan motor is faulty. Individual components are available for the fan assembly.

Removal and installation

Warning: The engine must be completely cool before carrying out this procedure.

3 Remove the radiator (see Section 5).

4 Unscrew the bolts securing the fan assembly to the radiator **(see illustration)**. Free the fan wiring connector from its clip on the bracket.

5 Unscrew the fan blade nut and remove the blade. Undo the three nuts on the front of the fan motor and separate the motor from its bracket.

6 Installation is the reverse of removal. Tighten the fan motor nuts to the torque setting specified at the beginning of the Chapter. Apply a suitable non-permanent thread locking compound to the fan blade nut and tighten it to the specified torque.

7 Install the radiator (see Section 5).

Cooling fan relay

Check

8 If the engine is overheating and the cooling fan isn't coming on, first check the cooling fan fuse (see Chapter 8). If the fuse is blown, check the fan circuit for a short to earth (see the wiring diagrams at the end of Chapter 8).

9 If the fuse is good, displace the relay box from its mount (see below), then release the brown connector clips and draw the brown

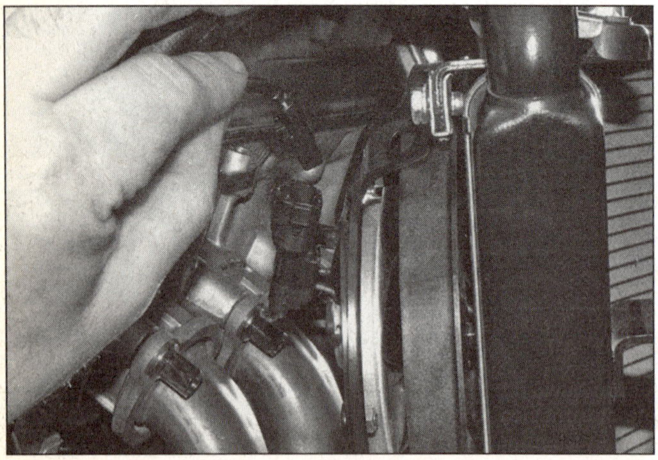

2.2 Disconnect the fan wiring connector

2.4 Unscrew the bolts (arrowed) and remove the fan assembly

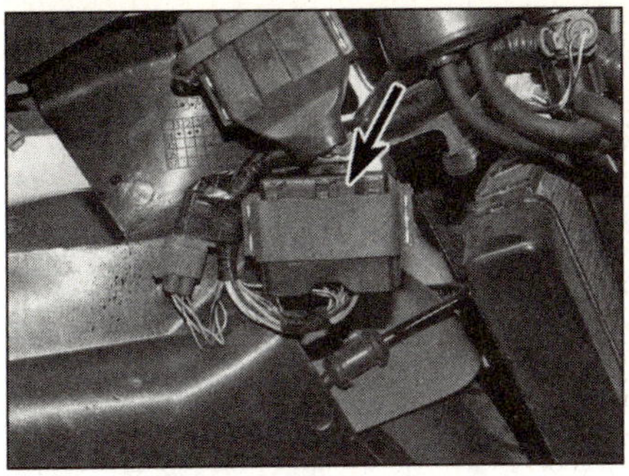

2.9a Relay box (arrowed) – RR-4 and RR-5 models

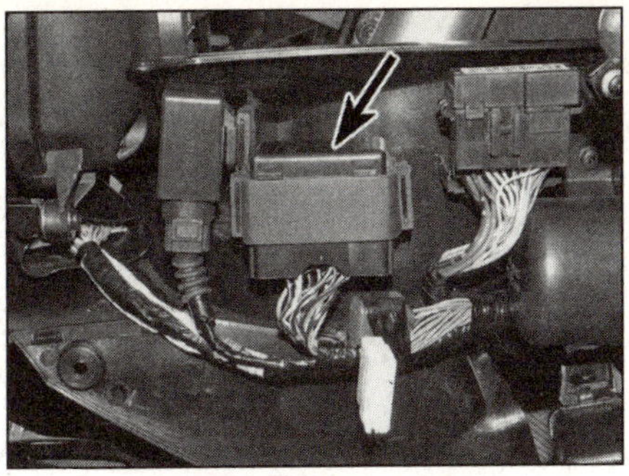

2.9b Relay box (arrowed) – RR-6 and RR-7 models

connector out of the box **(see illustrations)**. Pull the relay off its connector.

10 Set a multimeter to the ohms x 1 scale and connect it across the relay's A and B terminals **(see illustration)**. There should be no continuity (infinite resistance). Using a fully-charged 12 volt battery and two insulated jumper wires, connect the positive (+) terminal of the battery to the C terminal on the relay, and the negative (–) terminal to the D terminal on the relay. At this point the relay should be heard to click and the multimeter read 0 ohms (continuity). If this is the case the relay is proved good. If the relay does not click when battery voltage is applied and still indicates no continuity (infinite resistance) across its terminals, it is faulty and must be replaced with a new one.

11 If the relay is good, check for battery voltage at the blue/orange wire in the wiring connector with the ignition switch ON. If there is no voltage, check the wiring between the relay and the fusebox for continuity, referring to the relevant wiring diagram at the end of Chapter 8. If voltage is present, check that there is continuity to earth in the black/orange wire with the ignition switch OFF. If there is no continuity, check the wiring between the relay, the fan wiring connector, the fan then back to the connector and in the green wire to earth. If all is good check the grey/blue wire between the relay and the ECM (electronic control module), and the black/white wire to earth. There should be continuity in all wires.

12 If the fan is on the whole time, pull the relay off its connector. The fan should stop. If it does, the relay is defective and must be replaced with a new one.

13 If the fan works but is suspected of cutting in at the wrong temperature, check the ECT sensor (see Section 3).

Removal and installation

14 Remove the left-hand fairing side panel (see Chapter 7).

15 Displace the relay box from its mount, then release the clips and draw the brown connector out of the box **(see illustrations 2.9a, b and c)**. Pull the relay off its connector.

16 Installation is the reverse of removal.

3 Temperature display and ECT sensor

Temperature display

1 The circuit consists of the ECT sensor mounted in the thermostat housing and the digital display which is part of the instrument cluster LCD unit. If the system malfunctions check the instrument cluster fuse (see Chapter 8). When the ignition is first switched on all the digital display segments and modes should come on temporarily – this serves as an indication that the LCD is functioning correctly.

2 Under normal operating conditions, when the coolant temperature is below 34°C the display will show '- -'. The display will show the actual temperature from 35 to 132°C. Should coolant temperature reach 122°C the display will start to flash, and the red malfunction indicator light (MIL) and the temperature warning symbol will come on. If this occurs stop the engine and check the coolant level in the reservoir (see *Pre-ride checks*).

3 If the display is not working at all, check the instrument cluster power input (see Chapter 8). If the power lines are good, then either the printed circuit board (PCB) or the LCD display unit could be faulty.

4 If the display as a whole works but the coolant function doesn't or is thought to be inaccurate, check the ECT sensor (see below). If the sensor is good, remove the windshield (see Chapter 7) and check the wiring between the sensor and the instrument cluster for continuity. If the wiring is good the display is faulty.

5 The temperature display is part of the LCD unit in the instrument cluster PCB. No individual components are available for the instrument cluster PCB. If it is faulty, replace it with a new one (see Chapter 8).

ECT sensor

Check

6 Drain the cooling system (see Chapter 1). The sensor is mounted in the thermostat housing.

7 Remove the sensor (see Steps 10 and 11 below).

8 Fill a small heatproof container with coolant and place it on a stove. Using an ohmmeter, connect the positive (+) probe of the meter to the green/red wire terminal on the sensor **(see**

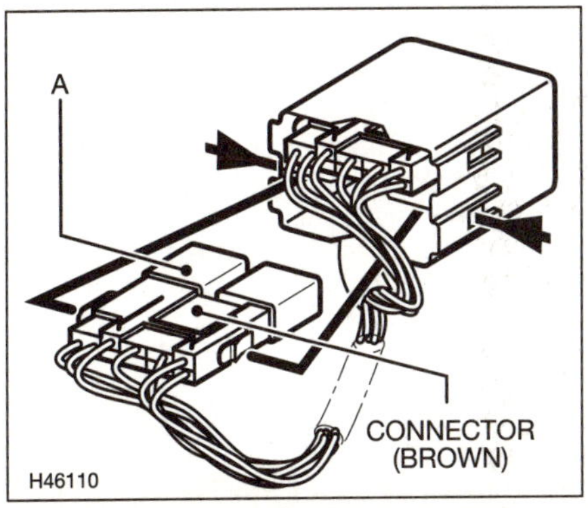

2.9c Release the brown connector from the box to access the cooling fan relay (A)

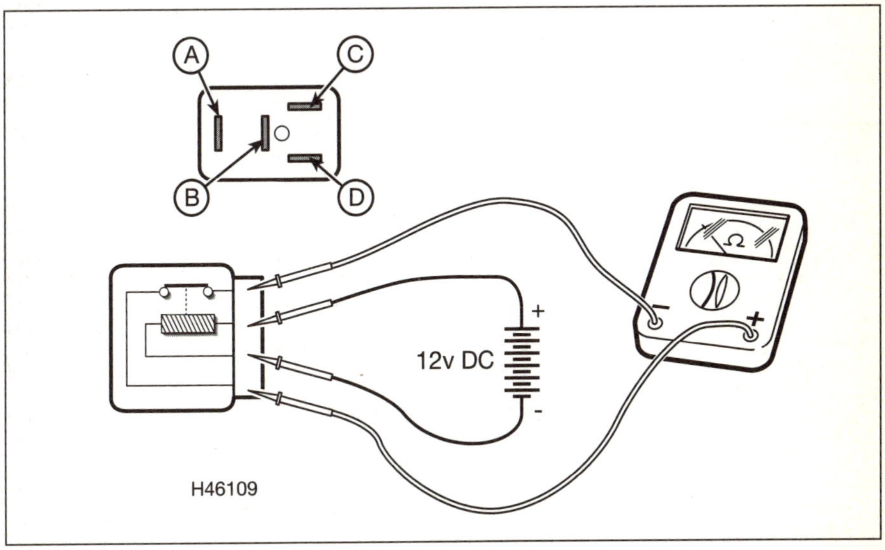

2.10 Fan relay test set-up

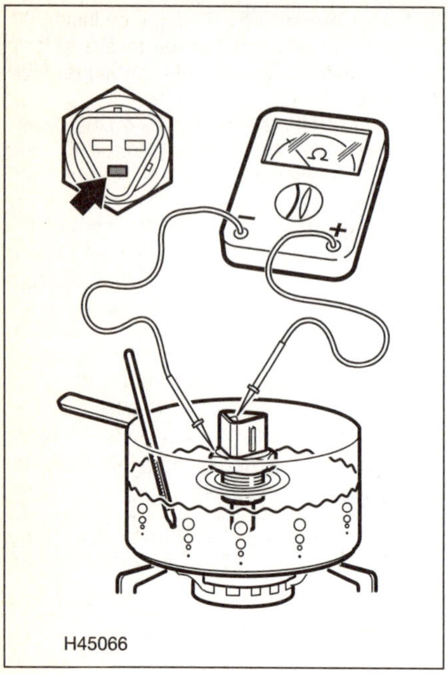

3.8 ECT sensor test set-up

illustration), and the negative (–) probe to the body of the sensor. Using some wire or other support suspend the sensor in the coolant so that just the sensing head up to the threads is submerged, and with the head a minimum of 40 mm above the bottom of the container. Also place a thermometer capable of reading temperatures up to 130°C in the coolant

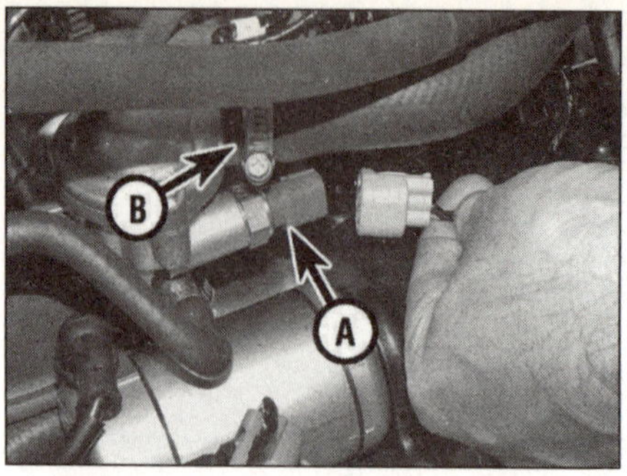

3.10 ECT sensor (A) and its wiring connector. To improve access detach the large bore hose (B) from the cover

so that its bulb is close to the sensor. **Note:** *None of the components should be allowed to directly touch the container.*

Warning: This must be done very carefully to avoid the risk of personal injury.

9 Begin to heat the coolant, stirring it gently. When the temperature reaches around 80°C, turn the heat down and maintain the temperature steady for three minutes. The meter reading should be as specified at the beginning of the Chapter. Turn the heat on again. When the temperature reaches around 120°C, again turn the heat down and maintain it for three minutes. The meter reading should again be as specified at the beginning of the Chapter. If the meter readings obtained are different by a margin of 10% or more, then the ECT sensor is faulty and must be replaced with a new one.

4.3a Unscrew the bolts (arrowed) and detach the cover . . .

4.3b . . . then withdraw the thermostat from the housing

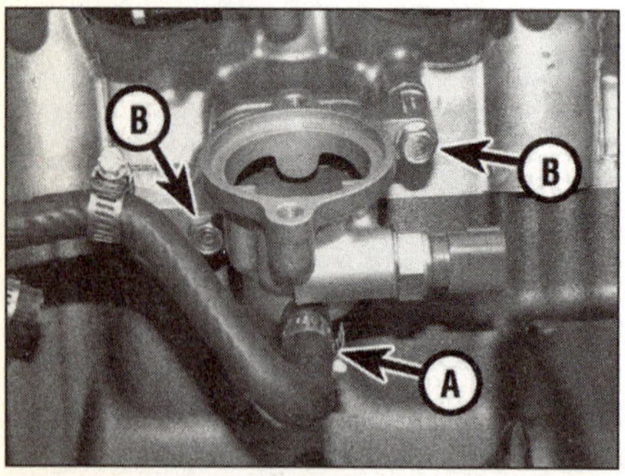

4.4a Detach the hose (A) from the housing. Housing mounting bolts (B)

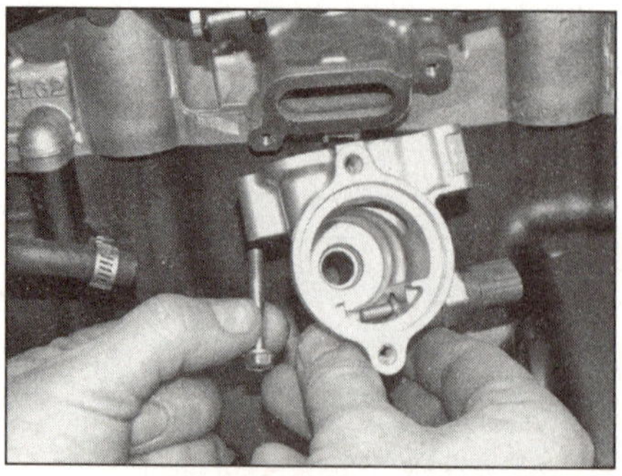

4.4b Unscrew the bolts and remove the housing

Removal and installation

Warning: The engine must be completely cool before carrying out this procedure.

10 Drain the cooling system (see Chapter 1). Raise, or for better access remove, the fuel tank (see Chapter 4). The sensor is mounted in the thermostat housing **(see illustration)**.

11 Disconnect the sensor wiring connector. Unscrew and remove the sensor, and discard the sealing washer. To improve access, slacken and move the clamp securing the large bore hose to the thermostat cover, and if required detach the hose.

12 Fit a new sealing washer onto the sensor. Install the sensor and tighten it to the torque setting specified at the beginning of the Chapter. Connect the wiring. If detached, fit the hose onto the thermostat cover and tighten its clamp.

13 Install the fuel tank (see Chapter 4). Refill the cooling system (see Chapter 1) and check the coolant level (see *Pre-ride checks*).

4 Thermostat and housing

1 The thermostat is automatic in operation and should give many years service without requiring attention. In the event of a failure, the valve will probably jam open, in which case the engine will take much longer than normal to warm up. Conversely, if the valve jams shut, the coolant will be unable to circulate and the engine will overheat. Neither condition is acceptable, and the fault must be investigated promptly.

Removal

Warning: The engine must be completely cool before carrying out this procedure.

2 Drain the cooling system (see Chapter 1). Remove the throttle bodies (see Chapter 4). The thermostat housing is on the back of the engine in the middle.

3 To remove the thermostat, unscrew the two bolts securing the cover and detach it from the housing **(see illustration)**. Withdraw the thermostat, noting how it fits **(see illustration)**.

4 To remove the thermostat housing, for ease of access to the bolt first remove the thermostat (Step 3). Disconnect the ECT sensor wiring connector **(see illustration 3.10)**. Slacken the clamp securing the hose to the housing and detach it **(see illustration)**. Unscrew the bolts securing the housing to the engine and remove the housing **(see illustration)**. Discard the O-ring.

Check

5 Examine the thermostat visually before carrying out the test. If it remains in the open position at room temperature, it should be replaced with a new one. Check the condition of the rubber seal around the thermostat and

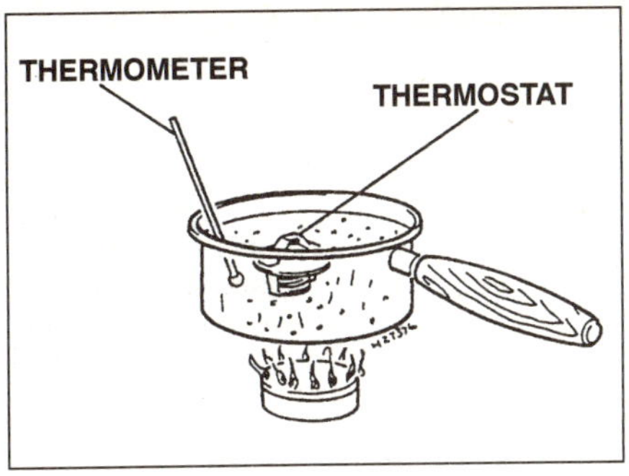

4.6 Thermostat testing set-up

replace it with a new one if it is damaged, deformed or deteriorated.

6 Suspend the thermostat by a piece of wire in a container of cold water. Place a thermometer capable of reading temperatures up to 110°C in the water so that the bulb is close to the thermostat **(see illustration)**. Heat the water, noting the temperature when the thermostat opens, and compare the result with the specifications given at the beginning of the Chapter. Also check the amount the valve opens after it has been heated for a few minutes and compare the measurement to the specifications. If the readings obtained differ from those given, the thermostat is faulty and must be replaced with a new one.

7 In the event of thermostat failure, if the thermostat is permanently closed, as an emergency measure only it can be removed and the machine used without it (this is better than leaving it in as the engine will overheat). If it is permanently open you are better to leave it in. In both cases take care when starting the engine from cold as it will take much longer than usual to warm up. Ensure that a new unit is installed as soon as possible.

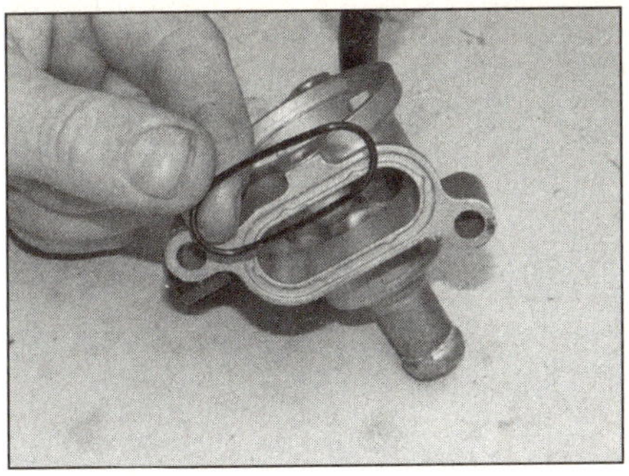

4.8 Fit a new O-ring into the groove

Installation

8 To install the thermostat housing, fit a new O-ring into the groove, using a dab of grease to keep it in place if required **(see illustration)**. Fit the housing and tighten the bolts **(see illustration 4.4b)**. Attach the hose to its union on the housing and tighten the clamp **(see illustration 4.4a)**. Connect the ECT sensor wiring connector **(see illustration 3.10)**.

9 To install the thermostat, first make sure the seal is fitted around it and that it is in good condition, otherwise use a new one. Smear some clean coolant over the seal. Install the thermostat with the hole facing back and make sure it locates correctly **(see illustration 4.3b)**. Fit the cover onto the housing, then install the bolts and tighten them to the torque setting specified at the beginning of the Chapter **(see illustration 4.3a)**.

10 Install the throttle bodies (see Chapter 4). Refill the cooling system (see Chapter 1) and check the coolant level (see *Pre-ride checks*).

5 Radiator

Note: *If the radiator is being removed as part of the engine removal procedure, detach the hoses from their unions on the engine rather than on the radiator and remove the radiator complete with its hoses. Note the routing of the hoses.*

Removal

Warning: The engine must be completely cool before carrying out this procedure.

1 Drain the cooling system (see Chapter 1). Remove the lower fairing and the fairing side panels (see Chapter 7). Remove the coolant reservoir (see Section 7).

2 Disconnect the fan wiring connector **(see illustration 2.2)**.

3 On RR-4 and RR-5 models unscrew the two bolts on the right-hand side which secure the reservoir bracket and if required the bolt securing the hose guide.

4 Slacken the clamps securing the hoses to the radiator and detach them **(see illustrations)**.

5 Unscrew and remove the radiator lower mounting bolt **(see illustration)**. Unscrew the radiator upper mounting bolt **(see illustration)**. Ease the radiator out to the right to free the mounting lug from its grommet, then remove the radiator taking care not to catch the fins on the bracket **(see illustration)**. Note the arrangement of the collars and rubber grommets in the radiator mounts. Replace the grommets with new ones if they are damaged, deformed or deteriorated.

6 Check the radiator for signs of damage and clear any dirt or debris that might obstruct air flow and inhibit cooling. If the radiator fins are badly damaged or broken the radiator must be replaced with a new one. To enable full examination and cleaning, remove the

5.4a Detach the hose (arrowed) from the right-hand side of the radiator . . .

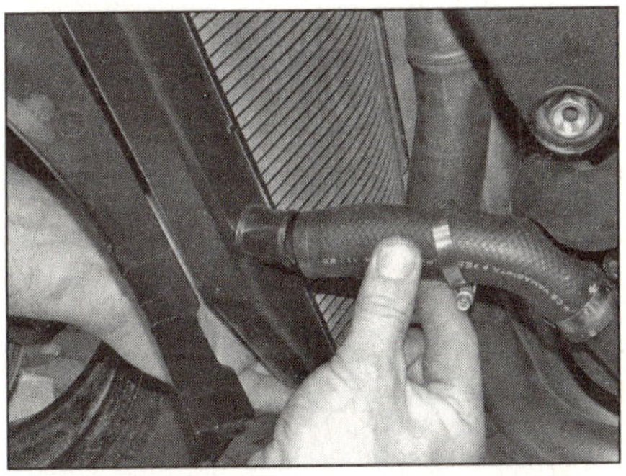

5.4b . . . and from the left-hand side

5.5a Unscrew the lower bolt (arrowed)

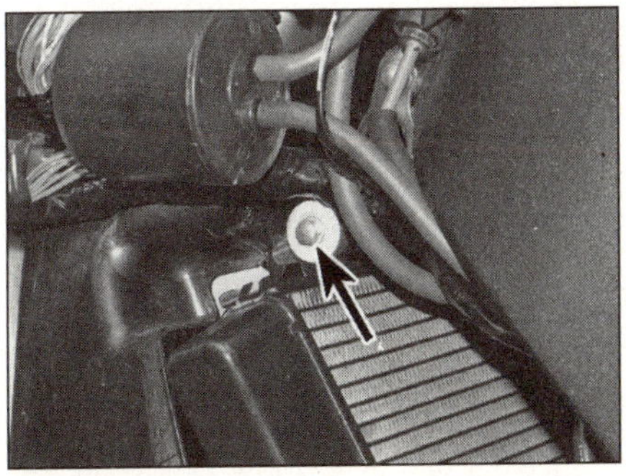

5.5b Unscrew the upper bolt (arrowed) . . .

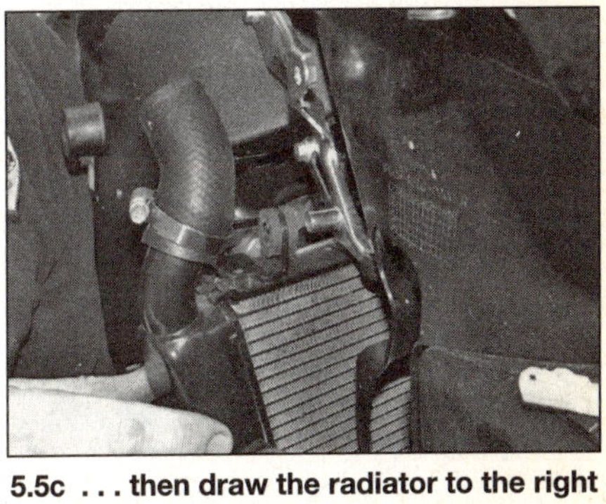

5.5c . . . then draw the radiator to the right to free the grommet from the lug

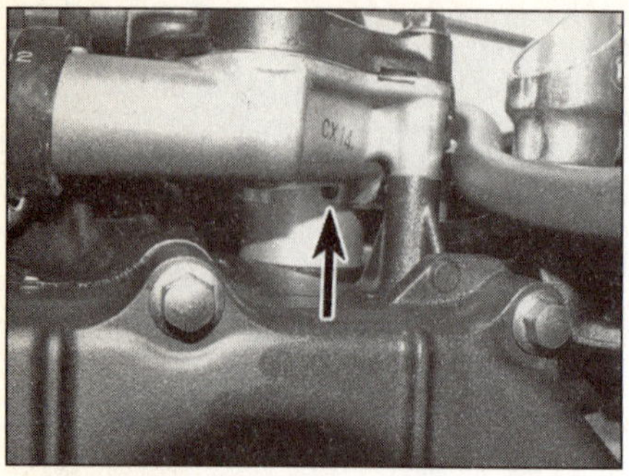

6.2 Check the drain hole (arrowed) for signs of leakage

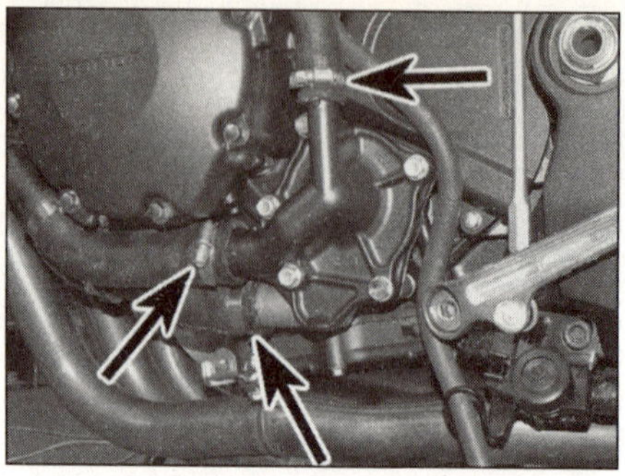

6.5a Slacken the clamps (arrowed) and detach the hoses

6.5b Unscrew the bolts . . .

cooling fan from the radiator (see Section 2) and detach the grille from the front; the grille is retained by four hooks, two on the bottom edge and one on each side.

Installation

7 Installation is the reverse of removal, noting the following.

- Ensure the coolant hoses are in good condition (see Chapter 1), and are securely retained by their clamps, using new ones if necessary.
- Make sure the rubber grommets are in place.
- Make sure the collars are correctly installed in the grommets.
- Make sure that the fan wiring is correctly connected.
- On completion refill the cooling system as described in Chapter 1 and check the coolant level (see *Pre-ride checks*).

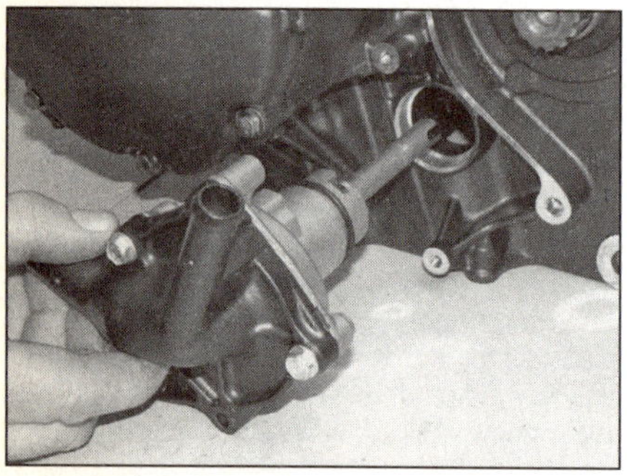

6.5c . . . and withdraw the pump

Pressure cap check

8 If problems such as overheating or loss of coolant occur, check the entire system as described in Chapter 1. The radiator cap opening pressure should be checked by a Honda dealer with the special tester required to do the job. If the cap is defective, replace it with a new one.

6 Water pump

Check

1 The water pump is located on the lower left-hand side of the engine. Remove the lower fairing (see Chapter 7). Visually check the area around the pump for signs of leakage.

2 To prevent leakage of water from the cooling system to the lubrication system and *vice versa*, two seals are fitted on the pump shaft. On the bottom of the pump housing there is also a drain hole **(see illustration)**. If either seal fails, the drain allows the coolant or oil to escape and prevents them mixing.

3 The seal on the water pump side is of the mechanical type which bears on the rear face of the impeller. The second seal, which is mounted behind the mechanical seal, is of the normal feathered lip type. If on inspection the drain shows signs of leakage, remove the pump and replace it with a new one – it comes as an assembly.

Removal

4 Drain the coolant (see Chapter 1).

5 Slacken the clamps securing the coolant hoses to the pump and detach the hoses, noting which fits where. Unscrew the top and bottom bolts, then draw the pump from the crankcase, noting how it fits **(see illustrations)**. It may be necessary to lever it out to overcome the O-ring on the pump body. Remove the O-ring from the rear of the body and discard it as a new one must be used **(see illustration 6.9)**.

6 To remove the cover, unscrew the remaining bolts – if the cover is stuck use a screwdriver in the cut-outs provided to lever it off **(see illustration)**. Remove the separator plate and the O-rings from the cover and pump **(see illustrations 6.8)**. Discard the O-rings as new ones must be used. Remove the dowels if they are loose.

7 Wiggle the water pump impeller back-and-forth and in-and-out **(see illustration)**. If there is excessive movement, replace the pump with a new one. Also check for corrosion or a build-up of scale in the pump body and clean or replace the pump as necessary.

Installation

8 Fit the dowels into the cover if removed. Smear one new O-ring with grease and fit it into the groove in the cover **(see illustration)**.

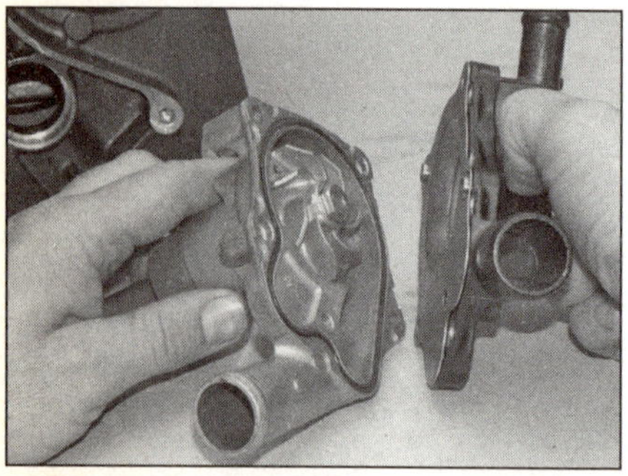

6.6 Unscrew the bolts and remove the cover

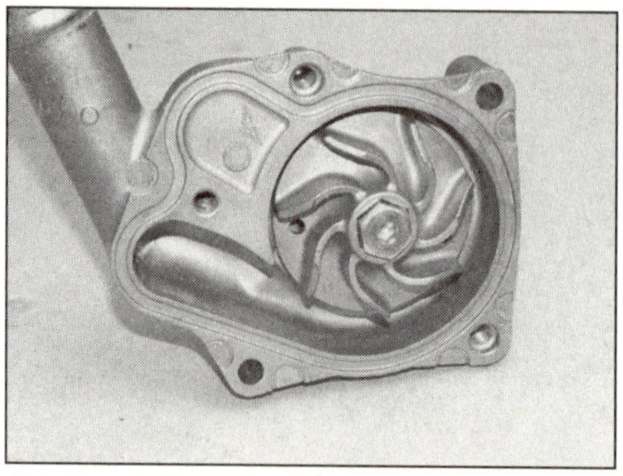

6.7 Check the pump impeller as described

6.8a Fit the O-ring into its groove . . .

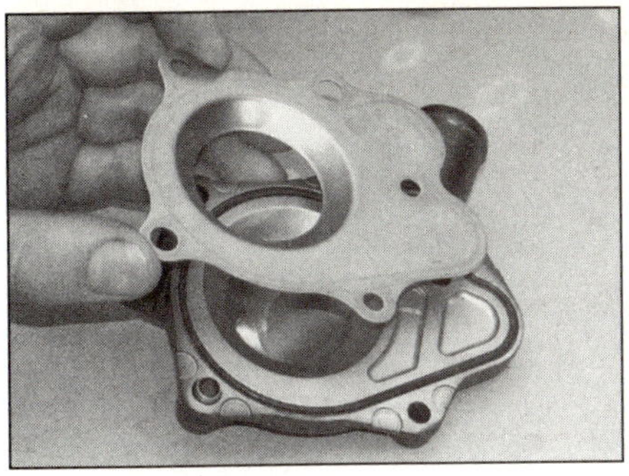
6.8b . . . then fit the separator

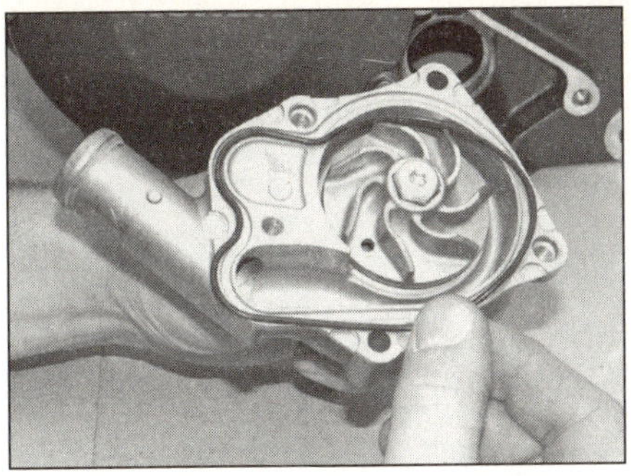
6.8c Fit the O-ring into the groove

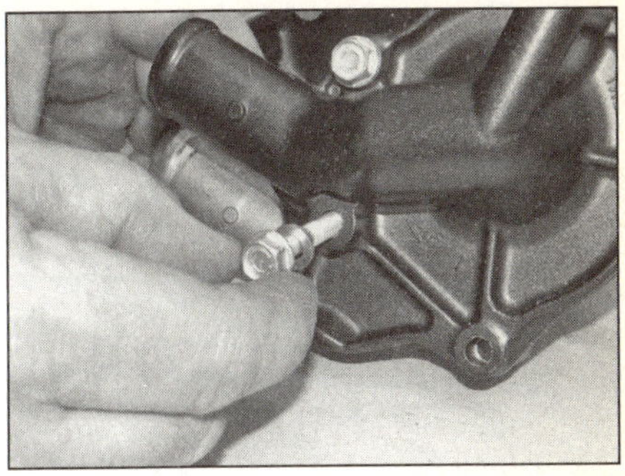
6.8d Use a new sealing washer on the bolt

Fit the separator plate onto the cover **(see illustration)**. Lubricate the other O-ring and fit it onto the groove in the housing. Fit the cover onto the housing **(see illustration 6.6)**. Install the three bolts, using a new sealing washer on the drain bolt, and tighten them to the torque setting specified at the beginning of the Chapter **(see illustration)**.

9 Apply a smear of engine oil to the new pump body O-ring and fit it into the groove in the body **(see illustration)**. Slide the pump into the crankcase, turning the shaft as required to align the slot in its end with the tab on the oil pump shaft **(see illustration 6.5c)**. Make sure the bolt holes are aligned. Install the mounting bolts and tighten them to the torque setting specified at the beginning of the Chapter **(see illustration 6.5b)**.

10 Fit the coolant hoses onto the pump cover and secure them with their clamps **(see illustration 6.5a)**.

11 Refill the cooling system (see Chapter 1) and check the coolant level (see *Pre-ride checks*).

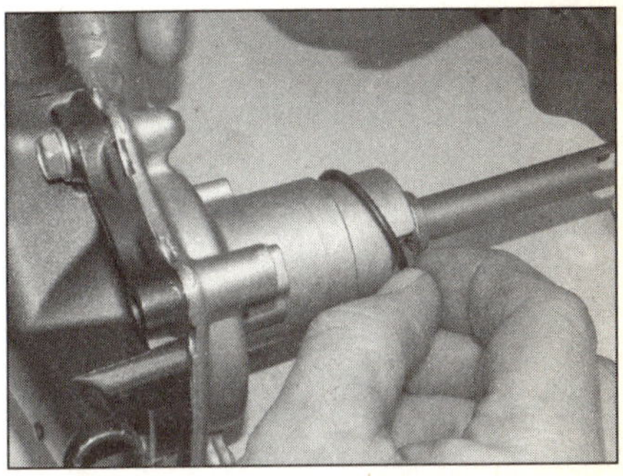
6.9 Fit a new O-ring onto the body

7 Coolant reservoir

Removal

1 The coolant reservoir is located on the right-hand side at the front of the frame. On RR-4 and RR-5 models remove the lower fairing and the right-hand fairing side panel (see Chapter 7). On RR-6 and RR-7 models remove the right-hand fairing side panel (see Chapter 7). Place a suitable container for catching the coolant below the reservoir.

2 Remove the reservoir filler cap **(see illustration)**. Disconnect the feed hose from the bottom of the reservoir and allow the reservoir to drain **(see illustration)**.

3 Unscrew the reservoir mounting bolt and manoeuvre the reservoir out, noting the routing of the breather/overflow hose from the neck **(see illustrations)**. Remove the hose if required.

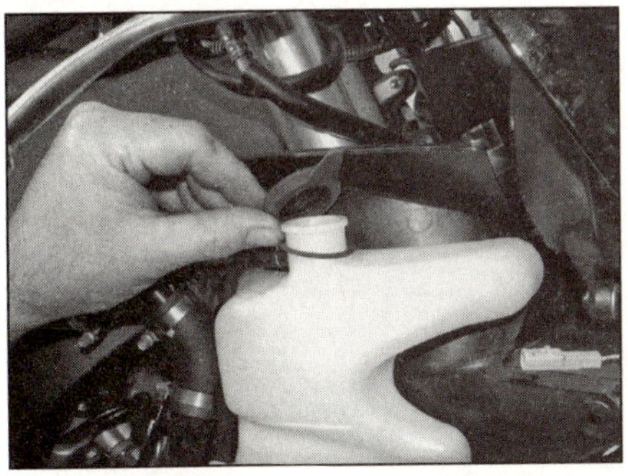
7.2a Remove the cap . . .

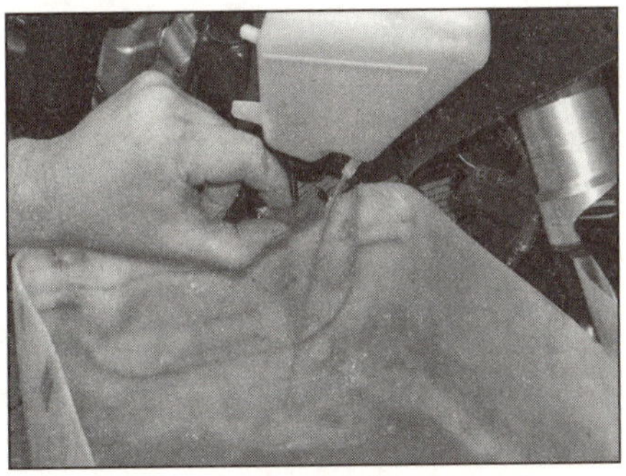
7.2b . . . and drain the reservoir

7.3a Reservoir mounting bolt (arrowed) - RR-4 and RR-5 models

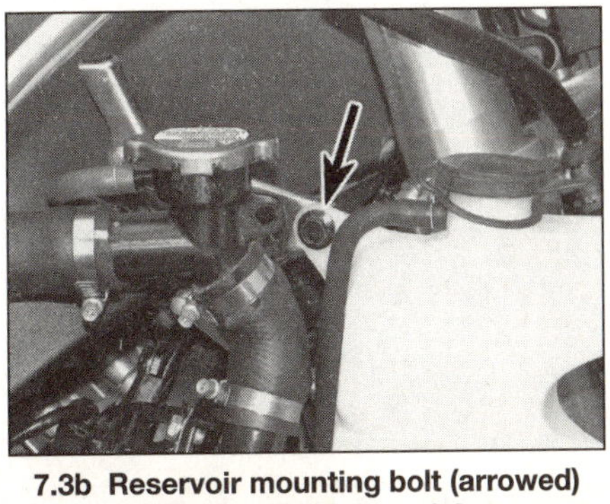
7.3b Reservoir mounting bolt (arrowed) - RR-6 and RR-7 models

Installation

4 Installation is the reverse of removal. Make sure the peg on the bottom of the reservoir locates in its grommet in the bracket. On completion refill the reservoir to the UPPER level line with the specified coolant mixture (see Chapter 1 and *Pre-ride checks*).

8 Coolant hoses and unions

Removal

1 Before removing a hose, drain the coolant (see Chapter 1).

2 Use a screwdriver to slacken the larger-bore hose clamps, then slide them back along the hose and clear of the union spigot. The smaller-bore hoses are secured by spring clamps which can be expanded by squeezing their ears together with pliers.

Caution: The radiator unions are fragile. Do not use excessive force when attempting to remove the hoses.

3 If a hose proves stubborn, release it by rotating it on its union before working it off. If all else fails, cut the hose with a sharp knife.

Whilst this means replacing the hose with a new one – it is preferable to buying a new radiator.

4 The inlet union to the engine is on the left-hand end of the cylinder block and can be removed by unscrewing its bolts, but only after lowering the engine out of the frame as access to the top bolt is restricted **(see illustration)**. If the union is removed, the O-ring must be replaced with a new one. The outlet from the cylinder head goes into the thermostat housing, which is covered in Section 4.

Installation

5 Slide the clamps onto the hose and then work the hose on to its union as far as the spigot where present.

HAYNES HiNT ***If the hose is difficult to push on its union, soften it by soaking it in very hot water, or alternatively a little soapy water on the union can be used as a lubricant.***

6 Rotate the hose on its unions to settle it in position before sliding the clamps into place and tightening them securely.

7 If the inlet union to the cylinder block has been removed, fit a new O-ring into the groove, using a dab of grease to hold it in place if necessary. Install the union and tighten the mounting bolts.

8 Refill the cooling system with fresh coolant (see Chapter 1) and check the coolant level (see *Pre-ride checks*).

8.4 Coolant inlet union (arrowed)

Chapter 4
Engine management system

Contents

Degrees of difficulty

Easy, suitable for novice with little experience	**Fairly easy,** suitable for beginner with some experience	**Fairly difficult,** suitable for competent DIY mechanic	**Difficult,** suitable for experienced DIY mechanic	**Very difficult,** suitable for expert DIY or professional

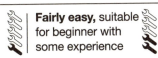

Specifications

General information

Cylinder numbering	1 to 4 from left to right
Firing order	1-2-4-3
Spark plugs	see Chapter 1

Fuel

Grade	Unleaded. Minimum 95 RON (Research Octane Number) for Europe. 91 RON for Mexico and Brazil. Minimum pump octane number 90 for the US
Fuel tank capacity (including reserve)	18.0 litres
Reserve volume	3.5 litres

Fuel injection system

Idle speed	1200 ± 100 rpm
Starter valve synchronisation – max. difference between bodies	20 mm Hg
Manifold absolute pressure at idle	150 to 250 mm Hg
Fuel pressure at specified idle speed*	50 psi (3.5 Bar)
Minimum fuel flow rate	189 cc every 10 seconds
Intake air duct control valve resistance	28 to 32 ohms @ 20°C

**Fuel pressure regulator vacuum hose disconnected and plugged*

Fuel injection system test data

Note: *All values given are only accurate at 20°C (68°F)*

Camshaft position (CMP) sensor	
Resistance	480 to 500 ohms
Minimum peak voltage output	0.7 volts
Crankshaft position (CKP) sensor	
Resistance	420 to 440 ohms
Minimum peak voltage output	0.7 volts
Engine coolant temperature (ECT) sensor resistance	2.3 to 2.6 K-ohms
Fuel injector resistance	10.5 to 14.5 ohms
Intake air temperature (IAT) sensor resistance	1 to 4 K-ohms
Oxygen sensor heater resistance	10 to 40 ohms

Exhaust gas control valve (EGCV)

Servo static resistance	5 K-ohms
Servo variable resistance	0 to 5 K-ohms

Emission control systems

PAIR system control valve resistance	20 to 24 ohms @ 20°C
EVAP system control valve resistance	30 to 34 ohms @ 20°C

Ignition timing

RR-4 and RR-5 models	8° 12' BTDC (F mark) at idle
RR-6 and RR-7 models	3.2° BTDC (F mark) at idle

Ignition HT coils

Primary winding resistance	approximately 1.6 ohms @ 20°C
Secondary winding resistance	approximately 13 K-ohms @ 20°C
Initial voltage (see text)	Battery voltage (approximately 12 volts)
Minimum peak voltage (see text)	100 volts

Torque settings

Engine coolant temperature (ECT) sensor	23 Nm
Exhaust downpipe nuts	12 Nm
Exhaust downpipe bolt	23 Nm
Exhaust clamp bolts	
Silencer to joint pipe clamp	10 Nm
Joint pipe to downpipe assembly bolt	18 Nm
Exhaust valve housing bolts	
RR-4 and RR-5 models	10 Nm
RR-6 and RR-7 models	5 Nm
Exhaust valve shaft nut	5 Nm
Fast idle system wax unit mounting screws	5 Nm
Footrest bracket to frame bolts	37 Nm
Fuel pump assembly mounting plate nuts	12 Nm
Fuel rail bolts	10 Nm
Fuel hoses	
Banjo bolt-to-fuel tank	22 Nm
Banjo union nuts-to-primary fuel rail	22 Nm
Union bolts-to-secondary fuel rail	10 Nm
Fuel tank front mounting bolts	26 Nm
Fuel tank rear mounting bolts	10 Nm
Oxygen sensor	44 Nm
Secondary fuel rail pressure check bolt	12 Nm
Starter valve base nuts	2 Nm
Throttle body intake adapter bolts	12 Nm
Timing inspection cap	18 Nm

1 General information and precautions

General information

Fuel system

The fuel supply system consists of the fuel tank with an internal fuel pump assembly incorporating the pressure regulator, filter and level sensor, the fuel hoses, the primary and secondary fuel rails, the primary and secondary injectors, the throttle bodies, and the throttle cables. The fuel pump is switched on and off via a relay. The injection system, known as PGM-DSFI, supplies fuel and air to the engine via 44 mm throttle bodies. There are two injectors per cylinder. The primary injectors are mounted in the throttle bodies below the throttle valve and operate all the time the engine is running. The secondary injectors are mounted in the top of the air filter housing and spray fuel into the air entering the throttle bodies above the throttle valves. These injectors operate when the throttle is opened wide at engine speeds over 5500 rpm. The injectors are operated by the Engine Control Module (ECM) using the information obtained from the various sensors it monitors (refer to Section 4 for more information on the operation of the fuel injection system).

All models have a low fuel warning light incorporated in the instrument cluster LCD, actuated by a level sensor which is part of the fuel pump inside the fuel tank. The warning light comes on when there is approximately 3.5 litres of fuel left.

Many of the fuel system service procedures are considered routine maintenance items and for that reason are covered in Chapter 1.

Ignition system

The transistorised electronic ignition system is combined with the fuel injection system, both being controlled by the ECM (engine control module). The ignition system comprises a crankshaft position sensor (CKP sensor), engine control module (ECM) and ignition coils.

The triggers on the starter clutch body (mounted on the end of the crankshaft) generate a signal in the CKP sensor as the crankshaft rotates. The CKP sensor sends that signal to the ECM which, in conjunction with information received from the throttle position sensor and engine coolant temperature sensor, calculates the ignition timing and supplies the ignition coils with the power necessary to produce a spark at the plugs. There is no provision for checking or adjusting the ignition timing.

The system uses four HT coils, one for each cylinder. The coils are of the plug top type known as 'stick coils', with the coil windings being incorporated in the spark plug cap, thus eliminating the need for HT leads.

The system incorporates a safety interlock circuit which will cut the ignition if the sidestand is extended whilst the engine is running and in gear, or if a gear is selected whilst the engine is running and the sidestand is down. It also prevents the engine from being started if the sidestand is down and the engine is in gear. The engine can be started with the sidestand up when it is in gear as long as the clutch lever is pulled in.

Many models are fitted with an immobiliser system (HISS – Honda Ignition Security System) which will not allow the engine to be started unless the correct key is used. The immobiliser system has its own fault diagnosis function.

Note that there is no provision for adjusting the ignition timing on these models.

Note: *Individual engine management system components can be checked but not repaired. If system troubles occur, and the faulty component can be isolated, the only cure for the problem in most cases is to replace the part with a new one. Keep in mind that most electronic parts, once purchased, cannot be returned. To avoid unnecessary expense, make very sure the faulty component has been positively identified before buying a new part.*

Precautions

Warning: Petrol (gasoline) is extremely flammable, so take extra precautions when you work on any part of the fuel system. Always remove the battery (see Chapter 8). Don't smoke or allow open flames or bare light bulbs near the work area, and don't work in a garage where a natural gas-type appliance is present. If you spill any fuel on your skin, rinse it off immediately with soap and water. When you perform any kind of work on the fuel system, wear safety glasses and have a fire extinguisher suitable for a class B type fire (flammable liquids) on hand.

With the fuel injection system, some residual pressure will remain in the fuel feed hoses and fuel rail assemblies after the motorcycle has been used. Before disconnecting any fuel hose, ensure the ignition is switched OFF then release fuel system pressure (see Section 2). It is vital that no dirt or debris is allowed to enter the fuel tank or the fuel rail assembly whilst the fuel hoses are disconnected. Any foreign matter in the fuel system components could result in injector damage or malfunction. Ensure the ignition is switched OFF before disconnecting or reconnecting any fuel injection system wiring connector. If a connector is disconnected or reconnected with the ignition switched ON, the engine control module (ECM) may be damaged.

Always perform service procedures in a well-ventilated area to prevent a build-up of fumes.

Never work in a building containing a gas appliance with a pilot light, or any other form of naked flame. Ensure that there are no naked light bulbs or any sources of flame or sparks nearby.

Do not smoke (or allow anyone else to smoke) while in the vicinity of petrol (gasoline) or of components containing it. Remember the possible presence of vapour from these sources and move well clear before smoking.

Check all electrical equipment belonging to the house, garage or workshop where work is being undertaken (see the Safety first! section of this manual). Remember that certain electrical appliances such as drills, cutters etc, create sparks in the normal course of operation and must not be used near petrol (gasoline) or any component containing it. Again, remember the possible presence of fumes before using electrical equipment.

Always mop up any spilt fuel and safely dispose of the rag used.

Any stored fuel that is drained off during servicing work must be kept in sealed containers that are suitable for holding petrol (gasoline), and clearly marked as such; the containers themselves should be kept in a safe place. Note that this last point applies equally to the fuel tank if it is removed from the machine; also remember to keep its filler cap closed at all times.

Read the *Safety first!* section of this manual carefully before starting work.

2 Fuel tank

Warning: Refer to the precautions given in Section 1 before starting work.

Raise

1 Make sure the fuel cap is secure. Remove the seats and the fuel tank cover (see Chapter 7). Disconnect the battery negative (–) lead (see Chapter 8).

2 Disconnect the fuel tank breather/overflow hose at the joint on the left-hand side of the bike **(see illustration)**.

2.2 Disconnect the hose at the joint

2.3a Unscrew the bolt on each side . . .

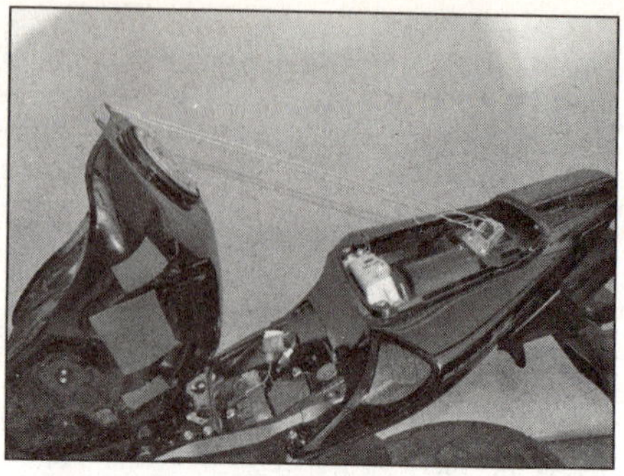

2.3b . . . then lift the tank up and secure it as shown

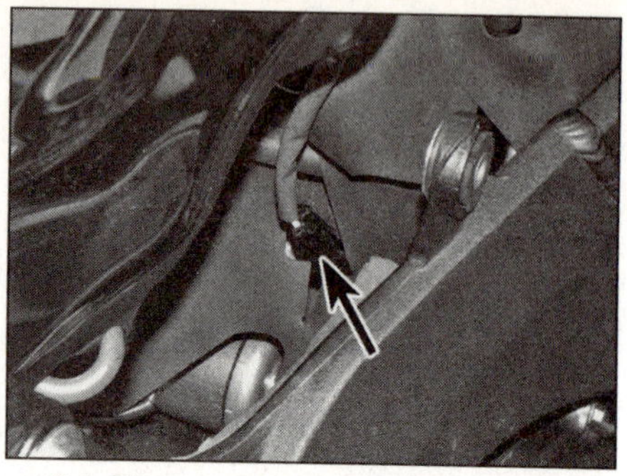

2.4 Disconnect the wiring connector (arrowed)

3 Unscrew the front mounting bolt on each side, noting the washers **(see illustration)**. Obtain a suitable length of cable or strong string to tie or hook between one of the holes at the front of the fuel tank front and the passenger seat retaining hook to hold it in the raised position. Lift the tank and pivot it back, then fit the cable or string to hold it **(see illustrations)**.

Removal

Note: *Removing the tank involves a certain amount of unavoidable fuel spillage, which is obviously dangerous. Refer to the precautions given in Section 1 before starting work, and have plenty of rag to hand. Once the tank has been removed, rest it on some soft rag to prevent damaging the paintwork or hose unions. Try to time the removal procedure with a near empty tank, which makes it much easier to lift. It is worth noting that self-sealing fuel hose connectors that fit in the fuel supply hose are commercially available through good accessory suppliers – these will make fuel tank removal a much easier task, eliminating fuel loss and having to obtain new sealing rings. If you decide to fit them, follow the manufacturer's installation instructions, and make sure they are capable of holding the pressure the system works at – this is listed in the Specifications at the beginning of the Chapter.*

4 Raise the tank as described above. Disconnect the fuel pump wiring connector **(see illustration)**.

5 Place a wad of rag for catching the residual fuel under the fuel supply hose union on the base of the pump, then slacken the banjo bolt **(see illustration)**. At this point some fuel will come out, so be ready with the rag to catch it. Unscrew the bolt and detach the hose, noting its alignment, and draw the hose out of its guide. Discard the sealing washers as new ones must be used.

6 Unscrew the tank pivot bolts and remove the collars, then carefully lift the tank off the frame and remove it **(see illustrations)**. Note the rubber mounts and remove them for safekeeping if required, noting the collars fitted from the inside in the front mounts **(see illustration)**.

7 Check all the tank rubbers and hoses for signs of damage or deterioration and replace them with new ones if necessary.

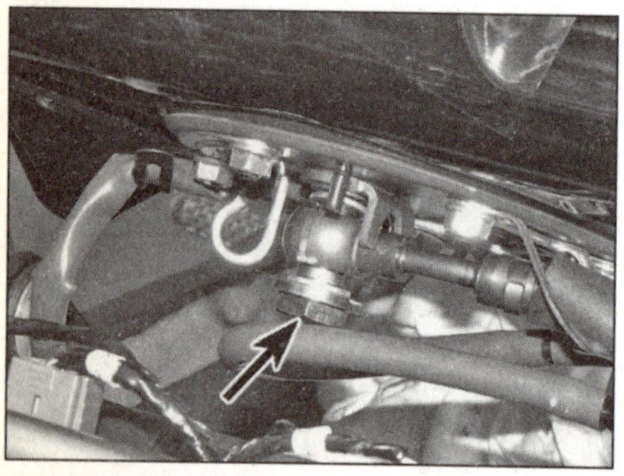

2.5 Fuel supply hose banjo bolt (arrowed). Note the alignment of the hose and the sealing washers

2.6a Unscrew the bolt on each side and remove the collars . . .

2.6b . . . then carefully lift the tank away

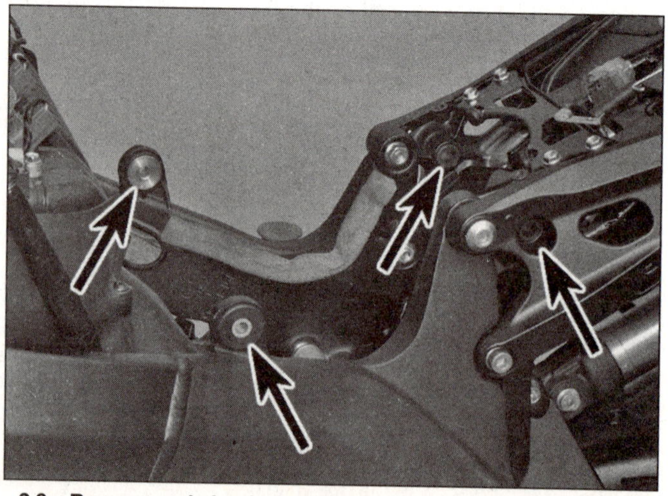

2.6c Remove and check the rubber mounts (arrowed) and their collars

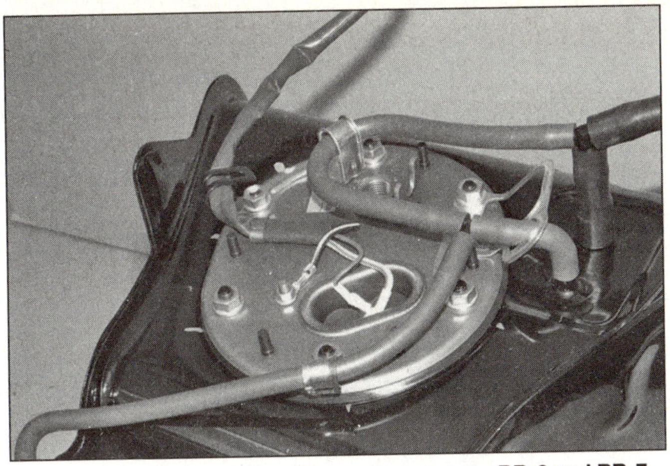

2.8 Breather and overflow hose arrangement – RR-6 and RR-7 model shown

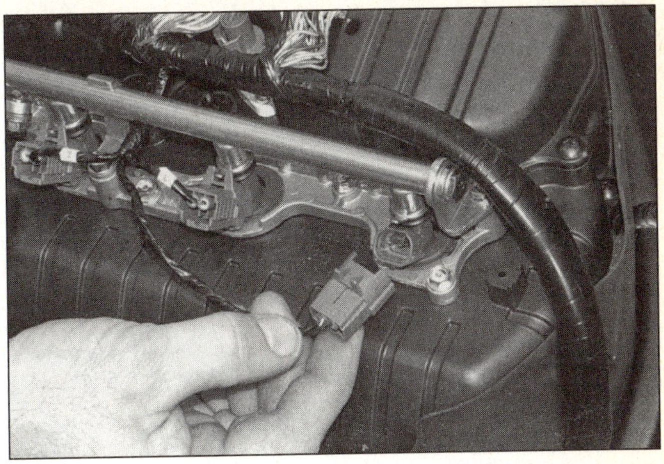

3.3a Disconnect the injector wiring connectors

Installation

8 If detached fit the breather and overflow hoses onto their unions, making sure they are correctly routed **(see illustration)**. Fit the mounting rubbers into their mounts if removed, not forgetting the collars on the front mounts, both of which fit from the inside **(see illustration 2.6c)**.
9 Depending on how the tank has been stood and how full it is there is the possibility of fuel having made its way into the breather pipe which could spurt out of the hose on the base when it is moved – be prepared with some rag for this. Once the tank is upright the pipe will fill itself with air.
10 Position the tank on the frame and insert the pivot bolts with their collars and tighten them finger-tight, then raise and support the tank as before **(see illustrations 2.6b and a)**.
11 Feed the fuel hose through its guide. Fit a new sealing washer on each side of the fuel hose union then fit the neck of the hose between the lugs and tighten the banjo bolt to the torque setting specified at the beginning of the Chapter **(see illustration 2.5)**.
12 Connect the fuel pump wiring connector **(see illustration 2.4)**. Make sure all the hoses are securely connected.
13 Remove the prop and pivot the tank down onto the frame, making sure the fuel supply and breather/overflow hoses do not get squashed or kinked. Fit the front mounting bolts and washers and tighten them to the specified torque **(see illustration 2.3a)**. Also tighten the rear bolts to the specified torque. Connect the breather/overflow hose at the joint on the left-hand side of the bike **(see illustration 2.2)**.
14 Start the engine and check that there is no sign of fuel leakage.

Repair

15 All repairs to the fuel tank should be carried out by a professional who has experience in this critical and potentially dangerous work. Even after cleaning and flushing of the fuel system, explosive fumes can remain and ignite during repair of the tank.
16 If the fuel tank is removed from the bike, it should not be placed in an area where sparks or open flames could ignite the fumes coming out of the tank. Be especially careful inside garages where a natural gas-type appliance is located, because the pilot light could cause an explosion.

3 Air filter housing and air intake system

Air filter housing

Removal

1 Raise or remove the fuel tank as required (see Section 2). If it has only been raised, disconnect its wiring connector **(see illustration 2.4)**.
2 Remove the air filters (see Chapter 1).
3 Disconnect the secondary fuel injector wiring connectors **(see illustration)**. Undo the wiring guide screw on the left-hand end of the secondary fuel rail and free the wiring **(see illustration)**. Unscrew the injector plate bolts and displace the injector assembly **(see illustration)**.

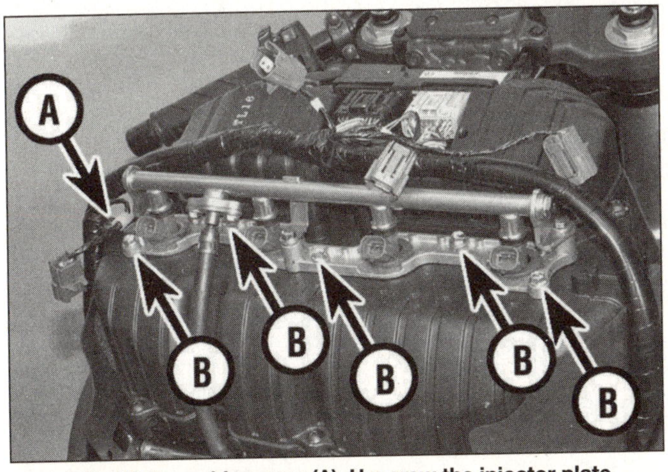

3.3b Wiring guide screw (A). Unscrew the injector plate bolts (B) . . .

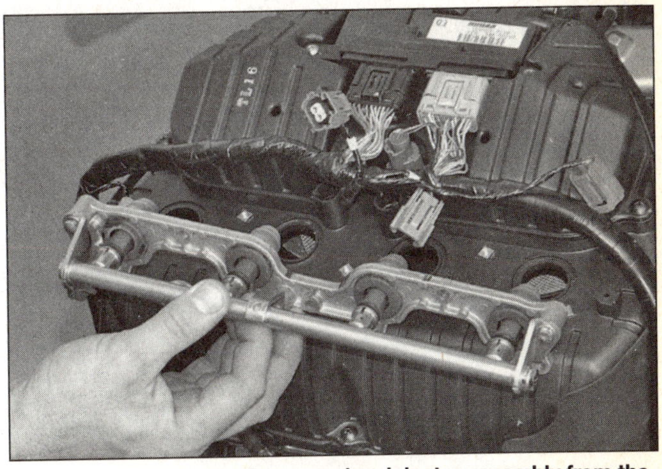

3.3c . . . then displace the secondary injector assembly from the housing

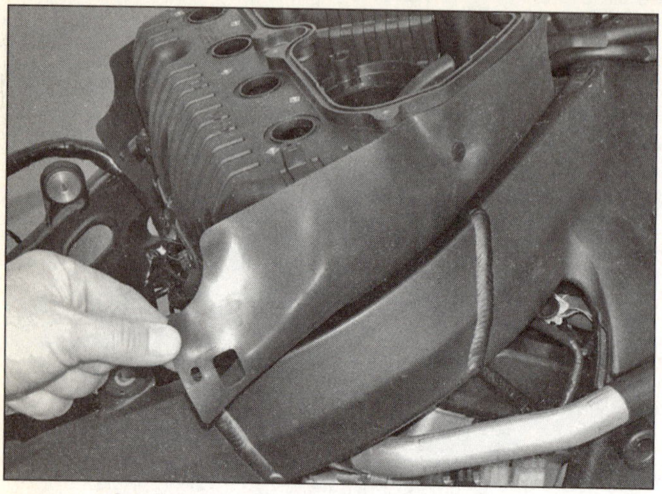

3.4 Release and remove the rubber shrouds

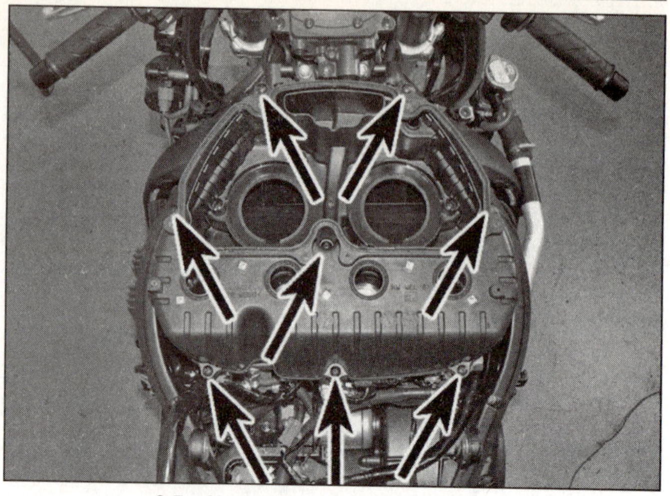

3.5a Undo the screws (arrowed) . . .

4 Draw the wiring back off the housing. Release the rubber shrouds from around the housing, noting how they fit and the routing of any wiring and hoses **(see illustration)**.

5 Undo the screws securing the upper section of the filter housing and remove it **(see illustrations)**.

6 Undo the air funnel/filter housing mounting screws and remove the funnels, noting which fits where **(see illustration)**.

7 Undo the screws securing the lower section of the filter housing to the air intake duct **(see illustration)**.

8 Displace the housing up off the throttle bodies and disconnect the crankcase breather hose and PAIR system supply hose **(see illustration)**. Remove the air filter housing. Cover the throttle bodies with a clean rag.

Installation

9 Installation is the reverse of removal. Check the condition of the throttle body and air intake seals and make sure they are in their groove. Check the condition of the PAIR and crankcase breather hoses and their clamps and use new ones if they are in any way damaged or deteriorated. Note that the air intake funnels are marked L and R (for left and right) to denote their position, and fit with the taller funnels above the middle (Nos. 2 and 3) throttle bodies **(see illustration)**. Make sure the secondary injector wiring connectors are securely connected.

Air intake duct

Removal

10 Remove the air filter housing (see above).

11 Either remove the radiator for best access, or displace it from its mounts and lower it, leaving the cooling system full and the hoses attached (see Chapter 3).

12 Undo the screw on each side that joins the front and rear sections of the duct **(see illustration)**.

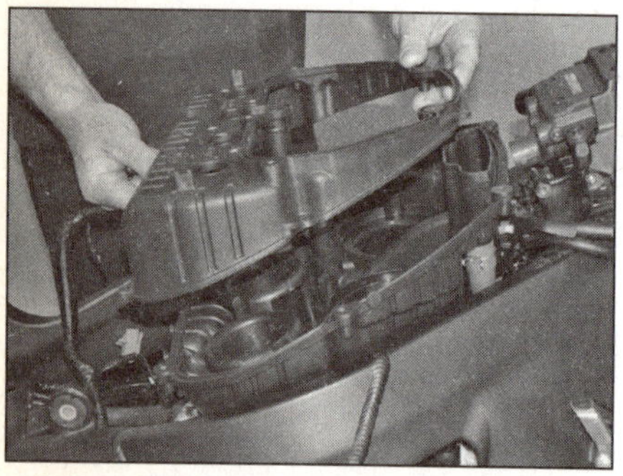

3.5b . . . and remove the upper section

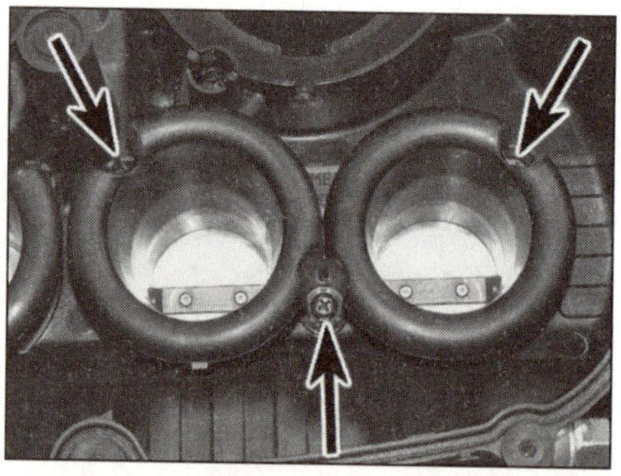

3.6 Undo the screws (arrowed) securing each pair of funnels and lift them out of the housing

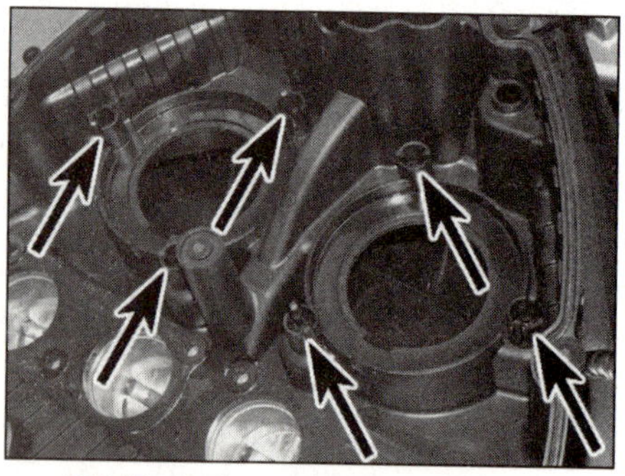

3.7 Undo the screws (arrowed) . . .

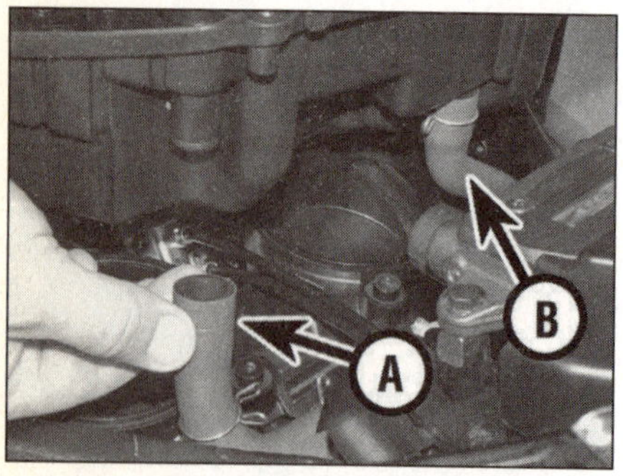

3.8 . . . then displace the housing and detach the crankcase breather hose (A) and the PAIR hose (B)

3.9 The taller funnels fit in the middle

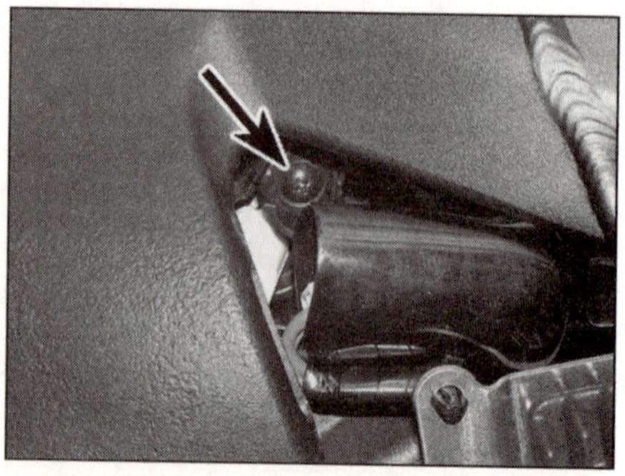

3.12 Undo the screw (arrowed) on each side

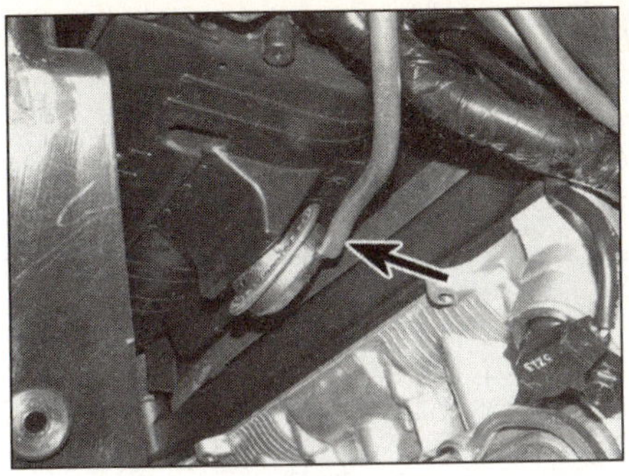

3.13 Detach the hose (arrowed) from the valve . . .

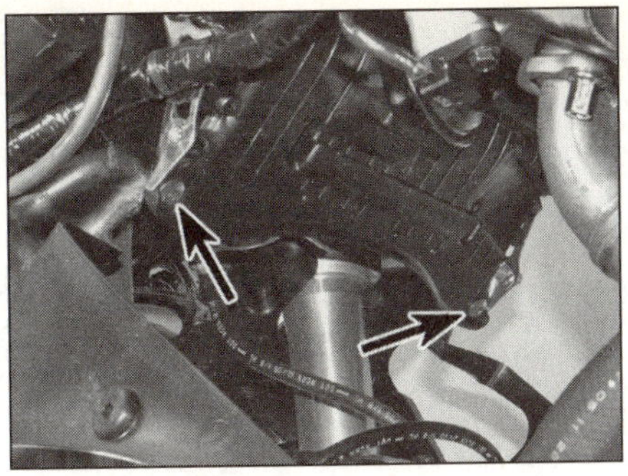

3.14a . . . undo the screws (arrowed) . . .

3.14b . . . then release the tab (arrowed) . . .

13 Detach the vacuum hose from the intake duct diaphragm valve on the underside of the front section **(see illustration)**.

14 Undo the screw securing each side of the front section **(see illustration)**. Release the tab that joins the two sections, then carefully manoeuvre the front section out **(see illustrations)**.

15 Manoeuvre the rear section out from under the throttle cables **(see illustration)**.

Inspection

16 Make sure the vacuum hose between the diaphragm valve and the control valve is in good condition and not split or cracked **(see illustration 3.13)**. Similarly check the vacuum hoses between the control valve and the vacuum chamber, and between the chamber and the throttle bodies **(see illustration 3.22)**. If a hose has a split the system will not work as it relies on vacuum. Make sure all hoses are securely connected to their unions.

17 Release the trim clips securing the front grille and remove the grille **(see illustrations)**. Make sure the intake flap opens and closes **(see illustration)**. If not undo the holder screws, detach the actuating rod and remove the flap. Check that the rod moves in and out of the diaphragm valve. If not replace the valve with a new one.

18 The diaphragm valve can also be checked by applying a vacuum to its union to see whether the rod moves **(see illustration)** – a specified vacuum at which the valve should actuate is not given, so start with a small one and gradually increase it. If the rod does not move the diaphragm may be split.

Installation

19 Installation is the reverse of removal. Make sure the vacuum hose is securely connected at each end.

Air intake control valve and vacuum chamber

Removal

20 Remove the left-hand fairing side panel (see Chapter 7).

21 To remove the control valve, disconnect its wiring connector, then detach the vacuum hoses, noting which fits where

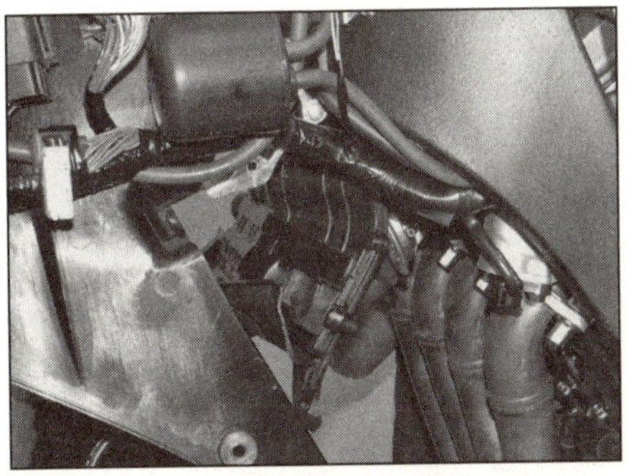

3.14c . . . and remove the front section

3.15 Draw the rear section out from under the cables

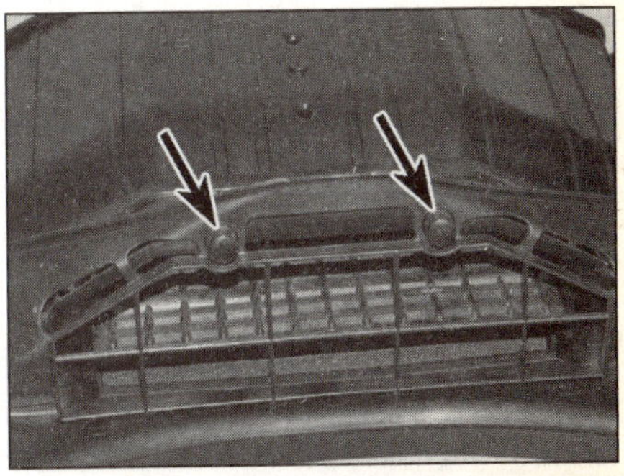

3.17a Release the trim clips (arrowed) and remove the grille

3.17b Check the action of the flap

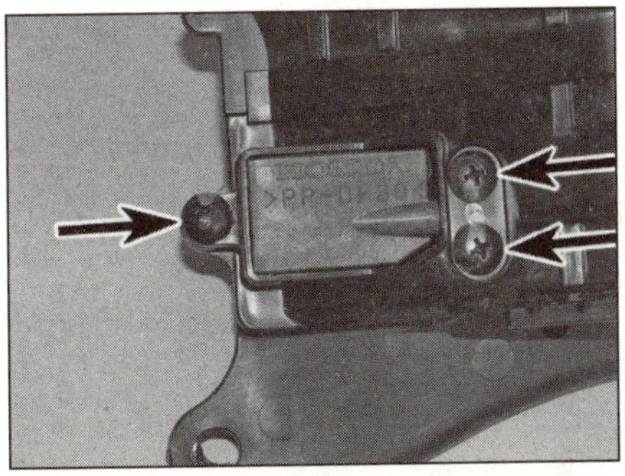

3.17c Undo the screws (arrowed) on each side

3.18 Check the diaphragm valve (arrowed) as described

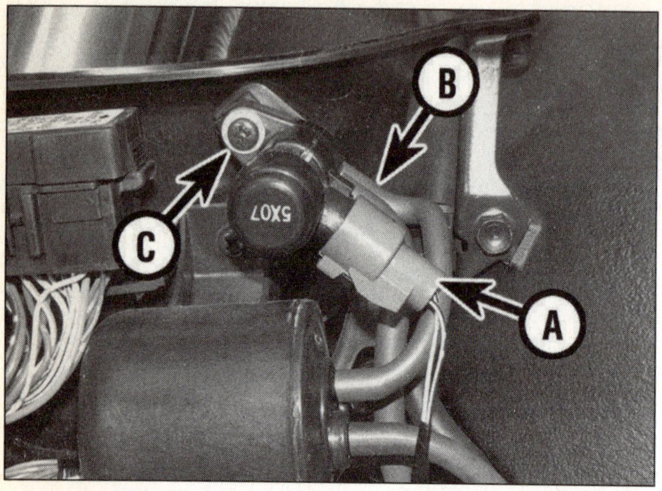

3.21 Control valve wiring connector (A), vacuum hoses (B) and mounting screw (C) – RR-6 and RR-7 model shown

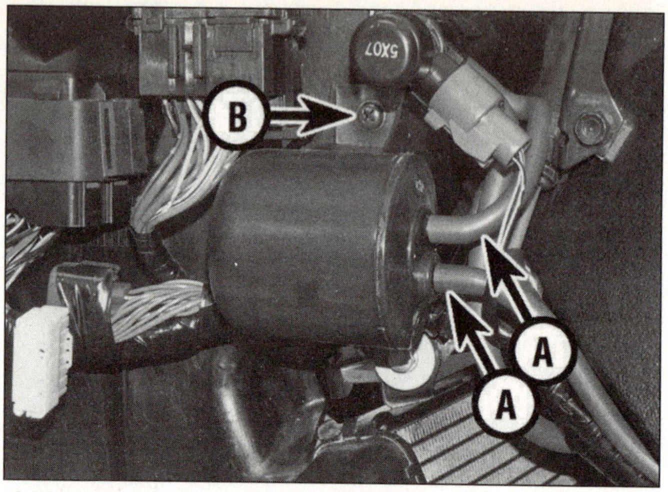

3.22 Vacuum chamber hoses (A) and mounting screw (B) – RR-6 and RR-7 model shown

(see illustration). Undo the screw or bolt (according to model) and remove the valve, noting how it locates.

22 To remove the vacuum chamber, detach the vacuum hoses, noting which fits where **(see illustration)**. Undo the screw or bolt (according to model) and remove the valve, noting how it locates.

Inspection

23 Check the operation of the control valve by blowing through the union A; no air should flow through the valve and out of union B **(see illustration)**. Now connect battery voltage (12 volts) across the valve terminals and repeat the check; air should now flow freely through the valve if it is functioning correctly.

24 Check the resistance of the control valve windings by connecting an ohmmeter between its connector terminals and compare the reading obtained to that given in the Specifications. Replace the valve with a new one if faulty.

25 Check the operation of the vacuum chamber one-way valve by blowing through the union A; no air should flow through the valve and out of union B **(see illustration)**. Now blow through union B; air should flow freely through the valve and out of union A if it is functioning correctly.

Installation

26 Installation is the reverse of removal. Make sure the vacuum hoses are securely connected at each end.

4 Fuel injection system description

1 All models are equipped with Honda's programmed dual stage fuel injection (PGM-DSFI) system. It is controlled by a management system with an engine control module (ECM) that operates both the injection and ignition systems **(see illustrations)**.

2 The engine control module (ECM) monitors signals from the following sensors.

- Throttle position (TP) sensor – informs the ECM of the throttle position, and the rate of throttle opening or closing.
- Engine coolant temperature (ECT) sensor – informs the ECM of engine temperature. It also actuates the temperature display and warning light (see Chapter 3).
- Manifold absolute pressure (MAP) sensor – informs the ECM of the engine load by monitoring the pressure in the throttle body inlet tracts.
- Intake air temperature (IAT) sensor – informs the ECM of the temperature of the air entering the throttle body.
- Camshaft position (CMP) sensor – informs the ECM of engine speed and camshaft position.
- Crankshaft position (CKP) sensor – informs the ECM of engine speed and crankshaft position.
- Speed sensor – informs the ECM of the motorcycle's road speed (see Chapter 8).
- Oxygen sensor (on models with catalytic converter) – informs the ECM of the oxygen content of the exhaust gases. The sensor is fitted to RR-4 and RR-5 Germany models and to all European RR-6 and RR-7 models.

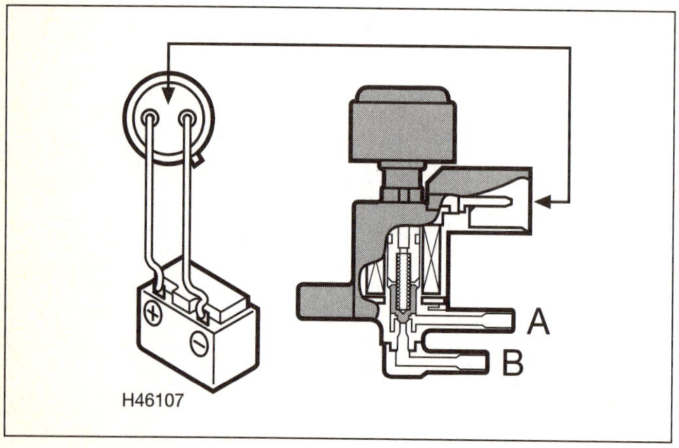

3.23 Control valve union location and battery connection

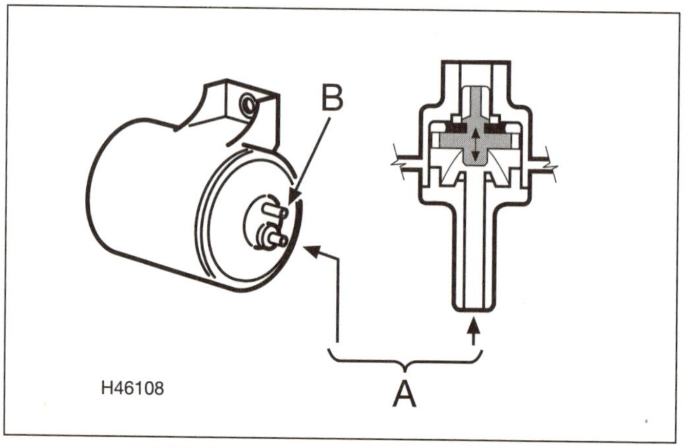

3.25 Vacuum chamber union location

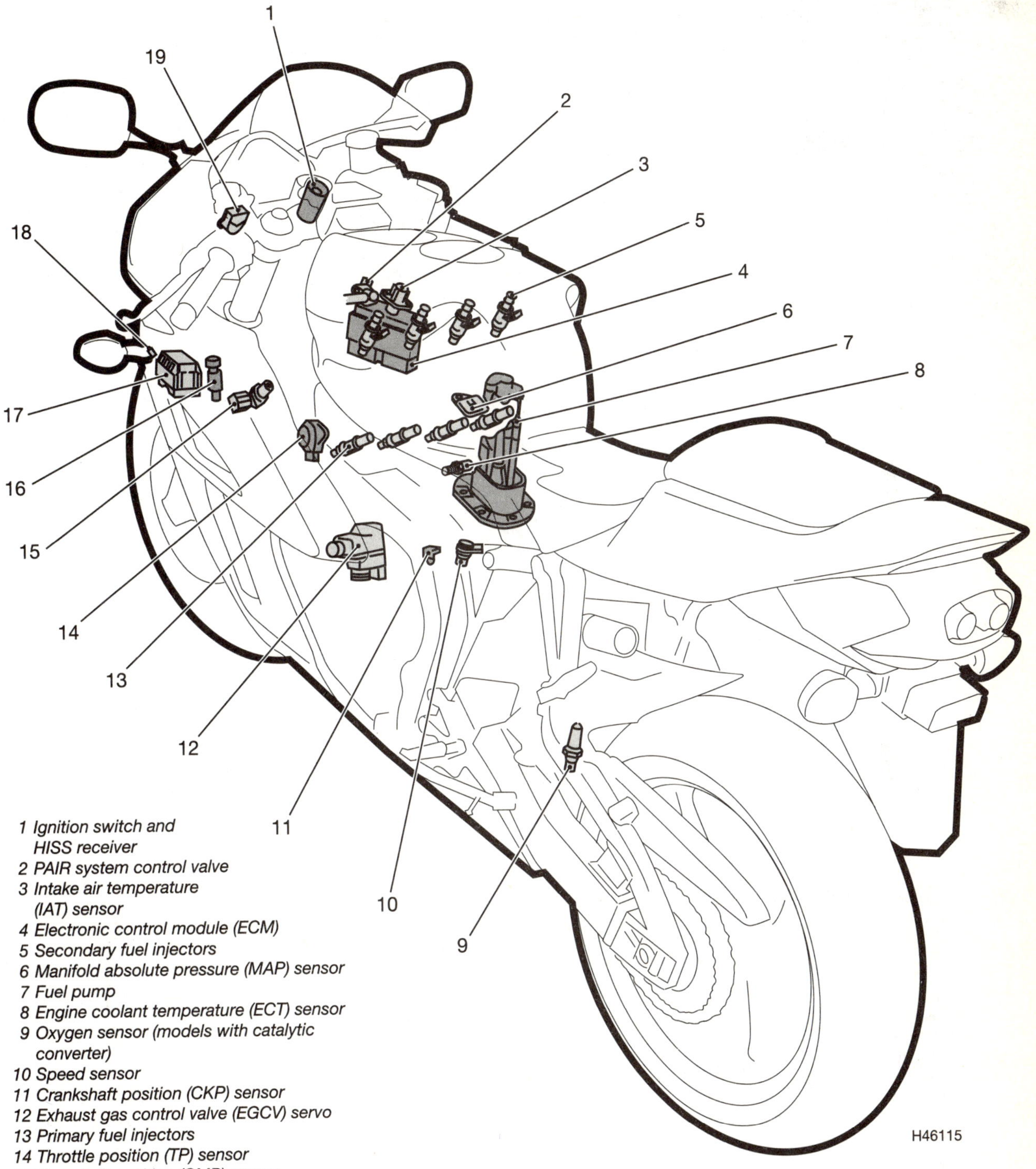

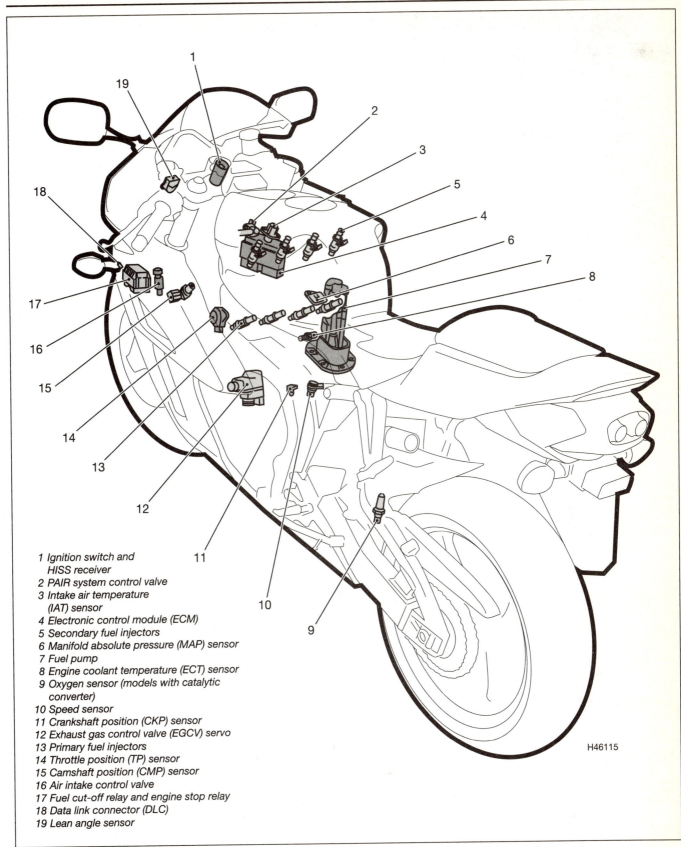

1 Ignition switch and HISS receiver
2 PAIR system control valve
3 Intake air temperature (IAT) sensor
4 Electronic control module (ECM)
5 Secondary fuel injectors
6 Manifold absolute pressure (MAP) sensor
7 Fuel pump
8 Engine coolant temperature (ECT) sensor
9 Oxygen sensor (models with catalytic converter)
10 Speed sensor
11 Crankshaft position (CKP) sensor
12 Exhaust gas control valve (EGCV) servo
13 Primary fuel injectors
14 Throttle position (TP) sensor
15 Camshaft position (CMP) sensor
16 Air intake control valve
17 Fuel cut-off relay and engine stop relay
18 Data link connector (DLC)
19 Lean angle sensor

4.1a Fuel injection and engine management system component location – RR-4 and RR-5 models

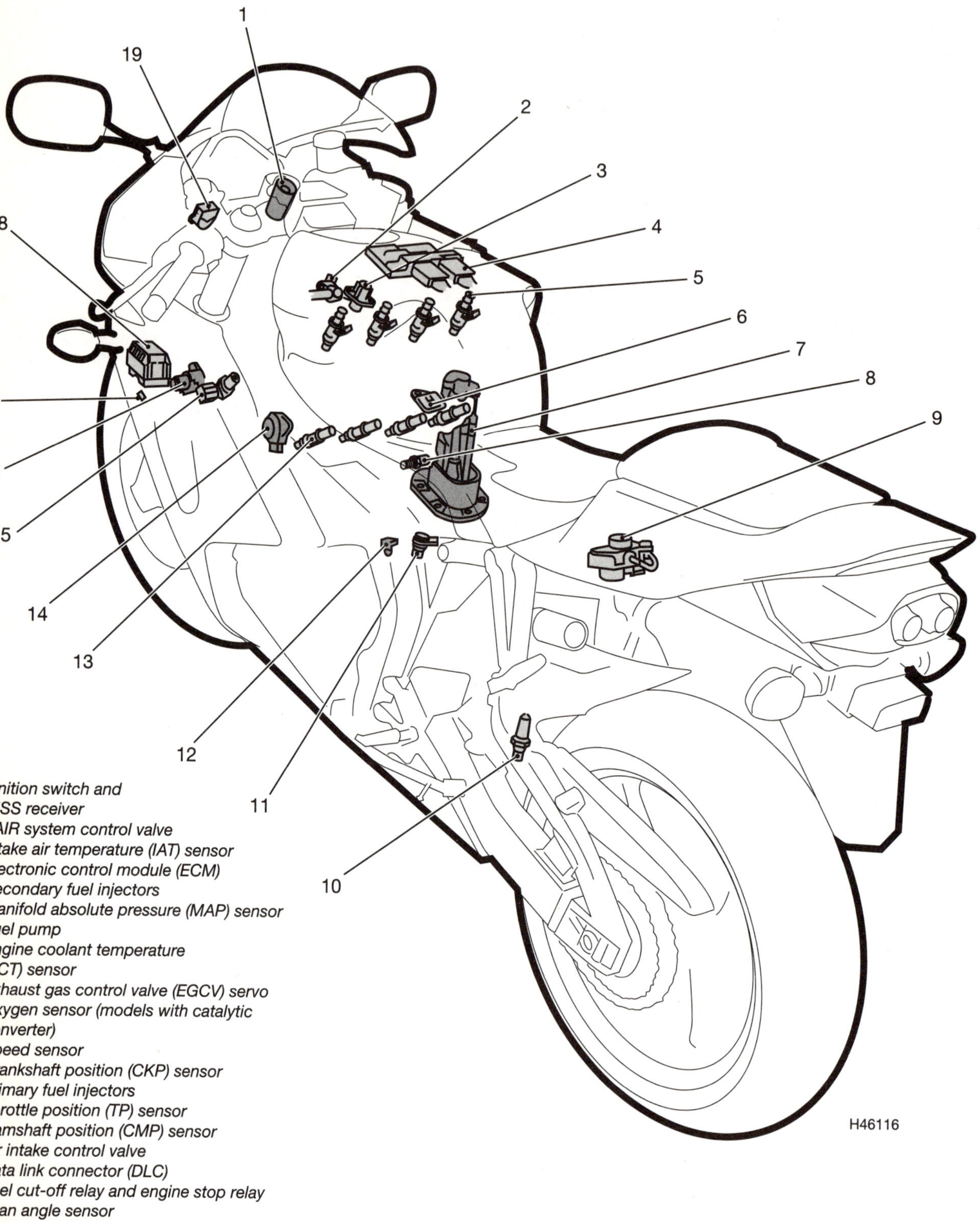

1 Ignition switch and HISS receiver
2 PAIR system control valve
3 Intake air temperature (IAT) sensor
4 Electronic control module (ECM)
5 Secondary fuel injectors
6 Manifold absolute pressure (MAP) sensor
7 Fuel pump
8 Engine coolant temperature (ECT) sensor
9 Exhaust gas control valve (EGCV) servo
10 Oxygen sensor (models with catalytic converter)
11 Speed sensor
12 Crankshaft position (CKP) sensor
13 Primary fuel injectors
14 Throttle position (TP) sensor
15 Camshaft position (CMP) sensor
16 Air intake control valve
17 Data link connector (DLC)
18 Fuel cut-off relay and engine stop relay
19 Lean angle sensor

4.1b Fuel injection and engine management system component location – RR-6 and RR-7 models

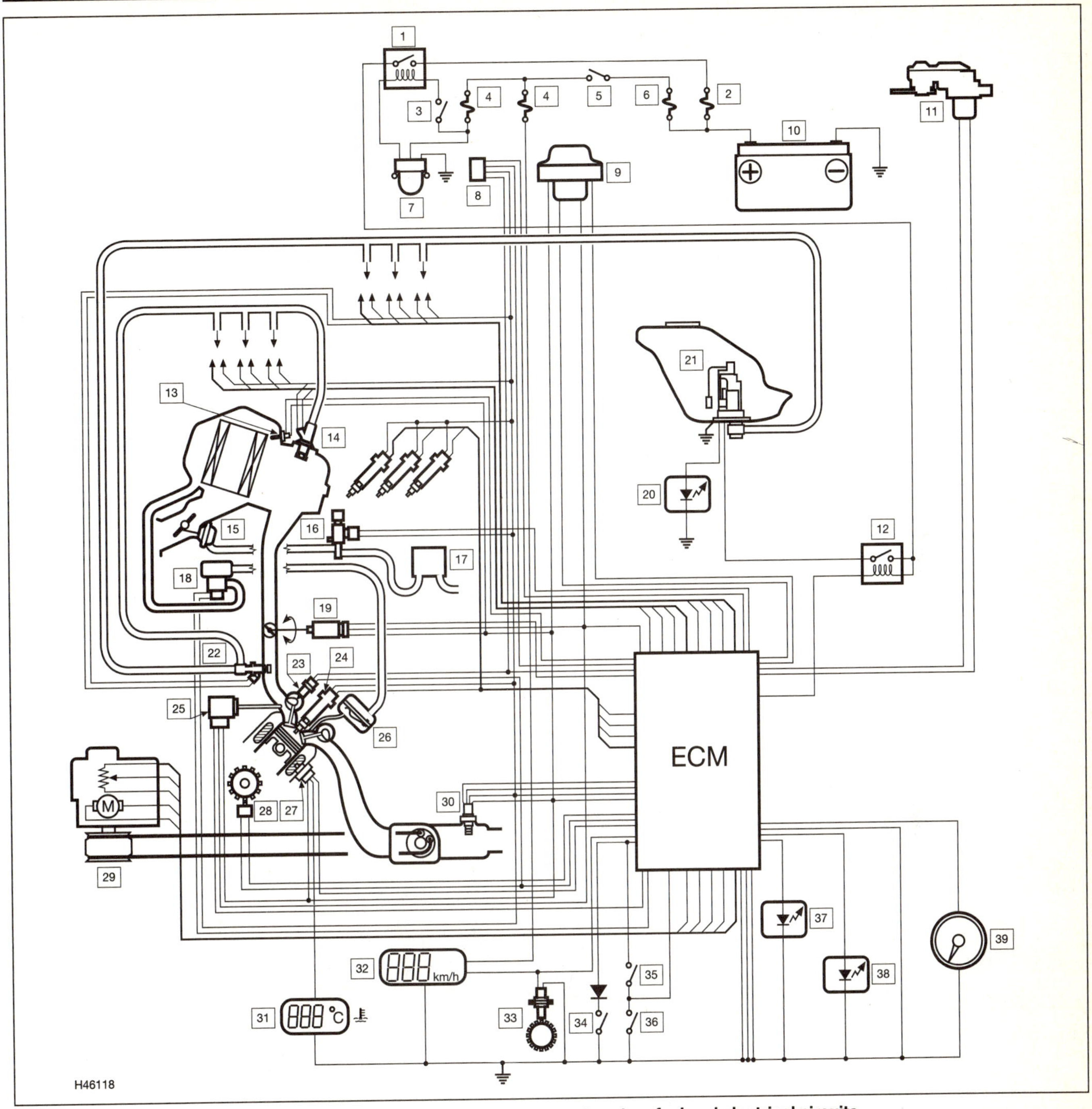

4.3 Fuel injection and engine management system fuel and electrical circuits

1 Engine stop relay
2 PGM fuse (20A)
3 Engine kill switch
4 Fuses (10A)
5 Ignition switch
6 Main fuse (30A)
7 Lean angle sensor
8 Data link connector (DLC)
9 HISS system immobiliser receiver (where fitted)
10 Battery
11 Honda electronic steering damper (HESD)
12 Fuel cut-off relay
13 Intake air temperature (IAT) sensor
14 Secondary fuel injector
15 Air intake duct diaphragm valve
16 Air intake control valve
17 Vacuum chamber
18 PAIR system control valve
19 Throttle position (TP) sensor
20 Fuel warning display
21 Fuel pump
22 Primary fuel injector
23 Camshaft position (CMP) sensor
24 Ignition coil
25 Manifold absolute pressure (MAP) sensor
26 PAIR system reed valve
27 Engine coolant temperature (ECT) sensor
28 Crankshaft position (CKP) sensor
29 Exhaust gas control valve (EGCV) servo
30 Oxygen sensor (models with catalytic converter)
31 Coolant temperature display (LCD)
32 Speedometer
33 Speed sensor
34 Neutral switch
35 Clutch switch
36 Sidestand switch
37 Malfunction indicator light (MIL)
38 HISS system immobiliser indicator
39 Tachometer

3 All the information from the sensors is analysed by the ECM, and from that it determines the appropriate ignition and fuelling requirements of the engine **(see illustration)**. The ECM controls each fuel injector by varying its pulse width – the length of time the injector is held open – to provide more or less fuel, as appropriate for cold starting, warm up, idle, cruising, and acceleration. The injection system is fully sequential, with each injector receiving its own signal from the ECM. Each cylinder is fed by two injectors. The primary injectors are mounted in the throttle bodies below the throttle valve and operate all the time the engine is running. The secondary injectors are mounted in the top of the air filter housing and spray fuel into the air entering the throttle bodies above the throttle valves. These injectors operate when the throttle is opened wide at engine speeds over 5500 rpm.

4 Cold starting and warm up idle speeds are controlled by an 'automatic fast idle system', which basically takes the place of a manual choke lever. A heat sensitive wax-filled unit that has engine coolant circulating around it actuates the starter valve arrangement in the throttle body assembly via a linkage rod. When the coolant is cold the wax unit is contracted and the starter valves are open. As the coolant heats up the wax expands, closing the starter valves. The starter valves allow additional air to bypass the throttle valves when the throttle is closed, and this increases the engine idle speed.

5 If there is an abnormality in any of the readings obtained from any sensor, the ECM enters its back-up mode. In this event, the ECM ignores the abnormal sensor signal, and assumes a pre-programmed value which will allow the engine to continue running (albeit at reduced efficiency). If the ECM enters this back-up mode, or when any faults occur, the malfunction indicator light (MIL) and the fuel injection system (FI) warning light in the instrument cluster will come on, and the relevant fault code will be stored in the ECM memory. The fault can be identified using the fault codes which can be accessed using the self-diagnosis function (see Section 5). However if there are certain faults detected in the injectors or the cam or crankshaft position sensors, the back-up mode becomes ineffective and the ECM will not allow the engine to run at all. Note that many European models have an immobiliser system (HISS – Honda Ignition Security System) which will not allow the engine to be started unless the correct key is used. A fault in this system should not be confused with a fuel injection system fault. The immobiliser system has its own fault diagnosis function (see Section 23).

5 Fuel injection system fault diagnosis

1 If the red malfunction indicator light (MIL) and the fuel injection system (FI) warning light on the instrument cluster illuminate when the motorcycle is running, a fault has occurred in the fuel injection/ignition system. The engine control module (ECM) will store the relevant fault code in its memory and this code can be read as follows using the self-diagnostic mode of the ECM. While the engine is running above 5000 rpm and the motorcycle is being ridden, the lights will come on and stay on. When the motorcycle is on its sidestand and the engine is running below 5000 rpm, the MIL will flash, the pattern of the flashes indicating the code for the fault the ECM has identified.

2 If the engine can be started, place the motorcycle on its sidestand then start the engine and allow it to idle. Whilst the engine is idling, observe the MIL and FI warning light on the instrument cluster.

3 If the engine cannot be started, place the motorcycle on its sidestand. With the kill switch in the run position turn the engine over on the starter motor for more then ten seconds and observe the MIL and FI warning light on the instrument cluster.

4 Alternatively, and to check for any stored fault codes even though the warning lights have not illuminated, remove the left-hand fairing side panel (see Chapter 7) to gain access to the fuel injection system data link connector (DLC), which is a 4-pin connector coming out of the wiring loom **(see illustrations)**. On RR-4 and RR-5 models disconnect the connector from its holder taped on the loom. On RR-6 and RR-7 models unfasten the connector from the loom and remove the blanking cap **(see illustration)**. Ensure the ignition is switched OFF then fit the Honda SCS service connector (Part No. 070PZ-ZY30100, available at reasonable cost from your dealer), or bridge the brown and green wire terminals of the connector with an auxiliary wire (do not confuse the brown wire with the adjacent brown/yellow wire) **(see illustration)**. With the terminals connected, make sure the kill switch is in the RUN position then turn the ignition ON and observe the red malfunction indicator light (MIL). If there are no stored fault codes, the MIL will come on and stay on. If there are stored fault codes, the MIL will flash.

5 The MIL uses long (1.3 second) and short (0.5 second) flashes to give out the fault code. A long flash is used to indicate the first digit of a double digit fault code (i.e. 10 and above). If a single digit fault code is being displayed (i.e. 0 – 9), there will be a number of short flashes equivalent to the code being displayed. For example, two long (1.3 sec) flashes followed by five short (0.5 sec) flashes indicates the fault code number 25. If there is more than one fault code, there will be a gap before the other codes are revealed (the codes will be revealed in order, starting with the lowest and finishing with the highest). Once all codes have been revealed, the ECM will continuously run through the code(s) stored in its memory, revealing each one in turn with a short gap between them. The fault codes are shown in the table opposite.

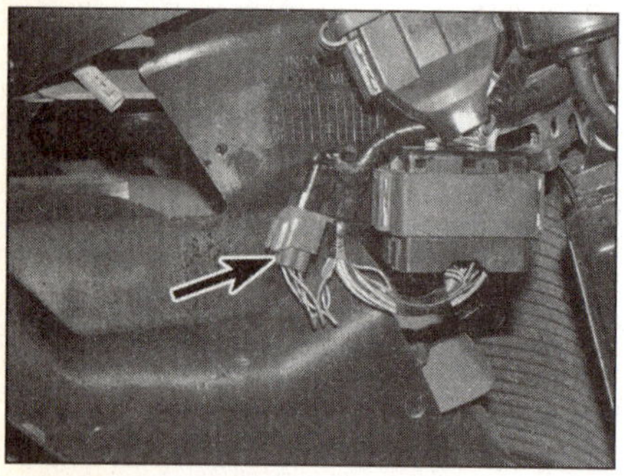

5.4a Data link connector (arrowed) – RR-4 and RR-5 models

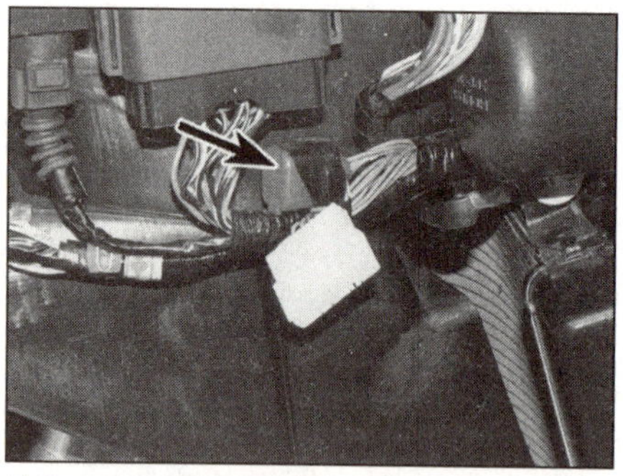

5.4b Data link connector (arrowed) – RR-6 and RR-7 models

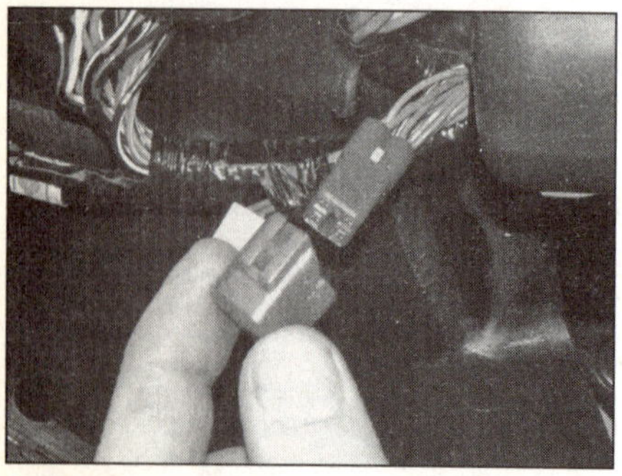

5.4c Release the connector and remove the cap

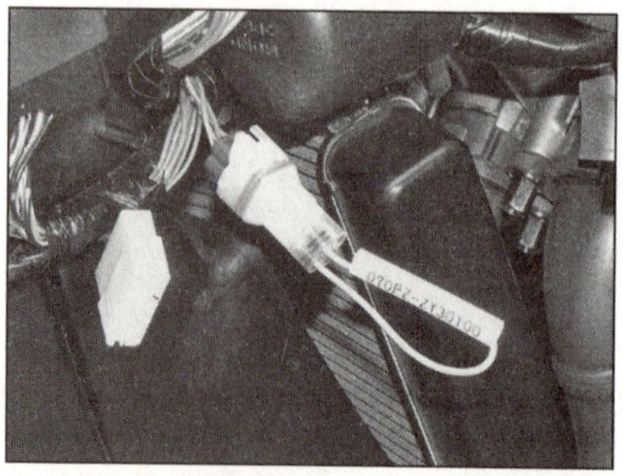

5.4d Honda service connector in place on DLC

Fault code (No. of flashes)	Symptoms	Possible causes
0 – no code (warning light off)	Engine does not start	Blown fuse (PGM or lean angle sensor)
		Faulty power supply to electronic control module (ECM)
		Short circuit in ECM output voltage (yellow/red) wire
		Faulty engine stop relay or wiring
		Faulty engine stop switch/open circuit on switch earth (ground) wire
		Faulty ignition switch
		Faulty lean angle sensor or wiring
		Faulty electronic control module (ECM)
0 – no code (warning light off)	Engine runs normally	Open or short circuit in warning light wiring
		Faulty electronic control module (ECM)
0 – no code (warning light constantly on)	Engine runs normally	Short circuit in data link connector or wiring
1	Engine runs normally	Faulty manifold absolute pressure (MAP) sensor or wiring
2	Engine runs normally	Faulty manifold absolute pressure (MAP) sensor or vacuum hose
7	Engine difficult to start at low temperatures	Faulty engine coolant temperature (ECT) sensor or wiring
8	Poor throttle response	Faulty throttle position (TP) sensor or wiring
9	Engine runs normally	Faulty intake air temperature (IAT) sensor or wiring
11	Engine operates normally	Faulty speed sensor or wiring
12	Engine does not start	Faulty No. 1 primary injector or wiring
13	Engine does not start	Faulty No. 2 primary injector or wiring
14	Engine does not start	Faulty No. 3 primary injector or wiring
15	Engine does not start	Faulty No. 4 primary injector or wiring
16	Engine does not start	Faulty No. 1 secondary injector or wiring
17	Engine does not start	Faulty No. 2 secondary injector or wiring
18	Engine does not start	Faulty camshaft position (CMP) sensor or wiring
19	Engine does not start	Faulty crankshaft position (CKP) sensor or wiring
34	Engine operates normally	Faulty potentiometer in exhaust gas control valve (EGCV) servo
35	Engine operates normally	Faulty exhaust gas control valve (EGCV) servo
48	Engine does not start	Faulty No. 3 secondary injector or wiring
49	Engine does not start	Faulty No. 4 secondary injector or wiring
51	Engine operates normally Steering damper inoperative	Faulty electronic steering damper (HESD) solenoid or wiring
The following codes are only applicable to models with a catalytic converter		
21	Engine operates normally	Faulty oxygen sensor or wiring
23	Engine operates normally	Faulty oxygen sensor or wiring, or faulty oxygen sensor heating element

Once all the codes have been revealed, switch off the ignition and (where necessary) remove the auxiliary wire from the data link connector. Identify the fault using the table above, then refer below for checking procedures.

6 Once the fault has been identified and corrected, it will be necessary to reset the system by removing the fault code from the ECM memory. To do this, ensure the ignition is switched OFF then fit the Honda SCS service connector or bridge the brown and green wire terminals of the data link connector (DLC) (see Step 3). Make sure the kill switch is in the RUN position, then turn the ignition switch ON. Disconnect the auxiliary wire from the DLC. When the wire is disconnected the malfunction indicator light should come on for about five seconds, during which time the auxiliary wire must be reconnected. The light should start to flash when it is reconnected, indicating that all fault codes have been erased. However if the light flashes twenty times the memory has not been erased and the procedure must be repeated. Turn off the ignition then remove the auxiliary wire. Check the MIL and FI warning light (in some cases it may be necessary to repeat the erasing procedure more than once) then install the fairing side panel.

7 While some of the sensors can be checked using home equipment, there are others which

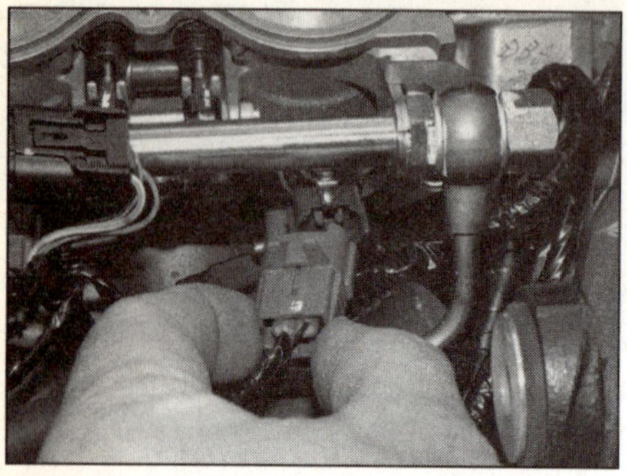

6.3a Disconnect the wiring connector . . .

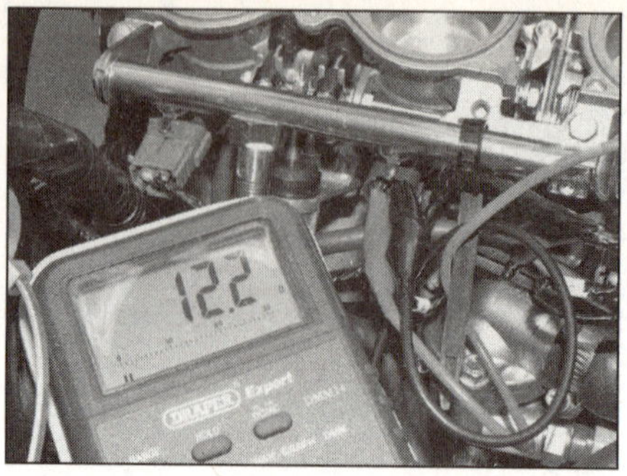

6.3b . . . and check the resistance between the terminals

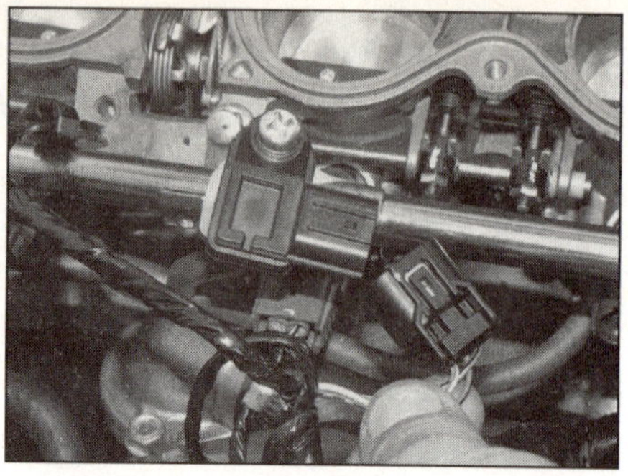

6.5a Disconnect the MAP sensor wiring connector

can only be tested using the Honda diagnostic system (HDS) tester which can be plugged into the system. If a fault appears, use the diagnostic function and fault code system described above to work out which component is faulty. First ensure that the relevant system wiring connectors are securely connected and free of corrosion – poor connections are the cause of the majority of problems. Also check the wiring itself for any obvious faults or breaks, and use a continuity tester to check the wiring between the component, its connectors and the ECM, referring to the wiring diagrams at the end of Chapter 8. Next refer to Section 6 to see if there are any other specific checks that can be made on that particular component. If this fails to reveal the cause of the problem, the motorcycle should be taken to a suitably-equipped Honda dealer for testing. They will have the tester which should locate the fault quickly and simply.

8 Also ensure that the fault is not due to poor maintenance – i.e. check that the air filter element is clean, that the spark plugs are in good condition, that the valve clearances are correctly adjusted, the cylinder compression pressures are correct, and the ignition timing is correct (refer to Chapters 1 and 2, and to Section 21). It is also worth removing the sensor(s) in question (see Section 6) and checking that the sensing tip or head is clean and not obstructed by anything **(see illustration 6.49)**. Where there is a vacuum hose to a sensor, make sure it is securely connected at both ends and has no cracks or splits.

6 Fuel injection components

Caution: Ensure the ignition is switched OFF before disconnecting/reconnecting any fuel injection system wiring connector. If a connector is disconnected/reconnected with the ignition switched ON the engine control module (ECM) could be damaged.

Fuel rails and injectors

Warning: Refer to the precautions given in Section 1 before starting work.

Check

1 Raise the fuel tank (see Section 2).

2 If the engine runs, start it and allow it to idle. Check the operation of each primary injector in the throttle bodies using a stethoscope or sounding rod; an injector will emit a 'clicking' noise when functioning. If any injector is silent, either the injector or its wiring harness is faulty. Check the secondary injectors in the top of the air filter housing in the same way, but note that engine must be running at over 5500 rpm before these injectors are active.

3 If the engine does not run, disconnect the wiring connector from each injector **(see illustration)**. Connect an ohmmeter between the terminals of each injector in turn and measure the resistance **(see illustration)**. Compare the reading for each injector to that given in the Specifications. Also check that there is no continuity to earth on the black/white wire terminal on the injector. If the resistance of any injector differs greatly from that specified, or there is continuity to earth, a new injector should be installed. Also check for battery voltage at the black/white wire terminal in the wiring connector. If there is no voltage, check the wiring. Check for continuity in the other wire in the connector – there should be no continuity to earth, but there should be continuity to the wire terminal in the ECM wiring connector.

Removal

Primary rail and injectors

4 Remove the air filter housing (see Section 3). If required, remove the throttle bodies (see Section 7) – this is not essential, but will improve access.

5 If the throttle bodies are in situ disconnect the wiring connector from each injector **(see illustration 6.3a)**, and from the MAP sensor **(see illustration)**. Counter-hold the hex on the fuel hose joint for the secondary injectors and unscrew the banjo union nut, noting the alignment of the hose and being prepared to catch any residual fuel with a rag **(see illustration)**. Detach the hose and discard the sealing washers – new ones must be used.

6 Counter-hold the hex on the fuel supply hose joint and unscrew the banjo union nut, noting the alignment of the hose and being prepared to catch any residual fuel with a rag **(see illustration)**. Detach the hose and discard the sealing washers – new ones must be used. Undo the screw securing the MAP sensor to the fuel rail **(see illustration)**.

6.5b Counter-hold the hex while unscrewing the secondary injector banjo bolt

6.6a Counter-hold the hex while unscrewing the fuel supply banjo bolt

6.6b Undo the screw and displace the MAP sensor

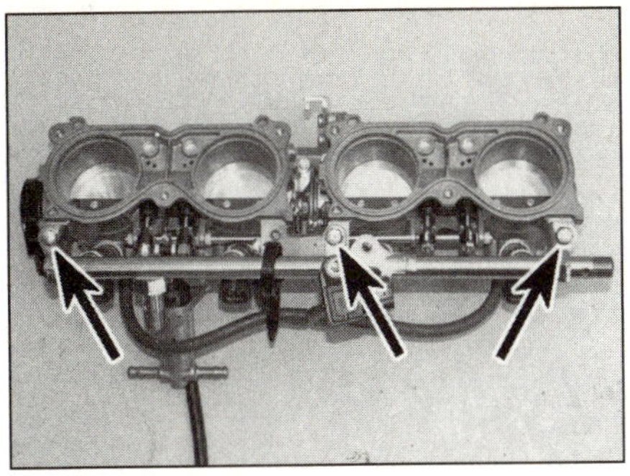

6.7a Unscrew the bolts (arrowed) . . .

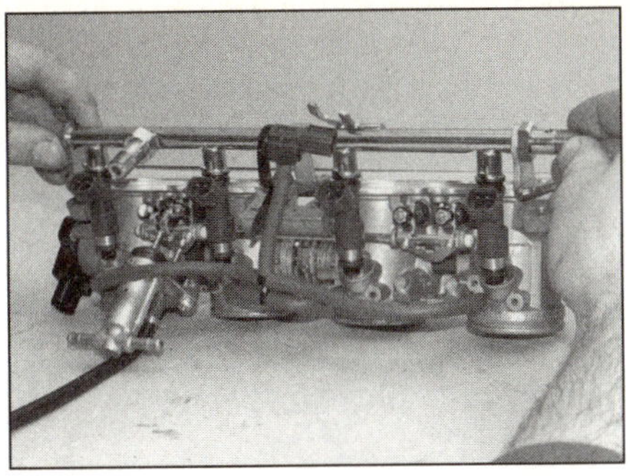

6.7b . . . and remove the fuel rail and injectors

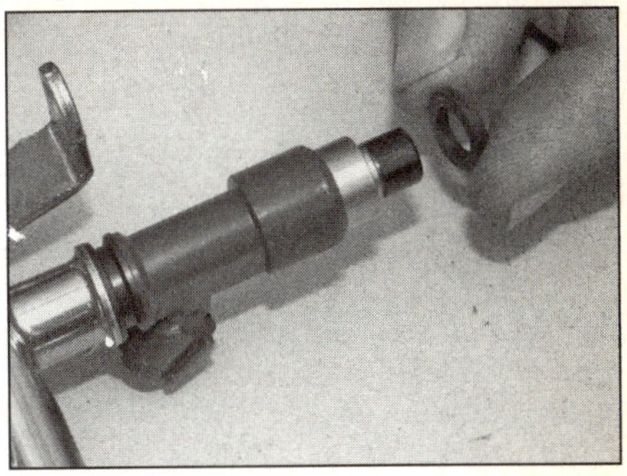

6.7c Remove the seal from each injector . . .

6.7d . . . or if not there from the throttle body

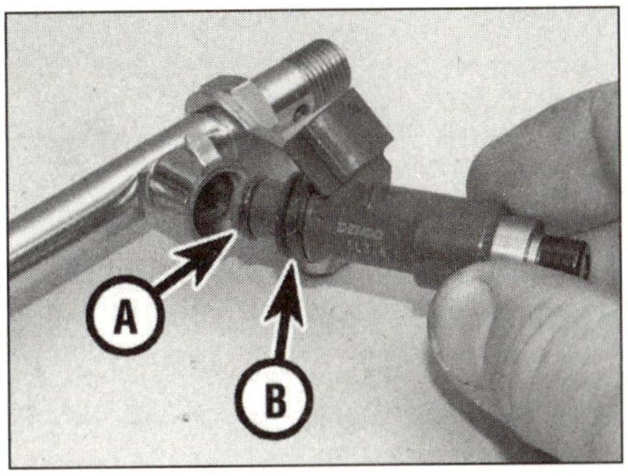

6.8 Ease the injector out and discard its O-ring (A). Check the cushion (B)

6.10 Unscrew the bolts (arrowed) and detach the fuel hose

7 Unscrew the fuel rail bolts **(see illustration)**. Carefully lift off the fuel rail assembly and injectors **(see illustration)**. Remove the seals from the injectors, or from the injector seats in the throttle bodies **(see illustrations)**. Discard them as new ones must be used.

8 If required remove the injectors from the fuel rail **(see illustration)**. Note the correct fitted positions of the O-ring and rubber cushion on each injector; the O-rings must be replaced with new ones, but the cushions can be reused as long as they are not damaged, deformed or deteriorated.

Secondary rail and injectors

9 Raise or remove the fuel tank (see Section 2).

10 Unscrew the bolts securing the fuel hose union to the rail, being prepared to catch any residual fuel with a rag **(see illustration)**. Discard the O-ring in the union as a new one must be used. Disconnect the wiring connector from each injector **(see illustration 3.3a)**.

11 If required (but note that the plate can stay in place and the rail and injectors be removed from it) unscrew the injector plate bolts and displace the complete injector assembly **(see illustrations 3.3b and c)**.

12 Unscrew the fuel rail bolts **(see illustration)**. Carefully lift off the fuel rail assembly and injectors **(see illustration)**. Remove the seals from the injectors, or from the injector seats in the plate **(see illustrations)**. The seals can be reused as long as they are in good condition.

13 If required remove the injectors from the fuel rail. Note the correct fitted positions of the O-ring and rubber cushion on each injector **(see illustration)**; the O-rings must be replaced with new ones, but the cushions can be reused as long as they are not damaged, deformed or deteriorated.

Installation

Note: *The primary injectors have brown bodies and the secondary injectors have blue bodies.*

14 If the injectors have been removed from

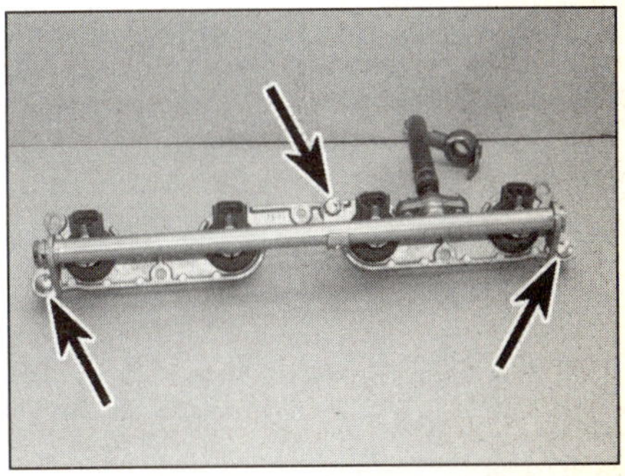

6.12a Unscrew the bolts (arrowed) . . .

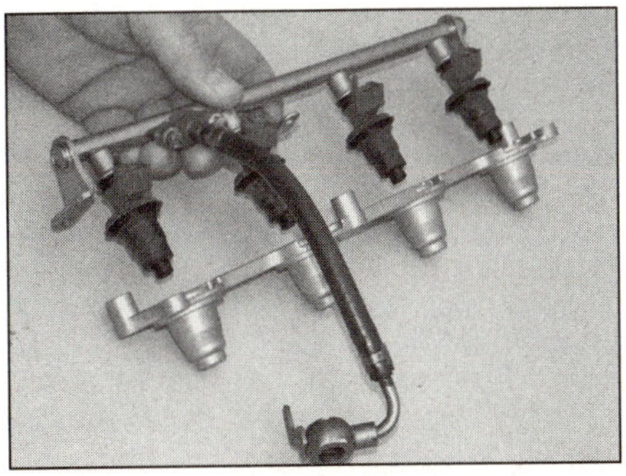

6.12b . . . and remove the fuel rail and injectors

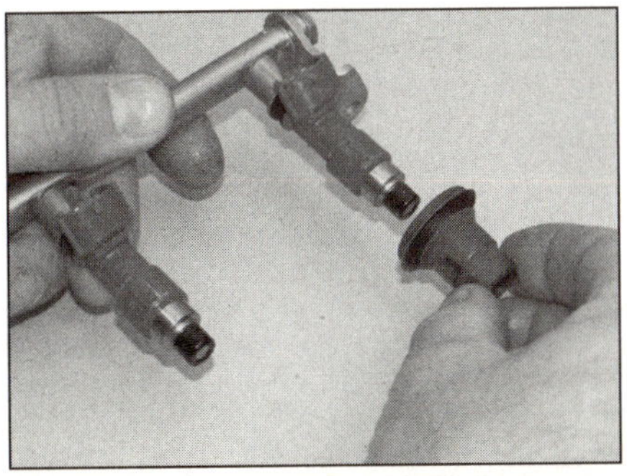

6.12c Remove the seals from the injectors or from the plate

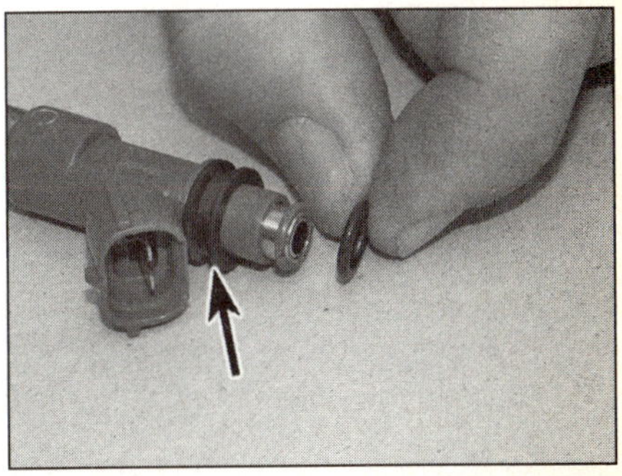

6.13 Ease the injector out and discard its O-ring. Check the cushion (arrowed)

6.16 Make sure each primary injector locates correctly in its throttle body

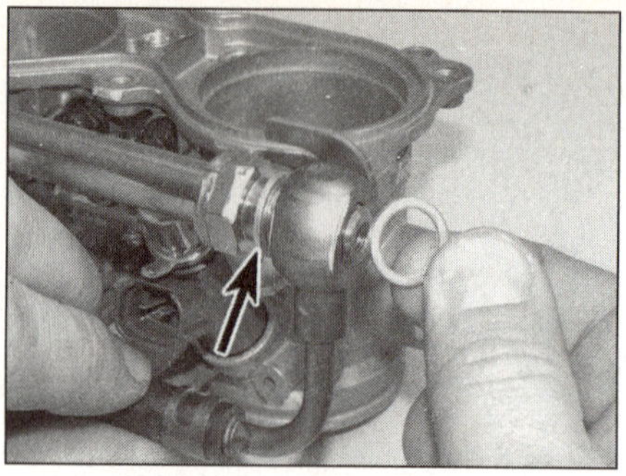

6.17a Always use new sealing washers . . .

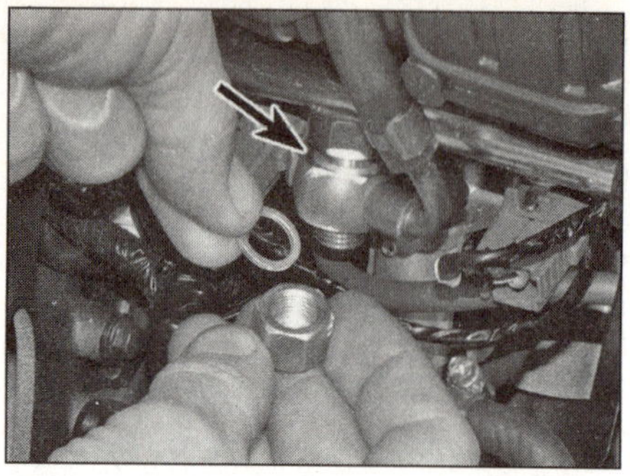

6.17b . . . on each side of the banjo unions

their rail, slide the cushion onto the top of each injector (using a new one if necessary), then fit a new O-ring lubricated with clean engine oil into the groove **(see illustration 6.13)**. Ease the injectors into the rail taking care not to damage the O-rings **(see illustration 6.8)**. Make sure the injectors are fitted so the wiring connector socket abuts the tab on the injector housing.

15 Fit the seal onto the bottom of each injector, using new ones for the primary rail injectors whatever the condition of the old ones, and if necessary for the secondary injectors **(see illustrations 6.7c and 6.12c)**.

16 Install the fuel rail assembly, making sure each injector enters its seat and the seals stay in place and locate correctly **(see illustration or 6.12b)**. Fit the fuel rail bolts and tighten them to the torque setting specified at the beginning of the Chapter **(see illustration and 6.7a or 6.12a)**. If removed install the secondary rail plate and tighten its bolts **(see illustration 3.3c and b)**.

17 Use new sealing washers on the primary rail fuel hose banjo unions **(see illustrations)**. Tighten the nuts to the specified torque setting, making sure you counter-hold the hex on each hose joint or the fuel rail could distort or break **(see illustrations 6.5b and 6.6a)**. Use a new O-ring on the secondary rail fuel hose union and tighten the union bolts to the torque setting specified at the beginning of the chapter **(see illustration 6.10)**.

18 Reconnect the injector wiring connectors – ensure they are connected correctly **(see illustration 6.3a or 3.3a)**.

19 Install the throttle bodies, air filter housing and fuel tank as required. Run the engine and check that the fuel system is working correctly before taking the machine out on the road.

Throttle position (TP) sensor

Check

20 The throttle sensor operation can only be checked using the Honda diagnostic system tester. Its power supply can be checked as follows. Raise the fuel tank (see Section 2). Disconnect the wiring connector from the sensor **(see illustration)**. Connect the positive (+) lead of a voltmeter to the yellow/red terminal of the sensor wiring connector, then connect the negative (–) lead to a good earth. Turn the ignition switch ON and check that a voltage of 4.75 to 5.25 volts is present. If it isn't, there is a fault in the yellow/red wire or the ECM. If voltage was present, now connect the negative lead to the grey/black wire terminal of the connector and check that the same voltage is present. If it isn't, there is a fault in the grey/black wire or the ECM. If there is voltage, check for continuity to earth in the yellow/red wire. If there is, trace the fault in the wire and repair it. If there isn't, and the sensor is proven good by the Honda tester, then the ECM is faulty.

Removal and installation

21 The throttle sensor is an integral part of the throttle body assembly and is not available separately **(see illustration)**. If the sensor is faulty, a complete new throttle body assembly will have to be installed, though it is worth checking with your Honda parts specialist whether anything can be done to avoid this.

Engine coolant temperature (ECT) sensor

Note: *The sensor also operates the coolant temperature display – refer to Chapter 3 to check this aspect of its function.*

Check

22 Raise or remove the fuel tank (See Section 2). The sensor is mounted in the thermostat housing on the back of the engine **(see illustration 6.26)**.

23 Disconnect the wiring connector from the sensor **(see illustration)**. With the engine cold, connect an ohmmeter between the blue/yellow and grey/black wire terminals on the sensor and measure its resistance. Compare the reading obtained to that given in the Specifications, noting that the specified value is valid at 20°C (68°F); the sensor resistance will increase at lower temperatures and decrease at higher temperatures. If the resistance reading differs greatly from that specified, the sensor is probably faulty.

24 If the sensor appears to be functioning correctly, check its power supply. Connect the positive (+) lead of a voltmeter to the blue/yellow wire terminal in the sensor wiring connector, then connect the negative (–) lead

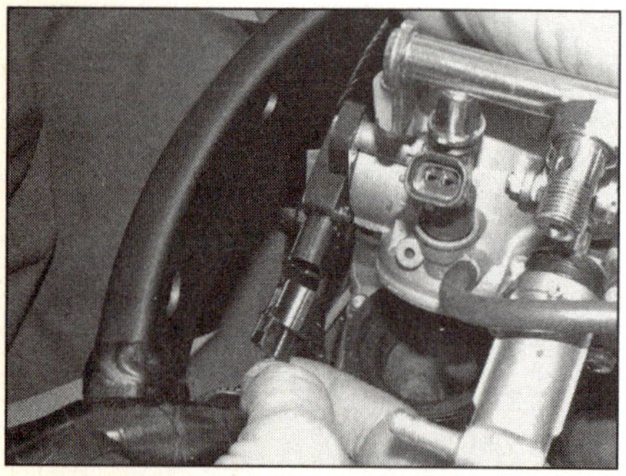

6.20 Disconnect the throttle position sensor wiring connector

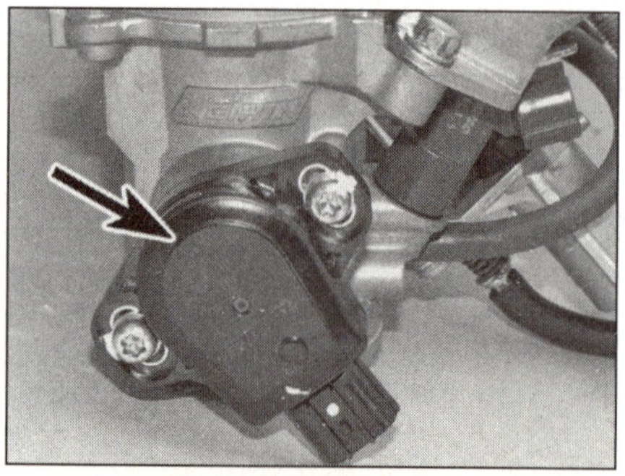

6.21 The TP sensor (arrowed) is an integral part of the throttle body assembly

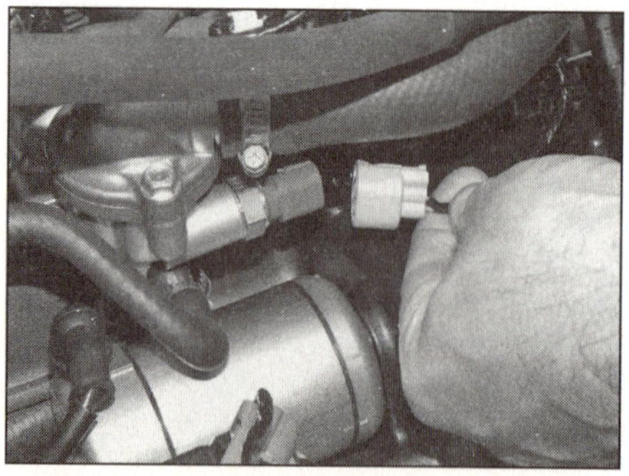

6.23 Disconnect the ECT sensor wiring connector

6.26 The sensor (arrowed) screws into the thermostat housing

to a good earth. Turn the ignition switch ON and check that a voltage of 4.75 to 5.25 volts is present. If it isn't, there is a fault in the blue/yellow wire or the ECM. If voltage was present, now connect the negative lead to the grey/black terminal of the connector and check that the same voltage is present. If it isn't, there is a fault in the grey/black wire or the ECM. If there is voltage, the ECM is probably faulty.

Removal

⚠ ***Warning: The engine must be completely cool before carrying out this procedure.***

25 Drain the cooling system (see Chapter 1). Raise the fuel tank (see Section 2). The sensor is mounted in the thermostat housing **(see illustration 6.26)**.

26 Disconnect the sensor wiring connector **(see illustration 6.23)**. Unscrew and remove the sensor **(see illustration)**. To improve access slacken and move the clamp securing the large bore hose to the thermostat cover, and if required detach the hose.

Installation

27 Fit a new sealing washer onto the sensor. Install the sensor and tighten it to the torque setting specified at the beginning of the Chapter. Connect the wiring **(see illustration 6.23)**. If detached fit the hose onto the thermostat cover and tighten its clamp **(see illustration 6.26)**.

28 Lower the fuel tank (see Section 2). Refill the cooling system (see Chapter 1).

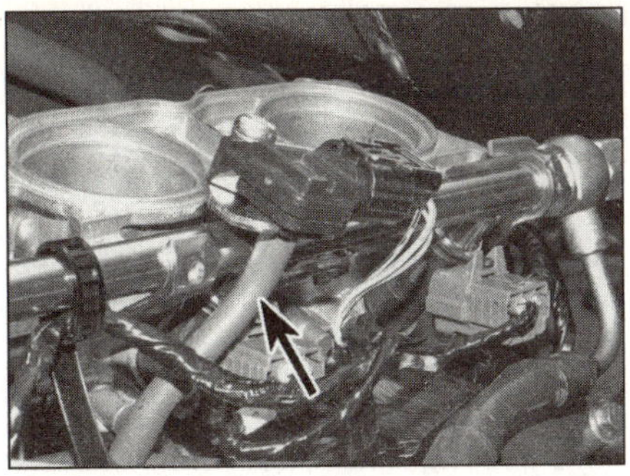

6.29 Make sure the MAP sensor vacuum hose (arrowed) and those it connects to are secure and in good condition

Manifold absolute pressure (MAP) sensor

Check

29 The MAP sensor is mounted on the primary fuel rail. The sensor can only be checked using the Honda diagnostic test pin box. However you can raise the fuel tank (see Section 2) and make sure that the vacuum hoses to it are securely fixed at both ends, and have no cracks or splits **(see illustration)**. If the necessary equipment is available, connect a vacuum gauge into the hose between the throttle bodies and the MAP sensor using an auxiliary three-way joint and some rubber hose, and with the engine idling check that the manifold absolute pressure is as specified at the beginning of the Chapter. If not, replace all the vacuum hoses with new ones. If the pressure is out of specification with new or good hoses, check for leaks between the air filter housing, the throttle bodies and the cylinder head.

30 The sensor power supply can be checked as follows. Raise the fuel tank (see Section 2). Disconnect the wiring connector from the sensor **(see illustration 6.5a)**. Connect the positive (+) lead of a voltmeter to the yellow/red terminal of the sensor wiring connector, then connect the negative (–) lead to a good earth. Turn the ignition switch ON and set the kill switch to Run and check that a voltage of 4.75 to 5.25 volts is present. If it isn't, there is a fault in the yellow/red wire or the ECM. Similarly check for the same voltage between the blue/black and the grey/black wire terminals of the connector. If there is voltage, check for continuity to earth in the blue/black wire. If there is, trace the fault in the wire and repair it. If there isn't, and the sensor is proven good by the Honda tester, then the ECM is faulty.

Removal and installation

31 Raise the fuel tank (see Section 2).

32 Disconnect the wiring connector and detach the vacuum hose from the sensor **(see illustration 6.5a)**. Undo the screw and remove the sensor **(see illustration 6.6b)**.

33 Installation is the reverse of removal.

Intake air temperature (IAT) sensor

Check

34 Raise the fuel tank (see Section 2). The sensor is mounted in the back of the air filter housing cover. Disconnect its wiring connector **(see illustration)**.

35 With the sensor cold, connect an ohmmeter across the sensor terminals and measure its resistance. Compare the reading obtained to that given in the Specifications noting that the specified value is valid at 20°C (68°F); the sensor resistance will increase at lower temperatures and decrease at higher temperatures. If the resistance reading differs greatly from that specified, the sensor is probably faulty.

36 If the sensor appears to be functioning correctly, check its power supply. Connect the positive (+) lead of a voltmeter to the grey/blue terminal of the sensor wiring connector, then connect the negative (–) lead to a good earth. Turn the ignition switch ON and check that a voltage of 4.75 to 5.25 volts is present. If it isn't, there is a fault in the grey/blue wire or the ECM. If voltage was present, now connect the negative lead to the grey/black terminal of the connector and check that the same voltage is present. If it isn't, there is a fault in the grey/black wire or the ECM. If there is voltage, the ECM is probably faulty.

Removal and installation

37 Remove the fuel tank cover (see Section 2). The sensor is mounted in the back of the air filter housing cover.

38 Disconnect the sensor wiring connector **(see illustration 6.34)**.

39 Undo the screws securing the sensor and remove it **(see illustration)**.

40 Installation is the reverse of removal.

Camshaft position (CMP) sensor

Check

41 Remove the fairing left-hand side panel (see Chapter 7).

42 Locate the sensor, which is on the left-hand end of the cylinder head at the front.

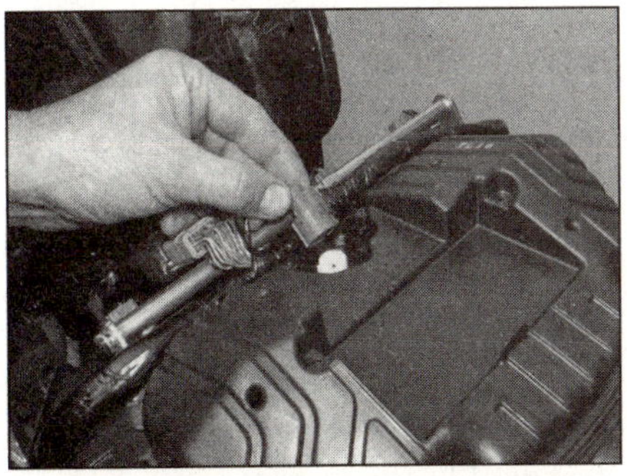

6.34 Disconnect the sensor wiring connector

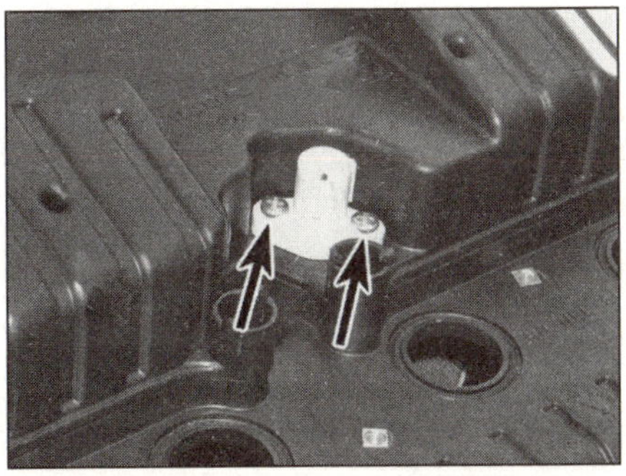

6.39 IAT sensor screws (arrowed)

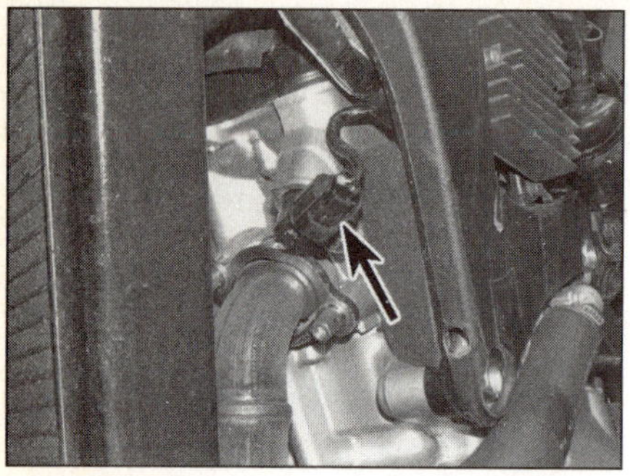

6.42a CMP sensor wiring connector (arrowed) – RR-4 and RR-5 models

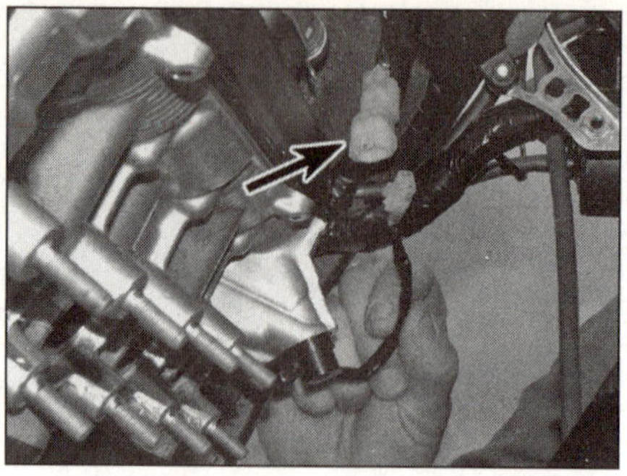

6.42b CMP sensor wiring connector (arrowed) – RR-6 and RR-7 models

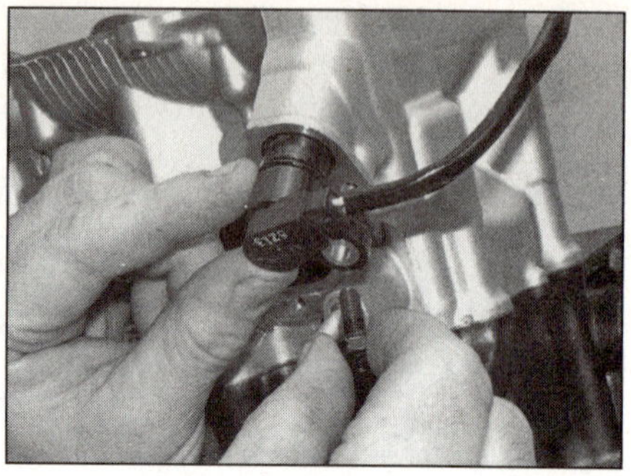

6.48a Unscrew the bolt and withdraw the sensor

Disconnect the sensor wiring connector **(see illustrations)**. Perform the following check(s).

43 Using an ohmmeter check for continuity first between the grey wire terminal on the sensor side of the connector and earth (ground) and then between the white/black wire terminal and earth. If there is continuity in either case the sensor is faulty. Measure the resistance of the sensor by connecting the meter, set to the ohms x 100 scale, to the terminals and compare the reading to that specified at the beginning of the chapter. If the value obtained differs greatly or is zero or infinity the sensor is faulty.

44 Connect the positive (+) lead of a voltmeter and peak voltage adapter arrangement* to the grey terminal on the sensor side of the connector and the negative (–) lead to the white/black terminal of the connector. Turn the engine over on the starter motor and note the voltage reading obtained. If this reading is below the specified minimum, the sensor is faulty.

***Note:** *Honda specify their own peak voltage adapter (Pt. No. 07HGJ-0020100) with an aftermarket digital multimeter having an impedance of 10 M-ohm/DCV minimum for this test.*

45 If the sensor functions correctly then the fault must be in the wiring harness or the ECM, and can be located by a Honda dealer with the test pin box.

Removal and installation

46 Remove the fairing left-hand side panel (see Chapter 7).

47 Locate the sensor, which is on the left-hand end of the cylinder head at the front. Disconnect the sensor wiring connector **(see illustration 6.42a or b)**.

48 Unscrew the bolt securing the sensor and draw it out of the head **(see illustration)**. Discard the O-ring **(see illustration)**.

49 Clean the sensor tip and fit a new O-ring smeared with oil into the groove in the sensor body **(see illustration)**. Fit the sensor into the cylinder head and secure it with the bolt **(see illustration 6.48a)**.

50 Reconnect the wiring connector **(see illustration 6.42a or b)**. Install the fairing side panel.

Crankshaft position (CKP) sensor

Check

51 Remove the fairing right-hand side panel (see Chapter 7). Trace the CKP sensor wiring from the top of the clutch cover and disconnect it at the red 2-pin wiring connector **(see illustrations)**. Perform the following checks.

52 Using an ohmmeter check for continuity first between the yellow wire terminal on the sensor side of the connector and earth (ground), and then between the white/black wire terminal and earth. If there is continuity in either case the sensor is faulty. Measure the resistance of the sensor by connecting the meter, set to the ohms x 100 scale, to the terminals and compare the reading to that specified at the beginning of the chapter. If the value obtained differs greatly or is zero or infinity the sensor is faulty.

53 Connect the positive (+) lead of a voltmeter and peak voltage adapter arrangement* to the yellow terminal on the sensor side of the connector and the negative (–) lead to the white/black terminal of the connector. Turn the engine over on the starter motor and note the voltage reading obtained. If this reading is below the specified minimum, the sensor is faulty.

***Note:** *Honda specify their own peak voltage adapter (Pt. No. 07HGJ-0020100) with an aftermarket digital multimeter having an impedance of 10 M-ohm/DCV minimum for this test.*

54 If the sensor functions correctly then the fault must be in the wiring harness or the ECM, and can be located by a Honda dealer with the test pin box.

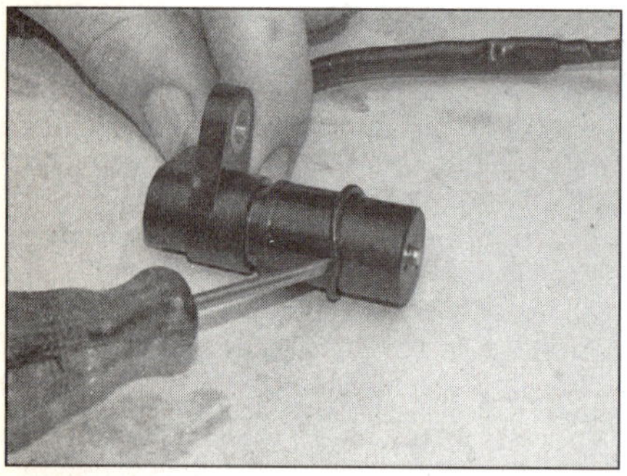

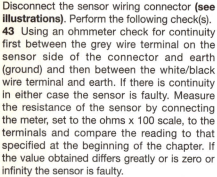

6.48b Remove the O-ring and discard it

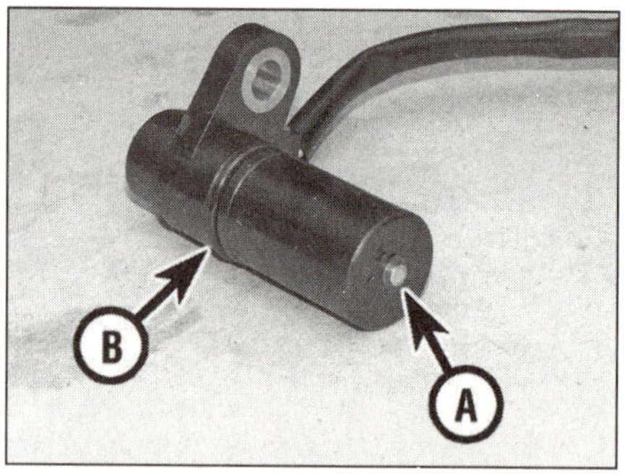

6.49 Make sure the sensor tip (A) is clean, then fit a new O-ring (B) into the groove

6.51a CKP sensor wiring connector (arrowed) – RR-4 and RR-5 models

6.51b CKP sensor wiring connector (arrowed) – RR-6 and RR-7 models

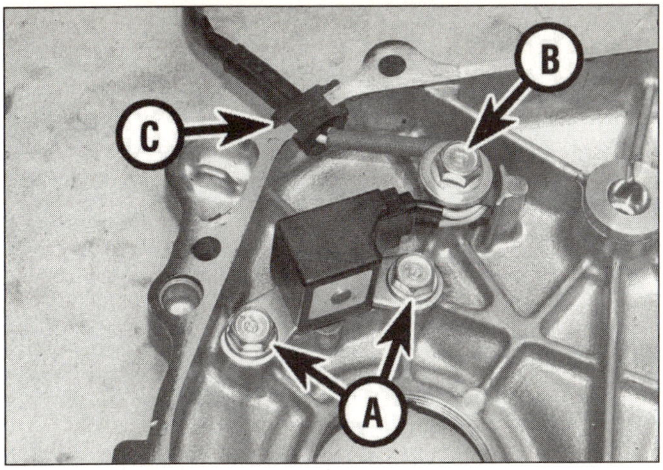

6.56 Unscrew the sensor bolts (A) and the wiring guide bolt (B), then free the wiring grommet (C)

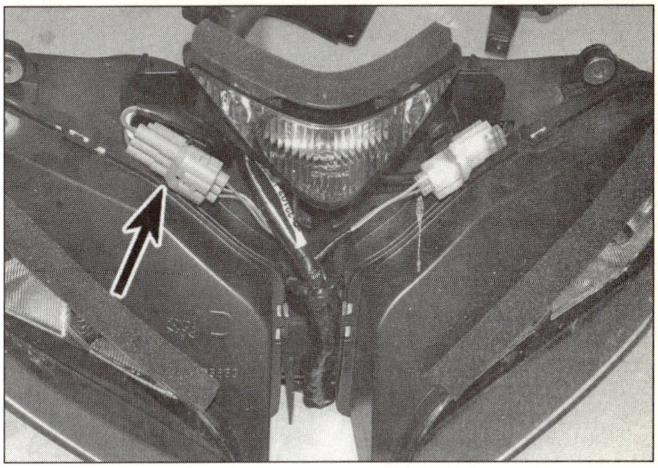

6.66a Disconnect the wiring connector (arrowed) . . .

Removal and installation

55 Remove the clutch cover (see Chapter 2, Section 14, Steps 1 to 4). The sensor is mounted inside it.

56 Undo the sensor mounting bolts and wiring guide bolt, then free the wiring grommet from the cover and remove the sensor **(see illustration)**.

57 Remove all traces of sealant from the sensor wiring grommet and clutch cover and apply a smear of fresh sealant to the grommet. Apply a suitable non-permanent thread locking compound to the sensor and wiring guide bolts.

58 Locate the grommet and sensor correctly in the cover and tighten the sensor bolts **(see illustration 6.56)**. Clean the sensor tip.

59 Install the clutch cover (see Chapter 2, Section 14, Steps 29 to 32).

Speed sensor

60 See Chapter 8, Section 16.

Lean angle sensor

Check

61 Position the motorcycle on an auxiliary stand so it is level. Remove the fairing (see Chapter 7) – the lean angle sensor is mounted above the headlight **(see illustration 6.66b)**. Remove the headlight and the wiring from the fairing (see Chapter 8). Remove the sensor from the headlight (see below). Reconnect the front wiring sub-loom to the main loom, and connect the sensor to the sub-loom.

62 With the ignition switch ON and the kill switch set to run, connect the negative (–) lead of a voltmeter to the green wire terminal of the lean angle sensor connector (with the connector still connected). Connect the voltmeter positive (+) lead first to the white/black wire terminal and check that battery voltage (approximately 12 volts) is present, then connect it to the red/white wire terminal and check that between 0 to 1 volt is present.

63 Hold the sensor horizontal and switch the ignition ON; the engine stop relay (in the relay box on the left-hand side – **see illustration 6.70a or b**) should click, indicating the power supply is closed (on). Slowly tilt the sensor to the left whilst listening to the engine stop relay; once the sensor reaches an angle of approximately 60° the relay should be heard to click, indicating the power supply is open (off). Switch the ignition OFF and return the sensor to the horizontal, then switch the ignition back ON again (engine stop relay should click again) and tilt the sensor to the right. The engine stop relay should be heard to click again once the sensor reaches an angle of around 60°.

64 If the voltage readings and/or relay performance are not as given, then it is likely the lean angle sensor is faulty.

Removal and installation

65 Remove the fairing, then remove the headlight from it (see Chapters 7 and 8) – the lean angle sensor is mounted above the headlight **(see illustration 6.66b)**.

66 Disconnect the lean angle sensor wiring connector **(see illustration)**. Undo the nuts and remove the sensor from its mounting studs, noting the washers **(see illustration)**.

67 Installation is the reverse of removal. Make sure the sensor is fitted with its UP mark facing upwards and with the wiring facing back **(see illustration)**.

6.66b . . . then unscrew the nuts (arrowed) and remove the lean angle sensor

6.67 Fit the sensor with the UP mark the correct way up

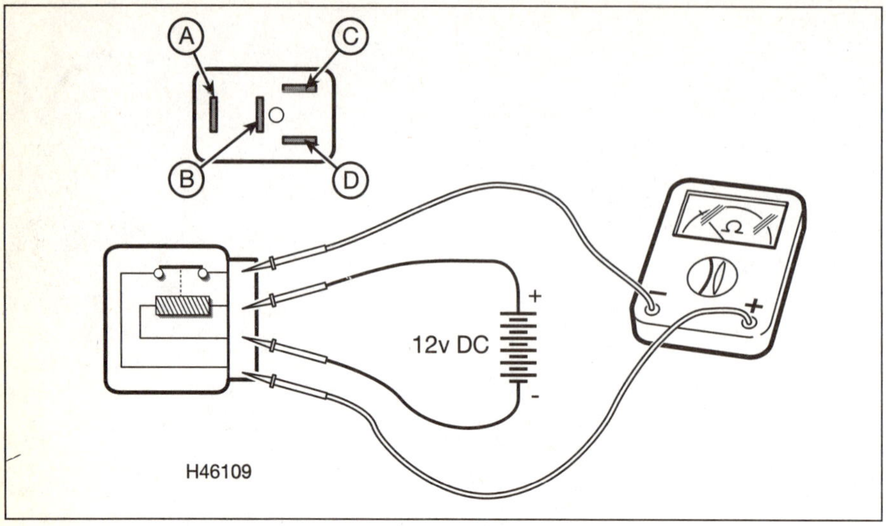

6.69 Relay terminal identification and test set-up

Engine stop relay

Check

68 Remove the relay (see below).

69 Connect an ohmmeter between the A and B terminals of the relay **(see illustration)**. Using a 12 volt battery and auxiliary wires, connect the battery positive (+) terminal to the C terminal of the relay and the negative (–) terminal to the D terminal and note the meter reading obtained. If the relay is operating correctly there should be continuity (zero resistance) when the battery is connected and no continuity (infinite resistance) when the battery is disconnected. If this is not the case, replace the relay with a new one.

Removal and installation

70 Remove the fairing left-hand side panel (see Chapter 7). The engine stop relay is in the relay box **(see illustrations)**.

71 Displace the relay box from its mount, then release the blue connector clips and draw the blue connector out of the box **(see illustration)**. Pull the relay off its connector.

72 Installation is the reverse of removal.

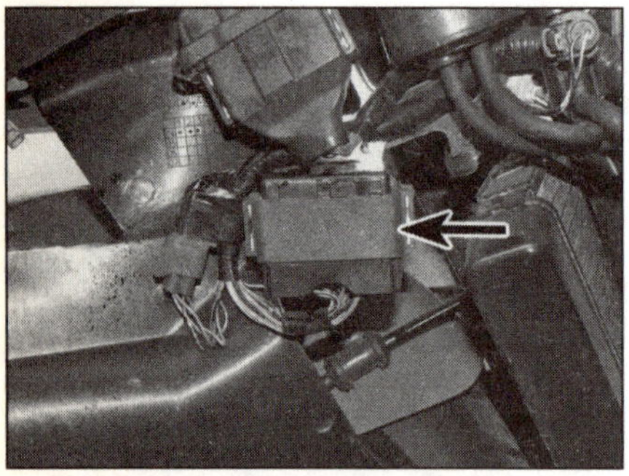

6.70a Relay box (arrowed) – RR-4 and RR-5 models

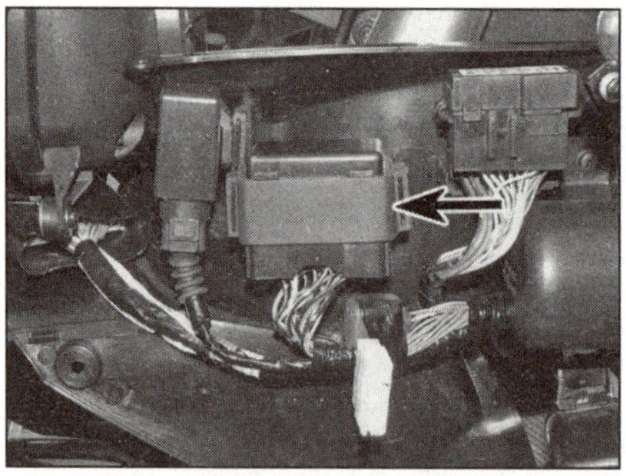

6.70b Relay box (arrowed) – RR-6 and RR-7 models

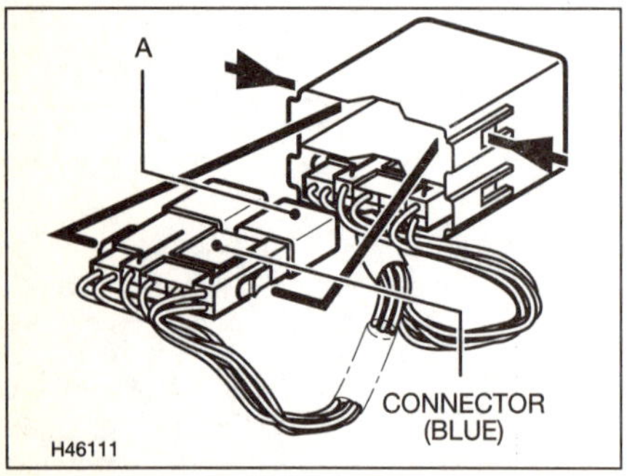

6.71 Release the blue connector from the box to access the engine stop relay (A)

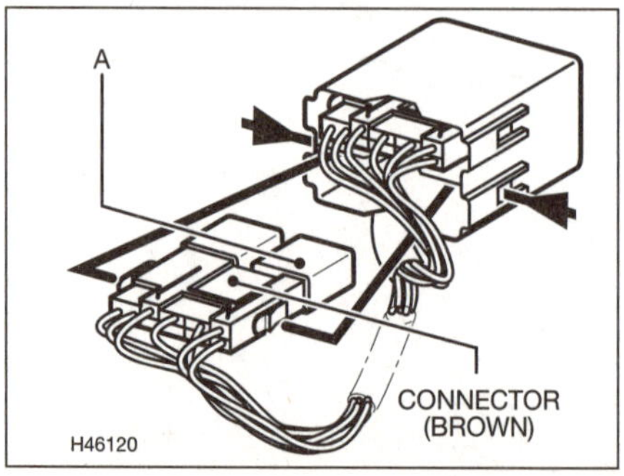

6.76 Release the brown connector from the box to access the fuel cut-off relay (A)

Fuel cut-off relay

Check

73 Remove the relay (see below).

74 Connect an ohmmeter between the A and B terminals of the relay **(see illustration 6.69)**. Using a 12 volt battery and auxiliary wires, connect the battery positive (+) terminal to the C terminal of the relay and the negative (–) terminal to the D terminal and note the meter reading obtained. If the relay is operating correctly there should be continuity (zero resistance) when the battery is connected and no continuity (infinite resistance) when the battery is disconnected. If this is not the case, replace the relay with a new one.

Removal and installation

75 Remove the fairing left-hand side panel (see Chapter 7). The fuel cut-off relay is in the relay box **(see illustration 6.70a or b)**.

76 Displace the relay box from its mount, then release the brown connector clips and draw the brown connector out of the box **(see illustration)**. Pull the relay off its connector.

77 Installation is the reverse of removal.

Engine control module (ECM)

Check

78 The engine control module (ECM) itself cannot be checked, but a process of elimination of other possible faulty components can point to it being faulty. However the power supply to the ECM can be tested as follows:

79 Access the ECM and disconnect its wiring connectors (see Steps 82 to 84). Turn the ignition switch ON and set the kill switch to RUN. The following checks are made on the wiring harness side of the connectors.

80 On RR-4 and RR-5 models connect the positive (+) probe of a voltmeter to terminal B15 in the light grey connector and the negative to a good earth (ground) **(see illustration)**. Repeat the check on terminal B16. There should be battery voltage (12V) in each case. If there is, check for continuity between the A4 terminal in the black connector and earth. Repeat the checks on terminals A18 and A19. There should be continuity in each case. If there is, replace the ECM with a known good one – if the fault is solved the ECM is faulty. If there is no continuity in any of the checks there is a break in the

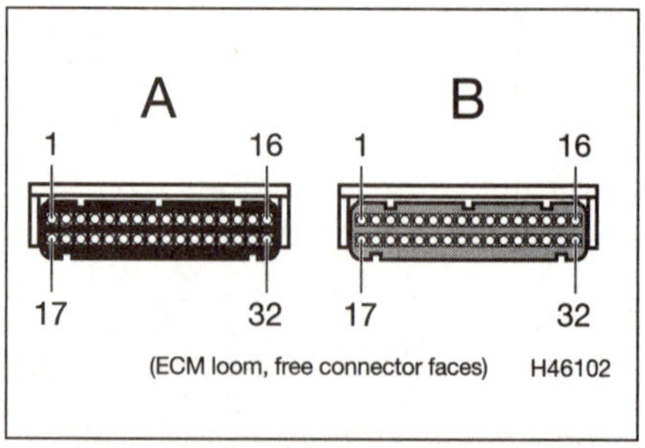

6.80 ECM terminal identification – RR-4 and RR-5 models

A Black connector *B Light grey connector*

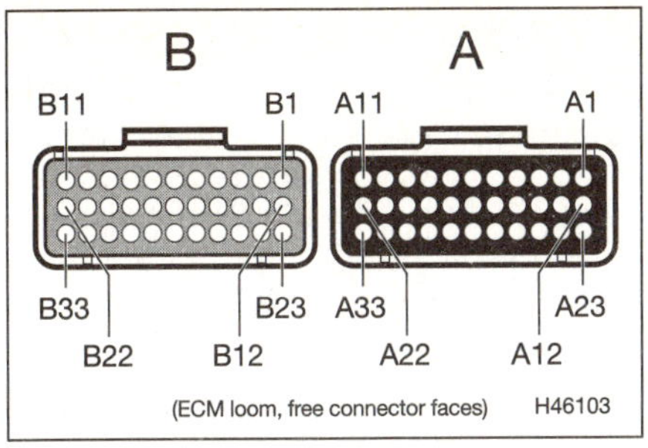

6.81 ECM terminal identification – RR-6 and RR-7 models

A Black connector B Grey connector

green/pink wire from that terminal. If there was no voltage at terminals B15 and B16 remove the engine stop relay (Steps 70 and 71) and check for battery voltage between the black (+) and red/blue (–) wire terminals with the ignition ON and the kill switch set to RUN. If there is no voltage check the lean angle sensor (Steps 61 to 64), and check the red/blue wire between the engine stop relay and lean sensor and the black wire between the relay and the kill switch for continuity. If there is voltage jump across the relay's red/white and black/white wire terminals in the connector using an auxiliary wire and check whether there is now voltage at terminals B15 and B16 in the light grey ECM connector. If there is check the engine stop relay (step 69). If not check the red/white wire between the starter relay and the engine stop relay for continuity, and the black white wire between the engine stop relay and the ECM.

81 On RR-6 and RR-7 models the tests are exactly the same but the terminals are differently numbered **(see illustration)**. Instead of terminals B15 and B16 in the grey connector use terminals A4 and A5 in the black connector, and instead of terminals A4, A18 and A19 in the black connector use terminals A23, A24 and A25 in the black connector.

Removal and installation

82 Make sure the ignition is OFF.

83 On RR-4 and RR-5 models remove the fairing right-hand side panel (see Chapter 7). Release the strap and lift the ECM out of its holder and disconnect the wiring connectors when accessible **(see illustration)**.

84 On RR-6 and RR-7 models remove the fuel tank cover (see Chapter 7). Undo the screws and remove the ECM holder **(see illustration)**. Lift the ECM and disconnect the wiring connectors **(see illustration)**.

85 Installation is the reverse of removal.

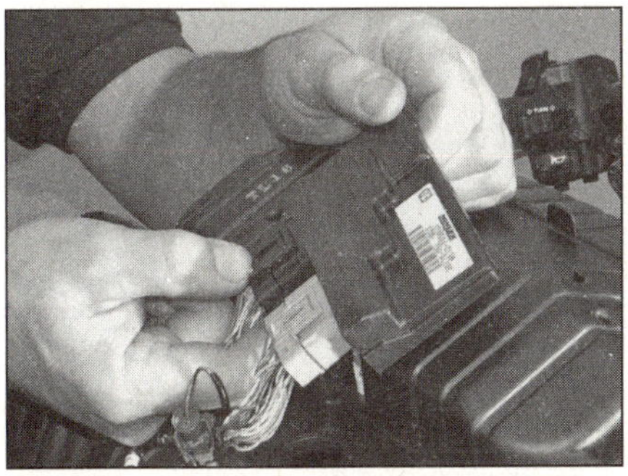

6.84b . . . then displace the ECM and disconnect the wiring connectors

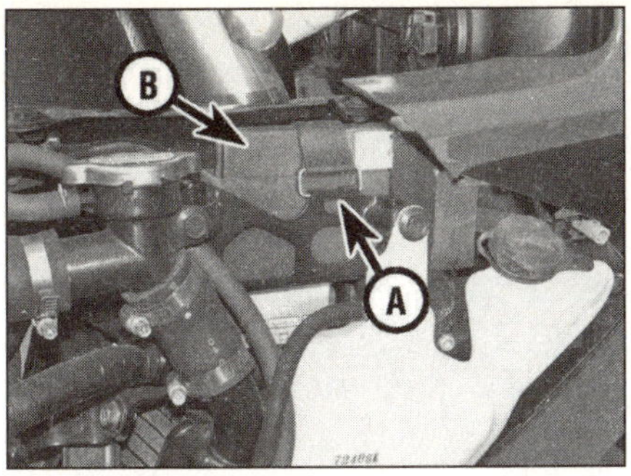

6.83 Release the strap (A) and lift the ECM (B) out

Oxygen sensor

Check

86 Apart from the wiring checks that are outlined in Section 5, the operation of the oxygen sensor can only be checked using the Honda diagnostic test pin box.

87 To check the sensor heater, on RR-4 and RR-5 models raise the fuel tank (see Section 2), and on RR-6 and RR-7 models remove the fairing right-hand side panel (see Chap-ter 7). Disconnect the sensor wiring connector (4-pin black connector taped to loom above starter motor on RR-4 and RR-5 models and 4-pin natural connector on RR-6 and RR-7 models **(see illustration)**). Connect an ohmmeter between the white and grey/black wire terminals on the sensor side of the connector and check that the resistance is between 10 and 40 ohms. Also check that there is no continuity to earth (ground) in the white wire. If the resistance is not as specified or if there is continuity to earth, replace the sensor with a new one. Otherwise check for battery voltage between the black/white (+) wire terminal and earth with the ignition ON. If there is no voltage, check the wiring, using the wiring diagrams at the end of Chapter 8. Otherwise have the sensor and its circuit tested by a Honda dealer equipped with the diagnostic tester.

6.87 Oxygen sensor wiring connector (arrowed) – RR-6 and RR-7 models

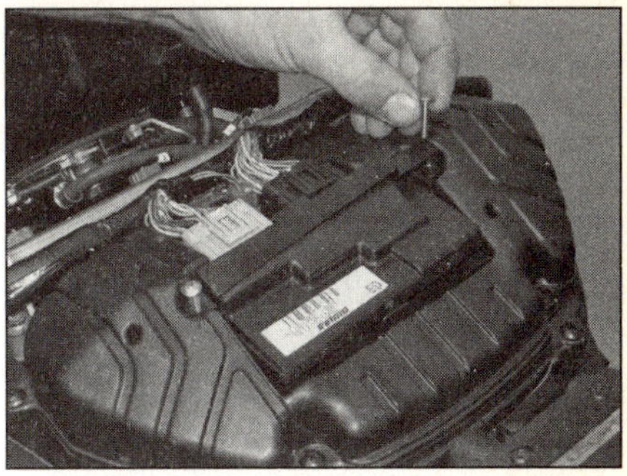

6.84a Undo the screws and remove the holder . . .

Removal and installation

Note: *The oxygen sensor is delicate and will not work if it is dropped or knocked, or if any cleaning materials are used on it. Ensure the exhaust system is cold before proceeding.*

88 On RR-4 and RR-5 models raise the fuel tank (see Section 2), and on RR-6 and RR-7 models remove the fairing right-hand side panel (see Chapter 7).

89 Trace the wiring from the sensor in the exhaust and disconnect it at the connector (4-pin black connector taped to loom above starter motor on RR-4 and RR-5 models and 4-pin natural connector on RR-6 and RR-7 models **(see illustration 6.87)**). Release the wiring from any clamp(s) and note its routing.

90 Unscrew the oxygen sensor and remove it from the exhaust system.

91 Installation is the reverse of removal. Tighten the sensor to the torque setting specified at the beginning of the Chapter.

7 Throttle bodies

Warning: Refer to the precautions given in Section 1 before starting work.

Removal

1 Remove the fairing side panels (see Chapter 7).

2 Remove the fuel tank and the air filter housing (Sections 2 and 3). Either drain the coolant (see Chapter 1), or prepare some hose clamps or blanking plugs for the fast idle system wax unit heating system hoses – there are two of them.

3 If required detach the fuel hoses from the primary rail as follows, but note that they can remain connected and the secondary rail can be removed along with the throttle body assembly. To remove the hoses counter-hold the hex on the fuel hose joint and unscrew the banjo union nut, noting the alignment of the hose and being prepared to catch any residual fuel with a rag **(see illustrations 6.5b and 6a)**. Detach the hose and discard the sealing washers – new ones must be used **(see illustrations 6.17a and b)**.

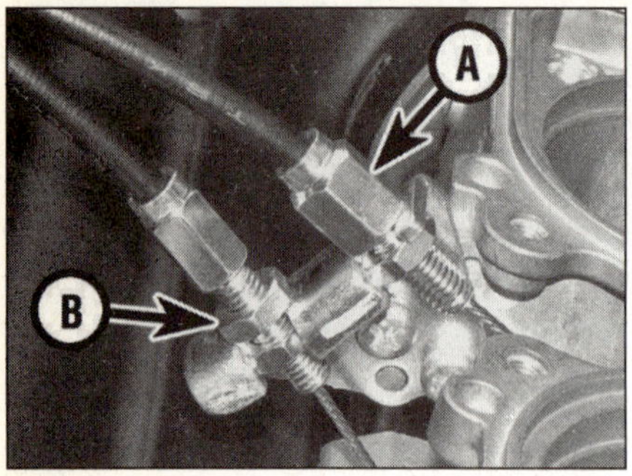

7.4 Unscrew the hex (A) to free the upper cable and the locknut (B) to free the lower cable

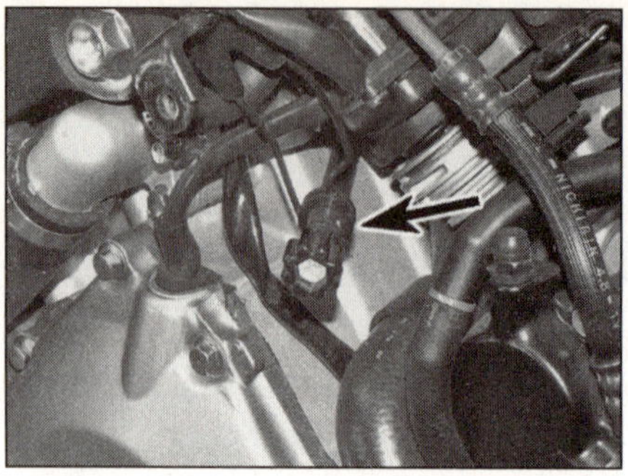

7.6 Free the idle speed adjuster from its holder (arrowed)

7.7 Detach the vacuum hose from its union

4 Free the upper throttle cable from the bracket by unscrewing the hex until the captive nut is free **(see illustration)**. Free the lower throttle cable by slackening the locknut and threading it up the cable until the captive nut is free.

5 Disconnect the wiring connector from each primary rail fuel injector **(see illustration 6.3a)**. Release the cable tie(s) from the primary fuel rail.

6 Release the idle speed adjuster from its clip on the coolant hose and feed it through to the base of the throttle body assembly **(see illustration)**.

7 Disconnect the air intake system vacuum chamber hose from the throttle bodies **(see illustration)**. On California models, disconnect the EVAP system solenoid valve vacuum hose from the five-way hose joint on the throttle body assembly.

8 Slacken the clamps securing the coolant hoses to the fast idle system wax unit **(see illustration)**. Detach the hoses, and if the coolant wasn't drained, clamp or plug the ends.

Caution: Do not snap the throttle cam/valves from fully open to fully closed once the cables have been disconnected because this can lead to engine idle speed problems.

9 Fully slacken the clamps on the cylinder head intake manifold rubbers using a long screwdriver, noting their orientation **(see illustration)**. Ease the throttle body assembly up off the manifold, noting that it may be quite a tight fit, and remove the assembly – do not use the fuel rail as a handle for removal **(see illustration)**. When accessible disconnect the throttle position sensor wiring connector **(see illustration 6.20)**. Free the throttle cable ends from the pulley, noting which fits where **(see illustration)**.

Caution: Tape over or stuff clean rag into each cylinder head intake after removing the throttle body assembly to prevent anything from falling in.

10 If the intake adapters on the cylinder head shown signs of cracking or deterioration new ones must be fitted. Note their orientation and how the clamps locate and are orientated before unscrewing the bolts and removing them, and on installation use new O-rings and tighten the bolts to the torque setting specified at the beginning of the Chapter **(see illustration)**. Also check the throttle body vacuum hoses for signs of damage or deterioration and replace any suspect hoses with new ones **(see illustration)**.

Caution: The throttle body assembly must be treated as a sealed unit. With the

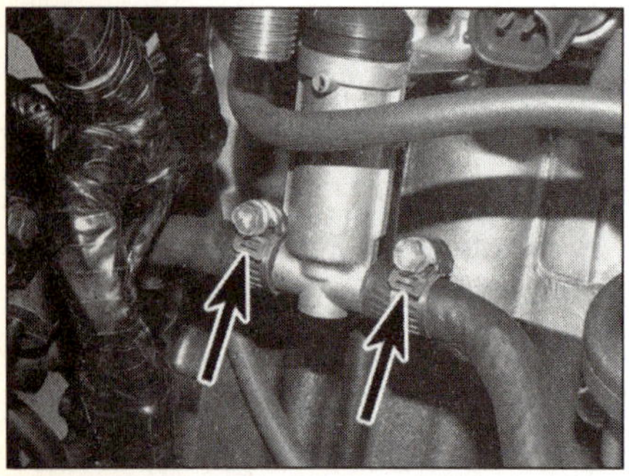

7.8 Slacken the clamps and detach the hoses

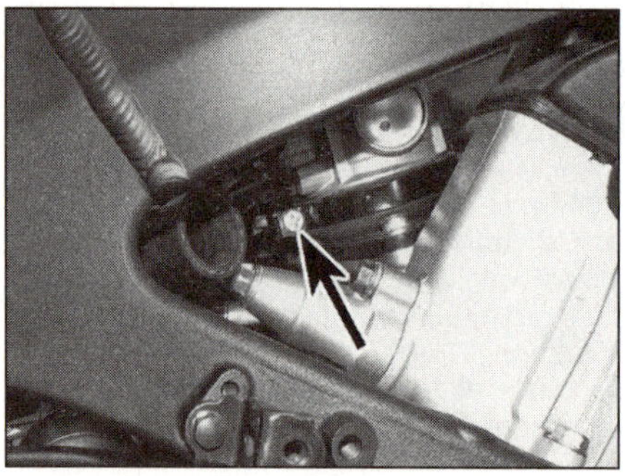

7.9a Slacken the screw (arrowed) on each clamp . . .

7.9b . . . then ease the throttle bodies up off the cylinder head . . .

7.9c . . . and detach the cable ends from the pulley

7.10a Intake adapter bolts (arrowed) – note the orientation of the clamps

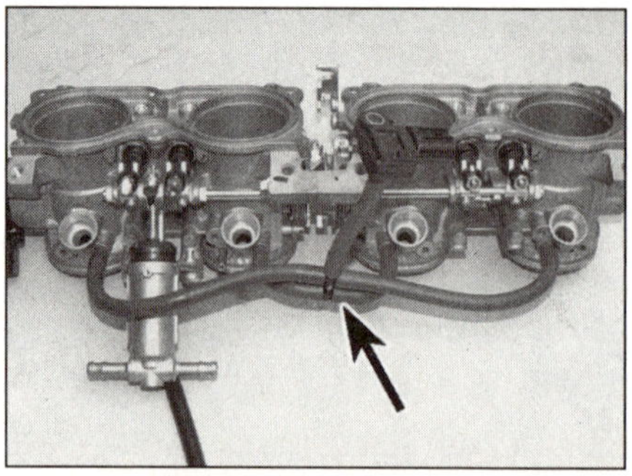

7.10b Vacuum hose location and routing – all models except California

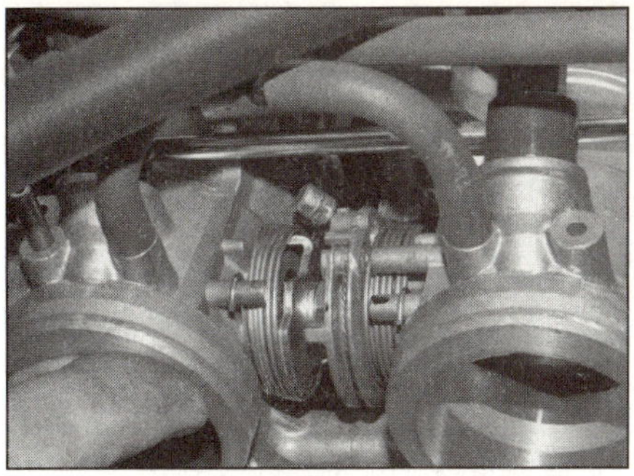

7.12a Connect the cable ends to the pulley . . .

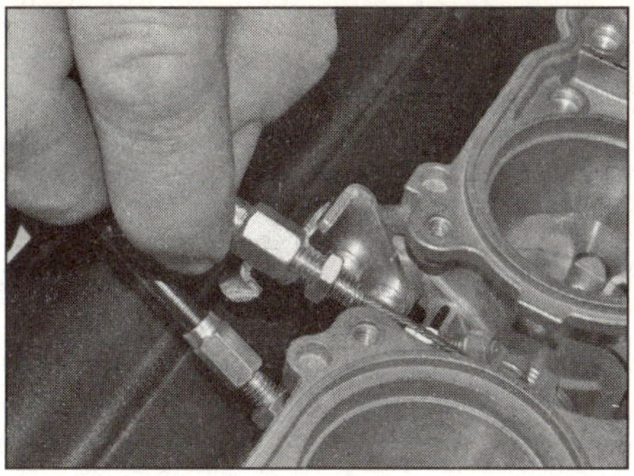

7.12b . . . then fit the upper cable . . .

7.12c . . . and tighten the hex onto the bracket . . .

exception of the fast idle system wax unit screws, NEVER loosen any of the white-painted nuts/bolts/screws on the assembly as these are pre-set at the factory to ensure correct synchronisation of the throttle valves. The only components on the assembly which are serviceable are the starter valves (see Section 8) and the various vacuum hoses.

Caution: NEVER use a solvent-based cleaner to clean the throttle body components. The throttle bores are covered with a molybdenum coating which could be removed by the cleaner.

Installation

11 Make sure the intake rubber clamp screws are correctly orientated as noted on removal **(see illustration 7.10a)**. Lubricate the inside of the rubbers with a light smear of engine oil to aid installation.

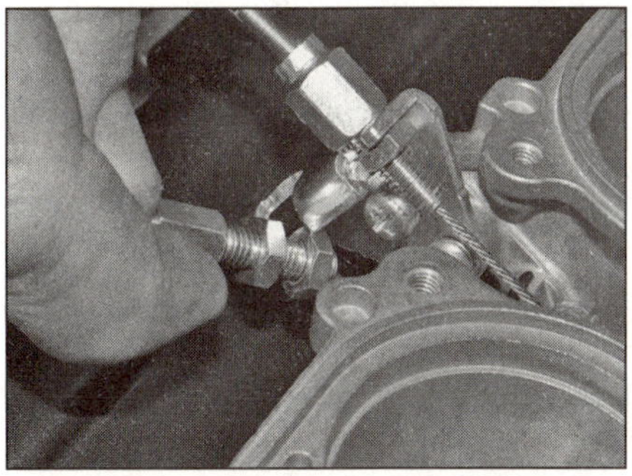

7.12d . . . then fit the lower cable

7.13b . . . and tighten the clamp screws

12 Connect the throttle cable ends to the pulley and feed the inner cables into their track **(see illustration)**. Fit the closing cable into the upper socket on the bracket on the throttle body and tighten the cable hex, making sure the nut is held in the bracket **(see illustrations)**. Fit the opening cable into the lower socket and thread the locknut down so the cable is secure and the captive nut is held in the bracket **(see illustration and 7.4)**. Check cable freeplay at the twistgrip and adjust if necessary (see Chapter 1).

13 Remove the tape/plugs from the intakes. Position the throttle body assembly on the intakes and connect the throttle position sensor wiring connector **(see illustrations 7.9b and 6.20)**, then push them down until they are fully engaged – do not use the fuel rail as a handle **(see illustration)**. Tighten the clamps so that the gap between the ends is 6 to 8 mm **(see illustration)**.

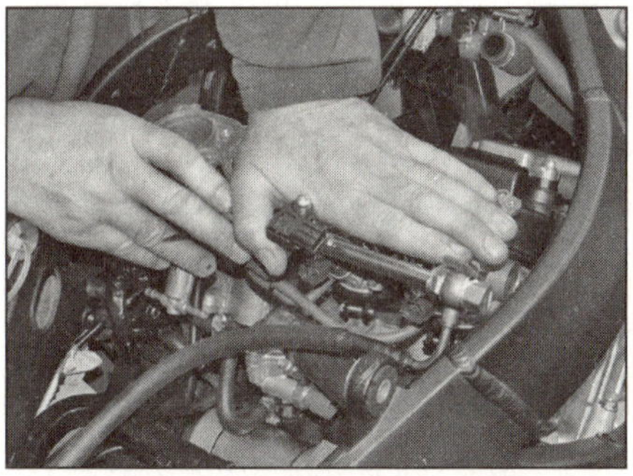

7.13a Push the assembly down into the adapters . . .

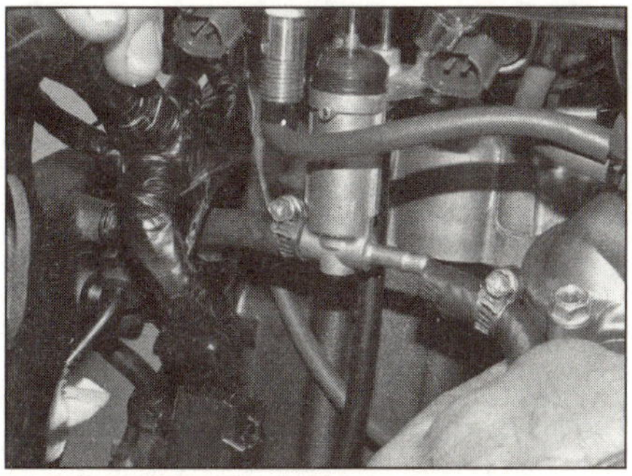

7.14 Fit the hoses and tighten the clamps

14 Fit the coolant hoses onto the wax unit and tighten the clamps securely **(see illustration)**.

15 Connect the injector wiring connectors, making sure they are all secure **(see illustration 6.3a)**. Secure the wiring with the cable tie(s).

16 Connect the vacuum chamber hose to its union on the throttle body assembly **(see illustration 7.7)**. On California models, connect the EVAP system solenoid valve vacuum hose to the five-way hose joint.

17 Fit the idle speed adjuster into its clip on the coolant hose **(see illustration 7.6)**.

18 If detached, use new sealing washers on the fuel hose banjo unions and tighten the nuts to the specified torque setting, making sure you counter-hold the hex on each hose joint or the fuel rail could distort or break **(see illustrations 6.17a and b, 6.5b and 6.6a)**.

19 If the cooling system was drained, do not forget to refill it (see Chapter 1). Otherwise, remove the clamps or plugs and just check the level and top up if necessary (see *Pre-ride checks*).

20 Install the air filter housing and the fuel tank (Sections 4 and 2). Install the fairing side panels (see Chapter 7).

8 Starter valves

Warning: Refer to the precautions given in Section 1 before starting work.

Note: *If the starter valves are removed they will have to be synchronized using vacuum gauges after installation to ensure accurate set-up.*

Removal

1 Remove the throttle bodies (see Section 7).

2 Remove the primary fuel rail and injectors (see Section 6).

3 Remove the fast idle system wax unit (see Section 9).

4 Undo the screws securing the arm for the

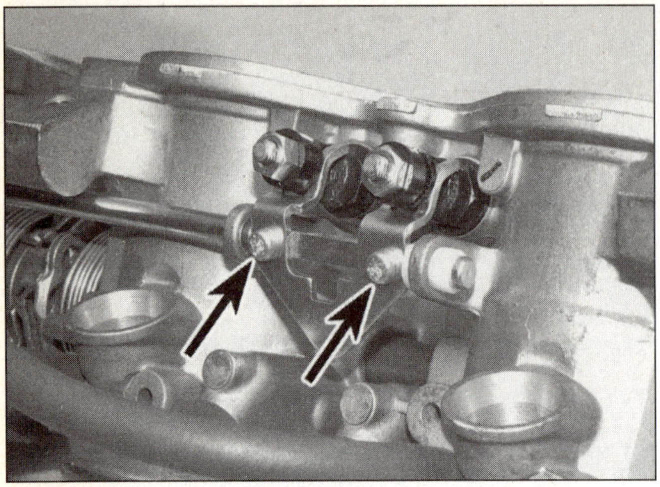

8.4 Undo the screws (arrowed) and remove the arm for Nos. 3 and 4 valves

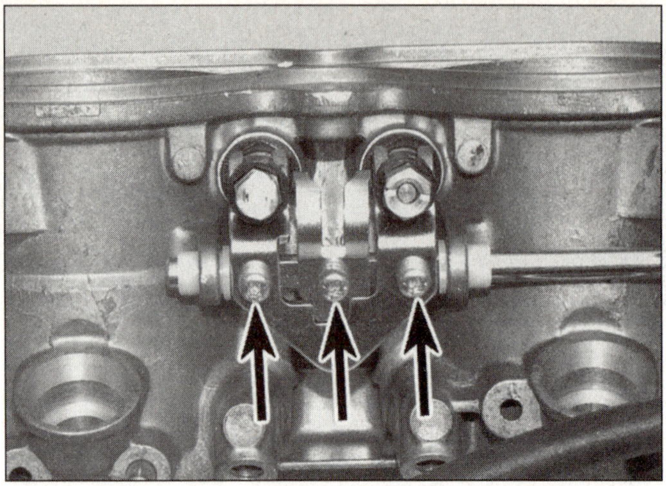

8.5 Undo the screws (arrowed) and remove the arms for Nos. 1 and 2 valves

Nos. 3 and 4 starter valves and remove the arm, noting how it fits **(see illustration)**. With the arms removed do not alter the setting of the synchronization nuts to ensure minimal adjustment on installation – note that the No. 1 valve is the base valve, and the nut is pre-set and locked at the factory and must not be disturbed.

5 Undo the screws securing the arms for the Nos. 1 and 2 starter valves and the screw securing the link arm for the wax unit and remove the arms, noting how they fit **(see illustration)**.

6 Unscrew the starter valve base nuts using a ring spanner or a deep socket and remove the four valves from the throttle body, keeping them in their correct fitted order **(see illustration)**.

7 Draw the shaft out (if required), noting the three collars in the bores that the shaft runs in. Remove the collars for safekeeping if they are loose.

8 Check all components for wear and damage and replace with new ones as necessary.

Installation

9 Clean the starter valves and throttle body passages using compressed air only. Do not use a throttle body/injector cleaner or any other solvent.

Caution: NEVER use a solvent-based cleaner to clean the throttle body components. The throttle bores are covered with a molybdenum coating which could be removed by the cleaner.

10 If removed, fit the collars into the shaft bores, noting that the bore adjacent the No. 3 starter valve does not have one, and making sure they are the correct way round. Slide the shaft in, making sure the collars stay in place.

11 Fit each starter valve into its original location and tighten the valve base nuts to the torque setting specified at the beginning of the Chapter **(see illustration)**. Check that each valve moves smoothly and easily in its bore by pulling on the valve end, and that it closes fully under spring pressure. Make sure the flats on each valve for the arm ends are vertical so they will locate correctly – if not turn the plunger so they are vertical.

12 Locate the arm for the Nos. 3 and 4 starter valves on the shaft and under the valve ends and secure it with the screws **(see illustration)**. Make sure the arm ends engage correctly with the flat sides on the valves.

13 Locate the arm for the Nos. 1 and 2 starter valves on the shaft and under the valve ends and secure it with the screws **(see illustration 8.5)**. Make sure the arm ends engage correctly with the flat sides on the valves. Also fit the link arm for the wax unit and secure it with the screw.

14 Check the operation of the starter valve shaft before continuing; it should move smoothly and easily, drawing all the valves out simultaneously as it turns, and return to the fully closed position under pressure of the return springs **(see illustration)**. If any of the valves are obviously out of synchronization with the No. 1 (base) valve (i.e. they start to move before or after it) turn the adjuster nut as required to approximate the setting.

15 Install the fast idle system wax unit (see Section 9).

16 Install the primary fuel injectors and rail (see Section 6), then install the throttle body

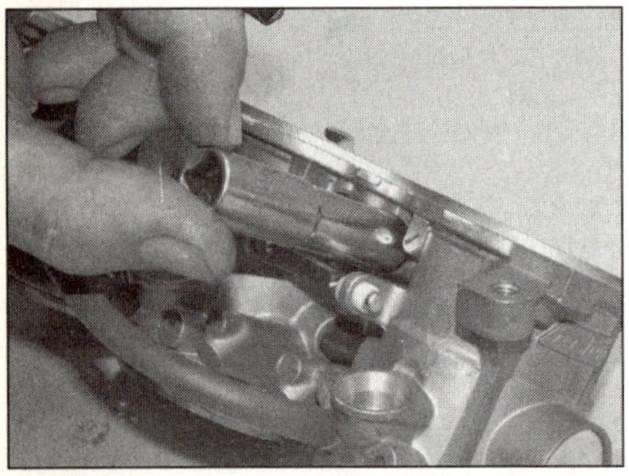

8.6 Unscrewing a starter valve using a deep socket

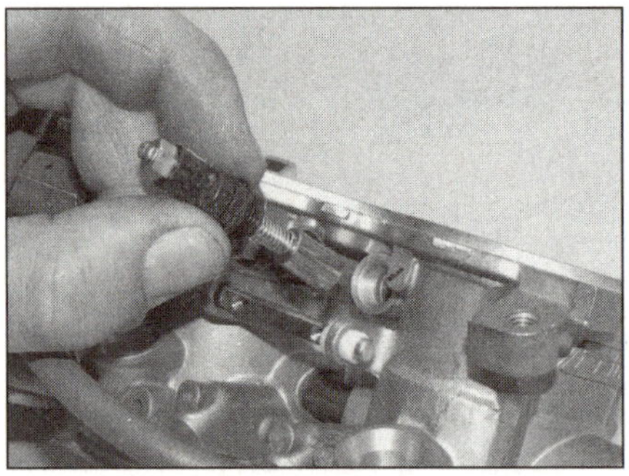

8.11 Fit the starter valves and tighten the nuts

8.12 Make sure the arm ends locate correctly against the flats

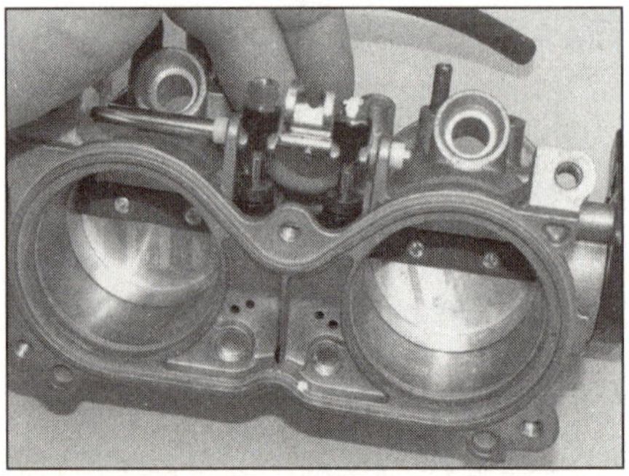

8.14 Check the operation of the starter valves as described

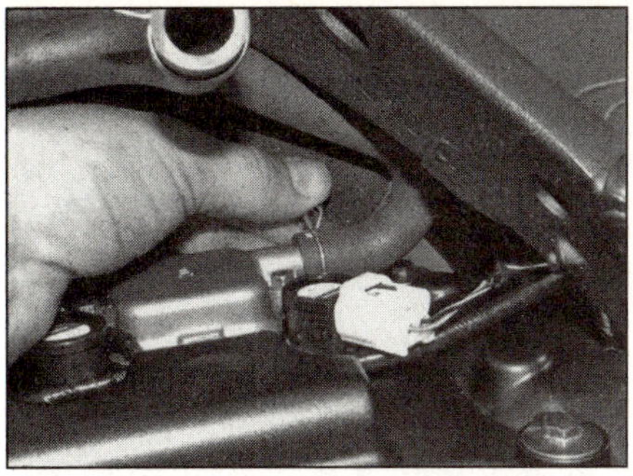

8.19 Release the clamps and detach the hoses from the reed valve covers

8.20 Detach the four opposed hoses from the joint (arrowed) and connect the gauge hoses to them

8.22a Checking starter valve synchronisation

assembly (Section 7). On completion check the starter valve synchronisation (see below).

Synchronisation

Warning: Do not allow exhaust gases to build up in the work area; either perform the check outside or use an exhaust gas extraction system.

Note: *Honda do not specify this as a service item, advising that it need only be carried out if the starter valves have been removed from the throttle body assembly. The procedure does not alter the setting of the throttle valves themselves (these are pre-set at the factory and fixed), but only the starter valves, which control the idle speed when the engine is cold and warming up. However on high mileage machines the linkage could wear and produce uneven idling when cold and warming up. If this is the case, then the synchronisation procedure should be carried out.*

17 Starter valve synchronisation is simply the process of adjusting the valves so they pass the same amount of fuel/air mixture to each cylinder on cold start and warm-up. This is done by measuring the vacuum produced in each intake duct. Starter valves that are out of synchronisation will result in uneven idling when cold starting and warming the engine. Before synchronising the starter valves, make sure the valve clearances are properly set (see Chapter 1).

18 To synchronise the starter valves, you will need a set of vacuum gauges suitable for a four cylinder engine, with the necessary adapters and hoses to fit the take-off points.

19 Start the engine and warm it up to normal temperature, then stop it. Raise the fuel tank and remove the air filter housing and the air duct (see Sections 2 and 3). Detach the air hoses from the PAIR system reed valve cover unions on the valve cover and fit blanking caps in their place **(see illustration)**. Refit the air filter housing.

20 Detach the four vacuum hoses from the five-way joint **(see illustration)**. Connect the gauge hoses to the vacuum hoses using suitable adapters making sure the No. 1 gauge goes to the No. 1 throttle body and so on. Make sure everything is a good fit because any air leaks will result in false readings.

21 Start the engine and adjust the idle speed (see Chapter 1). If using vacuum gauges fitted with damping adjustment, set this so that the needle flutter is just eliminated but so that they can still respond to small changes in pressure.

22 The vacuum readings for the Nos. 2, 3 and 4 cylinders should be the same as the No. 1 cylinder, or at least within the maximum difference specified at the beginning of the Chapter **(see illustration)**. The No. 1 cylinder starter valve is the base to which all the others are matched, and cannot itself be adjusted. If the vacuum readings vary, adjust the Nos. 2, 3 and 4 starter valves as required by turning the synchronisation nut on the end of the valve, until the readings are the same as No. 1 **(see illustration)**. **Note:** *Do not press hard on the nut whilst adjusting it, otherwise a false reading will be obtained.*

23 When the adjustment is complete, recheck the vacuum readings, then check and adjust the idle speed (see Chapter 1). Stop the engine.

24 Remove the vacuum gauges and the hose adapters. Fit the vacuum hoses on to the five-way joint **(see illustration 8.20)**. Remove the air filter housing, then fit the PAIR system hoses back onto the unions on the reed valve covers and secure them with the clamps **(see illustration 8.19)**. Install the air intake duct and air filter housing, and the fuel tank (see Sections 3 and 2).

9 Fast idle system wax unit

Warning: Refer to the precautions given in Section 1 before starting work.

Removal

1 Remove the throttle bodies (see Section 7).

2 Detach the vacuum hose from the No. 1 (left-hand) throttle body **(see illustration)**.

3 Undo the two screws securing the wax unit **(see illustration)**. Displace it upwards from its mount and release the pushrod pivot piece

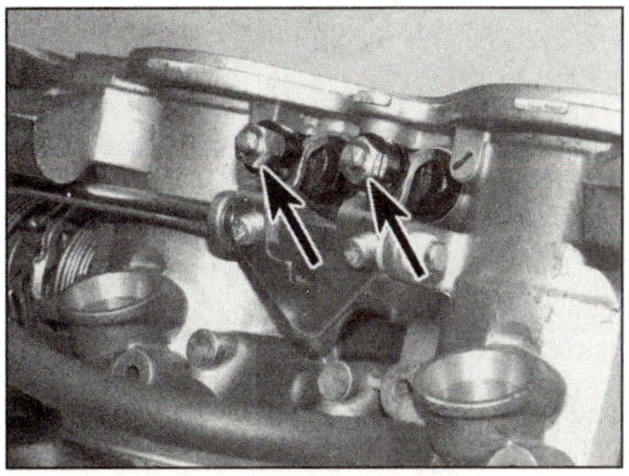

8.22b Nos. 3 and 4 starter valve adjustment nuts (arrowed)

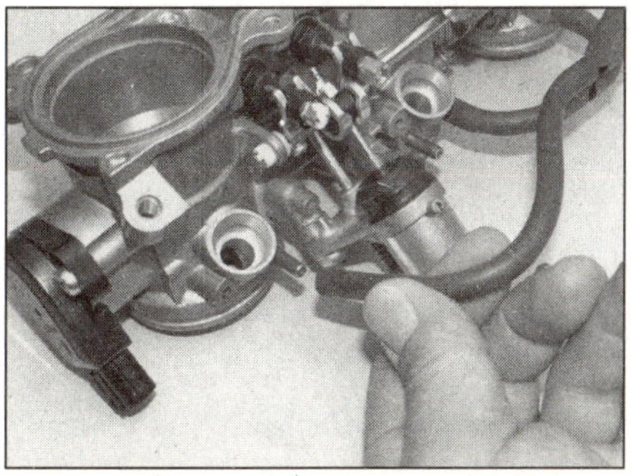

9.2 Detach the vacuum hose

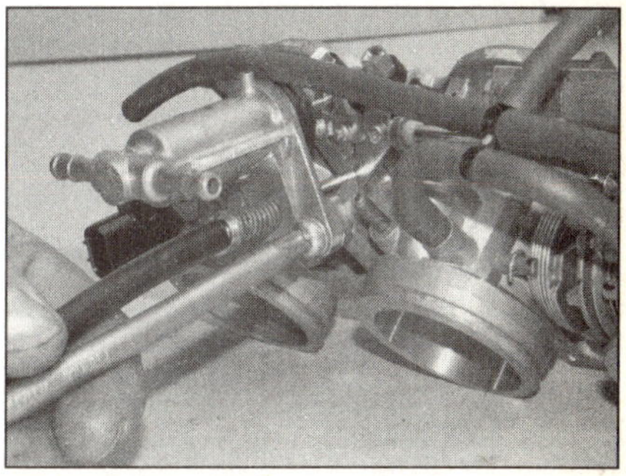

9.3a Undo the screws . . .

9.3b . . . and pivot the wax unit upwards

from the link arm, easing it out with a small screwdriver if necessary, then remove the wax unit **(see illustration)**.

Inspection

4 Visually inspect the unit for signs of damage.

5 If you suspect it is not working correctly, place it first in a cold place and check the position of the pushrod. Now gently heat it using a hairdryer or similar and check that the pushrod moves out of the unit. If it doesn't it is faulty and must be replaced with a new one.

Installation

6 Turn the starter valve shaft so that the valves are open, then fit the wax unit pushrod pivot piece into the link arm **(see illustration 9.3b)**.

7 Pivot the wax unit down onto its mount, then install the two screws and tighten them to the torque setting specified at the beginning of the Chapter **(see illustration 9.3a)**.

8 Fit the vacuum hose onto its union **(see illustration 9.2)**.

9 Install the throttle bodies (see Section 7).

10 Fuel pressure check

Warning: Refer to the precautions given in Section 1 before starting work.

Note: *A pressure gauge is required for this check. Honda specify the gauge Pt. No. 07406-0040002 or 3 (07406-004000A or B in the US) along with a special banjo bolt and two sealing washers for the gauge to thread onto (Pt. Nos. 90008-PD6-010, 90428-PD6-003 and 90430-PD-003). If a different gauge is used an adapter may be needed, either so it can thread onto the special banjo bolt, or that can be used in place of the special bolt. A gauge with a male end of the correct thread size and length could be used in place of the special bolt without an adapter. Two new sealing washers for the supply hose banjo bolt are also required.*

1 Remove the rider's seat and disconnect the battery negative (–) terminal (see Chapters 7 and 8). Raise the fuel tank (see Section 2).

10.2 Fuel pressure check bolt (arrowed)

2 Place some rag under and around the pressure check bolt in the right-hand end of the secondary fuel rail. Slacken the bolt until fuel comes out, but do not fully unscrew the bolt until all residual fuel pressure is released **(see illustration)**. Unscrew the bolt and catch any remaining fuel. Discard the sealing washer and obtain a new one.

3 Thread the gauge into the secondary rail. Securely tighten the gauge to ensure there are no fuel leaks. Mop up any spilt fuel.

4 Connect the battery negative (–) lead then start the engine and allow it to idle at the specified speed. Note the pressure present in the fuel system by reading the gauge, then turn the engine off. Compare the reading obtained to that given in the Specifications.

5 If the fuel pressure is higher than specified, the fuel pump is faulty and must be replaced with a new one.

6 If the fuel pressure is lower than specified, likely causes are.

- Leaking fuel hose union.
- Blocked fuel filter or strainer.
- Faulty fuel pressure regulator.
- Faulty fuel pump.

If necessary remove the fuel pump and clean the strainer. If the filter is blocked or the pressure regulator is faulty a new pump assembly must be installed (Section 11) – individual components are not available.

7 On completion, disconnect the battery negative (–) lead again. Remove the fuel gauge assembly, being prepared to catch any residual fuel, then install the original bolt using a new sealing washer, and tighten the bolt to the torque setting specified at the beginning of the Chapter.

8 Reconnect the battery then start the engine and check that there is no sign of fuel leakage. If all is well, lower the tank (see Section 2).

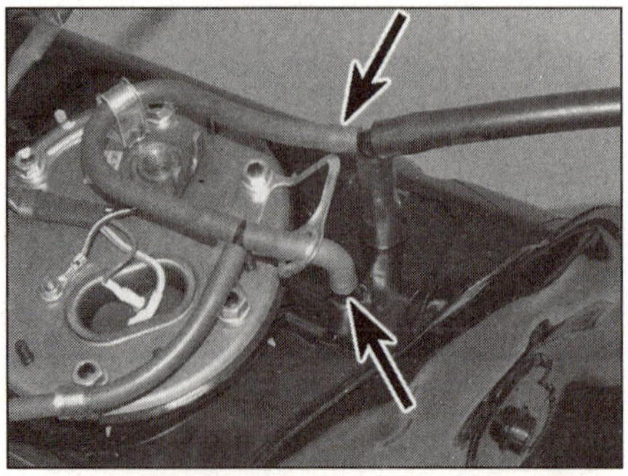

11.7a Note the positions of the guides then detach the hoses (arrowed) and unscrew the nuts – RR-6/7 shown

11 Fuel pump

Warning: Refer to the precautions given in Section 1 before starting work.

Check

1 The fuel pump is located inside the fuel tank. The fuel pump should run for a few seconds when the ignition is switched ON to pressurise the fuel system, and then cut out until the engine is started. If the pump is thought to be faulty, first check the fuses (see Chapter 8). If they are in good condition proceed as follows.

2 Raise and support the fuel tank (see Section 2).

3 Ensure the ignition is switched OFF then disconnect the fuel pump wiring connector **(see illustration 2.4)**. Connect the positive (+) lead of a voltmeter to the brown wire terminal on the loom side of the connector and the negative (–) lead to the green wire terminal. Switch the ignition ON whilst noting the reading obtained on the meter.

4 If battery voltage is present for a few seconds, the fuel pump circuit is operating correctly and the fuel pump itself is faulty and must be replaced with a new one.

5 If no reading is obtained, check the fuel pump circuit wiring for continuity and make sure all the connectors are free from corrosion and are securely connected. Repair/replace the wiring as necessary and clean the connectors using electrical contact cleaner. If this fails to reveal the fault, check the following components.

- Engine stop switch (see Chapter 8, Section 20).
- Fuel cut-off relay (see Section 6).
- Engine stop relay (see Section 6).
- Lean angle sensor (see Section 6).
- Engine control module (ECM) (see Section 6).

Removal

6 Remove the fuel tank (see Section 2), and place it upside down on some clean rag.

7 Detach the breather/overflow hoses from their unions **(see illustration)**. Unscrew the fuel pump mounting plate nuts and remove the hoses and guides, noting what fits where. Carefully remove the pump assembly from the tank along with the mounting plate seal, taking care not to knock

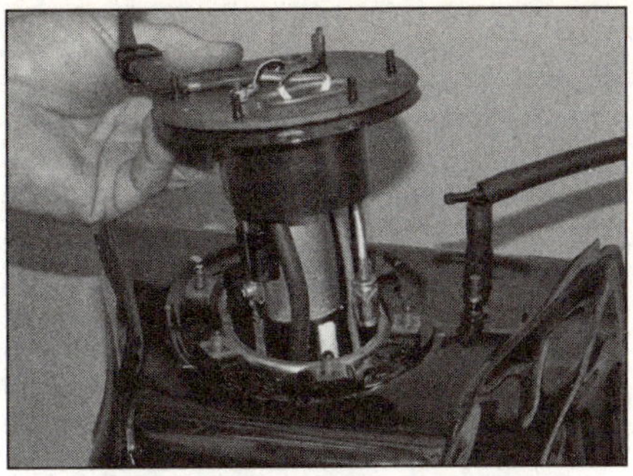

11.7b Carefully withdraw the pump assembly, noting its orientation

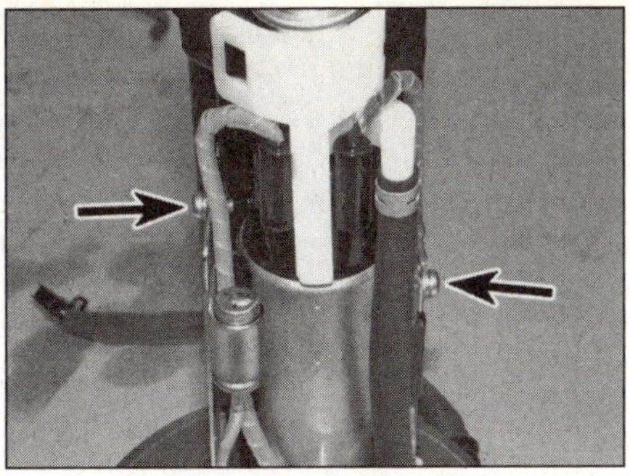

11.9a Make sure the terminal screws (arrowed) . . .

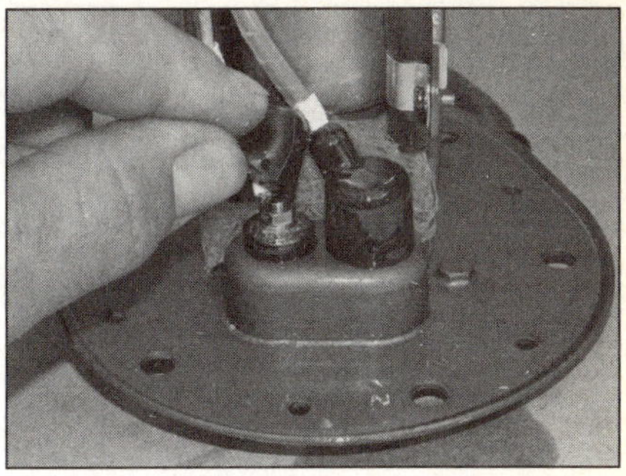

11.9b . . . and nuts on the pump . . .

11.9c . . . and the nut and connectors on the base are tight

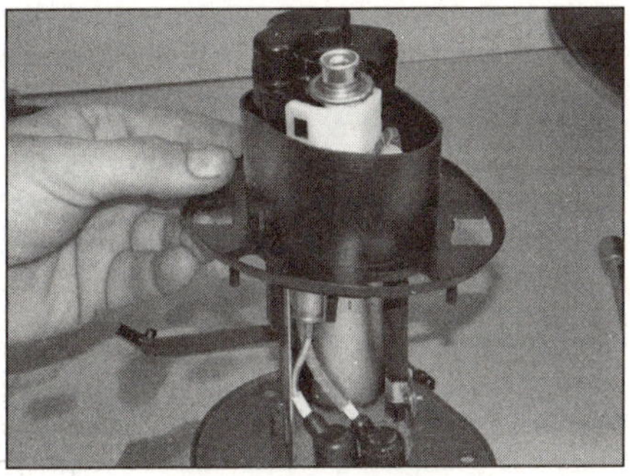

11.10a Fit the seal . . .

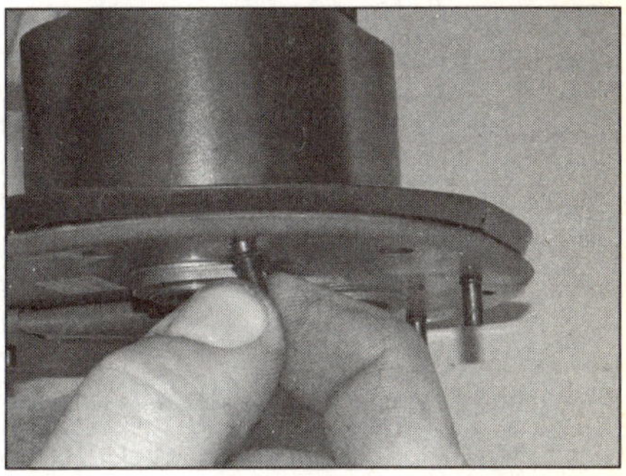

11.10b . . . and pull the pins through the holes

it against the rim of the tank **(see illustration)**. Remove the seal, noting how it fits, and discard it – a new one must be used on installation. The pump comes as a complete assembly and no individual components are available.

8 Check the strainer in the base of the pump housing for signs of dirt and clean it if necessary.

Installation

9 Make sure the wiring terminal screws, nuts and connectors are tight, both on the pump and the base **(see illustrations)**.

10 Ensure the mounting plate and tank surfaces are clean and dry. Fit the new seal onto the plate making sure its locating pins are all fitted correctly in the plate holes – the pins and holes are asymmetrical so it can only fit one way **(see illustration)**. Pull each pin from the underside to make sure its lip has pulled through the hole in the base **(see illustration)**.

11 Carefully manoeuvre the pump assembly into the tank, taking care not to knock it against the rim of the tank **(see illustration 11.7b)** – make sure the fuel hose union is at the front **(see illustration 11.7a)**.

12 Fit the nuts with the hoses and guides and tighten them finger-tight **(see illustration 11.7a)**. Now tighten them evenly and a little at a time in the numerical sequence shown to the torque setting specified at the beginning of the Chapter **(see illustration)**. Connect the breather/overflow hoses **(see illustration 11.7a)**.

13 Install the fuel tank (see Section 2).

12 Fuel warning light and sensor

Check

1 The circuit consists of the sensor, which is an integral part of the fuel pump assembly in the fuel tank, and the low fuel warning LED, which is part of the instrument cluster printed circuit board. If the system malfunctions first check that the fuses are good (see Chapter 8).

2 If the fuel warning light is permanently on irrespective of the amount of fuel in the tank, raise the fuel tank (see Section 2), and disconnect the fuel pump wiring connector **(see illustration 2.4)**. Turn the ignition ON. If the warning light is now off replace the fuel pump assembly with a new one. If it is still on, remove the windshield (see Chapter 7), and disconnect the instrument cluster wiring connector **(see illustration)**. Check the brown/black wire between the fuel pump connector and the instrument cluster connector for continuity. If there is, the instrument cluster PCB is faulty; if there isn't check the wiring and connectors for a break or dirty contact.

3 If the fuel warning light is permanently off irrespective of the amount of fuel in the tank, first check the instrument cluster (see Chapter 8). If it is good, raise the fuel tank (see Section 2), and disconnect the fuel pump wiring connector **(see illustration 2.4)**. Using a piece of wire jump across the brown/black and green wire terminals in the loom side of the connector. Turn the ignition ON. If the warning light is now on replace the fuel pump assembly with a new one. If it is still off, remove the windshield (see Chapter 7), and disconnect

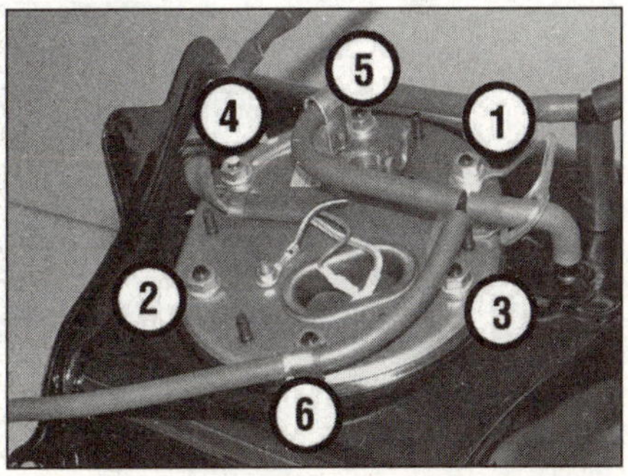

11.12 Tighten the nuts as described in the sequence shown

12.2 Disconnect the instrument wiring connector

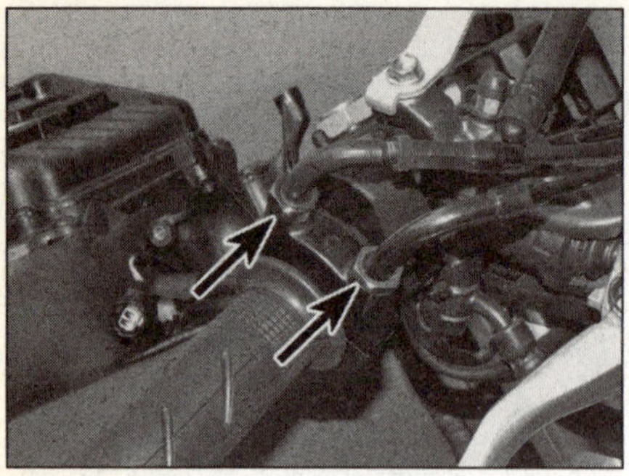

13.3a Unscrew the nuts (arrowed) . . .

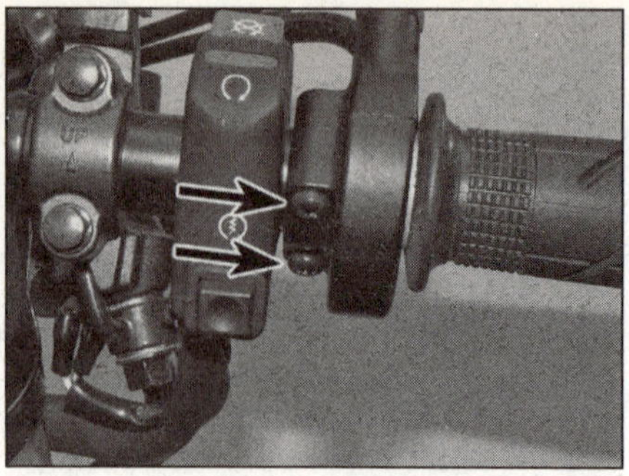

13.3b . . . then remove the housing screws (arrowed)

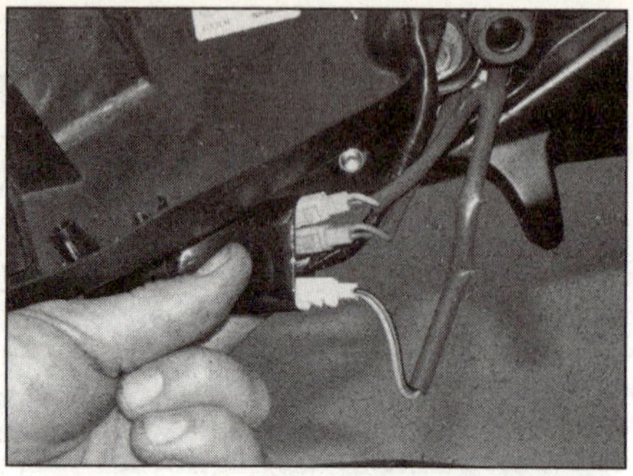

14.2a Disconnect the wiring connectors

the instrument cluster wiring connector **(see illustration 12.2)**. Check the brown/black wire between the fuel pump connector and the instrument cluster connector for continuity. If there is, the instrument cluster PCB is faulty; if there isn't check the wiring and connectors for a break or dirty contact.

4 If no faults are found, remove the pump (see Section 11) and check the pump wiring connectors **(see illustrations 11.9a, b and c)**.

Removal and installation

5 If the warning light is faulty refer to Chapter 8 for replacement of the instrument cluster PCB.

6 If the sensor is faulty replace the fuel pump assembly with a new one (see Section 11) – the sensor is not available separately.

13 Throttle cables

Warning: Refer to the precautions given in Section 1 before proceeding.

Removal

1 Remove the air filter housing (see Section 3). Mark each cable according to its location.

2 Refer to Section 11 and displace the throttle bodies – this procedure involves detaching the cables, and it is not possible to detach and fit the lower cable with the throttle bodies in place. Withdraw the cables from the frame noting their correct routing.

3 Unscrew the cable elbow nuts at the throttle pulley housing, then remove the housing screws and separate the halves **(see illustrations)**. Detach the cable nipples from the pulley, then remove the throttle closing cable from the housing. Thread the throttle opening cable elbow out of the housing and withdraw the cable. Mark each cable to ensure it is connected correctly on installation.

Installation

4 Fit the throttle opening cable elbow into the rear socket of the throttle pulley housing and thread the elbow into it without it becoming tight on the bottom of the threads – the elbow must stay loose so that it aligns itself – then thread the nut onto the elbow, again not so that it is tight **(see illustration 13.3a)**. Fit the closing cable into the front socket and tighten the nut finger-tight. Lubricate the cable nipples with multi-purpose grease and fit them into the throttle pulley. Assemble the housing onto the handlebar, making sure the pin locates in the hole, then fit the screws and tighten them **(see illustration 13.3b)**.

5 Feed the cables through to the throttle bodies, making sure they are correctly routed. The cables must not interfere with any other component and should not be kinked or bent sharply. Now tighten both cable elbow nuts on the housing.

6 Refer to Section 11 to connect the cables and install the throttle bodies.

7 Operate the throttle to check that it opens and closes freely.

8 Check and adjust the throttle cable freeplay (see Chapter 1). Turn the handlebars back-and-forth to make sure the cable doesn't cause the steering to bind.

9 Install the air filter housing (see Section 3).

10 Start the engine and check that the idle speed does not rise as the handlebars are turned. If it does, the throttle cable is routed incorrectly. Correct the problem before riding the motorcycle.

14 Exhaust system

Warning: If the engine has been running the exhaust system will be very hot. Allow the system to cool before carrying out any work.

Removal

Silencer

HAYNES HiNT *Exhaust system clamp bolts tend to become corroded and seized. It is advisable to spray them with WD40 or a similar product before attempting to slacken them.*

1 Remove the right-hand fairing side panel, the lower fairing and the seat cowling (see Chapter 7).

2 Disconnect the turn signal and licence plate light wiring connectors **(see illustration)**. Unscrew the bolts, and on RR-6 and RR-7 models the top screw, securing the turn signal/licence plate assembly and remove it **(see illustrations)**.

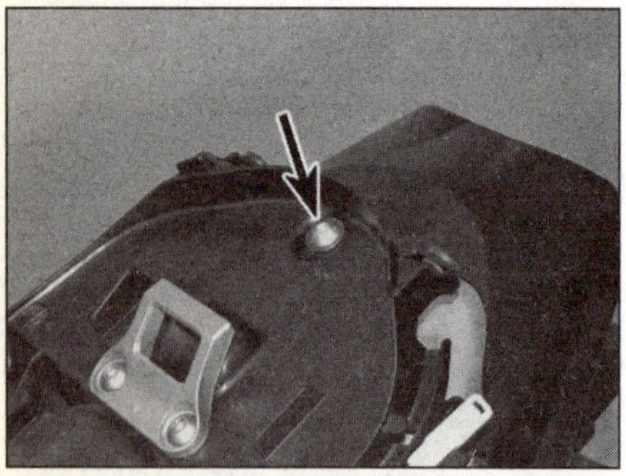

14.2b On RR-6 and RR-7 models undo the screw (arrowed)

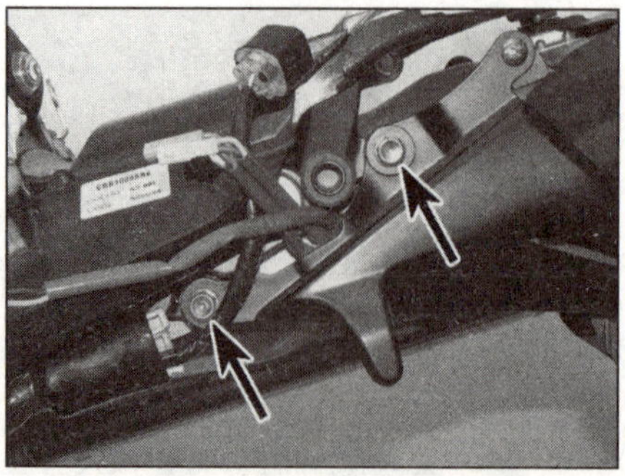

14.2c Unscrew the bolts (arrowed) . . .

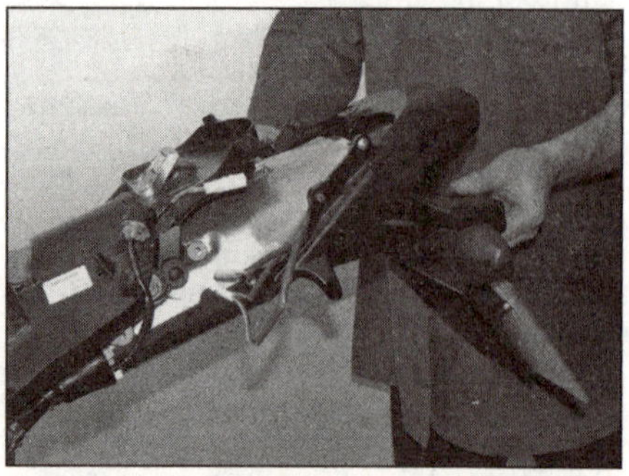

14.2d . . . and remove the assembly

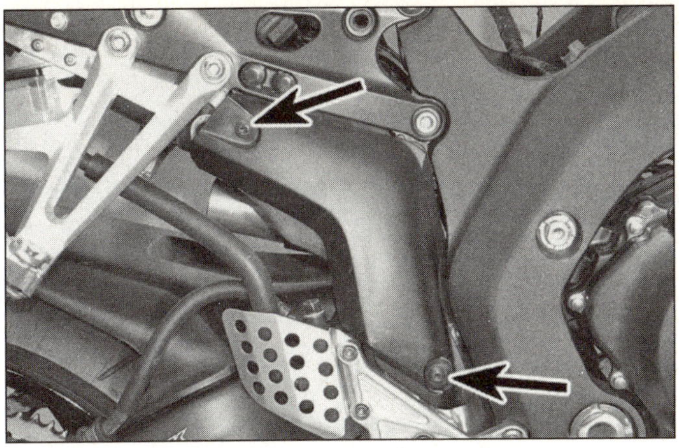

14.4a Undo the screws (arrowed) . . .

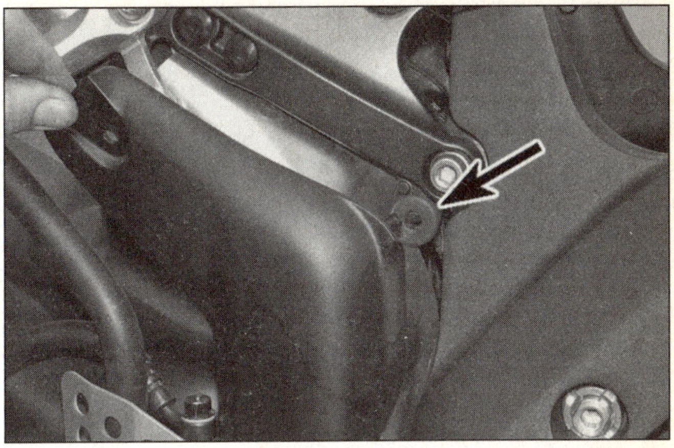

14.4b . . . and free the peg from the grommet (arrowed)

3 Displace the EGCV servo (see Section 15).
4 Undo the two screws securing the outer guard, noting the collar with the lower screw **(see illustration)**. Pull the guard away to release the peg from the grommet **(see illustration)**.
5 Disconnect the rear brake light switch wiring connector **(see illustrations)**. Release the wiring from its guide(s) and feed it down to the switch, noting its routing **(see illustrations)**. Unscrew the bolts securing the rider's footrest bracket, then release the assembly from the retainer on the inner guard and tie it up to the rear sub-frame, making sure no strain is placed on the hoses **(see illustration)**.
6 Unscrew the bolt securing the inner silencer guard and remove the guard, on RR-4 and RR-5 models noting how it engages with the retainer on the downpipe assembly **(see illustration)**.
7 Unscrew the bolt on the clamp securing the silencer to the joint pipe and remove the clamp, noting how it locates over the gasket and collar **(see illustration)**.
8 Unscrew the silencer mounting bolts **(see**

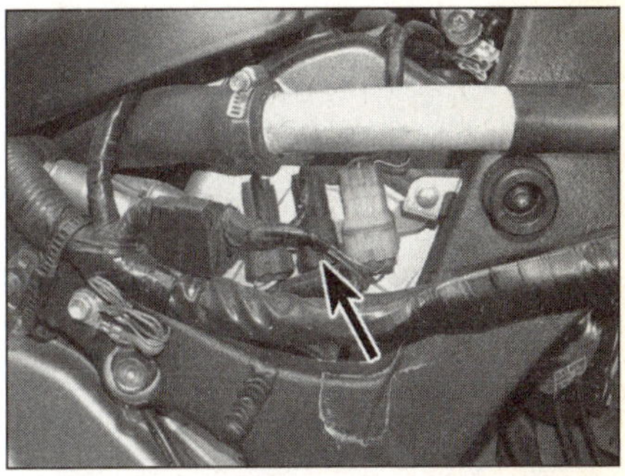

14.5a Rear brake light switch wiring connector (arrowed) – RR-4 and RR-5 models

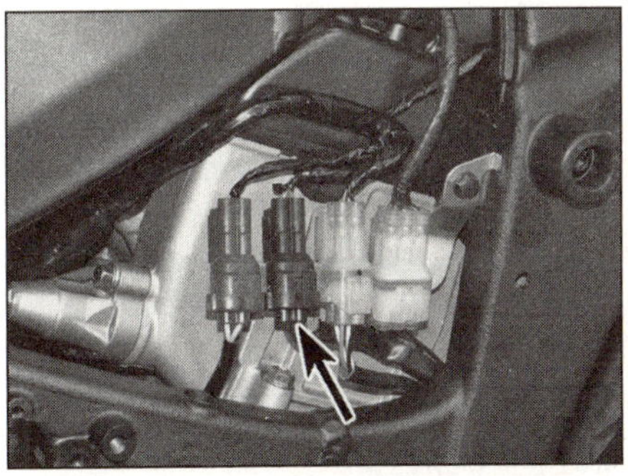

14.5b Rear brake light switch wiring connector (arrowed) – RR-6 and RR-7 models

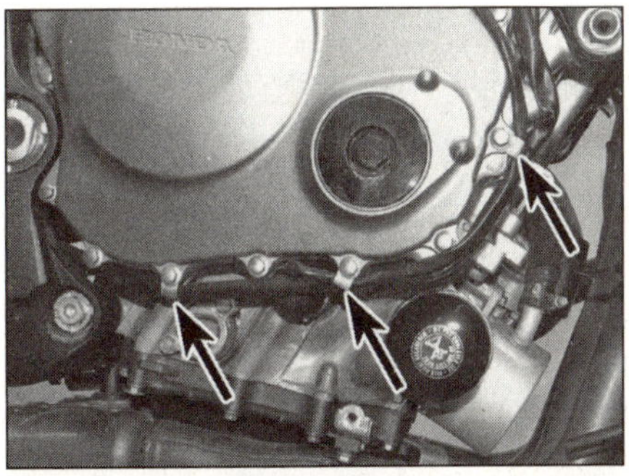

14.5c Wiring guides (arrowed) – RR-4 and RR-5 models

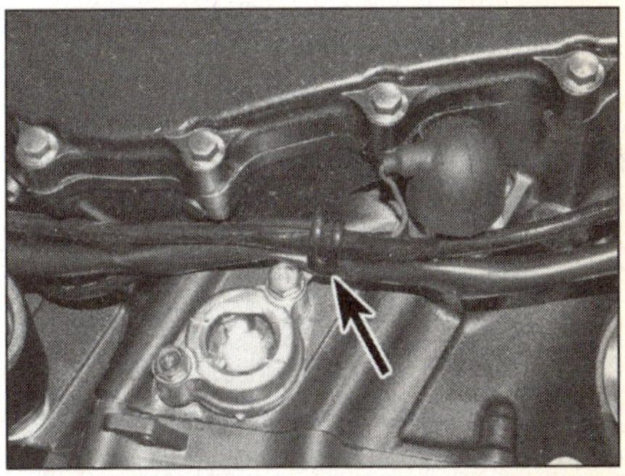

14.5d Wiring guide (arrowed) – RR-6 and RR-7 models

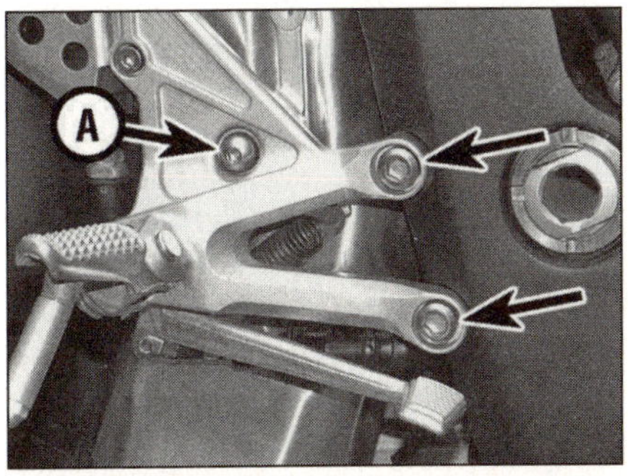

14.5e Footrest/master cylinder bracket bolts (arrowed) – bolt A on RR-6 and RR-7 models only

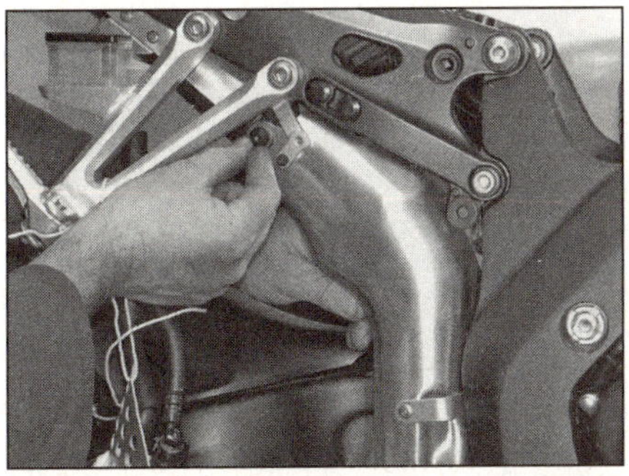

14.6 Unscrew the bolt and remove the inner guard

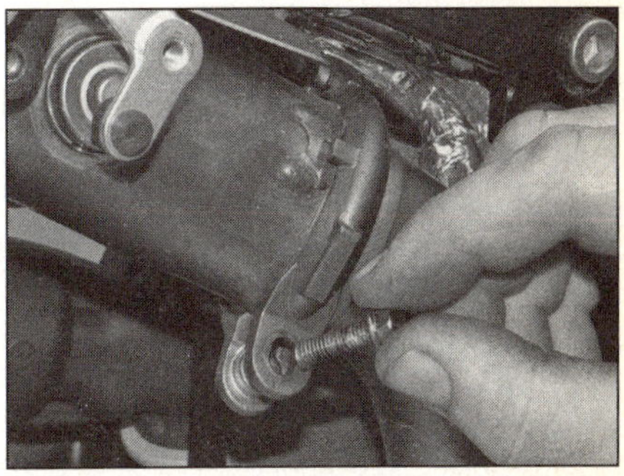

14.7 Unscrew the bolt and remove the clamp

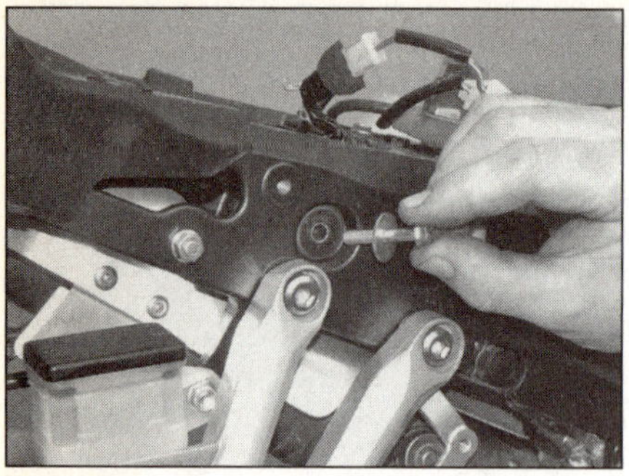

14.8a Unscrew the front bolt . . .

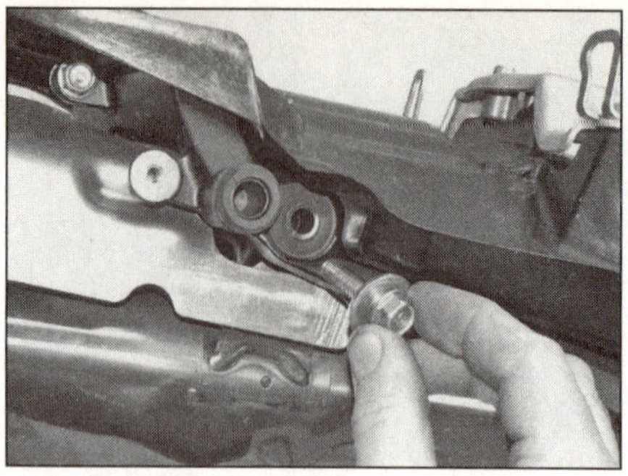

14.8b . . . and the rear bolt . . .

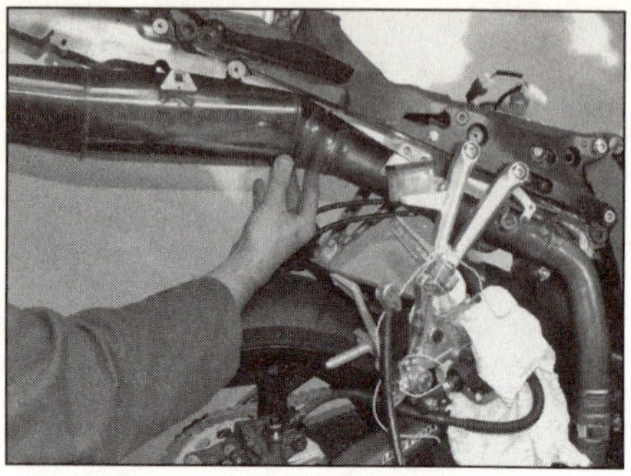

14.8c . . . and remove the silencer

illustrations). Ease the silencer up off the joint pipe and manoeuvre it off the back of the bike **(see illustration)**.

9 Remove the gasket and collar from the joint pipe and replace the gasket with a new one **(see illustrations)**.

10 If required detach the EGCV servo cables from the pulley (see Section 15).

11 Check the condition of the mounting bolts, washers, collars and rubbers and replace them with new ones if necessary.

Joint pipe

12 Remove the silencer.

13 Slacken the bolt on the clamp securing the joint pipe to the downpipe assembly and remove the pipe **(see illustrations)**.

14 If necessary remove the gasket from inside the bottom of the joint and replace it with a new one **(see illustration)**.

Downpipe assembly

15 Remove the lower fairing and both fairing side panels (see Chapter 7).

16 On RR-4 and RR-5 models with a catalytic converter raise the fuel tank (see Section 2). On all models with a catalytic converter disconnect the oxygen sensor wiring connector **(see illustration 6.87)**. Release the wiring from its guide(s) and feed it down to the switch, noting its routing.

17 For best access and to avoid the possibility of damage to the radiator fins drain the cooling system (see Chapter 1) and remove the radiator (see Chapter 3). Alternatively displace the radiator from its mounts, leaving just the hoses connected, and move it down, following the relevant Steps in Chapter 3.

18 Slacken the bolt on the clamp securing the downpipe assembly to the joint pipe **(see illustration 14.13a)**.

19 Unscrew the bolt securing the bottom of the downpipe assembly **(see illustration)**.

20 Unscrew the nuts securing the header pipes to the cylinder head **(see illustration)**.

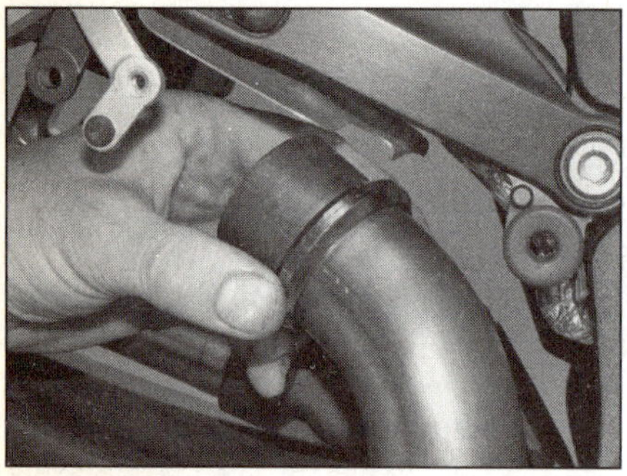

14.9a Remove the gasket . . .

14.9b . . . and the collar

14.13a Slacken the clamp bolt (arrowed) . . .

14.13b . . . and remove the pipe

14.14 Replace the gasket (arrowed) with a new one if necessary

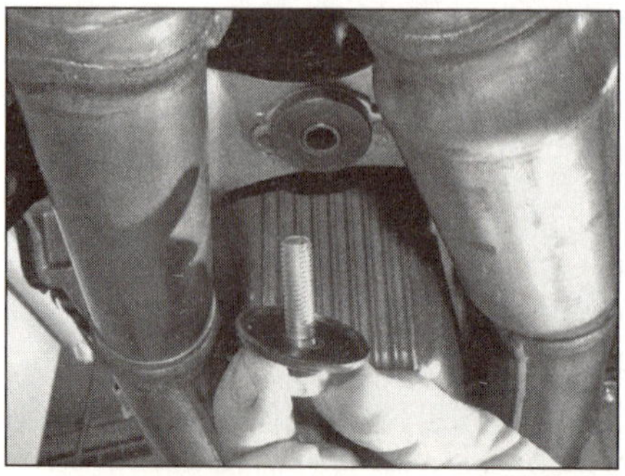

14.19 Unscrew the bolt on the underside

14.20 Unscrew the header pipe nuts and draw the flanges off . . .

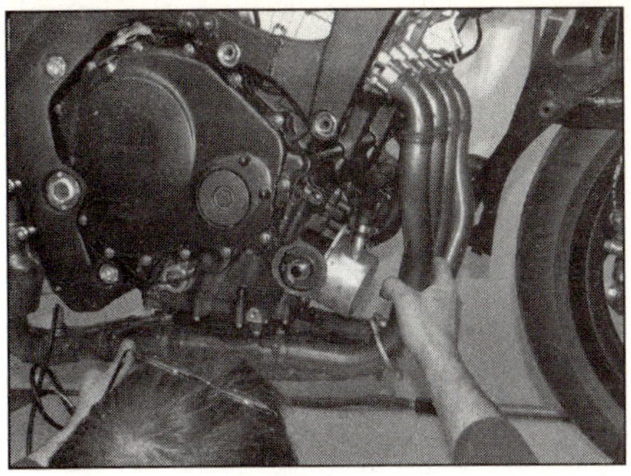

14.21 . . . then detach and remove the header pipes

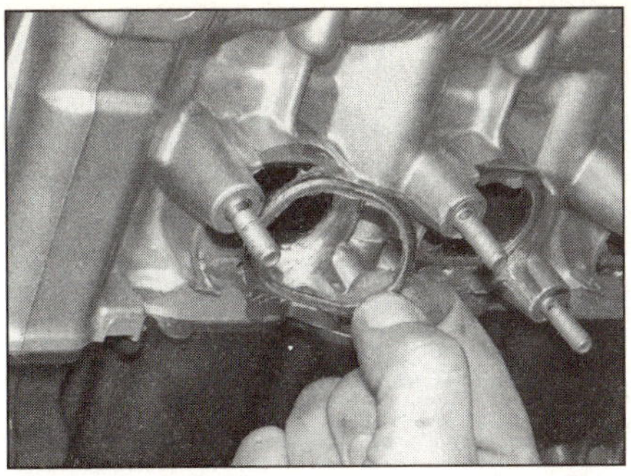

14.23a Use a new sealing ring in each port

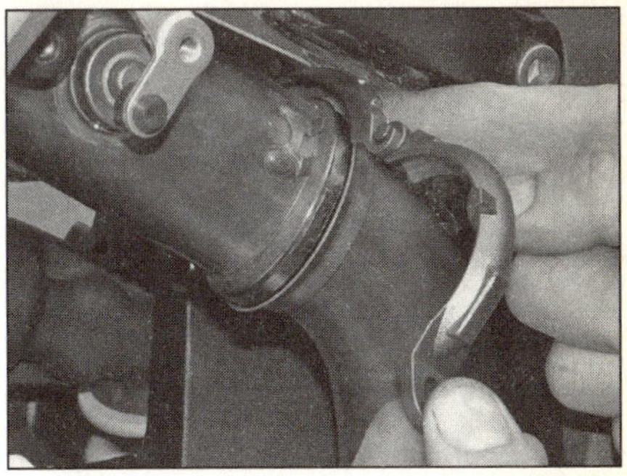

14.23b Make sure the clamp locates around the collar and gasket

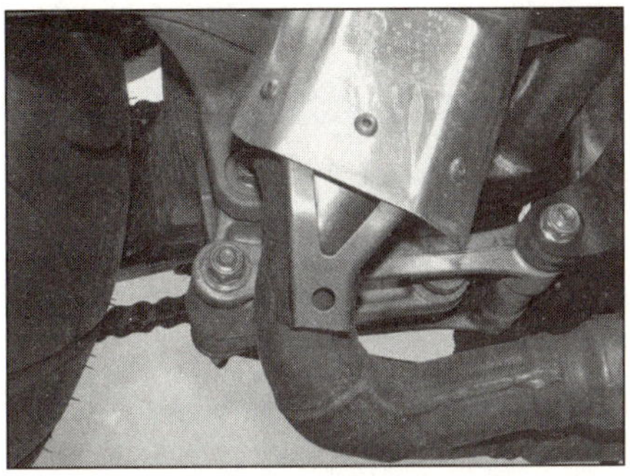

14.23c Make sure the bottom of the guard locates correctly

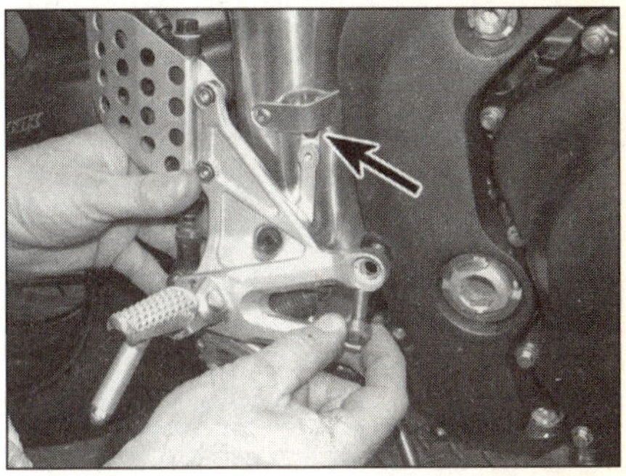

14.23d Make sure the lug locates behind the retainer (arrowed)

21 Draw the flanges off the studs and manoeuvre the downpipe assembly out of the head and the joint pipe and remove it **(see illustration)**. Remove the sealing ring from each port in the cylinder head and discard them as new ones must be used **(see illustration 14.23a)**. If necessary remove the gasket from inside the bottom of the joint pipe and replace it with a new one **(see illustration 14.14)**.

22 Check the condition of the mounting bolts, washers, collars and rubbers and replace them with new ones if necessary.

Installation

23 Installation is the reverse of removal, noting the following:

- Replace any damaged, deformed or deteriorated mounting rubbers with new ones.
- Use a new sealing ring in each cylinder head port, and dab them with grease to stick them in place **(see illustration 14.23a)**.
- When fitting the joint pipe onto the downpipe assembly fit it with the top end pointing out then pivot it round when the pipe is fully in place **(see illustration 14.13b)**.
- Apply a smear of copper grease to all nuts and bolts to prevent them from seizing up. When fitting the downpipe assembly bolt on RR-6 and RR-7 models make sure the dished side of the washer is facing up so it seats over the rubber bush **(see illustration 14.19)**.
- Leave all fasteners loose until the entire system has been installed, making alignment of the various sections easier.
- When fitting the silencer to joint pipe clamp make sure it locates over the collar and gasket **(see illustration 14.23b)**, and align it so the tab locates between the lugs on the silencer **(see illustration 14.7)**.
- Tighten the downpipe nuts first, then the downpipe and silencer mounting bolts, and tighten the clamp bolts last, and where given tighten them to the torque settings specified at the beginning of the Chapter.
- On RR-4 and RR-5 models make sure the bottom of the inner guard engages with the retainer on the downpipe assembly **(see illustration 14.23c)**.
- Make sure the footrest bracket locates correctly in its retainer on the inner guard **(see illustration 14.23d)**. Tighten the bracket to frame bolts to the specified torque.
- When fitting the outer guard note that the small shouldered bolt is for the upper mount.
- Do not forget to reconnect the rear brake light switch and, where fitted, the oxygen sensor wiring connector(s) **(see illustrations 14.5a and b and 6.87)**. Make sure the wiring is correctly routed and secured by its guide(s) **(see illustrations 14.5c and d)**.
- Run the engine and check the system for leaks, and also check the operation of the EGCV.

15 Exhaust gas control valve (EGCV)

1 The system controls the flow of gases through the exhaust system using a butterfly valve. The valves switch at pre-determined engine speeds, and are actuated by cables from a servo motor that is controlled by the ECM. Refer to Chapter 1 to check cable adjustment.

Servo motor

Check

2 To check the servo motor, first remove it (see below).

3 Using a fully charged 12V battery and some jumper leads, connect the positive (+) terminal of the battery to the red wire terminal on the servo connector, and the negative (–) terminal to the blue wire terminal. When the battery is connected, the servo should operate. Disconnect the battery immediately after the test. If the servo does not operate, replace it with a new one.

Caution: Disconnect the battery immediately after the test to prevent possible damage to the servo motor.

4 If the servo now operates, yet did not beforehand, check for voltage at the loom side of the wiring connector using a voltmeter – connect the positive (+) probe of the meter to the red wire terminal on the loom side of the connector, and the negative (–) terminal to the blue wire terminal. With the ignition ON there should be battery voltage. If not, check the connector for loose or corroded terminals, then check the wiring between the connector and the ECM connectors for continuity, referring to the Wiring Diagrams in Chapter 8. If the wiring is good, the ECM could be faulty.

5 Using an ohmmeter or multimeter set to the K-ohms scale check the static resistance between the yellow/red and green/orange wire terminals (RR-4 and RR-5 models) or the yellow/red and green wire terminals (RR-6 and RR-7 models) on the servo connector. Compare the reading to that specified at the beginning of the Chapter. Now check the variable resistance between the light green/pink and green/orange wire terminals (RR-4 and RR-5 models) or the brown and green wire terminals (RR-6 and RR-7 models) on the servo's connector while turning the

15.6a EGCV servo wiring connector (arrowed) – RR-4 and RR-5 models

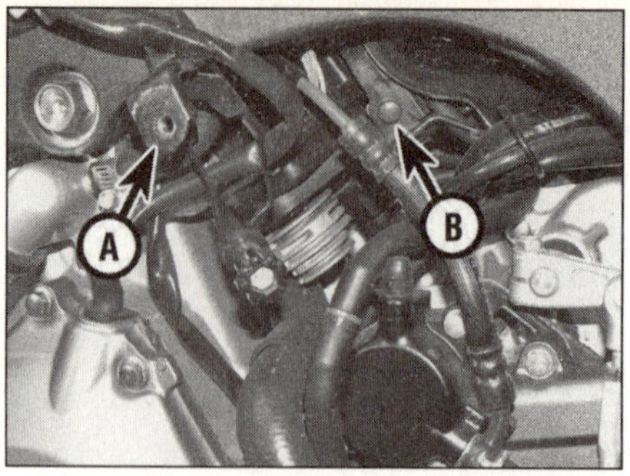

15.6b Fairing bracket (A). Servo mounting bolt (B)

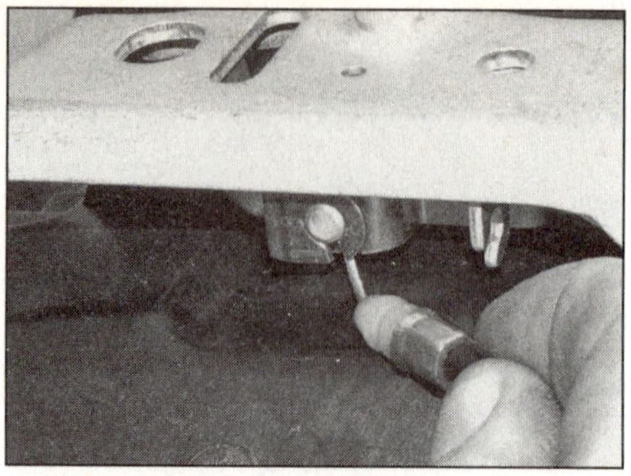

15.7a Detach the cable from the latch

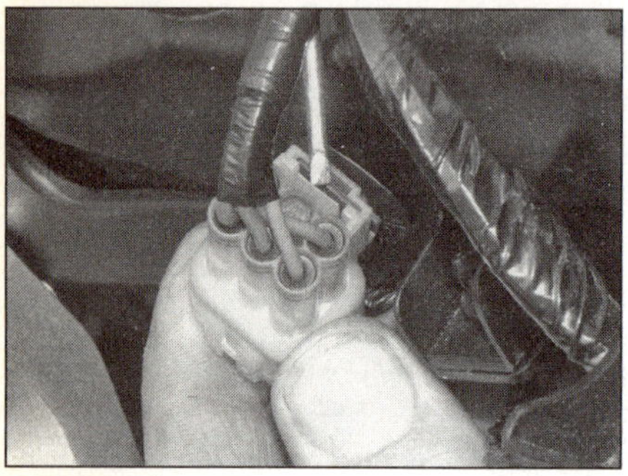

15.7b Release the wiring connector from its holder . . .

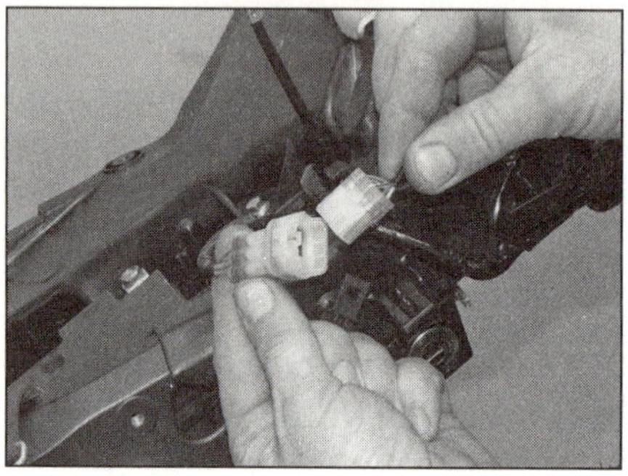

15.7c . . . then disconnect it

15.8a Undo the screws and remove the cover . . .

servo pulley by hand. Compare the reading range to that specified at the beginning of the Chapter. If the readings from either test are not within the range specified, replace the servo with a new one.

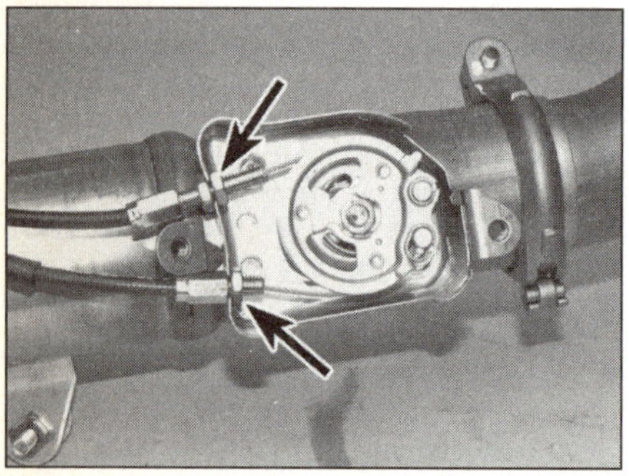

15.8b . . . then slacken the nuts (arrowed) and free the cables – RR-6 and RR-7 type shown

Removal

6 On RR-4 and RR-5 models raise or remove the fuel tank (see Section 2). Trace the wiring from the servo and disconnect it at the 6-pin wiring connector **(see illustration)**. Unscrew the bolt securing the fairing side panel bracket to the frame and displace the bracket, noting how it locates **(see illustration)**.

7 On RR-6 and RR-7 models remove the seat cowling (see Chapter 7). Free the seat lock cable from its bracket and detach the cable end from the latch **(see illustrations)**. Trace the wiring from the servo to the 6-pin wiring connector, then free the connector and disconnect it **(see illustration)**.

8 Unscrew the two exhaust control valve cover bolts and remove the cover **(see illustrations)**. Slacken the cable locknuts and free the cables from the housing.

9 On RR-4 and RR-5 models unscrew the bolt securing the servo and displace it, then mark each cable according to its location **(see illustration 15.6b)**. Free the outer cables from the holder and detach the cables from the pulley. If required unscrew the bolt securing the mounting bracket and remove the bracket, noting how it fits, and the collar in the rubber grommet.

10 On RR-6 and RR-7 models release the trim clip and unscrew the nut securing the seat lock/servo housing and remove the housing, drawing the seat lock cable with it, noting its routing, and how the bolt head locates **(see illustrations)**. Unscrew the bolt securing the servo and displace it, then mark each cable according to its location **(see illustrations)**. Free the outer cables from the holder and detach the cable ends from the pulley. Note the collars in the rubber grommets.

Installation

11 If you are installing the original servo, first connect the wiring connector **(see illus-**

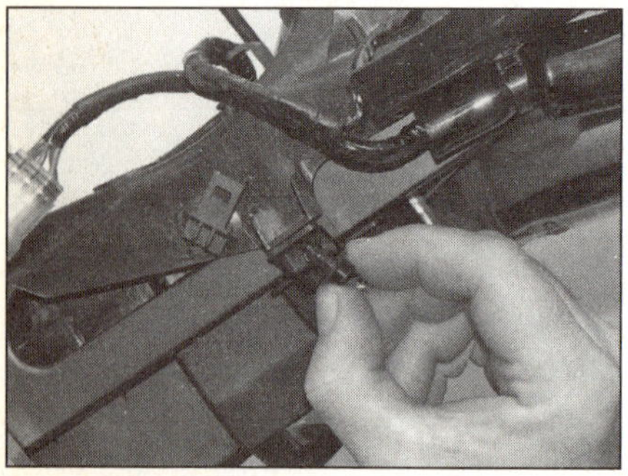

15.10a Release the trim clip . . .

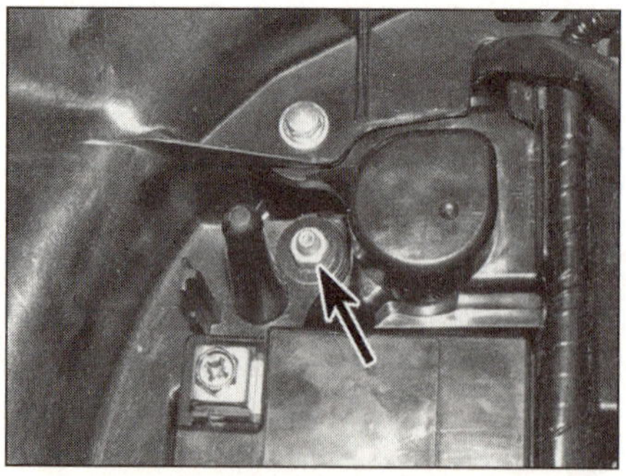

15.10b . . . then unscrew the nut (arrowed) . . .

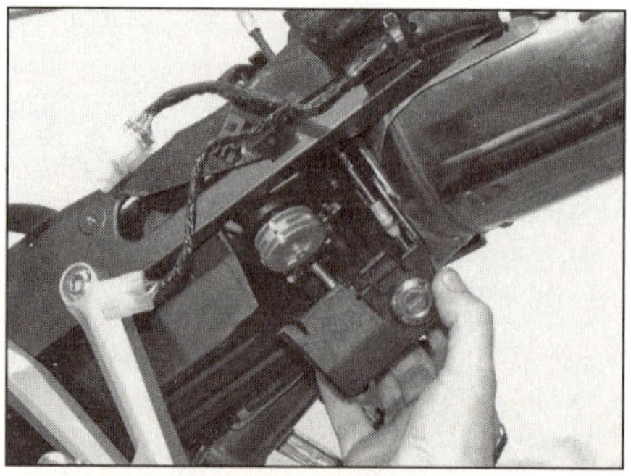

15.10c . . . and remove the housing

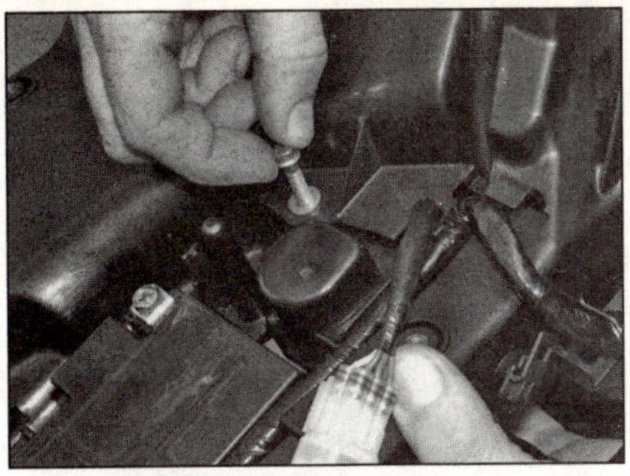

15.10d Unscrew the bolt . . .

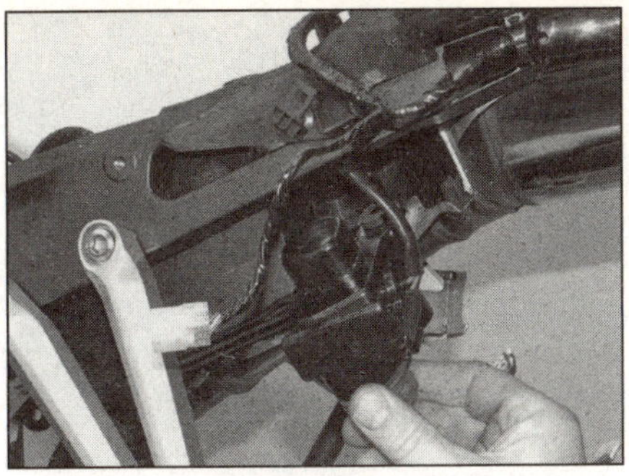

15.10e . . . then displace the servo and detach the cables

tration 15.6a or 15.7c). Now refer to Section 5, Step 4 and short the DLC connector terminals. Turn the ignition ON – the servo should turn, then stop. When it stops, insert a 3 x 28 mm (RR-4 and RR-5 models) or 3 x 18 mm (RR-6 and RR-7 models) bolt or equivalent pin into the hole in the top of the pulley to lock it in that position **(see illustration)**. Connect the cables to the pulley, making sure they are in their correct position as noted on removal. Remove the bolt or pin, then install the servo in a reverse of the removal procedure, and then adjust the cables (see Chapter 1).

12 If you are installing a new servo, first connect the cables to the pulley, making sure they are in their correct position as noted on removal. Install the servo in a reverse of the removal procedure, then adjust the cables (see Chapter 1).

Exhaust valve

Check

13 Unscrew the two exhaust control valve cover bolts and remove the cover **(see illustration 15.8a)**. Mark each cable according to its location. Slacken the cable locknuts and free the cables from the housing and the pulley **(see illustration 15.8b)**.

14 Turn the valve pulley by hand. If it doesn't turn smoothly and return under the force of the spring, remove the valve and check for a build-up of carbon deposits (see below).

15 Smear some grease onto the cable ends and attach them to the pulley (see below). Check the operation of the system and the cable freeplay (see Chapter 1).

16 Apply some copper grease to the exhaust valve cover bolt threads and fit the cover.

Removal

17 Remove the silencer (see Section 14). Unscrew the two exhaust control valve cover bolts and remove the cover **(see illustration 15.8a)**. Mark each cable according to its location. Slacken the cable locknuts and free the cables from the housing and the pulley **(see illustration 15.8b)**.

18 Bend back the tabs on the valve shaft nut lock washer. Counter-hold the pulley and unscrew the nut, then remove the lock washer, pulley, stopper arm (RR-4 and RR-5 models only), spring collar and return spring, noting how its ends locate.

19 Unscrew the bolts securing the housing and remove it.

20 Bend back the tabs on the butterfly valve lock washer, then undo the screws and remove the butterfly valve, noting which way round it fits.

21 Remove the cap from the outer bearing. Push the shaft through the silencer from the pulley side, removing the outer bearing as you do. Remove the inner bearing. Discard the bearings and bearing cap as new ones should be used.

22 Clean all components, including the bearing housings, and scrape off any carbon deposits.

Installation

23 Installation is the reverse of removal, noting the following:

- Fit the inner bearing first, then slide the shaft in from the right-hand side of the silencer, then fit the outer bearing.
- New lock washers should be used for the butterfly valve screws and shaft nut as the tabs will have weakened. Bend the tabs up against the screws and nut to lock them.
- Apply a smear of copper grease to the housing bolt threads, and tighten them to the torque setting specified at the beginning of the Chapter.
- Make sure the return spring ends locate correctly. Tighten the shaft nut to the specified torque. Rotate the valve by hand and check that it moves smoothly and returns under the force of the spring.
- Refer to Section 14 for silencer installation.
- Check and adjust cable freeplay (see Chapter 1). Also check the system for leaks.

Cable renewal

24 Mark each cable according to its location as a guide for fitting the new cables. Displace the servo (see above), then free the outer cables from the holder and detach the cables from the pulley.

25 Free the cables from the exhaust valve pulley and withdraw the cables from the machine, noting the correct routing of each cable and which fits where.

26 Lubricate the cable nipples with multi-purpose grease and fit them into the servo pulley. Fit the outer cables into the holder, making sure they locate correctly.

27 Feed the cables through to the exhaust, making sure they are correctly routed. The cables must not interfere with any other component and should not be kinked or bent sharply.

28 Lubricate the cable nipples with multi-purpose grease. Fit each cable into its socket in the pulley and in the housing – on RR-4 and RR-5 models the spring-loaded cable fits into the bottom of the housing, and on RR-6 and RR-7 models the cable with the single locknut fits into the bottom **(see illustration 15.8b)**.

29 Adjust the cable freeplay, then tighten the cable locknuts (see Chapter 1). Check the operation of the system.

30 Install the servo and fit the exhaust valve cover (see above).

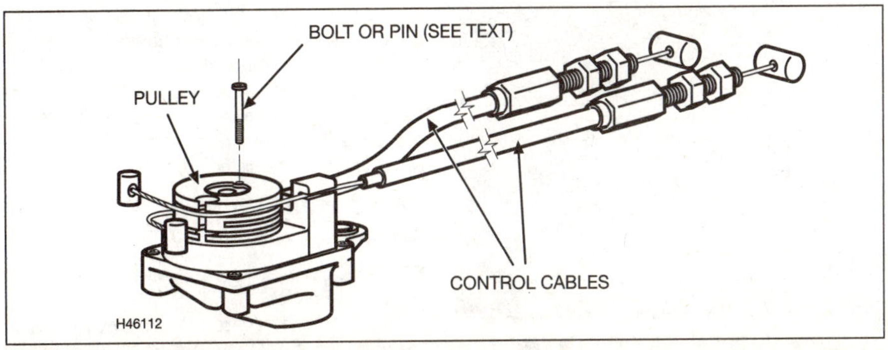

15.11 Lock the pulley using a bolt or pin and connect the cables – RR-6 and RR-7 type shown

16 Fuel system hoses

1 The fuel delivery, vacuum and PAIR system hoses should be replaced with new ones at the first sign of deterioration. On California models, also replace the EVAP emission control system hoses.

2 Remove the fuel tank and the air filter housing (see Sections 2 and 3).

3 Before detaching a hose, note any clamp that secures it and its routing between the components. Disconnect the vacuum hoses from the throttle bodies, the MAP sensor, air intake control valve and vacuum chamber, referring to the relevant Sections where necessary. Disconnect the PAIR system hoses from the control valve and reed valves, noting

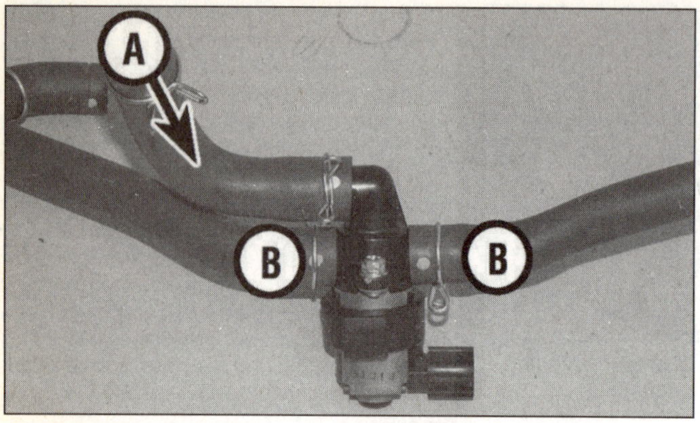

17.4a When blowing into hose (A) no air should flow out of hoses (B) – RR-4 and RR-5 type shown

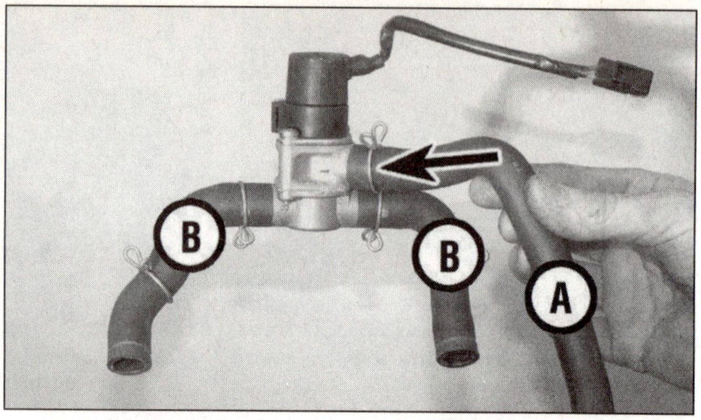

17.4b When blowing into hose (A) no air should flow out of hoses (B) – RR-6 and RR-7 type shown

the routing of each one and how it is secured (see Section 17). On California models refer to Section 18 for the EVAP system. **Note:** *It is advisable to make a sketch of the hoses before removing them to ensure they are correctly installed.* Make sure each new hose is correctly routed, not kinked or pinched, and fully pushed onto its union. Use new clamps if necessary where fitted.

4 The fuel supply hose runs from the fuel tank to the right-hand end of the primary fuel rail, then from near the left-hand end of the primary rail to the secondary rail. Unscrew the bolts securing the hose to the secondary rail, being prepared to catch any residual fuel with a rag **(see illustration 6.10)**. Discard the O-ring in the union as a new one must be used. Counter-hold the hex on each primary rail fuel hose joint and unscrew the banjo union nut, noting the alignment of the hose and being prepared to catch any residual fuel with a rag **(see illustrations 6.5b and 6.6a)**. Detach the hose and discard the sealing washers – new ones must be used.

5 Use a new O-ring and sealing washers when fitting the new hoses **(see illustrations 6.17a and b)**. Tighten the union bolts and nuts to the torque settings specified at the beginning of the chapter, counter-holding the hose joint hex when tightening each nut. Run the engine and check that the fuel system is working correctly before taking the machine out on the road.

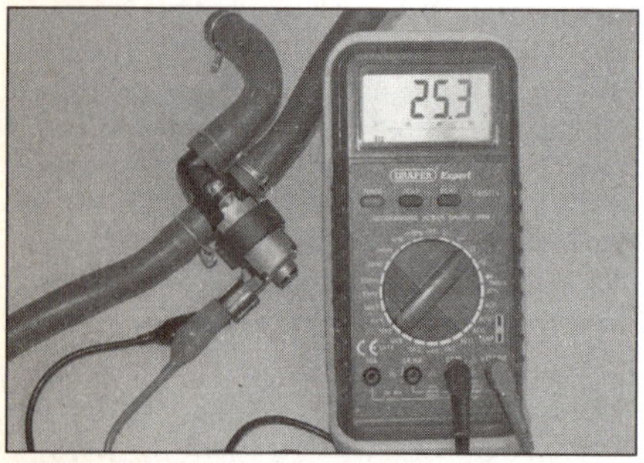

17.5 Check the resistance of the valve solenoid

17 Pulse secondary air (PAIR) system

General information

1 To reduce the amount of unburned hydrocarbons released in the exhaust gases, a pulse secondary air (PAIR) system is fitted. The system consists of the control valve (mounted under the front of the air filter housing), the reed valves (fitted in the valve cover) and the hoses linking them. The control valve is actuated electronically by the ECM.

2 Under certain operating conditions, a signal from the ECM opens up the PAIR control valve which then allows filtered air to be drawn through the reed valves and cylinder head passages and into the exhaust ports. The air mixes with the exhaust gases, causing any unburned particles of the fuel in the mixture to be burnt in the exhaust port/pipes. This process changes a considerable amount of hydrocarbons and carbon monoxide into relatively harmless carbon dioxide and water. The reed valves in the valve cover are fitted to prevent the flow of exhaust gases back up the cylinder head passages and into the air filter housing.

Testing

Control valve

3 Remove the valve from the motorcycle (see below).

4 Check the operation of the control valve by blowing through the air filter housing hose union; no air should flow through the reed valve hose unions **(see illustrations)**. Now connect battery voltage (12 volts) across the valve terminals and repeat the check; air should now flow freely through the valve if it is functioning correctly.

5 Check the resistance of the control valve solenoid by connecting an ohmmeter between its connector terminals and compare the reading obtained to that given in the Specifications **(see illustration)**. Replace the valve with a new one if faulty.

Reed valves

6 Remove the air filter housing and air intake duct (see Section 3). Disconnect the hose from each reed valve housing **(see illustration 8.19)**. Attach a clean auxiliary hose of the correct bore and about a foot long to one of the unions.

7 Check the valve by blowing and sucking on the auxiliary hose end. Air should flow through the hose only when blown down it and not when a vacuum is applied. If this is not the case the reed valve is faulty, though it is worth cleaning it as described below. Check the other valve in the same way.

Component renewal

Control valve and hoses

8 Remove the air filter housing and air intake duct (see Section 3).

9 Displace the control valve from its mount then disconnect the control valve wiring connector **(see illustrations)**.

17.9a Displace the control valve . . .

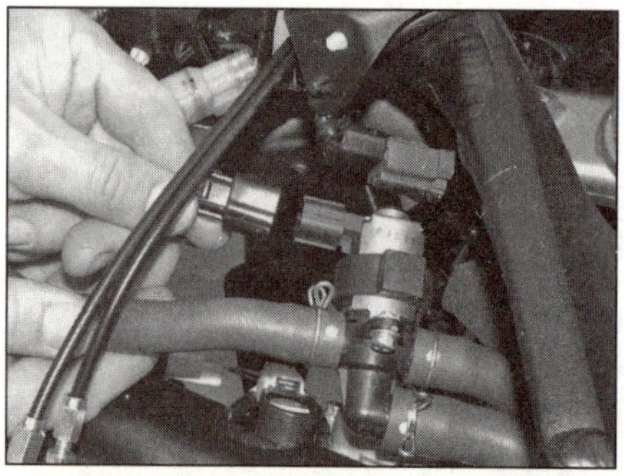

17.9b . . . and disconnect the wiring connector

17.13a Unscrew the bolts and remove the cover . . .

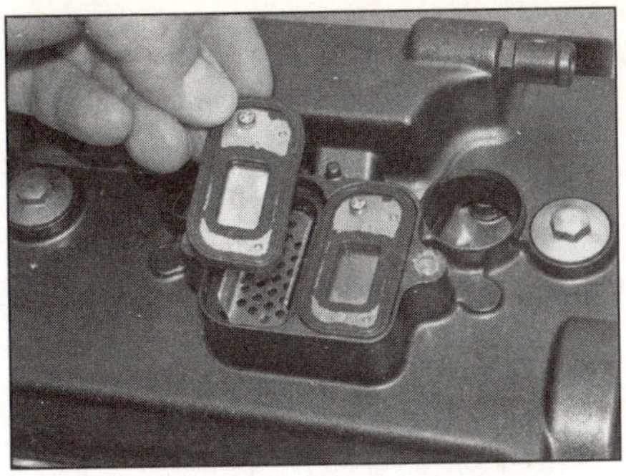

17.13b . . . then remove the reed valves . . .

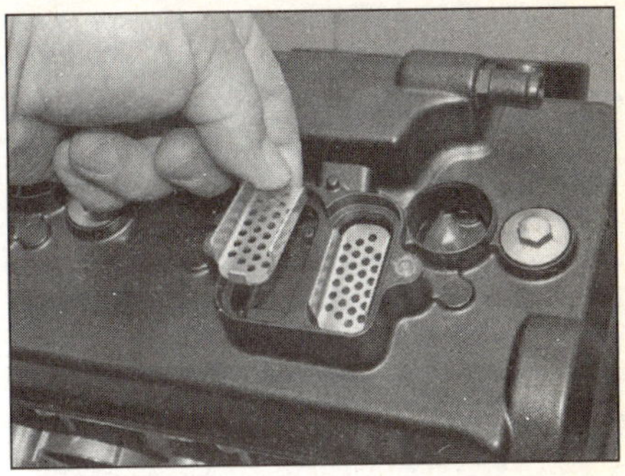

17.13c . . . and the base plates

10 Disconnect the hose from each reed valve housing **(see illustration 8.19)**. Remove the control valve with its hoses attached. Detach the hoses if required.
11 Installation is the reverse of removal.

Reed valves

12 Remove the air filter housing and air intake duct (see Section 3).
13 To remove either valve, first release the clamp and detach the air hose from its union **(see illustration 8.19)**. Unscrew the bolts securing the reed valve cover and remove the cover **(see illustration)**. Remove the reed valves and the base plates, noting which way around they fit **(see illustrations)**.
14 Installation is the reverse of removal. Make sure the reed valve components and housings are clean and correctly fitted.

18 Evaporative emission control (EVAP) system

Note: *This system is fitted to California market models only.*

General information

1 The evaporative emission control system (EVAP) is fitted to minimise the escape of fuel vapour into the atmosphere **(see illustration)**. The fuel tank is sealed and a charcoal canister collects the fuel vapours generated when the motorcycle is parked and stores them until they can be cleared from the canister, via the control valve, into the throttle body intake tracts to be burned by the engine during normal combustion. The purge control valve for the fuel tank vapour is opened and closed by the engine control module (ECM).
2 The valve should be tested if there is a problem starting the engine when it is hot.

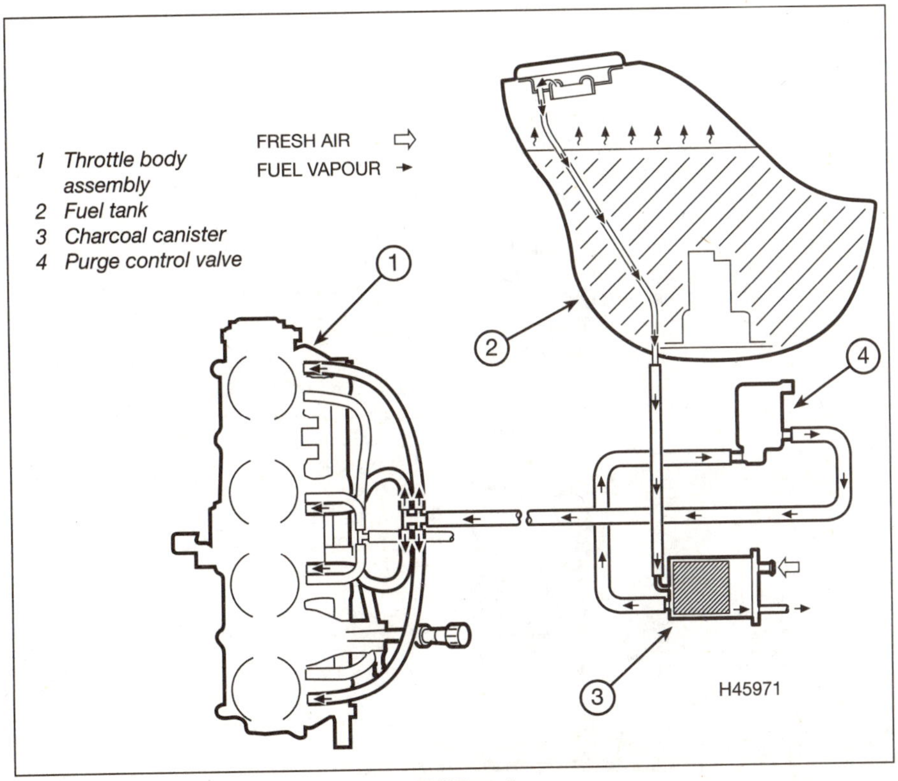

18.1 EVAP system

Testing

Purge control valve

3 Remove the valve from the motorcycle (see below).
4 Check the operation of the control valve by blowing through the intake (canister hose) union; air should not flow from the outlet hose union. Connect battery voltage (12 volts) across the valve terminals and repeat the check; air should flow from the outlet union if it is functioning correctly.
5 If an ohmmeter is available, check the resistance of the control valve windings and compare the reading obtained to that given in the Specifications. Renew the valve if the reading differs.
6 If the valve behaves as described, check for battery voltage using a multimeter across the terminals on the loom side of the valve wiring connector with the engine running. If no voltage is present check the wiring.

Charcoal canister

7 No testing of the canister is possible, if it is thought to be faulty a new one must be installed.

Component renewal

Purge control valve

8 The valve is mounted behind the engine, on the right-hand end of the canister mounting bracket.
9 Disconnect the wiring connector and hoses from the valve, noting which fits where, then unscrew the bolts and remove the valve.
10 Installation is the reverse of removal.

Charcoal canister

11 The canister is mounted behind the engine.
12 Disconnect the hoses, noting which fits where. Unscrew the canister mounting bolts and remove the canister.
13 Installation is the reverse of removal.

19 Catalytic converter

Note: *A catalytic converter is fitted as standard on RR-4 and RR-5 Germany market models and all RR-6 and RR-7 Europe market models, and may be available as standard or as an optional extra in some other markets.*

General information

1 A catalytic converter is incorporated in the exhaust system to minimise the level of exhaust pollutants released into the atmosphere.

2 The catalytic converter consists of a canister containing a fine mesh impregnated with a catalyst material, over which the hot exhaust gases pass. The catalyst speeds up the oxidation of harmful carbon monoxide, unburned hydrocarbons and soot, effectively reducing the quantity of harmful products released into the atmosphere via the exhaust gases.

3 The catalytic converter is of the closed-loop type with exhaust gas oxygen content information being fed back to the engine control module (ECM) by the oxygen sensor.

4 The oxygen sensor contains a heating element which is controlled by the ECM. When the engine is cold, the ECM switches on the heating element which warms the exhaust gases as they pass over the sensor. This brings the catalytic converter quickly up to its normal operating temperature and decreases the level of exhaust pollutants emitted whilst the engine warms up. Once the engine is sufficiently warmed up, the ECM switches off the heating element.

5 Refer to Section 14 for exhaust system removal and installation, and Section 6 for oxygen sensor removal and installation information.

Precautions

6 The catalytic converter is a reliable and simple device which needs no maintenance in itself, but there are some facts of which an owner should be aware if the converter is to function properly for its full service life.

- DO NOT use leaded or lead replacement petrol (gasoline) – the additives will coat the precious metals, reducing their converting efficiency and will eventually destroy the catalytic converter.
- Always keep the ignition and fuel systems well-maintained in accordance with the manufacturer's schedule – if the fuel/air mixture is suspected of being incorrect have it checked on an exhaust gas analyser.
- If the engine develops a misfire, do not ride the bike at all (or at least as little as possible) until the fault is cured.
- DO NOT use fuel or engine oil additives – these may contain substances harmful to the catalytic converter.
- DO NOT continue to use the bike if the engine burns oil to the extent of leaving a visible trail of blue smoke.
- Remember that the catalytic converter and oxygen sensor are FRAGILE – do not strike them with tools during servicing work.

20 Ignition system check

Warning: The energy levels in electronic systems can be very high. On no account should the ignition be switched on whilst the plugs or coils are being held. Shocks from the HT circuit can be most unpleasant. Secondly, it is vital that the engine is not turned over or run with any of the plug caps removed, and that the plugs are soundly earthed (grounded) when the system is checked for sparking. The ignition system components can be seriously damaged if the HT circuit becomes isolated.

1 As no means of adjustment is available, any failure of the system can be traced to failure of a system component or a simple wiring fault. Of the two possibilities, the latter is by far the most likely. In the event of failure, check the system in a logical fashion, as described below.

2 Make sure the ignition is OFF. Working on one ignition coil at a time, disconnect the wiring connector – to access them refer to Section 21, Step 2 **(see illustration)**. Pull the coil off the spark plug **(see illustration)**. Reconnect the wiring connector and connect the coil to a spare spark plug (preferably use a new plug). Earth the plug either against the front of the cylinder head, or to the crankcase earth using an auxiliary wire with a crocodile clip on each end, clipping one end to the spark plug threads. Do not earth the plug against the valve cover. If necessary, hold the spark plug with an insulated tool.

Warning: Do not remove any of the spark plugs from the engine to perform this check – atomised fuel being pumped out of the open spark plug hole could ignite, causing severe injury! Make sure the plugs are securely held against the engine – if they are not earthed when the engine is turned over, the ECM could be damaged.

3 Having observed the above precautions, check that the kill switch is in the RUN position and the transmission is in neutral, then turn the ignition switch ON and turn the engine over on the starter motor. If the system is in good condition a regular, fat blue spark should be evident at the plug electrode. If the spark appears thin or yellowish, or is non-existent, further investigation is necessary. Turn the ignition OFF and repeat the check for each coil.

4 Ignition faults can be divided into two categories, namely those where the ignition system has failed completely, and those which are due to a partial failure. The likely faults are listed below, starting with the most probable source of failure. Work through the list systematically, referring to the subsequent sections for full details of the necessary checks and tests. **Note:** *Before checking the following items ensure that the battery is fully charged and that all fuses are in good condition.*

- Loose, corroded or damaged wiring connections, broken or shorted wiring between any of the component parts of the ignition system (see Chapter 8).
- Faulty spark plug cap connection, faulty spark plug, dirty, worn or corroded plug electrodes.
- Faulty ignition (main) switch or engine kill switch (see Chapter 8).
- Faulty neutral, clutch or sidestand switch (see Chapter 8).
- Faulty crankshaft position (CKP) sensor (Section 6) or damaged triggers on starter clutch body (Chapter 2).
- Faulty engine stop relay (Section 6).
- Faulty ignition coil(s) (Section 21).
- Faulty electronic control module (Section 6).

5 If the above checks don't reveal the cause of the problem, have the ignition system tested by a Honda dealer.

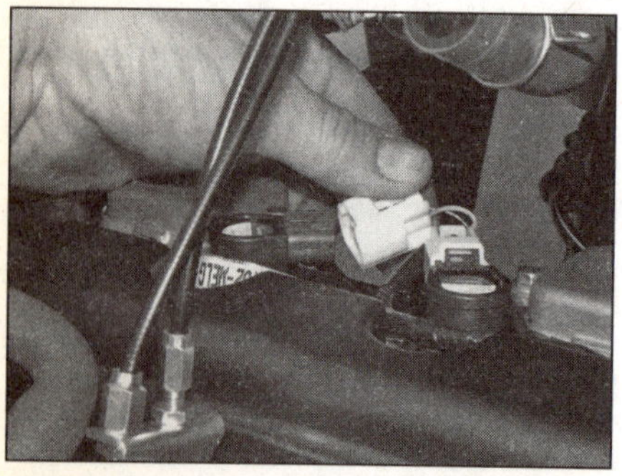

20.2a Disconnect the wiring connector . . .

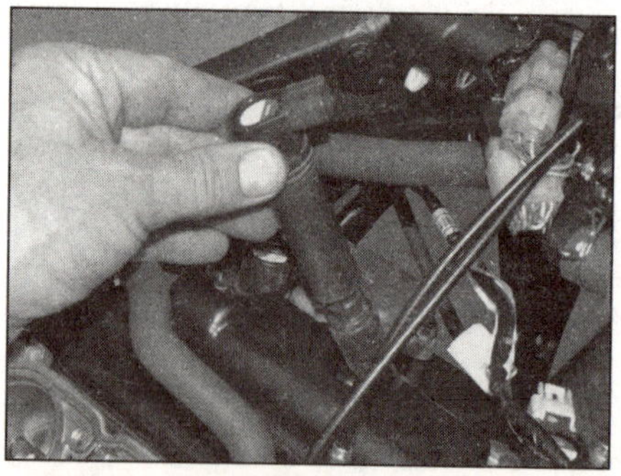

20.2b . . . and pull the coil off the spark plug

21 Ignition coils

Check

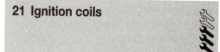

1 Remove the rider's seat (see Chapter 8). Disconnect the battery negative (–) lead.

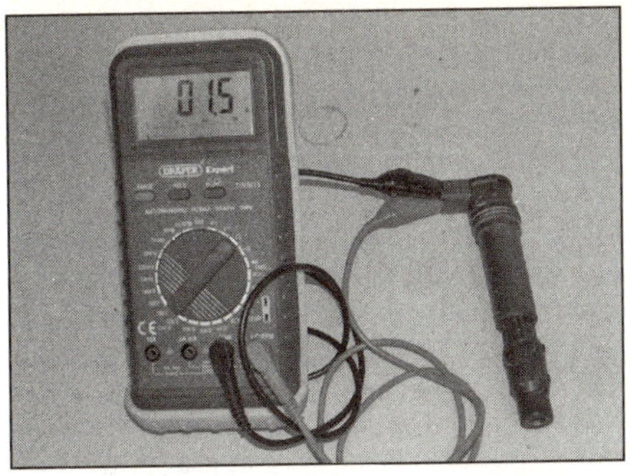

21.5 To test the coil primary resistance, connect the multimeter leads between the connector socket terminals

2 Remove the air filter housing and the air intake duct (see Section 3).

3 Check the coils visually for loose or damaged connectors and terminals, cracks and other damage. Clean the area around each coil to prevent any dirt falling into the spark plug channels.

4 Check that the cylinder location is marked on each coil wiring sleeve, then disconnect the wiring connector from the coil being tested **(see illustration 20.2a)**. Pull the coil off the spark plug **(see illustration 20.2b)**.

5 To check the condition of the primary windings, set a multimeter to the ohms x 1 scale. Connect one meter probe to one terminal in the coil socket and the other probe to the other terminal and measure the resistance **(see illustration)**. If the reading obtained is not within the range given in the Specifications, it is likely that the coil is defective. To confirm this, it must be tested as described below using the specified equipment, or by a Honda dealer.

6 To check the resistance of the secondary windings, set the meter to the K-ohm scale. Connect one meter probe to one of the terminals in the coil socket, and the other to the spark plug contact, using a steel rod or screwdriver as an extension if your probe is not long enough **(see illustration)**. If the reading obtained is not within the range given in the Specifications, it is likely that the coil is defective. To confirm this, the system must be tested by a Honda dealer.

22.4 Unscrew the timing inspection cap

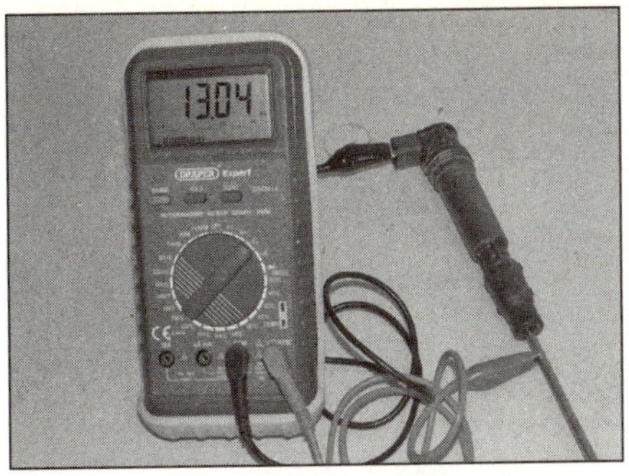

21.6 To test the coil secondary resistance, connect the multimeter leads between one terminal and the spark plug socket

Removal and installation

7 Remove the rider's seat (see Chapter 8). Disconnect the battery negative (-) lead.

8 Remove the air filter housing and the air intake duct (see Section 3).

9 Check that the cylinder location is marked on each coil wiring sleeve, then disconnect the wiring connector from the coil being removed **(see illustration 20.2a)**. Note the orientation of each coil (i.e. which way the wiring connector points), then pull the coil off the spark plug **(see illustration 20.2b)**.

10 Installation is the reverse of removal.

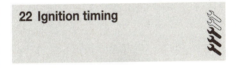

22 Ignition timing

General information

1 Since no provision exists for adjusting the ignition timing and since no component is subject to mechanical wear, there is no need for regular checks; only if investigating a fault such as a loss of power or a misfire should the ignition timing be checked.

2 The ignition timing is checked dynamically (engine running) using a stroboscopic lamp. The inexpensive neon lamps should be adequate in theory, but in practice may produce a pulse of such low intensity that the timing mark remains indistinct. If possible, one of the more precise xenon tube lamps should be used, powered by an external source of the appropriate voltage. Whatever type is used make sure it is capable of picking up the pulse from the low tension side of the coil rather than the high tension, as there are no HT leads on this machine. **Note:** *Do not use the machine's own battery as an incorrect reading may result from stray impulses within the machine's electrical system.*

22.5a Static timing mark alignment on RR-4 and RR-5 models (arrowed)

Check

3 Warm the engine up to normal operating temperature then stop it. Remove the lower fairing (see Chapter 7).

4 Unscrew the timing inspection cap from the clutch cover **(see illustration)**. Discard the O-ring as a new one must be used.

5 The dynamic timing mark on the rotor which indicates the firing point at idle speed for the No. 1 cylinder is the line next to the F mark on RR-4 and RR-5 models **(see illustration)** and mid-point between the lines next to the T and F marks on RR-6 and RR-7 models. The static timing mark with which this should align is the notch in the inspection hole rim.

> **HAYNES HiNT** ***The timing marks can be highlighted with white paint to make them more visible under the stroboscope light.***

6 Remove the air filter housing and air intake duct (see Section 3) – just displace the radiator from its mounts, leaving the hoses connected, rather than removing it completely. Connect the timing light to the No. 1 cylinder coil blue/black wire, then refit the duct and air filter housing.

7 Start the engine and aim the light at the static timing mark.

8 With the machine idling, the timing mark should align with the notch (see Step 5). Now increase engine speed to approximately 2500 rpm. At this point the dynamic timing mark should move anti-clockwise in relation to the static mark. This confirms the ignition is advancing.

9 As already stated, there is no means of adjustment of the ignition timing. If the ignition timing is incorrect, or suspected of being incorrect, one of the ignition system components is at fault, and the system must

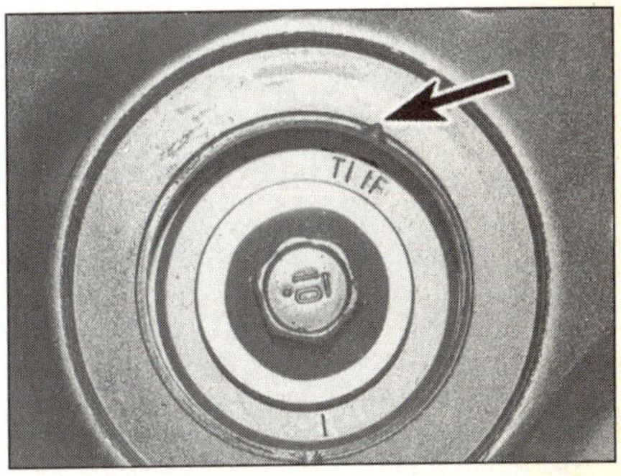

22.5b Static timing mark alignment on RR-6 and RR-7 models (arrowed)

be tested as described in the preceding Sections of this Chapter.

10 When the check is complete, install the timing inspection cap using a new O-ring, and smear it and the cap threads with grease **(see illustration 22.4)**. Tighten the cap to the torque setting specified at the beginning of the Chapter.

23 Immobiliser system

General information

1 An immobiliser system (known as HISS – Honda Ignition Security System) is fitted in certain markets as an anti-theft device. The system will only allow the machine to be started if the correct registered key is used to turn the ignition ON. The system consists of a transponder which is part of the ignition key, a receiver which is fitted around the ignition switch **(see illustration 23.52)**, and the electronic control module (ECM).

2 When the ignition is switched ON, the ECM sends power through the receiver to the transponder. The transponder sends a coded signal back through the receiver to the ECM. If the signal sent by the transponder matches the signal stored in the ECM memory, the HISS immobiliser indicator light in the instrument cluster comes on for two seconds, then goes out, and the ECM allows the engine to be started. If the key code signal is not recognised, or if there is a fault in the system, the indicator light stays on. If the light stays on, refer to the fault diagnosis and troubleshooting Sections below. Likewise if the light does not come on at all.

3 The ECM can store the codes for up to four registered keys. They keys should be kept separately (i.e. not on the same key-ring) as the proximity of another key to the one being used in the switch can lead to the signal from it being jammed, and the bike will not start. The key has a built in transponder which can be damaged if the key is dropped or knocked, gets too hot, is too close to a magnetic object, or is submerged in water for too long. If all the keys are lost, the ECM must be replaced with a new one, so always make sure you have at least one spare key. If a new key is obtained, it must be registered into the system before the bike can be started with the key.

Key registration procedure

With old ignition switch

Note: *The following procedures refer to the Honda special tool (Part No. 07XMZ-MBW0101) which is a wiring loom adapter that connects to a battery and plugs into the loom side of the crankshaft position (CKP) sensor wiring connector.*

4 Obtain a new key from a Honda dealer, and have it cut to match the original key.

5 Remove the right-hand fairing side panel (see Chapter 7). Trace the crankshaft position (CKP) sensor wiring from the top of the clutch cover and disconnect it at the red 2-pin wiring connector **(see illustration 6.51a or b)**. Connect the special tool wiring connector to the loom side of the connector, then connect the red coloured clip of the tool to the battery positive (+) terminal and the green coloured clip to the battery negative (–) terminal.

6 Turn the ignition switch ON using your original key. The immobiliser indicator light should come on and stay on (if it starts to flash after ten seconds, then there is a fault in the system, which will have gone into fault diagnosis, and the pattern of the flashes it emits should be matched with the fault code (see below)). Now disconnect the red clip from the battery positive terminal and leave it disconnected for at least two seconds, then reconnect it. The indicator should now come on for two seconds, then begin to flash repeatedly four times. This indicates that the system is in registration mode. At this point the registrations of all keys except the one in the switch will have been cancelled, so if you have another spare apart from the new one you want to register, this will also have to be registered.

7 Turn the ignition OFF and remove the original key, placing it well away from the receiver.

8 Insert the new key into the switch and turn it ON. The indicator should now come on for four seconds, then begin to flash repeatedly four times. This indicates that the system has registered the new key. Turn the ignition OFF and remove the key.

9 To register any other spare keys that will have been cancelled, repeat Step 8. Up to four keys can be registered.

10 On completion turn the ignition OFF, then remove the special tool and reconnect the crankshaft position (CKP) sensor wiring connector. Now turn the ignition ON using any of the registered keys to return the system to normal mode.

11 Check that all registered keys can start the motorcycle.

With a new ignition switch

12 Obtain a new switch and two (or more) new keys.

13 Remove the faulty switch (see Chapter 8), but retain the HISS receiver to fit with the new switch.

14 Remove the right-hand fairing side panel (see Chapter 7). Trace the crankshaft position (CKP) sensor wiring from the top of the clutch cover and disconnect it at the red 2-pin wiring connector **(see illustration 6.51a or b)**. Connect the special tool wiring connector (see **Note** above) to the loom side of the connector, then connect the red coloured clip of the tool to the battery positive (+) terminal and the green coloured clip to the battery negative (–) terminal.

15 Place one of the original registered keys for the faulty switch next to the receiver.

16 Connect the new ignition switch to its connector in the wiring loom, but keep it away from the receiver. Turn the new switch ON with one of the new keys. The immobiliser indicator light should come on and stay on, which means the ECM recognises the old key that is next to the receiver (if it starts to flash after ten seconds, then there is a fault in the system, which will have gone into fault diagnosis, and the pattern of the flashes it emits should be matched with the fault code (see below)). Now disconnect the red clip from the battery positive terminal and leave it disconnected for at least two seconds, then reconnect it. The indicator should now come on for two seconds, then begin to flash repeatedly four times. This indicates that the system is in registration mode. At this point the registrations of all keys except the one near the receiver will have been cancelled.

17 Turn the ignition OFF and remove the new key.

18 Install the new ignition switch, then fit the receiver onto it (see Chapter 8).

19 Insert the new key into the switch and turn it ON. The indicator should now come on for four seconds, then begin to flash repeatedly four times. This indicates that the system has registered the new key. If the indicator starts to flash after ten seconds, then there is a fault in the system, which will have gone into fault diagnosis, and the pattern of the flashes it emits should be matched with the fault code (see below). Turn the ignition OFF and disconnect the red clip of the special tool from the battery positive terminal.

20 Turn the ignition ON using the newly registered key. The indicator light should come on for two seconds, then go off.

21 Turn the ignition OFF and reconnect the red clip to the battery positive terminal.

22 Turn the ignition ON using the newly registered key. The indicator light should come on and stay on. Now disconnect the red clip from the battery positive terminal and leave it disconnected for at least two seconds, then reconnect it. The indicator should now come on for two seconds, then begin to flash repeatedly four times. This indicates that the system is in registration mode. At this point the registrations of all old keys (for the faulty switch) are cancelled.

23 Turn the ignition OFF and remove the key, placing it well away from the receiver.

24 Insert the second new unregistered key and turn the ignition ON. The indicator should now come on for four seconds, then begin to flash repeatedly four times. This indicates that the system has registered the second new key. Turn the ignition OFF and remove the key.

25 To register any other new spare keys, repeat Step 24. Up to four keys can be registered.

26 On completion turn the ignition OFF, then remove the special tool and reconnect the CKP sensor wiring connector. Now turn the ignition ON using any of the registered keys to return the system to normal mode.
27 Check that all newly registered keys can start the motorcycle.

With a new ECM (electronic control module)

28 Obtain a new ECM along with two new keys. Install the new ECM (see Section 6). Have the keys cut to match the original key for your ignition switch.
29 Insert a new key into the switch and turn it ON. The indicator should now come on for two seconds, then begin to flash repeatedly four times. This indicates that the system has registered the new key. If the indicator stays on for ten seconds then starts to flash, then there is a fault in the system, which will have gone into fault diagnosis, and the pattern of the flashes it emits should be matched with the fault code (see below).
30 Turn the ignition OFF and remove the key.
31 Insert the second new key and turn the ignition ON. The indicator should now come on for two seconds, then begin to flash repeatedly four times. This indicates that the system has registered the second new key.
32 Turn the ignition OFF and remove the key.
33 The new ECM will only register two new keys at this stage. If you have a third key to register, refer to Steps 4 to 10 to register it, noting that you will need the special tool mentioned therein.
34 Check that both newly registered keys can start the motorcycle.

Fault diagnosis

35 There are two fault diagnosis modes, one for faults which occur during normal use, and one for a fault that occurs when registering a new key. Make sure you refer to the correct table below when matching the fault code pattern.
36 If the indicator light has come on and stayed on during normal use, remove the right-hand fairing side panel (see Chapter 7). Trace the crankshaft position (CKP) sensor wiring from the top of the clutch cover and disconnect it at the red 2-pin wiring connector **(see illustration 6.51a or b)**. Connect the special tool wiring connector (see **Note** above) to the loom side of the connector, then connect the red coloured clip of the tool to the battery positive (+) terminal and the green coloured clip to the battery negative (–) terminal.
37 Turn the ignition switch ON. The indicator light will come on for ten seconds, then start to flash. This means it has entered diagnostic mode, and the pattern of the flashes indicates the fault that has occurred. The pattern repeats continuously. Match the pattern with the fault codes below, making sure you refer to the relevant table. If the indicator stays on after ten seconds and does not flash, then there is no fault logged in the system.

If fault is indicated during normal use		
Flash pattern	**Fault**	**Solution**
Two short, one long, one short	Faulty ECM	Install new ECM
Two short, two long	Faulty receiver or wiring	Follow Troubleshooting procedure below
One long, three short	Signal jammed by other key	Place other key well away from receiver
One long, two short, one long	Signal jammed by other key	Place other key well away from receiver

If fault is indicated during key registration		
Flash pattern	**Fault**	**Solution**
One short, one long, one short, one long	Key already registered	Use a new or cancelled key
Two short, two long	Faulty receiver or wiring	Follow *Troubleshooting* procedure below
One short, one long, two short	Key already registered on old ECM	Use a new key

Troubleshooting procedure

Indicator light does not come on when ignition switched ON

38 Check the fuses (see Chapter 8).
39 If the fuses are good, make sure the engine is in neutral then turn the ignition ON and check whether the neutral warning light has come on.
40 If the light has not come on, remove the windshield (see Chapter 7). Pull back the rubber boot on the instrument cluster wiring connector. Using a voltmeter, connect the positive (+) probe to the red/green wire terminal on the loom side of the instrument cluster connector and the negative (–) probe to the green wire terminal on the loom side of the connector. With the ignition ON there should be battery voltage. If voltage is present, the instrument cluster is faulty (see Chapter 8). If there is no voltage, check for continuity in the wiring, referring to the wiring diagrams at the end of Chapter 8. The green wire goes to earth (ground).
41 If the light has come on, refer to Section 6 to access the ECM and disconnect the ECM black wiring connector **(see illustration 6.84b)**. Using a voltmeter, connect the positive (+) probe to the white/red wire terminal on the loom side of the ECM connector and the negative (–) probe to earth (ground). Turn the ignition ON – there should be battery voltage.
42 If there was no voltage, using a voltmeter, connect the positive (+) probe to the white/red wire terminal on the instrument cluster connector and the negative (–) probe to earth. Turn the ignition ON – there should be no voltage for two seconds, then there should be battery voltage. If there is no voltage after two seconds, check for continuity in the white/red wire, and also in the green wire to earth, referring to the wiring diagrams at the end of Chapter 8. If voltage is present, the instrument cluster is faulty (see Chapter 8).
43 If there is voltage in Step 41, disconnect the ECM light grey wiring connector. Using a voltmeter, connect the positive (+) probe to the black/white (ECM) wire terminal on the loom side of the ECM connector and the negative (–) probe to earth (ground). Turn the ignition ON – there should be battery voltage. If there is no voltage, check for continuity in the black/white wire, and in the red/white wire between the battery and engine stop relay, referring to the wiring diagrams at the end of Chapter 8, and also check the 20A fuse (Chapter 8) and the engine stop relay (Section 6). If voltage is present, check for continuity to earth (ground) in the green/pink wire. If the wiring is good, check the ECM connector for loose, damaged or corroded terminals. If the connector is good, then the ECM could be faulty, and should be checked by a Honda dealer.

Indicator light stays on when ignition switched ON

44 Check that none of the other registered keys are close to the receiver. If they are, remove them and try the ignition again.
45 Turn the ignition ON with a spare key and check the indicator light, which should come on for two seconds, then go out. If it does, the first key is faulty. If it doesn't, perform the fault diagnosis procedure described above. If a fault code is displayed, use the appropriate table to determine the fault and the solution.
46 If no fault code is displayed, or the system does not go into fault diagnosis mode, refer to Section 6 to access the ECM and disconnect the ECM black wiring connector **(see illustration 6.84b)**. Using a voltmeter, connect the positive (+) probe to the white/red wire terminal on the loom side of the connector and the negative (–) probe to earth (ground). Turn the ignition ON – there should be battery voltage. If there is no voltage, check for continuity in the white/red wire between the ECM and the indicator unit.
47 If there is voltage, check for continuity

23.48 HISS receiver wiring connector (arrowed)

23.52 HISS receiver (A). Undo the screw (B) on each side

in the yellow and white/black wires between the ECM and the crankshaft position (CKP) sensor, referring to the wiring diagrams at the end of Chapter 8. If there is no continuity, trace the fault and repair or replace the wiring as necessary. If there is continuity, the ECM could be faulty and should be taken to a Honda dealer for assessment.

Fault code indicated by flash pattern

48 If the 'two short, two long' flash pattern has been indicated during the fault diagnosis procedure, remove the air filter housing (see Section 3). Trace the wiring from the receiver on the ignition switch and disconnect it at the 4-pin connector on the left-hand side of the steering head **(see illustration)**. Using a voltmeter, connect the positive (+) probe to the yellow/red wire terminal on the loom side of the receiver connector and the negative (–) probe to earth (ground). Turn the ignition ON – there should be approximately 5 volts present. If there is no voltage, check for continuity in the yellow/red wire between the ECM and the receiver, and repair or replace the wiring if there is no continuity.

49 If there is 5 volts present, check for continuity to earth (ground) in the grey/black wire on the loom side of the connector, and repair or replace the wiring if there is no continuity.

50 If the wiring is good, using a voltmeter, connect the positive (+) probe to the pink wire terminal on the loom side of the receiver connector and the negative (–) probe to earth (ground). Turn the ignition ON – there should be approximately 5 volts present. If there is, the receiver is faulty.

51 If there is no voltage, check for continuity in the blue/orange and pink wires between the ECM and the receiver, and repair or replace the wiring if there is no continuity between the connectors, or if there is continuity in either to earth (ground). If the wiring is good, the receiver is faulty.

Replacement

52 To replace the receiver, remove the air filter housing (see Section 3). Trace the wiring from the receiver on the ignition switch and disconnect it at the 4-pin connector on the left-hand side of the steering head **(see illustration 23.48)**. Feed the wiring back to the receiver, freeing it from any ties and noting its routing. Undo the screws and remove the receiver, noting how it fits **(see illustration)**. If you don't have the correct tools to easily access the screws, removing the fairing will help (see Chapter 7), otherwise follow the procedure for removing the top yoke in the ignition switch replacement section in Chapter 8.

53 To replace the ECM see Section 6.

Chapter 5
Frame and suspension

Contents

Section number

Degrees of difficulty

Easy, suitable for novice with little experience	**Fairly easy,** suitable for beginner with some experience	**Fairly difficult,** suitable for competent DIY mechanic	**Difficult,** suitable for experienced DIY mechanic	**Very difficult,** suitable for expert DIY or professional

Specifications

Front forks

Fork oil type	
European models	Honda Ultra Cushion 10W oil or equivalent 10W fork oil
US models	Pro-Honda SS-55 suspension fluid or equivalent 10W fork oil
Fork oil capacity	
RR-4 and RR-5 models	466 ± 2.5 cc
RR-6 and RR-7 models	471 ± 2.5 cc
Fork oil level*	
RR-4 and RR-5 models	90 mm
RR-6 and RR-7 models	86 mm
Fork spring free length (min)	
RR-4 and RR-5 models	
Standard	218.2 mm
Service limit	213.8 mm
RR-6 and RR-7 models	
Standard	215.2 mm
Service limit	210.9 mm
Fork tube runout limit	0.2 mm

**Oil level is measured from the top of the tube with the fork spring removed and the leg fully compressed.*

Steering head bearings

Bearing pre-load (see text)	
RR-4 and RR-5 models	12 to 19 N
RR-6 and RR-7 models	13 to 19 N

Steering damper (HESD)

Solenoid valve resistance	6 to 8 ohms

Torque settings

Clutch master cylinder clamp bolts	12 Nm
Drive chain slider bolts	9 Nm
Footrest bracket-to-frame bolts	37 Nm
Fork damper cartridge bolt	34 Nm
Fork top bolt	34 Nm
Fork yoke clamp bolts	
Top yoke bolts	23 Nm
Bottom yoke bolts	
RR-4 and RR-5 models	23 Nm
RR-6 and RR-7 models	26 Nm
Front brake master cylinder clamp bolts	12 Nm
Gearchange lever pivot bolt	22 Nm
Handlebar clamp bolts	26 Nm
Handlebar end-weight screws	10 Nm
Shock absorber bolts/nuts	44 Nm
Sidestand bracket bolts	54 Nm
Sidestand pivot bolt	10 Nm
Sidestand pivot bolt nut	29 Nm
Steering damper mounting bolts and linkage arm bolt	9 Nm
Steering head bearing adjuster nut	
RR-4 and RR-5 models	20 Nm
RR-6 and RR-7 models	27 Nm
Steering stem nut	103 Nm
Suspension linkage bolt nuts	44 Nm
Swingarm adjuster bolt	15 Nm
Swingarm adjuster bolt locknut	
Actual	64 Nm
Indicated (with special tool)	58 Nm
Swingarm pivot bolt nut	113 Nm

1 General information

All models have a box-section twin-spar aluminium frame which uses the engine as a stressed member.

Front suspension is by a pair of upside-down oil-damped telescopic forks that have a cartridge damper and are adjustable for spring pre-load and both rebound and compression damping.

Steering is damped by Honda's electronic steering damper (HESD), that adjusts the amount of damping according to the speed and rate of acceleration of the bike. Information is obtained from the speed sensor and used by the ECM, which then adjusts a valve in the damper to control the amount of fluid that can pass through. As the steering is turned a vane moves through an oil bath in the damper, sending oil from one side of the bath to the other via the valve.

At the rear, a box-section aluminium swingarm acts on a single shock absorber via a three-way linkage. The arrangement mimics the floating design used for the RC211V MotoGP bike by incorporating the upper shock absorber mount in the swingarm as opposed to it being bolted to the frame. The swingarm pivots through both the frame and the engine. The shock absorber is adjustable for spring pre-load and both rebound and compression damping.

2 Frame inspection and repair

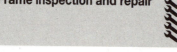

1 The frame should not require attention unless accident damage has occurred. In most cases, fitting a new frame is the only satisfactory remedy for such damage. A few frame specialists have the jigs and other equipment necessary for straightening frames to the required standard of accuracy, but even then there is no simple way of assessing to what extent the frame may have been over stressed.

2 After a high mileage, the frame should be examined closely for signs of cracking or splitting at the welded joints. Loose engine mounting bolts can cause ovaling or fracturing of the mounting points. Minor damage can often be repaired by specialised welding, depending on the extent and nature of the damage.

3 Remember that a frame that is out of alignment will cause handling problems. If, as the result of an accident, misalignment is suspected, it will be necessary to strip the machine completely so the frame can be thoroughly checked.

3 Footrests, brake pedal and gearchange lever

Footrests

Removal

1 Remove the split pin and washer from the bottom of the footrest pivot pin, then withdraw

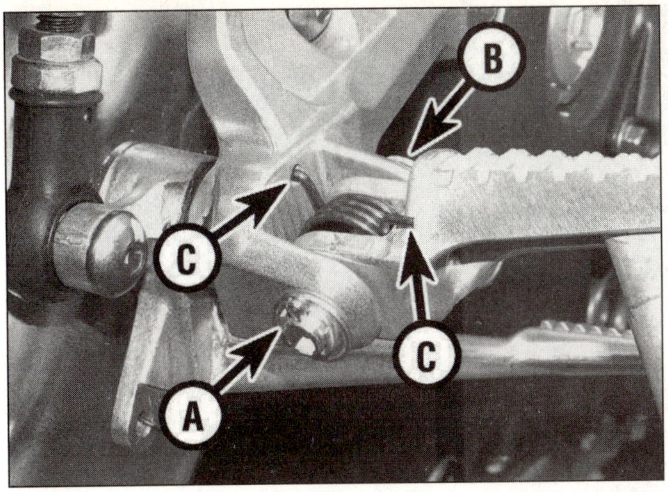

3.1a Split pin and washer (A), pivot pin (B), return spring ends (C) – rider's footrests

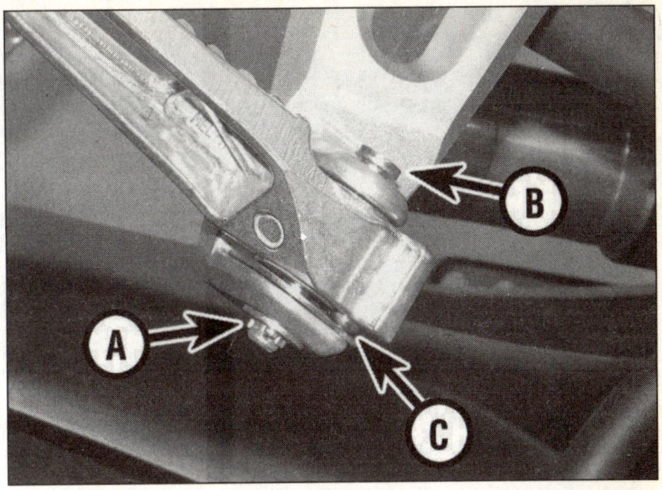

3.1b Split pin and washer (A), pivot pin (B), detent plate, ball and spring (C) – passenger footrests

the pivot pin and remove the footrest **(see illustrations)**. On the rider's footrests, note the fitting of the return spring. On the passenger footrests, note the fitting of the detent plate, ball and spring, and take care not to let the ball and spring ping away when removing the footrest.

Installation

2 Installation is the reverse of removal. Apply a small amount of copper-based grease to the pivot pin.

Brake pedal

Removal

3 Undo the two screws securing the outer exhaust guard, noting the collar with the lower screw **(see illustration)**. Pull the guard away to release the peg from the grommet **(see illustration)**.

4 Unscrew the bolts securing the rider's footrest bracket, then release the assembly from the retainer on the inner exhaust guard and turn it so the inside is accessible, making sure you don't strain the brake hoses or brake light switch wiring **(see illustration)**.

5 Remove the split pin from the bolt securing the brake pedal to the master cylinder pushrod, then unscrew the nut, withdraw the bolt and remove the washers **(see illustrations)**. Detach the pushrod from the pedal.

6 Unhook the brake pedal return spring and the brake light switch spring from the hook on the pedal **(see illustration)**.

7 Remove the circlip securing the brake pedal, then remove the washer **(see illustration 3.6)**. Slide the pedal off its pivot, and remove the wave washer.

Installation

8 Installation is the reverse of removal, noting the following:

- Apply grease to the pedal pivot and washers – clean off any old grease first.
- Slide the wave washer onto the pivot, followed by the pedal and the thrust washer. Make sure the circlip locates correctly in the

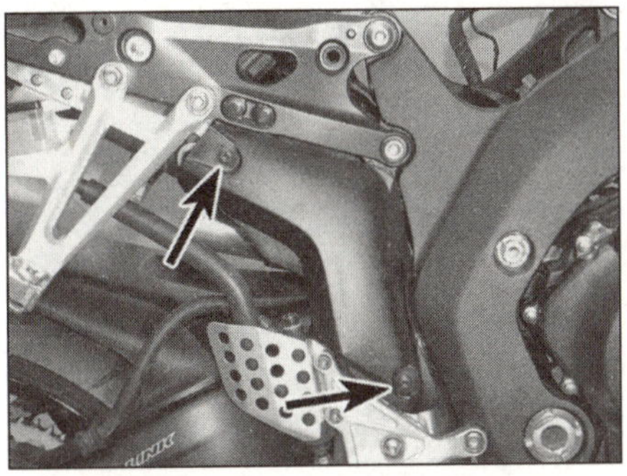

3.3a Undo the screws (arrowed) . . .

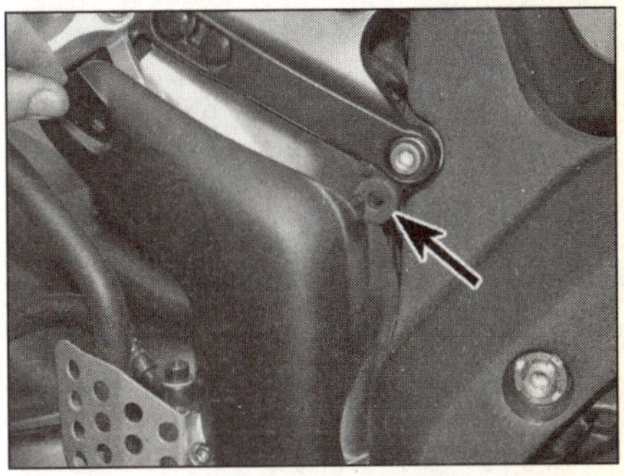

3.3b . . . and release the peg from the grommet (arrowed)

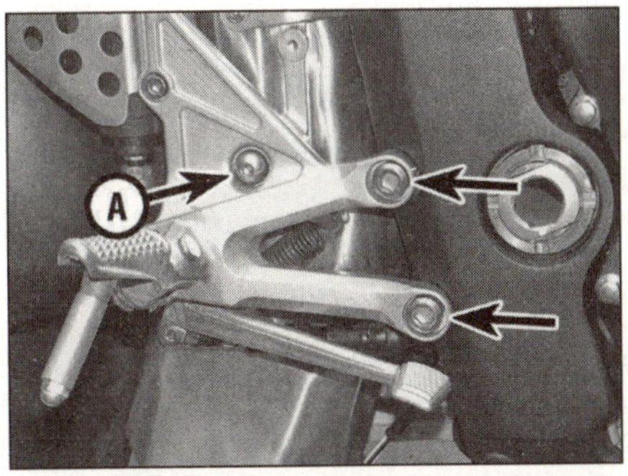

3.4 Footrest bracket bolts (arrowed) – bolt A on RR-6 and RR-7 models only

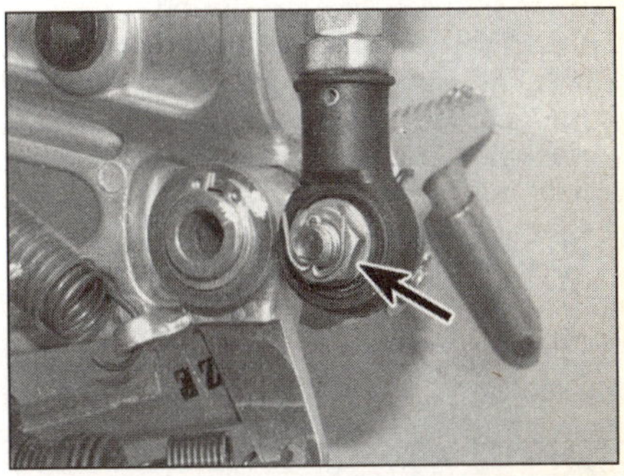

3.5a Remove the split pin then unscrew the nut (arrowed) and remove the washer

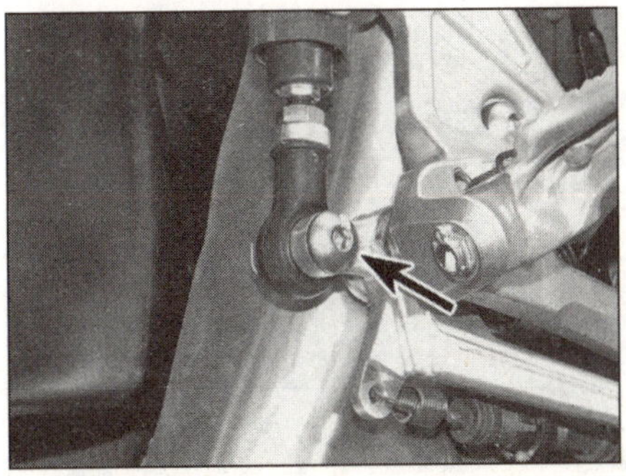

3.5b Withdraw the bolt (arrowed) with the washer

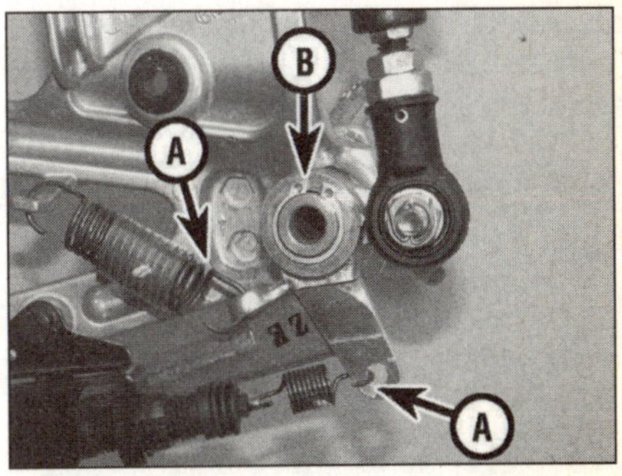

3.6 Unhook the springs (A), then remove the circlip (B) and slide the pedal off

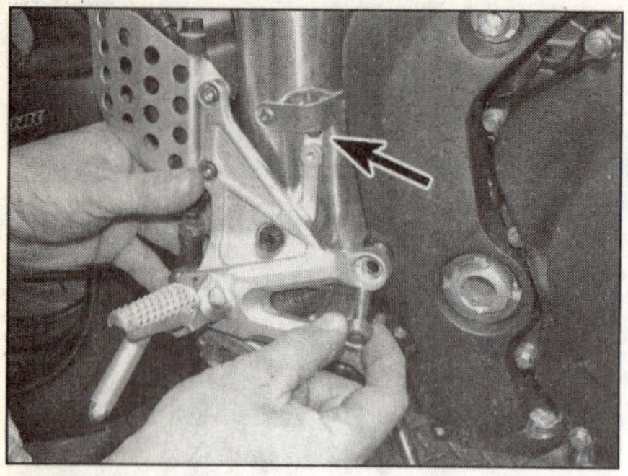

3.8 Make sure the lug locates behind the retainer (arrowed)

3.10 Slacken the locknuts (arrowed) and thread the rod out

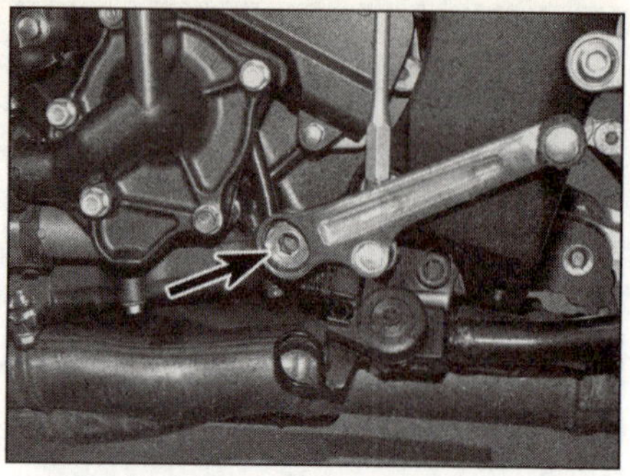

3.11 Unscrew the bolt (arrowed) and remove the lever

groove, and use a new one if the old one deformed when removed.
- Make sure the footrest bracket locates correctly in its retainer on the inner guard **(see illustration)**.
- Tighten the footrest bracket-to-frame bolts to the torque setting specified at the beginning of the Chapter.
- Use a new split pin on the bolt securing the brake pedal to the master cylinder pushrod.
- Check the operation of the rear brake light switch (see Chapter 1).

Gearchange lever and linkage

Removal

9 To avoid the possibility of damage, remove the lower fairing (see Chapter 7).

10 Counter-hold the gearchange lever linkage rod using a spanner on its flats and slacken the locknuts. Unscrew the rod and separate it from the lever and the arm – the rod is reverse-threaded on one end and will simultaneously unscrew from both lever and arm when turned in the one direction **(see illustration)**. Note how far the rod is threaded onto the lever and arm as this determines the height of the lever relative to the footrest.

11 Unscrew the gearchange lever pivot bolt and remove the lever, noting the wave washer and thrust washer **(see illustration)**.

Installation

12 Installation is the reverse of removal, noting the following:
- Apply grease to the pivot section on the bolt.
- Slide the wave washer onto the pivot section, followed by the lever and the thrust washer.
- Tighten the pivot bolt to the torque setting specified at the beginning of the Chapter.
- Adjust the gear lever height as required by screwing the linkage rod in or out of the lever and arm. Tighten the locknuts securely, counter-holding the rod.

4 Sidestand

Removal

1 The sidestand is attached to a bracket that bolts onto the frame. Springs anchored between the stand and its bracket ensure the stand is held in the retracted or extended position. Support the bike on an auxiliary stand. Remove the lower fairing (see Chapter 7).

2 To remove the sidestand without its bracket, first unscrew the sidestand switch bolt and displace the switch – there is no need to disconnect its wiring connector or remove it completely, just let it hang from its wiring **(see illustration)**. Unhook the stand springs, then unscrew the nut from the pivot bolt **(see illustration)**. Unscrew the pivot bolt and remove the stand.

3 To remove the complete sidestand assembly first remove the gearchange lever (see Section 3). Unscrew the sidestand switch bolt and displace the switch – there is no need to disconnect its wiring connector or remove it completely, just let it hang from its wiring **(see illustration 4.2a)**. Unscrew the sidestand bracket bolts and remove the stand assembly **(see illustration)**.

Installation

4 If the stand was removed without its bracket, apply grease to the pivot bolt shank and tighten the bolt to the torque setting specified at the beginning of the Chapter. Fit the nut and tighten it to the specified torque. Fit the sidestand switch **(see illustration 4.2a)**. Reconnect the springs and check that they hold the stand securely up when not in use – an accident is almost certain to occur if the stand extends while the machine is in motion **(see illustration 4.2b)**.

5 If the complete sidestand assembly was removed, clean the threads of the bracket bolts and apply a suitable non-permanent thread locking compound. Install the assembly and tighten the bolts to the torque setting specified at the beginning of the Chapter **(see illustration 4.3)**. Fit the sidestand switch **(see illustration 4.2a)**. Install the gearchange lever (see Section 3). Check the operation of the switch (see Chapter 1).

5 Handlebars and levers

1 As a precaution, remove the fuel tank cover (see Chapter 4) and the fairing (see Chapter 7). Though not actually necessary, this will

4.2a Sidestand switch bolt (arrowed)

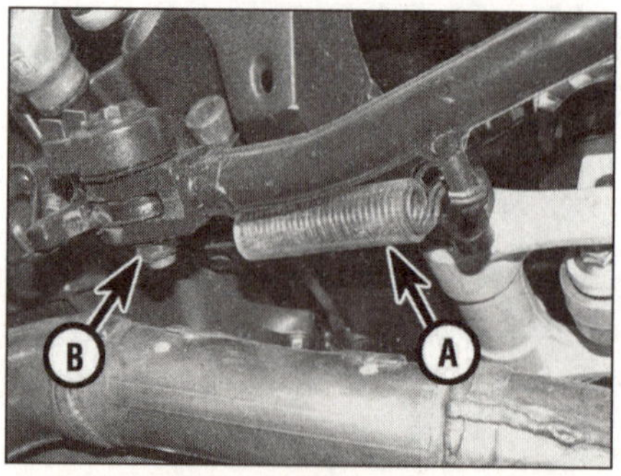

4.2b Unhook the springs (A). Stand pivot bolt nut (B)

4.3 Sidestand bracket bolts (arrowed)

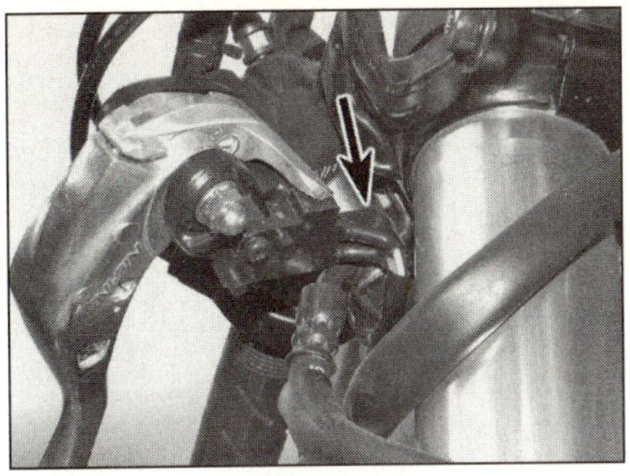

5.2a Disconnect the wiring connectors (arrowed)

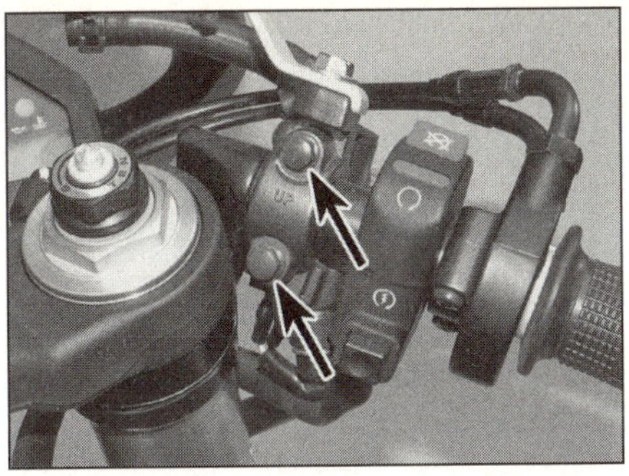

5.2b Unscrew the master cylinder clamp bolts (arrowed) and displace the assembly

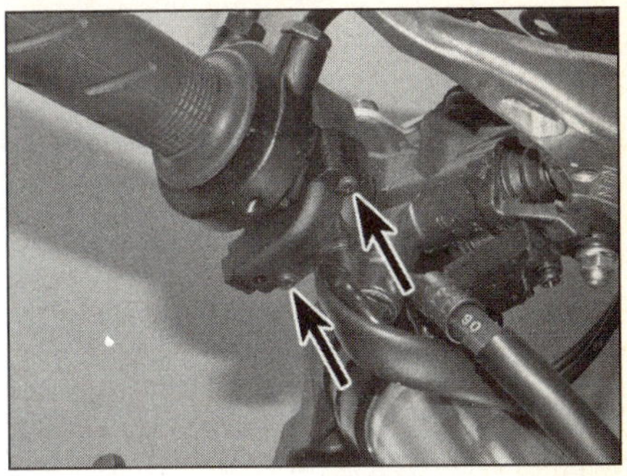

5.3 Undo the screws (arrowed) and detach the switch housing

5.4 Throttle pulley housing screws (arrowed)

5.5 Handlebar end-weight screw (arrowed)

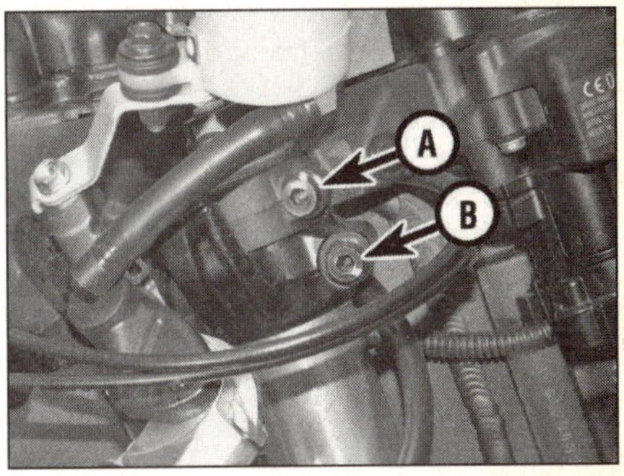

5.6 Slacken the fork clamp bolt (A) on each side. Handlebar clamp bolt (B)

prevent the possibility of damage should a tool slip.

Right handlebar removal

2 Disconnect the wires from the brake light switch **(see illustration)**. Unscrew the two master cylinder assembly clamp bolts and position the assembly clear of the handlebar, making sure no strain is placed on the hydraulic hose **(see illustration)**. Keep the master cylinder reservoir upright to prevent possible fluid leakage.

3 Unscrew the two handlebar switch housing screws and separate the halves **(see illustration)**.

4 Unscrew the throttle pulley housing screws and detach the rear of the housing **(see illustration)**.

5 Unscrew the handlebar end-weight retaining screw, then remove the weight and its rubber washer from the end of the handlebar **(see illustration)**.

6 Remove the steering damper (see Section 11). Slacken both fork clamp bolts in the top yoke **(see illustration)**.

7 Unscrew the steering stem nut and on RR-6 and RR-7 models remove the washer **(see illustration)**. Ease the yoke up and off the forks and lay it aside on some rag **(see illustration)**. To remove the top yoke from the bike rather than just displace it, remove the air filter housing (see Chapter 4), then trace the wiring from the ignition switch, and where fitted the HISS receiver, and disconnect it/them at the connector(s) **(see illustration 9.3)**. Release the wiring from any clips or ties and feed it through to the yoke.

8 Slacken the handlebar clamp bolt **(see illustration 5.6)**, then ease the handlebar up and off the fork **(see illustration)**. Slide the throttle twistgrip off the handlebar. Note the handlebar stopper ring in the fork groove **(see illustration 6.5c)**.

Left handlebar removal

9 Disconnect the wires from the clutch switch

5.7a Unscrew the nut . . .

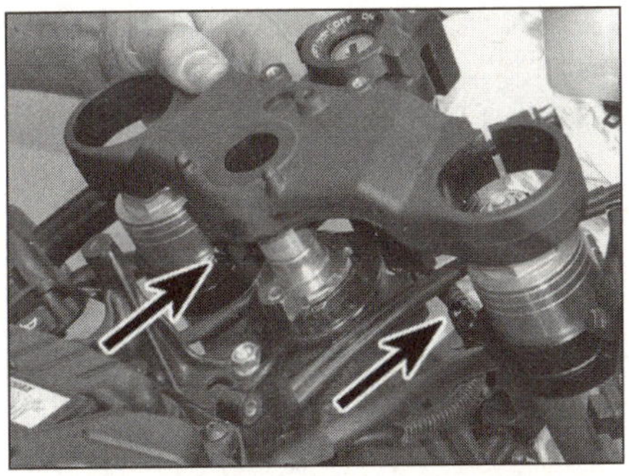

5.7b . . . and ease the yoke up and off the forks. Note the lug (arrowed) on each handlebar and how it locates in the underside of the yoke

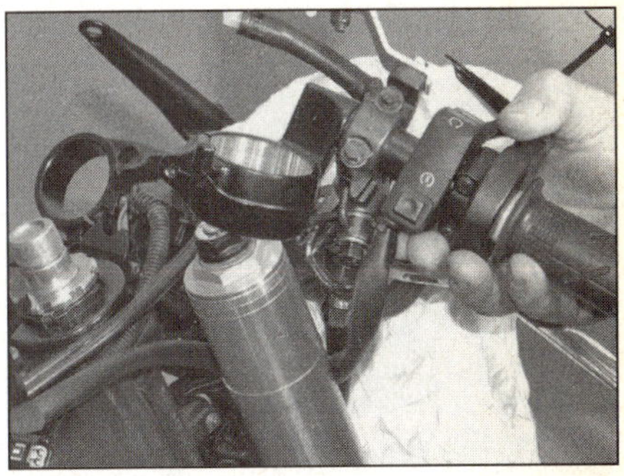

5.8 Slide the handlebar up and off the fork

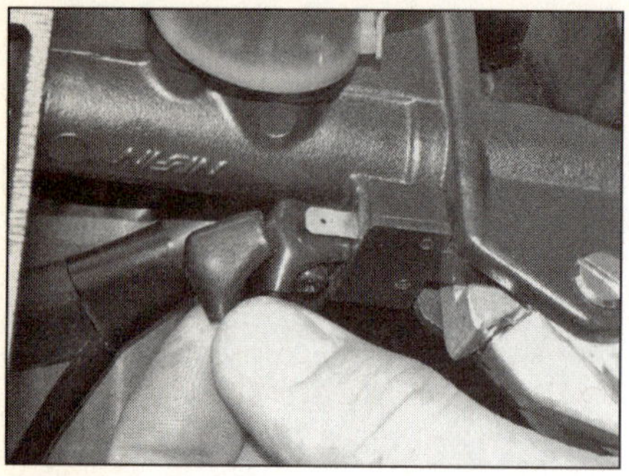

5.9a Disconnect the wiring connectors

5.9b Unscrew the master cylinder clamp bolts (arrowed) and displace the assembly

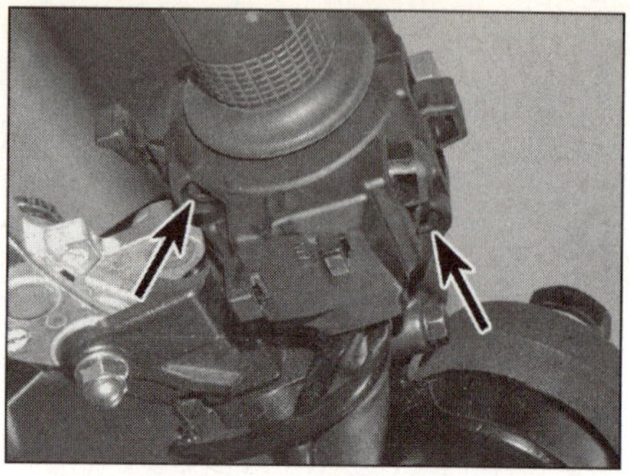

5.10 Undo the screws (arrowed) and detach the switch housing

(see illustration). Unscrew the two master cylinder assembly clamp bolts and position the assembly clear of the handlebar, making sure no strain is placed on the hydraulic hose **(see illustration)**. Keep the master cylinder reservoir upright to prevent possible fluid leakage.

10 Unscrew the two handlebar switch housing screws and separate the halves **(see illustration)**.

11 If required, unscrew the handlebar end-weight retaining screw, then remove the weight and its rubber washer from the end of the handlebar **(see illustration)**. Slide off the grip – if it has been glued on, you will probably have to slit it with a knife to remove it, which means replacing it with a new one. Also slide the switch housing end cover off.

12 Refer to Steps 6 and 7 and displace or remove the top yoke.

13 Slacken the handlebar clamp bolt **(see illustration 5.6)**, then ease the handlebar up and off the fork **(see illustration)**. Note the handlebar stopper ring in the fork groove **(see illustration 6.5c)**.

Handlebar weights

14 If a new handlebar is being installed, you need to transfer the inner weight from the old bar to the new one – to do this, reinstall the end-weight and tighten its screw. Squirt some lubricant (such as WD40) into the inner weight retainer tab hole, then press down on the tab using a screwdriver, then twist and pull on the end-weight, drawing the inner weight assembly out. Remove the end-weight and discard the retainer as a new one should be used. Check the condition of the rubbers on the inner weight and fit new ones if they are damaged, deformed or deteriorated.

Installation

15 Installation is the reverse of removal, noting the following.

- To fit new grips onto the throttle twistgrip and left handlebar, apply a suitable glue (Pro Honda handgrip cement or equivalent) to each, making sure they are clean, then rotate the grip when in place to evenly distribute the glue. Align the groove on the inside of the inner end of the right-hand grip with the index line on the throttle twistgrip. Allow the glue to fully dry before riding the bike.
- When installing the right handlebar, smear some grease onto the handlebar. Slide the throttle twistgrip and cable housing assembly onto the handlebar before fitting the handlebar onto the fork.
- Make sure the handlebar stopper ring is in its groove in the fork **(see illustration 6.5c)**. When fitting the handlebar onto the fork, slide it down over the ring as far as it will go so the ring seats up inside the bottom. Do not tighten the handlebar clamp bolts until the top yoke has been installed.
- When fitting the top yoke onto the forks, locate the lug on the top of each handlebar clamp in its hole in the underside of the yoke, so that the handlebars are set in the correct position **(see illustration 5.7b)**. Tighten the steering stem nut first, then the top yoke clamp bolts, then the handlebar clamp bolts, tightening them all to the torque settings specified at the beginning of the Chapter, and lifting the handlebar slightly if necessary so its top surface seats against the bottom of the yoke.
- If disconnected do not forget to connect the ignition switch and where fitted the HISS wiring connector(s) **(see illustration 9.3)**.
- When installing the handlebar inner weights, locate the tab on the retainer in the hole in the handlebar.
- When installing the handlebar end-weights, do not omit the rubber washers and align the boss with the cut-out on the inner weight inside the handlebar. Clean the threads of the end-weight retaining screws and apply a suitable non-permanent thread locking compound. Tighten them to the specified torque setting.
- Make sure the front brake and clutch master cylinder clamps are installed with the UP mark facing up **(see illustrations 5.2b and 5.9b)**, and with the clamp mating surfaces aligned with the punch mark on the top of the handlebar **(see illustration)**. Tighten the master cylinder clamp bolts to the specified torque setting, tightening the top bolt first.
- Make sure the pin in the bottom half of each switch housing locates in its hole in the handlebar. Tighten the front housing screw first, then the rear.
- Do not forget to reconnect the front brake light switch and clutch switch wiring connectors **(see illustrations 5.2a and 5.9a)**.

5.11 Handlebar end-weight screw (arrowed)

5.13 Slide the handlebar up and off the fork

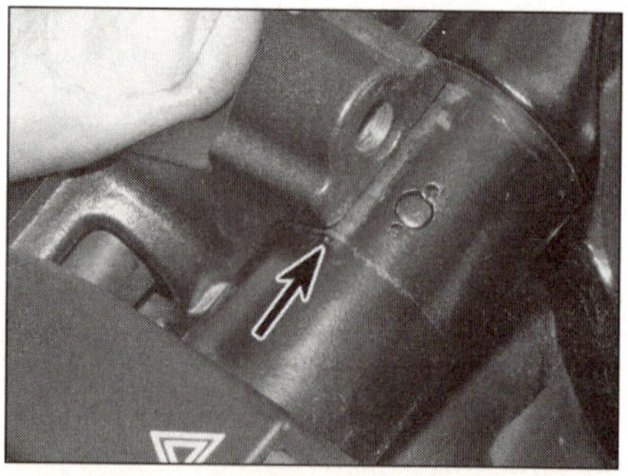

5.15 Align the clamp mating surfaces with the punch mark (arrowed)

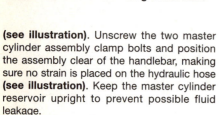

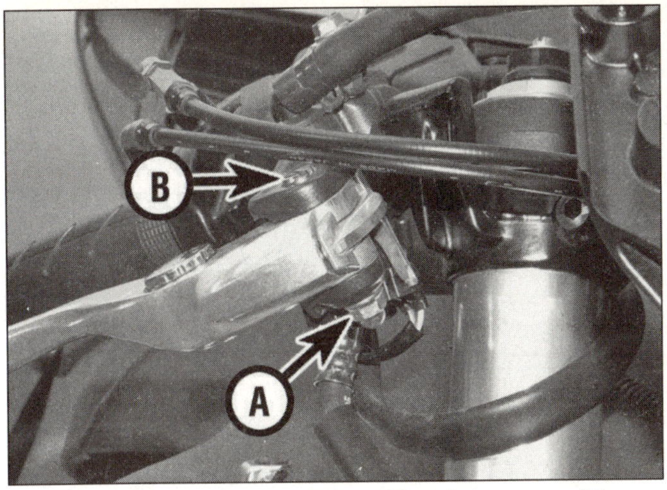

5.16a Front brake lever locknut (A) and pivot screw (B)

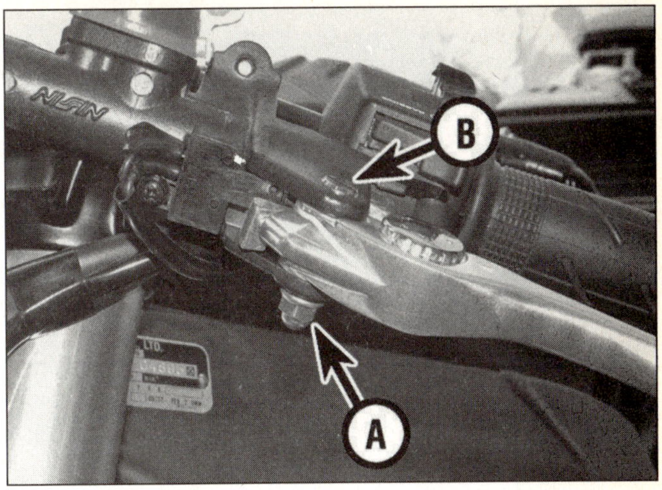

5.16b Clutch lever locknut (A) and pivot screw (B)

Levers

16 Undo the lever pivot screw locknut, then undo the pivot screw and remove the lever – there is a bush in the clutch lever that could drop out, so take care not to lose it **(see illustrations)**.

17 Installation is the reverse of removal. Apply silicone grease to all sliding surfaces and contact points. Apply a spray lubricant such as WD40, or a dry-film Teflon lubricant to the brake lever span adjuster mechanism. Fit the bush into the clutch lever, and locate the pushrod tip into its hole. Tighten the pivot screw lightly, then counter-hold it and tighten the nut.

6.4a Slacken the fork top bolt now if the fork is to be disassembled

6 Fork removal and installation

Removal

1 For best access and to prevent the possibility of damage, remove the fairing (see Chapter 7). Remove the front mudguard (see Chapter 7).

2 Remove the front wheel (see Chapter 6). Tie the front brake calipers and hoses back so that they are out of the way. Note the routing of any cables, hoses and wiring around the forks.

6.4b Note amount of protrusion above the yoke – the fork tube and top bolt mating surface (arrowed) sets the standard position

3 Removal of the clutch master cylinder is advised to improve access to the fork clamp bolts on the left-hand side. Remove the clutch switch **(see illustration 5.9a)**. Unscrew the two master cylinder assembly clamp bolts and position the assembly clear of the handlebar, making sure no strain is placed on the hydraulic hose **(see illustration 5.9b)**. Keep the master cylinder reservoir upright to prevent possible fluid leakage.

4 Working on one fork at a time, slacken the fork clamp bolt in the top yoke and the handlebar clamp bolt **(see illustration 5.6)**. If the fork is to be disassembled, or if the fork oil is being changed, slacken the fork top bolt now **(see illustration)**. Measure and note the amount of protrusion of the fork above the top yoke – as standard the top of the fork tube (not the top bolt) should be flush with the yoke surface **(see illustration)**.

5 Slacken the fork clamp bolts in the bottom yoke, and remove the fork by twisting it and pulling it downwards, guiding the handlebar off as you do **(see illustrations)**. Note the handlebar stopper ring in the groove in the fork and remove it for safekeeping if required **(see illustration)**.

6.5a Slacken the fork clamp bolts (arrowed) in the bottom yoke . . .

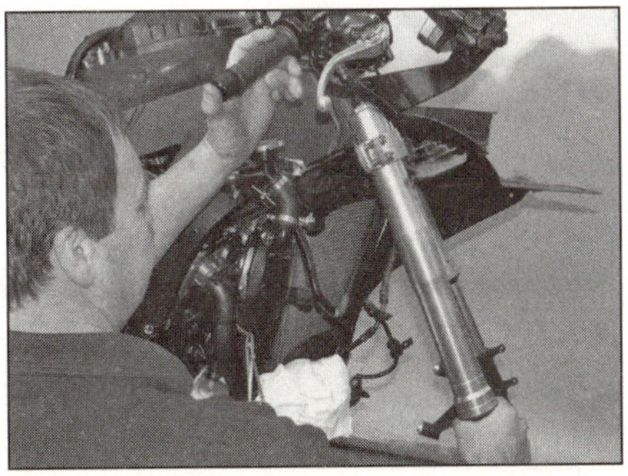

6.5b . . . then draw the fork down and out of the yokes guiding the handlebar off the top

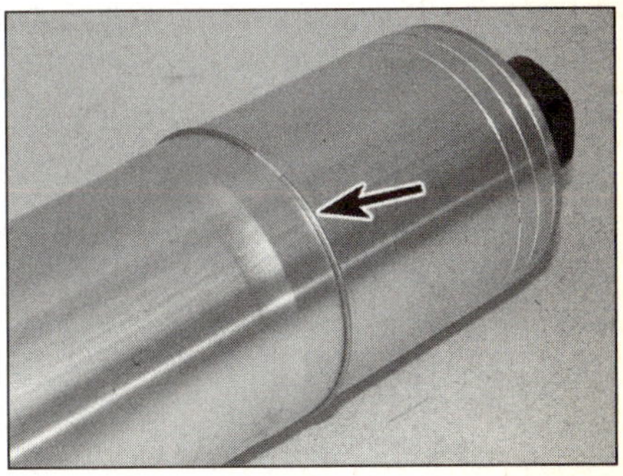

6.5c Remove the stopper ring (arrowed) for safekeeping

HAYNES HiNT ***If the fork legs are seized in the yokes, spray the area with penetrating oil and allow time for it to soak in before trying again.***

Installation

6 Remove all traces of corrosion from the fork tube and the yokes. If removed, fit the handlebar stopper ring into its groove **(see illustration 6.5c)**. Slide the fork up through the bottom yoke and the handlebar clamp and into the top yoke, making sure all cables, hoses and wiring are routed on the correct side of the fork **(see illustration 6.5b)**. Locate the lug on the top of the handlebar clamp in its hole in the underside of the yoke **(see illustration)**.

7 Set the amount of protrusion of the fork tube above the top yoke as noted on removal – Honda specify that the top of the fork tube (not the top bolt) should be flush with the upper surface of the yoke **(see illustration 6.4b)**.

8 Tighten the fork clamp bolts in the bottom yoke to the torque setting specified at the beginning of the Chapter **(see illustration 6.5a)**. If the fork has been dismantled or if the fork oil was changed, tighten the fork top bolt to the specified torque setting **(see illustration 6.4a)**. Now tighten the fork clamp bolt in the top yoke **(see illustration 5.6)**. Lift the handlebar slightly if necessary so its top surface seats against the bottom of the yoke, then tighten its clamp bolt to the specified torque.

9 Align the clutch master cylinder clamp mating surfaces with the punch mark on the top of the handlebar **(see illustration 5.15)**. Fit the clutch master cylinder with the UP mark facing up **(see illustration 5.9b)**, Tighten the master cylinder clamp bolts to the specified torque setting, tightening the top bolt first. Connect the switch wiring connectors **(see illustration 5.9a)**.

10 Install the front wheel (see Chapter 6) and the front mudguard (see Chapter 7).

11 Check the operation of the front forks and brakes before taking the machine out on the road.

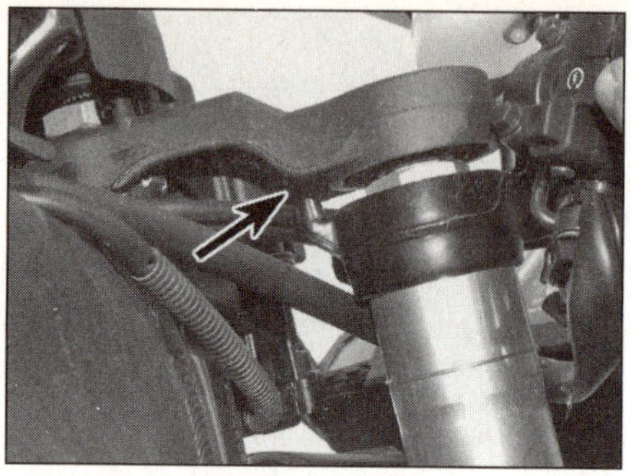

6.6 Locate the lug in the hole (arrowed)

7 Fork oil change

1 After a high mileage the fork oil will deteriorate and its damping and lubrication qualities will be impaired. Always change the oil in both fork legs.

2 Remove the fork; ensure that the top bolt is loosened while the leg is still clamped in the bottom yoke (see Section 6).

3 Refer to Section 14 and check the current pre-load setting so the fork can later be reset at the same amount.

4 Remove the handlebar stopper ring for safekeeping if not already done **(see illustration 6.5c)**.

5 Remove the snap-ring from the top of the damper rod adjuster piece **(see illustration)**. Remove the pre-load adjuster hex **(see illustration)**.

6 Remove the O-ring from the damper rod adjuster piece **(see illustration)**. Unscrew the fork top bolt from the top of the fork tube **(see illustration)**. The bolt will remain on the damper rod, held by the locknut on its top.

7 Slide the tube down gently until it seats on the bottom. Counter-hold the damper rod adjuster piece using a spanner on the flats, then unscrew the locknut above the top bolt and thread it off the damper rod **(see illustration)**. Remove the top bolt **(see illustration)**. Note how the cut-outs in the pre-load adjuster plate inside the top bolt locate over the ridges on the damper rod adjuster piece.

8 Remove the collar and the spacer, then

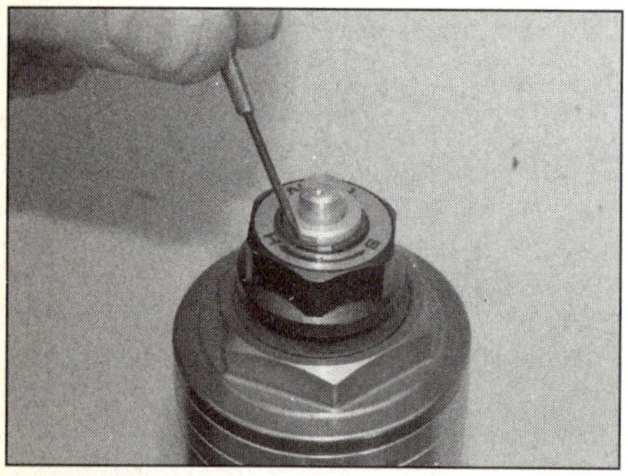

7.5a Remove the snap-ring . . .

7.5b . . . and the pre-load adjuster hex

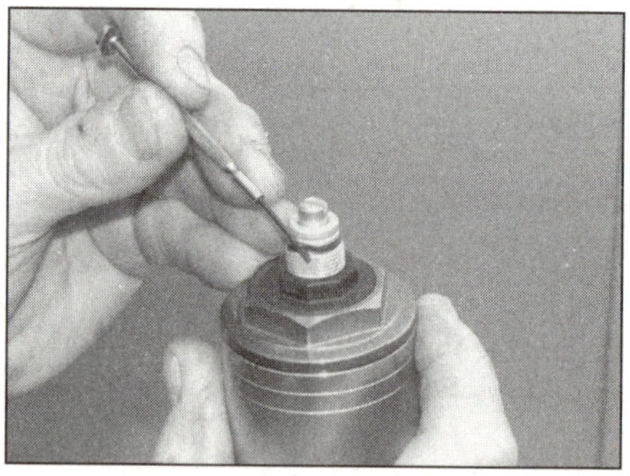

7.6a Remove the O-ring . . .

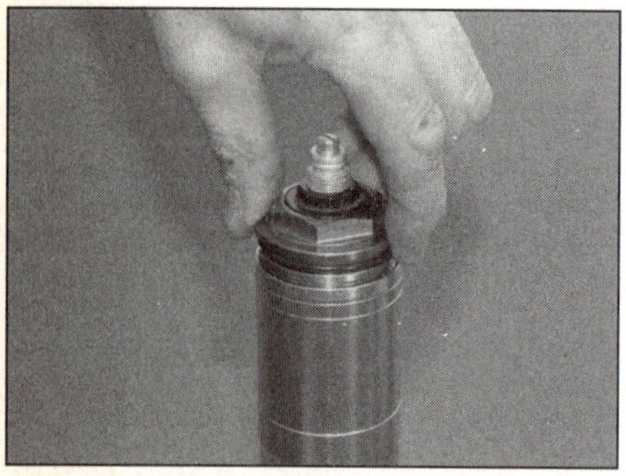

7.6b . . . then thread the top bolt out of the tube

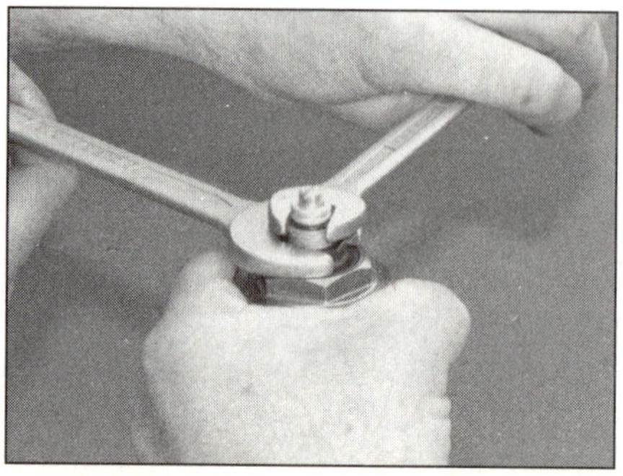

7.7a Unscrew the locknut . . .

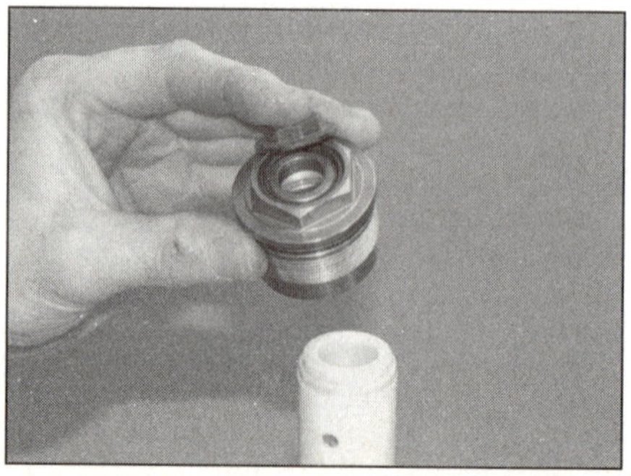

7.7b . . . and remove the top bolt

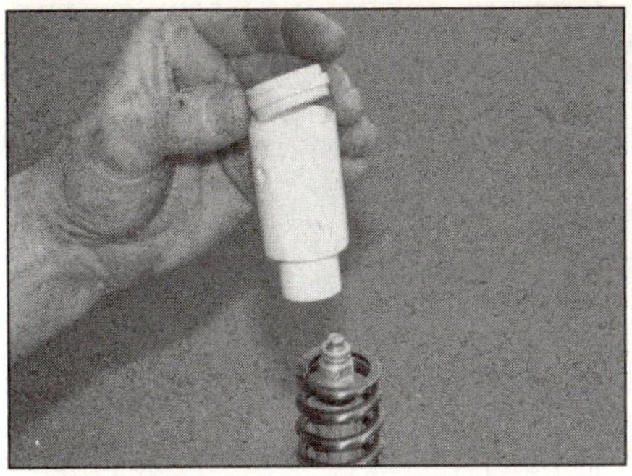

7.8a Remove the collar and spacer . . .

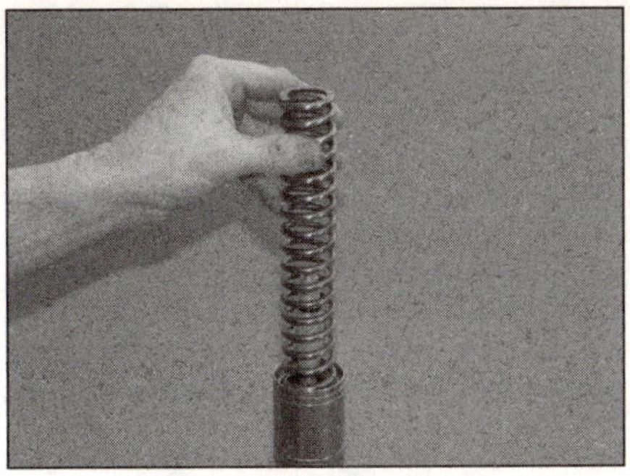

7.8b . . . and the spring

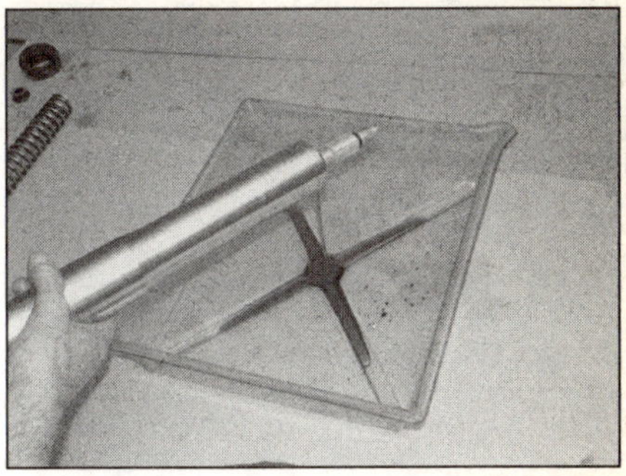

7.9a Invert the fork over a container and tip the oil out . . .

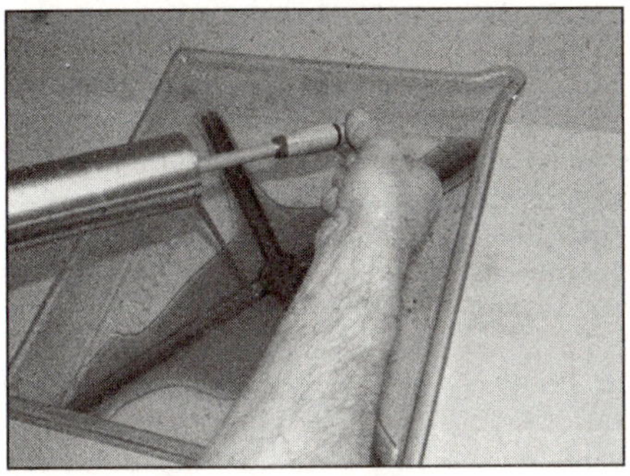

7.9b . . . then pump the tube and the rod to expel the rest

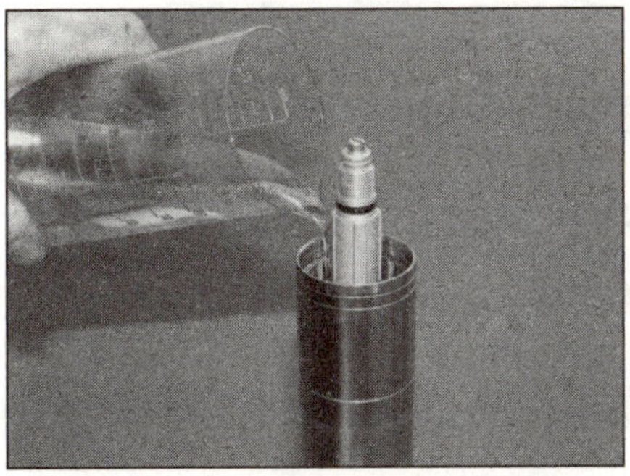

7.10a Pour the oil into the top of the tube and distribute and bleed it as described . . .

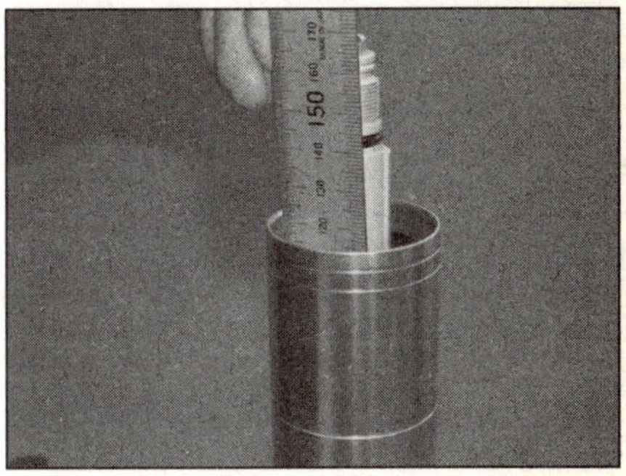

7.10b . . . then measure the level

withdraw the spring from the tube, noting which way up it fits **(see illustrations)**.

9 Invert the fork leg over a suitable container and pump the fork and damper rod vigorously several times to expel as much fork oil as possible **(see illustrations)**. Support the fork upside down in the container for a while to allow as much oil as possible to drain, then pump the fork and rod again. Wipe any excess oil off the spring and spacer. If the fork oil contains metal particles inspect the fork bushes for wear (see Section 8).

10 Stand the fork upright. Slowly pour in the specified quantity of the specified grade of fork oil **(see illustration)**. Fully extend the fork, then cover the top of the tube with your hand and compress the fork as much as possible – this helps to bleed any air. Extend the fork and repeat two or three times. Now pump the fork and damper rod slowly at least ten times each to distribute the oil evenly – take care not to overextend the fork when pumping. Fully compress the fork tube and damper rod onto the slider and let it sit for a few minutes, then measure the oil level from the top of the tube **(see illustration)**. Add or subtract oil until it is at the level specified at the beginning of this Chapter.

11 Pull the damper rod and fork tube out as far as possible then install the spring, with the tapered end at the top **(see illustration)**. Keeping the damper rod extended, fit the spacer, locating it in the top of the spring **(see illustration)**.

12 Keeping the damper rod extended push down on the spacer to compress the spring and slide a disc washer with a slot cut in it over the top of the spacer and under the hex on the bottom of the damper rod adjuster piece, then release the spacer – the washer will nestle up against the underside of the adjuster piece and keep the spring

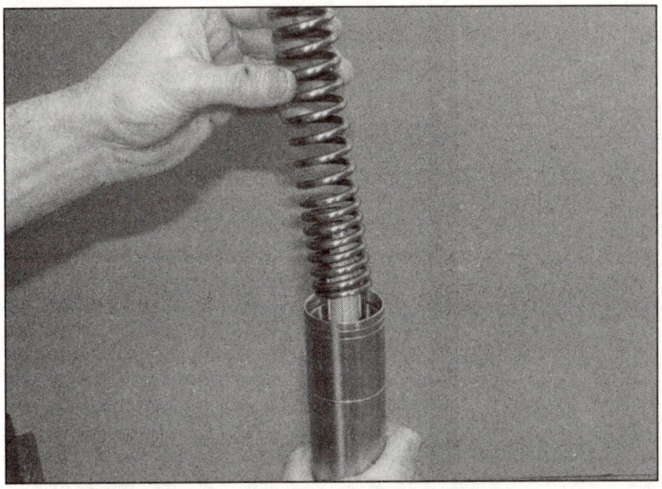

7.11a Fit the spring with its tapered end at the top and the closer-wound coils at the bottom

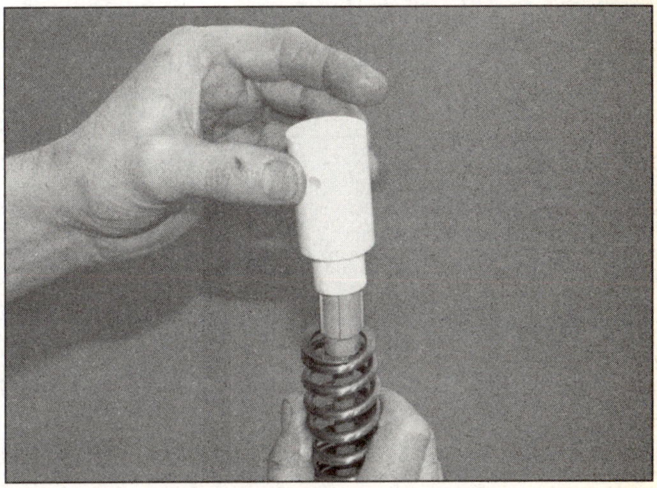

7.11b Fit the spacer into the spring

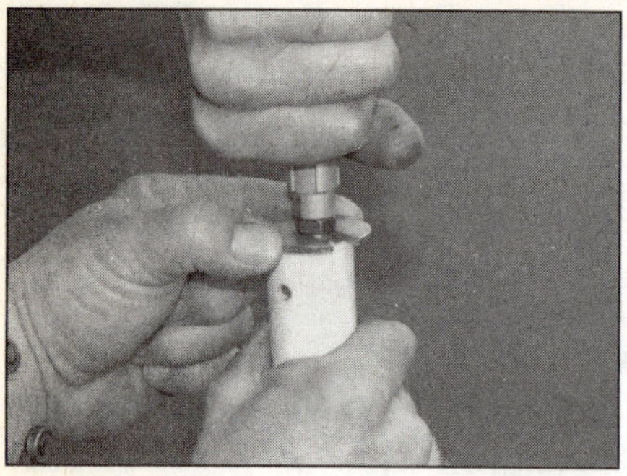

7.12a Compress the spring and slide in a slotted washer

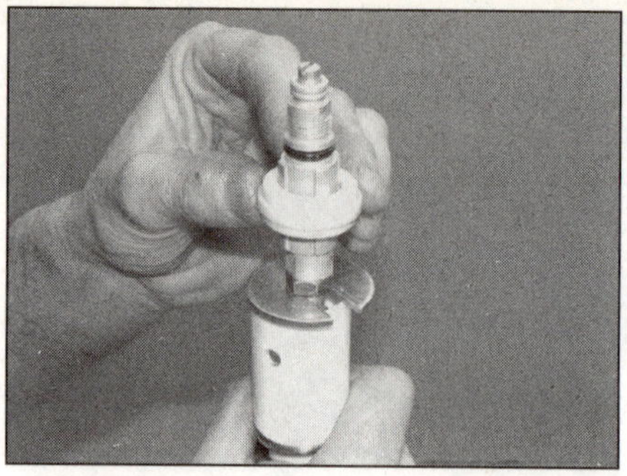

7.12b Fit the collar and rest it on the washer

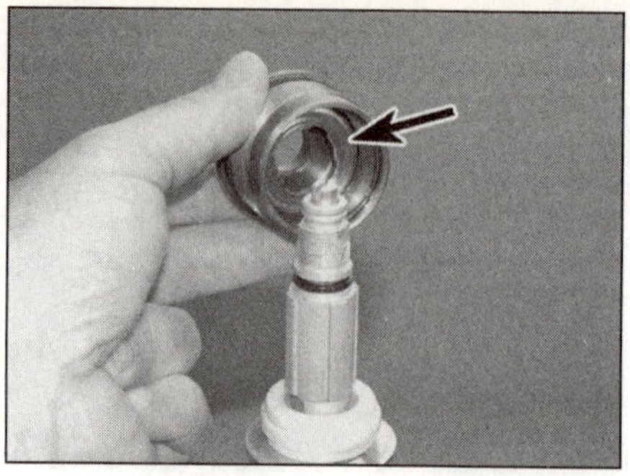

7.12c Align the cut-outs in the plate (arrowed) with the slots in the adjuster

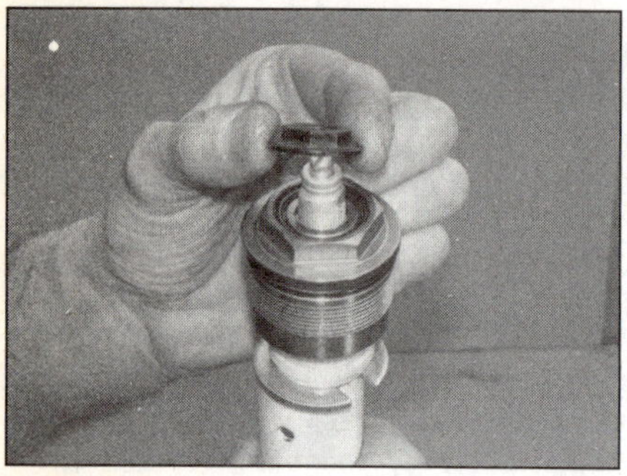

7.12d Thread the locknut on and tighten it as described

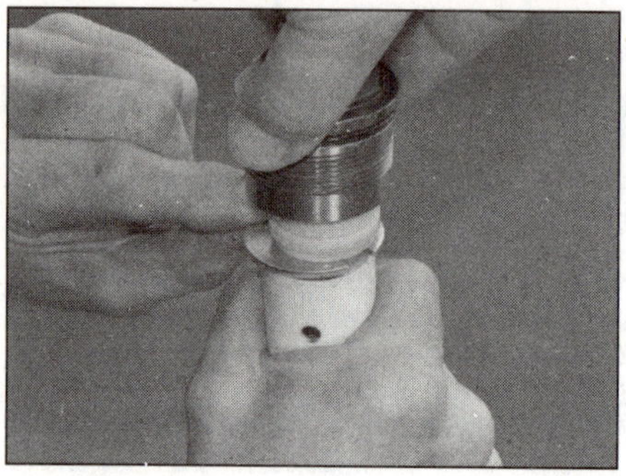

7.13 Remove the slotted washer and settle the components

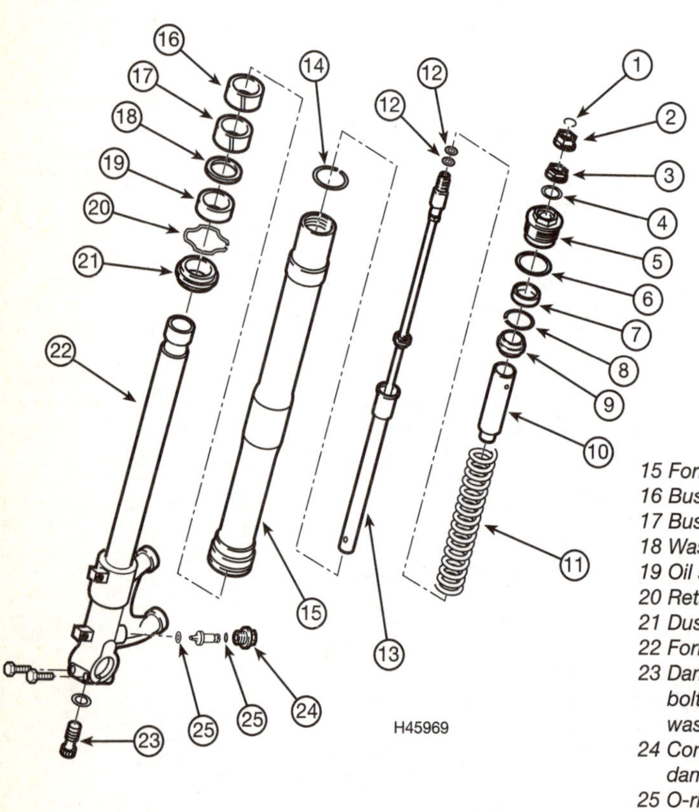

8.1 Front fork components

compressed **(see illustration)**. Make sure the washer is secure. Fit the collar and allow it to rest on the washer **(see illustration)**. Fit the top bolt onto the damper rod, aligning the cut-outs in the adjuster plate with the slots on the adjuster piece **(see illustration)**. Thread the locknut onto the damper rod **(see illustration)**. Counter-hold the damper rod adjuster piece using a spanner on the flats then tighten the locknut **(see illustration 7.7a)**.

13 Remove the slotted washer and allow the spacer to fit onto the collar and the collar to fit into the base of the top bolt **(see illustration)**. If the top bolt O-ring is damaged or deteriorated fit a new one. Smear some fork oil onto the O-ring. Extend the fork tube and thread the bolt into the top of the fork tube, and making sure it is not cross-threaded **(see illustration 7.6b)**. **Note:** *The top bolt can be tightened to the specified torque setting at this stage if the tube is held between the padded jaws of a vice, but do not risk distorting the tube by doing so. A better method is to tighten the top bolt when the fork has been installed in the bike and is held in the bottom yoke, but before the top yoke clamp bolt is tightened.*

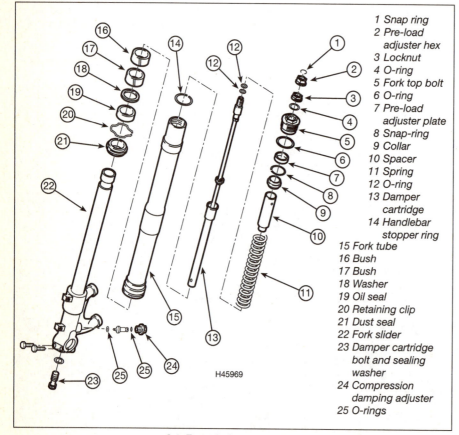

14 Fit a new O-ring into the larger groove in the top of the damper rod **(see illustration 7.6a)**. Fit the pre-load adjuster hex onto the top of the damper rod **(see illustration 7.5b)**. Fit the snap-ring into its groove in the top of the damper rod **(see illustration 7.5a)**. Set the pre-load as noted on removal.

15 Install the fork (see Section 6).

8 Fork overhaul

Special tool: *A damper cartridge holder tool (Pt. No. 07YMB-MCF0101) may be necessary (see Step 4).*

Disassembly

1 Remove the fork; ensure that the top bolt is loosened while the leg is still clamped in the bottom yoke (see Section 6). Always dismantle the fork legs separately to avoid interchanging parts and thus causing an accelerated rate of wear. Store all components in separate, clearly marked containers **(see illustration)**.

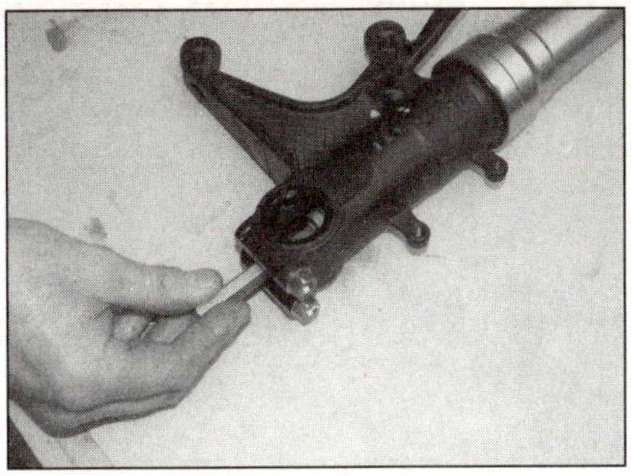

8.2 **Slacken the damper cartridge bolt**

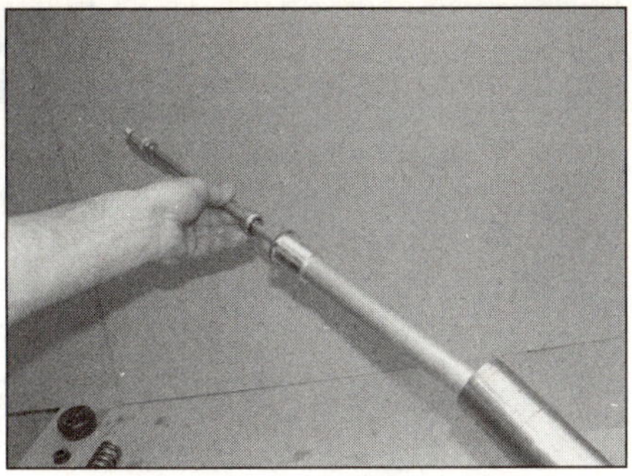

8.5 **Withdraw the damper cartridge**

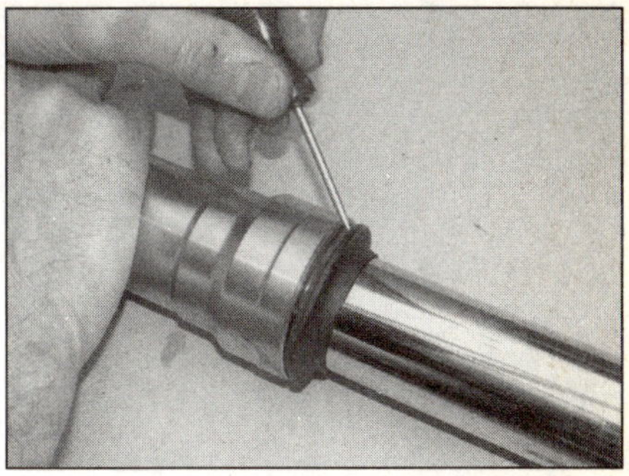

8.6 **Prise out the dust seal using a flat-bladed screwdriver**

2 Lay the fork flat on the bench with the caliper mounting lugs to the left, then hold the fork down and slacken the damper cartridge bolt in the base of the fork slider **(see illustration)**.

3 Refer to Section 7, Steps 3 to 9 and drain the oil form the fork.

4 Use a spanner on the compression damping adjuster flats to unscrew the adjuster from the base of the slider. Remove the damper cartridge bolt and its sealing washer from the bottom of the slider **(see illustration 8.23c)**. Discard the sealing washer as a new one must be used on reassembly. If the damper cartridge rotates inside the fork tube whilst attempting to unscrew the damper bolt, the service tool pt. no. 07YMB-MCF0101 can be used to hold the cartridge – the tool is passed down through the fork tube to engage the head of the damper body. An alternative method is to reinstall the fork spring, spacer and top bolt, compress the fork so that the spring exerts pressure on the cartridge body whilst the bolt is unscrewed.

5 Withdraw the damper cartridge from inside the fork tube **(see illustration)**.

6 Carefully prise out the dust seal from the bottom of the tube to gain access to the oil seal retaining clip **(see illustration)**.

7 Carefully prise out the retaining clip, taking care not to scratch the surface of the tube – slide the tube out of the slider slightly to keep any accidental damage above the seal area **(see illustration)**.

8 To separate the slider from the tube it is necessary to displace the bottom bush and oil seal. The top bush should not pass through the bottom bush, and this can be used to good effect. Grasp the slider in one hand and the tube in the other and compress them slightly, then pull them apart so that the bottom bush strikes the top bush **(see illustration)**. Repeat this operation until the top bush and seal are tapped out of the slider **(see illustration)**.

9 Remove the top bush from the slider by carefully levering its ends apart using a screwdriver **(see illustration)**. Slide the bottom bush, the oil seal washer, the oil seal, the retaining clip and the dust seal off the slider, noting which way up they fit **(see illustration 8.8b)**. Discard the oil seal and the dust seal as new ones must be used.

Inspection

10 Clean all parts in solvent and blow them dry with compressed air, if available. Check the fork slider for score marks, dents, pitting, scratches, flaking of it's surface and excessive or abnormal wear. Fit new tubes if any are found. Check the fork seal seat for nicks, gouges and scratches. If damage is evident, leaks will occur. Also check the oil seal washer for damage or distortion and fit a new one if necessary.

11 Check the fork slider for runout using

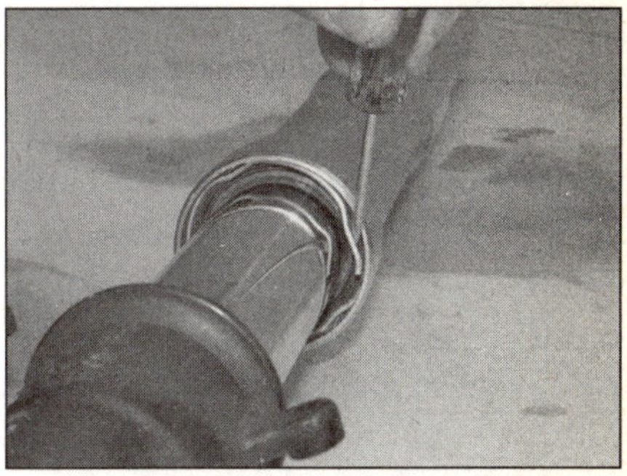

8.7 Prise out the retaining clip using a flat-bladed screwdriver

V-blocks and a dial gauge. If the amount of runout exceeds the service limit specified, a new tube should be fitted.

Warning: If the slider is bent or exceeds the runout limit, it should not be straightened; replace it with a new one.

12 Check the fork tube for dents and cracks. Check the fork seal seat and housing for nicks, gouges and scratches. If damage is evident, leaks will occur. Also check the oil seal washer for damage or distortion and fit a new one if necessary.

13 Check the spring for cracks and other damage. Measure the spring free length and compare the measurement to the specifications at the beginning of the Chapter

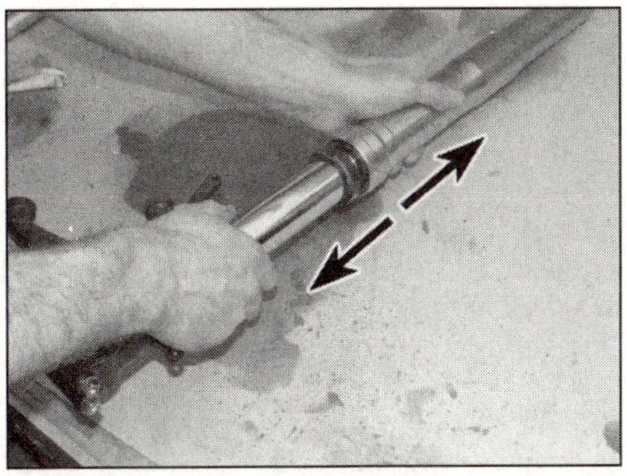

8.8a To separate the fork tube from the slider, pull them apart firmly several times . . .

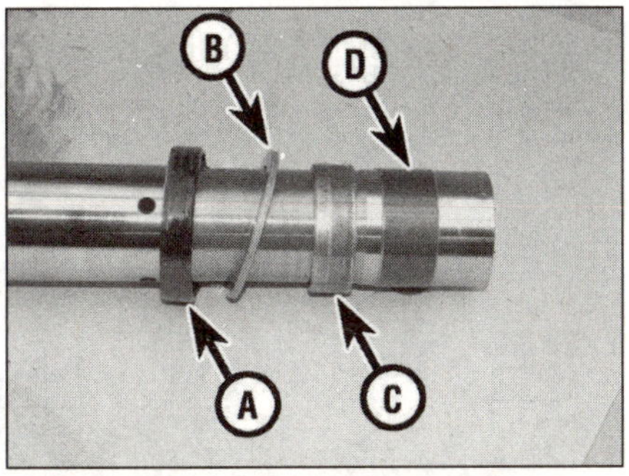

8.8b . . . the slide-hammer effect will displace the oil seal (A), washer (B) and bottom bush (C); top bush (D)

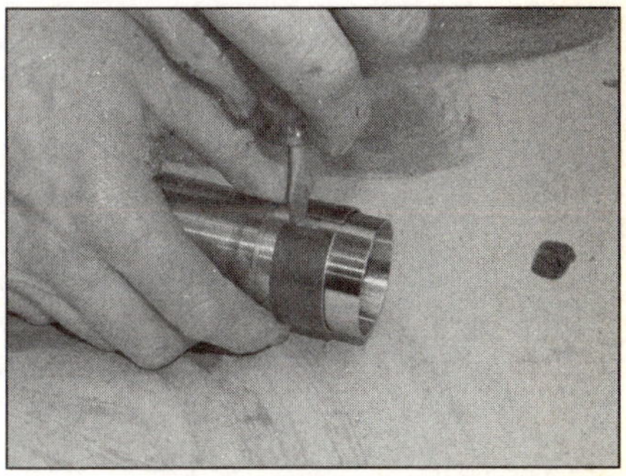

8.9 Remove the top bush

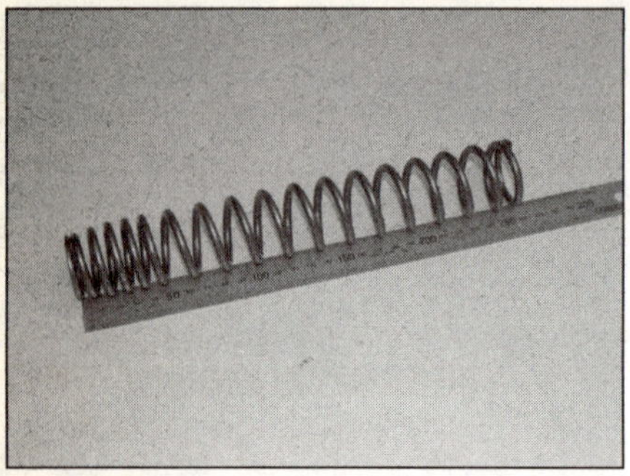

8.13 Measuring the fork spring free length

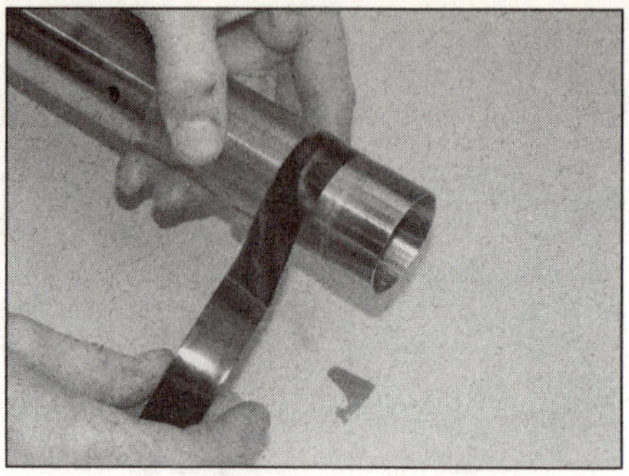

8.16a Wrap some tape over the ridges . . .

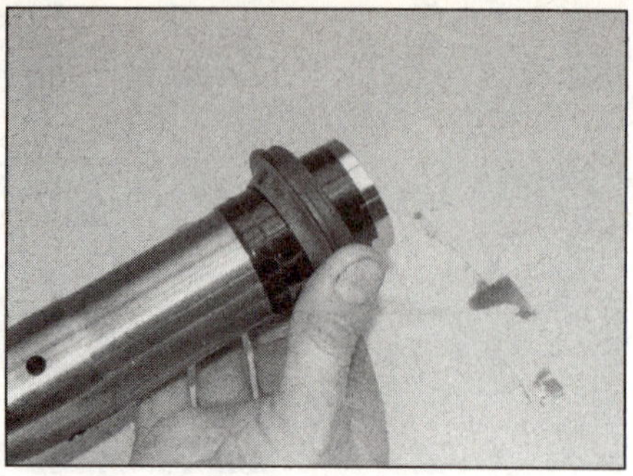

8.16b . . . then slide the dust seal . . .

(see illustration). If it is defective or sagged below the service limit, replace the springs in both forks with new ones. Never renew only one spring.

14 Examine the working surfaces of the two bushes (i.e. the outer surface of the top bush and the inner surface of the bottom bush); if the grey Teflon outer surface has been worn away to reveal the copper inner surface over more than 75% of the surface area, or if the bushes are scored or badly scuffed, they must be replaced with new ones.

15 Check the damper assembly for damage and wear. Pull the oil lock valve out of the top of the cartridge and check it for wear and damage. Holding the outside of the cartridge, pump the rod in and out. If any wear or damage is found, or if the rod does not move smoothly in the damper, a new damper assembly must be installed.

Reassembly

16 Wrap some insulating tape over the ridges on the end of the fork slider to protect the lips of the new oil seal as it is installed **(see illustration)**. Apply a smear of the specified clean fork oil to the lips of the dust seal, oil seal and the inner surface of each bush, then slide the new dust seal, the retaining clip, the oil seal, and the oil seal washer onto the fork slider, making sure the dust seal is the correct way round and that the marked side of the oil seal faces the dust seal **(see illustrations)**. Remove the insulating tape and slide the bottom bush onto the slider, then fit the top bush into its recess **(see illustrations)**.

17 Apply a smear of the specified clean fork oil to the outer surface of each bush, then carefully insert the slider fully into the fork tube **(see illustration)**.

18 Support the fork upside down, then press the bottom bush squarely into its recess in the fork tube as far as possible **(see illustration)**. Slide the oil seal washer on top of the bush, and keep the oil seal, the retaining clip and the

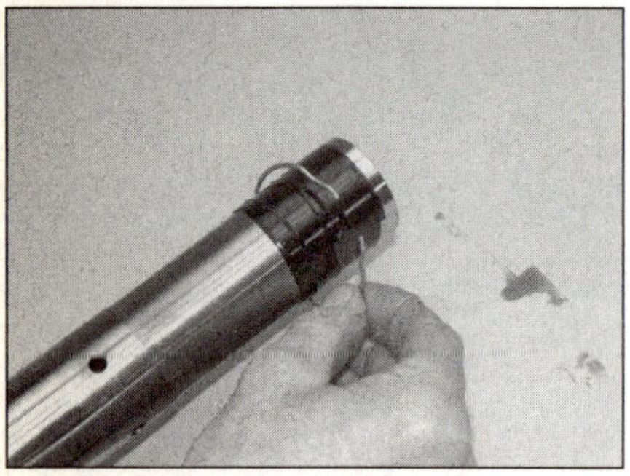

8.16c . . . the retaining clip . . .

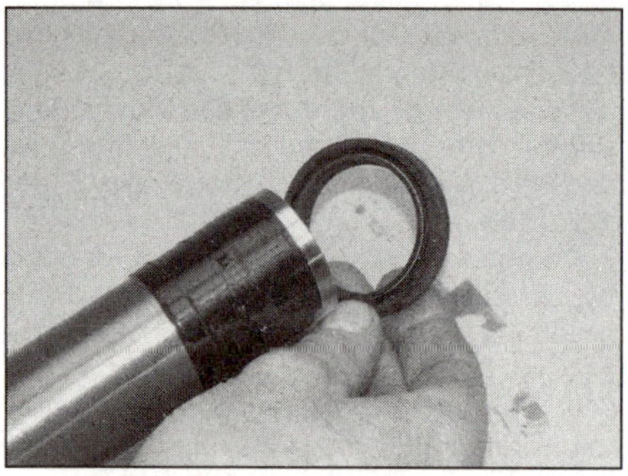

8.16d . . . the oil seal . . .

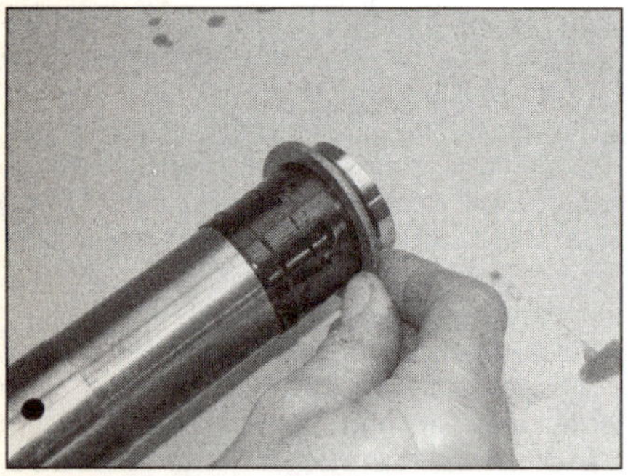

8.16e . . . and its washer onto the shaft

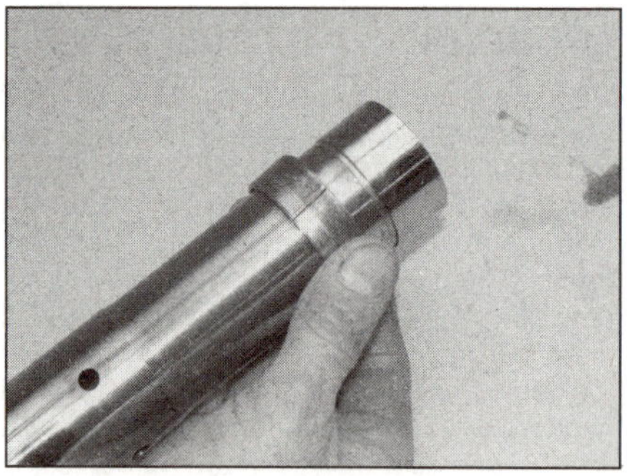

8.16f Slide the bottom bush on . . .

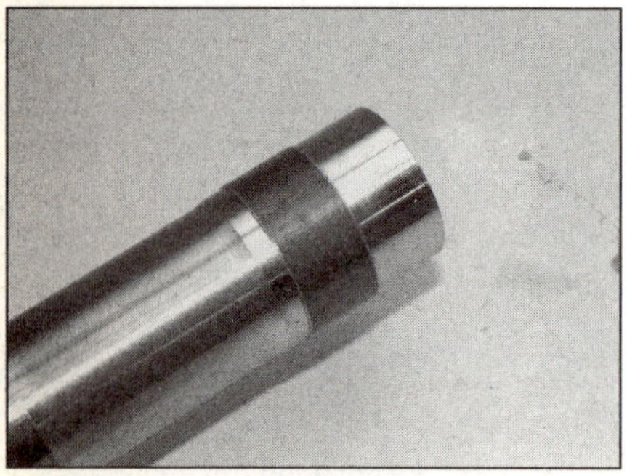

8.16g . . . then fit the top bush into its groove

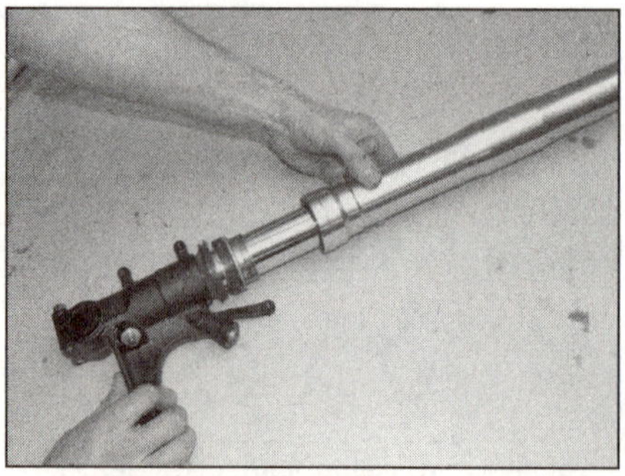

8.17 Fit the slider into the tube

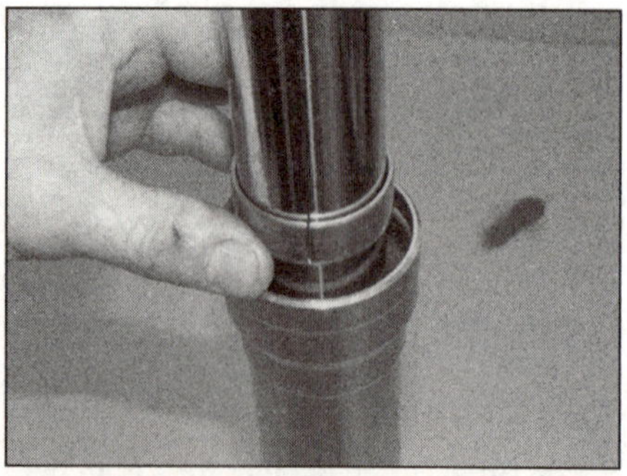

8.18a Fit the bottom bush into the base of the tube

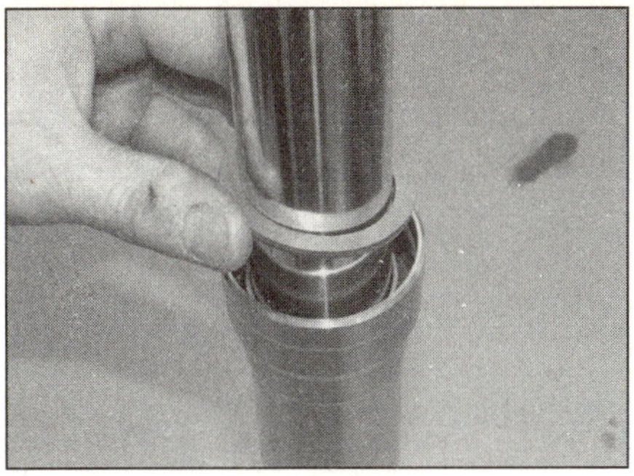

8.18b Locate the washer on top of the bush to protect it . . .

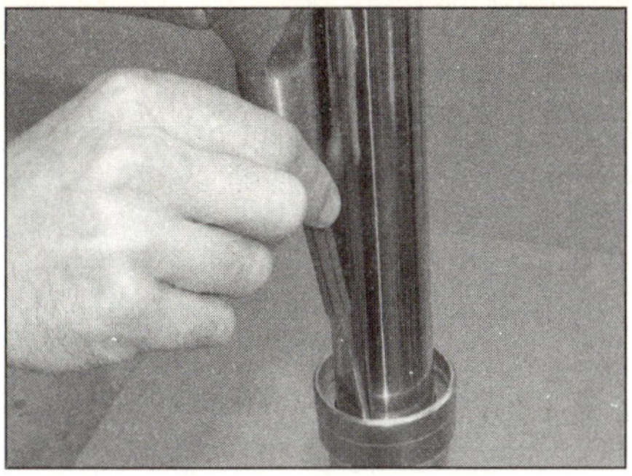

8.19 . . . and drive the bush into place

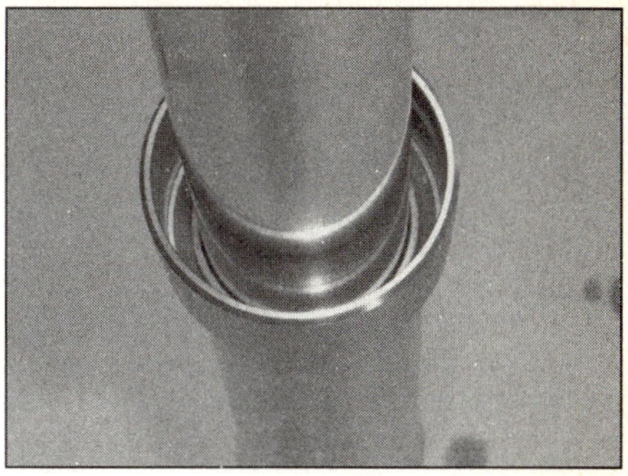

8.20 Make sure the bush is tapped fully home

dust seal out of the way by sliding them up the slider **(see illustration)**. If necessary, tape them to the slider to prevent them from falling down and interfering as the bush is drifted into place.

19 Using either the special service tool (part No. 07NMD-KZ3010A in the US or 07YMD-MCF0100 elsewhere) or a suitable drift, carefully drive the bottom bush fully into its recess – the oil seal washer prevents damaging the edges of the bush **(see illustration)**. If using a drift, wrap tape around it and the fork slider to prevent scratching the chrome. Make sure the bush enters the recess squarely. It is best to make sure that the fork slider is withdrawn as much as possible from the tube so that any accidental scratching is confined to the area that does not affect the oil seal.

20 Lift the washer to check the bush is seated fully and squarely in its recess in the slider, then wipe the recess clean and re-seat the washer **(see illustration)**.

21 Drive the oil seal into place as described in Step 19 until the retaining clip groove is visible **(see illustrations)**.

22 Once the oil seal is correctly seated, fit the retaining clip, making sure it is correctly located in its groove, then press the dust seal into position **(see illustrations)**.

23 Lay the fork flat on the bench with the caliper mounting lugs to the right. Slide the damper cartridge fully into the fork tube **(see illustration)**. Fit a new sealing washer onto the cartridge bolt and apply a few drops of a suitable non-permanent thread locking compound **(see illustration)**. Fit the bolt into the bottom of the slider and thread it into the cartridge, tightening it to the torque setting specified at the beginning of the Chapter **(see illustration)**. If the damper cartridge rotates inside the tube as you tighten the bolt, either use the holding tool described in Step 19 or wait until the fork is fully reassembled and tighten it then (the pressure of the spring on the cartridge will prevent it from turning).

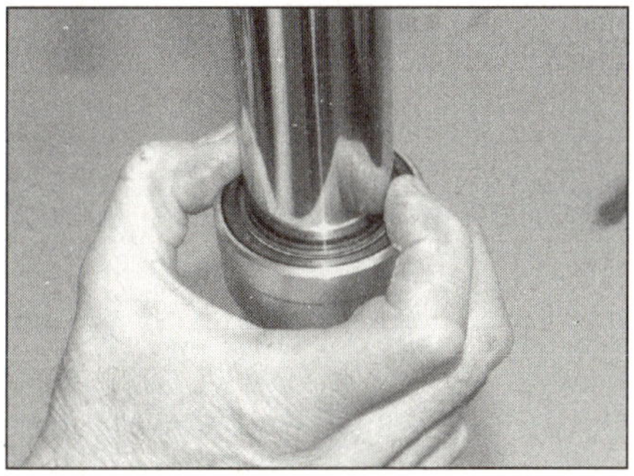

8.21a Fit the oil seal and drive it into place . . .

8.21b . . . until the retaining clip groove (arrowed) is exposed

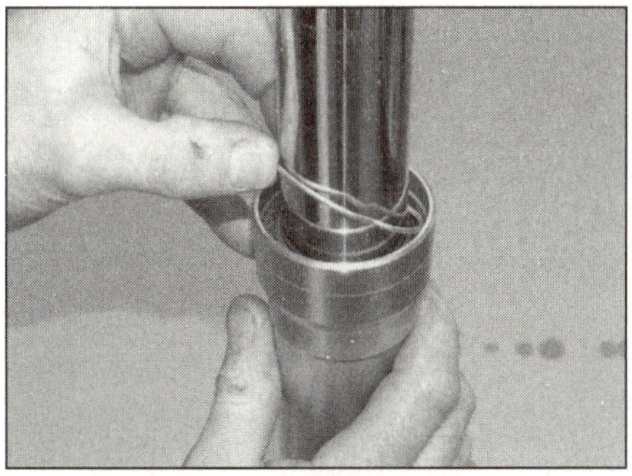

8.22a Fit the retaining clip . . .

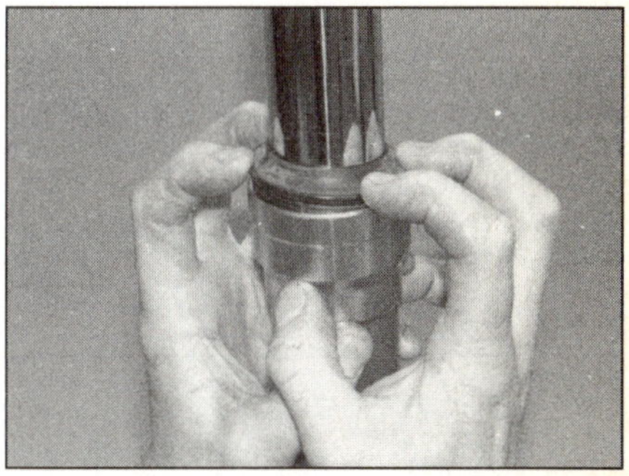

8.22b . . . and the dust seal

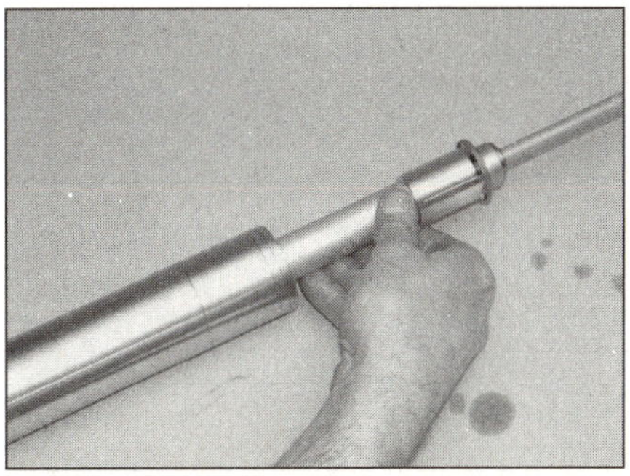

8.23a Slide the damper cartridge into the fork

8.23b Fit the bolt using threadlock and a new sealing washer . . .

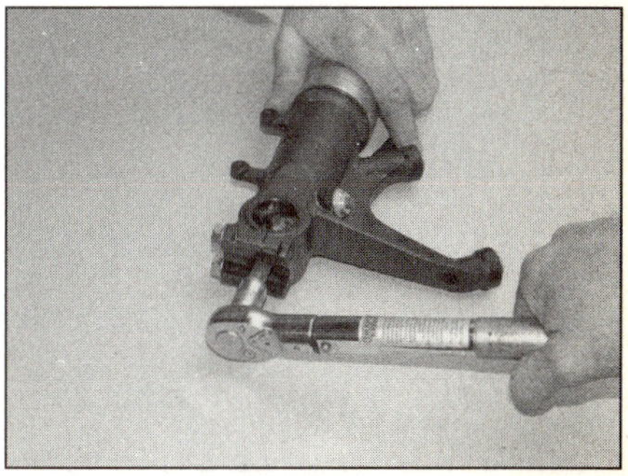

8.23c . . . and tighten it to the specified torque

9.2a Unscrew the bolts (arrowed) and remove the shield

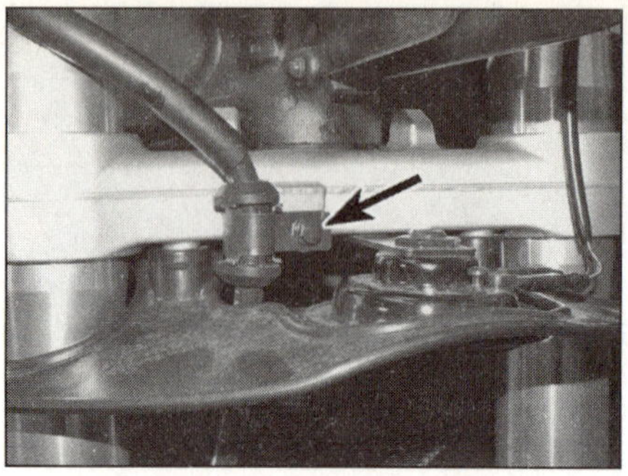

9.2b Unscrew the brake hose guide bolt (arrowed)

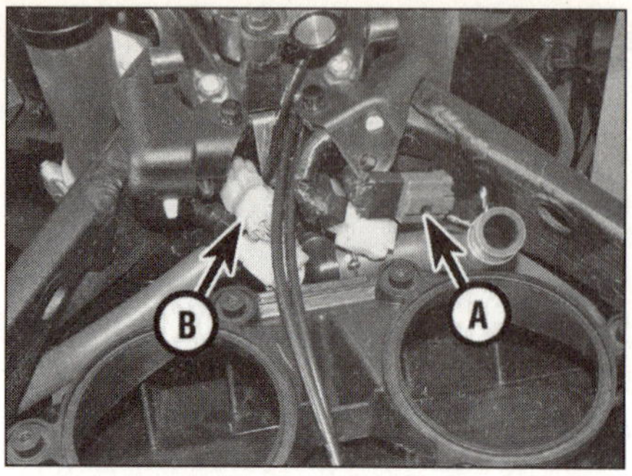

9.3 Ignition switch wiring connector (A). HISS receiver wiring connector (B)

24 Refer to Section 7, Steps 10 to 14 and fill the fork with oil and finish reassembly.

25 If the damper rod bolt requires tightening (see Step 23), place the fork upside down on the floor, using a rag to protect it, then have an assistant compress the fork so that maximum spring pressure is placed on the damper rod head while tightening the bolt to the specified torque setting.

26 Install the fork (see Section 6).

9 Steering stem

Removal

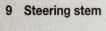

1 Remove the fairing and the fuel tank cover (see Chapter 7). Remove the front forks (see Section 6). Remove the steering damper (see Section 11).

2 Remove the horn (see Chapter 8). Unscrew the bolts and remove the shield from the bottom yoke **(see illustration)**. Unscrew the bolt securing the front brake hose holder to the bottom yoke and displace it **(see illustration)**. Take care not to strain or knock the brake hoses when removing the steering stem.

3 If the top yoke is being removed from the bike rather than just being displaced, remove the air filter housing (see Chapter 4), then trace the wiring from the ignition switch, and where fitted the HISS receiver, and disconnect it/them at the connector(s) **(see illustration)**. Release the wiring from any clips or ties and feed it through to the yoke.

4 Unscrew the steering stem nut and on RR-6 and RR-7 models remove the washer **(see illustration 5.7a)**. Lift the top yoke up off the steering stem and position it clear, using a rag to protect the tank or other components if it is only being displaced **(see illustration 5.7b)**.

5 Bend the lockwasher tabs out of the notches in the locknut **(see illustration)**. Unscrew the locknut using either your fingers (it shouldn't be tight), a C-spanner or a suitable drift located in one of the notches **(see illustration)**. Remove the lockwasher, bending up the remaining tabs to release it from the adjuster nut if necessary **(see illustration)**. Inspect the tabs for cracks or signs of fatigue. If there is any sign of damage, discard the lockwasher and use a new one; otherwise the old one can be re-used, but note that Honda recommend using a new one as a matter of course.

6 Support the bottom yoke and unscrew the adjuster nut using either a C-spanner, a peg-spanner or socket, or a drift located in one of the notches **(see illustration)**. Remove the grease seal from the steering stem **(see illustration)**. Gently lower the bottom yoke and steering stem out of the frame **(see illustration)**. Check the condition

9.5a Bend down the lockwasher tabs . . .

9.5b . . . then unscrew the locknut . . .

9.5c . . . and remove the lockwasher

9.6a Unscrew the adjuster nut . . .

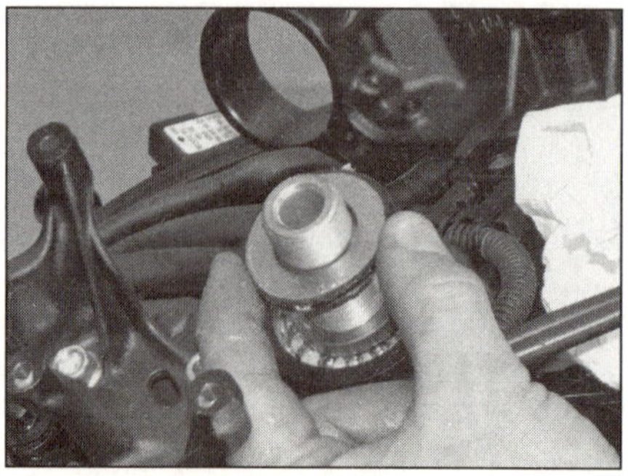

9.6b . . . and remove the grease seal . . .

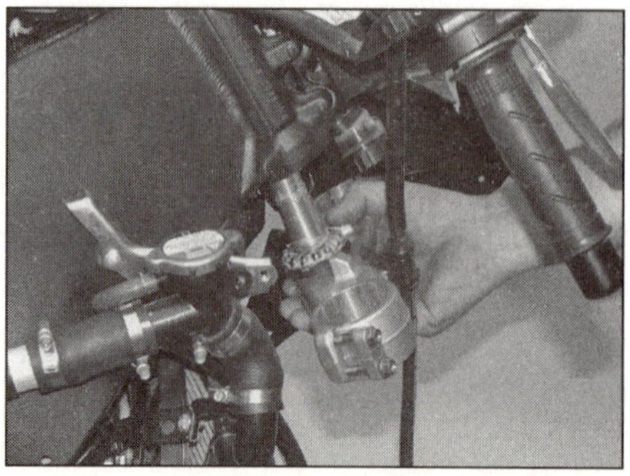

9.6c . . . then draw the bottom yoke/ steering stem out of the steering head

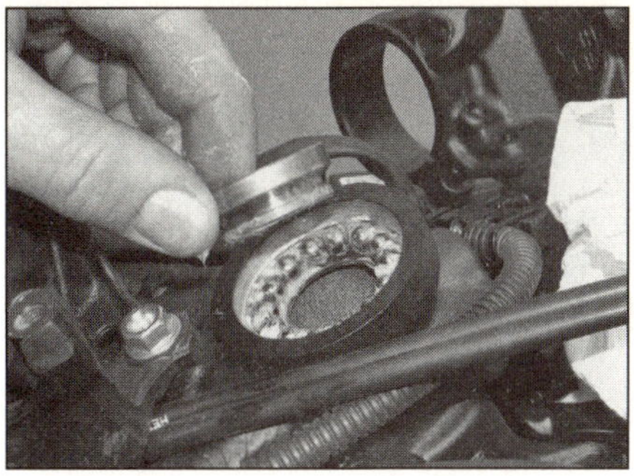

9.7a Remove the inner race . . .

9.7b . . . and the upper bearing

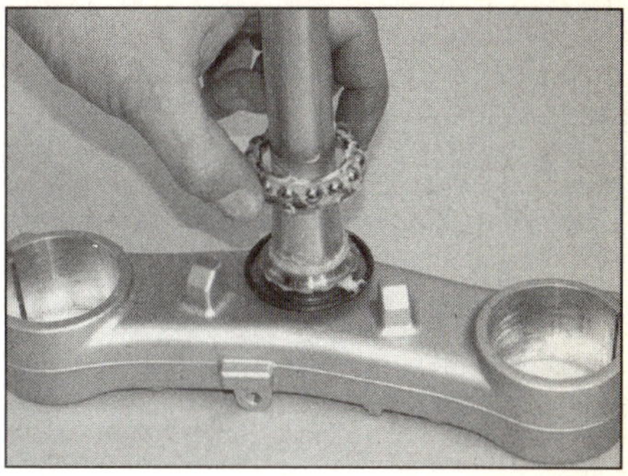

9.9 Fit the lower bearing onto the steering stem

of the grease seal and discard it if it is damaged.

7 Remove the inner race and bearing from the top of the steering head **(see illustrations)**. Remove the bearing from the base of the steering stem **(see illustration 9.9)**.

8 Remove all traces of old grease from the bearings and races and check them for wear or damage as described in Section 10. **Note:** *Do not attempt to remove the races from the steering head or the steering stem unless they are to be replaced with new ones (see Section 10).*

Installation

9 Smear a liberal quantity of Urea based multi-purpose grease with EP2 rating onto the bearing races, and work some grease well into both the upper and lower bearings. Also smear the grease seal lip, using a new seal if necessary. Fit the lower bearing onto the steering stem **(see illustration)**.

10 Carefully lift the steering stem/bottom yoke up through the steering head and support it there **(see illustration 9.6c)**. Fit the upper bearing and its inner race into the top of the steering head **(see illustrations 9.7b and a)**. Fit the grease seal **(see illustration 9.6b)**. Apply the Urea grease to the adjuster nut and thread the nut on the steering stem **(see illustration)**.

11 If the Honda service tool (Pt. No. 07916-3710101 or 3710100 according to country) or a suitable peg spanner (which can be made by cutting castellations into an old socket) is available, tighten the adjuster nut to the torque setting specified at the beginning of the Chapter for your model, then turn the steering stem through its full lock at least five times, then slacken the nut and tighten it again to the specified torque setting. Ensure that the steering stem is able to move freely from lock-to-lock following adjustment – it is best to check and if necessary reset the bearing adjustment as described in Chapter 1 after the forks and front wheel and all other components have been installed.

12 If the correct tools are not available, tighten the nut using a C-spanner or drift so that bearing play is eliminated, but the steering stem is able to move freely from lock-to-lock – refer to the procedure in Chapter 1 for details, and set the bearings after the forks and wheel are installed as their leverage and inertia need to be taken into account **(see illustration)**. Make sure the nut is tight enough to hold the steering stem in the head without any play, then install the forks and wheel, then refer to the procedure in Chapter 1.

Caution: Take great care not to apply excessive pressure because this will cause premature failure of the bearings.

13 With the bearings correctly adjusted, fit the new lockwasher onto the adjuster nut so that its two short tabs fit into the slots in the nut **(see illustration 9.5c)**. Hold the adjuster nut to prevent it from moving, then fit the locknut and tighten it finger-tight **(see illustration 9.5b)**. Tighten the locknut further (but no more than 90°) until its notches align with the remaining lockwasher tabs, making sure the adjuster nut does not turn as well (though that is unlikely). Secure the locknut in position by bending up the long lock washer tabs into its notches **(see illustration)**.

14 Fit the top yoke onto the steering stem **(see illustration 5.7b)**. Fit the steering stem nut, with its washer on RR-6 and RR-7 models, and tighten it finger-tight **(see illustration 5.7a)**. Temporarily install one of the forks to align the top and bottom yokes, and secure it by tightening the bottom yoke clamp bolts only (see Section 6). Now tighten the steering stem nut to the torque setting specified at the beginning of the Chapter.

15 Install the remaining components in a reverse of the removal procedure, referring to the relevant Sections or Chapters, and to the torque settings specified at the beginning of the Chapter.

16 Carry out a final check of the steering head bearing freeplay as described in Chapter 1, and if necessary re-adjust.

10 Steering head bearings

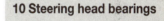

Inspection

1 Remove the steering stem (see Section 9).

2 Remove all traces of old grease from the bearings and races and check them for wear or damage.

3 The outer races in the top and bottom of the steering head should be polished and

9.10 Thread the adjuster nut onto the stem

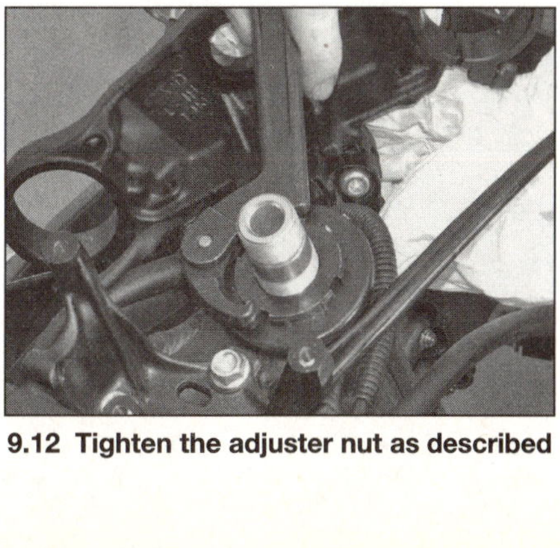

9.12 Tighten the adjuster nut as described

9.13 Bend the lockwasher tabs up into the notches in the locknut

10.3a Check the outer races in the top and bottom of the steering head

free from indentations **(see illustration)**. Inspect the bearing rollers for signs of wear, damage or discoloration, and examine the ball retainer cage for signs of cracks or splits. If there are any signs of wear on any of the above components both upper and lower bearing assemblies must be renewed as a set. Only remove the outer races in the steering head and the lower bearing inner race on the steering stem if they need to be replaced with new ones – do not reuse them once they have been removed **(see illustration)**.

Replacement

4 The outer races are an interference fit in the steering head – tap them from position using a suitable drift located in the recesses provided in the steering head that expose the lip of the race **(see illustrations)**. Tap firmly and evenly around each race to ensure that it is driven

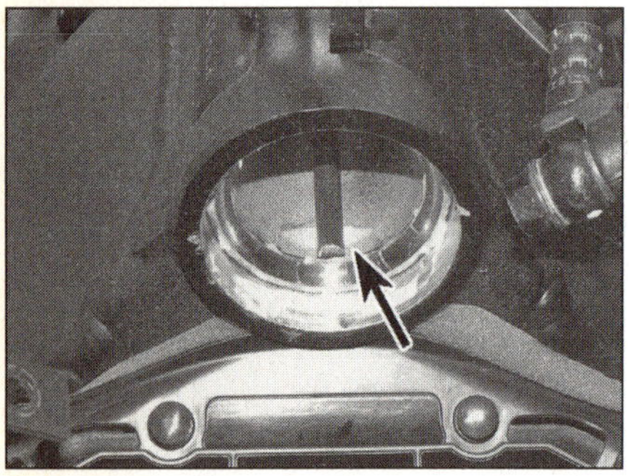

10.4b . . . locating it in the cut-outs (arrowed)

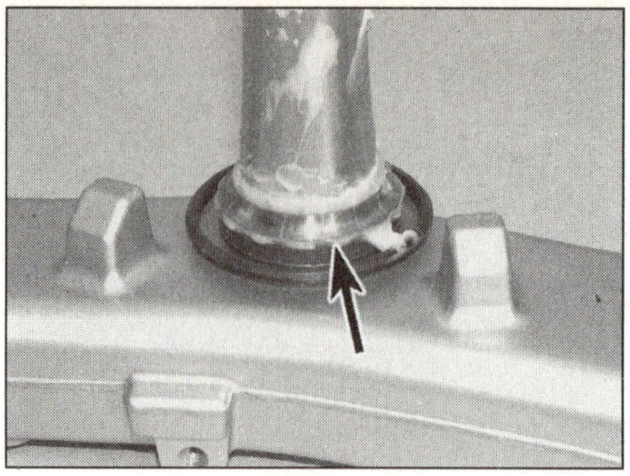

10.3b The lower bearing inner race (arrowed) is a press fit

out squarely. Curve the end of the drift slightly to improve access if necessary.

5 Alternatively, remove the races using a slide-hammer type bearing extractor; these can often be hired from tool shops.

6 Press the new outer races into the head using a drawbolt arrangement **(see illustration)**, or drive them in using a large diameter tubular

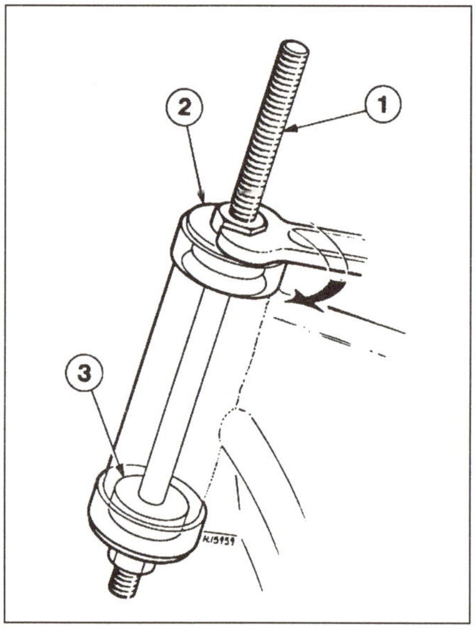

10.6 Drawbolt arrangement for fitting steering stem bearing races

1 *Long bolt or threaded bar*
2 *Thick washer*
3 *Guide for lower race*

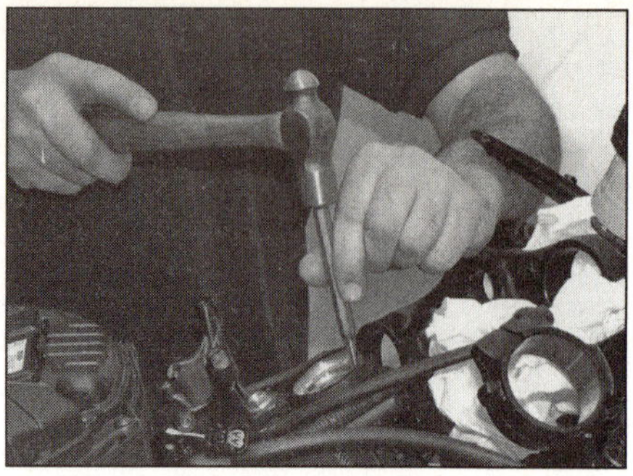

10.4a Drive the bearing races out with a brass drift . . .

drift. Ensure that the drawbolt washer or drift (as applicable) bears only on the outer edge of the race and does not contact the working surface. Alternatively, have the races installed by a Honda dealer equipped with the bearing race installation tools.

> **HAYNES HiNT** ***Installation of new bearing outer races is made much easier if the races are left overnight in the freezer. This causes them to contract slightly making them a looser fit. Alternatively, use a freeze spray.***

7 Only remove the lower bearing inner race from the steering stem if a new one is being fitted. To remove the race, use two screwdrivers placed on opposite sides to work it free, using blocks of wood to improve leverage and protect the yoke, or tap under it using a cold chisel **(see illustration)**. If you use the cold chisel method, first thread the steering stem nut onto the top then position the yoke on its front for stability – the nut will protect the threads from the transmitted force of the impact of the chisel **(see illustration)**. If the race is firmly in place it will be necessary to use a puller **(see illustration)**. Take the steering stem to a Honda dealer if required.

8 Remove the dust seal from the bottom of the stem and replace it with a new one. Smear the new one with grease.

9 Fit the new lower race onto the steering stem. Tap the new race into position using

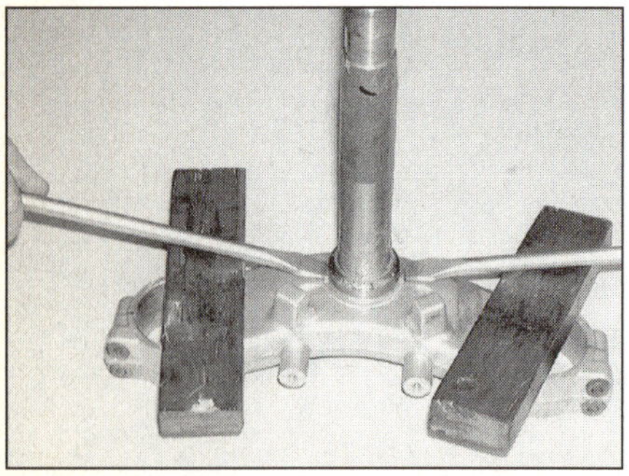

10.7a Remove the lower bearing using screwdrivers . . .

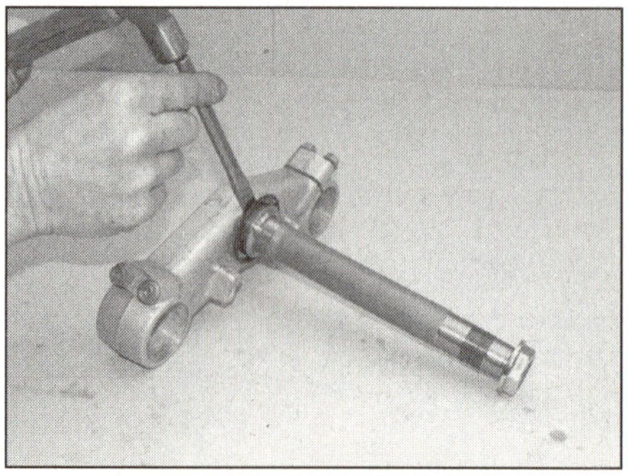

10.7b . . . a cold chisel . . .

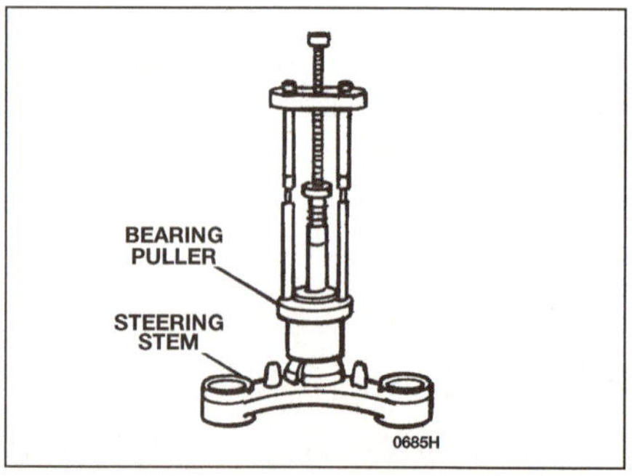

10.7c . . . or using a puller if necessary

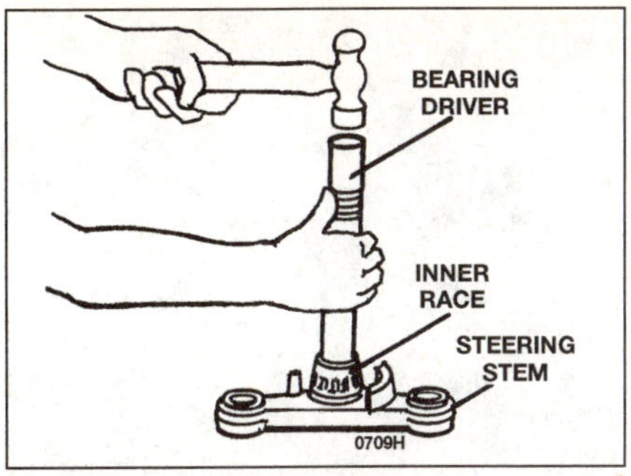

10.9 Drive the new inner race on using a suitable bearing driver or a length of pipe that bears only against the inner rim and not the bearing surface

11.12a Damper cover bolts (arrowed)

11.12b Linkage cover bolts (arrowed)

a length of tubing with an internal diameter slightly larger than the steering stem **(see illustration)**.

10 Install the steering stem (see Section 9).

11 Steering damper (HESD)

Inspection

1 The Honda Electronic Steering Damper (HESD) has a self-diagnostic feature linked to the engine management ECM – refer to Chapter 4, Section 5, for details on the fault code relevant to the HESD. If a fault is detected the system operates at its minimum damping capability as a fail-safe.

2 First make sure the wiring connector terminals are not corroded or broken and there are no loose connections. Also check for continuity in the wiring from the loom side of the connector to the ECM, referring to the Wiring Diagrams at the end of Chapter 8.

3 If the damper does not function correctly yet no fault is indicated by the malfunction indicator light (MIL), remove the damper (see below), and make sure that the steering problem is not due to worn, un-lubricated or over-tight steering head bearings (see Chapter 1 and if required Sections 9 and 10 of this chapter).

4 Refit the damper, making sure the linkage hardware between the top yoke and the damper is in good condition.

5 Two likely scenarios are that there is no increase in damping as vehicle speed increases, i.e. damping is always at its minimum, or that damping is always at its maximum whatever the speed. If so, the valve controlling the flow of damping fluid is stuck either fully open (minimum damping) or fully closed (maximum damping).

6 The damper has its own individual function test mode, allowing the maximum and minimum damping characteristics to be compared with the vehicle at a standstill. Remove the lower fairing (see Chapter 7). Raise the front wheel off the ground using an auxiliary stand. Always make sure that the bike is properly supported and secure.

7 Check minimum damping characteristics by turning the steering in a smooth and quick lock-to-lock movement.

8 Now set the HESD into its own function test mode by lowering the sidestand and selecting a gear. Open the throttle fully, and with it held open turn the ignition ON. The HESD indicator in the instrument display should start blinking, indicating that it is in function mode – it stays in this mode for ten seconds. Turn the steering as before during this time and compare the damping characteristics. If there is no change between the two tests replace the damper with a new one.

Fault code indicated

9 If the fault code is 11 flashes check the speed sensor (see Chapter 8).

10 If the fault code is 51 flashes, remove the damper (see below). Connect the probes of a multimeter or ohmmeter set to the ohms x 1 scale to the terminals of the damper wiring connector and measure the resistance of the solenoid valve. If it is not as specified at the beginning of the Chapter replace the damper with a new one. If the reading is as specified refer to Step 2.

Removal and installation

11 Remove the fuel tank cover (see Chapter 7).

12 Unscrew the two bolts and remove the damper cover **(see illustration)**. Unscrew the two bolts and remove the linkage cover **(see illustration)**.

13 Unscrew the damper mounting bolts **(see illustration)**. Unscrew the bolt and remove the washer securing the linkage arm to the top yoke and retrieve the washer from between the arm and the yoke **(see illustration)**.

14 Lift the damper off and disconnect the wiring connector **(see illustration)**. If required unscrew the nut securing the linkage arm and remove the arm and the washer.

15 Installation is the reverse of removal. Tighten the damper mounting bolts and linkage arm bolt to the torque setting specified at the beginning of the Chapter.

12 Rear shock absorber

Warning: Do not attempt to disassemble the shock absorber in the home workshop. It is nitrogen-charged under high

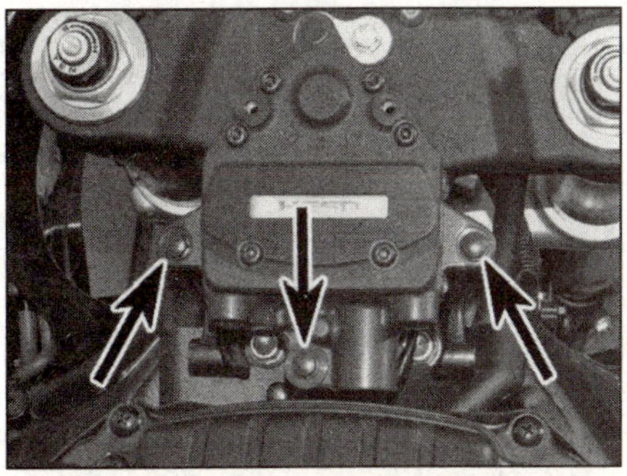

11.13a Unscrew the mounting bolts (arrowed) . . .

11.13b . . . then the linkage bolt, retrieving the washer

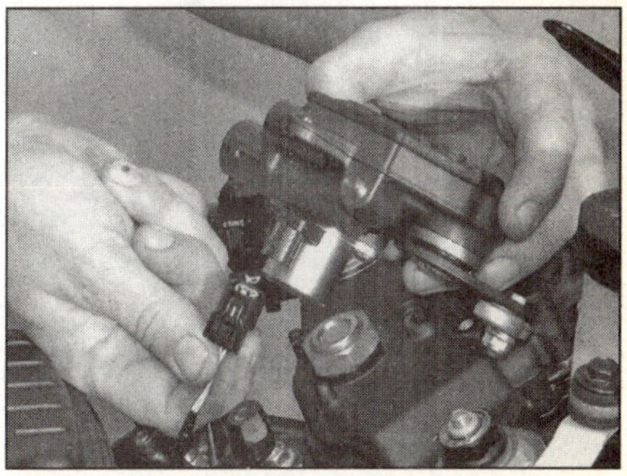

11.14 Disconnect the wiring connector and remove the damper

12.2 Unscrew the nut and withdraw the linkage rod-to-linkage arm bolt

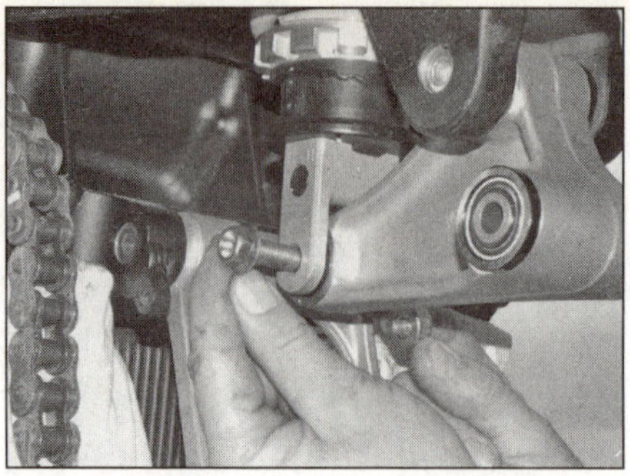

12.3 Unscrew the nut and withdraw the linkage arm-to-shock absorber bolt

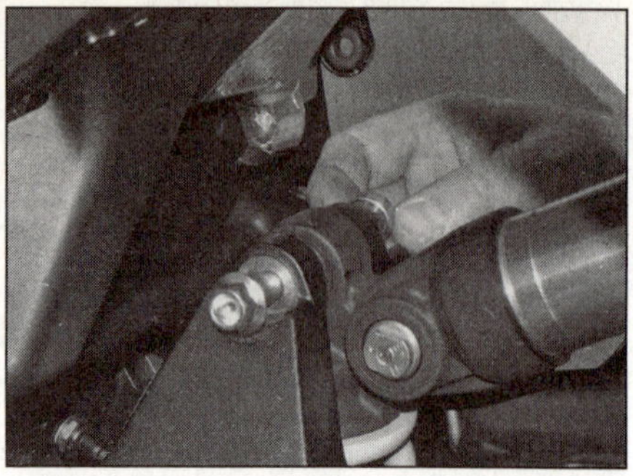

12.4a Unscrew the nut and withdraw the bolt . . .

pressure. Improper disassembly could result in serious injury.

Removal

Note: *If you are removing the suspension linkage as well, do so first (see Section 13).*

1 Support the motorcycle so that no weight is transmitted through any part of the rear suspension – tie the front brake lever to the handlebar to ensure the bike can't roll forward. Position a support under the rear wheel or swingarm so that it does not drop when the shock absorber is removed, but also making sure that the weight of the machine is off the rear suspension so that the shock is not compressed.

2 Unscrew the nut and withdraw the bolt securing the linkage rods to the linkage arm **(see illustration)**. Pivot the rod piece down.

3 Unscrew the nut and withdraw the bolt securing the linkage arm to the shock absorber **(see illustration)**.

4 Unscrew the nut on the bolt securing the top of the shock absorber to the swingarm **(see illustration)**. Support the shock from the bottom and withdraw the bolt, then remove the shock absorber pivoting the linkage arm back as you do to provide clearance **(see illustration)**.

Inspection

5 Inspect the shock absorber for obvious physical damage and oil leakage, and the coil spring for looseness, cracks or signs of fatigue **(see illustration)**.

6 Inspect the spherical bearing in the top of the shock absorber for wear or damage. If necessary lever out the grease seals, noting which way round they fit **(see illustration)**. Discard the seals as they must be replaced with new ones. Remove the stopper ring securing the bearing **(see illustration)**. Press the old bearing out from the right-hand side and the new bearing in from the left-hand side until it seats, referring to *Tools and Workshop Tips* in the Reference Section.

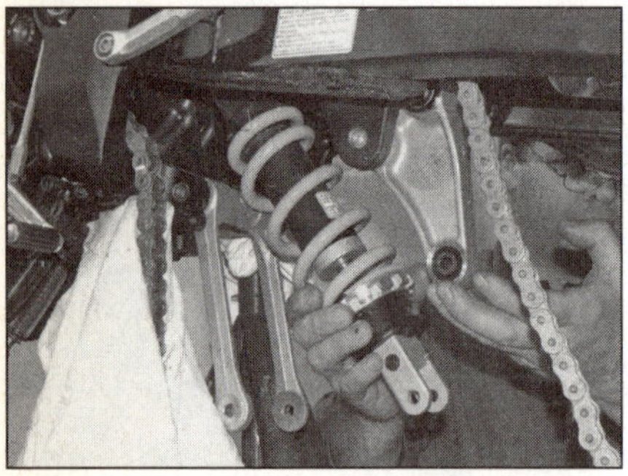

12.4b . . . and remove the shock absorber

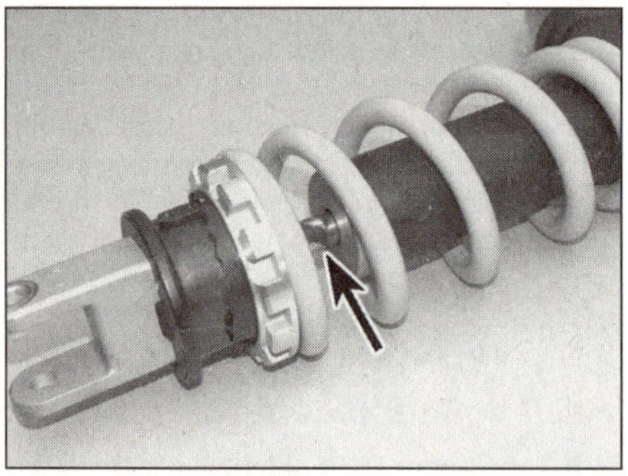

12.5 Check around the rod for signs of oil (arrowed)

7 Fit the stopper ring into its groove in the left-hand side **(see illustration 12.6b)**. Smear the new seals with grease and press them squarely into place with the marked flat side facing in towards the bearing, noting that the seal with the larger diameter goes into the left-hand side – use a thin-rimmed socket located in the dish of the seal to drive it in if necessary **(see illustration)**.

8 With the exception of the top pivot components, parts are not available for the shock absorber. If it is worn or damaged, it must be replaced with a new one. Before disposing of an old shock absorber, you should release the nitrogen gas from the reservoir. To do this, lever the blanking cap off the end of the reservoir using a screwdriver, then point the valve away from you and anyone else (direct it into the ground) and depress the valve. When all the pressure is released, remove the core of the valve using a valve core remover.

Warning: Be very careful when releasing the gas pressure – it is possible for fine debris particles to be released with it, and as the pressure is high these could damage you eyes if done carelessly. Always point the valve well away.

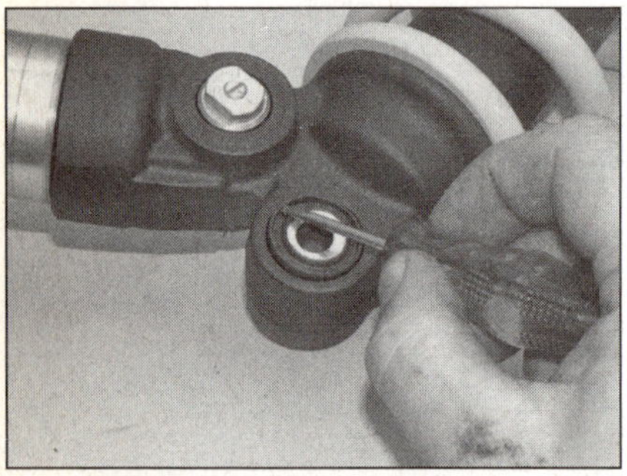

12.6a Lever the seals out

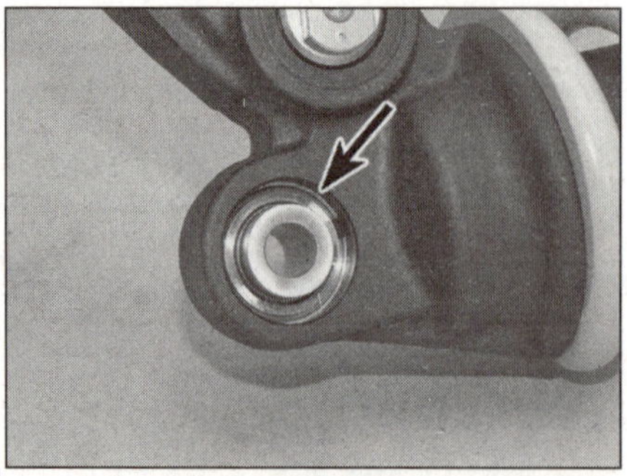

12.6b The bearing is retained by a ring (arrowed)

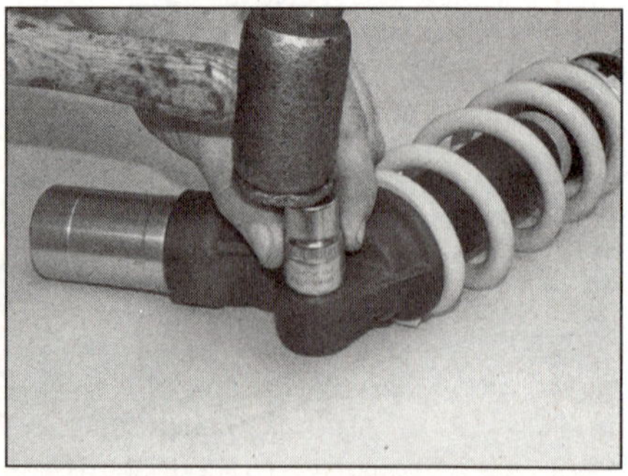

12.7 Fit the seals with the dished side on the outside and use a socket to drive them in if necessary

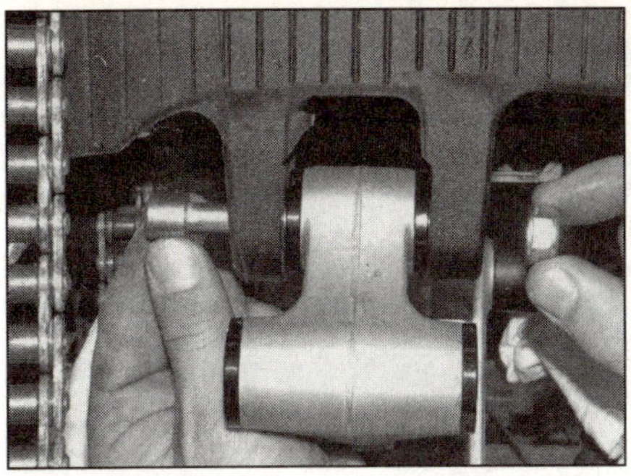
13.4 Unscrew the nut then withdraw the bolt and remove the arm

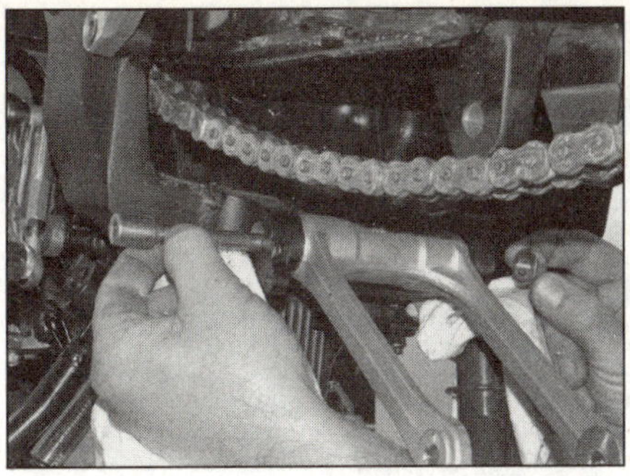
13.5 Unscrew the nut then withdraw the bolt and remove the linkage rod piece

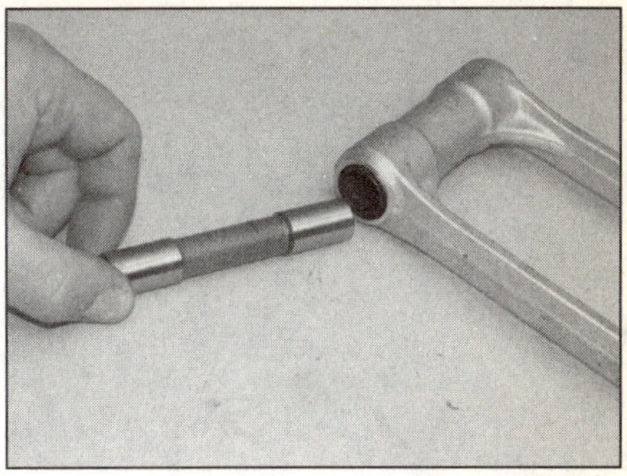
13.6a Withdraw the spacer . . .

Installation

9 Installation is the reverse of removal, noting the following:

- Apply multi-purpose grease with EP2 rating to the shock absorber and linkage plate and arm pivot points.
- Install the shock absorber with the damping adjuster screws facing the left-hand side.
- Install the bolts from the left-hand side.
- Tighten the nuts to the torque settings specified at the beginning of the Chapter.

13 Rear suspension linkage

Removal

1 Support the motorcycle so that no weight is transmitted through any part of the rear suspension – tie the front brake lever to the handlebar to ensure the bike can't roll forward. Position a support under the rear wheel or swingarm so that it does not drop when the linkage is removed, but also making sure that the weight of the machine is off the rear suspension so that the shock is not compressed.

2 Unscrew the nut and withdraw the bolt securing the linkage rods to the linkage arm **(see illustration 12.2)**. Pivot the rod piece down.

3 Unscrew the nut and withdraw the bolt securing the shock absorber to the linkage arm **(see illustration 12.3)**.

4 Unscrew the nut and withdraw the bolt securing the linkage arm to the swingarm and remove the arm, noting which way round it fits **(see illustration)**.

5 Unscrew the nut and withdraw bolt securing the linkage rod piece to the frame and remove the rod piece, noting which way round it fits **(see illustration)**.

Inspection

6 Withdraw the spacer from the linkage rod piece, then lever out the grease seals **(see illustrations)**.

7 Remove the thrust rings from the wider two mounts on the linkage arm, then withdraw the spacers and lever out the grease seals **(see illustrations)**. Hook the seals out from the narrow mount and remove the shouldered outer spacers **(see illustration)**. Remove the central spacer from the bearing if required, but note that the needles are not caged but loose, and so there is a danger of them dropping out **(see**

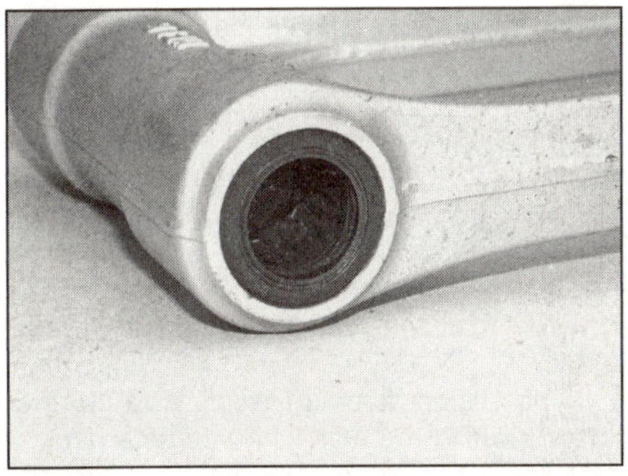
13.6b . . . to access the seals and bearings

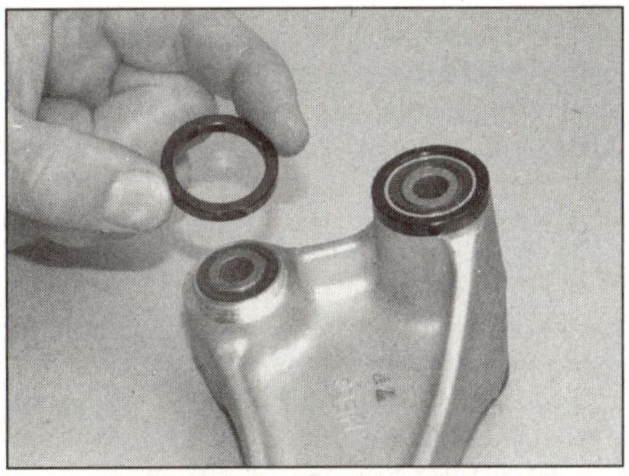
13.7a Remove the thrust rings . . .

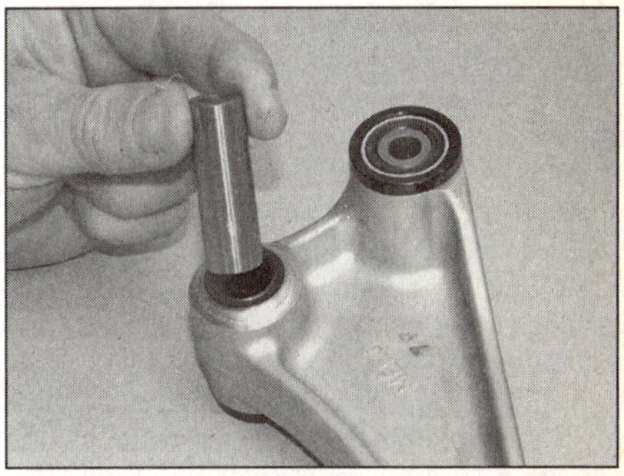
13.7b . . . then withdraw the spacers . . .

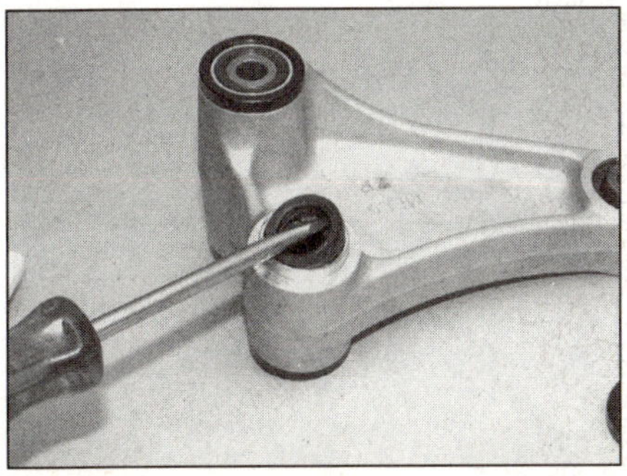
13.7c . . . and lever out the seals

13.7d Hook the seal out . . .

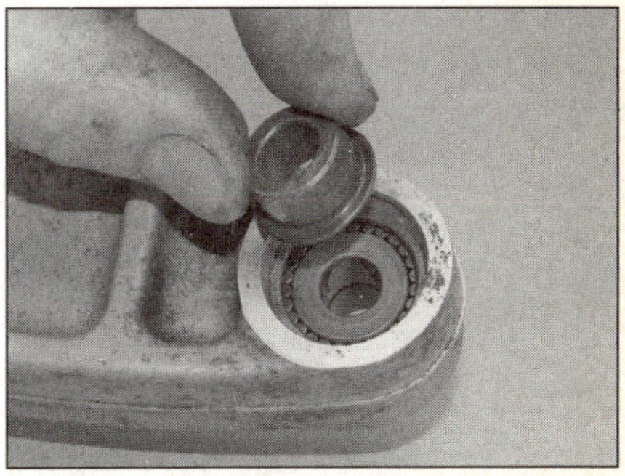
13.7e . . . and remove the shouldered spacer

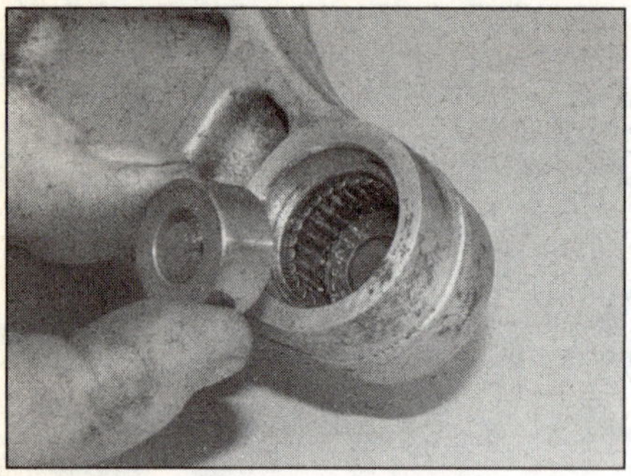

13.7f The central spacer holds the needles in place in the bearing

illustration) – in case they do, there should be 27 of them! If a new bearing is required it should come fitted with a central sleeve that can be pushed out when fitting the spacer in.

8 Discard the seals as new ones must be used. Thoroughly clean all components, removing all traces of dirt, corrosion and grease.

9 Inspect all components closely, looking for obvious signs of wear such as heavy scoring, or for damage such as cracks or distortion. Slip each spacer back into its bearing(s) and check that there is not an excessive amount of freeplay between the two components. Replace worn or damaged components with new ones as required.

10 Check the condition of the needle roller bearings in the linkage arm and rod piece **(see illustration)**. Refer to *Tools and Workshop Tips* (Section 5) in the Reference section for more information on bearings.

11 Worn bearings can be driven or drawn out of their bores, but note that removal will destroy them; new bearings should be obtained before work commences. The new bearings should be pressed or drawn into their bores rather than driven into position. In the absence of a press, a suitable drawbolt tool can be made up as described in *Tools and Workshop Tips* in the Reference section. When fitting the new bearings make sure the marked side faces out and they are central in their bores, with a 5.35 to 5.65 mm gap between each end and the rim of the bore for the shock absorber mount bearing, and a 4.8 to 5.2 mm gap for all the other bearings in the arm and rod piece.

12 Lubricate the needle bearings, spacers

13.10 Check the bearings

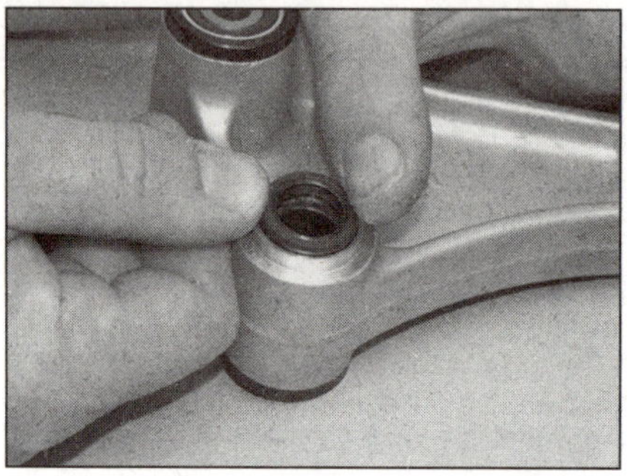

13.14 Press the new seals into place

and seals with a multi-purpose grease with EP2 rating.

13 Fit the seals onto the shouldered spacers for the narrow mount on the linkage arm, with the dished side facing out **(see illustration)**. Fit the spacers and seals against the central bearing spacer.

14 Press the new seals squarely into place in all the other mounts and in the linkage rod piece, with the marked flat side facing out **(see illustration)**. Install the spacers **(see illustrations 13.7b and 13.6a)**. Fit the thrust rings onto the linkage arm **(see illustration 13.7a)**.

Installation

15 Installation is the reverse of removal, noting the following:

- Apply molybdenum-disulphide grease to the pivot points.
- Insert all bolts from the left-hand side.
- Tighten the bolts to the torque setting specified at the beginning of the Chapter.

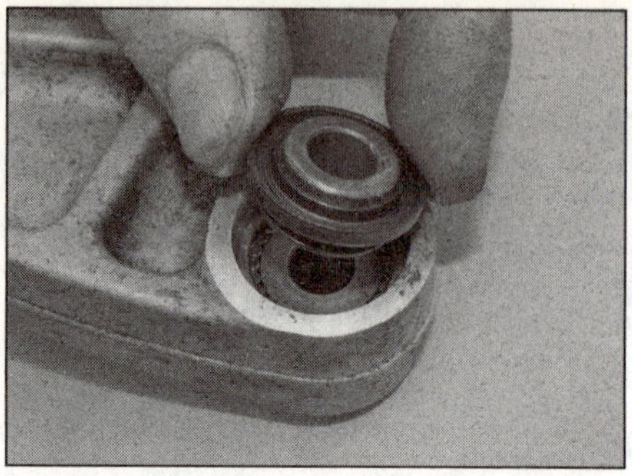

13.13 Fit the seal onto each spacer then fit them into the arm

14 Suspension adjustment

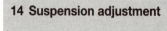

Front forks

1 The front forks are adjustable for spring pre-load and both rebound and compression damping. Always make sure both forks are set equally.

2 Spring pre-load is adjusted using a spanner on the adjuster flats **(see illustration)** – a spanner should be provided in the toolkit. Turn the adjuster clockwise to increase pre-load and anti-clockwise to decrease it. To set the standard position, turn the adjuster fully anti-clockwise until it stops, then turn it clockwise 7 full turns.

3 Rebound damping is adjusted using a screwdriver in the slot in the top of the damper rod protruding from the pre-load adjuster **(see illustration)**. Turn it clockwise to increase damping and anti-clockwise to decrease it. To set the standard position, turn the adjuster fully clockwise until it stops, then turn it anti-clockwise 2 turns on RR-4 and RR-5 models and 2 1/2 turns on RR-6 and RR-7 models, until the punch mark on the adjuster aligns with the reference mark on the directional arrow.

4 Compression damping is adjusted using a screwdriver in the slot in the adjuster which is on the bottom of the fork **(see illustration)**. Turn it clockwise to increase damping and anti-clockwise to decrease it. To set the standard

14.2 Fork pre-load adjuster (arrowed)

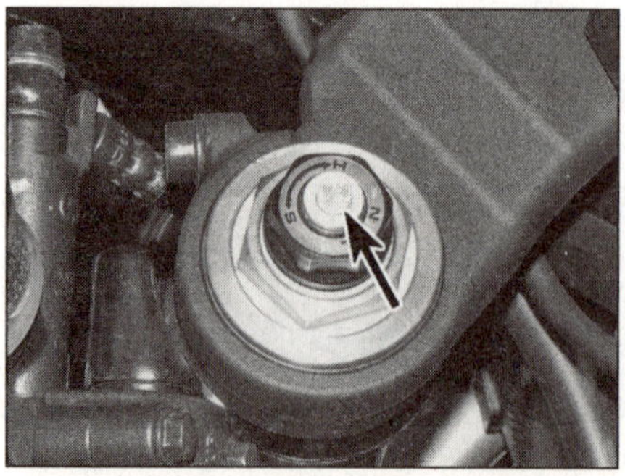

14.3 Fork rebound damping adjuster (arrowed)

14.4 Fork compression damping adjuster (arrowed)

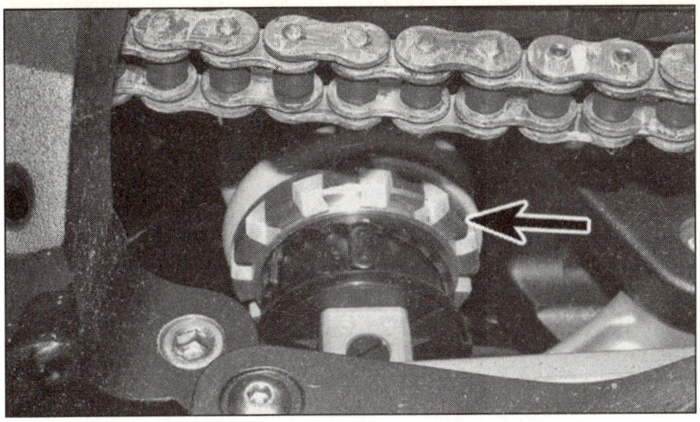

14.6 Shock pre-load adjuster (arrowed)

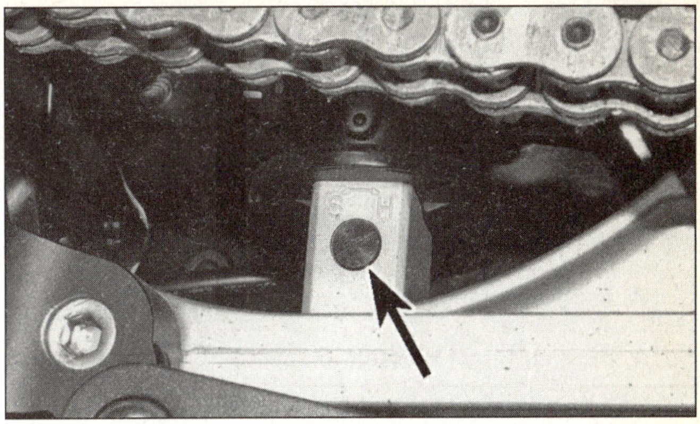

14.7 Shock rebound damping adjuster (arrowed)

position, turn the adjuster fully clockwise until it stops, then turn it anti-clockwise 2 turns on RR-4 and RR-5 models and 2 1/4 turns on RR-6 and RR-7 models until the punch mark on the adjuster aligns with the index mark on the housing.

Rear shock absorber

5 The shock absorber is adjustable for spring pre-load and both rebound and compression damping.

6 Spring pre-load is adjusted using a suitable C-spanner (one is provided in the toolkit) to turn the spring seat on the bottom of the shock absorber **(see illustration)**. There are ten positions. Position 1 is the lowest setting for light loads, position 4 the standard, and position 10 the highest, for heavy loads. Align the setting required with the adjustment stopper.

7 Rebound damping adjustment is made by turning the adjuster on the bottom of the shock absorber on the left-hand side using a flat-bladed screwdriver **(see illustration)**. To increase the damping, turn the adjuster clockwise. To decrease the damping, turn the adjuster anti-clockwise. To set the standard position, turn the adjuster clockwise until it stops, then turn it anti clockwise 2 1/2 turns on RR-4 and RR-5 models and 2 1/4 turns on RR-6 and RR-7 models until the punch mark on the adjuster aligns with the index mark on the shock absorber.

8 Compression damping adjustment is made by turning the adjuster on the top of the shock absorber on the left-hand side using a flat-bladed screwdriver **(see illustration)**. To increase the damping, turn the adjuster clockwise. To decrease the damping, turn the adjuster anti-clockwise. To set the standard position, turn the adjuster clockwise until it stops, then turn it anti clockwise 9 clicks on RR-4 and RR-5 models and 17 clicks on RR-6 and RR-7 models until the punch mark on the adjuster aligns with the index mark on the shock absorber.

15 Swingarm removal and installation

Special tools: *A peg spanner is required to slacken and tighten the adjuster bolt locknut. If the Honda service tool Pt. No. 07YMA-MCF0100 (MCFA100 in the US) is not available, a suitable one will have to obtained commercially or fabricated out of a piece of steel tubing, or an old socket* ***(see illustrations 15.7a)****. To unscrew the swingarm pivot bolt you need a large hex key, available, from an automotive or commercial vehicle tool supplier – sump keys are sometimes that big. Alternatively a tool can be fabricated using a bolt with two nuts that fit the hex in the end of the swingarm pivot bolt threaded onto it and locked very tightly together, or brazed or welded to it. Alternatively weld a bar onto a bolt or nut to act as a handle.*

14.8 Shock compression damping adjuster (arrowed)

Removal

1 Remove the front sprocket (see Chapter 6). Remove the rear wheel (see Chapter 6).

2 Unscrew the bolt securing the right-hand side of the hugger and the brake hose guide to the swingarm **(see illustration)**. Free the hose, noting how the tab on the guide locates in the hole in the swingarm, and tie the rear brake caliper to the frame, making sure no strain is placed on the hose **(see illustration)**.

3 If required unscrew the remaining bolts securing the rear hugger to the swingarm and remove it – this can be done after removing the swingarm if preferred **(see illustration)**.

4 If required unscrew the bolt(s) (if you have removed the hugger the front one will already have been removed) securing the rear section of the chainguard and remove the guard, then unscrew the bolt and release the trim clip

15.2a Unscrew the bolt (arrowed) . . .

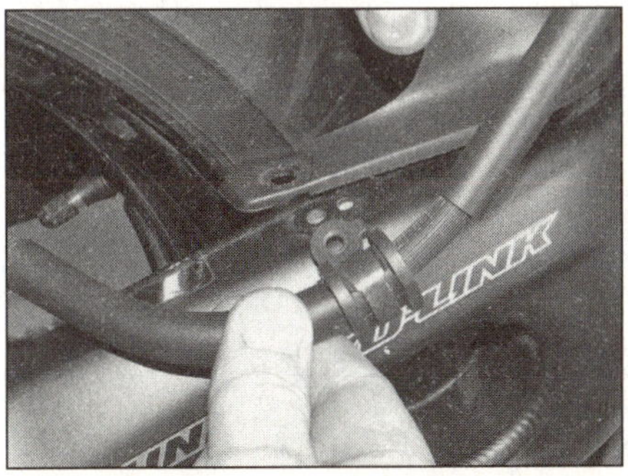

15.2b . . . and free the brake hose, noting how the guide locates

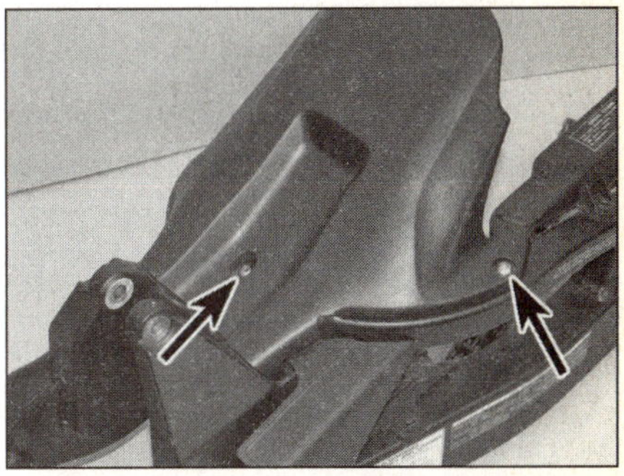

15.3 Unscrew the bolts (arrowed) and remove the hugger

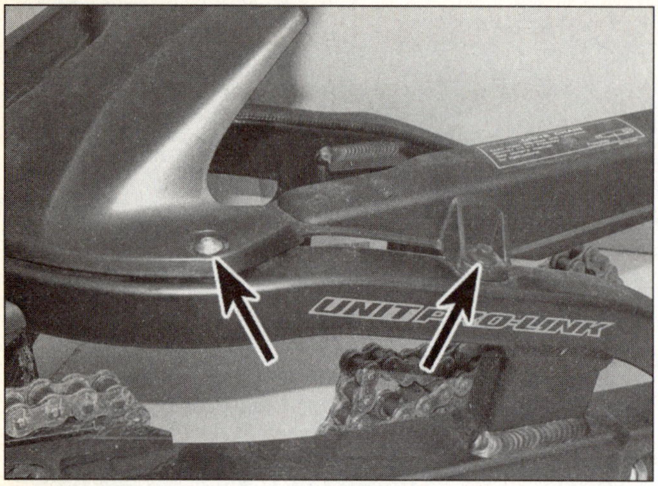

15.4a Unscrew the bolt(s) (arrowed) and remove the rear section

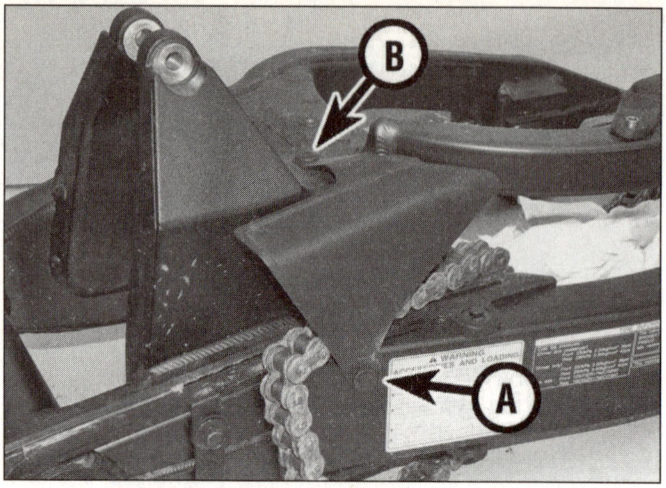

15.4b Unscrew the bolt (A) and release the trim clip (B) to remove the front section

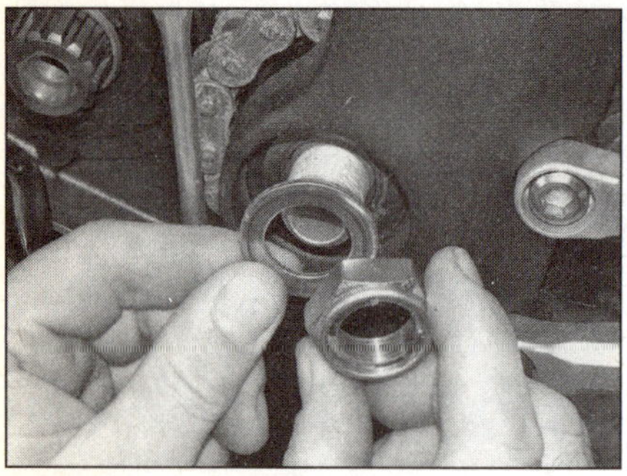

15.6 Unscrew the nut and remove the washer

securing the front section and remove the guard – this can be done after removing the swingarm if preferred **(see illustrations)**.

5 If required remove the shock absorber (see Section 12) and the suspension linkage arm (see Section 13). Alternatively just detach the linkage rod piece from the frame and remove the swingarm with the shock and linkage attached.

6 Unscrew the nut on the left-hand end of the pivot bolt and remove the washer **(see illustration)**.

7 Unscrew the adjuster bolt locknut on the right-hand end of the swingarm pivot using a suitable peg spanner (see **Special tools** above) **(see illustrations)**.

8 Unscrew the pivot bolt using a suitable tool (see **Special tools** above), thereby turning the adjuster bolt with which it engages, until the inner end of the adjuster bolt is clear of the swingarm and flush with the inside of the frame **(see illustration)**.

9 Withdraw the pivot bolt then manoeuvre the swingarm out of the frame **(see illustration)**. If required thread the adjuster bolt out of the frame **(see illustration)**.

10 Remove the chain slider from the swingarm if necessary, noting the collars that fit with the rear bolts **(see illustration)**. If it is badly worn or damaged, it should be replaced with a new

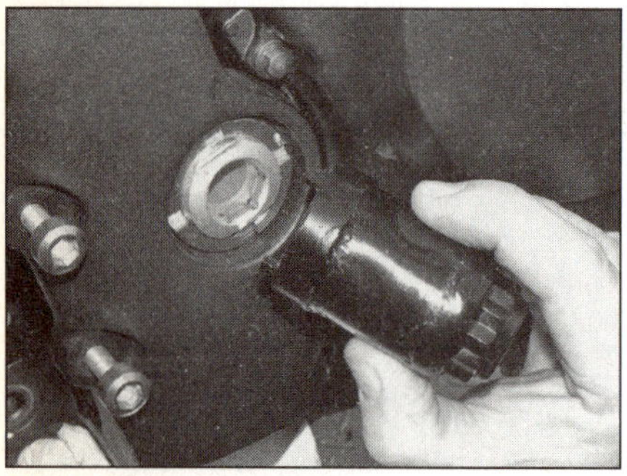

15.7a Using a home-made peg spanner . . .

15.7b . . . to unscrew the locknut

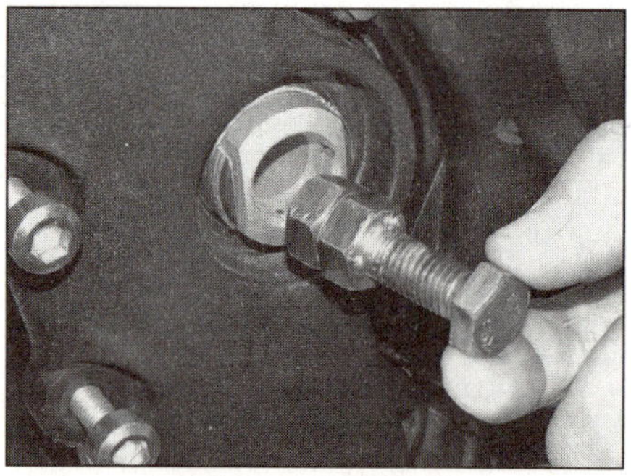

15.8 A home-made tool to fit into the head of the pivot bolt for unscrewing the adjuster bolt

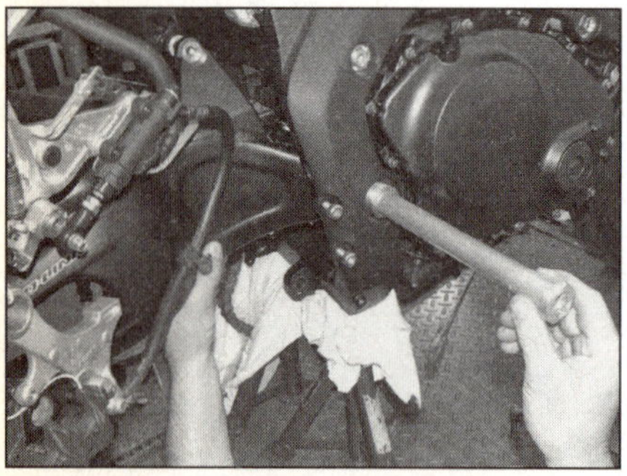

15.9a Withdraw the pivot bolt and remove the swingarm

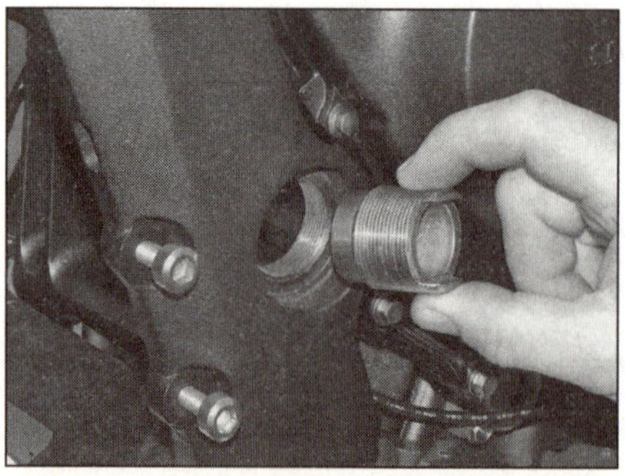

15.9b Remove the adjuster bolt if required

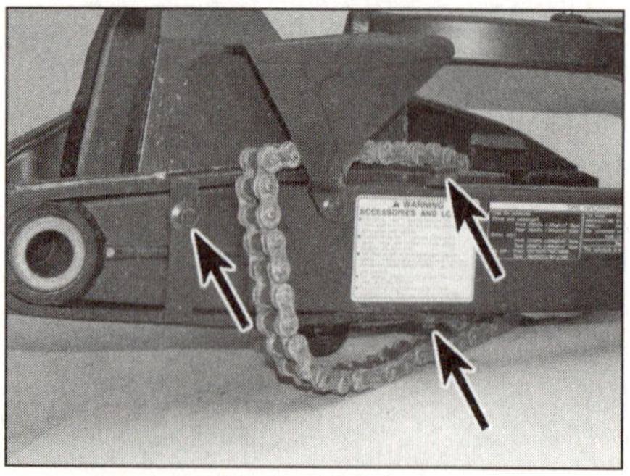

15.10 Chain slider bolts (arrowed)

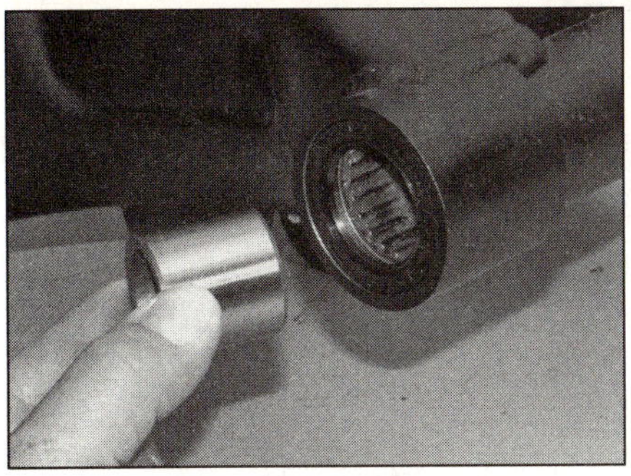
15.11a Remove the plain collar . . .

15.11b . . . and the shouldered collar

15.13 Make sure the adjuster bolt does not protrude from the inside of the frame

one – there are some wear limit arrows on the front. Inspect all pivot components for wear or damage as described in Section 16.

Installation

11 Remove the plain collar from the right-hand pivot and the shouldered collar from the left **(see illustrations)**. Clean off all old grease, then lubricate the grease seals, bearings, collars and the pivot bolt with multi-purpose grease with an EP2 rating. Fit the plain collar into the right-hand pivot and the shouldered collar into the left.

12 If removed, install the chain slider, making sure it locates correctly over the lug at the front and over the side mounting bolt lug **(see illustration 15.10)**. Apply a suitable non-permanent thread locking compound to the bolts, then fit them with their collars on the rear bolts and washer with the front bolt and tighten them to the torque setting specified at the beginning of the Chapter.

13 If removed thread the adjuster bolt into the frame **(see illustration 15.9b)**, setting it flush with the inside of the frame **(see illustration)**.

14 Offer up the swingarm and have an assistant hold it in place. Make sure the drive chain is looped over the front of the swingarm **(see illustration)**. Slide the pivot bolt through from the right-hand side **(see illustration 15.9a)**, and engage its flats with those on the adjuster bolt so they are locked together **(see illustration)**.

15 Using the same tool in the pivot bolt head as on removal tighten the adjuster bolt to the torque setting specified at the beginning of the Chapter **(see illustration 15.8)**. After tightening it make sure the flats on the bolt head are central in the adjuster bolt – any pressure on either side can make the locknut difficult to fit.

16 Thread the locknut onto the adjuster bolt **(see illustration 15.7b)**. Tighten the locknut to the specified torque setting using the Honda special tool or a peg spanner (see ***Special tools*** above) **(see illustration 15.7a)**. If you do not have the Honda special tool, which is offset and allows the adjuster bolt to be counter-held while tightening the locknut, it is advisable to make a reference mark between the adjuster bolt and the frame to make sure that it does not turn as the locknut is being tightened. If you have the special tool, tighten the locknut to the 'indicated' specified torque setting, which allows for the extra leverage provided by the offset. If you are using a standard or fabricated peg spanner tighten the locknut to the 'actual' specified torque setting.

17 Fit the washer and the nut onto the left-hand end of the pivot bolt and tighten it to the torque setting specified at the beginning of the Chapter **(see illustration 15.6)**.

18 Install the rear suspension linkage and shock absorber as required according to your removal method (see Sections 13 and 12).

19 Install the chainguard and rear hugger if removed **(see illustrations 15.4b and a and 15.3)**. Fit the brake hose guide, making sure the tab locates in the hole **(see illustration 15.2b and a)**.

20 Install the front sprocket (see Chapter 6).

21 Check and adjust the drive chain slack (see Chapter 1). Check the operation of the rear suspension and brake before taking the machine on the road.

16 Swingarm inspection and bearing replacement

Inspection

1 Remove the swingarm (see Section 15).

2 Thoroughly clean the swingarm, removing all traces of dirt, corrosion and grease.

3 Inspect the swingarm closely, looking for obvious signs of wear such as heavy scoring, and cracks or distortion due to accident damage. Any damaged or worn component must be replaced.

4 Check the swingarm pivot bolt for straightness by rolling it on a flat surface such as a piece of plate glass (first wipe off all old grease and remove any corrosion using steel wool). Replace the pivot bolt with a new one if it is bent.

Bearing check and replacement

5 Remove the plain collar from the right-hand pivot and the shouldered collar from the left **(see illustrations 15.11a and b)**. Lever the grease seal out from each side of each pivot, noting which size fits where **(see illustration)**.

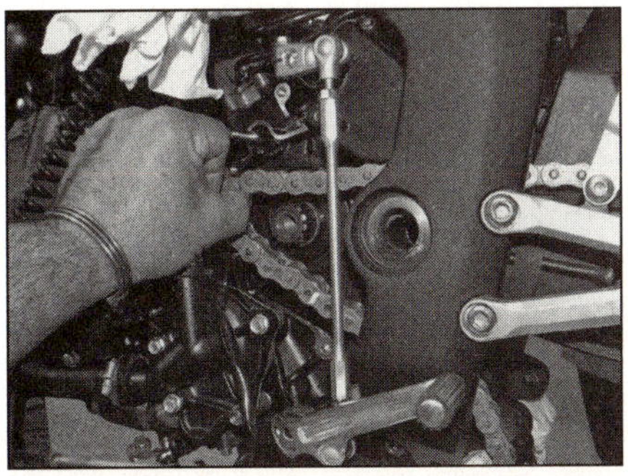
5.14a Make sure the drive chain is over the front and loop it round the output shaft

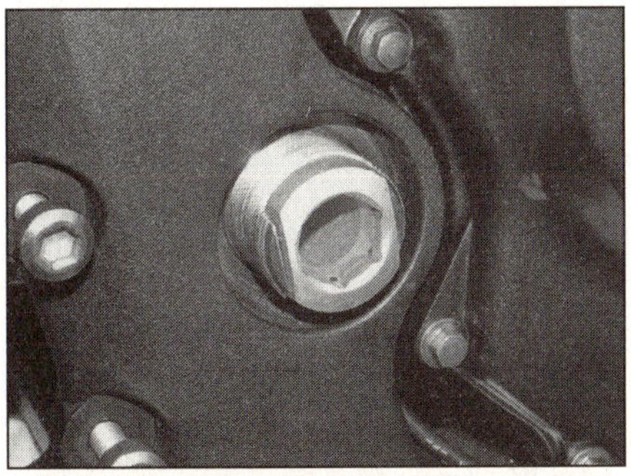
15.14b Engage the pivot bolt head in the adjuster bolt

16.5a Lever the seal out from each side of each pivot

16.5b Withdraw the spacer

New seals must be used, but keep the old ones laid out in order so the new seals can be matched for position. Withdraw the central spacer **(see illustration)**.

6 Refer to *Tools and Workshop Tips* in the Reference section and check the bearings – there is a needle bearing and a ball bearing in the right-hand pivot, and a needle bearing in the left-hand pivot **(see illustration)**. Clean and inspect them for wear or damage. If the bearings do not run smoothly and freely or if there is excessive freeplay, they must be replaced with new ones – refer to the Reference Section for removal and installation methods, noting that Honda specify the need for an hydraulic press. The bearings in the right-hand pivot are held by a circlip **(see illustration)**. Once disturbed, the bearings must be replaced with new ones if removed – they cannot be reused.

16.6a Check the bearings(s) in each pivot

7 When installing the new bearings, on the right-hand side press the ball bearing in until it seats, then press the needle bearing against it, with its marked side end facing out. Press the left-hand needle bearing in with its marked end facing out and so that its outer end is set in to a depth of 7 to 8 mm. Do not forget to fit the circlip into the groove in the right-hand side, using a new one if the old one deformed on removal **(see illustration 16.6b)**.

8 Lubricate the spacer, collars, bearings and grease seal lips with multi-purpose grease with an EP2 rating. Slide the spacer into the swingarm **(see illustration 16.5b)**. Press the new seals into place with their marked side facing outwards – the right-hand seal has a larger external diameter **(see illustration)**. Fit the plain collar into the right-hand pivot and the shouldered collar into the left **(see illustrations 15.11a and b)**.

16.6b A circlip (arrowed) secures the ball bearing

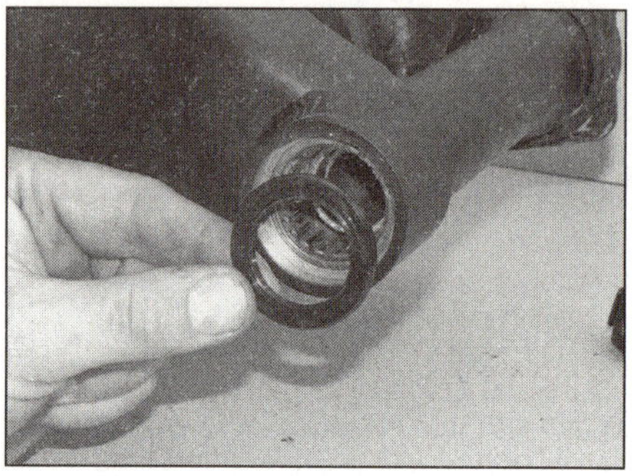

16.8 Make sure you select the correct seal for each pivot

Chapter 6
Brakes, wheels and final drive

Contents

Degrees of difficulty

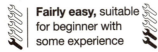

Easy, suitable for novice with little experience	**Fairly easy,** suitable for beginner with some experience	**Fairly difficult,** suitable for competent DIY mechanic	**Difficult,** suitable for experienced DIY mechanic	**Very difficult,** suitable for expert DIY or professional

Specifications

Front brakes

Brake fluid type	DOT 4
Caliper bore ID	
Upper bore	
Standard	32.080 to 32.130 mm
Service limit	32.140 mm
Lower bore	
Standard	30.280 to 30.330 mm
Service limit	30.340 mm
Caliper piston OD	
Upper piston	
Standard	31.967 to 32.000 mm
Service limit	31.957 mm
Lower piston	
Standard	30.167 to 30.200 mm
Service limit	30.157 mm
Master cylinder bore ID	
Standard	17.460 to 17.503 mm
Service limit	17.515 mm
Master cylinder piston OD	
Standard	17.321 to 17.367 mm
Service limit	17.309 mm
Disc thickness	
Front	
RR-4 and RR-5 models	
Standard	5.0 mm
Service limit	4.0 mm
RR-6 and RR-7 models	
Standard	4.5 mm
Service limit	3.5 mm
Rear	
Standard	5.0 mm
Service limit	4.0 mm
Disc maximum runout	0.3 mm

Rear brake

Brake fluid type	DOT 4
Caliper bore ID	
RR-4 and RR-5 models	
Standard	38.180 to 38.230 mm
Service limit	38.240 mm
RR-6 and RR-7 models	
Standard	30.230 to 30.280 mm
Service limit	30.29 mm
Caliper piston OD	
RR-4 and RR-5 models	
Standard	38.098 to 38.148 mm
Service limit	38.09 mm
RR-6 and RR-7 models	
Standard	30.082 to 30.115 mm
Service limit	30.14 mm
Master cylinder bore ID	
RR-4 and RR-5 models	
Standard	15.870 to 15.913 mm
Service limit	15.925 mm
RR-6 and RR-7 models	
Standard	14.000 to 14.043 mm
Service limit	14.055 mm
Master cylinder piston OD	
RR-4 and RR-5 models	
Standard	15.827 to 15.854 mm
Service limit	15.815 mm
RR-6 and RR-7 models	
Standard	13.957 to 13.984 mm
Service limit	13.945 mm
Disc thickness	
Standard	5.0 mm
Service limit	4.0 mm
Disc maximum runout	0.3 mm

Wheels

Maximum wheel runout (front and rear)	
Axial (side-to-side)	2.0 mm
Radial (out-of-round)	2.0 mm
Maximum axle runout (front and rear)	0.20 mm

Tyres

Tyre pressures	see *Pre-ride* checks
Tyre sizes*	
Front	120/70-ZR17 (58W) radial
Rear	190/50-ZR17 (73W) radial

**Refer to the owners handbook or the tyre information label on the swingarm for approved tyre brands.*

Final drive

Drive chain slack and lubricant	see Chapter 1
Drive chain type	
RK	RK50GFOZ1-114LJFZ (114 links)
DID	DID50VM2-114YB (114 links)
Joining link pin projection from side plate (unriveted)	
DID type chain	1.15 to 1.55 mm
RK type chain	1.20 to 1.40 mm
Joining link staked ends diameter	
DID type chain	5.50 to 5.80 mm
RK type chain	5.30 to 5.70 mm
Sprocket sizes	
Front (engine) sprocket	16T
Rear (wheel) sprocket	
RR-4 and RR-5 models	
Europe models	40T
US and Canada models	41T
RR-6 and RR-7 models	42T

Torque settings

Brake caliper bleed valves	
Front calipers	8 Nm
Front master cylinder	6 Nm
Rear caliper	6 Nm
Brake disc bolts	
Front	20 Nm
Rear	42 Nm
Brake hose banjo bolts	34 Nm
Front axle bolt	78 Nm
Front axle clamp bolts	22 Nm
Front brake caliper body joining bolts	23 Nm
Front brake caliper mounting bolts	45 Nm
Front brake master cylinder clamp bolts	12 Nm
Front brake pad retaining pins	16 Nm
Front sprocket bolt	54 Nm
Passenger footrest bracket bolts	37 Nm
Rear axle nut	113 Nm
Rear brake caliper front slider pin	27 Nm
Rear brake caliper mounting bolt/slider pin (RR-4 and RR-5 models)	23 Nm
Rear brake pad retaining pin	18 Nm
Rear master cylinder mounting bolts	10 Nm
Rear sprocket nuts	64 Nm

1 General information

All models covered in this manual have hydraulically operated disc brakes, with twin discs at the front and a single disc at the rear. On all models the front calipers have four opposed pistons, and the rear has a sliding caliper with a single piston.

The drive to the rear wheel is by chain and sprockets. The rear wheel hub incorporates a rubber 'cush-drive'.

All models are fitted with cast alloy wheels designed for tubeless tyres only.

***Caution:** Disc brake components rarely require disassembly. Do not disassemble components unless absolutely necessary.*

If an hydraulic brake hose is loosened or disconnected, the banjo union sealing washers must be replaced with new ones and the system must be bled upon reassembly. Do not use solvents on internal brake components. Solvents will cause the seals to swell and distort. Use only clean DOT 4 brake fluid for cleaning. Use care when working with brake fluid as it can injure your eyes and it will damage painted surfaces and plastic parts.

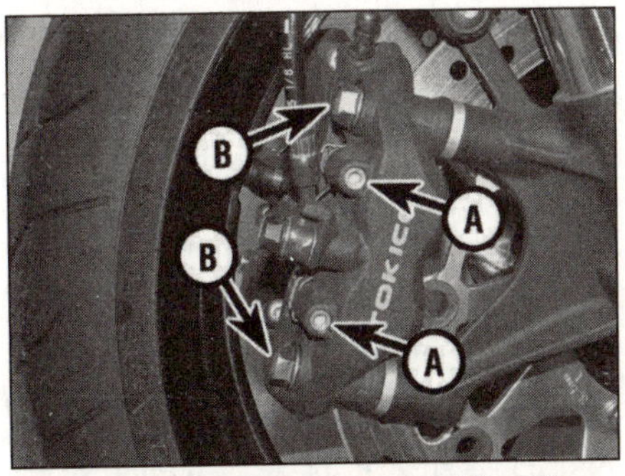

2.1a Brake pad retaining pins (A), caliper mounting bolts (B)

2.1b Free the hose from the mudguard

2.2a Unscrew the mounting bolts . . .

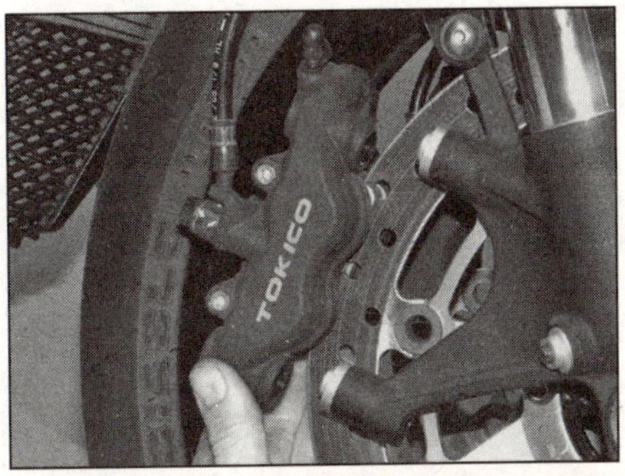
2.2b . . . and slide the caliper off the disc

2 Front brake pads

***Warning:** The dust created by the brake system may contain asbestos, which is harmful to your health. Never blow it out with compressed air and don't inhale any of it. An approved filtering mask should be worn when working on the brakes.*

Note: *Honda recommend using new caliper mounting bolts. This is because the bolts are pre-treated with a locking compound. It is possible, however, to clean up the old bolts and reinstall them using a suitable non-permanent thread locking compound that is commercially available.*

1 Slacken the pad retaining pins **(see illustration)**. Free the brake hose from the mudguard to give more freedom of movement if required – a bolt secures the splitter on the right-hand side and a nut secures the guide on the left **(see illustration)**.

2 Unscrew the caliper mounting bolts and slide the caliper off the disc **(see illustrations)**.

3 Unscrew and remove the pad pins, then remove the pads from the bottom of the

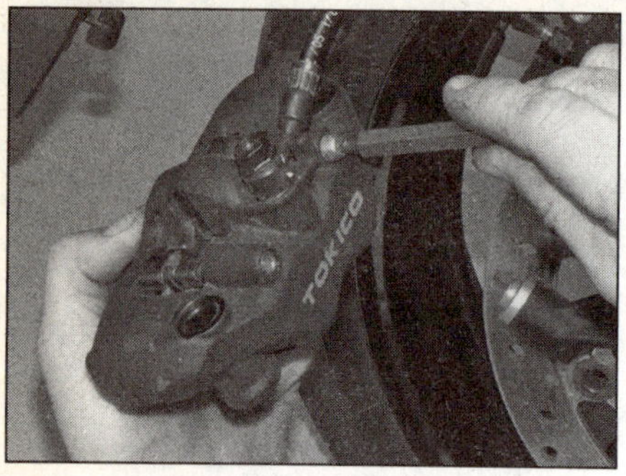

2.3a Unscrew the pins . . .

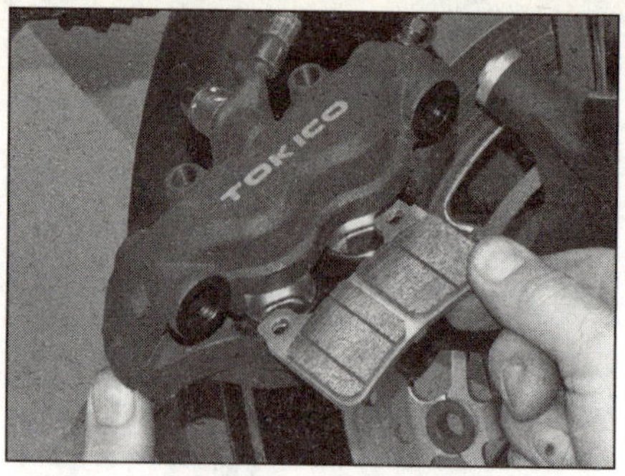

2.3b . . . and remove the pads from the bottom of the caliper

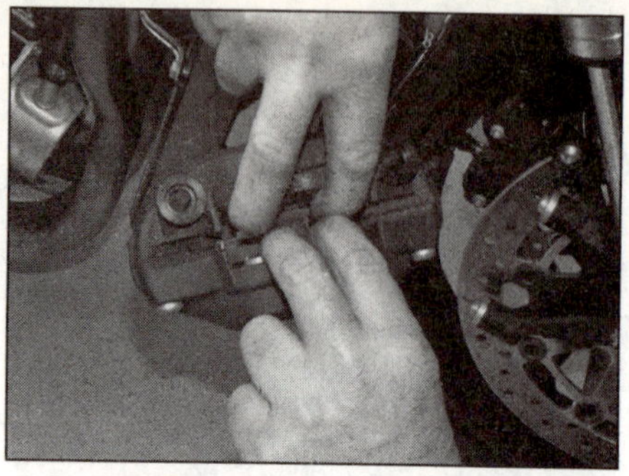

2.8a Press the pistons in as described to make space for the new pads

caliper **(see illustrations)**. The pad spring can stay in place unless you are overhauling the caliper – to remove the spring the pistons must be pushed all the way back into their bores to provide clearance (see Step 8) **(see illustration 2.10a)**. **Note:** *Do not operate the brake lever while the pads are out of the caliper. If required and fitted, remove the shim from the back of each pad, noting how it locates* ***(see illustration 2.10b)****.*

4 Inspect the surface of each pad for contamination and check that the friction material has not worn beyond its service limit (see Chapter 1, Section 3). If any pad is worn down to, or beyond, the service limit wear indicator (i.e. the wear indicator is no longer visible), is fouled with oil or grease, or heavily scored or damaged, fit a complete set of new pads. **Note:** *It is not possible to degrease the friction material; if the pads are contaminated in any way they must be replaced with new ones.*

2.8b A piston pushing tool

5 If the pads are in good condition clean them carefully, using a fine wire brush which is completely free of oil and grease to remove all traces of road dirt and corrosion. Using a pointed instrument, dig out any embedded particles of foreign matter. If required, spray with a dedicated brake cleaner to remove any dust.

6 Check the condition of the brake disc (see Section 4).

7 Remove all traces of corrosion from the pad pins and check them for wear and damage.

8 Clean around the exposed section of each piston to remove any dirt or debris that could cause the seals to be damaged. If new pads are being fitted, now push the pistons all the way back into the caliper to create room for them; if the old pads are still serviceable push the pistons in a little way. To push the pistons back use finger pressure or a piece of wood as leverage, or place the old pads back in the caliper and use a metal bar or a screwdriver inserted between them (but take care not to damage the friction surface if the pads are being reused), or use grips and a piece of wood, with rag or card to protect the caliper body **(see illustration)**. Alternatively obtain a proper piston-pushing tool from a good tool supplier **(see illustration)**. It may be necessary to remove the master cylinder reservoir cap, plate and diaphragm and siphon out some fluid (see *Pre-ride checks*). If the pistons are difficult to push back, remove the bleed valve cap, then attach a length of clear hose to the bleed valve and place the open end in a suitable container, then open the valve and try again (see Section 11). Take great care not to draw any air into the system. If in doubt, bleed the brakes afterwards.

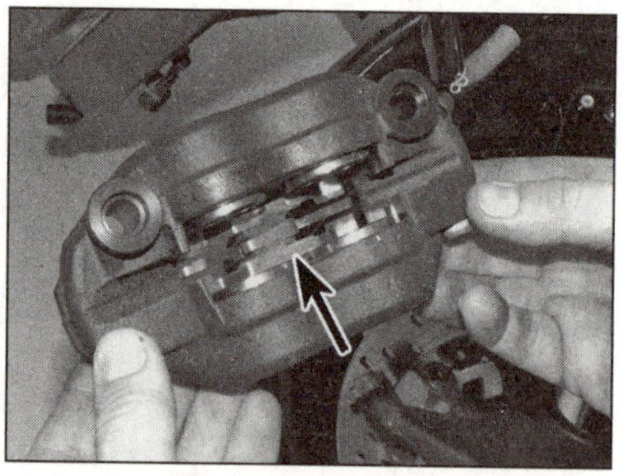

2.10a Make sure the pad spring (arrowed) is correctly in place

9 If any of the pistons appear seized, first block or hold the other pistons using wood or cable ties, then apply the brake lever and check whether the piston in question moves at all. If it moves out but can't be pushed back in the chances are there is some hidden corrosion stopping it. If it doesn't move at all, or to fully clean and inspect the pistons, disassemble the caliper and overhaul it (see Section 3).

10 If the pad spring was removed, make sure the pistons are fully recessed in their bores then fit the spring into the caliper **(see illustration)**. Where applicable fit the shim onto the back of each pad, making sure it locates correctly **(see illustrations)**. Fit the pads into the caliper so the friction material on each pad faces the other, and where applicable so the cut-away portion of the shim is at the lower end of the caliper **(see illustration)**. Press them up against the spring

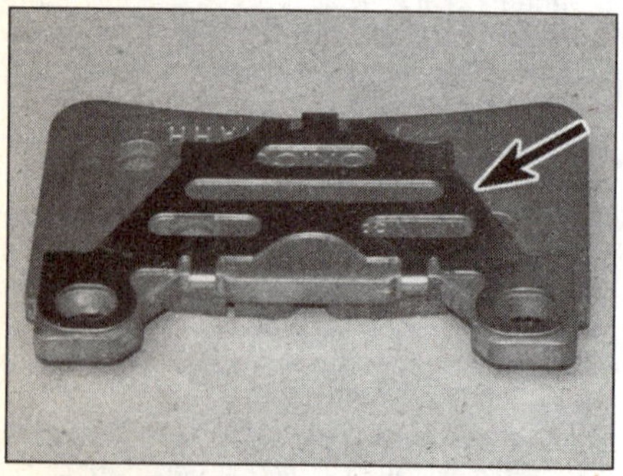

2.10b Make sure the shim (arrowed) is correctly in place – later type shim shown . . .

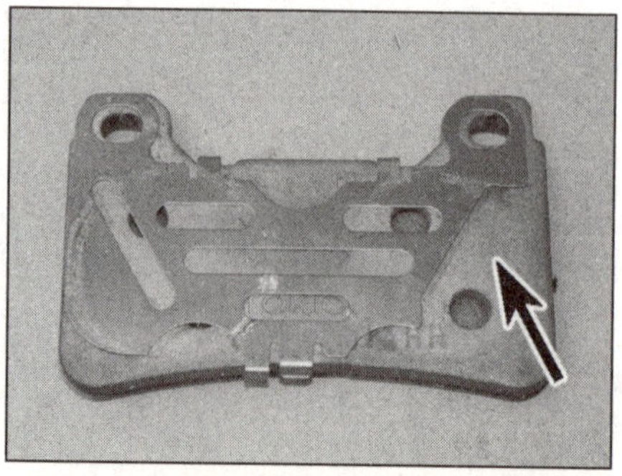

2.10c . . . some earlier shims have only one side cut away (arrowed) . . .

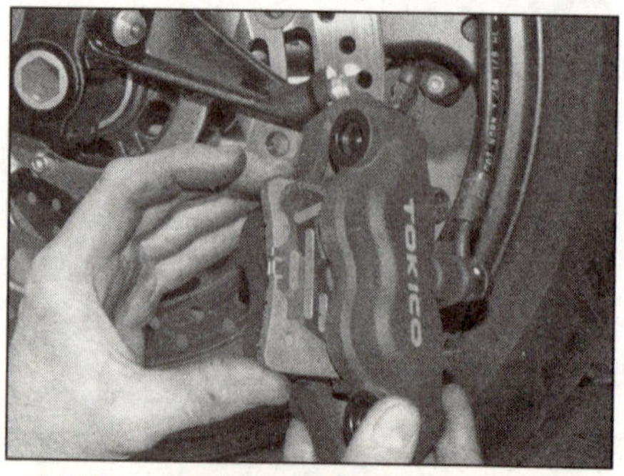

2.10d . . . and this must be at the lower end of the caliper

2.10e Insert the pads then slide the pins across

to align the holes, then insert the pad pins and tighten them finger-tight **(see illustration)**.

11 Slide the caliper onto the disc making sure the pads locate correctly on each side **(see illustration 2.2b)**. Clean the threads of the caliper mounting bolts and apply a suitable non-permanent thread locking compound, then tighten them to the torque setting specified at the beginning of the Chapter **(see illustration 2.2a)**. Fit the brake hose onto the mudguard if displaced **(see illustration 2.1b)**.

12 Tighten the pad pins to the torque setting specified at the beginning of this Chapter **(see illustration 2.1a)**.

13 Operate the brake lever until the pads contact with the disc. Check the level of fluid in the hydraulic reservoir and top-up if necessary (see *Pre-ride checks*).

14 Check the operation of the front brake before riding the motorcycle.

3 Front brake calipers

Warning: If a caliper is in need of an overhaul all old brake fluid should be flushed from the system. Also, the dust created by the brake system may contain asbestos, which is harmful to your health. Never blow it out with compressed air and do not inhale any of it. An approved filtering mask should be worn when working on the brakes. Overhaul of the brake calipers must be done in a spotlessly clean work area to avoid contamination and possible failure of the brake hydraulic system components. Do not, under any circumstances, use petroleum-based solvents to clean brake parts. Use clean DOT 4 brake fluid, dedicated brake cleaner or denatured alcohol only, as described. To prevent damage from spilled brake fluid, always cover paintwork when working on the braking system.

Removal

Note 1: *If the caliper is being overhauled (usually due to sticking pistons or fluid leaks) read through the entire procedure first and make sure that you have obtained all the new parts required, including some new DOT 4 brake fluid.*

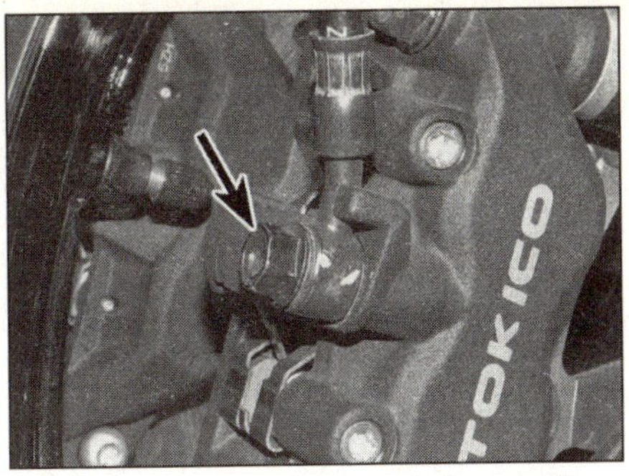

3.3 Brake hose banjo bolt (arrowed)

Note 2: *Honda recommend using new caliper mounting bolts. This is because the bolts are pre-treated with a locking compound. It is possible, however, to clean up the old bolts and reinstall them using a suitable non-permanent thread locking compound that is commercially available.*

1 If the caliper is being overhauled, slacken the brake pad retaining pins **(see illustration 2.1a)**. If the caliper is just being displaced from the forks as part of the wheel removal procedure, the brake pads can be left in place.

2 Free the brake hose from the mudguard to give more freedom of movement if required – a bolt secures the splitter on the right-hand side and a nut secures the guide on the left **(see illustration 2.1b)**.

3 If the caliper is being completely removed or overhauled, unscrew the brake hose banjo bolt and detach the banjo union, noting its alignment with the caliper **(see illustration)**.

4 Seal the banjo union and secure the hose in an upright position to minimise fluid loss Discard the sealing washers, as new ones must be fitted on reassembly.

5 If the caliper body is to be split into its halves for overhaul, loosen the caliper body joining bolts at this stage and retighten them lightly **(see illustration)** – the bolts are on the inner side of the caliper, so if you haven't got the necessary tools to access them you will have to slacken them with the caliper removed, in which case you may need an assistant to hold it, or use a vice with some protective card or a wad of rag.

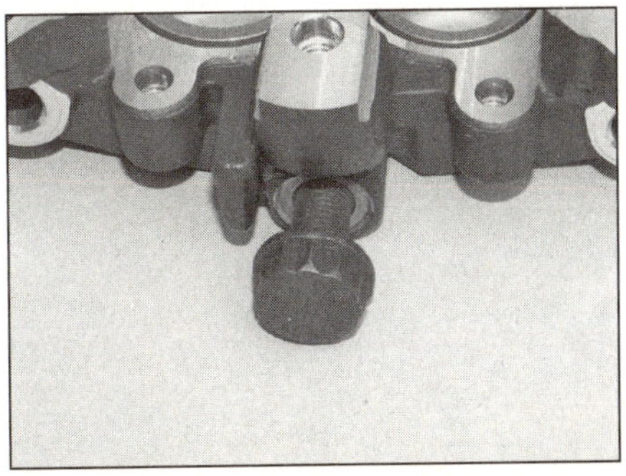

3.9a Block the fluid inlet using a suitable bolt

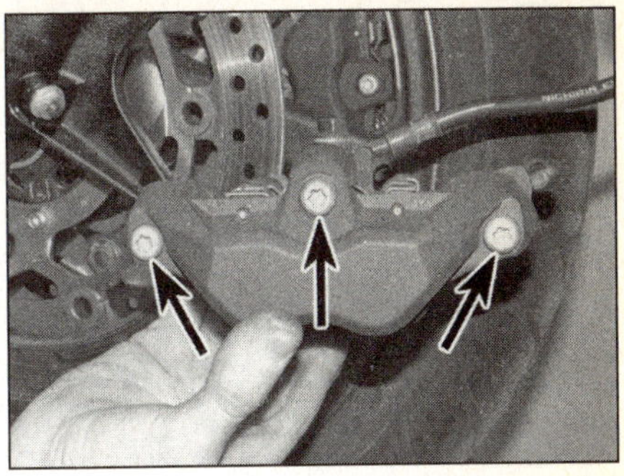

3.5 Caliper body joining bolts (arrowed)

6 Unscrew the caliper mounting bolts and slide the caliper off the disc **(see illustrations 2.2a and b)**. If the caliper is just being displaced, secure it to the motorcycle with a cable tie to avoid straining the brake hose. **Note:** *Do not operate the brake lever while either caliper is off the disc.* If the caliper is being overhauled, remove the brake pads (see Section 2).

Overhaul

7 Clean the exterior of the caliper with denatured alcohol or brake system cleaner. Have some clean rag ready to catch any spilled brake fluid.

8 Unscrew the caliper body joining bolts and separate the body halves, catching any residual fluid with the rag **(see illustration 3.5)**. Remove the caliper body O-ring from whichever body half it is in and discard it – fit a new one on reassembly **(see illustration 3.18a)**.

9 Place a caliper half piston-up on the bench. When working on the outer caliper half, make sure the bleed valve is tight, and find a suitable bolt to block the fluid inlet banjo bolt bore and thread it in **(see illustration)**. Get a wad of rag and hold it against the pistons as a cushion to protect your hand as the pistons are forced out. Apply compressed air gradually and progressively, starting with a fairly low pressure, to the fluid passage on the caliper joint and allow the pistons to ease out of their bores, controlling them with hand pressure and the rag **(see illustration)**. Make

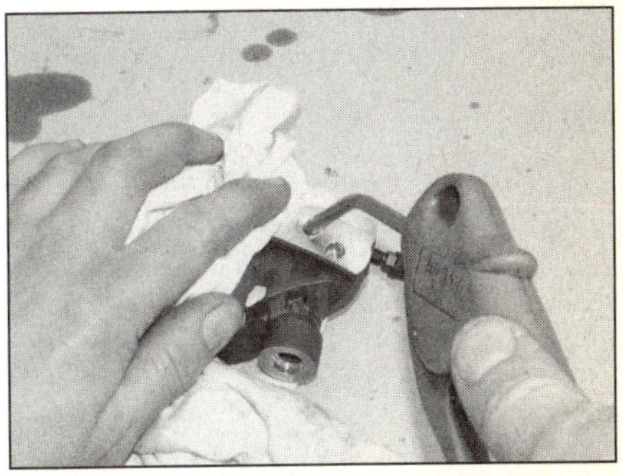

3.9b Apply compressed air to the fluid passage . . .

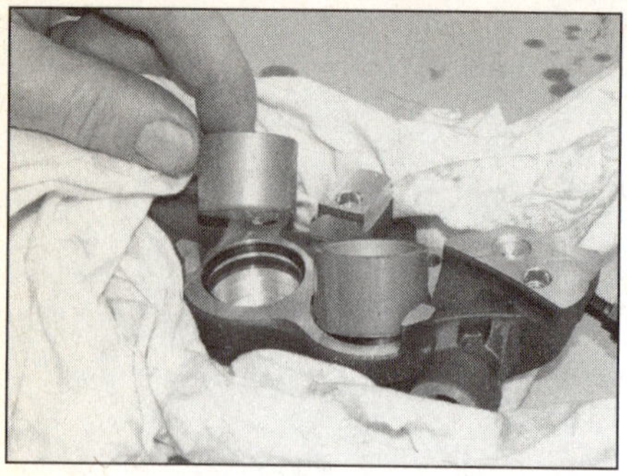

3.9c ... until the pistons are displaced

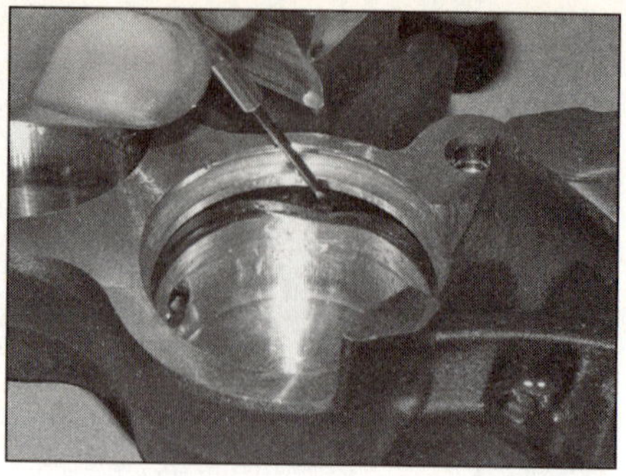

3.12 Remove the seals and discard them

sure the pistons are displaced evenly, using pressure to block one while the other moves if necessary **(see illustration)**. Repeat the procedure for the other caliper half.

10 If a piston is stuck in its bore due to corrosion the caliper should be replaced with a new one. Do not try to remove a piston by levering it out or by using pliers or other grips.

11 Mark each piston and the caliper body to ensure that the pistons can be matched to their original bores on reassembly. Note that two sizes of piston are used in each caliper (see Specifications at the beginning of this Chapter).

12 Remove the dust seals and the piston seals from the piston bores using a soft wooden or plastic tool to avoid scratching the bores **(see illustration)**. Discard the seals as new ones must be fitted on reassembly.

13 Clean the pistons and bores with clean brake fluid. If compressed air is available, blow it through the fluid galleries in the caliper to ensure they are clear (make sure it is filtered and unlubricated).

Caution: Do not, under any circumstances, use a petroleum-based solvent to clean brake parts.

14 Inspect the caliper bores and pistons for signs of corrosion, nicks and burrs and loss of plating. If surface defects are present, the pistons and/or the caliper assembly must be replaced with new ones. If the necessary measuring equipment is available, compare the dimensions of the caliper bores and pistons to those specified at the beginning of this Chapter, and obtain new pistons or a new caliper if necessary. If one caliper is in poor condition, the other front caliper and the master cylinder should also be checked.

15 Lubricate the new piston seals with clean brake fluid and fit them into their grooves in the caliper bores **(see illustrations)**. Note that there are two sizes of bore in each caliper and care must therefore be taken to ensure that the correct size seals are fitted to the correct bores (see Specifications). The same applies when fitting the new dust seals and pistons.

16 Lubricate the new dust seals with silicone grease and fit them into their grooves in the caliper bores **(see illustration)**.

17 Lubricate the pistons with clean brake fluid and fit them, closed-end first, into the caliper bores, taking care not to displace the seals **(see illustration)**. Using your thumbs, push the pistons all the way in, making sure they enter the bore squarely.

18 Lubricate the new caliper body O-ring with clean brake fluid and fit it into the outer half of the caliper body **(see illustration)**. Join the two halves of the caliper body together, ensuring that the O-ring stays in place **(see illustration)**. Clean the threads of the caliper body joining bolts and apply a suitable non-permanent thread locking compound, then tighten them evenly to the torque setting specified at the beginning of the Chapter, with the help of an assistant or using a vice with some protective rag to hold the caliper as you do **(see illustration 3.5)**.

Installation

19 If removed, install the brake pads (see Section 2).

20 Slide the caliper onto the brake disc, making sure the pads fit on each side of the disc **(see illustration 2.2b)**.

21 Clean the threads of the caliper mounting bolts and apply a suitable non-permanent

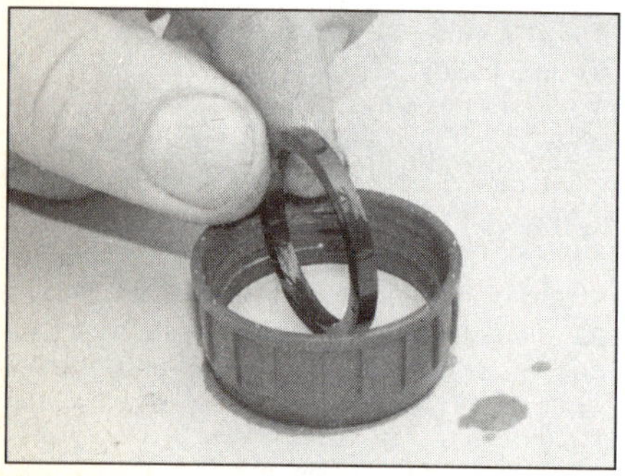

3.15a Lubricate the new piston seals with brake fluid ...

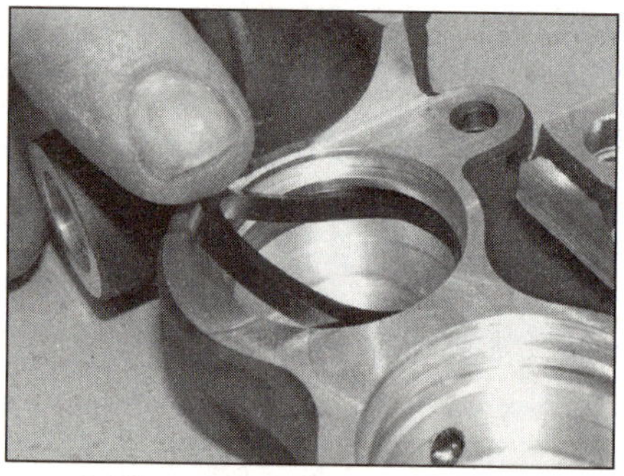

3.15b ... then fit them into their grooves ...

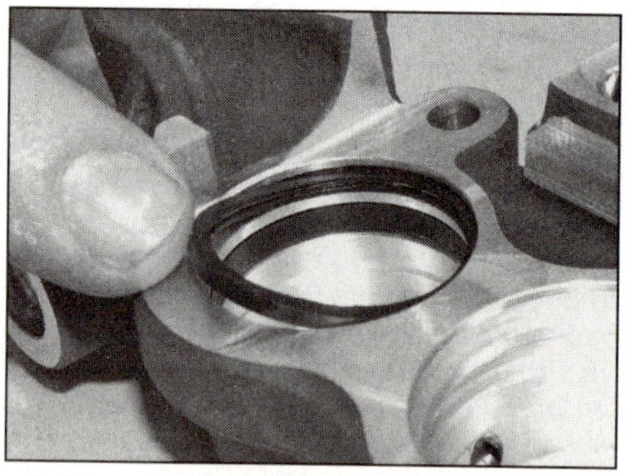

3.16 ... followed by the new dust seals

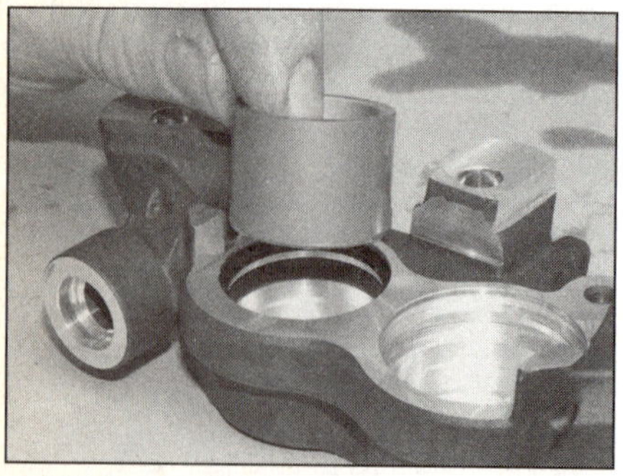

3.17 Fit the pistons and push them all the way in

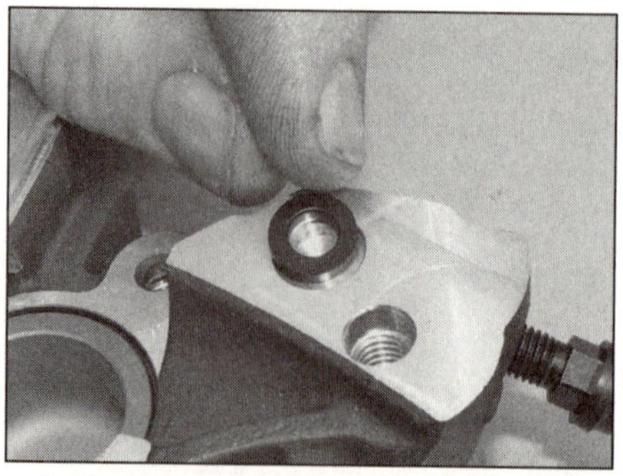

3.18a Fit the O-ring into its recess ...

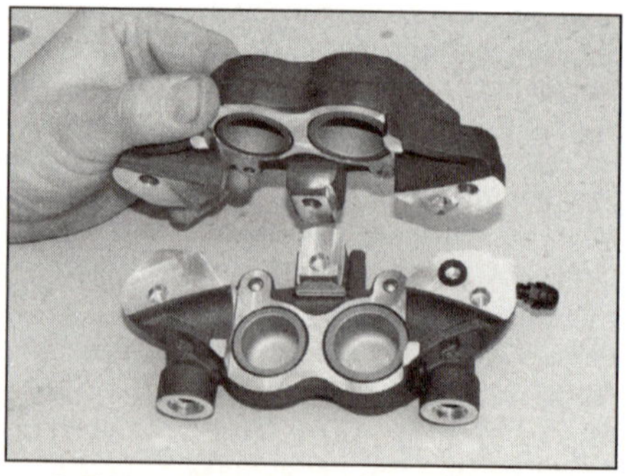

3.18b ... then join the caliper halves

thread locking compound, then tighten them to the torque setting specified at the beginning of the Chapter **(see illustration 2.2a)**.

22 If removed, connect the brake hose to the caliper, using new sealing washers on each side of the banjo fitting **(see illustration)**. Align the fitting as noted on removal **(see illustration 3.3)**. Tighten the banjo bolt to the specified torque setting.

23 Secure the brake hose assembly on the front mudguard **(see illustration 2.1b)**.

24 Top up the hydraulic reservoir with DOT 4 brake fluid (see *Pre-ride checks*) and bleed the system as described in Section 11. Check that there are no fluid leaks and test the operation of the front brake before riding the motorcycle.

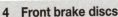

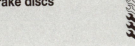

4 Front brake discs

Inspection

1 Inspect the surface of the disc for score marks and other damage. Light scratches are normal after use and won't affect brake operation, but deep grooves and heavy score marks will reduce braking efficiency and accelerate pad wear. If a disc is badly grooved it must be replaced with a new one.

2 The disc must not be machined or allowed to wear down to a thickness less than the service limit as listed in this Chapter's Specifications. The minimum thickness is also stamped on the disc **(see illustration)**. Check the thickness of the disc with a micrometer and replace it with a new one if necessary.

3 To check if the disc is warped, position the bike on an auxiliary stand with the front wheel raised off the ground. Mount a dial gauge to the fork leg, with the gauge plunger touching the surface of the disc about 10 mm from its outer edge **(see illustration)**. Rotate the wheel and watch the gauge

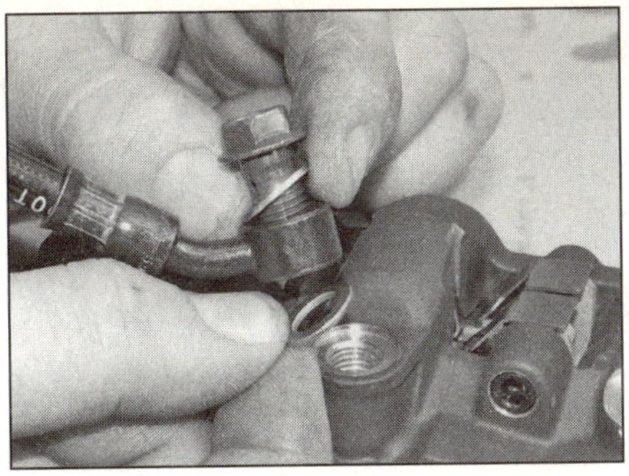

3.22 Always use new sealing washers

needle, comparing the reading with the limit listed in the Specifications at the beginning of this Chapter. If the runout is greater than the service limit, check the wheel bearings for play (see Chapter 1). If the bearings are worn, install new ones (see Section 16) and repeat this check. If the disc runout is still excessive, a new pair of discs will have to be fitted.

Removal

Note: *Honda recommend using new disc mounting bolts. This is because the bolts are pre-treated with a locking compound. It is possible, however, to clean up the old bolts and reinstall them using a suitable non-permanent thread locking compound that is commercially available.*

4 Remove the wheel (see Section 14).

Caution: Don't lay the wheel down and allow it to rest on the disc – the disc could become warped. Set the wheel on wood blocks so the wheel rim supports the weight of the wheel.

5 If you are not replacing the disc with a new one, mark the relationship of the disc to the wheel, so it can be installed in the same position and on the same side as originally fitted. Unscrew the disc retaining bolts, loosening them evenly and a little at a time in

4.2 The minimum thickness is marked on the disc

a criss-cross pattern to avoid distorting the disc, then remove the disc **(see illustration)**.

Installation

6 Before installing the disc, make sure there is no dirt or corrosion where the disc seats on the hub. If the disc does not sit flat when it is bolted down, it will appear to be warped when checked or when the front brake is used.

7 Install the disc on the wheel with its marked side facing out, aligning the previously applied matchmarks (if you're reinstalling the original disc), and making sure the arrow points in the direction of normal rotation.

8 Clean the threads of the disc mounting bolts, then apply a suitable non-permanent thread locking compound. Install the bolts and tighten them evenly and a little at a time in a criss-cross pattern to the torque setting specified at the beginning of this Chapter. Clean the disc using acetone or brake system cleaner. If a new disc has been installed, remove any protective coating from its working surfaces and fit new brake pads.

9 Install the front wheel (see Section 14).

10 Operate the brake lever several times to bring the pads into contact with the disc. Check the operation of the brake before riding the motorcycle.

4.3 Checking disc runout with a dial gauge

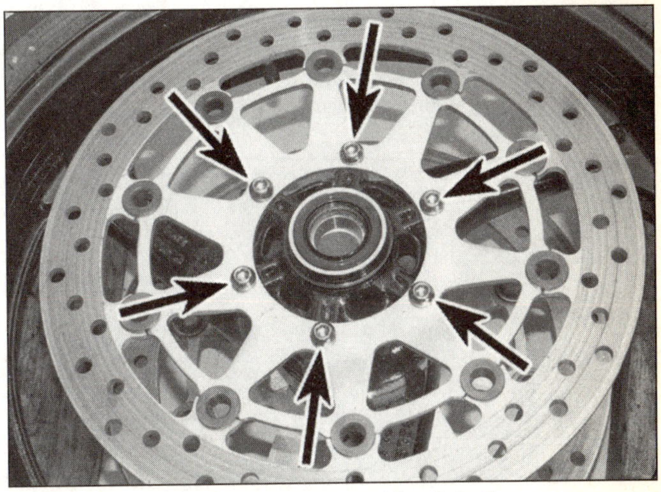

4.5 The disc is secured by six bolts

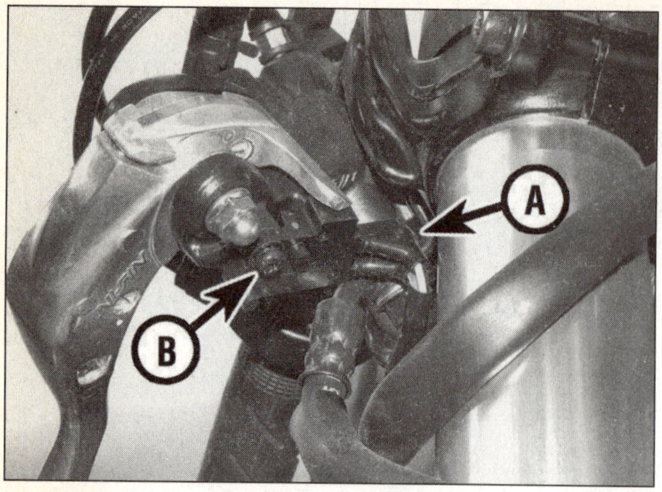

5.1 Disconnect the brake light switch wires (A). Switch mounting screw (B)

5.2 Unscrew the bolts (arrowed) and remove the master cylinder and its clamp

5 Front brake master cylinder

Warning: ***If the brake master cylinder is in need of an overhaul all old brake fluid should be flushed from the system. Overhaul must be done in a spotlessly clean work area to avoid contamination and possible failure of the brake hydraulic system components. Do not, under any circumstances, use petroleum-based solvents to clean brake parts. Use clean DOT 4 brake fluid, dedicated brake cleaner or denatured alcohol only, as described. To prevent damage from spilled brake fluid, always cover paintwork when working on the braking system.***

Removal

Note: *If the master cylinder is being overhauled (usually due to sticking or poor action, or fluid leaks) read through the entire procedure first and make sure that you have obtained all the new parts required, including some new DOT 4 brake fluid.*

1 Disconnect the electrical connectors from the brake light switch **(see illustration)**.

2 If the master cylinder is just being displaced, ensure the fluid reservoir cap is secure. Unscrew the master cylinder clamp bolts and remove the back of the clamp, noting how it fits, then position the master cylinder and reservoir assembly clear of the handlebar **(see illustration)**. Ensure no strain is placed on the hydraulic hose. Keep the reservoir upright to prevent air entering the system.

3 If the master cylinder is being overhauled, remove the brake lever (see Chapter 5).

4 On RR-4 and RR-5 models slacken the reservoir cap screws **(see illustration)**. On RR-6 and RR-7 models remove the reservoir cap clamp screw and clamp **(see illustration)**.

5 Unscrew the brake hose banjo bolt and detach the banjo union, noting its alignment with the master cylinder **(see illustration)**. Seal the banjo union and secure the hose in an upright position to minimise fluid loss. Discard the sealing washers as new ones must be fitted on reassembly.

6 Slacken the bolt securing the reservoir to the master cylinder **(see illustration)**. Unscrew the master cylinder clamp bolts and remove the back of the clamp, noting how it fits, then lift the master cylinder and reservoir away from the handlebar **(see illustration 5.2)**.

7 Remove the reservoir cap, the diaphragm plate and the diaphragm, and on RR-4 and

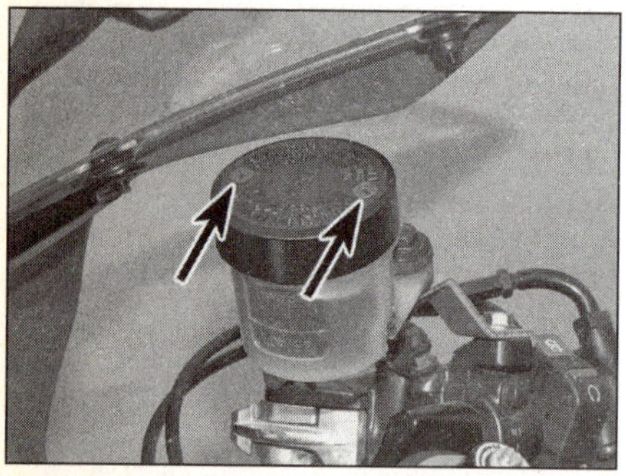

5.4a On RR-4 and RR-5 models slacken the cover screws

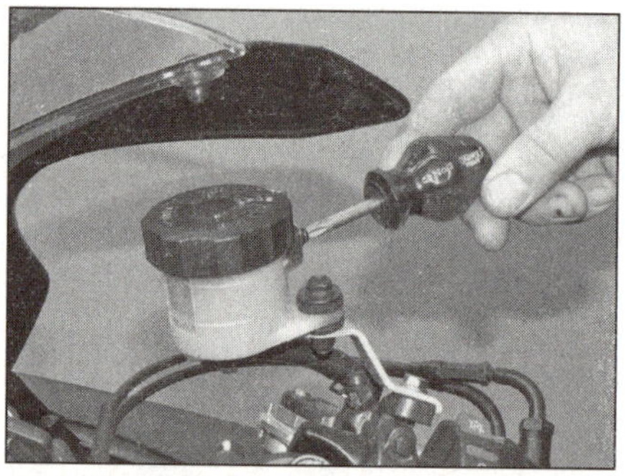

5.4b On RR-6 and RR-7 models undo the screw and remove the clamp

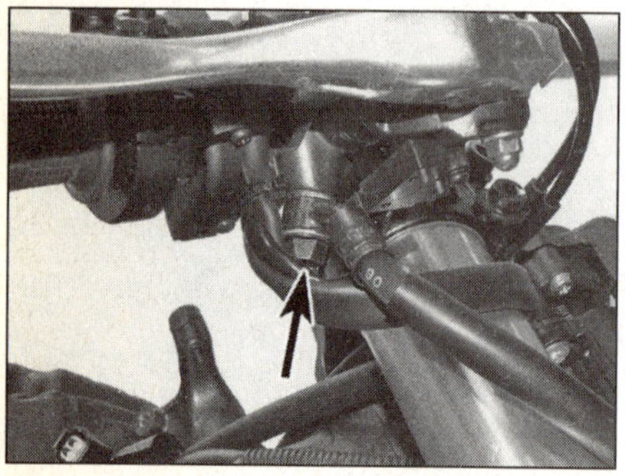

5.5 Brake hose banjo bolt (arrowed)

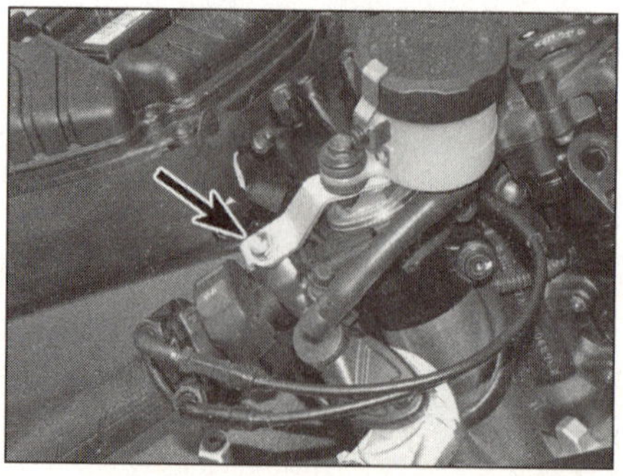

5.6 Slacken the reservoir bolt (arrowed)

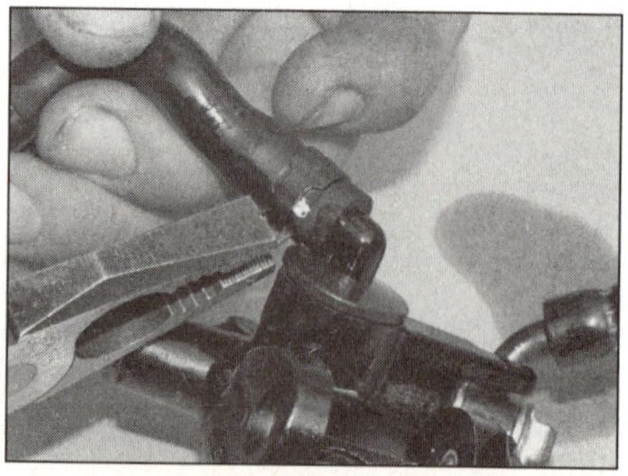

5.7 Release the clip and detach the hose

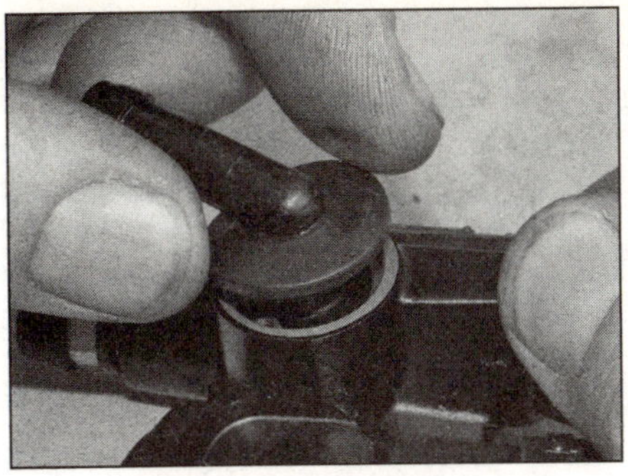

5.9a Lift the cap off . . .

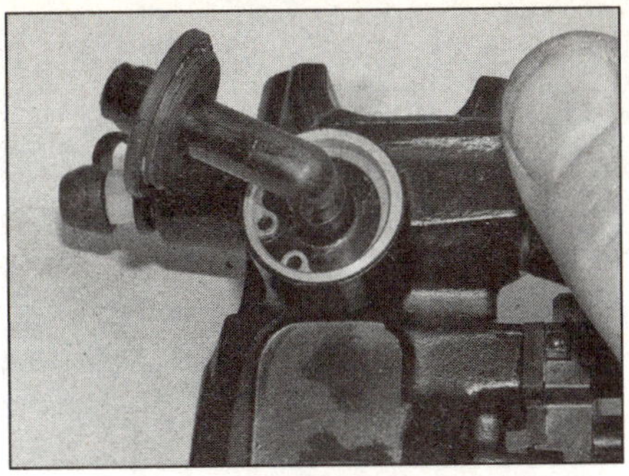

5.9b . . . to access the circlip

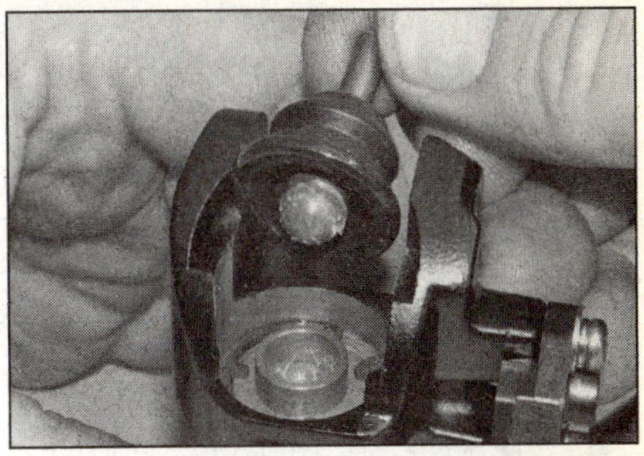

5.10 Remove the boot and pushrod where applicable from the end of the master cylinder piston . . .

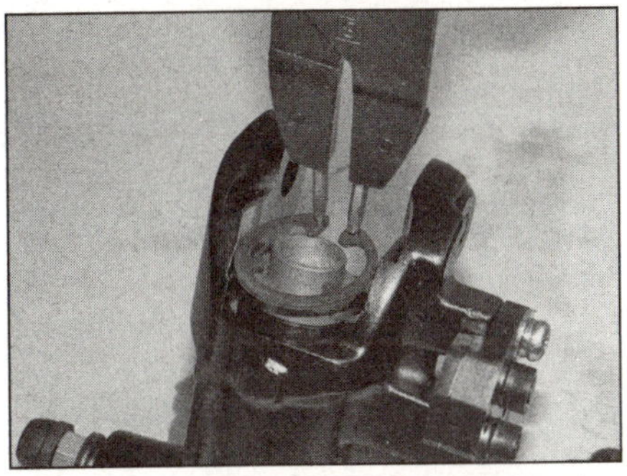

5.11a . . . then depress the piston and remove the circlip . . .

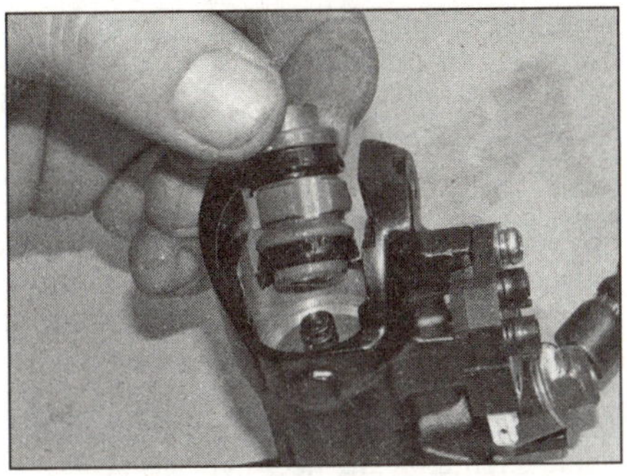

5.11b . . . then draw out the piston . . .

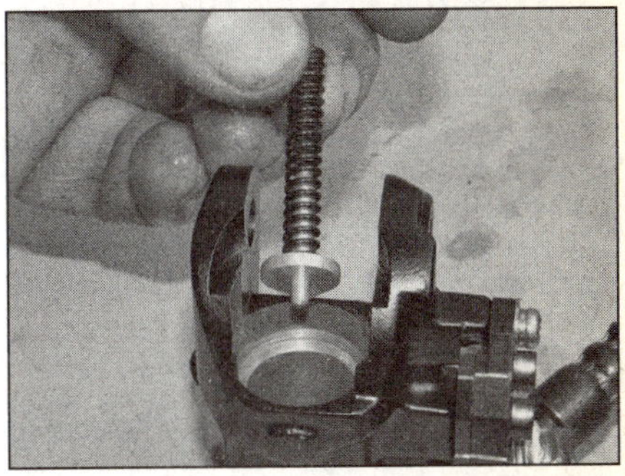

5.11c . . . and the spring

RR-5 models the float. Drain the brake fluid from the master cylinder and reservoir into a suitable container. Release the clip securing the reservoir hose to the union on the master cylinder and detach the hose **(see illustration)**. Wipe any remaining fluid out of the reservoir with a clean rag.

8 If required, undo the screw securing the brake light switch to the bottom of the master cylinder and remove the switch **(see illustration 5.1)**.

Overhaul

9 Lift the dust cap from the fluid reservoir hose union, then remove the circlip and detach the union from the master cylinder **(see illustrations)**. Discard the O-ring as a new one must be fitted on reassembly. Inspect the reservoir hose for cracks or splits and replace it with a new one if necessary.

10 Carefully remove the rubber boot from the master cylinder, bringing the pushrod with it **(see illustration)**.

11 Depress the piston and use circlip pliers to remove the circlip, then slide out the piston assembly, the spring and the spring guide, noting how they fit **(see illustrations)**. If they are difficult to remove, apply low pressure compressed air to the brake fluid outlet. Lay the parts out in the proper order to prevent confusion during reassembly.

12 Clean all parts with clean brake fluid. If compressed air is available, blow it through the fluid galleries to ensure they are clear (make sure the air is filtered and unlubricated).

Caution: Do not, under any circumstances, use a petroleum-based solvent to clean brake parts.

13 Check the master cylinder bore for corrosion, scratches, nicks and score marks. If the necessary measuring equipment is available, compare the dimensions of the piston and bore to those given in the Specifications at the beginning of this Chapter. If damage or wear is evident, the master cylinder must be replaced with a new one. If the master cylinder is in poor condition, then the calipers should be checked as well.

14 The dust boot, circlip, piston and its cup and seal, spring and spring guide are all included in a master cylinder rebuild kit, and all components except the piston, cup, seal and spring are available individually. Use all of the new parts, regardless of the apparent condition of the old ones. Lubricate the master cylinder bore with new brake fluid.

15 Smear the cup and seal with new brake fluid and if not already in place fit them into their grooves in the piston so their wider ends will fit into the master cylinder first **(see illustration)**. Fit the spring guide into the end of the spring **(see illustration)**. Fit the spring guide and spring into the master cylinder **(see illustration 5.11c)**. Lubricate the piston with clean brake fluid and slide it into the master cylinder and up against the spring **(see illustration 5.11b)**. Make sure the lips on the cup and seal do not turn inside out. Push the piston in to compress

5.15a Make sure the cup and seal are correctly installed on the piston

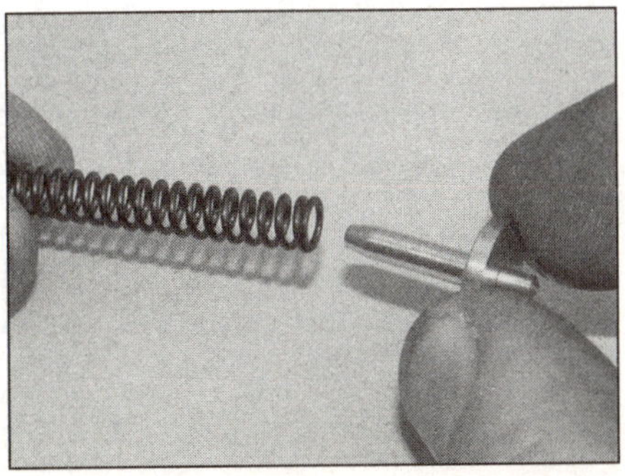

5.15b Fit the guide into the end of the spring

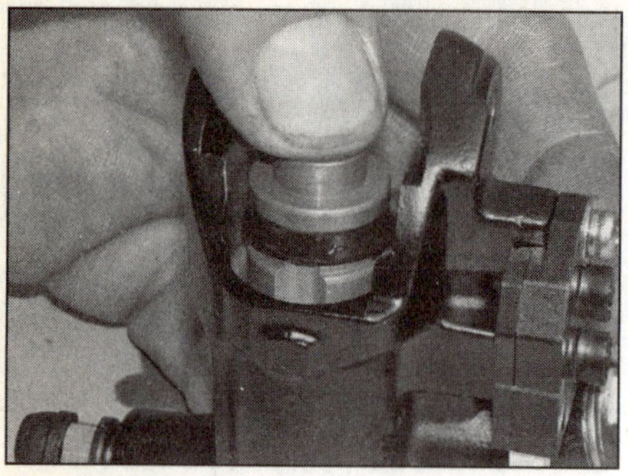

5.15c Push the piston into the bore . . .

5.15d . . . and hold it there while fitting the circlip

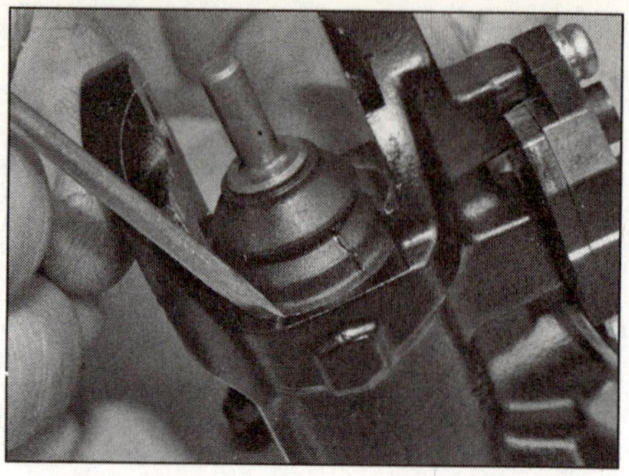

5.16 Feed the rim of the boot into the bore

the spring and install the new circlip **(see illustrations)**.

16 Smear the inner end of the pushrod with silicone grease. Fit the boot onto the pushrod so its narrow end lips locate in the groove **(see illustration 5.10)**. Locate the inner end of the pushrod in the end of the piston, then press the boot into the master cylinder **(see illustration)**.

17 Fit a new O-ring smeared with silicone grease onto the fluid reservoir hose union, then press the union into the master cylinder and secure it with the circlip **(see illustration 5.9b)**. Fit the dust cap over the circlip (see illustration 5.9a).

18 Inspect the reservoir diaphragm and fit a new one it if it is damaged or deteriorated.

Installation

19 If removed, fit the brake light switch onto the bottom of the master cylinder, making sure the pin locates in the hole, and tighten the screw **(see illustration 5.1)**.

20 Attach the master cylinder to the handlebar, aligning the switch housing side of the clamp joint with the punch mark on the top of the handlebar, then fit the back of the clamp with its UP mark facing up **(see illustration 5.2)**. Tighten the upper bolt to the torque setting specified at the beginning of this Chapter, followed by the lower bolt.

21 Locate the fluid reservoir on the master cylinder and tighten its bracket bolt **(see illustration 5.6)**. Connect the reservoir hose to the union on the master cylinder and secure it with the clip **(see illustration 5.7)**.

22 Connect the brake hose to the master cylinder, using new sealing washers on each side of the banjo fitting. Align the hose as noted on removal **(see illustration 5.5)**. Tighten the banjo bolt to the torque setting specified at the beginning of this Chapter.

6.1a Slacken the pin (arrowed) then unscrew the rear bolt/slider pin

6.1b Pivot the caliper up and remove the pads

6.2a Unscrew the pin (arrowed) . . .

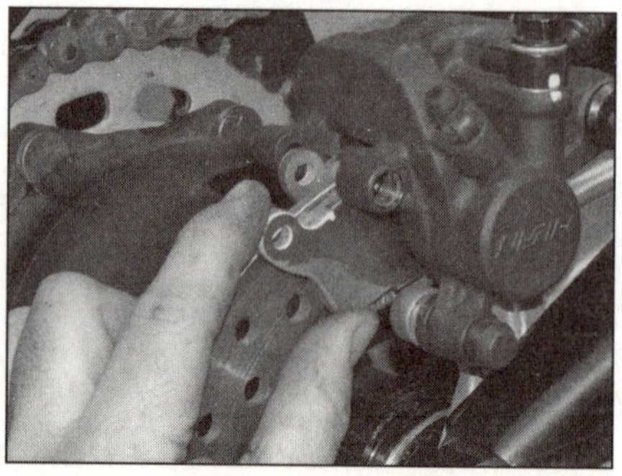

6.2b . . . then draw the pads out the back of the caliper

23 Install the brake lever (see Chapter 5).

24 Connect the brake light switch wiring **(see illustration 5.1)**.

25 Fill the fluid reservoir with new DOT 4 brake fluid (see *Pre-ride checks*). Refer to Section 11 and bleed the air from the system.

26 Check the operation of the front brake before riding the motorcycle.

6 Rear brake pads

Warning: The dust created by the brake system may contain asbestos, which is harmful to your health. Never blow it out with compressed air and don't inhale any of it. An approved filtering mask should be worn when working on the brakes.

Note: *Honda recommend using a new caliper mounting bolt/slider pin. This is because the bolts are pre-treated with a locking compound. It is possible, however, to clean up the old bolts and reinstall them using a suitable non-permanent thread locking compound that is commercially available.*

1 On RR-4 and RR-5 models slacken the pad retaining pin **(see illustration)**. Unscrew the caliper rear mounting bolt/slider pin. Unscrew the retaining pin then pivot the back of the caliper up off the disc and remove the pads, noting how they fit **(see illustration)**. Note the pad spring in the top of caliper and the pad guide on the caliper bracket and remove them if required for cleaning or replacement, noting how they fit. **Note:** *Do not operate the brake pedal while the pads are out of the caliper.* Check the condition of the O-ring on the pad pin and replace it with a new one if it is damaged, deformed or deteriorated.

2 On RR-6 and RR-7 models unscrew the pad retaining pin **(see illustration)**. Remove the pads, noting how they fit **(see illustration)**. **Note:** *Do not operate the brake pedal while the pads are out of the caliper.* Check the condition of the O-ring on the pad pin and replace it with a new one if it is damaged, deformed or deteriorated.

3 Where fitted and if required, remove the outer and inner shims from the back of each

6.3 Remove the shims, noting their arrangement

6.8 Push the piston back into the caliper as described

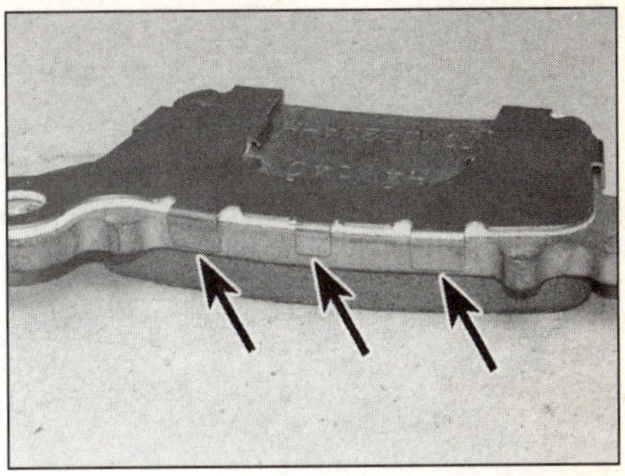

6.10 Make sure the shim tabs (arrowed) locate correctly all around

pad, noting how they fit – note that new pads should come with new shims where applicable, but make sure they do, especially if fitting after-market pads, before discarding the old ones **(see illustration)**.

4 Inspect the surface of each pad for contamination and check that the friction material has not worn beyond its service limit (see Chapter 1, Section 3). If either pad is worn down to, or beyond, the service limit wear indicator (i.e. the wear indicator is no longer visible), is fouled with oil or grease, or heavily scored or damaged, fit a set of new pads. **Note:** *It is not possible to degrease the friction material; if the pads are contaminated in any way they must be replaced with new ones.*

5 If the pads are in good condition clean them carefully, using a fine wire brush which is completely free of oil and grease to remove all traces of road dirt and corrosion. Using a pointed instrument, dig out any embedded particles of foreign matter. If required, spray with a dedicated brake cleaner to remove any dust.

6 Check the condition of the brake disc (see Section 8).

7 Remove all traces of corrosion from the pad pin and check it for wear and damage. Check the slider pin boots for cracks and splits and replace them with new ones if necessary (see Section 7).

8 Clean around the exposed section of the piston to remove any dirt or debris that could cause the seals to be damaged. If new pads are being fitted, now push the piston all the way back into the caliper to create room for them; if the old pads are still serviceable push the piston in a little way. On RR-4 and RR-5 models, to push the piston back use finger pressure or a piece of wood as leverage, or place the old pads back in the caliper and use a metal bar or a screwdriver inserted between them, or use grips and a piece of wood, with rag or card to protect the caliper body **(see illustration)**. Alternatively obtain a proper piston-pushing tool from a good tool supplier **(see illustration 2.8b)**. On RR-6 and RR-7 models slide a piece of card between the piston and the disc and push the caliper against the disc so that the piston is pressed all the way into the caliper body. It may be necessary to remove the master cylinder reservoir cap, plate and diaphragm and siphon out some fluid (see *Pre-ride checks*). If the piston is difficult to push back, remove the bleed valve cap, then attach a length of clear hose to the bleed valve and place the open end in a suitable container, then open the valve and try again (see Section 11). Take great care not to draw any air into the system. If in doubt, bleed the brake afterwards.

9 If the piston appears seized, apply the brake pedal and check whether the piston moves at all. If it moves out but can't be pushed back in, the chances are there is some hidden corrosion stopping it. If it doesn't move at all, or to fully clean and inspect the piston, disassemble the caliper and overhaul it (see Section 7).

10 Where applicable fit the shim(s) onto the back of each pad **(see illustration)**. Lightly smear the back of the pad backing material or shim and the edges of the backing material where it contacts the caliper body with copper-based grease, making sure that none gets on the friction material. Also smear the pad pin. Make sure the pad spring and guide are correctly fitted **(see illustrations 7.17a and b or 7.17c and d)**.

11 On RR-4 and RR-5 models apply a smear of silicone grease to the O-ring on the inner end of the pad pin, using a new one if necessary. Fit each pad into the caliper so that the friction material of each pad faces the disc and slide the pin through to hold them, tightening it finger-tight **(see illustration)**. Pivot the caliper down onto the disc, making sure the leading edges of the pads locate correctly against the guide **(see illustration)**.

6.11a Locate the pads in the caliper and slide the pin through . . .

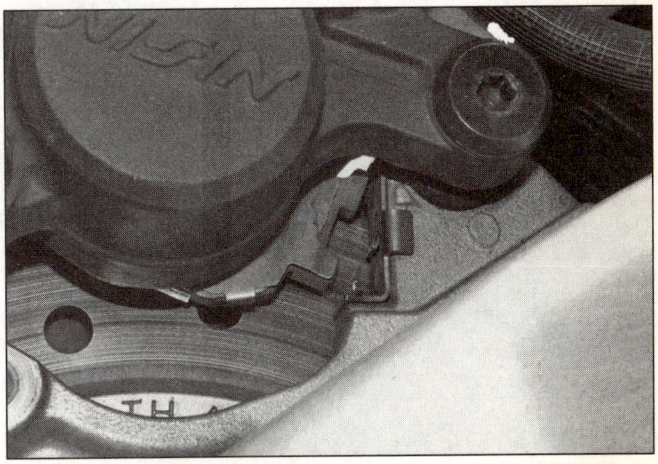

6.11b . . . then pivot the caliper down, making sure the pads seat in the bracket

6.12a Slide the pads into the caliper . . .

Clean the threads of the rear mounting bolt/slider pin and apply a suitable non-permanent thread locking compound, then tighten it to the torque setting specified at the beginning of the Chapter **(see illustration 6.1a)**.

12 On RR-6 and RR-7 models slide the pads into the caliper so that the friction material of each pad faces the disc, making sure the leading edges locate correctly against the guide on the bracket **(see illustration)**. Apply a smear of silicone grease to the O-ring on the inner end of the pad pin, using a new one if necessary. Push up on the end of each pad so the pads compress the spring and insert the pad pin when the holes are aligned **(see illustration)**. Tighten the pad pin to the specified torque setting.

13 Operate the brake pedal until the pads contact with the disc. Check the level of fluid in the hydraulic reservoir and top-up if necessary (see *Pre-ride checks*).

6.12b . . . then push their ends up and slide the pin through

14 Check the operation of the rear brake before riding the motorcycle.

7 Rear brake caliper

Warning: If the caliper is in need of overhaul all old brake fluid should be flushed from the system. Overhaul must be done in a spotlessly clean work area to avoid contamination and possible failure of the brake hydraulic system components. Do not, under any circumstances, use petroleum-based solvents to clean brake parts. Use clean DOT 4 brake fluid, dedicated brake cleaner or denatured alcohol only, as described. To prevent damage from spilled brake fluid, always cover paintwork when working on the braking system.

Removal

Note: *If the caliper is being overhauled (usually due to a sticking piston or fluid leak) read through the entire procedure first and make sure that you have obtained all the new parts required, including some new DOT 4 brake fluid.*

1 If the caliper is being completely removed or overhauled, unscrew the brake hose banjo bolt and detach the banjo union, noting its alignment with the caliper **(see illustrations)**. Seal the banjo union and secure the hose in an upright position to minimise fluid loss. Discard the sealing washers as new ones must be fitted on reassembly.

2 Unscrew the bolt securing the right-hand side of the hugger and the brake hose guide to the swingarm **(see illustration)**. Free the hose, noting how the tab on the guide locates in the hole in the swingarm **(see illustration)**.

3 On RR-4 and RR-5 models, if the caliper is being overhauled, remove the brake pads (see Section 6). Otherwise unscrew the caliper rear mounting bolt/slider pin **(see illustration 6.1a)**. Pivot the caliper up then slide it off the bracket and remove it **(see illustration)**.

4 On RR-6 and RR-7 models remove the brake pads (see Section 6). Remove the rear wheel (see Section 15). Slide the caliper off its bracket **(see illustration)**.

5 If required, remove the pad spring from the caliper and the pad guide from the bracket, noting how they fit **(see illustrations 7.17a and b or 7.17c and d)**.

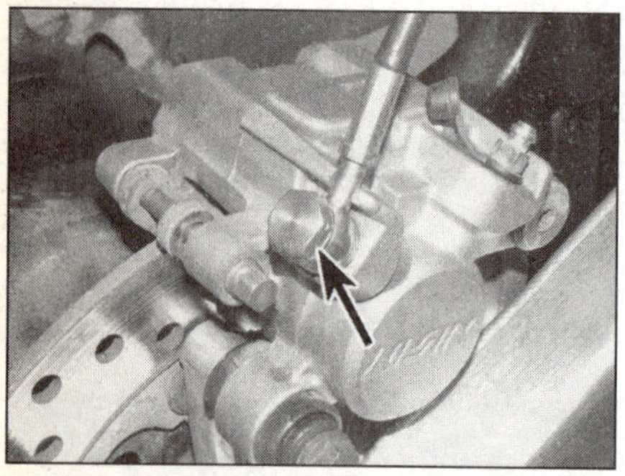

7.1a Brake hose banjo bolt (arrowed) – RR-4 and RR-5 models

7.1b Brake hose banjo bolt (arrowed) – RR-6 and RR-7 models

7.2a Unscrew the bolt (arrowed) . . .

7.2b . . . and free the hose guide, noting how it locates

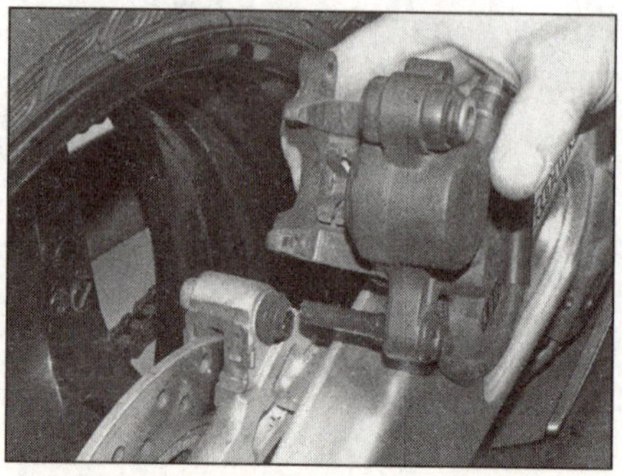

7.3 Pivot the caliper up and slide it out of the bracket

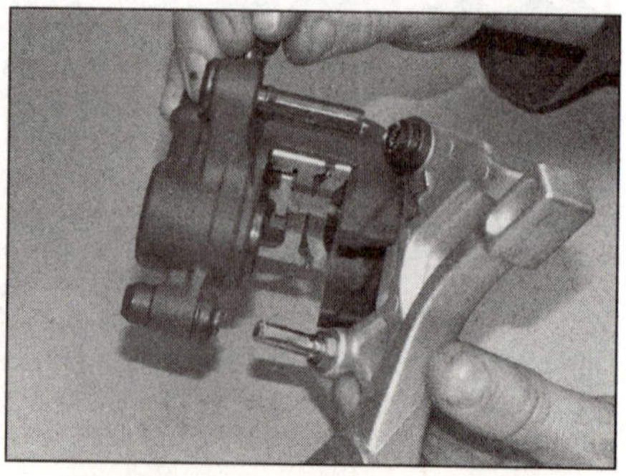

7.4 Slide the caliper off the bracket

7.7a Fit the wood, then apply the compressed air as described . . .

7.7b . . . until the piston is displaced

7.9 Remove the seals and discard them

Overhaul

6 Clean the exterior of the caliper with denatured alcohol or brake system cleaner. Have some clean rag ready to catch any spilled brake fluid.

7 Place a piece of wood between the piston and the caliper body – it should be just thick enough to stop the piston leaving the bore entirely **(see illustration)**. Apply compressed air gradually and progressively, starting with a fairly low pressure, to the fluid inlet on the caliper body and allow the piston to ease out of its bore, controlling it with the wood **(see illustration)**.

8 If the piston is stuck in its bore due to corrosion the caliper should be replaced with a new one. Do not try to remove a piston by levering it out or by using pliers or other grips.

9 Remove the dust seal and the piston seal from the piston bore using a soft wooden or plastic tool to avoid scratching the bores **(see illustration)**. Discard the seals as new ones must be fitted on reassembly.

10 Clean the piston and bore with clean brake fluid. If compressed air is available, blow it through the fluid passages in the caliper to ensure they are clear (make sure it is filtered and unlubricated).

Caution: Do not, under any circumstances, use a petroleum-based solvent to clean brake parts.

11 Inspect the caliper bore and piston for signs of corrosion, nicks and burrs and loss of plating. If surface defects are present, the piston and/or the caliper assembly must be replaced with new ones. If the necessary measuring equipment is available, compare the dimensions of the caliper bore and piston to the specifications at the beginning of this Chapter, and obtain a new piston or caliper if necessary. If the caliper is in poor condition, the master cylinder should also be checked.

12 On RR-4 and RR-5 models remove the collar from the rear slider pin boot **(see illustration)**. On all models remove the slider pin boots **(see illustrations)**. Clean off all traces of corrosion and hardened grease from the collar, boots and pins. Replace the rubber boots with new ones if they are damaged, deformed or deteriorated. Apply a smear of silicone-based grease to all the components. Fit the boots, making sure they locate correctly. On RR-4 and RR-5 models fit the collar into the rear boot, making sure each end of the boot locates in the groove in the collar.

13 Lubricate the new piston seal with clean brake fluid and fit it into its groove in the caliper bore **(see illustrations)**.

14 Lubricate the new dust seal with silicone grease and fit it into its groove in the caliper bore **(see illustration)**.

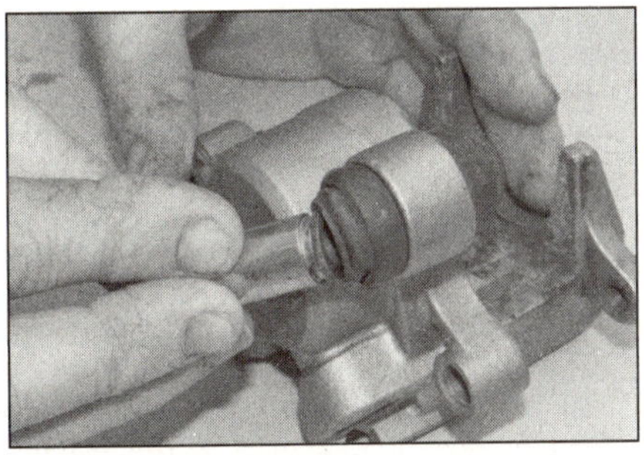

7.12a On RR-4 and RR-5 models remove the collar from the boot and the boot from the caliper . . .

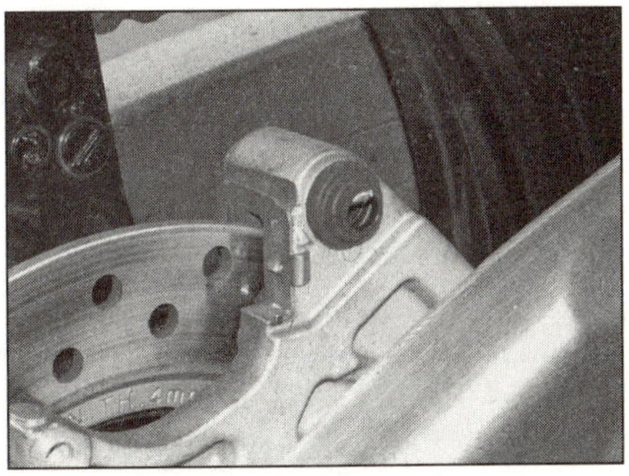

7.12b . . . and the bracket

7.12c On RR-6 and RR-7 models remove the boots from the caliper and bracket

7.13a Lubricate the new piston seal with brake fluid . . .

7.13b . . . then fit it into its groove . . .

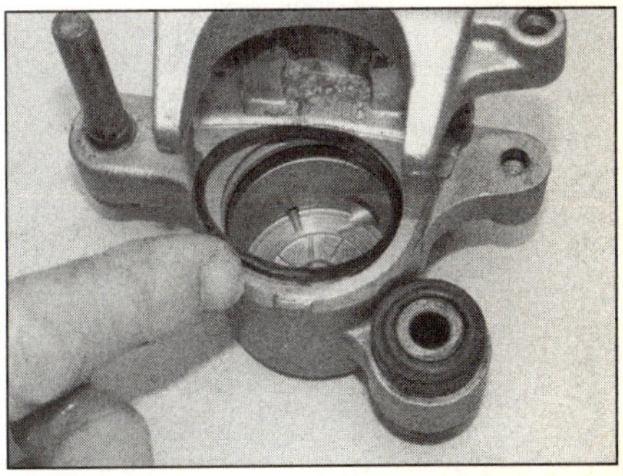

7.14 . . . followed by the new dust seal

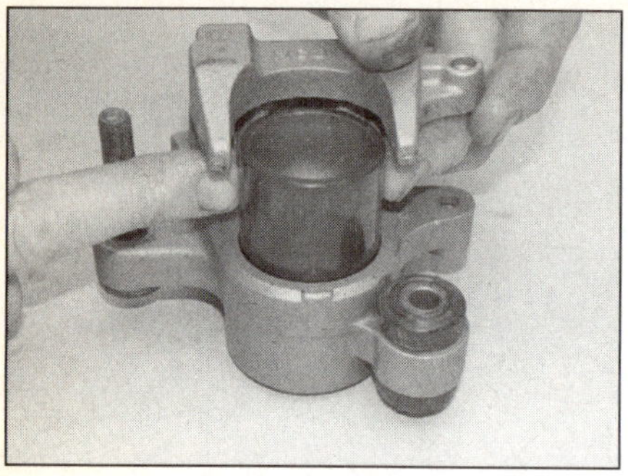

7.15a Fit the piston . . .

7.15b . . . and push it all the way in

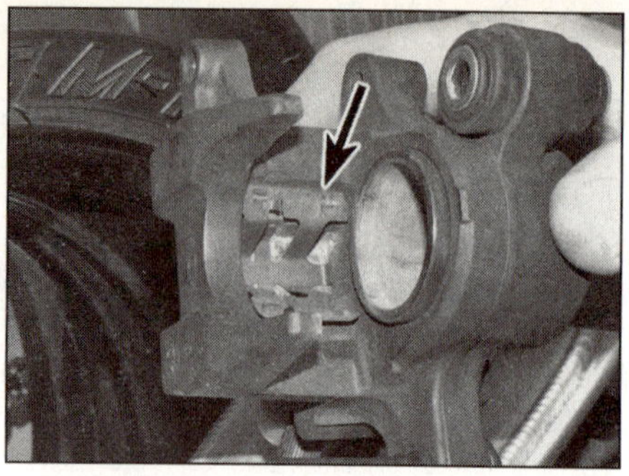

7.17a Pad spring (arrowed) . . .

15 Lubricate the piston with clean brake fluid and fit it, closed-end first, into the caliper bore, taking care not to displace the seals **(see illustration)**. Using your thumbs, push the piston all the way in, making sure it enters the bore squarely **(see illustration)**.

Installation

16 If the caliper has not been overhauled, refer to Step 12 and clean, check and re-grease the slider pins, boots and on RR-4 and RR-5 models the collar.

17 Make sure that the pad spring and pad guide are correctly fitted **(see illustrations)**.

18 On RR-4 and RR-5 models, if the caliper was overhauled, slide it onto the bracket **(see illustration 7.3)** and leave it with the rear pivoted up, then install the brake pads (see Section 6). If the caliper was just displaced, slide it onto the bracket, then pivot it down, making sure the pads locate on each side of the disc, and the front edges locate correctly against the guide **(see illustration 6.11b)**. Install the rear mounting bolt/slider pin and tighten it to the torque setting specified at the beginning of the Chapter **(see illustration 6.1a)**.

19 On RR-6 and RR-7 models, slide the caliper onto the bracket **(see illustration 7.4)**. Install the rear wheel (see Section 15). Install the brake pads (see Section 6).

20 If detached, connect the brake hose to the caliper, using new sealing washers on each side of the fitting **(see illustration)**. Align the hose as noted on removal **(see illustration 7.1a or b)**. Tighten the banjo bolt to the torque setting specified at the beginning of the Chapter.

21 If detached fit the brake hose guide, making sure the tab locates in the hole **(see illustrations 7.2b and a)**.

22 Top up the hydraulic reservoir with DOT 4 brake fluid (see *Pre-ride checks*) and bleed the system as described in Section 11. Check that there are no fluid leaks and test the operation of the rear brake before riding the motorcycle.

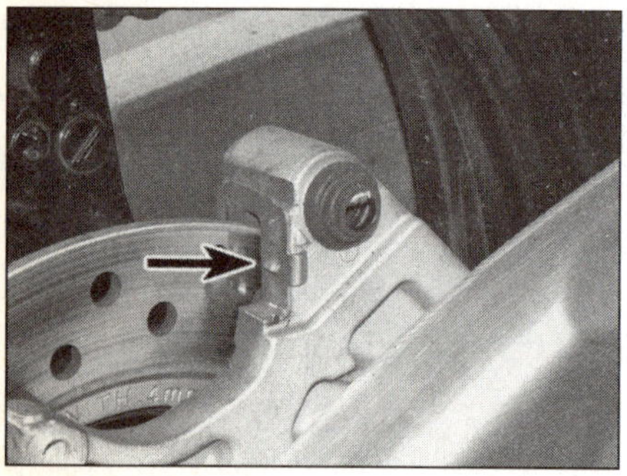

7.17b . . . and guide (arrowed) – RR-4 and RR-5 models

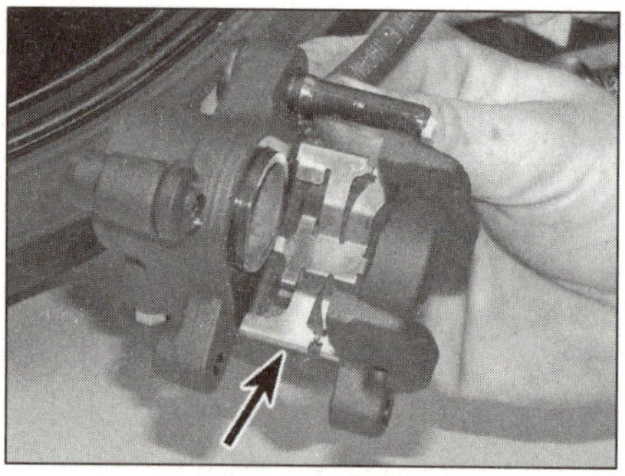

7.17c Pad spring (arrowed) . . .

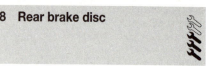

8 Rear brake disc

Inspection

1 Refer to Section 4 of this Chapter, noting that the dial gauge should be attached to the swingarm.

Removal

Note: *Honda recommend using new disc mounting bolts. This is because the bolts are pre-treated with a locking compound. It is possible, however, to clean up the old bolts and reinstall them using a suitable non-permanent thread locking compound that is commercially available.*

2 Remove the rear wheel (see Section 15).

Caution: Don't lay the wheel down and allow it to rest on the disc or sprocket – they could become warped. Set the wheel on wood blocks so the wheel rim supports the weight of the wheel.

3 If you are not replacing the disc with a new one, mark the relationship of the disc to the wheel so it can be installed in the same position. Unscrew the disc retaining bolts, loosening them evenly and a little at a time in a criss-cross pattern to avoid distorting the disc, then remove the disc **(see illustration)**.

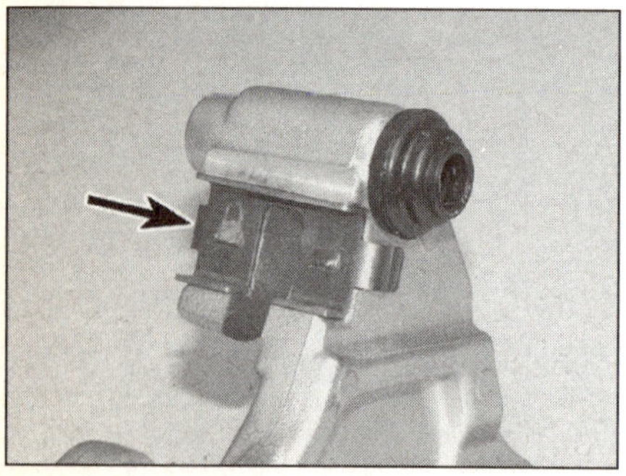

7.17d . . . and guide (arrowed) – RR-6 and RR-7 models

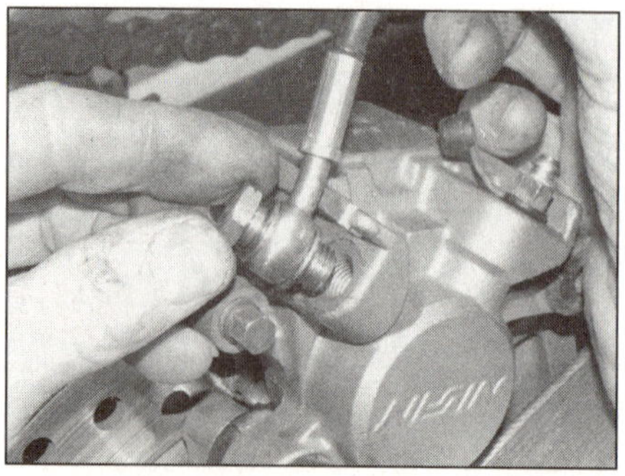

7.20 Always use new sealing washers

8.3 The disc is secured by four bolts

9.1a Remove the split pin (arrowed) then unscrew the nut . . .

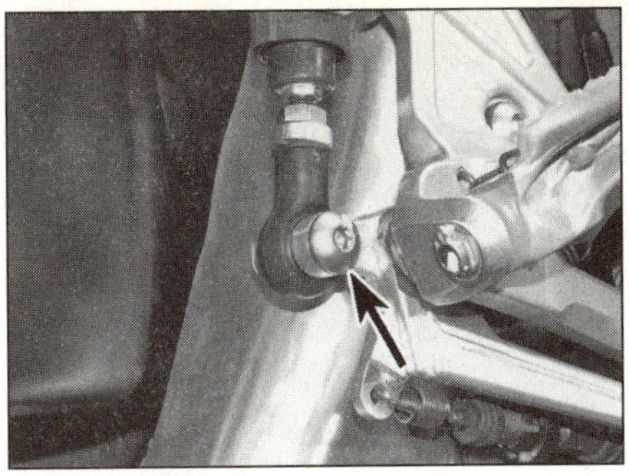

9.1b . . . withdraw the bolt (arrowed) and remove the washers

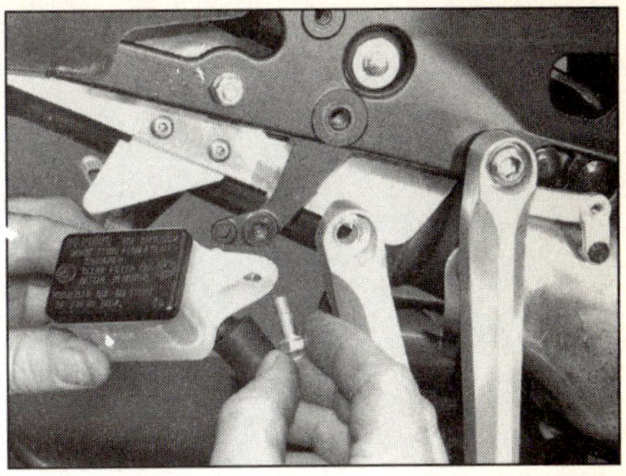

9.2 Detach and drain the fluid reservoir

Installation

4 Before installing the disc, make sure there is no dirt or corrosion where the disc seats on the hub. If the disc does not sit flat when it is bolted down, it will appear to be warped when checked or when the rear brake is used.

5 Install the disc on the wheel with its marked side facing out, aligning the previously applied matchmarks (if you're reinstalling the original disc).

6 Clean the threads of the disc mounting bolts, then apply a suitable non-permanent thread locking compound. Install the bolts and tighten them evenly and a little at a time in a criss-cross pattern to the torque setting specified at the beginning of this Chapter. Clean the disc using acetone or brake system cleaner. If a new disc has been installed, remove any protective coating from its working surfaces and fit new brake pads.

7 Install the rear wheel (see Section 15).

8 Operate the brake pedal several times to bring the pads into contact with the disc. Check the operation of the rear brake before riding the motorcycle.

9 Rear brake master cylinder

Warning: If the brake master cylinder is in need of overhaul all old brake fluid should be flushed from the system. Overhaul must be done in a spotlessly clean work area to avoid contamination and possible failure of the brake hydraulic system components. Do not, under any circumstances, use petroleum-based solvents to clean brake parts. Use clean DOT 4 brake fluid, dedicated brake cleaner or denatured alcohol only, as described. To prevent damage from spilled brake fluid, always cover paintwork when working on the braking system.

Removal

Note: *If the master cylinder is being overhauled (usually due to sticking or poor action, or fluid leaks) read through the entire procedure first and make sure that you have obtained all the new parts required, including some new DOT 4 brake fluid.*

1 Remove the split pin from the inner end of the pushrod joint piece bolt, then counter-hold the nut and unscrew the bolt, noting the washers **(see illustrations)**. Discard the split pin as a new one must be fitted on reassembly.

2 Unscrew the passenger footrest bracket rear bolt and slacken the front one, then pivot the bracket forwards **(see illustration)**. Undo the bolt securing the fluid reservoir to the frame, then undo the reservoir cover screws and remove the reservoir cover and diaphragm. Pour the brake fluid into a suitable container. Wipe any remaining fluid out of the reservoir with a clean rag.

3 Undo the brake hose banjo bolt and detach the banjo union, noting its alignment with the master cylinder **(see illustration)**. Once disconnected, seal the banjo union and secure the hose in an upright position to minimise fluid loss. Discard the sealing washers as new ones must be fitted on reassembly.

4 Undo the bolts securing the heel plate and master cylinder to the footrest bracket and remove the master cylinder along with the reservoir **(see illustration)**.

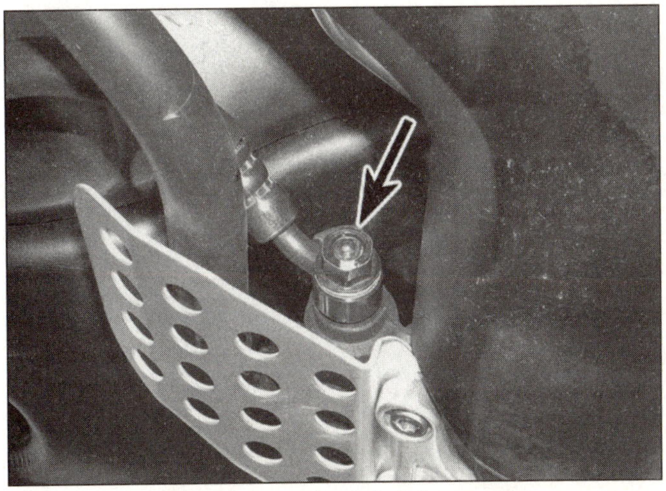

9.3 Brake hose banjo bolt (arrowed)

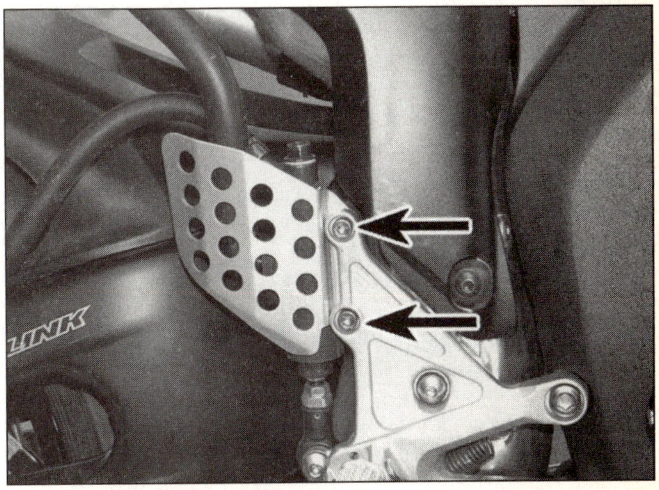

9.4 Master cylinder/heel plate bolts (arrowed)

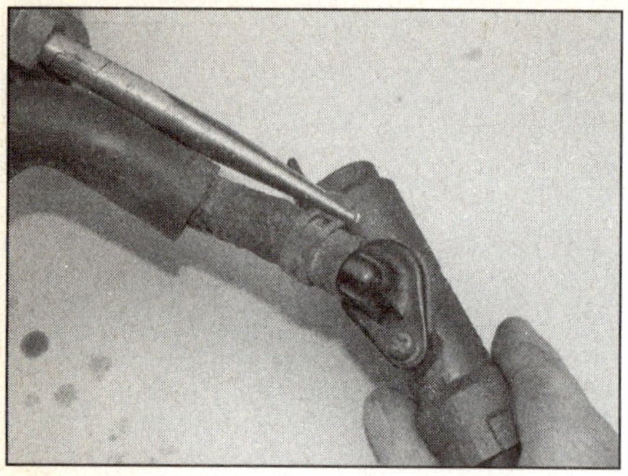

9.5 Release the clip and pull the hose off its union

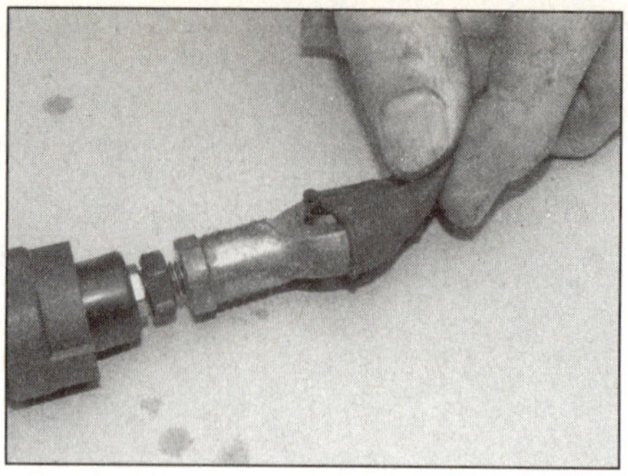

9.6a Remove the boot . . .

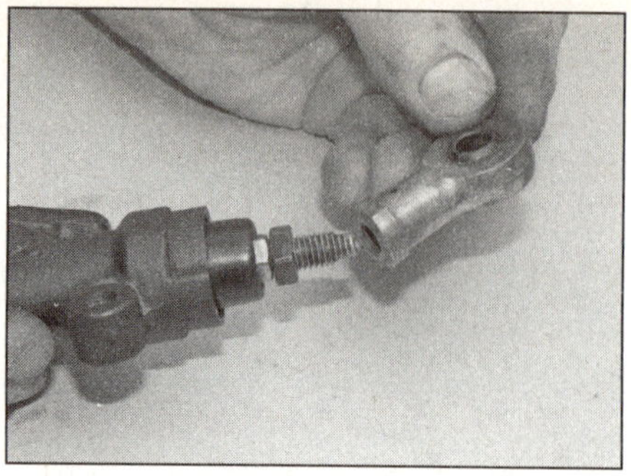

9.6b . . . then thread the joint piece . . .

Overhaul

5 Release the clip securing the reservoir hose to the union on the master cylinder and detach the hose, being prepared to catch any residual fluid **(see illustration)**.

6 If required remove the boot from the pushrod joint piece **(see illustration)**. Note how far the joint piece is threaded up the pushrod, then slacken its locknut and thread it off, followed by the locknut **(see illustrations)**.

7 Dislodge the rubber dust boot from the base of the master cylinder and from around the pushrod, noting how it locates **(see illustration)**. Push the pushrod in and, using circlip pliers, remove the circlip from its groove in the master cylinder and slide out the piston assembly and the spring, noting how they fit **(see illustrations)**. Lay the parts out in order as you remove them to prevent confusion during reassembly.

8 If required, undo the screw securing the fluid reservoir hose union and detach it from the master cylinder **(see illustration)**. Discard the O-ring as a new one must be used. Inspect the reservoir hose for cracks or splits and replace it with a new one if necessary.

9 Clean all parts with clean brake fluid. If compressed air is available, blow it through the fluid galleries to ensure they are clear (make sure the air is filtered and unlubricated).

Caution: Do not, under any circumstances, use a petroleum-based solvent to clean brake parts.

10 Check the master cylinder bore for corrosion, scratches, nicks and score marks **(see illustration)**. If the necessary measuring equipment is available, compare the dimensions of the piston and bore to those given in the Specifications at the beginning of this Chapter. If damage or wear is evident, the master cylinder must be replaced with a new one. If the master cylinder is in poor condition, then the caliper should be checked as well.

11 The dust boot, circlip, piston, seal, cup and spring are all included in the master cylinder rebuild kit. Use all of the new parts, regardless of the apparent condition of the old ones.

12 Smear the cup and seal with new brake fluid. If the seal is not already on the piston, fit it into its groove so the wider end will fit into

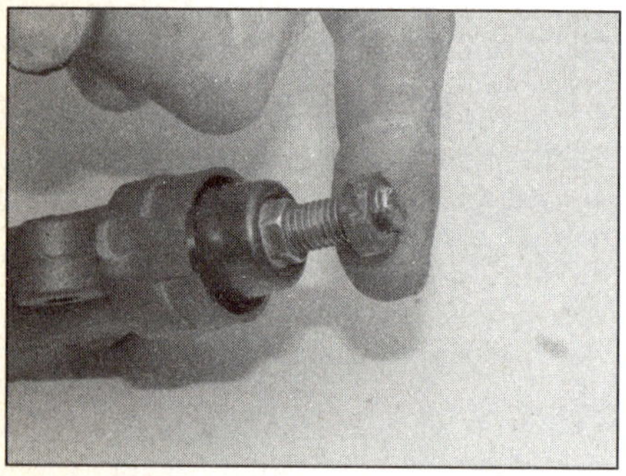

9.6c . . . and the locknut off

9.7a Remove the rubber boot . . .

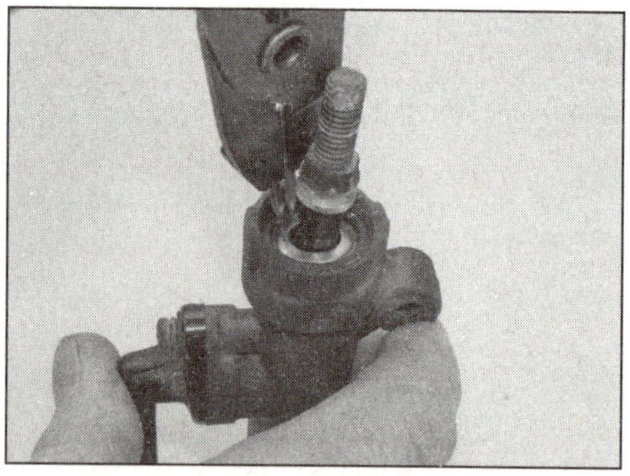

9.7b . . . then release the circlip . . .

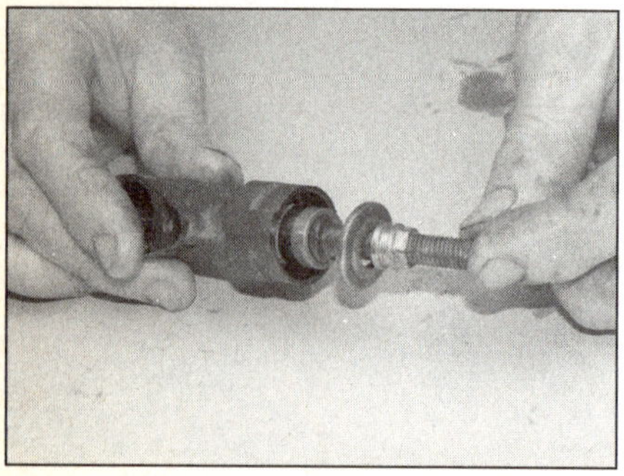

9.7c . . . and remove the pushrod, piston and spring

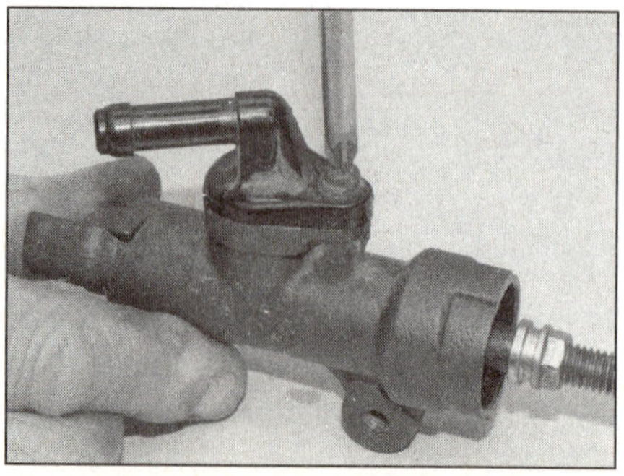

9.8 Undo the screw and remove the union

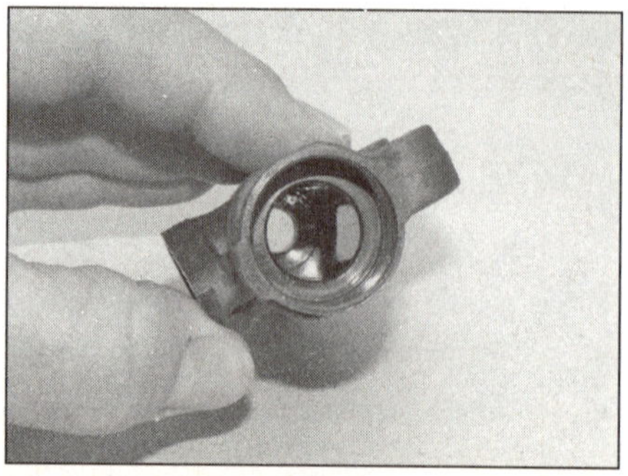

9.10 Check the cylinder for damage and wear

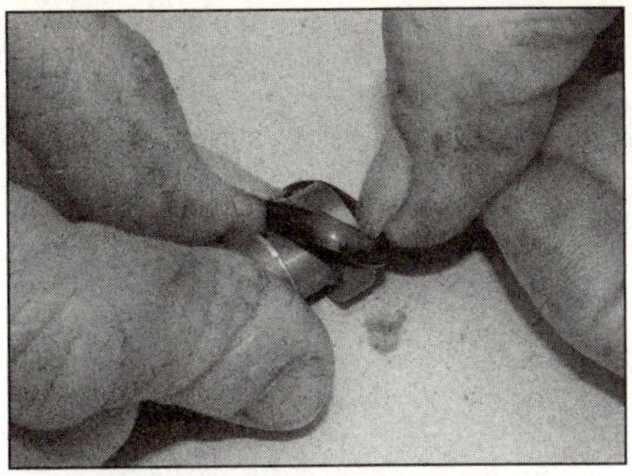

9.12a **Fit the seal on to the piston . . .**

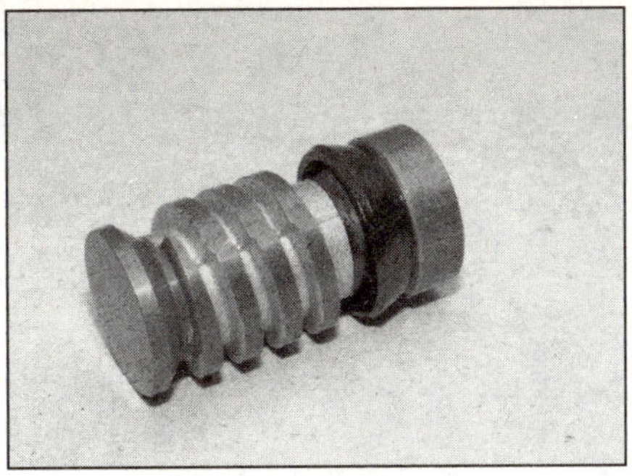

9.12b **. . . as shown**

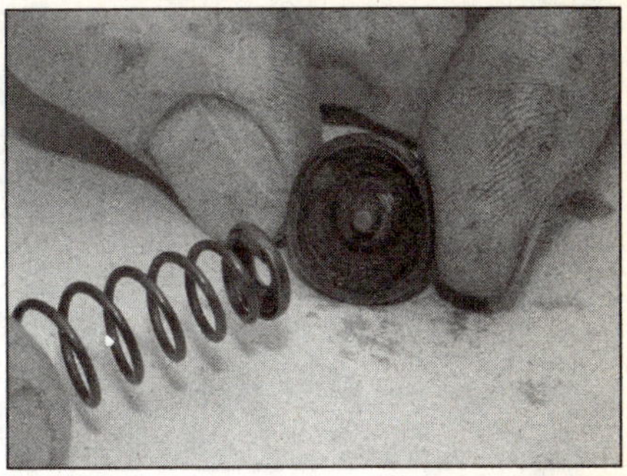

9.12c **Fit the cup onto the end of the spring, locating the peg in the hole**

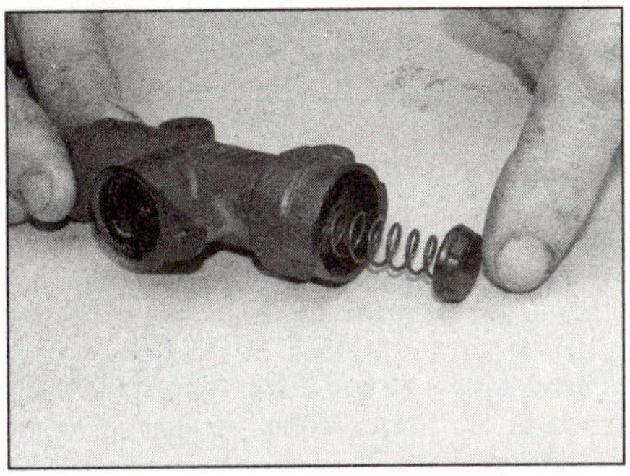

9.13 **Fit the spring making sure the cup locates correctly in the bore . . .**

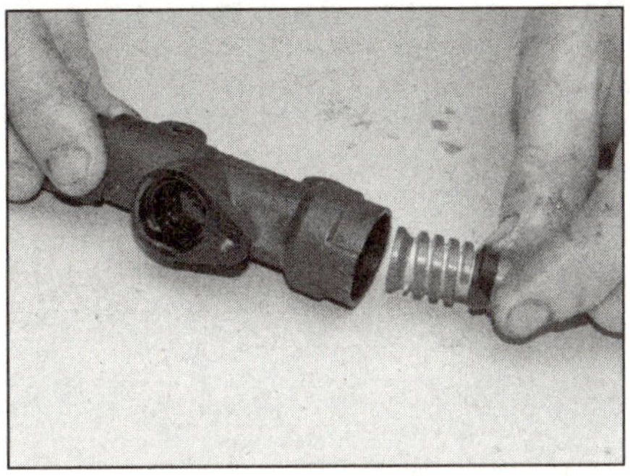

9.14 **. . . then push the piston in**

9.15a **Position the circlip on the washer . . .**

the master cylinder first **(see illustrations)**. Fit the cup onto the narrow end of the spring, locating the peg in the hole **(see illustration)**. Lubricate the master cylinder bore with new brake fluid.

13 Fit the spring wide-end first into the master cylinder and push the cup in, making sure its lips do not turn inside out **(see illustration)**.

14 Lubricate the piston with clean brake fluid and slide it into the master cylinder and up against the cup and spring **(see illustration)**. Make sure the lips on the seal do not turn inside out.

15 Smear some silicone grease onto the rounded end of the pushrod and locate it against the end of the piston **(see illustration 9.7c)**. Fit the new circlip around the pushrod **(see illustration)**. Push the piston in using the pushrod until the washer is beyond the circlip groove, then locate the circlip in the groove **(see illustration)**.

16 Fit a new fluid reservoir hose union O-ring smeared with brake fluid, then press the union into the master cylinder and secure it with the screw **(see illustrations)**.

17 Fit the rubber boot, making sure the lips

9.15b **. . . then depress the pushrod and fit the circlip into the groove**

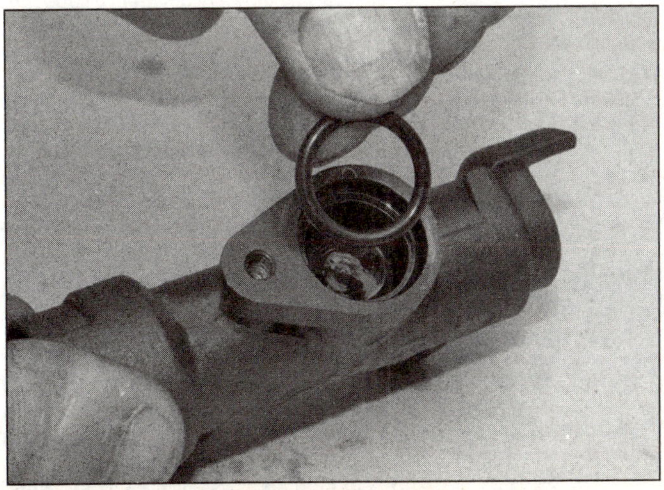

9.16a **Fit a new O-ring . . .**

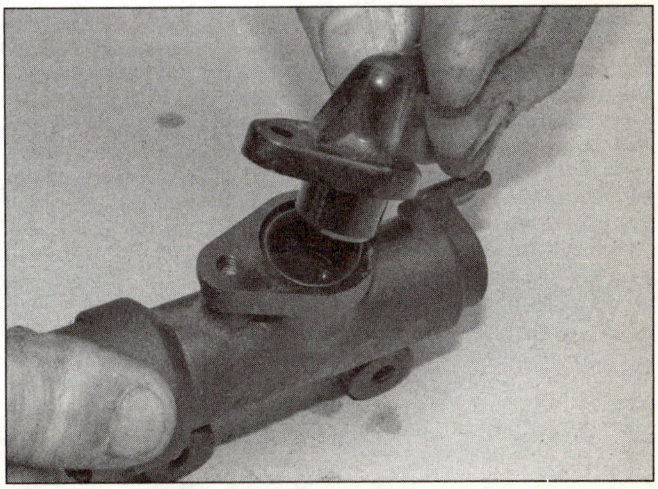

9.16b **. . . then press the union into place**

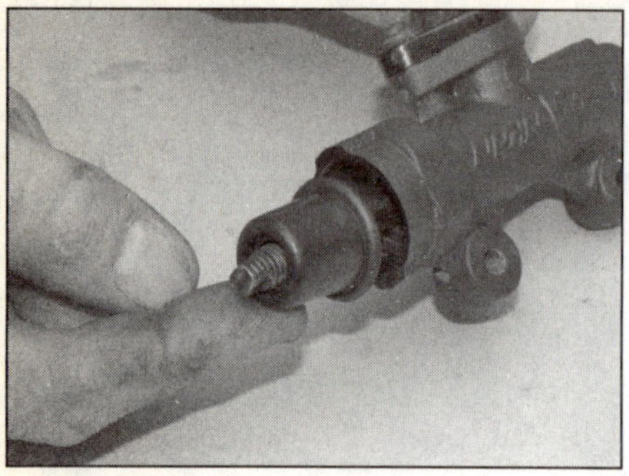

9.17a Fit the new boot . . .

9.17b . . . then press it into the cylinder . . .

9.17c . . . and make sure it is correctly located around the pushrod

are seated correctly in the master cylinder and around the pushrod **(see illustrations)**.

18 Thread the locknut and joint piece onto the master cylinder pushrod, setting them as noted on removal **(see illustrations 9.6c and b)** – Honda specify the distance between the centre of the joint piece eye and the lower mounting bolt hole should be 75 mm. Tighten the locknut securely against the joint piece. Fit the rubber boot **(see illustration 9.6a)**.

19 Connect the hose to the union on the master cylinder and secure it with the clip **(see illustration)**. Check that the hose is secured with a clip at the reservoir end as well. If the clips have weakened, use new ones.

Installation

20 Locate the master cylinder on the inside of the footrest bracket, then fit the heel plate and mounting bolts and tighten the bolts to the torque setting specified at the beginning of this Chapter **(see illustration 9.4)**.

21 Lubricate the joint piece eye with grease. Align the pushrod joint piece with the brake pedal, then insert the bolt with its washer and secure it with the washer, nut and a new split pin – do not over-tighten the nut **(see illustrations 9.1b and a)**. Bend the ends of the pin up to lock it. Check the brake pedal height (see Chapter 1, Section 3), and make sure the pedal pivots freely in the joint – if it doesn't the nut is too tight.

22 Align the brake hose as noted on removal and connect the hose to the master cylinder, using a new sealing washer on each side of the banjo fitting **(see illustration 9.3)**. Tighten the banjo bolt to the torque setting specified at the beginning of this Chapter.

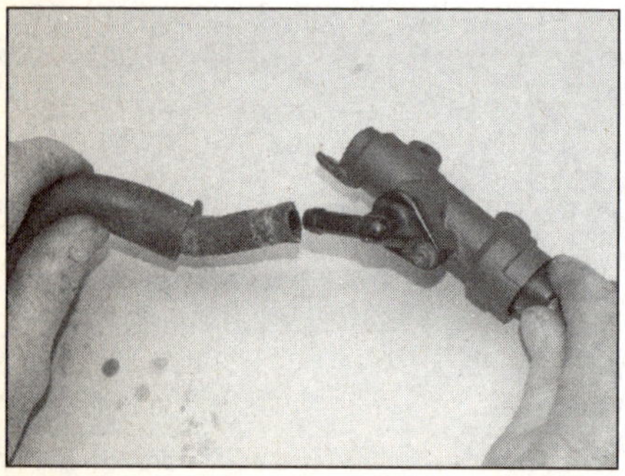

9.19 Fit the reservoir hose onto its union

23 Fit the fluid reservoir onto the frame, making sure the pin on the back locates in the hole **(see illustration 9.2)**. Locate the passenger footrest bracket and tighten its bolts to the specified torque.

24 Fill the fluid reservoir with new DOT 4 brake fluid (see *Pre-ride checks*). Refer to Section 11 and bleed the air from the system.

25 Check the operation of the rear brake carefully before riding the motorcycle.

10 Brake hoses and fittings

Inspection

1 Brake hose condition should be checked regularly and the hoses replaced with new ones at the specified interval (see Chapter 1).

2 Twist and flex the hoses while looking for cracks, bulges and seeping hydraulic fluid. Check extra carefully around the areas where the hoses connect with the banjo fittings, as these are common areas for hose failure.

3 Inspect the banjo fittings connected to the brake hoses. If the fittings are rusted, scratched or cracked, fit new hoses.

Removal and installation

4 The brake hoses have banjo fittings on each end. Cover the surrounding area with plenty of rags and unscrew the banjo bolt at each end of the hose, noting the alignment of the fitting with the master cylinder or brake caliper **(see illustrations 3.3, 5.5, 7.1a or b, and 9.3)**. Free the hose from any clips or guides and remove it, noting its routing. Discard the sealing washers. **Note:** *Do not operate the brake lever or pedal while a brake hose is disconnected.*

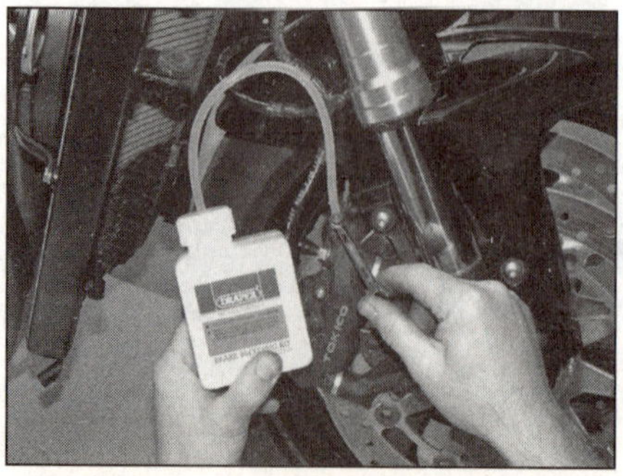

11.2 Set-up for bleeding the brakes

5 Position the new hose, making sure it isn't twisted or otherwise strained, and ensure that it is correctly routed through any clips or guides and is clear of all moving components.

6 Check that the fittings align correctly, then install the banjo bolts, using new sealing washers on both sides of the fittings **(see illustrations 3.22 and 7.20)**. Tighten the banjo bolts to the torque setting specified at the beginning of this Chapter.

7 Flush the old brake fluid from the system, refill with new DOT 4 brake fluid (see *Pre-ride checks*) and bleed the air from the system (see Section 11).

8 Check the operation of the brakes before riding the motorcycle.

11 Brake system bleeding and fluid change

Note: *If required use a commercially available vacuum-type brake bleeding tool* ***(see illustration 11.17)****. If bleeding the system using the conventional method does not work sufficiently well, it is advisable to obtain a bleeder and repeat the procedure detailed below, following the manufacturers instructions for using the tool.*

Bleeding

1 Bleeding the brakes is simply the process of removing air from the brake fluid reservoir, the hose and the brake caliper. Bleeding is necessary whenever a brake system hydraulic connection is loosened, after a component or hose is replaced with a new one, or when the master cylinder or caliper is overhauled. Leaks in the system may also allow air to enter, but leaking brake fluid will reveal their presence and warn you of the need for repair.

2 To bleed the brakes, you will need some new DOT 4 brake fluid, a length of clear vinyl or plastic hose, a small container partially filled with clean brake fluid, some rags, a spanner to fit the brake caliper bleed valve, and help from an assistant **(see illustration)**. The front master cylinder is fitted with a bleed

11.5a Front master cylinder bleed valve (arrowed)

11.5b Front brake caliper bleed valve (arrowed)

11.5c Rear brake caliper bleed valve (arrowed)

valve **(see illustration 11.5a)**. When bleeding the front brakes, start with the master cylinder (See Step 4), then do the right-hand caliper then the left-hand caliper.

3 Cover painted components to prevent damage in the event that brake fluid is spilled.

4 Refer to *Pre-ride checks* and remove the reservoir cap or cover, diaphragm plate and diaphragm, and on RR-4 and RR-5 models the front reservoir float, and slowly pump the brake lever (front brake) or pedal (rear brake) a few times, until no air bubbles can be seen floating up from the holes in the bottom of the reservoir. This bleeds the air from the master cylinder end of the line. Temporarily refit the reservoir cap or cover.

5 Pull the dust cap off the bleed valve **(see illustrations)**. Attach one end of the clear vinyl or plastic hose to the bleed valve and submerge the other end in the clean brake fluid in the container **(see illustration 11.2)**. **Note:** *To avoid damaging the bleed valve during the procedure, loosen it and then tighten it temporarily with a ring spanner before attaching the hose. With the hose attached, the valve can then be opened and closed either with an open-ended spanner, or by leaving the ring spanner located on the valve and fitting the hose above it.*

6 Check the fluid level in the reservoir. Do not allow the fluid level to drop below the lower mark during the procedure.

7 Carefully pump the brake lever or pedal three or four times and hold it in (front) or down (rear) while opening the bleed valve **(see illustration 11.2)**. When the valve is opened, brake fluid will flow out of the caliper into the clear tubing, and the lever will move toward the handlebar, or the pedal will move down. If there is air in the system there will be air bubbles in the brake fluid coming out of the caliper.

8 Tighten the bleed valve, then release the brake lever or pedal gradually. Top-up the reservoir and repeat the process until no air bubbles are visible in the brake fluid leaving the caliper, and the lever or pedal is firm when applied. On completion, disconnect the hose, then tighten the bleed valve to the torque setting specified at the beginning of this Chapter and install the dust cap.

HAYNES HiNT ***If it is not possible to produce a firm feel to the lever or pedal, the fluid may be aerated. Let the brake fluid in the system stabilise for a few hours and then repeat the procedure when the tiny bubbles in the system have settled out.***

9 Top-up the reservoir, then install the float (front reservoir on RR-4 and RR-5 models), diaphragm, diaphragm plate, and cap or cover (see *Pre-ride checks*). Wipe up any spilled brake fluid. Check the entire system for fluid leaks.

10 Check the operation of the brakes before riding the motorcycle.

Fluid change

11 Changing the brake fluid is a similar process to bleeding the brakes and requires the same materials plus a suitable tool for siphoning the fluid out of the reservoir. Also ensure that the container is large enough to take all the old fluid when it is flushed out of the system.

12 Follow Steps 3 and 5, then remove the reservoir cap or cover, diaphragm plate and diaphragm, and on RR-4 and RR-5 models the front reservoir float, and siphon the old fluid out of the reservoir. Fill the reservoir with new brake fluid, then carefully pump the brake lever or pedal three or four times and hold it in (front) or down (rear) while opening the caliper bleed valve. When the valve is opened, brake fluid will flow out of the caliper into the clear tubing, and the lever will move toward the handlebar, or the pedal will move down.

11.17 Drawing out brake fluid using a commercial vacuum-operated bleeding tool

13 Tighten the bleed valve, then release the brake lever or pedal gradually. Keep the reservoir topped-up with new fluid to above the LOWER level at all times or air may enter the system and greatly increase the length of the task. Repeat the process until new fluid can be seen emerging from the caliper bleed valve.

HAYNES HiNT ***Old brake fluid is invariably much darker in colour than new fluid, making it easy to see when all old fluid has been expelled from the system.***

14 Disconnect the hose, then make sure the bleed valve is tightened to the specified torque setting and install the dust cap.

15 Top-up the reservoir, then install the float (front reservoir on RR-4 and RR-5 models), diaphragm, diaphragm plate, and cap or cover (see *Pre-ride checks*). Wipe up any spilled brake fluid. Check the entire system for fluid leaks.

16 Check the operation of the brakes before riding the motorcycle.

Draining the system for overhaul

17 Draining the brake fluid is again a similar process to bleeding the brakes. The quickest and easiest way is to use a commercially available vacuum-type brake bleeding tool **(see illustration)** – follow the manufacturer's instructions. Otherwise follow the procedure described above for changing the fluid, but quite simply do not put any new fluid into the reservoir – the system fills itself with air instead.

12 Wheel inspection and repair

1 In order to carry out a proper inspection of the wheels, it is necessary to support the bike upright so that the wheel being inspected is raised off the ground. Position the motorcycle on an auxiliary stand. Clean the wheels

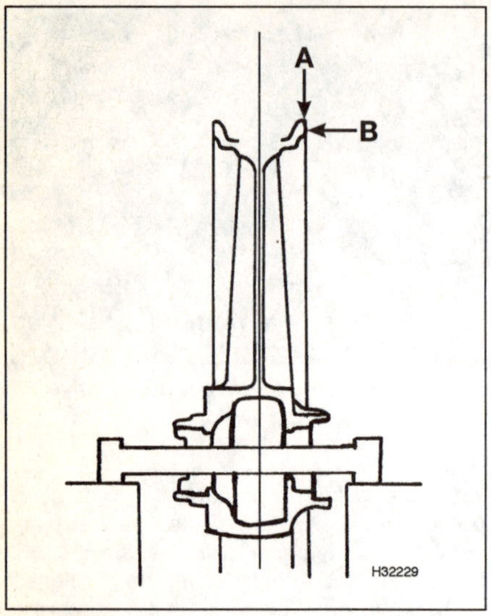

12.2 Check the wheel for radial (out-of-round) runout (A) and axial (side-to-side) runout (B)

thoroughly to remove mud and dirt that may interfere with the inspection procedure or mask defects. Make a general check of the wheels (see Chapter 1) and tyres (see *Pre-ride checks*).

2 Attach a dial gauge to the fork or the swingarm and position its tip against the side of the wheel rim. Spin the wheel slowly and check the axial (side-to-side) runout of the rim **(see illustration)**.

3 In order to accurately check radial (out of round) runout with the dial gauge, remove the wheel from the machine, and the tyre from the wheel. With the axle clamped in a vice and the dial gauge positioned on the top of the rim, the wheel can be rotated to check the runout **(see illustration 12.2)**.

4 An easier, though slightly less accurate, method is to attach a stiff wire pointer to the fork or the swingarm and position the end a fraction of an inch from the wheel rim where the wheel and tyre join. If the wheel is true, the distance from the pointer to the rim will be constant as the wheel is rotated. **Note:** *If wheel runout is excessive, check the wheel bearings very carefully before renewing the wheel.*

5 The wheels should also be inspected for cracks, flat spots on the rim and other damage. Look very closely for dents in the area where the tyre bead contacts the rim. Dents in this area may prevent complete sealing of the tyre against the rim, which leads to deflation of the tyre over a period of time. If damage is evident, or if runout in either direction is excessive, the wheel will have to be renewed. Never attempt to repair a damaged alloy wheel.

13 Wheel alignment check

1 Misalignment of the wheels due to a bent frame or forks can cause strange and possibly serious handling problems. If the frame or forks are at fault, repair by a frame specialist or renewal are the only options.

2 To check wheel alignment you will need an assistant, a length of string or a perfectly straight piece of wood and a ruler. A plumb bob or spirit level for checking that the wheels are vertical will also be required.

3 In order to make a proper check of the wheels it is necessary to support the bike in an upright position, using an auxiliary stand. First ensure that the chain adjuster markings coincide on each side of the swingarm (see Chapter 1, Section 1). Next, measure the width of both tyres at their widest points. Subtract the smaller measurement from the larger measurement, then divide the difference by two. The result is the amount of offset that should exist between the front and rear tyres on both sides of the machine.

4 If the string method is used, have your assistant hold one end of it about halfway between the floor and the rear axle, with the string touching the back edge of the rear tyre sidewall.

5 Run the other end of the string forward and pull it tight so that it is roughly parallel to the floor **(see illustration)**. Slowly bring the string into contact with the front edge of the rear tyre sidewall, then turn the front wheel until it is parallel with the string. Measure the distance from the front tyre sidewall to the string.

6 Repeat the procedure on the other side of the motorcycle. The distance from the front tyre sidewall to the string should be equal on both sides.

7 As previously mentioned, a perfectly straight length of wood or metal bar may be substituted for the string **(see illustration)**.

8 If the distance between the string and tyre is greater on one side, or if the rear wheel appears to be out of alignment, have your machine checked by a Honda dealer or frame specialist.

9 If the front-to-back alignment is correct, the wheels still may be out of alignment vertically.

10 Using a plumb bob or spirit level, check the rear wheel to make sure it is vertical. To do this, hold the string of the plumb bob against the tyre upper sidewall and allow the weight to settle just off the floor. If the string touches both the upper and lower tyre sidewalls and is perfectly straight, the wheel is vertical. If it is not, adjust the stand until it is.

11 Once the rear wheel is vertical, check the front wheel in the same manner. If both wheels are not perfectly vertical, the frame and/or major suspension components are bent.

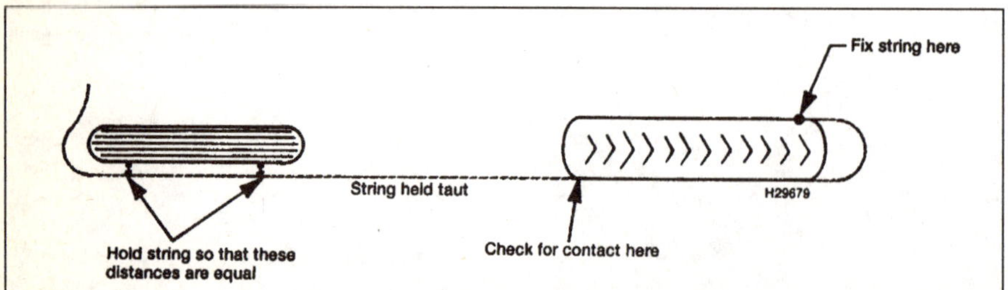

13.5 Wheel alignment check using string

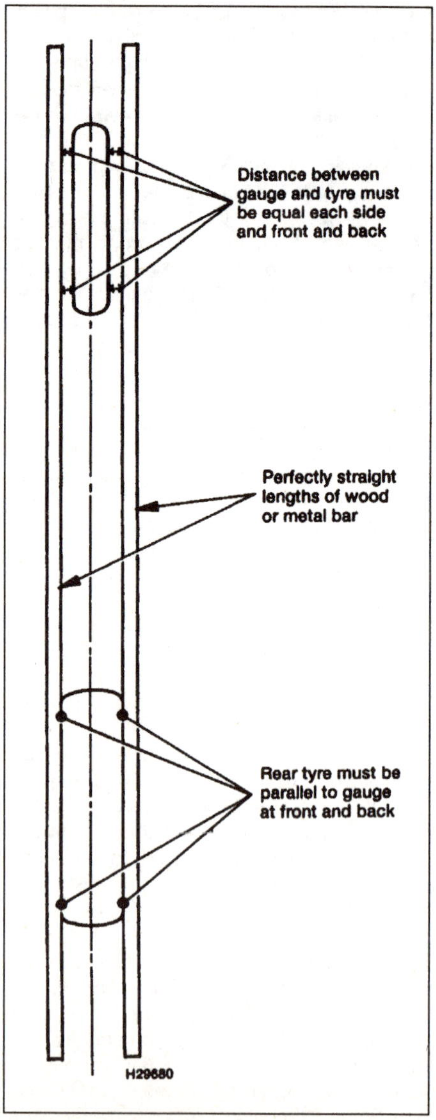

13.7 Wheel alignment check using a straight-edge

14.4 Slacken the axle clamp bolts (arrowed), then unscrew the axle bolt

14.5a Slacken the axle clamp bolts (arrowed) . . .

14.5b . . . then withdraw the axle and remove the wheel

14 Front wheel

Removal

1 Position the motorcycle on an auxiliary stand so that the front wheel is off the ground. Always make sure the motorcycle is properly supported. If a support is being placed under the engine, remove the lower fairing (see Chapter 7).

2 Displace the front brake calipers (see Section 3). Support the calipers with a cable tie or a bungee cord so that no strain is placed on the hydraulic hoses. There is no need to disconnect the hoses from the calipers. **Note:** *Do not operate the front brake lever with the calipers removed.*

3 If required, remove the front mudguard (see Chapter 7).

4 Slacken the axle clamp bolts on the bottom of the right-hand fork, then unscrew the axle bolt from the right-hand end of the axle **(see illustration)**.

5 Slacken the axle clamp bolts on the bottom of the left-hand fork **(see illustration)**. Take the weight of the wheel, then push the axle through from the right-hand side and withdraw it the left-hand side **(see illustration)**. Carefully lower the wheel and draw it forwards.

6 Remove the shouldered spacer from the right-hand side of the wheel and the plain spacer from the left-hand side **(see illustrations)**. Clean all old grease off the spacers, axle and seals.

Caution: Don't lay the wheel down and allow it to rest on a disc – the disc could become warped. Set the wheel on wood blocks so the disc doesn't support the weight of the wheel.

7 Check the axle for straightness by rolling it on a flat surface such as a piece of plate glass (first wipe off all old grease and remove any corrosion using steel wool). If the equipment is available, place the axle in V-blocks and measure the runout using a dial gauge. If the axle is bent or the runout exceeds the limit specified, replace it with a new one.

8 Check the condition of the grease seals and wheel bearings (see Section 16).

Installation

9 Apply a smear of grease to the inside of the wheel spacers, and also to the outside where they fit into the seals. Fit the shouldered spacer into the right-hand side of the wheel and the plain spacer into the left-hand side **(see illustration 14.6a and b)**. Each side of the wheel can be identified using the directional arrow cast into one of the spokes **(see illustration)**. The arrow denotes the normal direction of wheel rotation.

10 Manoeuvre the wheel into position between the fork sliders, making sure the directional arrows on the tyre, wheel and brake discs are pointing in the normal direction of rotation. Apply a thin coat of grease to the axle.

11 Lift the wheel into place, making sure the spacers remain in position. Slide the axle in from the left-hand side **(see illustration 14.5b)**.

12 Install the axle bolt and tighten it to the torque setting specified at the beginning of the Chapter **(see illustration 14.4)**. If the axle turns when tightening the bolt counter-hold it using large hex key or a suitable nut and bolt arrangement, such as the one photographed consisting of the correct nut for the axle head brazed onto a bolt that can be counter-held **(see illustration)**. A deep nut can be used on its own with care, by half inserting it into the axle head and counter-holding the exposed half.

13 Tighten the axle clamp bolts on the bottom of the right-hand fork to the specified torque setting **(see illustration 14.4)**.

14 Lower the front wheel to the ground, then install the brake calipers (see Section 3, and the Note therein regarding the caliper mounting bolts). If removed, install the front mudguard (see Chapter 7).

15 Apply the front brake a few times to bring the pads back into contact with the discs,

14.6a Remove the shouldered right-hand spacer . . .

14.6b . . . and the plain left-hand spacer

14.9 Note the directional arrow on the spoke

14.12 A tool made to counter-hold the axle head

15.3 Unscrew the axle nut and remove the washer and the adjustment marker (arrowed)

15.4a Withdraw the axle . . .

then with the brake applied pump the front forks a few times to settle all components in position. Now tighten the axle clamp bolts on the bottom of the left-hand fork to the specified torque **(see illustration 14.5a)**.

16 Check for correct operation of the front brake before riding the motorcycle. Check that there is at least 0.7 mm clearance between each front brake disc and the caliper bracket – make the check using a feeler gauge.

15 Rear wheel

Removal

1 Position the motorcycle on an auxiliary stand so that the rear wheel is off the ground. Always make sure the motorcycle is properly supported. Create some slack in the chain (see Chapter 1, Section 1).

2 On RR-4 and RR-5 models displace the rear brake caliper (see Section 7). On RR-6 and RR-7 models remove the brake pads (see Section 6).

3 Unscrew the axle nut and remove the washer **(see illustration)**. Remove the right-hand chain adjustment marker.

4 Take the weight of the wheel, then withdraw the axle from the left-hand side, bringing the left-hand chain adjustment marker with it, and lower the wheel to the ground **(see illustration)**. Remove the rear brake caliper bracket (complete with the caliper on RR-6 and RR-7 models), noting how it locates **(see illustration)**.

5 Disengage the chain from the sprocket and remove the wheel from the swingarm **(see illustration)**. If the axle is difficult to withdraw, drive it through making sure you don't damage the threads.

Caution: Do not lay the wheel down and allow it to rest on the disc or the sprocket – they could become warped. Set the wheel on wood blocks so the disc or the sprocket doesn't support the weight of the wheel. Do not operate the brake pedal with the wheel removed.

6 Remove the shouldered spacer from the left-hand side of the wheel and the plain spacer from the right-hand side **(see illustrations)**. Clean all old grease of the spacers, axle and seals.

7 Check the axle for straightness by rolling it on a flat surface such as a piece of plate glass (if the axle is corroded, first remove the corrosion with steel wool). If the equipment is available, place the axle in V-blocks and check the runout using a dial gauge. If the axle is bent or the runout exceeds the limit specified at the beginning of the Chapter, replace it with a new one.

8 Check the condition of the grease seals and wheel bearings (see Section 16).

Installation

9 Apply a smear of grease to the inside of the wheel spacers, and also to the outside where they fit into the seals. Fit the shouldered spacer into the left-hand side of the wheel and the plain spacer into the right-hand side **(see illustrations 15.6a and b)**. Apply a thin coat of grease to the axle.

10 Manoeuvre the wheel into position between the ends of the swingarm and

15.4b . . . and remove the caliper bracket

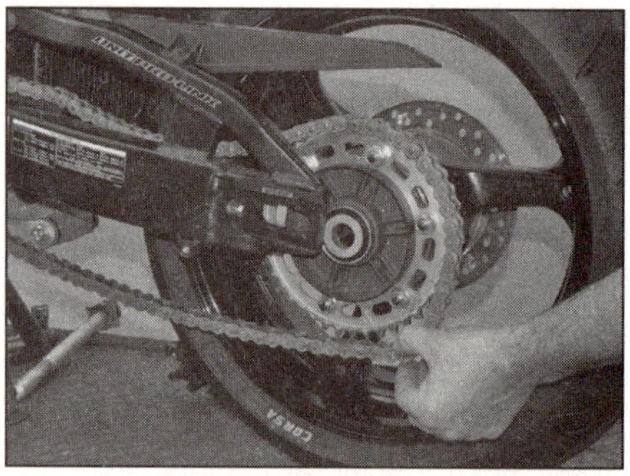

15.5 Disengage the chain and withdraw the wheel

15.6a Remove the shouldered left-hand spacer . . .

15.6b . . . and the plain right-hand spacer

engage the drive chain with the sprocket **(see illustration 15.5)**. Slide the brake caliper bracket between the wheel and the swingarm and locate it in its guide **(see illustrations)**.

11 Slide the left-hand chain adjustment marker onto the axle with the raised sections facing the axle head.

12 Lift the wheel into position and slide the axle in from the left **(see illustration 15.4a)**, making sure the spacers and caliper bracket remain correctly installed. Locate the flat edges of the axle head between the raised sections of the left-hand adjustment marker **(see illustration)**. Check that everything is correctly aligned. Fit the right-hand adjustment marker onto the end of the axle with its shaped sides at top and bottom **(see illustration)**. Fit the washer and axle nut but leave it loose **(see illustration 15.3)**.

13 On RR-4 and RR-5 models install the brake caliper (see Section 7). On RR-6 and RR-7 models install the brake pads (see Section 6). Operate the brake pedal several times to bring the pads into contact with the disc.

14 Move the bike off the auxiliary stand and onto its sidestand. Check and adjust the drive chain slack (see Chapter 1). On completion tighten the axle nut to the torque setting specified at the beginning of the Chapter.

15 Check the operation of the rear brake carefully before riding the bike.

16 Wheel bearings

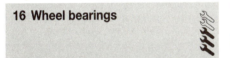

Note: *Always renew the wheel bearings in sets, never individually. Avoid using a high pressure cleaner on the wheel bearing area.*

Front wheel bearings

1 Remove the wheel (see Section 14). Remove the discs (see Section 4) to prevent them being damaged or distorted during bearing removal – if you do leave them in place, take care to support the wheel on wood blocks so that the wheel rim supports the weight of the wheel.

2 Lever out the bearing seal from each side of the hub using a flat-bladed screwdriver or a seal hook **(see illustration)**. Take care not to damage the hub. Discard the seals as new ones must be fitted on reassembly.

3 Inspect the bearings – check that the inner race turns smoothly and that the outer race is a tight fit in the hub (see *Tools and Workshop Tips* (Section 5) in the Reference Section). **Note:** *Do not remove the bearings unless they are going to be replaced with new ones.*

4 If the bearings are worn, drive one out using a suitable drift passed through the hub and located on the inner race – move the spacer to one side to expose the race, and tap evenly around the entire circumference to drive the bearing out squarely **(see illustrations)**. If it proves impossible to gain purchase on the inner race, remove the bearings using an internal expanding puller with slide-hammer attachment, which can be obtained commercially **(see illustration)**. Having removed the first bearing remove the spacer which fits between the bearings.

5 Turn the wheel over and remove the other bearing using the same procedure.

15.10a Slide the bracket into place . . .

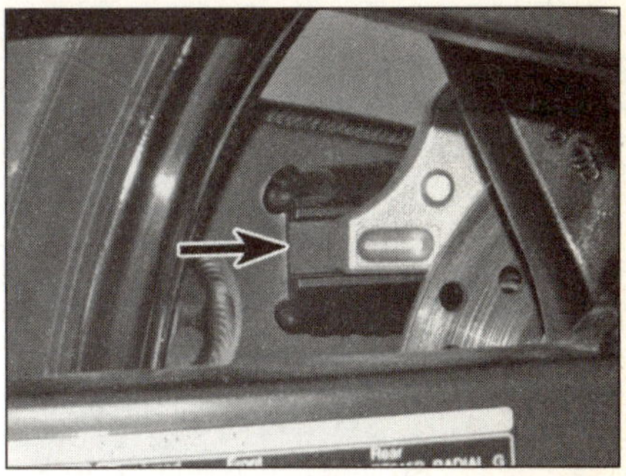
15.10b . . . locating the front section in the guide (arrowed) on the swingarm

15.12a Locate the axle head and adjustment marker as shown

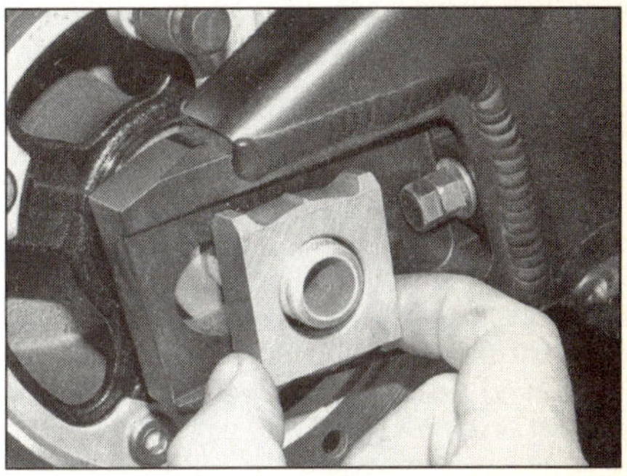
15.12b Slide the adjustment marker onto the axle

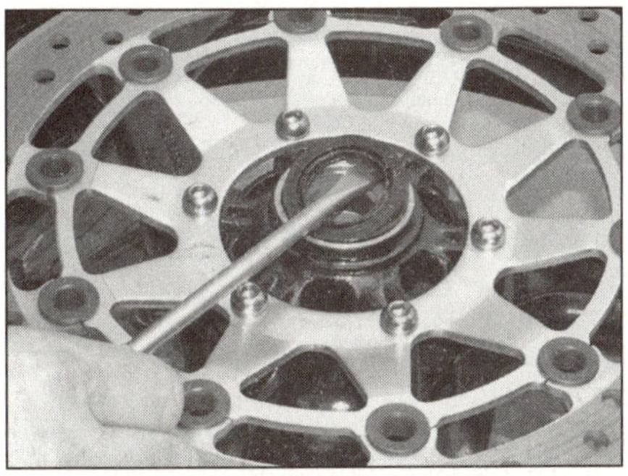
16.2 Lever out the bearing seals

16.4a Move the spacer aside to expose the inner race (arrowed) . . .

16.4b . . . then drive the bearing out using a drift

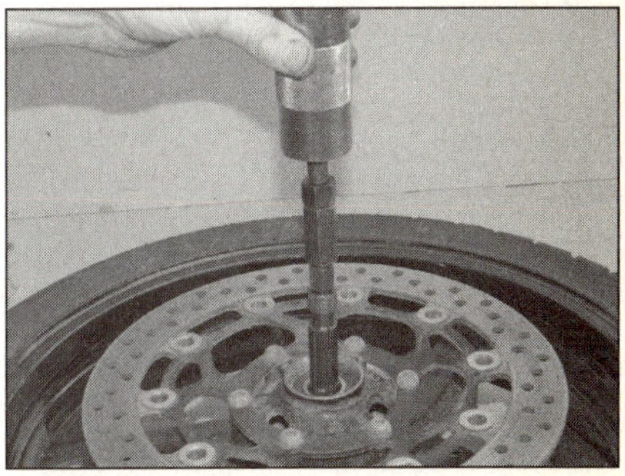
16.4c Using an expanding puller with slide-hammer attachment to pull out the bearings

16.7 Using a socket to drive the new bearing in

16.10 Press the seal into place setting it flush with the rim

16.12 Lift the sprocket coupling off the wheel

6 Thoroughly clean the hub area of the wheel with a suitable solvent and inspect the bearing seats for scoring and wear. If the seats are damaged, consult a Honda dealer before reassembling the wheel.

7 Drive the new bearings into the hub using a bearing driver or suitable socket **(see illustration)**. Ensure that the driver or socket bears only on the outer race.

8 Install the right-hand bearing first, with its marked side facing outwards. Ensure the bearing is fitted squarely and all the way into its seat.

9 Turn the wheel over then install the bearing spacer and the other new bearing.

10 Apply a smear of grease to the new seals, then press them into the hub **(see illustration)**. Level the seals with the rim of the hub with a small block of wood if necessary.

11 Clean the brake discs using acetone or brake system cleaner, then install the wheel (see Section 14).

Rear wheel bearings

12 Remove the wheel (see Section 15). Lift the sprocket coupling out of the hub **(see illustration)**. Remove the disc (see Section 8) to prevent it being damaged or distorted during bearing removal – if you do leave it in place, take care to support the wheel on wood blocks so that the wheel rim supports the weight of the wheel.

13 Lever out the bearing seal from the right-hand side of the hub using a flat-bladed screwdriver or a seal hook **(see illustration)**. Take care not to damage the hub. Discard the seal as a new one should be fitted on reassembly.

14 Inspect the bearings in both sides of the hub – check that the inner race turns smoothly and that the outer race is a tight fit in the hub (see *Tools and Workshop Tips* (Section 5) in the Reference section). **Note:** *Do not remove the bearings unless they are going to be replaced with new ones.*

15 If the bearings are worn, drive one out using a suitable drift located on the inner race – move the spacer to one side to expose the race, and tap evenly around the entire circumference to drive the bearing out squarely **(see illustrations)**. If it proves impossible to gain purchase on the inner race, remove the bearings using an internal expanding puller with slide-hammer attachment, which can be obtained commercially **(see illustration 16.4c)**. Having removed the first bearing remove the spacer which fits between the bearings.

16 Turn the wheel over and remove the remaining bearing using the same procedure.

17 Thoroughly clean the hub area of the wheel with a suitable solvent and inspect the bearing seats for scoring and wear. If the seats are damaged, consult a Honda dealer before reassembling the wheel.

18 Drive the new bearings into the hub using a bearing driver or suitable socket **(see illustration)**. Install the right-hand bearing first, with its marked side facing outwards. Ensure that the driver or socket bears only on the outer race. Ensure the bearing is fitted squarely and all the way into its seat.

19 Turn the wheel over then install the bearing spacer.

20 Install the other new bearing.

21 Apply a smear of grease to the new seal, then press it into the right-hand side of the hub. Level the seal with the rim of the hub using a small block of wood **(see illustration)**.

16.13 Lever out the bearing seal

16.15a Drive the bearing out using a drift . . .

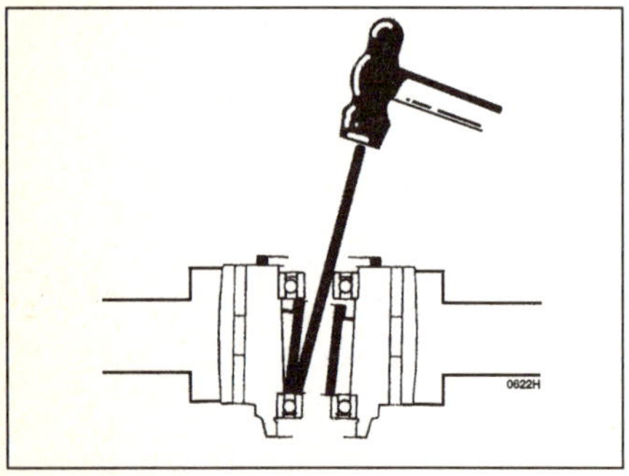

16.15b . . . locating it as shown

16.18 Using a socket to drive the new bearing in

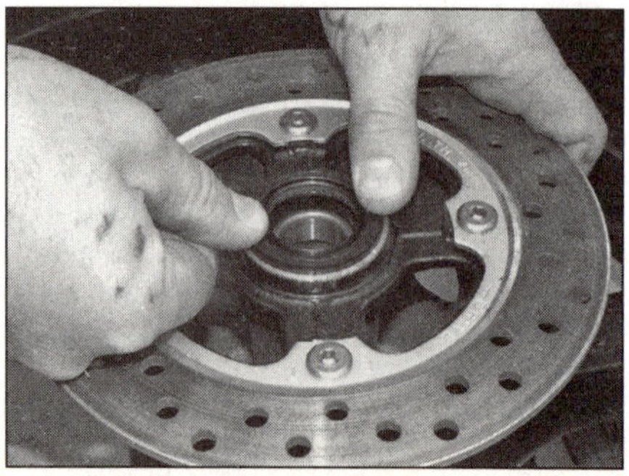

16.21 Press the seal into place and set it flush as shown

16.22 Fit a new O-ring if necessary

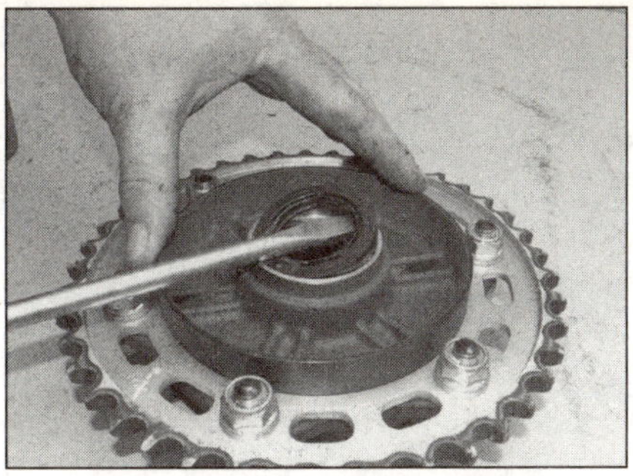
16.24 Lever out the bearing seal

16.25 Drive the spacer out of the bearings from the outside

22 Check the sprocket coupling/rubber dampers (see Section 20). Check the condition of the hub O-ring and clean it or replace it with a new one if necessary **(see illustration)**. Smear the O-ring with oil. Fit the sprocket coupling into the wheel **(see illustration 16.12)**. Clean the brake disc using acetone or brake system cleaner, then install the wheel (see Section 15).

Sprocket coupling bearings

23 Remove the rear wheel (see Section 15). Lift the sprocket coupling out of the hub **(see illustration 16.12)**.

24 Lever out the bearing seal on the outside of the coupling using a flat-bladed screwdriver or a seal hook **(see illustration)**. Take care not to damage the rim of the coupling. Discard the seal as a new one should be fitted on reassembly.

25 Place the sprocket coupling on the work surface, sprocket side up, and remove the bearing spacer, using a suitably sized socket to drive it out if it is tight **(see illustration)**.

26 Inspect the bearings – check that the inner races turn smoothly and that the outer races are a tight fit in the coupling (see *Tools and Workshop Tips* (Section 5) in the Reference Section). **Note:** *Do not remove the bearings unless they are going to be replaced with new ones.*

27 Support the coupling on blocks of wood, sprocket side down, and drive the bearings out from the inside using a bearing driver or socket **(see illustration)**.

28 Thoroughly clean the bearing seat with a suitable solvent and inspect the seat for scoring and wear. If the seat is damaged, consult a Honda dealer before reassembling the wheel.

29 Drive one bearing onto the spacer until it seats on the rim using a socket that bears on the inner race of the bearing.

30 Now drive the second bearing on using the same method until it seats against the first bearing.

31 Drive the new bearings and spacer as one into the hub using a bearing driver or suitable socket on the outer race of the outer bearing **(see illustration)**. Ensure that the driver or socket bears only on the outer race. Ensure the bearings are fitted squarely and all the way into the seat.

32 Apply a smear of grease to the new seal, then press it into the coupling **(see illustration)**. Level the seal with the rim of the coupling with a small block of wood.

33 Check the sprocket coupling/rubber dampers (see Section 20). Check the condition of the hub O-ring and clean it or replace it with a new one if necessary. Smear the O-ring with oil. Fit the sprocket coupling into the wheel and install the wheel (see Section 15).

16.27 Drive the bearings out from the inside

17 Tyres

General information

1 The wheels are designed to take tubeless tyres only. Tyre sizes are given in the Specifications at the beginning of this chapter.

16.31 Using a socket to drive the new bearings in

16.32 Fit the grease seal and press or tap it into place, setting it flush

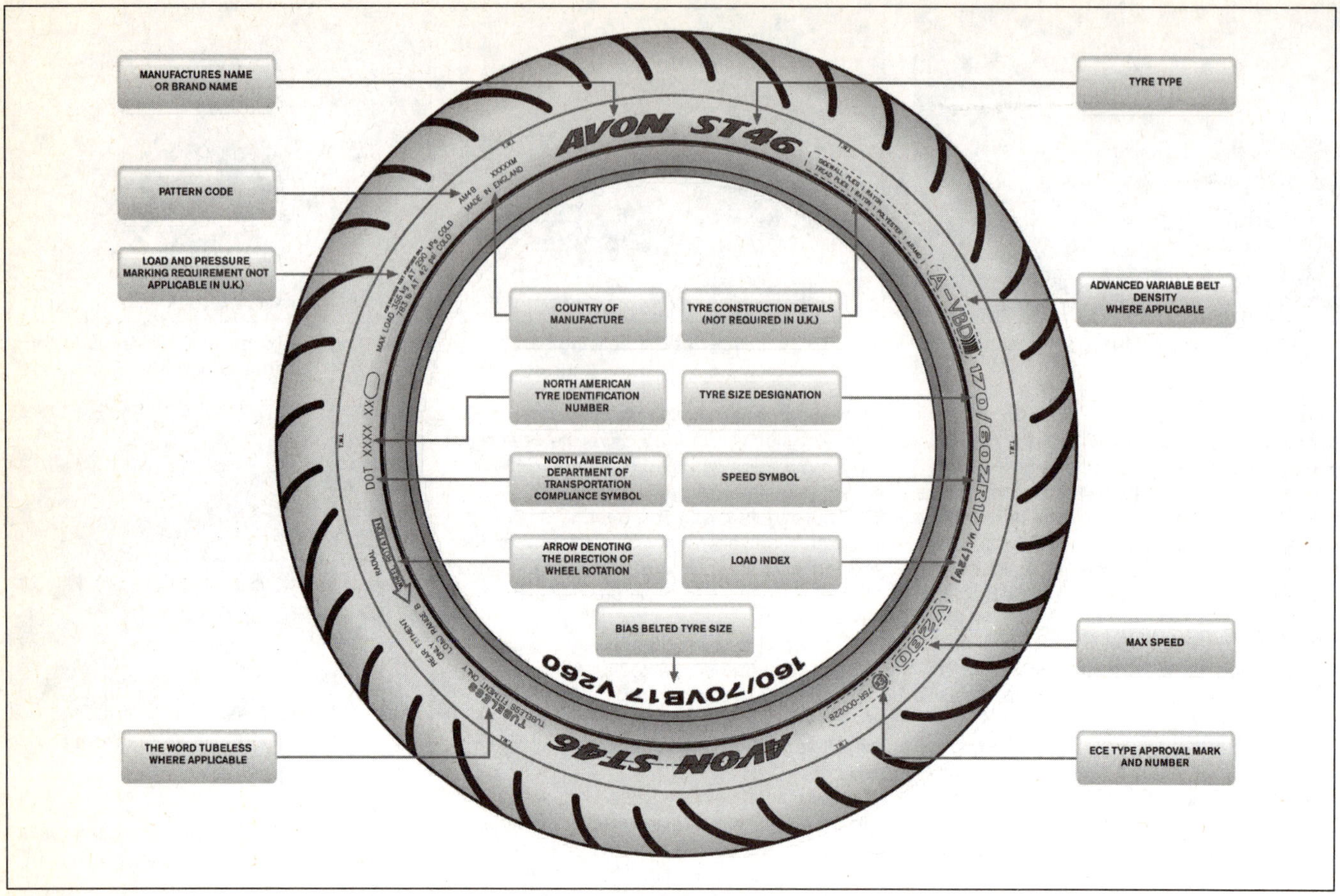

17.3 Common tyre sidewall markings

2 Refer to the *Pre-ride checks* listed at the beginning of this manual for tyre maintenance.

Fitting new tyres

3 When selecting new tyres, refer to the tyre information in the Owner's Handbook. Ensure that front and rear tyre types are compatible, the correct size and correct speed rating; if necessary seek advice from a Honda dealer or tyre fitting specialist **(see illustration)**.

4 It is recommended that tyres are fitted by a motorcycle tyre specialist rather than attempted in the home workshop. This is particularly relevant in the case of tubeless tyres because the force required to break the seal between the wheel rim and tyre bead is substantial, and is usually beyond the capabilities of an individual working with normal tyre levers. Additionally, the specialist will be able to balance the wheels after tyre fitting.

5 Note that punctured tubeless tyres can in some cases be repaired. Repairs must be carried out by a motorcycle tyre fitting specialist. Honda advise that a repaired tyre should not be used at speeds above 50 mph (80 kmh) for the first 24 hours, and not above 80 mph (130 kmh) thereafter.

18 Drive chain removal and installation

Note: *The original equipment drive chain fitted to these models has a staked-type soft link which can be split using either Honda service tool, Pt. No. 07HMH-MR1010C for US models or 07HMH-MR10103 for all other market models, or one of several commercially-available drive chain splitting/riveting tools. Such chains can be recognised by the soft link side plate's identification marks (and usually its different colour), as well as by the staked ends of the link's two pins which look as if they have been deeply centre-punched, instead of peened over as with all the other pins.*

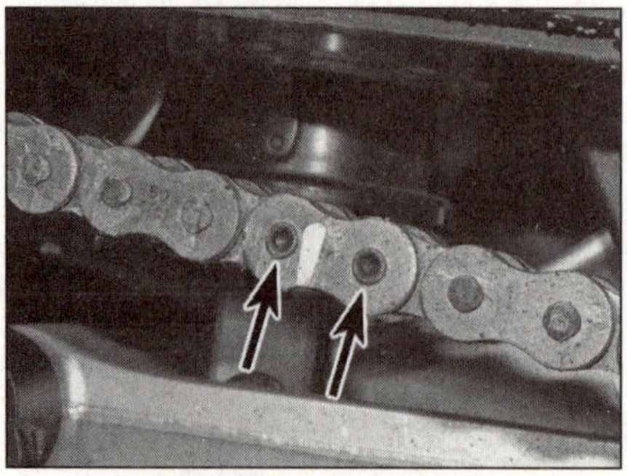

18.1 The soft link is identified by its different pin ends (arrowed)

Removal

1 Support the motorcycle on an auxiliary stand so that the rear wheel is off the ground. Position the soft link in a suitable position to work on by rotating the back wheel **(see illustration)**. Slacken the drive chain as described in Chapter 1, Section 1.

2 If required, unscrew the bolts securing the rear section of the chainguard and remove it **(see illustration)**.

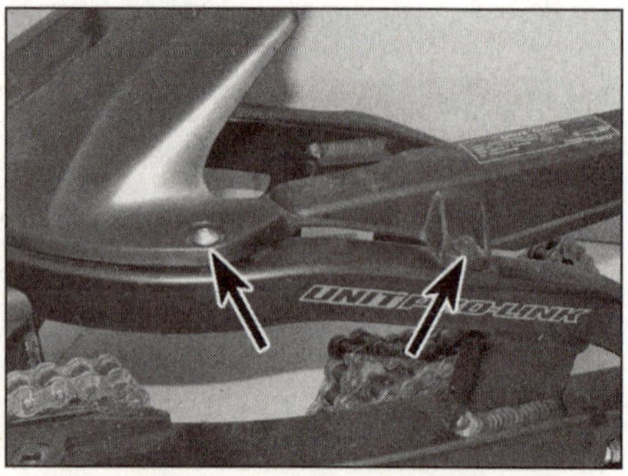

18.2 Unscrew the bolts (arrowed) and remove the guard if required

3 Remove the front sprocket cover (see Section 19).

4 Split the chain at the soft link using the chain splitter tool, following carefully the manufacturer's operating instructions (see also Section 8 of *Tools and Workshop Tips* in the Reference Section). Remove the chain from the bike, noting its routing around the swingarm.

Cleaning

5 Refer to Chapter 1, Section 1, for details of routine cleaning with the chain installed on the sprockets.

6 If the chain is extremely dirty remove it from the motorcycle and soak it in paraffin (kerosene) for approximately five or six minutes, then clean it using a soft brush.

Caution: Don't use gasoline (petrol), solvent or other cleaning fluids which might damage its internal sealing properties. Don't use high-pressure water. Remove the chain, wipe it off, then blow dry it with compressed air immediately. The entire process shouldn't take longer than ten minutes – if it does, the O-rings in the chain rollers could be damaged.

Installation

Warning: NEVER install a drive chain which uses a clip-type master (split) link. Use ONLY the correct service tools to secure the staked-type of master link – if you do not have access to such tools, have the chain replaced by a dealer service department or bike repair shop to be sure of having it securely installed.

7 Fit the drive chain through the swingarm and around the sprockets, leaving the two ends mid-way between the sprockets along the bottom run.

8 Refer to Section 8 of *Tools and Workshop Tips* in the Reference Section. Install the new soft link from the inside with the four O-rings correctly located between the link plate and side plate. Press on the new side plate with its identification marks facing out. If fitting a DID or RK chain, measure the amount that the soft link pins project from the side plate and check they are within the measurements specified at the beginning of the Chapter. Rivet the new link using the tool, following carefully the instructions of both the chain manufacturer and the tool manufacturer. DO NOT reuse old soft link components.

9 After riveting, check the staked pins for any signs of cracking. If there is any evidence of cracking, the soft link, O-rings and side plate must be replaced. Measure the diameter of the riveted ends in two directions and check that it is evenly riveted and within the measurements specified at the beginning of the Chapter. Check that the link pivots freely.

10 Install the sprocket cover (see Section 19).

11 Install the chainguard if removed **(see illustration 18.2)**.

12 On completion, adjust and lubricate the chain following the procedures described in Chapter 1.

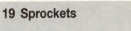

19 Sprockets

Front sprocket cover

1 On RR-4 and RR-5 models remove the lower fairing (see Chapter 7); removal is not necessary on RR-6 and RR-7 models, but is advised to prevent the possibility of damage. Unscrew the gearchange linkage arm pinch bolt and slide the arm off the shaft, noting how the slit in the arm aligns with the punch mark on the shaft **(see illustration)**.

2 Displace the clutch release cylinder (see Chapter 2). There is no need to detach the hydraulic hose. Withdraw the pushrod **(see illustration)**.

3 Unscrew the bolts securing the front sprocket cover and remove the cover, and then the guide plate **(see illustrations)** – if the guide plate sticks to the cover you must separate them as they cannot be removed together. Remove the gasket, and the dowels if they are loose **(see illustration 19.4)**.

4 Clean off all the old gasket. Fit the dowels, then locate a new gasket onto them **(see illustration)**. Fit the guide plate onto the dowels, then fit the cover and tighten its bolts **(see illustrations 19.3c, b and a)**.

5 Slide the clutch pushrod in **(see illustration 19.2)**. Install the clutch release cylinder (see Chapter 2). Slide the gearchange linkage arm onto the shaft, aligning the slit in the

19.1 Unscrew the bolt (arrowed) and slide the arm off the shaft, noting its alignment

19.2 Withdraw the clutch pushrod

19.3a Unscrew the bolts (arrowed) . . .

19.3b . . . and remove the cover . . .

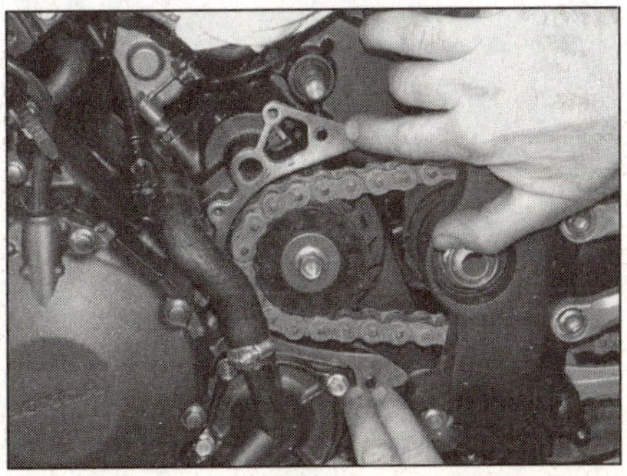

19.3c . . . and the guide plate

19.4 Locate the gasket over the dowels

19.10 Unscrew the bolt and remove the washer

19.12 Draw the sprocket off the shaft and disengage the chain

19.15 Install the bolt with its washer and tighten it to the specified torque

clamp with the punch mark on the shaft, then tighten the pinch bolt **(see illustration 19.1)**.
6 Install the lower fairing (see Chapter 7).

Sprocket check

7 Check the wear pattern on both sprockets (see Chapter 1, Section 1). If the sprocket teeth are worn excessively, replace the chain and both sprockets as a set. Whenever the sprockets are inspected, the drive chain should be inspected also. Always renew the chain and sprockets as a set – worn sprockets can ruin a new drive chain and *vice versa*.
8 Adjust and lubricate the chain following the procedures described in Chapter 1.

Sprocket removal and installation

Front sprocket

9 Remove the front sprocket cover (see Steps 1 to 3).
10 Have an assistant apply the rear brake, then unscrew the sprocket bolt and remove the washer **(see illustration)**.
11 Fully slacken the drive chain as described in Chapter 1, Section 1. If the rear sprocket is being removed as well, remove the rear wheel now to give full chain slack (see Section 15). Otherwise disengage the chain from the rear sprocket if required to provide more slack.
12 Slide the chain and sprocket off the shaft then slip the sprocket out of the chain **(see illustration)**. Clean all old chain grease and dirt from the sprocket area.
13 Engage the new sprocket with the chain, making sure the marked side is facing out, and slide it on the shaft.
14 If the rear wheel was removed, change the sprocket and install the wheel (see Section 15). If the chain was merely disengaged, fit it back onto the rear sprocket. Take up the slack in the chain.
15 Install the sprocket bolt with its washer **(see illustration 19.10)**. Tighten the bolt to the torque setting specified at the beginning of the Chapter, holding the rear brake on to prevent the sprocket turning **(see illustration)**.
16 Fit the sprocket cover (see Steps 4 to 6). Adjust and lubricate the chain following the procedures described in Chapter 1.

Rear sprocket

17 Remove the rear wheel (see Section 15).
18 Unscrew the nuts securing the sprocket to the hub assembly and remove the washers **(see illustration)**. Remove the sprocket, noting which way round it fits. Check the condition of the sprocket nuts – Honda advise that they should be renewed once disturbed.
19 Fit the sprocket onto the hub with the stamped mark facing out. Fit the washers with the chamfered side towards the sprocket, then fit the nuts and tighten them evenly and in a criss-cross sequence to the torque setting specified at the beginning of the Chapter.
20 Install the rear wheel (see Section 15).

19.18 Unscrew the nuts (arrowed), and remove the washers, noting which way round they fit

20.3 Check the rubber dampers as described

20 Rear sprocket coupling/ rubber dampers

1 Remove the rear wheel (see Section 15). Check for play between the sprocket coupling and the wheel hub by turning the sprocket. Any play indicates worn rubber damper segments.
Caution: Do not lay the wheel down on the disc as it could become warped. Lay the wheel on wooden blocks so that the disc is off the ground.
2 Lift the sprocket coupling away from the wheel leaving the rubber dampers in position **(see illustration 16.12)**. Note the spacer inside the coupling – it should be a tight fit. Check the coupling for cracks or any obvious signs of damage. Also check the sprocket nuts for wear or damage.
3 Lift the rubber damper segments from the wheel and check them for cracks, hardening and general deterioration **(see illustration)**. Replace them with a new set if necessary.
4 Check the condition of the hub O-ring – if it is damaged, deformed or deteriorated replace it with a new one and smear it with oil **(see illustration 16.22)**. Otherwise clean it and smear it with oil.
5 Checking and replacement procedures for the sprocket coupling bearings are in Section 16.
6 Installation is the reverse of removal. Make sure the spacer is correctly installed in the coupling.
7 Install the rear wheel (see Section 15).

Chapter 7
Bodywork

Contents

Section number

Degrees of difficulty

Easy, suitable for novice with little experience	**Fairly easy,** suitable for beginner with some experience	**Fairly difficult,** suitable for competent DIY mechanic	**Difficult,** suitable for experienced DIY mechanic	**Very difficult,** suitable for expert DIY or professional

1 General information

This Chapter covers the procedures necessary to remove and install the bodywork. Since many service and repair operations on these motorcycles require the removal of the body panels, the procedures are grouped here and referred to from other Chapters.

In the case of damage to the bodywork, it is usually necessary to remove the broken component and replace it with a new (or used) one. Note that there are however some companies that specialise in 'plastic welding' and there are a number of bodywork repair kits now available for motorcycles.

When attempting to remove any body panel, first study it closely, noting any fasteners and associated fittings, to be sure of returning everything to its correct place on installation. Refer to the beginning of Section 6 for more information on the types of trim clip used and how to release and refit them. In some cases the aid of an assistant will be required when removing panels, to help avoid the risk of damage to paintwork. Once the evident fasteners have been removed, try to withdraw the panel as described but DO NOT FORCE IT – if it will not release, check that all fasteners have been removed and try again.

When installing a body panel, first study it closely, noting any fasteners and associated fittings removed with it, to be sure of returning everything to its correct place. Check that all fasteners are in good condition, including the trim clips and damping/rubber mounts; replace any faulty fasteners with new ones before the panel is reassembled. Check also that all mounting brackets are straight and repair them or replace them with new ones if necessary before attempting to install the panel.

Tighten the fasteners securely, but be careful not to overtighten any of them or the panel may break (not always immediately) due to the uneven stress.

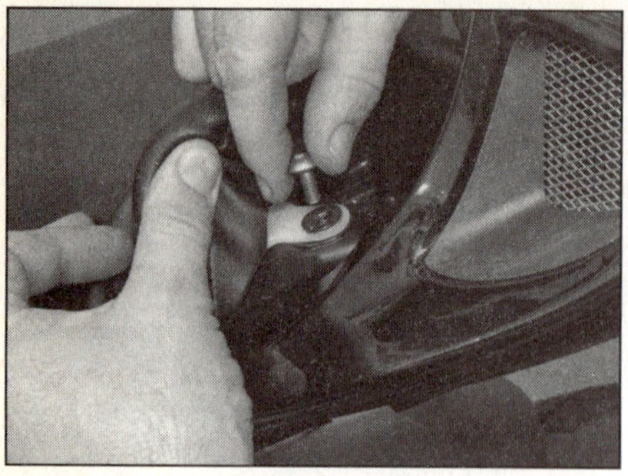

2.1a Unscrew the bolt on each side . . .

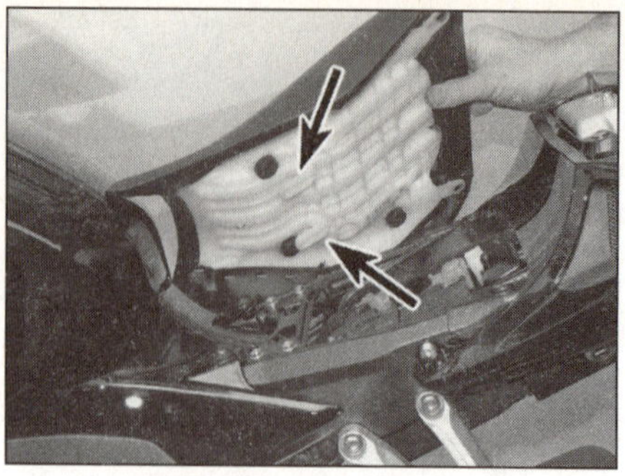

2.1b . . . then remove the seat, noting how its tabs (arrowed) locate

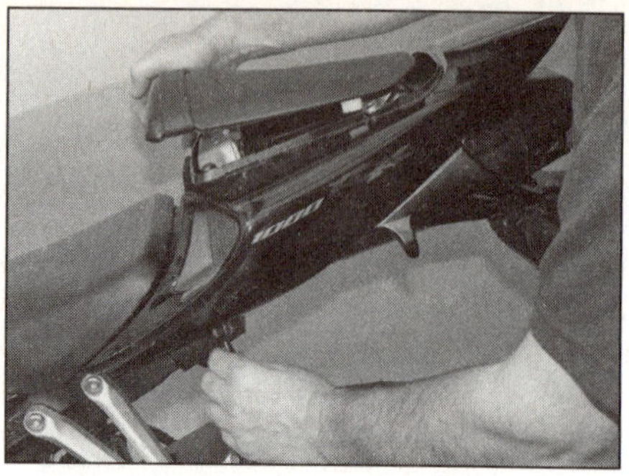

2.2a Unlock the seat and lift it up . . .

2 Seats

Removal

Rider's seat

1 Lift the seat padding on each rear corner, then unscrew the bolts and remove the collars **(see illustration)**. Draw the seat back and up to remove it, noting how it locates **(see illustration)**.

Passenger seat

2 Insert the ignition key into the seat lock (located under the left-hand side of the seat cowling and turn it clockwise to unlock the seat **(see illustration)**. Lift the front of the seat and draw it forward to disengage the tabs **(see illustration)**.

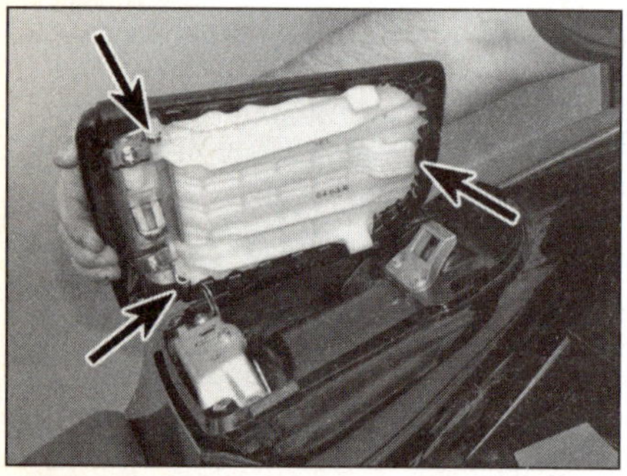

2.2b . . . noting how the hooks and tab (arrowed) locate

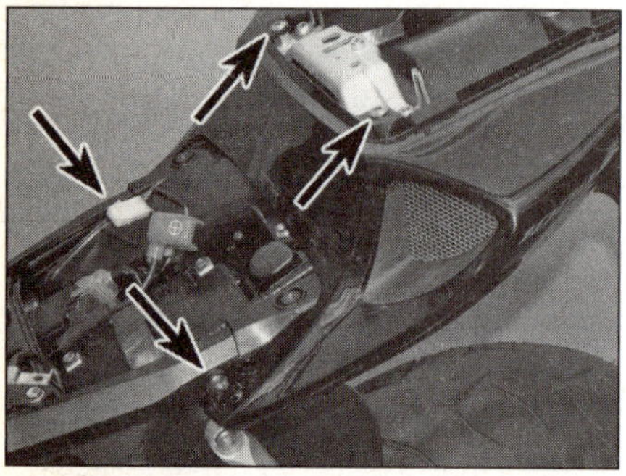

3.3 Undo the screws (arrowed) . . .

Installation

3 Installation is the reverse of removal. Make sure the tabs on the front of the rider's seat locate correctly under the bracket **(see illustration 2.1b)**. Fit the collars for the bolts. Make sure the two hooks at the front of the passenger seat and single tab at the back locate correctly, and push down on the front of the passenger seat to engage the latch **(see illustration 2.2b)**.

3 Seat cowling

1 Remove both seats (see Section 2).

2 Disconnect the tail light wiring connector **(see illustration)** – if you can't access it disconnect it after displacing the cowling.

3 Undo the four screws securing the cowling **(see illustration)**.

4 Carefully remove the cowling by pulling the sides out then drawing the cowling back and up off the bike, noting the two pegs at the back that locate in the grommets - do not worry about the amount the cowling has to flex to be removed as it is designed to do so, but do not flex it more than necessary **(see illustration)**.

5 Remove the tail light if required (see Chapter 8).

6 Installation is the reverse of removal. Make sure the pegs locate in the grommets at the back and the underside of the cowling is correctly located before tightening the screws.

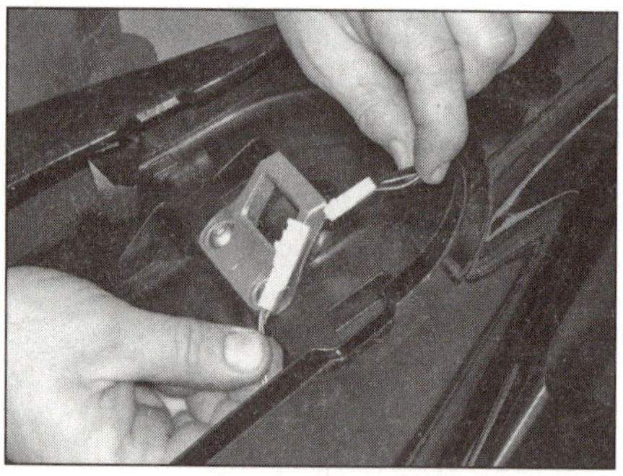

3.2 Disconnect the wiring connector

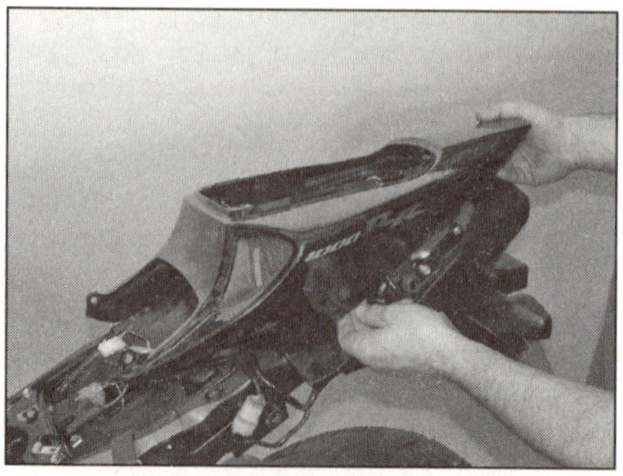

3.4 . . . and remove the cowling as described

4 Mirrors

1 Unscrew the two bolts and remove the mirror **(see illustration)**.

2 Installation is the reverse of removal.

5 Fuel tank cover

1 Remove the rider's seat (see Section 2).

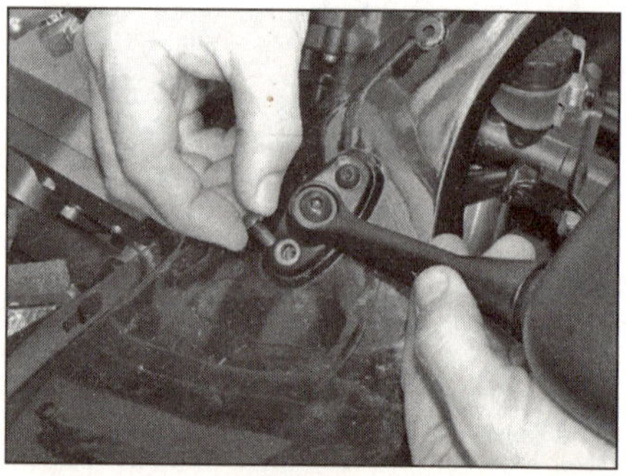

4.1 Unscrew the bolts and remove the mirror

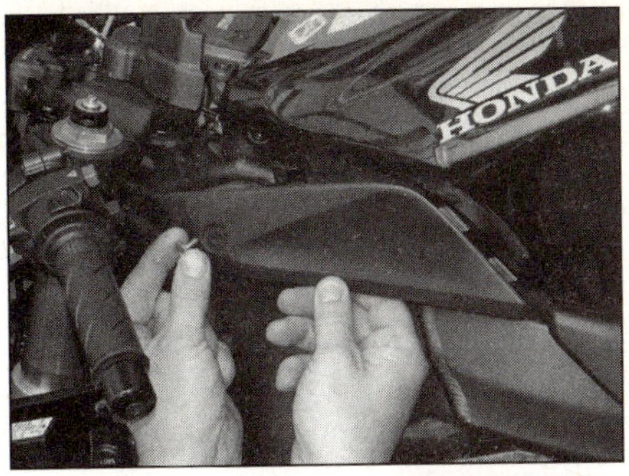

5.2 Undo the two screws and remove the front trim panel on each side

5.3a Undo the screw (arrowed) on each side at the front . . .

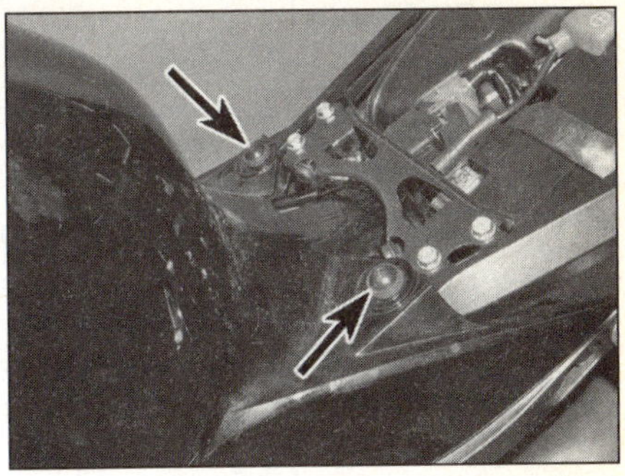

5.3b . . . and the two screws (arrowed) at the back . . .

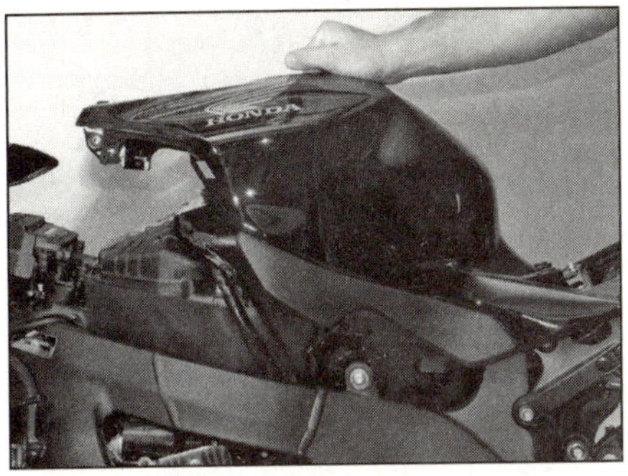

5.3c . . . and remove the tank cover

5.5 Lubricate the rubber seal rim so the cover fits easily over it

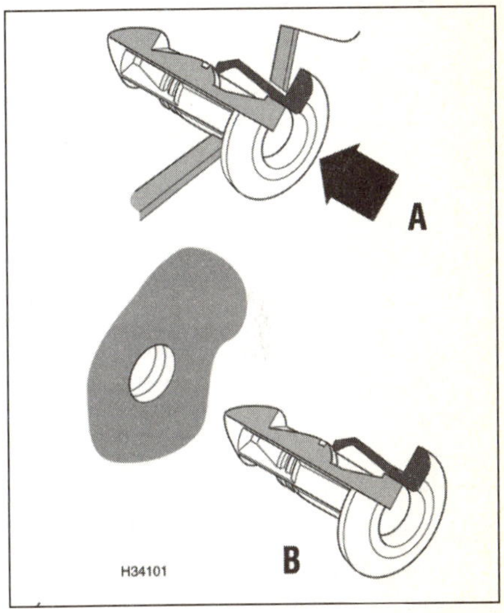

6.2a To remove the trim clip, push its centre pin (A) inwards and withdraw the clip from the panel (B)

2 Undo the screw securing the front trim panel on each side, then release the tabs from the fuel tank cover **(see illustration)**.

3 Undo the screw on each side at the front and the two at the back and remove the cover **(see illustrations)**.

4 If required undo the screws securing each rear trim panel, then release their tabs and remove them from the cover.

5 Installation is the reverse of removal. Make sure the trim panel tabs locate correctly. Spray or smear a suitable lubricant over the fuel cap rubber rim to ease installation, and make sure it doesn't deform when fitting the cover **(see illustration)**.

6 Fairing panels

Trim clips

1 Three types of plastic trim clip are used, so carefully note which fits where when removing the fairing panels.

2 The first type has a centre pin which you push into the body of the clip to allow the clip to be drawn out of the panel **(see illustration)**. To install the clip, first expand the pawls of the clip body and push the centre pin back out **(see illustration)**. Now fit the clip body into its hole, then push the centre pin in so that it is flush with the clip head. The clip should now be locked in place.

3 The second type of trim clip has a Phillips screw head. To release them unscrew the centre of the clip, then pull the body of the clip out of the panel **(see illustration)**. When installing them, unscrew the centre of the clip and insert it in the

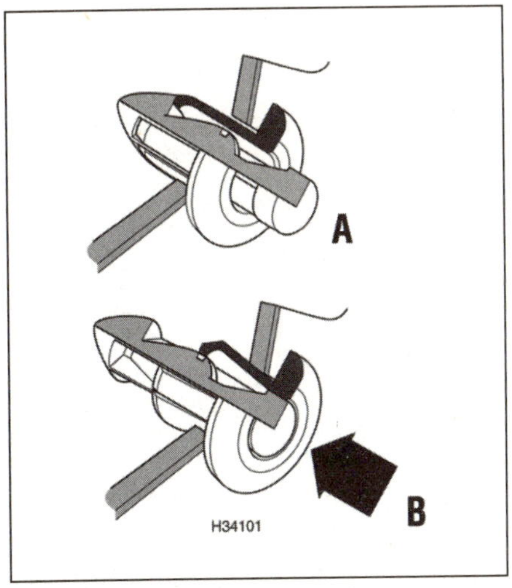

6.2b To install the trim clip, depress the pawls and push the centre pin outwards so that the clip can be inserted in the panel (A), then press the centre pin in level with the head of the clip to lock it in place (B)

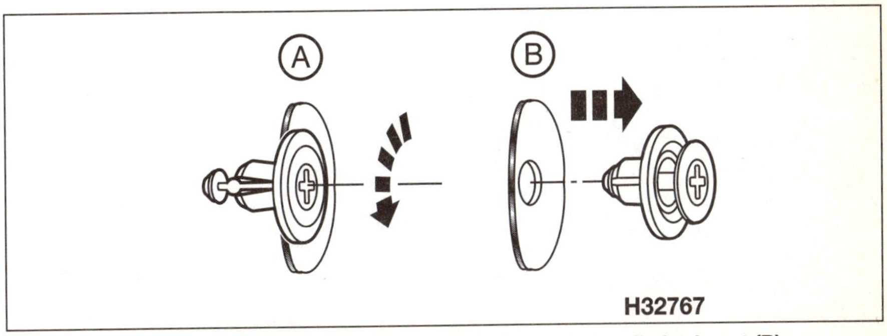

6.3a Unscrew the centre of the clip (A) then pull the clip body out (B)

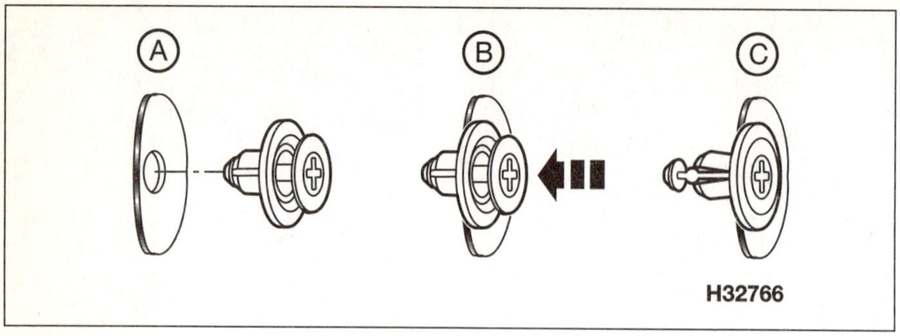

6.3b Fit the clip body into its hole (A), then push the centre into the body (B) so that its head is flush (C)

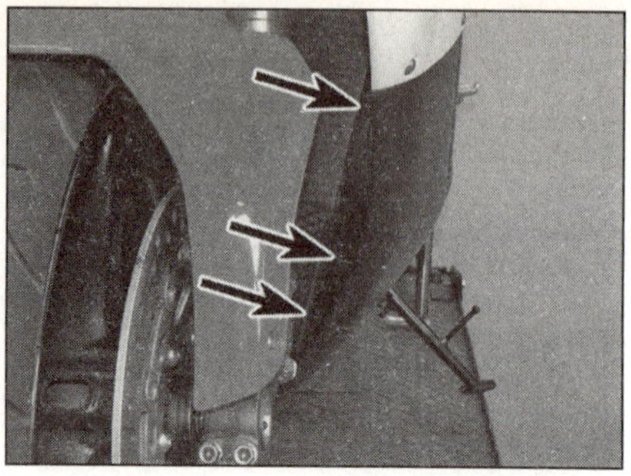

6.6 Release the trim clips (arrowed)

panel then push the centre fully into the body **(see illustration)**. As they are made of plastic, the threads easily become worn in which case the centres may not unscrew. If this happens, lever the centre out of the body using a small screwdriver and replace the trim clip with a new one.

4 The third has a protruding centre pin which you pull out of the body of the clip to allow the clip to be drawn out of the panel. To install the clip, fit the clip body into its hole, then push the centre pin in. The clip should now be locked in place.

Lower fairing

RR-4 and RR-5 models

Note: *Remove each side of the lower fairing individually. If access is only required to one side of the bike, the other panel can be left in place.*

5 Release the trim clips and undo the screw securing the panels on the underside.

6 Release the trim clips securing the lower fairing to the inner panels at the front **(see illustration)**.

7 Undo the three screws securing the lower fairing panel to the fairing side panel **(see illustration)**. Undo the two screws securing the lower fairing panel to the frame, then release the panel and remove it.

8 If required release the lower inner panel from the upper inner panel, noting how they engage.

9 Installation is the reverse of removal.

RR-6 and RR-7 models

Note: *Remove the lower fairing in one piece.*

10 Release the two front trim clips securing the lower fairing on the underside **(see illustration)**.

11 Undo the four screws on each side, then release the panel and carefully draw it out from under the bike **(see illustrations)**.

12 Installation is the reverse of removal.

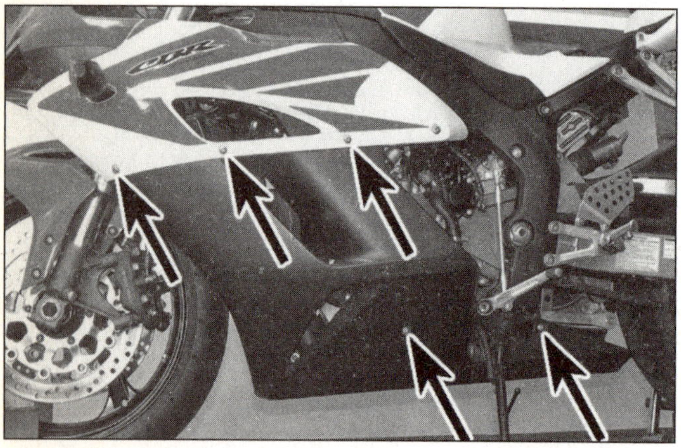

6.7 Undo the screws (arrowed) and remove the panel

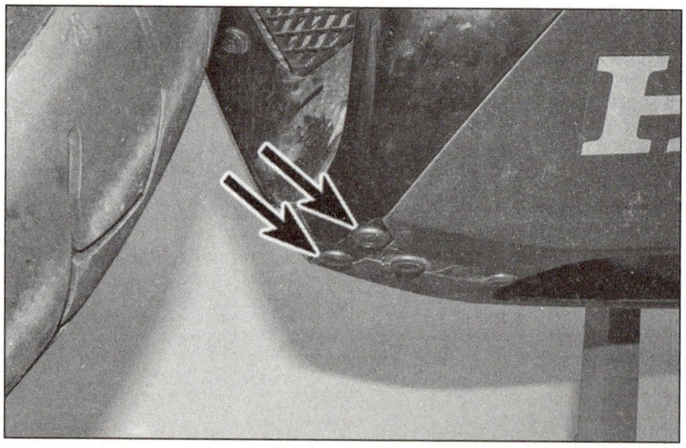

6.10 Release the trim clips (arrowed)

6.11a Undo the screws (arrowed) . . .

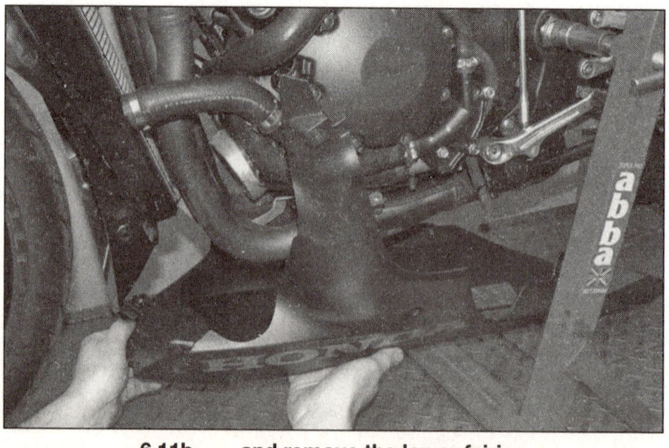

6.11b . . . and remove the lower fairing

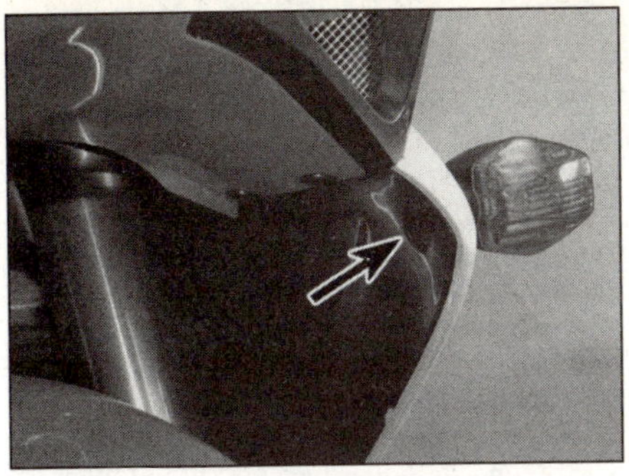

6.13 Release the trim clip (arrowed)

6.14 Fairing side panel screws (arrowed)

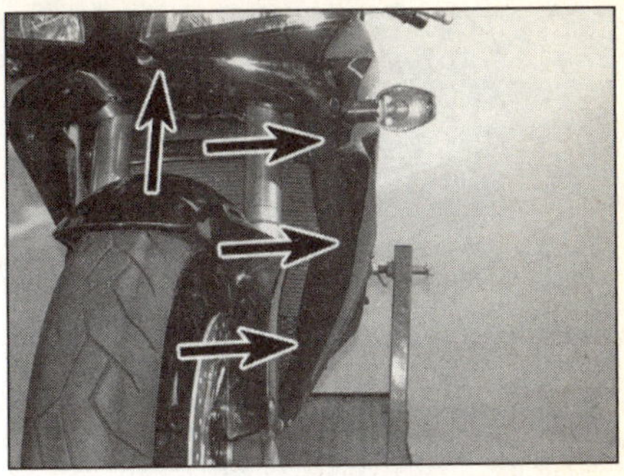

6.17a Undo the trim clips (arrowed) on the inner front side . . . .

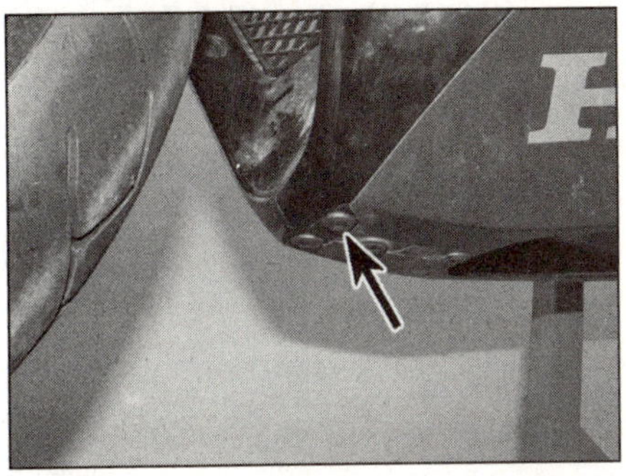

6.17b . . . and the trim clip (arrowed) on the underside – left-hand panel removal shown

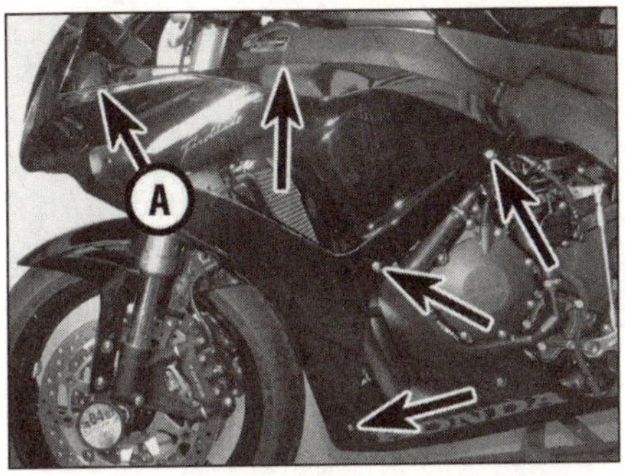

6.18 Trim clip (A). Side panel screws (arrowed)

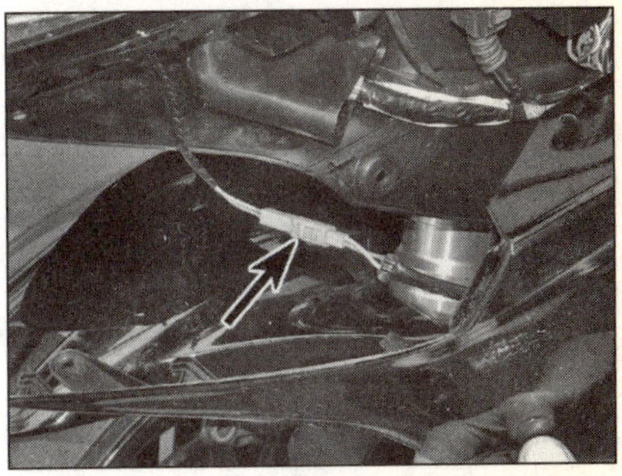

6.19 Disconnect the wiring connector (arrowed)

Fairing side panels

RR-4 and RR-5 models

13 Release the trim clip securing the panel to the upper inner panel **(see illustration)**.

14 Undo the two screws securing the fairing side panel to the main fairing, the three screws securing the side panel to the lower fairing, and the two screws securing the panel to the frame **(see illustration)**.

15 Carefully release the panel from the lower fairing and the main fairing - draw the panel back to release the slots from the hooks on the fairing. Disconnect the turn signal wiring connector when accessible and remove the panel.

16 Installation is the reverse of removal.

RR-6 and RR-7 models

17 Release the four trim clips on the inner front side and the one on the underside securing the panel to the inner panels **(see illustrations)**. Release the trim clip on the top **(see illustration 6.18)**.

18 Undo the two screws securing the fairing side panel to the lower fairing and the two screws securing the panel to the frame **(see illustration)**.

19 Carefully release the panel from the lower fairing and the main fairing - draw the panel back to release the slots from the hooks on the fairing. Disconnect the turn signal wiring connector when accessible and remove the panel **(see illustration)**.

20 If required release the lower inner panel from the upper inner panel, noting how they engage **(see illustration)**.

21 Installation is the reverse of removal.

Main fairing

22 Remove the fairing side panels (see above).

23 Remove the mirrors (see Section 4).

24 Remove the windshield (see Section 8).

25 Disconnect the instrument cluster and front wiring loom connectors **(see illustrations)**.

26 Release the trim clips on the underside to free the inner panels **(see illustrations)**. Remove the right-hand inner panel if required, noting how it fits - the left-hand panel can stay as it supports some electrical components

27 Carefully lift the fairing off the mirror mounts

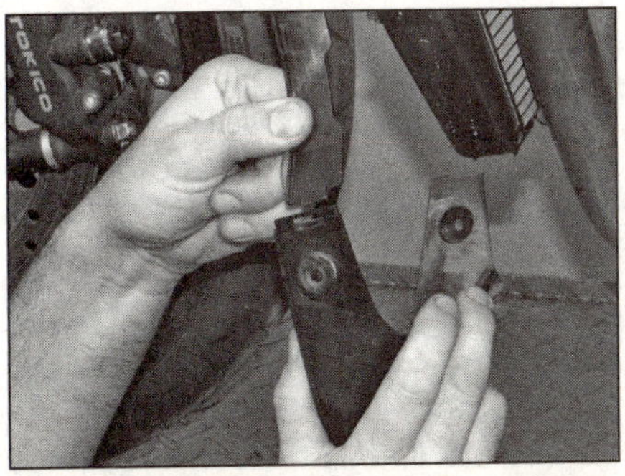

6.20 Release and remove the lower inner panel if required

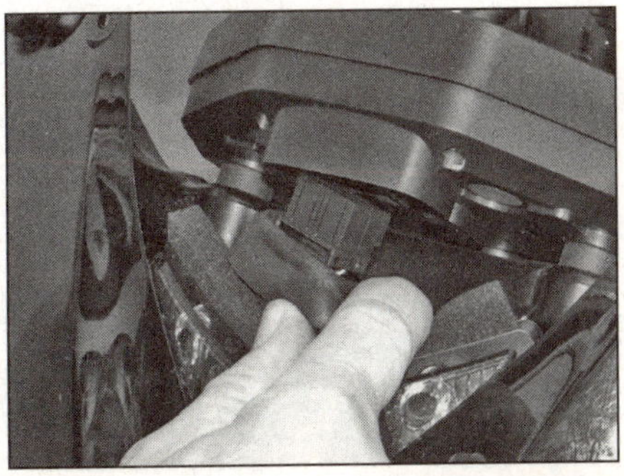

6.25a Disconnect the instrument wiring connector . . .

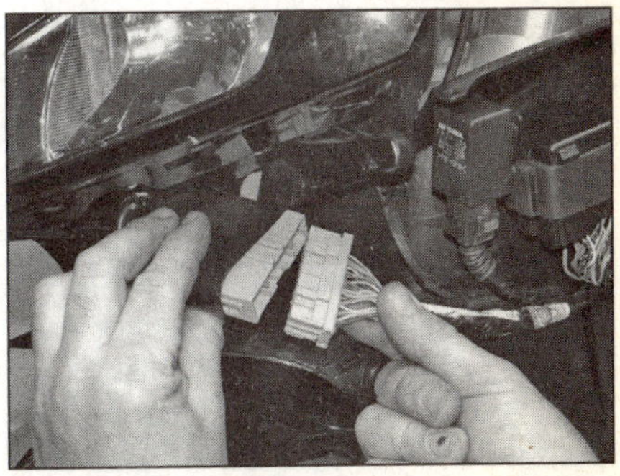

6.25b . . . and the front loom wiring connector

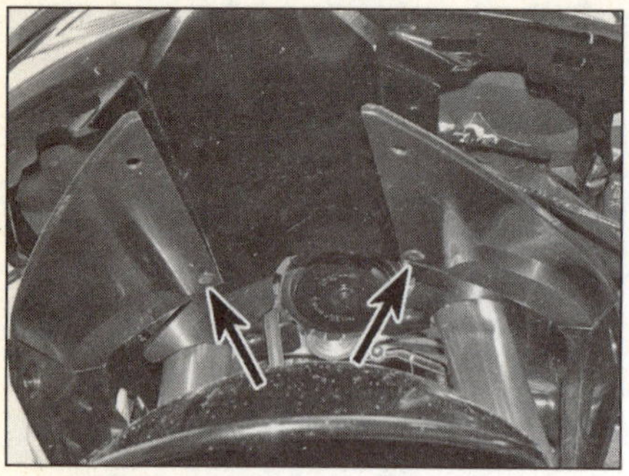

6.26a Release the trim clips (arrowed) . . .

6.27a Draw the main fairing forwards . . .

and draw it forwards, noting how the pegs locate in the grommets in the stay **(see illustrations)**.

28 If required remove the headlight assembly (see Chapter 8).

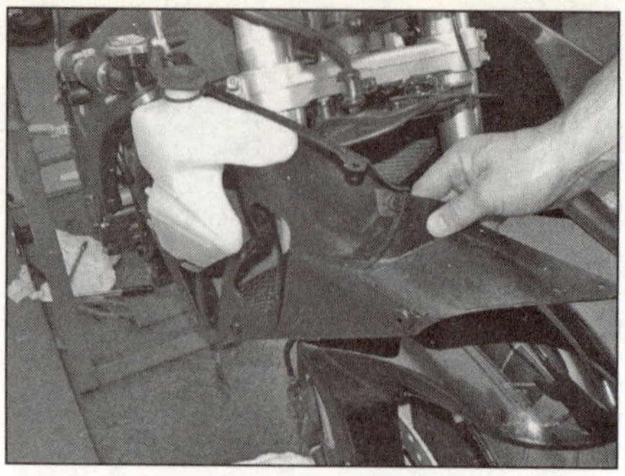

6.26b . . . and if required remove the right-hand inner panel

6.27b . . . noting how the pegs locate

29 Installation is the reverse of removal. Make sure the fairing pegs locate correctly in the grommets on the fairing stay **(see illustration 6.27b)**.

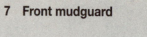

7 Front mudguard

1 Release the brake hose from each side of the mudguard - on the right-hand side a bolt secures the hose splitter **(see illustration)**, on the left-hand side a nut secures the hose guide on a stud.

2 Unscrew the bolts securing each side of the mudguard to each fork **(see illustration)**.

3 Draw the mudguard up and then forwards, squeezing the sides in to ensure the lug on the right-hand side and the stud on the left do not scratch the fork, and remove it **(see illustrations)**.

4 Installation is the reverse of removal.

8 Windshield

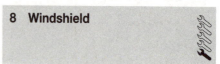

1 Slacken the mirror bolts.

2 Undo the screws securing the windshield, noting the washers **(see illustration)**. Carefully remove the windshield, noting how it engages with the main fairing **(see illustration)**.

3 Installation is the reverse of removal. Make sure the rubber wellnuts are in good condition and replace them with new ones if necessary

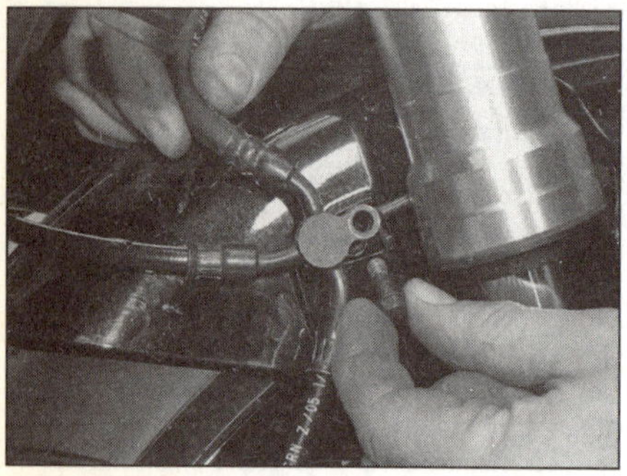

7.1 Release the brake hose from each side

7.2 Unscrew the bolts (arrowed) on each side . . .

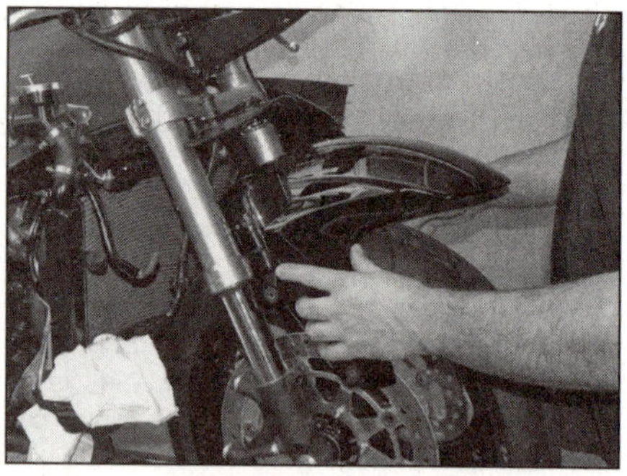

7.3a . . . and remove the mudguard . . .

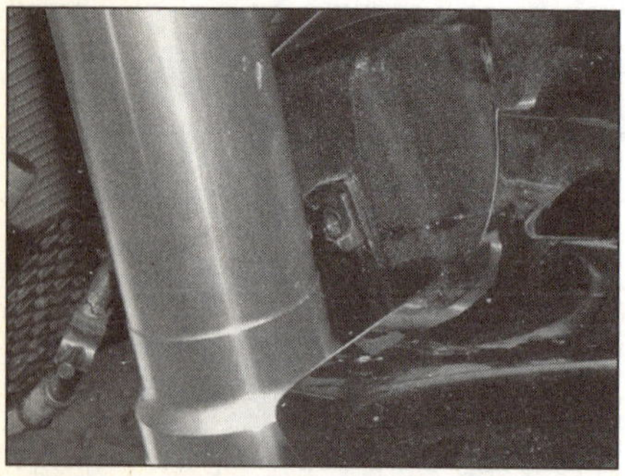

7.3b . . . squeezing the sides in to avoid scratching the fork

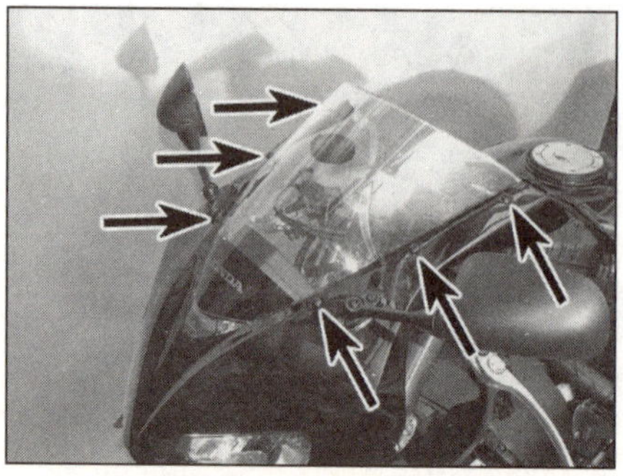

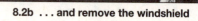

8.2a Undo the screws (arrowed) . . .

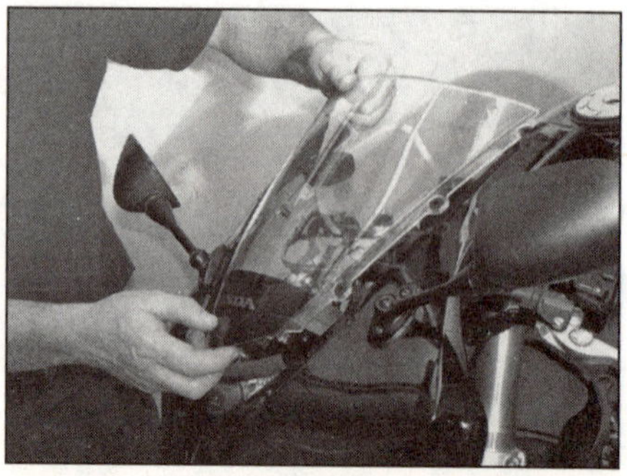

8.2b . . . and remove the windshield

Chapter 8
Electrical system

Contents

Degrees of difficulty

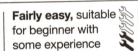

Easy, suitable for novice with little experience	**Fairly easy,** suitable for beginner with some experience	**Fairly difficult,** suitable for competent DIY mechanic	**Difficult,** suitable for experienced DIY mechanic	**Very difficult,** suitable for expert DIY or professional

Specifications

Battery

Capacity	12 V, 8.6 Ah
Voltage	
Fully-charged	13.0 to 13.2 V
Uncharged	below 12.4 V
Charging rate	
Normal	0.9 A for 5 to 10 hrs
Quick	4.5 A for 1 hr
Current leakage	2 mA (max)

Alternator

Stator coil resistance	0.1 to 1.0 ohms
Output	
RR-4 and RR-5 models	344 W @ 5000 rpm
RR-6 and RR-7 models	350 W @ 5000 rpm
Regulated voltage output	15.5V @ 5000 rpm

Starter motor

Brush length	
Standard	12.0 to 13.0 mm
Service limit (min)	6.5 mm

Instruments

Tachometer peak voltage (see Text)	10.5 V min.

Fuses

Main	30 A
PGM-FI (fuel injection system)	20 A
Others	10 A x 4, 20 A x 2

Bulbs

Headlights	55 W x 2 halogen H7
Sidelight	5 W
Brake/tail light	LED
Licence plate light	5 W
Turn signal lights	
European spec	21 W x 4
US and Canada spec	
Front	23/8 W x 2
Rear	23 W x 2
Instrument lights	LED
Turn signal indicator light	LED
HI beam indicator light	LED
Neutral indicator light	LED
PGM-FI malfunction indicator light	LED
Immobiliser indicator light	LED

Torque settings

Alternator rotor bolt	
RR-4 and RR-5 models	103 Nm
RR-6 and RR-7 models	113 Nm
Alternator stator and wiring clamp bolts	12 Nm
Fork clamp bolts (top yoke)	23 Nm
Ignition switch bolts	26 Nm
Neutral switch	12 Nm
Oil pressure switch	12 Nm
Sidestand switch bolt	10 Nm
Steering stem nut	103 Nm

1 General information

All models have a 12 volt electrical system charged by a three-phase alternator with a separate regulator/rectifier.

The regulator maintains the charging system output within the specified range to prevent overcharging, and the rectifier converts the ac (alternating current) output of the alternator to dc (direct current) to power the lights and other components and to charge the battery. The alternator rotor is mounted on the left-hand end of the crankshaft.

The starter motor is mounted on the top of the crankcase behind the cylinders. The starting system includes the motor, the battery, the relay and the various wires and switches. Some of the switches are part of a starter interlock system which prevents the engine from being started if the sidestand is down and the engine is in gear. The engine can be started with the sidestand up when it is in gear as long as the clutch lever is pulled in. The system will also cut the engine should the sidestand extend while the engine is running and in gear – see Chapter 1 for further information and checks on the system.

Note: *Keep in mind that electrical parts, once purchased, often cannot be returned. To avoid unnecessary expense, make very sure the faulty component has been positively identified before buying a replacement part.*

2 Electrical system fault finding

***Warning:** To prevent the risk of short circuits, the ignition (main) switch must always be OFF and the battery negative (–) terminal should be disconnected before any of the bike's other electrical components are disturbed. Don't forget to reconnect the terminal securely once work is finished or if battery power is needed for circuit testing.*

1 A typical electrical circuit consists of an electrical component, the switches, relays, etc, related to that component and the wiring and connectors that link the component to the battery and the frame. To aid in locating a problem in any electrical circuit, refer to the wiring diagrams at the end of this Chapter.

2.2a Common earth point (arrowed) – RR-4 and RR-5 models

2 Before tackling any troublesome electrical circuit, first study the wiring diagram thoroughly to get a complete picture of what makes up that individual circuit. Trouble spots, for instance, can often be narrowed down by noting if other components related to that circuit are operating properly or not. If several components or circuits fail at one time, chances are the fault lies either in the fuse or in the common earth (ground) connection, as several circuits are often routed through the same fuse and earth (ground) connections. Earthing points are recognisable by a wire or wires routing into a connector that is either screwed or bolted directly to the frame or is secured to the engine by one of its bolts **(see illustrations)**. Make sure the terminal is tight and corrosion-free.

3 Electrical problems often stem from simple causes, such as loose or corroded connections or a blown fuse. Prior to any electrical fault

2.2b Common earth point (arrowed) – RR-6 and RR-7 models

3.2 Disconnect the negative lead first, then disconnect the positive lead (arrowed)

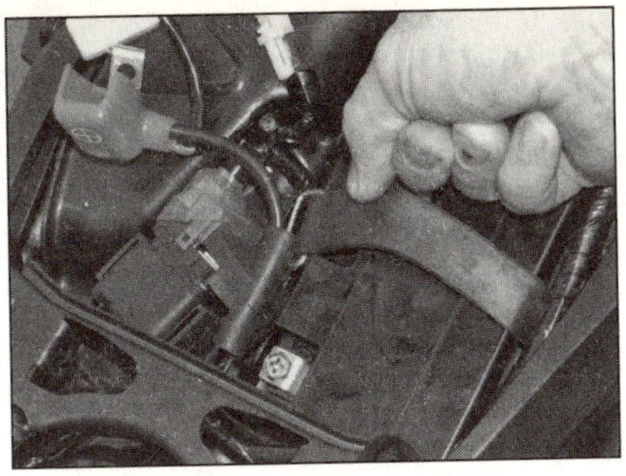

3.3a Release the battery strap . . .

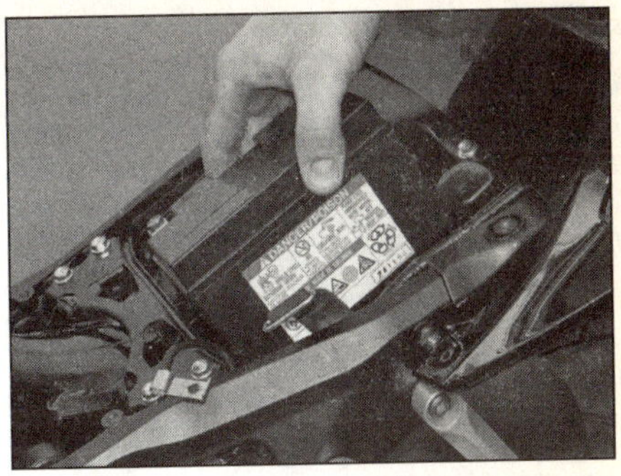

3.3b . . . and remove the battery

finding, always visually check the condition of the fuse, wires and connections in the problem circuit. Intermittent failures can be especially frustrating, since you can't always duplicate the failure when it's convenient to test. In such situations, a good practice is to clean all connections in the affected circuit, whether or not they appear to be good. All of the connections and wires should also be wiggled to check for looseness which can cause intermittent failure.

4 If testing instruments are going to be used, use the wiring diagram to plan where you will make the necessary connections in order to accurately pinpoint the trouble spot.

5 The basic tools needed for electrical fault finding include a battery and bulb test circuit or a continuity tester, a test light, and a jumper wire. A multimeter capable of reading volts, ohms and amps is a very useful alternative and performs the functions of all of the above, and is necessary for performing more extensive tests and checks where specific voltage, current or resistance values are needed.

> **HAYNES HiNT** ***Refer to Fault Finding Equipment in the Reference section for details of how to use electrical test equipment.***

3 Battery removal and installation

Caution: Be extremely careful when handling or working around the battery. The electrolyte is very caustic and an explosive gas (hydrogen) is given off when the battery is charging.

Removal and installation

1 Make sure the ignition is switched OFF. Remove the rider's seat (see Chapter 7).

2 Unscrew the negative (–) terminal bolt first and disconnect the lead from the battery **(see illustration)**. Lift up the red insulating cover to access the positive (+) terminal, then unscrew the bolt and disconnect the lead.

3 Release the battery strap **(see illustration)**. Lift the battery from the bike **(see illustration)**.

4 On installation, clean the battery terminals and lead ends with a wire brush, emery paper or steel wool. Reconnect the leads, connecting the positive (+) terminal first.

> **HAYNES HiNT** ***Battery corrosion can be kept to a minimum by applying a layer of battery terminal grease or petroleum jelly (Vaseline) to the terminals after the leads have been connected. DO NOT use a mineral based grease.***

5 Fit the battery strap. Install the seat (see Chapter 7).

Inspection and maintenance

6 The battery is of the maintenance free (sealed) type, therefore requiring no regular maintenance. However, the following checks should still be performed.

7 Check the battery terminals and leads are tight and free of corrosion. If corrosion is evident, clean the terminals as described in Step 4, then protect them from further corrosion (see ***Haynes Hint***).

8 Keep the battery case clean to prevent current leakage, which can discharge the battery over a period of time (especially when it sits unused). Wash the outside of the case with a solution of baking soda and water. Rinse the battery thoroughly, then dry it.

9 Look for cracks in the case and replace the battery with a new one if any are found. If acid has been spilled on the frame or battery box, neutralise it with a baking soda and water solution, dry it thoroughly, then touch up any damaged paint.

10 If the motorcycle sits unused for long periods of time, disconnect the cables from the battery terminals, negative (–) terminal first. Refer to Section 4 and charge the battery once every month to six weeks.

11 Check the condition of the battery by measuring the voltage present at the battery terminals. Connect the voltmeter positive (+) probe to the battery positive (+) terminal, and the negative (–) probe to the battery negative (–) terminal. When fully-charged there should be 13.0 to 13.2 volts present. If the voltage falls below 12.4 volts remove the battery (see above), and recharge it as described below in Section 4.

4 Battery charging

Caution: Be extremely careful when handling or working around the battery. The electrolyte is very caustic and an explosive gas (hydrogen) is given off when the battery is charging.

1 Remove the battery (see Section 3). Connect the charger to the battery, making sure that the positive (+) lead on the charger is connected to the positive (+) terminal on the battery, and the negative (–) lead is connected to the negative (–) terminal.

2 Honda recommend that the battery is charged at the normal rate specified at the beginning of the Chapter. A higher 'quick charge' rate is also specified, but note that exceed this could cause the battery to overheat, buckling the plates and rendering it useless. Few owners will have access to an expensive current controlled charger, so if a normal domestic charger is used check that after a possible initial peak, the charge rate falls to a safe level **(see illustration)**. If the battery becomes hot during charging **stop**. Further charging will cause damage.

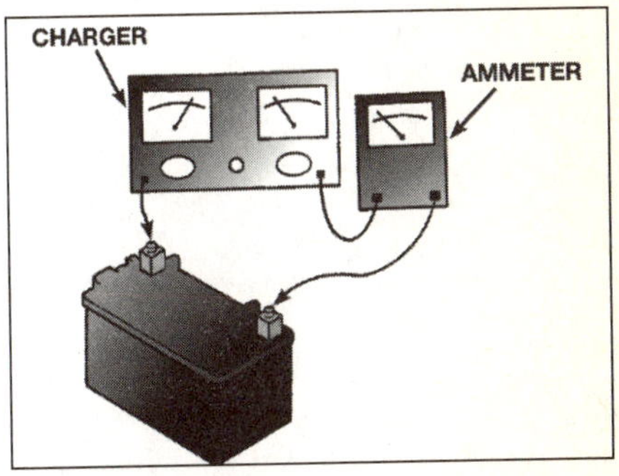

4.2 If the charger doesn't have an ammeter built in, connect one in series as shown. DO NOT connect the ammeter between the battery terminals or it will be ruined

Note: *In emergencies the battery can be charged at the quick rate specified. However, this is not recommended and the normal charging rate is by far the safer method of charging the battery.*

3 If the recharged battery discharges rapidly if left disconnected it is likely that an internal short caused by physical damage or sulphation has occurred. A new battery will be required. A sound item will tend to lose its charge at about 1% per day.

4 Install the battery (see Section 3).

5 If the motorcycle sits unused for long periods of time, charge the battery once every month to six weeks and leave it disconnected.

5 Fuses

1 The electrical system is protected by fuses of different ratings. All except the main fuse and the PGM-FI (fuel injection system) fuse, are housed in the fusebox, which is located behind the fairing left-hand side panel **(see illustrations)** – remove the panel to access it (see Chapter 7). The main fuse is integral with the starter relay **(see illustration 26.2a or b)** – remove the rider's seat to access it (see Chapter 7). The PGM-FI fuel injection system fuse is located in its own housing near the starter relay **(see illustration)**.

2 To access the fusebox fuses unclip the fusebox lid, which on RR-4 and RR-5 models is under the rubber cover **(see illustration)**. To access the main fuse, disconnect the starter relay wiring connector **(see illustration)**. To access the PGM-FI fuse unclip the fuseholder cap **(see illustration 5.1c)**.

3 The fuses can be removed and checked visually. If you can't pull the fuse out with your fingertips, use a pair of suitable pliers. A blown fuse is easily identified by a break in the element **(see illustration)**. Each fuse is clearly marked with its rating and must only be replaced by a fuse of the correct rating. A spare fuse of each rating except the main fuse is housed in the fusebox, and a spare main fuse is housed in the starter relay holder. If a spare fuse is used, always replace it with a new one so that a spare of each rating is carried on the bike at all times.

Warning: Never put in a fuse of a higher rating or bridge the terminals with any other substitute, however temporary it may be. Serious damage may be done to the circuit, or a fire may start.

4 If the new fuse blows immediately check the wiring circuit very carefully for evidence of a short-circuit. Look for bare wires and chafed, melted or burned insulation.

5 Occasionally a fuse will blow or cause an open-circuit for no obvious reason. Corrosion of the fuse ends and fusebox terminals may occur and cause poor fuse contact. If this happens, remove the corrosion with a wire brush or emery paper, then spray the fuse end and terminals with electrical contact cleaner.

6 Lighting system check

1 The battery provides power for operation of the lights. If a light fails first check the bulb (see relevant Section), and the bulb terminals in the holder. If none of the lights work, always check battery voltage before proceeding. Low battery voltage indicates either a faulty battery or a defective charging system. Refer to Section 3 for battery checks and Section 29 for charging system tests. Also, check the condition of the fuses – if there is more than one problem at the same time, it is likely to be a fault relating to a multi-function component, such as one of the fuses governing more than one circuit, or the ignition switch. When checking for a blown filament in a bulb, it is advisable to back up a visual check with a continuity test of the filament as it is not always apparent that a bulb has blown. When testing for continuity, remember that on single terminal bulbs it is the metal body of the bulb that is the earth (ground).

Headlight

2 All models have two single filament bulbs – the left-hand bulb works on LO beam and both bulbs work on HI beam. If either or both headlight beams fail to work, first check the fuse (see Section 5), and then the bulb(s) (see Section 7). If they are good, use jumper wires

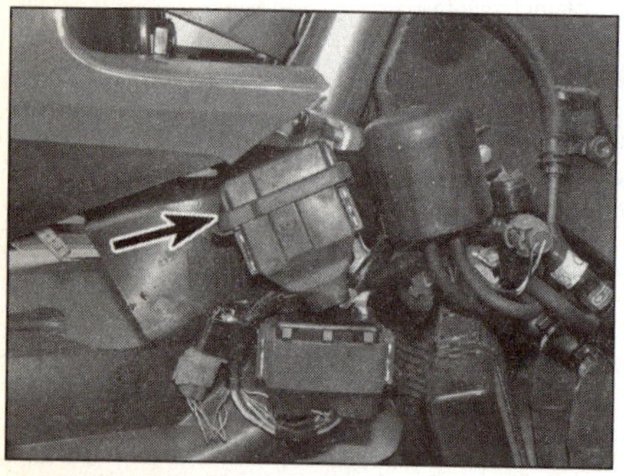

5.1a Fusebox (arrowed) – RR-4 and RR-5 models

5.1b Fusebox (arrowed) – RR-6 and RR-7 models

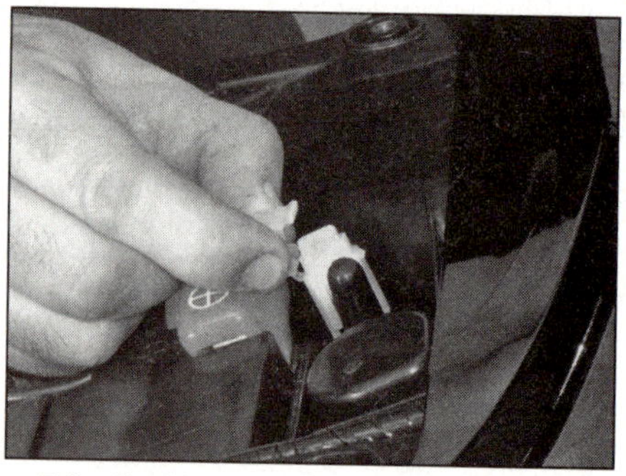

5.1c Fuel injection system fuse holder

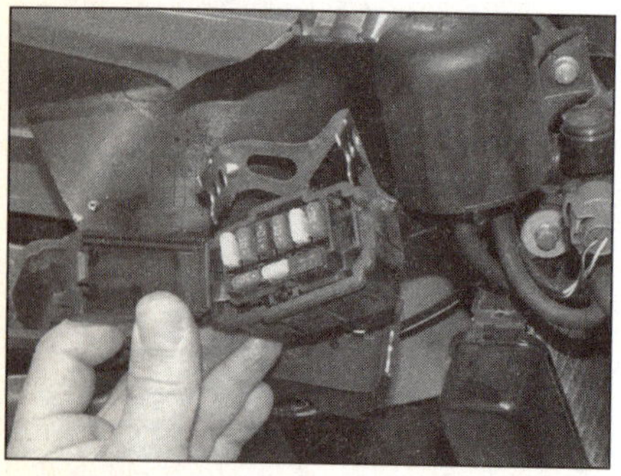

5.2a Unclip the lid to access the fuses

5.2b The main fuse (arrowed) is under the starter relay wiring connector

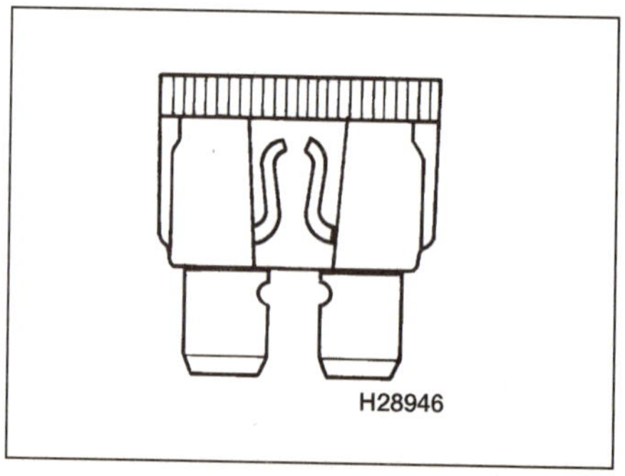

5.3 A blown fuse can be identified by a break in its element

to connect the bulb in question directly to the battery terminals. If the light comes on, the problem lies in the wiring or connectors, the HI beam relay or the dimmer switch. Refer to Section 20 for the switch testing procedures, and also to the wiring diagrams at the end of this Chapter.

3 If the HI beam does not work and the relay is suspected of being faulty, it can be tested as follows. Remove the left-hand fairing side panel (see Chapter 7). The relay is in the relay box **(see illustrations)**. Displace the relay box from its mount, then release the blue connector clips and draw the blue connector out of the box **(see illustration)**. Pull the relay off its connector and move it to the bench for testing. Set a multimeter to the ohms x 1 scale and connect it across the relay's black/red and blue wire terminals. There should be no continuity (infinite resistance). Using a fully-charged 12 volt battery and two insulated jumper wires, connect the positive (+) terminal of the battery to the white wire terminal on the relay, and the negative (–) terminal to the green wire terminal. At this point the relay should be heard to click and the meter read 0 ohms (continuity). If this is the case the relay is good. If the relay does not click when battery voltage is applied and indicates no continuity (infinite resistance) across its terminals, it is faulty and must be replaced with a new one.

4 If the relay is good, check for battery voltage at the black/red wire terminal on the relay wiring connector with the ignition ON. If there is no voltage, check the wiring between the relay wiring connector and the ignition switch, via the fusebox, and check the dimmer switch (see Section 20) and the ignition switch (see Section 19). If voltage is present, check that there is continuity to the headlight wiring connector in the blue (becoming black/blue) wire, and continuity to earth (ground) in the black wire from the headlight connector. Also check for battery voltage at the white wire terminal on the relay wiring connector with the ignition ON, and the dimmer switch set to HI. If voltage is present, check for continuity to earth (ground) in the green wire from the relay wiring connector. Repair or renew the wiring or connectors as necessary.

5 If the LO beam does not work, check for battery voltage at the black/white wire terminal on the headlight wiring connector with the ignition ON **(see illustration 7.1a)**. If voltage is present, check for continuity to earth (ground) in the black wire from the wiring connector. Repair or renew the wiring or connectors as necessary.

Tail light

6 If the tail light fails to work, first check the fuse (see Section 5). If the fuse is good, remove the passenger seat (see Chapter 7), then disconnect the tail light wiring connector and check for battery voltage at the brown/white wire terminal on the loom side of the connector with the ignition switch ON **(see illustration)**. If voltage is present, check for continuity to earth (ground) in the green wire from the wiring connector. If no voltage is indicated, check the wiring and connectors between the tail light and the ignition switch, via the fusebox, then check the ignition switch itself (see Section 19). Refer to the wiring diagrams at the end of this Chapter.

7 If the power, wiring and connectors are good, or if only one or some of the tail light LEDs have failed leaving others working, then the tail light unit is faulty and must be replaced with a new one – individual LEDs are not available.

Brake light

8 If the brake light fails to work, first check the fuse (see Section 5). If the fuse is good, remove the passenger seat (see Chapter 7), then disconnect the tail light wiring connector **(see illustration 6.6)** and check for battery voltage at the green/yellow wire terminal on the loom side of the connector, first with the front brake lever on, then with the rear brake pedal on. If voltage is present with one brake on but not the other, then the switch or its wiring is faulty. If voltage is present in both cases, check for continuity to earth (ground) in the green wire from the wiring connector. If no voltage is indicated, check the wiring and connectors between the brake light and the brake switches, the fusebox, and the ignition switch, then check the switches themselves. Refer to Section 14 for the switch testing procedures, and also to the wiring diagrams at the end of this Chapter.

9 If the power, wiring and connectors are good, or if only one or some of the brake light LEDs have failed leaving others working, then the tail light unit is faulty and must be replaced with a new one – individual LEDs are not available.

Sidelight and licence plate light

10 If the bulb fails to work, first check the fuse (see Section 5). If the fuse is good, remove the bulb (see Section 7 or 9), and test it by connecting it directly to the battery terminals using jumper wires. Alternatively use a continuity tester to check for continuity in the filament. If the bulb comes on or the filament shows continuity, the problem lies in the wiring or connectors. Otherwise the bulb is faulty and must be replaced with a new one.

11 If the bulb is good, check for battery voltage at the brown/white wire terminal on the loom side of the wiring connector with the ignition switch ON. If voltage is present, check for continuity to earth (ground) in the green wire from the wiring connector. If no voltage is indicated, check the wiring and connectors in the circuit. If other lights in the system have not come on as well, check the wiring via the fusebox and the ignition switch, and check the switch itself. Refer to Section 19 for the switch testing procedure, and also to the wiring diagrams at the end of this Chapter.

Turn signals

12 See Section 11.

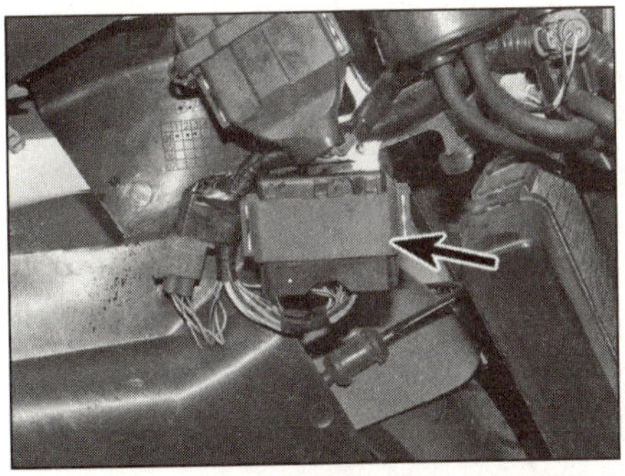

6.3a Relay box (arrowed) – RR-4 and RR-5 models

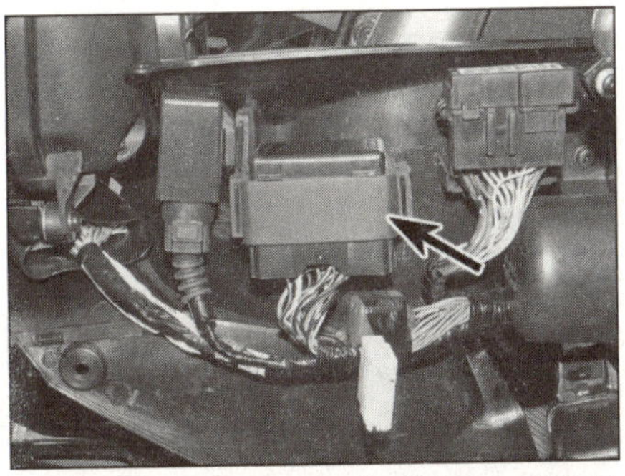

6.3b Relay box (arrowed) – RR-6 and RR-7 models

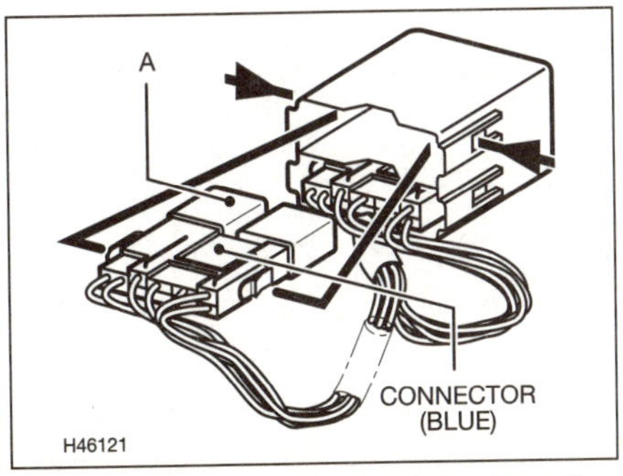

6.3c Release the blue connector from the box to access the headlight HI beam relay (A)

6.6 Tail light wiring connector

7.1a Disconnect the wiring connector . . .

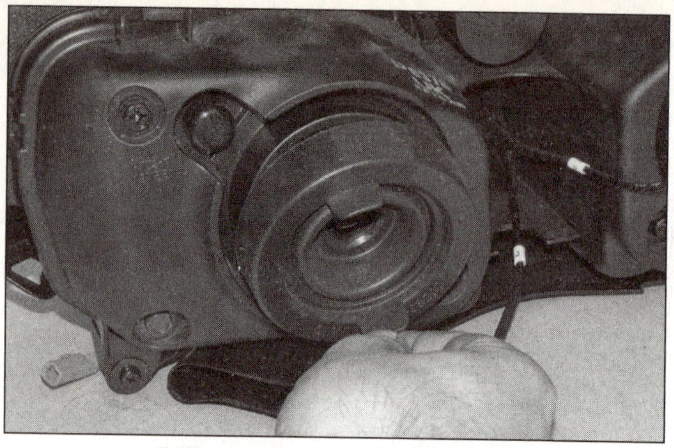

7.1b . . . and remove the dust cover

7 Headlight bulb and sidelight bulb

Note: *The headlight bulbs are of the quartz-halogen type. Do not touch the bulb glass as skin acids will shorten the bulb's service life. If the bulb is accidentally touched, it should be wiped carefully when cold with a rag soaked in methylated spirit and dried before fitting.*

Headlight

1 Reaching behind the back of the headlight, disconnect the wiring connector from the bulb in question, then remove the rubber dust cover, noting how it fits **(see illustrations)**.

2 Release the bulb retaining clip, noting how it fits, then remove the bulb **(see illustrations)**.

3 Carefully pull the bulb off the socket adapter, then fit the new bulb onto the adapter, bearing in mind the information in the **Note** above **(see illustration)**.

4 Fit the new bulb into the headlight, making sure it locates correctly, and secure it in position with the retaining clip.

> **HAYNES HiNT** ***Always use a paper towel or dry cloth when handling new bulbs to prevent injury if the bulb should break and to increase bulb life.***

5 Install the dust cover, making sure it is correctly seated and with the arrow at the top, and connect the wiring connector.

6 Check the operation of the headlight.

Sidelight

7 Undo the screws and remove the lens **(see illustrations)**. Carefully pull the bulb out of the holder **(see illustration)**.

8 Fit the new bulb in the bulbholder. Make sure the rubber seal is in good condition and correctly seated, then install the lens – do not over-tighten the screws as it is easy to strip the threads or crack the lens.

9 Check the operation of the sidelight.

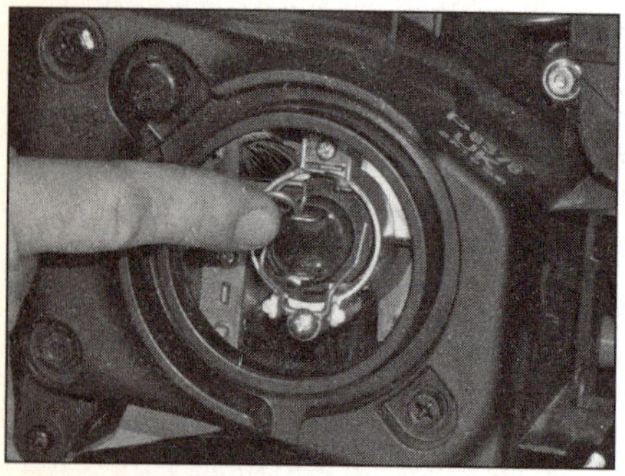

7.2a Release the clip . . .

7.2b . . . and remove the bulb

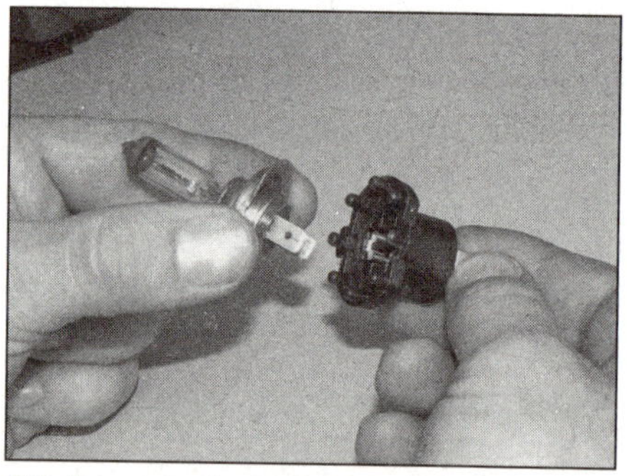

7.3 Separate the bulb from its adapter and fit a new one

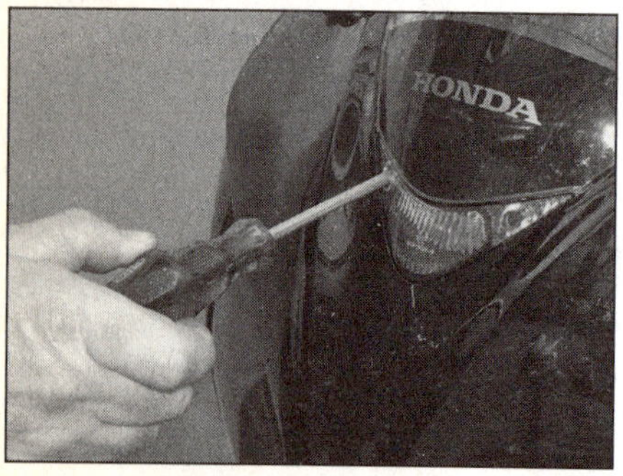

7.7a Undo the screws . . .

7.7b . . . then remove the lens . . .

7.7c . . . and replace the bulb with a new one

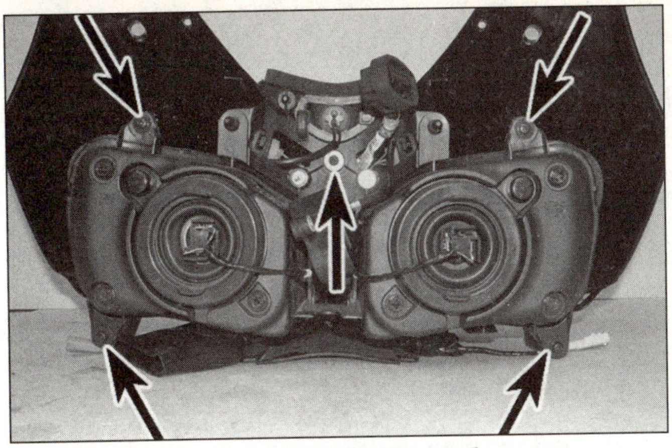

8.2a Undo the screws (arrowed) . . .

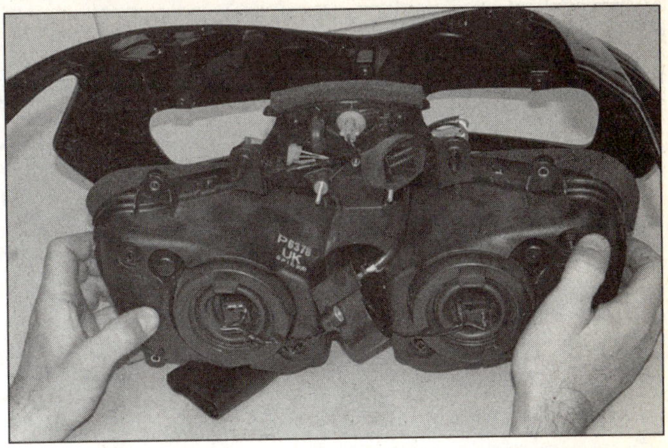

8.2b . . . and remove the headlight from the fairing

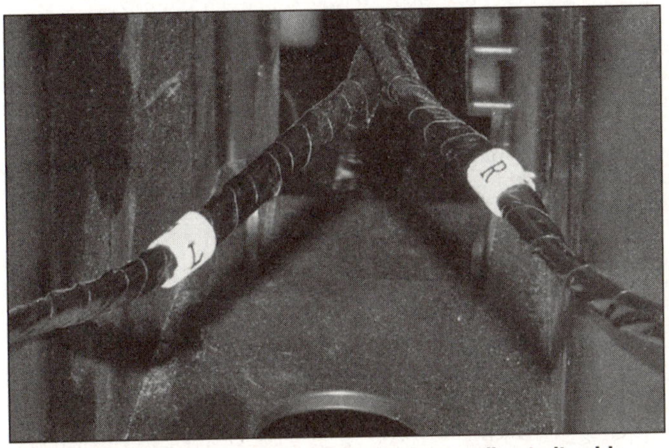

8.4 Each wiring connector is marked according to its side

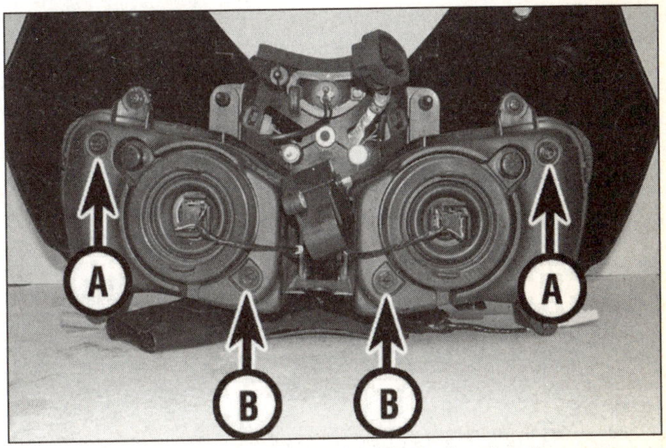

8.6 Vertical alignment adjusters (A). Horizontal alignment adjusters (B)

8 Headlight

Removal

1 Remove the fairing (see Chapter 7). Remove the lean angle sensor (see Chapter 4).

2 Undo the screws securing the headlight assembly to the fairing and lift it out **(see illustrations)**. On RR-4 and RR-5 note the turn signal relay located between the headlight units.

3 If required disconnect the headlight wiring connectors and remove the bulbs (see Section 7), and remove the sidelight bulbholder by twisting it anti-clockwise. Remove the wiring sub-loom, noting the routing of the various wires.

Installation

4 Installation is the reverse of removal. Make sure all the wiring is correctly routed, connected and secured – the headlight connectors are marked L and R **(see illustration)**. Check the operation of the headlight and sidelight. Check the headlight aim.

Headlight aim

Note: *An improperly adjusted headlight may cause problems for oncoming traffic or provide poor, unsafe illumination of the road ahead. Before adjusting the headlight aim, be sure to consult with local traffic laws and regulations – for UK models refer to MOT Test Checks in the Reference section.*

5 The headlight beam can adjusted both horizontally and vertically. Before making any adjustment, check that the tyre pressures are correct and the suspension is adjusted as required. Make any adjustments to the headlight aim with the machine on level ground, with the fuel tank half full and with an assistant sitting on the seat. If the bike is usually ridden with a passenger on the back, have a second assistant to do this.

6 Vertical adjustment is made by turning the adjuster screw on the top outer corner of the relevant beam unit **(see illustration)**. Turn it clockwise to move the beam up, and anti-clockwise to move it down.

7 Horizontal adjustment is made by turning the adjuster screw on the bottom inner corner of the relevant beam unit **(see illustration 8.6)**. For the LO beam (left-hand unit) turn the adjuster clockwise to move the beam to the right, and anti-clockwise to move it to the left. For the HI beam (right-hand unit) turn the adjuster clockwise to move the beam to the left, and anti-clockwise to move it to the right.

9 Brake/tail light LEDs and licence plate bulb

Brake/tail light LEDs

1 If one or more of the LEDs within the brake or tail light unit has failed, replace the entire tail light assembly with a new one – individual LEDs are not available (see Section 10).

Licence plate light bulb

Note: *It is a good idea to use a paper towel or dry cloth when handling the new bulb to*

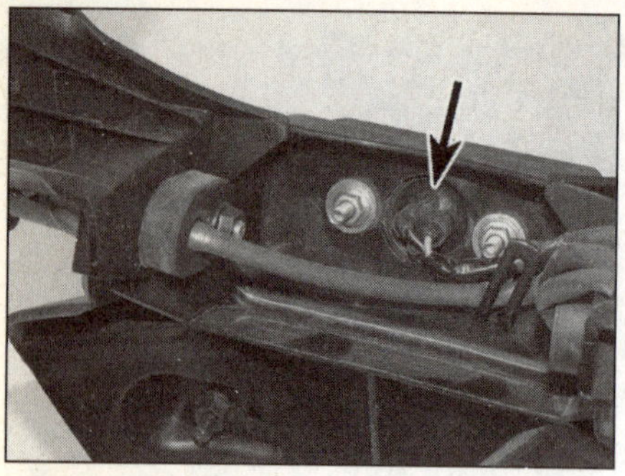

9.2 Licence plate bulbholder (arrowed)

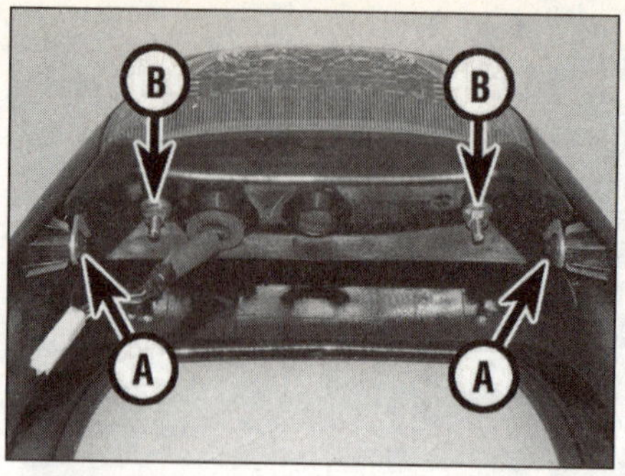

10.2 Undo the screws (A) and remove the tail light, then remove the nuts (B) and separate the light from its holder

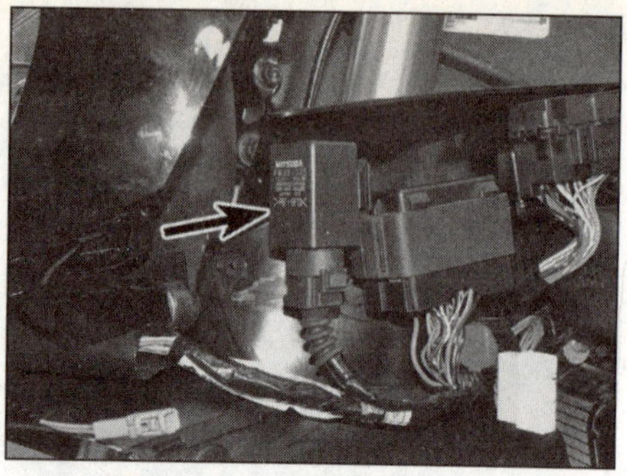

11.2 Turn signal relay (arrowed) – RR-6 and RR-7 models

prevent injury if it breaks, and to increase bulb life.

2 Reaching up under the mudguard, release the wiring from the clamp **(see illustration)**.

3 Turn the bulbholder anti-clockwise to release it. Carefully pull the bulb out of its socket and replace it with a new one.

4 Fit the bulbholder and turn it clockwise, then secure the wiring in the clamp.

10 Tail light

Removal

1 Remove the seat cowling (see Chapter 7).

2 Undo the two screws securing the tail light holder in the seat cowling and draw the tail light out, noting how the tabs on the top locate **(see illustration)**.

3 Unscrew the nuts and remove the collars, then separate the tail light from its holder and the side brackets, taking care as you draw the wiring through.

Installation

4 Installation is the reverse of removal. Check the operation of the tail and brake lights.

11 Turn signal circuit check

Note: *On US and Canada models the front turn signals also function as running lights and have dual filament bulbs. When checking for faults, refer to the wiring diagram at the end of this Chapter.*

1 Most turn signal problems are the result of a burned out bulb or corroded socket. This is especially true when the turn signals function properly in one direction, but fail to flash in the other direction. If this is the case, first check the bulbs, the sockets and the wiring connectors. If all the turn signals fail to work, first check the fuse (see Section 5), and then the relay (see below). If they are good, the problem lies in the wiring or connectors, or the switch. Refer to Section 20 for the switch testing procedures, and also to the wiring diagrams at the end of this Chapter.

2 To check the relay, on RR-4 and RR-5 models remove the headlight (see Section 8) – the relay is located between the two lenses at the front. Support the headlight next to the front of the bike on the left-hand side and reconnect the front sub-loom wiring connector. On RR-6 and RR-7 models remove the left-hand fairing side panel (see Chapter 7) – the relay is clipped to the inner fairing panel **(see illustration)**.

3 Disconnect the relay wiring connector. Check for battery voltage at the white/green wire terminal on the loom side of the connector with the ignition ON. If no voltage is present, check the wiring from the relay to the ignition (main) switch (via the fusebox) for continuity.

4 If voltage was present, short between the white/green and grey wire terminals on the connector using a jumper wire. On RR-6 and RR-7 models support the fairing side panel next to the bike and reconnect the turn signal wiring connector. Turn the ignition ON and operate the turn signal switch. If the lights come on, the relay is faulty and must be replaced with a new one.

5 If the lights do not come on, check the grey wire for continuity to the left-hand switch housing, and repair or renew the wiring or connectors as required.

6 If all is good so far, or if the lights came on one side but not the other, check the wiring between the left-hand switch housing and the turn signals themselves. Repair or renew the wiring or connectors as necessary.

12 Turn signal bulbs

1 Remove the screw securing the lens and detach the lens from the housing, noting how it fits **(see illustrations)**. Check the rubber lens seal and fit a new one if it is damaged, deformed or deteriorated.

2 Push the bulb into the holder and twist it anti-clockwise to remove it **(see illustration)**. Check the socket terminals for corrosion and clean them if necessary.

3 Line up the pins of the new bulb with the slots in the socket, then push the bulb in and turn it clockwise until it locks into place. **Note:** *It is a good idea to use a paper towel or dry cloth when handling the new bulb to prevent injury if the bulb should break and to increase bulb life.*

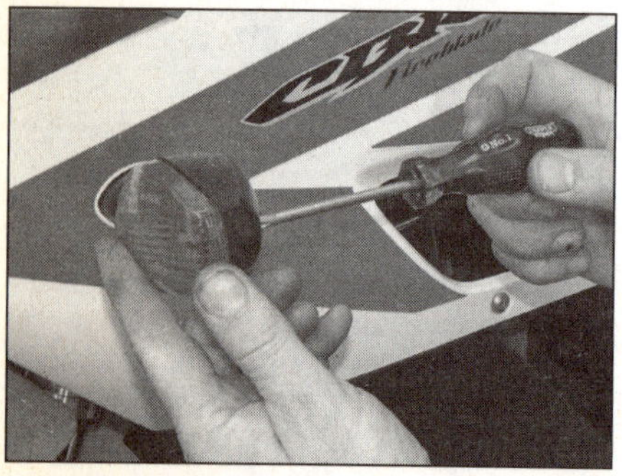

12.1a Undo the screw and remove the lens (on some models the screw is on the front)

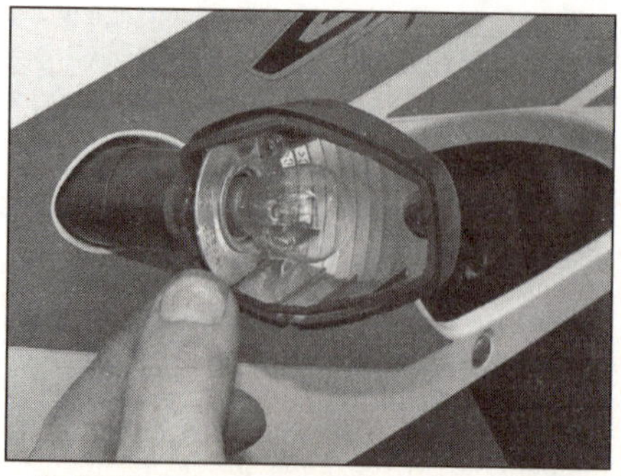

12.1b Check the condition of the rubber seal

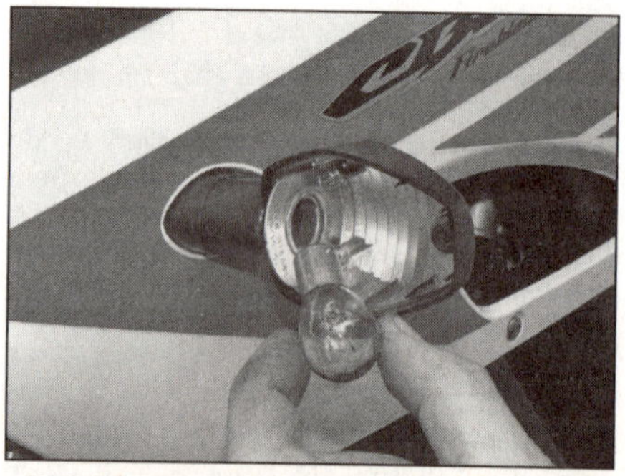

12.2 Release the bulb and replace it with a new one

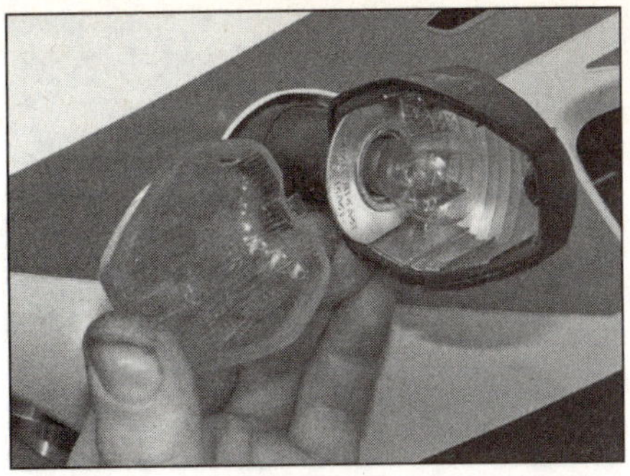

12.4 Make sure the tab locates correctly

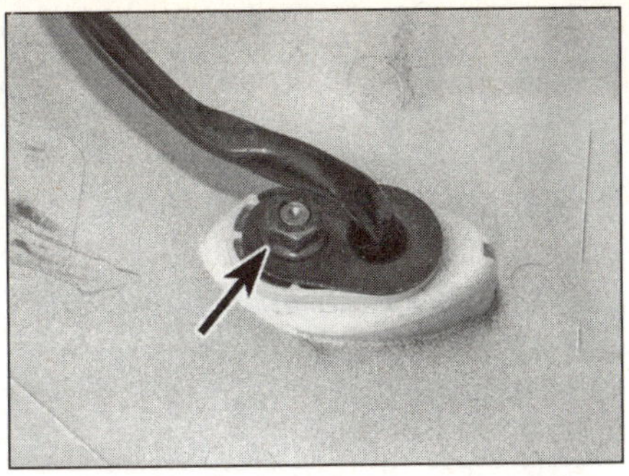

13.2 Front turn signal nut (arrowed)

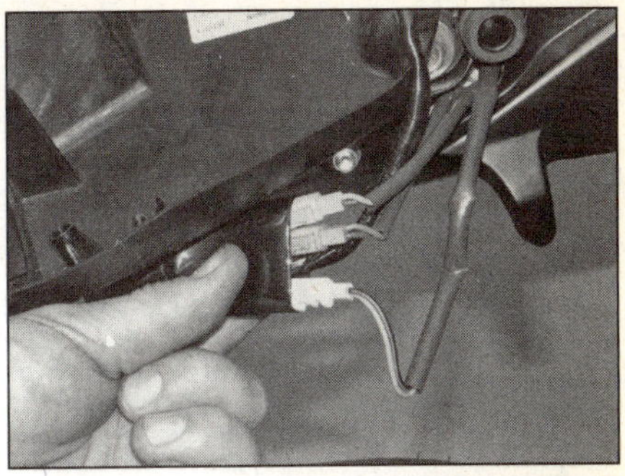

13.4 Disconnect the wiring connectors

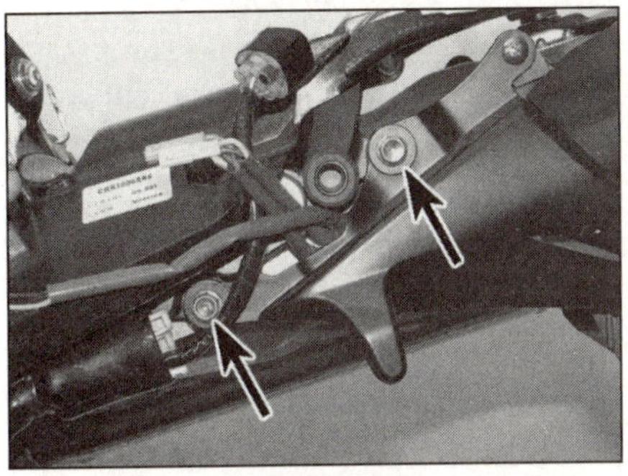

13.5a Unscrew the bolts (arrowed) on each side . . .

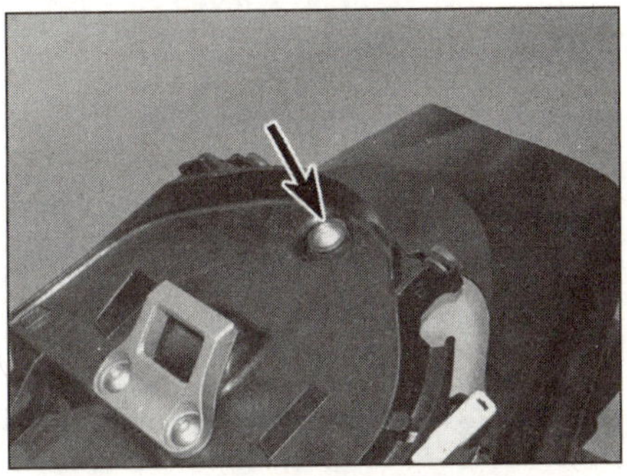

13.5b . . . and on RR-6 and RR-7 models the screw (arrowed) on the top . . .

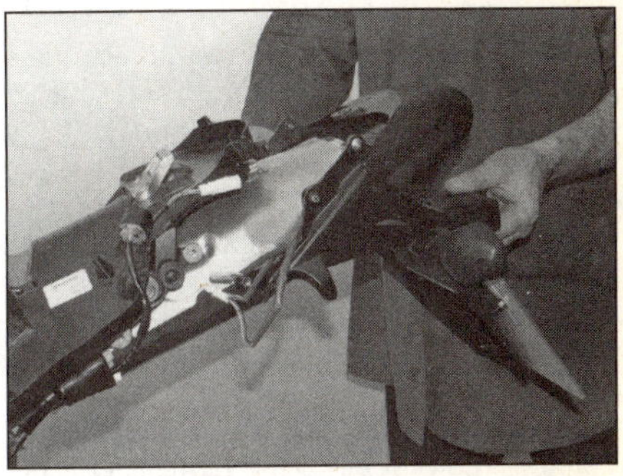

13.5c . . . and remove the rear mudguard/ licence plate assembly

4 Make sure the lens seal is properly seated and does not get pinched **(see illustration 12.1b)**. Fit the lens onto the housing, locating the tab in the cutout in the housing, and install the screw **(see illustration)**. Do not overtighten the screw as it is easy to strip the threads or crack the lens.

13 Turn signal assemblies

Front turn signals

1 Remove the fairing side panel (see Chapter 7).

2 Unscrew the nut securing the stem to the inside of the fairing and remove the mounting plate, and on RR-6 and RR-7 models the rubber mount **(see illustration)**. Remove the turn signal, taking care as you draw the wiring through.

Rear turn signals

3 Remove the seat cowling (see Chapter 7).

4 Disconnect the turn signal and licence plate light wiring connectors **(see illustration)**.

5 Unscrew the bolts, and on RR-6 and RR-7 models the top screw, securing the turn signal/licence plate assembly and remove it **(see illustrations)**.

6 On RR-4 and RR-5 models release the turn signal wiring from its guides – remove the trim cover if required **(see illustration)**. Unscrew the nut securing the turn signal stem and remove the turn signal, taking care as you draw the wiring through.

7 On RR-6 and RR-7 models release the turn signal wiring from its clamps. Unscrew the nut securing the turn signal stem and remove the mounting plate and the rubber mount **(see illustration)**. Remove the turn signal, taking care as you draw the wiring through.

14 Brake light switches

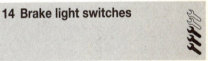

Circuit check

1 Before checking the switches, and if not already done, check the brake light circuit (see Section 6).

2 The front brake light switch is mounted on the underside of the brake master cylinder. Disconnect the wiring connectors from the switch **(see illustration)**. Using a continuity tester, connect the probes to the terminals of

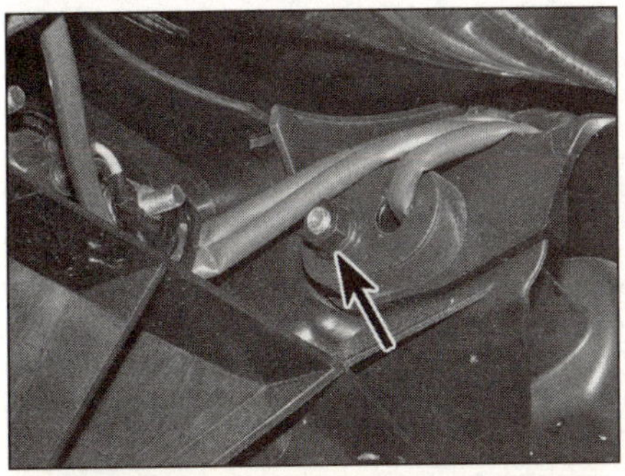

13.6 Release the wiring then unscrew the nut (arrowed) – RR-4 and RR-5

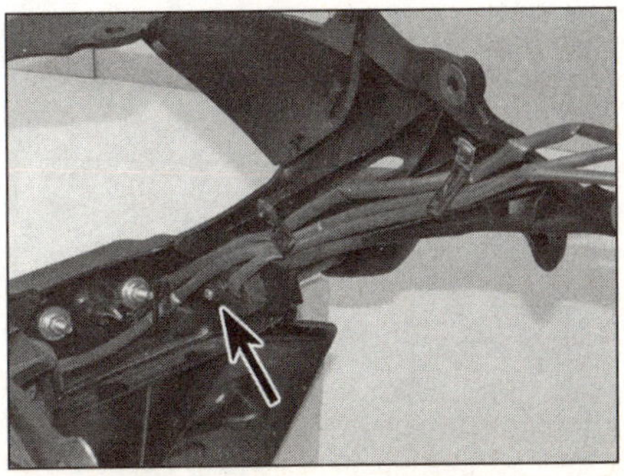

13.7 Release the wiring then unscrew the nut (arrowed) – RR-6 and RR-7

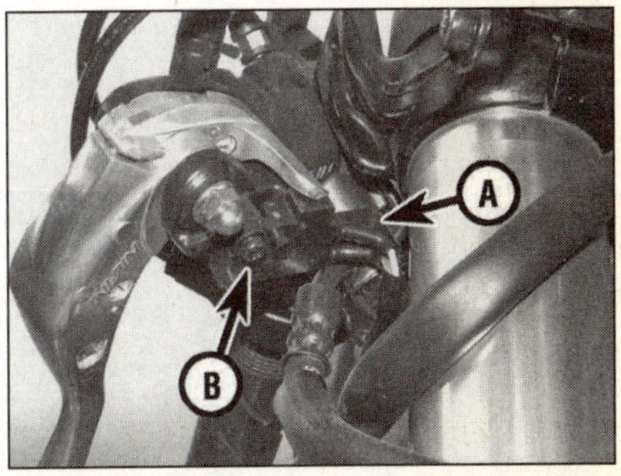

14.2 Front brake switch wiring connectors (A) and mounting screw (B)

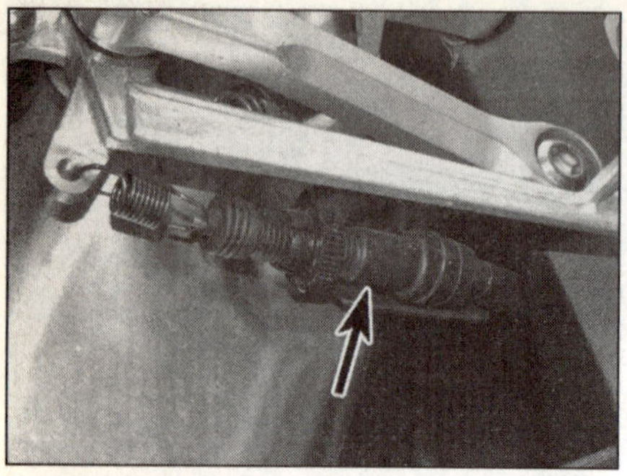

14.3a Rear brake light switch (arrowed)

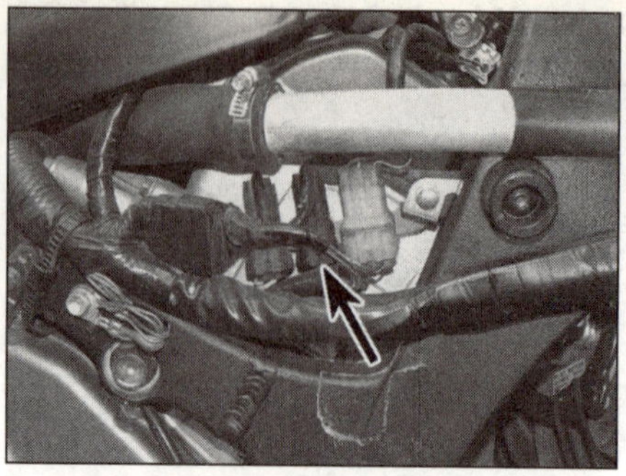

14.3b Rear brake light switch wiring connector (arrowed) – RR-4 and RR-5 models

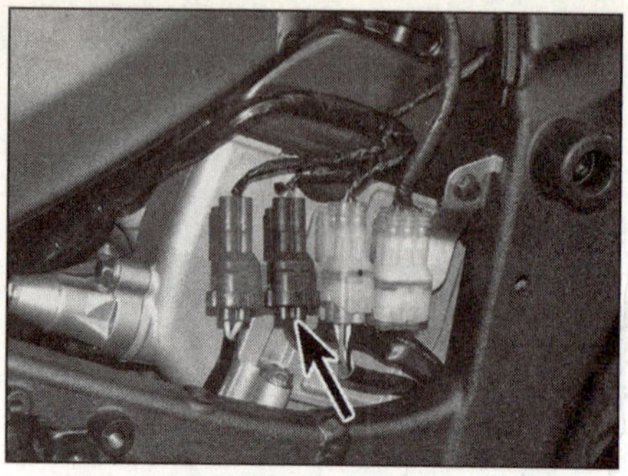

14.3c Rear brake light switch wiring connector (arrowed) – RR-6 and RR-7 models

the switch. With the brake lever at rest, there should be no continuity. With the brake lever applied, there should be continuity. If the switch does not behave as described, replace it with a new one.

3 The rear brake light switch is mounted on the inside of the right-hand rider's footrest bracket **(see illustration)**. Remove the fairing right-hand side panel (see Chapter 7) to access the wiring connector and disconnect it **(see illustrations)**. Using a continuity tester, connect the probes to the terminals on the switch side of the wiring connector. With the brake pedal at rest, there should be no continuity. With the brake pedal applied, there should be continuity. If the switch does not behave as described, replace it with a new one, although check first that the switch is adjusted correctly (see Step 10).

4 If the switches are good, check for voltage at the white/green wire on the loom side of the connector with the ignition switch ON – there should be battery voltage. If there's no voltage present, check the wiring between the connector and the ignition switch via the fusebox (see the wiring diagrams at the end of this Chapter). If voltage is present, check the green/yellow wire for continuity to the brake light LED wiring connector. Repair or renew the wiring as necessary.

Switch replacement

Front brake lever switch

5 The switch is mounted on the underside of the brake master cylinder. Disconnect the wiring connectors from the switch **(see illustration 14.2)**.

6 Undo the single screw securing the switch to the master cylinder and remove the switch.

7 Installation is the reverse of removal. Make sure the peg on the switch is correctly located in its hole before tightening the screw. The switch isn't adjustable.

Rear brake pedal switch

8 The rear brake light switch is mounted on the inside of the rider's right-hand footrest bracket **(see illustration 14.3a)**. Remove the fairing right-hand side panel (see Chapter 7) to access the wiring connector and disconnect it **(see illustration 14.3b or c)**. Feed the wiring down to the switch, noting its routing and releasing it from its clamp(s).

9 Detach the end of the switch spring from the brake pedal **(see illustration 14.3a)**. Thread the switch out of its adjuster nut, then pull the nut out of the bracket.

10 Installation is the reverse of removal. Make sure the brake light is activated just before the rear brake pedal takes effect. If adjustment is necessary, hold the switch body and turn the adjuster nut as required until the brake light is activated correctly – if the brake light comes on too late or not at all, turn the ring clockwise (when looked at from the front) so the switch threads out of the bracket. If the brake light comes on too soon or is permanently on, turn the ring anti-clockwise so the switch threads into the bracket.

15 Instrument cluster removal and installation

Removal

1 Remove the main fairing (see Chapter 7).

2 Undo the screws and remove the washers, then lift the instrument cluster off the bracket, noting how it locates **(see illustrations)**. Note the rubber grommets fitted in the mounts.

Installation

3 Installation is the reverse of removal. Check the rubber grommets for damage, deformation and deterioration and replace them with new ones if necessary. Make sure the pegs locate correctly in the grommets. Make sure that the wiring connector is secure when installing the fairing.

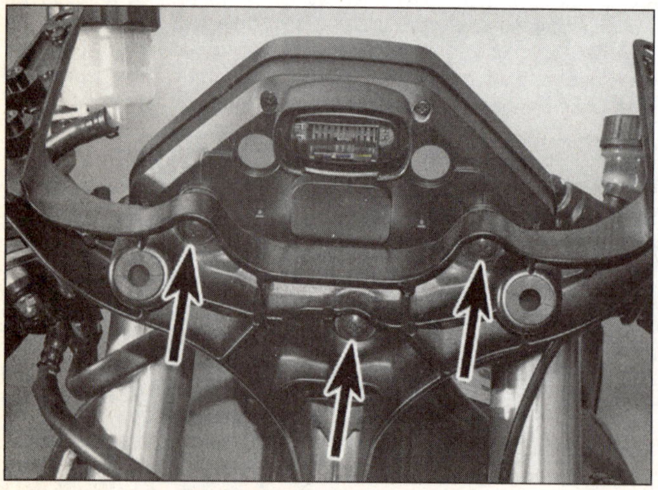

15.2a Undo the screws (arrowed) . . .

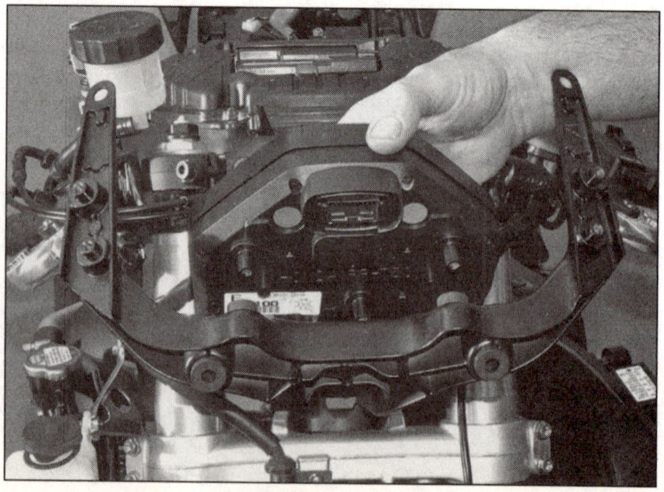

15.2b . . . and remove the instrument cluster

16 Instruments and speed sensor check

Instrument cluster power check

1 If none of the instruments or displays are working, first check the fuse (see Section 5).

2 If the fuse is good, remove the windshield and the fairing left-hand side panel (see Chapter 7) and check the instrument cluster and front loom wiring connectors for loose or broken connections **(see illustrations)**.

3 To check the power input wire, check for battery voltage between the brown/white wire terminal on the wiring loom side of the instrument connector and a good earth (ground) with the ignition switch ON. There should be battery voltage. If there is no voltage, refer to the wiring diagrams and check the black/brown wire between the instrument cluster and the fusebox for loose or broken connections or a damaged wire.

4 To check the back-up power wire, check for battery voltage between the red/green wire terminal on the wiring loom side of the connector and a good earth (ground) with the ignition switch OFF. There should be battery voltage. If there is no voltage, refer to the wiring diagrams and check the red/green wire between the instrument cluster and the fusebox for loose or broken connections or a damaged wire, then check the red wire from the fusebox to the main fuse and battery.

5 If there is voltage, and to check the earth (ground) wires, check for continuity between the green/black wire terminal on the loom side of the wiring connector and earth (ground), and between the green wire terminal and earth. If there is no continuity, check the circuit for loose or broken connections or a damaged wire and repair as necessary.

6 If all power input and earth wires are good, but there is no display or instrument function, then the printed circuit board (PCB), which contains the LCD display, is faulty. Disassemble the instrument cluster and replace the PCB with a new one (see Steps 18 to 21).

Speedometer and speed sensor

7 First check the fuse (see Section 5).

8 If the fuse is good, remove the windshield and the fairing left-hand side panel (see Chapter 7), and check the instrument cluster and front loom wiring connectors for loose or broken connections **(see illustrations 16.2a and b)**.

9 Raise the fuel tank (see Chapter 4). Trace the wiring from the speed sensor, which is mounted on the crankcase behind the cylinders, and disconnect it at the 3-pin connector **(see illustrations)**. Check the connector for loose terminals. With the ignition switch ON, check for battery voltage between the brown/white (+) and green/black (-) wire terminals on the wiring

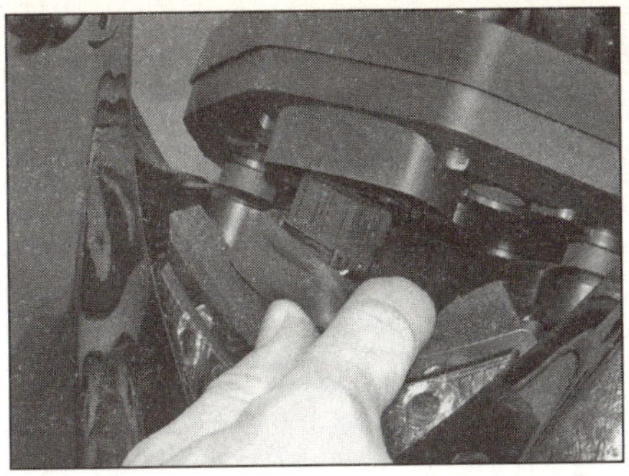

16.2a Instrument cluster wiring connector

loom side of the connector. If there is no voltage refer to the wiring diagrams and check the wires for continuity and repair any loose or broken connection or damaged wire.

10 If there is voltage, reconnect the wiring connector, then place the machine on an auxiliary stand so the rear wheel is off the ground. Connect a voltmeter between the pink (+) and green/black (-) wire terminals – make sure the probes make good contact when inserted into the connector. With the ignition switch ON, turn the rear wheel by hand and check that a fluctuating voltage reading between 0 and 5 volts is obtained. If no reading is obtained, refer to Step 5 and check the instrument cluster earth wires. If the wiring is good, then the speed sensor is faulty and must be replaced with a new one (see Steps 22 to 25).

11 If a reading is obtained, remove the windshield (see Chapter 7), then pull back the rubber boot and disconnect the instrument cluster wiring connector **(see illustration 16.2a)**. Check the connector for loose or broken connections, then repeat the check in Step 10, but connect the meter between the pink and green/black wire terminals on the loom side of the cluster wiring connector. If no fluctuating voltage is obtained, check for continuity in the wiring between the speed sensor wiring connector and the instrument cluster wiring connector, and for continuity to earth in the green/black wire, referring to the wiring diagrams.

12 If the wiring is all good, the printed circuit board (PCB), which contains the LCD display, is faulty. Disassemble the instrument cluster

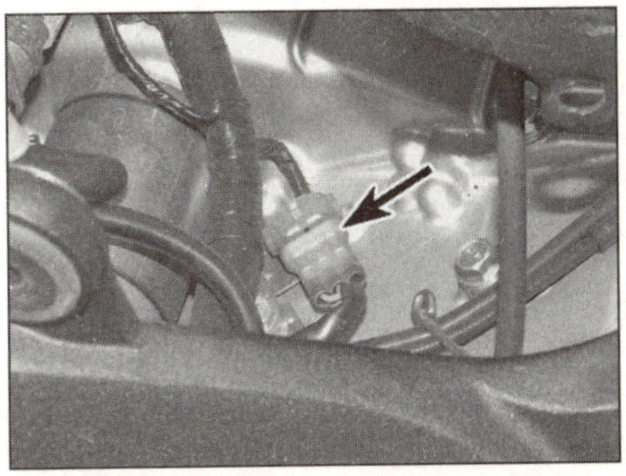

16.9a Speed sensor wiring connector (arrowed) – RR-4 and RR-5 models

16.2b Front loom wiring connector

and replace the PCB with a new one (see Steps 18 to 21).

Tachometer

13 Check that when the ignition is switched on the tachometer needle makes a full swing round the dial and returns to zero. If not check the power input (see Steps 1 to 6).

14 To check the tachometer input peak voltage Honda specify to use the peak voltage adapter (Pt. No. 07HGJ-0020100) with an aftermarket digital multimeter having an impedance of 10 M-ohm/DCV minimum, for this test. Remove the windshield (see Chapter 7). Connect the positive (+) lead of the voltmeter and peak voltage adapter arrangement to the yellow/green wire terminal on the loom side of the instrument wiring connector and the negative (–) lead to a good earth (ground). Start the engine and measure the tachometer input peak voltage, which should be at least 10.5 volts. If the peak voltage is normal, check the instrument cluster earth wires (see Step 5). If they are good then the tachometer is faulty. Disassemble the instrument cluster and replace the PCB with a new one (see Steps 18 to 21).

15 If there is no reading, on RR-4 and RR-5 models remove the fairing right-hand side panel, and on RR-5 and RR-6 models remove the fuel tank cover (see Chapter 7), and disconnect the ECM grey wiring connector (see Chapter 4). Check for continuity in the yellow/green wire between the ECM wiring connector and the instrument cluster wiring connector. If there is no continuity there is a break in the wire or faulty connector. Refer to the wiring diagrams and trace and rectify the

16.9b Speed sensor wiring connector – RR-6 and RR-7 models

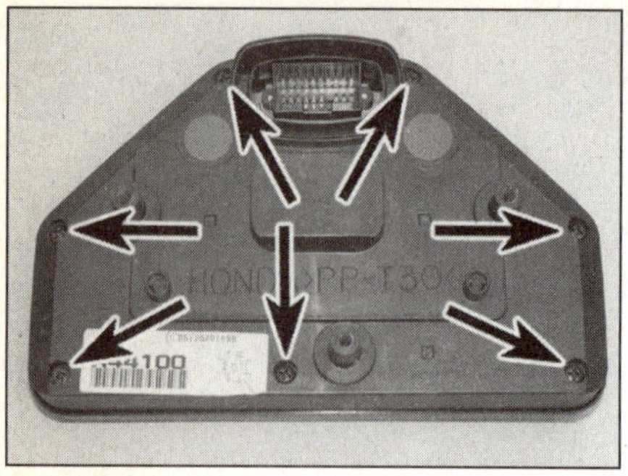

16.19a Undo the screws (arrowed) . . .

16.19b . . . and remove the cover

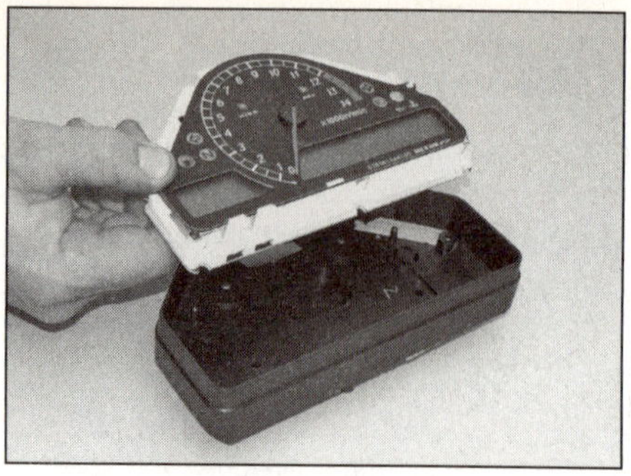

16.20 Remove the PCB, noting how it locates

fault. If the wiring is good the ECM could be faulty (see Chapter 4).

LCD display

16 If the display is not working at all, check the instrument cluster power input (see above) and earth wires. If the wires are good, then the printed circuit board (PCB), which contains the LCD display, is faulty. Disassemble the instrument cluster and replace the PCB with a new one (see Steps 18 to 21).

17 If an individual display is not working, refer to Chapter 3 for the coolant temperature and warning display, Chapter 4 for the low fuel warning, and Section 18 for the oil pressure warning. If the clock doesn't work, first check the fuse (see Section 5). If any fault points to the LCD unit being faulty, replace the instrument cluster PCB with a new one (see Steps 18 to 21).

PCB replacement

18 Remove the instrument cluster (see Section 15).

19 Undo the rear cover screws, then turn the instruments over and lift the front cover off **(see illustrations)**.

20 Lift the PCB out of the rear cover **(see illustration)**.

21 Installation is the reverse of removal. Do not over-tighten the screws.

Speed sensor replacement

22 The speed sensor is mounted on the crankcase behind the cylinders. Raise the fuel tank (see Chapter 4) and access the sensor from the top.

23 Trace the wiring from the sensor and disconnect it at the 3-pin connector **(see illustration 16.9a or b)**. On RR-6 and RR-7 models release the starter motor and earth cables from the wiring harness guide, then detach the guide from its clip and from the frame **(see illustrations)**.

24 Unscrew the sensor mounting bolt and remove the sensor **(see illustration)**. Check the condition of its O-ring and replace it with a new one if is damaged **(see illustration)**. Plug the sensor orifice with clean rag to prevent anything falling into the engine.

25 Installation is the reverse of removal, using a new O-ring if necessary, and not forgetting the wiring clamp with the bolt.

17 Instrument and warning light bulbs

1 All instrument and warning lights are LEDs, which are part of the instrument cluster printed circuit board and are not available individually. If one of the LEDs fails disassemble the instrument cluster and replace the PCB with a new one (see Section 16, Steps 18 to 21).

18 Oil pressure switch

Check

1 The oil pressure warning light should come on when the ignition (main) switch is turned ON and go out a few seconds after the engine is started. If the oil pressure warning light does not go out or comes on whilst the engine

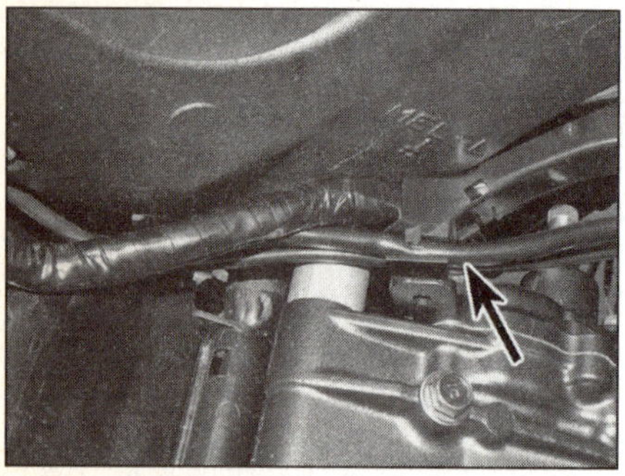

16.23a Release the cables . . .

16.23b . . . then lift the guide of its clip (arrowed) . . .

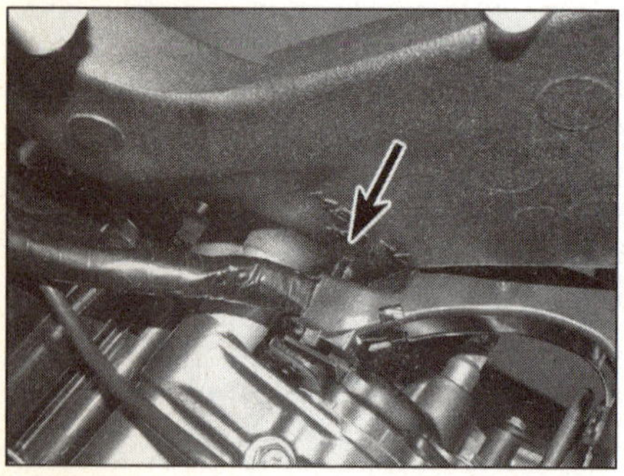

16.23c . . . and detach it from the frame

16.24a Undo the bolt and withdraw the sensor

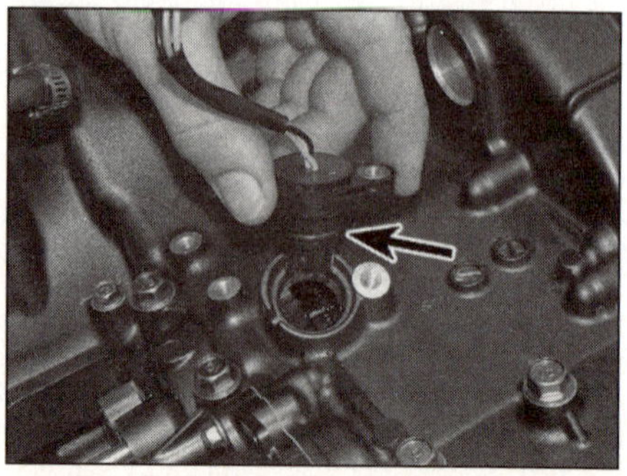

16.24b Replace the O-ring (arrowed) with a new one if necessary

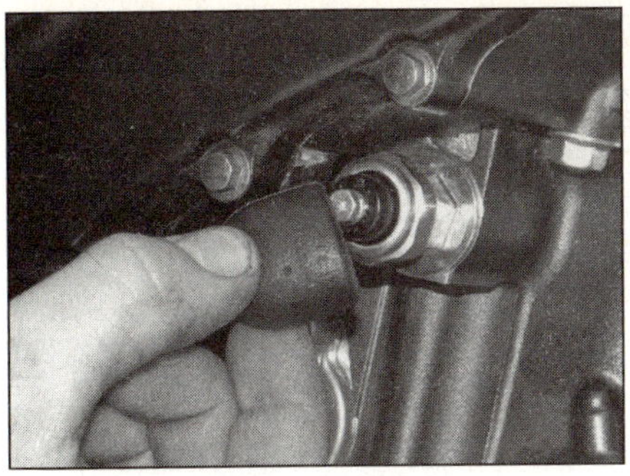

18.3a Pull back the rubber cover . . .

is running, stop the engine immediately and carry out an oil level check (see *Pre-ride checks*), and if the level is correct, an oil pressure check (see Chapter 2).

2 If the oil pressure warning light does not come on when the ignition is turned ON, but the LCD display otherwise appears to be functioning, remove the lower fairing (see Chapter 7).

3 The oil pressure switch is screwed into the crankcase on the right-hand side. Pull the rubber cover off the switch and remove the screw securing the wiring connector **(see illustrations)**. With the ignition switched ON, earth (ground) the wire on the crankcase and check that the warning light comes on. If the light comes on, the switch is defective and must be replaced with a new one.

4 If the light still does not come on, check the fuse (see Section 5), then check for voltage at the wire terminal. If there is no voltage present, check the wire between the switch, the instrument cluster and fusebox for continuity (see the wiring diagrams at the end of this Chapter).

5 If the warning light does not go out when the engine is started or comes on whilst the engine is running, yet the oil pressure is satisfactory, detach the wire from the oil pressure switch (see above). With the wire detached and the ignition switched ON the light should be out. If it is illuminated, the wire between the switch and instrument cluster is earthed (grounded) at some point. If the wiring is good, the switch must be assumed faulty and replaced with a new one.

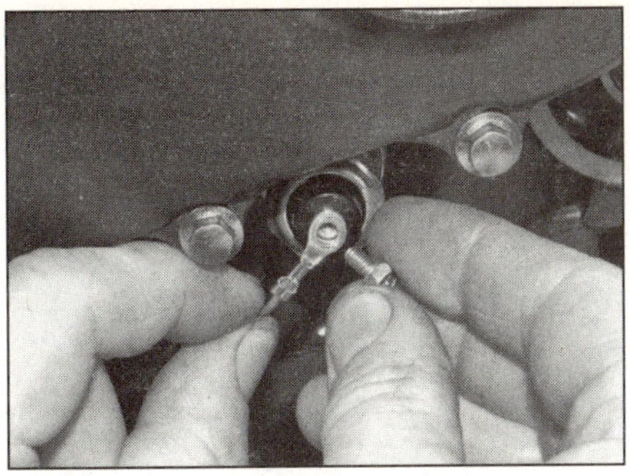

18.3b . . . then undo the terminal screw and detach the wiring

Removal

6 The oil pressure switch is screwed into the crankcase on the right-hand side. Remove the lower fairing (see Chapter 7).

7 Pull the rubber cover off the switch, then undo the screw securing the wiring connector **(see illustrations 18.3a and b)**.

8 Counter-hold the hex on the crankcase adapter the switch threads into then unscrew the switch and withdraw it from the crankcase **(see illustration)**.

Installation

9 Apply a suitable sealant to the upper portion of the switch threads near the switch body, leaving the bottom 3 to 4 mm of thread clean. Install the switch in the crankcase, then counter-hold the adapter hex and tighten the switch to the torque setting specified at the beginning of the Chapter **(see illustration 18.8)**. Attach the wiring connector and secure it with the screw, then fit the rubber cover **(see illustrations 18.3b and a)**.

10 Run the engine and check that the switch operates correctly and without leakage.

11 Install the lower fairing panel.

19 Ignition (main) switch

Warning: To prevent the risk of short circuits, disconnect the battery negative (–) lead before making any ignition (main) switch checks.

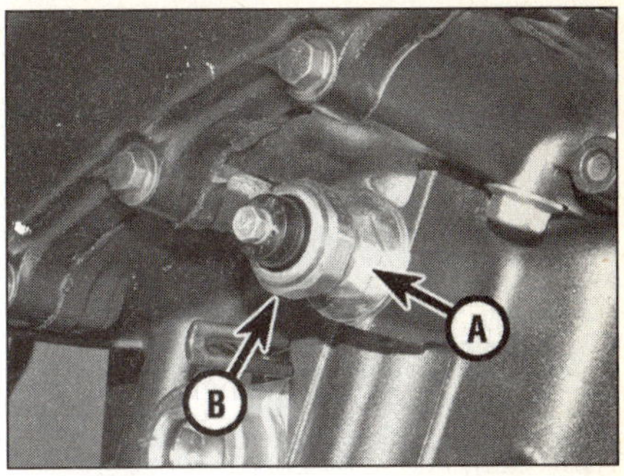

18.8 Counter-hold the adapter (A) and unscrew the switch (B)

Check

1 Remove the air filter housing (see Chapter 4). Trace the wiring from the ignition switch and disconnect it at the connector – release the trim clip and remove the connector cover if required **(see illustration)**.

2 Using an ohmmeter or a continuity tester, check the continuity of the connector terminal pairs (see the wiring diagrams at the end of this Chapter). Continuity should exist between the terminals connected by a solid line on the diagram when the switch is in the indicated position.

3 If the switch fails any of the tests, replace it with a new one.

Removal

4 Remove the fairing and the air filter housing (see Chapters 7 and 4).

5 Trace the wiring from the ignition switch and disconnect it at the connector – release the trim clip and remove the connector cover if required **(see illustration 19.1)**. Feed the wiring back to the switch, freeing it from any clips and ties and noting its routing.

6 On models fitted with the HISS immobiliser system, undo the screws securing the receiver around the ignition switch and displace it, noting how it fits **(see illustration)**.

7 Displace the clutch master cylinder (see Chapter 2) – there is no need to detach the hydraulic hose. Slacken the fork clamp bolts in the top yoke **(see illustration)**. Unscrew the steering stem nut and on

19.1 Ignition switch wiring connector (arrowed)

19.6 Immobiliser receiver screws (arrowed)

19.7a Slacken the clamp screw (arrowed) . . .

19.7b . . . then unscrew the nut and remove the washer where fitted . . .

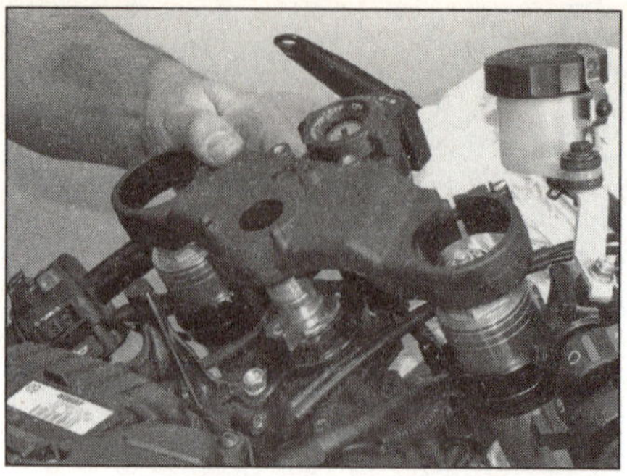

19.7c . . . and lift the top yoke off the forks

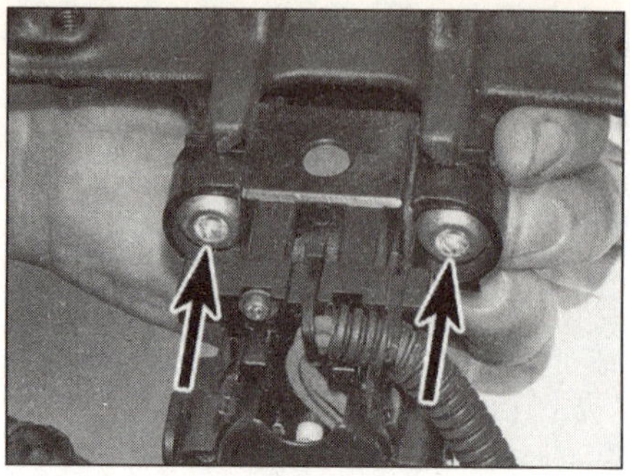

19.8 Ignition switch one-way security bolts (arrowed)

RR-6 models remove the washer **(see illustration)**. Gently ease the top yoke up off the fork tubes and remove it **(see illustration)**.

8 One-way security bolts (which can be done up but not undone using conventional tools) are fitted **(see illustration)** – drive the heads around using a punch or unscrew them using grips.

9 If required separate the contact plate from the bottom of the switch.

Installation

10 Installation is the reverse of removal. Tighten the ignition switch bolts to the torque setting specified at the beginning of the Chapter, using new ones if necessary. Also tighten the steering stem nut and then the fork clamp bolts to the specified torque. Make sure the wiring connector is correctly routed and securely connected.

20 Handlebar switches

Check

1 Generally speaking, the switches are reliable and trouble-free. Most troubles, when they do occur, are caused by dirty or corroded contacts, but wear and breakage of internal parts is a possibility that should not be overlooked. If breakage does occur, the entire switch and related wiring harness will have to be replaced with a new one, as individual parts are not available.

2 The switches can be checked for continuity using an ohmmeter or a continuity test light. Always disconnect the battery negative (–) lead, which will prevent the possibility of a short circuit, before making the checks.

3 Remove the air filter housing (see Chapter 4). Trace the wiring from the ignition switch and disconnect it at the connector – release the trim clip and remove the connector cover if required **(see illustration)**.

4 Check for continuity between the terminals of the switch connector with the switch in the various positions (i.e. switch off – no continuity, switch on – continuity) – see the wiring diagrams at the end of this Chapter. Continuity should exist between the terminals connected by a solid line on the diagram when the switch is in the indicated position.

5 If the continuity check indicates a problem exists, displace the switch housing (Step 8), and spray the switch contacts with electrical contact cleaner (there is no need to remove the switch completely). If they are accessible, the contacts can be scraped clean with a knife or polished with crocus cloth. If switch components are damaged or broken, it will be obvious when the switch is disassembled.

Removal and installation

6 Remove the air filter housing (see Chapter 4). Trace the wiring from the ignition switch and disconnect it at the connector – release the trim clip and remove the connector cover if required **(see illustration 20.3)**. Feed the wiring back to the switch, freeing it from any clips and ties and noting its routing.

7 If removing the right-hand switch disconnect the wires from the brake light switch **(see illustration 14.2)**. If removing the left-hand switch disconnect the wires from the clutch switch **(see illustration 23.2)**.

8 Unscrew the two handlebar switch screws and free the switch from the handlebar by separating the halves **(see illustrations)**.

9 Installation is the reverse of removal. Make sure the locating pin in the switch housing locates in the hole in the handlebar.

21 Neutral switch

Check

1 Before checking the electrical circuit, check the fuse (see Section 5).

2 The switch is located in the back of the engine. Detach the wiring connector from

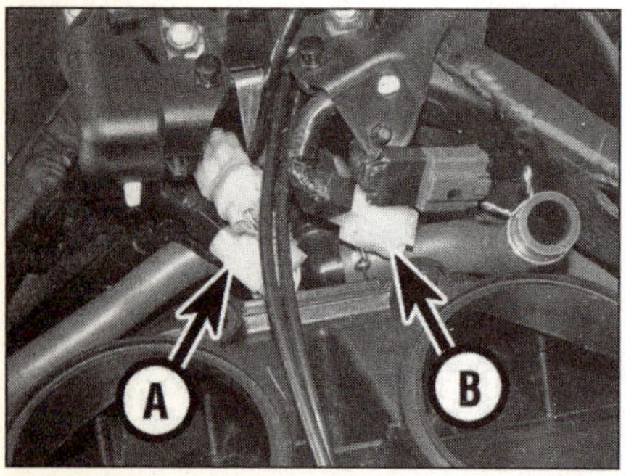

20.3 Left-hand switch wiring connector (A), the right-hand switch wiring connector (B)

20.8a Left-hand switch housing screws (arrowed)

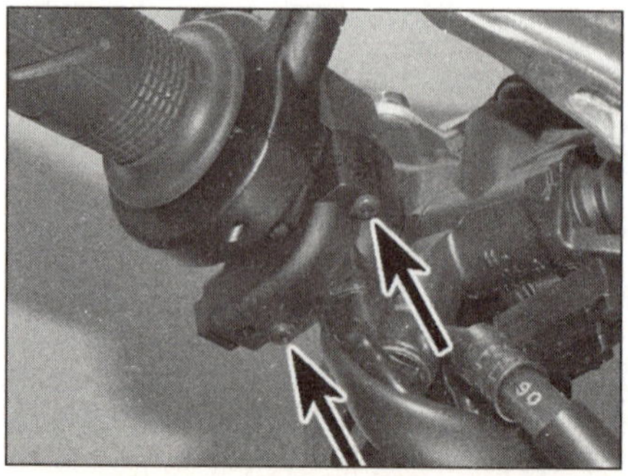

20.8b Right-hand switch housing screws (arrowed)

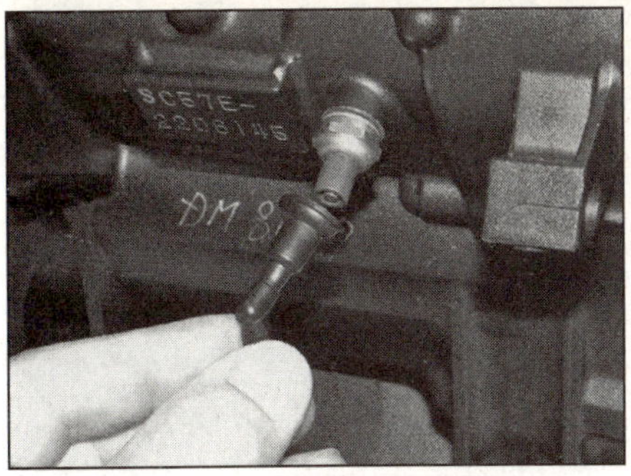

21.2 Pull the wiring connector off the switch

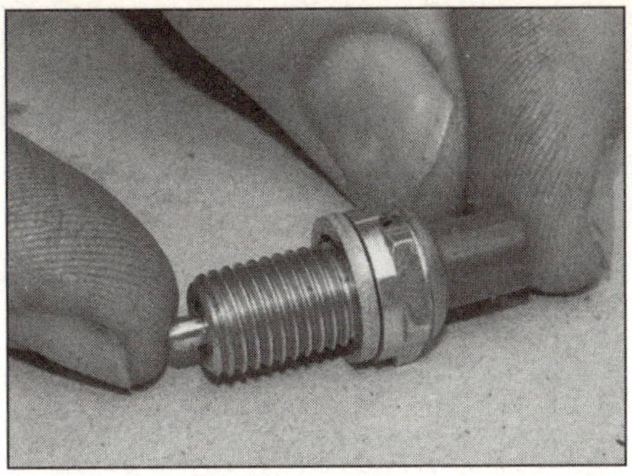
21.4 Make sure the plunger moves in and out smoothly and freely

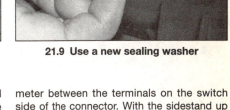

21.9 Use a new sealing washer

the switch **(see illustration)**. Make sure the transmission is in neutral.

3 With the connector disconnected and the ignition switch ON, the neutral light should be out. If not, the wire between the connector and instrument cluster must be earthed (grounded) at some point.

4 Check for continuity between the switch terminal and the crankcase. With the transmission in neutral, there should be continuity. With the transmission in gear, there should be no continuity. If the tests prove otherwise, then remove the switch (see below) and check whether the plunger is bent or damaged, or just stuck **(see illustration)**. Replace the switch with a new one if necessary.

5 If the continuity tests prove the switch is good, check for voltage at the wire terminal. If there's no voltage present, check the wire between the switch, the instrument cluster and fusebox (see the wiring diagrams at the end of this Chapter). If all is good, the LCD unit in the instrument cluster could be faulty (see Section 16).

Removal and installation

6 The switch is located in the back of the engine.

7 Detach the wiring connector from the switch **(see illustration 21.2)**.

8 Clean the area around the switch, then unscrew it from the crankcase **(see illustration 21.9)**. Discard the sealing washer as a new one should be used.

9 Install the switch using a new washer and tighten it to the torque setting specified at the beginning of the Chapter **(see illustration)**.

10 Connect the wiring connector and check the operation of the neutral light **(see illustration 21.2)**.

22 Sidestand switch

Check

1 The sidestand switch is mounted on the stand pivot. The switch is part of the starter interlock safety circuit which prevents or stops the engine running if the transmission is in gear whilst the sidestand is down, and prevents the engine from starting if the transmission is in gear unless the sidestand is up and the clutch is pulled in. Before checking the electrical circuit, check the fuse (see Section 5).

2 On RR-4 and RR-5 models remove the left-hand lower fairing and fairing left-hand side panel (see Chapter 7), then trace the wiring from the switch and disconnect at the green 2-pin wiring connector inside the rubber boot – release the cable tie from the boot **(see illustration)**. On RR-6 and RR-7 models trace the wiring from the switch and disconnect at the black 2-pin wiring connector **(see illustration)**.

3 Check the operation of the switch using an ohmmeter or continuity test light. Connect the meter between the terminals on the switch side of the connector. With the sidestand up there should be continuity (zero resistance) between the terminals, and with the stand down there should be no continuity (infinite resistance).

4 If the switch does not perform as expected, it is faulty and must be replaced with a new one.

5 If the switch is good, check the wiring and connectors between the various components in the starter safety circuit using a continuity tester (see the wiring diagrams at the end of this Chapter). Also check for voltage at the green/white wire terminal on the loom side of the connector with the ignition ON – there should be battery voltage. Repair or renew the wiring as required.

Removal

6 The sidestand switch is mounted on the stand pivot. On RR-4 and RR-5 models remove the left-hand lower fairing and fairing side panel (see Chapter 7), then trace the wiring from the switch and disconnect at the green 2-pin wiring connector inside the rubber boot – release the cable tie from the boot **(see illustration 22.2a)**. On RR-6 and RR-7 models trace the wiring from the switch and disconnect at the black 2-pin wiring connector **(see illustration 22.2b)**. Feed the wiring back to the switch, freeing it from any clips and ties and noting its routing.

7 Unscrew the switch bolt and remove the switch from the stand, noting how it fits **(see illustration)**. Honda specify that the switch

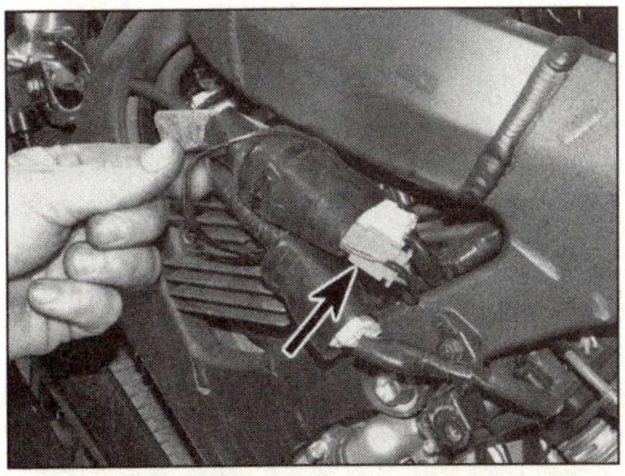
22.2a Sidestand switch wiring connector (arrowed) – RR-4 and RR-5 models

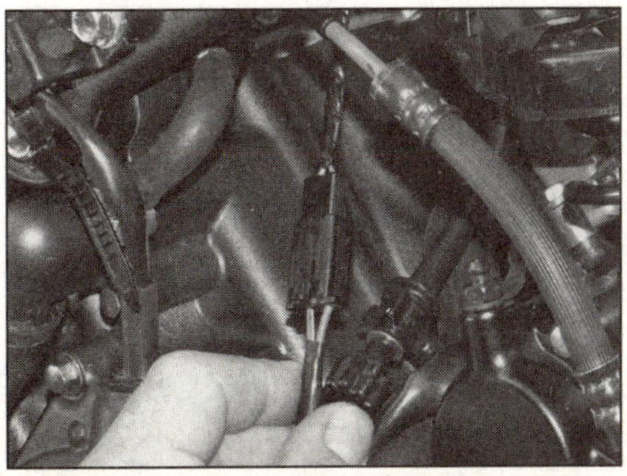
22.2b Sidestand switch wiring connector – RR-6 and RR-7 models

22.7 Sidestand switch mounting bolt (arrowed)

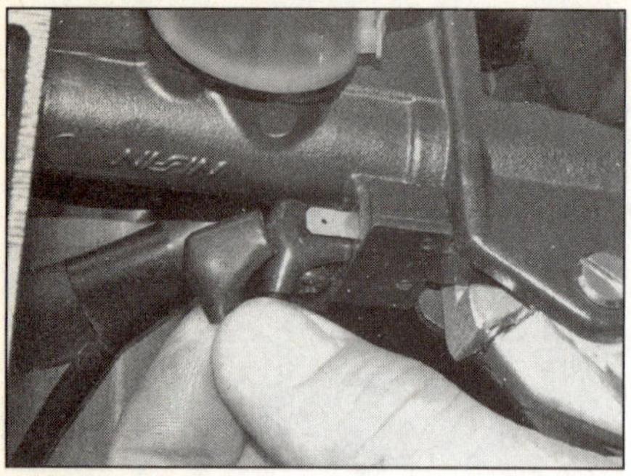
23.2 Disconnect the clutch switch wiring connectors

bolt be replaced with a new one every time it is disturbed – the new bolt has a locking compound already applied to its threads. However there is nothing to stop you cleaning up the threads on the old bolt and applying a suitable non-permanent thread locking compound on installation.

Installation

8 Fit the new switch onto the sidestand, making sure the pin locates in the hole, and the lug on the stand bracket locates into the cutout in the switch body. Secure the switch with a new or cleaned and threadlocked bolt and tighten it to the torque setting specified at the beginning of the Chapter **(see illustration 22.7)**.

9 Feed the wiring up to its connector, making sure it is correctly routed and secured by any clips.

10 Reconnect the wiring connector and check the operation of the sidestand switch **(see illustration 22.2a or b)**.

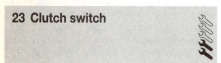

23 Clutch switch

Check

1 The clutch switch is mounted on the front of the master cylinder. The switch is part of the starter interlock safety circuit which prevents or stops the engine running if the transmission is in gear whilst the sidestand is down, and prevents the engine from starting if the transmission is in gear unless the sidestand is up and the clutch lever is pulled in. The switch isn't adjustable.

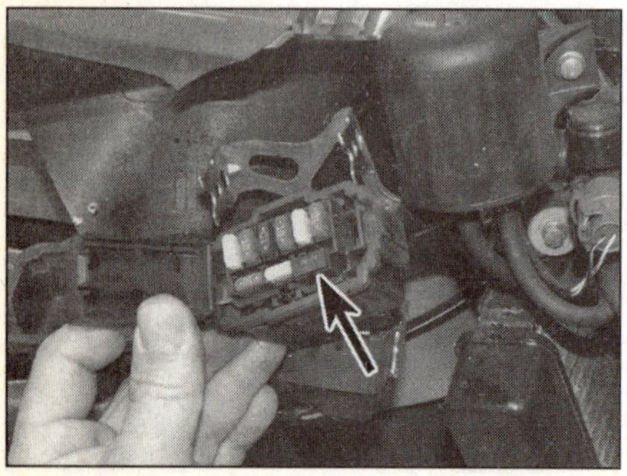
24.2 The diode block (arrowed)

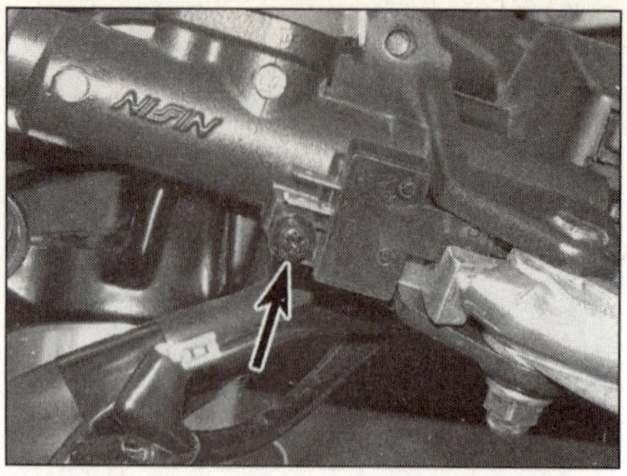
23.6 Clutch switch screw (arrowed)

2 To check the switch, disconnect the wiring connectors from it **(see illustration)**. Connect the probes of an ohmmeter or a continuity tester to the two switch terminals. With the clutch lever pulled in, continuity should be indicated. With the clutch lever out, no continuity (infinite resistance) should be indicated.

3 If the switch is good, check the other components in the starter circuit as described in the relevant sections of this Chapter. If all components are good, check the wiring between the various components (see the wiring diagrams at the end of this Chapter).

Removal and installation

4 The clutch switch is mounted on the front of the master cylinder.

5 Disconnect the wiring connectors from the switch **(see illustration 23.2)**.

6 Undo the single screw securing the switch and remove it, noting how it fits **(see illustration)**.

7 Installation is the reverse of removal. Make sure the switch is correctly located before tightening its screw.

24 Diode block

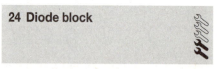

1 The diode block plugs into a connector in the fusebox, which is located behind the fairing left-hand side panel **(see illustration 5.1a or b)**. The diode block contains two diodes which are part of the starter interlock safety circuit that prevents or stops the engine running if the transmission is in gear whilst the sidestand is down, and prevents the engine from starting if the transmission is in gear unless the sidestand is up and the clutch lever is pulled in.

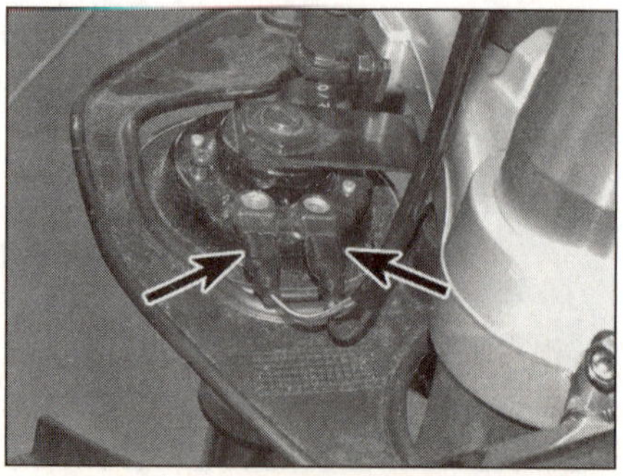
25.2 Disconnect the wiring connectors (arrowed)

2 Remove the fairing left-hand side panel (see Chapter 7), then open the fusebox lid. Pull the diode block out of its socket **(see illustration)**.

3 Using an ohmmeter or continuity tester, connect the positive (+) probe to one of the outer terminals of the diode block and the negative (–) probe to the middle terminal of the block. The diode being tested should show continuity. Now reverse the probes. The diode should show no continuity. Repeat the tests between the other outer terminal and the middle terminal. The same results should be achieved. If it doesn't behave as stated, replace the diode block with a new one.

4 If the diode block is good, push it back into its socket, then check the other components in the starter circuit as described in the relevant sections of this Chapter. If all components are good, check the wiring between the various components (see the wiring diagrams at the end of this Chapter).

25 Horn

Check

1 The horn is mounted under the bottom yoke.

2 Disconnect the wiring connectors from the horn **(see illustration)**. Check them for loose wires. Using two jumper wires, apply voltage from a fully-charged 12V battery directly to the terminals on the horn. If the horn doesn't sound, replace it with a new one.

3 If there is no sound check for voltage at the black wire connector with the ignition ON and the horn button pressed. If voltage is present, check the black/green wire for continuity to earth.

4 If no voltage was present, check the black wire for continuity between the horn and the switch, and the white/green wire from the switch to the fusebox, and then to the ignition switch (see the wiring diagrams at the end of this Chapter). With the ignition switch ON, check that there is voltage at the white/green wire to the horn button in the left-hand switch gear. If there is, the problem lies between the switch and the horn. If there isn't, the problem lies between the ignition switch and the horn switch via the fusebox.

5 If all the wiring and connectors are good, check the button contacts in the switch housing (see Section 20).

25.7 Horn mounting bolt (arrowed)

26.2a Starter relay (arrowed) – RR-4 and RR-5 models

26.2b Starter relay (arrowed) – RR-6 and RR-7 models

Replacement

6 The horn is mounted under the bottom yoke.

7 Unplug the wiring connectors from the horn **(see illustration 25.2)**. Unscrew the bolt securing the horn **(see illustration)**.

8 Install the horn and tighten the bolt. Connect the wiring to the horn. Check that it works.

26 Starter relay

Check

1 If the starter circuit is faulty, first check the fuse (see Section 5).

2 The starter relay is located under the rider's seat **(see illustrations)** – remove the rider's seat (see Chapter 7).

3 Lift the rubber terminal cover and unscrew the bolt securing the starter motor lead, identified by the letter M (the other lead, marked B, is the battery lead) **(see illustrations)**; position the lead away from the relay terminal. With the ignition switch ON, the engine kill switch in the RUN position, and the transmission in neutral, press the starter switch. The relay should be heard to click.

4 If the relay doesn't click, switch off the ignition and remove the relay as described below; test it as follows.

5 Set a multimeter to the ohms x 1 scale and connect it across the relay's starter motor and battery lead terminals. There should be no continuity. Using a fully-charged 12 volt battery and two insulated jumper wires, connect the positive (+) terminal of the battery to the yellow/red wire terminal of the relay, and the negative (–) terminal to the green/red wire terminal of the relay. At this point the relay should be heard to click and the multimeter read 0 ohms (continuity). If this is the case the relay is proved good. If the relay does not click when battery voltage is applied and indicates no continuity (infinite resistance) across its terminals, it is faulty and must be replaced with a new one.

6 If the relay is good, check for continuity in the main lead from the battery to the relay. Also check that the terminals and connectors at each end of the lead are tight and corrosion-free.

7 Next check for battery voltage at the yellow/red wire terminal on the relay wiring connector with the ignition ON, the kill switch in the RUN position and the starter button pressed. If there is no voltage, check the wiring between the relay wiring connector and the starter button.

8 If voltage is present, check that there is continuity to earth in the green/red wire with the transmission in neutral (note that there will be a very slight resistance due to the diodes in the starter interlock circuit. If not check the wiring and connectors between the relay, the fusebox and the neutral switch, then if that is good check the switch itself and the diode block.

9 Now shift the transmission into gear, raise the sidestand and pull the clutch lever in and check for continuity to earth again. If there is no continuity, check the clutch switch and sidestand switch as described in the relevant sections of this Chapter. If all components are good, check the wiring between the various components (see the wiring diagrams at the end of this Chapter).

Replacement

10 The starter relay is located under the rider's seat **(see illustration 26.2a or b)** – remove the rider's seat (see Chapter 7).

11 Disconnect the battery terminals, remembering to disconnect the negative (–) terminal first.

12 Disconnect the relay wiring connector **(see illustration)**. Lift the insulating cover and unscrew the bolts securing the starter motor and battery leads to the relay and detach the leads **(see illustration 26.3a)**. Remove the relay from its rubber sleeve. If the relay is being replaced with a new one, remove the main fuse and its spare from the relay.

13 Installation is the reverse of removal. Connect the lead from the battery to the terminal marked B and the lead from the starter motor to the terminal marked M, and make sure the terminal bolts are securely tightened **(see illustration 26.3b)**. Do not forget to fit the main fuse and its spare into the relay, if removed. Connect the negative (–) lead last when reconnecting the battery.

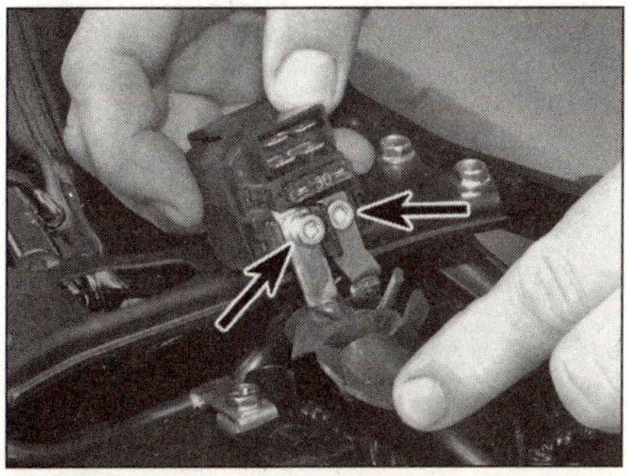

26.3a Lift the rubber cover to access the terminals (arrowed) . . .

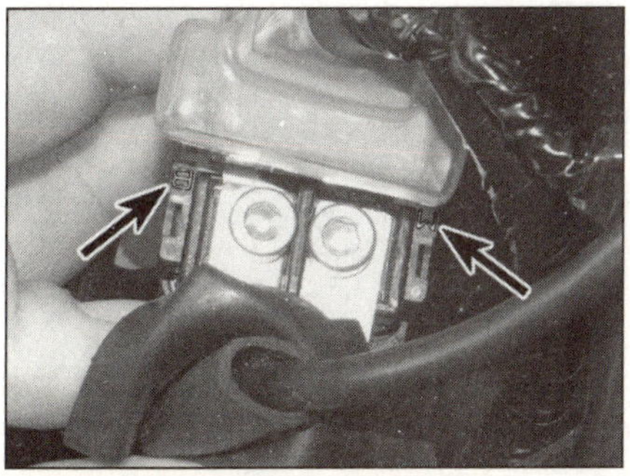

26.3b . . . which are lettered for identification

26.12 Disconnect the wiring connector

27.4 Pull back the terminal cover then unscrew the nut (arrowed) and detach the lead

27.5a Unscrew the two bolts (arrowed), noting the earth lead . . .

27 Starter motor removal and installation

Removal

1 Remove the rider's seat (see Chapter 7). Disconnect the battery negative (–) lead. The starter motor is mounted on the crankcase behind the cylinders.

2 Raise or remove the fuel tank (see Chapter 4).

3 On RR-6 and RR-7 models disconnect the speed sensor wiring connector **(see illustration 16.9b)**. Release the starter motor and earth cables from the wiring harness guide, then detach the guide from its clip and from the frame **(see illustrations 16.23a, b and c)**.

4 Peel back the rubber terminal cover on the starter motor **(see illustration)**. Unscrew the nut securing the starter lead to the motor and detach the lead.

5 Unscrew the two bolts securing the starter motor to the crankcase, noting the earth lead secured by the rear bolt, and on RR-6 and RR-7 models the harness guide clip secured by both bolts **(see illustration)**. Slide the starter motor out and remove it **(see illustration)**.

6 Remove the O-ring on the end of the starter motor and discard it as a new one must be used **(see illustration 27.7)**.

Installation

7 Fit a new O-ring onto the end of the starter motor, making sure it is seated in its groove **(see illustration)**. Apply a smear of engine oil to the O-ring.

8 Manoeuvre the motor into position and slide it into the crankcase **(see illustration 27.5b)**. Ensure that the starter motor teeth mesh correctly with those of the starter idle/reduction gear. Install the mounting bolts, not forgetting the wiring harness guide clip on RR-6 and RR-7 models, and on all models to secure the earth lead with the rear bolt, and tighten them **(see illustration 27.5a)**.

9 Connect the starter lead to the motor and secure it with the nut **(see illustration 27.4)**. Fit the rubber cover over the terminal.

10 On RR-6 and RR-7 models fit the wiring harness guide into the frame and onto its clip **(see illustrations 16.23c and b)**. Fit the starter motor and earth cables into the guide **(see illustration 16.23a)**. Connect the speed sensor wiring connector **(see illustration 16.9b)**.

11 Install the fuel tank (see Chapter 4).

12 Connect the battery negative (–) lead and install the rider's seat (see Chapter 7).

28 Starter motor overhaul

Check

1 Remove the starter motor (see Section 27). Cover the body in some rag and clamp the motor in a soft-jawed vice – do not overtighten it.

2 Using a fully-charged 12 volt battery and two insulated jumper wires, connect the positive (+) terminal of the battery to the protruding terminal on the starter motor, and the negative (–) terminal to one of the motor's mounting lugs. At this point the starter motor should spin. If this is the case the motor is proved good, though it is worth disassembling it and checking it if you suspect it of not working properly under load.

Disassembly

3 Remove the starter motor (see Section 27).

4 Note any alignment marks between the main housing and the front and rear covers, or make your own if they aren't clear **(see illustration)**.

5 Unscrew the two long bolts, noting the

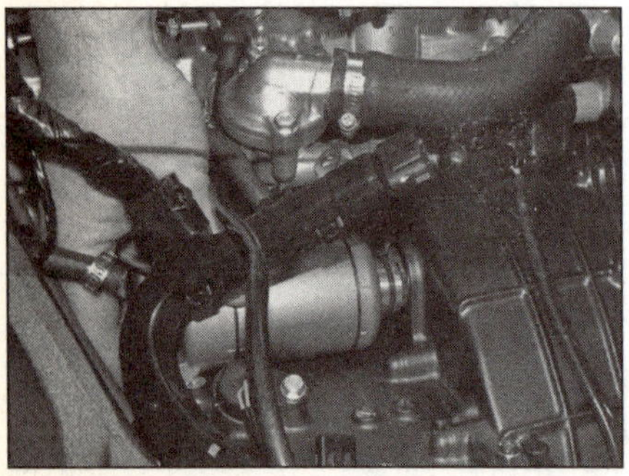

27.5b . . . and remove the starter motor

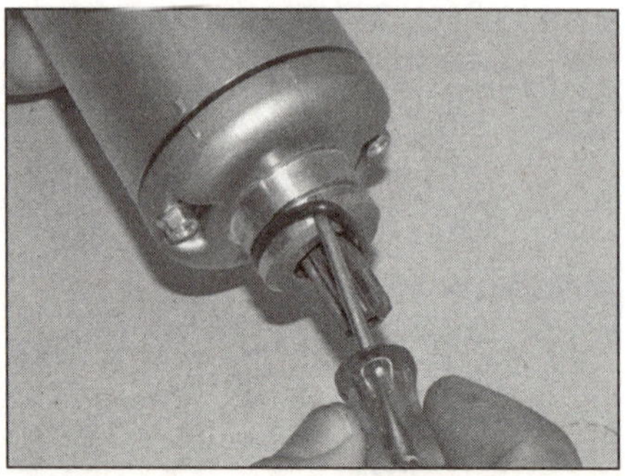

27.7 Fit a new O-ring and lubricate it

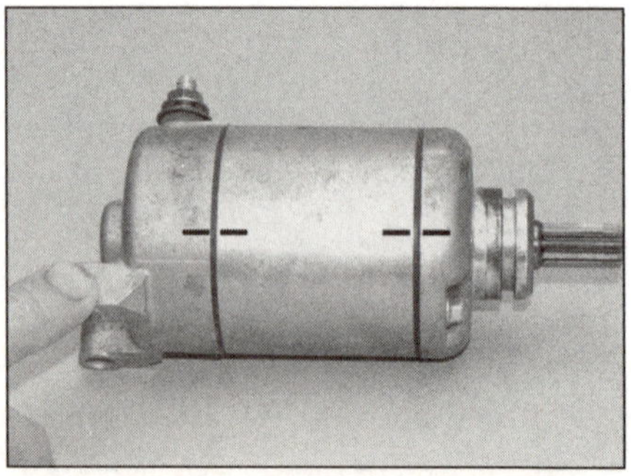

28.4 Note the alignment marks between the housing and the covers

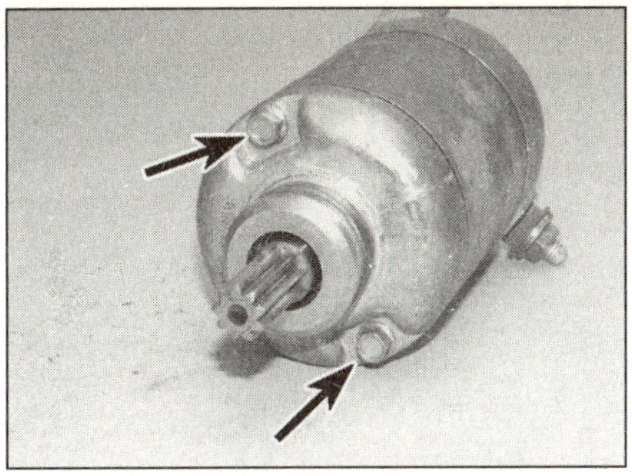

28.5a Unscrew and remove the two bolts (arrowed) . . .

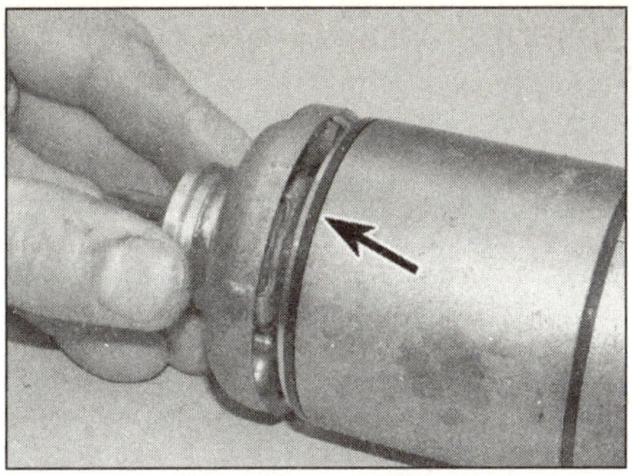

28.5b . . . then remove the front cover and sealing ring (arrowed)

28.5c Remove the tabbed washer . . .

O-rings, then remove the front cover from the motor along with its sealing ring **(see illustrations)**. Discard the sealing ring as a new one must be used. Remove the tabbed washer from the cover and slide the insulating washer and shim(s) from the front end of the armature, noting the number of shims and their correct fitted order **(see illustrations)**.

6 Remove the rear cover from the motor along with its sealing ring **(see illustration)**. Discard the sealing ring as a new one must be used. Remove the shim(s) from the rear end of the armature noting how many are fitted **(see illustration 28.21a)**.

7 Withdraw the armature from the main housing noting that there will some resistance from the pull of the magnets set in the housing.

8 At this stage check for continuity between the terminal bolt and the brush on the insulated base – there should be continuity (zero resistance) **(see illustration)**. Check for continuity between the terminal bolt and the cover – there should be no continuity (infinite resistance) **(see illustration)**. Also check for continuity between the uninsulated brush and the brushplate – there should be continuity (zero resistance). If there is no continuity when there should be or *vice versa*, identify the faulty component and replace it with a new one.

9 Noting the correct fitted location of each component, unscrew the nut from the terminal bolt and remove the plain washer, the one large and two small insulating washers **(see illustration)**. Remove the brushplate assembly and terminal bolt from the main housing, noting how it locates **(see illustration)**. Remove the O-ring and the insulator from the bolt **(see illustration)**.

28.5d . . . and the insulating washer and shim(s)

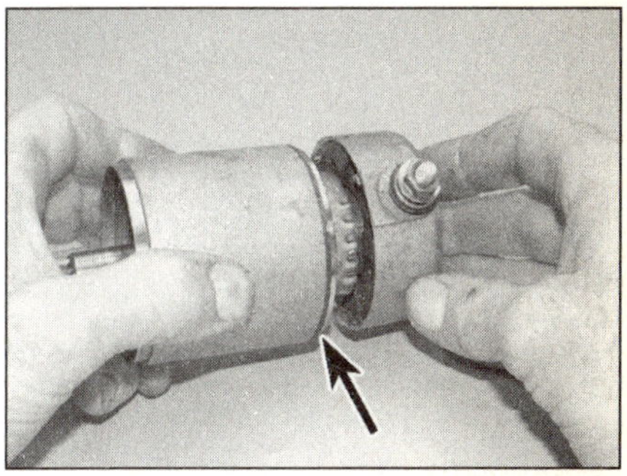

28.6 Remove the rear cover and its sealing ring (arrowed)

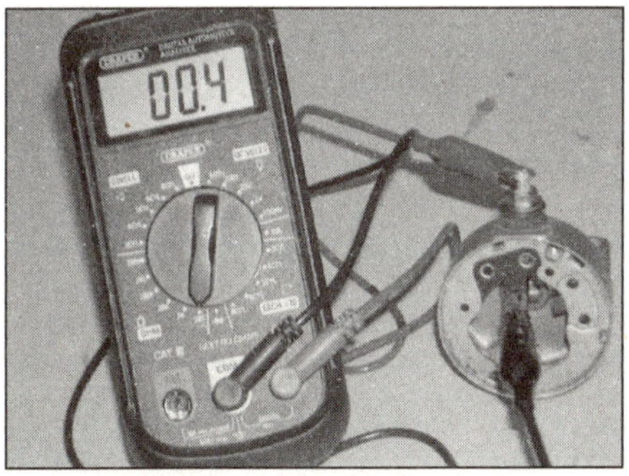

28.8a Check for continuity between the terminal and its brush . . .

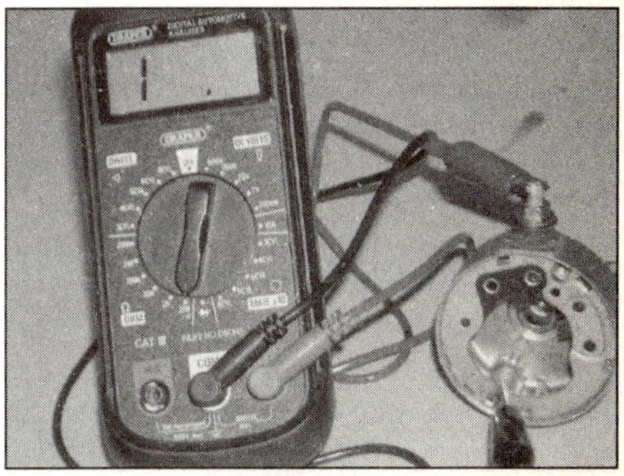

28.8b . . . and between the terminal and the cover

28.9a Unscrew the nut (arrowed) and remove the plain washer and the large and small insulating washers

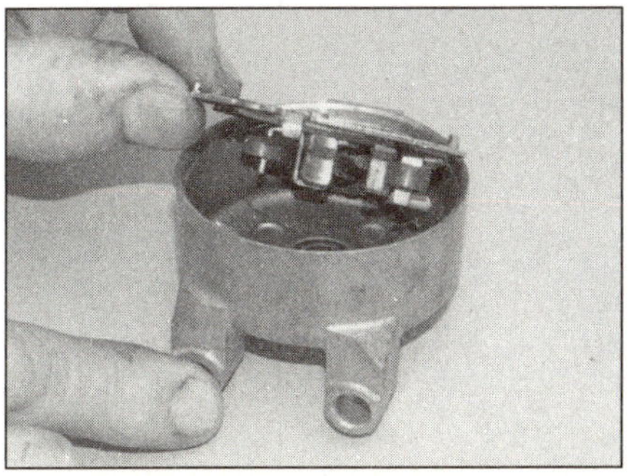

28.9b Remove the brushplate assembly . . .

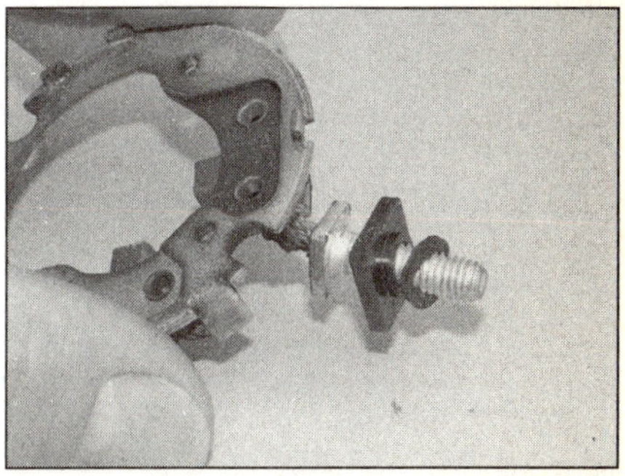

28.9c . . . then remove the O-ring and the insulator

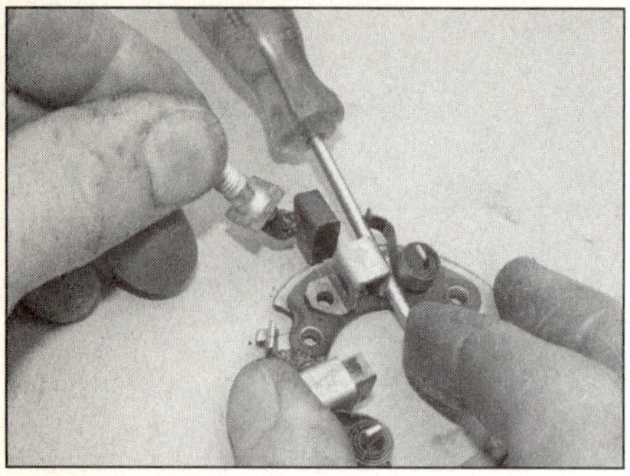

28.10 Move the brush springs aside and slide the brushes out

28.13b . . . and no continuity between the bars and the shaft

10 Move each brush spring end aside and slide the brushes out **(see illustration)**.

Inspection

11 The parts of the starter motor that are most likely to require attention are the brushes. Measure the length of each brush and compare the results to the length listed in this Chapter's Specifications **(see illustration)**. If either of the brushes are worn beyond the service limit, fit a new brush and brushplate assembly. If the brushes are not worn excessively, nor cracked, chipped, or otherwise damaged, they may be reused.

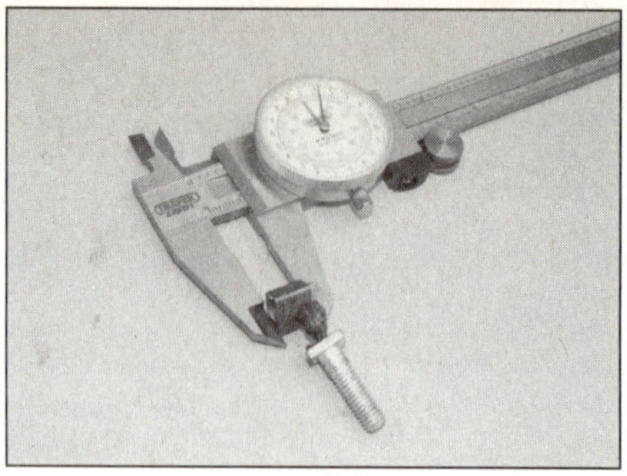

28.11 Measure the length of each brush

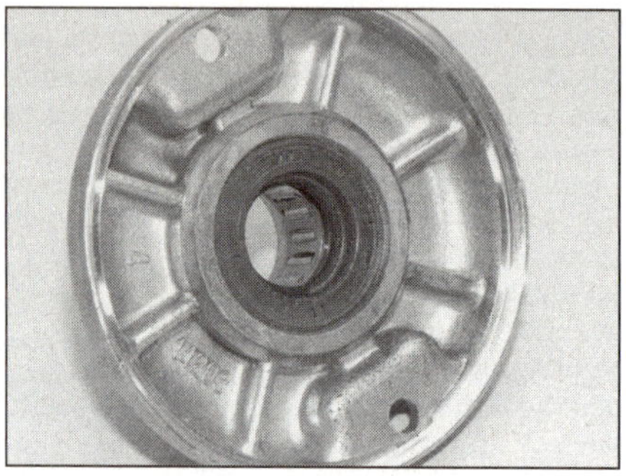

28.15a Check the bearing and seal in the front cover . . .

12 Inspect the commutator bars on the armature for scoring, scratches and discoloration. The commutator can be cleaned and polished with crocus cloth, but do not use sandpaper or emery paper. After cleaning, wipe away any residue with a cloth soaked in electrical system cleaner or denatured alcohol.

13 Using an ohmmeter or a continuity test light, check for continuity between the commutator bars **(see illustration)**. Continuity should exist between each bar and all of the others. Also, check for continuity between the commutator bars and the armature shaft **(see illustration)**. There should be no continuity

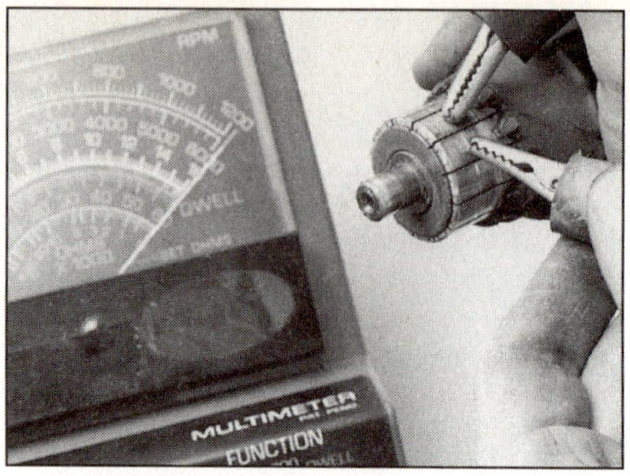

28.13a There should be continuity between the bars . . .

(infinite resistance) between the commutator and the shaft. If the checks indicate otherwise, the armature is defective and a new starter motor must be obtained – the armature is not available separately.

14 Check the front end of the armature shaft for worn, cracked, chipped and broken teeth. If the shaft is damaged or worn, a new starter motor must be obtained – the armature is not available separately.

15 Inspect the front and rear covers for signs of cracks or wear. Check the oil seal and the needle bearing in the front cover and the bush in the rear cover for wear and damage – the seal, bearing, bush and covers are not listed as being available separately so if necessary a new starter motor must be fitted **(see illustrations)**.

16 Inspect the magnets in the main housing and the housing itself for cracks.

17 Inspect the insulating washers, O-ring, and sealing rings for signs of damage, deformation and deterioration and replace them with new ones if necessary.

Reassembly

18 Slide the brushes back into position in their housings and locate the brush spring ends onto the outer ends of the brushes **(see illustration)**.

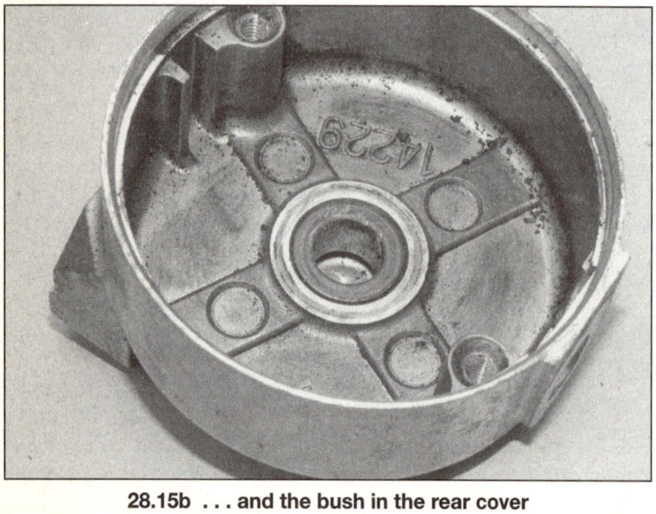

28.15b . . . and the bush in the rear cover

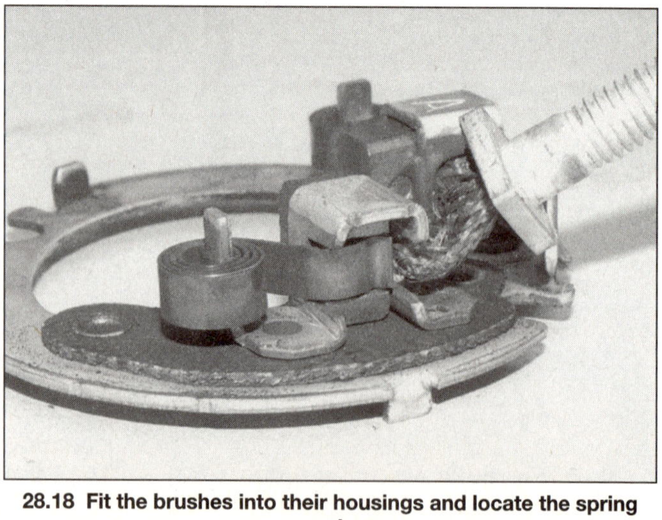

28.18 Fit the brushes into their housings and locate the spring ends

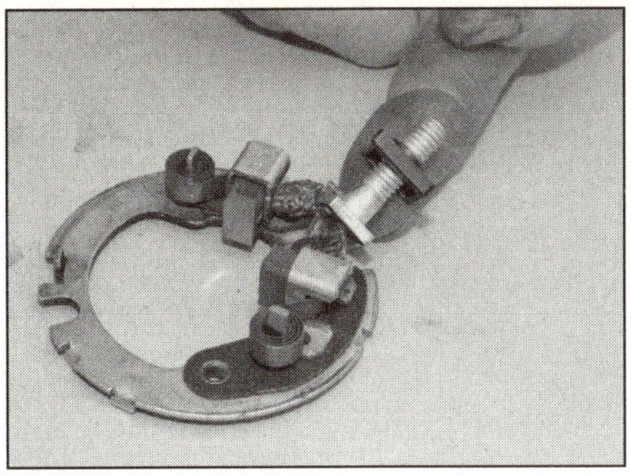

28.19a Fit the insulator onto the bolt . . .

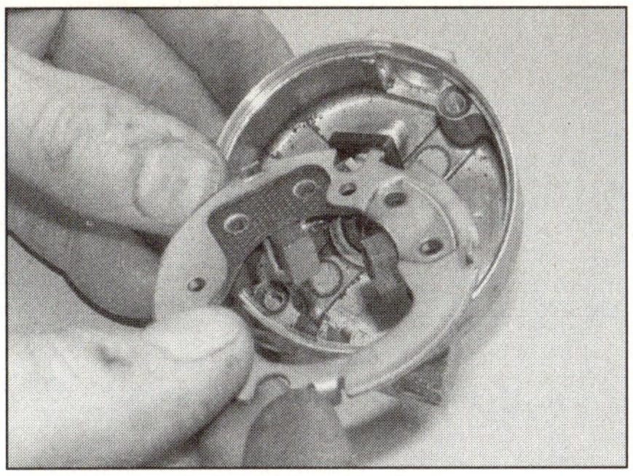

28.19b . . . fit the brushplate into the rear cover . . .

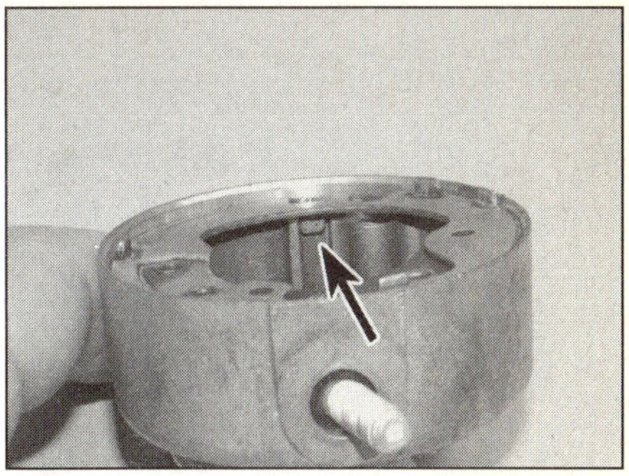

28.19c . . . locating the tab in the groove (arrowed)

19 Fit the insulator onto the terminal bolt **(see illustration)**. Insert the terminal bolt through its hole in the rear cover then fit the brushplate into the cover, making sure its tab is correctly located in the groove in the cover **(see illustration)**. Fit the O-ring down over the bolt and press it into place between the bolt and the cover **(see illustrations)**. Slide the small insulating washers onto the terminal bolt, followed by the large insulating washer and the plain washer **(see illustration 28.9a)**. Fit the nut onto the terminal bolt and tighten it securely.

20 At this stage check again for continuity between the terminal bolt and the brush on the insulated base – there should be continuity (zero resistance) **(see illustration 28.8a)**. Check for continuity between the terminal bolt and the cover – there should be no continuity (infinite resistance) **(see illustration 28.8b)**. Also check for continuity between the uninsulated brush and the brushplate – there should be continuity (zero resistance). If there is no continuity when there should be or *vice versa*, identify the faulty component and replace it with a new one.

21 Fit the shim(s) onto the rear of the armature shaft **(see illustration)**. Apply a smear of grease to the end of the shaft. Insert the armature into the brushplate at an angle so that the brushes locate against the commutator, then straighten the armature, pushing the brushes back into their housings against the springs, and slide it into the rear cover so that the shaft end locates in its bush **(see illustration)**.

22 Fit the sealing ring onto the rear of the main housing **(see illustration)**. Grasp both the armature and the rear cover in one hand and hold them together – this will prevent the armature being drawn out by the magnets in the housing. Note however that you should take care not to let the housing be drawn forcibly onto the armature by the magnets. Carefully allow the housing to be drawn onto the armature, making sure the end with the cut-out faces the rear cover and aligns with the brushplate outer tab **(see illustrations)** – aligning the marks between the cover and housing will help (see Step 4).

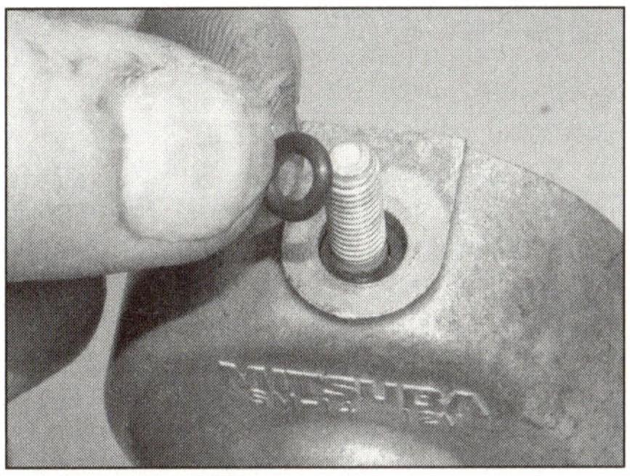

28.19d Fit the O-ring over the bolt . . .

28.19e . . . then slide it down and press it into place

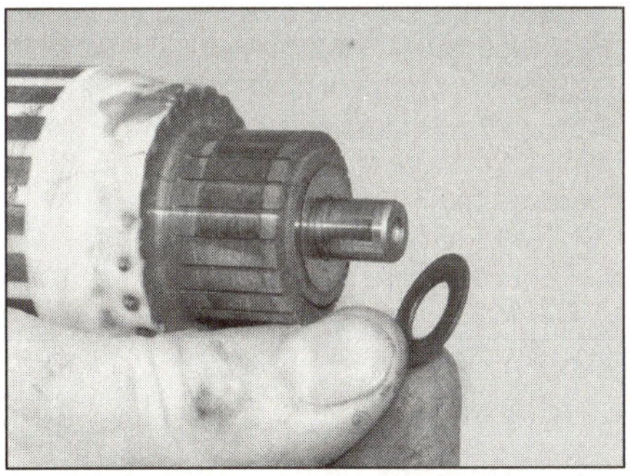

28.21a Fit the shim(s) onto the shaft . . .

28.21b . . . then fit the armature into the rear cover making sure the brushes locate correctly onto the commutator

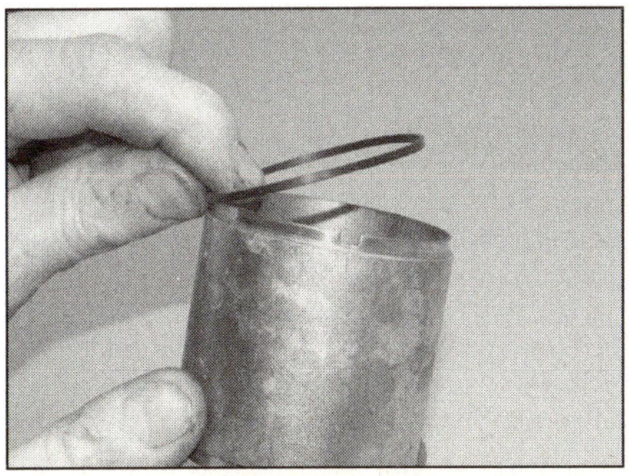

28.22a Fit a new sealing ring onto the rear of the housing . . .

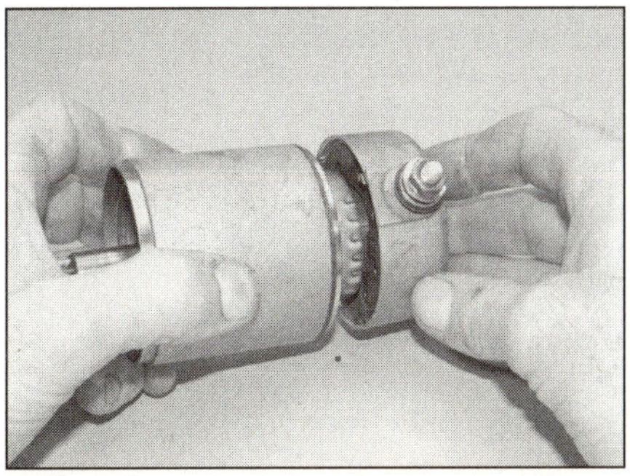

28.22b . . . then fit the housing onto the armature . . .

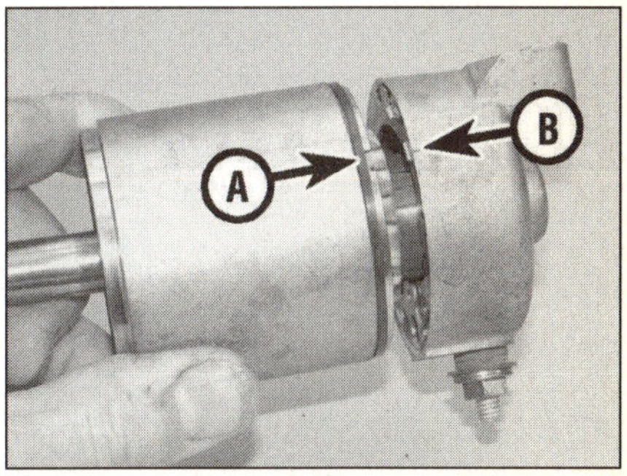

28.22c . . . locating the cut-out (A) over the tab (B)

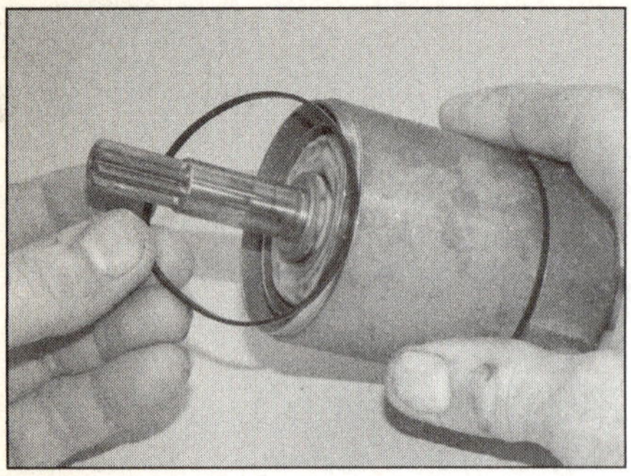

28.24 Fit a new sealing ring onto the front of the housing

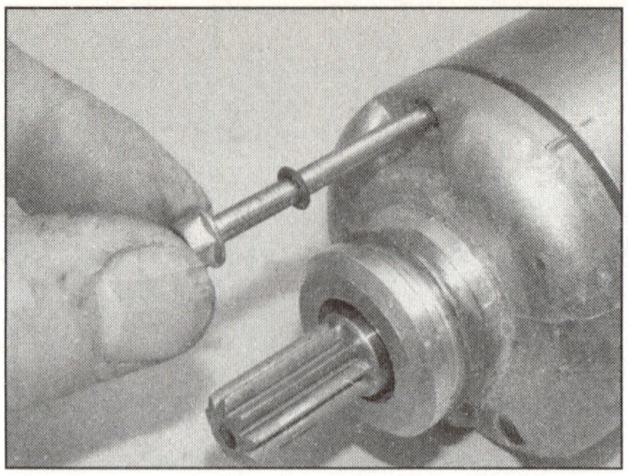

28.25 Fit the long bolts with their O-rings

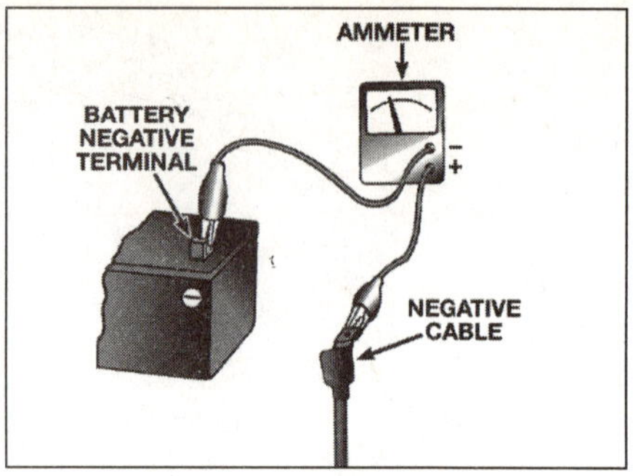

29.5 Checking the charging system leakage rate – connect the meter as shown

23 Apply a smear of grease to the front cover oil seal lip. Fit the tabbed washer into the cover so that its teeth are correctly located between the cover ribs **(see illustration 28.5c)**.

24 Fit the sealing ring onto the front of the housing **(see illustration)**. Slide the shim(s) onto the front end of the armature shaft then fit the insulating washer **(see illustration 28.5d)**. Slide the front cover into position, aligning the marks made on removal **(see illustration 28.5b)**.

25 Check the marks made on removal are correctly aligned then fit the long bolts, not forgetting the O-rings (using new ones if necessary) and tighten them **(see illustration)**.

26 Install the starter motor (see Section 27).

29 Charging system testing

1 If the performance of the charging system is suspect, the system as a whole should be checked first, followed by testing of the individual components. **Note:** *Before beginning the checks, make sure the battery is fully charged and that all system connections are clean and tight.*

2 Checking the output of the charging system and the performance of the various components within the charging system requires the use of a multimeter (with voltage, current, resistance checking facilities). If a multimeter is not available, the job of checking the charging system should be left to a Honda dealer.

3 When making the checks, follow the procedures carefully to prevent incorrect connections or short circuits resulting in irreparable damage to electrical system components.

Leakage test

Caution: Always connect an ammeter in series, never in parallel with the battery, otherwise it will be damaged. Do not turn the ignition ON or operate the starter motor when the ammeter is connected – a sudden surge in current will blow the meter's fuse.

4 Ensure the ignition is OFF, then remove the rider's seat and disconnect the battery negative (-) lead (see Section 3).

5 Set the multimeter to the Amps function and connect its negative (-) probe to the battery negative (-) terminal, and positive (+) probe to the disconnected negative (-) lead **(see illustration)**. Always set the meter to a high amps range initially and then bring it down to the mA (milli Amps) range; if there is a high current flow in the circuit it may blow the meter's fuse.

6 Battery current leakage should not exceed the maximum limit (see Specifications). If a higher leakage rate is shown there is a short circuit in the wiring, although if an after-market immobiliser or alarm is fitted, its current draw should be taken into account. Disconnect the meter and reconnect the battery negative (-) lead.

7 If leakage is indicated, refer to Wiring Diagrams at the end of this Chapter to systematically disconnect individual electrical components and repeat the test until the source is identified.

Output test

8 Remove the rider's seat (see Chapter 7), then start the engine and warm it up.

9 To check the regulated (DC) voltage output, allow the engine to idle with the headlight main beam (HI) turned ON. Connect a multimeter set to the 0-20 volts DC scale across the terminals of the battery with the positive (+) meter probe to battery positive (+) terminal and the negative (-) meter probe to battery negative (-) terminal (see Section 3).

10 Slowly increase the engine speed to 5000 rpm and note the reading obtained. Compare the result with the Specification at the beginning of this Chapter. If the regulated voltage output is outside the specification, check the alternator and the regulator/rectifier (see Sections 30 and 31).

HAYNES HiNT ***Clues to a faulty regulator are constantly blowing bulbs, with brightness varying considerably with engine speed, and battery overheating.***

30 Alternator

Check

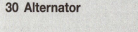

1 Remove the left-hand fairing side panel (see Chapter 7).

2 Release the wiring boot cable tie. Disconnect the white 3-pin alternator wiring connector with the three yellow wires **(see illustrations)**. Check the connector terminals for corrosion and security.

3 Using a multimeter set to the ohms x 1 (ohmmeter) scale measure the resistance between each of the yellow wires on the alternator side of the connector, taking a total of three readings, then check for continuity between each terminal and ground (earth). If the stator coil windings are in good condition

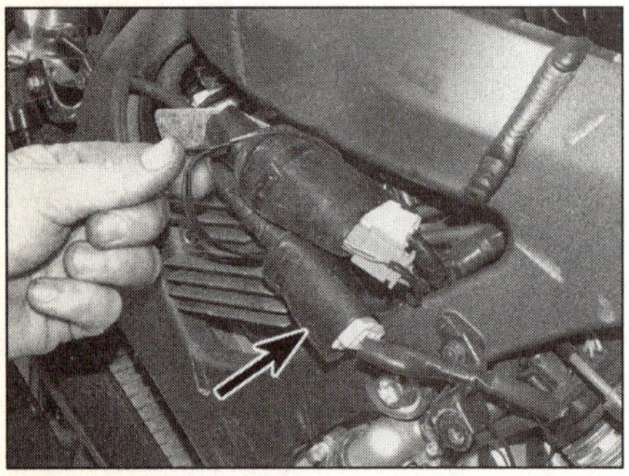

30.2a Alternator wiring connector – RR-4 and RR-5 models

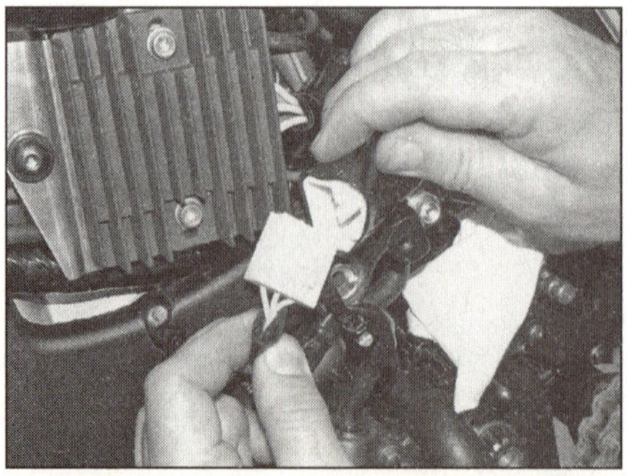

30.2b Disconnecting the alternator wiring connector – RR-6 and RR-7 models

30.7 Alternator cover bolts (arrowed)

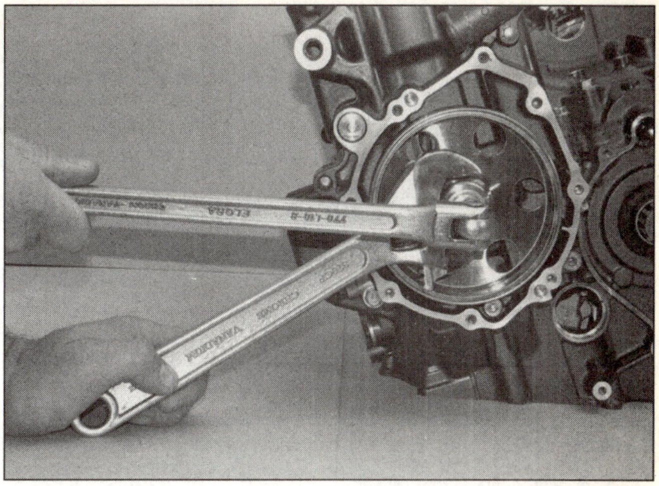

30.8 Using a spanner to hold the rotor while unscrewing the bolt

the three readings should be within the range shown in the Specifications at the start of this Chapter, and there should be no continuity (infinite resistance) between any of the terminals and ground (earth). If not, the alternator stator coil assembly is at fault and should be replaced with a new one. **Note:** *Before condemning the stator coils, check the fault is not due to damaged wiring between the connector and the coils.*

Removal

Special tool: *A centre-bolt type rotor puller will be required to remove the rotor from the crankshaft (see Step 9).*

4 Remove the lower fairing and the fairing left-hand side panel (see Chapter 7).

5 Either drain the engine oil (see Chapter 1), or place a container under the engine to catch the oil that will come out when the alternator cover is removed. If you have an auxiliary stand place the bike on it so that it is level – this minimises oil loss. If you do not have an auxiliary stand it is best to drain the oil.

6 Release the wiring boot cable tie. Disconnect the white 3-pin alternator wiring connector with the three yellow wires **(see illustration 30.2a or b)**. Feed the wiring down to the alternator cover, releasing it from any ties and noting its routing.

7 Working in a criss-cross pattern, evenly slacken the alternator cover bolts **(see illustration)**. Draw the cover off the engine, noting that it will be restrained by the force of the rotor magnets, and be prepared to catch any residual oil. Remove the dowels from either the cover or the crankcase if they are loose.

8 To remove the rotor bolt it is necessary to stop the rotor from turning using either a commercially available rotor strap, or by counter-holding the flats on the rotor boss using a suitable, preferably offset, spanner **(see illustration)**. Unscrew the bolt. Note the washer fitted with the bolt.

9 To remove the rotor from the shaft it is necessary to use a centre-bolt type rotor puller; either the Honda service tool Pt. No. 07733-0020001 or an aftermarket alternative – do not attempt removal using a legged puller. Thread the rotor puller into the centre of the rotor and turn it until the rotor is displaced from the shaft, holding the rotor to prevent the engine turning **(see illustrations)**.

10 To remove the stator from the cover, unscrew its bolts, and the bolt securing the wiring clamp, then remove the assembly, noting how the rubber wiring grommet fits **(see illustration)**.

30.9a Thread the puller into the rotor . . .

30.9b . . . then hold the rotor and turn the puller, using a bar for leverage

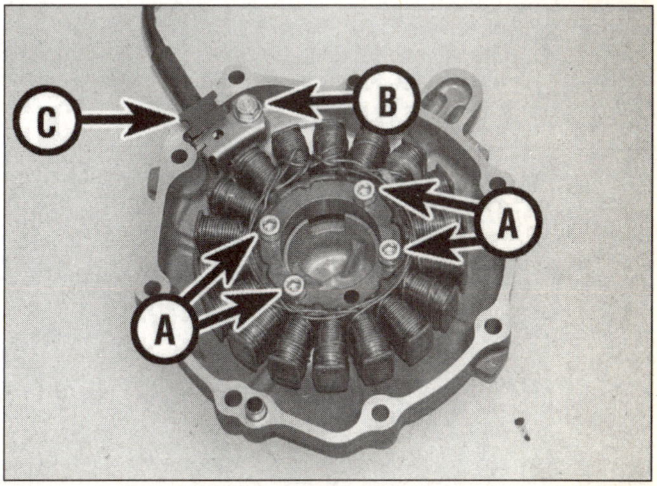

30.10 Unscrew the stator bolts (A) and the wiring clamp bolt (B) and free the grommet (C)

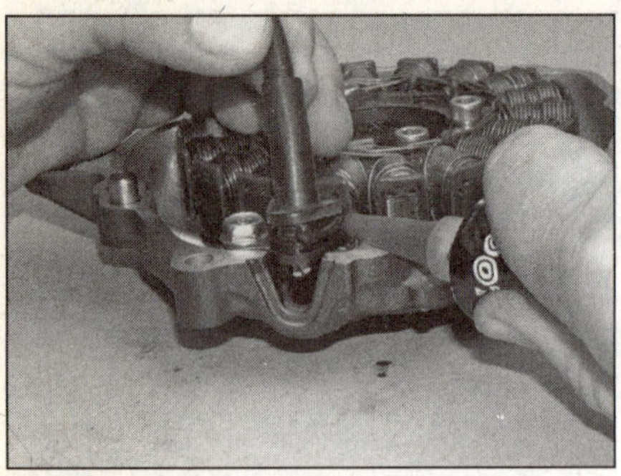
30.11 Apply sealant to the grommet

30.13 Slide the rotor onto the shaft

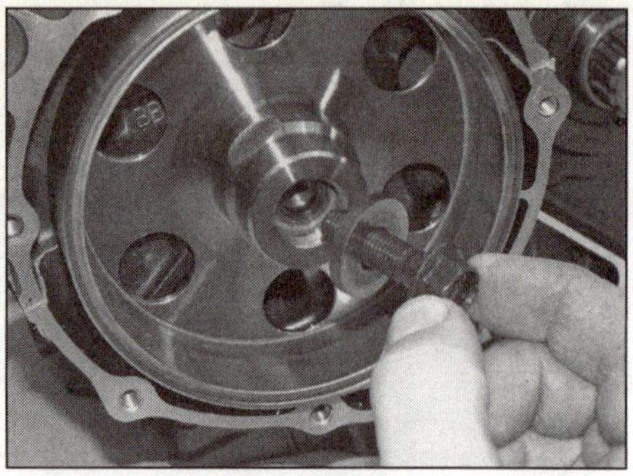
30.14a Lubricate the bolt then install it with its washer . . .

30.14b . . . and tighten it to the specified torque

30.15a Apply sealant to the mating surface

Installation

11 Fit the stator into the cover, aligning the rubber wiring grommet with the groove **(see illustration 30.10)**. Install the bolts and tighten them to the torque setting specified at the beginning of the Chapter. Apply a suitable sealant to the wiring grommet, then press it into the cut-out in the cover **(see illustration)**. Secure the wiring with its clamp and tighten the bolt.

12 Clean the tapered end of the crankshaft and the corresponding mating surface on the inside of the rotor with a suitable solvent.

13 Make sure that no metal objects have attached themselves to the magnet on the inside of the rotor. Slide the rotor onto the shaft **(see illustration)**.

14 Apply some clean oil to the rotor bolt threads and the underside of the head **(see illustration)**. Install the rotor bolt with its washer and tighten it to the torque setting specified at the beginning of the Chapter, using the method employed on removal to prevent the rotor from turning **(see illustration)**.

15 Apply a smear of suitable sealant to the mating surface of the alternator cover **(see illustration)**. Fit the dowels into the cover or crankcase if removed **(see illustration)**. Install the alternator cover, noting that the rotor magnets will forcibly draw the cover/stator on, making sure the dowels locate **(see illustration)**. Tighten the cover bolts evenly in a criss-cross sequence.

16 Reconnect the wiring at the connector and secure it in the boot **(see illustration 30.2a or b)**.

17 Fill the engine with the correct quantity of oil, or top it up to the correct level, according to your removal method (see Chapter 1 and *Pre-ride checks*). Install the fairing side panel and lower fairing (see Chapter 7).

31 Regulator/rectifier

Check

1 Remove the fairing left-hand side panel (see Chapter 7).

2 Release the wiring boot cable tie. Disconnect the regulator/rectifier wiring connectors **(see**

30.15b Make sure the dowels (arrowed) are in place . . .

30.15c . . . then fit the cover

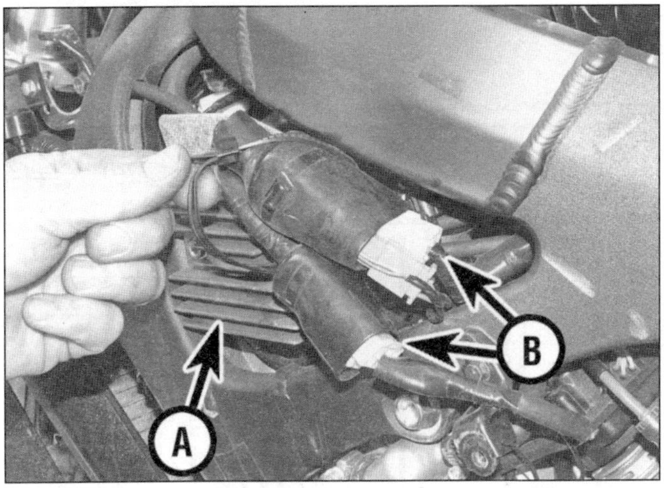

31.2a Regulator/rectifier (A) and its wiring connectors (B) – RR-4 and RR-5 models

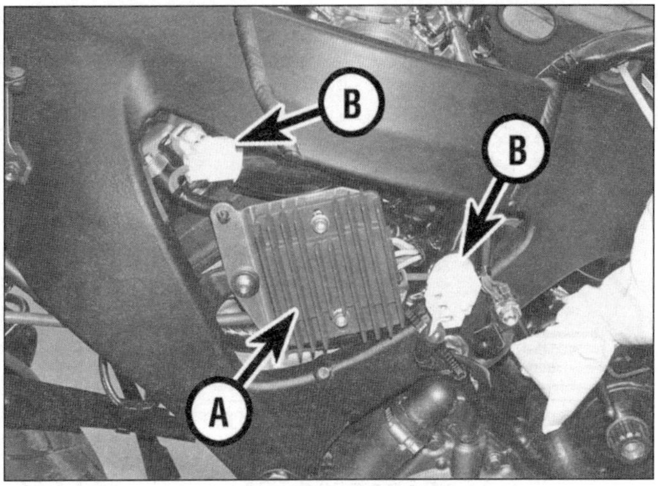

31.2b Regulator/rectifier (A) and its wiring connectors (B) – RR-6 and RR-7 models

illustrations). Check the connector terminals for corrosion and security.

3 Set the multimeter to the 0 to 20 dc volts setting. Connect the meter positive (+) probe to the red wire terminal on the loom side of the connector and the negative (–) probe to a suitable ground (earth) and check for voltage. Full battery voltage should be present at all times.

4 Switch the multimeter to the resistance (ohms) scale. Check for continuity between the green wire terminal on the loom side of the connector and ground (earth). There should be continuity to earth.

5 Set the multimeter to the ohms x 1 (ohmmeter) scale and measure the resistance between each of the yellow wires on the alternator side of the connector, taking a total of three readings, then check for continuity between each terminal and ground (earth). The three readings should be within the range shown in the Specifications for the alternator stator coil at the start of this Chapter, and there should be no continuity (infinite resistance) between any of the terminals and ground (earth).

6 If the above checks do not provide the expected results check the wiring and connectors between the battery, regulator/rectifier and alternator for shorts, breaks, and loose or corroded terminals (see the wiring diagrams at the end of this chapter).

7 If the wiring checks out, the regulator/rectifier unit is probably faulty. Honda provide no test data for the unit itself. Take it to a Honda dealer for confirmation of its condition before replacing it with a new one.

Removal and installation

8 Remove the left-hand fairing side panel (see Chapter 7).

9 Release the wiring boot cable tie. Disconnect the regulator/rectifier wiring connectors **(see illustration 31.2a or b)**.

10 Unscrew the two bolts securing the regulator/rectifier to the frame and remove it, along with its heat shield on RR-4 and RR-5 models.

11 Fit the new unit and tighten its bolts. Connect the wiring connectors and secure them in the rubber boots.

12 Install the fairing side panel (see Chapter 7).

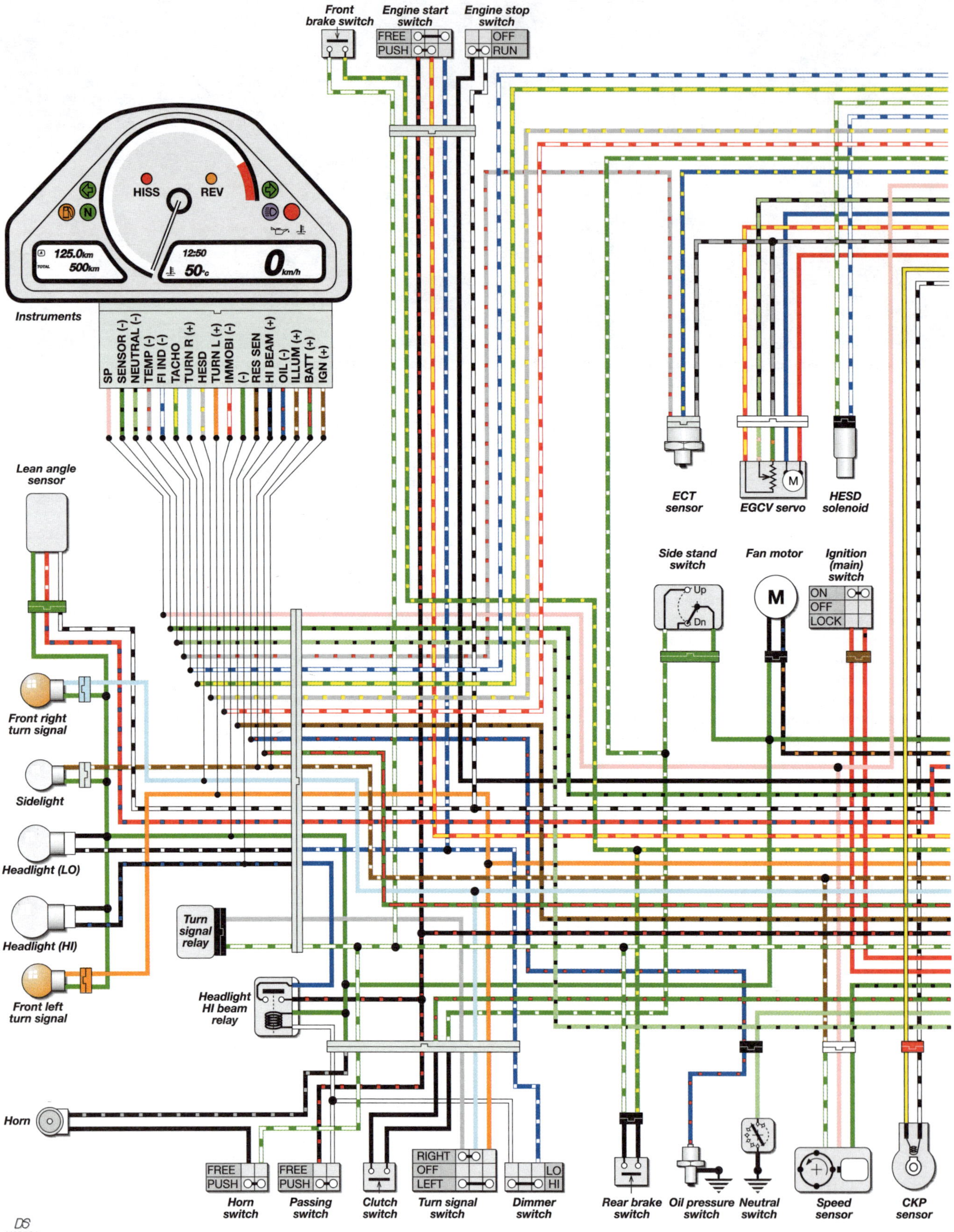
Front brake switch
Engine start switch
FREE
PUSH
Engine stop switch
OFF
RUN
HISS
REV
N
125.0km
TOTAL
500km
12:50
50°c
0km/h
Instruments
SP
SENSOR (-)
NEUTRAL (-)
TEMP (-)
FI IND (-)
TACHO
TURN R (+)
HESD
TURN L (+)
IMMOBI (-)
(-)
RES SEN
HI BEAM (+)
OIL (-)
ILLUM (+)
BATT (+)
IGN (+)
ECT sensor
EGCV servo
M
HESD solenoid
Lean angle sensor
Side stand switch
Up
Dn
Fan motor
M
Ignition (main) switch
ON
OFF
LOCK
Front right turn signal
Sidelight
Headlight (LO)
Headlight (HI)
Turn signal relay
Front left turn signal
Headlight HI beam relay
Horn
FREE
PUSH
Horn switch
FREE
PUSH
Passing switch
Clutch switch
RIGHT
OFF
LEFT
Turn signal switch
LO
HI
Dimmer switch
Rear brake switch
Oil pressure switch
Neutral switch
Speed sensor
CKP sensor
H33501

Europe CBR1000 RR-4 and RR-5

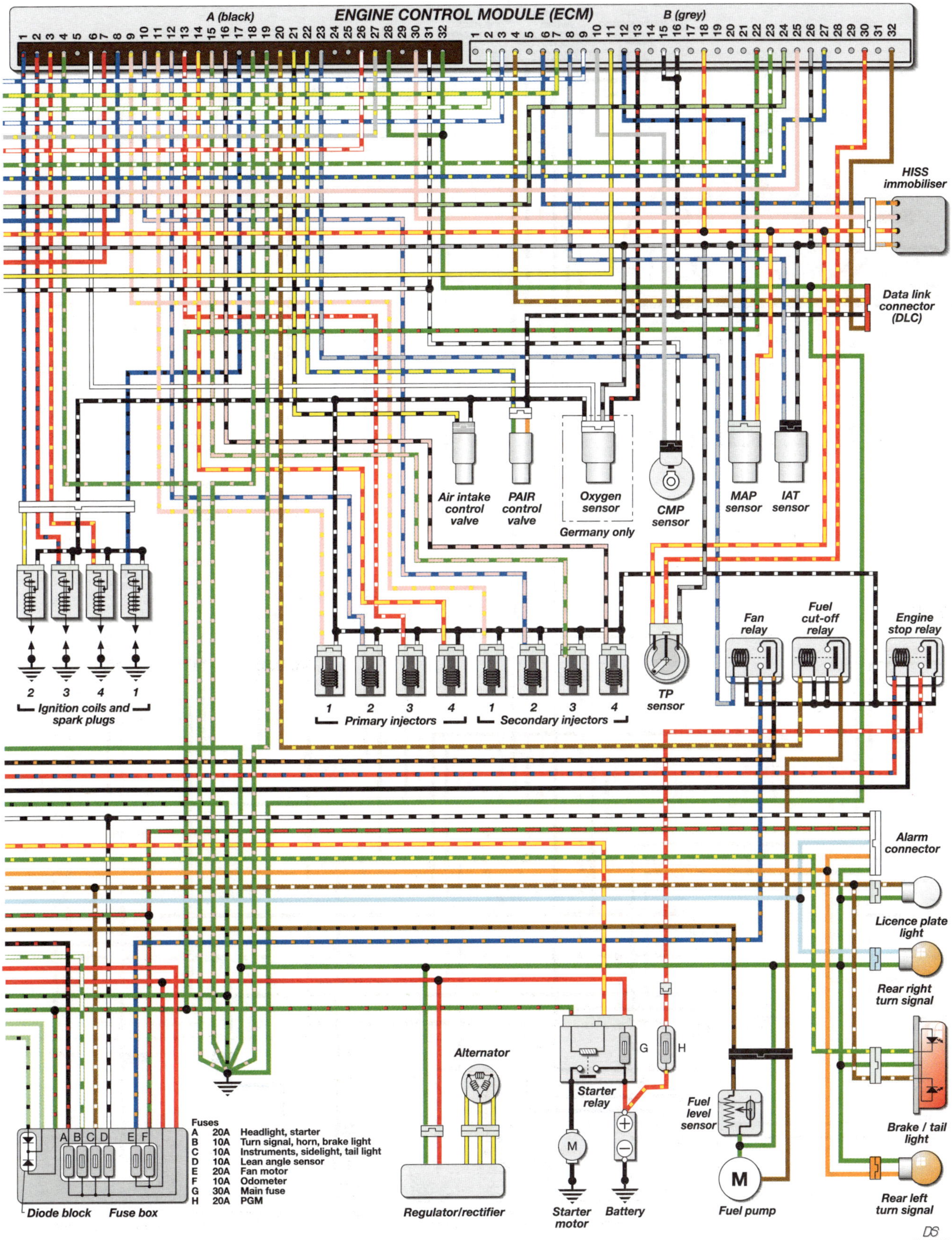
ENGINE CONTROL MODULE (ECM)
A (black)
B (grey)
1 2 3 4 5 6 7 8 9 10 11 12 13 14 15 16 17 18 19 20 21 22 23 24 25 26 27 28 29 30 31 32
1 2 3 4 5 6 7 8 9 10 11 12 13 14 15 16 17 18 19 20 21 22 23 24 25 26 27 28 29 30 31 32
HISS immobiliser
Data link connector (DLC)
Air intake control valve
PAIR control valve
Oxygen sensor
Germany only
CMP sensor
MAP sensor
IAT sensor
2 3 4 1
Ignition coils and spark plugs
1 2 3 4
Primary injectors
1 2 3 4
Secondary injectors
TP sensor
Fan relay
Fuel cut-off relay
Engine stop relay
Alarm connector
Licence plate light
Rear right turn signal
Brake / tail light
Rear left turn signal
Alternator
G
H
Starter relay
Fuel level sensor
M
Fuel pump
Regulator/rectifier
Starter motor
Battery
A B C D E F
Diode block
Fuse box
Fuses
A 20A Headlight, starter
B 10A Turn signal, horn, brake light
C 10A Instruments, sidelight, tail light
D 10A Lean angle sensor
E 20A Fan motor
F 10A Odometer
G 30A Main fuse
H 20A PGM
H33502

Europe CBR1000 RR-4 and RR-5

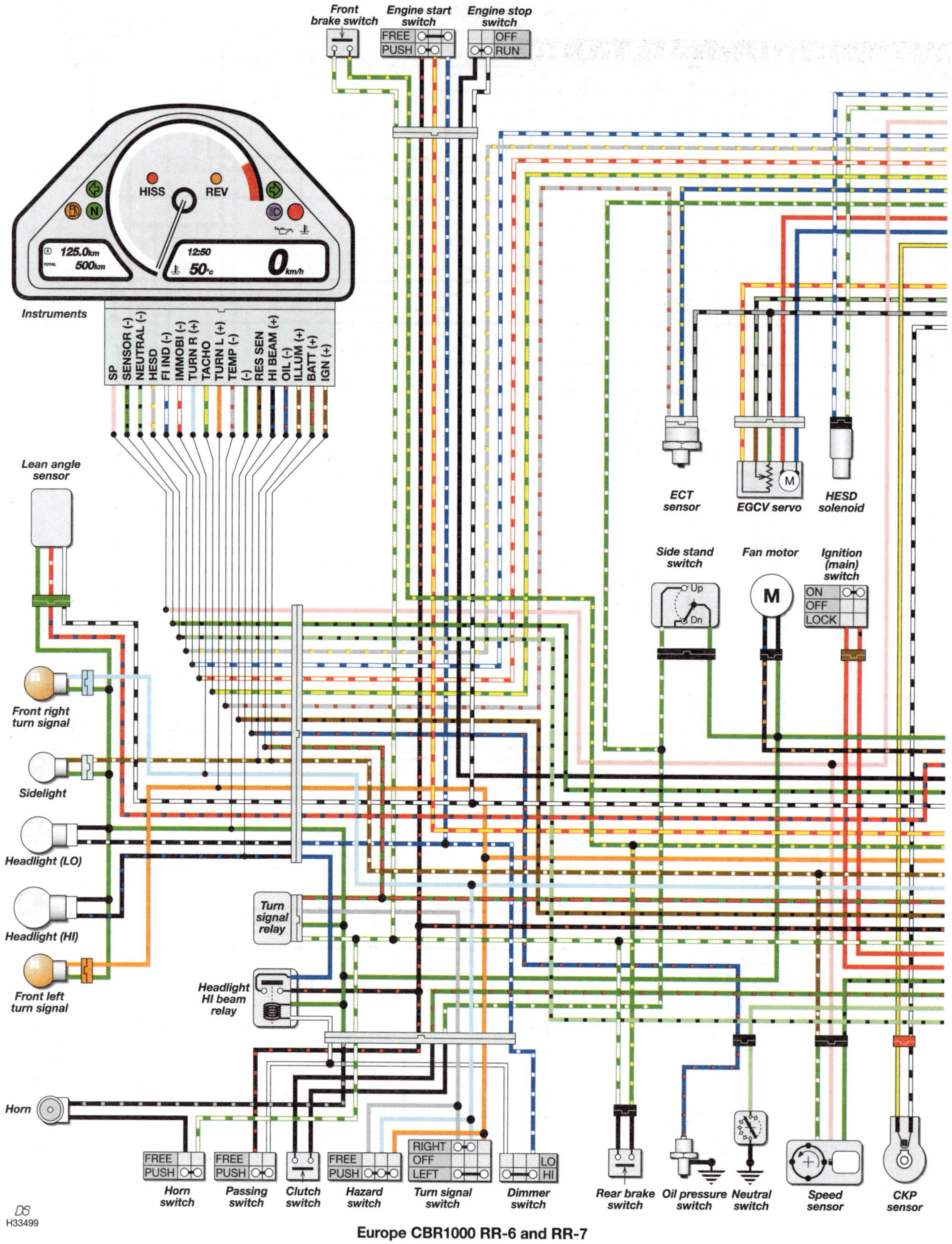
Front brake switch
Engine start switch
FREE
PUSH
Engine stop switch
OFF
RUN
HISS
REV
125.0km
500km
12:50
50°c
0km/h
Instruments
SP
SENSOR (-)
NEUTRAL (-)
HESD
FI IND (-)
IMMOBI (-)
TURN R (+)
TACHO
TURN L (+)
TEMP (-)
(-)
RES SEN
HI BEAM (+)
OIL (-)
ILLUM (+)
BATT (+)
IGN (+)
Lean angle sensor
Front right turn signal
Sidelight
Headlight (LO)
Headlight (HI)
Front left turn signal
Turn signal relay
Headlight HI beam relay
Horn
ECT sensor
EGCV servo
HESD solenoid
Side stand switch
Up
Dn
Fan motor
M
Ignition (main) switch
ON
OFF
LOCK
FREE
PUSH
Horn switch
FREE
PUSH
Passing switch
Clutch switch
FREE
PUSH
Hazard switch
RIGHT
OFF
LEFT
Turn signal switch
LO
HI
Dimmer switch
Rear brake switch
Oil pressure switch
Neutral switch
Speed sensor
CKP sensor
H33499

Europe CBR1000 RR-6 and RR-7

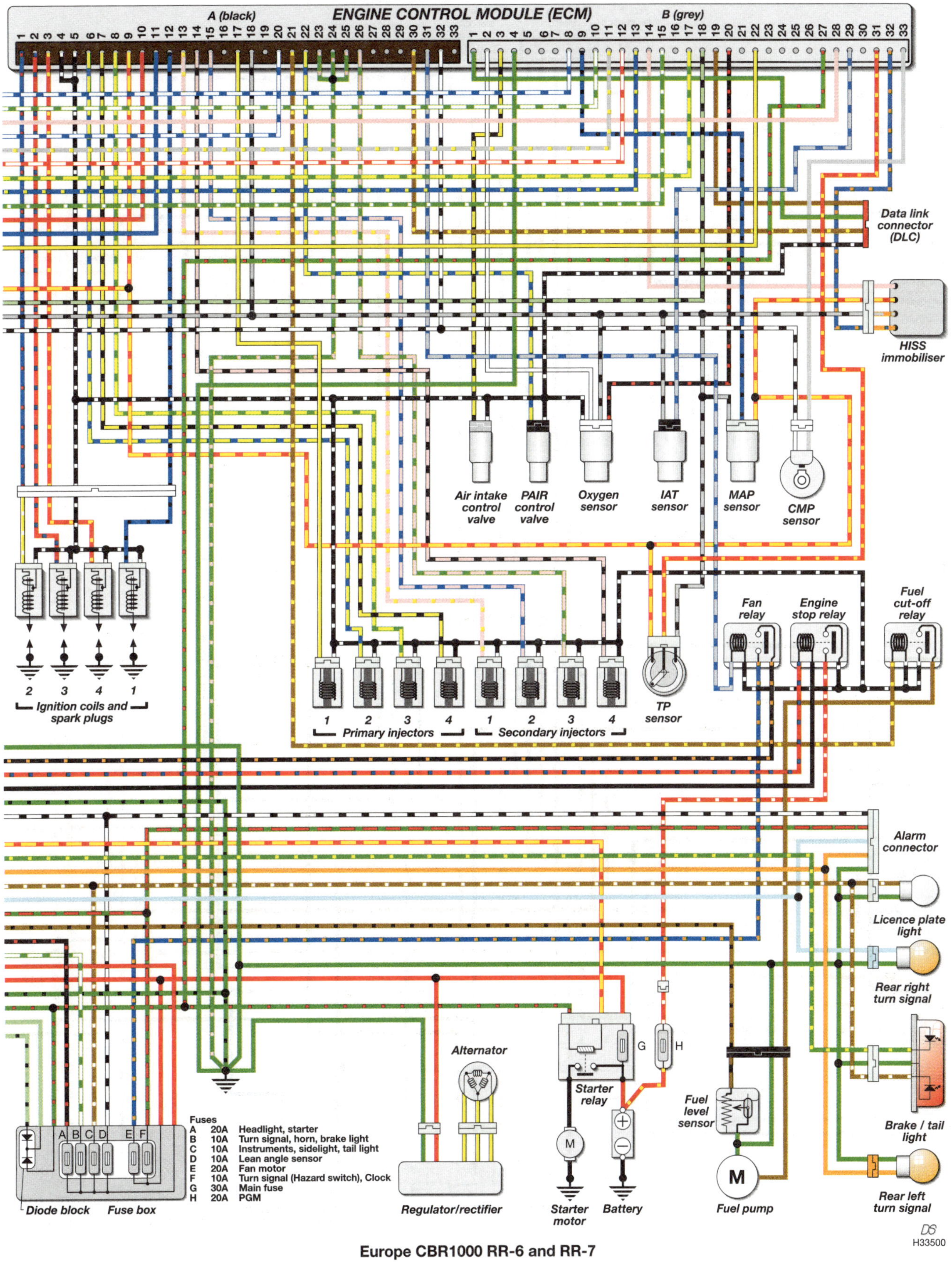
ENGINE CONTROL MODULE (ECM)
A (black)
B (grey)
Data link connector (DLC)
HISS immobiliser
Air intake control valve
PAIR control valve
Oxygen sensor
IAT sensor
MAP sensor
CMP sensor
Fan relay
Engine stop relay
Fuel cut-off relay
TP sensor
2 3 4 1
Ignition coils and spark plugs
1 2 3 4
Primary injectors
1 2 3 4
Secondary injectors
Alarm connector
Licence plate light
Rear right turn signal
Brake / tail light
Rear left turn signal
Alternator
Starter relay
G
H
Fuel level sensor
Fuel pump
Starter motor
Battery
Regulator/rectifier
Diode block
Fuse box
A B C D E F
Fuses
A 20A Headlight, starter
B 10A Turn signal, horn, brake light
C 10A Instruments, sidelight, tail light
D 10A Lean angle sensor
E 20A Fan motor
F 10A Turn signal (Hazard switch), Clock
G 30A Main fuse
H 20A PGM
DS
H33500

Europe CBR1000 RR-6 and RR-7

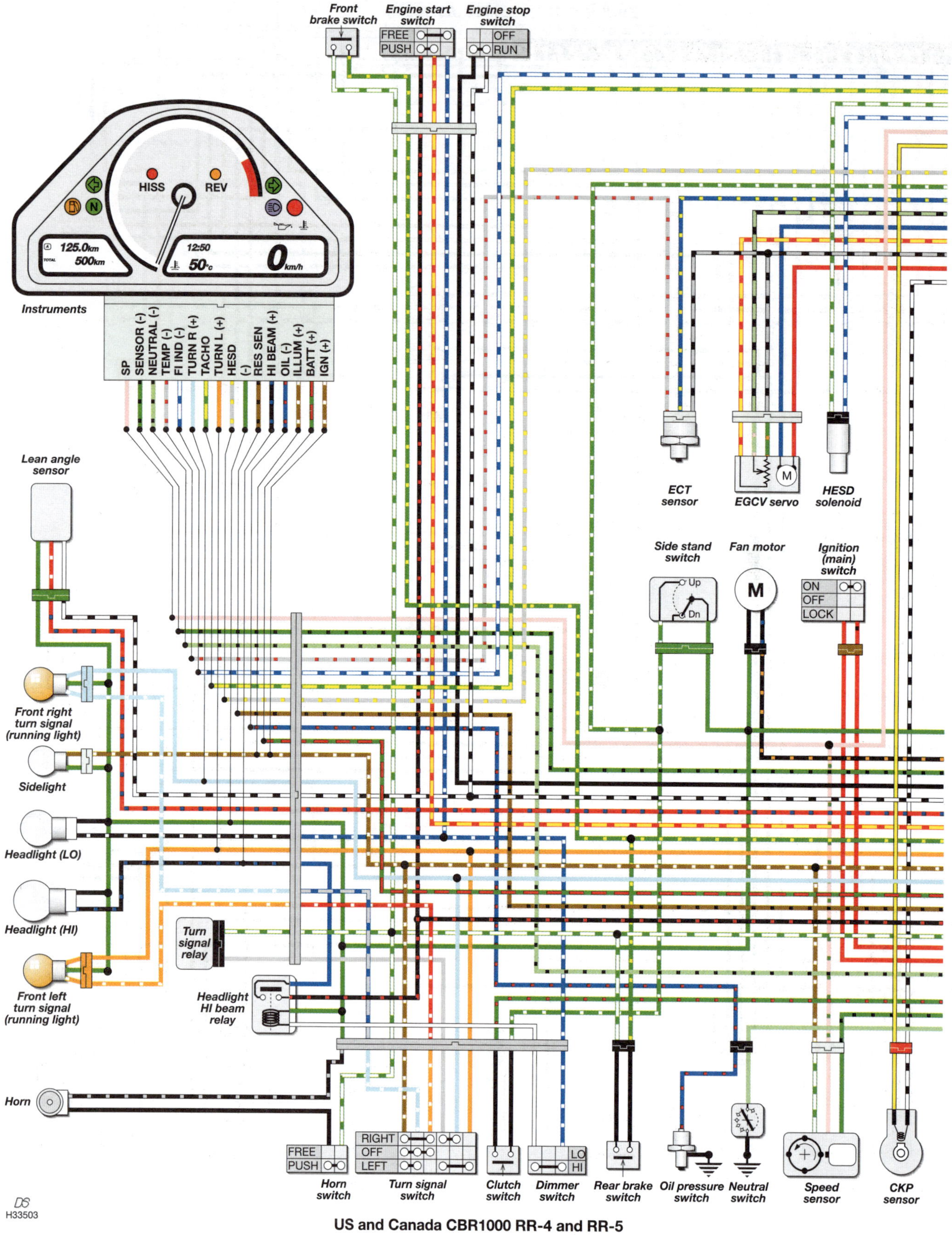
Front brake switch
Engine start switch
FREE
PUSH
Engine stop switch
OFF
RUN
HISS
REV
125.0km
500km
12:50
50°c
0 km/h
Instruments
SP
SENSOR (-)
NEUTRAL (-)
TEMP (-)
FI IND (-)
TURN R (+)
TACHO
TURN L (+)
HESD
(-)
RES SEN
HI BEAM (+)
OIL (-)
ILLUM (+)
BATT (+)
IGN (+)
Lean angle sensor
ECT sensor
EGCV servo
HESD solenoid
Side stand switch
Up
Dn
Fan motor
Ignition (main) switch
ON
OFF
LOCK
Front right turn signal (running light)
Sidelight
Headlight (LO)
Headlight (HI)
Turn signal relay
Front left turn signal (running light)
Headlight HI beam relay
Horn
FREE
PUSH
Horn switch
RIGHT
OFF
LEFT
Turn signal switch
Clutch switch
LO
HI
Dimmer switch
Rear brake switch
Oil pressure switch
Neutral switch
Speed sensor
CKP sensor
DS
H33503

US and Canada CBR1000 RR-4 and RR-5

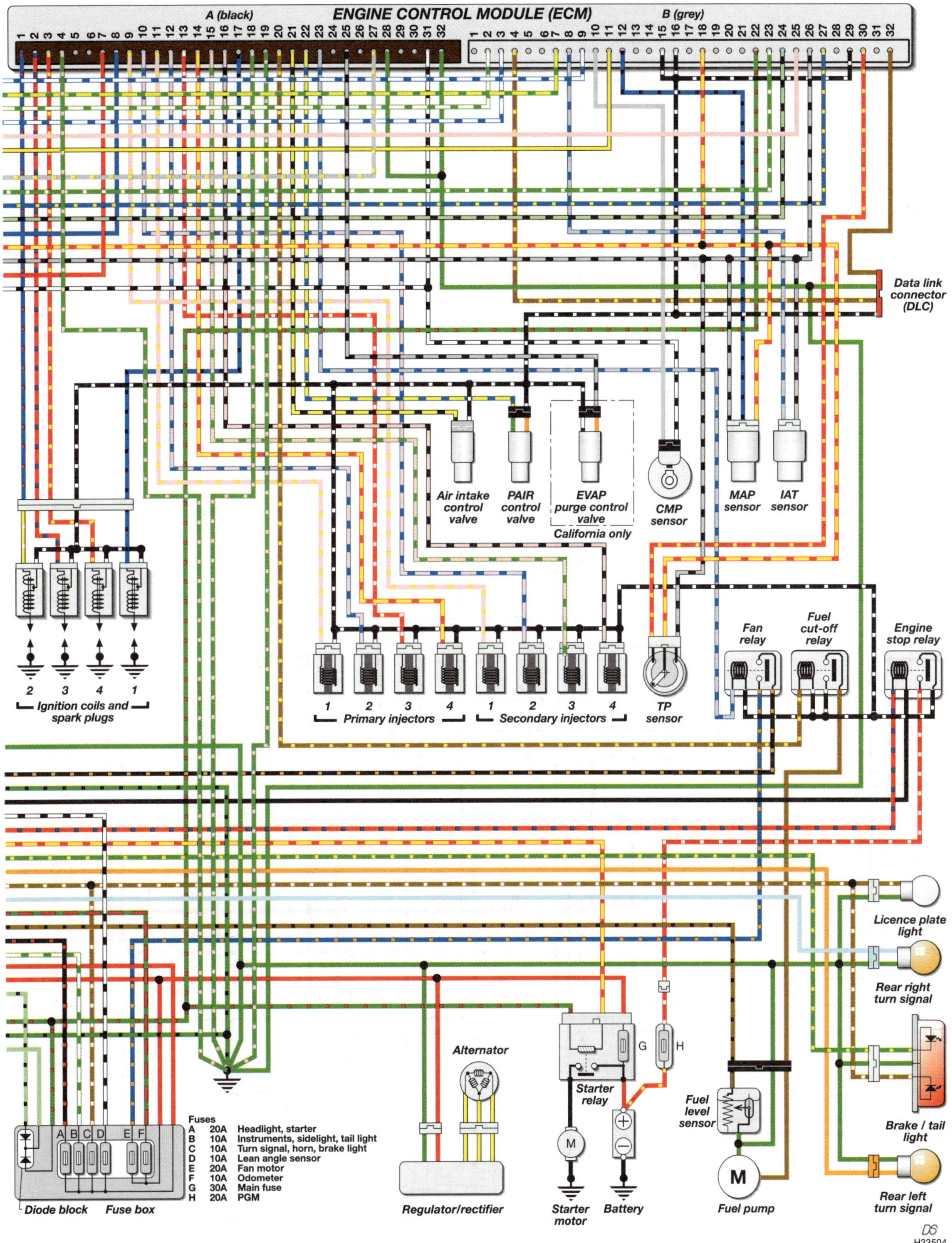
ENGINE CONTROL MODULE (ECM)
A (black)
B (grey)
Data link connector (DLC)
Air intake control valve
PAIR control valve
EVAP purge control valve
California only
CMP sensor
MAP sensor
IAT sensor
Ignition coils and spark plugs
Primary injectors
Secondary injectors
TP sensor
Fan relay
Fuel cut-off relay
Engine stop relay
Licence plate light
Rear right turn signal
Brake / tail light
Rear left turn signal
Alternator
Regulator/rectifier
Starter relay
Starter motor
Battery
Fuel level sensor
Fuel pump
Diode block
Fuse box
Fuses
A 20A Headlight, starter
B 10A Instruments, sidelight, tail light
C 10A Turn signal, horn, brake light
D 10A Lean angle sensor
E 20A Fan motor
F 10A Odometer
G 30A Main fuse
H 20A PGM
DS
H33504

US and Canada CBR1000 RR-4 and RR-5

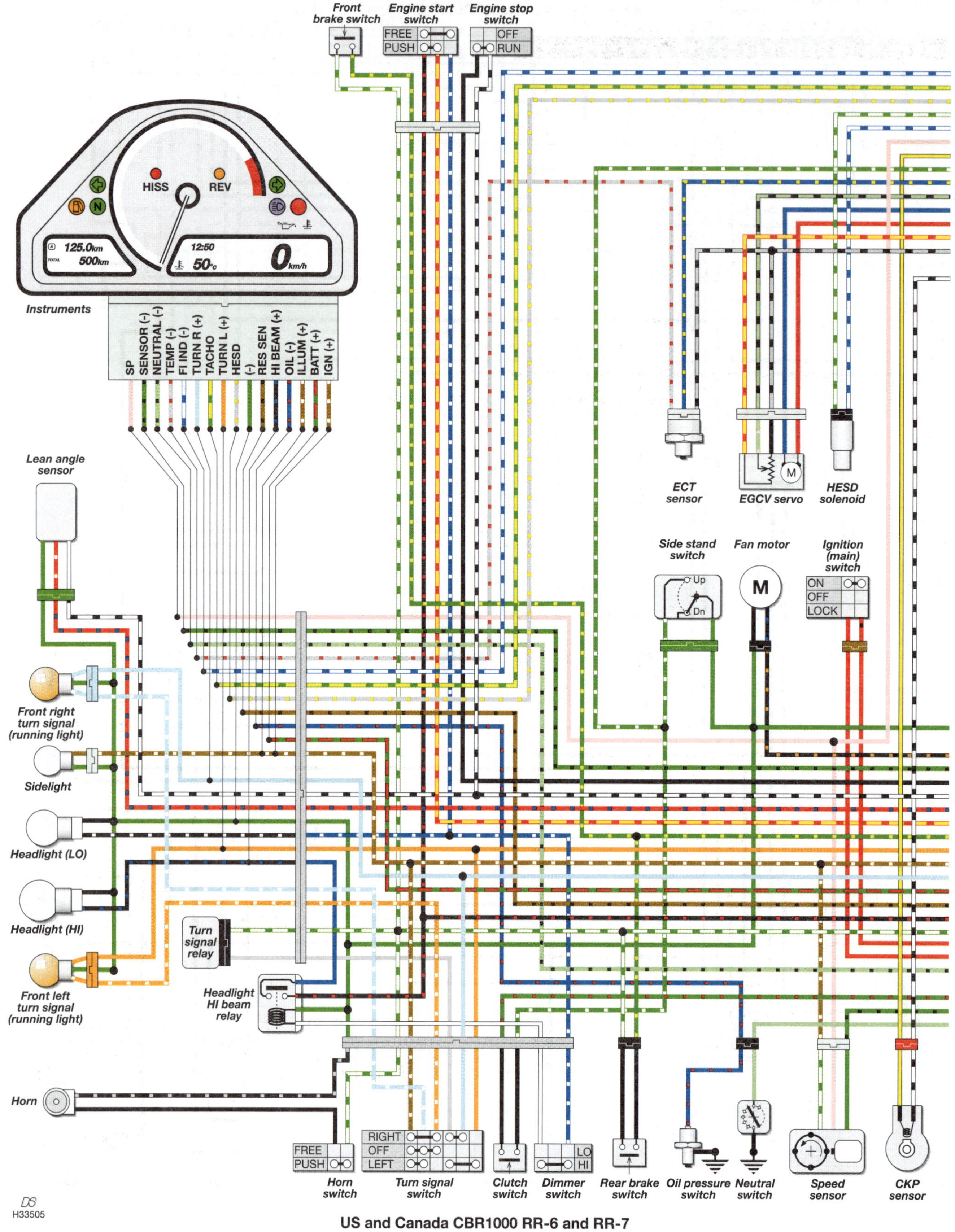

US and Canada CBR1000 RR-6 and RR-7

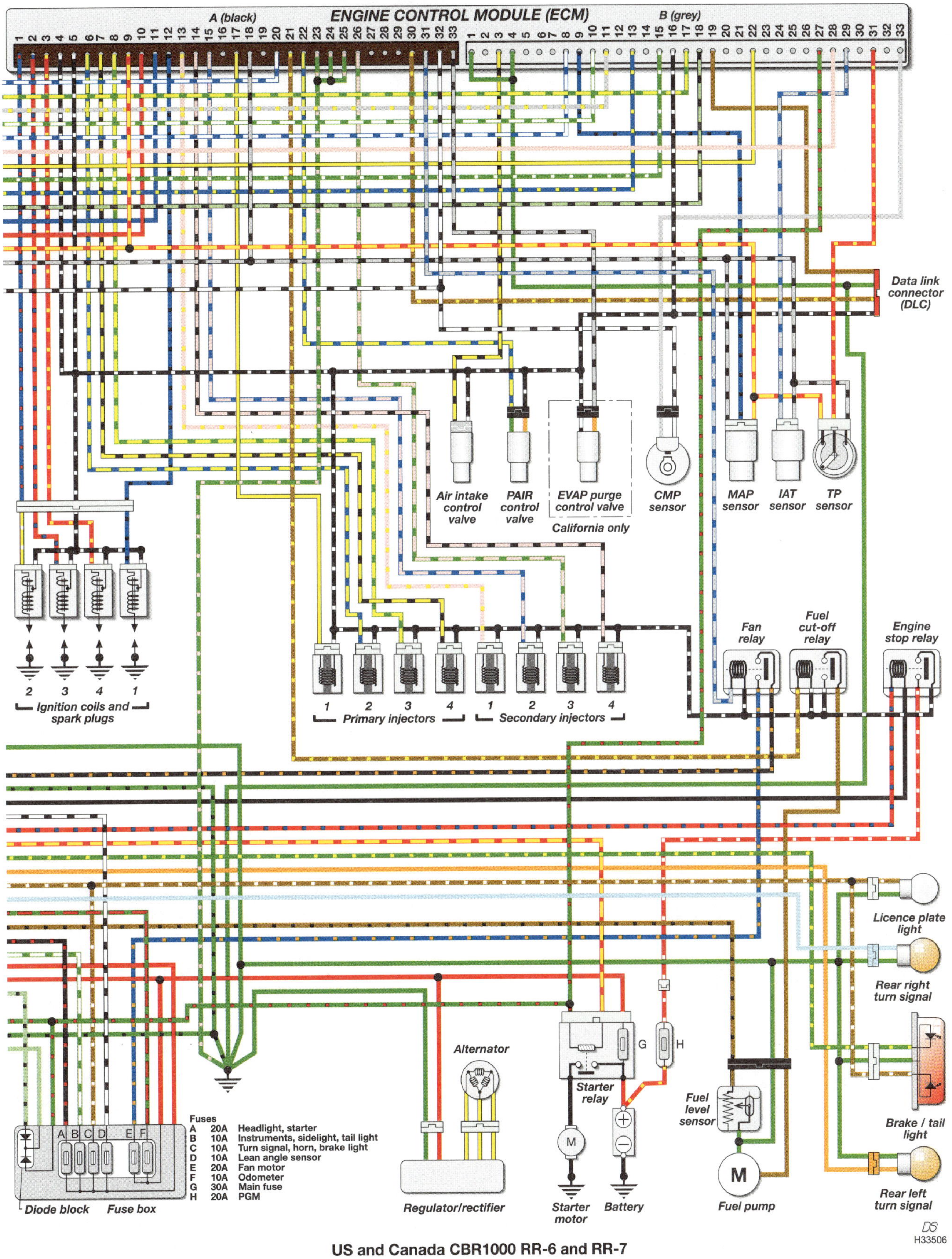

US and Canada CBR1000 RR-6 and RR-7

Reference

Tools and Workshop Tips

Buying tools

A toolkit is a fundamental requirement for servicing and repairing a motorcycle. Although there will be an initial expense in building up enough tools for servicing, this will soon be offset by the savings made by doing the job yourself. As experience and confidence grow, additional tools can be added to enable the repair and overhaul of the motorcycle. Many of the specialist tools are expensive and not often used so it may be preferable to hire them, or for a group of friends or motorcycle club to join in the purchase.

As a rule, it is better to buy more expensive, good quality tools. Cheaper tools are likely to wear out faster and need to be renewed more often, nullifying the original saving.

Warning: To avoid the risk of a poor quality tool breaking in use, causing injury or damage to the component being worked on, always aim to purchase tools which meet the relevant national safety standards.

The following lists of tools do not represent the manufacturer's service tools, but serve as a guide to help the owner decide which tools are needed for this level of work. In addition, items such as an electric drill, hacksaw, files, soldering iron and a workbench equipped with a vice, may be needed. Although not classed as tools, a selection of bolts, screws, nuts, washers and pieces of tubing always come in useful.

For more information about tools, refer to the Haynes *Motorcycle Workshop Practice Techbook* (Bk. No. 3470).

Manufacturer's service tools

Inevitably certain tasks require the use of a service tool. Where possible an alternative tool or method of approach is recommended, but sometimes there is no option if personal injury or damage to the component is to be avoided. Where required, service tools are referred to in the relevant procedure.

Service tools can usually only be purchased from a motorcycle dealer and are identified by a part number. Some of the commonly-used tools, such as rotor pullers, are available in aftermarket form from mail-order motorcycle tool and accessory suppliers.

Maintenance and minor repair tools

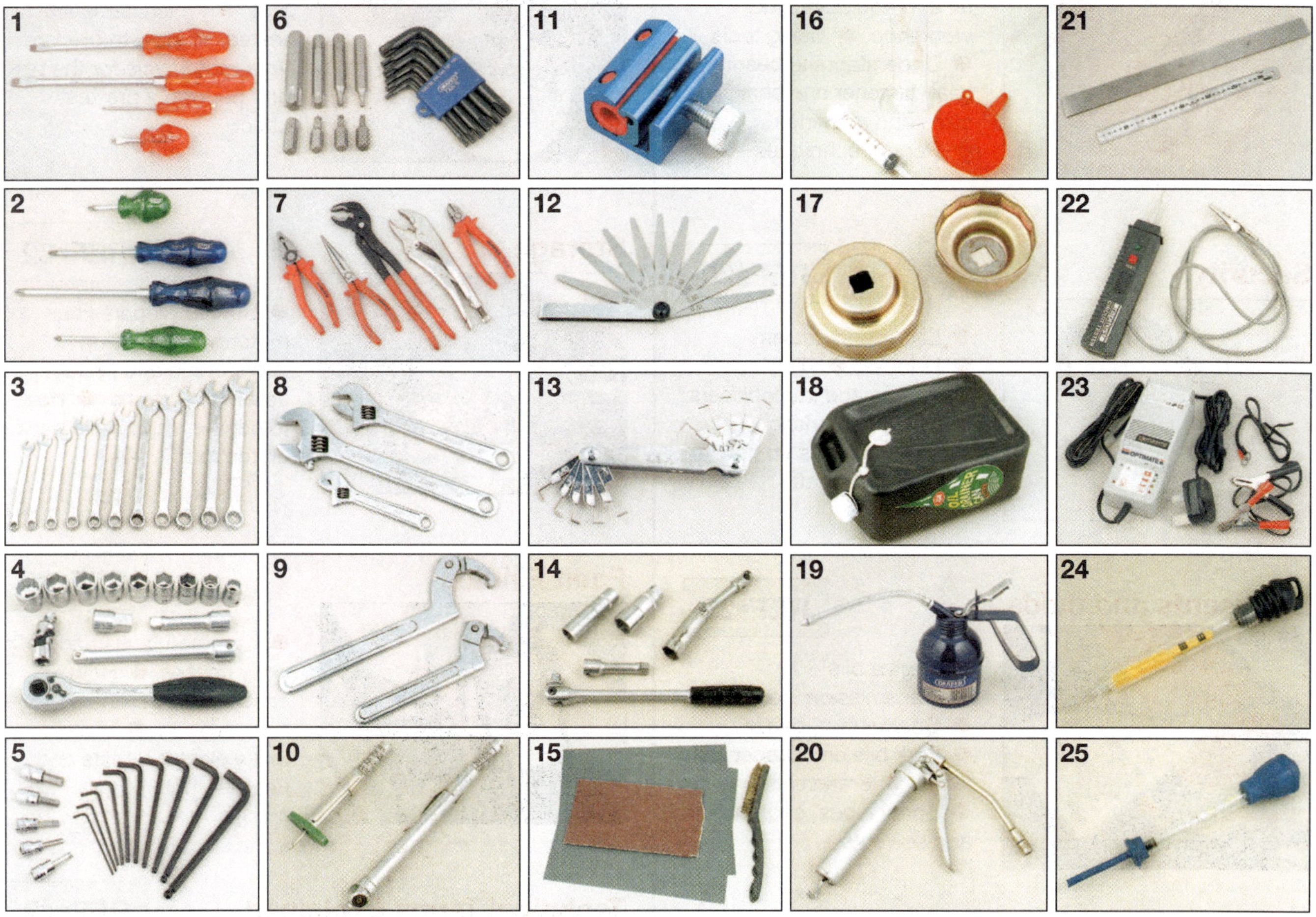

1 *Set of flat-bladed screwdrivers*
2 *Set of Phillips head screwdrivers*
3 *Combination open-end and ring spanners*
4 *Socket set (3/8 inch or 1/2 inch drive)*
5 *Set of Allen keys or bits*
6 *Set of Torx keys or bits*
7 *Pliers, cutters and self-locking grips (Mole grips)*
8 *Adjustable spanners*
9 *C-spanners*
10 *Tread depth gauge and tyre pressure gauge*
11 *Cable oiler clamp*
12 *Feeler gauges*
13 *Spark plug gap measuring tool*
14 *Spark plug spanner or deep plug sockets*
15 *Wire brush and emery paper*
16 *Calibrated syringe, measuring vessel and funnel*
17 *Oil filter adapters*
18 *Oil drainer can or tray*
19 *Pump type oil can*
20 *Grease gun*
21 *Straight-edge and steel rule*
22 *Continuity tester*
23 *Battery charger*
24 *Hydrometer (for battery specific gravity check)*
25 *Anti-freeze tester (for liquid-cooled engines)*

Repair and overhaul tools

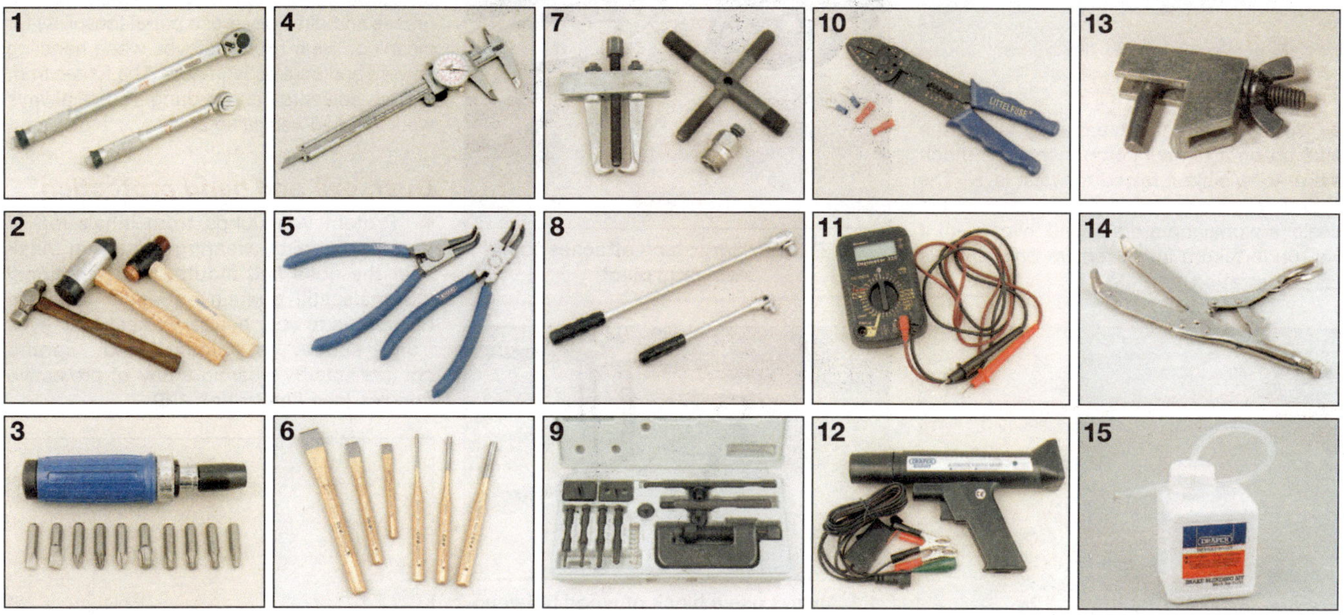

1 *Torque wrench (small and mid-ranges)*
2 *Conventional, plastic or soft-faced hammers*
3 *Impact driver set*
4 *Vernier gauge*
5 *Circlip pliers (internal and external, or combination)*
6 *Set of cold chisels and punches*
7 *Selection of pullers*
8 *Breaker bars*
9 *Chain breaking/ riveting tool set*
10 *Wire stripper and crimper tool*
11 *Multimeter (measures amps, volts and ohms)*
12 *Stroboscope (for dynamic timing checks)*
13 *Hose clamp (wingnut type shown)*
14 *Clutch holding tool*
15 *One-man brake/clutch bleeder kit*

Specialist tools

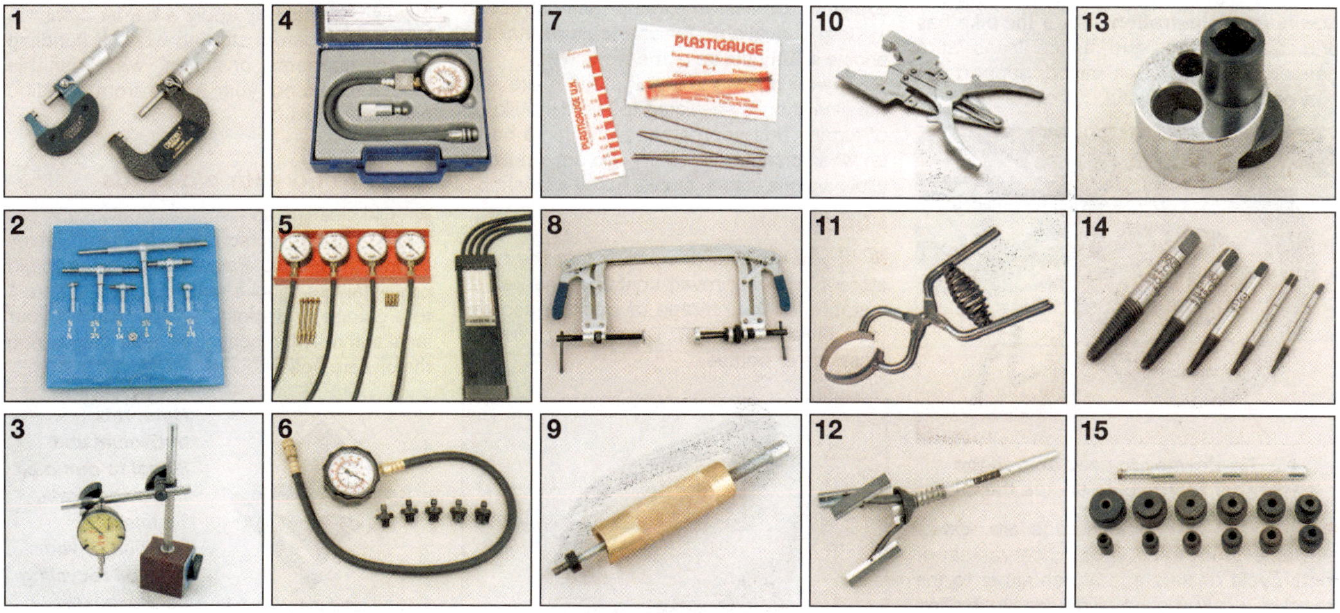

1 *Micrometers (external type)*
2 *Telescoping gauges*
3 *Dial gauge*
4 *Cylinder compression gauge*
5 *Vacuum gauges (left) or manometer (right)*
6 *Oil pressure gauge*
7 *Plastigauge kit*
8 *Valve spring compressor (4-stroke engines)*
9 *Piston pin drawbolt tool*
10 *Piston ring removal and installation tool*
11 *Piston ring clamp*
12 *Cylinder bore hone (stone type shown)*
13 *Stud extractor*
14 *Screw extractor set*
15 *Bearing driver set*

1 Workshop equipment and facilities

The workbench

- Work is made much easier by raising the bike up on a ramp - components are much more accessible if raised to waist level. The hydraulic or pneumatic types seen in the dealer's workshop are a sound investment if you undertake a lot of repairs or overhauls **(see illustration 1.1)**.

1.1 Hydraulic motorcycle ramp

- If raised off ground level, the bike must be supported on the ramp to avoid it falling. Most ramps incorporate a front wheel locating clamp which can be adjusted to suit different diameter wheels. When tightening the clamp, take care not to mark the wheel rim or damage the tyre - use wood blocks on each side to prevent this.
- Secure the bike to the ramp using tie-downs **(see illustration 1.2)**. If the bike has only a sidestand, and hence leans at a dangerous angle when raised, support the bike on an auxiliary stand.

1.2 Tie-downs are used around the passenger footrests to secure the bike

- Auxiliary (paddock) stands are widely available from mail order companies or motorcycle dealers and attach either to the wheel axle or swingarm pivot **(see illustration 1.3)**. If the motorcycle has a centrestand, you can support it under the crankcase to prevent it toppling whilst either wheel is removed **(see illustration 1.4)**.

1.3 This auxiliary stand attaches to the swingarm pivot

1.4 Always use a block of wood between the engine and jack head when supporting the engine in this way

Fumes and fire

- Refer to the Safety first! page at the beginning of the manual for full details. Make sure your workshop is equipped with a fire extinguisher suitable for fuel-related fires (Class B fire - flammable liquids) - it is not sufficient to have a water-filled extinguisher.
- Always ensure adequate ventilation is available. Unless an exhaust gas extraction system is available for use, ensure that the engine is run outside of the workshop.
- If working on the fuel system, make sure the workshop is ventilated to avoid a build-up of fumes. This applies equally to fume build-up when charging a battery. Do not smoke or allow anyone else to smoke in the workshop.

Fluids

- If you need to drain fuel from the tank, store it in an approved container marked as suitable for the storage of petrol (gasoline) **(see illustration 1.5)**. Do not store fuel in glass jars or bottles.

1.5 Use an approved can only for storing petrol (gasoline)

- Use proprietary engine degreasers or solvents which have a high flash-point, such as paraffin (kerosene), for cleaning off oil, grease and dirt - never use petrol (gasoline) for cleaning. Wear rubber gloves when handling solvent and engine degreaser. The fumes from certain solvents can be dangerous - always work in a well-ventilated area.

Dust, eye and hand protection

- Protect your lungs from inhalation of dust particles by wearing a filtering mask over the nose and mouth. Many frictional materials still contain asbestos which is dangerous to your health. Protect your eyes from spouts of liquid and sprung components by wearing a pair of protective goggles **(see illustration 1.6)**.

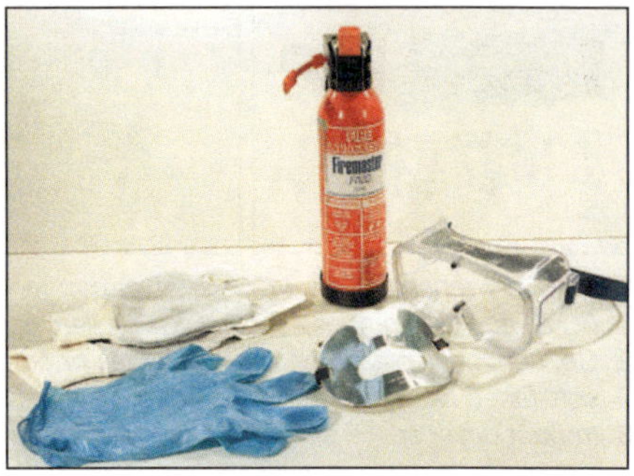

1.6 A fire extinguisher, goggles, mask and protective gloves should be at hand in the workshop

- Protect your hands from contact with solvents, fuel and oils by wearing rubber gloves. Alternatively apply a barrier cream to your hands before starting work. If handling hot components or fluids, wear suitable gloves to protect your hands from scalding and burns.

What to do with old fluids

- Old cleaning solvent, fuel, coolant and oils should not be poured down domestic drains or onto the ground. Package the fluid up in old oil containers, label it accordingly, and take it to a garage or disposal facility. Contact your local authority for location of such sites or ring the oil care hotline.

OIL CARE
FOLLOW THE CODE
OIL BANK LINE
0800 66 33 66
www.oilbankline.org.uk

Note: It is antisocial and illegal to dump oil down the drain. To find the location of your local oil recycling bank, call this number free.

In the USA, note that any oil supplier must accept used oil for recycling.

2 Fasteners - screws, bolts and nuts

Fastener types and applications

Bolts and screws

● Fastener head types are either of hexagonal, Torx or splined design, with internal and external versions of each type **(see illustrations 2.1 and 2.2);** splined head fasteners are not in common use on motorcycles. The conventional slotted or Phillips head design is used for certain screws. Bolt or screw length is always measured from the underside of the head to the end of the item **(see illustration 2.11)**.

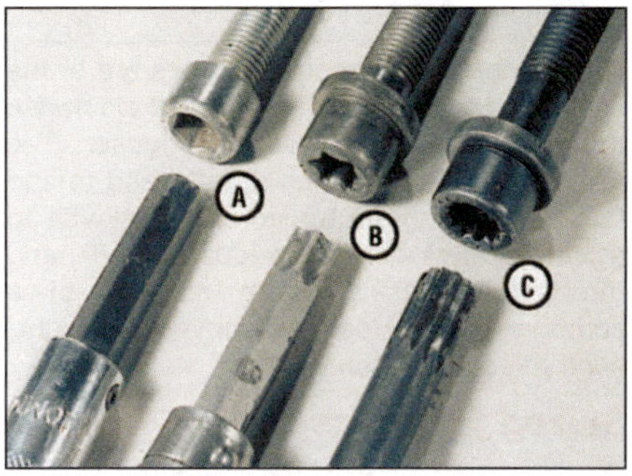

2.1 Internal hexagon/Allen (A), Torx (B) and splined (C) fasteners, with corresponding bits

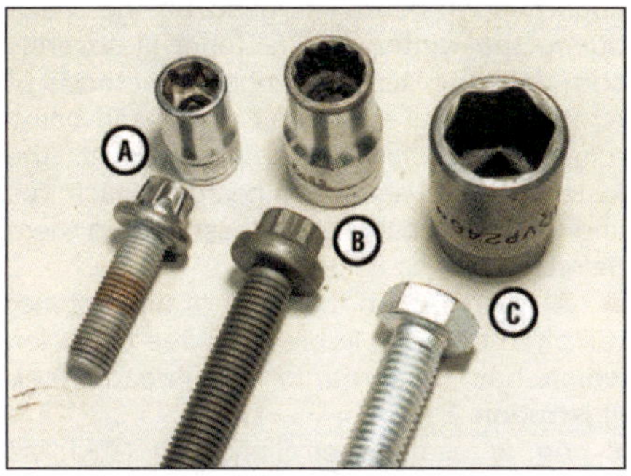

2.2 External Torx (A), splined (B) and hexagon (C) fasteners, with corresponding sockets

● Certain fasteners on the motorcycle have a tensile marking on their heads, the higher the marking the stronger the fastener. High tensile fasteners generally carry a 10 or higher marking. Never replace a high tensile fastener with one of a lower tensile strength.

Washers (see illustration 2.3)

● Plain washers are used between a fastener head and a component to prevent damage to the component or to spread the load when torque is applied. Plain washers can also be used as spacers or shims in certain assemblies. Copper or aluminium plain washers are often used as sealing washers on drain plugs.

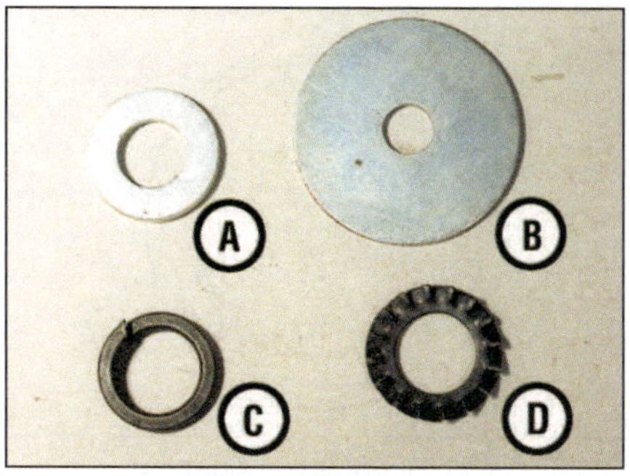

2.3 Plain washer (A), penny washer (B), spring washer (C) and serrated washer (D)

● The split-ring spring washer works by applying axial tension between the fastener head and component. If flattened, it is fatigued and must be renewed. If a plain (flat) washer is used on the fastener, position the spring washer between the fastener and the plain washer.

● Serrated star type washers dig into the fastener and component faces, preventing loosening. They are often used on electrical earth (ground) connections to the frame.

● Cone type washers (sometimes called Belleville) are conical and when tightened apply axial tension between the fastener head and component. They must be installed with the dished side against the component and often carry an OUTSIDE marking on their outer face. If flattened, they are fatigued and must be renewed.

● Tab washers are used to lock plain nuts or bolts on a shaft. A portion of the tab washer is bent up hard against one flat of the nut or bolt to prevent it loosening. Due to the tab washer being deformed in use, a new tab washer should be used every time it is disturbed.

● Wave washers are used to take up endfloat on a shaft. They provide light springing and prevent excessive side-to-side play of a component. Can be found on rocker arm shafts.

Nuts and split pins

● Conventional plain nuts are usually six-sided **(see illustration 2.4)**. They are sized by thread diameter and pitch. High tensile nuts carry a number on one end to denote their tensile strength.

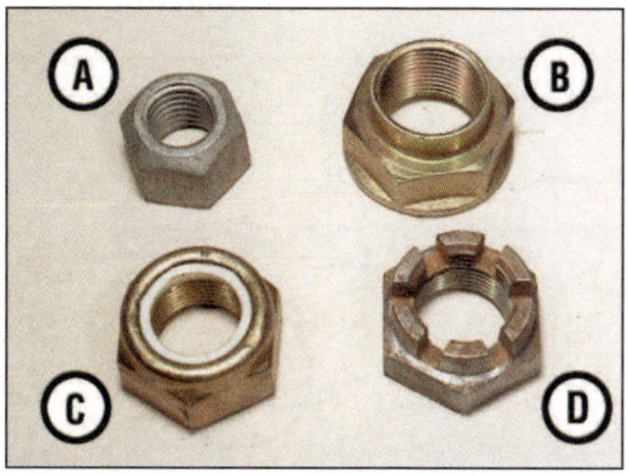

2.4 Plain nut (A), shouldered locknut (B), nylon insert nut (C) and castellated nut (D)

● Self-locking nuts either have a nylon insert, or two spring metal tabs, or a shoulder which is staked into a groove in the shaft - their advantage over conventional plain nuts is a resistance to loosening due to vibration. The nylon insert type can be used a number of times, but must be renewed when the friction of the nylon insert is reduced, ie when the nut spins freely on the shaft. The spring tab type can be reused unless the tabs are damaged. The shouldered type must be renewed every time it is disturbed.

● Split pins (cotter pins) are used to lock a castellated nut to a shaft or to prevent slackening of a plain nut. Common applications are wheel axles and brake torque arms. Because the split pin arms are deformed to lock around the nut a new split pin must always be used on installation - always fit the correct size split pin which will fit snugly in the shaft hole. Make sure the split pin arms are correctly located around the nut **(see illustrations 2.5 and 2.6)**.

2.5 Bend split pin (cotter pin) arms as shown (arrows) to secure a castellated nut

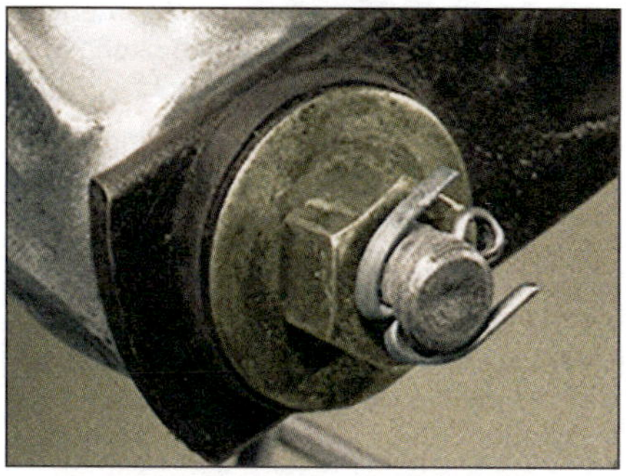

2.6 Bend split pin (cotter pin) arms as shown to secure a plain nut

Caution: If the castellated nut slots do not align with the shaft hole after tightening to the torque setting, tighten the nut until the next slot aligns with the hole - never slacken the nut to align its slot.

● R-pins (shaped like the letter R), or slip pins as they are sometimes called, are sprung and can be reused if they are otherwise in good condition. Always install R-pins with their closed end facing forwards **(see illustration 2.7)**.

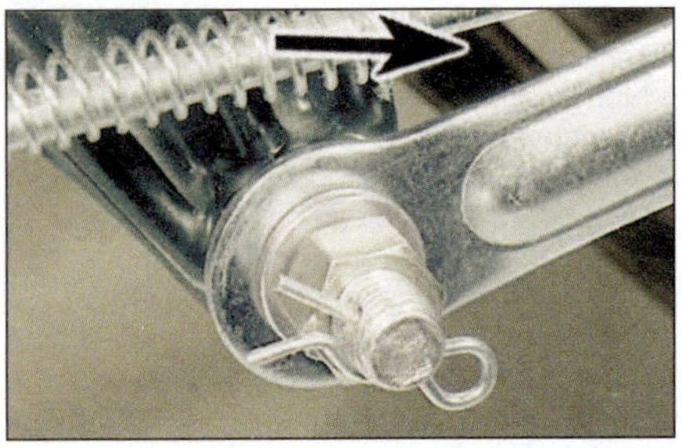

2.7 Correct fitting of R-pin. Arrow indicates forward direction

Circlips (see illustration 2.8)

● Circlips (sometimes called snap-rings) are used to retain components on a shaft or in a housing and have corresponding external or internal ears to permit removal. Parallel-sided (machined) circlips can be installed either way round in their groove, whereas stamped circlips (which have a chamfered edge on one face) must be installed with the chamfer facing away from the direction of thrust load **(see illustration 2.9)**.

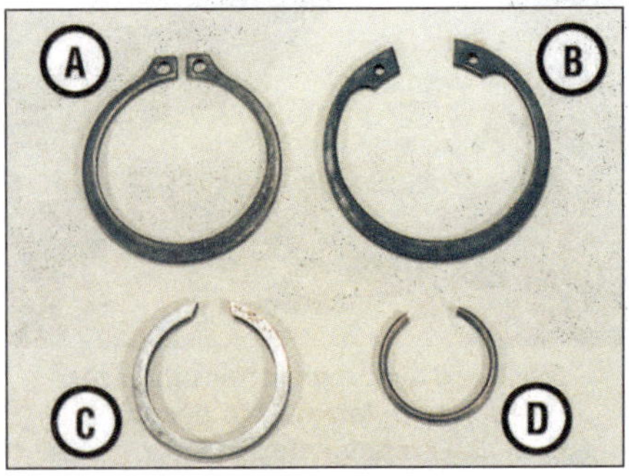

2.8 External stamped circlip (A), internal stamped circlip (B), machined circlip (C) and wire circlip (D)

● Always use circlip pliers to remove and install circlips; expand or compress them just enough to remove them. After installation, rotate the circlip in its groove to ensure it is securely seated. If installing a circlip on a splined shaft, always align its opening with a shaft channel to ensure the circlip ends are well supported and unlikely to catch **(see illustration 2.10)**.

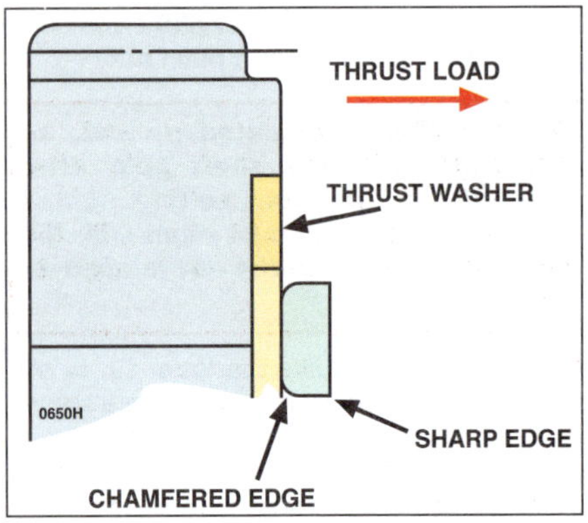

2.9 Correct fitting of a stamped circlip

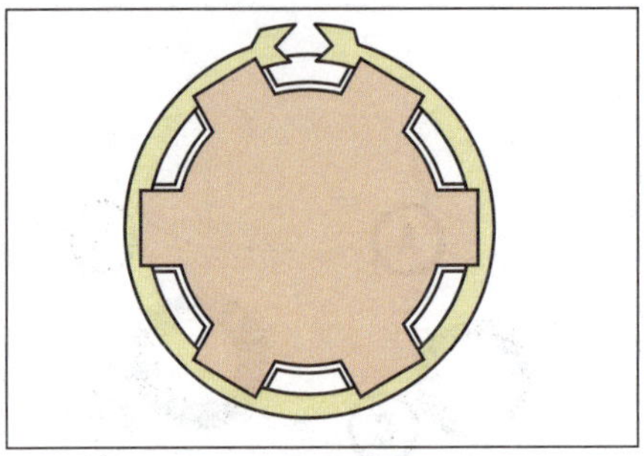

2.10 Align circlip opening with shaft channel

● Circlips can wear due to the thrust of components and become loose in their grooves, with the subsequent danger of becoming dislodged in operation. For this reason, renewal is advised every time a circlip is disturbed.

● Wire circlips are commonly used as piston pin retaining clips. If a removal tang is provided, long-nosed pliers can be used to dislodge them, otherwise careful use of a small flat-bladed screwdriver is necessary. Wire circlips should be renewed every time they are disturbed.

Thread diameter and pitch

● Diameter of a male thread (screw, bolt or stud) is the outside diameter of the threaded portion **(see illustration 2.11)**. Most motorcycle manufacturers use the ISO (International Standards Organisation) metric system expressed in millimetres, eg M6 refers to a 6 mm diameter thread. Sizing is the same for nuts, except that the thread diameter is measured across the valleys of the nut.

● Pitch is the distance between the peaks of the thread **(see illustration 2.11)**. It is expressed in millimetres, thus a common bolt size may be expressed as 6.0 x 1.0 mm (6 mm thread diameter and 1 mm pitch). Generally pitch increases in proportion to thread diameter, although there are always exceptions.

● Thread diameter and pitch are related for conventional fastener applications and the accompanying table can be used as a guide. Additionally, the AF (Across Flats), spanner or socket size dimension of the bolt or nut **(see illustration 2.11)** is linked to thread and pitch specification. Thread pitch can be measured with a thread gauge **(see illustration 2.12)**.

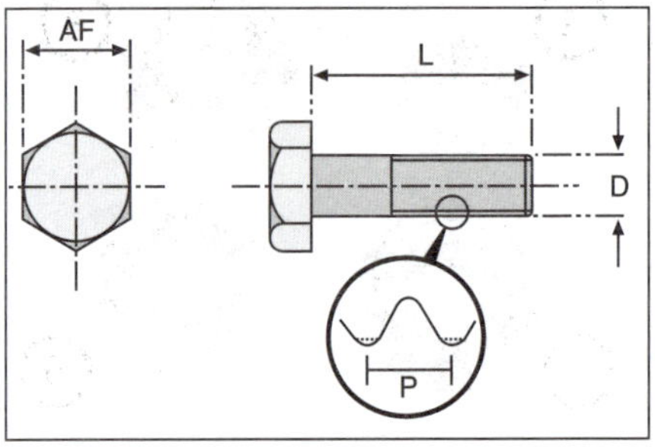

2.11 Fastener length (L), thread diameter (D), thread pitch (P) and head size (AF)

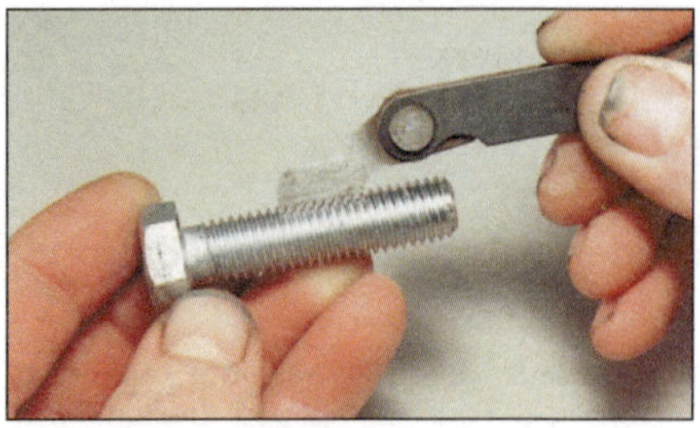

2.12 Using a thread gauge to measure pitch

AF size	Thread diameter x pitch (mm)
8 mm	M5 x 0.8
8 mm	M6 x 1.0
10 mm	M6 x 1.0
12 mm	M8 x 1.25
14 mm	M10 x 1.25
17 mm	M12 x 1.25

● The threads of most fasteners are of the right-hand type, ie they are turned clockwise to tighten and anti-clockwise to loosen. The reverse situation applies to left-hand thread fasteners, which are turned anti-clockwise to tighten and clockwise to loosen. Left-hand threads are used where rotation of a component might loosen a conventional right-hand thread fastener.

Seized fasteners

● Corrosion of external fasteners due to water or reaction between two dissimilar metals can occur over a period of time. It will build up sooner in wet conditions or in countries where salt is used on the roads during the winter. If a fastener is severely corroded it is likely that normal methods of removal will fail and result in its head being ruined. When you attempt removal, the fastener thread should be heard to crack free and unscrew easily - if it doesn't, stop there before damaging something.

● A smart tap on the head of the fastener will often succeed in breaking free corrosion which has occurred in the threads **(see illustration 2.13)**.

● An aerosol penetrating fluid (such as WD-40) applied the night beforehand may work its way down into the thread and ease removal. Depending on the location, you may be able to make up a Plasticine well around the fastener head and fill it with penetrating fluid.

2.13 A sharp tap on the head of a fastener will often break free a corroded thread

● If you are working on an engine internal component, corrosion will most likely not be a problem due to the well lubricated environment. However, components can be very tight and an impact driver is a useful tool in freeing them **(see illustration 2.14)**.

2.14 Using an impact driver to free a fastener

● Where corrosion has occurred between dissimilar metals (eg steel and aluminium alloy), the application of heat to the fastener head will create a disproportionate expansion rate between the two metals and break the seizure caused by the corrosion. Whether heat can be applied depends on the location of the fastener - any surrounding components likely to be damaged must first be removed **(see illustration 2.15)**. Heat can be applied using a paint stripper heat gun or clothes iron, or by immersing the component in boiling water - wear protective gloves to prevent scalding or burns to the hands.

2.15 Using heat to free a seized fastener

● As a last resort, it is possible to use a hammer and cold chisel to work the fastener head unscrewed **(see illustration 2.16)**. This will damage the fastener, but more importantly extreme care must be taken not to damage the surrounding component.

Caution: Remember that the component being secured is generally of more value than the bolt, nut or screw - when the fastener is freed, do not unscrew it with force, instead work the fastener back and forth when resistance is felt to prevent thread damage.

2.16 Using a hammer and chisel to free a seized fastener

Broken fasteners and damaged heads

● If the shank of a broken bolt or screw is accessible you can grip it with self-locking grips. The knurled wheel type stud extractor tool or self-gripping stud puller tool is particularly useful for removing the long studs which screw into the cylinder mouth surface of the crankcase or bolts and screws from which the head has broken off **(see illustration 2.17)**. Studs can also be removed by locking two nuts together on the threaded end of the stud and using a spanner on the lower nut **(see illustration 2.18)**.

2.17 Using a stud extractor tool to remove a broken crankcase stud

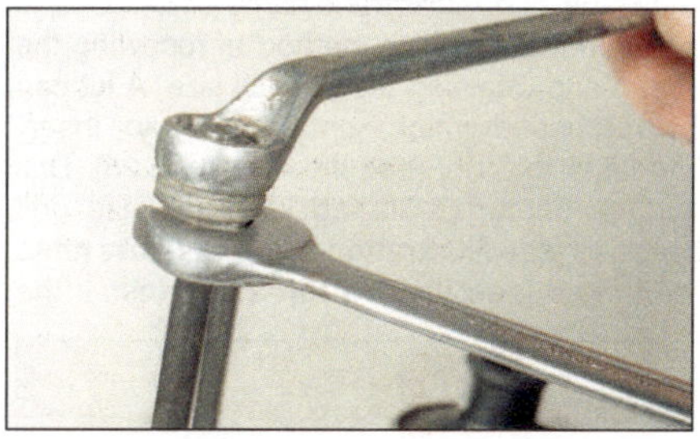

2.18 Two nuts can be locked together to unscrew a stud from a component

● A bolt or screw which has broken off below or level with the casing must be extracted using a screw extractor set. Centre punch the fastener to centralise the drill bit, then drill a hole in the fastener **(see illustration 2.19)**. Select a drill bit which is approximately half to three-quarters the

2.19 When using a screw extractor, first drill a hole in the fastener . . .

diameter of the fastener and drill to a depth which will accommodate the extractor. Use the largest size extractor possible, but avoid leaving too small a wall thickness otherwise the extractor will merely force the fastener walls outwards wedging it in the casing thread.

● If a spiral type extractor is used, thread it anti-clockwise into the fastener. As it is screwed in, it will grip the fastener and unscrew it from the casing **(see illustration 2.20)**.

2.20 . . . then thread the extractor anti-clockwise into the fastener

● If a taper type extractor is used, tap it into the fastener so that it is firmly wedged in place. Unscrew the extractor (anti-clockwise) to draw the fastener out.

Warning: Stud extractors are very hard and may break off in the fastener if care is not taken - ask an engineer about spark erosion if this happens.

● Alternatively, the broken bolt/screw can be drilled out and the hole retapped for an oversize bolt/screw or a diamond-section thread insert. It is essential that the drilling is carried out squarely and to the correct depth, otherwise the casing may be ruined - if in doubt, entrust the work to an engineer.

● Bolts and nuts with rounded corners cause the correct size spanner or socket to slip when force is applied. Of the types of spanner/socket available always use a six-point type rather than an eight or twelve-point type - better grip

2.21 Comparison of surface drive ring spanner (left) with 12-point type (right)

is obtained. Surface drive spanners grip the middle of the hex flats, rather than the corners, and are thus good in cases of damaged heads **(see illustration 2.21)**.

- Slotted-head or Phillips-head screws are often damaged by the use of the wrong size screwdriver. Allen-head and Torx-head screws are much less likely to sustain damage. If enough of the screw head is exposed you can use a hacksaw to cut a slot in its head and then use a conventional flat-bladed screwdriver to remove it. Alternatively use a hammer and cold chisel to tap the head of the fastener around to slacken it. Always replace damaged fasteners with new ones, preferably Torx or Allen-head type.

HAYNES HiNT

A dab of valve grinding compound between the screw head and screw-driver tip will often give a good grip.

Thread repair

- Threads (particularly those in aluminium alloy components) can be damaged by overtightening, being assembled with dirt in the threads, or from a component working loose and vibrating. Eventually the thread will fail completely, and it will be impossible to tighten the fastener.
- If a thread is damaged or clogged with old locking compound it can be renovated with a thread repair tool (thread chaser) **(see illustrations 2.22 and 2.23);** special thread

2.22 A thread repair tool being used to correct an internal thread

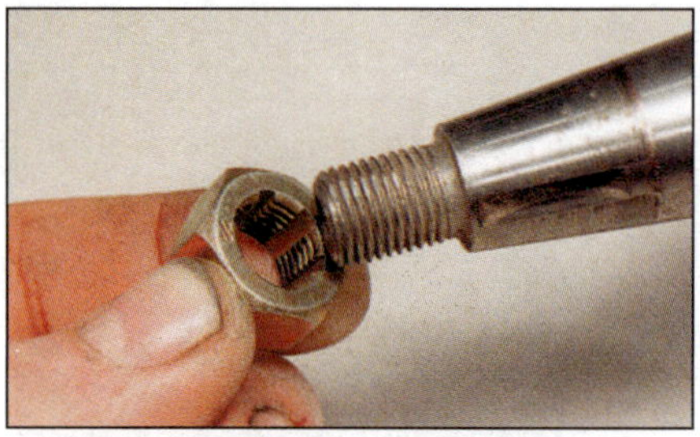

2.23 A thread repair tool being used to correct an external thread

chasers are available for spark plug hole threads. The tool will not cut a new thread, but clean and true the original thread. Make sure that you use the correct diameter and pitch tool. Similarly, external threads can be cleaned up with a die or a thread restorer file **(see illustration 2.24)**.

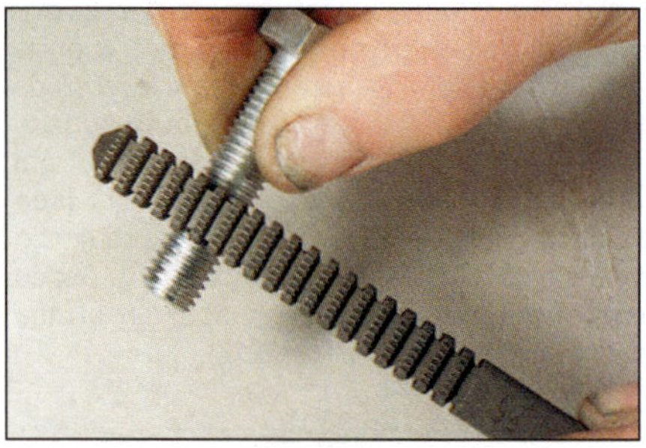

2.24 Using a thread restorer file

- It is possible to drill out the old thread and retap the component to the next thread size. This will work where there is enough surrounding material and a new bolt or screw can be obtained. Sometimes, however, this is not possible - such as where the bolt/screw passes through another component which must also be suitably modified, also in cases where a spark plug or oil drain plug cannot be obtained in a larger diameter thread size.
- The diamond-section thread insert (often known by its popular trade name of Heli-Coil) is a simple and effective method of renewing the thread and retaining the original size. A kit can be purchased which contains the tap, insert and installing tool **(see illustration 2.25)**. Drill out the damaged thread with the size drill specified **(see illustration 2.26)**. Carefully retap the thread **(see illustration 2.27)**. Install the

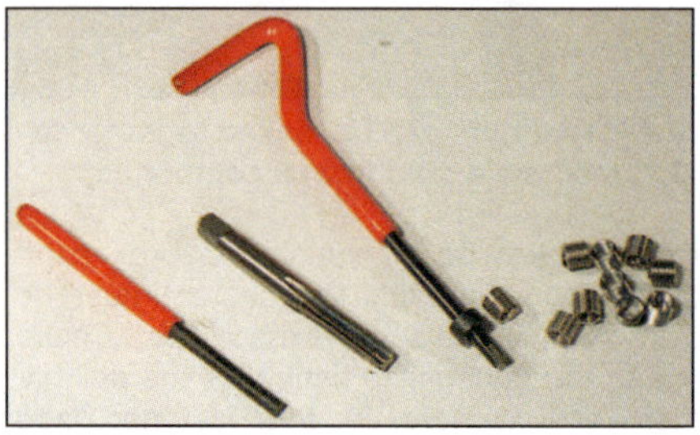

2.25 Obtain a thread insert kit to suit the thread diameter and pitch required

2.26 To install a thread insert, first drill out the original thread . . .

2.27 . . . tap a new thread . . .

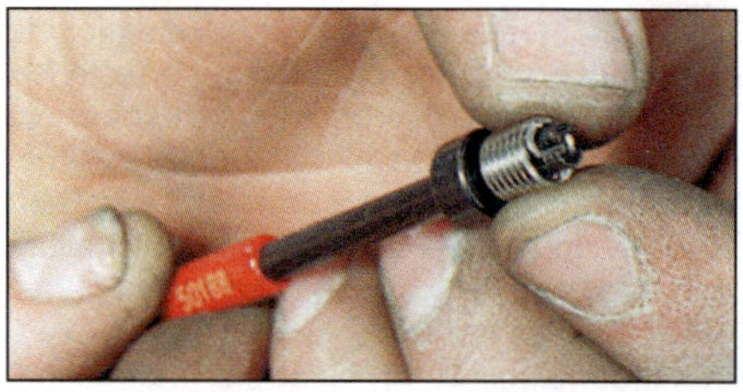

2.28 . . . fit insert on the installing tool . . .

2.29 . . . and thread into the component . . .

2.30 . . . break off the tang when complete

insert on the installing tool and thread it slowly into place using a light downward pressure **(see illustrations 2.28 and 2.29)**. When positioned between a 1/4 and 1/2 turn below the surface withdraw the installing tool and use the break-off tool to press down on the tang, breaking it off **(see illustration 2.30)**.

- There are epoxy thread repair kits on the market which can rebuild stripped internal threads, although this repair should not be used on high load-bearing components.

Thread locking and sealing compounds

- Locking compounds are used in locations where the fastener is prone to loosening due to vibration or on important safety-related items which might cause loss of control of the motorcycle if they fail. It is also used where important fasteners cannot be secured by other means such as lockwashers or split pins.
- Before applying locking compound, make sure that the threads (internal and external) are clean and dry with all old compound removed. Select a compound to suit the component being secured - a non-permanent general locking and sealing type is suitable for most applications, but a high strength type is needed for permanent fixing of studs in castings. Apply a drop or two of the compound to the first few threads of the fastener, then thread it into place and tighten to the specified torque. Do not apply excessive thread locking compound otherwise the thread may be damaged on subsequent removal.
- Certain fasteners are impregnated with a dry film type coating of locking compound on their threads. Always renew this type of fastener if disturbed.
- Anti-seize compounds, such as copper-based greases, can be applied to protect threads from seizure due to extreme heat and corrosion. A common instance is spark plug threads and exhaust system fasteners.

3 Measuring tools and gauges

Feeler gauges

- Feeler gauges (or blades) are used for measuring small gaps and clearances **(see illustration 3.1)**. They can also be used to measure endfloat (sideplay) of a component on a shaft where access is not possible with a dial gauge.
- Feeler gauge sets should be treated with care and not bent or damaged. They are etched with their size on one face. Keep them clean and very lightly oiled to prevent corrosion build-up.

3.1 Feeler gauges are used for measuring small gaps and clearances - thickness is marked on one face of gauge

- When measuring a clearance, select a gauge which is a light sliding fit between the two components. You may need to use two gauges together to measure the clearance accurately.

Micrometers

- A micrometer is a precision tool capable of measuring to 0.01 or 0.001 of a millimetre. It should always be stored in its case and not in the general toolbox. It must be kept clean and never dropped, otherwise its frame or measuring anvils could be distorted resulting in inaccurate readings.
- External micrometers are used for measuring outside diameters of components and have many more applications than internal micrometers. Micrometers are available in different size ranges, eg 0 to 25 mm, 25 to 50 mm, and upwards in 25 mm steps; some large micrometers have interchangeable anvils to allow a range of measurements to be taken. Generally the largest precision measurement you are likely to take on a motorcycle is the piston diameter.
- Internal micrometers (or bore micrometers) are used for measuring inside diameters, such as valve guides and cylinder bores. Telescoping gauges and small hole gauges are used in conjunction with an external micrometer, whereas the more expensive internal micrometers have their own measuring device.

External micrometer

Note: *The conventional analogue type instrument is described. Although much easier to read, digital micrometers are considerably more expensive.*

- Always check the calibration of the micrometer before use. With the anvils closed (0 to 25 mm type) or set over a test gauge (for the larger types) the scale should read zero **(see illustration 3.2)**; make sure that the anvils (and test piece) are clean first. Any discrepancy can be adjusted by referring to the instructions supplied with the tool. Remember that the micrometer is a precision measuring tool - don't force the anvils closed, use the ratchet (4) on the end of the micrometer to close it. In this way, a measured force is always applied.

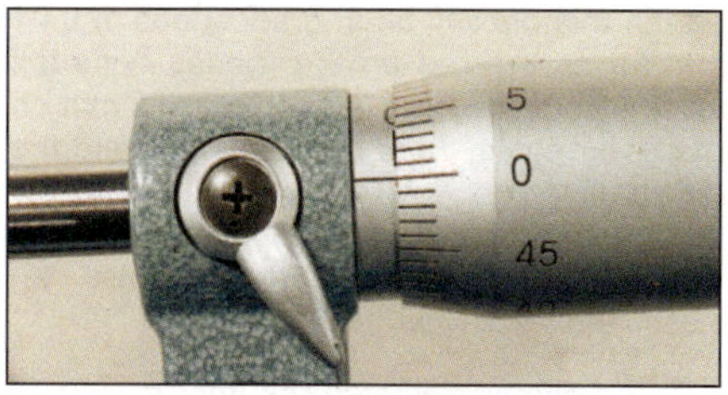

3.2 Check micrometer calibration before use

- To use, first make sure that the item being measured is clean. Place the anvil of the micrometer (1) against the item and use the thimble (2) to bring the spindle (3) lightly into contact with the other side of the item **(see illustration 3.3)**. Don't tighten the thimble down because this will damage the micrometer - instead use the ratchet (4) on the end of the micrometer. The ratchet mechanism applies a measured force preventing damage to the instrument.
- The micrometer is read by referring to the linear scale on the sleeve and the annular scale on the thimble. Read off the sleeve first to obtain the base measurement, then add the fine measurement from the thimble to obtain the overall reading. The linear scale on the sleeve represents the measuring range of the micrometer (eg 0 to 25 mm). The annular scale

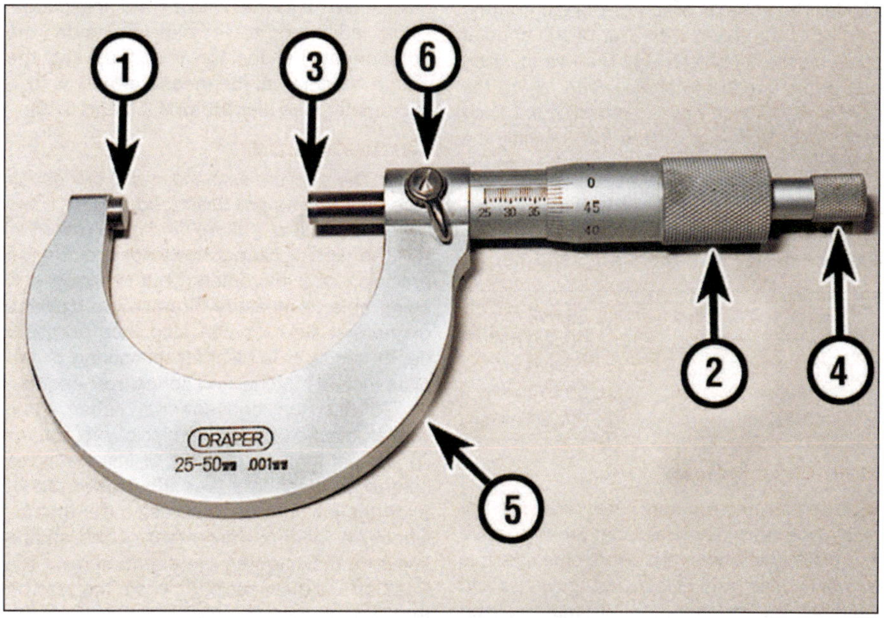

3.3 Micrometer component parts

1 Anvil	*3 Spindle*	*5 Frame*
2 Thimble	*4 Ratchet*	*6 Locking lever*

on the thimble will be in graduations of 0.01 mm (or as marked on the frame) - one full revolution of the thimble will move 0.5 mm on the linear scale. Take the reading where the datum line on the sleeve intersects the thimble's scale. Always position the eye directly above the scale otherwise an inaccurate reading will result.

In the example shown the item measures 2.95 mm **(see illustration 3.4)**:

Linear scale	2.00 mm
Linear scale	0.50 mm
Annular scale	0.45 mm
Total figure	**2.95 mm**

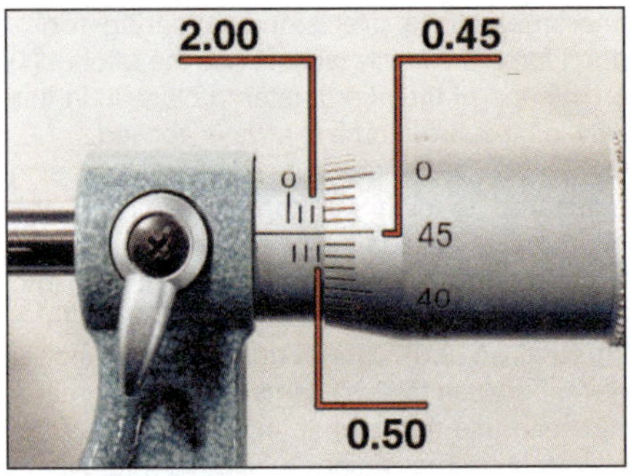

3.4 Micrometer reading of 2.95 mm

Most micrometers have a locking lever (6) on the frame to hold the setting in place, allowing the item to be removed from the micrometer.

- Some micrometers have a vernier scale on their sleeve, providing an even finer measurement to be taken, in 0.001 increments of a millimetre. Take the sleeve and thimble measurement as described above, then check which graduation on the vernier scale aligns with that of the annular scale on the thimble **Note:** *The eye must be perpendicular to the scale when taking the vernier reading - if necessary rotate the body of the micrometer to ensure this.* Multiply the vernier scale figure by 0.001 and add it to the base and fine measurement figures.

In the example shown the item measures 46.994 mm **(see illustrations 3.5 and 3.6)**:

Linear scale (base)	46.000 mm
Linear scale (base)	00.500 mm
Annular scale (fine)	00.490 mm
Vernier scale	00.004 mm
Total figure	**46.994 mm**

Internal micrometer

- Internal micrometers are available for measuring bore diameters, but are expensive and unlikely to be available for home use. It is suggested that a set of telescoping gauges and small hole gauges, both of which must be used with an external micrometer, will suffice for taking internal measurements on a motorcycle.
- Telescoping gauges can be used to measure internal diameters of components. Select a gauge with the correct size range, make sure its ends are clean and insert it into the bore. Expand the gauge, then lock its position and withdraw it from the bore **(see illustration 3.7)**. Measure across the gauge ends with a micrometer **(see illustration 3.8)**.
- Very small diameter bores (such as valve guides) are measured with a small hole gauge. Once adjusted to a slip-fit inside the component, its position is locked and the gauge withdrawn for measurement with a micrometer **(see illustrations 3.9 and 3.10)**.

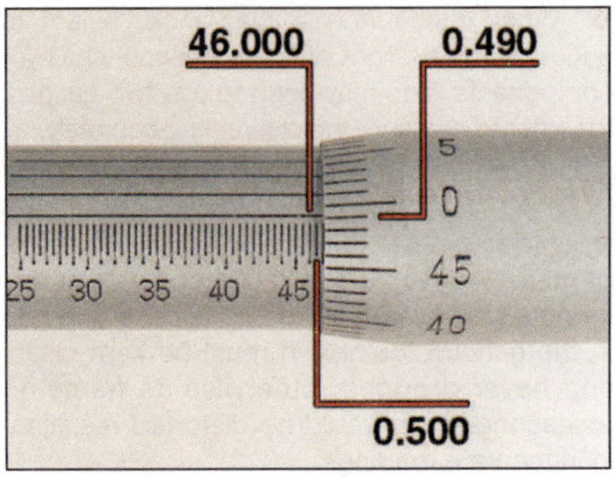

3.5 Micrometer reading of 46.99 mm on linear and annular scales . . .

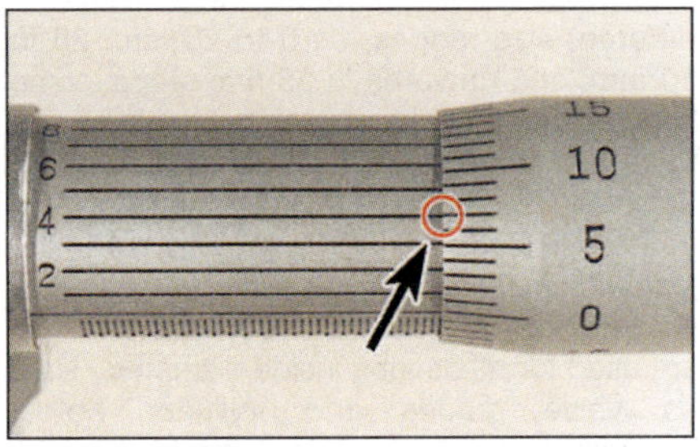

3.6 . . . and 0.004 mm on vernier scale

Vernier caliper

Note: *The conventional linear and dial gauge type instruments are described. Digital types are easier to read, but are far more expensive.*

- The vernier caliper does not provide the precision of a micrometer, but is versatile in being able to measure internal and external diameters. Some types also incorporate a depth gauge. It is ideal for measuring clutch plate friction material and spring free lengths.
- To use the conventional linear scale vernier, slacken off the vernier clamp screws (1) and set its jaws over (2), or inside (3), the item to be measured **(see illustration 3.11)**. Slide the jaw into contact, using the thumb-wheel (4) for fine movement of the sliding scale (5) then tighten the clamp screws (1). Read off the main scale (6) where the zero on the sliding scale (5) intersects it, taking the whole number to the left of the zero; this provides the base measurement. View along the sliding scale and select the division which lines up exactly with any of the divisions on the main scale, noting that the divisions usually represents 0.02 of a millimetre. Add this fine measurement to the base measurement to obtain the total reading.

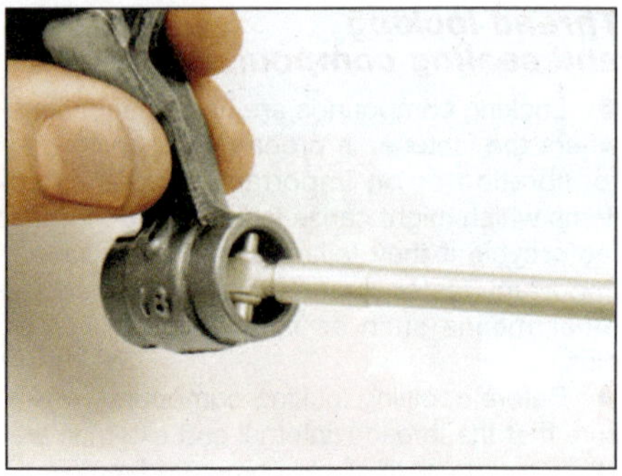

3.7 Expand the telescoping gauge in the bore, lock its position . . .

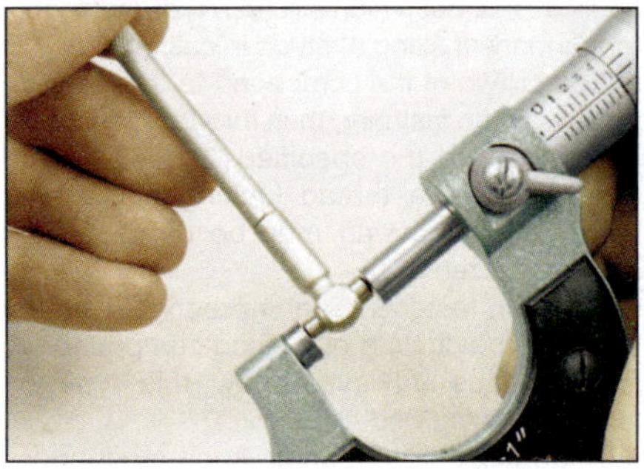

3.8 . . . then measure the gauge with a micrometer

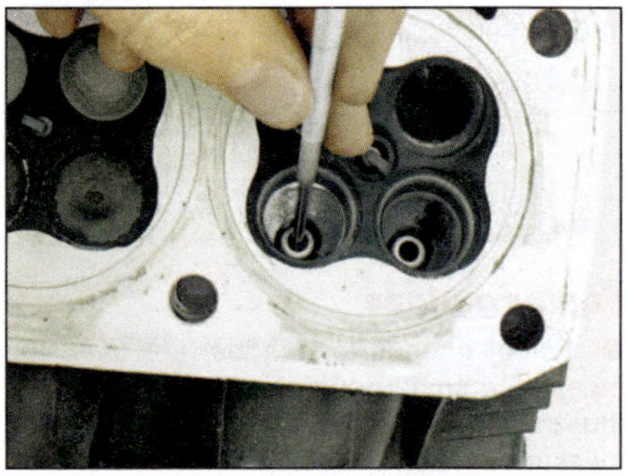

3.9 Expand the small hole gauge in the bore, lock its position . . .

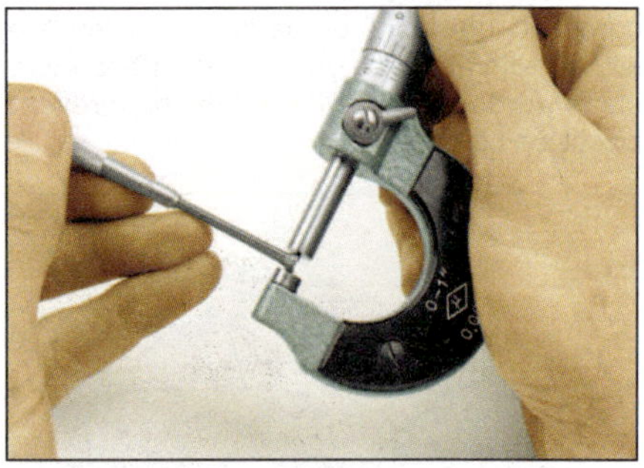

3.10 . . . then measure the gauge with a micrometer

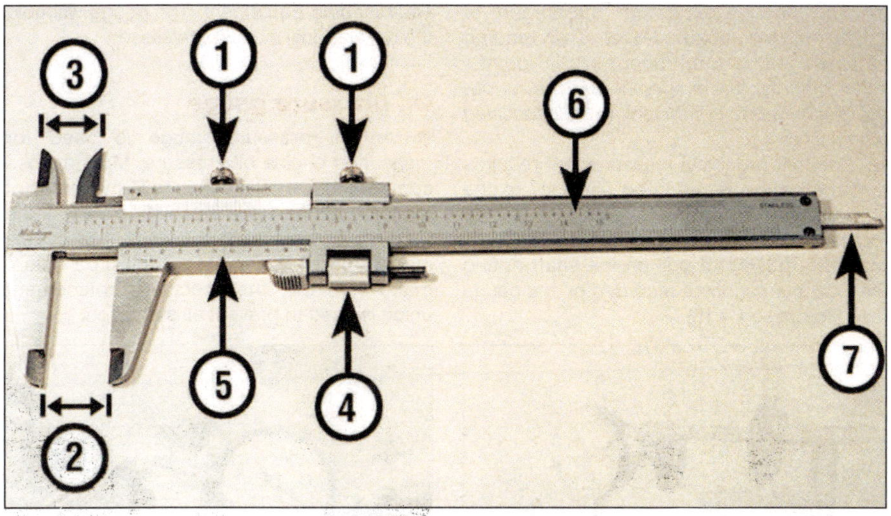

3.11 Vernier component parts (linear gauge)

1 Clamp screws
2 External jaws
3 Internal jaws
4 Thumbwheel
5 Sliding scale
6 Main scale
7 Depth gauge

In the example shown the item measures 55.92 mm **(see illustration 3.12)**:

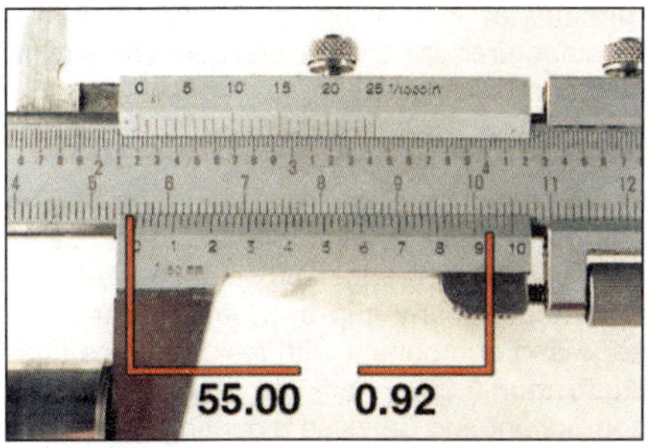

3.12 Vernier gauge reading of 55.92 mm

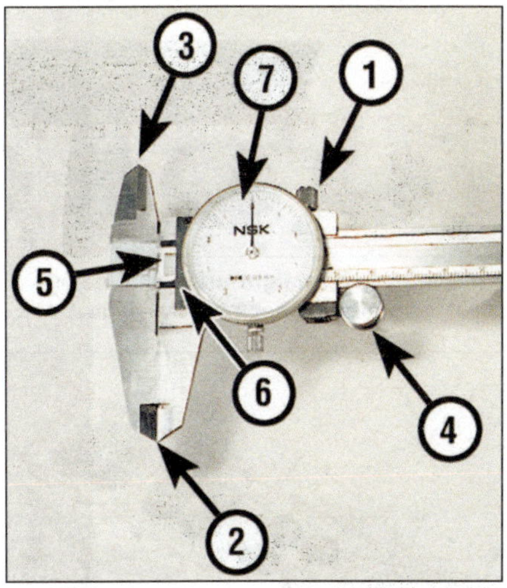

3.13 Vernier component parts (dial gauge)

1 Clamp screw
2 External jaws
3 Internal jaws
4 Thumbwheel
5 Main scale
6 Sliding scale
7 Dial gauge

Base measurement	55.00 mm
Fine measurement	00.92 mm
Total figure	**55.92 mm**

- Some vernier calipers are equipped with a dial gauge for fine measurement. Before use, check that the jaws are clean, then close them fully and check that the dial gauge reads zero. If necessary adjust the gauge ring accordingly. Slacken the vernier clamp screw (1) and set its jaws over (2), or inside (3), the item to be measured **(see illustration 3.13)**. Slide the jaws into contact, using the thumbwheel (4) for fine movement. Read off the main scale (5) where the edge of the sliding scale (6) intersects it, taking the whole number to the left of the zero; this provides the base measurement. Read off the needle position on the dial gauge (7) scale to provide the fine measurement; each division represents 0.05 of a millimetre. Add this fine measurement to the base measurement to obtain the total reading.

In the example shown the item measures 55.95 mm **(see illustration 3.14)**:

Base measurement	55.00 mm
Fine measurement	00.95 mm
Total figure	**55.95 mm**

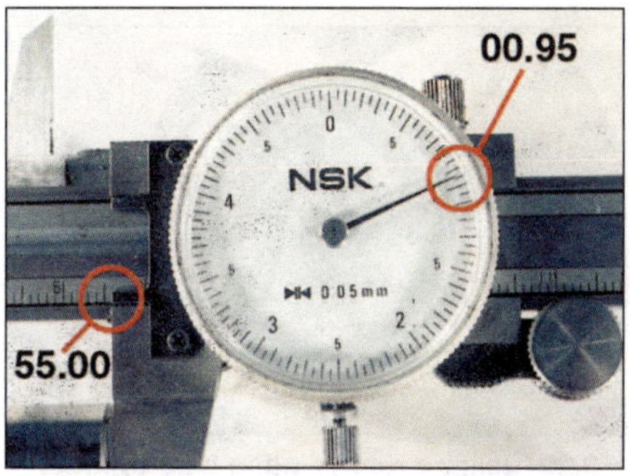

3.14 Vernier gauge reading of 55.95 mm

Plastigauge

- Plastigauge is a plastic material which can be compressed between two surfaces to measure the oil clearance between them. The width of the compressed Plastigauge is measured against a calibrated scale to determine the clearance.
- Common uses of Plastigauge are for measuring the clearance between crankshaft journal and main bearing inserts, between crankshaft journal and big-end bearing inserts, and between camshaft and bearing surfaces. The following example describes big-end oil clearance measurement.
- Handle the Plastigauge material carefully to prevent distortion. Using a sharp knife, cut a length which corresponds with the width of the bearing being measured and place it carefully across the journal so that it is parallel with the shaft **(see illustration 3.15)**. Carefully install both bearing shells and the connecting rod. Without rotating the rod on the journal tighten its bolts or nuts (as applicable) to the specified torque. The connecting rod and bearings are then disassembled and the crushed Plastigauge examined.

3.15 Plastigauge placed across shaft journal

- Using the scale provided in the Plastigauge kit, measure the width of the material to determine the oil clearance **(see illustration 3.16)**. Always remove all traces of Plastigauge after use using your fingernails.

Caution: Arriving at the correct clearance demands that the assembly is torqued correctly, according to the settings and sequence (where applicable) provided by the motorcycle manufacturer.

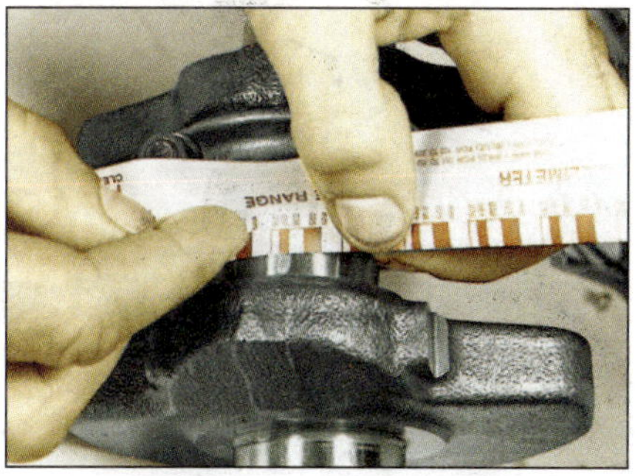

3.16 Measuring the width of the crushed Plastigauge

Dial gauge or DTI (Dial Test Indicator)

● A dial gauge can be used to accurately measure small amounts of movement. Typical uses are measuring shaft runout or shaft endfloat (sideplay) and setting piston position for ignition timing on two-strokes. A dial gauge set usually comes with a range of different probes and adapters and mounting equipment.

● The gauge needle must point to zero when at rest. Rotate the ring around its periphery to zero the gauge.

● Check that the gauge is capable of reading the extent of movement in the work. Most gauges have a small dial set in the face which records whole millimetres of movement as well as the fine scale around the face periphery which is calibrated in 0.01 mm divisions. Read off the small dial first to obtain the base measurement, then add the measurement from the fine scale to obtain the total reading.

In the example shown the gauge reads 1.48 mm **(see illustration 3.17)**:

Base measurement	1.00 mm
Fine measurement	0.48 mm
Total figure	**1.48 mm**

3.17 Dial gauge reading of 1.48 mm

● If measuring shaft runout, the shaft must be supported in vee-blocks and the gauge mounted on a stand perpendicular to the shaft. Rest the tip of the gauge against the centre of the shaft and rotate the shaft slowly whilst watching the gauge reading **(see illustration 3.18)**. Take several measurements along the length of the shaft and record the maximum gauge reading as the amount of runout in the shaft. **Note:** *The reading obtained will be total runout at that point - some manufacturers specify that the runout figure is halved to compare with their specified runout limit.*

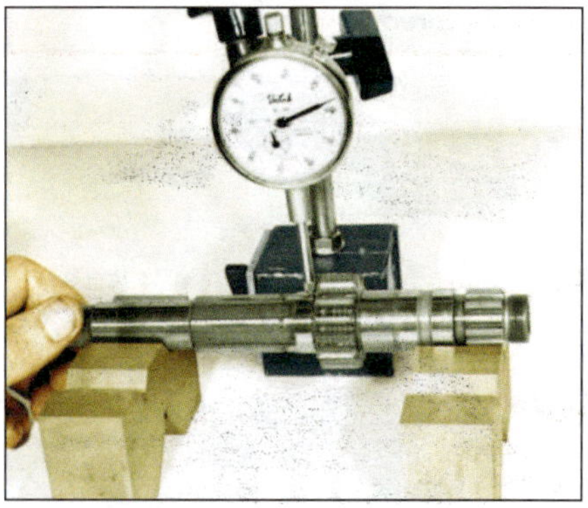

3.18 Using a dial gauge to measure shaft runout

● Endfloat (sideplay) measurement requires that the gauge is mounted securely to the surrounding component with its probe touching the end of the shaft. Using hand pressure, push and pull on the shaft noting the maximum endfloat recorded on the gauge **(see illustration 3.19)**.

3.19 Using a dial gauge to measure shaft endfloat

● A dial gauge with suitable adapters can be used to determine piston position BTDC on two-stroke engines for the purposes of ignition timing. The gauge, adapter and suitable length probe are installed in the place of the spark plug and the gauge zeroed at TDC. If the piston position is specified as 1.14 mm BTDC, rotate the engine back to 2.00 mm BTDC, then slowly forwards to 1.14 mm BTDC.

Cylinder compression gauges

● A compression gauge is used for measuring cylinder compression. Either the rubber-cone type or the threaded adapter type can be used. The latter is preferred to ensure a perfect seal against the cylinder head. A 0 to 300 psi (0 to 20 Bar) type gauge (for petrol/gasoline engines) will be suitable for motorcycles.

● The spark plug is removed and the gauge either held hard against the cylinder head (cone type) or the gauge adapter screwed into the cylinder head (threaded type) **(see illustration 3.20)**. Cylinder compression is measured with the engine turning over, but not running - carry out the compression test as described in *Fault Finding Equipment*. The gauge will hold the reading until manually released.

3.20 Using a rubber-cone type cylinder compression gauge

Oil pressure gauge

● An oil pressure gauge is used for measuring engine oil pressure. Most gauges come with a set of adapters to fit the thread of the take-off point **(see illustration 3.21)**. If the take-off point specified by the motorcycle manufacturer is an external oil pipe union, make sure that the specified replacement union is used to prevent oil starvation.

3.21 Oil pressure gauge and take-off point adapter (arrow)

● Oil pressure is measured with the engine running (at a specific rpm) and often the manufacturer will specify pressure limits for a cold and hot engine.

Straight-edge and surface plate

● If checking the gasket face of a component for warpage, place a steel rule or precision straight-edge across the gasket face and measure any gap between the straight-edge and component with feeler gauges **(see illustration 3.22)**. Check diagonally across the component and between mounting holes **(see illustration 3.23)**.

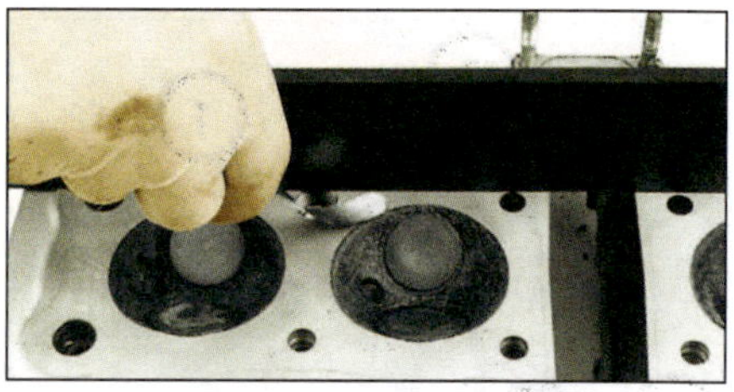

3.22 Use a straight-edge and feeler gauges to check for warpage

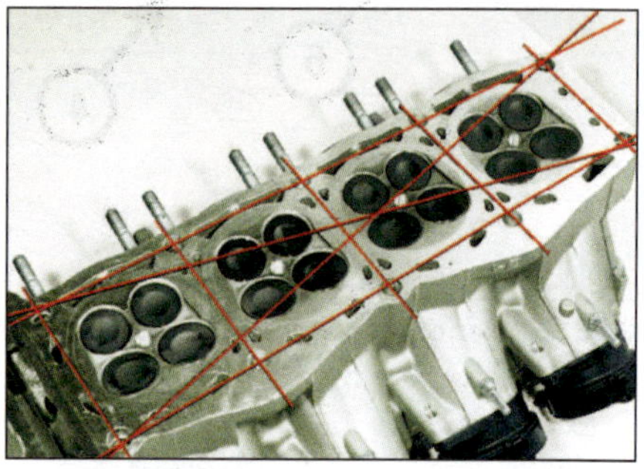

3.23 Check for warpage in these directions

● Checking individual components for warpage, such as clutch plain (metal) plates, requires a perfectly flat plate or piece or plate glass and feeler gauges.

4 Torque and leverage

What is torque?

● Torque describes the twisting force about a shaft. The amount of torque applied is determined by the distance from the centre of the shaft to the end of the lever and the amount of force being applied to the end of the lever; distance multiplied by force equals torque.
● The manufacturer applies a measured torque to a bolt or nut to ensure that it will not slacken in use and to hold two components securely together without movement in the joint. The actual torque setting depends on the thread size, bolt or nut material and the composition of the components being held.
● Too little torque may cause the fastener to loosen due to vibration, whereas too much torque will distort the joint faces of the component or cause the fastener to shear off. Always stick to the specified torque setting.

Using a torque wrench

● Check the calibration of the torque wrench and make sure it has a suitable range for the job. Torque wrenches are available in Nm (Newton-metres), kgf m (kilograms-force metre), lbf ft (pounds-feet), lbf in (inch-pounds). Do not confuse lbf ft with lbf in.
● Adjust the tool to the desired torque on the scale **(see illustration 4.1)**. If your torque wrench is not calibrated in the units specified, carefully convert the figure (see *Conversion Factors*). A manufacturer sometimes gives a torque setting as a range (8 to 10 Nm) rather than a single figure - in this case set the tool midway between the two settings. The same torque may be expressed as 9 Nm ± 1 Nm. Some torque wrenches have a method of locking the setting so that it isn't inadvertently altered during use.

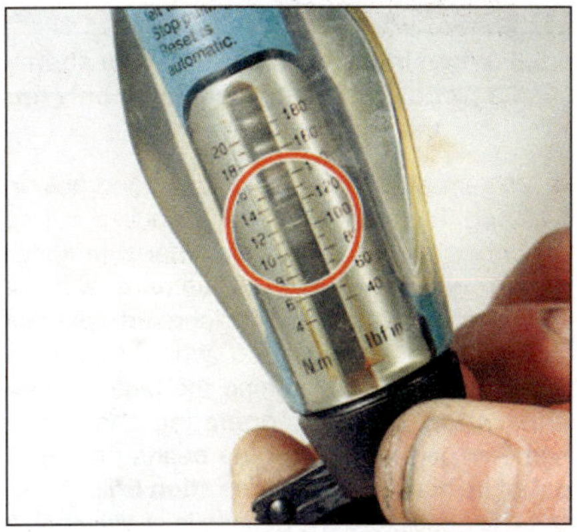

4.1 Set the torque wrench index mark to the setting required, in this case 12 Nm

● Install the bolts/nuts in their correct location and secure them lightly. Their threads must be clean and free of any old locking compound. Unless specified the threads and flange should be dry - oiled threads are necessary in certain circumstances and the manufacturer will take this into account in the specified torque figure. Similarly, the manufacturer may also specify the application of thread-locking compound.
● Tighten the fasteners in the specified sequence until the torque wrench clicks, indicating that the torque setting has been reached. Apply the torque again to double-check the setting. Where different thread diameter fasteners secure the component, as a rule tighten the larger diameter ones first.
● When the torque wrench has been finished with, release the lock (where applicable) and fully back off its setting to zero - do not leave the torque wrench tensioned. Also, do not use a torque wrench for slackening a fastener.

Angle-tightening

● Manufacturers often specify a figure in degrees for final tightening of a fastener. This usually follows tightening to a specific torque setting.
● A degree disc can be set and attached to the socket **(see illustration 4.2)** or a protractor can be used to mark the angle of movement on the bolt/nut head and the surrounding casting **(see illustration 4.3)**.

4.2 Angle tightening can be accomplished with a torque-angle gauge . . .

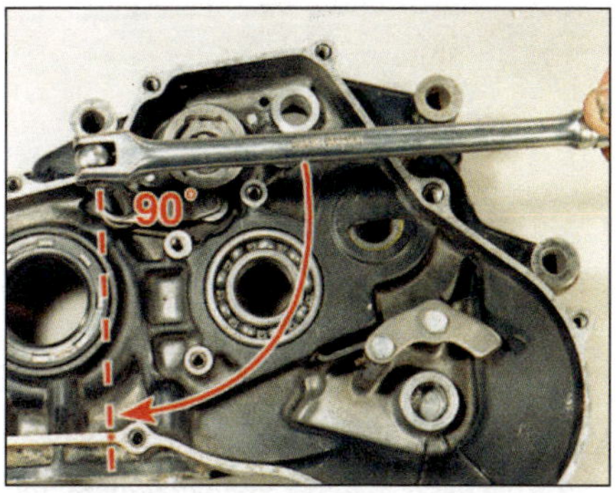

4.3 . . . or by marking the angle on the surrounding component

Loosening sequences

● Where more than one bolt/nut secures a component, loosen each fastener evenly a little at a time. In this way, not all the stress of the joint is held by one fastener and the components are not likely to distort.
● If a tightening sequence is provided, work in the REVERSE of this, but if not, work from the outside in, in a criss-cross sequence **(see illustration 4.4)**.

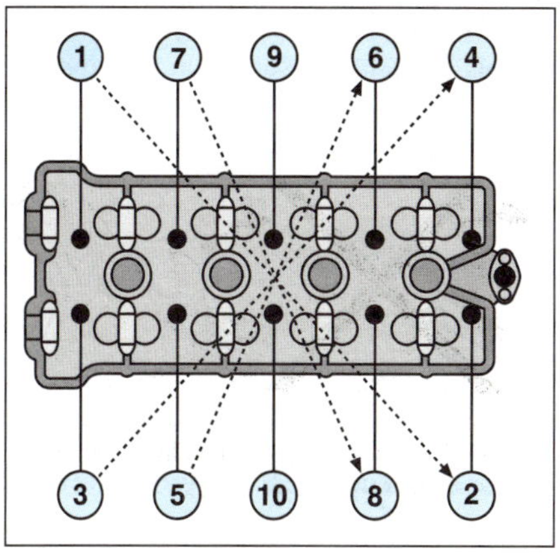

4.4 When slackening, work from the outside inwards

Tightening sequences

● If a component is held by more than one fastener it is important that the retaining bolts/nuts are tightened evenly to prevent uneven stress build-up and distortion of sealing faces. This is especially important on high-compression joints such as the cylinder head.
● A sequence is usually provided by the manufacturer, either in a diagram or actually marked in the casting. If not, always start in the centre and work outwards in a criss-cross pattern **(see illustration 4.5)**. Start off by securing all bolts/nuts finger-tight, then set the torque wrench and tighten each fastener by a small amount in sequence until the final torque is reached. By following this practice,

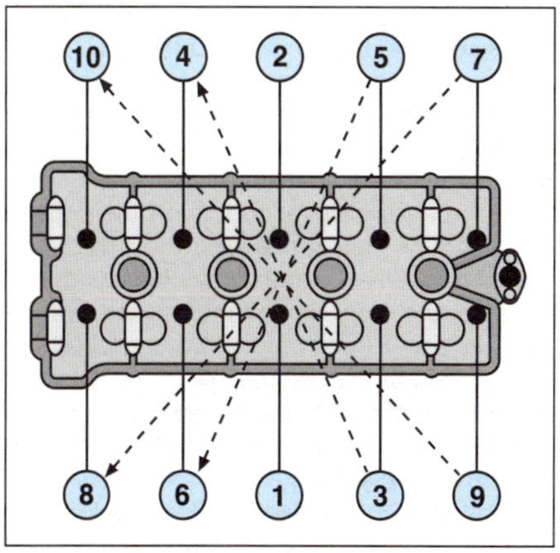

4.5 When tightening, work from the inside outwards

the joint will be held evenly and will not be distorted. Important joints, such as the cylinder head and big-end fasteners often have two- or three-stage torque settings.

Applying leverage

- Use tools at the correct angle. Position a socket wrench or spanner on the bolt/nut so that you pull it towards you when loosening. If this can't be done, push the spanner without curling your fingers around it **(see illustration 4.6)** - the spanner may slip or the fastener loosen suddenly, resulting in your fingers being crushed against a component.

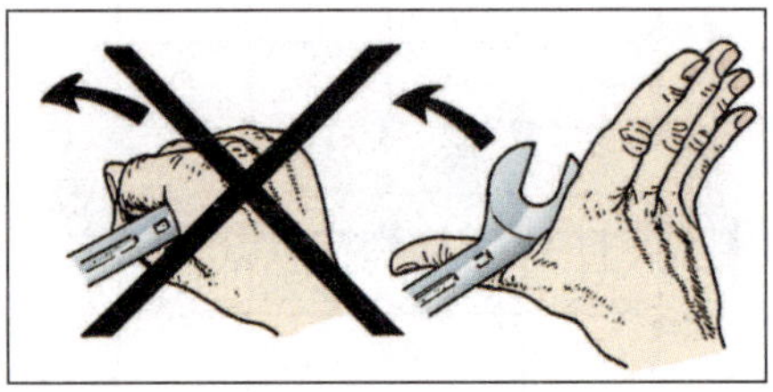

4.6 If you can't pull on the spanner to loosen a fastener, push with your hand open

- Additional leverage is gained by extending the length of the lever. The best way to do this is to use a breaker bar instead of the regular length tool, or to slip a length of tubing over the end of the spanner or socket wrench.
- If additional leverage will not work, the fastener head is either damaged or firmly corroded in place (see *Fasteners*).

5 Bearings

Bearing removal and installation

Drivers and sockets

- Before removing a bearing, always inspect the casing to see which way it must be driven out - some casings will have retaining plates or a cast step. Also check for any identifying markings on the bearing and if installed to a certain depth, measure this at this stage. Some roller bearings are sealed on one side - take note of the original fitted position.
- Bearings can be driven out of a casing using a bearing driver tool (with the correct size head) or a socket of the correct diameter. Select the driver head or socket so that it contacts the outer race of the bearing, not the balls/rollers or inner race. Always support the casing around the bearing housing with wood blocks, otherwise there is a risk of fracture. The bearing is driven out with a few blows on the driver or socket from a heavy mallet. Unless access is severely restricted (as with wheel bearings), a pin-punch is not recommended unless it is moved around the bearing to keep it square in its housing.
- The same equipment can be used to install bearings. Make sure the bearing housing is supported on wood blocks and line up the bearing in its housing. Fit the bearing as noted on removal - generally they are installed with their marked side facing outwards. Tap the bearing squarely into its housing using a driver or socket which bears only on the bearing's outer race - contact with the bearing balls/rollers or inner race will destroy it **(see illustrations 5.1 and 5.2)**.
- Check that the bearing inner race and balls/rollers rotate freely.

5.1 Using a bearing driver against the bearing's outer race

5.2 Using a large socket against the bearing's outer race

Pullers and slide-hammers

- Where a bearing is pressed on a shaft a puller will be required to extract it **(see illustration 5.3)**. Make sure that the puller clamp or legs fit securely behind the bearing and are unlikely to slip out. If pulling a bearing off a gear shaft for example, you may have to locate the puller behind a gear pinion if there is no access to the race and draw the gear pinion off the shaft as well **(see illustration 5.4)**.

5.3 This bearing puller clamps behind the bearing and pressure is applied to the shaft end to draw the bearing off

Caution: Ensure that the puller's centre bolt locates securely against the end of the shaft and will not slip when pressure is applied. Also ensure that puller does not damage the shaft end.

5.4 Where no access is available to the rear of the bearing, it is sometimes possible to draw off the adjacent component

- Operate the puller so that its centre bolt exerts pressure on the shaft end and draws the bearing off the shaft.
- When installing the bearing on the shaft, tap only on the bearing's inner race - contact with the balls/rollers or outer race with destroy the bearing. Use a socket or length of tubing as a drift which fits over the shaft end **(see illustration 5.5)**.

5.5 When installing a bearing on a shaft use a piece of tubing which bears only on the bearing's inner race

- Where a bearing locates in a blind hole in a casing, it cannot be driven or pulled out as described above. A slide-hammer with knife-edged bearing puller attachment will be required. The puller attachment passes through the bearing and when tightened expands to fit firmly behind the bearing **(see illustration 5.6)**. By operating the slide-hammer part of the tool the bearing is jarred out of its housing **(see illustration 5.7)**.
- It is possible, if the bearing is of reasonable weight, for it to drop out of its housing if the casing is heated as described opposite. If this

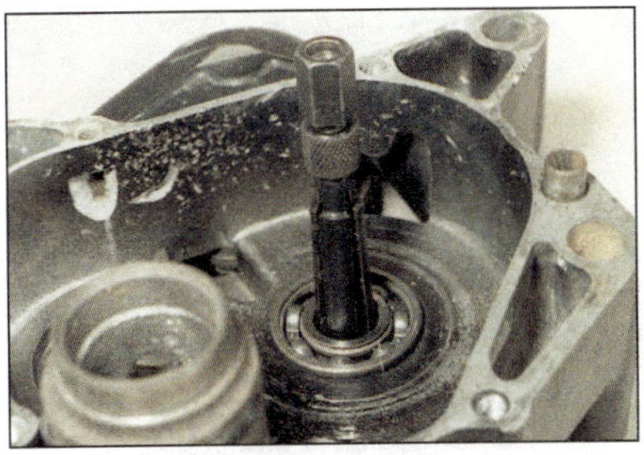

5.6 **Expand the bearing puller so that it locks behind the bearing . . .**

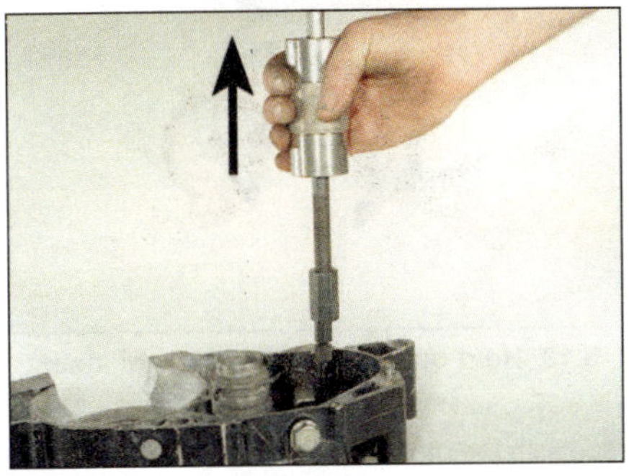

5.7 **. . . attach the slide hammer to the bearing puller**

method is attempted, first prepare a work surface which will enable the casing to be tapped face down to help dislodge the bearing - a wood surface is ideal since it will not damage the casing's gasket surface. Wearing protective gloves, tap the heated casing several times against the work surface to dislodge the bearing under its own weight **(see illustration 5.8)**.

5.8 **Tapping a casing face down on wood blocks can often dislodge a bearing**

● Bearings can be installed in blind holes using the driver or socket method described above.

Drawbolts

● Where a bearing or bush is set in the eye of a component, such as a suspension linkage arm or connecting rod small-end, removal by drift may damage the component. Furthermore, a rubber bushing in a shock absorber eye cannot successfully be driven out of position. If access is available to a engineering press, the task is straightforward. If not, a drawbolt can be fabricated to extract the bearing or bush.

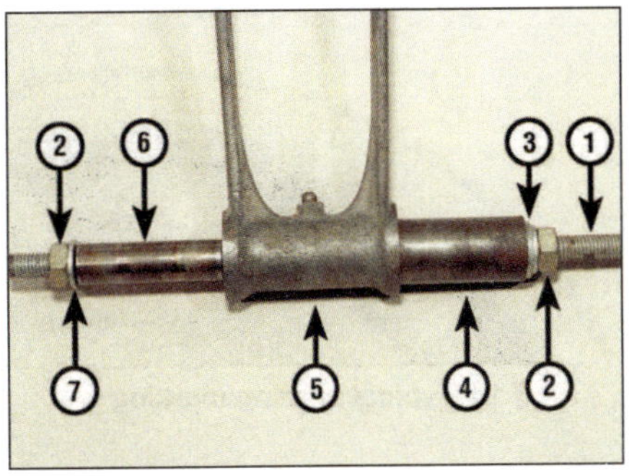

5.9 **Drawbolt component parts assembled on a suspension arm**

1 Bolt or length of threaded bar
2 Nuts
3 Washer (external diameter greater than tubing internal diameter)
4 Tubing (internal diameter sufficient to accommodate bearing)
5 Suspension arm with bearing
6 Tubing (external diameter slightly smaller than bearing)
7 Washer (external diameter slightly smaller than bearing)

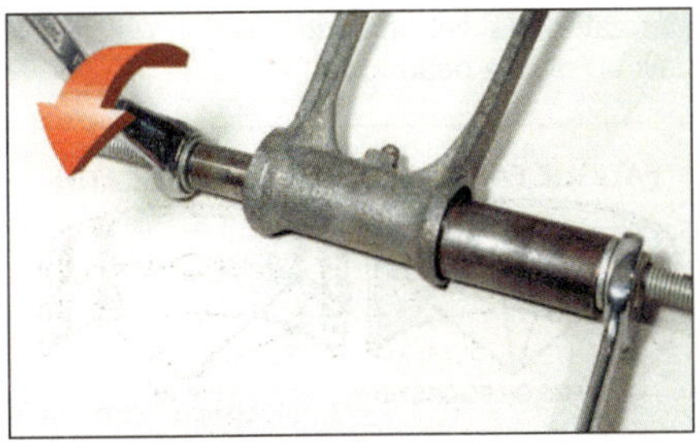

5.10 **Drawing the bearing out of the suspension arm**

● To extract the bearing/bush you will need a long bolt with nut (or piece of threaded bar with two nuts), a piece of tubing which has an internal diameter larger than the bearing/bush, another piece of tubing which has an external diameter slightly smaller than the bearing/ bush, and a selection of washers **(see illustrations 5.9 and 5.10)**. Note that the pieces of tubing must be of the same length, or longer, than the bearing/bush.

● The same kit (without the pieces of tubing) can be used to draw the new bearing/bush back into place **(see illustration 5.11)**.

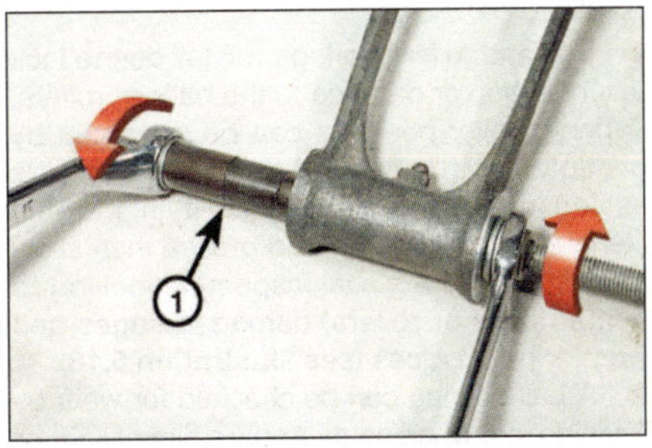

5.11 **Installing a new bearing (1) in the suspension arm**

Temperature change

● If the bearing's outer race is a tight fit in the casing, the aluminium casing can be heated to release its grip on the bearing. Aluminium will expand at a greater rate than the steel bearing outer race. There are several ways to do this, but avoid any localised extreme heat (such as a blow torch) - aluminium alloy has a low melting point.

● Approved methods of heating a casing are using a domestic oven (heated to 100°C) or immersing the casing in boiling water **(see illustration 5.12)**. Low temperature range localised heat sources such as a paint stripper heat gun or clothes iron can also be used **(see illustration 5.13)**. Alternatively, soak a rag in boiling water, wring it out and wrap it around the bearing housing.

> ***Warning: All of these methods require care in use to prevent scalding and burns to the hands. Wear protective gloves when handling hot components.***

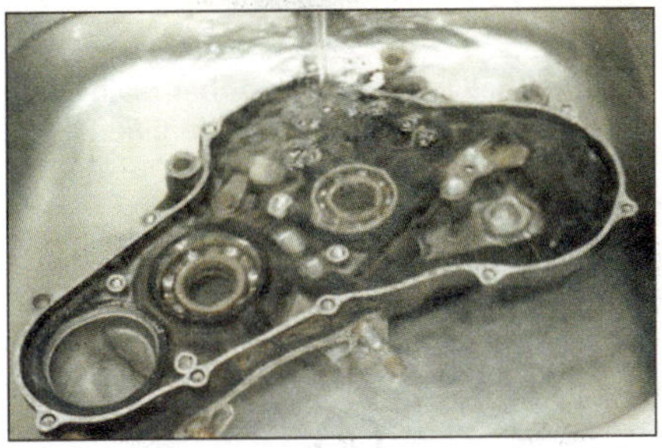

5.12 **A casing can be immersed in a sink of boiling water to aid bearing removal**

5.13 **Using a localised heat source to aid bearing removal**

● If heating the whole casing note that plastic components, such as the neutral switch, may suffer - remove them beforehand.

● After heating, remove the bearing as described above. You may find that the expansion is sufficient for the bearing to fall out of the casing under its own weight or with a light tap on the driver or socket.

● If necessary, the casing can be heated to aid bearing installation, and this is sometimes the recommended procedure if the motorcycle manufacturer has designed the housing and bearing fit with this intention.

● Installation of bearings can be eased by placing them in a freezer the night before installation. The steel bearing will contract slightly, allowing easy insertion in its housing. This is often useful when installing steering head outer races in the frame.

Bearing types and markings

● Plain shell bearings, ball bearings, needle roller bearings and tapered roller bearings will all be found on motorcycles **(see illustrations 5.14 and 5.15)**. The ball and roller types are usually caged between an inner and outer race, but uncaged variations may be found.

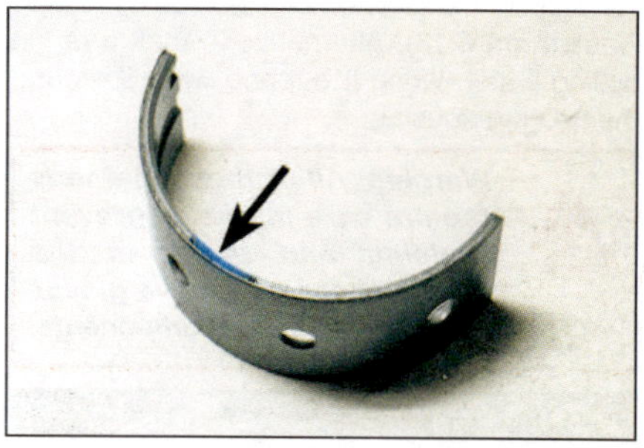

5.14 Shell bearings are either plain or grooved. They are usually identified by colour code (arrow)

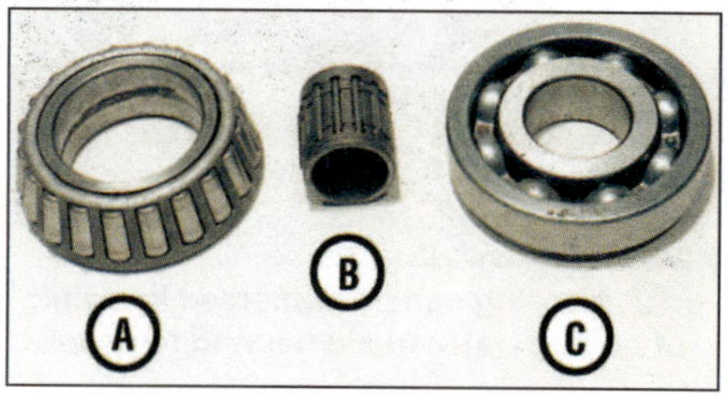

5.15 Tapered roller bearing (A), needle roller bearing (B) and ball journal bearing (C)

● Shell bearings (often called inserts) are usually found at the crankshaft main and connecting rod big-end where they are good at coping with high loads. They are made of a phosphor-bronze material and are impregnated with self-lubricating properties.

● Ball bearings and needle roller bearings consist of a steel inner and outer race with the balls or rollers between the races. They require constant lubrication by oil or grease and are good at coping with axial loads. Taper roller bearings consist of rollers set in a tapered cage set on the inner race; the outer race is separate. They are good at coping with axial loads and prevent movement along the shaft - a typical application is in the steering head.

● Bearing manufacturers produce bearings to ISO size standards and stamp one face of the bearing to indicate its internal and external diameter, load capacity and type **(see illustration 5.16)**.

● Metal bushes are usually of phosphor-bronze material. Rubber bushes are used in suspension mounting eyes. Fibre bushes have also been used in suspension pivots.

5.16 Typical bearing marking

Bearing fault finding

● If a bearing outer race has spun in its housing, the housing material will be damaged. You can use a bearing locking compound to bond the outer race in place if damage is not too severe.

● Shell bearings will fail due to damage of their working surface, as a result of lack of lubrication, corrosion or abrasive particles in the oil **(see illustration 5.17)**. Small particles of dirt in the oil may embed in the bearing material whereas larger particles will score the bearing and shaft journal. If a number of short journeys are made, insufficient heat will be generated to drive off condensation which has built up on the bearings.

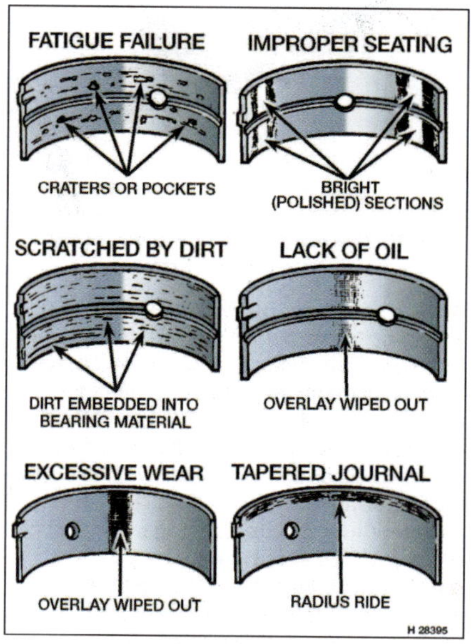

5.17 Typical bearing failures

● Ball and roller bearings will fail due to lack of lubrication or damage to the balls or rollers. Tapered-roller bearings can be damaged by overloading them. Unless the bearing is sealed on both sides, wash it in paraffin (kerosene) to remove all old grease then allow it to dry. Make a visual inspection looking to dented balls or rollers, damaged cages and worn or pitted races **(see illustration 5.18)**.

● A ball bearing can be checked for wear by listening to it when spun. Apply a film of light oil to the bearing and hold it close to the ear - hold the outer race with one hand and spin the inner

5.18 Example of ball journal bearing with damaged balls and cages

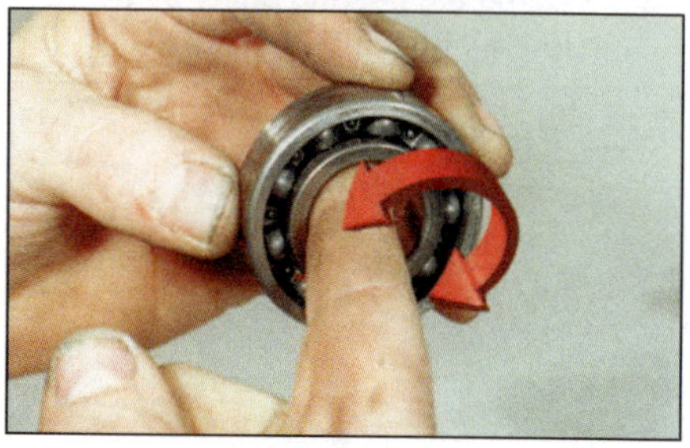

5.19 Hold outer race and listen to inner race when spun

race with the other hand **(see illustration 5.19)**. The bearing should be almost silent when spun; if it grates or rattles it is worn.

6 Oil seals

Oil seal removal and installation

● Oil seals should be renewed every time a component is dismantled. This is because the seal lips will become set to the sealing surface and will not necessarily reseal.

● Oil seals can be prised out of position using a large flat-bladed screwdriver **(see illustration 6.1)**. In the case of crankcase seals, check first that the seal is not lipped on the inside, preventing its removal with the crankcases joined.

6.1 Prise out oil seals with a large flat-bladed screwdriver

● New seals are usually installed with their marked face (containing the seal reference code) outwards and the spring side towards the fluid being retained. In certain cases, such as a two-stroke engine crankshaft seal, a double lipped seal may be used due to there being fluid or gas on each side of the joint.

- Use a bearing driver or socket which bears only on the outer hard edge of the seal to install it in the casing - tapping on the inner edge will damage the sealing lip.

Oil seal types and markings

- Oil seals are usually of the single-lipped type. Double-lipped seals are found where a liquid or gas is on both sides of the joint.
- Oil seals can harden and lose their sealing ability if the motorcycle has been in storage for a long period - renewal is the only solution.
- Oil seal manufacturers also conform to the ISO markings for seal size - these are moulded into the outer face of the seal **(see illustration 6.2)**.

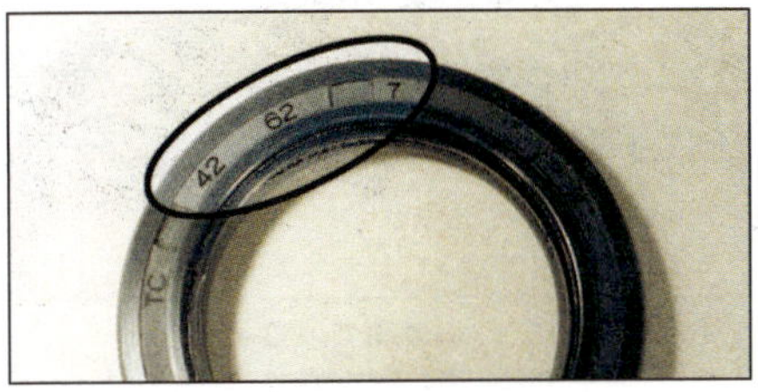

6.2 These oil seal markings indicate inside diameter, outside diameter and seal thickness

7 Gaskets and sealants

Types of gasket and sealant

- Gaskets are used to seal the mating surfaces between components and keep lubricants, fluids, vacuum or pressure contained within the assembly. Aluminium gaskets are sometimes found at the cylinder joints, but most gaskets are paper-based. If the mating surfaces of the components being joined are undamaged the gasket can be installed dry, although a dab of sealant or grease will be useful to hold it in place during assembly.
- RTV (Room Temperature Vulcanising) silicone rubber sealants cure when exposed to moisture in the atmosphere. These sealants are good at filling pits or irregular gasket faces, but will tend to be forced out of the joint under very high torque. They can be used to replace a paper gasket, but first make sure that the width of the paper gasket is not essential to the shimming of internal components. RTV sealants should not be used on components containing petrol (gasoline).
- Non-hardening, semi-hardening and hard setting liquid gasket compounds can be used with a gasket or between a metal-to-metal joint. Select the sealant to suit the application: universal non-hardening sealant can be used on virtually all joints; semi-hardening on joint faces which are rough or damaged; hard setting sealant on joints which require a permanent bond and are subjected to high temperature and pressure. **Note:** *Check first if the paper gasket has a bead of sealant impregnated in its surface before applying additional sealant.*
- When choosing a sealant, make sure it is suitable for the application, particularly if being applied in a high-temperature area or in the vicinity of fuel. Certain manufacturers produce sealants in either clear, silver or black colours to match the finish of the engine. This has a particular application on motorcycles where much of the engine is exposed.
- Do not over-apply sealant. That which is squeezed out on the outside of the joint can be wiped off, whereas an excess of sealant on the inside can break off and clog oilways.

Breaking a sealed joint

- Age, heat, pressure and the use of hard setting sealant can cause two components to stick together so tightly that they are difficult to separate using finger pressure alone. Do not resort to using levers unless there is a pry point provided for this purpose **(see illustration 7.1)** or else the gasket surfaces will be damaged.
- Use a soft-faced hammer **(see illustration 7.2)** or a wood block and conventional hammer to strike the component near the mating surface. Avoid hammering against cast extremities since they may break off. If this method fails, try using a wood wedge between the two components.

Caution: If the joint will not separate, double-check that you have removed all the fasteners.

7.1 If a pry point is provided, apply gently pressure with a flat-bladed screwdriver

7.2 Tap around the joint with a soft-faced mallet if necessary - don't strike cooling fins

Removal of old gasket and sealant

- Paper gaskets will most likely come away complete, leaving only a few traces stuck on the sealing faces of the components. It is imperative that all traces are removed to ensure correct sealing of the new gasket.
- Very carefully scrape all traces of gasket away making sure that the sealing surfaces are not gouged or scored by the scraper **(see illustrations 7.3, 7.4 and 7.5)**. Stubborn deposits can be removed by spraying with an aerosol gasket remover. Final preparation of

HAYNES HiNT

Most components have one or two hollow locating dowels between the two gasket faces. If a dowel cannot be removed, do not resort to gripping it with pliers - it will almost certainly be distorted. Install a close-fitting socket or Phillips screwdriver into the dowel and then grip the outer edge of the dowel to free it.

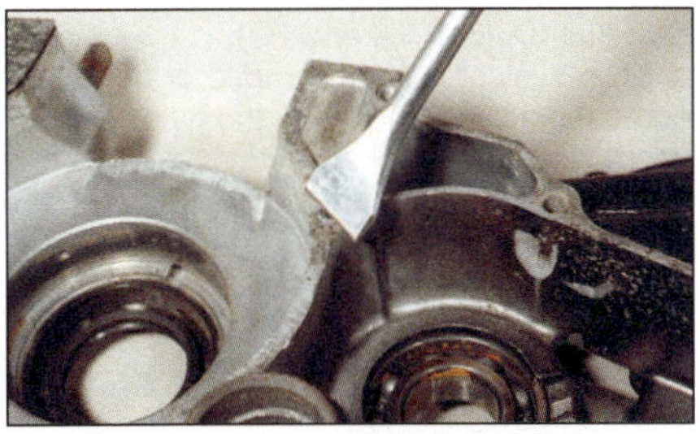

7.3 Paper gaskets can be scraped off with a gasket scraper tool . . .

7.4 . . . a knife blade . . .

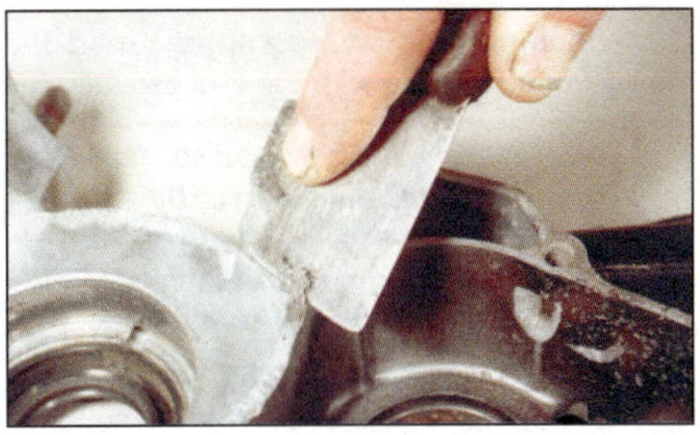

7.5 . . . or a household scraper

7.6 Fine abrasive paper is wrapped around a flat file to clean up the gasket face

7.7 A kitchen scourer can be used on stubborn deposits

the gasket surface can be made with very fine abrasive paper or a plastic kitchen scourer **(see illustrations 7.6 and 7.7)**.

- Old sealant can be scraped or peeled off components, depending on the type originally used. Note that gasket removal compounds are available to avoid scraping the components clean; make sure the gasket remover suits the type of sealant used.

8 Chains

Breaking and joining final drive chains

- Drive chains for all but small bikes are continuous and do not have a clip-type connecting link. The chain must be broken using a chain breaker tool and the new chain securely riveted together using a new soft rivet-type link. Never use a clip-type connecting link instead of a rivet-type link, except in an emergency. Various chain breaking and riveting tools are available, either as separate tools or combined as illustrated in the accompanying photographs - read the instructions supplied with the tool carefully.

Warning: The need to rivet the new link pins correctly cannot be overstressed - loss of control of the motorcycle is very likely to result if the chain breaks in use.

- Rotate the chain and look for the soft link. The soft link pins look like they have been

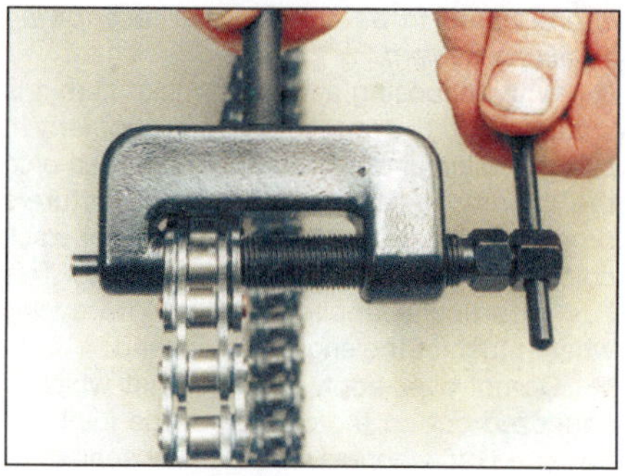

8.1 Tighten the chain breaker to push the pin out of the link . . .

8.2 . . . withdraw the pin, remove the tool . . .

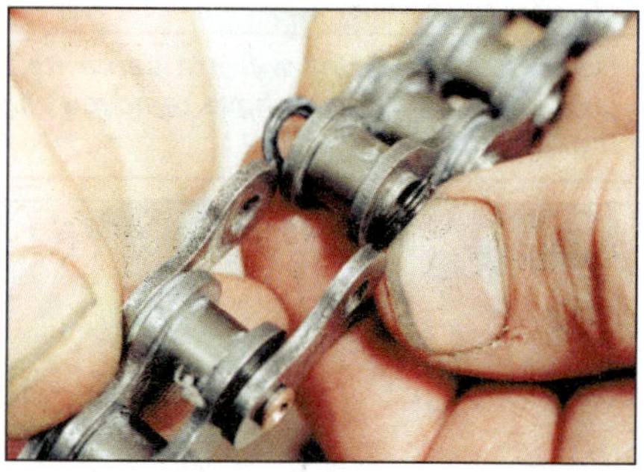

8.3 . . . and separate the chain link

deeply centre-punched instead of peened over like all the other pins **(see illustration 8.9)** and its sideplate may be a different colour. Position the soft link midway between the sprockets and assemble the chain breaker tool over one of the soft link pins **(see illustration 8.1)**. Operate the tool to push the pin out through the chain **(see illustration 8.2)**. On an O-ring chain, remove the O-rings **(see illustration 8.3)**. Carry out the same procedure on the other soft link pin.

Caution: Certain soft link pins (particularly on the larger chains) may require their ends to be filed or ground off before they can be pressed out using the tool.

- Check that you have the correct size and strength (standard or heavy duty) new soft link - do not reuse the old link. Look for the size marking on the chain sideplates **(see illustration 8.10)**.
- Position the chain ends so that they are engaged over the rear sprocket. On an O-ring

8.4 Insert the new soft link, with O-rings, through the chain ends . . .

8.5 . . . install the O-rings over the pin ends . . .

8.6 . . . followed by the sideplate

chain, install a new O-ring over each pin of the link and insert the link through the two chain ends **(see illustration 8.4)**. Install a new O-ring over the end of each pin, followed by the sideplate (with the chain manufacturer's marking facing outwards) **(see illustrations 8.5 and 8.6)**. On an unsealed chain, insert the link through the two chain ends, then install the sideplate with the chain manufacturer's marking facing outwards.

- Note that it may not be possible to install the sideplate using finger pressure alone. If using a joining tool, assemble it so that the plates of the tool clamp the link and press the sideplate over the pins **(see illustration 8.7)**. Otherwise, use two small sockets placed over

8.7 Push the sideplate into position using a clamp

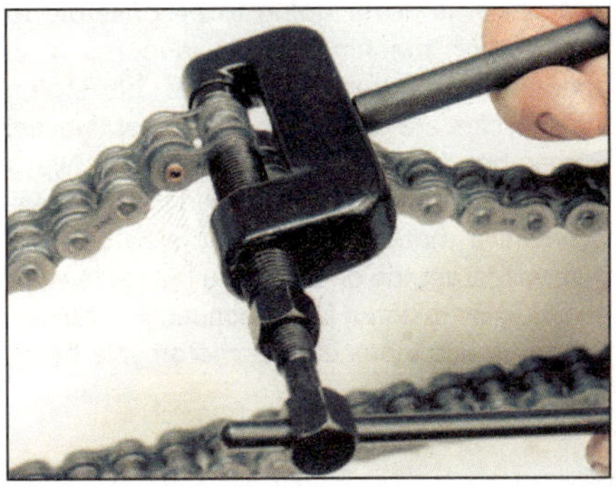

8.8 Assemble the chain riveting tool over one pin at a time and tighten it fully

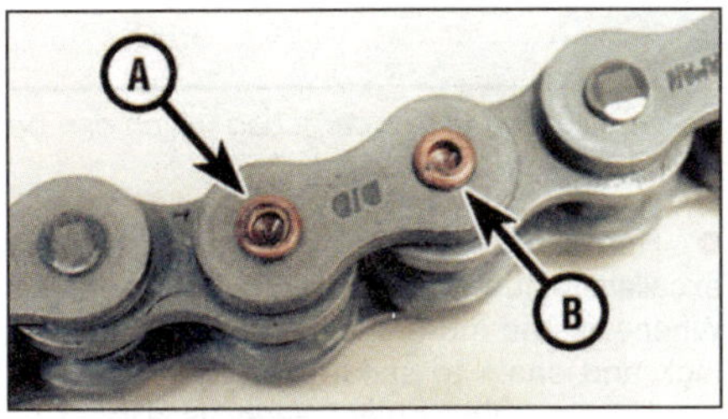

8.9 Pin end correctly riveted (A), pin end unriveted (B)

the rivet ends and two pieces of the wood between a G-clamp. Operate the clamp to press the sideplate over the pins.

- Assemble the joining tool over one pin (following the maker's instructions) and tighten the tool down to spread the pin end securely **(see illustrations 8.8 and 8.9)**. Do the same on the other pin.

> ***Warning: Check that the pin ends are secure and that there is no danger of the sideplate coming loose. If the pin ends are cracked the soft link must be renewed.***

Final drive chain sizing

- Chains are sized using a three digit number, followed by a suffix to denote the chain type **(see illustration 8.10)**. Chain type is either standard or heavy duty (thicker sideplates), and also unsealed or O-ring/X-ring type.
- The first digit of the number relates to the pitch of the chain, ie the distance from the centre of one pin to the centre of the next pin **(see illustration 8.11)**. Pitch is expressed in eighths of an inch, as follows:

8.10 Typical chain size and type marking

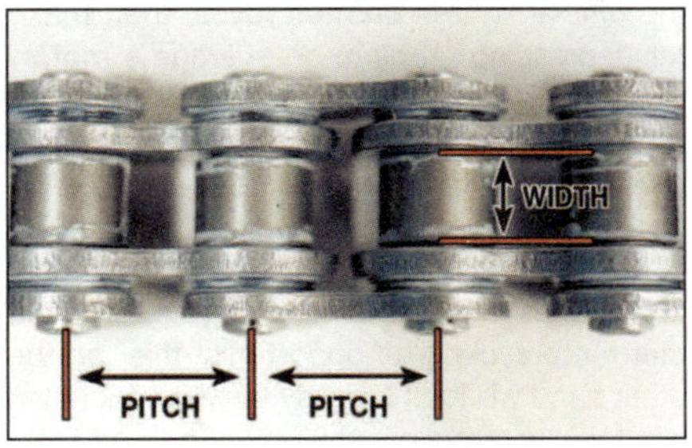

8.11 Chain dimensions

Sizes commencing with a 4 (eg 428) have a pitch of 1/2 inch (12.7 mm)

Sizes commencing with a 5 (eg 520) have a pitch of 5/8 inch (15.9 mm)

Sizes commencing with a 6 (eg 630) have a pitch of 3/4 inch (19.1 mm)

- The second and third digits of the chain size relate to the width of the rollers, again in imperial units, eg the 525 shown has 5/16 inch (7.94 mm) rollers **(see illustration 8.11)**.

9 Hoses

Clamping to prevent flow

- Small-bore flexible hoses can be clamped to prevent fluid flow whilst a component is worked on. Whichever method is used, ensure that the hose material is not permanently distorted or damaged by the clamp.

a) *A brake hose clamp available from auto accessory shops **(see illustration 9.1)**.*
b) *A wingnut type hose clamp **(see illustration 9.2)**.*

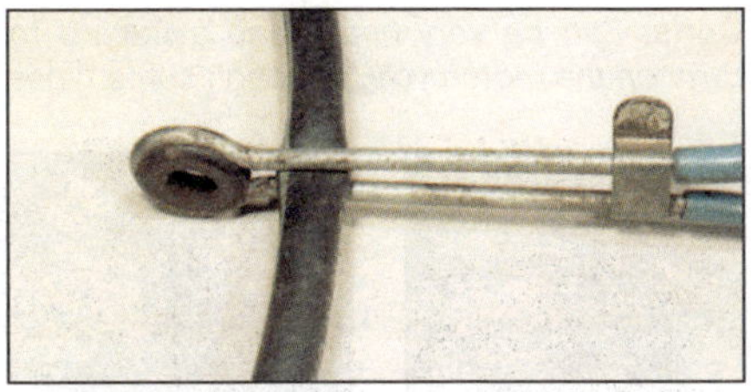

9.1 Hoses can be clamped with an automotive brake hose clamp . . .

9.2 . . . a wingnut type hose clamp . . .

c) *Two sockets placed each side of the hose and held with straight-jawed self-locking grips **(see illustration 9.3)**.*
d) *Thick card each side of the hose held between straight-jawed self-locking grips **(see illustration 9.4)**.*

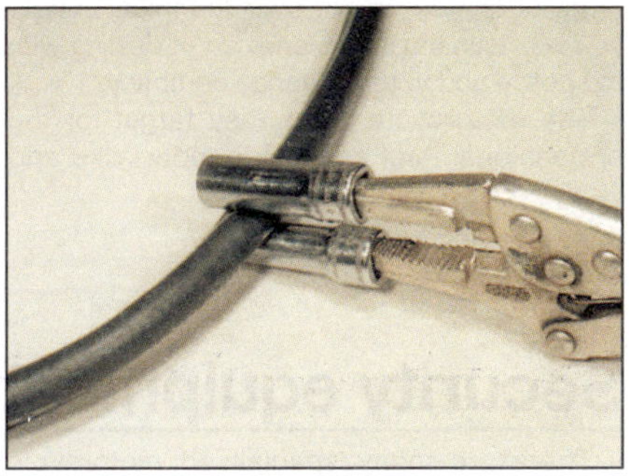

9.3 . . . two sockets and a pair of self-locking grips . . .

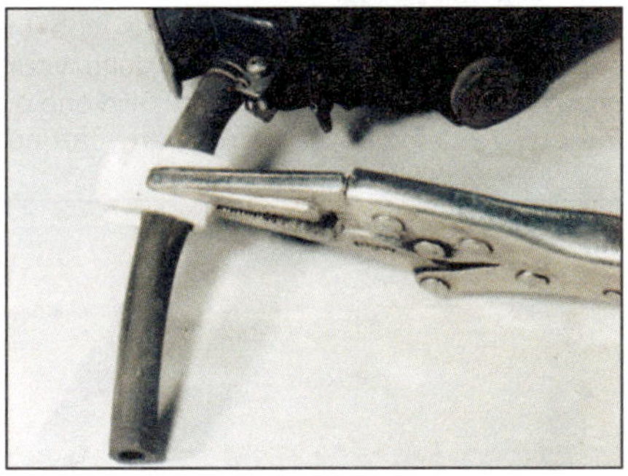

9.4 . . . or thick card and self-locking grips

Freeing and fitting hoses

- Always make sure the hose clamp is moved well clear of the hose end. Grip the hose with your hand and rotate it whilst pulling it off the union. If the hose has hardened due to age and will not move, slit it with a sharp knife and peel its ends off the union **(see illustration 9.5)**.
- Resist the temptation to use grease or soap on the unions to aid installation; although it helps the hose slip over the union it will equally aid the escape of fluid from the joint. It is preferable to soften the hose ends in hot water and wet the inside surface of the hose with water or a fluid which will evaporate.

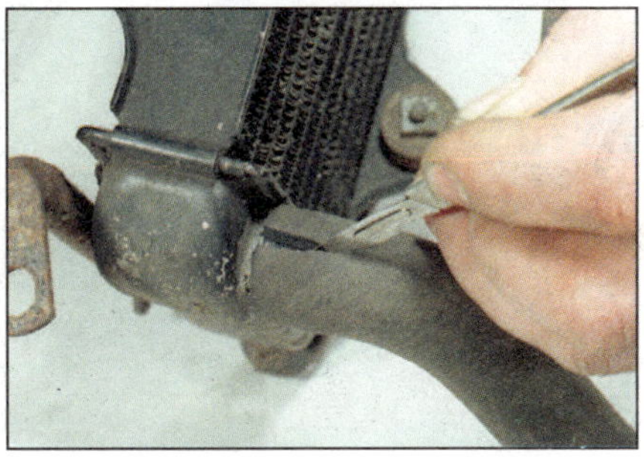

9.5 Cutting a coolant hose free with a sharp knife

Introduction

In less time than it takes to read this introduction, a thief could steal your motorcycle. Returning only to find your bike has gone is one of the worst feelings in the world. Even if the motorcycle is insured against theft, once you've got over the initial shock, you will have the inconvenience of dealing with the police and your insurance company.

The motorcycle is an easy target for the professional thief and the joyrider alike and the official figures on motorcycle theft make for depressing reading; on average a motorcycle is stolen every 16 minutes in the UK!

Motorcycle thefts fall into two categories, those stolen 'to order' and those taken by opportunists. The thief stealing to order will be on the look out for a specific make and model and will go to extraordinary lengths to obtain that motorcycle. The opportunist thief on the other hand will look for easy targets which can be stolen with the minimum of effort and risk.

Whilst it is never going to be possible to make your machine 100% secure, it is estimated that around half of all stolen motorcycles are taken by opportunist thieves. Remember that the opportunist thief is always on the look out for the easy option: if there are two similar motorcycles parked side-by-side, they will target the one with the lowest level of security. By taking a few precautions, you can reduce the chances of your motorcycle being stolen.

Security equipment

There are many specialised motorcycle security devices available and the following text summarises their applications and their good and bad points.

Once you have decided on the type of security equipment which best suits your needs, we recommended that you read one of the many equipment tests regularly carried out by the motorcycle press. These tests compare the products from all the major manufacturers and give impartial ratings on their effectiveness, value-for-money and ease of use.

Ensure the lock and chain you buy is of good quality and long enough to shackle your bike to a solid object

No one item of security equipment can provide complete protection. It is highly recommended that two or more of the items described below are combined to increase the security of your motorcycle (a lock and chain plus an alarm system is just about ideal). The more security measures fitted to the bike, the less likely it is to be stolen.

Lock and chain

Pros: *Very flexible to use; can be used to secure the motorcycle to almost any immovable object. On some locks and chains, the lock can be used on its own as a disc lock (see below).*

Cons: *Can be very heavy and awkward to carry on the motorcycle, although some types will be supplied with a carry bag which can be strapped to the pillion seat.*

- Heavy-duty chains and locks are an excellent security measure **(see illustration 1)**. Whenever the motorcycle is parked, use the lock and chain to secure the machine to a solid, immovable object such as a post or railings. This will prevent the machine from being ridden away or being lifted into the back of a van.

- When fitting the chain, always ensure the chain is routed around the motorcycle frame or swingarm **(see illustrations 2 and 3)**. Never merely pass the chain around one of the wheel rims; a thief may unbolt the wheel and lift the rest of the machine into a van, leaving you with just the wheel! Try to avoid having excess chain free, thus making it difficult to use cutting tools, and keep the chain and lock off the ground to prevent thieves attacking it with a cold chisel. Position the lock so that its lock barrel is facing downwards; this will make it harder for the thief to attack the lock mechanism.

Pass the chain through the bike's frame, rather than just through a wheel . . .

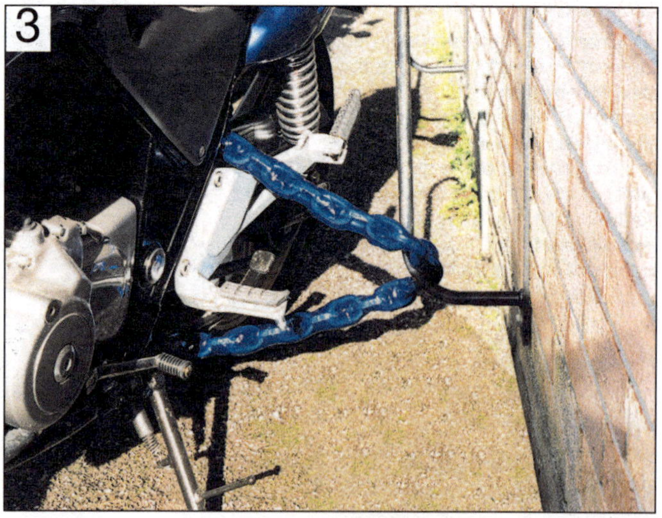

. . . and loop it around a solid object

U-locks

Pros: *Highly effective deterrent which can be used to secure the bike to a post or railings. Most U-locks come with a carrier which allows the lock to be easily carried on the bike.*

Cons: *Not as flexible to use as a lock and chain.*

- These are solid locks which are similar in use to a lock and chain. U-locks are lighter than a lock and chain but not so flexible to use. The length and shape of the lock shackle limit the objects to which the bike can be secured **(see illustration 4)**.

4

U-locks can be used to secure the bike to a solid object – ensure you purchase one which is long enough

Disc locks

Pros: *Small, light and very easy to carry; most can be stored underneath the seat.*

Cons: *Does not prevent the motorcycle being lifted into a van. Can be very embarrassing if you forget to remove the lock before attempting to ride off!*

5

A typical disc lock attached through one of the holes in the disc

- Disc locks are designed to be attached to the front brake disc. The lock passes through one of the holes in the disc and prevents the wheel rotating by jamming against the fork/brake caliper **(see illustration 5)**. Some are equipped with an alarm siren which sounds if the disc lock is moved; this not only acts as a theft deterrent but also as a handy reminder if you try to move the bike with the lock still fitted.

- Combining the disc lock with a length of cable which can be looped around a post or railings provides an additional measure of security **(see illustration 6)**.

Alarms and immobilisers

Pros: *Once installed it is completely hassle-free to use. If the system is 'Thatcham' or 'Sold Secure-approved', insurance companies may give you a discount.*

Cons: *Can be expensive to buy and complex to install. No system will prevent the motorcycle from being lifted into a van and taken away.*

- Electronic alarms and immobilisers are available to suit a variety of budgets. There are three different types of system available: pure alarms, pure immobilisers, and the more expensive systems which are combined alarm/immobilisers **(see illustration 7)**.
- An alarm system is designed to emit an audible warning if the motorcycle is being tampered with.
- An immobiliser prevents the motorcycle being started and ridden away by disabling its electrical systems.
- When purchasing an alarm/immobiliser system, check the cost of installing the system unless you are able to do it yourself. If the motorcycle is not used regularly, another consideration is the current drain of the system. All alarm/immobiliser systems are powered by the motorcycle's battery; purchasing a system with a very low current drain could prevent the battery losing its charge whilst the motorcycle is not being used.

6

A disc lock combined with a security cable provides additional protection

7

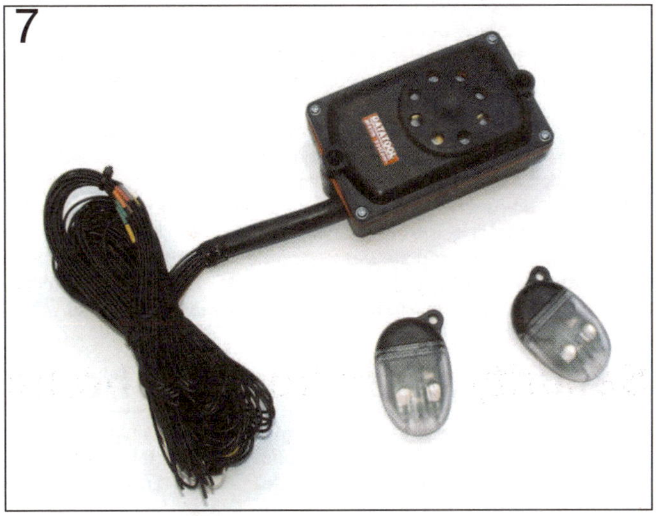

A typical alarm/immobiliser system

Indelible markings can be applied to most areas of the bike – always apply the manufacturer's sticker to warn off thieves

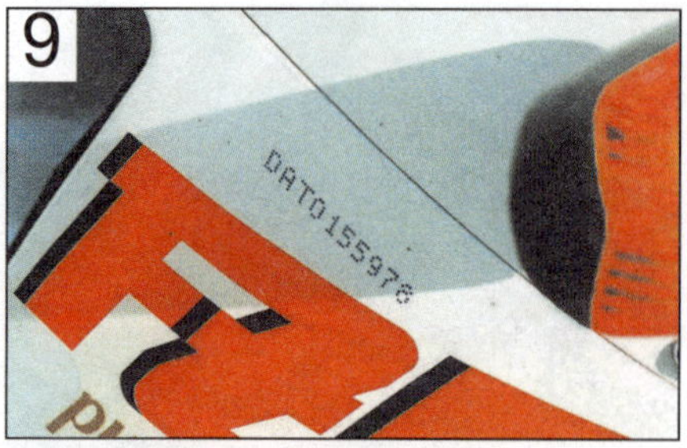

Chemically-etched code numbers can be applied to main body panels . . .

. . . again, always ensure that the kit manufacturer's sticker is applied in a prominent position

Security marking kits

Pros: *Very cheap and effective deterrent. Many insurance companies will give you a discount on your insurance premium if a recognised security marking kit is used on your motorcycle.*

Cons: *Does not prevent the motorcycle being stolen by joyriders.*

● There are many different types of security marking kits available. The idea is to mark as many parts of the motorcycle as possible with a unique security number **(see illustrations 8, 9 and 10)**. A form will be included with the kit to register your personal details and those of the motorcycle with the kit manufacturer. This register is made available to the police to help them trace the rightful owner of any motorcycle or components which they recover should all other forms of identification have been removed. Always apply the warning stickers provided with the kit to deter thieves.

Ground anchors, wheel clamps and security posts

Pros: *An excellent form of security which will deter all but the most determined of thieves.*

Cons: *Awkward to install and can be expensive.*

● Whilst the motorcycle is at home, it is a good idea to attach it securely to the floor or a solid wall, even if it is kept in a securely locked garage. Various types of ground anchors, security posts and wheel clamps are available for this purpose **(see illustration 11)**. These security devices are either bolted to a solid concrete or brick structure or can be cemented into the ground.

Permanent ground anchors provide an excellent level of security when the bike is at home

Security at home

A high percentage of motorcycle thefts are from the owner's home. Here are some things to consider whenever your motorcycle is at home:

✔ Where possible, always keep the motorcycle in a securely locked garage. Never rely solely on the standard lock on the garage door, these are usual hopelessly inadequate. Fit an additional locking mechanism to the door and consider having the garage alarmed. A security light, activated by a movement sensor, is also a good investment.

✔ Always secure the motorcycle to the ground or a wall, even if it is inside a securely locked garage.

✔ Do not regularly leave the motorcycle outside your home, try to keep it out of sight wherever possible. If a garage is not available, fit a motorcycle cover over the bike to disguise its true identity.

✔ It is not uncommon for thieves to follow a motorcyclist home to find out where the bike is kept. They will then return at a later date. Be aware of this whenever you are returning home on your motorcycle. If you suspect you are being followed, do not return home, instead ride to a garage or shop and stop as a precaution.

✔ When selling a motorcycle, do not provide your home address or the location where the bike is normally kept. Arrange to meet the buyer at a location away from your home. Thieves have been known to pose as potential buyers to find out where motorcycles are kept and then return later to steal them.

Security away from the home

As well as fitting security equipment to your motorcycle here are a few general rules to follow whenever you park your motorcycle.

✔ Park in a busy, public place.

✔ Use car parks which incorporate security features, such as CCTV.

✔ At night, park in a well-lit area, preferably directly underneath a street light.

✔ Engage the steering lock.

✔ Secure the motorcycle to a solid, immovable object such as a post or railings with an additional lock. If this is not possible, secure the bike to a friend's motorcycle. Some public parking places provide security loops for motorcycles.

✔ Never leave your helmet or luggage attached to the motorcycle. Take them with you at all times.

Lubricants and fluids

A wide range of lubricants, fluids and cleaning agents is available for motor-cycles. This is a guide as to what is available, its applications and properties.

Four-stroke engine oil

● Engine oil is without doubt the most important component of any four-stroke engine. Modern motorcycle engines place a lot of demands on their oil and choosing the right type is essential. Using an unsuitable oil will lead to an increased rate of engine wear and could result in serious engine damage. Before purchasing oil, always check the recommended oil specification given by the manufacturer. The manufacturer will state a recommended 'type or classification' and also a specific 'viscosity' range for engine oil.

● The oil 'type or classification' is identified by its API (American Petroleum Institute) rating. The API rating will be in the form of two letters, e.g. SG. The S identifies the oil as being suitable for use in a petrol (gasoline) engine (S stands for spark ignition) and the second letter, ranging from A to J, identifies the oil's performance rating. The later this letter, the higher the specification of the oil; for example API SG oil exceeds the requirements of API SF oil. **Note:** *On some oils there may also be a second rating consisting of another two letters, the first letter being C, e.g. API SF/CD. This rating indicates the oil is also suitable for use in a diesel engines (the C stands for compression ignition) and is thus of no relevance for motorcycle use.*

● The 'viscosity' of the oil is identified by its SAE (Society of Automotive Engineers) rating. All modern engines require multigrade oils and the SAE rating will consist of two numbers, the first followed by a W, e.g. 10W/40. The first number indicates the viscosity rating of the oil at low temperatures (W stands for winter – tested at –20°C) and the second number represents the viscosity of the oil at high temperatures (tested at 100°C). The lower the number, the thinner the oil. For example an oil with an SAE 10W/40 rating will give better cold starting and running than an SAE 15W/40 oil.

● As well as ensuring the 'type' and 'viscosity' of the oil match the recommendations, another consideration to make when buying engine oil is whether to purchase a standard mineral-based oil, a semi-synthetic oil (also known as a synthetic blend or synthetic-based oil) or a fully-synthetic oil. Although all oils will have a similar rating and viscosity, their cost will vary considerably; mineral-based oils are the cheapest, the fully-synthetic oils the most expensive with the semi-synthetic oils falling somewhere in-between. This decision is very much up to the owner, but it should be noted that modern synthetic oils have far better lubricating and cleaning qualities than traditional mineral-based oils and tend to retain these properties for far longer. Bearing in mind the operating conditions inside a modern, high-revving motorcycle engine it is highly recommended that a fully synthetic oil is used. The extra expense at each service could save you money in the long term by preventing premature engine wear.

● As a final note always ensure that the oil is specifically designed for use in motorcycle engines. Engine oils designed primarily for use in car engines sometimes contain additives or friction modifiers which could cause clutch slip on a motorcycle fitted with a wet-clutch.

Two-stroke engine oil

● Modern two-stroke engines, with their high power outputs, place high demands on their oil. If engine seizure is to be avoided it is essential that a high-quality oil is used. Two-stroke oils differ hugely from four-stroke oils. The oil lubricates only the crankshaft and piston(s) (the transmission has its own lubricating oil) and is used on a total-loss basis where it is burnt completely during the combustion process.

● The Japanese have recently introduced a classification system for two-stroke oils, the JASO rating. This rating is in the form of two letters, either FA, FB or FC – FA is the lowest classification and FC the highest. Ensure the oil being used meets or exceeds the recommended rating specified by the manufacturer.

● As well as ensuring the oil rating matches the recommendation, another consideration to make when buying engine oil is whether to purchase a standard mineral-based oil, a semi-synthetic oil (also known as a synthetic blend or synthetic-based oil) or a fully-synthetic oil. The cost of each type of oil varies considerably; mineral-based oils are the cheapest, the fully-synthetic oils the most expensive with the semi-synthetic oils falling somewhere in-between. This decision is very much up to the owner, but it should be noted that modern synthetic oils have far better lubricating properties and burn cleaner than traditional mineral-based oils. It is therefore recommended that a fully synthetic oil is used. The extra expense could save you money in the long term by preventing premature engine wear, engine performance will be improved, carbon deposits and exhaust smoke will be reduced.

● Always ensure that the oil is specifically designed for use in an injector system. Many high quality two-stroke oils are designed for competition use and need to be pre-mixed with fuel. These oils are of a much higher viscosity and are not designed to flow through the injector pumps used on road-going two-stroke motorcycles.

Transmission (gear) oil

● On a two-stroke engine, the transmission and clutch are lubricated by their own separate oil bath which must be changed in accordance with the Maintenance Schedule.

● Although the engine and transmission units of most four-strokes use a common lubrication supply, there are some exceptions where the engine and gearbox have separate oil reservoirs and a dry clutch is used.

● Motorcycle manufacturers will either recommend a monograde transmission oil or a four-stroke multigrade engine oil to lubricate the transmission.

● Transmission oils, or gear oils as they are often called, are designed specifically for use in transmission systems. The viscosity of these oils is represented by an SAE number, but the scale of measurement applied is different to that used to grade engine oils. As a rough guide a SAE90 gear oil will be of the same viscosity as an SAE50 engine oil.

Shaft drive oil

● On models equipped with shaft final drive, the shaft drive gears are will have their own oil supply. The manufacturer will state a recommended 'type or classification' and also a specific 'viscosity' range in the same manner as for four-stroke engine oil.

● Gear oil classification is given by the number which follows the API GL (GL standing for gear lubricant) rating, the higher the number, the higher the specification of the oil, e.g. API GL5 oil is a higher specification than API GL4 oil. Ensure the oil meets or exceeds the classification specified and is of the correct viscosity. The viscosity of gear oils is also represented by an SAE number but the scale of measurement used is different to that used to grade engine oils. As a rough guide an SAE90 gear oil will be of the same viscosity as an SAE50 engine oil.

● If the use of an EP (Extreme Pressure) gear oil is specified, ensure the oil purchased is suitable.

Fork oil and suspension fluid

● Conventional telescopic front forks are hydraulic and require fork oil to work. To ensure the forks function correctly, the fork oil must be changed in accordance with the Maintenance Schedule.

● Fork oil is available in a variety of viscosities, identified by their SAE rating; fork oil ratings vary from light (SAE 5) to heavy (SAE 30). When purchasing fork oil, ensure the viscosity rating matches that specified by the manufacturer.

● Some lubricant manufacturers also produce a range of high-quality suspension fluids which are very similar to fork oil but are designed mainly for competition use. These fluids may have a different viscosity rating system which is not to be confused with the SAE rating of normal fork oil. Refer to the manufacturer's instructions if in any doubt.

Brake and clutch fluid

● All disc brake systems and some clutch systems are hydraulically operated. To ensure correct operation, the hydraulic fluid must be changed in accordance with the Maintenance Schedule.

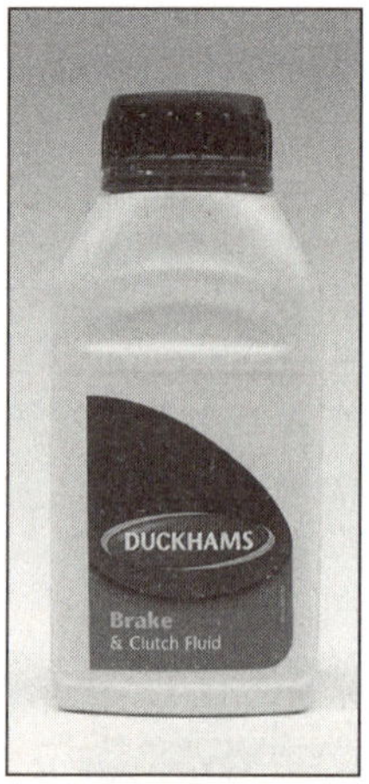

● Brake and clutch fluid is classified by its DOT rating with most motorcycle manufacturers specifying DOT 3 or 4 fluid. Both fluid types are glycol-based and can be mixed together without adverse effect; DOT 4 fluid exceeds the requirements of DOT 3 fluid. Although it is safe to use DOT 4 fluid in a system designed for use with DOT 3 fluid, never use DOT 3 fluid in a system which specifies the use of DOT 4 as this will adversely affect the system's performance. The type required for the system will be marked on the fluid reservoir cap.

● Some manufacturers also produce a DOT 5 hydraulic fluid. DOT 5 hydraulic fluid is silicone-based and is not compatible with the glycol-based DOT 3 and 4 fluids. Never mix DOT 5 fluid with DOT 3 or 4 fluid as this will seriously affect the performance of the hydraulic system.

Coolant/antifreeze

● When purchasing coolant/antifreeze, always ensure it is suitable for use in an aluminium engine and contains corrosion inhibitors to prevent possible blockages of the internal coolant passages of the system. As a general rule, most coolants are designed to be used neat and should not be diluted whereas antifreeze can be mixed with distilled water to provide a coolant solution of the required strength. Refer to the manufacturer's instructions on the bottle.

● Ensure the coolant is changed in accordance with the Maintenance Schedule.

Chain lube

● Chain lube is an aerosol-type spray lubricant specifically designed for use on motorcycle final drive chains. Chain lube has two functions, to minimise friction between the final drive chain and sprockets and to prevent corrosion of the chain. Regular use of a good-quality chain lube will extend the life of the drive chain and sprockets and thus maximise the power being transmitted from the transmission to the rear wheel.

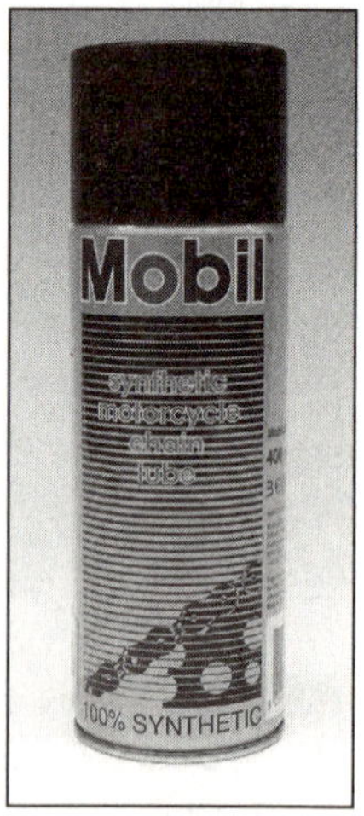

● When using chain lube, always allow some time for the solvents in the lube to evaporate before riding the motorcycle. This will minimise the amount of lube which will 'fling' off from the chain when the motorcycle is used. If the motorcycle is equipped with an 'O-ring' chain, ensure the chain lube is labelled as being suitable for use on 'O-ring' chains.

Degreasers and solvents

- There are many different types of solvents and degreasers available to remove the grime and grease which accumulate around the motorcycle during normal use. Degreasers and solvents are usually available as an aerosol-type spray or as a liquid which you apply with a brush. Always closely follow the manufacturer's instructions and wear eye protection during use. Be aware that many solvents are flammable and may give off noxious fumes; take adequate precautions when using them (*see Safety First!*).
- For general cleaning, use one of the many solvents or degreasers available from most motorcycle accessory shops. These solvents are usually applied then left for a certain time before being washed off with water.

Brake cleaner is a solvent specifically designed to remove all traces of oil, grease and dust from braking system components. Brake cleaner is designed to evaporate quickly and leaves behind no residue.

Carburettor cleaner is an aerosol-type solvent specifically designed to clear carburettor blockages and break down the hard deposits and gum often found inside carburettors during overhaul.

Contact cleaner is an aerosol-type solvent designed for cleaning electrical components. The cleaner will remove all traces of oil and dirt from components such as switch contacts or fouled spark plugs and then dry, leaving behind no residue.

Gasket remover is an aerosol-type solvent designed for removing stubborn gaskets from engine components during overhaul. Gasket remover will minimise the amount of scraping required to remove the gasket and therefore reduce the risk of damage to the mating surface.

Spray lubricants

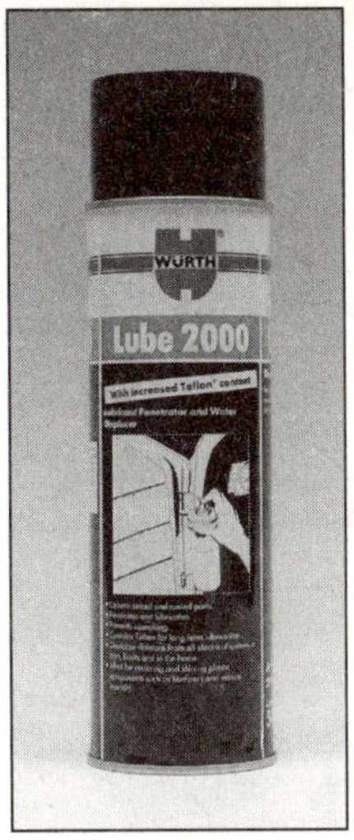

- Aerosol-based spray lubricants are widely available and are excellent for lubricating lever pivots and exposed cables and switches. Try to use a lubricant which is of the dry-film type as the fluid evaporates, leaving behind a dry-film of lubricant. Lubricants which leave behind an oily residue will attract dust and dirt which will increase the rate of wear of the cable/lever.
- Most lubricants also act as a moisture dispersant and a penetrating fluid. This means they can also be used to 'dry out' electrical components such as wiring connectors or switches as well as helping to free seized fasteners.

Greases

- Grease is used to lubricate many of the pivot-points. A good-quality multi-purpose grease is suitable for most applications but some manufacturers will specify the use of specialist greases for use on components such as swingarm and suspension linkage bushes. These specialist greases can be purchased from most motorcycle (or car) accessory shops; commonly specified types include molybdenum disulphide grease, lithium-based grease, graphite-based grease, silicone-based grease and high-temperature copper-based grease.

Gasket sealing compounds

- Gasket sealing compounds can be used in conjunction with gaskets, to improve their sealing capabilities, or on their own to seal metal-to-metal joints. Depending on their type, sealing compounds either set hard or stay relatively soft and pliable.

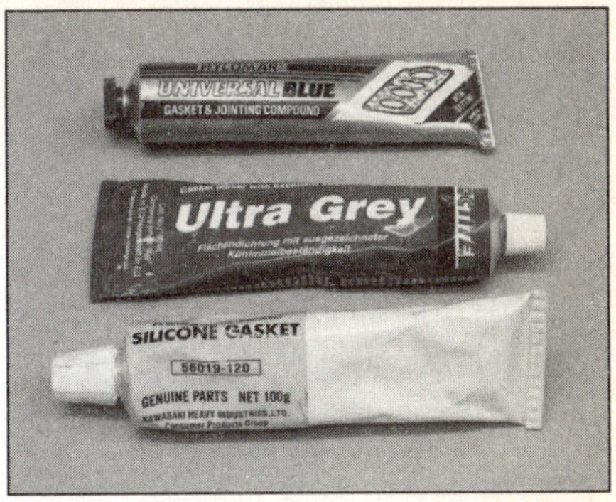

- When purchasing a gasket sealing compound, ensure that it is designed specifically for use on an internal combustion engine. General multi-purpose sealants available from DIY stores may appear visibly similar but they are not designed to withstand the extreme heat or contact with fuel and oil encountered when used on an engine (*see 'Tools and Workshop Tips' for further information*).

Thread locking compound

- Thread locking compounds are used to secure certain threaded fasteners in position to prevent them from loosening due to vibration. Thread locking compounds can be purchased from most motorcycle (and car) accessory shops. Ensure the threads of the both components are completely clean and dry before sparingly applying the locking compound (*see 'Tools and Workshop Tips' for further information*).

Fuel additives

- Fuel additives which protect and clean the fuel system components are widely available. These additives are designed to remove all traces of deposits that build up on the carburettors/injectors and prevent wear, helping the fuel system to operate more efficiently. If a fuel additive is being used, check that it is suitable for use with your motorcycle, especially if your motorcycle is equipped with a catalytic converter.

- Octane boosters are also available. These additives are designed to improve the performance of highly-tuned engines being run on normal pump-fuel and are of no real use on standard motorcycles.

Conversion factors

Length (distance)

Inches (in)	x 25.4	= Millimetres (mm)	x 0.0394	= Inches (in)
Feet (ft)	x 0.305	= Metres (m)	x 3.281	= Feet (ft)
Miles	x 1.609	= Kilometres (km)	x 0.621	= Miles

Volume (capacity)

Cubic inches (cu in; in^3)	x 16.387	= Cubic centimetres (cc; cm^3)	x 0.061	= Cubic inches (cu in; in^3)
Imperial pints (Imp pt)	x 0.568	= Litres (l)	x 1.76	= Imperial pints (Imp pt)
Imperial quarts (Imp qt)	x 1.137	= Litres (l)	x 0.88	= Imperial quarts (Imp qt)
Imperial quarts (Imp qt)	x 1.201	= US quarts (US qt)	x 0.833	= Imperial quarts (Imp qt)
US quarts (US qt)	x 0.946	= Litres (l)	x 1.057	= US quarts (US qt)
Imperial gallons (Imp gal)	x 4.546	= Litres (l)	x 0.22	= Imperial gallons (Imp gal)
Imperial gallons (Imp gal)	x 1.201	= US gallons (US gal)	x 0.833	= Imperial gallons (Imp gal)
US gallons (US gal)	x 3.785	= Litres (l)	x 0.264	= US gallons (US gal)

Mass (weight)

Ounces (oz)	x 28.35	= Grams (g)	x 0.035	= Ounces (oz)
Pounds (lb)	x 0.454	= Kilograms (kg)	x 2.205	= Pounds (lb)

Force

Ounces-force (ozf; oz)	x 0.278	= Newtons (N)	x 3.6	= Ounces-force (ozf; oz)
Pounds-force (lbf; lb)	x 4.448	= Newtons (N)	x 0.225	= Pounds-force (lbf; lb)
Newtons (N)	x 0.1	= Kilograms-force (kgf; kg)	x 9.81	= Newtons (N)

Pressure

Pounds-force per square inch (psi; lbf/in^2; lb/in^2)	x 0.070	= Kilograms-force per square centimetre (kgf/cm^2; kg/cm^2)	x 14.223	= Pounds-force per square inch (psi; lbf/in^2; lb/in^2)
Pounds-force per square inch (psi; lbf/in^2; lb/in^2)	x 0.068	= Atmospheres (atm)	x 14.696	= Pounds-force per square inch (psi; lbf/in^2; lb/in^2)
Pounds-force per square inch (psi; lbf/in^2; lb/in^2)	x 0.069	= Bars	x 14.5	= Pounds-force per square inch (psi; lbf/in^2; lb/in^2)
Pounds-force per square inch (psi; lbf/in^2; lb/in^2)	x 6.895	= Kilopascals (kPa)	x 0.145	= Pounds-force per square inch (psi; lbf/in^2; lb/in^2)
Kilopascals (kPa)	x 0.01	= Kilograms-force per square centimetre (kgf/cm^2; kg/cm^2)	x 98.1	= Kilopascals (kPa)
Millibar (mbar)	x 100	= Pascals (Pa)	x 0.01	= Millibar (mbar)
Millibar (mbar)	x 0.0145	= Pounds-force per square inch (psi; lbf/in^2; lb/in^2)	x 68.947	= Millibar (mbar)
Millibar (mbar)	x 0.75	= Millimetres of mercury (mmHg)	x 1.333	= Millibar (mbar)
Millibar (mbar)	x 0.401	= Inches of water (inH_2O)	x 2.491	= Millibar (mbar)
Millimetres of mercury (mmHg)	x 0.535	= Inches of water (inH_2O)	x 1.868	= Millimetres of mercury (mmHg)
Inches of water (inH_2O)	x 0.036	= Pounds-force per square inch (psi; lbf/in^2; lb/in^2)	x 27.68	= Inches of water (inH_2O)

Torque (moment of force)

Pounds-force inches (lbf in; lb in)	x 1.152	= Kilograms-force centimetre (kgf cm; kg cm)	x 0.868	= Pounds-force inches (lbf in; lb in)
Pounds-force inches (lbf in; lb in)	x 0.113	= Newton metres (Nm)	x 8.85	= Pounds-force inches (lbf in; lb in)
Pounds-force inches (lbf in; lb in)	x 0.083	= Pounds-force feet (lbf ft; lb ft)	x 12	= Pounds-force inches (lbf in; lb in)
Pounds-force feet (lbf ft; lb ft)	x 0.138	= Kilograms-force metres (kgf m; kg m)	x 7.233	= Pounds-force feet (lbf ft; lb ft)
Pounds-force feet (lbf ft; lb ft)	x 1.356	= Newton metres (Nm)	x 0.738	= Pounds-force feet (lbf ft; lb ft)
Newton metres (Nm)	x 0.102	= Kilograms-force metres (kgf m; kg m)	x 9.804	= Newton metres (Nm)

Power

Horsepower (hp)	x 745.7	= Watts (W)	x 0.0013	= Horsepower (hp)

Velocity (speed)

Miles per hour (miles/hr; mph)	x 1.609	= Kilometres per hour (km/hr; kph)	x 0.621	= Miles per hour (miles/hr; mph)

Fuel consumption*

Miles per gallon (mpg)	x 0.354	= Kilometres per litre (km/l)	x 2.825	= Miles per gallon (mpg)

Temperature

Degrees Fahrenheit = (°C x 1.8) + 32

Degrees Celsius (Degrees Centigrade; °C) = (°F - 32) x 0.56

** It is common practice to convert from miles per gallon (mpg) to litres/100 kilometres (l/100km), where mpg x l/100 km = 282*

About the MOT Test

In the UK, all vehicles more than three years old are subject to an annual test to ensure that they meet minimum safety requirements. A current test certificate must be issued before a machine can be used on public roads, and is required before a road fund licence can be issued. Riding without a current test certificate will also invalidate your insurance.

For most owners, the MOT test is an annual cause for anxiety, and this is largely due to owners not being sure what needs to be checked prior to submitting the motorcycle for testing. The simple answer is that a fully roadworthy motorcycle will have no difficulty in passing the test.

This is a guide to getting your motorcycle through the MOT test. Obviously it will not be possible to examine the motorcycle to the same standard as the professional MOT tester, particularly in view of the equipment required for some of the checks. However, working through the following procedures will enable you to identify any problem areas before submitting the motorcycle for the test.

It has only been possible to summarise the test requirements here, based on the regulations in force at the time of printing. Test standards are becoming increasingly stringent, although there are some exemptions for older vehicles. More information about the MOT test can be obtained from the TSO publications, *How Safe is your Motorcycle* and *The MOT Inspection Manual for Motorcycle Testing*.

Many of the checks require that one of the wheels is raised off the ground. If the motorcycle doesn't have a centre stand, note that an auxiliary stand will be required. Additionally, the help of an assistant may prove useful.

Certain exceptions apply to machines under 50 cc, machines without a lighting system, and Classic bikes - if in doubt about any of the requirements listed below seek confirmation from an MOT tester prior to submitting the motorcycle for the test.

Check that the frame number is clearly visible.

HAYNES HiNT ***If a component is in borderline condition, the tester has discretion in deciding whether to pass or fail it. If the motorcycle presented is clean and evidently well cared for, the tester may be more inclined to pass a borderline component than if the motorcycle is scruffy and apparently neglected.***

Electrical System

Lights, turn signals, horn and reflector

✔ With the ignition on, check the operation of the following electrical components. **Note:** *The electrical components on certain small-capacity machines are powered by the generator, requiring that the engine is run for this check.*

a) Headlight and tail light. Check that both illuminate in the low and high beam switch positions.

b) Position lights. Check that the front position (or sidelight) and tail light illuminate in this switch position.

c) Turn signals. Check that all flash at the correct rate, and that the warning light(s) function correctly. Check that the turn signal switch works correctly.

d) Hazard warning system (where fitted). Check that all four turn signals flash in this switch position.

e) Brake stop light. Check that the light comes on when the front and rear brakes are independently applied. Models first used on or after 1st April 1986 must have a brake light switch on each brake.

f) Horn. Check that the sound is continuous and of reasonable volume.

✔ Check that there is a red reflector on the rear of the machine, either mounted separately or as part of the tail light lens.

✔ Check the condition of the headlight, tail light and turn signal lenses.

Headlight beam height

✔ The MOT tester will perform a headlight beam height check using specialised beam setting equipment **(see illustration 1)**. This equipment will not be available to the home mechanic, but if you suspect that the headlight is incorrectly set or may have been maladjusted in the past, you can perform a rough test as follows.

✔ Position the bike in a straight line facing a brick wall. The bike must be off its stand, upright and with a rider seated. Measure the height from the ground to the centre of the headlight and mark a horizontal line on the wall at this height. Position the motorcycle 3.8 metres from the wall and draw a vertical line up the wall central to the centreline of the motorcycle. Switch to dipped beam and check that the beam pattern falls slightly lower than the horizontal line and to the left of the vertical line **(see illustration 2)**.

1

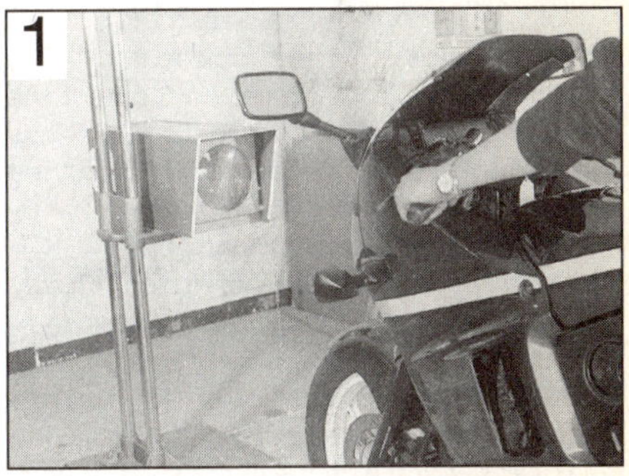

Headlight beam height checking equipment

2

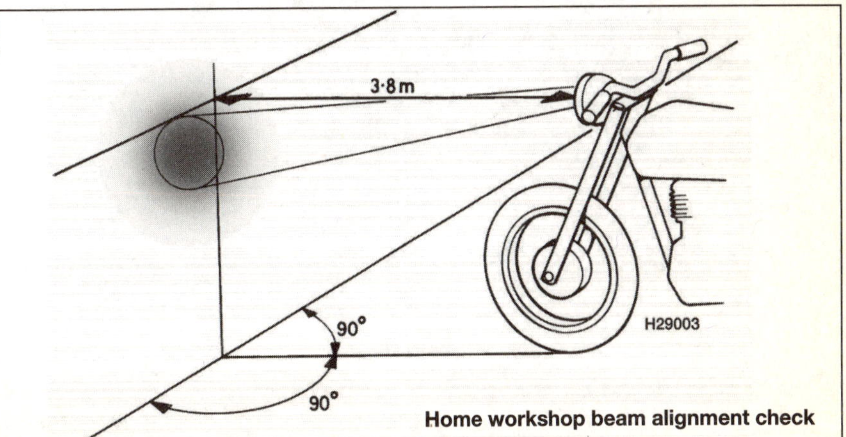

Home workshop beam alignment check

Exhaust System and Final Drive

Exhaust

✔ Check that the exhaust mountings are secure and that the system does not foul any of the rear suspension components.

✔ Start the motorcycle. When the revs are increased, check that the exhaust is neither holed nor leaking from any of its joints. On a linked system, check that the collector box is not leaking due to corrosion.

✔ Note that the exhaust decibel level ("loudness" of the exhaust) is assessed at the discretion of the tester. If the motorcycle was first used on or after 1st January 1985 the silencer must carry the BSAU 193 stamp, or a marking relating to its make and model, or be of OE (original equipment) manufacture. If the silencer is marked NOT FOR ROAD USE, RACING USE ONLY or similar, it will fail the MOT.

Final drive

✔ On chain or belt drive machines, check that the chain/belt is in good condition and does not have excessive slack. Also check that the sprocket is securely mounted on the rear wheel hub. Check that the chain/belt guard is in place.

✔ On shaft drive bikes, check for oil leaking from the drive unit and fouling the rear tyre.

Steering and Suspension

Steering

✔ With the front wheel raised off the ground, rotate the steering from lock to lock. The handlebar or switches must not contact the fuel tank or be close enough to trap the rider's hand. Problems can be caused by damaged lock stops on the lower yoke and frame, or by the fitting of non-standard handlebars.

✔ When performing the lock to lock check, also ensure that the steering moves freely without drag or notchiness. Steering movement can be impaired by poorly routed cables, or by overtight head bearings or worn bearings. The tester will perform a check of the steering head bearing lower race by mounting the front wheel on a surface plate, then performing a lock to lock check with the weight of the machine on the lower bearing **(see illustration 3)**.

✔ Grasp the fork sliders (lower legs) and attempt to push and pull on the forks **(see illustration 4)**. Any play in the steering head bearings will be felt. Note that in extreme cases, wear of the front fork bushes can be misinterpreted for head bearing play.

3 **Front wheel mounted on a surface plate for steering head bearing lower race check**

✔ Check that the handlebars are securely mounted.

✔ Check that the handlebar grip rubbers are secure. They should by bonded to the bar left end and to the throttle cable pulley on the right end.

Front suspension

✔ With the motorcycle off the stand, hold the front brake on and pump the front forks up and down **(see illustration 5)**. Check that they are adequately damped.

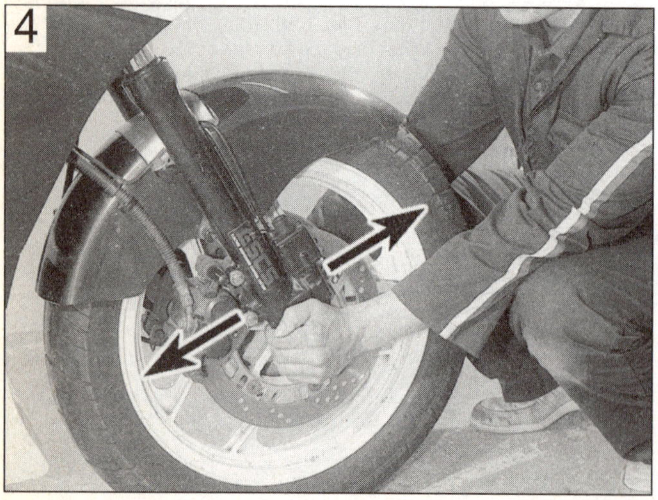

4 **Checking the steering head bearings for freeplay**

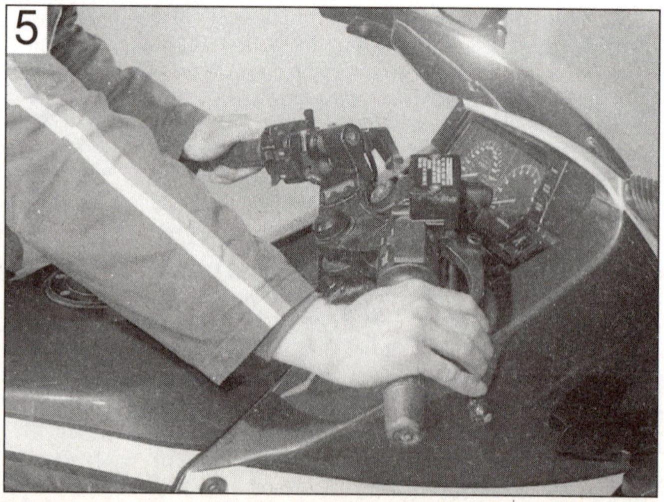

5 **Hold the front brake on and pump the front forks up and down to check operation**

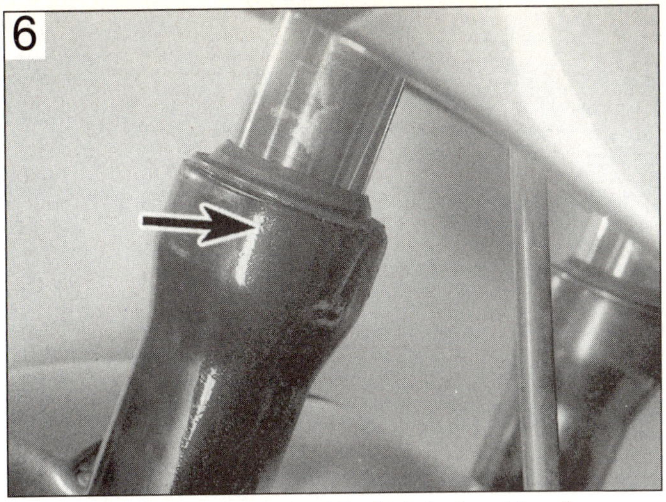

Inspect the area around the fork dust seal for oil leakage (arrow)

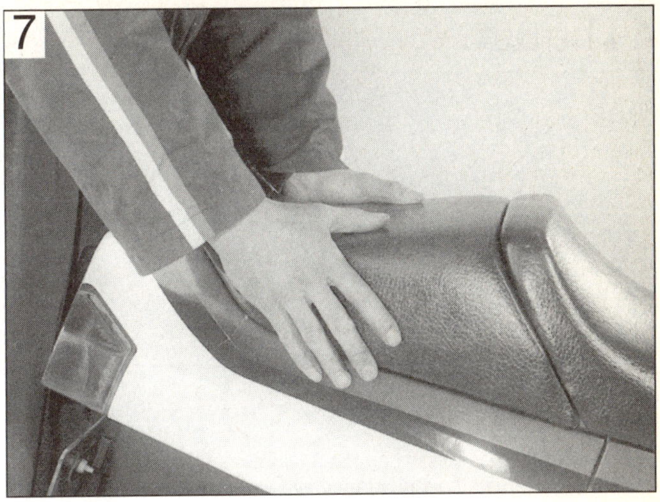

Bounce the rear of the motorcycle to check rear suspension operation

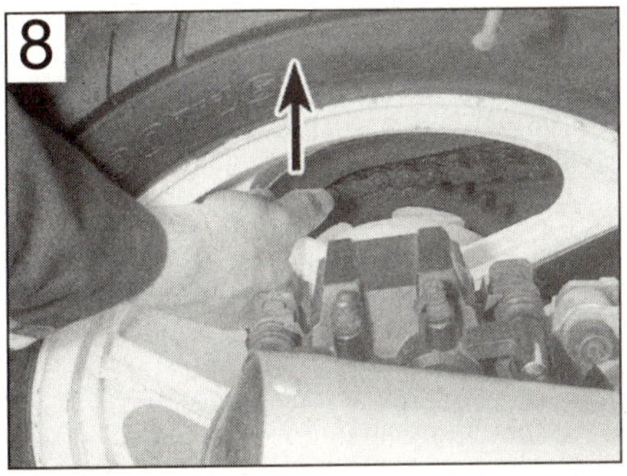

Checking for rear suspension linkage play

✔ Inspect the area above and around the front fork oil seals **(see illustration 6)**. There should be no sign of oil on the fork tube (stanchion) nor leaking down the slider (lower leg). On models so equipped, check that there is no oil leaking from the anti-dive units.

✔ On models with swingarm front suspension, check that there is no freeplay in the linkage when moved from side to side.

Rear suspension

✔ With the motorcycle off the stand and an assistant supporting the motorcycle by its handlebars, bounce the rear suspension **(see illustration 7)**. Check that the suspension components do not foul on any of the cycle parts and check that the shock absorber(s) provide adequate damping.

✔ Visually inspect the shock absorber(s) and check that there is no sign of oil leakage from its damper. This is somewhat restricted on certain single shock models due to the location of the shock absorber.

✔ With the rear wheel raised off the ground, grasp the wheel at the highest point and attempt to pull it up **(see illustration 8)**. Any play in the swingarm pivot or suspension linkage bearings will be felt as movement. **Note:** *Do not confuse play with actual suspension movement.* Failure to lubricate suspension linkage bearings can lead to bearing failure **(see illustration 9)**.

✔ With the rear wheel raised off the ground, grasp the swingarm ends and attempt to move the swingarm from side to side and forwards and backwards - any play indicates wear of the swingarm pivot bearings **(see illustration 10)**.

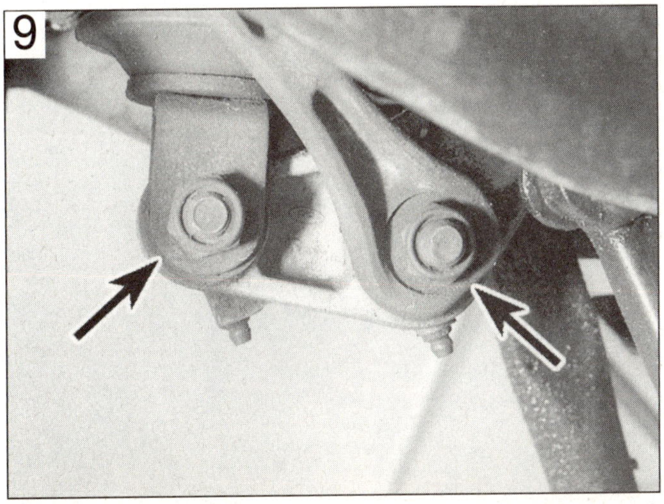

Worn suspension linkage pivots (arrows) are usually the cause of play in the rear suspension

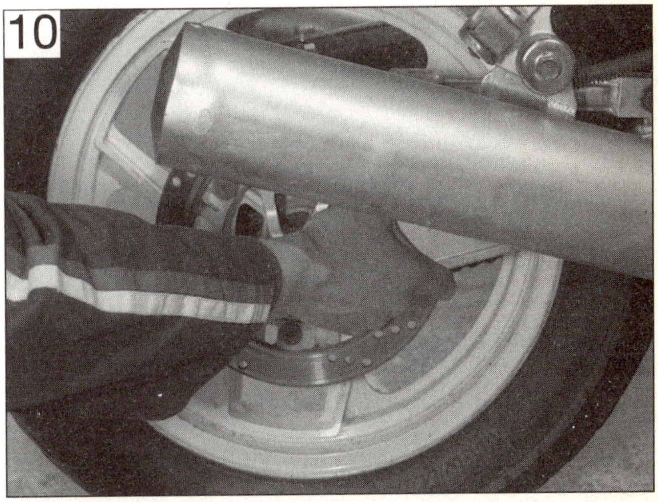

Grasp the swingarm at the ends to check for play in its pivot bearings

11

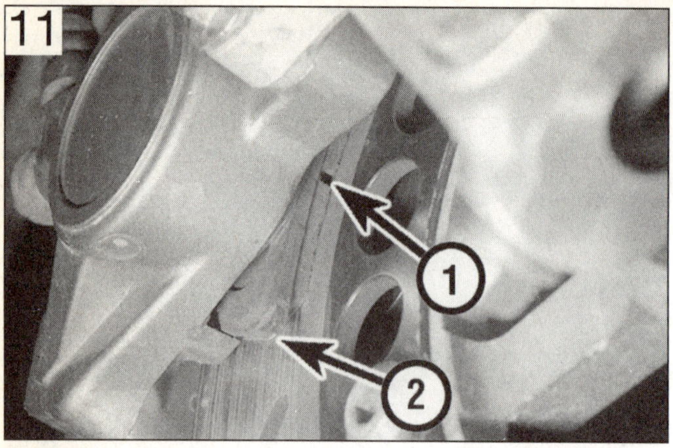

Brake pad wear can usually be viewed without removing the caliper. Most pads have wear indicator grooves (1) and some also have indicator tangs (2)

12

On drum brakes, check the angle of the operating lever with the brake fully applied. Most drum brakes have a wear indicator pointer and scale.

Brakes, Wheels and Tyres

Brakes

✔ With the wheel raised off the ground, apply the brake then free it off, and check that the wheel is about to revolve freely without brake drag.

✔ On disc brakes, examine the disc itself. Check that it is securely mounted and not cracked.

✔ On disc brakes, view the pad material through the caliper mouth and check that the pads are not worn down beyond the limit **(see illustration 11)**.

✔ On drum brakes, check that when the brake is applied the angle between the operating lever and cable or rod is not too great **(see illustration 12)**. Check also that the operating lever doesn't foul any other components.

✔ On disc brakes, examine the flexible hoses from top to bottom. Have an assistant hold the brake on so that the fluid in the hose is under pressure, and check that there is no sign of fluid leakage, bulges or cracking. If there are any metal brake pipes or unions, check that these are free from corrosion and damage. Where a brake-linked anti-dive system is fitted, check the hoses to the anti-dive in a similar manner.

✔ Check that the rear brake torque arm is secure and that its fasteners are secured by self-locking nuts or castellated nuts with split-pins or R-pins **(see illustration 13)**.

✔ On models with ABS, check that the self-check warning light in the instrument panel works.

✔ The MOT tester will perform a test of the motorcycle's braking efficiency based on a calculation of rider and motorcycle weight. Although this cannot be carried out at home, you can at least ensure that the braking systems are properly maintained. For hydraulic disc brakes, check the fluid level, lever/pedal feel (bleed of air if its spongy) and pad material. For drum brakes, check adjustment, cable or rod operation and shoe lining thickness.

Wheels and tyres

✔ Check the wheel condition. Cast wheels should be free from cracks and if of the built-up design, all fasteners should be secure. Spoked wheels should be checked for broken, corroded, loose or bent spokes.

✔ With the wheel raised off the ground, spin the wheel and visually check that the tyre and wheel run true. Check that the tyre does not foul the suspension or mudguards.

✔ With the wheel raised off the ground, grasp the wheel and attempt to move it about the axle (spindle) **(see illustration 14)**. Any play felt here indicates wheel bearing failure.

13

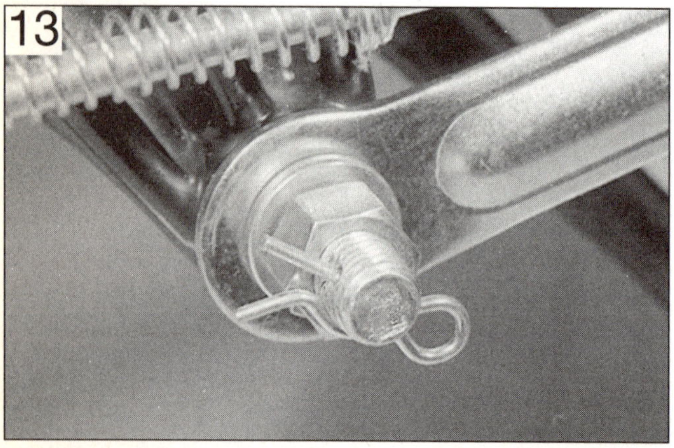

Brake torque arm must be properly secured at both ends

14

Check for wheel bearing play by trying to move the wheel about the axle (spindle)

Checking the tyre tread depth

Tyre direction of rotation arrow can be found on tyre sidewall

Castellated type wheel axle (spindle) nut must be secured by a split pin or R-pin

Two straightedges are used to check wheel alignment

✔ Check the tyre tread depth, tread condition and sidewall condition **(see illustration 15)**.

✔ Check the tyre type. Front and rear tyre types must be compatible and be suitable for road use. Tyres marked NOT FOR ROAD USE, COMPETITION USE ONLY or similar, will fail the MOT.

✔ If the tyre sidewall carries a direction of rotation arrow, this must be pointing in the direction of normal wheel rotation **(see illustration 16)**.

✔ Check that the wheel axle (spindle) nuts (where applicable) are properly secured. A self-locking nut or castellated nut with a split-pin or R-pin can be used **(see illustration 17)**.

✔ Wheel alignment is checked with the motorcycle off the stand and a rider seated. With the front wheel pointing straight ahead, two perfectly straight lengths of metal or wood and placed against the sidewalls of both tyres **(see illustration 18)**. The gap each side of the front tyre must be equidistant on both sides. Incorrect wheel alignment may be due to a cocked rear wheel (often as the result of poor chain adjustment) or in extreme cases, a bent frame.

General checks and condition

✔ Check the security of all major fasteners, bodypanels, seat, fairings (where fitted) and mudguards.

✔ Check that the rider and pillion footrests, handlebar levers and brake pedal are securely mounted.

✔ Check for corrosion on the frame or any load-bearing components. If severe, this may affect the structure, particularly under stress.

Sidecars

A motorcycle fitted with a sidecar requires additional checks relating to the stability of the machine and security of attachment and swivel joints, plus specific wheel alignment (toe-in) requirements. Additionally, tyre and lighting requirements differ from conventional motorcycle use. Owners are advised to check MOT test requirements with an official test centre.

Preparing for storage

Before you start

If repairs or an overhaul is needed, see that this is carried out now rather than left until you want to ride the bike again.

Give the bike a good wash and scrub all dirt from its underside. Make sure the bike dries completely before preparing for storage.

Engine

- Remove the spark plug(s) and lubricate the cylinder bores with approximately a teaspoon of motor oil using a spout-type oil can **(see illustration 1)**. Reinstall the spark plug(s). Crank the engine over a couple of times to coat the piston rings and bores with oil. If the bike has a kickstart, use this to turn the engine over. If not, flick the kill switch to the OFF position and crank the engine over on the starter **(see illustration 2)**. If the nature on the ignition system prevents the starter operating with the kill switch in the OFF position, remove the spark plugs and fit them back in their caps; ensure that the plugs are earthed (grounded) against the cylinder head when the starter is operated **(see illustration 3)**.

Warning: It is important that the plugs are earthed (grounded) away from the spark plug holes otherwise there is a risk of atomised fuel from the cylinders igniting.

> HAYNES HiNT *On a single cylinder four-stroke engine, you can seal the combustion chamber completely by positioning the piston at TDC on the compression stroke.*

- Drain the carburettor(s) otherwise there is a risk of jets becoming blocked by gum deposits from the fuel **(see illustration 4)**.
- If the bike is going into long-term storage, consider adding a fuel stabiliser to the fuel in the tank. If the tank is drained completely, corrosion of its internal surfaces may occur if left unprotected for a long period. The tank can be treated with a rust preventative especially for this purpose. Alternatively, remove the tank and pour half a litre of motor oil into it, install the filler cap and shake the tank to coat its internals with oil before draining off the excess. The same effect can also be achieved by spraying WD40 or a similar water-dispersant around the inside of the tank via its flexible nozzle.
- Make sure the cooling system contains the correct mix of antifreeze. Antifreeze also contains important corrosion inhibitors.
- The air intakes and exhaust can be sealed off by covering or plugging the openings. Ensure that you do not seal in any condensation; run the engine until it is hot,

1
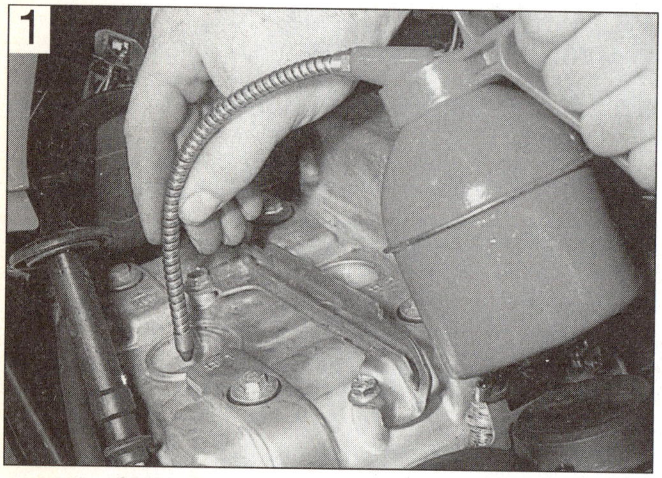
Squirt a drop of motor oil into each cylinder

2

Flick the kill switch to OFF . . .

3

. . . and ensure that the metal bodies of the plugs (arrows) are earthed against the cylinder head

4
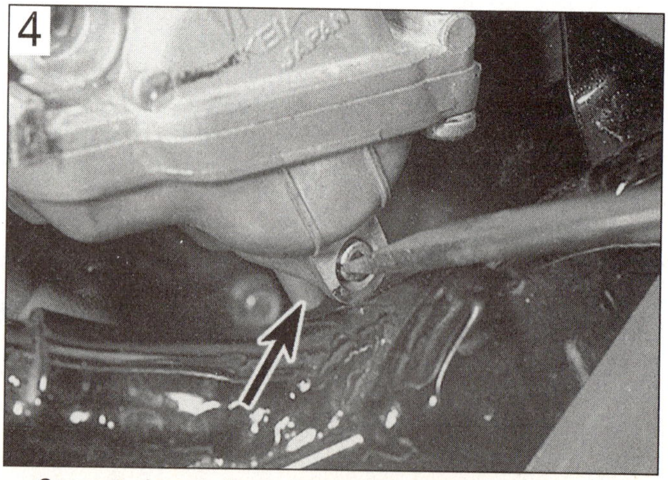
Connect a hose to the carburettor float chamber drain stub (arrow) and unscrew the drain screw

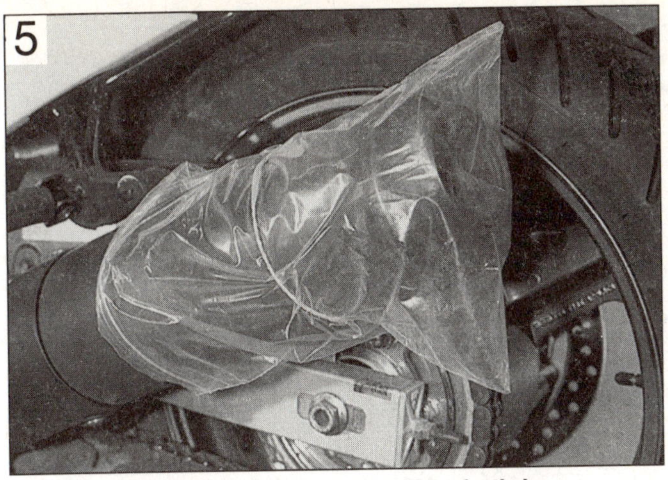

Exhausts can be sealed off with a plastic bag

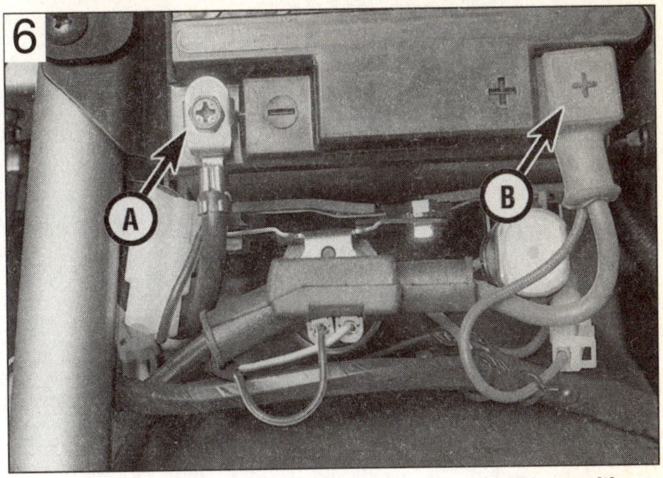

Disconnect the negative lead (A) first, followed by the positive lead (B)

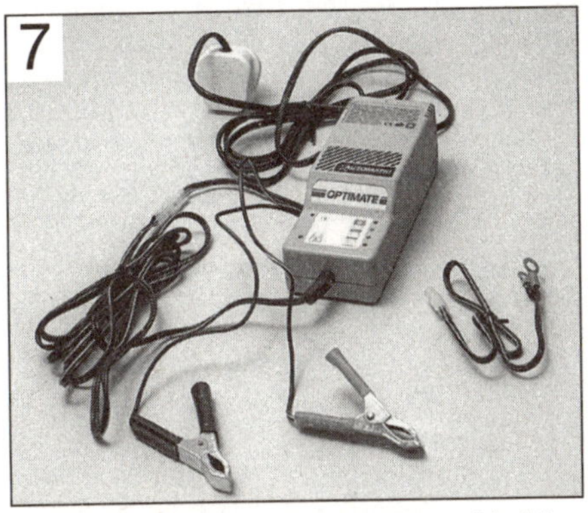

Use a suitable battery charger - this kit also assess battery condition

then switch off and allow to cool. Tape a piece of thick plastic over the silencer end(s) **(see illustration 5)**. Note that some advocate pouring a tablespoon of motor oil into the silencer(s) before sealing them off.

Battery

- Remove it from the bike - in extreme cases of cold the battery may freeze and crack its case **(see illustration 6)**.
- Check the electrolyte level and top up if necessary (conventional refillable batteries). Clean the terminals.
- Store the battery off the motorcycle and away from any sources of fire. Position a wooden block under the battery if it is to sit on the ground.
- Give the battery a trickle charge for a few hours every month **(see illustration 7)**.

Tyres

- Place the bike on its centrestand or an auxiliary stand which will support the motorcycle in an upright position. Position wood blocks under the tyres to keep them off the ground and to provide insulation from damp. If the bike is being put into long-term storage, ideally both tyres should be off the ground; not only will this protect the tyres, but will also ensure that no load is placed on the steering head or wheel bearings.
- Deflate each tyre by 5 to 10 psi, no more or the beads may unseat from the rim, making subsequent inflation difficult on tubeless tyres.

Pivots and controls

- Lubricate all lever, pedal, stand and footrest pivot points. If grease nipples are fitted to the rear suspension components, apply lubricant to the pivots.
- Lubricate all control cables.

Cycle components

- Apply a wax protectant to all painted and plastic components. Wipe off any excess, but don't polish to a shine. Where fitted, clean the screen with soap and water.
- Coat metal parts with Vaseline (petroleum jelly). When applying this to the fork tubes, do not compress the forks otherwise the seals will rot from contact with the Vaseline.
- Apply a vinyl cleaner to the seat.

Storage conditions

- Aim to store the bike in a shed or garage which does not leak and is free from damp.
- Drape an old blanket or bedspread over the bike to protect it from dust and direct contact with sunlight (which will fade paint). This also hides the bike from prying eyes. Beware of tight-fitting plastic covers which may allow condensation to form and settle on the bike.

Getting back on the road

Engine and transmission

- Change the oil and replace the oil filter. If this was done prior to storage, check that the oil hasn't emulsified - a thick whitish substance which occurs through condensation.
- Remove the spark plugs. Using a spout-type oil can, squirt a few drops of oil into the cylinder(s). This will provide initial lubrication as the piston rings and bores comes back into contact. Service the spark plugs, or fit new ones, and install them in the engine.
- Check that the clutch isn't stuck on. The plates can stick together if left standing for some time, preventing clutch operation. Engage a gear and try rocking the bike back and forth with the clutch lever held against the handlebar. If this doesn't work on cable-operated clutches, hold the clutch lever back against the handlebar with a strong elastic band or cable tie for a couple of hours **(see illustration 8)**.
- If the air intakes or silencer end(s) were blocked off, remove the bung or cover used.
- If the fuel tank was coated with a rust

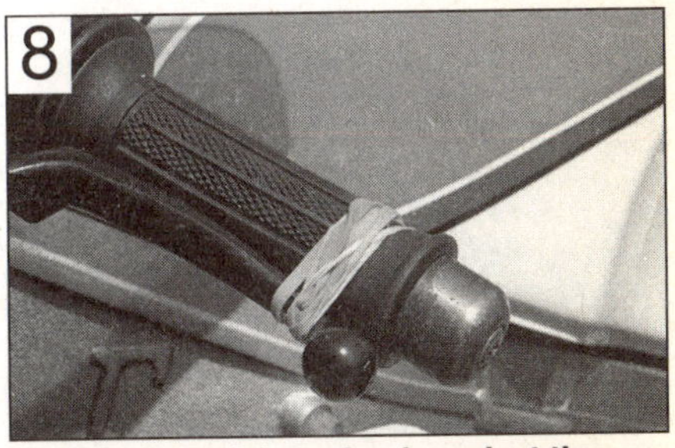

Hold clutch lever back against the handlebar with elastic bands or a cable tie

preventative, oil or a stabiliser added to the fuel, drain and flush the tank and dispose of the fuel sensibly. If no action was taken with the fuel tank prior to storage, it is advised that the old fuel is disposed of since it will go off over a period of time. Refill the fuel tank with fresh fuel.

Frame and running gear

● Oil all pivot points and cables.

● Check the tyre pressures. They will definitely need inflating if pressures were reduced for storage.

● Lubricate the final drive chain (where applicable).

● Remove any protective coating applied to the fork tubes (stanchions) since this may well destroy the fork seals. If the fork tubes weren't protected and have picked up rust spots, remove them with very fine abrasive paper and refinish with metal polish.

● Check that both brakes operate correctly. Apply each brake hard and check that it's not possible to move the motorcycle forwards, then check that the brake frees off again once released. Brake caliper pistons can stick due to corrosion around the piston head, or on the sliding caliper types, due to corrosion of the slider pins. If the brake doesn't free after repeated operation, take the caliper off for examination. Similarly drum brakes can stick due to a seized operating cam, cable or rod linkage.

● If the motorcycle has been in long-term storage, renew the brake fluid and clutch fluid (where applicable).

● Depending on where the bike has been stored, the wiring, cables and hoses may have been nibbled by rodents. Make a visual check and investigate disturbed wiring loom tape.

Battery

● If the battery has been previously removal and given top up charges it can simply be reconnected. Remember to connect the positive cable first and the negative cable last.

● On conventional refillable batteries, if the battery has not received any attention, remove it from the motorcycle and check its electrolyte level. Top up if necessary then charge the battery. If the battery fails to hold a charge and a visual checks show heavy white sulphation of the plates, the battery is probably defective and must be renewed. This is particularly likely if the battery is old. Confirm battery condition with a specific gravity check.

● On sealed (MF) batteries, if the battery has not received any attention, remove it from the motorcycle and charge it according to the information on the battery case - if the battery fails to hold a charge it must be renewed.

Starting procedure

● If a kickstart is fitted, turn the engine over a couple of times with the ignition OFF to distribute oil around the engine. If no kickstart is fitted, flick the engine kill switch OFF and the ignition ON and crank the engine over a couple of times to work oil around the upper cylinder components. If the nature of the ignition system is such that the starter won't work with the kill switch OFF, remove the spark plugs, fit them back into their caps and earth (ground) their bodies on the cylinder head. Reinstall the spark plugs afterwards.

● Switch the kill switch to RUN, operate the choke and start the engine. If the engine won't start don't continue cranking the engine - not only will this flatten the battery, but the starter motor will overheat. Switch the ignition off and try again later. If the engine refuses to start, go through the fault finding procedures in this manual. **Note:** *If the bike has been in storage for a long time, old fuel or a carburettor blockage may be the problem. Gum deposits in carburettors can block jets - if a carburettor cleaner doesn't prove successful the carburettors must be dismantled for cleaning.*

● Once the engine has started, check that the lights, turn signals and horn work properly.

● Treat the bike gently for the first ride and check all fluid levels on completion. Settle the bike back into the maintenance schedule.

This Section provides an easy reference-guide to the more common faults that are likely to afflict your machine. Obviously, the opportunities are almost limitless for faults to occur as a result of obscure failures, and to try and cover all eventualities would require a book. Indeed, a number have been written on the subject.

Successful troubleshooting is not a mysterious 'black art' but the application of a bit of knowledge combined with a systematic and logical approach to the problem. Approach any troubleshooting by first accurately identifying the symptom and then checking through the list of possible causes, starting with the simplest or most obvious and progressing in stages to the most complex.

Take nothing for granted, but above all apply liberal quantities of common sense.

The main symptom of a fault is given in the text as a major heading below which are listed the various systems or areas which may contain the fault. Details of each possible cause for a fault and the remedial action to be taken are given, in brief, in the paragraphs below each heading. Further information should be sought in the relevant Chapter.

1 Engine doesn't start or is difficult to start

Starter motor doesn't rotate

- ☐ Engine kill switch OFF.
- ☐ Fuse blown. Check main fuse and PGM-FI fuse (Chapter 8).
- ☐ Battery voltage low. Check and recharge battery (Chapter 8).
- ☐ Starter motor defective. Make sure the wiring to the starter is secure. Make sure the starter relay clicks when the start button is pushed. If the relay clicks, then the fault is in the wiring or motor (see Chapter 8).
- ☐ Starter switch not contacting. The contacts could be wet, corroded or dirty. Disassemble and clean the switch (Chapter 8).
- ☐ Wiring open or shorted. Check all wiring connections and harnesses to make sure that they are dry, tight and not corroded. Also check for broken or frayed wires that can cause a short to ground (earth) (see *Wiring diagrams*, Chapter 8).
- ☐ Ignition (main) switch defective. Check the switch and replace with a new one if it is defective (see Chapter 8).
- ☐ Engine kill switch defective. Check for wet, dirty or corroded contacts. Clean or replace the switch with a new one as necessary (see Chapter 8).
- ☐ Faulty neutral switch, sidestand switch or clutch switch. Check the wiring to each switch and the switch itself (see Chapter 8).
- ☐ Faulty diode (Chapter 8).
- ☐ Fuel injection system shutdown due to system fault (Chapter 4).

Starter motor rotates but engine does not turn over

- ☐ Starter clutch defective. Inspect and repair or replace with a new one (see Chapter 2).
- ☐ Damaged idler or starter gears. Inspect and replace the damaged parts (see Chapter 2).

Starter works but engine won't turn over (seized)

- ☐ Seized engine caused by one or more internally damaged components. Failure due to wear, abuse or lack of lubrication. Damage can include seized valves, followers, camshafts, pistons, crankshaft, connecting rod bearings, or transmission gears or bearings. Refer to Chapter 2 for engine disassembly.

No fuel flow

- ☐ No fuel in tank.
- ☐ Fuel tank breather hose obstructed.
- ☐ Faulty fuel cut-off relay. Check the relay (see Chapter 4).
- ☐ Fuel pump faulty, or the fuel filter is blocked (see Chapter 4).
- ☐ Fuel hose clogged. Remove the fuel hose and carefully blow through it. Check the fuel filter for damage.
- ☐ Fuel rail or injector clogged. For all of the injectors to be clogged, either a very bad batch of fuel with an unusual additive has been used, or some other foreign material has entered the tank. Check the fuel filter. In some cases, if a machine has been unused for several months, the fuel turns to a varnish-like liquid which can cause an injector needle to stick to its seat. Drain the tank and fuel system (Chapter 4).

Engine flooded

- ☐ Injector needle valve worn or stuck open. A piece of dirt, rust or other debris can cause the needle to seat improperly, causing excess fuel to be admitted to the throttle body. In this case, the injector should be cleaned and the needle and seat inspected (see Chapter 4). If the needle and seat are worn, then the leaking will persist and the parts should be renewed.
- ☐ Starting technique incorrect. Under normal circumstances (i.e. if all the components of the fuel injection system are good) the machine should start with the throttle closed.

No spark or weak spark

- ☐ Ignition switch OFF.
- ☐ Engine kill switch turned to the OFF position or engine stop relay defective.
- ☐ Ignition or kill switch shorted. This is usually caused by water, corrosion, damage or excessive wear. The switches can be disassembled and cleaned with electrical contact cleaner. If cleaning does not help, replace the switches (see Chapter 8).
- ☐ Battery voltage low. Check and recharge the battery as necessary (Chapter 8).
- ☐ Ignition coils not making good contact. Make sure that the caps fit snugly over the plug ends.
- ☐ Spark plugs dirty, defective or worn out. Locate reason for fouled plugs using spark plug condition chart on the inside back cover and follow the plug maintenance procedures (see Chapter 1).
- ☐ Incorrect spark plugs. Wrong type or heat range. Check and install correct plugs (see Chapter 1).
- ☐ Ignition coil defective. Test and renew if necessary (Chapter 4).
- ☐ Fuel injection system shutdown due to system fault (Chapter 4).
- ☐ Camshaft position (CMP) sensor defective (see Chapter 4).
- ☐ Crankshaft position (CKP) sensor defective (see Chapter 4).
- ☐ Engine control module (ECM) defective (see Chapter 4).
- ☐ Wiring shorted or broken between:
  - a) Ignition (main) switch and engine kill switch (or blown fuse)
  - b) ECM and engine kill switch
  - c) ECM and ignition coils
  - d) ECM and CKP
- ☐ Make sure that all wiring connections are clean, dry and tight. Look for chafed and broken wires (see Chapters 4 and 8).

Compression low

- ☐ Spark plugs loose. Remove the plugs and inspect their threads. Reinstall and tighten securely (see Chapter 1).
- ☐ Cylinder head not sufficiently tightened down. If a cylinder head is suspected of being loose, then there's a chance that the gasket or head is damaged if the problem has persisted for any length of time. The head bolts should be tightened to the proper torque and in the correct sequence (Chapter 2).
- ☐ Improper valve clearance. This means that the valve is not closing completely and compression pressure is leaking past the valve. Check and adjust the valve clearances (Chapter 1).
- ☐ Cylinder and/or piston worn. Excessive wear will cause compression pressure to leak past the rings. This is usually accompanied by worn rings as well. A top-end overhaul is necessary (Chapter 2).
- ☐ Piston rings worn, weak, broken, or sticking. Broken or sticking piston rings usually indicate a lubrication or fuelling problem that causes excess carbon deposits to form on the pistons and rings. Top-end overhaul is necessary (Chapter 2).
- ☐ Piston ring-to-groove clearance excessive. This is caused by excessive wear of the piston ring lands. Piston renewal is necessary (Chapter 2).
- ☐ Cylinder head gasket damaged. If a head is allowed to become loose, or if excessive carbon build-up on the piston crown and combustion chamber causes extremely high compression, the head gasket may leak. Retorquing the head is not always sufficient to restore the seal, so a new gasket is necessary (Chapter 2).
- ☐ Cylinder head warped. This is caused by overheating or improperly tightened head bolts. Machine shop resurfacing or head renewal is necessary (Chapter 2).
- ☐ Valve spring broken or weak. Caused by component failure or wear; the springs must be renewed (Chapter 2).
- ☐ Valve not seating properly. This is caused by a bent valve (from over-revving or improper valve adjustment), burned valve or seat (improper fuelling) or an accumulation of carbon deposits on the seat. The valves must be cleaned and/or renewed and the seats serviced (Chapter 2).

1 Engine doesn't start or is difficult to start (continued)

Stalls after starting

- ☐ Faulty fast idle system. Check the operation of the wax unit and starter valves (see Chapter 4).
- ☐ Engine idle speed incorrect. Turn idle adjusting screw until the engine idles at the specified rpm (Chapter 1).
- ☐ Ignition malfunction (see Chapter 4).
- ☐ Fuel injection system malfunction (see Chapter 4).
- ☐ Fuel contaminated. The fuel can be contaminated with either dirt or water, or can change chemically if the machine has been unused for several months. Drain the tank and fuel system (Chapter 4).
- ☐ Intake air leak. Check for loose throttle body-to-intake manifold connections, loose or damaged PAIR vacuum hose or loose vacuum hoses on the throttle body (Chapter 4).

Rough idle

- ☐ Idle speed incorrect (see Chapter 1).
- ☐ Ignition fault (see Chapter 4).
- ☐ Starter valves not synchronised. Adjust them as described in Chapter 4.
- ☐ Fuel injection system malfunction (see Chapter 4).
- ☐ Fuel contaminated. The fuel can be contaminated with either dirt or water, or can change chemically if the machine has been unused for several months. Drain the tank and the fuel system (Chapter 4).
- ☐ Intake air leak. Check for loose throttle body-to-intake manifold connections, loose or damaged PAIR vacuum hose or loose vacuum hoses on the throttle body (Chapter 4).
- ☐ Air filter clogged. Clean the air filter element or replace it with a new one (Chapter 1).

2 Poor running at low speeds

Spark weak

- ☐ Battery voltage low. Check and recharge battery (see Chapter 8).
- ☐ Ignition coils not making good contact. Make sure that the caps fit snugly over the plug ends.
- ☐ Spark plugs dirty, defective or worn out. Locate reason for fouled plugs using spark plug condition chart on the inside back cover and follow the plug maintenance procedures (see Chapter 1).
- ☐ Incorrect spark plugs. Wrong type or heat range. Check and install correct plugs (see Chapter 1).
- ☐ Ignition coil defective. Test and renew if necessary (see Chapter 4).

Fuel/air mixture incorrect

- ☐ Fuel tank breather hose obstructed.
- ☐ Fuel pump faulty, or the fuel filter is blocked (see Chapter 4).
- ☐ Fuel hose clogged. Remove the fuel hose and carefully blow through it. Check the fuel filter for damage.
- ☐ Fuel rail or injector clogged. For all of the injectors to be clogged, either a very bad batch of fuel with an unusual additive has been used, or some other foreign material has entered the tank. Check the fuel filter. In some cases, if a machine has been unused for several months, the fuel turns to a varnish-like liquid which can cause an injector needle to stick to its seat. Drain the tank and fuel system (Chapter 4).
- ☐ Intake air leak. Check for loose throttle body-to-intake manifold connections, loose or damaged PAIR vacuum hose or loose vacuum hoses on throttle body (Chapter 4).
- ☐ Air filter clogged. Clean the air filter elements or renew them (Chapter 1).

Compression low

- ☐ Spark plugs loose. Remove the plugs and inspect their threads. Reinstall and tighten securely (see Chapter 1).
- ☐ Cylinder head not sufficiently tightened down. If a cylinder head is suspected of being loose, then there's a chance that the gasket or head is damaged if the problem has persisted for any length of time. The head bolts should be tightened to the proper torque and in the correct sequence (Chapter 2).
- ☐ Improper valve clearance. This means that the valve is not closing completely and compression pressure is leaking past the valve. Check and adjust the valve clearances (Chapter 1).
- ☐ Cylinder and/or piston worn. Excessive wear will cause compression pressure to leak past the rings. This is usually accompanied by worn rings as well. A top-end overhaul is necessary (Chapter 2).
- ☐ Piston rings worn, weak, broken, or sticking. Broken or sticking piston rings usually indicate a lubrication or fuelling problem that causes excess carbon deposits to form on the pistons and rings. Top-end overhaul is necessary (Chapter 2).
- ☐ Piston ring-to-groove clearance excessive. This is caused by excessive wear of the piston ring lands. Piston renewal is necessary (Chapter 2).
- ☐ Cylinder head gasket damaged. If the head is allowed to become loose, or if excessive carbon build-up on the piston crown and combustion chamber causes extremely high compression, the head gasket may leak. Retorquing the head is not always sufficient to restore the seal, so a new gasket is necessary (Chapter 2).
- ☐ Cylinder head warped. This is caused by overheating or improperly tightened head bolts. Machine shop resurfacing or head renewal is necessary (Chapter 2).
- ☐ Valve spring broken or weak. Caused by component failure or wear; the springs must be renewed (Chapter 2).
- ☐ Valve not seating properly. This is caused by a bent valve (from over-revving or improper valve adjustment), burned valve or seat (improper fuelling) or an accumulation of carbon deposits on the seat (from fuelling or lubrication problems). The valves must be cleaned and/or renewed and the seats serviced (Chapter 2).

Poor acceleration

- ☐ Timing not advancing. The crankshaft position sensor (CKP) or the engine control module (ECM) may be defective (see Chapter 4). If so, they must be renewed.
- ☐ Engine oil viscosity too high. Using a heavier oil than that recommended in Chapter 1 can damage the oil pump or lubrication system and cause drag on the engine.
- ☐ Brakes dragging. Usually caused by debris which has entered the brake caliper piston seals, or from a warped disc or bent axle (see Chapter 6).

3 Poor running or no power at high speed

Firing incorrect

- ☐ Ignition coils not making good contact. Make sure that the caps fit snugly over the plug ends and that the wiring is secure.
- ☐ Spark plugs dirty, defective or worn out. Locate reason for fouled plugs using spark plug condition chart on the inside back cover and follow the plug maintenance procedures (see Chapter 1).
- ☐ Incorrect spark plugs. Wrong type or heat range. Check and install correct plugs (see Chapter 1).
- ☐ Ignition coil defective. Test and renew if necessary (see Chapter 4).
- ☐ Faulty ECM (engine control module) (see Chapter 4).

Fuel/air mixture incorrect

- ☐ Fuel tank breather hose obstructed.
- ☐ Fuel pump faulty, or the fuel filter is blocked (see Chapter 4).
- ☐ Fuel hose clogged. Remove the fuel hose and carefully blow through it. Check the fuel filter for damage.
- ☐ Fuel rail or injector clogged. For all of the injectors to be clogged, either a very bad batch of fuel with an unusual additive has been used, or some other foreign material has entered the tank. Check the fuel filter. In some cases, if a machine has been unused for several months, the fuel turns to a varnish-like liquid which can cause an injector needle to stick to its seat. Drain the tank and fuel system (Chapter 4).
- ☐ Intake air leak. Check for loose throttle body-to-intake manifold connections, loose or damaged PAIR vacuum hose or loose vacuum hoses on throttle body (Chapter 4).
- ☐ Air filter clogged. Clean the air filter element or replace it with a new one (Chapter 1).

Compression low

- ☐ Spark plugs loose. Remove the plugs and inspect their threads. Reinstall and tighten securely (see Chapter 1).
- ☐ Cylinder head not sufficiently tightened down. If a cylinder head is suspected of being loose, then there's a chance that the gasket or head is damaged if the problem has persisted for any length of time. The head bolts should be tightened to the proper torque and in the correct sequence (Chapter 2).
- ☐ Improper valve clearance. This means that the valve is not closing completely and compression pressure is leaking past the valve. Check and adjust the valve clearances (Chapter 1).
- ☐ Cylinder and/or piston worn. Excessive wear will cause compression pressure to leak past the rings. This is usually accompanied by worn rings as well. A top-end overhaul is necessary (Chapter 2).
- ☐ Piston rings worn, weak, broken, or sticking. Broken or sticking piston rings usually indicate a lubrication or fuelling problem that causes excess carbon deposits to form on the pistons and rings. Top-end overhaul is necessary (Chapter 2).
- ☐ Piston ring-to-groove clearance excessive. This is caused by excessive wear of the piston ring lands. Piston renewal is necessary (Chapter 2).
- ☐ Cylinder head gasket damaged. If a head is allowed to become loose, or if excessive carbon build-up on the piston crown and combustion chamber causes extremely high compression, the head gasket may leak. Retorquing the head is not always sufficient to restore the seal, so a new gasket is necessary (Chapter 2).
- ☐ Cylinder head warped. This is caused by overheating or improperly tightened head bolts. Machine shop resurfacing or head renewal is necessary (Chapter 2).
- ☐ Valve spring broken or weak. Caused by component failure or wear; the springs must be replaced with new ones (Chapter 2).
- ☐ Valve not seating properly. This is caused by a bent valve (from over-revving or improper valve adjustment), burned valve or seat (improper fuelling) or an accumulation of carbon deposits on the seat (from fuelling or lubrication problems). The valves must be cleaned and/or renewed and the seats serviced (Chapter 2).

Knocking or pinking

- ☐ Carbon build-up in combustion chamber. Use of a fuel additive that will dissolve the adhesive bonding the carbon particles to the piston crown and chamber is the easiest way to remove the build-up. Otherwise, the cylinder head will have to be removed and decarbonised (Chapter 2).
- ☐ Incorrect or poor quality fuel. Old or improper grades of fuel can cause detonation. This causes the piston to rattle, thus the knocking or pinking sound. Drain old fuel and always use the recommended fuel grade.
- ☐ Spark plug heat range incorrect. Uncontrolled detonation indicates the plug heat range is too hot. The plug in effect becomes a glow plug, raising cylinder temperatures. Install the proper heat range plug (Chapter 1).
- ☐ Improper air/fuel mixture. This will cause the cylinders to run hot, which leads to detonation. A blockage in the fuel system or an air leak can cause this imbalance (see Chapter 4).

Miscellaneous causes

- ☐ Throttle valve doesn't open fully. Adjust the throttle twistgrip freeplay (see Chapter 1).
- ☐ Clutch slipping due loose or worn clutch components (see Chapter 2).
- ☐ Timing not advancing. The crankshaft position sensor (CKP) or the engine control module (ECM) may be defective (see Chapter 4). If so, they must be replaced with new ones.
- ☐ Engine oil viscosity too high. Using a heavier oil than the one recommended in Chapter 1 can damage the oil pump or lubrication system and cause drag on the engine.
- ☐ Brakes dragging. Usually caused by debris which has entered the brake caliper piston seals, or from a warped disc or bent axle (see Chapter 6).

4 Overheating

Engine overheats

- ☐ Coolant level low. Check and add coolant (see *Pre-ride checks*).
- ☐ Leak in cooling system. Check cooling system hoses and radiator for leaks and other damage. Repair or renew parts as necessary (see Chapter 3).
- ☐ Faulty thermostat. Check and renew as described in Chapter 3.
- ☐ Faulty radiator cap. Remove the cap and have it pressure tested.
- ☐ Coolant passages clogged. Have the entire system drained and flushed, then refill with fresh coolant.
- ☐ Water pump defective. Remove the pump and check the components (see Chapter 3).
- ☐ Clogged or damaged radiator fins (see Chapter 3).
- ☐ Faulty cooling fan, ECT sensor or fan relay (see Chapter 3).

Firing incorrect

- ☐ Wrongly connected ignition coil wiring.
- ☐ Spark plugs dirty, defective or worn out. Locate reason for fouled plugs using spark plug condition chart on the inside back cover and follow the plug maintenance procedures (see Chapter 1).
- ☐ Incorrect spark plugs. Wrong type or heat range. Check and install correct plugs (see Chapter 1).
- ☐ Ignition coil defective. Test and replace with a new one if necessary (see Chapter 5).
- ☐ Faulty ECM (engine control module) (see Chapter 4).

Fuel/air mixture incorrect

- ☐ Fuel tank breather hose obstructed.
- ☐ Fuel pump faulty, or the fuel filter blocked (see Chapter 4).
- ☐ Fuel hose clogged. Remove the fuel hose and carefully blow through it. Check the fuel filter for damage.
- ☐ Fuel rail or injector clogged. For all of the injectors to be clogged, either a very bad batch of fuel with an unusual additive has been used, or some other foreign material has entered the tank. Check the fuel filter. In some cases, if a machine has been unused for several months, the fuel turns to a varnish-like liquid which can cause an injector needle to stick to its seat. Drain the tank and fuel system (Chapter 4).
- ☐ Intake air leak. Check for loose throttle body-to-intake manifold connections, loose or damaged PAIR vacuum hose or loose vacuum hoses on throttle body (Chapter 4).
- ☐ Air filter clogged. Clean the air filter elements or renew them (Chapter 1).

Compression too high

- ☐ Carbon build-up in combustion chamber. Use of a fuel additive that will dissolve the adhesive bonding the carbon particles to the piston crown and chamber is the easiest way to remove the build-up. Otherwise, the cylinder head will have to be removed and decarbonised (Chapter 2).
- ☐ Improperly machined head surface or installation of incorrect gasket during engine assembly.

Engine load excessive

- ☐ Clutch slipping due loose or worn clutch components (see Chapter 2).
- ☐ Engine oil level too high. Too much oil will cause pressurisation of the crankcase and inefficient engine operation. Check Specifications and drain to proper level (see *Pre-ride checks*).
- ☐ Engine oil viscosity too high. Using a heavier oil than the one recommended in Chapter 1 can damage the oil pump or lubrication system as well as cause drag on the engine.
- ☐ Brakes dragging. Usually caused by debris which has entered the brake caliper piston seals, or from a warped disc or bent axle (see Chapter 6).

Lubrication inadequate

- ☐ Engine oil level too low. Friction caused by intermittent lack of lubrication or from oil that is overworked can cause overheating. The oil provides a definite cooling function in the engine. Check the oil level (see *Pre-ride checks*).
- ☐ Low engine oil pressure. Check the pressure (see Chapter 2).
- ☐ Blocked oil filter or strainer (see Chapter 1).
- ☐ Poor quality engine oil or incorrect viscosity or type. Oil is rated not only according to viscosity but also according to type. Some oils are not rated high enough for use in this engine. Check the Specifications section and change to the correct oil (Chapter 1).

Miscellaneous causes

- ☐ Modification to exhaust system. Most aftermarket exhaust systems cause the engine to run leaner, which make them run hotter. When installing an accessory exhaust system, always check with the manufacturer/supplier as to whether the ECM requires re-mapping.

5 Clutch problems

Clutch slipping

- ☐ Clutch plates worn or warped. Overhaul the clutch assembly (see Chapter 2).
- ☐ Clutch springs broken or weak. Old or heat-damaged (from slipping clutch) springs should be renewed (Chapter 2).
- ☐ Clutch centre or housing unevenly worn. This causes improper engagement of the plates. Replace the damaged or worn parts (see Chapter 2).
- ☐ Clutch release mechanism fault. Check the pushrod and release cylinder components (see Chapter 2).
- ☐ Incorrect type of oil. Use of oils designed for car engines which include friction modifiers can cause clutch slip in a wet clutch application.

Clutch not disengaging completely

- ☐ Clutch fluid level low (see *Pre-ride checks*).
- ☐ Clutch master cylinder seals or release cylinder seals worn (see Chapter 2).
- ☐ Clutch plates warped or damaged. This will cause clutch drag, which in turn will cause the machine to creep. Overhaul the clutch assembly (see Chapter 2).
- ☐ Clutch springs fatigued or broken. Check and renew the springs (see Chapter 2).
- ☐ Engine oil deteriorated. Old, thin oil will not provide proper lubrication for the plates, causing the clutch to drag. Renew the oil and filter (see Chapter 1).
- ☐ Engine oil viscosity too high. Using a heavier oil than recommended in Chapter 1 can cause the plates to stick together. Change to the correct weight oil.
- ☐ Clutch housing bearing seized on the transmission input shaft. Lack of lubrication, severe wear or damage can cause the bearing to seize. Overhaul of the clutch, and perhaps transmission, may be necessary to repair the damage (see Chapter 2).
- ☐ Loose clutch centre nut. Causes housing and centre misalignment putting a drag on the engine. Engagement adjustment continually varies. Overhaul the clutch assembly (see Chapter 2).

6 Gearchange problems

Doesn't go into gear or lever doesn't return

- ☐ Clutch not disengaging (see above).
- ☐ Gearchange mechanism stopper arm spring weak or broken, or arm roller broken or worn. Replace the spring or arm with a new one (see Chapter 2).
- ☐ Selector fork(s) bent, worn or seized. Renew the forks (see Chapter 2).
- ☐ Gear(s) stuck on shaft. Most often caused by a lack of lubrication or excessive wear in transmission bearings and bushes. Strip and rebuild the gearshafts (see Chapter 2).
- ☐ Selector drum binding. Caused by lubrication failure or excessive wear. Replace the drum and/or its bearing with a new one (see Chapter 2).
- ☐ Gearchange mechanism centralising spring weak or broken (see Chapter 2).
- ☐ Gearchange lever linkage rod incorrectly adjusted (see Chapter 6).

Jumps out of gear

- ☐ Selector fork(s) worn (see Chapter 2).
- ☐ Selector fork groove(s) in selector drum worn (see Chapter 2).
- ☐ Selector pawls or pins worn (see Chapter 2).
- ☐ Gear pinion dogs or dog slots worn or damaged. Strip and rebuild the gearshafts (see Chapter 2).

Overselects

- ☐ Gearchange mechanism stopper arm spring weak or broken, or arm roller broken or worn. Renew the spring or arm (see Chapter 2).
- ☐ Gearchange mechanism centralising spring weak or broken (see Chapter 2).

7 Abnormal engine noise

Knocking or pinking

- ☐ Carbon build-up in combustion chamber. Use of a fuel additive that will dissolve the adhesive bonding the carbon particles to the piston crown and chamber is the easiest way to remove the build-up. Otherwise, the cylinder head will have to be removed and decarbonised (Chapter 2).
- ☐ Incorrect or poor quality fuel. Old or improper grades of fuel can cause detonation. This causes the piston to rattle, thus the knocking or pinking sound. Drain old fuel and always use the recommended fuel grade.
- ☐ Spark plug heat range incorrect. Uncontrolled detonation indicates the plug heat range is too hot. The plug in effect becomes a glow plug, raising cylinder temperatures. Install the proper heat range plug (Chapter 1).
- ☐ Improper air/fuel mixture. This will cause the cylinders to run hot, which leads to detonation. A blockage in the fuel system or an air leak can cause this imbalance (see Chapter 4).

Piston slap or rattling

- ☐ Cylinder-to-piston clearance excessive. Cylinder and/or piston worn, usually accompanied by worn rings as well. Inspect and measure components and rebore if necessary (see Chapter 2).
- ☐ Piston ring(s) worn, broken or sticking. Overhaul the top-end (see Chapter 2).
- ☐ Piston pin, piston pin bore or connecting rod small-end worn from high mileage or seized due to lack of lubrication (see Chapter 2).
- ☐ Piston seizure damage. Usually from lack of lubrication or overheating. Inspect the piston and bores and rebore if necessary (see Chapter 2).
- ☐ Connecting rod big-end clearance excessive. Caused by excessive wear or lack of lubrication. Replace worn parts.
- ☐ Connecting rod bent. Caused by over-revving, trying to start a badly flooded engine or from ingesting a foreign object into the combustion chamber. Replace the damaged parts (Chapter 2).

Valve noise

- ☐ Incorrect valve clearances – check and adjust (see Chapter 1).
- ☐ Valve spring broken or weak. Check and replace weak valve springs with new ones (see Chapter 2).
- ☐ Camshaft or camshaft journals in the cylinder head worn or damaged. Lubrication failure at high rpm is usually the cause of damage due to insufficient oil or failure to change the oil at the recommended intervals. Since there are no replaceable bearings in the head, the head itself will have to be replaced with a new one (see Chapter 2).

Other noise

- ☐ Cylinder head gasket leaking. Check around the joint for blowing with the engine running.
- ☐ Exhaust pipe leaking at cylinder head connection. Caused by incorrect fit of pipe(s), loose exhaust flange or damaged gasket. All exhaust system fasteners should be tightened evenly and carefully to avoid leaks (see Chapter 4).
- ☐ Crankshaft runout excessive. Caused by a bent crankshaft (from over-revving) or damage from an upper cylinder component failure.
- ☐ Engine mounting bolts loose – ensure all the bolts are tightened to the specified torque settings (see Chapter 2).
- ☐ Crankshaft bearings worn (see Chapter 2).
- ☐ Cam chain rattle, due to worn chain or defective tensioner. Also worn chain tensioner/guide blades (see Chapter 2).
- ☐ Gear whine or clatter from the front of the engine. Too little or too much backlash between the balancer shaft gear and its drive gear on the crankshaft. Carry out the dynamic backlash adjustment procedure (see Chapter 2).

8 Abnormal driveline noise

Clutch noise

- ☐ Clutch housing/friction plate clearance excessive (see Chapter 2).
- ☐ Wear between the clutch housing splines and input shaft splines (see Chapter 2).
- ☐ Worn release bearing (see Chapter 2).

Transmission noise

- ☐ Bearings worn. Also includes the possibility that the shafts are worn. Overhaul the transmission see (Chapter 2).
- ☐ Gears worn or chipped (see Chapter 2).
- ☐ Metal chips jammed in gear teeth. Probably pieces from a broken clutch, gear or selector mechanism that were picked up by the gears. This will cause early bearing failure (see Chapter 2).
- ☐ Engine oil level too low. Causes a howl from transmission. Also affects engine power and clutch operation (see *Pre-ride checks*).

Final drive noise

- ☐ Chain not adjusted properly (Chapter 1).
- ☐ Front or rear sprocket loose. Tighten fasteners (Chapter 6).
- ☐ Sprockets and/or chain worn. Fit new sprockets and chain (Chapter 6).
- ☐ Rear sprocket warped. Fit a new sprocket (Chapter 6).
- ☐ Rubber dampers in rear wheel worn (Chapter 6).

9 Abnormal frame and suspension noise

Front end noise

- ☐ Low fluid level or improper viscosity oil in forks. This can sound like spurting and is usually accompanied by irregular fork action (Chapter 5).
- ☐ Spring weak or broken. Makes a clicking or scraping sound. Fork oil, when drained, will have a lot of metal particles in it (Chapter 5).
- ☐ Steering head bearings loose or damaged. Clicks when braking. Check and adjust or replace with new ones as necessary (Chapters 1 and 5).
- ☐ Fork yoke clamp bolts loose – ensure all the bolts are tightened to the specified torque (Chapter 6).
- ☐ Forks bent. Good possibility if machine has been dropped. Replace the sliders or tubes with new ones as required (Chapter 5).
- ☐ Front axle or axle pinch bolts loose. Tighten them to the specified torque (Chapter 6).
- ☐ Loose or worn wheel bearings. Check and replace with new ones as needed (Chapters 1 and 6).
- ☐ Faulty steering damper (see Chapter 5).

Shock absorber noise

- ☐ Fluid level incorrect. Indicates a leak caused by defective seal. Shock will be covered with oil. Replace shock with a new one or seek advice on repair from a suspension specialist (Chapter 5).
- ☐ Defective shock absorber with internal damage. This is in the body of the shock and can't be remedied. The shock must be replaced with a new one or returned to a suspension specialist for rebuild (Chapter 5).
- ☐ Bent or damaged shock body. Replace the shock with a new one (Chapter 5).
- ☐ Loose or worn suspension linkage components. Check and replace bearings as necessary (Chapter 5).

Brake noise

- ☐ Squeal caused by pad shim not installed or positioned correctly (where fitted) (Chapter 6).
- ☐ Squeal caused by dust on brake pads. Usually found in combination with glazed pads. Renew the pads (Chapter 6).
- ☐ Pads glazed. Caused by excessive heat from prolonged hard use or from contamination. DO NOT use sandpaper, emery cloth, carborundum cloth or any other abrasive to roughen the pad surfaces as abrasives will stay in the pad material and damage the disc. A very fine flat file can be used, but new pads is the best remedy (Chapter 6).
- ☐ Contamination of brake pads. Oil or brake fluid can cause the brake pads to chatter or squeal. Fit new pads. Identify the cause of the contamination, especially check the caliper piston seals for leaking fluid. Clean disc thoroughly with brake system cleaner (Chapter 6).
- ☐ Disc warped. Can cause a chattering, clicking or intermittent squeal. Usually accompanied by a pulsating lever and uneven braking. Replace the disc(s) (Chapter 6).
- ☐ Loose or worn wheel bearings. Check and replace (Chapters 1 and 6).

10 Oil pressure warning light comes on

Engine lubrication system

- ☐ Engine oil level low. Inspect for leak or other problem causing low oil level and add recommended oil (see *Pre-ride checks*).
- ☐ Engine oil pump defective, blocked oil strainer gauze or failed pressure regulator. Carry out an oil pressure check (Chapter 2).
- ☐ Engine oil viscosity too low. Very old, thin oil or an improper weight of oil used in the engine. Change to correct oil (Chapter 1).
- ☐ Camshaft or crankshaft journals worn. Excessive wear causing drop in oil pressure. Abnormal wear could be caused by oil starvation at high rpm from low oil level or improper weight or type of oil (Chapter 1).

Electrical system

- ☐ Oil pressure switch defective. Check the switch according to the procedure in Chapter 8. Replace it with a new one it if it is defective.
- ☐ Oil pressure warning LED or symbol defective. Check for pinched, shorted, disconnected or damaged wiring (Chapter 8).

11 Excessive exhaust smoke

White smoke

- ☐ Piston rings worn or broken, causing oil from the crankcase to be pulled past the piston into the combustion chamber. Replace the rings with new ones (Chapter 2).
- ☐ Cylinders worn or scored. Caused by overheating or oil starvation. Rebore the cylinders (Chapter 2).
- ☐ Valve stem oil seal damaged or worn. Replace the oil seals with new ones (Chapter 2).
- ☐ Valve guide worn. Perform a complete valve job (Chapter 2).
- ☐ Engine oil level too high, which causes the oil to be forced past the rings. Drain oil to the proper level (see *Pre-ride checks*).
- ☐ Head gasket broken between oil return and cylinder. Causes oil to be pulled into the combustion chamber. Replace the head gasket with a new one and check the head for warpage (Chapter 2).
- ☐ Abnormal crankcase pressurisation which forces oil past the rings, usually caused by a clogged breather.

Black smoke

- ☐ Air filter clogged. Clean the air filter elements or renew them (Chapter 1).
- ☐ Fuel injection system malfunction (Chapter 4).

Brown smoke

- ☐ Air filters poorly sealed or not installed (Chapter 1).
- ☐ Fuel injection system malfunction (Chapter 4).

12 Poor handling or stability

Handlebar hard to turn

- ☐ Steering head bearing adjuster nut too tight. Check adjustment as described in Chapter 1.
- ☐ Bearings damaged. Roughness can be felt as the bars are turned from side-to-side. Replace the bearings with new ones (Chapter 5).
- ☐ Races dented or worn. Denting results from wear in only one position (e.g., straight ahead), from a collision or hitting a pothole or from dropping the machine. Replace the bearings with new ones (Chapter 5).
- ☐ Steering stem lubrication inadequate. Causes are grease getting hard from age or being washed out by high pressure car washes. Disassemble steering head and repack bearings (Chapter 5).
- ☐ Steering stem bent. Caused by a collision, hitting a pothole or by dropping the machine. Replace damaged part. Don't try to straighten the steering stem (Chapter 5).
- ☐ Front tyre air pressure too low (see Pre-ride checks).
- ☐ Faulty steering damper (see Chapter 5).

12 Poor handling or stability (continued)

Handlebar shakes or vibrates excessively

- ☐ Tyres worn or out of balance (Pre-ride checks and Chapter 6).
- ☐ Swingarm bearings worn. Replace the bearings with new ones (Chapter 5).
- ☐ Failed steering damper (Chapter 5).
- ☐ Wheel rim(s) warped or damaged. Inspect wheels for runout (Chapter 6).
- ☐ Wheel bearings worn. Worn front or rear wheel bearings can cause poor tracking. Worn front bearings will cause wobble (Chapters 1 and 6).
- ☐ Fork yoke clamp bolts or handlebar clamp bolts loose. Tighten them to the specified torque (Chapter 5).
- ☐ Engine mounting bolts loose. Will cause excessive vibration with increased engine rpm – ensure all the bolts are tightened to the specified torque settings (see Chapter 2).

Machine pulls to one side

- ☐ Frame bent. Definitely suspect this if the machine has been dropped. May or may not be accompanied by cracking near the steering head, swingarm mountings or engine mountings. Replace the frame with a new one (Chapter 5).
- ☐ Wheels out of alignment. Insufficient attention to wheel alignment when adjusting drive chain slack (Chapter 1). Caused by improper location of axle spacers following wheel removal (Chapter 6). Bent steering stem or frame following accident damage.
- ☐ Forks bent. Disassemble the forks and replace the damaged parts (Chapter 5).
- ☐ Swingarm bent or twisted. Replace the arm with a new one (Chapter 5).
- ☐ Fork oil level uneven. Check and add or drain as necessary (Chapter 5).

Poor shock absorbing qualities

- ☐ Too hard:
  - a) Suspension settings incorrect (Chapter 5).
  - b) Fork oil level excessive (Chapter 5).
  - c) Fork oil viscosity too high. Use a lighter oil (see the Specifications in Chapter 5).
  - d) Fork tube bent. Causes a harsh, sticking feeling (Chapter 5).
  - e) Fork internal damage (Chapter 5).
  - f) Shock shaft or body bent or damaged (Chapter 5).
  - g) Shock internal damage (Chapter 5).
  - h) Tyre pressure too high (Pre-ride checks).
- ☐ Too soft:
  - a) Suspension settings incorrect (Chapter 5).
  - b) Fork oil level too low (Chapter 5).
  - c) Fork oil viscosity too light (Chapter 5).
  - d) Fork springs weak or broken (Chapter 5).
  - e) Fork or shock oil leaking (Chapter 5).
  - f) Shock internal damage (Chapter 5).

13 Braking problems

Brakes are spongy, don't hold

- ☐ Low brake fluid level (see Pre-ride checks).
- ☐ Air in hydraulic system. Caused by inattention to master cylinder fluid level or by leakage. Locate problem and bleed brakes (Chapter 6).
- ☐ Pads or disc worn (Chapters 1 and 6).
- ☐ Contaminated pads. Caused by contamination with oil, grease, brake fluid, etc. Fit new pads. Identify the cause of the contamination, especially check the caliper piston seals for leaking fluid. Clean disc thoroughly with brake system cleaner (Chapter 6).
- ☐ Brake fluid deteriorated. Fluid is old or contaminated. Drain system, replenish with new fluid and bleed the system (Chapter 6).
- ☐ Master cylinder internal seals worn or damaged causing fluid to bypass (Chapter 6).
- ☐ Master cylinder bore scratched by foreign material or broken spring. Fit a new master cylinder (Chapter 6).
- ☐ Disc warped. Replace disc(s) (Chapter 6).

Brake lever or pedal pulsates

- ☐ Disc warped. Replace disc with new one (Chapter 6).
- ☐ Brake caliper bolts loose – tighten the bolts to the specified torque (Chapter 6).
- ☐ Wheel warped or otherwise damaged (Chapter 6).
- ☐ Wheel bearings damaged or worn (Chapters 1 and 6).

Brakes drag

- ☐ Master cylinder piston seized. Caused by wear or damage to piston or cylinder bore (Chapter 6).
- ☐ Lever balky or stuck. Check pivot and lubricate (Chapter 5).
- ☐ Brake caliper piston seized in bore. Caused by corrosion or ingestion of dirt past deteriorated seal (Chapter 6).
- ☐ Brake caliper piston seized in bore. Caused by corrosion or ingestion of dirt past deteriorated seal (Chapter 6).
- ☐ Brake caliper slider pins sticking – rear caliper (Chapter 6).
- ☐ Pads improperly installed (Chapter 6).
- ☐ Brake caliper incorrectly installed (Chapter 6).

14 Electrical problems

Battery dead or weak

- ☐ Battery faulty. Caused by sulphated plates which are shorted through sedimentation. Confirm with battery condition check (Chapter 8).
- ☐ Broken battery terminal making only occasional contact.
- ☐ Battery leads making poor contact (Chapter 8).
- ☐ Load excessive. Caused by addition of high wattage lights or other electrical accessories.
- ☐ Ignition (main) switch defective. Switch either grounds (earths) internally or fails to shut off system. Renew the switch (Chapter 8).
- ☐ Regulator/rectifier defective (Chapter 8).
- ☐ Alternator stator coil open or shorted (Chapter 8).
- ☐ Charging system fault. Check for excessive current leakage (Chapter 8).
- ☐ Wiring faulty. Wiring grounded (earthed) or connections loose in ignition, charging or lighting circuits (Chapter 8).

Battery overcharged

- ☐ Regulator/rectifier defective. Overcharging is noticed when battery gets excessively warm (Chapter 8).
- ☐ Battery faulty. Confirm with battery condition check (Chapter 8).
- ☐ Battery amperage too low, wrong type or size of battery. Install manufacturer's specified amp-hour battery to handle charging load (Chapter 8).

Checking engine compression

- Low compression will result in exhaust smoke, heavy oil consumption, poor starting and poor performance. A compression test will provide useful information about an engine's condition and if performed regularly, can give warning of trouble before any other symptoms become apparent.
- A compression gauge will be required, along with an adapter to suit the spark plug hole thread size. Note that the screw-in type gauge/adapter set up is preferable to the rubber cone type.
- Before carrying out the test, first check the valve clearances as described in Chapter 1.

1 Run the engine until it reaches normal operating temperature, then stop it and remove the spark plug(s), taking care not to scald your hands on the hot components.

2 Install the gauge adapter and compression gauge in No. 1 cylinder spark plug hole **(see illustration 1)**.

Screw the compression gauge adapter into the spark plug hole, then screw the gauge into the adapter

3 On kickstart-equipped motorcycles, make sure the ignition switch is OFF, then open the throttle fully and kick the engine over a couple of times until the gauge reading stabilises.

4 On motorcycles with electric start only, the procedure will differ depending on the nature of the ignition system. Flick the engine kill switch (engine stop switch) to OFF and turn the ignition switch ON; open the throttle fully and crank the engine over on the starter motor for a couple of revolutions until the gauge reading stabilises. If the starter will not operate with the kill switch OFF, turn the ignition switch OFF and refer to the next paragraph.

5 Install the plugs back in their coils. Earth the plug either against the front of the cylinder head (not against the valve cover), or to the crankcase earth using an auxiliary wire with a crocodile clip on each end, clipping one end to the spark plug threads; this is essential to prevent damage to the ignition system **(see illustration 2)**. Position the plugs well away from the plug holes otherwise there is a risk of atomised fuel escaping from the plug holes and igniting. As a safety precaution, cover the cylinder head cover with rag. Turn the ignition switch and kill switch ON, open the throttle fully and crank the engine over on the starter motor for a couple of revolutions until the gauge reading stabilises.

All spark plugs must be earthed (grounded)

6 After one or two revolutions the pressure should build up to a maximum figure and then stabilise. Take a note of this reading and on multi-cylinder engines repeat the test on the remaining cylinders.

7 The correct pressures are given in Chapter 2 Specifications. If the results fall within the specified range and on multi-cylinder engines all are relatively equal, the engine is in good condition. If there is a marked difference between the readings, or if the readings are lower than specified, inspection of the top-end components will be required.

8 Low compression pressure may be due to worn cylinder bores, pistons or rings, failure of the cylinder head gasket, worn valve seals, or poor valve seating.

9 To distinguish between cylinder/piston wear and valve leakage, pour a small quantity of oil into the bore to temporarily seal the piston rings, then repeat the compression tests **(see illustration 3)**. If the readings show a noticeable increase in pressure this confirms that the cylinder bore, piston, or rings are worn. If, however, no change is indicated, the cylinder head gasket or valves should be examined.

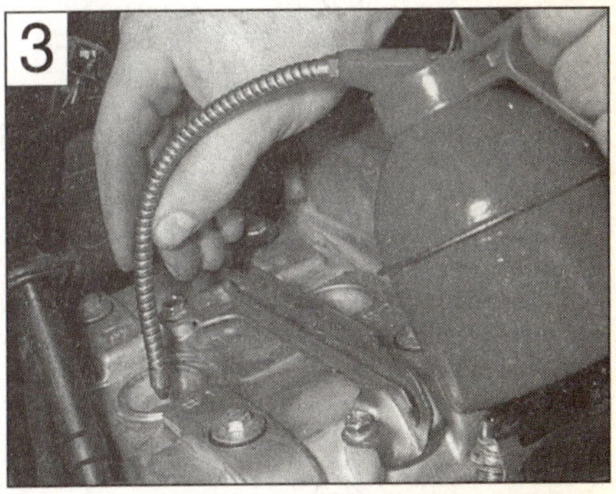

Bores can be temporarily sealed with a squirt of motor oil

10 High compression pressure indicates excessive carbon build-up in the combustion chamber and on the piston crown. If this is the case the cylinder head should be removed and the deposits removed. Note that excessive carbon build-up is less likely with the used on modern fuels.

Checking battery open-circuit voltage

Warning: The gases produced by the battery are explosive - never smoke or create any sparks in the vicinity of the battery. Never allow the electrolyte to contact your skin or clothing - if it does, wash it off and seek immediate medical attention.

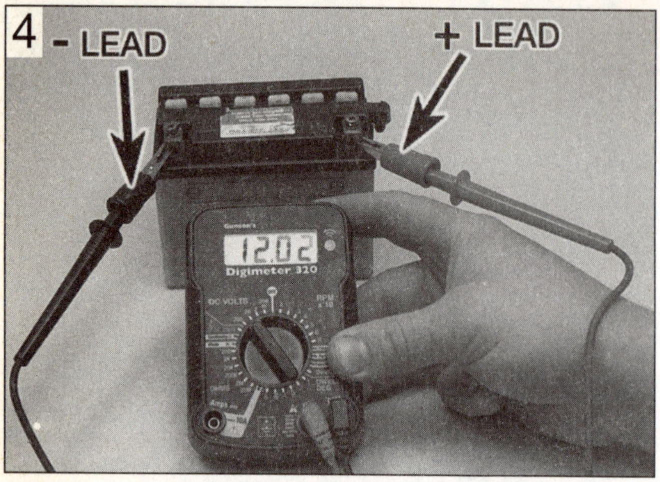

Measuring open-circuit battery voltage

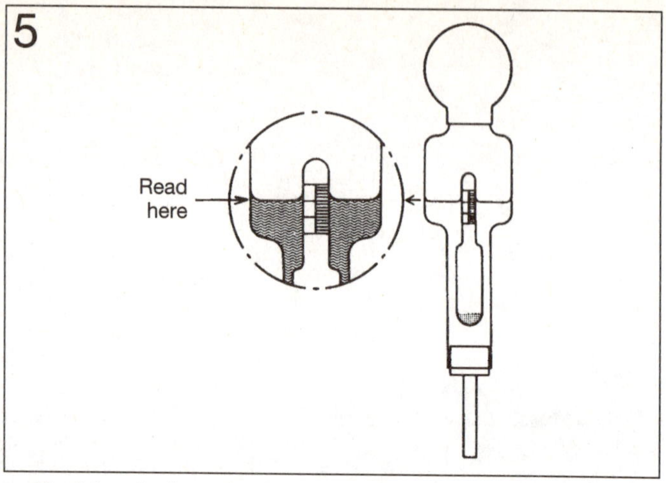

Float-type hydrometer for measuring battery specific gravity

● Before any electrical fault is investigated the battery should be checked.

● You'll need a dc voltmeter or multimeter to check battery voltage. Check that the leads are inserted in the correct terminals on the meter, red lead to positive (+ve), black lead to negative (-ve). Incorrect connections can damage the meter.

● A sound fully-charged 12 volt battery should produce between 12.3 and 12.6 volts across its terminals (12.8 volts for a maintenance-free battery). On machines with a 6 volt battery, voltage should be between 6.1 and 6.3 volts.

1 Set a multimeter to the 0 to 20 volts dc range and connect its probes across the battery terminals. Connect the meter's positive (+ve) probe, usually red, to the battery positive (+ve) terminal, followed by the meter's negative (-ve) probe, usually black, to the battery negative terminal (-ve) **(see illustration 4)**.

2 If battery voltage is low (below 10 volts on a 12 volt battery or below 4 volts on a six volt battery), charge the battery and test the voltage again. If the battery repeatedly goes flat, investigate the motorcycle's charging system.

Checking battery specific gravity (SG)

Warning: The gases produced by the battery are explosive - never smoke or create any sparks in the vicinity of the battery. Never allow the electrolyte to contact your skin or clothing - if it does, wash it off and seek immediate medical attention.

● The specific gravity check gives an indication of a battery's state of charge.

● A hydrometer is used for measuring specific gravity. Make sure you purchase one which has a small enough hose to insert in the aperture of a motorcycle battery.

● Specific gravity is simply a measure of the electrolyte's density compared with that of water. Water has an SG of 1.000 and fully-charged battery electrolyte is about 26% heavier, at 1.260.

● Specific gravity checks are not possible on maintenance-free batteries. Testing the open-circuit voltage is the only means of determining their state of charge.

1 To measure SG, remove the battery from the motorcycle and remove the first cell cap. Draw some electrolyte into the hydrometer and note the reading **(see illustration 5)**. Return the electrolyte to the cell and install the cap.

2 The reading should be in the region of 1.260 to 1.280. If SG is below 1.200 the battery needs charging. Note that SG will vary with temperature; it should be measured at 20°C (68°F). Add 0.007 to the reading for every 10°C above 20°C, and subtract 0.007 from the reading for every 10°C below 20°C. Add 0.004 to the reading for every 10°F above 68°F, and subtract 0.004 from the reading for every 10°F below 68°F.

3 When the check is complete, rinse the hydrometer thoroughly with clean water.

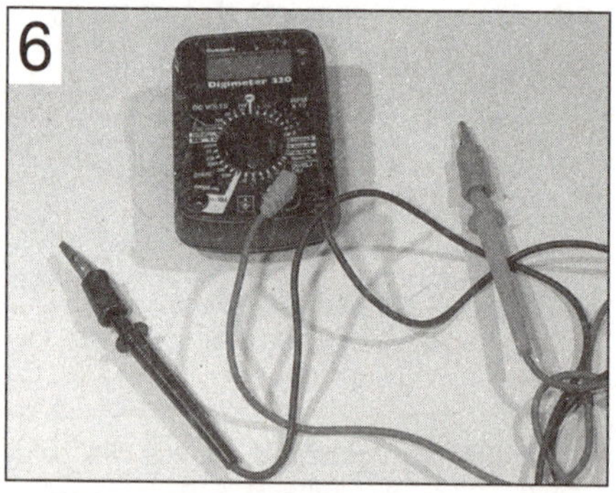

Digital multimeter can be used for all electrical tests

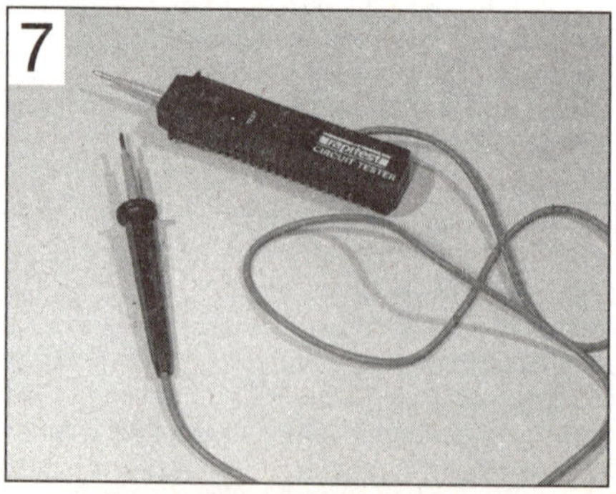

Battery-powered continuity tester

Checking for continuity

● The term continuity describes the uninterrupted flow of electricity through an electrical circuit. A continuity check will determine whether an **open-circuit** situation exists.

● Continuity can be checked with an ohmmeter, multimeter, continuity tester or battery and bulb test circuit **(see illustrations 6, 7 and 8)**.

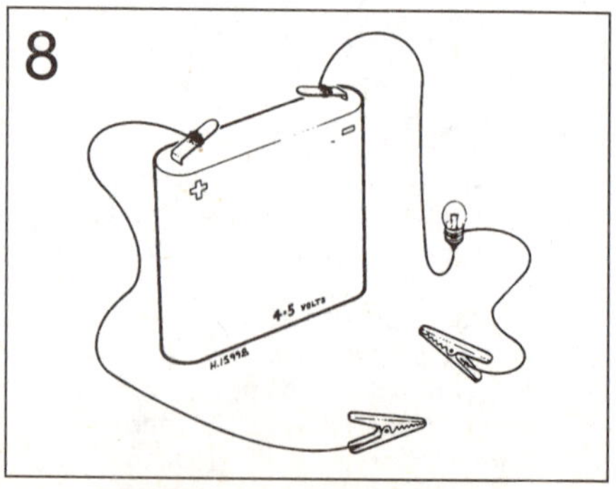

Battery and bulb test circuit

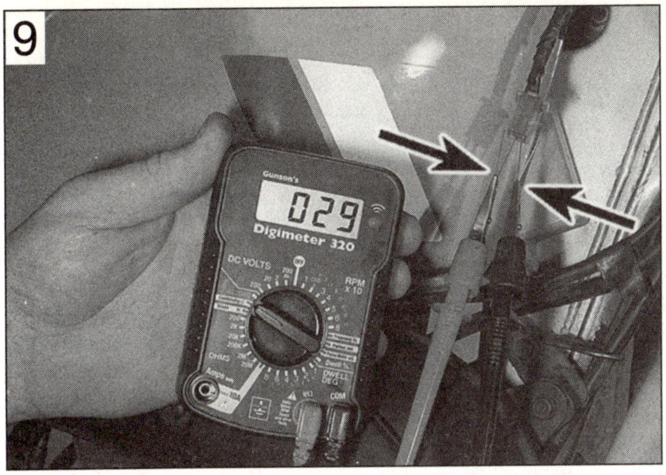

Continuity check of front brake light switch using a meter - note split pins used to access connector terminals

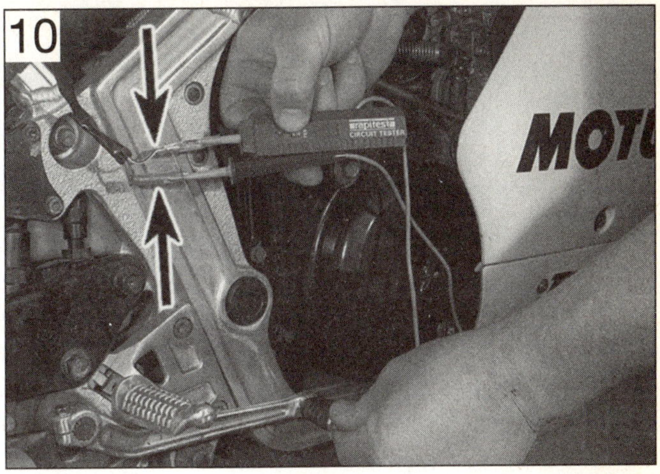

Continuity check of rear brake light switch using a continuity tester

- All of these instruments are self-powered by a battery, therefore the checks are made with the ignition OFF.
- As a safety precaution, always disconnect the battery negative (-ve) lead before making checks, particularly if ignition switch checks are being made.
- If using a meter, select the appropriate ohms scale and check that the meter reads infinity (∞). Touch the meter probes together and check that meter reads zero; where necessary adjust the meter so that it reads zero.
- After using a meter, always switch it OFF to conserve its battery.

Switch checks

1 If a switch is at fault, trace its wiring up to the wiring connectors. Separate the wire connectors and inspect them for security and condition. A build-up of dirt or corrosion here will most likely be the cause of the problem - clean up and apply a water dispersant such as WD40.

2 If using a test meter, set the meter to the ohms x 10 scale and connect its probes across the wires from the switch **(see illustration 9)**. Simple ON/OFF type switches, such as brake light switches, only have two wires whereas combination switches, like the ignition switch, have many internal links. Study the wiring diagram to ensure that you are connecting across the correct pair of wires. Continuity (low or no measurable resistance - 0 ohms) should be indicated with the switch ON and no continuity (high resistance) with it OFF.

3 Note that the polarity of the test probes doesn't matter for continuity checks, although care should be taken to follow specific test procedures if a diode or solid-state component is being checked.

4 A continuity tester or battery and bulb circuit can be used in the same way. Connect its probes as described above **(see illustration 10)**. The light should come on to indicate continuity in the ON switch position, but should extinguish in the OFF position.

Wiring checks

- Many electrical faults are caused by damaged wiring, often due to incorrect routing or chaffing on frame components.
- Loose, wet or corroded wire connectors can also be the cause of electrical problems, especially in exposed locations.

1 A continuity check can be made on a single length of wire by disconnecting it at each end and connecting a meter or continuity tester across both ends of the wire **(see illustration 11)**.

2 Continuity (low or no resistance - 0 ohms) should be indicated if the wire is good. If no continuity (high resistance) is shown, suspect a broken wire.

Checking for voltage

- A voltage check can determine whether current is reaching a component.
- Voltage can be checked with a dc voltmeter, multimeter set on the dc volts scale, test light or buzzer **(see illustrations 12 and 13)**. A meter has the advantage of being able to measure actual voltage.
- When using a meter, check that its leads are inserted in the correct terminals on the meter, red to positive (+ve), black to negative (-ve). Incorrect connections can damage the meter.
- A voltmeter (or multimeter set to the dc volts scale) should always be connected in parallel (across the load). Connecting it in series will not harm the meter, but the reading will not be meaningful.
- Voltage checks are made with the ignition ON.

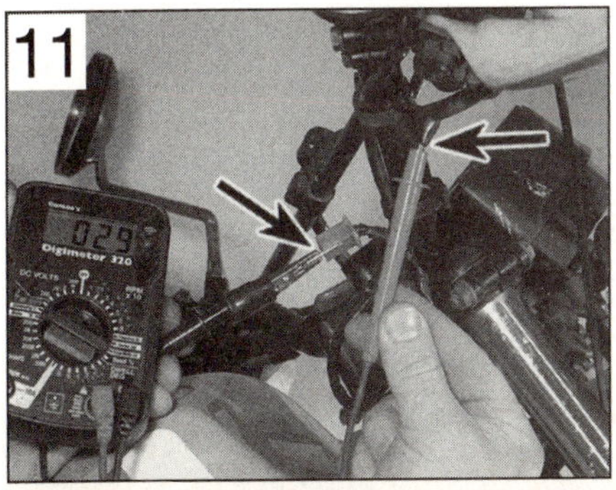

Continuity check of front brake light switch sub-harness

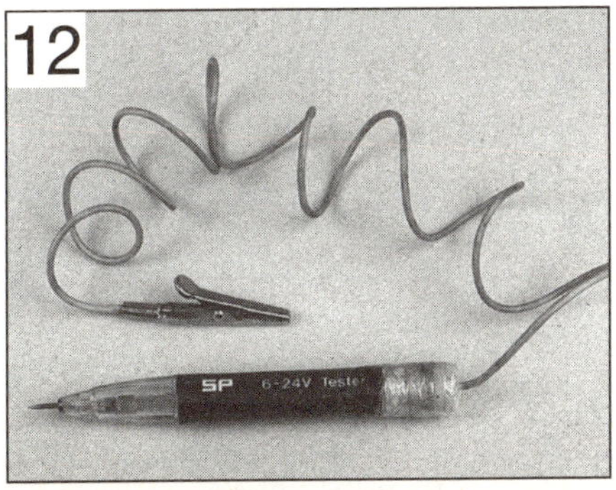

A simple test light can be used for voltage checks

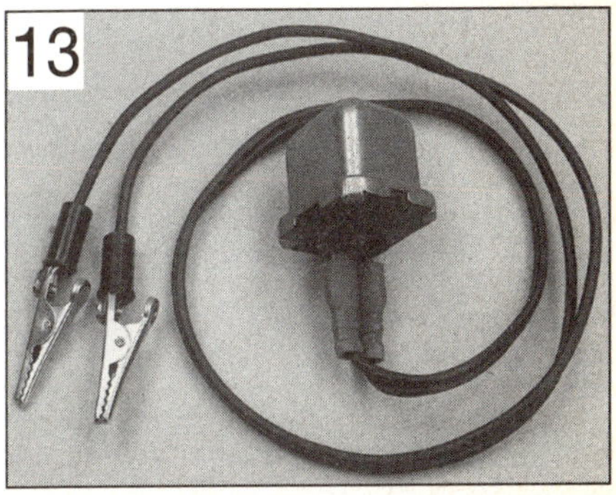

A buzzer is useful for voltage checks

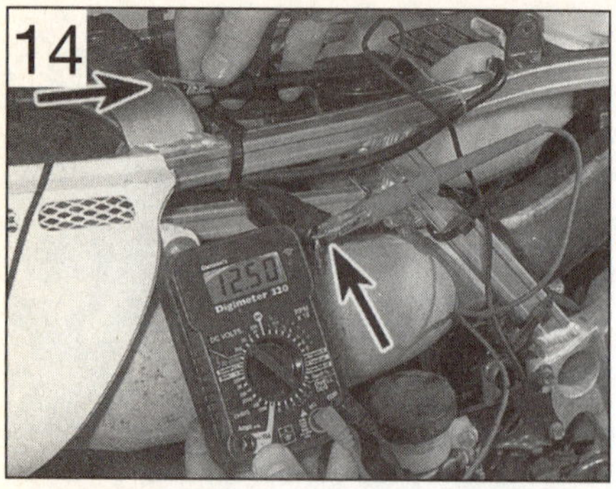

Checking for voltage at the rear brake light power supply wire using a meter . . .

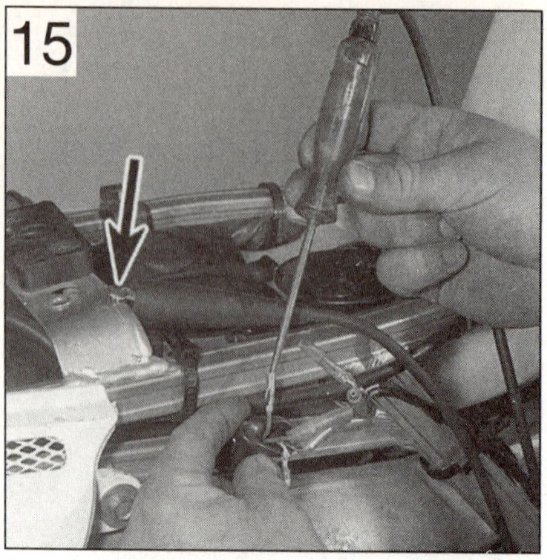

. . . or a test light - note the earth connection to the frame (arrow)

1 First identify the relevant wiring circuit by referring to the wiring diagram at the end of this manual. If other electrical components share the same power supply (ie are fed from the same fuse), take note whether they are working correctly - this is useful information in deciding where to start checking the circuit.

2 If using a meter, check first that the meter leads are plugged into the correct terminals on the meter (see above). Set the meter to the dc volts function, at a range suitable for the battery voltage. Connect the meter red probe (+ve) to the power supply wire and the black probe to a good metal earth (ground) on the motorcycle's frame or directly to the battery negative (-ve) terminal **(see illustration 14)**. Battery voltage should be shown on the meter with the ignition switched ON.

3 If using a test light or buzzer, connect its positive (+ve) probe to the power supply terminal and its negative (-ve) probe to a good earth (ground) on the motorcycle's frame or directly to the battery negative (-ve) terminal **(see illustration 15)**. With the ignition ON, the test light should illuminate or the buzzer sound.

4 If no voltage is indicated, work back towards the fuse continuing to check for voltage. When you reach a point where there is voltage, you know the problem lies between that point and your last check point.

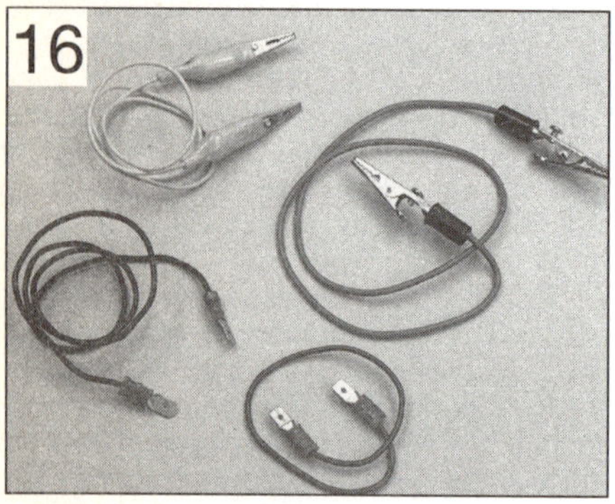

A selection of jumper wires for making earth (ground) checks

Checking the earth (ground)

- Earth connections are made either directly to the engine or frame (such as sensors, neutral switch etc. which only have a positive feed) or by a separate wire into the earth circuit of the wiring harness. Alternatively a short earth wire is sometimes run directly from the component to the motorcycle's frame.
- Corrosion is often the cause of a poor earth connection.
- If total failure is experienced, check the security of the main earth lead from the negative (-ve) terminal of the battery and also the main earth (ground) point on the wiring harness. If corroded, dismantle the connection and clean all surfaces back to bare metal.

1 To check the earth on a component, use an insulated jumper wire to temporarily bypass its earth connection **(see illustration 16)**. Connect one end of the jumper wire between the earth terminal or metal body of the component and the other end to the motorcycle's frame.

2 If the circuit works with the jumper wire installed, the original earth circuit is faulty. Check the wiring for open-circuits or poor connections. Clean up direct earth connections, removing all traces of corrosion and remake the joint. Apply petroleum jelly to the joint to prevent future corrosion.

Tracing a short-circuit

- A short-circuit occurs where current shorts to earth (ground) bypassing the circuit components. This usually results in a blown fuse.
- A short-circuit is most likely to occur where the insulation has worn through due to wiring chafing on a component, allowing a direct path to earth (ground) on the frame.

1 Remove any bodypanels necessary to access the circuit wiring.

2 Check that all electrical switches in the circuit are OFF, then remove the circuit fuse and connect a test light, buzzer or voltmeter (set to the dc scale) across the fuse terminals. No voltage should be shown.

3 Move the wiring from side to side whilst observing the test light or meter. When the test light comes on, buzzer sounds or meter shows voltage, you have found the cause of the short. It will usually shown up as damaged or burned insulation.

4 Note that the same test can be performed on each component in the circuit, even the switch.

A

ABS (Anti-lock braking system) A system, usually electronically controlled, that senses incipient wheel lockup during braking and relieves hydraulic pressure at wheel which is about to skid.
Aftermarket Components suitable for the motorcycle, but not produced by the motorcycle manufacturer.
Allen key A hexagonal wrench which fits into a recessed hexagonal hole.
Alternating current (ac) Current produced by an alternator. Requires converting to direct current by a rectifier for charging purposes.
Alternator Converts mechanical energy from the engine into electrical energy to charge the battery and power the electrical system.
Ampere (amp) A unit of measurement for the flow of electrical current. Current = Volts ÷ Ohms.
Ampere-hour (Ah) Measure of battery capacity.
Angle-tightening A torque expressed in degrees. Often follows a conventional tightening torque for cylinder head or main bearing fasteners **(see illustration)**.

Angle-tightening cylinder head bolts

Antifreeze A substance (usually ethylene glycol) mixed with water, and added to the cooling system, to prevent freezing of the coolant in winter. Antifreeze also contains chemicals to inhibit corrosion and the formation of rust and other deposits that would tend to clog the radiator and coolant passages and reduce cooling efficiency.
Anti-dive System attached to the fork lower leg (slider) to prevent fork dive when braking hard.
Anti-seize compound A coating that reduces the risk of seizing on fasteners that are subjected to high temperatures, such as exhaust clamp bolts and nuts.
API American Petroleum Institute. A quality standard for 4-stroke motor oils.
Asbestos A natural fibrous mineral with great heat resistance, commonly used in the composition of brake friction materials. Asbestos is a health hazard and the dust created by brake systems should never be inhaled or ingested.
ATF Automatic Transmission Fluid. Often used in front forks.
ATU Automatic Timing Unit. Mechanical device for advancing the ignition timing on early engines.
ATV All Terrain Vehicle. Often called a Quad.
Axial play Side-to-side movement.
Axle A shaft on which a wheel revolves. Also known as a spindle.

B

Backlash The amount of movement between meshed components when one component is held still. Usually applies to gear teeth.
Ball bearing A bearing consisting of a hardened inner and outer race with hardened steel balls between the two races.
Bearings Used between two working surfaces to prevent wear of the components and a build-up of heat. Four types of bearing are commonly used on motorcycles: plain shell bearings, ball bearings, tapered roller bearings and needle roller bearings.
Bevel gears Used to turn the drive through 90°. Typical applications are shaft final drive and camshaft drive **(see illustration)**.

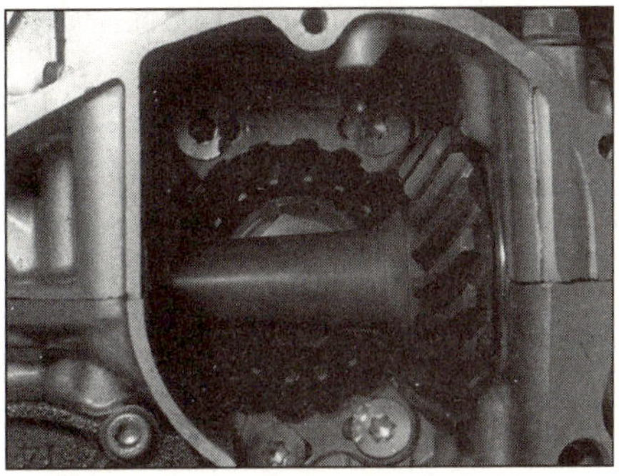
Bevel gears are used to turn the drive through 90°

BHP Brake Horsepower. The British measurement for engine power output. Power output is now usually expressed in kilowatts (kW).
Bias-belted tyre Similar construction to radial tyre, but with outer belt running at an angle to the wheel rim.
Big-end bearing The bearing in the end of the connecting rod that's attached to the crankshaft.
Bleeding The process of removing air from an hydraulic system via a bleed nipple or bleed screw.
Bottom-end A description of an engine's crankcase components and all components contained there-in.
BTDC Before Top Dead Centre in terms of piston position. Ignition timing is often expressed in terms of degrees or millimetres BTDC.
Bush A cylindrical metal or rubber component used between two moving parts.
Burr Rough edge left on a component after machining or as a result of excessive wear.

C

Cam chain The chain which takes drive from the crankshaft to the camshaft(s).
Canister The main component in an evaporative emission control system (California market only); contains activated charcoal granules to trap vapours from the fuel system rather than allowing them to vent to the atmosphere.
Castellated Resembling the parapets along the top of a castle wall. For example, a castellated wheel axle or spindle nut.
Catalytic converter A device in the exhaust system of some machines which converts certain pollutants in the exhaust gases into less harmful substances.
Charging system Description of the components which charge the battery, ie the alternator, rectifer and regulator.
Circlip A ring-shaped clip used to prevent endwise movement of cylindrical parts and shafts. An internal circlip is installed in a groove in a housing; an external circlip fits into a groove on the outside of a cylindrical piece such as a shaft. Also known as a snap-ring.
Clearance The amount of space between two parts. For example, between a piston and a cylinder, between a bearing and a journal, etc.
Coil spring A spiral of elastic steel found in various sizes throughout a vehicle, for example as a springing medium in the suspension and in the valve train.
Compression Reduction in volume, and increase in pressure and temperature, of a gas, caused by squeezing it into a smaller space.
Compression damping Controls the speed the suspension compresses when hitting a bump.
Compression ratio The relationship between cylinder volume when the piston is at top dead centre and cylinder volume when the piston is at bottom dead centre.
Continuity The uninterrupted path in the flow of electricity. Little or no measurable resistance.
Continuity tester Self-powered bleeper or test light which indicates continuity.
Cp Candlepower. Bulb rating commonly found on US motorcycles.
Crossply tyre Tyre plies arranged in a criss-cross pattern. Usually four or six plies used, hence 4PR or 6PR in tyre size codes.
Cush drive Rubber damper segments fitted between the rear wheel and final drive sprocket to absorb transmission shocks **(see illustration)**.

Cush drive rubbers dampen out transmission shocks

D

Degree disc Calibrated disc for measuring piston position. Expressed in degrees.
Dial gauge Clock-type gauge with adapters for measuring runout and piston position. Expressed in mm or inches.
Diaphragm The rubber membrane in a master cylinder or carburettor which seals the upper chamber.
Diaphragm spring A single sprung plate often used in clutches.
Direct current (dc) Current produced by a dc generator.

Decarbonisation The process of removing carbon deposits - typically from the combustion chamber, valves and exhaust port/system.
Detonation Destructive and damaging explosion of fuel/air mixture in combustion chamber instead of controlled burning.
Diode An electrical valve which only allows current to flow in one direction. Commonly used in rectifiers and starter interlock systems.
Disc valve (or rotary valve) A induction system used on some two-stroke engines.
Double-overhead camshaft (DOHC) An engine that uses two overhead camshafts, one for the intake valves and one for the exhaust valves.
Drivebelt A toothed belt used to transmit drive to the rear wheel on some motorcycles. A drivebelt has also been used to drive the camshafts. Drivebelts are usually made of Kevlar.
Driveshaft Any shaft used to transmit motion. Commonly used when referring to the final driveshaft on shaft drive motorcycles.

E

Earth return The return path of an electrical circuit, utilising the motorcycle's frame.
ECU (Electronic Control Unit) A computer which controls (for instance) an ignition system, or an anti-lock braking system.
EGO Exhaust Gas Oxygen sensor. Sometimes called a Lambda sensor.
Electrolyte The fluid in a lead-acid battery.
EMS (Engine Management System) A computer controlled system which manages the fuel injection and the ignition systems in an integrated fashion.
Endfloat The amount of lengthways movement between two parts. As applied to a crankshaft, the distance that the crankshaft can move side-to-side in the crankcase.
Endless chain A chain having no joining link. Common use for cam chains and final drive chains.
EP (Extreme Pressure) Oil type used in locations where high loads are applied, such as between gear teeth.
Evaporative emission control system Describes a charcoal filled canister which stores fuel vapours from the tank rather than allowing them to vent to the atmosphere. Usually only fitted to California models and referred to as an EVAP system.
Expansion chamber Section of two-stroke engine exhaust system so designed to improve engine efficiency and boost power.

F

Feeler blade or gauge A thin strip or blade of hardened steel, ground to an exact thickness, used to check or measure clearances between parts.
Final drive Description of the drive from the transmission to the rear wheel. Usually by chain or shaft, but sometimes by belt.
Firing order The order in which the engine cylinders fire, or deliver their power strokes, beginning with the number one cylinder.
Flooding Term used to describe a high fuel level in the carburettor float chambers, leading to fuel overflow. Also refers to excess fuel in the combustion chamber due to incorrect starting technique.
Free length The no-load state of a component when measured. Clutch, valve and fork spring lengths are measured at rest, without any preload.
Freeplay The amount of travel before any action takes place. The looseness in a linkage, or an assembly of parts, between the initial application of force and actual movement. For example, the distance the rear brake pedal moves before the rear brake is actuated.
Fuel injection The fuel/air mixture is metered electronically and directed into the engine intake ports (indirect injection) or into the cylinders (direct injection). Sensors supply information on engine speed and conditions.
Fuel/air mixture The charge of fuel and air going into the engine. See **Stoichiometric ratio.**
Fuse An electrical device which protects a circuit against accidental overload. The typical fuse contains a soft piece of metal which is calibrated to melt at a predetermined current flow (expressed as amps) and break the circuit.

G

Gap The distance the spark must travel in jumping from the centre electrode to the side electrode in a spark plug. Also refers to the distance between the ignition rotor and the pickup coil in an electronic ignition system.
Gasket Any thin, soft material - usually cork, cardboard, asbestos or soft metal - installed between two metal surfaces to ensure a good seal. For instance, the cylinder head gasket seals the joint between the block and the cylinder head.
Gauge An instrument panel display used to monitor engine conditions. A gauge with a movable pointer on a dial or a fixed scale is an analogue gauge. A gauge with a numerical readout is called a digital gauge.
Gear ratios The drive ratio of a pair of gears in a gearbox, calculated on their number of teeth.
Glaze-busting see **Honing**
Grinding Process for renovating the valve face and valve seat contact area in the cylinder head.
Gudgeon pin The shaft which connects the connecting rod small-end with the piston. Often called a piston pin or wrist pin.

H

Helical gears Gear teeth are slightly curved and produce less gear noise that straight-cut gears. Often used for primary drives.

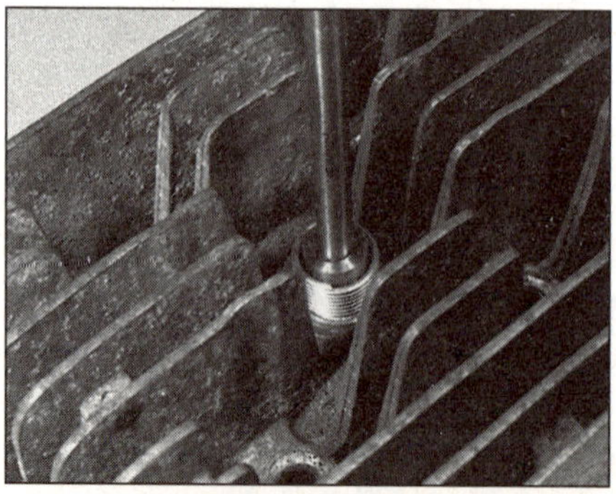

Installing a Helicoil thread insert in a cylinder head

Helicoil A thread insert repair system. Commonly used as a repair for stripped spark plug threads **(see illustration).**
Honing A process used to break down the glaze on a cylinder bore (also called glaze-busting). Can also be carried out to roughen a rebored cylinder to aid ring bedding-in.
HT (High Tension) Description of the electrical circuit from the secondary winding of the ignition coil to the spark plug.
Hydraulic A liquid filled system used to transmit pressure from one component to another. Common uses on motorcycles are brakes and clutches.
Hydrometer An instrument for measuring the specific gravity of a lead-acid battery.
Hygroscopic Water absorbing. In motorcycle applications, braking efficiency will be reduced if DOT 3 or 4 hydraulic fluid absorbs water from the air - care must be taken to keep new brake fluid in tightly sealed containers.

I

lbf ft Pounds-force feet. An imperial unit of torque. Sometimes written as ft-lbs.
lbf in Pound-force inch. An imperial unit of torque, applied to components where a very low torque is required. Sometimes written as in-lbs.
IC Abbreviation for Integrated Circuit.
Ignition advance Means of increasing the timing of the spark at higher engine speeds. Done by mechanical means (ATU) on early engines or electronically by the ignition control unit on later engines.
Ignition timing The moment at which the spark plug fires, expressed in the number of crankshaft degrees before the piston reaches the top of its stroke, or in the number of millimetres before the piston reaches the top of its stroke.
Infinity (∞) Description of an open-circuit electrical state, where no continuity exists.
Inverted forks (upside down forks) The sliders or lower legs are held in the yokes and the fork tubes or stanchions are connected to the wheel axle (spindle). Less unsprung weight and stiffer construction than conventional forks.

J

JASO Quality standard for 2-stroke oils.
Joule The unit of electrical energy.
Journal The bearing surface of a shaft.

K

Kickstart Mechanical means of turning the engine over for starting purposes. Only usually fitted to mopeds, small capacity motorcycles and off-road motorcycles.
Kill switch Handebar-mounted switch for emergency ignition cut-out. Cuts the ignition circuit on all models, and additionally prevent starter motor operation on others.
km Symbol for kilometre.
kmh Abbreviation for kilometres per hour.

L

Lambda (λ) sensor A sensor fitted in the exhaust system to measure the exhaust gas oxygen content (excess air factor).

Lapping see **Grinding**.
LCD Abbreviation for Liquid Crystal Display.
LED Abbreviation for Light Emitting Diode.
Liner A steel cylinder liner inserted in a aluminium alloy cylinder block.
Locknut A nut used to lock an adjustment nut, or other threaded component, in place.
Lockstops The lugs on the lower triple clamp (yoke) which abut those on the frame, preventing handlebar-to-fuel tank contact.
Lockwasher A form of washer designed to prevent an attaching nut from working loose.
LT Low Tension Description of the electrical circuit from the power supply to the primary winding of the ignition coil.

M

Main bearings The bearings between the crankshaft and crankcase.
Maintenance-free (MF) battery A sealed battery which cannot be topped up.
Manometer Mercury-filled calibrated tubes used to measure intake tract vacuum. Used to synchronise carburettors on multi-cylinder engines.
Micrometer A precision measuring instrument that measures component outside diameters **(see illustration)**.

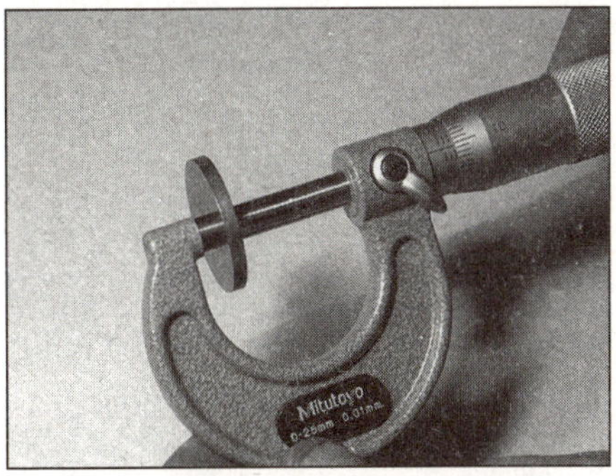

Tappet shims are measured with a micrometer

MON (Motor Octane Number) A measure of a fuel's resistance to knock.
Monograde oil An oil with a single viscosity, eg SAE80W.
Monoshock A single suspension unit linking the swingarm or suspension linkage to the frame.
mph Abbreviation for miles per hour.
Multigrade oil Having a wide viscosity range (eg 10W40). The W stands for Winter, thus the viscosity ranges from SAE10 when cold to SAE40 when hot.
Multimeter An electrical test instrument with the capability to measure voltage, current and resistance. Some meters also incorporate a continuity tester and buzzer.

N

Needle roller bearing Inner race of caged needle rollers and hardened outer race. Examples of uncaged needle rollers can be found on some engines. Commonly used in rear suspension applications and in two-stroke engines.
Nm Newton metres.
NOx Oxides of Nitrogen. A common toxic pollutant emitted by petrol engines at higher temperatures.

O

Octane The measure of a fuel's resistance to knock.
OE (Original Equipment) Relates to components fitted to a motorcycle as standard or replacement parts supplied by the motorcycle manufacturer.
Ohm The unit of electrical resistance. Ohms = Volts ÷ Current.
Ohmmeter An instrument for measuring electrical resistance.
Oil cooler System for diverting engine oil outside of the engine to a radiator for cooling purposes.
Oil injection A system of two-stroke engine lubrication where oil is pump-fed to the engine in accordance with throttle position.
Open-circuit An electrical condition where there is a break in the flow of electricity - no continuity (high resistance).
O-ring A type of sealing ring made of a special rubber-like material; in use, the O-ring is compressed into a groove to provide the sealing action.
Oversize (OS) Term used for piston and ring size options fitted to a rebored cylinder.
Overhead cam (sohc) engine An engine with single camshaft located on top of the cylinder head.
Overhead valve (ohv) engine An engine with the valves located in the cylinder head, but with the camshaft located in the engine block or crankcase.
Oxygen sensor A device installed in the exhaust system which senses the oxygen content in the exhaust and converts this information into an electric current. Also called a Lambda sensor.

P

Plastigauge A thin strip of plastic thread, available in different sizes, used for measuring clearances. For example, a strip of Plastigauge is laid across a bearing journal. The parts are assembled and dismantled; the width of the crushed strip indicates the clearance between journal and bearing.
Polarity Either negative or positive earth (ground), determined by which battery lead is connected to the frame (earth return). Modern motorcycles are usually negative earth.
Pre-ignition A situation where the fuel/air mixture ignites before the spark plug fires. Often due to a hot spot in the combustion chamber caused by carbon build-up. Engine has a tendency to 'run-on'.
Pre-load (suspension) The amount a spring is compressed when in the unloaded state. Preload can be applied by gas, spacer or mechanical adjuster.
Premix The method of engine lubrication on older two-stroke engines. Engine oil is mixed with the petrol in the fuel tank in a specific ratio. The fuel/oil mix is sometimes referred to as "petroil".
Primary drive Description of the drive from the crankshaft to the clutch. Usually by gear or chain.
PS Pfedestärke - a German interpretation of BHP.
PSI Pounds-force per square inch. Imperial measurement of tyre pressure and cylinder pressure measurement.
PTFE Polytetrafluroethylene. A low friction substance.
Pulse secondary air injection system A process of promoting the burning of excess fuel present in the exhaust gases by routing fresh air into the exhaust ports.

Q

Quartz halogen bulb Tungsten filament surrounded by a halogen gas. Typically used for the headlight **(see illustration)**.

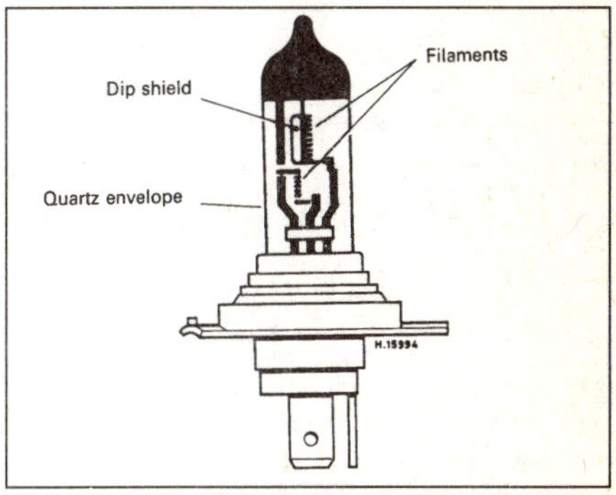

Quartz halogen headlight bulb construction

R

Rack-and-pinion A pinion gear on the end of a shaft that mates with a rack (think of a geared wheel opened up and laid flat). Sometimes used in clutch operating systems.
Radial play Up and down movement about a shaft.
Radial ply tyres Tyre plies run across the tyre (from bead to bead) and around the circumference of the tyre. Less resistant to tread distortion than other tyre types.
Radiator A liquid-to-air heat transfer device designed to reduce the temperature of the coolant in a liquid cooled engine.
Rake A feature of steering geometry - the angle of the steering head in relation to the vertical **(see illustration)**.

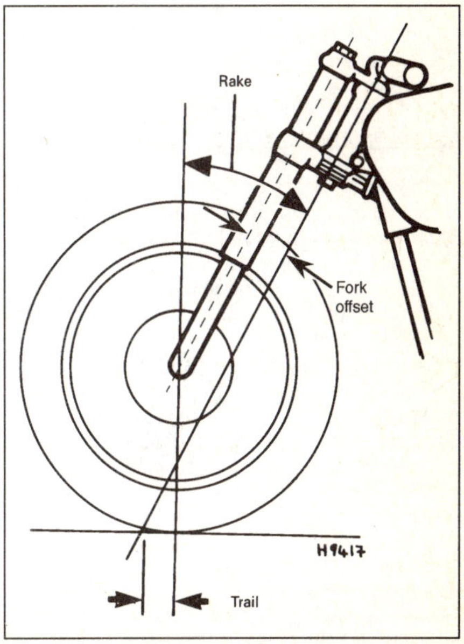

Steering geometry

Rebore Providing a new working surface to the cylinder bore by boring out the old surface. Necessitates the use of oversize piston and rings.
Rebound damping A means of controlling the oscillation of a suspension unit spring after it has been compressed. Resists the spring's natural tendency to bounce back after being compressed.
Rectifier Device for converting the ac output of an alternator into dc for battery charging.
Reed valve An induction system commonly used on two-stroke engines.
Regulator Device for maintaining the charging voltage from the generator or alternator within a specified range.
Relay A electrical device used to switch heavy current on and off by using a low current auxiliary circuit.
Resistance Measured in ohms. An electrical component's ability to pass electrical current.
RON (Research Octane Number) A measure of a fuel's resistance to knock.
rpm revolutions per minute.
Runout The amount of wobble (in-and-out movement) of a wheel or shaft as it's rotated. The amount a shaft rotates `out-of-true'. The out-of-round condition of a rotating part.

S

SAE (Society of Automotive Engineers) A standard for the viscosity of a fluid.
Sealant A liquid or paste used to prevent leakage at a joint. Sometimes used in conjunction with a gasket.
Service limit Term for the point where a component is no longer useable and must be renewed.
Shaft drive A method of transmitting drive from the transmission to the rear wheel.
Shell bearings Plain bearings consisting of two shell halves. Most often used as big-end and main bearings in a four-stroke engine. Often called bearing inserts.
Shim Thin spacer, commonly used to adjust the clearance or relative positions between two parts. For example, shims inserted into or under tappets or followers to control valve clearances. Clearance is adjusted by changing the thickness of the shim.
Short-circuit An electrical condition where current shorts to earth (ground) bypassing the circuit components.
Skimming Process to correct warpage or repair a damaged surface, eg on brake discs or drums.
Slide-hammer A special puller that screws into or hooks onto a component such as a shaft or bearing; a heavy sliding handle on the shaft bottoms against the end of the shaft to knock the component free.
Small-end bearing The bearing in the upper end of the connecting rod at its joint with the gudgeon pin.
Spalling Damage to camshaft lobes or bearing journals shown as pitting of the working surface.
Specific gravity (SG) The state of charge of the electrolyte in a lead-acid battery. A measure of the electrolyte's density compared with water.
Straight-cut gears Common type gear used on gearbox shafts and for oil pump and water pump drives.
Stanchion The inner sliding part of the front forks, held by the yokes. Often called a fork tube.
Stoichiometric ratio The optimum chemical air/fuel ratio for a petrol engine, said to be 14.7 parts of air to 1 part of fuel.
Sulphuric acid The liquid (electrolyte) used in a lead-acid battery. Poisonous and extremely corrosive.
Surface grinding (lapping) Process to correct a warped gasket face, commonly used on cylinder heads.

T

Tapered-roller bearing Tapered inner race of caged needle rollers and separate tapered outer race. Examples of taper roller bearings can be found on steering heads.
Tappet A cylindrical component which transmits motion from the cam to the valve stem, either directly or via a pushrod and rocker arm. Also called a cam follower.
TCS Traction Control System. An electronically-controlled system which senses wheel spin and reduces engine speed accordingly.
TDC Top Dead Centre denotes that the piston is at its highest point in the cylinder.
Thread-locking compound Solution applied to fastener threads to prevent slackening. Select type to suit application.
Thrust washer A washer positioned between two moving components on a shaft. For example, between gear pinions on gearshaft.
Timing chain See **Cam Chain.**
Timing light Stroboscopic lamp for carrying out ignition timing checks with the engine running.
Top-end A description of an engine's cylinder block, head and valve gear components.
Torque Turning or twisting force about a shaft.
Torque setting A prescribed tightness specified by the motorcycle manufacturer to ensure that the bolt or nut is secured correctly. Undertightening can result in the bolt or nut coming loose or a surface not being sealed. Overtightening can result in stripped threads, distortion or damage to the component being retained.
Torx key A six-point wrench.
Tracer A stripe of a second colour applied to a wire insulator to distinguish that wire from another one with the same colour insulator. For example, Br/W is often used to denote a brown insulator with a white tracer.
Trail A feature of steering geometry. Distance from the steering head axis to the tyre's central contact point.
Triple clamps The cast components which extend from the steering head and support the fork stanchions or tubes. Often called fork yokes.
Turbocharger A centrifugal device, driven by exhaust gases, that pressurises the intake air. Normally used to increase the power output from a given engine displacement.
TWI Abbreviation for Tyre Wear Indicator. Indicates the location of the tread depth indicator bars on tyres.

U

Universal joint or U-joint (UJ) A double-pivoted connection for transmitting power from a driving to a driven shaft through an angle. Typically found in shaft drive assemblies.
Unsprung weight Anything not supported by the bike's suspension (ie the wheel, tyres, brakes, final drive and bottom (moving) part of the suspension).

V

Vacuum gauges Clock-type gauges for measuring intake tract vacuum. Used for carburettor synchronisation on multi-cylinder engines.
Valve A device through which the flow of liquid, gas or vacuum may be stopped, started or regulated by a moveable part that opens, shuts or partially obstructs one or more ports or passageways. The intake and exhaust valves in the cylinder head are of the poppet type.
Valve clearance The clearance between the valve tip (the end of the valve stem) and the rocker arm or tappet/follower. The valve clearance is measured when the valve is closed. The correct clearance is important - if too small the valve won't close fully and will burn out, whereas if too large noisy operation will result.
Valve lift The amount a valve is lifted off its seat by the camshaft lobe.
Valve timing The exact setting for the opening and closing of the valves in relation to piston position.
Vernier caliper A precision measuring instrument that measures inside and outside dimensions. Not quite as accurate as a micrometer, but more convenient.
VIN Vehicle Identification Number. Term for the bike's engine and frame numbers.
Viscosity The thickness of a liquid or its resistance to flow.
Volt A unit for expressing electrical "pressure" in a circuit. Volts = current x ohms.

W

Water pump A mechanically-driven device for moving coolant around the engine.
Watt A unit for expressing electrical power. Watts = volts x current.
Wear limit see **Service limit**
Wet liner A liquid-cooled engine design where the pistons run in liners which are directly surrounded by coolant **(see illustration)**.

Wet liner arrangement

Wheelbase Distance from the centre of the front wheel to the centre of the rear wheel.
Wiring harness or loom Describes the electrical wires running the length of the motorcycle and enclosed in tape or plastic sheathing. Wiring coming off the main harness is usually referred to as a sub harness.
Woodruff key A key of semi-circular or square section used to locate a gear to a shaft. Often used to locate the alternator rotor on the crankshaft.
Wrist pin Another name for gudgeon or piston pin.